EDUCATIONAL PSYCHOLOGY

Developing Learners

EDUCATIONAL PSYCHOLOGY
Developing Learners

Fifth Edition

Jeanne Ellis Ormrod

University of Northern Colorado (Emerita)
University of New Hampshire

PEARSON

Merrill
Prentice Hall

Upper Saddle River, New Jersey
Columbus, Ohio

Library of Congress Cataloging-in-Publication Data
Ormrod, Jeanne Ellis.
    Educational psychology : developing learners / Jeanne Ellis Ormrod.—5th ed.
        p. cm.
    Includes bibliographical references and index.
    ISBN 0-13-119087-3 (pbk.)
    1. Educational psychology. 2. Teaching. 3. Learning. 4. Classroom management. I.
Title.

LB1051.O66 2006
370.15—dc22

2004061775

Vice President and Executive Publisher: Jeffery W. Johnston
Publisher: Kevin M. Davis
Development Editor: Autumn Crisp Benson
Editorial Assistant: Margaret Bowen
Production Editor: Mary Harlan
Copy Editor: Sue Snyder Kopp
Design Coordinator: Diane C. Lorenzo
Photo Coordinator: Valerie Schultz

Text and Cover Design: Kristina D. Holmes
Cover Image: Index Stock
Illustrations: Carlisle Publishers Services
Production Manager: Laura Messerly
Director of Marketing: Ann Castel Davis
Marketing Manager: Autumn Purdy
Marketing Coordinator: Tyra Poole

This book was set in Berkeley by Carlisle Communications, Ltd. It was printed and bound by Courier Kendallville, Inc. The cover was printed by Coral Graphic Services, Inc.

Photo Credits: Bill Aron/PhotoEdit, pp. 328, 432; Bill Bachmann/Photo Researchers, Inc., p. 395; Billy E. Barnes/PhotoEdit, p. 528; David Buffington/Getty Images, Inc.–Photodisc, p. 260; Susan Burger, pp. 76, 131, 172, 173, 213, 273, 301, 309, 509, 524; Jim Carter/Photo Researchers, Inc., p. 109; Myrleen Ferguson Cate/PhotoEdit, p. 36; CNRI/Science Photo Library/Photo Researchers, Inc., p. 23; Elizabeth Crews/Elizabeth Crews Photography, p. 448; Scott Cunningham/Merrill, pp. 18, 50, 60, 63, 85, 138, 153, 182, 190, 217, 239, 330, 368, 396, 420, 472, 489, 494, 496, 522, 556, 583, 586; Bob Daemmrich/The Image Works, pp. 127, 227; Bob Daemmrich/Stock Boston, p. 225; Mary Kate Denny/Getty Images Inc.–Stone Allstock, p. 147; Mary Kate Denny/PhotoEdit, pp. 318, 504; Tony Freeman/PhotoEdit, pp. 102, 228, 322; Catrina Genovese/Omni–Photo Communications, Inc., p. 538; Getty Images, p. 176; Getty Images, Inc.–Photodisc, p. 245; Jeff Greenberg/PhotoEdit, pp. 21, 341; Charles Gupton/Stock Boston, p. 377; Ken Hammond/USDA Natural Resources Conservation Service, p. 294; Will Hart/PhotoEdit, pp. 185, 461, 485, 563; Richard Hutchings/PhotoEdit, pp. 170, 435; Bonnie Kamin/PhotoEdit, p. 398; Mark Lewis/Getty Images Inc.–Stone Allstock, p. 211; Anthony Magnacca/Merrill, pp. 2, 6, 165, 353, 501, 544, 577; Will McIntyre/Photo Researchers, Inc., p. 133; Will & Deni McIntyre/Photo Researchers, Inc., p. 381; Lawrence Migdale/Photo Researchers, Inc., p. 370; Michael Newman/PhotoEdit, pp. 111, 442, 532, 554; Michael Provest/Silver Burdett Ginn, p. 298; Kevin Radford/SuperStock, Inc., p. 222; Mark Richards/PhotoEdit, p. 46; Elena Rooraid/PhotoEdit, p. 358; Andy Sacks/Getty Images Inc.–Stone Allstock, p. 118; James L. Shaffer, p. 167; Frank Siteman/Index Stock Imagery, Inc., p. 310; Elliot Smith/Image State/International Stock Photography Ltd., p. 157; courtesy of Vanderbilt University, p. 284; Tom Watson/Merrill, pp. 10, 315; Patrick White/Merrill, pp. 254, 257, 364, 422, 482, 570; James D. Wilson/Getty Images, Inc.–Liaison, p. 246; David Young-Wolff/Getty Images Inc.–Stone Allstock, p. 390; David Young-Wolff/PhotoEdit, pp. 33, 141, 229, 333, 384, 407, 439, 451, 467.

The Praxis Series: Professional Assessments for Beginning Teachers is a registered trademark of Educational Testing Service (ETS). Praxis® is a trademark of ETS. This publication is not endorsed or approved by ETS.

Pearson Education Ltd.
Pearson Education Singapore Pte. Ltd.
Pearson Education Canada, Ltd.
Pearson Education–Japan

Pearson Education Australia Pty. Limited
Pearson Education North Asia Ltd.
Pearson Educación de Mexico, S.A. de C.V.
Pearson Education Malaysia Pte. Ltd.

10 9 8 7 6 5 4 3 2 1
ISBN: 0-13-119087-3

Preface

As teachers, we play a critical role in the lives of children and adolescents. Some of us help them learn to read and write. Some of us help them express themselves through physical movement, the visual arts, or music. Some of us help them understand their physical and social worlds through an exploration of science, mathematics, geography, history, or literature. But regardless of the subject matter we teach, we help the generation that follows us to become knowledgeable, self-confident, and productive citizens.

In my mind, teaching is the most rewarding profession we could possibly choose. Yet it is often a challenging profession as well. Students don't always come to us ready or willing to learn. How can we help them develop the knowledge and skills they need to become productive adults? What strategies can we use to motivate them? What tasks and instructional materials are appropriate for children at different developmental levels? Over the years, researchers, theorists, and practitioners have worked together to answer such questions. We are in the fortunate position of being able to benefit from the many insights they offer.

I have been teaching educational psychology since 1974, and I've loved every minute of it. How children and adolescents learn and think, how they change as they grow and develop, why they do the things they do, how they are often very different from one another—our understanding of all these things has innumerable implications for classroom practice and, ultimately, for the lives of young people.

I have written this textbook in much the same way that I teach my college classes. Because I want the field of educational psychology to captivate you the way it has captivated me, I have tried to make the book interesting, meaningful, and thought-provoking as well as informative. I have a definite philosophy about how future teachers can best learn and apply educational psychology—a philosophy that has guided me as I have written all five editions of the book. More specifically, I believe that you can construct a more accurate and useful understanding of the principles of educational psychology when you:

- Focus on core principles of the discipline
- Relate the principles to your own learning and behavior
- Use the principles to understand the learning and behavior of children and adolescents
- Consistently apply the principles to classroom practice

I have incorporated numerous features into the book that will encourage you to do all of these things. I hope that you will learn a great deal from what educational psychology has to offer, not only about the students you will be teaching but also about yourself—a human being who continues to learn and develop even as an adult.

A Focus on Core Ideas and Helping Readers Understand Those Ideas Deeply

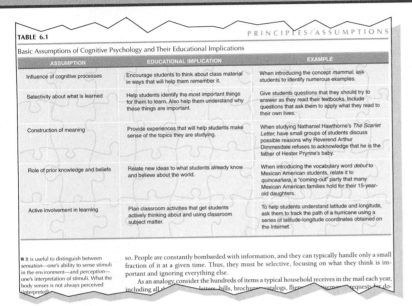

TABLE 6.1

PRINCIPLES/ASSUMPTIONS

Basic Assumptions of Cognitive Psychology and Their Educational Implications

ASSUMPTION	EDUCATIONAL IMPLICATION	EXAMPLE
Influence of cognitive processes	Encourage students to think about class material in ways that will help them remember it.	When introducing the concept *mammal*, ask students to identify numerous examples.
Selectivity about what is learned	Help students identify the most important things for them to learn. Also help them understand why these things are important.	Give students questions that they should try to answer as they read their textbooks. Include questions that ask them to apply what they read to their own lives.
Construction of meaning	Provide experiences that will help students make sense of the topics they are studying.	When studying Nathaniel Hawthorne's *The Scarlet Letter*, have small groups of students discuss possible reasons why Reverend Arthur Dimmesdale refuses to acknowledge that he is the father of Hester Prynne's baby.
Role of prior knowledge and beliefs	Relate new ideas to what students already know and believe about the world.	When introducing the vocabulary word *debut* to Mexican American students, relate it to *quinceañera*, a "coming-out" party that many Mexican American families hold for their 15-year-old daughters.
Active involvement in learning	Plan classroom activities that get students actively thinking about and using classroom subject matter.	To help students understand latitude and longitude, ask them to track the path of a hurricane using a series of latitude-longitude coordinates obtained on the Internet.

■ It is useful to distinguish between *sensation*—one's ability to sense stimuli in the environment—and *perception*—one's interpretation of stimuli. What the body senses is not always perceived (interpreted).

so. People are constantly bombarded with information, and they can typically handle only a small fraction of it at a given time. Thus, they must be selective, focusing on what they think is important and ignoring everything else.

As an analogy, consider the hundreds of items a typical household receives in the mail each year, including all the ... letters, bills, brochures, catalogs, fliers, ... isements, requests for do-

A FOCUS ON UNDERLYING ASSUMPTIONS AND CORE IDEAS

Rather than superficially explore every aspect of educational psychology, this text offers in-depth treatment of the fundamental concepts and principles that have broad applicability to classroom practice. Throughout the text, principles and core concepts are identified, discussed in depth, and then summarized in *Principles/Assumptions* tables. Each table includes educational implications and concrete examples.

HELPING READERS SEE HOW CORE IDEAS OPERATE IN THEIR OWN LEARNING

A central goal of this text has always been to help readers discover more about themselves as thinkers and learners. A key component of this aspect of the text is the *Experiencing Firsthand* exercises embedded throughout the book. These help readers to discover important points firsthand and to construct a more complete, meaningful understanding of educational psychology. In addition, as you look through the text you will discover other features, including reflective margin notes and embedded questions, that help readers understand their own learning.

Research clearly indicates that meaningful learning is more effective than rote learning (Ausubel, Novak, & Hanesian, 1978; Bransford & Johnson, 1972; Mayer, 1996). It is especially effective when learners relate new ideas not only to the things they already know but also to *themselves* (e.g., Rogers, Kuiper, & Kirker, 1977). For instance, in Figure 6.6 Nadia explains the four seasons in terms of the things *she* does during each season.

As illustrations of the effectiveness of meaningful learning, try the following two exercises.

Experiencing FIRSTHAND · · · · · · · · · · · · · · · Two Letter Strings, Two Pictures

1. Study each of the following strings of letters until you can remember them perfectly:

   AIIRODFMLAWRS   FAMILIARWORDS

2. Study each of the two pictures to the right until you can reproduce them accurately from memory.

· · · · · · ·

Figures are from "Comprehension and Memory for Pictures" by G. H. Bower, M. B. Karlin, and A. Dueck, 1975, *Memory and Cognition, 3*, p. 217. Reprinted by permission of Psychonomic Society, Inc.

No doubt the second letter string was easier to learn because you could relate it to something you already knew: "familiar words." How easily were you able to learn the two pictures? Do you think you could draw them from memory a week from now? Do you think you would be able to remember them more easily if they had meaningful titles such as "a midget playing a trombone in a telephone booth" and "an early bird who caught a very strong worm"? The answer to the latter question is a very definite yes: Meaningful labels enhance people's memory for simple line drawings (Bower, Karlin, & Dueck, 1975).

Some students approach school assignments with meaningful learning in mind: They turn to what they already know to make sense of new information. These students are apt to be the high achievers in the classroom. Other students instead use rote learning strategies, such as repeating something over and over to themselves without really thinking about what they are saying. As you might guess, these students learn less successfully (Britton, Stimson, Stennett, & Gülgöz, 1998; Novak, 1998; Van Rossum & Schenk, 1984).

Yet we ... ... when ... meaning ...

CREATING A PRODUCTIVE CLASSROOM ENVIRONMENT

Creating Conditions in Which Students Can Effectively Learn

Physically arrange the classroom in a way that facilitates teacher-student interactions and keeps distracting influences to a minimum.
An elementary school teacher has arranged the twenty-eight student desks in his classroom into seven clusters of four desks each. The four-student clusters become base groups for many of the classroom's cooperative learning activities. The teacher occasionally asks students to move their chairs into a large circle for whole-class discussions.

Show students that you care about and respect them as human beings, and give them some say about what happens in the classroom.
A high school teacher realizes that she is continually admonishing one particular student for his off-task behavior. To establish a more positive relationship with the student, she makes a point to greet him warmly in the hallway before school every day. At the end of one day in which his behavior has been especially disruptive, she catches him briefly to express her concern, and the two agree to meet the following morning to discuss ways of helping him stay on task more regularly.

Set reasonable limits for student behavior.
After describing the objectives of an instrumental music class on the first day of school, a junior high school teacher tells students,

"There is one rule for this class to which I will hold firm. You must not engage in any behavior that will interfere with your own learning or with that of your classmates."

Plan classroom activities that encourage on-task behavior.
Before each class, a creative writing teacher writes the day's topic on the chalkboard. Her students know that when they arrive at class, they are to take out pencil and paper and begin an essay addressing that topic.

Show students you are continually aware of what they're doing.
While meeting with each reading group in one corner of the classroom, an elementary school teacher sits with his back to the wall so he can keep an eye on those students who are working together at the science table or independently at their desks.

Modify your plans for instruction when necessary.
A teacher discovers that students quickly complete the activity she thought would take them an entire class period. She wraps up the activity after fifteen minutes and then begins the lesson she had originally planned for the following day.

HELPING READERS UNDERSTAND HOW CORE IDEAS TRANSLATE INTO CLASSROOM PRACTICE

Throughout this text, psychological concepts and principles are consistently applied to classroom practice. Applications are summarized and illustrated in a number of features, including the *Principles/Assumptions* tables. At least twice in every chapter, teaching strategies are collected and presented together in *Into the Classroom* features. A new feature, *Creating a Productive Classroom Environment*, focuses specifically on helping readers see how core concepts throughout the text relate to classroom management. This feature reinforces the idea that classroom management should not be thought of as an isolated task but should be integrated with the other principles in the text. All of these features provide practical strategies and concrete examples for a variety of subject areas and grade levels.

A Focus on Helping Students Truly See and Better Understand Children and Adolescents

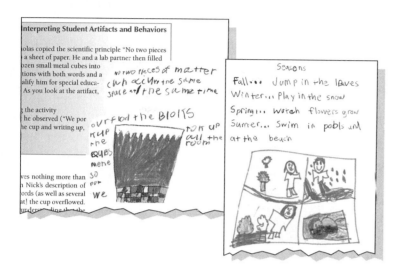

REAL STUDENTS AND THEIR WORK

Another central goal of this text is to situate the concepts and principles of educational psychology in real students and classrooms. Case studies begin and end each chapter, and there are other separate vignettes embedded throughout the book. And unique to educational psychology texts, the book makes frequent use of real artifacts from children's journals, sketchbooks, and school assignments. The text now also contains, on two CDs, video artifacts of students, teachers, and classrooms.

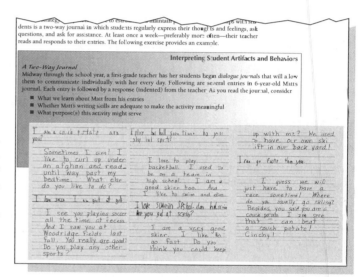

INTERPRETING STUDENT ARTIFACTS AND BEHAVIORS

This feature gives readers practice in evaluating and interpreting student work. Not only does the *Interpreting Student Artifacts and Behaviors* feature provide readers with additional authentic illustrations of chapter content, but it also offers readers an opportunity to apply their knowledge of educational psychology content in an authentic context. And since interpreting real children's work is a core assessment task of those who work with and educate children, this feature gives readers direct, concrete practice in assessment.

DEVELOPMENTAL TRENDS

Another new feature in this edition is the *Developmental Trends* table. This text is the only educational psychology textbook to discuss development and its implications for understanding and applying core educational psychology concepts throughout the book. These tables (at least one in each of Chapters 2 through 16) summarize age-typical characteristics of four grade levels (K–2, 3–5, 6–8, and 9–12) and provide suggested strategies for practice. As you can see from the examples on pages 206 and 498, this feature helps students focus on developmental differences and helps them match practice to developmental level.

Extensive and Integrated Coverage of Diversity

DIVERSITY COVERED IN EVERY CHAPTER

This text has the most extensive, practical coverage of diversity available in an introduction to educational psychology text. It offers truly integrated coverage of diversity by devoting an entire section to diversity in *every* chapter. (For example, see pages 217–219 and 507–510.) These sections reinforce the idea that teachers must take the diverse characteristics and needs of students into account in every aspect of learning and instruction.

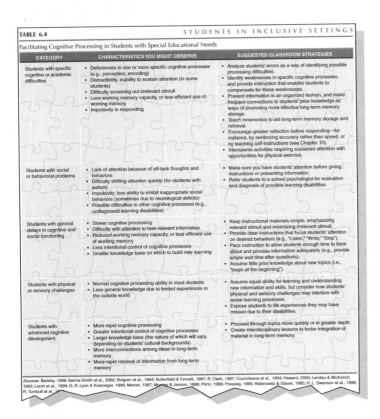

TABLE 6.4

STUDENTS IN INCLUSIVE SETTINGS

Facilitating Cognitive Processing in Students with Special Educational Needs

CATEGORY	CHARACTERISTICS YOU MIGHT OBSERVE	SUGGESTED CLASSROOM STRATEGIES
Students with specific cognitive or academic difficulties	• Deficiencies in one or more specific cognitive processes (e.g., perception, encoding) • Distractibility, inability to sustain attention (in some students) • Difficulty screening out irrelevant stimuli • Less working memory capacity, or less efficient use of working memory • Impulsivity in responding	• Analyze students' errors as a way of identifying possible processing difficulties. • Identify weaknesses in specific cognitive processes, and provide instruction that enables students to compensate for these weaknesses. • Present information in an organized fashion, and make frequent connections to students' prior knowledge as ways of promoting more effective long-term memory storage. • Teach mnemonics to aid long-term memory storage and retrieval. • Encourage greater reflection before responding—for instance, by reinforcing accuracy rather than speed, or by teaching self-instructions (see Chapter 10). • Intersperse activities requiring sustained attention with opportunities for physical exercise.
Students with social or behavioral problems	• Lack of attention because of off-task thoughts and behaviors • Difficulty shifting attention quickly (for students with autism) • Impulsivity; less ability to inhibit inappropriate social behaviors (sometimes due to neurological deficits) • Possible difficulties in other cognitive processes (e.g., undiagnosed learning disabilities)	• Make sure you have students' attention before giving instructions or presenting information. • Refer students to a school psychologist for evaluation and diagnosis of possible learning disabilities.
Students with general delays in cognitive and social functioning	• Slower cognitive processing • Difficulty with attention to task-relevant information • Reduced working memory capacity, or less efficient use of working memory • Less intentional control of cognitive processes • Smaller knowledge base on which to build new learning	• Keep instructional materials simple, emphasizing relevant stimuli and minimizing irrelevant stimuli. • Provide clear instructions that focus students' attention on desired behaviors (e.g., "Listen," "Write," "Stop"). • Pace instruction to allow students enough time to think about and process information adequately (e.g., provide ample wait time after questions). • Assume little prior knowledge about new topics (i.e., "begin at the beginning").
Students with physical or sensory challenges	• Normal cognitive processing ability in most students • Less general knowledge due to limited experiences in the outside world	• Assume equal ability for learning and understanding new information and skills, but consider how students' physical and sensory challenges may interfere with some learning processes. • Expose students to life experiences they may have missed due to their disabilities.
Students with advanced cognitive development	• More rapid cognitive processing • Greater intentional control of cognitive processes • Larger knowledge base (the nature of which will vary, depending on students' cultural backgrounds) • More interconnections among ideas in long-term memory • More rapid retrieval of information from long-term memory	• Proceed through topics more quickly or in greater depth. • Create interdisciplinary lessons to foster integration of material in long-term memory.

Sources: Barkley, 1998; Beirne-Smith et al., 2002; Bulgren et al., 1994; Butterfield & Ferretti, 1987; B. Clark, 1997; Courchesne et al., 1994; Heward, 2000; Landau & McAninch, 1993; Lorch et al., 1999; G. R. Lyon & Krasnegor, 1996; Mercer, 1997; Morgan & Jenson, 1988; Piirto, 1999; Pressley, 1995; Rabinowitz & Glaser, 1985; H. L. Swanson et al., 1998; R. Turnbull et al.,

---

(e.g., learning disabilities, ineffective study skills, brain injury) have been ruled out as the cause of the decline.

Poor coping skills. A student has little ability to deal effectively with frustration, takes the smallest affront personally, and has trouble "bouncing back" after minor disappointments.

Lack of anger control. A student frequently responds with uncontrolled anger to even the slightest injustice and may misdirect anger at innocent bystanders.

Sense of superiority, self-centeredness, and lack of empathy. A student depicts himself or herself as "smarter" or in some other way better than peers, is preoccupied with his or her own needs, and has little regard for the needs of others.

Lengthy grudges. A student is unforgiving of others' transgressions, even after considerable time has elapsed.

Violent themes in drawings and written work. Violence predominates in a student's artwork, stories, and journal entries.

Prejudice. A student has a long record of seriously inappropriate behavior extending over several years.

Association with violent peers. A student associates regularly with a gang or other antisocial peer group.

Inappropriate role models. A student may speak with admiration about Hitler, Satan, or some other malevolent figure.

Excessive alcohol or drug use. A student who abuses alcohol or drugs may have reduced self-control; in some cases substance abuse signals significant mental illness.

Inappropriate access to firearms. A student has easy access to guns and ammunition and may regularly practice using them.

Threats of violence. A student has openly expressed an intent to harm someone else. *This warning sign alone requires immediate action.*

extreme violence is *very rare* in schools; unreasonable paranoia about potential school violence will prevent us from working effectively with students. Second, the great majority of students who exhibit one or a few of the warning signs on the list will *not* become violent. And most importantly, we must *never* use the warning signs as a reason to unfairly accuse, isolate, or punish a student (Dwyer et al., 1998). These signs provide a means of getting students help if they need it, not of excluding them from the education that all children and adolescents deserve.

TAKING STUDENT DIVERSITY INTO ACCOUNT

As we plan for a productive classroom environment, we must always take the diverse characteristics and needs of our students into account. For example, we should make an extra effort to establish a supportive classroom climate when working with students from ethnic minority groups or with students from lower-income neighborhoods. We must also be aware that some cultural and ethnic groups may have views about "appropriate" and "inappropriate" behaviors that are different from our own. Finally, we may often have to make special accommodations for students with special educational needs. Let's look briefly at each of these issues.

STUDENTS IN INCLUSIVE STETINGS

The text is also the only educational text to address needs of students with exceptionalities in every chapter. Each chapter ends with a discussion of accommodating students with special needs and with the feature *Students in Inclusive Settings*. This feature familiarizes readers with the characteristics teachers might observe in children and adolescents with special needs and then provides concrete classroom adaptation and inclusion strategies.

EXPANDED COVERAGE OF DIVERSITY

Throughout the fifth edition, coverage of diversity has been expanded and deepened. In particular, coverage of children from low-socioeconomic (SES) backgrounds has been substantially expanded throughout the text. For example, a new section on factors affecting the school success of students from low-SES backgrounds has been added to Chapter 4, and a new section discussing socioeconomic group differences in motivation has been added to Chapter 12.

Some of the other new and expanded diversity content includes

- Diversity in personal, social, and moral development (Chapter 3)
- Teachers' cultural lenses (Chapter 4)

- Students with multiple cultural affiliations (Chapter 4)
- Roles of biology, socialization, and self-socialization in promoting gender differences (Chapter 4)
- Gender differences in academic and social domains (Chapter 4)
- Temperament (Chapter 5)
- Accommodating diversity in cognitive processes (Chapter 6)
- Diversity in motivation and affect (Chapter 11)
- Ethnic group differences in motivation (Chapter 12)
- Taking group differences into account when working with parents (Chapter 14)

CHANGES IN THE FIFTH EDITION

Most of the content from the fourth edition remains in the fifth edition, although a few topics (adaptive behaviors, Maslow's hierarchy of needs, an in-depth discussion of taxonomies) have migrated to the *Study Guide and Reader*. I have moved intelligence and temperament to Chapter 5 to create an "Individual Differences and Special Educational Needs" chapter. I have moved discussions of creativity and dispositions to Chapters 8 and 12, respectively, where they seemed to be a better fit. I have reorganized much of Chapters 15 and 16: Classroom assessment strategies are now in Chapter 15, and some topics previously in that chapter—test scores, standardized tests, high-stakes testing, accountability, confidentiality, communication about assessment results, and cultural bias—are now in Chapter 16.

I've updated every chapter of the book to be in line with current research, theory, and practices, and I've added new student artifacts to illustrate concepts and ideas. More significant changes include: (a) increased coverage of child and adolescent development; (b) greater integration of classroom management with discussions of development, learning, and motivation; (c) additional new and expanded topics; and (d) the addition of two *Video Examples* compact disks (CDs).

Child and Adolescent Development   In previous editions of the book, much of the discussion of development was confined to Chapters 2 and 3. Here in the fifth edition, I've made a concerted effort to address developmental issues throughout the book. This change is most noticeable in the *Developmental Trends* tables that appear in Chapters 2 through 16, but you will also see it in the running text—for instance, in new sections on "Developmental Trends in Storage Processes for Declarative Information" (Chapter 6) and "Developmental Trends in Achievement Goals" (Chapter 12).

Classroom Management   In previous editions, I addressed classroom management largely in Chapter 14, although a few sections in Chapters 3, 9, 10, 11, and 12 were also relevant to management concerns. In this edition, I've more explicitly highlighted classroom management strategies in *Creating a Productive Classroom Environment* features in Chapters 3 through 5 and Chapters 9 through 12, as well as in Chapter 14. Chapter 14 also has several new sections related to classroom management: "Forming and Maintaining Productive Teacher-Student Relationships," "Enforcing Rules Consistently and Equitably," "Taking Individual and Developmental Differences into Account," and "Addressing Aggression and Violence at School."

Other New and Expanded Topics   In addition to the increased coverage of development and classroom management, the book includes many smaller changes. I have added four new case studies: "*The Scarlet Letter*" (Chapter 3), "Why Jack Wasn't in School" (Chapter 4), "Tim" (Chapter 5), and "B in History" (Chapter 16). I have added new sections on play (Chapter 2); social construction of meaning (Chapter 2); cognitive tools (Chapter 2); a critique of information processing theory (Chapter 2); self-socialization (Chapter 3); effects of group membership and

achievements on students' sense of self (Chapter 3); developmental trends in morality and prosocial behavior (Chapter 3); cultural differences in personal space and teasing (Chapter 4); cultural lenses (Chapter 4); students with multiple cultural affiliations (Chapter 4); roles of biology, socialization, and self-socialization in promoting gender differences (Chapter 4); behaviors learned through modeling (Chapter 10); fostering high self-efficacy (Chapter 10); teacher self-efficacy (Chapter 10); promoting self-regulation in students at risk (Chapter 10); how emotion (*affect*) is related to motivation, learning, and cognition (Chapter 11); the "TARGET" mnemonic for motivational strategies (Table 12.4 in Chapter 12); taking group differences into account when working with parents (Chapter 14); including students in the grading process (Chapter 16); and school readiness tests (Chapter 16).

Meanwhile, I have expanded discussions of brain development (Chapter 2); peer influences (Chapter 3); diversity in personal, social, and moral development (Chapter 3); gender differences in academic and social domains (Chapter 4); factors affecting the school success of students from low socioeconomic backgrounds (Chapter 4); temperament (Chapter 5); learning and the brain (Chapter 6); accommodating diversity in cognitive processes (Chapter 6); conceptual change (Chapter 7); factors influencing students' use of effective study strategies (Chapter 8); effects of self-efficacy (Chapter 10); self-regulated learning (Chapter 10); making the transition from elementary school to middle or secondary school (Chapter 11); diversity in motivation and affect (Chapter 11); expectancies and values (Chapter 12); interest (Chapter 12); achievement goals (Chapter 12); social goals (Chapter 12); dispositions (Chapter 12); student attributions (Chapter 12); teacher expectations and attributions (Chapter 12); ethnic and socioeconomic-group differences in motivation (Chapter 12); content area standards (Chapters 13 and 15); online research (Chapter 13); effects of assessment practices on learning (Chapter 15); cheating (Chapter 15); and high-stakes testing (including the No Child Left Behind Act, Chapter 16).

Video Examples CDs   New to the fifth edition are two compact disks (CDs) entitled *Video Examples to Accompany Educational Psychology: Developing Learners*. Volume 1, "Observing Children and Adolescents," includes 19 video segments of children and adolescents (ages 6 to 17) engaging in learning and problem-solving tasks and discussing such topics as their learning strategies, interpersonal relationships, emotions, and motivation. Volume 2, "Observing Classrooms in Action," includes 11 video segments of lessons and activities in elementary, middle school, and high school classrooms; these segments illustrate a variety of teaching strategies and classroom management styles. In many places throughout the book, I direct your attention to portions of one or more video segments that relate to the concepts, principles, or classroom strategies we are discussing; in such instances, a "CD" icon such as the one to the right will appear in the margin.

SUPPLEMENTARY MATERIALS

In addition to the *Video Examples* CDs, numerous supplements to the textbook are available to enhance your learning and development as a teacher.

Study Guide and Reader   This resource provides many support mechanisms to help you learn and study more effectively, including focus questions to consider as you read the text, a chapter glossary, application exercises to give you practice in applying concepts and principles of educational psychology to classroom settings, answers to selected margin notes, sample test questions, and many supplementary readings. It will also give you guidance on using the *Video Examples* CDs, the table "Matching Book and Ancillary Content to the Praxis™ *Principles of Learning and Teaching* Tests" (Appendix C) in the text, and the Companion Website.

Companion Website   You can find the Companion Website for *Educational Psychology: Developing Learners* at **www.prenhall.com/ormrod**. For each chapter of the book, the Companion Website presents Key Questions that identify the chapter's central issues, a chapter glossary, key concepts linked to Internet destinations, and quick self-tests (multiple-choice and essay questions that let you self-assess what you've learned). The Companion Website also provides a syllabus manager that your instructor may use to post and occasionally update the course syllabus, as well as an interactive "Message Board" through which you and your classmates can engage in discussions about chapter content.

Videotapes and Multimedia Guide   Videos are a highly effective means of visually demonstrating concepts and principles in educational psychology. The nine videotapes that accompany this textbook portray a wide variety of teachers, students, and classrooms in action. Seven videos present numerous case studies in many content domains and at a variety of grade levels. Two additional videos are *A Private Universe* (which examines learner misconceptions in science) and Constance Kamii's *Double-Column Addition: A Teacher Uses Piaget's Theory* (which depicts a constructivist approach to teaching mathematics). Opportunities to react to these videos in class discussions will further enhance your ability to think analytically and identify good teaching practices. Your instructor will have a *Multimedia Guide* to help guide and enrich your interpretation and understanding of what you see in the videos.

Student Artifact Library   Available on the Companion Website is a large collection of artifacts from actual elementary, middle, and secondary school classrooms. Many of these artifacts are examples of students' work: short stories, essays, problem solutions, drawings, and so on. Others are assignments, classroom activities, scoring rubrics, letters to parents, and the like, that teachers have developed. You and your instructor can apply concepts and principles of educational psychology in analyzing and interpreting these artifacts.

ASCD/Merrill Web Site   A partnership between the Association for Supervision and Curriculum Development (ASCD) and Merrill Education has led to the development of www.EducatorLearningCenter.com, a Web site that includes articles from the journal *Educational Leadership,* lesson plans and strategies, excerpts from Merrill texts, videos, case studies, listservs that allow pre-service and in-service teachers to exchange ideas, and other resources to assist both novice and experienced teachers. A four-month subscription to this virtual "library" of resources is packaged with Merrill Education textbooks when specifically ordered by the instructor.

Instructor's Manual   Available to your instructor are suggestions for learning activities, additional "Experiencing Firsthand" exercises, supplementary lectures, case study analyses, discussion topics, group activities, and additional media resources. These have been carefully selected to provide opportunities to support, enrich, and expand on what you read in the textbook.

Transparencies   More than 100 acetate transparencies for in-class use include summative outlines and graphic organizers of essential concepts. These transparencies are designed to help you understand, organize, and remember the concepts and principles you are studying.

Test Bank   Many instructors use the test questions that accompany this textbook. Some items (lower-level questions) will simply ask you to identify or explain concepts and principles you have learned. But many others (higher-level questions) will ask you to apply those same concepts and principles to specific classroom situations—that is, to actual student behaviors and teaching strategies. The lower-level questions assess your basic knowledge of educational psychology. But ultimately, it is the higher-level questions that will assess your ability to use principles of educational psychology in your own teaching practice.

Multimedia Presentation Software   The multimedia presentation software is a series of DVDs that contain every ancillary offered with the text and are organized around PowerPoint presentations. This technology enables professors to use any available ancillary in a classroom setting and to show appropriate video clips or present examples or problems to help facilitate classroom discussions or to supplement lectures. Professors can also create their own PowerPoint presentations or modify existing ones.

ACKNOWLEDGMENTS

Although I am listed as the sole author of this textbook, I have been fortunate to have had a great deal of assistance in writing it. First and foremost, this book would not be what it is today without an ongoing partnership with my editor, Kevin Davis. Kevin first came on board as development editor for the book in 1989, but his innovative ideas and tireless devotion to creating high-quality textbooks for preservice and practicing teachers have led to several promotions at Merrill/Prentice Hall. Now, as

Assistant Vice President and Publisher, Kevin continues to stand by my side, offering new suggestions and insights and insisting that I stretch my talents further with each new edition of the book. He has limitless ideas on how we can continue to make *Educational Psychology* and its ancillary materials ever more meaningful, user-friendly, and supportive to students and instructors alike, and he provides the guidance (scaffolding) I need to accomplish tasks that initially seem so impossible. After spending countless hours working with Kevin over the past fifteen years, I can say that he is not only my editor but also a very good friend.

I am equally indebted to Autumn Benson, formerly Kevin's editorial assistant and now development editor for the fifth edition. Autumn has been there day in and day out for the past several years to answer questions about the many "little" things that need doing, and I know I can count on her to provide timely feedback and suggestions for improving whatever product I am working on at the time.

Three previous development editors have also been instrumental in shaping the book's evolution over previous editions. Julie Peters, development editor for the fourth edition, continually kept me focused on the big picture: how we can best help students and instructors in their efforts to understand, communicate about, and apply principles of educational psychology. Not only did she keep me on task, but she also brightened many a day with encouraging words and a great sense of humor. Linda Montgomery brought to the third edition creative ideas, a commitment to excellence, and extensive experience as both an elementary school teacher and an editor. And Linda Peterson, who saw me through the first and second editions, helped define much of the pedagogy of the book and, with her continuing insistence on *application, application, application,* kept my focus on the things that future teachers really need to know.

Others at Merrill/Prentice Hall have also contributed in important ways. As production editor, Mary Harlan has coordinated and overseen the very complex process of transforming a manuscript into a book, simultaneously keeping track of a million little things that needed to be done, graciously accommodating my requests for last-minute changes, and thankfully catching numerous anomalies and omissions. Copy editor Sue Kopp has looked closely at every word, finding places where I've been unclear or inconsistent, and often suggested better ways of communicating my ideas. Photo coordinator Valerie Schultz has found many photographs that have given life to the words on the page. As marketing director, Ann Davis has brought incredible energy and innovation to Merrill's efforts to get the word out about the book. When I reflect on my many visits to Columbus for planning meetings with the Merrill staff, as well as visits to New Orleans, Chicago, San Diego, and other locations for recent conventions, dinners with Ann and Kevin Davis have always been highlights of my trips.

In addition to the folks at Merrill/Prentice Hall, numerous colleagues across the country have given the book and its ancillaries a balance of perspectives that no single author could possibly do on her own. Drs. Margie Garanzini-Daiber and Peggy Cohen provided ideas for the *Students in Inclusive Settings* tables

that were introduced in the second edition. Dr. Ann Turnbull offered helpful suggestions for enhancing my discussion of students with special needs in the third edition. For the current edition, Dr. Theodore Christ of the University of Southern Mississippi has developed a Companion Website that will support readers in their efforts to assess their own learning, communicate with one another, and expand their knowledge of various topics in the book by visiting relevant sites on the World Wide Web. Also for this fifth edition, Dr. Jayne Downey of Montana State University has come on board as co-author of the *Instructor's Manual* and *Multimedia Guide*; widely praised by students, Jayne has drawn on her own teaching experiences to greatly enrich the content of these ancillary materials.

Many other colleagues have strengthened the final product considerably by reviewing one or more versions of the book. Reviewers for the first four editions were: Joyce Alexander, Indiana University; Eric Anderman, University of Kentucky; Margaret D. Anderson, SUNY–Cortland; J. C. Barton, Tennessee Technical University; Timothy A. Bender, Southwest Missouri State University; Phyllis Blumenfeld, University of Michigan; Randy L. Brown, University of Central Oklahoma; Stephen L. Benton, Kansas State University; Karen L. Block, University of Pittsburgh; Kathryn J. Biacindo, California State University–Fresno; Barbara Bishop, Eastern New Mexico University; Robert Braswell, Winthrop College; Kay S. Bull, Oklahoma State University; Margaret W. Cohen, University of Missouri–St. Louis; Theodore Coladarci, University of Maine; Roberta Corrigan, University of Wisconsin–Milwaukee; Richard D. Craig, Towson State University; José Cruz, Jr., The Ohio State University; Peggy Dettmer, Kansas State University; Joan Dixon, Gonzaga University; Leland K. Doebler, University of Montevallo; Catherine Emilhovich, SUNY–Buffalo; Joanne B. Engel, Oregon State University; Kathy Farber, Bowling Green State University; William R. Fisk, Clemson University; Victoria Fleming, Miami University of Ohio; M. Arthur Garmon, Western Michigan University; Roberta J. Garza, Pan American University–Brownsville; Cheryl Greenberg, University of North Carolina–Greensboro; Richard Hamilton, University of Houston; Jennifer Mistretta Hampston, Youngstown State University; Arthur Hernandez, University of Texas–San Antonio; Frederick C. Howe, Buffalo State College; Dinah Jackson, University of Northern Colorado; Janina M. Jolley, Clarion University of Pennsylvania; Caroline Kaczala, Cleveland State University; CarolAnne M. Kardash, University of Missouri–Columbia; Nancy F. Knapp, University of Georgia; Mary Lou Koran, University of Florida; Randy Lennon, University of Northern Colorado; Pamela Manners, Troy State University; Hermine H. Marshall, San Francisco State University; Teresa McDevitt, University of Northern Colorado; Sharon McNeely, Northeastern Illinois University; Michael Meloth, University of Colorado–Boulder; Bruce P. Mortenson, Louisiana State University; Janet Moursund, University of Oregon; Gary A. Negin, California State University; Joe Olmi, The University of Southern Mississippi; Helena Osana, Concordia University; Judy Pierce, Western Kentucky University; James R. Pullen, Central Missouri State University; Gary F. Render, University of Wyoming; Robert S. Ristow, Western Illinois University; Gregg Schraw, University of Nebraska–Lincoln; Dale H. Schunk, University of North Carolina–Greensboro; Mark Seng, University of Texas; Glenn E. Snelbecker, Temple University; Johnna Shapiro, University of California–Davis; Harry L. Steger, Boise State University; Bruce Torff, Hofstra University; Ann Turnbull, University of Kansas; Julianne C. Turner, University of Notre Dame; Enedina Vazquez, New Mexico State University; Alice A. Walker, SUNY–Cortland; Mary Wellman, Rhode Island College; Jane A. Wolfle, Bowling Green State University; and Karen Zabrucky, Georgia State University. Coming on board for the fifth edition were these reviewers: Eric M. Anderman, University of Kentucky; Linda M. Anderson, Michigan State University; Phyllis Blumenfeld, University of Michigan; Roberta Corrigan, University of Wisconsin–Milwaukee; Mary Gauvain, University of California–Riverside; P. Karen Murphy, The Pennsylvania State University; and Helena Osana, Concordia University.

On the home front, Ann Shump helps me on a part-time basis, gathering artifacts and permissions for the book and Student Artifact Library. Ann knows everyone in town, or at least it seems so, and her gentle yet persistent ways have encouraged many teachers and children to contribute their work to help me elucidate important principles and strategies. Furthermore, some of my own students and teacher interns—especially Jenny Bressler, Kathryn Broadhead, Ryan Francoeur, Gerry Holly, Michele Minichiello, Shelly Lamb, Kim Sandman, Melissa Tillman, Nick Valente, and Brian Zottoli—have agreed to let me use their interviews, essays, and experiences as examples. Teachers and administrators in several school districts, and especially in New Hampshire's Oyster River School District, have allowed me to share their strategies with my readers; I thank Liz Birnam, Berneen Bratt, Don Burger, Tom Carroll, Barbara Dee, Jackie Filion, Sarah Gagnon, Dinah Jackson, Sheila Johnson, Don Lafferty, Carol Lincoln, Sharon McManus, Linda Mengers, Mark Nichols, Susan O'Byrne, Ann Reilly, Gwen Ross, and my daughter Tina (now a second-grade teacher herself).

Many young people, too, deserve thanks for letting me use their work. In particular, I want to acknowledge the contributions of the following present and former students: Andrew and Katie Belcher; Noah and Shea Davis; Zachary Derr; Amaryth, Andrew, and Anthony Gass; Ben and Darcy Geraud; Dana Gogolin; Colin Hedges; Erin Islo; Charlotte Jeppsen; Laura Linton; Michael McShane; Frederik Meissner; Meghan Milligan; Alex, Jeff, and Tina Ormrod; Patrick Paddock; Isabelle Peters; Ian Rhoads; Corey Ross; Ashton and Haley Russo; Connor Sheehan; Matt and Melinda Shump; Andrew Teplitz; Emma Thompson; Grace Tober; Grant Valentine; and Geoff Wuehrmann; also Kyle and his grandfather, who so generously allowed me to use Kyle's writing samples in Chapter 2.

Last but certainly not least, I must thank my husband and children, who have for many years forgiven my countless hours spent either buried in my books and journals or else glued to my computer. Without their continuing support and understanding of what has, for me, become a passion, this book would never have seen the light of day.

J. E. O.

EDUCATOR LEARNING CENTER:
AN INVALUABLE ONLINE RESOURCE

Merrill Education and the Association for Supervision and Curriculum Development (ASCD) invite you to take advantage of a new online resource, one that provides access to the top research and proven strategies associated with ASCD and Merrill—the Educator Learning Center. At **www.educatorlearningcenter.com**, you will find resources that will enhance readers' understanding of course topics and of current educational issues, in addition to being invaluable for further research.

How the Educator Learning Center Will Help Readers Become Better Teachers

With the combined resources of Merrill Education and ASCD, instructors and students will find a wealth of tools and materials to better prepare them for the classroom.

Research

- More than 600 articles from the ASCD journal *Educational Leadership* discuss everyday issues faced by practicing teachers.
- A direct link on the site to Research Navigator™ provides access to many of the leading education journals, as well as extensive content detailing the research process.
- Excerpts from Merrill Education texts provide insights on important topics of instructional methods, diverse populations, assessment, classroom management, technology, and refining classroom practice.

Classroom Practice

- Hundreds of lesson plans and teaching strategies are categorized by content area and age range.
- Case studies and classroom video footage provide virtual field experience for reflection.
- Computer simulations and other electronic tools keep future teachers abreast of today's classrooms and current technologies.

Look into the Value of Educator Learning Center Yourself

A four-month subscription to Educator Learning Center is $25 but is **FREE** when packaged with any Merrill Education text. In order for your students to have access to this site, you must use this special value-pack ISBN number **WHEN** placing your textbook order with the bookstore: **0-13-154823-9**. Your students will then receive a copy of the text packaged with a free ASCD pincode. To preview the value of this website to you and your students, please go to **www.educatorlearningcenter.com** and click on "Demo."

Brief Contents

Contents

Chapter 9   Behaviorist Views of Learning   294

610 ## Chapter 10   Social Cognitive Views of Learning   328

610 ## Chapter 11   Motivation and Affect   364

610 ## Chapter 12   Cognitive Factors in Motivation   390

PART III   CLASSROOM STRATEGIES

Chapter 13 Instructional Strategies   432

Chapter 14 Creating a Productive Learning Environment   482

Chapter 15 Classroom Assessment Strategies   522

Special Topics

CLASSROOM MANAGEMENT AND TEACHER-STUDENT RELATIONSHIPS

CULTURAL AND ETHNIC DIFFERENCES

EDUCATIONAL PSYCHOLOGY

Developing Learners

Educational Psychology and Teacher Decision Making

$\mathcal{E}$ach time I walk through the front door of a school building, I am reminded of how exciting and energizing it is to interact and work with children and adolescents. Watching young people acquire an understanding of the world around them, derive pleasure from literature and music, collaborate with peers in accomplishing common goals, and gain increasing confidence in their own abilities—all of these things make teaching one of the most rewarding professions on the planet.

Yet teaching is also a very complex, challenging enterprise. Picture yourself standing in front of a class of twenty-five children or adolescents. Your goal is that your students *learn* something—perhaps how to distinguish between nouns and pronouns, interpret bar graphs, dribble a basketball, or diagnose the problem in a malfunctioning automobile engine. It appears, however, that the students are less interested in accomplishing the task than you are. Some are attending to your lesson, but many others are not. Sarah and Marta, the best of friends, are whispering and giggling. Clifton and Lenesa seem lost in their thoughts. Danny, Joe, and Friedrich are poking and shoving one another, and their behaviors seem to be escalating into a major conflict. At the back of the room, Nicole is slumped deep in her chair with her arms crossed and a you-can't-make-me-do-it expression on her face.

Certainly, effective teaching involves presenting a topic or skill in such a way that students can understand and master it. But it involves many other things as well. For instance, teachers must get students' attention (consider Clifton and Lenesa), motivate students to *want* to learn the subject matter (consider Nicole), and transform existing interpersonal relationships—some friendly, some not—into a cohesive, respectful, and productive learning community. Furthermore, effective teaching requires determining where students are currently "at" in their learning and development—what they know and don't know, what they can and cannot do, what cognitive and social skills they have and have not acquired, and so on. And it requires accommodating students' diverse backgrounds, beliefs, and family circumstances, as well as the physical, cognitive, and behavioral disabilities that some students may have.

Mastering the multifaceted nature of teaching takes time and practice, of course. But it also takes knowledge about developmental trends, individual and group differences, and human learning and motivational processes, as well as an understanding of how to translate such knowledge into effective classroom practice. The field of **educational psychology**, which applies psychological principles and theories to instructional practice, provides a solid foundation in such knowledge and understanding.

In this first chapter we will begin our exploration of educational psychology by addressing the following questions:

* What misconceptions do future teachers often have about children, learning, motivation, and instruction?
* What resources can teachers draw on to help them make good decisions in the classroom?
* How can practicing teachers continue to improve throughout their professional teaching careers?
* What basic principles can facilitate learning about and studying virtually any topic, including educational psychology itself?

We will begin our exploration of such issues by looking at 6-year-old Lupita and her teacher, Ms. Padilla.

CASE STUDY: *Hidden Treasure*

Six-year-old Lupita has just enrolled in Ms. Padilla's kindergarten classroom. The daughter of migrant workers, Lupita has been raised in Mexico by her grandmother, who has had limited financial resources and been able to provide very few playthings such as toys, puzzles, crayons, and scissors. Ms. Padilla rarely calls on Lupita in class because of her apparent lack of academic skills. By midyear, Ms. Padilla is thinking about holding Lupita back for a second year of kindergarten.

Lupita is always quiet and well behaved in class; in fact, she's so quiet that Ms. Padilla sometimes forgets she's there. Yet a researcher's video camera captures a different side to Lupita. On one occasion Lupita is quick to finish her Spanish assignment and so starts to

■ **educational psychology** Discipline encompassing the nature of learning, development, motivation, diversity, and assessment, especially as these topics relate to classroom practice.

work on a puzzle during her free time. A classmate approaches, and he and Lupita begin playing with a box of toys. A teacher aide asks the boy whether he has finished his Spanish assignment, implying that he should return to complete it, but the boy does not understand the aide's subtle message. Lupita gently persuades the boy to go back and finish his work. She then returns to her puzzle and successfully fits most of it together. Two classmates having difficulty with their own puzzles request Lupita's assistance, and she competently and patiently shows them how to assemble puzzles and how to help each other.

Ms. Padilla is amazed when she views the videotape, which shows Lupita to be a competent girl with strong teaching and leadership skills. Ms. Padilla readily admits, "I had written her off . . . her and three others. They had met my expectations and I just wasn't looking for anything else." Ms. Padilla and her aides begin working closely with Lupita on academic skills, and they often allow her to take a leadership role in group activities. At the end of the school year, Lupita obtains achievement test scores indicating exceptional competence in language skills and mathematics, and she is promoted to first grade. (based on a case study in Carrasco, 1981.)

▚ Why might the teacher have initially underestimated Lupita's academic skills? Might Lupita's background be a reason? Might her classroom behavior be a reason?

▚ What might have happened to Lupita if her behavior with classmates had gone unnoticed? How might her academic life have been different?

TEACHING AS DECISION MAKING

Over the years, Ms. Padilla has almost certainly had kindergartners who lacked some of the basic knowledge and skills—color and shape names, counting, the alphabet, and so on—on which early academic success depends. Some of these children have probably come from lower-income, minority-group backgrounds, just as Lupita has. And in Ms. Padilla's experience, children who can answer questions and contribute to class discussions usually speak up or raise their hands, but Lupita is quiet and restrained, so much so that she's almost invisible. With such data in hand, Ms. Padilla initially draws the conclusion that Lupita may not have mastered the knowledge and skills she will need to be successful in first grade the following year.

On a typical day teachers take on a variety of roles, including subject matter experts, tutors, consultants, motivators, behavior managers, confidantes, mediators, and evaluators. But above all, teachers are *decision makers*: They must continually choose among many possible strategies for helping students learn, develop, and achieve. In fact, some researchers (C. M. Clark & Peterson, 1986) have estimated that classroom teachers must make a nontrivial instructional decision approximately once every two minutes!

Some teacher decisions, such as how to decorate a class bulletin board or which words to include on a weekly spelling list, may be small, relatively inconsequential ones. But many other decisions can have a significant influence on students' learning, development, and long-term success. Let's consider what might have happened if Lupita's social skills and proficiency with puzzles had not been captured on videotape. Quite possibly, Lupita would have remained "forgotten" throughout much of the school year, getting little assistance on academic skills, few opportunities to practice her already strong leadership abilities, and little recognition of her many strengths. The teacher's actions, or rather *inactions*, may have led to a self-fulfilling prophecy: Lupita would *not* have had the skills she needed for first grade. As you will discover when you read Chapter 12, teachers' expectations for students can affect students' learning and achievement, in part because those expectations affect what and how much teachers do to *help* students learn and achieve.

Wise educational decisions are not made in a vacuum. Instead, they are based on hard data about which instructional strategies are effective and which are not, a solid understanding of how children learn and develop, and accurate information about what every student currently knows and can do. Psychological and educational research studies provide the hard data about effective and ineffective classroom strategies and offer insights about the nature of human learning and development. Psychological theories help us make sense of those data and so enhance our understanding of how children learn and develop. And regular, ongoing classroom assessments inform us about every student's current knowledge and skills. In the following sections, we look at each of these resources for educational decision making.

USING RESEARCH IN CLASSROOM DECISION MAKING

You yourself have been a student for many years now, and in the process you have undoubtedly learned a great deal about how young people learn and develop and about how teachers can best help them achieve. But exactly how much *do* you know? To help you find out, I've developed a short pretest, Ormrod's Own Psychological Survey (OOPS).

Experiencing FIRSTHAND · · · · · · · · · · · · · ·Ormrod's Own Psychological Survey (OOPS)

Decide whether each of the following statements is *true* or *false.*

True/False

_____   1. Most children 5 years of age and older are natural learners; they know the best way to learn something without having to be taught how to learn it.

_____   2. When we compare boys and girls, we find that the two groups are, on average, similar in their mathematical and verbal abilities.

_____   3. The best way to learn and remember a new fact is to repeat it over and over again.

_____   4. Although students initially have many misconceptions about the world, they quickly revise their thinking once their teacher presents information that contradicts what they believe.

_____   5. Students often misjudge how much they know about a topic.

_____   6. Taking notes during a lecture usually interferes with learning more than it helps.

_____   7. When a teacher rewards one student for appropriate behavior, the behavior of other students may also improve.

_____   8. Anxiety sometimes helps students learn and perform more successfully in the classroom.

_____   9. When we have children tutor their classmates in academic subject matter, we help only the students being tutored; the students doing the tutoring gain very little from the interaction.

_____   10. The ways in which teachers assess students' learning influence what and how the students actually learn.

· · · · · · ·

Now let's see how well you did on the OOPS. The answers, along with an explanation for each one, are as follows:

1. *Most children 5 years of age and older are natural learners; they know the best way to learn something without having to be taught how to learn it.* FALSE—Many students of all ages are relatively naive about how they can best learn something, and they often use inefficient strategies when they study. For example, most elementary students and a substantial number of high school students don't engage in **elaboration** as they study classroom material; that is, they don't analyze, interpret, or otherwise add their own ideas to the things they need to learn. (To illustrate, many students are apt to take the information presented in a history textbook at face value; they rarely take time to consider why historical figures made the decisions they did or how some events might have led to others.) Yet elaboration is one of the most effective ways of learning new information: Students learn the information more quickly and remember it better. We will look at developmental trends in elaboration as we discuss cognitive development in Chapter 2. We'll also explore the very important role that elaboration plays in long-term memory as we discuss cognitive processes in Chapter 6.

2. *When we compare boys and girls, we find that the two groups are, on average, similar in their mathematical and verbal abilities.* TRUE—Despite commonly held beliefs to the contrary, boys and girls tend to be similar in their ability to perform both mathematical and verbal academic tasks. Any differences in the average performance of boys and girls in these areas are usually too small for teachers to worry about. We will explore gender differences—and similarities as well—in Chapter 4.

■ How often do you elaborate when you read your textbooks?

■ **elaboration** Cognitive process in which learners expand on new information based on what they already know.

As teachers, we will continually be making decisions about how best to help students learn, develop, and achieve.

3. *The best way to learn and remember a new fact is to repeat it over and over again.* FALSE—Although repeating information over and over again is better than doing nothing at all, repetition is a relatively *ineffective* way to learn. Students learn information more easily and remember it longer when they connect it with the things they already know and when they elaborate on it. Chapter 6 describes several cognitive processes that promote students' long-term retention of school subject matter.

4. *Although students initially have many misconceptions about the world, they quickly revise their thinking once their teacher presents information that contradicts what they believe.* FALSE—As you will discover in Chapter 7, students typically have many misconceptions about the world (e.g., they may believe that rivers always run south rather than north or that the earth is round only in the sense that a pancake is round). They often hold strongly to these misconceptions even in the face of contradictory evidence or instruction. As teachers, one of our biggest challenges is to help students discard their erroneous beliefs in favor of more accurate and useful perspectives; strategies for promoting such *conceptual change* appear in Chapter 7.

5. *Students often misjudge how much they know about a topic.* TRUE—Contrary to popular opinion, students are usually *not* the best judges of what they do and do not know. For example, many students think that if they've spent a long time studying a textbook chapter, they must know its contents very well. Yet if they have spent most of their study time inefficiently (perhaps by "reading" without paying attention to meaning or by mindlessly copying definitions), they may know far less than they think they do. We will consider this *illusion of knowing* further in Chapter 8.

6. *Taking notes during a lecture usually interferes with learning more than it helps.* FALSE— In general, students who take notes learn more material from a lecture than students who don't take notes. Note taking appears to facilitate learning in at least two ways: It helps students put, or *store,* information into memory more effectively, and it allows them to review that information at a later time. Chapter 8 presents research concerning the effectiveness of note taking and other study strategies.

7. *When a teacher rewards one student for appropriate behavior, the behavior of other students may also improve.* TRUE—When teachers reward one student for behaving in a particular way, other students who have observed that student being rewarded sometimes begin to behave in a similar way. We will identify numerous roles that observation plays in learning as we explore social cognitive theory in Chapter 10.

8. *Anxiety sometimes helps students learn and perform more successfully in the classroom.* TRUE—Many people think that anxiety is always a bad thing. Yet for some classroom tasks, and especially for relatively easy tasks, a moderate level of anxiety actually *improves* students' learning and performance. We will consider the effects of anxiety and other emotions in Chapter 11.

9. *When we have children tutor their classmates in academic subject matter, we help only the students being tutored; the students doing the tutoring gain very little from the interaction.* FALSE—When students teach one another, the tutors often benefit as much as the students being tutored. For instance, in one research study, fourth graders who were doing relatively poorly in mathematics served as arithmetic tutors for first and second graders; the tutors themselves showed a substantial improvement in arithmetic skills (Inglis & Biemiller, 1997). We will look more closely at the effects of peer tutoring in Chapter 13.

10. *The ways in which teachers assess students' learning influence what and how the students actually learn.* TRUE—What and how students learn depend, in part, on how they expect their learning to be assessed. For example, students typically spend more time studying the things they think will be on a test than the things they think the test won't cover. And they are more likely to organize and integrate class material as they study if they expect assessment activities to require such organization and integration. Chapter 15 describes the effects of classroom assessment practices on students' learning.

TABLE 1.1   COMPARE/CONTRAST

Questions We Might Answer with Descriptive, Correlational, and Experimental Studies

DESCRIPTIVE STUDIES	CORRELATIONAL STUDIES	EXPERIMENTAL STUDIES
What percentage of high school students can think abstractly?	Are older students more capable of abstract thought than younger students?	Can abstract thinking skills be improved through specially designed educational programs?
What kinds of aggressive behaviors do we see in our schools, and with what frequencies do we see them?	Are students more likely to be aggressive at school if their parents are physically violent at home?	Which method is most effective in reducing aggressive behavior—reinforcing appropriate behavior, punishing aggressive behavior, or a combination of both?
How pervasive are gender stereotypes in books commonly used to teach reading in the elementary grades?	Are better readers also better spellers?	Which of two reading programs produces greater gains in reading comprehension?
How well have our nation's students performed on a recent standardized achievement test?	Do students who get the highest scores on multiple-choice tests also get the highest scores on essays dealing with the same material?	Do different kinds of tests (e.g., multiple choice vs. essay tests) encourage students to study in different ways and therefore affect what students actually learn?

How many of the OOPS items did you answer correctly? Did some of the false items seem convincing enough that you marked them true? Did some of the true items contradict certain beliefs you had? If either of these was the case, you are hardly alone. College students often agree with statements that seem obvious but are, in fact, completely wrong (Gage, 1991; Lennon, Ormrod, Burger, & Warren, 1990). Furthermore, many students in teacher education classes reject research findings when those findings appear to contradict their own personal beliefs and experiences (Borko & Putnam, 1996; Holt-Reynolds, 1992; Wideen, Mayer-Smith, & Moon, 1998).

■ Keep an open mind as you read this book. When you encounter ideas that at first seem incorrect, try to think of personal experiences and observations that support those ideas.

Drawing Conclusions from Research

It's easy to be persuaded by "common sense" and assume that what seems logical must be reality. Yet common sense and logic do not always tell us the true story about how people actually learn and develop, nor do they always give us accurate information about how best to help students succeed in the classroom. Educational psychologists believe that knowledge about teaching and learning should come from a more objective source of information—that is, from psychological and educational research.

Most of the ideas presented in this book are based either directly or indirectly on the results of research studies. Let's take a look at three major types of research—descriptive, correlational, and experimental—and at the kinds of conclusions we can draw from each one.

Descriptive Studies   A **descriptive study** does exactly what its name implies: It *describes* a situation. Descriptive studies might give us information about the characteristics of students, teachers, or schools; they might also provide information about how often certain events or behaviors occur. Descriptive studies allow us to draw conclusions about the way things are—the current state of affairs. The left column of Table 1.1 lists some examples of questions we could answer with descriptive studies.

Some descriptive studies are primarily *quantitative* in nature: They yield numbers that reflect percentages, frequencies, or averages related to certain characteristics or phenomena. For example, we are apt to get quantitative information from questionnaires and standardized tests. Other descriptive studies are more *qualitative*: They yield nonnumeric information—perhaps in the form of verbal reports, written documents, pictures, or maps—that captures a complex situation in a way that cannot be reduced to numbers. For example, we might get a great deal of qualitative information from one-on-one interviews or in-depth case studies of particular children, classrooms, or cultural groups.

■ **descriptive study** Study that enables researchers to draw conclusions about the current state of affairs.

Correlational Studies   A **correlational study** explores possible relationships among different things. For instance, it might tell us how closely two human characteristics are associated with one another, or it might give us information about the consistency with which certain human

■ **correlational study** Study that explores possible relationships among variables.

■ Correlations are often described numerically with a statistic known as a *correlation coefficient*. Correlation coefficients are described in Appendix A.

behaviors occur in conjunction with certain environmental conditions. In general, correlational studies enable us to draw conclusions about **correlation**: the extent to which two characteristics or phenomena tend to be found together or to change together.

The middle column of Table 1.1 lists some examples of questions we might answer with correlational studies. Notice how each of these questions asks about a relationship between two variables—between age and abstract thought, between student aggression and parental violence, between reading and spelling, or between multiple-choice and essay test scores.

Correlations between two variables allow us to make *predictions* about one variable if we know the status of the other. For example, if we find that older students are more capable of abstract thought than younger students, we can predict that tenth graders will benefit more from an abstract discussion of democratic government than fourth graders. If we find a correlation between multiple-choice and essay test scores, we can predict that those students who have done well on essays in a biology class will probably also do well on a national test covering the same topics in a multiple-choice format.

Experimental Studies   Descriptive and correlational studies describe things as they exist naturally in the environment. In contrast, an **experimental study**, or **experiment**, is a study in which the researcher somehow changes, or *manipulates*, one or more aspects of the environment (often called *independent variables*) and then measures the effects of such changes on something else. In educational research the "something else" being affected (often called the *dependent variable*) is usually some aspect of student behavior—perhaps performance on achievement tests, skill in executing a complex physical movement, persistence in trying to solve difficult mathematics problems, or ability to interact appropriately with peers. When carefully designed, experimental studies enable us to draw conclusions about *causation*—about *why* behaviors occur.

The right column of Table 1.1 lists examples of questions that might be answered through experimental studies. Notice how each question addresses a cause-effect relationship—the effect of educational programs on abstract thinking, the effect of reinforcement and punishment on aggressive behavior, the effect of a reading program on the development of reading comprehension, or the effect of test questions on students' learning.

■ Can you think of other questions that each type of research might address?

As you can see from the examples in the table, the difference between correlational and experimental research is an important one: Whereas correlational studies let us draw conclusions about associations, only experimental studies enable us to draw conclusions about cause and effect. The following section describes how one phenomenon in particular—visual-spatial thinking—has been studied with both correlational and experimental research studies and considers the conclusions we can draw from each type of study.

An Example: Research on Visual-Spatial Thinking   **Visual-spatial thinking** is the ability to imagine and mentally manipulate two- and three-dimensional figures. The exercise that follows provides three examples.

Experiencing FIRSTHAND · · · · · · · · · · · · · · · Three Examples of Visual-Spatial Thinking

1. The figure on the left is a flag. Which one or more of the three figures on the right represent(s) the *same* side of the flag? Which one or more of them represent(s) the *flip* side?

■ **correlation** Extent to which two variables are associated, such that when one variable increases, the other either increases or decreases somewhat predictably.

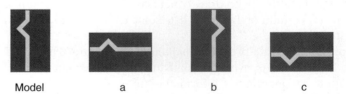

Model   a   b   c

■ **experimental study (experiment)** Study that involves the manipulation of one variable to determine its possible effect on another variable, allowing conclusions about cause-effect relationships.

2. When the figure on the left is folded along the dotted lines, it becomes a three-dimensional object. Which one or more of the four figures on the right represent(s) how this object might appear from different perspectives?

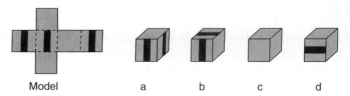

Model   a   b   c   d

■ **visual-spatial thinking** Ability to imagine and mentally manipulate two- and three-dimensional figures.

3. When the object on the left is rotated in three-dimensional space, it can look like one or more of the objects on the right. Which one(s)?

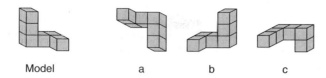

Model   a   b   c

tated to look like either a or c.

rection from which it is viewed, the object might look like either a or d. (3) The object can be ro-

Answer key: (1) Flags *a* and *b* are the flip side; flag *c* is the same side. (2) Depending on the di-

Three tasks modeled, respectively, after Thurstone & Jeffrey, 1956; G. K. Bennett, Seashore, & Wesman, 1982; and R. N. Shepard & Metzler, 1971.

· · · · · · ·

Visual-spatial thinking appears to be related to some aspects of mathematics achievement, although the nature of the connection is not totally clear (Friedman, 1995; Hegarty & Kozhevnikov, 1999; Threadgill-Sowder, 1985). Many correlational studies have found a relationship between gender and visual-spatial thinking: On average, boys have slightly better visual-spatial thinking skills than girls (Halpern & LaMay, 2000; Lippa, 2002). Are males genetically more capable of visual-spatial thought? Do parents encourage their sons to think in "visual-spatial" ways more frequently than they encourage their daughters? Do the typical childhood experiences of boys promote greater development of visual-spatial thinking ability? Unfortunately, correlational studies, although they demonstrate that a relationship exists, can never tell us for certain *why* it exists; they don't tell us whether genetics, parental encouragement, childhood experiences, a combination of such factors, or perhaps something else altogether is the cause of the relationship we see.

An experimental study by Sprafkin, Serbin, Denier, and Connor (1983) points to one probable cause of the gender difference in visual-spatial thinking. These researchers hypothesized that typical "male" toys (e.g., wooden blocks, Legos, trucks) provide greater opportunities for children to explore visual-spatial relationships than do typical "female" toys (e.g., dolls, board games). To test their hypothesis, they randomly selected half of the boys and girls enrolled in a preschool to be members of an experimental group, or **treatment group**, leaving the remaining children as an untrained **control group**. Children in both groups took a test of visual-spatial thinking, revealing that the treatment and control groups were equal (on average) in visual-spatial ability. During the next six weeks, the experimental group participated in twelve sessions involving instruction and structured play opportunities with blocks, building toys, puzzles, dominoes, and various other materials requiring visual-spatial thought. At the end of the six-week period, these specially trained children obtained higher average scores on a test of visual-spatial thinking than the untrained, control group children.

From this study with preschool children, we can draw a conclusion about a cause-effect relationship: We can say that structured exposure to certain types of toys promotes increased visual-spatial thinking ability. Other characteristics of the two groups of children were the same; for example, both groups began with equivalent visual-spatial thinking ability, and all the children attended the same preschool. Furthermore, because the children were randomly assigned to the training and nontraining conditions, we can assume that both groups were approximately the same (on average) in terms of such other factors as general intelligence, prior exposure to different types of toys, and home environment. Because the researchers eliminated other possible explanations for the differences they observed in the two groups of preschoolers, they could reasonably draw a conclusion about a cause-effect relationship: Increased exposure to certain types of toys fosters the development of visual-spatial thinking skills.

A Cautionary Note   To draw conclusions about causal relationships, we must eliminate other possible explanations for the outcomes we observe. As an example, imagine that Hometown School District wants to find out which of two reading programs, *Reading Is Great* (RIG) or *Reading and You* (RAY), leads to better reading in third grade. The district asks each of its third-grade teachers to choose one of these two reading programs and use it throughout a particular school year. The district then compares the end-of-year achievement test scores of students in the RIG and RAY classrooms and finds that RIG students have gotten substantially higher reading

■ Here the researchers separated the possible variables affecting visual-spatial thinking and kept all but one of them constant. Chapter 2 describes this process of *separating and controlling variables.*

■ **treatment group** People in a research study who are given a particular experimental treatment (e.g., a particular method of instruction).

■ **control group** People in a research study who are given either no treatment or a presumably ineffective (*placebo*) treatment.

Early exposure to certain types of toys encourages greater visual-spatial thinking ability for both boys and girls.

comprehension scores than RAY students. We might quickly jump to the conclusion that RIG promotes better reading comprehension than RAY—in other words, that a cause-effect relationship exists between instructional method and reading comprehension. But is this really so?

The fact is, the school district hasn't eliminated all other possible explanations for the difference in students' reading comprehension scores. Remember, the third-grade teachers selected the instructional program they used. Why did some teachers choose RIG and others choose RAY? Were the teachers who chose RIG different in some way from the teachers who chose RAY? Had RIG teachers taken more graduate courses in reading instruction, did they have higher expectations for their students, or did they devote more class time to reading instruction? If the RIG and RAY teachers were different from each other in any of these ways—or perhaps different in some other way we might not happen to think of—then the district hasn't eliminated an alternative explanation for why the RIG students have developed better reading skills than the RAY students. A better way to study the causal influence of reading program on reading comprehension would be to randomly assign teachers to the RIG and RAY programs, thereby making the two groups of teachers roughly equivalent in areas such as graduate level coursework, expectations for students, and class time devoted to reading instruction.

Be careful that you don't jump too quickly to conclusions about what factors are affecting students' learning, development, and behavior in particular situations. Scrutinize descriptions of research carefully, always with this question in mind: *Have the researchers ruled out other possible explanations for their results?* Only when the answer to this question is an undeniable *yes* should you draw a conclusion about a cause-effect relationship.

APPLYING PSYCHOLOGICAL THEORIES IN CLASSROOM DECISION MAKING

As researchers learn more and more about how things are (descriptive studies), what variables are associated with one another (correlational studies), and what events cause what outcomes (experimental studies), they begin to develop **theories** that integrate and explain their findings. Such theories are rarely set in stone. Rather, they are continually expanded and modified as additional data come to light, and in some cases one theory may be abandoned in favor of another that better explains the phenomena researchers have observed.

Throughout the book we will examine theories related to development, learning, thinking, behavior, and motivation. Although these theories will inevitably change in the future, they can be quite useful even in their present, "unfinished" forms. They help us pull together thousands of research studies into concise, integrated understandings of how children typically develop and learn, and they allow us to make inferences and predictions about how students in classrooms are apt to perform and achieve in particular situations. In general, theories can help us to both *explain* and *predict* human behavior, and so they will give us numerous ideas and insights about how best to help children and adolescents achieve academic and social success at school.

IMPORTANCE OF REGULAR ASSESSMENTS IN CLASSROOM DECISION MAKING

Most teachers regularly assess what their students know and can do, perhaps in the form of assignments, projects, presentations, and quizzes. But effective teachers don't limit themselves to such formal, planned evaluations. They continually observe their students in a variety of contexts—in the classroom, in the cafeteria, on the playground, on field trips, during extracurricular activities, with family members at parent-teacher conferences and school open houses—for clues about what students might be thinking, believing, feeling, and learning. Students' comments, questions, facial expressions, body language, work habits, and interactions with friends and classmates can provide valuable insights into their learning, development, and motivation. For instance, in our opening case study, Lupita's behavior during free time—her facility with puzzles, her correct interpretation of an aide's subtle message, and her skill in guiding and persuading her peers—reveals a great deal about her cognitive and social development.

■ **theory** Integrated set of concepts and principles developed to explain a particular phenomenon.

We will explore the topic of assessment in depth in Chapters 15 and 16, yet you will find implications for assessment in every chapter. Throughout this book, *Interpreting Student Artifacts and Behaviors* features will invite you to look below the surface of what children produce, say, and do and to form hypotheses about their knowledge, abilities, thoughts, and feelings. To get your feet wet in the process of assessment, try the following exercise.

Interpreting Student Artifacts and Behaviors

The Pet Who Came to Dinner
Seven-year-old Justin wrote the story shown here. As you read it, consider what you might conclude about

- Justin's progress in writing
- Justin's family
- The nature of Justin's home life

Clearly, Justin has learned how to spell some words but has not yet learned many others; for example, he spells *once* as "owans" or "ouns," *drink* as "briak," *water* as "wodr," *rushed* as "rust," and *started* as "stor did." Overall, he knows which alphabet letters represent which sounds in speech. However, he sometimes reverses the letter *d* so that it looks like a *b*, and he occasionally leaves out a sound when he spells a word (notice how his spelling of *drink* begins with *b* and omits the *n* sound). He has learned some common English spelling patterns; for instance, his misspelling of *snoring* ("soreing") includes a silent *e* (which is present in the word *snore*) and a correct spelling of the *-ing* ending. He has learned appropriate uses for periods and apostrophes, but he does not always know when one sentence should end and another should begin. He has learned to tell a simple story, but he does so merely by listing a series of seemingly unrelated events, and he has not yet learned that the title of a story should appear in a line by itself, centered at the top of the page.

Justin's story tells us a few things about his family and home life as well. For instance, it appears that he lives with both his mother and father. The family gives at least some attention to nutrition (it serves "melk" at dinner) and has sufficient financial resources to provide dessert ("dasrt") after the main course. Justin also talks about the pet reading the newspaper ("nuwspapr"), suggesting that reading is a familiar activity in the home.

Are such inferences about Justin accurate? Not necessarily. The conclusions we reach about our students are, like theories of development and learning, at best only reasonable guesses based on the evidence at hand. As such, we must think of them as *hypotheses* to be tested further rather than as indisputable *facts*. Nevertheless, they can give us guidance in the decisions we must continually make to help students learn, grow, and thrive.

ACCOMMODATING DIVERSITY IN THE CLASSROOM

In the opening case study, Lupita's background (e.g., her lower-income family, her Mexican heritage) almost certainly has implications for instructional strategies and other classroom practices. For instance, many Mexican immigrants feel more comfortable working cooperatively with, rather than competitively against, their peers (recall Lupita's willingness to help classmates with puzzles). And they are more accustomed to observing events quietly and unobtrusively than to asking adults for explanations (recall Lupita's "invisibility" in classroom activities). Thus, we might guess that cooperative learning groups and clear, concrete demonstrations would be especially effective for students with Mexican backgrounds.

All children are unique individuals who bring different strengths, weaknesses, and cultural traditions to the classroom, and as teachers, we must take such diversity into account when identifying strategies for working with each student. Some differences may reflect **group differences**—whether students are male or female, belong to one or another ethnic group, come from a middle-income or lower-income home, live in an urban or rural environment, and so on. Yet

- **group differences** Consistently observed differences (on average) among diverse groups of students (e.g., students of different genders or ethnic backgrounds).

TABLE 1.2   STUDENTS IN INCLUSIVE SETTINGS

Categories of Students with Special Educational Needs

GENERAL CATEGORY	DESCRIPTION	SPECIFIC CATEGORY(IES) INCLUDED	EXAMPLE
Students with specific cognitive or academic difficulties	These students exhibit an uneven pattern of academic performance; they may have unusual difficulty with certain kinds of tasks yet perform quite successfully on other tasks.	• Learning disabilities • Attention-deficit hyperactivity disorder (ADHD) • Speech and communication disorders	James has exceptional difficulty learning to read but seems to grasp ideas in science and mathematics quite easily.
Students with social or behavioral problems	These students exhibit social, emotional, or behavioral difficulties serious enough to interfere significantly with their academic performance.	• Emotional and behavioral disorders • Autism	Amy has frequent aggressive outbursts during which she hits or kicks whomever happens to be near her. She rarely interacts with either her teacher or her classmates in a socially acceptable manner.
Students with general delays in cognitive and social functioning	These students exhibit low achievement in virtually all academic areas, and they have social skills typical of much younger children.	• Mental retardation	Although Margaret is 11 years old, her academic skills are similar to those of a 7-year-old, and she often blurts out whatever is on her mind without considering how other people might react to her comments.
Students with physical and sensory challenges	These students have disabilities caused by diagnosed physical or medical problems.	• Physical and health impairments • Visual impairments • Hearing loss • Severe and multiple disabilities	After sustaining a brain injury in a car accident, Jonathan tires easily, and he has trouble remembering some of the things he studies in class.
Students with advanced cognitive development	These students have unusually high ability in one or more areas.	• Giftedness	Mike shows exceptional skill and creativity in writing; for instance, he has won several local and statewide writing contests.

diversity also emerges from **individual differences**—variability in intelligence, personality, physical agility, and the like—that are seen within any single group. As long as we use what we know about group and individual differences to form *tentative hypotheses* (rather than hard-and-fast conclusions) about what strategies are apt to be effective with each student, and as long as we continue to *modify* those hypotheses and strategies as we learn more about each student, we will be able to maximize our effectiveness in the classroom.

In many cases we will be able to accommodate students' unique characteristics within the context of general classroom practices and activities. Yet some students are different enough that they require specially adapted instructional materials or practices to help them maximize their learning and development. Now, more than ever before, many of these **students with special needs** are in general education classrooms, a practice called **inclusion**. Regardless of the grade level or subject matter you plan to teach, you should expect to have students with a wide variety of special needs in your classroom at one time or another.

We will explore group differences, individual differences, and special needs in depth in Chapters 4 and 5. However, student diversity is such an important topic that I include a section on it in *every* chapter of the book. Discussions of differences between boys and girls and among various ethnic groups will be commonplace, and we will often address the particular needs of students from lower-income families. Furthermore, every chapter includes a *Students in Inclusive Settings* table that provides instructional strategies for students within five general categories of special needs. These categories are described and illustrated in Table 1.2. Keep in mind, however, that categorizing students with special needs in *any* way is a controversial issue (more about this point in Chapter 5). Ultimately, we must remember that all of our students, including those with special needs, can benefit from having instruction tailored to their unique characteristics.

■ **individual differences** Variability in abilities and characteristics (intelligence, personality, etc.) among students at a particular age.

■ **students with special needs** Students different enough from their peers that they require specially adapted instructional materials and practices.

■ **inclusion** Practice of educating all students, including those with severe and multiple disabilities, in neighborhood schools and general education classrooms.

DEVELOPING AS A TEACHER

As a beginning teacher, you may initially find your role a bit overwhelming. After all, you may have twenty-five to thirty students (possibly even more) in your classroom at any one time, and they are all apt to have different backgrounds, ability levels, and needs. In such a situation your role as decision maker will be a challenging one indeed. So in the first few weeks or months, you may need to rely heavily on the standard lessons that curriculum development specialists provide (Berliner, 1988). But as you gain experience, you will eventually be able to make decisions about routine situations and problems quickly and efficiently, giving you the time and energy to think creatively and flexibly about how best to teach your students (Borko & Putnam, 1996; Sternberg, 1996a).

The chapters that follow describe many ways you can help your students learn and develop. But it is equally important that *you* learn and develop as well, especially in your role as a teacher. Following are several strategies for doing so:

◎ *Continue to take courses in teacher education.*   Additional coursework in teaching is one surefire way of keeping up-to-date on the latest theoretical perspectives and research results related to classroom practice. In general, both preservice teacher education and on-the-job professional development definitely *do* enhance teaching effectiveness (Darling-Hammond, 1995; Guskey & Sparks, 2002).

◎ *Learn as much as you can about the subject matter you teach.*   When we look at effective teachers—for example, those who are flexible in their approaches to instruction, help students develop a thorough understanding of classroom subject matter, and convey obvious enthusiasm for whatever they are teaching—we typically find teachers who know their subject matter extremely well (Borko & Putnam, 1996; Cochran & Jones, 1998; Phillip, Flores, Sowder, & Schappelle, 1994; Windschitl, 2002).

◎ *Learn as much as you can about specific strategies for teaching your particular subject matter.*   In addition to knowing general teaching strategies, it is also helpful to develop strategies specific to the topic you are teaching; a repertoire of such strategies is known as **pedagogical content knowledge**. Effective teachers typically have a large number of strategies for teaching various topics and skills (Borko & Putnam, 1996; Brophy, 1991; Cochran & Jones, 1998; L. S. Shulman, 1986). Furthermore, they can usually anticipate—and so can also address—the difficulties students will have, as well as the kinds of errors students will make, in the process of mastering a skill or body of knowledge (Borko & Putnam, 1996; D. C. Smith & Neale, 1991). Some teachers keep journals or other records of the strategies they develop and use in particular situations and then reuse these strategies as needed (Berliner, 1988).

◎ *Believe that you can make a difference in students' lives.*   In Chapter 10 we will consider the nature of **self-efficacy**: the extent to which people believe they are capable of executing certain behaviors or reaching certain goals. Students are more likely to try to learn something if they believe they *can* learn it—in other words, if they have high self-efficacy. But you, too, must have high self-efficacy. Believing that you can be a good teacher will help you persist in the face of occasional setbacks and ultimately be effective in the classroom (Ashton, 1985). Students who achieve at high levels are apt to be those whose teachers have confidence in what they *themselves* can do for their students (Ashton, 1985; J. A. Langer, 2000; Tschannen-Moran, Woolfolk Hoy, & Hoy, 1998).

Teaching, like any other complex skill, takes time and practice to master. And you, like any other learner, will inevitably make a few mistakes, especially at the beginning. But you *will* improve over time. If you base classroom decisions on documented principles and sound educational practice, you can undoubtedly make a difference in the lives of your students. In Figure 1.1, 12-year-old Grace explains just how much of a difference a single teacher can make.

◎ *Continually reflect on and critically examine your assumptions, inferences, and teaching practices.*   In Chapter 8 we will address **critical thinking**, the process of evaluating the accuracy and worth of one's information and lines of reasoning. Our focus there will be on encouraging students to think critically about classroom subject matter. Yet it is essential that *we* think critically as well, both about why our students might be behaving in particular ways and achieving

■ **pedagogical content knowledge** Knowledge about effective methods of teaching a specific content area.

■ **self-efficacy** Belief that one is capable of executing certain behaviors or reaching certain goals.

■ **critical thinking** Process of evaluating the accuracy and worth of information and lines of reasoning.

FIGURE 1.1 Twelve-year-old Grace describes her favorite teacher.

I know a great teacher and his name is Mr. Shipley. Mr. Shipley was my 6th grade teacher for Science, Social Studies, and Flex (or Study hall). This man is my favorite teacher for many reasons.

I had Science during First period and since, I don't think that it is the most interesting subject, I would often get bored and lose interest in what he was saying. But every so often Mr. Shipley would do something crazy and funny to kind-of snap me out of my daze and put me back into class. I thank him for that!

Mr. Shipley was always understanding and he seemed to have a special bond with kids. I was in his study hall and during that period, 6th period, the 7th graders had lunch. That is a free time to do whatever you want, so the 7th graders would wander down to talk to him. (Of course they'd ask for a Jolly Rancher from his famous stash in his desk!) I admire and was amazed to see how he continued to bring students from years past, down to him.

Not only was Mr. Shipley funny, understanding, and just a great, all around great teacher, he believed in me. Mr. Shipley had faith in me and that is something I knew my other teachers had, but rarely expressed. I always got an A or A+ in his classes and Language Arts, but Math was a struggle

for me. I always ended up with a B+ in that class. But I tried harder and harder to get that B+ up to an A, but I just couldn't. So each time grade card time rolled around, I'd wind up with all A's and A+'s except for Math, a B+. I worked so hard all year for a 4.0 (straight A's) but wound up with an average of 3.899. Mr. Shipley always told me that I'd "get 'em next time." And I did! I am now in 7th grade with a 4.0, straight A's! Even in Math. I also made the tennis team, 1st doubles, Mr. Shipley believed in me All The Way! So, I owe a lot to him.

Mr. Shipley - the funny man, the understander, the believer: My favorite teacher!

at particular levels and also about how our own classroom practices may be influencing their behavior and achievement. Effective teachers engage in **reflective teaching**: They continually examine and critique their assumptions, inferences, and instructional practices, and they regularly adjust their beliefs and strategies in the face of new evidence (T. Hogan, Rabinowitz, & Craven, 2003; Silverberg, 2003).

◎ *Conduct your own research.* The research literature on learning, motivation, development, and instructional practice grows by leaps and bounds every year. Nevertheless, teachers sometimes encounter problems in the classroom that existing research findings don't address. In such circumstances we have an alternative: We can conduct our own research. When we conduct systematic studies of issues and problems in our own schools, with the goal of seeking more effective interventions in the lives of our students, we are conducting **action research**.

Action research is becoming an increasingly popular endeavor among teachers, educational administrators, and other educational professionals. It takes a variety of forms; for example, it might involve assessing the effectiveness of a new teaching technique, gathering information about students' opinions on a schoolwide issue, or conducting an in-depth case study of a particular student (Cochran-Smith & Lytle, 1993; Mills, 2003). Many colleges and universities now offer courses in action research. You can also find inexpensive paperback books on the topic (e.g., Mills, 2003; Stringer, 2004).

◎ *Learn as much as you can about the culture(s) of the community in which you are working.* In the following chapters (and especially in Chapter 4), we will identify numerous ways in which students from diverse cultural groups may think and behave differently than *you* did as a child. Yet a textbook can give only a sample of these many possible differences. You can more effectively become aware of students' cultural beliefs and practices if you participate in local community activities and converse regularly with community members (McCarty & Watahomigie, 1998; Rogoff, 2003; H. L. Smith, 1998).

Throughout the book you'll find *Into the Classroom* and *Creating a Productive Classroom Environment* boxes that identify and illustrate concrete strategies for classroom practice. The first of these, "Becoming a More Effective Teacher," appears on the next page. Let's turn our attention now to a more immediate concern: studying educational psychology effectively.

STUDYING EDUCATIONAL PSYCHOLOGY EFFECTIVELY

As you read this book, you will gain many insights about how you can help your students more effectively learn the things you want to teach them. At the same time, I hope you will also gain insights about how *you yourself* can learn course material. But rather than wait until we begin our discussion of learning in Chapter 6, let's look briefly at three principles of effective learning that you can apply as you read and study this book:

■ **reflective teaching** Regular, ongoing examination and critique of one's assumptions and instructional strategies, and revision of them as necessary to enhance students' learning and development.

■ **action research** Research conducted by teachers and other school personnel to address issues and problems in their own schools or classrooms.

Becoming a More Effective Teacher

 Use some of the standard lessons that curriculum development specialists provide, especially in your first few weeks or months in the classroom.

A science teacher consults the teaching manual that accompanies her class textbook for ideas about how to make science come alive for her students.

 As you gain experience, modify standard lessons and create your own lessons to better meet students' needs and accomplish your instructional goals.

When a high school social studies teacher begins using a new geography textbook, he peruses the accompanying teacher's manual. He notices that the manual's lesson plans focus almost exclusively on meaningless memorization of geographic concepts and principles. Rather than use these lessons, he develops classroom activities of his own that will encourage his students to apply geography to real-life situations.

 Keep a journal of the instructional strategies you use and their relative effectiveness.

As a way of winding down at bedtime, a new teacher reflects on his day in the classroom. He picks up the notebook and pen on his bedside table and jots down notes about the strategies that did and did not work well in class that day.

 Seek the advice and suggestions of your more experienced colleagues.

A fourth-grade teacher is teaching her students long division, but after a week they still don't understand the process. In the teacher's lounge she consults with two fellow teachers for ideas about how she might approach the topic differently.

 Continue your education, both formally and informally.

A middle school science teacher takes advantage of a tour package to Costa Rica designed specifically for teachers. There she will study the plants, animals, and ecology of the rain forest. She will also take many pictures and collect numerous specimens that she can show her students.

 Conduct your own research to answer questions about your students and about the effectiveness of your teaching practices.

Over the course of the school year, a second-grade school teacher alternates among three different approaches to teaching the weekly spelling words. At the end of the school year, he compares his students' spelling quiz scores for each of the three methods and sees that one approach led to noticeably higher scores than the other two.

 Remember that teaching, like any other complex skill, takes time and practice to master.

A teacher continues to try new instructional techniques described in professional journals. As he does so, he adds to his repertoire of effective teaching strategies and becomes increasingly able to adjust his methods to the diverse population of students in his classroom.

◎ *Students learn more effectively when they relate new information to what they already know.* Try to connect the ideas you read in this book with things you are already familiar with. For example, connect new ideas with your own past experiences, with your previous course work, with things you have observed in schools, or with your general knowledge about the world. I'll occasionally help you with this process by asking you to reflect on your prior experience, knowledge, and beliefs related to a topic. One of the readings in the *Study Guide and Reader*, "Common Themes Throughout the Book," can also help you by pointing out a few central ideas that continually pop up in the book in different forms.

■ See "Common Themes Throughout the Book" in the *Study Guide and Reader* for key concepts that can help you interrelate many ideas in the book.

◎ *Students learn more effectively when they elaborate on new information.* As you learned earlier, elaboration is a process of adding one's own ideas to new information. In most situations elaboration enables us to learn information with greater understanding, remember it better, and apply it more readily when we need it. So try to think *beyond* the information you read. Generate new examples of concepts. Draw inferences from the research findings presented. Identify your own educational applications of various principles and theories.

One of the most effective ways to elaborate on the ideas you see in a textbook is to see those ideas in action, and the compact disks (CDs) *Video Examples to Accompany Educational Psychology: Developing Learners* will help you do just that. These CDs contain video clips of children and adolescents discussing a variety of topics (Volume 1) and numerous clips of actual classroom lessons (Volume 2). Throughout this book I will draw your attention to specific clips that relate to concepts and theories we are discussing.

■ View the video clips on the video CDs to help you tie concepts and theories of educational psychology to real children, adolescents, and classroom lessons.

◎ *Students learn more effectively when they periodically check to make sure they have learned.* There are times when even the best of us don't concentrate on what we're reading—when we are actually thinking about something else as our eyes go down the page. So stop once in a while (perhaps once every two or three pages) to make sure you have really learned and understood

■ How frequently do you apply these principles when you study?

the things you've been reading. Try to summarize the material. Ask yourself questions about it. Make sure everything makes logical sense to you. Don't become a victim of that *illusion of knowing* I mentioned earlier.

Perhaps you are a student who has been following these principles for years. But in case such learning strategies are relatively new for you, I've provided margin notes (designated by a dark blue square) to help you learn and study as you read this book. These notes give suggestions for how you might think about the material in nearby paragraphs. With practice, the strategies I recommend should eventually become second nature to you as you read and study in all your classes.

Furthermore, the case studies in each chapter can help you relate chapter content to concrete classroom situations. An opening case study introduces you to a variety of concepts and principles and is frequently referred to in the chapter. A case study and questions at the end of each chapter ask you to apply concepts and principles you have just learned. You will find my own analyses of the ending cases in Appendix B.

■ You can find chapter summaries in the *Study Guide and Reader* that accompanies this textbook.

An additional feature of every chapter is "The Big Picture," a section that synthesizes chapter content and highlights key ideas. In "The Big Picture" section that follows, I identify the most important points of Chapter 1.

THE BIG PICTURE

As teachers, we must make innumerable daily decisions about how to teach, interact with, and respond to the students in our classrooms. Although we may sometimes be able to use common sense in making these decisions, such "sense" can lead us to draw unwarranted and possibly inaccurate conclusions. We are most likely to make good decisions—those that maximize students' learning and development over the long run—when we base them both on knowledge of current theories and research and on a good grasp of each student's strengths, weaknesses, and background experiences relevant to the subject matter at hand.

Effective teachers think critically and reflectively about their assumptions, beliefs, and classroom strategies; and they continue to modify what they think and do as they acquire new informa-

tion. Such information comes from a variety of sources: from both formal and informal assessments of students' progress, from consultations with parents and colleagues, from advancements in theory and research, and occasionally from their own research.

Teaching is a multifaceted process that often seems overwhelming to new teachers. Keep in mind, however, that even the most masterful of teachers had to begin their teaching careers as novices, and they probably entered their first classroom with the same concerns and uncertainties that you may be having now. Be confident that with time, practice, a solid understanding of how children and adolescents learn and develop, a large toolkit of instructional strategies, and each student's best interests at heart, you, too, can make a significant difference in young people's lives.

CASE STUDY: *More Harm Than Good?*

Mr. Gualtieri, a high school mathematics teacher, begins his class one Monday with an important announcement: "I've just obtained some new instructional software programs for the school's computer laboratory. These programs will give you practice in solving mathematical word problems. I strongly encourage you to stay after school once or twice a week to get extra practice on the computer whenever you're having trouble with the homework assignments I give you."

Mr. Gualtieri is firmly convinced that the new instructional software will help his students perform better in mathematics. To test his hypothesis, he keeps a record of which students report to the computer lab after school and which students do not. He then looks at how well the two groups of students perform on his next classroom test. Much to his surprise, he discovers that, on average, the students who have stayed after school to use the computer software have gotten *lower* scores than those who did not stay after school. "How can this be?" he puzzles. "Is the computer software actually doing more harm than good?"

- Is the computer software somehow making mathematics more difficult for students? Or is there another possible explanation for the students' lower scores?

- Which kind of study has Mr. Gualtieri conducted: descriptive, correlational, or experimental?

- Did Mr. Gualtieri make a good or a bad decision in advising his students to use the computer software? Is there any way to answer this question from the information he has obtained?

Once you have answered these questions, compare your responses with those presented in Appendix B.

KEY CONCEPTS

educational psychology (p. 3)
elaboration (p. 5)
descriptive study (p. 7)
correlational study (p. 7)
correlation (p. 8)
experimental study (experiment) (p. 8)
visual-spatial thinking (p. 8)

treatment group (p. 9)
conrol group (p. 9)
theory (p. 10)
group differences (p. 11)
individual differences (p. 12)
students with special needs (p. 12)
inclusion (p. 12)

pedagogical content knowledge (p. 13)
self-efficacy (p. 13)
critical thinking (p. 13)
reflective teaching (p. 14)
action research (p. 14)

PRAXIS Turn to Appendix C, "Matching Book and Ancillary Content to the Praxis Principles of Learning and Teaching Tests," to discover sections of this chapter that may be especially applicable to the Praxis tests.

Companion Website

Now go to our Companion Website at www. pren-hall.com/ormrod to assess your understanding of chapter content with "Multiple-Choice Questions," apply comprehension in "Essay Questions," broaden your knowledge of educational psychology with related "Web Links," gain greater insight about classroom learning in "Learning in the Content Areas," and analyze and assess classroom work in the "Student Artifact Library."

2

Cognitive and Linguistic Development

*T*hink, *for a moment,* about your own experiences in the early elementary grades. What topics did you study, and what instructional strategies did your teachers use to teach those topics? Now think about your high school years. In what ways were the subject matter and instructional methods different from those in elementary school? Certainly many differences come to mind. For instance, in the early elementary grades you probably focused on basic knowledge and skills: learning letter-sound correspondences, reading simple prose, using correct capitalization and punctuation, adding and subtracting two-digit numbers, and so on. Your teachers probably provided a great deal of structure and guidance, giving you small, concrete tasks that would enable you to practice and eventually master certain information and procedures. By high school, however, you were studying complex topics—biological classifications, historical events, symbolism in literature and poetry, and so on—that were abstract and multifaceted, and your teachers put much of the burden of mastering those topics on *you.*

Such differences reflect the fact that classroom instruction must be *developmentally appropriate.* It must take into account the physical, cognitive, social, and emotional characteristics and abilities that a particular age-group is likely to have. It must also be geared toward helping students move forward toward adultlike levels of competence and independence. Even though teachers typically work with only a single age-group over the course of only one academic year, they are most effective when they understand how the tasks and activities within that academic year fit in with and contribute to students' overall academic and personal growth.

In Chapters 2 and 3, we will explore the nature of child and adolescent development. Our focus in this chapter will be on general principles of development and on the cognitive and linguistic capabilities that children acquire over time. In the process, we will address the following questions:

- What general principles characterize child and adolescent development?
- In what ways do children's brains change as they grow older, and what implications do such changes have for teachers?
- What insights do three theories of cognitive development—those of Jean Piaget, Lev Vygotsky, and information processing theorists—offer for classroom practice?
- What language capabilities can we typically expect for students at different grade levels?
- How are students likely to differ from one another in their cognitive and linguistic development, and how can we accommodate such differences?

In Chapter 3 we will turn our attention to the development of self-perceptions, social skills, peer relationships, and moral understandings.

CASE STUDY: *Economic Activities*

The students in Mr. Sand's advanced high school geography course are struggling with their reading assignments, and they readily share their frustration with their teacher.

"The textbook is really *hard.* I can't understand it at all!" Lucy whines.

"Same here!" Mike shouts out. "I'm really trying, Mr. Sand, but most of the time I have no idea what I'm reading." Many other students nod their heads in agreement.

"OK," Mr. Sand responds. "Let's see if we can figure out why you might be having trouble. Look at the section called 'Economic Activity' on page 55, which was part of last night's reading."

The class peruses this excerpt from the book:

Economic activities are those in which human beings engage to acquire food and satisfy other wants. They are the most basic of all activities and are found wherever there are people. Economic activity is divided into four sections. *Primary activity* involves the direct harvesting of the earth's resources. Fishing off the coast of Peru, pumping oil from wells in Libya, extracting iron ore from mines in Minnesota, harvesting trees for lumber in Chile, and growing wheat in China are all examples of primary production. The commodities that result from those activities acquire value from the effort required in production and from consumer demand.

The processing of commodities is classified as a *secondary activity.* In this sector items are increased in value by having their forms changed to enhance their usefulness. Thus, a primary commodity such as cotton might be processed into fabric, and that fabric might be cut and assembled as apparel. Textile manufacturing and apparel manufacturing are both secondary activities.

An economic activity in which a service is performed is classified as a *tertiary activity*. Wholesaling and retailing are tertiary activities by which primary and secondary projects are made available to consumers. Other tertiary activities include governmental, banking, educational, medical, and legal services, as well as journalism and the arts.

The service economy of the technologically most developed countries has become so large and complex that a fourth sector of *quarternary activity* is sometimes included. Institutions and corporations that provide information are in the quarternary sector. (Clawson & Fisher, 1998, p. 55)

"Tell me the kinds of problems you had when you read this passage," Mr. Sand suggests. "Then maybe I can help you understand it better."

The students eagerly describe their difficulties.

"I never heard of some of the words. What's *tertiary* mean? What's *quarternary*?"

"Yeah. And what are *commodities*?"

"There's too much to learn. Do you expect us to memorize *all* of this stuff?"

"OK, I see your point," Mr. Sand responds. "I guess this stuff can be pretty abstract. No, I don't want you to memorize it all. What's most important is that you get the main idea, which in this case is that different levels of economic activity build on one another. Here, let me show you what I mean. We start out with primary activities, which involve direct use of natural resources." Mr. Sand writes "Primary activity—using natural resources" on the chalkboard. "Who can give me some examples of natural resources we use right here in Pennsylvania?"

"Coal," Sam suggests.

"Milk," Kristen adds.

"And vegetables," Nikki says.

"Excellent examples!" Mr. Sand exclaims. "Now in secondary activities, people change those items into other things that can be used." Mr. Sand writes "Secondary activity—changing natural resources into other products" on the board. "Let's identify some possible examples for this one."

Why are the students having trouble reading their textbook? What characteristics of the text seem to be interfering with their understanding?

What strategies does Mr. Sand use to help the students understand the passage about economic activities?

BASIC PRINCIPLES OF HUMAN DEVELOPMENT

The college-level textbook Mr. Sand has chosen for his advanced geography class is very difficult for his high school students. As he points out, the book's content is quite abstract—it is almost completely removed from the concrete, everyday world his students regularly encounter. The book also uses words—*tertiary*, *quarternary*, *commodities*, and so on—that are not part of the students' existing vocabularies. Without further information, it is difficult to know whether Mr. Sand's choice of textbooks is developmentally appropriate, both cognitively and linguistically, for the students in his class. But Mr. Sand does do a couple of things that probably *are* appropriate for his students' developmental levels. First, he describes what his students need to do as they read and think about chapter content; in particular, he tells them to find the main ideas in what they are reading. Second, he shows them two things to do as they study: write down key concepts and generate new examples.

As we study various theories of cognitive and linguistic development in the pages ahead, we will gain additional insights about the case. But before we look at specific developmental theories, let's consider four principles that seem to hold true regardless of the aspect of development we're talking about. Keep these principles in mind as you read Chapters 2 and 3:

◎ *Development proceeds in a somewhat orderly and predictable pattern.* Human development is often characterized by **developmental milestones** that occur in a predictable sequence. For example, children typically learn to walk only after they have already learned to sit up and crawl. They learn the stereotypical behaviors of males and females—for example, that men are more likely to become doctors and women to become nurses—only after they have learned to distinguish between men and women. They begin to think logically about abstract ideas only after they

■ You can find information about physical development in the supplementary reading "Physical Development Across Childhood and Adolescence" in the *Study Guide and Reader*.

■ **developmental milestone**
Appearance of a new, developmentally more advanced behavior.

have learned to think logically about concrete objects and observable events. To some extent, then, we see **universals** in development: We see similar patterns in how children change over time regardless of the specific environment in which they are being raised.

◎ *Different children develop at different rates.* Descriptive research in child and adolescent development tells us the average ages at which various developmental milestones are reached. For example, the average child can draw circular shapes at age 3, starts using repetition as a way of learning information at age 7, and begins puberty at age 10 (for girls) or 11½ (for boys) (McDevitt & Ormrod, 2004). But not all children reach developmental milestones at the average age; some reach them earlier, some later. Accordingly, we will see considerable variability in students' developmental accomplishments at any single grade level.

Descriptive research of child development tells us the *average* age at which various developmental milestones are reached. But we must remember that individual children develop at different rates.

Determining the approximate ages at which children can perform certain behaviors and think in certain ways allows us to form general expectations about the capabilities of children at a particular age level and to design our educational curriculum and instructional strategies around these expectations. At the same time, we should never jump to conclusions about what any individual student can and cannot do on the basis of age alone.

◎ *Periods of relatively rapid growth (spurts) may appear between periods of slower growth (plateaus).* Development does not always proceed at a constant rate. For example, during the early elementary school years, children gain an average of two or three inches in height per year; during their adolescent growth spurt, they may grow as much as five inches per year (Berk, 2003; A. C. Harris, 1986). Toddlers may speak with a limited vocabulary and one-word "sentences" for several months, yet sometime around their second birthday a virtual explosion in language development occurs, with vocabulary expanding rapidly and sentences becoming longer and longer within just a few weeks.

Some theorists use such patterns of uneven growth and change as evidence for distinct, qualitatively different periods in development. In a **stage theory**, development is characterized as progressing through a predictable sequence of stages, with earlier stages providing the foundation for, and so being prerequisite to, later ones. We will encounter stage theories in our discussions of both cognitive and moral development.

◎ *Development is continually affected by both nature (heredity) and nurture (environment).* Virtually all aspects of development are affected either directly or indirectly by a child's genetic makeup. Not all inherited characteristics appear at birth; heredity continues to control a child's growth through the process of **maturation**, an unfolding of genetically controlled changes as the child develops. For example, motor skills such as walking, running, and jumping develop primarily as a result of neurological development, increased strength, and increased muscular control—changes that are largely determined by inherited biological "instructions." Furthermore, children are genetically endowed with particular ways of responding to their physical and social environments, and such **temperaments** influence their tendency to be calm or irritable, outgoing or shy, adventuresome or cautious, cheerful or fearful (Kagan, 1998; B. K. Keogh, 2003). (We'll look at temperamental differences more closely in Chapter 5.)

Yet the environment plays an equally critical role in most aspects of development. For example, although children's heights and body builds are primarily inherited characteristics, the nutritional value of their food also affects physical growth. Although children's behaviors are partly the result of inherited temperaments, the ways in which their environment encourages them to behave are just as influential, and probably more so. And the families and cultures in which children are raised affect the particular cognitive abilities, social skills, and moral values they acquire.

Heredity and environment typically interact in their effects, such that we can probably never disentangle the unique influences of nature and nurture on development (Gottlieb, 2000; Kolb, Gibb, & Robinson, 2003; Lippa, 2002). For some characteristics and abilities, inherited predispositions set a **sensitive period** (you may also see the term *critical period*), a point in development during which a growing child can be especially influenced by environmental conditions. As we will discover later in the chapter, some theorists have found evidence that children learn a language more easily when they are exposed to it in their early years rather than in adolescence or adulthood. Others speculate about possible sensitive periods in brain development, as we shall see in the following section.

■ The extent to which development is affected by *nature versus nurture* continues to be a source of controversy among developmental theorists. In your own opinion, how much are human characteristics influenced by heredity? by environment?

■ **universals** Similar patterns in how children change and progress over time regardless of their specific environment.

■ **stage theory** Theory that depicts development as a series of relatively discrete periods (*stages*).

■ **maturation** Unfolding of genetically controlled changes as a child develops.

■ **temperament** Genetic predisposition to respond in particular ways to one's physical and social environments.

■ **sensitive period** Age range during which a certain aspect of a child's development is especially susceptible to environmental conditions.

FIGURE 2.1   Neurons and their interconnections

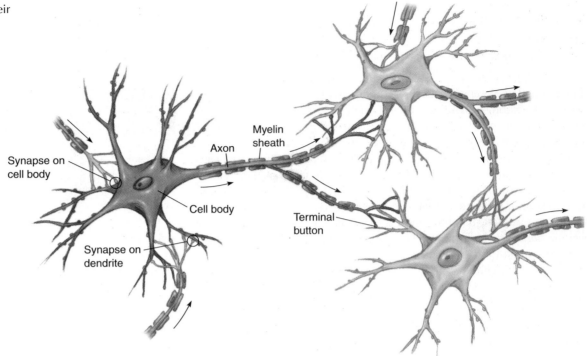

ROLE OF THE BRAIN IN COGNITIVE DEVELOPMENT

The human brain is an incredibly complicated organ that includes somewhere in the neighborhood of one hundred billion nerve cells (Goodman & Tessier-Lavigne, 1997). These nerve cells, known as **neurons**, are microscopic in size and interconnected in innumerable ways. Some neurons receive information from the rest of the body, others synthesize and interpret that information, and still others send messages that tell the body how to respond to its present circumstances.

Although neurons vary in size and shape, all of them have several features in common (see Figure 2.1). First, like other cells in the body, they have a *cell body* that contains the cell's nucleus and is responsible for the cell's health and well-being. Furthermore, they have a number of branchlike structures, called *dendrites*, that receive messages from other neurons. They also have an *axon*, a long, armlike structure that transmits information on to additional neurons. The end of the axon may branch out many times, and the ends of its tiny branches have *terminal buttons* that contain certain chemical substances (more about these substances in a moment). For some (but not all) neurons, much of the axon has a white, fatty coating called a *myelin sheath*.

When a neuron's dendrites are stimulated by other neurons (either those in the brain or those extending from other parts of the body), the dendrites become electrically charged. If the total charge reaches a certain level, the neuron "fires," sending an electrical impulse along its axon to the terminal buttons. If the axon has a myelin sheath, the impulse travels quite rapidly because it leaps from one gap in the myelin to the next, almost as if it were playing leap frog. If the axon does not have a myelin sheath, the impulse travels more slowly.

Curiously, neurons don't actually touch one another. Instead, they send chemical messages to their neighbors across tiny spaces known as **synapses**. When an electrical impulse moves down a neuron's axon, it signals the terminal buttons to release chemicals known as **neurotransmitters**. These chemicals travel across the synapses and stimulate the dendrites or cell bodies of neighboring neurons. Any single neuron may have synaptic connections with hundreds or even thousands of other neurons (Goodman & Tessier-Lavigne, 1997; Lichtman, 2001; R. F. Thompson, 1985).

Groups of neurons in different parts of the brain seem to specialize in different things. Complex, conscious thinking takes place primarily in the upper and outer parts of the brain that are collectively known as the **cortex**, which rests on top of the brain like a thick, bumpy toupee (Kimberg, D'Esposito, & Farah, 1997; Nadel & Jacobs, 1998; E. E. Smith, 2000). The portion of the cortex located near the forehead, called the *frontal cortex*, is largely responsible for a wide variety of very "human" activities, including attention, reasoning, planning, decision making, controlled movements, and inhibition of irrelevant thoughts and inappropriate actions. Other parts

■ **neuron** Cell in the brain or another part of the nervous system that transmits information to other cells.

■ **synapse** Junction between two neurons that allows transmission of messages from one to the other.

■ **neurotransmitter** Chemical substance through which one neuron sends a message to another.

■ **cortex** Upper part of the brain; site of conscious and higher-level thinking processes.

of the cortex are important as well; for instance, they are actively involved in interpreting visual and auditory information, thinking about the spatial characteristics of objects and events, and keeping track of general knowledge about the world.

With such basics about the brain in mind, let's consider three key points about the brain's role in cognitive development:

◎ *Most learning probably involves changes in neurons and synapses.* Many theorists and re-searchers believe that the physiological basis for most learning and much of cognitive develop-ment lies in changes in the interconnections among neurons. In particular, learning often involves strengthening existing synapses or forming new ones, perhaps through increasing the number and complexity of dendrites at the "receiving" ends of neurons (Byrnes & Fox, 1998; Greenough, Black, & Wallace. 1987; Merzenich, 2001; Rosenzweig, 1986). In some instances, however, cognitive advancements actually involve *eliminating* synapses. Development requires not only that children think and do certain things but also that they *not* think or do other things—in other words, that they inhibit tendencies to think or behave in particular ways (Bruer & Greenough, 2001; Byrnes, 2001; Dempster, 1992; Haier, 2001).

◎ *Developmental changes in the brain enable increasingly complex and efficient thought.* At birth the human brain is about one-fourth the size it will be in adulthood, but by age 3 it has reached three-fourths of its adult size (M. H. Johnson & de Haan, 2001; Kolb & Whishaw, 1990). The cortex is the least mature part of the brain at birth, and changes in the cortex that occur in infancy and early childhood probably account for many advancements in young children's abil-ity to think and reason.

Neurons begin to form synapses well before a child is born. But shortly after birth the rate of synapse formation increases dramatically. Neurons sprout new dendrites in every direction, and so they come into contact with many of their neighbors, especially in the first two or three years of life. Much of this early **synaptogenesis** appears to be driven primarily by genetic programming rather than by learning experiences. Thanks to synaptogenesis, children in the elementary grades have many more synapses than adults do (Bruer, 1999).

Theorists speculate that by generating a large number of synapses in the early years, children have the potential to adapt to a wide variety of conditions and circumstances. As they encounter different stimuli and experiences in their daily lives, some synapses come in quite handy and are used repeatedly. Other synapses are largely useless, and these gradually fade away through a process known as **synaptic pruning**. Synaptic pruning is a good thing, not a bad one, as it elim-inates "nuisance" synapses that are inconsistent with typical environmental events and behav-ioral patterns (Bruer & Greenough, 2001; Byrnes, 2001). In some parts of the brain, intensive synaptic pruning occurs fairly early (e.g., in the preschool or early elementary years). In other parts it begins later and extends into adolescence and beyond (Bortfeld & Whitehurst, 2001; Bruer, 1999; Huttenlocher & Dabholkar, 1997; M. H. Johnson & de Haan, 2001).

Even as synaptic pruning is occurring, however, children and adolescents—in fact, people of all ages—continue to form new synapses in response to their experiences (R. D. Brown & Bjork-lund, 1998; Fischer & Rose, 1996; O'Boyle & Gill, 1998). In this sense, certainly, a person is *never* too old to acquire new knowledge and skills.

Another important developmental process in the brain is **myelination**. When neurons first develop, their axons have no myelin coating. As they acquire this myelin over time, they fire much more quickly, greatly enhancing the brain's overall efficiency. Myelination continues throughout childhood, adolescence, and early adulthood, especially in the cortex (Merzenich, 2001; Paus et al., 1999).

In addition, the onset of puberty is marked by significant changes in hormone levels, which affect the continuing maturation of brain structures and possibly also affect the production and effectiveness of neurotransmitters (Achenbach, 1974; Eisenberg, Martin, & Fabes, 1996; Walker, 2002). Theorists have speculated that such changes may affect young people's functioning in a variety of areas, including attention, planning, and impulse control.

◎ *The brain remains adaptable throughout life.* Some well-meaning educators have proposed that the proliferation of synapses in the preschool and early elementary years points to a sensi-tive period in brain development, and they urge us to maximize children's educational experi-ences specifically during this time period. But before you, too, jump to this conclusion, consider this: Although adequate nutrition and everyday forms of stimulation are critical for normal brain

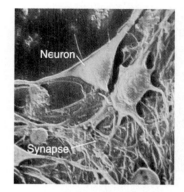

Learning is, at least in part, a process of forming and modifying connections (synapses) among brain cells (neurons). This photo shows neurons in the cortex of the human brain.

■ **synaptogenesis** Universal process in early brain development in which many new synapses spontaneously appear.

■ **synaptic pruning** Universal process in brain development in which many previously formed synapses wither away.

■ **myelination** Growth of a fatty sheath (myelin) around neurons, enabling faster transmission of messages.

development, there is no evidence that intensive, "enriching" experiences in the early years enhance brain power over the long run (Bruer, 1999; R. A. Thompson & Nelson, 2001). If infants don't have normal exposure to patterns of light (e.g., if they are born with cataracts), they may soon lose the ability to see normally, and if children don't hear spoken language until age 5, they may never acquire the language's subtle grammatical complexities (Bialystok, 1994a; Bruer, 1999; Levay, Wiesel, & Hubel, 1980). But exposure to patterned light and spoken language are *normal* experiences, not exceptional ones. There is *no* evidence to indicate that sensitive periods exist for traditional academic subjects such as reading, writing, or mathematics (Bruer, 1999; Geary, 1998; Greenough et al., 1987).

Ultimately, cognitive development is, and must be, a long-term endeavor. The early years are important for development, to be sure, but so are the later years, and we should remain optimistic about the cognitive abilities that students can acquire *throughout* the elementary and secondary grade levels (R. D. Brown & Bjorklund, 1998; Bruer, 1999; Byrnes & Fox, 1998).

Even as researchers pin down how the brain develops with age, current knowledge of brain physiology doesn't begin to tell us everything we need to know about cognitive development or how to foster it. For instance, brain research cannot tell us what information and skills are most important for children to acquire in a particular community and culture (L. Bloom & Tinker, 2001; D. J. Chalmers, 1996; Gardner, 2000). Nor does it provide many clues about the instructional strategies that are most likely to promote children's mental growth (Byrnes, 2001; Mayer, 1998). For answers to such questions, we must look elsewhere, and in particular to psychological theories of cognitive development.

Over the years, psychologists have offered numerous explanations of how and why children's thinking processes change over time. Three theories—those of Jean Piaget, Lev Vygotsky, and information processing theorists—have been especially influential, and so we will examine them in the upcoming sections. As you will see, each of these theories approaches cognitive development from a different angle, and each can give us considerable guidance about how best to foster students' cognitive growth.

PIAGET'S THEORY OF COGNITIVE DEVELOPMENT

Experiencing FIRSTHAND ·Beads, Beings, and Basketballs

Take a moment to solve these three problems:

1. To the left are ten wooden beads. Eight are brown and two are white.
   Are there more brown beads or more wooden beads?
2. If all children are human beings,
   And if all human beings are living creatures,
   Then must all children be living creatures?
3. If all children are basketballs,
   And if all basketballs are jellybeans,
   Then must all children be jellybeans?

· · · · · · ·

You undoubtedly found the first problem ridiculously easy; there are, of course, more wooden beads than brown beads. You may have found the second problem a little more difficult but were probably able to conclude fairly quickly that, yes, all children must be living creatures. The third problem is a bit tricky: It follows the same line of reasoning as the second but the conclusion it leads to—all children must be jellybeans—contradicts what is true in reality.

In the early 1920s the Swiss biologist Jean Piaget began studying children's responses to problems similar to these. He found, for instance, that 4-year-olds often have difficulty with the "beads" problem—they are likely to say that there are more *brown* beads than wooden beads—but that 7-year-olds almost always answer the question correctly. He found, too, that 10-year-olds have an easier time with logic problems that involve real-world phenomena (problems like the "living creatures" problem) than with problems that involve hypothetical and contrary-to-fact ideas (problems like the "jellybeans" problem); only adolescents can effectively deal with the latter kinds of problems. Through a variety of thought-provoking questions and tasks, Piaget and his research colleagues learned a great deal about how children think and learn about the world around them (e.g., Inhelder & Piaget, 1958; Piaget, 1928, 1952, 1959, 1970, 1980).

■ Have you encountered Piaget's theory in other courses? What do you already know about his theory?

Piaget's Basic Assumptions

Piaget introduced a number of ideas and concepts to describe and explain the changes in logical thinking he observed in children and adolescents:

◎ *Children are active and motivated learners.* Piaget believed that children do not just passively observe and remember the things they see and hear. Instead, they are naturally curious about the world and actively seek out information to help them understand and make sense of it. They continually experiment with the objects they encounter, manipulating them and observing the effects of their actions. You can see an example of such curiosity and experimentation when 2-year-old Maddie discovers an intriguing new object in the "Cognitive Development: Early Childhood" clip on Video CD 1.

◎ *Children construct knowledge from their experiences.* Children's knowledge is not limited to a collection of isolated pieces of information. Instead, children pull their experiences together into an integrated view of how the world operates. For example, by observing that food, toys, and other objects always fall down (never up) when released, children begin to construct a rudimentary understanding of gravity. As they interact with family pets, visit zoos, look at picture books, and so on, they develop an increasingly complex understanding of animals. Because Piaget proposed that children construct their own beliefs and understandings from their experiences, his theory is sometimes called a *constructivist* theory or, more generally, **constructivism**.

In Piaget's terminology, the things that children learn and can do are organized as **schemes**— groups of similar actions or thoughts. Initially, schemes are largely behavioral in nature, but over time they become increasingly mental and, eventually, abstract. To illustrate, an infant may have a scheme for putting things in her mouth; she calls on this scheme when dealing with a variety of objects, including her thumb, her toys, and her blanket. A 7-year-old may have a scheme for identifying snakes that includes their long, thin bodies, their lack of legs, and their slithery nature. A 13-year-old may have a scheme for what constitutes *fashion*, allowing her to classify her peers as being either "totally awesome" or "complete dorks."

Over time, children's schemes are modified with experience and become increasingly integrated with one another. For instance, children begin to recognize the hierarchical interrelationships of some schemes: They learn that poodles and cocker spaniels are both dogs, that dogs and cats are both animals, and so on. Children's progressively more organized body of knowledge and thought processes allow them to think in increasingly complex and logical ways.

◎ *Children learn through the two complementary processes of assimilation and accommodation.* Although children's schemes change over time, the processes by which children develop them remain the same. Piaget proposed that learning and cognitive development occur as the result of two complementary processes: assimilation and accommodation. **Assimilation** entails dealing with an object or event in a way that is consistent with an existing scheme. For example, an infant may assimilate a new teddy bear into her putting-things-in-the-mouth scheme. A 7-year-old may quickly identify a new slithery object in the backyard as a snake. A 13-year-old may readily label a classmate's clothing as being either quite fashionable or "soooo yesterday."

But sometimes children cannot easily relate to a new object or event with existing schemes. In these situations one of two forms of **accommodation** will occur: Children will either modify an existing scheme to account for the new object or event or else form an entirely new scheme to deal with it. For example, the infant may have to open her mouth wider than usual to accommodate a teddy bear's fat paw. The 13-year-old may have to revise her existing scheme of fashion according to changes in what's hot and what's not. The 7-year-old may find a long, thin, slithery thing that can't possibly be a snake because it has four legs. After some research, he will develop a new scheme—*salamander*—for this creature.

Assimilation and accommodation typically work hand in hand as children develop their knowledge and understanding of the world. Children interpret each new event within the context of their existing knowledge (assimilation) but at the same time may modify their knowledge as a result of the new event (accommodation). Accommodation rarely happens without assimilation: Our students can benefit from (accommodate to) new experiences only when they can relate those experiences to their current knowledge and beliefs.

■ Observe Maddie experiment with a new object in the "Cognitive Development: Early Childhood" clip on Video CD 1.

■ **constructivism** Theoretical perspective proposing that learners construct (rather than absorb) a body of knowledge from their experiences.

■ **scheme** Organized group of similar actions or thoughts.

■ **assimilation** Dealing with a new event in a way that is consistent with an existing scheme.

■ **accommodation** Dealing with a new event by either modifying an existing scheme or forming a new one.

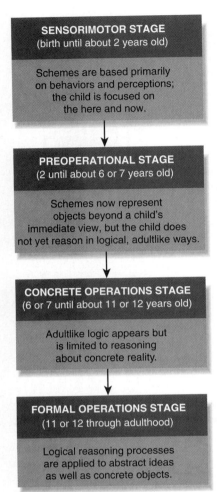

FIGURE 2.2   Piaget's stages of cognitive development

◎   *Interaction with one's physical and social environments is essential for cognitive development.* According to Piaget, active experimentation with the physical world is essential for cognitive growth. By exploring and manipulating physical objects—"fiddling" with sand and water, measuring things, playing games with balls and bats, experimenting in a science lab, and so on—children learn the nature of such characteristics as volume and weight, discover principles related to force and gravity, acquire a better understanding of cause-effect relationships, and so on. Thus, Piaget's theory leads us to conclude that *discovery learning* should be an important aspect of classroom instruction. We'll look at discovery learning more closely in Chapter 13.

In Piaget's view, social interaction is equally critical for cognitive development. Through interaction with other people, children begin to realize that different individuals see things differently and that their own view of the world is not necessarily a completely accurate or logical one. To illustrate, a 5-year-old may have difficulty seeing the world from anyone's perspective but his own. Through social interactions, both pleasant (e.g., a conversation) and unpleasant (e.g., an argument), he begins to realize that his own perspective is a unique one not shared by others. Similarly, a 9-year-old may recognize the logical inconsistencies in what she says and does only after someone else points them out. And through discussions with peers or adults about social and political issues, a high school student may modify some initially abstract and idealistic notions about how the world "should" be to reflect the constraints the real world imposes.

◎   *The process of equilibration promotes progression toward increasingly complex thought.* According to Piaget, when children can comfortably explain new events with existing schemes, they are in a state of **equilibrium**. But this equilibrium doesn't continue indefinitely. As children grow, they often encounter events they cannot adequately address with their existing knowledge and beliefs. Such inexplicable events create **disequilibrium**, a sort of mental "discomfort" that leads them to reexamine their current understandings. By replacing, reorganizing, or better integrating their schemes (in other words, through accommodation), children eventually are able to understand and explain previously puzzling events. The movement from equilibrium to disequilibrium and back to equilibrium again is known as **equilibration**. Equilibration and children's intrinsic desire to achieve equilibrium promote the development of more complex levels of thought and knowledge.

As an example, let's return to the "beads" problem I gave you earlier. Imagine that we show the ten wooden beads (eight brown and two white) to 4-year-old Abby and ask her, "Are there more brown beads or more wooden beads?" Abby tells us there are more brown beads and seems quite comfortable with this response; she is in equilibrium. Apparently Abby is having trouble thinking of the brown beads as belonging to two categories (*brown* and *wooden*) at the same time and so is actually comparing the brown beads to the beads left over (the white ones). So we ask her to count the brown beads (she counts eight of them) and then to count the wooden beads (she counts ten). "So then, Abby," we say, "there are *eight* brown beads and *ten* wooden beads. Are there more brown beads or more wooden beads?" If Abby can recognize the inconsistency in her reasoning—that eight cannot possibly be more than ten—she will experience disequilibrium. At this point, she may reorganize her thinking to accommodate the idea that some beads are both brown and wooden and so should simultaneously be included in both categories.

◎   *Cognitive development is stagelike in nature.* According to Piaget, children cannot think and reason as adults do until their brains have developed sufficiently to allow such thinking. Piaget speculated that major changes take place when children are about 2 years old, again when they are 6 or 7, and again around puberty. Changes at each of these times allow new abilities to emerge, such that children progress through a sequence of increasingly advanced levels of thought, as we shall see now.

Piaget's Stages of Cognitive Development

Piaget proposed that as a result of both maturation and experience, children proceed through four stages of cognitive development (see Figure 2.2). Although each stage builds on any preceding stages, it is also qualitatively different from its predecessors, in that it encompasses new abilities and ways of thinking about the world. The age ranges associated with the stages are *averages*; some children reach a stage a bit earlier, others a bit later. Also, children can be in *transition* from one stage to the next, displaying characteristics of two adjacent stages at the same time.

For reasons described later, many psychologists question whether cognitive development is as stagelike as Piaget proposed. Nevertheless, Piaget's stages provide insights into the nature of children's thinking at different age levels, and so we will look at them more closely.

Sensorimotor Stage (birth until 2 years)   Imagine that we show a colorful stuffed clown to 6-month-old Karen. Karen reaches for it in much the same way that she reaches for her teddy bear and her stacking blocks; in other words, she has a reaching-and-grasping scheme into which she assimilates this new object. Karen then drops the clown and watches it fall to the floor, applying her letting-go and visually-following-a-moving-object schemes in the process. Now imagine that we put Karen's clown inside a box so that she can no longer see it. Karen seems to forget the clown and turns to play with something else, acting as if she cannot think about a clown she cannot actually see.

Piaget proposed that for much of the **sensorimotor stage**, children focus on what they are doing and seeing at the moment, and so their schemes are based primarily on behaviors and perceptions. Yet important cognitive capabilities emerge during this stage, especially as children begin to experiment with their environments through trial and error. For example, shortly before their first birthday, children develop *object permanence*, the realization that objects continue to exist even when removed from view. After repeatedly observing that certain actions lead to certain consequences, children at this stage also begin to develop an understanding of *cause-effect relationships*.

Toward the end of the second year, **symbolic thought** emerges: Children can represent objects and events in the outside world in terms of internal, mental entities, *symbols*. Often these symbols take the form of words that children hear around them and use in their early, one-word "sentences." For instance, at this point, Karen will be able to think about a clown without having one directly in front of her, in part because she knows the word *clown*.

Preoperational Stage (2 years until 6 or 7 years)   In the early part of the **preoperational stage**, children's language skills virtually explode, and their rapidly increasing vocabularies enable them to represent and think about a wide variety of objects and events. Language also provides the basis for a new form of social interaction—verbal communication. Children can now express their thoughts and receive information in a way that previously was not possible.

At the same time, preoperational thinking has some definite limitations, especially when compared with concrete operational thinking (see Table 2.1). For example, children in this stage exhibit **preoperational egocentrism**, an inability to view situations from another person's perspective. They may have trouble understanding why they must share school supplies with a classmate or why they must be careful not to hurt someone else's feelings. Young children may also exhibit egocentrism through **egocentric speech**, saying things without taking into account what a listener is likely to know and not know about a topic.

Preoperational thinking can also be illogical (at least from an adult's point of view), especially during the preschool years. Recall 4-year-old Abby's insistence that the ten wooden beads included more brown beads than wooden beads; her reasoning reflects *single classification*. And consider the following situation:

> We show 5-year-old Nathan the three glasses in Figure 2.3. We ask him whether Glasses A and B contain the same amount of water, and he replies confidently that they do. We then pour the water from Glass B into Glass C and ask him whether A and C have the same amount. Nathan replies, "No, that glass [pointing to Glass A] has more because it's taller."

Nathan's response reflects lack of **conservation**: He does not realize that because no water has been added or taken away, the amount of water in the two glasses must be equivalent. Young children such as Nathan often confuse changes in appearance with changes in amount.

As children approach the later part of the preoperational stage, perhaps around age 5, they sometimes draw more logical conclusions about classification and conservation problems. However, they base their conclusions on hunches and intuition rather than on any conscious

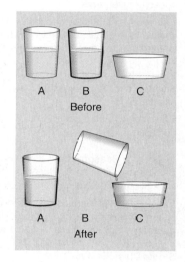

FIGURE 2.3 Conservation of liquid: Do Glasses A and C contain the same amount of water?

■ **sensorimotor stage** Piaget's first stage of cognitive development, in which schemes are based on behaviors and perceptions.

■ **symbolic thought** Ability to represent and think about external objects and events in one's mind.

■ **preoperational stage** Piaget's second stage of cognitive development, in which children can think about objects beyond their immediate view but do not yet reason in logical, adultlike ways.

■ **preoperational egocentrism** Inability of children in Piaget's preoperational stage to view situations from another's perspective.

■ **egocentric speech** Act of speaking without taking the perspective and knowledge of the listener into account.

■ **conservation** Realization that if nothing is added or taken away, amount stays the same regardless of alterations in shape or arrangement.

TABLE 2.1

Preoperational Versus Concrete Operational Thought

PREOPERATIONAL THOUGHT	CONCRETE OPERATIONAL THOUGHT
Preoperational Egocentrism Students think their own perspective is the only one possible. *Example:* A student tells a story without considering what prior knowledge the listener is likely to have.	**Differentiation of One's Own Perspective from the Perspectives of Others** Students recognize that others see things differently than they do and that their own ideas may be incorrect. *Example:* A student seeks validation of his own thoughts (e.g., "Did I get that right?").
Lack of Conservation Students believe that amount (e.g., number, mass) changes when a substance is reshaped or rearranged, even though nothing has been added or taken away. *Example:* A student asserts that two rows of five pennies similarly spaced have equal amounts; but when one row is spread out and so longer than the other, she says that it has more pennies.	**Conservation** Students recognize that amount stays the same if nothing has been added or taken away, even if the substance is reshaped or rearranged. *Example:* A student asserts that two rows of five pennies have the same number of pennies regardless of their spacing.
Irreversibility Students don't recognize that certain processes can be undone, or reversed. *Example:* A student treats addition and subtraction as two unrelated processes.	**Reversibility** Students understand that certain processes can be reversed. *Example:* A student recognizes that subtraction is the reverse of addition; for instance, she realizes that $7 - 4 = 3$ essentially "undoes" $3 + 4 = 7$.
Inability to Reason About Transformations Students focus on static situations; they have difficulty thinking about change processes. *Example:* A student refuses to believe that a caterpillar can turn into a butterfly, instead insisting that the caterpillar crawls away and the butterfly comes to replace it (K. R. Harris, 1986).	**Ability to Reason About Transformations** Students can reason about change and its effects. *Example:* A student understands that a caterpillar becomes a butterfly through the process of metamorphosis.
Single Classification Students can classify objects in only one way at any given time. *Example:* A student denies that a mother can also be a doctor.	**Multiple Classification** Students recognize that objects may belong to several categories simultaneously. *Example:* A student acknowledges that a mother can also be a doctor, a spouse, and an artist.
Transductive Reasoning Students reason by combining unrelated facts; for instance, they infer a cause-effect relationship simply because two events occur close together in time and space. *Example:* A student believes that clouds make the moon grow (Piaget, 1928).	**Deductive Reasoning** Students can draw a logical inference from two or more pieces of information. *Example:* A student deduces that if all children are human beings and if all human beings are living things, then all children must be living things.

■ Observe Kent's conservation of number in the "Cognitive Development: Middle Childhood" clip on Video CD 1.

■ **concrete operations stage** Piaget's third stage of cognitive development, in which adultlike logic appears but is limited to concrete reality.

■ **deductive reasoning** Drawing a logical inference about something that must be true, given other information that has already been presented as true.

awareness of underlying logical principles, and so they cannot yet explain *why* their conclusions are correct. As children move into the concrete operations stage, they become increasingly able to make logical inferences and explain their reasoning.

Concrete Operations Stage (6 or 7 years until 11 or 12 years)   Piaget proposed that as children enter the **concrete operations stage**, their thought processes become organized into larger systems of mental processes—*operations*—that allow them to think more logically (see Table 2.1). They now realize that their own thoughts and feelings may reflect personal opinions rather than reality. They also show conservation: They readily understand that amount stays the same, despite changes in shape or arrangement, if nothing is added or taken away (for example, see 10-year-old Kent's conservation of number in the "Cognitive Development: Middle Childhood" clip on Video CD 1). And they demonstrate **deductive reasoning**: They can draw logical inferences from information they are given.

Children continue to refine their newly acquired thinking capabilities for several years. For instance, some forms of conservation, such as conservation of liquid and conservation of number (the latter illustrated by the "pennies" problem in Table 2.1 and the "M&Ms" task in the

"Cognitive Development: Middle Childhood" video clip), appear at age 6 or 7. Others don't emerge until later. Consider the problem in Figure 2.4. Using a balance scale, an adult shows a child that two balls of clay have the same weight. One ball is removed from the scale and smashed into a pancake shape. Does the pancake weigh the same as the unsmashed ball, or are the weights different? Children typically do not achieve conservation of weight—they don't realize that the flattened pancake weighs the same as the round ball it was earlier—until sometime between 9 and 12 (Sund, 1976).

Although students displaying concrete operational thought show many signs of logical thinking, their cognitive development is not yet complete (see Table 2.2). For instance, they have trouble understanding abstract ideas and struggle with problems involving multiple hypotheses or variables. Such capabilities emerge in the final stage, formal operations.

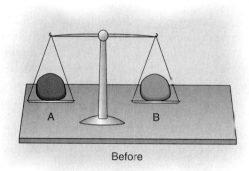

Before

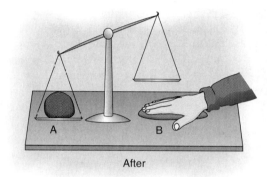

After

FIGURE 2.4 Conservation of weight: Ball A and Ball B initially weigh the same. When Ball B is flattened into a pancake shape, how does its weight now compare with that of Ball A?

TABLE 2.2

COMPARE/CONTRAST

Concrete Operational Versus Formal Operational Thought

CONCRETE OPERATIONAL THOUGHT	FORMAL OPERATIONAL THOUGHT
Dependence on Concrete Reality Students can reason logically about things they can observe; they are unable to reason about abstract, hypothetical, or contrary-to-fact ideas. *Example:* A student has difficulty with the concept of negative numbers, wondering how something can possibly be less than zero.	**Ability to Reason About Abstract, Hypothetical, and Contrary-to-Fact Ideas** Students can reason about things that are not tied directly to concrete, observable reality. *Example:* A student understands negative numbers and is able to use them effectively in mathematical procedures.
Inability to Formulate and Test Multiple Hypotheses When seeking an explanation for a scientific phenomenon, students identify and test only one hypothesis. *Example:* When asked what makes a pendulum swing faster or more slowly, a student says that the weight of the pendulum is the determining factor.	**Formulation and Testing of Multiple Hypotheses** Students seeking an explanation for a scientific phenomenon formulate and test several hypotheses about possible cause-effect relationships. *Example:* When asked what makes a pendulum swing faster or more slowly, a student says that weight, length, and strength of the initial push are all possible explanations.
Inability to Separate and Control Variables When attempting to confirm or disconfirm a particular hypothesis about cause-effect relationships, students change two or more variables simultaneously and so confound their possible effects. *Example:* In testing possible factors influencing the oscillation rate of a pendulum, a student adds more weight to the pendulum while at the same time also shortening the length of the pendulum.	**Separation and Control of Variables** When attempting to confirm or disconfirm a particular hypothesis, students test one variable at a time while holding all other variables constant. *Example:* In testing factors that influence a pendulum's oscillation rate, a student tests the effect of weight while keeping pendulum length and strength of push constant; the student then tests the effect of length while keeping weight and push constant.
Lack of Proportional Reasoning Students do not understand the general nature of proportions. *Example:* A student cannot make sense of the procedure a teacher demonstrates for converting fractions to ratios.	**Proportional Reasoning** Students understand proportions and can use them effectively in mathematical problem solving. *Example:* A student works easily with proportions, fractions, decimals, and ratios.

Erin
Poetry
Class.
5th
Grade

Dear God, Help Us

The black of war
Darkens the day,
There is no point,
I say.
Why do all these poor men die
Fighting those
Who could be friends.
Gun shots sound through the air
Only to bring sadness and despair.
Why do leaders sit around,
While innocent men
Fall to the ground.
When the grass is painted red,
you know
Some man has lost his head.
When you're in a war
you're guarenteed to come out sore.
While you are lying in pain,
slowly,
You'll become insane
The men you kill shouldn't die,
Their souls shouldn't float in the sky.
As a solider gasps
One more time,
He should know
His honor is
Divine.

FIGURE 2.5 As students become increasingly able to reason about abstract, hypothetical, and contrary-to-fact ideas, they also become increasingly idealistic about how the world should be.

(poetry by Erin, age 11)

■ **formal operations stage** Piaget's fourth and final stage of cognitive development, in which logical reasoning processes are applied to abstract ideas as well as to concrete objects.

Formal Operations Stage (11 or 12 years through adulthood) In the poem in Figure 2.5, 11-year-old Erin uses several abstract ideas—for instance, *war darkens the day*, *honor is divine*—as she laments the pointlessness of war. Children and adolescents in the **formal operations stage** can think about concepts that have little or no basis in concrete reality. Furthermore, they recognize that what is logically valid is different from what is true in the real world; for example, if all children are basketballs and all basketballs are jellybeans, then all children must be jellybeans, even though in the real world children *aren't* jellybeans. Several abilities essential for sophisticated scientific and mathematical reasoning—formulating and testing multiple hypotheses, separating and controlling variables, and proportional reasoning—also emerge in the formal operations stage (see Table 2.2).

Let's consider how, from Piaget's perspective, students' capabilities in mathematics are likely to improve once formal operational thinking develops. Abstract problems, such as mathematical word problems, should become easier to solve. Students should become capable of understanding such concepts as *negative number*, *pi* (π), and *infinity*; for instance, they should now comprehend how temperature can be below zero and how two parallel lines will never touch even if they go on forever. And because they can now understand proportions, they can use fractions, ratios, and decimals when solving problems.

Scientific reasoning is also likely to improve once students are capable of formal operational thought. Three formal operational abilities—reasoning logically about hypothetical ideas, formulating and testing hypotheses, and separating and controlling variables—together allow formal operations individuals to use a *scientific method*, in which several possible explanations for an observed phenomenon are proposed and tested in a systematic manner. As an example, consider the pendulum problem in the exercise that follows.

Experiencing FIRSTHAND ·Pendulum Problem

In the absence of other forces, an object suspended by a rope or string—a pendulum—swings at a constant rate (a playground swing and the pendulum of a grandfather clock are two everyday examples). Some pendulums swing back and forth rather slowly, others more quickly. What characteristics of a pendulum determine how fast it swings? Write down at least three hypotheses about the variable(s) that might affect a pendulum's oscillation rate.

Now gather several small, heavy objects (an eraser, a bolt, and a fishing sinker are three possibilities) and a piece of string. Tie one of the objects to one end of the string, and set your pendulum in motion. Conduct one or more experiments to test each of your hypotheses.

What can you conclude? What variable or variables affect the rate with which a pendulum swings?

· · · · · · ·

What hypotheses did you generate? Perhaps you considered the weight of the object, the length of the string, the force with which the pendulum is pushed, and the height from which the object is first released; you may have formed additional hypotheses as well.

Did you then test each hypothesis in a systematic fashion? A student capable of formal operational thinking *separates* and *controls variables*, testing one at a time while holding all others constant (recall our discussion of this issue in Chapter 1). For example, if you were testing the hypothesis that weight makes a difference, you might have tried objects of different weights while keeping constant the length of the string, the force with which you pushed each object, and the height from which you released or pushed it. Similarly, if you hypothesized that the length of the string was a critical factor, you might have varied the length while continuing to use the same object and setting the pendulum in motion in the same manner. If you carefully separated and controlled each variable, then you would have come to the correct conclusion: Only length affects a pendulum's oscillation rate. The "Designing Experiments" clip on Video CD 2 shows the difficulty that four seventh graders have with the pendulum problem: They repeatedly vary both length and weight until their teacher nudges them toward the realization that this approach prevents them from drawing a firm conclusion.

Because students capable of formal operational reasoning can deal with hypothetical and contrary-to-fact ideas, they can envision how the world might be different from—and better than—the way it actually is. As a result, they may exhibit considerable idealism about social and political issues. Many secondary school students begin to show concern about world problems and to devote energy to worthy causes, such as the environment or world hunger. However, they may offer recommendations for change that seem logical but aren't practical in today's world. For example, a teenager might argue that racism would disappear overnight if people would just begin to love one another, or suggest that a nation should eliminate its armed forces and weaponry as a way of moving toward world peace. Piaget proposed that adolescent idealism reflects **formal operational egocentrism**, an inability to separate one's own logical abstractions from the perspectives of others and from practical considerations. Only through experience do adolescents eventually begin to temper their optimism with some realism about what is possible in a given time frame and with limited resources.

Now that you've learned something about each of Piaget's stages, put your understanding to the test in the following assessment exercise.

■ Observe seventh graders' difficulty separating and controlling variables in the "Designing Experiments" clip on Video CD 2.

Interpreting Student Artifacts and Behaviors

Army of Noses
Twelve-year-old friends Zach and Fred wrote a series of comic books featuring "nose" people as the main characters. Below, two pages from one of Zach's books depict an army of noses (led by Napoleon Nose), a time warp trap, and villain Dark Fang's evil new weapon. As you examine Zach's pages, identify

- The logical reasoning abilities the boys exhibit
- The Piagetian stage with which such reasoning is associated

In his story Zach is, of course, portraying a situation that is contrary to fact: Noses don't exist separate from the people who own them, and they certainly don't act and think as people do. Furthermore, Zach's notion of a *time warp* is abstract and hypothetical in nature. Such thinking processes are associated with the formal operations stage.

Current Perspectives on Piaget's Theory

Piaget's theory has sparked a great deal of research about children's cognitive development. In general, this research supports Piaget's proposed *sequence* in which different abilities emerge (Flavell, 1996; Siegler & Richards, 1982). For example, the ability to reason about abstract ideas emerges only after children are already capable of reasoning about concrete objects and events, and the order in which various conservation tasks are mastered is much as Piaget described. Researchers question the *ages* at which various abilities actually appear, however. They are also finding that students' logical reasoning capabilities may vary considerably depending on their previous knowledge and experiences. And although they agree with some of Piaget's basic assumptions, they are less certain about others.

■ **formal operational egocentrism**
Inability of adolescents in Piaget's formal operations stage to separate their own abstract logic from the perspectives of others and from practical considerations.

Capabilities of Different Age-Groups Infants and preschoolers are apparently more competent than Piaget's descriptions of the sensorimotor and preoperational stages suggest. For instance, infants show preliminary signs of object permanence as early as 2½ months old (Baillargeon, 2004). And 3- and 4-year-olds don't always show egocentrism; if we ask them to show us their artwork, they hold it so that we (rather than they) can see it, and they can often recognize the emotions that others are feeling (Lennon, Eisenberg, & Carroll, 1983; Newcombe & Huttenlocher, 1992; Siegler, 1998). Preschoolers can also draw logical deductions (e.g., by making inferences when listening to stories), and under some circumstances they are capable of conservation and multiple classification (Donaldson, 1978; Gelman & Baillargeon, 1983; Rosser, 1994).

Piaget may have underestimated the capabilities of elementary school students as well. Many elementary students occasionally show some ability to think abstractly and hypothetically (S. Carey, 1985; Metz, 1995). Also, some older elementary school children can separate and control variables, especially when given hints about the importance of controlling all variables except the one they are testing (Danner & Day, 1977; Metz, 1995).

Yet Piaget probably *over*estimated what adolescents can do. Formal operational thinking processes emerge much more gradually than Piaget suggested, and adolescents don't use them as regularly as Piaget would have us believe (Byrnes, 1988; Karplus, Pulos, & Stage, 1983; Kuhn, Garcia-Mila, Zohar, & Andersen, 1995; Pascarella & Terenzini, 1991). Furthermore, students may demonstrate formal operational thought in one content domain while thinking more concretely in another. Evidence of formal operations typically emerges in the physical sciences earlier than in such subjects as history and geography; students often have difficulty thinking about abstract and hypothetical ideas in history and geography until well into the high school years (Lovell, 1979; Tamburrini, 1982). Recall, for example, how in the opening case study, Mr. Sand's high school geography students have considerable difficulty understanding an abstract college textbook.

FIGURE 2.6 What are some possible reasons that Herb is catching more fish than the others? Based on Pulos & Linn, 1981.

Effects of Prior Knowledge and Experience It is becoming increasingly apparent that the ability to think logically about a situation or topic depends, in part, on a student's knowledge and background experiences. Four-year-olds begin to show conservation after having experience with conservation tasks, especially if they can actively manipulate the task materials and discuss their reasoning with someone who already exhibits conservation (D. Field, 1987; Mayer, 1992; F. B. Murray, 1978). Similarly, concrete manipulatives can help children as young as 9 grasp the nature of proportions (Fujimura, 2001). Children ages 10 and 11 can solve logical problems involving hypothetical ideas if they are taught relevant problem-solving strategies, and they become increasingly able to separate and control variables when they have numerous experiences that require them to do so (S. Lee, 1985; Schauble, 1990). Junior high and high school students, and adults as well, often apply formal operational thought to topics about which they have a great deal of knowledge and yet think concretely about topics with which they are unfamiliar (Girotto & Light, 1993; M. C. Linn, Clement, Pulos, & Sullivan, 1989; Schliemann & Carraher, 1993).

As an illustration of how knowledge affects formal operational thinking, consider the fishing pond in Figure 2.6. In a study by Pulos and Linn (1981), 13-year-olds were shown a similar picture and told, "These four children go fishing every week, and one child, Herb, always catches the most fish. The other children wonder why." If you look at the picture, it is obvious that Herb differs from the other children in several ways, including the kind of bait he uses, the length of his fishing rod, and his location by the pond. Students who were avid fishermen more effectively separated and controlled variables for this situation than they did for the pendulum problem described earlier, whereas the reverse was true for nonfishermen (Pulos & Linn, 1981). In the "Cognitive Development: Middle Childhood" and "Cognitive Development: Late Adolescence" clips on Video CD 1, 10-year-old Kent and 14-year-old Alicia both look at the picture in Figure 2.6. Notice how Kent, who appears to have some experience with

■ Observe how experience with fishing affects Kent's and Alicia's ability to identify relevant variables in the middle childhood and late adolescence "Cognitive Development" clips on Video CD 1.

fishing, considers several relevant variables. In contrast, Alicia, who is older but admittedly a nonfisherman, considers only two:

Kent: He has live . . . live worms, I think. Fish like live worms more, I guess 'cause they're live and they'd rather have that than the lures, plastic worms. . . . Because he might be more patient or that might be a good side of the place. Maybe since Bill has a boombox thing [referring to the radio], I don't think they would really like that because . . . and he doesn't really have anything that's extra. . . . But he's the standing one. I don't get that. But Bill, that could scare the fish away to Herb because he's closer. . . .

Alicia: Because of the spot he's standing in, probably. . . . I don't know anything about fishing. Oh, OK! He actually has live worms for bait. The other girl's using saltine crackers [she misreads *crickets*]. . . . She's using plastic worms, he's using lures, and she's using crackers and he's actually using live worms. So obviously the fish like the live worms the best.

Reconsidering Piaget's Basic Assumptions   Some of Piaget's basic assumptions— for instance, that children construct their own knowledge about the world, that they must relate new experiences to what they already know, and that encountering puzzling phenomena can sometimes spur them to revise their understandings—have stood the test of time. However, interaction with the physical environment, while certainly valuable, may be less critical than Piaget believed. For instance, children with significant physical disabilities, who cannot actively experiment with physical objects, learn a great deal about the world simply by observing what happens around them (Bebko, Burke, Craven, & Sarlo, 1992; Brainerd, 2003). In contrast, social interaction—not only with peers but with adults as well—is probably even more influential than Piaget realized (Callanan & Oakes, 1992; Gauvain, 2001). Lev Vygotsky's theory, which we turn to next, describes the many ways in which interaction with both adults and peers can foster cognitive growth.

Piaget probably underestimated the capabilities of children in the elementary grades; for instance, elementary school children sometimes exhibit abstract thinking. Nevertheless, concrete experiences—such as observing chicks hatching in an incubator—provide a good foundation on which abstract ideas can build.

Can cognitive development truly be characterized as a series of stages? A few contemporary theorists have offered stage theories that may more adequately account for current findings about children's logical thinking (e.g., Case & Okamoto, 1996; Fischer & Bidell, 1991). But most now believe that cognitive development can more accurately be described in terms of gradual *trends* rather than discrete stages. They further suggest that Piaget's stages may better describe how children *can* think, rather than how they typically *do* think, and that the nature of cognitive development may be somewhat specific to different contexts, content areas, and cultures (Flavell, 1994; Klaczynski, 2001; Rogoff, 2003; Rosser, 1994; Siegler, 1998). Later in the chapter, when we consider information processing theory, we will identify several general developmental trends in children's ability to think and learn in the classroom.

Despite such concerns, the many tasks that Piaget created to study children's reasoning abilities (conservation, classification, separation and control of variables, etc.) can give us valuable insights about the logic students use when thinking about their world. And educators have found many of Piaget's ideas—egocentrism, disequilibrium, the progression from concrete to abstract thought—quite useful in instructional settings. The Into the Classroom feature "Applying Piaget's Theory" offers several suggestions for putting Piaget's theory into practice in the classroom.

VYGOTSKY'S THEORY OF COGNITIVE DEVELOPMENT

Lev Vygotsky conducted numerous studies of children's thinking from the 1920s until his premature death from tuberculosis in 1934 at the age of 37. Many Western psychologists did not fully appreciate the usefulness of his work until several decades later, when his major writings were translated into English (e.g., Vygotsky, 1962, 1978, 1987, 1997). Although Vygotsky never had the chance to develop his theory fully, his ideas are clearly evident in our views of child development, learning, and instructional practices today.

Applying Piaget's Theory

 Provide hands-on experiences with physical objects, especially when working with elementary school students. Allow and encourage students to explore and manipulate things.

A kindergarten teacher and his students work with small objects (e.g., blocks, buttons, pennies) to explore such basic elements of arithmetic as conservation of number and the reversibility of addition and subtraction.

 When students show signs of egocentric thought, express confusion or explain that others think differently.

A first grader asks, "What's this?" about an object that is out of the teacher's view. The teacher responds, "What's *what*? I can't see the thing you're looking at."

 Ask students to explain their reasoning, and challenge illogical explanations.

When learning about pendulums, cooperative groups in a seventh-grade science class experiment with three variables (weight, length, and height from which the pendulum is first dropped) to see which variables determine the rate at which a pendulum swings. When a student in one group asserts that weight affects oscillation rate, her teacher points out that her group has simultaneously varied both weight and length in her experiments. (This example is depicted in the "Designing Experiments" clip on Video CD 2.)

 Be sure students have certain capabilities for mathematical and scientific reasoning (e.g., conservation of number, reversibility, proportional reasoning, separation and control of variables) before requiring them to perform complex tasks that depend on these capabilities.

In a unit on fractions in a sixth-grade math class, students express confusion about why ⅔, ⅘, and ⁸⁄₁₂ are all equivalent. Before beginning a lesson about how to add and subtract fractions with different denominators—processes that require an understanding of such equivalencies—their teacher uses concrete objects (e.g., sliced pizza pies, plastic rods that can be broken into small segments) to help students understand how two different fractions can be equal.

Relate abstract and hypothetical ideas to concrete objects and observable events.

To illustrate the idea that heavy and light objects fall at the same speed, a high school science teacher has students drop objects of various weights from a second-story window.

Vygotsky's Basic Assumptions

As you should recall, Piaget proposed that through assimilation and accommodation, children develop increasingly advanced and integrated schemes over time. In Piaget's view, cognitive development is largely an individual enterprise; growing children do most of the mental work themselves.

In contrast, Vygotsky believed that the adults in a society foster children's cognitive development in an intentional and somewhat systematic manner. Adults continually engage children in meaningful and challenging activities and help them perform those activities successfully. Because Vygotsky emphasized the importance of society and culture for promoting cognitive growth, his theory is sometimes referred to as the **sociocultural perspective**. The following major assumptions provide a summary of this perspective:

◎   *Through both informal conversations and formal schooling, adults convey to children the ways in which their culture interprets and responds to the world.* Let's return again to the opening case study. The geography textbook Mr. Sand's class is using describes four kinds of economic activities: primary, secondary, tertiary, and quarternary. By presenting these four concepts, the text shows the students how geographers conceptualize and categorize (i.e., how they think about) economic activities. Vygotsky proposed that as adults interact with children, they share the *meanings* they attach to objects, events and, more generally, human experience. In the process, they transform, or *mediate*, the situations that children encounter. Meanings are conveyed through a variety of mechanisms, including language (spoken words, writing, etc.), symbols, mathematics, art, music, literature, and so on.

Informal conversations are one common method by which adults pass along culturally relevant ways of interpreting situations. But no less important is formal education, where teachers systematically impart the ideas, concepts, and terminology used in various academic disciplines (Vygotsky, 1962). Although Vygotsky, like Piaget, saw value in allowing children to make some discoveries themselves, he also saw value in having adults describe the discoveries of previous generations (Karpov & Haywood, 1998).

To the extent that specific cultures pass along unique concepts, ideas, and beliefs, children of different cultural backgrounds will acquire somewhat different knowledge, skills, and ways of thinking. Thus, Vygotsky's theory leads us to expect greater diversity among children, at least in

■ For another theoretical perspective on how society influences children's development, see the supplementary reading "An Ecological Systems Perspective of Child Development" in the *Study Guide and Reader* that accompanies this book.

■ **sociocultural perspective** Theoretical perspective emphasizing the importance of society and culture for promoting cognitive development.

cognitive development, than Piaget's theory does. For example, some cultures use a wide variety of maps (road maps, maps of subway systems, shopping mall layouts) and expose children to them early and frequently, whereas other cultures rarely if ever use maps (Trawick-Smith, 2003; Whiting & Edwards, 1988).

◎   *Thought and language become increasingly interdependent in the first few years of life.* For us as adults, thought and language are closely interconnected. We often think by using the specific words our language provides; for example, when we think about household pets, our thoughts contain words such as *dog* and *cat*. In addition, we usually express our thoughts when we converse with others: as we sometimes put it, we "speak our minds."

But Vygotsky proposed that thought and language are separate functions for infants and young toddlers. In these early years, thinking occurs independently of language, and when language appears, it is first used primarily as a means of communication rather than as a mechanism of thought. Sometime around age 2, thought and language become intertwined: Children begin to express their thoughts when they speak, and they begin to think in words.

When thought and language first merge, children often talk to themselves, a phenomenon known as **self-talk** (also known as *private speech*). Recall Piaget's notion of *egocentric speech*, based on his observation that young children often say things without taking into account the listener's perspective. Vygotsky proposed that on such occasions children may be talking to themselves rather than to others. Self-talk serves an important function in cognitive development: By talking to themselves, children learn to guide and direct their own behaviors through difficult tasks and complex maneuvers in much the same way that adults may have previously guided them. Self-talk eventually evolves into **inner speech**, in which children "talk" to themselves mentally rather than aloud. They continue to direct themselves verbally through tasks and activities, but others can no longer see and hear them do it.

These excerpts from 5-year-old Luisa's "Caterpillar Number Book" show how kindergartners might practice writing and using numbers. Such an activity reflects elements of both Vygotsky's theory (numbers are basic *cognitive tools* within our culture) and Piaget's theory (young children learn more effectively through concrete, hands-on experiences).

Recent research has supported Vygotsky's views regarding the progression and role of self-talk and inner speech. The frequency of children's audible self-talk decreases with age, but this decrease is at first accompanied by an increase in whispered mumbling and silent lip movements, presumably reflecting a transition to inner speech (Bivens & Berk, 1990; R. E. Owens, 1996; Winsler & Naglieri, 2003). Furthermore, self-talk increases when children are performing more challenging tasks at which they must exert considerable effort to be successful (Berk, 1994; Schimmoeller, 1998).

◎   *Complex mental processes begin as social activities; as children develop, they gradually internalize processes they use in social contexts and begin to use them independently.* Vygotsky proposed that many thought processes have their roots in social interactions. As children discuss objects and events with adults and other knowledgeable individuals—often within the context of the everyday activities of their culture—they gradually incorporate into their own thinking the ways in which people around them talk about and interpret the world, and they begin to use the words, concepts, symbols, and strategies that are typical for their culture. In essence, they are acquiring the **cognitive tools** of their culture (Vygotsky called them *signs*) that will enable them to interpret, organize, and respond to tasks and problems more effectively.

Let's return once again to Mr. Sand's classroom. The textbook introduces concepts (e.g., *primary*, *secondary*, *tertiary*, and *quarternary activities*) that social scientists have developed to help them understand how various economic enterprises build on one another. When Mr. Sand discovers that students are having trouble understanding these concepts, he initiates a discussion of a study strategy—relating new ideas to prior knowledge—that students can use when reading challenging textbook passages on their own in the future. (Unfortunately, he does so fairly late in the game, after his students have experienced considerable frustration with the assignment.)

The process through which social activities evolve into internal mental activities is called **internalization**. The self-talk and inner speech we spoke of earlier illustrate the internalization process in action: Over time, children gradually internalize adults' directions so that they are eventually giving *themselves* directions. Yet keep in mind that children do not necessarily internalize *exactly* what they see and hear in a social context. Rather, internalization often involves transforming ideas and processes to make them uniquely one's own. For instance, different students in Mr. Sand's class may interpret *tertiary activity* somewhat differently, and they are apt to apply the new study strategy in idiosyncratic ways.

Not all mental processes emerge as children interact with adults, however; some also develop as children interact with peers. As an example, children frequently argue with one another about

■ **self-talk** Process of talking to oneself as a way of guiding oneself through a task.

■ **inner speech** Process of "talking" to oneself mentally rather than aloud.

■ **cognitive tool** Concept, symbol, strategy, or other culture-based mechanism that helps people think and act more effectively.

■ **internalization** Process through which social activities evolve into mental activities.

After looking closely at this cricket, the children voice varying opinions about whether to keep it and, if so, how best to care for it. According to Vygotsky, the process of considering various points of view first occurs at a social level. Gradually, children internalize the "arguing" process and become capable of looking at a situation from multiple perspectives by themselves.

a variety of matters—how best to carry out an activity, what games to play, who did what to whom, and so on. According to Vygotsky, childhood arguments help children discover that there are often several ways to view the same situation. Eventually, children can, in essence, internalize the "arguing" process, developing the ability to look at a situation from several different angles *on their own*.

◎ *Children can perform more challenging tasks when assisted by more advanced and competent individuals.* Vygotsky distinguished between two kinds of abilities that children are apt to have at any particular point in their development. A child's **actual developmental level** is the upper limit of tasks he or she can perform independently, without help from anyone else. A child's **level of potential development** is the upper limit of tasks he or she can perform with the assistance of a more competent individual. To get a true sense of children's cognitive development, Vygotsky suggested, we should assess their capabilities both when performing alone and when performing with assistance.

Children can typically do more difficult things in collaboration with adults than they can do on their own. For instance, as we saw in the opening case study, they can read more complex prose with the assistance of a teacher than they are likely to read independently. When learning how to swing a baseball bat, they are often more successful when adults initially guide their swing. And notice how a student who cannot independently solve division problems with remainders begins to learn the correct procedure through an interaction with her teacher:

Teacher: [writes 6)‾44‾ on the board] 44 divided by 6. What number times 6 is close to 44?
Child: 6.
Teacher: What's 6 times 6? [writes 6]
Child: 36.
Teacher: 36. Can you get one that's any closer? [erasing the 6]
Child: 8.
Teacher: What's 6 times 8?
Child: 64 . . . 48.
Teacher: 48. Too big. Can you think of something . . .
Child: 6 times 7 is 42. (Pettito, 1985, p. 251)

◎ *Challenging tasks promote maximum cognitive growth.* The range of tasks children cannot yet perform independently but *can* perform with the help and guidance of others is, in Vygotsky's terminology, the **zone of proximal development (ZPD)**. A child's zone of proximal development includes learning and problem-solving abilities that are just beginning to develop—abilities that are in an immature, "embryonic" form. Naturally, any child's ZPD will change over time; as some tasks are mastered, other, more complex ones appear on the horizon to take their place.

Vygotsky proposed that children learn very little from performing tasks they can already do independently. Instead, they develop primarily by attempting tasks they can accomplish only in collaboration with a more competent individual—that is, when they attempt tasks within their zone of proximal development. In a nutshell, it is the challenges in life, not the easy successes, that promote cognitive development.

As teachers, then, we should assign some tasks that students can perform successfully only with help from others. In some cases such assistance must come from more skilled individuals, such as adults or older students. In other situations, however, students of equal ability can work together to jointly accomplish difficult assignments. Students with different zones of proximal development may sometimes need different tasks and assignments—a strong case for providing as much individualized instruction as possible.

◎ *Play allows children to stretch themselves cognitively.* As a kindergartner, my son Jeff often played "restaurant" with his friend Scott. In a corner of our basement, the boys created a restaurant "kitchen" with a toy sink and stove and stocked it with plastic dishes, cooking utensils, and "food" items. They created a separate dining area with child-sized tables and chairs and made menus for their customers. On one occasion they invited both sets of parents to "dine" at the restaurant, taking our orders, serving us our food, and eventually giving us our bills. (Fortunately, they seemed quite happy with the few pennies we paid them for our "meals.")

■ **actual developmental level** Upper limit of tasks one can perform independently.

■ **level of potential development** Upper limit of tasks one can perform with the assistance of a more competent individual.

■ **zone of proximal development (ZPD)** Range of tasks that a child can perform with the help and guidance of others but cannot yet perform independently.

In their restaurant play, the two boys took on several adult roles (restaurant manager, waiter, cook) and practiced a variety of adultlike behaviors. In real life such a scenario would, of course, be impossible: Very few 5-year-old children have the cooking, reading, writing, mathematical, or organizational skills necessary to run a restaurant. Yet the element of make-believe brought these tasks within the boys' reach. In Vygotsky's words:

> In play a child is always above his average age, above his daily behavior, in play it is as though he were a head taller than himself. (Vygotsky, 1978, p. 102)

Furthermore, as children play, their behaviors must conform to certain standards or expectations. In the early elementary school years, children often act in accordance with how a "daddy," "teacher," or "waiter' would behave. In the organized group games and sports that come later, children must follow a specific set of rules. By adhering to such restrictions on their behavior, children learn to plan ahead, to think before they act, and to engage in self-restraint—skills critical for successful participation in the adult world.

Play, then, is hardly a waste of time. Instead, it provides a valuable training ground for the adult world, and perhaps for this reason it is seen in virtually all cultures worldwide.

Current Perspectives on Vygotsky's Theory

Vygotsky focused more on the processes through which children develop than on the abilities that children of particular ages are apt to have. Furthermore, his descriptions of developmental processes were often imprecise and lacking in detail (Gauvain, 2001; Haenan, 1996; Wertsch, 1984). For such reasons, Vygotsky's theory has been more difficult for researchers to test and either verify or disprove than has Piaget's theory.

Nevertheless, contemporary theorists and educators have found Vygotsky's ideas quite insightful and helpful. First and foremost, his theory points out the many ways in which *culture* influences cognitive development. A society's culture ensures that each new generation benefits from the wisdom that preceding generations have accumulated. It guides children in certain directions by encouraging them to pay attention to particular stimuli (and not to others) and to engage in particular activities (and not in others). And it provides a lens through which children come to construct culturally appropriate interpretations of their experiences. We see obvious effects of culture in many of children's everyday activities—in the books they read, the jokes they tell, the roles they enact in pretend play, the extracurricular activities they pursue—but we must remember that culture permeates children's unobservable thinking processes as well.

The Into the Classroom feature "Applying Vygotsky's Theory" presents concrete examples of how teachers might make use of Vygotsky's ideas. In the next few pages, we'll consider several ways in which contemporary theorists and educators have built upon the foundation that Vygotsky laid. In later chapters we will continue to apply Vygotsky's theory—for instance, as we discuss authentic activities (Chapters 7 and 13), self-instructions (Chapter 10), reciprocal teaching (Chapter 13), and dynamic assessment (Chapter 15).

Social Construction of Meaning   As mentioned earlier, Vygotsky proposed that adults help children attach meaning to the objects and events around them. More recently, theorists have elaborated on this idea. They point out that an adult often helps a child make sense of the world through joint discussion of a phenomenon or event they have mutually experienced (Eacott, 1999; Feuerstein, 1990; Feuerstein, Klein, & Tannenbaum, 1991; John-Steiner & Mahn, 1996). Such an interaction, sometimes called a **mediated learning experience**, encourages the child to think about the phenomenon or event in particular ways: to attach labels to it, recognize principles that underlie it, draw certain conclusions from it, and so on.

In addition to co-constructing meanings with adults, children often talk among themselves to make sense of their experiences. School provides an ideal setting in which young learners can toss around ideas and perhaps reach consensus about how best to interpret and understand an issue or problem. As an example, let's consider a discussion in Keisha Coleman's third-grade class. The students are debating how they might solve the problem $-10 + 10 = ?$. They are using a number line like the following to facilitate their discussion:

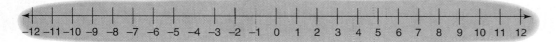

■ **mediated learning experience**
Interaction in which an adult helps a child make sense of a phenomenon or event.

Applying Vygotsky's Theory

 Encourage students to talk themselves through difficult tasks.

As his students work on complex mathematical equations such as this one,

$$x = \frac{2(4 \times 9)^2 + 3}{6}$$

a junior high school mathematics teacher gives students a mnemonic (*"Please excuse my dear Aunt Sally"*) they might repeat to themselves to remember the order in which they should perform various operations (*parentheses, exponents, multiplication and divison, addition and subtraction*).

 Provide cognitive tools that students can use to make difficult tasks easier.

A high school chemistry teacher places two equal-size inflated balloons into two beakers of water, one heated to 25°C and the other heated to 50°C. The students all agree that the balloon placed in the warmer water expands more. "Now how much more did the 50-degree balloon expand?" the teacher asks. "Let's use Charles's law to figure it out."

 Present some tasks that students can perform successfully only with assistance.

A fifth-grade teacher assigns students their first research paper, knowing that he will have to give them a great deal of guidance as they work on it.

Provide sufficient support (scaffolding) to enable students to perform challenging tasks successfully;

gradually withdraw the support as they become more proficient.

An elementary physical education teacher begins a lesson on tumbling by demonstrating forward and backward rolls in slow motion and physically guiding her students through the correct movements. As the students become more skillful, she stands back from the mat and gives verbal feedback about how to improve.

 Have students work in small groups to accomplish complex tasks.

A middle school art teacher asks his students to work in groups of four or five to design large murals that depict various ecosystems— rain forest, desert, grassland, tundra, and so on—and the kinds of plant and animal species that live in each one. The groups then paint their murals on the walls in the school corridors.

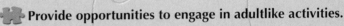 **Provide opportunities to engage in adultlike activities.**

A high school publishes a monthly school newspaper with news articles, editorials, cartoons, announcements of upcoming events, advertisements for local businesses, and classified ads. Students assume various roles, including reporters, cartoonists, marketers, editors, proofreaders, photocopiers, and distributors.

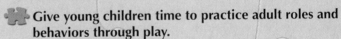 **Give young children time to practice adult roles and behaviors through play.**

A kindergarten teacher equips his classroom with many household items (dress-up clothes, cooking utensils, a toy telephone, etc.) so that students can play house during free-play time.

Several students, including Tessa, agree that the solution is "zero" but disagree about how to use the number line to arrive at that answer. Excerpts from a discussion between Tessa and her classmate Chang (as facilitated by Ms. Coleman) follow:

Tessa: You have to count numbers to the right. If you count numbers to the right, then you couldn't get to zero. You'd have to count to the left.

[Ms. Coleman]: Could you explain a little bit more about what you mean by that? I'm not quite sure I follow you. . . .

Tessa: Because if you went that way [points to the right] then it would have to be a higher number. . . .

Chang: I disagree with what she's trying to say. . . . Tessa says if you're counting right, then the number is—I don't really understand. She said, "If you count right, then the number has to go smaller." I don't know what she's talking about. Negative ten plus ten is zero. . . . What do you mean by counting to the right?

Tessa: If you count from ten up, you can't get zero. If you count from ten left, you can get zero.

Chang: Well, negative ten is a negative number—smaller than zero.

Tessa: I know.

Chang: Then why do you say you can't get to zero when you're adding to negative ten, which is smaller than zero?

Tessa: OHHHH! NOW I GET IT! This is positive. . . . You have to count right.

[Ms. Coleman]: You're saying in order to get to zero, you have to count to the right? From where, Tessa?

Tessa: Negative 10. (P. L. Peterson, 1992, pp. 165–166)

The class continues in its efforts to pin down precisely how to use the number line to solve the problem. Eventually, Tessa offers a revised and more complete explanation. Pointing to the appropriate location on the number line, she says, "You start at negative 10. Then you add 1, 2, 3, 4, 5, 6, 7, 8, 9, 10." She moves her finger one number to the right for each number she counts. She reaches the zero point on the number line when she counts "10" and concludes, "That equals zero" (P. L. Peterson, 1992, p. 168).

Notice that at no time does Ms. Coleman impose her own interpretations on either the problem itself or on what Tessa and Chang have to say about the problem. Instead, she lets the two children struggle to make sense of the problem and, eventually, to agree on how best to solve it.

Many contemporary theorists have become convinced of the value of joint meaning-making discussions in helping children acquire more complex understandings of their physical, social, and academic worlds (e.g., Hatano & Inagaki, 1993; Hiebert et al., 1997; Lampert, 1990; Sosniak & Stodolsky, 1994). We will pursue this idea, generally known as **social constructivism**, in more depth in Chapter 7.

Cognitive Tools   No other species can compare to human beings in its use of tools to facilitate daily living. Tools such as hammers, knives, and scissors—as well as books, diagrams, maps, computers, and even paper and pencil—greatly enhance our ability to solve problems, communicate with one another and, more generally, thrive and prosper.

Not all tools are concrete objects, however. Many take the form of concepts, symbols, study strategies, and other ways of thinking and learning about the world. For instance, students often become better musicians when they can read music and understand what *keys*, *chords*, and *thirds* are. They can more easily attack mathematical and scientific problems when they work with symbols such as H_2O, *NaCl*, π, and x^3.

Writing is one area in which providing cognitive tools seems to make an appreciable difference in what students are capable of doing (Scardamalia & Bereiter, 1985). As an illustration, in teacher Sharon McManus's combined third- and fourth-grade classroom, students use several tools that either directly or indirectly help them plan and focus their writing and make their stories and essays graphic, interesting, and easy to understand. In Figure 2.7 we see how a boy named Kyle shows considerable improvement in writing from September of his third-grade year to December of his fourth-grade year. As Ms. McManus has used this approach over the past several years, she has seen many of her students internalize the tools they have been using—eventually using them almost without thinking—and has seen the quality of writing improve dramatically in children of all ability levels and backgrounds. Kyle, for instance, has learning disabilities, and until his grandparents gained custody of him at age 8, he lived an unstable, transient life with a single mother who had significant substance abuse problems.

Scaffolding   Theorists have given considerable thought to the kinds of assistance that can help children complete challenging tasks and activities. The term **scaffolding** is often used here: Adults and other more competent individuals provide some form of guidance or structure that enables children to perform tasks in their zone of proximal development. To understand this concept, let's first think about how scaffolding is used in the construction of a new building. The *scaffold* is an external structure that provides support for the workers (e.g., a place where they can stand) until the building itself is strong enough to support them. As the building gains stability, the scaffold becomes less necessary and so is gradually removed.

In much the same way, an adult guiding a child through a new task may provide an initial scaffold to support the child's early efforts. In the teacher-student dialogue about division presented earlier, the teacher provided clues about how to proceed, such as searching for the multiple of 6 closest to, but still less than, 44. Similarly, Sharon McManus gave Kyle a structure ("web") to help him brainstorm his ideas about hockey (see Figure 2.7). As a child becomes capable of working without such support, the adult gradually removes it, a process known as *fading*.

As teachers, we can provide a variety of support mechanisms to help students master tasks within their zone of proximal development. Following are examples:

- Work with students to develop a plan for dealing with a new task.
- Demonstrate the proper performance of the task in a way that students can easily imitate.
- Divide a complex task into several smaller, simpler tasks.
- Provide structure or guidelines about how the task should be accomplished.

■ What task in your zone of proximal development have you recently performed? Who scaffolded your efforts so that you could successfully complete it?

■ **social constructivism** Theoretical perspective that focuses on people's collective efforts to impose meaning on the world.

■ **scaffolding** Support mechanism that helps a learner successfully perform a task within his or her ZPD.

FIGURE 2.7 In writing a narrative about hockey, Kyle uses several cognitive tools, all of which revolve around essential elements of good writing. Notice how the quality of Kyle's writing improves from September of his third-grade year to December of his fourth-grade year.

The "Framing a Paper" form shown in Item 2 and three evaluation criteria presented in Item 3 are from the program *Empowering Young Writers®* developed and copyrighted by Frederick M. Jervis and Janis P. Williams of The Center for Constructive Change, 16 Strafford Avenue, Durham, NH 03824 (603–868–5433). They are reprinted by permission.

The first day was uasoum
I liked it very/munch
becase we play a lot
of games but it was
hot that day and I was
swatiting and the lunch
was daring good The End

1. In September of third grade, Kyle writes only a single paragraph, with little in the way of a story line. (The last word on the first line is his version of *awesome*.)

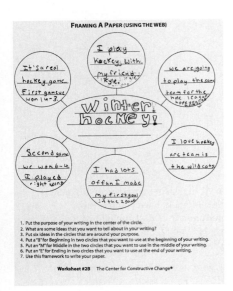

FRAMING A PAPER (USING THE WEB)

1. Put the purpose of your writing in the center of the circle.
2. What are some ideas that you want to tell about in your writing?
3. Put six ideas in the circles that are around your purpose.
4. Put a "B" for Beginning in two circles that you want to use at the beginning of your writing.
5. Put an "M" for Middle in the two circles that you want to use in the middle of your writing.
6. Put an "E" for Ending in two circles that you want to use at the end of your writing.
7. Use this framework to write your paper.

Worksheet #2B The Center for Constructive Change®

2. By December of fourth grade, Kyle has learned how to frame his compositions using a variety of structures. Here he uses a *web* format to brainstorm the things he wants to say about a hockey game.

Winter Hockey

I love hockey and winter becase hockey is my favriot sport and winter is my favriot season becase I was bon in winter thats why.

It is a pain to put my stuff on. So my grampy helped me put my stuff on. He put my pads, sholder pads, helmett, all other stuff. Than I got their and I played hockey and I thought it was so fun we won 14–3. I was so proud. When I got home. I said to my nanny and grampy we won are first game my nanny and grampy sal d good job. I was so Exsited! that are team won.

Next game Andrew was their and he was dribiling up to the net he fake d and shot and he got the goal! We were banging are stick agentce the boards. Than joe came up and shoot and got the goal to! Than the score was 3–3 than I went up to the goal and I shoot at the goal and I mad the goal and everybody was saying lets go Kyle lets go letsgo! 4–3 than sam came up and got a goal. Than 5–4 than Andrew again shoot than we won the game Than it was practice and we practicet stoping. It was awesome great and we got are T-shirts.

Hockey is the best sport ever I hope you like it as much as I do.

3. After organizing his ideas, Kyle writes a first draft of his story. Then both he and his teacher evaluate this draft using a variety of criteria (e.g., "uses examples and comparisons," "uses one or more of the five senses," "variety in language and sentence structure"), and his teacher also evaluates his self-evaluation.

House Hockey

I love Hockey and I love winter. Hockey is my favorite sport and winter is My favorite season because I was born in winter that's why.

It is a pain to put my stuff on so my grampy helped me put my stuff on, my pads, sholuder pads, helmet and all other stuff. Then I got there and I played hockey. I thought it was so fun, we won 14–3. I was so proud When I got home I said to my nanny and grampy "we won our first game." my nanny and grampy said "Good job." I was so Excited that our team won!!!

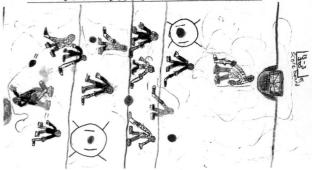

My coach's is Greg Quret, and coach Parker. Next game Andrew was there and he was dribbling up to the net. He faked and shot and he got the goal! We were banging our sticks against the boards. Than Joe came up and shot and got the goal too! Then the score was 3–3. I went up to the

goal and I made the goal! Every body was saying "Lets go Kyle, lets go! 4–3! Then Sam came up and got a goal to make it 5–4. Then Andrew again shot then we won the game!

Then it was practice and we practice stopping. It was awesome, great and we got our T shirts.

Hockey is the best sport ever. I hope you like it as much as I do I was born to play hockey It makes me me feel great when I play hockey. Hockey is the fastest and most exciting game on earth!

The End

4. Making use of the evaluation results, Kyle writes and illustrates his final draft.

- Provide a calculator, computer software (word processing program, spreadsheet, etc.), or other technology that makes some aspects of the task easier.
- Ask questions that get students thinking in appropriate ways about the task.
- Keep students' attention focused on the relevant aspects of the task.
- Keep students motivated to complete the task.
- Remind students what their goal is in performing the task (e.g., what a problem solution should look like).
- Give frequent feedback about how students are progressing. (Gallimore & Tharp, 1990; Good, McCaslin, & Reys, 1992; Lajoie & Derry, 1993; P. F. Merrill et al., 1996; Rogoff, 1990; Rosenshine & Meister, 1992; D. Wood, Bruner, & Ross, 1976)

As students develop increasing competence, we can gradually withdraw some of these support mechanisms, eventually allowing students to perform the task independently. In a manner of speaking, when we remove such scaffolding, we allow and encourage students to stand on their own two feet.

Guided Participation   When you were a young child, did you sometimes help your mother, father, or an older sibling bake things in the kitchen? Did the cook let you pour, measure, and mix ingredients when you were old enough to do so? Did the cook also give you directions or suggestions as you performed these tasks?

Older family members often allow young children to perform household tasks (cooking, cleaning, painting, and so on) while providing guidance about how to do these tasks appropriately. Teachers, too, often introduce students to adult tasks within a structured and supportive context. For instance, they might ask students to conduct laboratory experiments, write letters to government officials, or search the Internet for specific information, while always providing the support the students need to accomplish such tasks successfully.

When we guide or assist our students as they perform adultlike activities, we engage them in **guided participation** in the world of adults (Rogoff, 2003). As we guide them, we might also use some of the language that adults frequently use in such contexts; for example, when students conduct scientific experiments, we should use words such as *hypothesis*, *evidence*, and *theory* as we help them evaluate their procedures and results (Perkins, 1992).

Apprenticeships   In some instances adults work with children and adolescents in formal or informal **apprenticeships**, one-on-one relationships in which the adults teach the young people new skills, guide their initial efforts, and present increasingly difficult tasks as proficiency improves and the zone of proximal development changes (Rogoff, 1990, 1991). Many cultures use apprenticeships as a way of gradually introducing children to particular skills and trades—perhaps weaving, tailoring, or midwifery—in the adult community (Lave & Wenger, 1991; Rogoff, 1990). Apprenticeships are also common in teaching a child how to play a musical instrument (D. J. Elliott, 1995).

Through an apprenticeship, a student often learns not only how to perform a task but also how to *think about* a task; such a situation is sometimes called a **cognitive apprenticeship** (J. S. Brown, Collins, & Duguid, 1989; John-Steiner, 1997; W. Roth & Bowen, 1995). For instance, a student and a teacher might work together to accomplish a challenging task or solve a difficult problem (perhaps collecting data samples in biology fieldwork, solving a mathematical brain teaser, or translating a difficult passage from German to English). In the process of talking about various aspects of the task or problem, the teacher and student together analyze the situation and develop the best approach to take, and the teacher models effective ways of thinking about and mentally processing the situation.

Although apprenticeships can differ widely from one context to another, they typically have some or all of these features (A. Collins, Brown, & Newman, 1989):

- *Modeling.*   The teacher demonstrates the task, simultaneously thinking aloud about the process, while the student observes and listens.
- *Coaching.*   As the student performs the task, the teacher gives frequent suggestions, hints, and feedback.
- *Scaffolding.*   The teacher provides various forms of support for the student, perhaps by simplifying the task, breaking it into smaller and more manageable components, or providing less complicated equipment.

■ **guided participation** A child's performance, with guidance and support, of an activity in the adult world.

■ **apprenticeship** Situation in which a learner works intensively with an expert to learn how to accomplish complex tasks.

■ **cognitive apprenticeship** Mentorship in which a teacher and a student work together on a challenging task and the teacher gives guidance about how to think about the task.

- *Articulation.*　The student explains what he or she is doing and why, allowing the teacher to examine the student's knowledge, reasoning, and problem-solving strategies.
- *Reflection.*　The teacher asks the student to compare his or her performance with that of experts, or perhaps with an ideal model of how the task should be done.
- *Increasing complexity and diversity of tasks.*　As the student gains greater proficiency, the teacher presents more complex, challenging, and varied tasks to complete.
- *Exploration.*　The teacher encourages the student to frame questions and problems on his or her own and thereby expand and refine acquired skills.

Apprenticeships are clearly labor-intensive; as such, their use in the classroom is not always practical or logistically feasible (e.g., De Corte, Greer, & Verschaffel, 1996). Yet many theorists believe that involvement in adult activities is important to help children tie their newly acquired skills and thinking abilities to the specific contexts in which they are likely to need them later on. We'll explore this idea in more depth in our discussion of *transfer* in Chapter 8.

Peer Interaction　Contemporary theorists suggest that interacting with peers plays somewhat different roles in development than interacting with adults. Adults usually have more experience and expertise than age-mates do, and they tend to be more skillful teachers; accordingly, they are often the partners of choice when children are trying to master complex new tasks and procedures (Gauvain, 2001; Radziszewska & Rogoff, 1988). Yet working with peers has its own advantages, three of which we have already noted. First, by discussing various perspectives on a situation or problem, children can often construct a more complete understanding of a topic. Second, to the extent that their discussions involve debate and disagreement, children may internalize the arguing process and become capable of independently looking at a situation from multiple angles. Third, children can often accomplish more difficult tasks when they work together rather than alone; in such situations they are essentially providing scaffolding for one another's efforts. A fourth advantage, which we haven't yet considered, is that children learn valuable social behaviors—how to plan a joint enterprise, how to coordinate differing roles, and so on—when they work on cognitive tasks with their peers (Gauvain, 2001).

In recent years researchers and practitioners alike have become increasingly convinced that interactive approaches to instruction, in which students work collaboratively rather than in isolation, can be highly effective in promoting both cognitive development and classroom achievement. In Chapter 7 we'll consider the advantages and effects of peer interaction for classroom learning and achievement, and in Chapter 13 we'll examine instructional strategies that promote such interaction.

As we have seen, Vygotsky and his followers have suggested several possible mechanisms—for instance, internalization, mediated learning experiences, and cognitive apprenticeships—through which children might acquire increasingly sophisticated cognitive processes. Meanwhile, other developmental theorists have tried to pin down the specific nature of children's cognitive processes at different ages. Some have looked at the development of reasoning and logic (as Piaget did), whereas others have examined processes involved in attention, learning, and memory. The perspective that many of these researchers have taken—information processing theory—is our next topic of discussion.

AN INFORMATION PROCESSING VIEW OF COGNITIVE DEVELOPMENT

Stop for a moment to consider what you yourself have observed about children of different ages. Do you think children become better at paying attention as they grow older? Do you think older children remember more than younger children, or vice versa? In what ways do high school students learn and study differently from elementary students?

Such questions are addressed by **information processing theory**, an approach to cognitive development that emerged in the late 1950s and early 1960s and has continued to evolve in the decades that have followed. Initially, many information processing theorists speculated that human beings think in ways similar to how computers operate, but in recent years they have discovered that human thought is much more complex, and much less straightforward, than computer processes. Much of information processing theory now has a *constructivist* flavor similar to that of Piaget's and Vygotsky's theories: Children actively construct their understandings of the world, rather than simply receiving and absorbing knowledge from the outside world in the relatively "mindless" way a computer does.

■ **information processing theory**
Theoretical perspective focusing on the specific ways in which learners mentally think about (process) new information and events.

Information processing theory is actually a collection of theories that emphasize the development of **cognitive processes**—processes through which children acquire, interpret, remember, manipulate, and make use of information. Most information processing theorists reject Piaget's notion of discrete developmental stages. Instead, they believe that children's cognitive processes and abilities develop through more steady and gradual *trends*; for instance, they propose that children learn faster, remember more, and can think about increasingly complex tasks as they grow. In the next few pages, we examine developmental trends in children's attention, learning strategies, knowledge, and metacognition.

Attention

Two trends in cognitive development relate to children's attention and its impact on learning:

■ Observe Maddie's short attention span in the "Cognitive Development: Early Childhood" clip on Video CD 1.

◎ *Children become less distractible over time.* Young children's attention often moves quickly from one thing to another, and it is easily drawn to objects and events unrelated to the task at hand (e.g., notice how quickly Maddie loses interest in the conservation task near the end of the "Cognitive Development: Early Childhood" clip on Video CD 1). But as children grow older, they become better able to focus their attention on a particular task and keep it there, and they are less distracted by irrelevant thoughts and events (S. M. Carlson & Moses, 2001; Dempster & Corkill, 1999; Lane & Pearson, 1982). For example, in one experiment (Higgins & Turnure, 1984), children at several grade levels were given a difficult learning task. Some children worked on the task in a quiet room, others worked in a room with a little background noise, and still others worked with a great deal of background noise. Preschool and second-grade children learned most quickly under the quiet conditions and most slowly under the very noisy conditions. But the sixth graders were able to learn just as easily in the noisy room as in the quiet room. Apparently, the older children could ignore the noise, whereas the younger children could not.

◎ *How and what children learn depend increasingly on what they actually intend to learn.* Try the following exercise before you read further.

Experiencing FIRSTHAND ·Six Cards

Look at the six cards below. Try to remember the *colors* of the cards and the order in which each color appears. Study them for about 15 seconds, and then cover them with your hand.

Now that you have covered the six cards, answer these questions:

■ In which spot is the yellow card? the green card? the blue card? the pink card?
■ Where is the cake? the flowers? the guitar? the pair of scissors?

Modeled after a task used by Maccoby & Hagen, 1965.

· · · · · · ·

How accurately did you remember the colors of the cards? How accurately did you remember the objects pictured on the cards? If you are like most adults, you had better success remembering what you intended to learn (the colors) than what you did *not* intend to learn (the objects).

Perhaps because of their distractibility, younger children often remember many things unrelated to what they are supposed to be doing or learning (DeMarie-Dreblow & Miller, 1988; Hagen & Stanovich, 1977; P. Miller & Seier, 1994). For example, when students in grades 1 through 7 were asked to perform a series of tasks similar to the "Six Cards" exercise, older students remembered the background colors more accurately than younger students. Yet the older students were no better than the younger ones at remembering the objects pictured on the cards; in fact,

■ **cognitive processes** Ways in which one thinks about (processes) information.

the oldest group in the study remembered the *fewest* number of objects (Maccoby & Hagen, 1965). Older children, then, are better at learning and remembering the things they *want* to learn; they are not necessarily better at learning irrelevant information.

Learning Strategies

Preschoolers often recognize the need to remember something but seem to have little idea of how to go about learning it, apart from looking or pointing at it (Kail, 1990; Wellman, 1988). As children grow older, however, they develop a number of **learning strategies**—specific, intentional methods of learning information—that help them learn and remember things. Following are several commonly observed trends in the development of learning strategies:

◎   *Rehearsal increases during the elementary school years.* What do you do if you need to remember a telephone number for a few minutes? Do you repeat it to yourself over and over again as a way of keeping it in your memory until you dial it? This process of **rehearsal** is rare in kindergarten children but increases in frequency and sophistication throughout the elementary school years (Bjorklund & Coyle, 1995; Gathercole & Hitch, 1993; Kail, 1990). As you will discover in Chapter 6, rehearsal is a relatively *ineffective* way of learning and remembering information for the long run (just how long do you remember those phone numbers you rehearse?), but it is certainly better than no strategy at all.

◎   *Organization improves throughout the elementary and secondary grades.* Before you read further, try the following learning exercise.

Experiencing FIRSTHAND ·Mental Maneuver

Read the twelve words below *one time only*. Then cover up the page, and write the words down in the order they come to mind.

shirt	table	hat
carrot	bed	squash
pants	potatoes	stool
chair	shoe	bean

· · · · · · ·

In what order did you remember the words? Did you recall them in their original order, or did you rearrange them somehow? If you are like most people, you grouped the words into three categories—clothing, vegetables, and furniture—and remembered one category at a time. In other words, you imposed **organization** on the information. In three of the four "Memory and Metacognition" clips on Video CD 1, you can watch 6-year-old Brent, 12-year-old Colin, and 16-year-old Hilary organize these twelve words into categories. For example, Brent first recalls two vegetables, then a piece of furniture, then three items of clothing: "Beans, squash, stool, shirt, pants, hat . . . . I forget."

Research consistently shows that organized information is learned more easily and remembered more completely than unorganized information (see Chapter 6). As children grow older, they more frequently and effectively organize the information they receive. This tendency to organize begins in early childhood and continues to develop well into the high school years (Bjorklund, Schneider, Cassel, & Ashley, 1994; M. Carr, Kurtz, Schneider, Turner, & Borkowski, 1989; DeLoache & Todd, 1988; Hacker, 1998a; Plumert, 1994).

◎   *Elaboration emerges around puberty and increases throughout adolescence.* If I tell you that I lived in Colorado for many years, you will probably conclude that I lived in or near the Rocky Mountains. You might also infer that perhaps I did a lot of skiing, hiking, or camping. In this situation you are learning more than the information I actually gave you; you are also learning some information that you yourself are supplying. This process of using what you already know to expand on new information is called **elaboration**. In our "Economic Activities" case study, Mr. Sand encourages his students to elaborate by generating their own examples of economic concepts.

Elaboration clearly helps students learn and remember classroom material more effectively than they would otherwise (more about this in Chapter 6). Children begin to elaborate on their experiences as early as the preschool years (Fivush, Haden, & Adam, 1995). Yet as a

■ Observe how Brent, Colin, and Hilary organize a word list in the early childhood, early adolescence, and late adolescence "Memory and Metacognition" clips on Video CD 1.

■ **learning strategy** One or more cognitive processes used intentionally for a particular learning task.

■ **rehearsal** Cognitive process in which information is repeated over and over as a possible way of learning and remembering it.

■ **organization** Cognitive process in which learners find connections (e.g., by forming categories, identifying hierarchies, determining cause-effect relationships) among the various pieces of information they need to learn.

■ **elaboration** Cognitive process in which learners expand on new information based on what they already know.

strategy that children *intentionally* use to help them learn and make sense of new information, elaboration appears relatively late in development (usually around puberty) and gradually increases throughout the teenage years (Flavell, Miller, & Miller, 1993; Schneider & Pressley, 1989). Even in high school, it is primarily high-achieving students who use their existing knowledge to help themselves learn (Barnett, 2001; Pressley, 1982; E. Wood, Motz, & Willoughby, 1997). Low-achieving high school students often depend on more superficial, less "thoughtful" strategies (such as rehearsal) in their attempts to remember what they are studying.

Both organization and elaboration are *constructive* in nature: Learners take new information, rearrange it or add to it based on what they already know, and so construct an understanding that is uniquely their own.

◎ *Learning strategies become increasingly efficient and effective.* Children often have several strategies at their disposal at any one time, and they may use different strategies on different occasions (Kuhn, 2001b; Siegler, 1996). When children first acquire new learning strategies, they use them infrequently, effortfully, and often ineffectively. But with time and practice, they become increasingly adept at applying their strategies quickly, effeciently, and flexibly as they tackle challenging classroom learning tasks. As they gain competence and confidence with more sophisticated strategies, they gradually leave their less efficient ones behind (P. A. Alexander, Graham, & Harris, 1998; Flavell et al., 1993; Siegler, 1998).

Often, by looking closely at what students say and write, we can get a sense of the kinds of strategies they are and aren't using. As an example, try the following exercise.

> ■ We will examine rehearsal, organization, and elaboration in greater depth in Chapter 6.

Interpreting Student Artifacts and Behaviors

Dutch Cheese

Ten-year-old Sean wrote this research report about Dutch cheese. At the bottom of the report, he has pasted (1) a picture of Edam cheese, (2) a map of the Netherlands (with dairy regions circled in felt tip pen), and (3) a photocopied picture of a Dutch cheese market; the numbers in his paper are intended to direct the reader to these three items. As you read Sean's report, speculate about

- Strategies he used when reading about his topic and writing his paper
- Strategies he did *not* use that might have made the report better and enhanced his learning

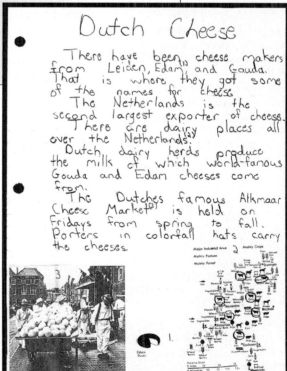

Sean has taken a somewhat superficial approach to reading and writing about Dutch cheese. It appears that he has simply taken a few facts he has read (perhaps paraphrasing them, perhaps reproducing them verbatim) without organizing or elaborating on them in any way that might help him remember them better. One exception to this pattern is his circling of dairy regions on the map of the Netherlands, indicating an effort to integrate (organize) a little bit of what he has learned. Middle school students often write reports in a superficial manner, listing facts rather than pulling them together in a cohesive, organized, and elaborated fashion (Bereiter & Scardamalia, 1987; McCutchen, 1996).

Knowledge

Children's knowledge of specific topics and of the world in general—their **knowledge base**—changes in at least two ways as they develop:

◎ *Children's growing knowledge base enhances their ability to learn new things.* Children's knowledge about the world grows by leaps and bounds every year. This increasing knowledge base is one reason why adults and older children learn new things more easily than younger children: They have more existing knowledge to help them understand and elaborate on new ideas and events (Flavell et al., 1993; Halford, 1989; Kail, 1990). As an example, consider the case of an Inuit (Eskimo) man named Tor.

> ■ **knowledge base** One's knowledge about specific topics and the world in general.

As children grow older, they become increasingly able to draw inferences from what they see, in part because they have a larger and better integrated knowledge base to help them interpret their experiences.

Experiencing FIRSTHAND · · · · · · · · · · · · · · ·Tor of the Targa

Tor, a young man of the Targa tribe, was out hunting in the ancient hunting territory of his people. He had been away from his village for many days. The weather was bad and he had not yet managed to locate his prey. Because of the extreme temperature he knew he must soon return but it was a matter of honor among his people to track and kill the prey single-handed. Only when this was achieved could a boy be considered a man. Those who failed were made to eat and keep company with the old men and the women until they could accomplish this task.

Suddenly, in the distance, Tor could make out the outline of a possible prey. It was alone and not too much bigger than Tor, who could take him single-handed. But as he drew nearer, a hunter from a neighboring tribe came into view, also stalking the prey. The intruder was older than Tor and had around his neck evidence of his past success at the hunt. "Yes," thought Tor, "he is truly a man." Tor was undecided. Should he challenge the intruder or return home empty handed? To return would mean bitter defeat. The other young men of the tribe would laugh at his failure. He decided to creep up on the intruder and wait his chance. (A. L. Brown, Smiley, Day, Townsend, & Lawton, 1977, p. 1460)

■ On what kind of terrain was Tor hunting?
■ What was the weather like?
■ What kind of prey might Tor have been stalking?

· · · · · · ·

You probably used your knowledge about Inuits to speculate that Tor was hunting polar bears or seals on snow and ice, possibly in freezing temperatures or a bad blizzard. But notice that the story itself didn't tell you any of these things; you had to *infer* them. Like you, older children often know a great deal about how Inuit people live and can use that information to help them to elaborate on, and so better understand and remember, this very ambiguous story about Tor. Younger children are less likely to make connections between a new situation and what they already know (A. L. Brown et al., 1977).

■ Might you see better performance in "low-ability" students if you encourage them to work with a topic they know a lot about?

In cases where children have more knowledge than adults, then children are often the more effective learners (Chi, 1978; Rabinowitz & Glaser, 1985). For example, when my son Alex and I used to read books about lizards together, Alex always remembered more than I did because he was a self-proclaimed "lizard expert" and I myself knew very little about reptiles of any sort.

◎   *Children's knowledge becomes increasingly integrated.* As we have seen, older children are more likely to organize and elaborate on new information. As learning strategies, both organization and elaboration involve making connections among ideas. As a result, the knowledge base of older children includes many associations and interrelationships among concepts and ideas; that of younger children is more likely to consist of separate, isolated facts (Bjorklund, 1987; Flavell et al., 1993). The more integrated knowledge base of older children is probably one reason that, as Piaget discovered, they can think more logically and draw inferences more readily.

Metacognition

As an adult with many years of formal education behind you, you have probably learned a great deal about how you think and learn. For example, you may have learned that you cannot absorb everything in a textbook the first time you read it, or that you remember information better when you elaborate on it, rather than when you simply repeat it over and over meaninglessly.

The term **metacognition** refers both to the knowledge people have about their own cognitive processes and to their intentional use of certain cognitive processes to facilitate learning and memory. As children develop, their metacognitive knowledge and skills improve in the following ways:

◎   *Children become more aware of the limitations of their memories.* Young children tend to be overly optimistic about how much they can remember. As they grow older and encounter a greater variety of learning tasks, they discover that some things are more difficult to learn than others (Bjorklund & Green, 1992; Flavell et al., 1993). They also begin to realize that their memories are not perfect—that they cannot possibly remember everything they see or hear.

■ **metacognition** One's knowledge and beliefs about one's own cognitive processes and one's resulting attempts to regulate those cognitive processes to maximize learning and memory.

Let's consider an experiment with elementary school children (Flavell, Friedrichs, & Hoyt, 1970) as an example. Children in four age-groups (ranging from preschool to fourth grade) were shown strips of paper with pictures of one to ten objects. The children were asked to predict how many of the objects they could remember over a short period of time. The average predictions of each age-group and the average number of objects the different groups actually *did* remember were as follows:

Age-Group	Predicted Number	Actual Number
Preschool	7.2	3.5
Kindergarten	8.0	3.6
Grade 2	6.0	4.4
Grade 4	6.1	5.5

Notice how all four age-groups predicted that they would remember more objects than they actually could. But the older children were more realistic about the limitations of their memories than the younger ones. The kindergartners predicted they would remember eight objects, but they actually remembered fewer than four!

In the "Memory and Metacognition" clips on Video CD 1, you can observe similar overestimations by 6-year-old Brent and 10-year-old David: Both predict they will recall all twelve words presented, but Brent remembers just six and David recalls only three. In contrast, 12-year-old Colin and 16-year-old Hilary predict their performance quite accurately.

■ In the four "Memory and Metacognition" clips on Video CD 1, observe how older children are more realistic about how much they can remember.

◎ *Children become better able to identify the things they do and do not know.* Young children (e.g., those in the early elementary grades) often think they know or understand something before they actually do. As a result, they don't study new material as much as they should, and they often don't ask questions when they receive incomplete or confusing information (Markman, 1977; McDevitt, Spivey, Sheehan, Lennon, & Story, 1990).

Yet even high school and college students sometimes have difficulty assessing their own knowledge accurately. For example, they often think they can spell words they actually cannot spell (Adams,& Adams, 1960; Ormrod & Wagner, 1987). And they often overestimate how well they will perform on an exam (Hacker, Bol, Horgan, & Rakow, 2000). My own students occasionally come to me expressing frustration about doing poorly on an exam. "I knew the material so well!" they tell me. But when we sit down and begin to talk about the exam material, it usually becomes clear that in fact they have only a very vague understanding of some ideas and an incorrect understanding of others.

◎ *Children become more knowledgeable about effective learning strategies.* As mentioned earlier, children show greater use of such learning strategies as rehearsal, organization, and elaboration as they grow older. With experience they also become increasingly aware of which strategies are effective in different situations (Lovett & Flavell, 1990; Short, Schatschneider, & Friebert, 1993; Wellman, 1985). For example, consider the simple idea that when you don't learn something the first time you try, you need to study it again. This is a strategy that 8-year-olds use but 6-year-olds do not (Masur, McIntyre, & Flavell, 1973). In a similar way, tenth graders are more aware than eighth graders of the advantages of using elaboration to learn new information (Waters, 1982). Even so, many students of all ages (college students included) seem relatively uninformed about which learning strategies work most effectively in different situations (Ormrod & Jenkins, 1989; J. W. Thomas, 1993b; Waters, 1982). Consider one high-achieving high school student's reflections in the following exercise.

Interpreting Student Artifacts and Behaviors

What Do You Do . . . ?

In recent years I have sometimes asked students in my educational psychology classes to interview elementary or high school students about study strategies. One of my students, Kathryn Broadhead, reported the following conversation with a high-achieving 16-year-old sophomore (I'll call him Mitch) who was taking several challenging high school classes. As you read the conversation, consider

■ The kinds of strategies Mitch uses and the learning tasks for which he uses each one
■ Mitch's awareness of what he does (mentally) when he studies and learns

Kathryn:	What do you do when you need to remember something?
Mitch:	I guess just repetition. "Repetition is the master of all teachers." I forgot who said that.
Kathryn:	How do you study for a test? What kinds of things do you do in your head when you study?
Mitch:	I study differently for each subject. I don't study for math . . . never have, never will. It comes easily. Once I learn it the first time, I know it. English [literature] is more of asking questions. The more questions I have, the better I understand. Writing just comes naturally. History, well, that's mostly repetition. That's mainly where it [repetition] comes in . . . history, foreign languages [Latin and Spanish], and science.

Mitch claims that he uses only repetition (i.e., rehearsal) when he studies and believes this to be the most effective strategy ("the master of all teachers"). He is apparently using this strategy primarily for history, foreign languages, and science, however. For English literature he says he asks questions; we can reasonably guess that his questions reflect his attempt to better understand (e.g., elaborate on) what he is reading. Mitch has little awareness of how he approaches math ("it comes easily") or writing (it "just comes naturally"). The facility he has with math and writing suggests a well-integrated knowledge base in these areas, such that he can easily understand and elaborate on new material and so can readily recall the ideas and skills he may need for mathematical problems and writing tasks.

As teachers, we must remember that our students are likely to be less efficient learners than we are. A variety of factors that affect their ability to learn—attention, intention to learn, prior knowledge, awareness and use of effective learning strategies, and so on—develop gradually throughout the school years. We cannot expect that our students will always learn as quickly, or even in the same way, as we do.

Learning strategies make such a difference in students' classroom achievement that we shouldn't leave the development of these strategies to chance. As we ask students to study and learn classroom subject matter, we should also give them suggestions about *how* they might study and learn it. Such an approach is consistent not only with information processing theory but also with Vygotsky's proposal that adults can better promote children's cognitive development by talking about how they themselves think about challenging tasks. Chapter 8 explores the nature of metacognitive knowledge and skills in more detail and provides suggestions for promoting students' metacognitive development.

Critiquing Information Processing Theory

The Into the Classroom feature "Applying Information Processing Theory" illustrates just a few of the many implications this perspective has for classroom practice. Information processing theory is still a work-in-progress, in that theorists continue to modify it as new research data come in. In its present form, it has some limitations. First, although it helps us understand the strategies children use in learning about and understanding new topics, it doesn't explain why children often approach similar learning tasks in very different ways (Klaczynski, 2001). Second, to date it has largely overlooked the effects of children's social and cultural environments on their cognitive development (Gauvain, 2001).

Perhaps a more serious criticism—one we should level at Piaget's and Vygotsky's theories as well as information processing theory—is that current perspectives of cognitive development don't yet adequately account for *why* children advance in their cognitive abilities (Gauvain, 2001; Siegler, 1998). For instance, why do children become less distractible with age? Through what means do they learn about and master such learning strategies as rehearsal, organization, and elaboration? Psychologists have made some progress on this front, to be sure; for instance, children's decreasing distractibility may be partly due to brain maturation (see our earlier discussion of brain development), and their use of more complex learning strategies may result from specific training in such strategies (see Chapter 8). However, we do not yet have a detailed understanding of how maturation and the environment work in concert to transform newborn infants into cognitively sophisticated adults.

Ultimately, we can better understand and promote children's cognitive development when we pull together the concepts and research findings of multiple theoretical perspectives. For example, whereas information processing theorists can tell us the nature of children's learning strategies, sociocultural theorists who build on Vygotsky's work can tell us how adults might help

Applying Information Processing Theory

 Minimize distractions, especially when working with young children.

As his class begins a writing assignment, a first-grade teacher asks his students to put all objects except pencil and paper inside their desks.

 Base instruction on what students already know.

A music teacher introduces a new topic by saying, "You've already learned the scale in C major. Today we're going to study the scale in C minor and see how it is both similar to and different from C major."

 Encourage learning strategies appropriate for the subject matter and age-group.

A third-grade teacher encourages her students to study their spelling words by repeating the letters of each word over and over to themselves and by writing each word several times. Meanwhile, a high school history teacher asks her students to think about why certain historical events may have happened as they did; for example, she encourages them to speculate about the personal motives, economic circumstances, and political and social issues that may have influenced people's decisions at the time.

 Identify situations in which various learning strategies are apt to be useful.

A sixth-grade teacher says to his class, "We've studied several features of the planets in our solar system—size, color, composition, distance from the sun, and duration of revolution around the sun. This sounds like a situation where a two-dimensional chart might help us organize the information."

 Give students many opportunities to assess their own learning efforts and identify what they do and do not know.

A junior high school health teacher has students read a textbook chapter at home and then gives them a nongraded quiz to help them identify parts of the chapter they may need to read again.

children acquire such strategies (Freund, 1990; Gauvain, 2001). Imagine a teacher who wants to help students elaborate on—and so learn more effectively from—what they read in textbooks. This teacher might scaffold students' elaboration on a particular textbook chapter within the context of a group discussion, as Mr. Sand does in the opening case study. With experiences such as this, students may gradually internalize the elaboration process.

No matter which theoretical perspective we take—that of Piaget, Vygotsky, or information processing theorists—we find that children's language capabilities play a key role in their cognitive development. Piaget suggested that words help children mentally represent and think about external objects and events and that language in general is critical for the social interactions that enable children to think less egocentrically and more logically. In Vygotsky's view, verbal interaction and self-talk provide the means through which children gradually internalize and adopt the social processes and ways of thinking of the people around them. From an information processing point of view, much of the knowledge that children acquire about their world comes to them through conversations, explanations, books, and other verbal formats; furthermore, many of their learning strategies (e.g., rehearsal, organization, elaboration) involve words to some degree. We can better understand cognitive development, then, when we also know something about linguistic development.

LINGUISTIC DEVELOPMENT

Using human language effectively is a very complex endeavor. We must know thousands of words and put them together in particular ways. We must be able to articulate such vowel sounds as "ay" and "ee" and such consonants and consonant blends as "buh," "duh," and "struh." To be truly effective communicators, we also must follow certain social conventions; for instance, we should respond to someone else's greeting (e.g., "How are you?") with a greeting of our own (e.g., "Fine, thanks, and how about you?"), and we should let a conversation partner finish a sentence before we speak.

As teachers, we need to know what linguistic knowledge and skills students of different ages tend to have so that we can form realistic expectations for their performance. In the pages that follow, we will briefly examine theoretical perspectives on language development and then look at how various aspects of language change over time. We will also consider research findings related to second-language learning and bilingualism. Much of our focus will be on spoken language; you can learn more about the development of written language (reading and writing) in the chapter "Learning in the Content Areas" in the *Study Guide and Reader* that accompanies this book.

To communicate effectively, children must master many aspects of language; for instance, they must know the meanings of thousands of words, learn complex rules for putting words together, and acquire social conventions for interacting in culturally appropriate ways with adults and peers. Such knowledge and skills continue to develop throughout the school years, often with the guidance of teachers.

Theoretical Perspectives on Language Development

Many theorists believe that human beings are born with a predisposition to learn language—that, to some degree, our knowledge of language is "built-in" (N. Chomsky, 1972; Gopnik, 1997; Karmiloff-Smith, 1993; Lenneberg, 1967). Although we almost certainly are not born knowing any *particular* language, we apparently inherit some constraints regarding the form our language must take. Theorists describe several sources of evidence to support this idea. First, most languages seem to share certain characteristics, such as similar rules for forming negatives and asking questions (N. Chomsky, 1965). Second, all members of a particular society acquire what is more or less the *same* language, despite widely differing early childhood experiences and a general lack of systematic instruction in appropriate language use (Crain, 1993; Cromer, 1993). And third, in some aspects of language development, there appear to be *sensitive periods* during which children benefit more from exposure to their first language. For instance, children have an easier time mastering a language's various verb tenses and learning how to pronounce words flawlessly when they are immersed in the language within the first five to ten years of life (Bialystok, 1994a; Bortfeld & Whitehurst, 2001; Bruer, 1999; Newport, 1993).

But environment, too, must obviously play a role in language development. Children can learn a language only if the people around them converse in that language. It may be that children acquire language, at least in part, because it enables them to accomplish certain goals—perhaps to influence another person's behavior, obtain a desired object, and so on (Bates & MacWhinney, 1987; Budwig, 1995). Yet children do not directly "absorb" the language spoken around them; instead, they appear to use what they hear to *construct* their own understanding of the language, including knowledge about what words mean, rules governing how words can be combined into meaningful sentences, and so on (Cairns, 1996; Cromer, 1993; Karmiloff-Smith, 1993).

Trends in Language Development

Children begin using recognizable words sometime around their first birthday and are putting these words together by their second birthday. During the preschool years they become capable of forming longer and more complex sentences. By the time they begin school at age 5 or 6, they use language that seems adultlike in many respects. Yet their language capabilities continue to develop and mature throughout their childhood and adolescence. Examples of linguistic abilities at different grade levels are shown in Table 2.3. In the following sections, we'll briefly examine several aspects of linguistic development—vocabulary, syntax, listening comprehension, oral communication, and metalinguistic awareness—and their implications for teachers.

Development of Vocabulary   One obvious change in students' language during the school years is the increase in their vocabulary (see Table 2.3). Children learn some words through direct vocabulary instruction at school, but they probably learn many more by inferring meaning from the contexts in which they hear or read the words (Nippold, 1988; Owens, 1996; Pinker, 1987).

Students' knowledge of word meanings, known as **semantics**, is not always an all-or-none thing. Sometimes their initial understandings are vague and imprecise. One common error is *undergeneralization:* The meaning attached to a word is too restricted. For instance, I once asked my son Jeff, then age 6, to tell me what an *animal* is, and he replied, "It has a head, tail, feet, paws, eyes, noses, ears, lots of hair." Like Jeff, young elementary school children often restrict their meaning of *animal* primarily to mammals, such as dogs and horses, and insist that fish, birds, and insects are *not* animals (S. Carey, 1985; Saltz, 1971). Another common error is *overgeneralization:* The meaning attached to a word is too broad, and so the word is sometimes used when it doesn't apply. For instance, when I asked Jeff to give me examples of *insects*, he included black widow spiders in his list. Jeff overgeneralized: All insects have six legs, so eight-legged spiders do not qualify.

With age, experience, and instruction, students continue to refine their understandings of words, and many initially concrete definitions become more abstract. For example, when Jeff was 4, he defined *summer* as the time of year when school is out and it's hot outside. But when he was in middle school, after he had developed a capacity for abstract reasoning and had studied the seasons in his science class, he was able to define *summer in terms of the earth's tilt relative to the sun*—a far more abstract notion.

■ **semantics** *Meanings of words and word combinations.*

TABLE 2.3

Examples of Linguistic Characteristics and Abilities at Different Grade Levels

GRADE LEVEL	AGE-TYPICAL CHARACTERISTICS	SUGGESTED STRATEGIES
K–2	• Knowlege of 8,000–14,000 words by age 6 • Difficulty understanding complex sentences (e.g., those with multiple clauses) • Overdependence on word order and context (instead of syntax) when interpreting messages • Superficial understanding of being a "good listener" (e.g., just sitting quietly) • Literal interpretations of messages and requests (e.g., not realizing that "Goodness, this class is noisy" means "Be quiet") • Increasing ability to tell a story • Mastery of most sounds; some difficulty pronouncing *r*, *th*, *dr*, *sl*, and *str* • Occasional use of regular word endings (*-s*, *-ed*, *-er*) with irregular words (*sheeps*, *goed*, *gooder*) • Basic etiquette in conversations (e.g., taking turns, answering questions) • Reluctance to initiate conversations with adults (for many students from Asian and Mexican American backgrounds)	• Read age-appropriate storybooks as a way of enhancing vocabulary. • Give corrective feedback when students' use of words indicates inaccurate understanding. • Work on listening skills (e.g., sitting quietly, paying attention, trying to understand and remember). • Ask follow-up questions to make sure students accurately understand important messages. • Ask students to construct narratives about recent events (e.g., "Tell me about your camping trip last weekend").
3–5	• Increasing understanding of temporal words (e.g., *before*, *after*) and comparatives (e.g., *bigger*, *as big as*) • Occasional confusion about when to use *the* versus *a* • Incomplete knowledge of irregular word forms • Increasing awareness of when sentences are and are not grammatically correct • Pronunciation of sounds mastered by age 9 • Sustained conversations about concrete topics • Increasing ability to take listeners' prior knowledge into account during explanations • Construction of stories with plots and cause-effect relationships • Linguistic creativity and word play (e.g., rhymes, word games)	• Teach irregular word forms (e.g., the past tense of *ring* is *rang*, the past tense of *bring* is *brought*). • Begin instruction about parts of speech. • Use group discussions as a way to explore academic subject matter. • Have students develop short stories to present orally or in writing. • When articulation problems are evident in the upper elementary grades, consult with a speech-language pathologist. • Encourage jokes and rhymes that capitalize on double meanings and homonyms (i.e., soundalike words).
6–8	• Knowledge of about 50,000 words at age 12 • Increasing awareness of the terminology used in various academic disciplines • Confusion about when to use various connectives (*but*, *yet*, *although*, *unless*) • Ability to understand complex, multiclause sentences • Emerging ability to look beyond literal interpretations; comprehension of simple proverbs • Emerging ability to carry on lengthy conversations about abstract topics • Significant growth in metalinguistic awareness	• Assign reading materials that introduce new vocabulary. • Introduce some of the terminology used by experts in various academic disciplines (e.g., *simile* in language arts, *molecule* in science). • Conduct structured debates to explore controversial issues. • Present proverbs, and ask students to consider their underlying meanings. • Explore the nature of words and language as entities in and of themselves.
9–12	• Knowledge of about 80,000 words • Acquisition of many vocabulary words specifically related to various academic disciplines • Subtle refinements in syntax, mostly as a result of formal instruction • Mastery of a wide variety of connectives (e.g., *although*, *however*, *nevertheless*) • General ability to understand figurative language (e.g., metaphors, proverbs, hyperbole)	• Consistently use the terminology associated with various academic disciplines. • Distinguish between similar abstract words (e.g., *weather* vs. *climate*, *velocity* vs. *acceleration*). • Explore complex syntactic structures (e.g., multiple embedded clauses). • Consider the underlying meanings and messages in poetry and fiction. • When students have a native dialect other than Standard English, encourage them to use it in informal conversations and creative writing; encourage Standard English for more formal situations.

Sources: Bowey, 1986; L. Bradley & Bryant, 1991; S. Carey, 1978; Delgado-Gaitar, 1994; Karmiloff-Smith, 1979; Maratsos, 1998; McDevitt et al., 1990; McDevitt & Ford, 1987; Nippold, 1988; O'Grady, 1997; Owens, 1996; Reich, 1986; Sheldon, 1974; Stanovich, 2000; Swanborn & de Glopper, 1999; Thelen & Smith, 1998).

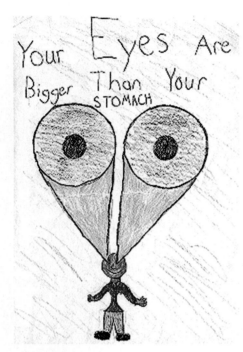

FIGURE 2.8 Adults typically use the expression "Your eyes are bigger than your stomach" figuratively, perhaps to describe a situation in which someone has ordered more food than can possibly be eaten. Here, however, 8-year-old Jeff interprets the expression quite literally.

To some extent, we must obviously tailor our lessons and reading materials to our students' vocabulary, yet we must not restrict instruction only to words that students already know. One way to promote students' semantic development is to teach vocabulary words and definitions directly, for instance, by having students define new vocabulary in their own words and use it in a variety of contexts. We should also correct any misconceptions (e.g., under- or overgeneralizations) that reveal themselves in students' speech. And we must encourage students to *read, read, read*: Children and adolescents learn many new words through their reading activities (Stanovich, 2000; Swanborn & de Glopper, 1999). The discussion of concept learning in Chapter 7 presents additional ways of teaching word meanings.

Development of Syntax   Rules of **syntax** allow us to put words together into grammatically correct sentences. These rules are incredibly complex, but for the most part, we aren't consciously aware of them (N. Chomsky, 1972; N. C. Ellis, 1994). By the time children begin school, they have already acquired many syntactic rules. Their understanding and use of complex constructions (e.g., passive sentences, sentences with multiple clauses) continue to evolve throughout the elementary years, and even more subtle aspects of syntax appear in the middle school and high school grades (see Table 2.3). By sixth or seventh grade, students use more complex syntax in their writing than in their speech (Owens, 1996).

In the later grades most syntactical development probably occurs as the result of formal language instruction—perhaps courses in language arts, English composition, and foreign language (Maratsos, 1998). Thus, we should continue instruction and practice in grammar and composition throughout the high school years. Our students are more likely to improve their speech and writing when they have ample opportunities to express their ideas orally and on paper and when they receive direct feedback about ambiguities and grammatical errors in their speech and writing.

Development of Listening Comprehension   Students' ability to comprehend what they hear is obviously influenced by their knowledge of vocabulary and syntax, but other factors contribute as well. For instance, children's conceptions of what listening comprehension *is* seem to change during the elementary school years. Children in the early elementary grades believe they are good listeners if they simply sit quietly without interrupting the teacher; not until about age 11 do they realize that good listening also requires *understanding* what is said (McDevitt et al., 1990). Elementary school children also differ in their beliefs about what to do when they don't understand something the teacher says. Many children, younger ones especially, apparently believe it is inappropriate to ask for clarification, perhaps because they have previously been discouraged from asking questions at school or at home (McDevitt, 1990; McDevitt et al., 1990). Such a belief is especially common when children's cultures have taught them that initiating conversation with an adult is disrespectful, as is true in many Asian and Mexican American communities (Delgado-Gaitan, 1994; Grant & Gomez, 2001).

Furthermore, young children's comprehension of what they hear is influenced by the context in which they hear it. Using various nonverbal contextual clues, they recognize that what is said in a situation is sometimes different from what is actually meant. For example, they may realize that a teacher who asks "Whose jacket is lying on the floor?" is actually requesting the jacket's owner to pick it up and put it where it belongs. Unfortunately, younger children are sometimes so dependent on context that they don't listen carefully enough to understand a spoken message accurately. They may "hear" what they *think* we mean, based on their beliefs about our intentions, rather than hearing what we really do mean (Donaldson, 1978). It is important, then, not only to ask students whether they understand what they hear but also to check for that understanding by asking them to rephrase a message in their own words.

As children get older, they become less dependent on context to understand what others say to them. They also become increasingly able to look beyond the literal meanings of messages (Owens, 1996; Winner, 1988). Children in the early elementary grades take the words they hear at face value—for instance, interpreting the expression "Your eyes are bigger than your stomach" quite literally (see Figure 2.8). And they have little success drawing generalizations from such proverbs as "Look before you leap" or "Don't put the cart before the horse." In the middle childhood and late adolescence "Cognitive Development" clips on Video CD 1, you can observe how

■ **syntax** Set of rules that one uses (often unconsciously) to put words together into sentences.

children's ability to understand proverbs improves with age. For example, whereas 10-year-old Kent seems baffled by the old adage "A rolling stone gathers no moss," 14-year-old Alicia offers a reasonable explanation: "Maybe when you go through things too fast, you don't . . . collect anything from it." Students' ability to interpret proverbs in a generalized, abstract fashion continues to develop even in the high school years (Owens, 1996).

Development of Oral Communication Skills   During the preschool and early elementary years, many children have difficulty pronouncing sounds such as *s* and *th* (see Table 2.3). Most students master the sounds of English by age 8 or 9; if pronunciation difficulties continue after that time, consultation with the school's speech pathologist about remediation strategies is probably in order.

Correct pronunciation is not the only thing students need in order to communicate effectively. They must also consider the characteristics (e.g., age, prior knowledge, perspectives) of people receiving their message. As noted earlier, young children sometimes say things without really considering the listener's point of view (Piaget called this *egocentric speech*). Even students in the upper elementary grades sometimes neglect to take into account what prior information their listeners are apt to have (Glucksberg & Krauss, 1967; McDevitt & Ford, 1987). As teachers, we must let students know when we don't understand them—for instance, by asking them to explain whom they are talking about when they refer to people we don't know and by expressing confusion when they describe events and ideas ambiguously.

Another component of effective oral communication is **pragmatics**, the social conventions governing appropriate verbal interactions with others. Pragmatics include not only rules of etiquette—taking turns when conversing with others, saying goodbye when leaving, and so on—but also strategies for beginning and ending conversations, changing the subject, telling stories, and arguing effectively. Children continue to refine their knowledge of pragmatics throughout the elementary grades (Owens, 1996); my own observation has been that this process continues into the middle and high school years (often even longer). When students haven't mastered certain social conventions—for instance, when they interrupt frequently or change the subject without warning—others may find their behavior irritating or strange; a lack of pragmatic skills, then, can seriously interfere with students' relationships with peers. It is important to observe students' pragmatic skills as they interact both with us and with their classmates and to give students guided practice in any skills they may be lacking.

Development of Metalinguistic Awareness   Throughout the school years students exhibit a tendency to "play" with language by reciting rhymes, chants, jokes, puns, and so on (Christie & Johnsen, 1983; Owens, 1996). Such wordplay is almost certainly beneficial; for instance, rhymes help students discover the relationships between sounds and letters, and jokes and puns may help students come to realize that words and phrases often have more than one meaning (L. Bradley & Bryant, 1991; Cazden, 1976). In the latter case students are developing their **metalinguistic awareness**, the ability to think about the nature of language itself.

Metalinguistic awareness seems to emerge slowly over time. During the elementary years students gradually become capable of determining when sentences are grammatically acceptable and when they are not (Bowey, 1986). As they move into the upper elementary and middle school grades, they begin to consider the various functions of words in a sentence (nouns, verbs, adjectives, etc.); such growth is almost certainly due in large part to the formal instruction they receive about parts of speech. High school students enhance their metalinguistic awareness still further as they consider the figurative nature of words—the nonliteral meanings of proverbs, the symbolism in poems and literature, and so on. Studying a second language also promotes metalinguistic awareness, as we shall see now.

Learning a Second Language

As the adult workplace becomes increasingly international in scope, the need is greater than ever for children to learn one or more languages in addition to their native tongue. As noted previously, there may be a sensitive period for learning language, thus making exposure to language in early childhood very important. But not all theorists are convinced that an early sensitive period exists for learning a *second* language (for diverse perspectives, see Hakuta, 2001; Hakuta, Bialystok, & Wiley, 2003; Merzenich, 2001). In general, early exposure to a second language appears to be

■ Observe the progression in understanding proverbs in the middle childhood and late adolescence "Cognitive Development" clips on Video CD 1.

■ **pragmatics** Knowledge about culture-specific social conventions guiding verbal interactions.

■ **metalinguistic awareness** Extent to which one is able to think about the nature of language.

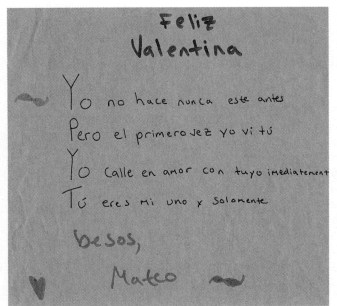

Learning a second language has both cognitive and social benefits. Here Matt, an eighth grader, uses his rudimentary knowledge of Spanish to create a Valentine's Day card.

■ Observe a bilingual teacher as she both talks and signs in the "Bilingual Classroom" clip on Video CD 2.

■ **immersion** Approach to second-language instruction in which students hear and speak that language almost exclusively in the classroom.

■ **bilingual education** Approach to second-language instruction in which students are instructed in academic subject areas in their native language while simultaneously being taught to speak and write in the second language.

important for mastering correct pronunciation, especially if the language is very different from a child's native tongue, and perhaps also for mastering complex grammatical constructions (T. K. Au, Knightly, Jun, & Oh, 2002; Bialystok, 1994a, 1994b; Neville & Bavelier, 2001). Aside from such possible limitations, children and adolescents can probably acquire fluency in a second language regardless of when they begin instruction.

Although there may be no hard-and-fast sensitive period for learning a second language, beginning second-language instruction in the early years has definite advantages. For one thing, it appears that learning a second language facilitates achievement in such other academic areas as reading, vocabulary, and grammar (Diaz, 1983; Reich, 1986). Instruction in a foreign language also sensitizes young children to the international and multicultural nature of the world. Students who learn a second language during the elementary school years express more positive attitudes toward people who speak that language and are more likely to enroll in foreign language classes in high school (Reich, 1986).

Bilingualism   At least 50 percent of the world's children are *bilingual*; that is, they speak two (sometimes three or more) languages fluently (Hoff-Ginsberg, 1997). Some bilingual children have been raised in families in which two languages are spoken regularly. Others have lived for a time in a community where one language is spoken and then moved to a community where a different language is spoken. Still others live in a bilingual society—for example, in Canada (where both English and French are spoken), Wales (where both English and Welsh are spoken), and certain ethnic communities in the United States (where a language such as Spanish or Chinese is spoken along with English). Bilingualism does not necessarily involve two *spoken* languages; for example, in the "Bilingual Classroom" clip on Video CD 2, one language is English and the other is American Sign Language.

Research reveals clear advantages to being bilingual. When children are truly fluent in both languages, they tend to perform better on tasks requiring complex cognitive functioning (e.g., on intelligence tests or on tasks requiring creativity). They also appear to have greater metalinguistic awareness—a better understanding of the nature of language itself (Bialystok, 2001; Diaz & Klingler, 1991; Garcia, 1994; C. E. Moran & Hakuta, 1995). In addition, bilingualism has social benefits in the classroom: In cases where different students speak only one of two different languages (perhaps some speaking only English and others speaking only Spanish), teaching students one another's languages increases student interaction (A. Doyle, 1982).

Promoting bilingualism. It appears that the best approach to teaching a second language depends on the circumstances. For English-speaking students learning a second language while still living in their native country, total **immersion** in the second language—hearing and speaking it almost exclusively within the classroom—is the method of choice. Total immersion helps students become proficient in a second language relatively quickly, and any adverse effects of such immersion on students' achievement in other areas of the curriculum appear to be short-lived (Collier, 1992; Cunningham & Graham, 2000; Krashen, 1996; W. P. Thomas, Collier, & Abbott, 1993).

In contrast, for non-English-speaking students who have recently immigrated to an English-speaking country, total immersion in English may actually be detrimental to their academic progress. For these students, **bilingual education**—where students receive instruction in academic subject areas in their native language while simultaneously being taught to speak and write in English—leads to higher academic achievement (e.g., in reading, mathematics, and social studies), greater self-esteem, and a better attitude toward school (Marsh, Hau, & Kong, 2002; C. E. Snow, 1990; S. C. Wright & Taylor, 1995).

Why does immersion work better for some students while bilingual education is better for others? As noted earlier, language is critical for children's cognitive development, promoting social interaction and providing a symbolic means through which they can mentally represent and think about their world. We therefore need a method of teaching a second language without losing the first language in the process. When students whose first language is English continue to live in their native country while being immersed in another language at school, they still have many opportunities—at home, with their friends, and in the local community—to use and continue developing their English. But recent immigrants to an English-speaking country often have little opportunity outside their immediate families to use their native language. If these students are taught exclusively in English, they may very well lose proficiency in one language (their native tongue) before developing proficiency in another (Pérez, 1998; Willig, 1985; S. C. Wright, Taylor, & Macarthur, 2000).

Given the many advantages of second-language learning and bilingualism, we should think seriously about promoting bilingualism in *all* students. Doing so would not only promote students' cognitive and linguistic development but also enhance communication, interaction, and interpersonal understanding among students with diverse linguistic and cultural backgrounds.

CONSIDERING DIVERSITY IN COGNITIVE AND LINGUISTIC DEVELOPMENT

Although the *order* in which various cognitive and linguistic abilities emerge tends to be fairly predictable, the *rate* at which they emerge may differ considerably from one child to the next (e.g., see Figure 2.9). Thus, we are apt to find considerable diversity in any particular age-group. For instance, from the perspective of Piaget's theory, we may see signs of both preoperational and concrete operational thinking in the primary grades, as well as evidence of both concrete and formal operational thinking at the middle school and high school levels. From Vygotsky's point of view, we will inevitably have students with different zones of proximal development: Tasks that are easy for some students may be quite challenging for others. And from an information processing perspective, we will find diversity in students' learning strategies and in the background knowledge and experiences they bring to bear on classroom subject matter.

Children's cognitive development may also differ somewhat depending on the cultures in which they've been raised. For instance, some of the logical reasoning abilities Piaget described (e.g., conservation, separation and control of variables) and some of the learning strategies (e.g., rehearsal) information processing theorists have identified appear earlier in children raised in Western countries than in children raised in some developing countries, presumably because such cognitive processes are more highly valued and more systematically promoted in Western culture (Berk, 2003; N. S. Cole, 1990; Trawick-Smith, 2003). When we consider cognitive abilities that other cultures value more than we do (e.g., the ability to judge the right amount of clay to use in making a pot or the ability to locate food in a barren desert), children in Western society are the ones who lag behind (Kearins, 1981; Price-Williams, Gordon, & Ramirez, 1969; Rogoff & Waddell, 1982).

We will find diversity in students' language capabilities as well. Students will vary considerably in the size of their vocabulary and in their knowledge of complex syntactical structures. Some students may express themselves using a **dialect**—a form of English characteristic of a particular ethnic group or region of the country—different from the one that we ourselves use. Other students may have **limited English proficiency (LEP):** They will be fluent in their native language but not in English and so will have difficulty communicating with and understanding others. Finally, students are likely to have acquired various social conventions about human interaction and dialogue (i.e., various pragmatic skills) depending on the families and cultures in which they've been raised. We will identify strategies for accommodating such differences in Chapter 4.

As teachers, we must continually be aware of the specific cognitive and linguistic abilities and weaknesses that individual students possess and then tailor instruction accordingly. For example, students will display more advanced reasoning skills when we ask them to deal with topics with which they are familiar. And as we have seen, students with limited English proficiency will achieve at higher levels in a bilingual education program.

Accommodating Students with Special Needs

We are especially likely to see differences in cognitive and linguistic development in students who have special educational needs. We may have a few students who show especially advanced cognitive development (e.g., students who are gifted); we may also have one or two who have not yet acquired the cognitive abilities typical of their age-group (e.g., students with mental

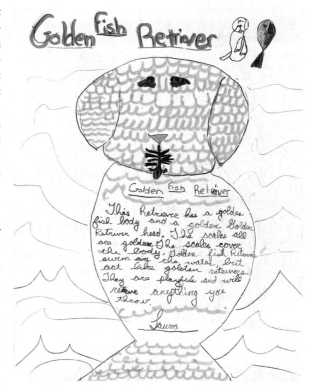

FIGURE 2.9 Students exhibit considerable diversity in the age at which they acquire formal operational capabilities. Here 10-year-old Laura shows some ability to envision alternatives to reality. In Piaget's theory such an ability appears, on average, at age 11 or 12.

■ **dialect** Form of a language characteristic of a particular region or ethnic group.

■ **limited English proficiency (LEP)** Limited ability to understand and communicate in oral or written English, usually because English is not one's native language.

retardation). We may have students with exceptional difficulties in specific aspects of cognition despite otherwise normal cognitive development (e.g., students with learning disabilities or attention-deficit hyperactivity disorder). Finally, we may have students who display impairments in speech that significantly interfere with their classroom performance (e.g., students with speech and communication disorders). Chapter 5 looks more closely at students with these types of special needs.

Table 2.4 presents specific characteristics related to cognitive and linguistic development that we may see in students with a variety of special needs. It also presents strategies for helping such students achieve academic success.

TABLE 2.4   STUDENTS IN INCLUSIVE SETTINGS

Promoting Cognitive and Linguistic Development in Students with Special Educational Needs

Category	Characteristics You Might Observe	Suggested Classroom Strategies
Students with specific cognitive or academic difficulties	• Distractibility, difficulty paying and maintaining attention • Delays in internalization of self-talk (some students with attention-deficit hyperactivity disorder) • Few effective learning strategies • Possible difficulties with abstract reasoning • Difficulties in listening comprehension • Difficulties in expressive language (e.g., in syntax)	• Make sure you have students' attention before giving instructions or presenting information. • Keep distracting stimuli to a minimum. • Teach learning strategies within the context of classroom lessons. • Encourage students to use self-talk to help themselves handle challenging situations. • Seek assistance from a speech pathologist when students have unusual difficulties with listening comprehension or spoken language.
Students with social or behavioral problems	• Lack of attention, as reflected in restlessness or daydreaming • Delayed language development (some students with autism) • Uneven performance on cognitive tasks (some students with autism)	• Capture students' attention by gearing instruction toward their personal interests. • Provide intensive instruction and practice for any delayed cognitive or linguistic skills. (Also use strategies presented above for students with specific cognitive or academic difficulties.)
Students with general delays in cognitive and social functioning	• Reasoning abilities characteristic of younger children (e.g., preoperational thought in the upper elementary grades, inability to think abstractly in the secondary grades) • Lack of learning strategies such as rehearsal and organization • Less developed knowledge base to which new information can be related • Delayed language development (e.g., in vocabulary, listening comprehension)	• Present new information in a concrete, hands-on fashion. • Teach simple learning strategies (e.g., rehearsal) within the context of classroom lessons. • Give instructions in concrete and specific terms.
Students with physical or sensory challenges	• Less developed knowledge base to which new information can be related, due to limited experiences in the outside world • Possible cognitive or language deficiencies or both (if brain damage is present) • Delayed language development (if students have long-term hearing loss and have had only limited exposure to sign language) • Difficulties with articulation (if students have limited muscular control or are congenitally deaf)	• Provide the basic life experiences that students may have missed because of their disabilities. • Identify any specific cognitive or language deficiencies, and adjust instruction and assessment practices accordingly. • Provide intensive instruction in the cognitive and language skills that students are lacking.
Students with advanced cognitive development	• Appearance of formal operational thinking (e.g., abstract thought) at an earlier age • Tendency for many regular classroom tasks to be below students' zone of proximal development • Greater knowledge base to which new information can be related • Advanced vocabulary • More sophisticated expressive language	• Provide opportunities through which students can explore classroom topics in greater depth or complexity. • Provide opportunities for students to proceed through the curriculum at a more rapid pace.

Sources: Beirne-Smith, Ittenbach, & Patton, 2002; Berk & Potts, 1991; Butterfield & Ferretti, 1987; Carter & Ormrod, 1982; Cone, Wilson, Bradley, & Reese, 1985; Diaz & Berk, 1995; A. W. Gottfried, Gottfried, Bathurst, & Guerin, 1994; M. Harris, 1992; Mastropieri, Scruggs, & Butcher, 1997; Mercer, 1997; Morgan & Jenson, 1988; Piirto, 1999; Pressley, 1995; R. Turnbull, Turnbull, Shank, & Smith, 2004; Winner, 1997.

THE BIG PICTURE

At first glance, the three perspectives of cognitive development we've examined in this chapter seem quite different from one another. Piaget's theory portrays cognitive development as a sequence of relatively discrete stages, each with its own set of abilities and limitations. In contrast, information processing theorists describe cognitive development in terms of gradual changes in cognitive processes and metacognitive awareness. And Vygotsky's approach looks more at the social factors that foster cognitive development than at specific changes in children's thinking. Furthermore, our discussion of language development has focused not on thinking and reasoning processes or the environmental conditions that promote them, but instead on the development of specific language skills and abilities.

Despite the varying directions in which this chapter has gone, several common themes have appeared frequently in one form or another:

◎ *Children tend to think in qualitatively different ways at different ages.* Qualitative changes in children's thinking processes are obvious elements of both Piaget's theory and information processing theory. Piaget portrayed these changes as reflecting four distinct stages of thought and reasoning capabilities, whereas information processing theorists have instead proposed that young children lack many learning strategies (e.g., organization, elaboration) and the metacognitive sophistication (e.g., knowing *when* they know something) that adolescents have. Yet Vygotsky's theory, too, implies qualitative change: As children gradually internalize the various processes they encounter in social interactions, they continually acquire distinctly new ways of thinking about situations and tasks. Some trends in language development—for instance, the gradual realization that good listening means understanding the speaker rather than simply sitting quietly, and the progression from literal to figurative interpretations of proverbs and common expressions—reflect qualitative changes as well.

◎ *Children actively construct their knowledge.* All three perspectives of cognitive development portray children not as passive receptacles for incoming information, but as active, constructive *builders* of knowledge. Piaget described cognitive development as a process of constructing one's own understanding of the world. Vygotsky and his followers have suggested that children and adults often work together to make sense of and find meaning in events. And information processing theorists have proposed that children use such constructive learning processes as organization and elaboration to help them learn and remember classroom subject matter. Constructive processes are presumed to occur in language development—for instance, in acquiring word meanings and syntactical rules—as well. Chapter 7 explores the process of knowledge construction in greater depth.

◎ *Development builds upon prior acquisitions.* Children rarely learn new information and skills in isolation from their existing knowledge; instead, they use what they know to acquire more complex understandings and processes. For instance, Piaget proposed that children adapt to their world through the two processes of assimilation and accommodation, both of which involve relating new experiences to previously developed schemes. Information processing theorists also stress the importance of prior knowledge: The more children already know about the world, the greater their ability to understand, elaborate on, and remember new information.

◎ *Challenging situations and tasks promote development.* We see the importance of challenge most clearly in Vygotsky's *zone of proximal development.* Yet challenge plays a role in other perspectives as well. From Piaget's view, children modify their schemes and develop new ones only when they cannot easily interpret new events using their existing schemes—that is, when they experience disequilibrium. From an information processing view, children are more apt to use sophisticated learning strategies when

Challenges promote cognitive and linguistic development. CALVIN AND HOBBES © 1995 Watterson. Reprinted with permission of UNIVERSAL PRESS SYNDICATE. All rights reserved.

new learning tasks require such strategies, and they become more realistic about what they can reasonably remember as they encounter increasingly complex subject matter.

◎ *Social interaction is critical for development.* Social interaction is a key element in both Vygotsky's and Piaget's theories. In Vygotsky's view, social interactions provide the very foundation for cognitive advancement: Children internalize the processes they use when they converse with others until, ultimately, they can use those processes independently. And both Piaget and Vygotsky pointed out that when children disagree and argue with one another, they begin to appreciate that a situation can often be viewed from multiple perspectives. Language development, too, depends heavily on social interaction: Children can learn to understand and produce language only if they encounter the language of others. Of course, a child's social world has ramifications far beyond cognitive and linguistic development; we will look at its effects on children's personal, social, and moral development in Chapter 3.

CASE STUDY: *In the Eye of the Beholder*

Ms. Kontos is teaching a unit on vision to her fifth-grade class. She shows her students a diagram of the various parts of the human eye: lens, cornea, retina, and so on. She then explains that people can see objects because light from the sun or another light source bounces off those objects and into the eye. To illustrate this idea, she shows them the picture to the right:

"Do you all understand how our eyes work?" she asks. Her students nod that they do.

The next day Ms. Kontos gives her students this picture:

She asks them to draw how light travels so that the child can see the tree. More than half of the students draw lines something like this:

Obviously, most of Ms. Kontos's students have not really learned what she thought she had taught them.

◆ What went wrong? Can you explain the students' inability to learn within the context of Piaget's theory of cognitive development? Can you explain it using some of Vygotsky's ideas? Can you explain it from an information processing perspective?

◆ In what ways might students' language capabilities have been insufficient to enable them to understand?

◆ What things might Ms. Kontos have done differently?

Once you have answered these questions, compare your responses with those presented in Appendix B.

KEY CONCEPTS

developmental milestone (p. 20)
universals (in development) (p. 21)
stage theory (p. 21)
maturation (p. 21)
temperament (p. 21)
sensitive period (p. 21)
neuron (p. 22)
synapse (p. 22)
neurotransmitter (p. 22)
cortex (p. 22)
synaptogenesis (p. 23)
synaptic pruning (p. 23)
myelination (p. 23)
constructivism (p. 25)
scheme (p. 25)
assimilation (p. 25)
accommodation (p. 25)
equilibrium (p. 26)
disequilibrium (p. 26)
equilibration (p. 26)

sensorimotor stage (p. 27)
symbolic thought (p. 27)
preoperational stage (p. 27)
preoperational egocentrism (p. 27)
egocentric speech (p. 27)
conservation (p. 27)
concrete operations stage (p. 28)
deductive reasoning (p. 28)
formal operations stage (p. 30)
formal operational egocentrism (p. 31)
sociocultural perspective (p. 34)
self-talk (private speech) (p. 35)
inner speech (p. 35)
cognitive tool (p. 35)
internalization (p. 35)
actual developmental level (p. 36)
level of potential development (p. 36)
zone of proximal development (ZPD) (p. 36)
mediated learning experience (p. 37)
social constructivism (p. 39)

scaffolding (p. 39)
guided participation (p. 41)
apprenticeship (p. 41)
cognitive apprenticeship (p. 41)
information processing theory (p. 42)
cognitive processes (p. 43)
learning strategy (p. 44)
rehearsal (p. 44)
organization (p. 44)
elaboration (p. 44)
knowledge base (p. 45)
metacognition (p. 46)
semantics (p. 50)
syntax (p. 52)
pragmatics (p. 53)
metalinguistic awareness (p. 53)
immersion (p. 54)
bilingual education (p. 54)
dialect (p. 55)
limited English proficiency (LEP) (p. 55)

PRAXIS Turn to Appendix C, "Matching Book and Ancillary Content to the Praxis Principles of Learning and Teaching Tests," to discover sections of this chapter that may be especially applicable to the Praxis tests.

Companion Website

Now go to our Companion Website at **www.prenhall.com/ormrod** to assess your understanding of chapter content with "Multiple-Choice Questions," apply comprehension in "Essay Questions," broaden your knowledge of educational psychology with related "Web Links," gain greater insight about classroom learning in "Learning in the Content Areas," and analyze and assess classroom work in the "Student Artifact Library."

3

Development of Self, Social Skills, and Morality

*S*chool is not just a place where children and adolescents acquire cognitive and linguistic skills. It is also a place where they acquire beliefs about themselves, strategies for getting along with other people, and perspectives about right and wrong. In other words, school is a place where young people grow personally, socially, and morally as well as academically.

In this chapter we will address questions such as these:

- What aspects of the environment are especially influential in students' personal, social, and moral development?
- How do students' beliefs about themselves affect their classroom behavior and academic achievement? How can we help students think positively and optimistically about themselves and their abilities?
- How do peer relationships change with age? How can we help students make friends and interact effectively with others?
- In what ways do students' moral reasoning and behavior change over time, and how can we promote their moral development?

As we address such questions, we will find that children's personal, social, and moral understandings depend considerably on their thinking and reasoning capabilities. At various points throughout the chapter, then, we will be drawing on things we learned about cognitive development in Chapter 2.

CASE STUDY: *The Bad Apple*

Adam seems to cause problems wherever he goes. In the classroom he is rude and defiant. On a typical school day, he comes to class late, slouches in his seat, rests his feet on his desk, yells obscenities at classmates and his teacher, and stubbornly refuses to participate in classroom activities.

Away from his teacher's watchful eye, Adam's behavior is even worse. He shoves and pushes students in the hall, steals lunches from smaller boys in the cafeteria, and frequently initiates physical fights on the school grounds.

For obvious reasons, no one at school likes Adam very much. His classmates say he's a bully, and their parents describe him as a "bad apple," rotten to the core. Even his teacher, who tries to find the best in all of her students, has seen few redeeming qualities in Adam and is beginning to write him off as a lost cause.

Adam doesn't seem to be bothered by the hostile feelings he generates. He's counting the days until he can legally drop out of school.

- Why does Adam behave the way he does? What possible factors in his environment—perhaps at home, at school, or among his peers—might have contributed to his aggressiveness, impulsiveness, and apparent self-centeredness?

- How might a teacher help Adam develop more appropriate and productive behaviors?

ENVIRONMENTAL INFLUENCES ON PERSONAL, SOCIAL, AND MORAL DEVELOPMENT

You may have formed several hypotheses about why Adam behaves as he does. Perhaps a parent encourages aggressive behavior, or at least does nothing to *discourage* it. Perhaps Adam's family can't afford to provide breakfast at home or lunch at school, or perhaps family members have never taught Adam that stealing infringes on the rights of others. Perhaps Adam lives in a high-crime neighborhood in which violence is commonplace and aggression is the best means of self-defense. At school, perhaps previous teachers have tolerated Adam's obscene language. Perhaps classmates have learned to stay away from him because of his inappropriate social skills, and he now finds that pushing, shoving, and picking fights are the only ways he can get their attention.

Although children seem to inherit predispositions to behave in certain ways (more about differences in *temperament* in Chapter 5), Adam almost certainly wasn't born with a predisposition to be noncooperative and antisocial. Instead, the hypotheses we've just generated indicate that aspects of his environment are probably at the root of his nonproductive behaviors. Let's look at three general environmental factors—parents, culture, and peers—that appear to influence students' personal, social, and moral development. We will then consider how children interpret and integrate environmental messages through the process of self-socialization.

Effects of Parenting

The behaviors of parents and other caregivers influence children's personalities and behaviors almost from the beginning. For example, when parents and their infants form a strong, affectionate bond (a process called **attachment**), infants are apt to develop into amiable, independent, self-confident, and cooperative children who adjust easily to the classroom environment and establish productive relationships with teachers and peers. In contrast, those who do not become closely attached to a parent or some other individual early in life can be immature, dependent, unpopular, and prone to disruptive and aggressive behaviors later on (Hartup, 1989; S. Shulman, Elicker, & Sroufe, 1994; Sroufe, Carlson, & Shulman, 1993). Attachment to an adult caregiver remains important even in adolescence: Although teenagers often disagree with their parents, those who are well adjusted tend to do so within the context of an affectionate, supportive parent-child relationship (J. P. Allen et al., 2003).

General patterns of childrearing—*parenting styles*—also appear to play a role in children's personal, social, and moral development. For most children the ideal situation appears to be **authoritative parenting**, in which parents provide a loving and supportive home, hold high expectations and standards for performance, explain why behaviors are or are not acceptable, enforce household rules consistently, and include children in decision making. Children from authoritative homes are happy, energetic, self-confident, and likeable; they make friends easily and show self-control and concern for the rights and needs of others (Baumrind, 1989; W. A. Collins, Maccoby, Steinberg, Hetherington, & Bornstein, 2000; Lamborn, Mounts, Steinberg, & Dornbusch, 1991; Rohner, 1998). In contrast, children from very controlling homes tend to be unhappy, anxious, and lacking in social skills; those from very permissive homes tend to be selfish, unmotivated, impulsive, and disobedient (Baumrind, 1989; Maccoby & Martin, 1983). Children whose parents use harsh disciplinary methods can be defiant, explosive, and unpredictable; those from exceptionally abusive homes tend to have emotional difficulties and low self-esteem and can be oppositional and aggressive (Maughan & Cicchetti, 2002; Nix et al., 1999; R. A. Thompson & Wyatt, 1999). Thinking back to the opening case study, we might wonder whether Adam's impulsiveness, self-centeredness, and aggressiveness are, at least in part, a result of ineffective parenting.

Keep in mind, however, that research on parenting is typically correlational in nature: It shows relationships between parenting styles and children's characteristics but does not necessarily indicate that certain parenting behaviors *cause* certain characteristics in children. Many children do well despite unhappy conditions at home (Masten & Coatsworth, 1998; R. A. Thompson & Wyatt, 1999). In some cases parents' behaviors are probably the result of how their children treat *them*; for instance, temperamentally lively or irritable children may require more parental control than restrained, easygoing ones (Clarke-Stewart, 1998; J. R. Harris, 1998; Stice & Barrera, 1995). Keep in mind, too, that some parents may have learned only ineffective parenting strategies from their *own* parents, and others may have challenges in their lives—perhaps mental illness, marital conflict, or serious financial problems—that hamper their ability to nurture and support their children (e.g., Serbin & Karp, 2003; Werner & Smith, 1982).

As teachers, we can serve as valuable resources to parents by offering possible strategies for promoting their children's development. With newsletters, parent-teacher conferences, and parent discussion groups, we can share ways of helping children acquire age-appropriate behaviors. The important thing is to communicate information without pointing accusatory fingers or being judgmental about parenting behaviors.

Effects of Culture

The term **culture** refers to the behaviors and belief systems that characterize a long-standing social group. Culture is a pervasive part of children's social environment—it permeates their

■ For more information about parenting styles, see the supplementary reading "Parenting Styles and Children's Behavior" in the *Study Guide and Reader* that accompanies this book.

■ **attachment** Strong, affectionate bond formed between a child and another individual.

■ **authoritative parenting** Parenting style characterized by emotional warmth, high standards for behavior, explanation and consistent enforcement of rules, and inclusion of children in decision making.

■ **culture** Behaviors and belief systems of a long-standing social group.

social interactions, as well as the toys, books, television shows, and other manmade objects and media they encounter—and provides an overall framework in which children determine what things are true and not true, rational and irrational, normal and abnormal, good and bad (Shweder et al., 1998).

Just as members of a cultural group pass along many concepts and other cognitive tools to help children make sense of their experiences (recall our discussion of Vygotsky's theory in Chapter 2), so, too, do they work hard to help growing children adopt the behaviors and beliefs the group holds dear. Beginning early in life, most children learn that there are some things they can or should do and other things they definitely should *not* do, and they acquire a cultural "lens" for viewing social situations and tasks. For instance, in mainstream Western society, many parents teach their toddlers not to hit other children, first-grade teachers ask their students to sit quietly rather than interrupt when an adult is speaking, and high school teachers expect students to turn in homework assignments on time. In doing such things, these adults also teach youngsters important cultural beliefs: that physical aggression is an unacceptable way to interact with playmates, that children should defer to and show respect for adults, and that punctuality will get students ahead in life.

The process of molding behavior and beliefs so that children fit in with their cultural group is called **socialization.** Sometimes adults' socialization efforts are obvious. For instance, the message is clear when an adult tells Johnny, "You know it's not nice to hit other children," and puts Johnny in time-out for his aggressive behavior. At other times socialization is more subtle. For example, adults communicate cultural values and beliefs by encouraging and modeling certain activities ("Let's give some of our clothes and toys to the homeless shelter") and discouraging others ("Stay away from that neighborhood; there are drug dealers on every corner").

Not all cultures endorse the same behaviors and values, of course, and even adults within a *single* culture may encourage somewhat different behaviors and beliefs. In Chapter 4 we will discover how children of various ethnic and socioeconomic groups, as well as boys and girls within a particular group, are often socialized quite differently.

Children typically learn their earliest lessons about their culture's standards and expectations from parents and other family members, who teach them personal hygiene, table manners, rudimentary interpersonal skills (e.g., saying "please" and "thank you"), and so on. Yet teachers become equally important socialization agents once children reach school age. For example, in mainstream Western society, teachers typically expect and encourage behaviors such as the following (Helton & Oakland, 1977; R. D. Hess & Holloway, 1984):

- Obeying school rules
- Behaving in an orderly fashion
- Showing respect for authority figures
- Controlling impulses
- Following instructions
- Working independently
- Completing assigned tasks
- Helping and cooperating with classmates
- Striving for academic excellence
- Delaying satisfaction of immediate needs and desires in order to reach long-term goals

When behaviors expected of students at school differ from those expected at home, or when belief systems presented by teachers are inconsistent with those of children's parents, children may become confused, nonproductive, and sometimes even angry or resistant (R. D. Hess & Holloway, 1984; Kumar, Gheen, & Kaplan, 2002). In other words, children may experience some **culture shock** when they begin school.

As teachers, we must especially encourage our students to exhibit those behaviors essential for long-term school success—behaviors such as obeying school rules, following instructions, and working independently. For example, when we expect students to work independently, even those students who have not had this expectation placed on them at home show improved work habits (J. L. Epstein, 1983). At the same time, students will need our guidance, support, and patience when our expectations differ from those of their family or cultural group.

■ Society and culture involve several "layers" of influence that contribute to children's and adolescents' development in a variety of ways. To explore this idea in depth, see the supplementary reading "An Ecological Systems Perspective of Child Development" in the *Study Guide and Reader* that accompanies this book.

Children may experience some culture shock when they begin school, especially if behaviors expected at school are very different from those expected at home.

■ **socialization** Process of molding a child's behavior to be appropriate for his or her cultural group.

■ **culture shock** Sense of confusion when a student encounters a culture with behavioral expectations very different from those previously learned.

Young adolescents often strive to look cool in the eyes of their peers, as this drawing by 11-year-old Marci illustrates.

Peer Influences

Parents, teachers, and other adults are hardly the only ones who influence young people's personal, social, and moral development. Peers, too, are important socialization agents. Children and adolescents socialize one another in several ways (Erwin, 1993; Ginsburg, Gottman, & Parker, 1986; J. R. Harris, 1998; A. M. Ryan, 2000). They define options for leisure time, perhaps getting together in a study group or smoking cigarettes on the corner. They offer new ideas and perspectives, perhaps demonstrating how to do an "Ollie" on a skateboard or presenting arguments for becoming a vegetarian. They serve as role models and provide standards for acceptable behavior, showing what is possible, what is admirable, what is cool. They reinforce one another for acting in ways deemed appropriate for their age, gender, or ethnic group. And they sanction one another for stepping beyond acceptable bounds, perhaps through ridicule, gossip, or ostracism. Such **peer pressure** has its greatest effects during the junior high school years, and teenagers who have weak emotional bonds to their families seem to be especially vulnerable (Berndt, Laychak, & Park, 1990; Erwin, 1993; R. M. Ryan & Lynch, 1989; Urdan & Maehr, 1995).

Many peers encourage such desirable qualities as truthfulness, fairness, cooperation, and abstinence from drugs and alcohol (Berndt & Keefe, 1996; Damon, 1988; McCallum & Bracken, 1993). Others, however, encourage aggression, criminal activity, and other antisocial behaviors (Berndt, Hawkins, & Jiao, 1999; Espelage, Holt, & Henkel, 2003; D. C. Gottfredson, 2001). Some peers encourage academic achievement, yet others convey the message that academic achievement is undesirable, perhaps by making fun of "brainy" students or by encouraging such behaviors as cheating on homework, cutting class, and skipping school (Berndt, 1992; B. B. Brown, 1993; A. M. Ryan, 2001). In fact, in some ethnic minority groups, a student who achieves good grades is "acting White"—a label some students want to avoid at all costs (B. B. Brown, 1993; W. E. Cross, Strauss, & Fhagen-Smith, 1999; Ogbu, 1992). Consider what happened to the professional basketball player Kareem Abdul-Jabbar when, as a 9-year-old African American student, he enrolled in a new school:

> I got there and immediately found I could read better than anyone in the school. . . . When the nuns found this out they paid me a lot of attention, once even asking me, a fourth grader, to read to the seventh grade. When the kids found this out I became a target. . . . I got all A's and was hated for it; I spoke correctly and was called a punk. I had to learn a new language simply to be able to deal with the threats. I had good manners and was a good little boy and paid for it with my hide. (Abdul-Jabbar & Knobles, 1983, p. 16)

Although peer pressure certainly is a factor affecting development, its effects on children's behaviors have probably been overrated (Berndt & Keefe, 1996). Most children and adolescents acquire a strong set of values and behavioral standards from their families, and they do not necessarily discard these values and standards in the company of peers (B. B. Brown, 1990; W. A. Collins et al., 2000; Galambos, Barker, & Almeida, 2003). Furthermore, they tend to choose friends who are similar to themselves in motives, styles of behavior, academic achievement, and leisure-time activities (W. A. Collins et al., 2000; Kindermann, McCollam, & Gibson, 1996; A. M. Ryan, 2001).

In some cases students lead "double lives" that enable them to attain academic success while maintaining peer acceptance; for example, although they attend class and do their homework faithfully, they may feign disinterest in scholarly activities, disrupt class with jokes or goofy behaviors, and express surprise at receiving high grades (B. B. Brown, 1993; Covington, 1992). As teachers, we can help such students maintain their "image" by sometimes allowing them to demonstrate their achievements to us privately—through written assignments or in one-on-one conversations—instead of in front of their classmates.

Self-Socialization

As we have seen, young people get many messages—sometimes consistent, sometimes not—from parents, teachers, peers, and others about how they should behave and what they should think. But rarely do they passively adopt others' opinions as their own. Instead, they evaluate the advice they get, choose some role models over others, weigh the pros and cons of "going along

■ **peer pressure** Phenomenon whereby age-mates strongly encourage some behaviors and discourage others.

with the crowd," and gradually develop their own views about which behaviors are and are not appropriate for themselves. This tendency for children and adolescents to participate actively in their *own* socialization is known as **self-socialization** (B. B. Brown, 1990; F. M. Deutsch, Ruble, Fleming, & Brooks-Gunn, 1988; Durkin, 1995; M. Lewis, 1991).

The decisions that youngsters make about which individuals and sources of information to rely on depend on their developmental levels and life experiences. Parents are dominating forces in the lives of most children in the primary grades. Peers become increasingly important as children grow and develop, not necessarily replacing parents but certainly offering compelling models of how to dress, which music to listen to, and how to spend leisure time. Despite the increasing influence of peers, however, parents typically remain strong sources of support and persuasion, especially with respect to core values. Most adolescents continue to see their relationships with parents and other family members as important and valuable throughout the secondary school grades (Cauce, Mason, Gonzales, Hiraga, & Liu, 1994; Furman & Buhrmester, 1992; Neubauer, Mansel, Avrahami, & Nathan, 1994).

The process of self-socialization is just one example of how children's personal, social, and moral development—like their cognitive development—involves *construction*, rather than simple absorption, of knowledge and understandings. We find another example in the development of children's *sense of self*, a topic we turn to now.

DEVELOPMENT OF A SENSE OF SELF

Experiencing FIRSTHAND ·Describing Yourself

On a sheet of paper, list ten adjectives or phrases that describe the kind of person you think you are.

· · · · · · ·

How did you describe yourself? Are you a good student? Are you physically attractive? Are you friendly? likable? moody? intelligent? test-anxious? strong? uncoordinated? Your answers to these questions tell you something about your **sense of self**—your perceptions, beliefs, judgments, and feelings about who you are as a person. Many theorists distinguish between two aspects of the sense of self: *self-concept* (assessments of one's own characteristics, strengths, and weaknesses) and *self-esteem* (judgments and feelings about one's own value and worth). In everyday usage, however, the two terms overlap considerably and are often used interchangeably (Byrne, 2002; Harter, 1999).

Students tend to have an overall, general feeling of *self-worth*: They believe either that they are good, capable individuals or that they are somehow inept or unworthy. At the same time, they are usually aware that they have both strengths and weaknesses—that they do some things well and other things poorly. Children in the primary grades make a general distinction between two aspects of themselves, how competent they are at day-to-day tasks and how well they are liked by friends and family. They make finer and finer distinctions as they grow older. In the upper elementary grades, they realize that they may be more or less competent or "good" in their academic work, athletic activities, classroom behavior, acceptance by peers, and physical attractiveness. By adolescence, they also make general self-assessments about their ability to make friends, their competence at adultlike work tasks, and their romantic appeal (Davis-Kean & Sandler, 2001; Harter, 1999).

Students may even have differing beliefs about themselves that are specific to certain tasks and situations within a particular domain. For instance, although Consuela may not consider herself to be very good at team sports—she's not very skillful and has little endurance—she may be confident that she's a good figure skater. And although Mark might think of himself as generally shy around people he's never met, he's aware that he's quite friendly with people he knows well. When we talk about people's self-beliefs in such specific areas, we are talking about *self-efficacy*—their beliefs about whether they are capable of achieving certain goals or outcomes. We'll examine this concept more closely in Chapter 10.

Students tend to behave in ways that mirror their beliefs about themselves, and those who have positive self-views are more likely to succeed academically, socially, and physically (Guay, Marsh, & Boivin, 2003; Ma & Kishor, 1997; Pintrich & Garcia, 1994; Valentine, Cooper, Bettencourt, & DuBois, 2002). Those who see themselves as "good students" are more apt to pay attention, follow directions in class, use effective learning strategies, work independently and persistently to solve difficult problems, and enroll in challenging courses. In contrast, those who believe they are

Tina drew this self-portrait in second grade. For children and adolescents alike, self-perceived physical attractiveness often plays a significant role in their overall self-esteem (Harter, 1999).

■ **self-socialization** Tendency to integrate personal observations and others' input into self-constructed standards for behavior and to choose actions accordingly.

■ **sense of self** Perceptions, beliefs, judgments, and feelings about oneself (includes *self-concept* and *self-esteem*).

"poor students" are apt to misbehave in class, study infrequently or not at all, ignore homework assignments, and avoid taking difficult subjects. Along a similar vein, students who see themselves as friendly and likable are apt to seek the company of their classmates and perhaps run for student council, whereas those who believe they are disliked by classmates may keep to themselves or act with hostility and aggression toward their peers. Students with a high sense of physical competence will go out for extracurricular athletics, whereas those who see themselves as total klutzes probably will not.

Students' beliefs about themselves are, like their beliefs about the world, largely self-constructed (Harter, 1999), and so there is room for error in their self-assessments. When students appraise themselves fairly accurately, they are in a good position to choose age-appropriate activities and work toward realistic goals (R. F. Baumeister, Campbell, Krueger, & Vohs, 2003; Harter, 1999). A slightly inflated self-assessment can be beneficial as well, in that it encourages students to set challenging yet potentially reachable goals (Assor & Connell, 1992; Phillips & Zimmerman, 1990). However, self-concepts that are *too* inflated may give some students an unwarranted sense of superiority over classmates and lead them to bully or in other ways act aggressively toward peers (R. F. Baumeister et al., 2003; R. F. Baumeister, Smart, & Boden, 1996). And as you might guess, significant *under*estimates lead students to avoid the many challenges that are apt to enhance their cognitive and social growth (Assor & Connell, 1992; D. Phillips & Zimmerman, 1990).

Factors Influencing the Development of Self-Views

Simply telling students they are "good" or "smart" or "popular" is unlikely to make much of a dent in low self-esteem (Damon, 1991; Katz, 1993; Marsh & Craven, 1997). Furthermore, vague, abstract statements such as "You're special" have little meaning in the concrete realities of young children (McMillan, Singh, & Simonetta, 1994). However, at least three factors definitely *do* influence the kinds of self-concepts that students form: students' previous performance, the behaviors of other individuals and, in some cases, the achievements of a larger group to which students belong. Each one offers insights as to how, as teachers, we can enhance our students' sense of self.

Previous Performance   As we have seen, students' self-concepts influence how they behave. Yet the reverse is true as well: Students' self-assessments depend on how successful their actions have been in the past (Damon, 1991; Guay et al., 2003). Students are more likely to believe they have an aptitude for mathematics if they have been successful in previous math classes, to believe they are likable individuals if they have been able to make and keep friends, or to believe they are capable athletes if they have been victorious in athletic competitions.

The interplay between self-perceptions and behavior can create a vicious cycle: A poor self-concept leads to less productive behavior, which leads to fewer successes, which perpetuates the poor self-concept. (This might be the case for Adam in our opening case study.) To break the cycle, we must make sure that students have numerous opportunities to succeed at academic, social, and physical tasks, or at least to show significant improvement in those tasks (Damon, 1991; Katz, 1993; Leary, 1999; Marsh & Craven, 1997). For example, we can gear assignments to their developmental levels and cognitive capabilities. We can make sure they have mastered the necessary prerequisite knowledge and skills *before* we assign new tasks. But we must remember that success in very *easy* activities is unlikely to have much of an impact, as Figure 3.1 humorously illustrates. Instead, we should assign challenging tasks, giving students the structure and support (the scaffolding) they need to accomplish them successfully.

Behaviors of Others   Other people's behaviors influence students' self-perceptions in at least two ways. First, how students evaluate their own performance depends to some extent on how it compares to the performance of those around them, and especially to that of peers (Guay, Boivin, & Hodges, 1999; Marsh & Hau, 2003; Nicholls, 1984). Older students in particular tend to judge themselves in comparison with classmates: Those who see themselves achieving at higher levels than others are apt to develop more positive self-perceptions than those who consistently find themselves falling short. To help students develop a positive sense of self, then, we probably want to minimize competition and other situations in which they might compare themselves unfavorably with others.

Second, students' self-perceptions are affected by how others behave *toward* them (Harter, 1996; Hartup, 1989; R. M. Ryan & Lynch, 1989). Through their behaviors, adults and peers com-

DOONESBURY
BY GARRY TRUDEAU

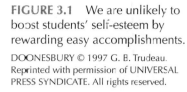

FIGURE 3.1 We are unlikely to boost students' self-esteem by rewarding easy accomplishments.

municate their evaluations of a student and their beliefs about his or her worth as a person. For example, when parents and teachers have high expectations and offer support and encouragement for the attainment of challenging goals, students tend to have more positive self-concepts and greater confidence in their own academic capabilities (Dweck, 2000; Eccles, Jacobs, Harold-Goldsmith, Jayaratne, & Yee, 1989; M. J. Harris & Rosenthal, 1985). Meanwhile, peers communicate information about students' social and athletic competence—perhaps by seeking out a student's companionship, ridiculing a student in front of others, and so on (Harter, 1999).

As teachers, we cannot always control how other people treat our students. But we can make sure that *we* respond to students in ways that will boost rather than lower self-esteem. Students who misbehave usually capture our attention more readily than those who behave appropriately, so it is often easier to criticize undesirable behavior than to praise desirable behavior. We must therefore make a concerted effort to catch students in the act of doing something well and praise them accordingly. We must be specific about what we are praising, because we will usually be more successful in improving particular aspects of our students' self-concepts than in improving their overall sense of self-worth (Marsh, 1990b). More generally, we must treat students with respect—for example, by asking them about their personal views and opinions about academic subject matter, seeking their input in important classroom decisions, and communicating a genuine interest in their well-being (see Chapter 14).

We do not necessarily want to convince students that they are more capable than they really are, however. Students can improve in areas of academic or athletic weakness and acquire more productive social behaviors only if we let them know when they are doing something ineffective or inappropriate. It is inevitable, then, that we occasionally give negative feedback. The trick is to give that negative feedback while also communicating respect and affection for students as human beings. For example, when students make mistakes in their academic work, we can point out that errors are a natural part of the learning process and can provide valuable information about how to improve in knowledge and skills (Clifford, 1990). When students behave inappropriately in the classroom, we can communicate that although we like them, we disapprove of their present actions. As an example, we might say, "You're generally a very kind person, Gail, but you hurt Jenny's feelings just now by making fun of her new outfit."

Group Membership and Achievements   In our discussion so far, we've focused on how students view themselves as individuals. But membership in one or more groups can also impact students' sense of self (Harter, 1999). For example, if you think back to your own school years, perhaps you can recall taking pride in something your entire class accomplished, feeling good about a community service project completed through an extracurricular club, or reveling in the state championship earned by one of your school's athletic teams. More generally, students are more likely to have high self-esteem if they are members of successful groups.

School groups are not the only important ones in students' lives. Some cultures encourage children to take pride in the accomplishments of their families as well as, or perhaps even *instead of*, their own accomplishments (Olneck, 1995; Pang, 1995). In addition, many children are both

■ Have you ever heard a student say something that threatens a classmate's self-esteem? How might a teacher intervene in such a situation?

aware and proud of their ethnic group and willingly adopt some of the group's behaviors; that is, they have a strong **ethnic identity** (Phinney, 1989; Sheets & Hollins, 1999). Although occasionally students' ethnic identities can lead them to reject mainstream values, including academic achievement (recall our earlier discussion of acting "White"), for the most part students with a strong and positive ethnic identity do well in school both academically and socially (Chavous et al., 2003; Spencer, Noll, Stoltzfus, & Harpalani, 2001). Furthermore, pride in one's ethnic heritage can serve as an emotional "buffer" against the insults and discrimination that students from minority groups sometimes encounter (Caldwell, Zimmerman, Bernat, Sellers, & Notaro, 2002; W. E. Cross et al., 1999; DuBois, Burk-Braxton, Swenson, Tevendale, & Hardesty, 2002). Consider this statement by Eva, an African American high school student, as an example:

> I'm proud to be black and everything. But, um, I'm aware of, you know, racist acts and racist things that are happening in the world, but I use that as no excuse, you know. I feel as though I can succeed. . . . I just know that I'm not gonna let [racism] stop me. . . . Being black is good. I'm proud to be black but you also gotta face reality. And what's going on, you know, black people are not really getting anywhere in life, but I know I will and I don't know—I just know I will. (Way, 1998, p. 257)

Obviously, then, we can foster self-esteem by focusing students' attention on the accomplishments of the many groups in which they are members, including those that exist outside school walls. We will identify strategies for doing so when, in later chapters, we consider how to create a more multicultural classroom environment (Chapter 4) and an overall sense of community at school (Chapter 14).

Developmental Changes in Sense of Self

We have already seen one way in which self-perceptions change with age: Children increasingly differentiate among the many "parts" of themselves—the academic part, the social part, the physical appearance part, and so on. But developmentalists have long recognized that children's and adolescents' beliefs and feelings about themselves change in other ways as well. One early developmentalist, Erik Erikson, proposed that people's views of both themselves and others change significantly not only in childhood and adolescence but throughout the lifespan. Figure 3.2 presents Erikson's classic theory of eight psychosocial stages. In the following sections, we look at what more contemporary researchers have learned about developmental changes in children's and adolescents' sense of self.

Childhood   Elementary school children tend to think of themselves in terms of concrete, easily observable characteristics and behaviors (D. Hart, 1988; Harter, 1983). For example, when my son Alex was 9, he described himself this way:

> I have brown hair, brown eyes. I like wearing short-sleeved shirts. My hair is curly. I was adopted. I was born in Denver. I like all sorts of critters. The major sport I like is baseball. I do fairly well in school. I have a lizard, and I'm going to get a second one.

In racially and culturally diverse communities, where different skin colors, languages, customs, and so on are obvious, children may also classify themselves as belonging to one or another racial or ethnic group (Phinney, 1990; Sheets, 1999).

In the preschool and primary grades, most children have positive self-concepts and high self-esteem; often they believe they are more capable than they really *are* and that they can easily overcome initial failures (Harter, 1999; Lockhart, Chang, & Story, 2002; Paris & Cunningham, 1996). Such overestimations are probably due to young children's tendency to base self-assessments on their continuing improvement in "big boy" and "big girl" tasks, rather than on their performance relative to others. A small amount of overconfidence can be beneficial, in that it motivates children to attempt and persist at new and challenging activities (Bjorklund & Green, 1992).

As children have more opportunities to compare themselves with peers during the elementary grades, and as they become cognitively more able to *make* such comparisons, their self-assessments become increasingly realistic (Chapman, Tunmer, & Prochnow, 2000; Harter, 1999). They also begin to pull together their many self-observations into generalizations about the kinds of people they are—perhaps "friendly," "good at sports," "smart," or "dumb"—and, for good or for bad, such generalizations lead to increasingly stable self-concepts (D. A. Cole et al., 2001; Harter, 1999). At

■ **ethnic identity** Awareness of one's membership in a particular ethnic or cultural group and willingness to adopt behaviors characteristic of the group.

FIGURE 3.2   Erikson's eight stages of psychosocial development

Erik Erikson (1963, 1972) described eight stages through which people proceed over the course of development. Each stage presents a unique developmental task, and how an individual addresses it influences the person's overall development. Although contemporary developmental theorists suggest that the age ranges for accomplishing the developmental tasks are probably more flexible than Erikson proposed, they find value in many of his ideas.

Trust versus mistrust (infancy). According to Erikson, the major developmental task in infancy is to learn whether or not other people, especially primary caregivers, regularly satisfy basic needs. If caregivers are consistent sources of food, comfort, and affection, an infant learns *trust*—that others are dependable and reliable. If they are neglectful, or perhaps even abusive, the infant instead learns *mistrust*—that the world is an undependable, unpredictable, and possibly dangerous place.

Autonomy versus shame and doubt (toddler years). As they gain increased muscular coordination and mobility, toddlers become capable of satisfying some of their own needs. They begin to feed themselves, wash and dress themselves, and use the bathroom. If caregivers encourage self-sufficient behavior, toddlers develop a sense of *autonomy*—a sense of being able to handle many problems on their own. But if caregivers demand too much too soon, refuse to let children perform tasks of which they are capable, or ridicule early attempts at self-sufficiency, children may instead develop *shame and doubt* about their ability to handle problems.

Initiative versus guilt (preschool years). Preschoolers are increasingly able to accomplish tasks on their own, and with this growing independence come many choices about activities to be pursued. Sometimes children take on projects they can readily accomplish, but at other times they undertake projects that are beyond their capabilities or that interfere with other people's plans and activities. If parents and preschool teachers encourage and support children's efforts, while also helping them make realistic and appropriate choices, children develop *initiative*—independence in planning and undertaking activities.[a] But if, instead, adults discourage the pursuit of independent activities or dismiss them as silly and bothersome, children develop *guilt* about their needs and desires.

Industry versus inferiority (elementary school years). Erikson viewed the elementary school years as critical for the development of self-confidence. Ideally, elementary school provides many opportunities for children to achieve the recognition of teachers, parents, and peers by producing things—drawing pictures, solving addition problems, writing sentences, and so on. If children are encouraged to make and do things and are then praised for their accomplishments, they begin to demonstrate *industry* by being diligent, persevering at tasks until completed, and putting work before pleasure. If children are instead ridiculed or punished for their efforts or if they find they are incapable of meeting their teachers' and parents' expectations, they develop feelings of *inferiority* about their capabilities.

Identity versus role confusion (adolescence). As they make the transition from childhood to adulthood, adolescents ponder the roles they will play in the adult world. Initially, they are apt to experience some *role confusion*—mixed ideas and feelings about the specific ways in which they will fit into society—and may experiment with a variety of behaviors and activities (e.g., tinkering with cars, baby-sitting for neighbors, affiliating with certain political or religious groups). Eventually, Erikson proposed, most adolescents achieve a sense of *identity* regarding who they are and where their lives are headed.[b]

Intimacy versus isolation (young adulthood). Once people have established their identities, they are ready to make long-term commitments to others. They become capable of forming *intimate,* reciprocal relationships (e.g., through marriage or close friendships) and willingly make the sacrifices and compromises that such relationships require.[c] If people cannot form these intimate relationships (perhaps because of their reluctance or inability to forego the satisfaction of their own needs), then a sense of *isolation* may result.

Generativity versus stagnation (middle age). During middle age the primary developmental task is one of contributing to society and helping to guide future generations. When a person makes a contribution during this period, perhaps by raising a family or working toward the betterment of society, a sense of *generativity*—a sense of productivity and accomplishment—results. In contrast, a person who is self-centered and unable or unwilling to help society move forward develops a feeling of *stagnation*—a dissatisfaction with the relative lack of productivity.

Integrity versus despair (retirement years). The final developmental task is retrospection: People look back on their lives and accomplishments. They develop feelings of contentment and *integrity* if they believe that they have led a happy, productive life. They may instead develop a sense of *despair* if they look back on a life of disappointments and unachieved goals.

---

[a]Erikson did not take into account the important role that culture plays in development. Many cultures intentionally discourage autonomy, initiative, and self-assertiveness in young children, sometimes as a way of protecting them from the very real dangers of their environments (X. Chen, Rubin, & Sun, 1992; Dennis, Cole, Zahn-Waxler, & Mizuta, 2002; Harwood, Miller, & Irizarry, 1995; G. J. Powell, 1983).

[b]Most people probably do not achieve a sense of identify as early or as easily as Erikson suggested (see the section "Late Adolescence" beginning on p. 70).

[c]Erikson based his stages primarily on work with men; for many women, a focus on intimacy occurs simultaneously with, and in some cases may even precede, a focus on identity (Josselson, 1988).

this point, too, children value some characteristics and abilities more highly than others, and their success in highly valued ones has a strong impact on their overall self-esteem (Harter, 1999).

Early Adolescence   As students approach adolescence and gain a greater capability for abstract thought, they increasingly think of themselves in terms of general traits. Consider my daughter Tina's self-description when she was in sixth grade:

> I'm cool. I'm awesome. I'm way cool. I'm twelve. I'm boy crazy. I go to Brentwood Middle School. I'm popular with my fans. I play viola. My best friend is Lindsay. I have a gerbil named Taj. I'm adopted. I'm beautiful.

Although Tina listed several concrete features about herself (her school, her best friend, her gerbil), she had clearly developed a fairly abstract self-perception. Tina's focus on coolness, popularity, and beauty, rather than on intelligence or academic achievement (or, I might add, modesty), is fairly typical: Social acceptance and physical appearance are far more important to most young adolescents than academic competence (D. Hart, 1988; Harter, 1999). Students' self-concepts and self-esteem often drop as they make the transition from elementary school to middle school or junior high, with the drop being more pronounced for girls (D. A. Cole et al., 2001; Harter, 1999; Wigfield & Eccles, 1994). The physiological changes that occur with puberty may be a factor: Although students' self-concepts depend more and more on their beliefs about their appearance and popularity, boys and girls alike tend to think of themselves as being somewhat less attractive once they reach adolescence (T. A. Bender, 1997; Cornell et al., 1990; Harter, 1990). The changing school environment probably also has a negative impact. Traditional junior high schools often differ from elementary schools in several ways (Eccles & Midgley, 1989). For one thing, students don't have the opportunity to form the close-knit, supportive relationships with teachers that many of them had in elementary school. Students may also discover that their school grades are based more on competitive criteria—that is, on how well they perform in comparison with their classmates. Furthermore, at a time when they probably have an increased need for close friendships, students may find themselves in classes with many people they don't know. With all of these unsettling changes occurring simultaneously, it is not surprising that we see a temporary drop in young adolescents' self-esteem. (We'll return to this troublesome transition time in Chapter 11.)

Two additional phenomena characterize the self-perceptions of young adolescents. First, these students often believe that in any social situation, everyone else's attention is focused squarely on them—a phenomenon known as the **imaginary audience** (Elkind, 1981; Lapsley, 1993; R. M. Ryan & Kuczkowski, 1994). Because they believe themselves to be the center of attention, young teenagers (girls especially) are often preoccupied with their physical appearance and can be quite self-critical, assuming that everyone else is equally observant and critical. Concerned about how others may evaluate them and wanting desperately to "fit in," they can be quite conforming, rigidly imitating peers' choices in dress, music, slang, and behavior (Hartup, 1983; Owens, 1996). Thus, self-socialization goes full throttle at this point.

A second noteworthy phenomenon in early adolescence is the emergence of the **personal fable:** Young teenagers often believe themselves to be unlike anyone else (Elkind, 1981; Lapsley, 1993). They may think that their own feelings are completely unique—that those around them have never experienced such emotions—and so no one else, least of all parents and teachers, can possibly know how they feel. Furthermore, they may have a sense of invulnerability and immortality, believing themselves immune to the normal dangers of life. Thus, many adolescents take seemingly foolish risks, such as experimenting with drugs and alcohol, having unprotected sexual intercourse, or driving at high speeds (Arnett, 1995; DeRidder, 1993; Jacobs & Klaczynski, 2002; S. P. Thomas, Groër, & Droppleman, 1993).

Although the imagery audience and personal fable slowly decline after early adolescence, certain aspects of them remain throughout the high school years. For example, some teens, especially boys, persist in risky behaviors, and so through automobile accidents, drug overdoses, and the like, they are twice as likely to die as girls (Frankenberger, 2000; Lapsley, 1993; Nell, 2002).

Late Adolescence   The majority of older adolescents have sufficiently recovered from the "double whammy" of puberty and a changing school environment that they enjoy positive self-concepts

Musical ♪ ♫ ♩
Equestrian
Lovable ♥ ♥ ♥ ♥ ♥
Imaginative
Noble
Dancer
Animal-lover

As students get older, they increasingly include abstract qualities in their self-descriptions. In this self-description, 12-year-old Melinda identifies several abstract characteristics: musical, lovable, imaginative, noble, and animal-lover.

■ **imaginary audience** Belief that one is the center of attention in any social situation.

■ **personal fable** Belief that one is completely unlike anyone else and so cannot be understood by others.

FOR BETTER OR FOR WORSE / Lynn Johnston

Such an excessive concern about appearance illustrates a phenomenon known as the *imaginary audience*: Elizabeth believes she is the focus of everyone else's attention.

© Lynn Johnston Productions, Inc./Distributed by United Feature Syndicate, Inc.

and overall mental health (Harter, 1999; S. I. Powers, Hauser, & Kilner, 1989). Yet they may struggle with the seeming inconsistencies in their self-perceptions, as one ninth grader explained:

> I really don't understand how I can switch so fast from being cheerful with my friends, then coming home and feeling anxious, and then getting frustrated and sarcastic with my parents. Which one is the *real* me? (Harter, 1999, p. 67)

Eventually (perhaps around eleventh grade), they integrate their various self-perceptions into a complex, multifaceted self-concept that reconciles apparent contradictions; for instance, they may realize that diverse emotions mean they are "moody" and that their inconsistent behaviors on different occasions mean they are "flexible" (Harter, 1999). Also, their sense of self increasingly incorporates a general sense of **identity**: a self-constructed definition of who they are, what things they find important, and what goals they want to accomplish in life. Memberships in various groups—perhaps informal cliques at school, organized clubs or teams, or ethnic neighborhoods or communities—often play a key role in adolescents' identities (Phinney, 1989; Wigfield, Eccles, & Pintrich, 1996). Not only do such groups help teens define who they are, but these groups also endorse values and goals that teens may adopt for themselves.

In their ongoing search for a long-term identity, adolescents may take on temporary "identities," aligning themselves strongly with a particular peer group, adhering rigidly to a single brand of clothing, or insisting on a certain hairstyle. For example, as a 15-year-old, my son Alex described himself as a "skater"—someone for whom skateboarding becomes a way of life as well as a form of transportation—and insisted on wearing the oversized shirts and hip-hugging, baggy pants (revealing several inches' worth of boxer shorts) that came with the territory. Older adolescents, especially those from ethnic minority groups, may also experiment with varying forms of an ethnic identity. Some teens, for instance, may initially adopt a fairly intense, inflexible, and perhaps hostile ethnic identity before eventually retreating to a more relaxed, open-minded, and productive one (W. E. Cross et al., 1999).

Erik Erikson proposed that most people achieve a sense of identity by the end of adolescence (see Figure 3.2). But more recent evidence indicates that even by the high school years, only a small minority of teenagers in Western cultures have begun to think seriously about the eventual role they will play in society and to identify lifelong goals (Archer, 1982; Durkin, 1995; Marcia, 1980, 1988). Most adolescents need considerable time to explore various options related to careers, political beliefs, religious affiliations, and so on before they achieve a true sense of their adult identity. Marcia (1980) has described four distinct patterns of behavior that may characterize the status of an adolescent's search for identity:

- *Identity diffusion.* The adolescent has made no commitment to a particular career path or ideological belief system. Some haphazard experimentation with particular roles or beliefs may have taken place, but the individual has not yet embarked on a serious exploration of issues related to self-definition.
- *Foreclosure.* The adolescent has made a firm commitment to an occupation, a particular set of beliefs, or both. The choices have been based largely on what others (especially parents) have prescribed, without an earnest exploration of other possibilities.
- *Moratorium.* The adolescent has no strong commitment to a particular career or set of beliefs but is actively exploring and considering a variety of professions and ideologies. In essence, the individual is undergoing an identity crisis.

ME! ■ **identity** Self-constructed definition of who one thinks one is and what things are important in life.

- *Identity achievement.*   After going through a period of moratorium, the adolescent has emerged with a commitment to particular political or religious beliefs, a clear choice of occupation, or both.

The ideal situation is to proceed through a period of moratorium—an exploration that may continue into early adulthood—before finally settling on a clear identity (Berzonsky, 1988; Marcia, 1988). Foreclosure—identity choice *without* prior exploration—rules out potentially more productive alternatives, and identity diffusion leaves young people without a clear sense of direction in life.

Table 3.1 presents developmental changes in children's and adolescents' sense of self and offers ideas for how we, as teachers, can enhance their self-perceptions at different grade levels. We must keep in mind, however, that students' self-esteem depends not only on what we do but also (perhaps more importantly) on what *peers* do. We turn now to social development, with a particular focus on interpersonal relationships and social skills with peers.

SOCIAL DEVELOPMENT

Let's return to the case study presented at the beginning of the chapter. Adam engages in several socially inappropriate behaviors: He pushes other students in the corridor, picks fights in the school yard, and yells obscenities in class. As a result, his peers want little to do with him, and his teacher has just about given up on him.

TABLE 3.1   DEVELOPMENTAL TRENDS

Sense of Self at Different Grade Levels

GRADE LEVEL	AGE-TYPICAL CHARACTERISTICS	SUGGESTED STRATEGIES
K–2	• Self-concept limited to concrete, easily observable characteristics • Tendency to overestimate abilities and chances of future success	• Encourage students to "stretch" themselves by tackling the challenging tasks they think they can accomplish; provide sufficient scaffolding to make success possible.
3–5	• Increasing awareness of, and differentiation among, particular strengths and weaknesses • Association of such emotions as pride and shame with various self-perceptions	• Focus students' attention on their improvement over time. • Encourage pride in individual and group achievements, but be aware that students from some ethnic groups may prefer that attention be given only to group achievement (see Chapter 4). • Provide opportunities for students to look at one another's work only when *all* of them have something to be proud of.
6–8	• Increasingly abstract conceptions of oneself • For many, a decline in self-esteem after the transition to middle or junior high school • Heightened sensitivity to what others may think (imaginary audience) • Excessive belief in one's own uniqueness, often accompanied by risk taking and a sense of invulnerability from normal dangers (personal fable)	• After students make the transition to middle school or junior high, be especially supportive and optimistic about their abilities and potential for success. • Be patient when students show exceptional self-consciousness; give them strategies for presenting themselves to others in a positive light. • Show no tolerance for risk-taking behaviors on school grounds.
9–12	• Continuing risk-taking behavior, especially in males • Gradual increase in self-esteem • Search for the "real me" and an adult identity • Increasing integration of diverse self-perceptions into an overall, multifaceted sense of self	• When discussing the potential consequences of risky behaviors, present the facts but don't make students so anxious or upset that they can't effectively learn and remember (e.g., avoid scare tactics). • Give students opportunities to examine and try out a variety of adultlike roles.

Sources: Dweck, 2000; Elkind, 1981; Harter, 1999; Lockhart et al. 2002; Marcia, 1980; Nell, 2002.

As students grow older, they should be acquiring more effective strategies for getting along with others. They should also be growing more perceptive about how those around them are likely to think, act, and react—that is, more adept at *social cognition*. In the next few pages, we will learn more about peer relationships and social cognition. We will then identify strategies for fostering students' social skills and promoting interaction across diverse groups.

Peer Relationships

School is very much a "social" place: Students interact regularly with one another, and most of them actively seek out friendly relationships with classmates. In fact, for many students, interacting with and gaining the acceptance of peers are more important than classroom learning and achievement (B. B. Brown, 1993; Dowson & McInerney, 2001; W. Doyle, 1986a). For example, in the "Motivation: Late Adolescence" clip on Video CD 1, when 15-year-old Greg is asked what he most likes about school, he quickly responds, "Lunch ... . all the social aspects ... . friends and cliques."

■ Observe Greg's preference for the social aspects of school in the "Motivation: Late Adolescence" clip on Video CD 1.

Peer relationships, especially friendships, serve several functions in children's and adolescents' personal and social development. First, as we noted earlier, peers are powerful socialization agents who encourage what are, at least in their own minds, appropriate ways of behaving. Second, peer interactions provide an arena for learning and practicing social skills. In most peer relationships children participate as equal partners; in doing so, they begin to develop skills in negotiation, persuasion, cooperation, compromise, emotional control, and conflict resolution (Asher & Parker, 1989; Erwin, 1993; Gauvain, 2001; Maxwell, Jarrett, & Dickerson, 1998; Sutton-Smith, 1979).

Furthermore, peers often provide social and emotional support. As preschoolers, children see their age-mates primarily as sources of recreation, but as they grow older, they find that friends can provide comfort and safety—a group with whom to eat lunch, a "safe haven" from playground bullies, and so on (Berndt, 2002; Pellegrini & Bartini, 2000; Youniss & Volpe, 1978). Once children reach puberty, they rely increasingly on their peers for emotional support, especially in times of trouble or confusion (Levitt, Guacci-Franco, & Levitt, 1993; R. M. Ryan, Stiller, & Lynch, 1994). Although some students adjust quite successfully on their own, as a general rule those students who have the acceptance and support of their peers have higher self-esteem, fewer emotional problems (e.g., depression), and higher school achievement (Buhrmester, 1992; Guay et al., 1999; Levitt et al., 1999; R. M. Ryan et al., 1994; Wentzel, 1999).

Many adolescents (especially girls) may reveal their innermost thoughts and feelings to their friends (Basinger, Gibbs, & Fuller, 1995; Levitt et al., 1993; A. J. Rose, 2002). Friends often understand a teenager's perspective—the preoccupation with physical appearance, the concerns about the opposite sex, and so on—when no one else seems to. By sharing their thoughts and feelings with one another, students may discover they aren't as unique as they once thought and gradually abandon the personal fable I spoke of earlier (Elkind, 1981).

Some peers are, of course, more influential than others. Here we will look at three types of peer relationships: friendships, larger social groups, and romantic relationships. We will then consider the nature and effects of popularity and social isolation.

Friendships   Close friends tend to be similar in age and are usually of the same sex, although some children and adolescents have close friends of the opposite sex as well (Gottman, 1986; Hartup, 1992; Kovacs, Parker, & Hoffman, 1996; Maccoby, 2002). Friends also tend to be of the same race; cross-race friendships are more common when the number of available peers is relatively small, as it may be in small classes or rural communities (Hallinan & Teixeira, 1987; Roopnarine, Lasker, Sacks, & Stores, 1998).

Friends find activities that are mutually meaningful and enjoyable, and over time they acquire a common set of experiences that enable them to share certain perspectives on life (Gottman, 1986; Suttles, 1970). Friends care for and help one another, and ultimately how they *feel* about one another is more important than what they *do* with one another (J. L. Epstein, 1986; Rubin, Bukowski, & Parker, 1998). Because friends have an emotional investment in their relationship, they work hard to look at a situation from one another's point of view and to resolve any disputes that threaten to separate them; as a result, they develop increased perspective-taking and conflict resolution skills (Basinger et al., 1995; DeVries, 1997; Newcomb & Bagwell, 1995). Close friendships foster self-esteem and, especially at the secondary school level, provide a sense of identity for students—a sense that they "belong" to a particular group (Berndt, 1992; Knapp & Woolverton, 1995).

As children get older, and especially as they reach adolescence, they increasingly think of friends as people to be trusted and relied on. Yet to some degree, even first graders realize that friends provide more than recreation, as this description by 6-year-old Katie (who depicts herself and friend Meghan playing with dolls) illustrates.

■ Observe developmental trends in the importance of friends in the three "Friendships" clips on Video CD 1.

■ Were you part of a social group in adolescence? If so, how would you characterize it?

The three "Friendships" clips on Video CD 1 reveal how friends become increasing important as students get older. For 8-year-old Kate, having friends primarily means being nice, having companionship, and helping one another. But for 13-year-old Ryan and 17-year-old Paul, friends are also people they can trust, rely on, and confide in.

Larger Social Groups   Most children and adolescents frequently interact and enjoy being with peers besides their close friends. Over time, many form larger social groups that regularly get together (Eisenberg et al. 1996; Gottman & Mettetal, 1986). Initially, such groups are usually comprised of a single sex, but in adolescence they often include both boys and girls (Gottman & Mettetal, 1986; J. R. Harris, 1995).

Once children or adolescents gel as a group, they prefer other group members over nonmembers, and they develop feelings of loyalty to individuals within the group. In some cases they also develop feelings of hostility and rivalry toward members of other groups (J. R. Harris, 1998; Sherif, Harvey, White, Hood, & Sherif, 1961). If you look back on your own adolescent years, you may recall that you and your friends attached names to members of different groups—perhaps "brains," "jocks," "druggies," or "geeks"—and you probably viewed some of these groups unfavorably (Eckert, 1989; J. R. Harris, 1995). Even children in the primary grades know that social groups can vary considerably in social status (Bigler, Brown, & Markell, 2001; Nesdale & Flesser, 2001).

As students reach puberty, larger groups become an especially prominent feature of their social worlds. Researchers have described several distinct types of groups during the adolescent years: cliques, crowds, subcultures, and gangs. **Cliques** are moderately stable friendship groups of perhaps three to ten individuals, and such groups provide the setting for most voluntary social interactions (Crockett, Losoff, & Peterson, 1984; J. L. Epstein, 1986; Kindermann et al., 1996). Clique boundaries tend to be fairly rigid and exclusive (some people are "in," others are "out"), and memberships in various cliques often affect students' social status (Wigfield et al., 1996).

Crowds are considerably larger than cliques and may not have the tight-knit cohesiveness and carefully drawn boundaries of a clique. Their members tend to share common interests (e.g., "brains" study a lot, "jocks" are active in sports), attitudes about academic achievement, and (occasionally) ethnic background (L. Steinberg, 1996). Sometimes a crowd takes the form of a **subculture**, a group that resists a powerful dominant culture by adopting a significantly different way of life (J. S. Epstein, 1998). Some subcultures are relatively benign; for example, the baggy-pants "skaters" with whom my son Alex affiliated spent much of their free time riding their skateboards and addressing almost everyone as "dude." Other subcultures are more worrisome, such as those that endorse racist and anti-Semitic behaviors (e.g., "skinheads") and those that practice Satanic worship and rituals (C. C. Clark, 1992). Adolescents are more likely to affiliate with subcultures when they feel alienated from the dominant culture (perhaps that of their school or that of society more generally) and want to distinguish themselves from it in some way (C. C. Clark, 1992; J. R. Harris, 1998).

A **gang** is a cohesive social group characterized by initiation rites, distinctive colors and symbols, ownership of a specific "territory," and feuds with one or more rival groups (A. Campbell, 1984). Typically, gangs are governed by strict rules for behavior, with stiff penalties for rule violations. Adolescents (and sometimes younger children as well) affiliate with gangs for a variety of reasons (A. Campbell, 1984; C. C. Clark, 1992; Parks, 1995; Simons, Whitbeck, Conger, & Conger, 1991). Some do so as a way of demonstrating loyalty to their family, friends, or neighborhood. Some seek the status and prestige that gang membership brings. Some have poor academic records and perceive the gang as an alternative arena in which they might gain recognition for their accomplishments. Many members of gangs have had troubled relationships with their families, or they have been consistently rejected by peers, and so they turn to gangs to get the emotional support they can find nowhere else. As teachers, we can definitely make a difference in the lives of any gang members who might be in our classes (S. G. Freedman, 1990; Parks, 1995). We must, first and foremost, show these students that we truly care about them and their well-being; for instance, we can be willing listeners in times of trouble and can provide the support students need to achieve both academic and social success. We must also have some knowledge of students' backgrounds—their cultural values, economic circumstances, and so on—so that we can better understand the issues with which they may be dealing.

In the upper high school grades, a greater capacity for abstract thought may allow students to think of other people more as unique individuals and less as members of specific categories.

■ **clique** Moderately stable friendship group of perhaps three to ten members.

■ **crowd** Large, loose-knit social group that shares common interests and attitudes.

■ **subculture** Group that resists the ways of the dominant culture and adopts its own norms for behavior.

■ **gang** Cohesive social group characterized by initiation rites, distinctive colors and symbols, territorial orientation, and feuds with rival groups.

Many older adolescents gain new awareness of the characteristics they share with people from diverse backgrounds. Perhaps as a result, ties to specific peer groups tend to dissipate, hostilities between groups soften, and young people become more flexible about the people with whom they associate (B. B. Brown, Eicher, & Petrie, 1986; Gavin & Fuhrman, 1989; Larkin, 1979; Shrum & Cheek, 1987).

Romantic Relationships   Many children talk of love and romance even in kindergarten and the primary grades; for instance, they may claim to have "boyfriends" or "girlfriends." And the opposite sex is the subject of some curiosity throughout the elementary school years; for example, in the "Friendships: Middle Childhood" clip on Video CD 1, 8-year-old Kate mentions that she and her friends "try to catch boys."

■ Note Kate's interest in boys in the "Friendships: Middle Childhood" clip on Video CD 1.

With the onset of adolescence, the biological changes of puberty are accompanied by new, often unsettling, feelings and sexual desires. Not surprisingly, then, romance is often on adolescents' minds and is a frequent topic of conversation at school (B. B. Brown, Feiring, & Furman, 1999). From a developmental standpoint, romantic relationships have definite benefits: They can address students' needs for companionship, affection, and security; and they provide an opportunity to experiment with new social skills and interpersonal behaviors (Furman & Simon, 1999; B. C. Miller & Benson, 1999). At the same time, romance can wreak havoc with adolescents' emotions. Adolescents have more extreme mood swings than younger children or adults, and, for many, this instability may be partly due to the excitement and frustrations of being romantically involved or *not* involved (Arnett, 1999; Larson, Clore, & Wood, 1999).

Initially, "romances" often exist more in students' minds than in reality (Gottman & Mettetal, 1986). Consider Sandy's recollection of her first foray into couplehood:

> In about fifth and sixth grade, all our little group that we had . . . was like, "OK," you know, "we're getting ready for junior high," you know, "it's time we all have to get a boyfriend." So I remember, it was funny, Carol, like, there were two guys who were just the heartthrobs of our class, you know . . . so, um, I guess it was Carol and Cindy really, they were, like, sort of the leaders of our group, you know, they were the, yeah, they were just the leaders, and they got Tim and Joe, each of those you know. Carol had Tim and Cindy had Joe. And then, you know, everyone else, then it kind of went down the line, everyone else found someone. I remember thinking, "Well, who am I gonna get? I don't even like anybody," you know. I remember, you know, all sitting around, we were saying, "OK, who can we find for Sandy?" you know, looking, so finally we decided, you know, we were trying to decide between Al and Dave and so finally I took Dave. (Eckert, 1989, p. 84)

For many students, thoughts of romance emerge early. Here is just one of many notes 5-year-old Isabelle wrote about a classmate named Will.

Middle school students' romantic thoughts may also involve crushes on people who are out of reach—perhaps favorite teachers, movie idols, or rock stars (B. B. Brown, 1999; B. C. Miller & Benson, 1999).

Eventually, however, many adolescents begin to date, especially if their friends are also dating. Their early choices in dating partners are often based on physical attractiveness or social status, and dates may involve only limited and superficial interaction (Furman, Brown, & Feiring, 1999; Pellegrini, 2002). As students move into the high school grades, some form more intense, affectionate, and long-term relationships with members of the opposite sex, and these relationships often (but by no means always) lead to some degree of sexual intimacy (B. B. Brown, 1999; J. Connolly & Goldberg, 1999). The age of first sexual intercourse has decreased steadily over the last few decades, perhaps in part because the media often communicate the message that sexual activity among unmarried partners is acceptable (Brooks-Gunn & Paikoff, 1993; Larson et al., 1999). In the United States the average age of first sexual intercourse is now around age 16, and the majority of adolescents are sexually active by 18, but the age varies considerably as a function of gender (boys begin earlier) and cultural background (Hofferth, 1990; Katchadourian, 1990; Lippa, 2002; D. S. Moore & Erickson, 1985).

As they reach high school (perhaps even earlier), some students find themselves attracted to their own sex either instead of or in addition to the opposite sex. Adolescence is a particularly confusing time for homosexual and bisexual students. Some students actively try to ignore or stifle what they perceive to be deviant urges. Others accept their sexual yearnings yet struggle to form an identity while feeling different and isolated from peers (Morrow, 1997; C. J. Patterson, 1995). Many gay, lesbian, and bisexual students describe feelings of anger and depression, some entertain thoughts of suicide, and a higher than average proportion drop out of school (Elia, 1994; C. J. Patterson, 1995).

Teenagers often have mixed feelings about their early sexual experiences (Alapack, 1991), and those around them—parents, teachers, peers—are often uncertain about how to handle the topic (Katchadourian, 1990). When parents and teachers do broach the topic of sexuality, they often raise it in conjunction with *problems*, such as irresponsible behavior, substance abuse, disease, and unwanted pregnancy. They rarely raise the topic of homosexuality except within the context of acquired immune deficiency syndrome (AIDS) and other risks (M. B. Harris, 1997).

As teachers, the extent to which we talk about sexuality with our students must, in part, be dictated by the policies of the school and the values of the community in which we work. At the same time, especially if we are teaching at the middle school or high school level, we must be aware that romantic and sexual relationships, whether real or imagined, are a considerable source of excitement, frustration, confusion, and distraction for students; and we must lend a sympathetic and open-minded ear to those students who seek our counsel and support.

■ What were your perceptions of the "popular" students at your school?

Truly popular students have good social skills.

Popularity and Social Isolation   When my daughter Tina was in junior high school, she sometimes told me, "No one likes the popular kids." Her remark was, of course, self-contradictory, and I usually told her so, but in fact it was consistent with research findings. When students are asked to identify their most popular age-mates, they identify peers who have dominant social status at school (perhaps those who belong to a prestigious social group) but in many cases are aggressive or stuck-up (Parkhurst & Hopmeyer, 1998). Truly **popular students**—those whom many others choose as people they'd like to do things with—may or may not hold high-status positions, but they are kind and trustworthy (Parkhurst & Hopmeyer, 1998). Students who are popular in this way typically have good social skills; for instance, they know how to initiate and sustain conversations, are sensitive to the subtle social and emotional cues that others give them, and adjust their behavior to changing circumstances. They also tend to show genuine concern for their peers; for instance, they are more likely to help, share, cooperate, and empathize with others (Caprara, Barbaranelli, Pastorelli, Bandura, & Zimbardo, 2000; Crick & Dodge, 1994; Mostow, Izard, Fine, & Trantacosta, 2002; Wentzel & Asher, 1995).

In addition to asking students whom they would most like to do something with, researchers often ask them to identify classmates whom they would *least* like to do something with. Those who are frequently selected are known as **rejected students**. Students from minority groups often find themselves the targets of derogatory remarks and other forms of racism and discrimination, as do students from low-income families (Nieto, 1995; Olneck, 1995; Pang, 1995; Phelan, Yu, & Davidson, 1994). And students with few social skills—for example, those who are impulsive or aggressive and those who continually try to draw attention to themselves (remember Adam in the opening case)—typically experience peer rejection (Asher & Renshaw, 1981; Bolger & Patterson, 2001; Eisenberg, Pidada, & Liew, 2001; Pellegrini, Bartini, & Brooks, 1999).

Researchers have described a third category as well. **Neglected students** are those whom classmates rarely choose as someone they would either most like or least like to do something with (Asher & Renshaw, 1981). Neglected students tend to be quiet and keep to themselves. Some prefer to be alone, others may be very shy or may not know how to go about initiating interaction, and still others may be quite content with having only one or two close friends (Gazelle & Ladd, 2003; Guay et al., 1999; Rubin & Krasnor, 1986). For some students, "neglected" status is a relatively temporary situation. Others are out of the social loop for extended periods, and these students are at greater risk for depression (Gazelle & Ladd, 2003).

As teachers, we can help offset the hard feelings that peer rejection or neglect may engender by being particularly warm and attentive to socially isolated students (Wentzel, 1999). We can also assist with social skills. Because of their social isolation, rejected and neglected students have fewer opportunities to develop the social skills that many of them desperately need (Coie & Cillessen, 1993). When they do interact with their peers, their behaviors may be counterproductive, leaving them more isolated than ever. Consider the plight of a seventh-grader named Michelle:

> Michelle is an extremely bright student, and her academic accomplishments have earned her much teacher praise over the years. But despite her many scholastic successes, Michelle has few friends. To draw attention to herself, she talks incessantly about her academic achievements. Her classmates interpret such bragging as a sign of undeserved arrogance, and so they insult her frequently as a way of knocking her down a peg or two. In self-defense, Michelle begins hurling insults at her classmates as soon as she sees them—beating them to the punch, so to speak.

■ **popular students** Students whom many peers like and perceive to be kind and trustworthy.

■ **rejected students** Students whom many peers identify as being undesirable social partners.

■ **neglected students** Students about whom most peers have no strong feelings, either positive or negative.

When students routinely offend or alienate others (as Michelle does), their peers seldom give them the constructive feedback that allows them to improve their behavior on future occasions, and so it may be up to us, as teachers, to give them that guidance.

Of course, children differ in the value they place on peer relationships. In the following exercise, we look at what one student has to say about friends.

■ Think back to our discussion of self-concept. What do Michelle's behaviors tell us about her self-perceptions of social competence?

Interpreting Student Artifacts and Behaviors

Friends

In the writing sample to the right, 7-year-old Andrew explains what he thinks friends are for. As you read his essay, consider

- What he thinks friends are for
- How successful he appears to be in making and keeping friends

> Freinds c ur for you when youare lonLey and Sad. they PLay with. you, they are nice; they are mean; they tell stories And the things they Do. they Walk you to the nursce,

---

Andrew appears to see friends partly as companions and sources of entertainment (they're for "when you are lonley," "they play with you," "they tell stories") and partly as people who provide support ("they walk you to the nursce"). He recognizes that friendships can be rocky at times (friends may be "nice" or "mean"), but overall he finds value in spending time with friends. The fact that Andrew sees more positives than negatives in his peers suggests that he has one or more good friends. In fact, Andrew is quite popular with his classmates.

One important ingredient in establishing and maintaining positive interpersonal relationships is the way children and adolescents *think* about people and their behaviors. This ingredient is known as *social cognition*.

Social Cognition

As we discovered in Chapter 2, children and adolescents become increasingly able to understand and think logically about the physical world and academic subject matter. Their cognitive development enables them to make better sense of their social world as well; in particular, they become more able to understand the perspectives and interpret the behaviors of other people. When students consider how the people around them are likely to think, act, and react, they are engaging in **social cognition**.

At any particular age level, students vary considerably in their interest in and awareness of other people's thoughts and feelings. Those who *do* consider such matters are more socially skillful, make friends more easily, and have better self-understanding (Bosacki, 2000; Izard et al., 2001). Here we look at two aspects of social cognition that influence students' ability to get along with peers; perspective taking and social information processing.

GOLEMAN'S EMOTIONAL INTELLIGENCE

Perspective Taking   To truly understand and get along with other people, students must be able to step into other people's shoes—that is, to look at the world from other viewpoints. The following situation provides an example.

Experiencing FIRSTHAND ·Last Picked

Kenny and Mark are co-captains of the soccer team. They have one person left to choose for the team. Without saying anything, Mark winks at Kenny and looks at Tom, who is one of the remaining children left to be chosen for the team. Mark looks back at Kenny and smiles. Kenny nods and chooses Tom to be on their team. Tom sees Mark and Kenny winking and smiling at each other. Tom, who is usually one of the last to be picked for team sports, wonders why Kenny wants him to be on his team. . . .

- Why did Mark smile at Kenny?
- Why did Kenny nod?
- Why did Kenny choose Tom to be on the team? How do you know this?
- Do you think that Tom has any idea of why Kenny chose him to be on the team? How do you know this? . . .
- How do you think Tom feels? (Bosacki, 2000, p. 711; format adapted)

· · · · · · ·

■ **social cognition** Process of thinking about how other people are likely to think, act, and react.

TABLE 3.2

Perspective Taking and Theory of Mind at Different Grade Levels

GRADE LEVEL	AGE-TYPICAL CHARACTERISTICS	SUGGESTED STRATEGIES
K–2	• Awareness that mental events are not physical entities • Awareness that others' knowledge and thoughts may be different from one's own • Ability to draw inferences about people's thoughts, feelings, and intentions from their behaviors, albeit in a simplistic manner (e.g., "She's sad")	• Talk frequently about people's thoughts, feelings, and motives; use words such as *think*, *remember*, *feel*, and *want*. • Ask questions about thoughts, feelings, and motives during storybook readings.
3–5	• Growing recognition that others interpret (rather than simply absorb) experiences and so may misconstrue events • Realization that other people's actions may hide their true feelings	• As students read literature, ask them to consider why various characters might behave as they do. • Have students consider what people might have been thinking and feeling during events in history. • Help students resolve interpersonal conflicts by asking them to consider one another's perspectives and to develop a solution that addresses everyone's needs.
6–8	• Increasing interest in other people's thoughts and feelings • Recognition that people may have multiple and possibly conflicting motives and emotions • Ability to think *recursively* about one's own and others' thoughts (see discussion in section "Early Adolescence")	• Encourage students to look at historical and current events from the perspective of various historical figures and cultural groups. • In discussions of literature, talk about other people's complex (and sometimes conflicting) motives.
9–12	• Recognition that people are products of their environment and that past events and present circumstances influence personality and behavior • Awareness that people are not always aware of why they act as they do	• Explore the possible origins of people's perspectives and motives in discussions of real and fictional events. • Schedule debates in which students must present convincing arguments for perspectives opposite to their own. • Offer units or courses in psychology, with a focus on such "internal" activities as cognition, motivation, and emotion.

Sources: Astington & Pelletier, 1996; Bosacki, 2000; Brophy & Alleman, 1996; Brophy & VanSledright, 1997; Eisenberg, Carlo, Murphy, & Van Court, 1995; Flanagan & Tucker, 1999; Flavell, 2000; Flavell, Green, & Flavell, 1995; Flavell & Miller, 1998; Flavell et al., 1993; Harter & Whitesell, 1989; Perner & Wimmer, 1985; Ruffman, Slade, & Crowe, 2002; Schult, 2002; Selman, 1980; Wellman, 1990; Wellman, Cross, & Watson, 2001; Wellman, Phillips, & Rodriguez, 2000; Woolfe, Want, & Siegal, 2002; Woolley, 1995.

■ **perspective taking** Ability to look at a situation from someone's else viewpoint.

■ **theory of mind** Understanding of one's own and other people's mental and psychological states (thoughts, feelings, etc.).

To answer these questions, you must look at the situation from the perspectives of three individuals: Kenny, Mark, and Tom. Such **perspective taking** helps people make sense of actions that might otherwise be puzzling and choose responses that are most likely to achieve desired results and maintain positive interpersonal relationships.

As you should recall from Chapter 2, Jean Piaget proposed that with age, children become better able to look at the world from other people's viewpoints. You should also recall that from an information processing perspective, *metacognition* improves with age: As children grow older, they become increasingly aware of their own thought processes. In fact, as children learn more about their own thinking, they also become more adept at drawing inferences about what *other* people are thinking. More generally, children develop a **theory of mind** that encompasses increasingly complex understandings of people's mental and psychological states—thoughts, beliefs, feelings, motives, and so on. Their theory of mind enables them to interpret and predict the behaviors of the important people in their lives and, as a result, to interact effectively with those individuals (e.g., Flavell, 2000; Gopnik & Meltzoff, 1997; Wellman & Gelman, 1998). Table 3.2 presents ways in which a student's theory of mind is apt to change over the course of childhood and adolescence. In the following sections, we look at some of the changes more closely.

Childhood. As you might guess from what you have learned about cognitive development, young children tend to think of other people in a fairly concrete fashion and focus on observable characteristics and behaviors; Andrew's essay about friends is a case in point. However, they do have some awareness of other people's inner worlds. As early as age 4 or 5, they realize that what *they* know may be different from what *other people* know (Wellman, Cross, & Watson, 2001; Wimmer & Perner, 1983); thus, they are beginning to lose the preoperational egocentrism of which Piaget spoke. By age 5, they also have some ability to draw inferences about other people's mental states—for instance, to deduce that people who behave in certain ways have certain feelings or intentions (Astington & Pelletier, 1996; Flavell, 2000; Schult, 2002; Wellman et al., 2000). In the "Emotions: Middle Childhood" clip on Video CD 1, 10-year-old Daniel shows an understanding that people often (but not always) reveal their emotions in their facial expressions and body language; for instance, they may smile when happy, frown when angry, or walk with drooping shoulders when sad. (In contrast, in the early adolescence and late adolescence "Emotions" clips, respectively, 13-year-old Crystal and 15-year-old Greg are aware of more subtle cues. For instance, people may get "hyper" or "won't stop talking" when they're happy, may "hide their face" or "don't talk" when sad, or "don't want you to be around them" when angry.)

As children progress through the elementary grades, they draw more sophisticated inferences about other people's mental states. For instance, they may realize that people's actions do not always reflect their thoughts and feelings (e.g., someone who appears happy may actually feel sad) and that people sometimes have mixed feelings about a situation (Flavell et al., 1993; Gnepp, 1989; Selman, 1980). Children understand, too, that people interpret events—rather than simply "recording" them in an objective manner—and that others may view a situation differently than they themselves do (M. Chandler & Boyes, 1982; Flavell et al., 1993). In other words, children increasingly understand that thinking and learning are active, constructive processes (Flavell et al., 1995; Wellman, 1990).

■ Observe examples of social cognition in the three "Emotions" clips on Video CD 1.

Early adolescence. As children move into early adolescence, they begin to appreciate that people can have ambivalent feelings about events and other individuals (Donaldson & Westerman, 1986; Flavell & Miller, 1998; Harter & Whitesell, 1989). They also become aware that people may simultaneously have multiple, and possibly conflicting, intentions (Chandler, 1987). As an example, let's return to the "Last Picked" exercise you did earlier. You may have suspected that Tom has mixed feelings about being chosen for the team. He may think that he's a poor athlete (he's often one of the last picked) and so may wonder why Mark and Kenny have chosen him. He may also wonder what Mark's smile means: It could mean that Mark is delighted to find a capable player still available to be picked, yet it might instead signal a malicious intention to make Tom look foolish on the soccer field. Despite his misgivings, Tom may be happy to have a chance to play one of his favorite games. Young adolescents become increasingly thoughtful about such matters (Bosacki, 2000).

Courtesy of their expanding cognitive abilities, memory capacity, and social awareness, young adolescents become able to engage in *recursive thinking* (Oppenheimer, 1986; Perner & Wimmer, 1985): They can think about what other people might be thinking about them and eventually can reflect on other people's thoughts about themselves through multiple iterations (e.g., "You think that I think that you think . . . "). This is not to say that adolescents (or adults, for that matter) always use this capacity. In fact, thinking only about one's own perspective, without regard for the perspective of others, is a common phenomenon in the early adolescent years (recall our earlier discussion of the *imaginary audience*). As teachers, then, we may often need to remind young teenagers to consider why others might reasonably think and behave as they do.

Late adolescence. Older adolescents can draw on a rich knowledge base derived from numerous social experiences, and so they become ever more skillful at drawing inferences about people's psychological characteristics, intentions, and needs (Eisenberg et al., 1995; Paget, Kritt, & Bergemann, 1984). In addition, they are more attuned to the complex dynamics—not only thoughts, feelings, and present circumstances but also past experiences—that influence behavior (C. A. Flanagan & Tucker, 1999; Selman, 1980). And they realize that other people are not always aware of why they act as they do (Selman, 1980). What we see emerging in the high school years, then, is a budding psychologist: an individual who can be quite astute in deciphering and explaining the motives and actions of others.

We sometimes see glimmers of students' perspective-taking ability in their written work. As an example, try the following exercise.

Interpreting Student Artifacts and Behaviors

Looking Through Others' Eyes

The following two artifacts were created during history lessons about slavery during colonial America. The reaction paper on the left was written by 10-year-old Charmaine, whose fifth-grade class had been watching *Roots*, a miniseries about a young African man (Kunta Kinte) who is captured and brought to America to be a slave. The "diary" on the right was written by 14-year-old Craig, whose ninth-grade history teacher asked his class to write journal entries that might capture the life of a colonial plantation owner. As you read the two artifacts:

■ Look for evidence of perspective taking
■ Identify specific abilities that reflect development of a theory of mind

Roots I ON THE BOAT TO AMERICA

I could feel the pain Kunta-Kinte was having. Once I had a paper cut and when in the ocean it hurt more than a wasp sting, and that was just paper cut. I can't even imagine the pain or fright that Kunta-Kinte had being taken from his family and home. Or his parents' hurt finding out that their first son was being taken to be a slave, their son that had just become a man. I also am horrified about how they treated women. Belly-warmers! The makes angre!

My Diary

July 1, 1700
Dear Diary - Today was a scorcher. I could not stand it and I was not even working. The slaves looked so hot. I even felt for them. And it is affecting my tobacco. It's too hot too early in the season. The tobacco plants are not growing quickly enough. I can only hope that it rains. Also today Robert Smith invited me to a ball at his house in two days. In 5 days I am going to have my masked ball. We mailed out the invitations two days ago. My wife, Beth, and I thought of a great idea of a masked ball. We will hire our own band.

July 2, 1700
Dear Diary - It was another scorcher. I wish it would cool down. I don't think the slaves can handle it. It looked like some of them would faint. I had them drink more water. Later in the day a nice breeze came up. Then I gave them the rest of the day off. Also today we planned a trip to Richmond. . . .

July 5, 1700
Dear Diary - Today we had to wake up before the sun had risen. After a breakfast of hot cakes, eggs, and sausage, we headed back home. We got there at the end of the morning. When I got back it was very, very hot. One of the slaves fainted so I gave them the rest of the day off, fearing revolt. I also gave them extra food and water. It makes me think that they are only people too. I know that this is unheard of but it really makes me think.

Charmaine certainly shows some perspective-taking ability: She talks about Kunta Kinte's "pain" and "fright" and about his parents' "hurt" at losing their firstborn son. She acknowledges that she cannot fully grasp Kunta Kinte's physical pain, as her own experience with pain has been limited to having a paper cut in saltwater. In recognizing that people's ability to take the perspective of another may be limited by the extent to which they've had similar experiences, Charmaine shows an understanding that people (herself included) are to some degree products of their past environments.

Craig, too, is able to put himself in another person's shoes. In fact, he tries to imagine someone else (a plantation owner) taking *other people's* perspectives (those of slaves). Such "two-tiered" perspective taking is, in a way, similar to recursive thinking, but in this case it is a matter of thinking "I think that you think that someone else thinks . . . " Like Charmaine, Craig realizes that people are products of their environment: The plantation owner struggles with the prevailing attitude during colonial times that slaves were not really human beings ("It makes me think they are only people too. I know that this is unheard of but it really makes me think").

How can we promote greater perspective taking in students? One strategy is to create opportunities for students to encounter multiple—and perhaps equally legitimate—perspectives and beliefs. Another is to talk frequently about people's thoughts, feelings, and motives (Ruffman et al., 2002; Woolfe et al., 2002). In the process, we must, of course, use age-appropriate language (J. Chalmers & Townsend, 1990; Wittmer & Honig, 1994). With first graders, such words might be *think*, *want*, *excitement*, or *sadness*. With fifth graders, they might be *misunderstand*, *frustration*, or *mixed feelings*. High school students have the cognitive and social reasoning capabilities to understand descriptions that use fairly abstract and complex psychological terms, such as *being passive aggressive* or *having an inner moral compass*. These and other strategies are presented in the right-hand column of Table 3.2.

Having students take other people's perspectives in writing assignments (as Charmaine and Craig did) can also be helpful. Often such assignments are most effective when used in combination with in-class discussions that spur students to reflect more deeply about interpersonal situations. The following report from an elementary school teacher illustrates the importance of persistence in asking students to think about the effects of their actions on others:

> During gym lesson five of the boys misbehaved and were dismissed from class. They acted out their anger by insulting the gym teacher and the other staff greatly by answering back, shouting and even swearing, and throwing eggs at the school buildings.... When the boys came to my class they were very upset.... I told them I was not going to blame them at this point but I wanted them to write an essay at home about what had happened.... [The essays] were written sincerely in the sense that they described clearly what they had done but to my surprise without any regret or tendency to see the staff members' point of view. Having read the essays I decided to discuss the event in class.... The children defined the problem and thought about the feelings of those involved. I spent a considerable time asking them to consider the staff members' feelings, whether they knew of somebody who worked in a place similar to the gym, which in fact they did, how that person felt, etc. Gradually, the boys' vehemence subsided. I never blamed them so that they wouldn't become defensive, because then I thought I might lose them. Instead, I tried to improve their understanding of the opinions and feelings of other people, which might differ from their own.... The boys improved their behavior in gym class, and this never happened again. (Adalbjarnardottir & Selman, 1997, pp. 423–424)

Social Information Processing   Children have a lot to think about when they consider what other people are thinking, feeling, and doing. This idea of **social information processing**—the mental processes involved in understanding and responding to social events—is simply a more "social" version of the information processing theory described in Chapter 2. Among other things, social information processing involves paying *attention* to some of people's behaviors in a social situation and trying to interpret and make sense of those behaviors through *elaboration* (Crick & Dodge, 1996; Dodge, 1986). For example, when students interact with classmates, they might focus on certain remarks, facial expressions, and body language and try to figure out what a classmate really *means* by, say, a thoughtless comment or sheepish grin. They then combine their interpretations with their previous knowledge and experiences to identify one or more possible responses and choose what is, in their eyes, a productive course of action.

Social information processing theory is especially helpful in understanding why some students are unusually aggressive toward their peers, as we shall see now.

Aggression and Social Cognition   In the opening case study, Adam exhibits a variety of aggressive behaviors, including pushing and shoving, yelling obscenities, and starting fights. More generally, **aggressive behavior** is an action intentionally taken to hurt another person either physically (perhaps by hitting, shoving, or fighting) or psychologically (perhaps by embarrassing, insulting, or ostracizing). **Physical aggression**—actions such as hitting and shoving, which can potentially cause bodily injury—is more common in boys. **Relational aggression**—actions such as ostracizing a peer or spreading rumors, which can adversely affect friendships and other interpersonal relationships—is more common in girls (Crick, Grotpeter, & Bigbee, 2002; D. C. French, Jansen, & Pidada, 2002; Pellegrini, 2002). As a general rule, aggression declines over the course of childhood and adolescence, but it increases for a short time after students make the transition from elementary school to middle school or junior high (Pellegrini, 2002).

Researchers have identified two distinct groups of aggressive students (Crick & Dodge, 1996; Poulin & Boivin, 1999; Vitaro, Gendreau, Tremblay, & Oligny, 1998). Those who engage in **proactive aggression** deliberately initiate aggressive behaviors as a means of obtaining desired goals. Those who engage in **reactive aggression** act aggressively primarily in response to frustration or

- **social information processing** Mental processes involved in understanding and responding to social events.

- **aggressive behavior** Action intentionally taken to hurt another either physically or psychologically.

- **physical aggression** Action that can potentially cause bodily injury.

- **relational aggression** Action that can adversely affect interpersonal relationships.

- **proactive aggression** Deliberate aggression against another as a means of obtaining a desired goal.

- **reactive aggression** Aggressive response to frustration or provocation.

Chapter 1
The Bully

"Mom, do I have to go to school?"
"Yes, you do Kevin."
"But what if there are bullies?"
"There will not be bullies."
"Fine, I'll go to school."
I got on the bus.
"Hey you, come here."
"No."
"I'll give you my bike if you come here!"
"No!"
"Why?"
"'Cause I have my own."
"Yeah, right. Why should I believe you?"
"I do not know."
"Because you are a liar."
"No, I am not."
"Yes, you are."
"No, I am not."
"Yes, you are."
"Fine, I am."

Many children and adolescents encounter bullies at school and elsewhere. This excerpt is from the first chapter in "The Biggest Bully Ever," a story in which 7-year-old Michael describes an encounter with a bully on the school bus. In the second (final) chapter of his story, Michael describes how he and his friends defended themselves against the bully's behaviors.

■ **hostile attributional bias** Tendency to interpret others' behaviors as reflecting hostile or aggressive intentions.

provocation. Of the two groups, students who exhibit proactive aggression are more likely to have difficulty maintaining friendships with others (Poulin & Boivin, 1999). They may also direct considerable aggression toward particular children; those who do so are often known as *bullies* (G. R. Patterson, Littman, & Bricker, 1967; Pellegrini et al., 1999; D. Schwartz, Dodge, Pettit, & Bates, 1997). Their hapless victims often are children who are immature, anxious, friendless, and lacking in self-confidence—some also have disabilities—and so are relatively defenseless (Hodges, Malone, & Perry, 1997; Juvonen, Nishina, & Graham, 2000; Little, 2002; Marsh, Parada, Yeung, & Healey, 2001; D. Schwartz, McFadyen-Ketchum, Dodge, Pettit, & Bates, 1999).

Some children and adolescents are genetically more predisposed to aggression than their peers, and others may exhibit heightened aggression as a result of neurological damage (Raine & Scerbo, 1991; D. C. Rowe, Almeida, & Jacobson, 1999). Yet cognitive and motivational factors play a key role in aggressive behavior as well, and several of these factors, described in the following paragraphs, relate to our preceding discussion of social cognition.

Poor perspective-taking ability. Students who are highly aggressive tend to have limited ability to look at situations from other people's perspectives or to empathize with their victims (Coie & Dodge, 1998; Damon & Hart, 1988; R. F. Marcus, 1980).

Misinterpretation of social cues. Students who are either physically or relationally aggressive toward peers tend to interpret others' behaviors as reflecting hostile intentions, especially when such behaviors have ambiguous meanings (Crick et al., 2002; Dodge et al., 2003; Graham & Hudley, 1994; Orobio de Castro, Veerman, Koops, Bosch, & Monshouwer, 2002). This **hostile attributional bias** is especially prevalent in students who are prone to *reactive* aggression (Crick & Dodge, 1996).

Prevalence of self-serving goals. For most students, establishing and maintaining interpersonal relationships is a high priority. For aggressive students, however, more self-serving goals—perhaps maintaining an inflated self-image, seeking revenge, or gaining power and dominance—often take precedence (R. F. Baumeister et al., 1996; G. Bender, 2001; Crick & Dodge, 1996; Erdley & Asher, 1996; Pellegrini, 2002).

Poor social problem-solving skills. Aggressive students often have limited ability to generate effective solutions to social dilemmas. They may have little knowledge of how to persuade, negotiate, or compromise, and so they resort to hitting, shoving, barging into play activities, and other ineffective strategies (Lochman & Dodge, 1994; Neel, Jenkins, & Meadows, 1990; D. Schwartz et al., 1998; Shure & Spivack, 1980).

Beliefs about the appropriateness and effectiveness of aggression. Many aggressive students believe that violence and other forms of aggression are perfectly acceptable ways of resolving conflicts and retaliating for others' misdeeds. For instance, they may believe they need to teach someone a "lesson" (Astor, 1994; Boldizar, Perry, & Perry, 1989; E. Staub, 1995; Zelli, Dodge, Lochman, & Laird, 1999). Those who display high rates of *proactive* aggression are also apt to believe that aggressive action will yield positive results—for instance, that it will enhance their social status (Dodge, Lochman, Harnish, Bates, & Pettit, 1997; C. H. Hart, Ladd, & Burleson, 1990; Pellegrini & Bartini, 2000). Not surprisingly, aggressive students tend to associate with one another, thus confirming one another's beliefs that aggression is appropriate (Espelage et al., 2003; Farmer et al., 2002).

Without intervention, many aggressive children (especially those who exhibit proactive aggression) show a continuing pattern of aggression and violence as they grow older (Dodge et al., 2003; Eron, 1980; Kupersmidt & Coie, 1990; Vitaro et al., 1998). The specific strategies we use to help aggressive students behave more appropriately must, of course, be tailored to the cognitions and motives that underlie their aggression (Crick & Dodge, 1996). Such strategies as encouraging perspective taking, helping students interpret social situations more accurately, and teaching effective social problem-solving skills are all potentially useful in reducing aggression and other disruptive behaviors (Cunningham & Cunningham, 1998; Guerra & Slaby, 1990; Hudley & Graham, 1993).

It is important to note, however, that interventions with individual students are apt to be effective only if their school is a relatively peaceful one. At some schools violence and aggression are commonplace, and students may believe that acting aggressively is the only way to ensure that they don't become victims of *someone else's* aggression. Unfortunately, they may be right: Putting on a tough, seemingly invulnerable appearance (sometimes known as "frontin' it") can be critical for their survival (Williams, 2001a). Such a situation is, of course, hardly conducive to effective learning and academic achievement. We will look at strategies for addressing school-wide aggression and violence in Chapter 14.

As teachers, we can draw on our understanding of social cognition (including perspective taking and social information processing) as we work to help all students—including aggressive ones—interact effectively and form friendships with their classmates. In the next section we apply what we've learned to identify strategies for fostering the development of social skills.

Fostering Social Skills

Because schools and classrooms present complex social situations, they provide an ideal context in which social skills can develop (M. Deutsch, 1993; S. N. Elliott & Busse, 1991). Furthermore, students with good social skills tend to be more academically successful, perhaps in part because they are better able to gain the support of teachers and peers when they need assistance and support (H. A. Davis, 2003; Patrick, Anderman, & Ryan, 2002).

We can do many things to help students acquire effective ways of interacting with others and forming productive interpersonal relationships. The Creating a Productive Classroom Environment feature "Promoting Effective Interpersonal Relationships" presents several examples. Following are more general strategies:

◎ *Provide numerous opportunities for social interaction.* Students gain considerable information about which social behaviors are and are not effective simply by interacting with one another. For instance, students' play activities—whether the fantasy play of preschoolers and kindergartners or the rule-based games of older children and adolescents—can promote cooperation, sharing, perspective taking, and conflict resolution skills (Creasey, Jarvis, & Berk, 1998; Gottman, 1986; Rubin, 1982). Students are, of course, more likely to learn effective social skills when they have opportunities to interact with peers who exhibit socially appropriate behaviors, rather than with those who are disruptive and aggressive (Dishion, McCord, & Poulin, 1999).

CREATING A PRODUCTIVE CLASSROOM ENVIRONMENT

Promoting Effective Interpersonal Relationships

 Give students numerous opportunities to interact with one another in pairs or small groups.

A middle school teacher has students work in groups of three on a complex library research project. She structures the assignment so that each group member has a clearly defined role to perform.

 When students have interpersonal conflicts, provide guidance that helps them work out their difficulties to everyone's satisfaction.

When several second graders argue about whose turn it is to use the classroom computer, their teacher encourages them to work out a plan that will allow fair and equitable use of the computer each week.

 Foster perspective taking.

A fourth-grade teacher prepares his class for the arrival of a new student, first by discussing the feelings of uncertainty, apprehension, and loneliness the student is apt to have and then by helping the class identify steps it can take to make the student feel at home.

 Help students learn to interpret others' behaviors and intentions accurately and to identify appropriate responses to a variety of social situations.

A special education teacher meets weekly with three boys who have a history of lashing out at others at the slightest provocation. Through a series of role-playing activities, she has the boys enact various scenarios in which one student inconveniences or causes harm to another, and she asks them to brainstorm possible motives behind the "aggressive" behaviors. The group also discusses and practices courses of action that productively resolve each situation and preserve positive peer relationships.

 Promote social interaction among diverse groups.

A junior high school science teacher decides how students will be paired for weekly lab activities. She changes the pairings every month and frequently pairs students from different ethnic backgrounds.

 Consistently model respect for diversity.

A high school English teacher listens patiently and attentively as a student with a speech impediment stumbles over his words. At one point, she gives a stern look to a classmate who is giggling at the student's plight.

◎   *Plan cooperative activities.* When students participate in cooperative games, rather than in competitive ones, their aggressive behaviors toward one another decrease (Bay-Hinitz, Peterson, & Quilitch, 1994). Further, when they engage in cooperative classroom assignments, they can learn and practice help-giving, help-seeking, and conflict resolution skills, and they develop a better sense of justice and fairness regarding their peers (Damon, 1988; Lickona, 1991; N. M. Webb & Farivar, 1994). Chapter 13 offers several suggestions for conducting effective cooperative learning activities.

◎   *Help students interpret social situations in an accurate and productive way.* Students will interact more appropriately with others if they can accurately interpret others' behaviors and intentions (Graham, 1997; Guerra & Slaby, 1990). For example, in one research study involving third- through fifth-grade boys (Hudley & Graham, 1993), students attended a series of training sessions in which, through role playing, discussions of personal experiences, brainstorming, and similar activities, they practiced making inferences about other people's intentions and identifying appropriate courses of action. They also learned several guidelines to remind them of how to behave in various situations; for example, they might think to themselves, "When I don't have the information to tell what he meant, I should act as if it were an accident" (p. 128). Following the training, the students were less likely to presume hostile intent or endorse aggressive retaliation in interpersonal situations, and their teachers rated them as less aggressive than control-group students.

◎   *Teach specific social skills, provide opportunities for students to practice them, and give feedback.* We can teach students appropriate ways of behaving both through explicit verbal instructions and through modeling desired behaviors. Such instruction is especially likely to be effective when we also ask students to practice their newly learned social skills (perhaps through role playing) and give them concrete feedback about how they are doing (S. N. Elliott & Busse, 1991; Themann & Goldstein, 2001; S. Vaughn, 1991; Zirpoli & Melloy, 2001).

◎   *Label and praise appropriate behaviors when they occur.* We should identify and praise the specific social skills we see students exhibit (Vorrath, 1985; Wittmer & Honig, 1994). For example, we might say, "Thank you for being so helpful" or "I'm glad you two were able to cooperate so well as you worked on your project."

◎   *Describe students as having desirable social behaviors.* We can openly describe students as being helpful, courteous, or generous (Grusec & Redler, 1980; Wittmer & Honig, 1994). For example, 8-year-olds who are told, "You're the kind of person who likes to help others whenever you can," are more likely to share their belongings with others at a later date (Grusec & Redler, 1980).

◎   *Teach social problem-solving strategies.* Some students lack productive strategies for solving social problems; for example, they may barge into a game without asking or respond aggressively to any provocation. One strategy we can teach such students is to think carefully about a situation before responding and then talk themselves through the appropriate behaviors for dealing with it. A second strategy, for the classroom as a whole, is *mediation training*, which teaches students how to mediate conflicts among classmates by asking the opposing sides to express their differing points of view and then work together to devise a reasonable resolution. We'll discuss both of these strategies in more depth when we consider self-regulation in Chapter 10.

◎   *Establish and enforce firm rules for acceptable classroom behavior.* In addition to encouraging appropriate social behaviors, we must actively *discourage* such inappropriate behaviors as inconsiderateness, aggression, and prejudicial remarks (Bierman, Miller, & Stabb, 1987; Braukmann, Kirigin, & Wolf, 1981; Schofield, 1995). We must have clear guidelines for classroom behavior and impose consequences when such guidelines are not followed (see Chapters 9 and 14). By establishing and enforcing firm rules about aggressive and other antisocial behaviors while simultaneously teaching appropriate social skills, we will often see noticeable improvements in behavior.

Even when students are able to relate effectively with one another, we may find that many of them interact almost exclusively within a small, close-knit group or clique and that a few others remain socially isolated. Yet students have much of value to learn from classmates very different from themselves. So let's also consider how we can promote social interaction among diverse groups of students.

Promoting Social Interaction Among Diverse Groups

Simply putting students in the same school building is rarely sufficient to promote interaction among diverse groups of students. Students often divide themselves along ethnic lines when they eat lunch and interact in the school yard (Schofield, 1995). Immigrant students rarely interact with long-term residents, and newcomers to a school are often socially isolated (Olneck, 1995; Pérez, 1998). Many students with special needs are neglected or rejected by their classmates (Hymel, 1986; Juvonen & Hiner, 1991; Yuker, 1988).

As teachers, we must often take proactive steps to broaden the base of students' social interactions. Some of the strategies just listed for fostering social skills can be effective for promoting social interaction among diverse groups; for example, activities that involve cooperation rather than competition often reduce hostile attitudes toward members of other groups (Devine, 1995; Oskamp, 2000). Following are several additional strategies:

Assigning partners to students with special needs may encourage new friendships to develop.

◎ *Set up situations in which students can form new friendships.* We can do many simple things to help students get to know one another. We can arrange situations that compel them to work or play together; for example, we can develop structured cooperative learning activities in which all group members must share equal responsibility, or we can provide play equipment that requires the participation of several students (Banks, 1994; Schofield, 1995). We can assign a partner to a student with special needs—a classmate who can provide assistance when needed, perhaps reading to a student with a visual impairment, tutoring a student with a learning disability, or taking notes for a student with a physical impairment. Even the very simple practice of giving students assigned seats in class and occasionally changing the assignments increases the number of friends they make (Schofield, 1995).

◎ *Minimize or eliminate barriers to social interaction.* Students are less likely to interact with peers when physical, linguistic, or social barriers keep them from doing so. For example, I am reminded of a junior high girl who could not negotiate the cafeteria steps with her wheelchair and so always ended up eating lunch alone. Obviously, we must campaign for the removal of any physical impediments to the mobility of students with special needs. We can also teach groups of students who speak different languages (including American Sign Language) some basic vocabulary and simple phrases in one another's native tongues. Social barriers may begin to crumble if we vigorously address the prejudices and tensions that sometimes separate diverse ethnic groups; we will identify specific strategies for doing so in Chapter 4.

◎ *Encourage and facilitate participation in extracurricular activities.* Extracurricular activities provide additional opportunities for students to interact and work cooperatively with a wide range of peers (Genova & Walberg, 1984; Mahoney, Cairns, & Farmer, 2003; Schofield, 1995). Furthermore, participation in activities can help students find common grounds for communication, as one high school explains:

> If you feel like you have something to do after school, it's really neat. You get to talk to people in the hall, like, "Oh, is that meeting today?" Or, "What are we doing next week?" It gives you a feeling of, I have people who are in the same club as me. (Certo, Cauley, & Chafin, 2002, p. 20)

We must be careful, however, that no single group of students dominates in membership or leadership in any particular activity (Sleeter & Grant, 1999). And to ensure equal access to activities, schools may need to make arrangements for after-school transportation for those students who need it (Schofield, 1995).

◎ *Develop nondisabled students' understanding of students with special needs.* Nondisabled students sometimes feel resentment or anger about inappropriate behaviors that they believe a classmate with special needs should be able to control (Juvonen, 1991). For example, they are less likely to be tolerant of students with cognitive difficulties or emotional and behavioral disorders than they are of students with obvious physical disabilities (B. Cook & Semmel, 1999; Morrison, Furlong, & Smith, 1994; Yuker, 1988). Although we must respect individual students' right to privacy about medical and psychiatric conditions, we can certainly sensitize nondisabled students to the kinds of difficulties that students with special needs may have as a result of a

Extracurricular activities not only provide a means through which students can interact with peers but also can be a source of success for students who struggle with academic tasks. Here 7-year-old Daniel, who has attention and cognitive-processing deficits that make reading and writing quite difficult, expresses his love of baseball.

disability. At the same time, we must also show nondisabled students—and, ideally, give them opportunities to discover on their own—the many ways in which students with disabilities are normal children with the same thoughts, feelings, and needs as anyone else their age.

◎ *Help change the reputations of formerly antisocial students.* Unfortunately, students' bad reputations often live on long after their behavior has changed for the better. Even when students show dramatic improvements in behavior, their classmates may continue to dislike and reject them (Bierman et al., 1987; Juvonen & Hiner, 1991; Juvonen & Weiner, 1993). In the case of formerly aggressive students, the perception of many peers is "once a bully, always a bully." So when we work to improve the behaviors of antisocial students, we must work to improve their reputations as well. For example, we might encourage their active involvement in extracurricular activities or place them in structured cooperative learning groups where they can use their newly developed social skills. We should also demonstrate through our words and actions that *we* like and appreciate them; when we do so, our attitudes are apt to be contagious (Chang, 2003). In one way or another, we must help students discover that formerly antisocial classmates have changed and are worth getting to know better.

◎ *Encourage a general feeling of respect for others.* Teachers who effectively cultivate friendships among diverse groups are often those who communicate a consistent message over and over: We must all respect one another as human beings (A. P. Turnbull, Pereira, & Blue-Banning, 2000). Fernando Arias, a high school vocational education teacher, has put it this way:

> In our school, our philosophy is that we treat everybody the way we'd like to be treated. . . . Our school is a unique situation where we have pregnant young ladies who go to our school. We have special education children. We have the regular kids, and we have the drop-out recovery program . . . we're all equal. We all have an equal chance. And we have members of every gang at our school, and we hardly have any fights, and there are close to about 300 gangs in our city. We all get along. It's one big family unit it seems like. (A. P. Turnbull et al., 2000, p. 67)

Truly productive interpersonal relationships depend on students' ability to respect one another's rights and privileges and to support classmates who are going through hard times. Such capabilities are aspects of students' moral and prosocial development, a domain we turn to now.

MORAL AND PROSOCIAL DEVELOPMENT

Some social skills are aimed at benefiting others more than oneself; such **prosocial behaviors** include sharing, helping, and comforting. The domain of **morality** encompasses prosocial behavior, as well as such traits as honesty, fairness, and respect for other people's needs and rights. In our opening case study, Adam engages in behaviors that violate basic moral standards, including stealing lunches and trying to inflict harm on classmates.

Students' beliefs about moral and immoral behavior—their beliefs about right and wrong—affect their behavior at school. For example, we will see fewer instances of theft or violence when students respect the property and safety of their classmates and fewer cases of cheating when students believe that cheating is morally unacceptable. By acting morally and prosocially, students gain greater support from their teachers and classmates and thereby achieve greater academic and social success over the long run (Caprara et al., 2000).

Students' beliefs about morality also affect how they think about and respond to the topics they study in school. For instance, their moral values are apt to influence their reactions when they read descriptions of the Holocaust during World War II or discuss recent acts of terrorism around the world. Their sense of human dignity may enter in when they read the anti-Semitic statements that some characters in Shakespeare's *The Merchant of Venice* make about a Jewish money-lender. And beliefs about fairness and respect for the rights of others certainly come into play in any discussions about good sportsmanship on the athletic field. Students simply cannot avoid moral issues at school.

As teachers, we play a significant role in the moral and prosocial development of our students. Consider the teacher who prepares a class for the arrival of a new student, first by discussing the feelings of uncertainty, apprehension, and loneliness the student is likely to have, and then by helping the class identify steps it can take to make the student feel at home. This teacher is facilitating perspective taking and setting the stage for students to behave prosocially toward the newcomer. Now consider the teacher who ignores acts of selfishness and aggression in class and around the school building, perhaps using the rationale that students should always work things out among

Crucial!

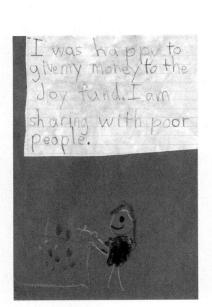

On a page in her "Happiness Book," 6-year-old Jaquita expresses her pleasure in behaving prosocially.

I was happy to give my money to the Joy fund. I am sharing with poor people.

■ **prosocial behavior** Behavior directed toward promoting the well-being of another.

■ **morality** One's general standards about right and wrong.

TABLE 3.3 DEVELOPMENTAL TRENDS

Moral Reasoning and Prosocial Behavior at Different Grade Levels

GRADE LEVEL	AGE-TYPICAL CHARACTERISTICS	SUGGESTED STRATEGIES
K–2	• Awareness that other people have desires, goals, and intentions different from one's own • Some empathy for, and attempts to comfort, people in distress, especially people that students know well • Ability to distinguish between behaviors that violate human rights and dignity versus those that violate social conventions • Some awareness that behaviors causing physical or psychological harm are morally wrong • Guilt about misbehaviors that cause obvious harm or damage • Greater concern for one's own needs than for those of others • Emerging concerns about possession and ownership; some reluctance to share	• Encourage students to comfort others when they can. • Model sympathetic responses; explain what you are doing and why you are doing it. • Make standards for behavior very clear. • When students misbehave, give reasons why such behaviors are not acceptable, focusing on the harm and distress they have caused for others (i.e., use *induction*; see discussion on p. 94). • Recognize that some selfish behavior is typical for the age-group.
3–5	• Knowledge of social conventions for appropriate behavior • Increasing empathy for unknown individuals who are suffering or needy • Recognition that one should strive to meet others' needs as well as one's own; growing appreciation for cooperation and compromise • Feelings of shame as well as guilt for moral wrongdoings • Increase in the desire to help others as an objective in and of itself	• Talk about how rules enable classrooms and other group situations to run more smoothly. • Explain how students can often meet their own needs while helping others (e.g., when asking students to be "reading buddies" for younger children, explain that doing so will help them become better readers themselves). • Use prosocial adjectives (e.g., *kind*, *helpful*) when praising altruistic behavior.
6–8	• Some tendency to think of rules and conventions as standards that should be followed for their own sake • Interest in pleasing and helping others, but with a tendency to oversimplify what "helping" requires • Tendency to believe that distressed individuals (e.g., the homeless) are entirely responsible for their own fate	• When imposing discipline for moral transgressions, remember that induction may be especially important for students who have deficits in empathy and moral reasoning. • Make prosocial behavior (e.g., giving, sharing, caring for others) a high priority in the classroom. • Involve students in group projects that will benefit their school or community.
9–12	• Understanding that rules and conventions help society run more smoothly • Increasing concern about doing one's duty and abiding by the rules of society as a whole rather than simply pleasing certain authority figures • Genuine empathy for those in distress • Belief that society has an obligation to help others in need	• Explore moral issues in social studies, science, and literature. • Encourage community service to engender feelings of commitment to helping others. Ask students to reflect on their experiences through group discussions or written essays. • Assign autobiographies and other literature that depict heroic figures who have actively worked to help others.

Sources: Damon, 1988; Eisenberg, 1982; Eisenberg & Fabes, 1998; Eisenberg, Lennon, & Pasternack, 1986; Farver & Branstetter, 1994; C. A. Flanagan & Faison, 2001; Gibbs, 1995; D. Hart & Fegley, 1995; Helwig & Jasiobedzka, 2001; Helwig et al.,2001; Hoffman, 1975, 1991; Kohlberg, 1984; Krebs & Van Hesteren, 1994; Kurtines, Berman, Ittel, & Williamson, 1995; Laupa & Turiel, 1995; Nucci & Weber, 1995; Rushton, 1980; Smetana & Braeges, 1990; Turiel, 1983, 1998; Yates & Youniss, 1996; Yau & Smetana, 2003; Youniss & Yates, 1999; Zahn-Waxler, Radke-Yarrow, Wagner, & Chapman, 1992.

themselves. This teacher is doing little to promote students' social and moral growth and in fact may inadvertently be sending them the message that antisocial behavior is quite acceptable.

In the pages that follow, we will explore the multidimensional nature of moral and prosocial development, looking first at general developmental trends, then at two specific theories of moral reasoning (those of Lawrence Kohlberg and Carol Gilligan), and finally at factors and strategies that can nudge children and adolescents toward more advanced moral reasoning and behavior.

Developmental Trends in Morality and Prosocial Behavior

Most children behave more morally and prosocially as they grow older; for example, they become increasingly generous with age (Eisenberg, 1982; Rushton, 1980). Table 3.3 describes the forms that morality and prosocial behavior are apt to take at various grade levels. Some of the entries in the table reflect the following developmental trends:

◎ *Children begin using internal standards to evaluate behavior at an early age.* Even preschoolers have some understanding that behaviors causing physical or psychological harm are inappropriate (Helwig, Zelazo, & Wilson, 2001; J. M. Kim & Turiel, 1996). By age 4, most children understand that causing harm to another person is wrong regardless of what authority figures might tell them and regardless of what consequences certain behaviors may or may not bring (Laupa & Turiel, 1995; Smetana, 1981; Tisak, 1993).

◎ *Children increasingly distinguish between moral and conventional transgressions.* Society discourages some behaviors—**moral transgressions**—because they cause damage or harm, violate human rights, or run counter to basic principles of equality, freedom, or justice. It discourages other behaviors—**conventional transgressions**—because, although not unethical, they violate widely held understandings about how one should act (e.g., children shouldn't talk back to adults or burp at meals). Conventional transgressions are usually culturally defined; for instance, although burping is frowned upon in mainstream Western culture, people in some cultures burp as a compliment to the cook. In contrast, many moral transgressions are universal across cultures.

Even preschoolers realize that not all actions are wrong in the same way and that violations of moral standards are more serious than other misbehaviors (Nucci & Weber, 1995; Turiel, 1983; Yau & Smetana, 2003). Children's awareness of social conventions is minimal in early childhood but increases throughout the elementary school years (Helwig & Jasiobedzka, 2001; Laupa & Turiel, 1995; Nucci & Nucci, 1982; Turiel, 1983). However, children and adults do not always agree about which behaviors constitute moral transgressions, which ones fall into the conventional domain, and which ones are simply a matter of personal choice. For instance, whereas adults typically view drug use as a moral transgression, teenagers often think it is acceptable as long as it doesn't harm other people (Berkowitz, Guerra, & Nucci, 1991).

◎ *Children's understanding of fairness evolves throughout early and middle childhood.* The ability to share with others depends on children's sense of **distributive justice**, their beliefs about what constitutes a person's fair share of a desired commodity (e.g., food or toys). Children's notions of distributive justice change with age (Damon, 1977, 1980). Preschoolers' beliefs about what's fair are based on their own needs and desires; thus, it would be perfectly "fair" to give oneself a large handful of candy and give others smaller amounts. In the early elementary grades, children base their judgments about fairness on strict equality: Everyone gets the same amount. Sometime around age 8, children begin to take merit and special needs into account; for instance, children who contribute more to a group's efforts should reap a greater portion of the group's rewards, and people who are exceptionally poor might receive more resources than others.

◎ *Children's capacity to respond emotionally to others' harm and distress increases over the school years.* How do you feel when you inadvertently cause inconvenience for someone else? when you hurt someone else's feelings? when a friend suddenly and unexpectedly loses a close family member? Perhaps such feelings as guilt, shame, and empathy come to mind. All of these emotions are associated with moral and prosocial development (Eisenberg & Fabes, 1991; Hoffman, 1991; Kochanska, Gross, Lin, & Nichols, 2002; Turiel, 1998).

Children begin to show signs of **guilt**—a feeling of discomfort when they know they have inflicted damage or caused distress—well before they reach school age (Kochanska et al., 2002). By the time they reach the middle elementary grades, most of them also feel **shame**: They feel embarrassed or humiliated when they fail to meet the standards for moral behavior that adults have set for them (Damon, 1988). Both guilt and shame, though unpleasant emotions, are good signs that children are developing a sense of right and wrong.

Guilt and shame emerge when children believe they have done something wrong. In contrast, empathy—experiencing the same feelings as someone in unfortunate circumstances—appears in the absence of wrongdoing. The ability to empathize continues to develop throughout the elementary school years and often into the high school years as well (Eisenberg, 1982; Eisenberg et al., 1986, 1995). At the primary grade levels, students show empathy mostly to people they know, such as friends and classmates. But by the upper elementary school grades, they may also begin to feel empathy for people they *don't* know—perhaps for the poor, the homeless, or those in catastrophic circumstances (Damon, 1988; Eisenberg, 1982; Hoffman, 1991).

◎ *Children increasingly take circumstances into account in their evaluations of behavior.* As children get older, they are more likely to consider motives, intentions, and other situational

■ **moral transgression** Action that causes harm or infringes on the needs and rights of others.

■ **conventional transgression** Action that violates a culture's general expectations regarding socially appropriate behavior.

■ **distributive justice** Beliefs about what constitutes people's fair share of a commodity.

■ **guilt** Feeling of discomfort when one knows one has caused someone else pain or distress.

■ **shame** Feeling of embarrassment or humiliation after failing to meet standards for moral behavior that adults have set.

■ **empathy** Experience of sharing the same feelings as someone in unfortunate circumstances.

factors when deciding what's morally right and wrong (Helwig et al., 2001; Piaget, 1932/1960; Thorkildsen. 1995; Turiel, 1998). For example, they are more apt to think of lying as immoral if it causes someone else harm than if it has no adverse effect—that is, if it is just a "white lie" (Turiel, Smetana, & Killen, 1991). And although most adolescents in mainstream Western culture endorse such civil liberties as freedom of speech and freedom of religion *in principle*, they recognize that such liberties must sometimes be restricted to protect others from harm (Helwig, 1995).

In general, children and adolescents become more able to reason flexibly and abstractly about moral issues as they grow older. Lawrence Kohlberg has proposed a series of stages that capture some of the changes in their moral reasoning. We look at his theory now.

Development of Moral Reasoning: Kohlberg's Theory

Experiencing FIRSTHAND · Heinz's Dilemma

> In Europe, a woman was near death from a rare form of cancer. There was one drug that the doctors thought might save her, a form of radium that a druggist in the same town had recently discovered. The druggist was charging $2,000, ten times what the drug cost him to make. The sick woman's husband, Heinz, went to everyone he knew to borrow the money, but he could only get together about half of what the drug cost. He told the druggist that his wife was dying and asked him to sell it cheaper or let him pay later. But the druggist said no. So Heinz got desperate and broke into the man's store to steal the drug for his wife. (Kohlberg, 1984, p. 186)

> - Should Heinz have stolen the drug? What would *you* have done if you were Heinz? Which is worse, stealing something that belongs to someone else or letting another person die a preventable death? Why?

· · · · · · ·

The story you just read is a **moral dilemma**, a situation to which there is no clear-cut right or wrong response. Following are three solutions to Heinz's dilemma offered by elementary and secondary school students. I have given the students fictitious names so that we can talk about them more easily.

> *James (a fifth grader):* Maybe his wife is an important person and runs a store, and the man buys stuff from her and can't get it any other place. The police would blame the owner that he didn't save the wife. He didn't save an important person, and that's just like killing with a gun or a knife. You can get the electric chair for that. (Kohlberg, 1981, pp. 265–266)

> *Jesse (a high school student):* If he cares enough for her to steal for her, he should steal it. If not he should let her die. It's up to him. (Kohlberg, 1981, p. 132)

> *Jules (a high school student):* In that particular situation Heinz was right to do it. In the eyes of the law he would not be doing the right thing, but in the eyes of the moral law he would. If he had exhausted every other alternative I think it would be worth it to save a life. (Kohlberg, 1984, pp. 446–447)

Each boy offers a different reason to justify why Heinz should steal the lifesaving drug. James bases his decision on the possible advantages and disadvantages of stealing or not stealing the drug for Heinz alone; he does not consider the perspective of the dying woman at all. Likewise, Jesse takes a self-serving view, proposing that the decision to either steal or not steal the drug depends on how much Heinz loves his wife. Only Jules considers the value of human life in justifying why Heinz should break the law.

After obtaining hundreds of responses to moral dilemmas, Lawrence Kohlberg proposed that the development of moral reasoning is characterized by a series of stages (e.g., Colby, Kohlberg, Gibbs, & Lieberman, 1983; Kohlberg, 1963, 1976, 1984). These stages, as in any stage theory, form an invariant sequence: Each stage builds upon the foundation laid by earlier stages, and so an individual must progress through them in order, without skipping any. Kohlberg grouped his stages into three *levels* of morality: preconventional, conventional, and postconventional. These three levels and the two stages within each one are described in Table 3.4.

As you can see from the table, **preconventional morality** is the earliest and least mature form of moral reasoning, in that the child has not yet adopted or internalized society's conventions regarding what is right or wrong—hence the label *preconventional*. James's response to the Heinz dilemma is a good example of preconventional (Stage 1) thinking: He considers the

**hopes
goals
dreams
happiness
    broken
    destroyed
    eliminated
    exterminated
no steps forward
no evolution
no prosperity
no hope
But
maybe
perhaps
except
if we
help
together
we stand
a chance.**

In this poem Matt, a middle school student, shows empathy for victims of the Holocaust.

■ **moral dilemma** Situation in which there is no clear-cut answer regarding the morally correct action.

■ **preconventional morality** Lack of internalized standards about right and wrong; making decisions based solely on what is best for oneself.

TABLE 3.4   COMPARE/CONTRAST

Kohlberg's Three Levels and Six Stages of Moral Reasoning

LEVEL	AGE RANGE	STAGE	NATURE OF MORAL REASONING
Level I: Preconventional morality	Seen in preschool children, most elementary school students, some junior high school students, and a few high school students	Stage 1: Punishment-avoidance and obedience	People make decisions based on what is best for themselves, without regard for others' needs or feelings. They obey rules only if established by more powerful individuals; they may disobey if they aren't likely to get caught. "Wrong" behaviors are those that will be punished.
		Stage 2: Exchange of favors	People recognize that others also have needs. They may try to satisfy others' needs if their own needs are also met ("you scratch my back, I'll scratch yours"). They continue to define right and wrong primarily in terms of consequences to themselves.
Level II: Conventional morality	Seen in a few older elementary school students, some junior high school students, and many high school students (Stage 4 typically does not appear before high school)	Stage 3: Good boy/good girl	People make decisions based on what actions will please others, especially authority figures (e.g., teachers, popular peers). They are concerned about maintaining relationships through sharing, trust, and loyalty, and they take other people's perspectives and intentions into account when making decisions.
		Stage 4: Law and order	People look to society as a whole for guidelines about right or wrong. They know rules are necessary for keeping society running smoothly and believe it is their "duty" to obey them. However, they perceive rules to be inflexible; they don't necessarily recognize that as society's needs change, rules should change as well.
Level III: Postconventional morality	Rarely seen before college (Stage 6 is extremely rare even in adults)	Stage 5: Social contract	People recognize that rules represent agreements among many individuals about appropriate behavior. Rules are seen as useful mechanisms that maintain the general social order and protect individual rights, rather than as absolute dictates that must be obeyed simply because they are "the law." People also recognize the flexibility of rules; rules that no longer serve society's best interests can and should be changed.
		Stage 6: Universal ethical principle	People adhere to a few abstract, universal principles (e.g., equality of all people, respect for human dignity, commitment to justice) that transcend specific norms and rules. They answer to a strong inner conscience and willingly disobey laws that violate their own ethical principles. Stage 6 is an "ideal" stage that few people ever reach.

Sources: Colby & Kohlberg, 1984; Colby et al., 1983; Kohlberg, 1976, 1984, 1986; Reimer, Paolitto, & Hersh, 1983; Snarey, 1995.

■ **conventional morality** Acceptance of society's conventions regarding right and wrong.

■ **postconventional morality** Behaving in accordance with self-developed, abstract principles regarding right and wrong.

consequences of Heinz's actions only for Heinz himself. Kohlberg also classified Jesse's response as a preconventional (Stage 2) response. Jesse is beginning to recognize the importance of saving someone else's life, but the decision to do so ultimately depends on whether or not Heinz loves his wife; in other words, it depends on *his* feelings alone.

Conventional morality is characterized by an acceptance of society's conventions concerning right and wrong: The individual obeys rules and follows society's norms even when there are no consequences for obedience or disobedience. Adherence to rules and conventions is somewhat rigid, however; a rule's appropriateness or fairness is seldom questioned. In contrast, people who exhibit **postconventional morality** view rules as useful but changeable mechanisms that maintain the general social order and protect human rights, rather than as absolute dictates that must be obeyed without question. They live by their own abstract principles about right and wrong—principles that typically include such basic human rights as life, liberty, and justice. They may disobey rules inconsistent with their principles, as we see in Jules's (Stage 5) response to the Heinz dilemma: "In the eyes of the law he would not be doing the right thing, but in the eyes of the moral law he would."

The "Moral Reasoning" clip on Video CD 1 shows four children's reasoning about a dilemma in which a boy named Steve cheats on a history test because work commitments have prevented him from studying. All four children conclude that Steve should not cheat on the test but give varying reasons. The first two (younger) children, concerned only with the negative consequences for Steve, exhibit preconventional reasoning: "He'll get kicked out," "The teacher might find out." The last two (older) children are instead concerned with society's expectations for behavior and so exhibit conventional reasoning: "He would be getting somebody else's grade instead of *his* grade," "He should have been paying attention earlier in the course."

Kohlberg drew on two aspects of Piaget's theory (Piaget's stages of cognitive development and the concept of *disequilibrium*) to explain the progression to higher stages of moral reasoning. First, Kohlberg proposed that advancements in moral reasoning depend on cognitive development. Stages 4 through 6 involve formal operational thinking (e.g., the importance of laws for helping society run smoothly is a fairly abstract idea) and so typically do not appear until adolescence. Progression to an advanced stage of cognitive development does not guarantee moral development, however. In Kohlberg's mind, individuals move from one stage to the next only after experiencing disequilibrium: They must realize that their existing beliefs cannot adequately address the events and dilemmas they encounter. With time and experience, individuals become increasingly aware of the weaknesses of a particular stage of moral reasoning, especially if their moral judgments are challenged by people reasoning at the next higher stage (e.g., a Stage 3 student who agrees to let a popular cheerleader copy his homework may begin to question his decision if a Stage 4 student argues that the cheerleader would learn more by doing her own homework). By struggling with such challenges, children and adolescents may begin to restructure their thoughts about morality and gradually move from one stage to the next.

A great deal of research on moral development has followed on the heels of Kohlberg's work. Some of it supports Kohlberg's sequence of moral reasoning: Generally speaking, people seem to make advancements in the order that Kohlberg proposed (Boom, Brugman, & van der Heijden, 2001; Colby & Kohlberg, 1984; Snarey, 1995; Stewart & Pascual-Leone, 1992). Furthermore, challenges to children's reasoning do seem to promote their moral development (more about this point later). Nevertheless, contemporary psychologists have identified several weaknesses in Kohlberg's theory. First, Kohlberg underestimated young children, who, as we discovered earlier, acquire some internal standards of right and wrong long before they begin kindergarten. Second, Kohlberg addressed both moral issues (e.g., causing harm) and social conventions (e.g., having rules to help society run smoothly) in the stages he described, but as we have seen, children view these two domains differently. Third, moral development appears to involve *trends* rather than a progression through distinct stages. Kohlberg himself acknowledged that youngsters may, at any single age, show reasoning across a three-stage span. It appears that children and adolescents gradually acquire several different standards that guide their moral decision making in different situations; such standards include the need to address their own personal interests, a desire to abide by society's rules and conventions, and, eventually, an appreciation for abstract ideals regarding human rights and society's overall needs (Rest, Narvaez, Bebeau, & Thoma, 1999). With age, youngsters increasingly apply more advanced standards, but even a fairly primitive one—satisfying one's own needs without regard for others—may occasionally dominate in certain situations (Rest et al., 1999; Turiel, 1998).

Despite such weaknesses, Kohlberg's theory offers valuable insights into the nature and development of children's and adolescents' moral thinking. Most importantly, it shows us that children's moral reasoning does not simply result from adults handing down particular moral values and preachings, but instead emerges out of children's own, personally constructed beliefs (hence, Kohlberg's theory is very much a *constructivist* approach). Kohlberg's theory also highlights the importance of social interaction in creating disequilibrium and nudging students toward more advanced moral views.

Possible Gender Differences in Moral Reasoning: Gilligan's Theory

Consider this quirk in Kohlberg's research: Subjects in his early studies were predominantly males. Carol Gilligan (1982, 1987) believes that Kohlberg's theory does not adequately describe female moral development. His stages emphasize issues of fairness and justice but omit

■ Observe preconventional and conventional responses in the "Moral Reasoning" clip on Video CD 1.

other aspects of morality, especially compassion and caring for those in need, that Gilligan suggests are more characteristic of the moral reasoning and behavior of females. She argues that females are socialized to stress interpersonal relationships and to take responsibility for the well-being of others to a greater extent than males; therefore, females develop a morality that emphasizes a greater concern for other's welfare. The dilemma that follows illustrates a morality based on compassion.

Experiencing FIRSTHAND ·The Porcupine Dilemma

> A group of industrious, prudent moles have spent the summer digging a burrow where they will spend the winter. A lazy, improvident porcupine who has not prepared a winter shelter approaches the moles and pleads to share their burrow. The moles take pity on the porcupine and agree to let him in. Unfortunately, the moles did not anticipate the problem the porcupine's sharp quills would pose in close quarters. Once the porcupine has moved in, the moles are constantly being stabbed. The question is, what should the moles do? (Meyers, 1987, p. 141, adapted from Gilligan, 1985)

· · · · · · ·

According to Gilligan, males are apt to view the problem as that of someone's rights being violated. They might point out that the burrow belongs to the moles, who can legitimately throw the porcupine out. If the porcupine refuses to leave, some may argue that the moles are well within their rights to kill him. In contrast, females are more likely to show compassion and caring when addressing the dilemma. They might suggest that the moles cover the porcupine with a blanket, so that his quills won't annoy anyone (Meyers, 1987).

Gilligan raises a good point: Males and females are often socialized quite differently, as you will discover in Chapter 4. Furthermore, by including compassion for other human beings as well as consideration for their rights, she broadens our conception of what morality *is* (L. J. Walker, 1995). But in fact, most research studies do *not* find major gender differences in moral reasoning (Eisenberg et al., 1996; Nunner-Winkler, 1984; L. J. Walker, 1991). And as Gilligan herself has acknowledged, males and females alike reveal concern for both justice and compassion in their moral reasoning (L. M. Brown, Tappan, & Gilligan, 1995; Gilligan & Attanucci, 1988; Turiel, 1998).

Determinants of Moral and Prosocial Behavior

Both Kohlberg's and Gilligan's theories focus on moral reasoning. But ultimately, it is more important that children and adolescents *behave* morally and prosocially—that they act in ways that respect and preserve others' rights and well-being. Most children and adolescents act more morally and prosocially as they grow older. Researchers have identified several factors, described in the following paragraphs, that influence moral behavior.

Level of moral reasoning. On average, people who exhibit more advanced moral reasoning behave more morally as well (Blasi, 1980; Eisenberg, Zhou, & Koller, 2001; Reimer et al., 1983). For example, students who, from Kohlberg's perspective, reason at higher stages are less likely to cheat or insult others, more likely to help people in need, and more likely to disobey orders that would cause harm to another (F. H. Davidson, 1976; Kohlberg, 1975; Kohlberg & Candee, 1984; P. A. Miller, Eisenberg, Fabes, & Shell, 1996).

Guilt, perspective taking, and empathy. Guilt can be a powerful motivator: When children feel guilty about damage or distress they have caused, they may work hard to repair the damage, soothe hurt feelings, and in other respects "make things right" (Eisenberg, 1995; Harter, 1999). But guilt is limited to situations in which children themselves have caused harm. Truly prosocial children—those who help others even in the absence of their own wrongdoing—typically have considerable capacity for perspective taking and empathy (Damon, 1988; Eisenberg, Zhou, & Koller, 2001; Hoffman, 1991). Empathy is especially likely to spur prosocial behavior when it leads to **sympathy**, whereby children not only assume another person's feelings but also have concerns for the individual's well-being (Batson, 1991; Eisenberg & Fabes, 1998; Turiel, 1998).

■ **sympathy** Feeling of sorrow or concern for another person's problems or distress.

Personal motives. When children behave prosocially, their own needs and goals often come into play as well. For instance, although children may want to do the right thing, they may also be concerned about whether others will approve of their actions and about what positive or negative consequences might result. Children are more apt to behave in accordance with their moral standards if the benefits are high (e.g., they gain others' approval or respect) and the personal costs are low (e.g., an act of altruism involves little sacrifice) (Batson & Thompson, 2001; Eisenberg, 1987; Narváez & Rest, 1995).

Self-perceptions. In adolescence some young people begin to integrate a commitment to moral values into their overall sense of identity (Arnold, 2000; Blasi, 1995; Youniss & Yates, 1999). They think of themselves as generally moral, caring individuals who are concerned about the rights and well-being of others. Their acts of altruism and compassion are not limited to their friends and acquaintances but also extend to the community at large. For example, in one study (D. Hart & Fegley, 1995), researchers conducted in-depth interviews with inner-city Hispanic and African American teenagers who showed an exceptional commitment to helping others (by volunteering many hours at Special Olympics, a neighborhood political organization, a nursing home, etc.). These teens did not necessarily display more advanced moral reasoning (as defined by Kohlberg's stages) than their peers, but they were more likely to describe themselves in terms of moral traits and goals (e.g., helping others) and to mention certain ideals toward which they were striving.

■ In the "Describing Yourself" exercise earlier in the chapter, did you list any characteristics that might suggest a strong moral identity?

Promoting Moral and Prosocial Development in the Classroom

Some well-meaning individuals have suggested that society is in a sharp moral decline and urge parents and educators to impart desirable moral traits (honesty, integrity, loyalty, responsibility, etc.) through lectures at home and in school, as well as through firm control of children's behavior. In fact, there is no evidence that the present generation of young people is in any way less moral or prosocial than previous generations (Turiel, 1998). Furthermore, lecturing students about morally appropriate behavior and imposing firm control on their actions do little to instill a particular set of moral values (Damon, 1988; Higgins, 1995; Turiel, 1998). Nor does reading stories with a moral message have much of an impact (Narváez, 2002).

Some strategies *can* make a difference, however. The Into the Classroom feature "Promoting Moral and Prosocial Development" presents a few examples. Following are several general suggestions based on research findings:

INTO THE CLASSROOM

Promoting Moral and Prosocial Development

Encourage prosocial behavior, and acknowledge and reward it when it occurs.

A kindergarten teacher commends a student for consoling a classmate whose feelings have been hurt.

Talk about reasons why some behaviors are inappropriate, emphasizing the harm or inconvenience those behaviors have caused.

A second-grade teacher explains to Sarah that because she has thoughtlessly left her chewing gum on Margaret's chair, Margaret's mother must now pay to have Margaret's new pants professionally cleaned. The teacher, Sarah, and Margaret work out an arrangement through which Sarah can make amends for the inconvenience and expense to Margaret and her family.

Model moral and prosocial behavior.

A junior high school teacher mentions that he will be working at a Habitat for Humanity project on Saturday and asks if any of his students would like to join him.

Incorporate moral issues and dilemmas into classroom discussions.

When discussing the Vietnam War, a high school history teacher mentions that many young men in the United States escaped the draft by going to Canada. She asks her students to decide whether they think such behavior was appropriate and to explain their reasoning.

Be sensitive to cultural differences when addressing inappropriate behaviors.

A teacher sees one of her students inadvertently knock a classmate's jacket off its hook. The teacher mentions the incident to the student, but he denies that he had anything to do with the fallen jacket. Remembering that in this student's culture, lying is an acceptable way of saving face, the teacher doesn't immediately chastise the student; instead, she asks him to do her the "favor" of returning the jacket to its hook. Later she talks with the student privately about the importance of taking responsibility for his actions and explains that in her classroom, misrepresenting the facts is unacceptable.

◎   *Give reasons why some behaviors are unacceptable.* Although it is important to impose consequences for immoral and antisocial behaviors, punishment by itself often focuses children's attention primarily on their own hurt and distress (Hoffman, 1975). To promote moral development, we must instead focus students' attention on the hurt and distress their behaviors have caused *others.* Thus, we should give them reasons why certain behaviors are unacceptable—an approach known as **induction** (Hoffman, 1970, 1975). For example, we might describe how a behavior harms someone else either physically ("Having your hair pulled the way you just pulled Mai's can really be painful") or emotionally ("You hurt John's feelings when you call him names like that"). We might also show students how they have caused someone else inconvenience ("Because you ruined Marie's jacket, her parents are making her work around the house to earn the money for a new one"). Still another approach is to explain someone else's perspective, intention, or motive ("This science project you've just ridiculed may not be as fancy as yours, but I know that Camren spent many hours working on it and is quite proud of what he's done").

Induction is victim-centered: It helps students focus on the distress of others and recognize that they themselves have been the cause (Hoffman, 1970). The consistent use of induction in disciplining children, particularly when accompanied by *mild* punishment for misbehavior, appears to promote cooperation with rules and facilitate the development of such prosocial characteristics as empathy, compassion, and altruism (Baumrind, 1971; G. H. Brody & Shaffer, 1982; Hoffman, 1975; Maccoby & Martin, 1983; Rushton, 1980).

◎   *Provide practice in recognizing others' emotional states.* We will have less need to explain someone else's feelings if students can identify those feelings on their own. Yet some students, young ones especially, are poor judges of others' emotional states (recall our earlier discussion of social cognition). With young children, we can orally label a classmate's feelings as "sad," "disappointed," or "angry" (J. Chalmers & Townsend, 1990; Wittmer & Honig, 1994). At higher grade levels we might ask students to describe to one another exactly how they feel about particular misbehaviors directed toward them (Doescher & Sugawara, 1989). Or we might ask them how they themselves would feel in a peer's circumstances (Hoffman, 1991). As teachers, we also should describe our own emotional reactions to any inappropriate behaviors (Damon, 1988).

◎   *Encourage perspective taking, empathy, and prosocial behavior.* In any classroom, both the academic curriculum and day-to-day events offer many opportunities for perspective taking, empathy, and prosocial behavior. For instance, we can ask students to imagine how people must have felt during particularly traumatic and stressful events in history, or possibly even have them role-play such events (Brophy & Alleman, 1996; Brophy & VanSledright, 1997). In discussions of current events, we can expose students to situations in which other people's needs are far greater than their own. And we can encourage, acknowledge, and reward such prosocial behaviors as sharing, cooperation, and comforting others.

◎   *Expose students to numerous models of moral behavior.* Children and adolescents are more likely to exhibit moral and prosocial behavior when they see others behaving in moral rather than immoral ways. For instance, when youngsters see adults or peers being generous and showing concern for others, they tend to do likewise (Rushton, 1980; C. C. Wilson, Piazza, & Nagle, 1990). When they watch television shows that emphasize perspective taking and prosocial actions (e.g., *Sesame Street, Mister Rogers' Neighborhood, Barney & Friends*), they are more inclined to exhibit such behaviors themselves (Hearold, 1986; Rushton, 1980; Singer & Singer, 1994). Powerful models can be found in literature as well (Ellenwood & Ryan, 1991). For example, in Harper Lee's *To Kill a Mockingbird,* set in the highly segregated and racially charged Alabama of the 1930s, a lawyer defends an obviously innocent African American man charged with raping a white woman; in doing so, he exemplifies a willingness to fight for high moral principles in the face of strong social pressure to let the man hang for the crime. In John Gunther's *Death Be Not Proud,* a young boy is generous and considerate despite his impending death from cancer.

As teachers, we are highly visible models who teach by what we do as well as by what we say. When we model compassion and consideration for the feelings of others, such behaviors may rub off on our students. When we are instead self-centered and place our own needs before those of others, our students may follow suit.

◎   *Engage students in discussions of moral issues and dilemmas.* Kohlberg proposed that children develop morally when they are challenged by moral dilemmas they cannot adequately deal with at their current stage of moral reasoning. Research confirms his belief: Classroom

■ We will look at modeling in more detail in Chapter 10.

■ **induction**   Explanation of why a certain behavior is unacceptable, often with a focus on the pain or distress that someone has caused another.

discussions of controversial topics and moral issues appear to promote increased perspective taking and the transition to more advanced moral reasoning (DeVries & Zan, 1996; D. W. Johnson & Johnson, 1988; Power, Higgins, & Kohlberg, 1989; Schlaefli, Rest, & Thoma, 1985).

Social and moral dilemmas often arise within the school curriculum. Consider the following questions that might emerge in discussions related to history, social studies, science, or literature:

- Is it appropriate to engage in armed conflict, and hence to kill others, when two groups of people disagree about political or religious issues?
- Is military retaliation for acts of terrorism justified even when it may involve killing innocent people?
- How can a capitalistic society encourage free enterprise while at the same time protecting the rights of citizens and the ecology of the environment?
- Should laboratory rats be used to study the effects of cancer-producing agents?
- Was Hamlet justified in killing Claudius to avenge the murder of his father?

Social and moral issues do not always have right or wrong answers. As teachers, we can encourage student discussions of such issues in a variety of ways (Reimer et al., 1983). First, we can provide a trusting and nonthreatening classroom atmosphere in which students feel free to express their ideas without censure or embarrassment. Second, we can help students identify all aspects of a dilemma, including the needs and perspectives of the various individuals involved. Third, we can help students explore their reasons for thinking as they do; that is, we can help them clarify and examine the principles on which they are basing their moral judgments. We should keep in mind, too, that students are more apt to consider diverse perspectives on an issue if we keep our own opinions to ourselves, especially in the early stages of discussion.

■ Chapter 13 offers additional suggestions for conducting effective classroom discussions.

◎ *Engage students in community service.* As we have seen, adolescents are more likely to act in moral and prosocial ways when they have integrated a commitment to moral ideals into their overall sense of identity. Such integration is more probable when students become actively involved in service to others even before they reach puberty (Youniss & Yates, 1999). Through ongoing community service activities—food and clothing drives, visits to homes for the elderly, community cleanup efforts, and so on—elementary and secondary students alike learn that they have the skills and the responsibility for helping those less fortunate than themselves and in other ways making the world a better place in which to live. In the process, they also begin to think of themselves as concerned, compassionate, and moral citizens (Youniss & Yates, 1999).

CONSIDERING DIVERSITY IN SENSE OF SELF, SOCIAL DEVELOPMENT, AND MORALITY

Throughout the chapter we've identified numerous ways in which students think and act differently at different ages. We are apt to see considerable diversity *within* an age-group as well. Some of this diversity is, of course, due to temperament, health, family circumstances, and other individual variables. But researchers have also identified significant group differences—in particular, differences among various ethnic groups, between boys and girls, and among different socioeconomic groups.

Ethnic Differences

One area in which we will often find ethnic differences is students' sense of self. For instance, as we have seen, some cultures encourage children to take pride in the achievements of their families and social groups (rather than in personal accomplishments), and some adolescents have a strong sense of ethnic identity. Not all students from ethnic minority groups affiliate strongly with those groups, however, and some students (especially students with multiple cultural heritages) fluctuate in the strength of their ethnic identity depending on the context and situation (W. E. Cross et al., 1999; A. M. Lopez, 2003; Yip & Fuligni, 2002). We may find, too, that members of some minority groups, while having high self-esteem in general, may have little faith in their ability to achieve academic success (Covington, 1992; Elrich, 1994; Graham, 1994; van Laar, 2000). For some students from minority-group backgrounds, we need to make a special effort to foster positive self-perceptions, certainly by providing enough support to ensure success on academic tasks and perhaps also by giving students reasons to take pride in their cultural heritage (Phinney, 1989; S. C. Wright & Taylor, 1995).

Encourage all!

Interpersonal skills and relationships may also vary somewhat for students from different backgrounds. Some ethnic groups (e.g., African Americans living along the South Carolina coast and many Navajos in the American Southwest) place particular emphasis on maintaining group harmony and resolving interpersonal conflicts peacefully, and children from these groups may be especially adept at negotiation and peace making (Guthrie, 2001; Witmer, 1996). Although teasing and ridicule are discouraged in mainstream Western culture, these are common ways of teaching children to "keep their cool" and handle criticism in certain other cultures, such as in some communities in northern Canada and in the South Pacific (Rogoff, 2003). Although children and adolescents of all cultures enjoy the company of their peers, Asian Americans spend less leisure time with friends, and are more likely to choose friends who value academic achievement, than young people from other groups (L. Steinberg, 1996). Children who have recently immigrated from a non-English-speaking country may have relatively little interaction with peers primarily because they have limited ability to communicate with other children in their neighborhoods and classrooms (A. Doyle, 1982).

Conceptions of moral and immoral behavior are also likely to differ somewhat depending on students' backgrounds. Although lying is generally discouraged in mainstream Western society, it is a legitimate way of saving face in certain cultures (Triandis, 1995). Some ethnic groups (including many from Asia and South America) value loyalty and foster prosocial behavior more than others do (Greenfield, 1994; Markus & Kitayama, 1991; P. B. Smith & Bond, 1994; Triandis, 1995). Whereas some ethnic groups emphasize the importance of being considerate of other people (e.g., "Please be quiet so that your sister can study"), others emphasize the importance of tolerating inconsiderate behavior (e.g., "Please try not to let your brother's radio bother you when you study") (Fuller, 2001; Grossman, 1994). Although virtually all cultures espouse the importance of both individual rights and responsibility for others, many cultural groups tend to place greater emphasis on one than on the other (J. G. Miller & Bersoff, 1992; Shweder, Mahapatra, & Miller, 1987; Snarey, 1995; Turiel, 1998). As teachers, we must remember that our students' notions of moral behavior may sometimes be quite different from our own. At the same time, of course, we should never accept behavior that violates such basic principles as equality or respect for the rights and well-being of others.

Gender Differences

Some researchers find gender differences in overall self-esteem, with boys rating themselves more highly than girls, especially in adolescence. Adolescent boys also have more positive self-perceptions about their physical attractiveness than do adolescent girls. Most students' self-perceptions tend to be consistent with stereotypes about what males and females are "good at." Even when actual ability levels are the same, boys tend to rate themselves more highly in mathematics and sports, and girls tend to rate themselves more highly in reading and literature (D. A. Cole et al., 2001; Eccles, Wigfield, & Schiefele, 1998; Harter, 1999; Herbert, Stipek, & Miles, 2003; Wigfield et al., 1996).

Gender differences have also been observed in interpersonal behaviors. Boys tend to hang out in large groups, whereas girls tend to favor smaller, more intimate gatherings with close friends (Maccoby, 2002). Girls reveal more about themselves to others than boys do, and they are more apt to feel guilt and empathy for others' misfortunes (Lippa, 2002; A. J. Rose, 2002; Zahn-Waxler & Robinson, 1995). And as noted earlier, aggression tends to take different forms in boys (who are prone to physical aggression) and girls (who are more apt to engage in relational aggression in which they disrupt friendships and tarnish others' reputations).

Socioeconomic Differences

Children and adolescents from all walks of life grow up facing challenges—perhaps they must deal with a serious illness, a single-parent home, or neighborhood violence—but those from low-income families often have more than their share. Perhaps as a result of such challenges, these children and adolescents tend to have lower self-esteem, and are more apt to suffer from depression, than their wealthier peers (Becker & Luthar, 2002; Seaton et al., 1999).

By no means do low-income circumstances always lead to adverse outcomes, however. Many children and adolescents raised in low-income homes enjoy positive self-concepts, good interpersonal skills, and strong moral standards (D. Hart & Fegley, 1995; Masten & Coatsworth,

1998). In fact, supportive teachers and other adults can make a world of difference for these young people, as we will discover in our discussion of *resilient students* in Chapter 4.

Accommodating Students with Special Needs

Some students will have special educational needs related to their personal, social, or moral development. Many students with special needs will have lower self-esteem than their classmates (Brown-Mizuno, 1990; T. Bryan, 1991; Marsh & Craven, 1997). Students with mental retardation will typically have limited understanding of how to behave in social situations (Greenspan & Granfield, 1992). Students with emotional and behavioral disorders may have poor perspective-taking and social problem-solving abilities and so may have few if any friends (Harter, Whitesell, & Junkin, 1998; Lind, 1994). And students with a variety of disabilities—especially those with ADHD, autism, emotional and behavioral disorders, or mental retardation—may have trouble drawing accurate inferences from others' behaviors and body language (C. Gray & Garaud, 1993; Leffert, Siperstein, & Millikan, 1999; Lochman & Dodge, 1994; Milch-Reich, Campbell, Pelham, Connelly, & Geva, 1999). These and other characteristics, along with suggested classroom strategies, are presented in Table 3.5.

TABLE 3.5   STUDENTS IN INCLUSIVE SETTINGS

Promoting Personal, Social, and Moral Development in Students with Special Educational Needs

CATEGORY	CHARACTERISTICS YOU MIGHT OBSERVE	SUGGESTED CLASSROOM STRATEGIES
Students with specific cognitive or academic difficulties	• Low self-esteem related to areas of academic difficulty • Greater susceptibility to peer pressure (for students with learning disabilities or ADHD) • Difficulty in perspective taking or accurately interpreting social situations (for some students with learning disabilities or ADHD) • In some cases, poor social skills and few friendships; tendency to act without considering possible consequences of one's actions (especially if students have ADHD)	• Promote academic success (e.g., by providing extra scaffolding for classroom tasks). • Give students the opportunity to "show off" the things they do well. • Use induction to promote perspective taking (e.g., focus students' attention on how their behaviors have caused harm or distress to others). • Teach any missing social skills.
Students with social or behavioral problems	• Rejection by peers; few friendships • Difficulty in perspective taking and recognizing others' emotional states • Deficits in ability to interpret social cues (e.g., perceiving hostile intent in innocent interactions) • Poor social skills and social problem-solving ability; limited awareness of how insufficient their social skills really are • Poor impulse control; difficulty controlling emotions • Less empathy for others	• Explicitly teach social skills, provide opportunities to practice them, and give feedback. • Establish and enforce firm rules regarding acceptable classroom behavior. • Label and praise appropriate behaviors. • Teach social problem-solving strategies (e.g., through mediation training; see Chapter 10). • Provide opportunities for students to make new friends (e.g., through structured and well-monitored cooperative learning activities). • Help students recognize the outward signs of various emotions. • Use induction to promote empathy and perspective taking.
Students with general delays in cognitive and social functioning	• Generally low self-esteem • Social skills typical of younger children • Difficulty identifying and interpreting social cues • Concrete, often preconventional, ideas of right and wrong	• Scaffold academic success. • Teach social skills, provide opportunities to practice them, and give feedback. • Specify rules for classroom behavior in explicit, concrete terms. • Label and praise appropriate behaviors.
Students with physical or sensory challenges	• Fewer friends and possible social isolation • Fewer opportunities to develop appropriate social skills	• Maximize opportunities for students to interact with their classmates. • Assign "buddies"—classmates who can assist students with tasks they cannot perform themselves due to a disability. • Teach any missing social skills.

(continued)

Promoting Personal, Social, and Moral Development in Students with Special Educational Needs

CATEGORY	CHARACTERISTICS YOU MIGHT OBSERVE	SUGGESTED CLASSROOM STRATEGIES
Students with advanced cognitive development	• Above-average social development and emotional adjustment (although some extremely gifted students may have difficulty because they are so *very* different from their peers) • High self-esteem with regard to academic tasks (more typical of males than females) • Conflicts between the need to demonstrate abilities, on the one hand, and to gain peer acceptance, on the other (especially for females) • For some students, more advanced moral reasoning • Concerns about moral and ethical issues at a younger age than peers • Greater perspective taking	• Be sensitive to students' concerns about how their exceptional abilities may affect their relationships with classmates. • Engage students in conversations about ethical issues and moral dilemmas. • Involve students in projects that address social problems at a community, national, or international level.

Sources: Barkley, 1998; Beirne-Smith et al., 2002; Bierman et al., 1987; Cartledge & Milburn, 1995; Coie & Cillessen, 1993; Dempster & Corkill, 1999; Flavell et al., 1993; Gresham & MacMillan, 1997; Grinberg & McLean-Heywood, 1999; Harter et al., 1998; Heward, 2003; J. N. Hughes, 1988; Juvonen & Weiner, 1993; B. K. Keogh & MacMillan, 1996; Lind, 1994; Maker & Schiever, 1989; Marsh & Craven, 1997; Mercer, 1997; Milch-Reich et al., 1999; Neel et al., 1990; Piirto, 1999; Schonert-Reichl, 1993; Schumaker & Hazel, 1984; R. Turnbull et al., 2004; Winner, 1997; Wong, 1991a; Zeaman & House, 1979; Zirpoli & Melloy, 2001.

THE BIG PICTURE

At earlier points in the chapter, we've considered how children and adolescents are apt to change with respect to sense of self, perspective taking and theory of mind, and moral reasoning and behavior. Let's recap now by summarizing the characteristics we are likely to see in students of different ages. We'll then identify several general themes that have appeared repeatedly throughout the chapter.

CHARACTERISTICS OF DIFFERENT AGE-GROUPS

The following paragraphs pull together what we've learned about personal, social, and moral development to summarize students' characteristics in the elementary, middle school, and high school years.

Elementary school years.   Many children first come to school quite optimistic—often overly so—about what they can do. As they spend more time at school, they encounter a wide variety of academic tasks and social situations and have many opportunities to compare their performance to that of their peers, and so they gain an increasing understanding of their strengths and weaknesses. As they mature physically and socially, their social circles increase, and friends become frequent companions and sources of entertainment. Most elementary school students can look at events from other people's perspectives, understand that behaviors that cause harm or are unfair to others are fundamentally wrong, and show a growing capacity for empathy.

Middle school years.   After students make the transition to middle school, many show a decline in self-esteem, probably as a result of the many physical, social, and academic changes they encounter in a very short period of time. At this point, students tend to believe they are unlike anyone else (the personal fable) and have a heightened awareness of what others think of them

(the imaginary audience). Friendships become more important and supportive; social groups become more rigid and exclusive. Students increasingly understand the complexity of others' thoughts and feelings, and such perspective taking enhances their interpersonal relationships. Although some students may act prosocially primarily to gain approval, others are motivated by true feelings of empathy for a person in need.

High school years.   By high school, many students are beginning to form an identity that encompasses who they are as people, what things they find important, and what goals they hope to achieve. They now see their peers more as complex individuals than as stereotypical members of a particular group, their social groups are less rigid and exclusive, and many of them form romantic bonds with others. Most high school students have internalized society's views (or perhaps the views of a particular subgroup) of what is right and wrong. But by and large, they still see rules as absolute and inflexible entities, rather than as socially constructed, changeable mechanisms for protecting human rights and promoting the advancement of society. Their personal, social, and moral development is by no means complete when they graduate from high school; they will continue to refine their sense of self, social skills, and moral understandings well into the adult years.

GENERAL THEMES IN PERSONAL, SOCIAL, AND MORAL DEVELOPMENT

Despite the diversity of topics addressed in this chapter, several general themes have been evident throughout:

◎   *Standards for acceptable behavior, along with reasons why these standards must be upheld, are essential for optimal development.* Well-adjusted children are often those who grow up in an authoritative environment in which rules are set for appropriate behavior, reasons for the rules are spelled out, and negative consequences are imposed for rule infractions. Perspective taking and moral development are promoted when punishment is accompanied by induction—by a description of how one's misbehavior has caused physical or emotional harm to someone else. As teachers, we must communicate clearly to students what behaviors are and are not acceptable at school and explain why certain behaviors will not be tolerated.

◎   *Interaction with others, especially peers, provides the impetus for many personal, social, and moral advancements.* Social interaction is critical not only for children's cognitive and linguistic development (see Chapter 2) but also for personal, social, and moral development. For example, students learn a great deal about their own strengths and weaknesses by observing the behaviors of others. Relationships with peers provide an arena in which to practice existing social skills and experiment with new ones. Conversations about controversial topics and moral issues are critical for the development of perspective taking and moral reasoning; thus, class discussions and other opportunities for social interaction should be frequent occurrences at school.

◎   *Development is best fostered within the context of a warm, supportive environment.* We first saw the importance of a loving yet firm environment in our discussion of authoritative parenting. We also discovered the very important role that positive feedback plays in the development of students' sense of self. And we learned that students are more likely to express their ideas about moral issues in a classroom in which they feel free to express their ideas openly and honestly.

◎   *Students' personal, social, and moral understandings are self-constructed.* Just as children and adolescents construct their own knowledge and beliefs about the physical world, so, too, do they construct their own beliefs about themselves (e.g., their self-concepts and identities), the nature of other people (e.g., their interpretations of peers' motives and intentions), and morality (e.g., their definitions of right and wrong). As teachers, we must create numerous opportunities for students to construct their own understandings of their personal, social, and moral worlds. The final case study provides an example.

CASE STUDY: *The Scarlet Letter*

For the past several days, Ms. Southam's eleventh-grade English class has been reading Nathaniel Hawthorne's *The Scarlet Letter*. The novel, set in seventeenth century Boston, focuses largely on two characters who have been carrying on an illicit love affair: Hester Prynne (a young woman who has not seen or heard from her husband for the past two years) and the Reverend Arthur Dimmesdale (a pious and well-respected local preacher). When Hester becomes pregnant, she is imprisoned for adultery and soon bears a child. The class is currently discussing Chapter 3, in which the governor and town leaders (including Dimmesdale) are urging Hester to name the baby's father. (You can observe the following interaction in the "Scarlet Letter" clip on Video CD 2.)

■ Observe the lesson firsthand in the "Scarlet Letter" clip on Video CD 2.

Ms. Southam:	The father of the baby . . . how do you know it's Dimmesdale . . . the Reverend Arthur Dimmesdale? Why not the Reverend John Wilson or Governor Bellingham? . . . What are the clues in the text in Chapter 3? . . . Nicole?
Nicole:	He acts very withdrawn. He doesn't even want to be involved with the situation. He wants the other guy to question her, because he doesn't want to look her in the face and ask her to name *him*.
Ms. Southam:	OK. Anything else? . . .
Student:	The baby.
Ms. Southam:	What about the baby?
Student:	She starts to cry, and her eyes follow him.
Ms. Southam:	That is one of my absolutely favorite little Hawthornisms. . . . (Ms. Southam reads a paragraph in the novel that describes Dimmesdale's character.) In your logs, jot down some of the important characteristics of that description. What's the diction that strikes you as being essential to understanding Dimmesdale's character? How do you see him? If you were going to draw a portrait of him, what would you make sure he had? . . . Just write some things, or draw a picture if you'd like. (Ms. Southam walks around the room, monitoring what students are doing until they appear to have finished writing.)
Ms. Southam:	What pictures do you have in your minds of this man . . . if you were directing a film of *The Scarlet Letter*?

Mike:	I don't have a person in mind, just characteristics. About five-foot-ten, short, well-groomed hair, well dressed. He looks really nervous and inexperienced. Guilty look on his face. Always nervous, shaking a lot.
Ms. Southam:	He's got a guilty look on his face. His lips always trembling, always shaking.
Mike:	He's very unsure about himself.
Matt:	Sweating really bad. Always going like this. (He shows how Dimmesdale might be wiping his forehead.) He does . . . he has his hanky. . . .
Ms. Southam:	Actually, we don't see him mopping his brow, but we do see him doing what? What's the action? Do you remember? If you go to the text, he's holding his hand over his heart, as though he's somehow suffering some pain.
Student:	Wire-framed glasses. . . . I don't know why. He's like. . . .
Mike:	He's kind of like a nerd-type guy. . . . Short pants. Michael J. Fox's dad . . . (Mike is referring to a nerdish character in the film *Back to the Future*.)
Ms. Southam:	With the short pants and everything.
Student:	Yeah, George McFly. (Student identifies the nerdish character's name in the film.)
Ms. Southam:	George McFly in his younger years. But at the same time . . . I don't know if it was somebody in this class or somebody in another class when we had all these pictures up here on the wall that characterize this woman, I guess it was one of the guys in fourth period. . . . He said, "Well, she was sure *worth* it." Worth risking your immortal soul for, you know? . . . Obviously she's sinned, but so has he, right? And if she was worth it, don't we also have to see him as somehow having been worthy of her risking *her* soul for this?
Student:	Maybe he's got a good personality. . . .
Ms. Southam:	He apparently is, you know, a spellbinding preacher. He really can grab the crowd.
Student:	It's his eyes. Yeah, the eyes.
Ms. Southam:	Those brown, melancholy eyes. Yeah, those brown, melancholy eyes. Absolutely.

What elements of a theory of mind and perspective taking are evident in the students' comments?

What strategies does the teacher use to foster perspective taking, as well as social cognition more generally, as the students read the novel?

Once you have answered these questions, compare your responses with those presented in Appendix B.

KEY CONCEPTS

attachment (p. 62)

authoritative parenting (p. 62)

culture (p. 62)

socialization (p. 63)

culture shock (p. 63)

peer pressure (p. 64)

self-socialization (p. 65)

sense of self (p. 65)

ethnic identity (p. 68)

imaginary audience (p. 70)

personal fable (p. 70)

identity (p. 71)

clique (p. 74)

crowd (p. 74)

subculture (p. 74)

gang (p. 74)

popular students (p. 76)

rejected students (p. 76)

neglected students (p. 76)

social cognition (p. 77)

perspective taking (p. 78)

theory of mind (p. 78)

social information processing (p. 81)

aggressive behavior (p. 81)

physical aggression (p. 81)

relational aggression (p. 81)

proactive aggression (p. 81)

reactive aggression (p. 81)

hostile attributional bias (p. 82)

prosocial behavior (p. 86)

morality (p. 86)

moral transgression (p. 88)

conventional transgression (p. 88)

distributive justice (p. 88)

guilt (p. 88)

shame (p. 88)

empathy (p. 88)

moral dilemma (p. 89)

preconventional morality (p. 89)

conventional morality (p. 90)

postconventional morality (p. 90)

sympathy (p. 92)

induction (p. 94)

PRAXIS Turn to Appendix C, "Matching Book and Ancillary Content to the Praxis Principles of Learning and Teaching Tests," to discover sections of this chapter that may be especially applicable to the Praxis tests.

Now go to our Companion Website at **www.prenhall. com/ormrod** to assess your understanding of chapter content with "Multiple-Choice Questions," apply comprehension in "Essay Questions," broaden your knowledge of educational psychology with related "Web Links," gain greater insight about classroom learning in "Learning in the Content Areas," and analyze and assess classroom work in the "Student Artifact Library."

Group Differences

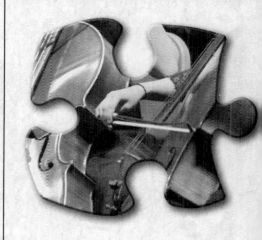

In preceding chapters we've talked about how different cultural groups nurture somewhat different beliefs, cognitive tools, reasoning skills, linguistic practices, interpersonal behaviors, and moral values. We've talked about possible differences between boys and girls in self-perceptions, risk-taking behavior, and aggression. And near the end of Chapter 3, we got a brief glimpse of how children from low-income families may face greater challenges than their wealthier peers. In this chapter we will look more closely at **group differences**, the differences we are apt to see *on average* among students from diverse cultural and ethnic groups, between boys and girls, and among students with different socioeconomic backgrounds. We will also look at students at risk, a particular group for which the guidance and support of teachers may be especially important. As we proceed through the chapter, we will address questions such as these:

* To what extent will knowledge about group differences enable us to draw conclusions about particular students?
* In what ways are students from various cultural and ethnic groups apt to be alike and different from one another? What implications do their differences have for classroom practice?
* In what ways are males and females alike and different? What can we do to provide equitable educational opportunities for both boys and girls?
* How can we accommodate the unique needs of students from lower socioeconomic groups?
* What characteristics can help us identify students at risk for school failure, and how can we help these students achieve academic success?

CASE STUDY: *Why Jack Wasn't in School*

Jack was a Native American seventh grader who lived on the Navajo reservation in the American Southwest. In this rural agricultural area, he had to travel almost 100 miles each day to go to school. He enjoyed school, worked hard in his studies, and got along well with his classmates. But Jack had been absent from school all week. In fact, he had been absent from home as well, and his family (which didn't have a telephone) wasn't sure exactly where he was.

Jack's English teacher described the situation to Donna Deyhle, an educator who had known Jack for many years:

> "That seventh grader was away from home for 5 days, and his parents don't care! . . . Almost one-third of my Navajo students were absent this week. Their parents just don't support their education. How can I teach when they are not in my classes?" (Deyhle & LeCompte, 1999, p. 127)

A few days later, Jack's sister explained why her parents had eventually begun to look for Jack:

> "He went to see Rambo II with friends and never came home. If he was in trouble we would know. But now the family needs him to herd sheep tomorrow." (Deyhle & LeCompte, 1999, p. 127)

It was spring—time for the family to plant crops and shear the sheep—and all family members needed to help out.

Jack's whereabouts were soon discovered, as Donna later reported:

> "That evening Jack and his parents stopped by [my] home on their way home from town. . . . With proper Navajo courtesy they waited in their car until [I] acknowledged their presence and invited them inside. As they unfolded from the car, Jack's dad said, "We found him." His mother turned in his direction and said teasingly, "Now maybe school will look easy!" Jack stayed at home for several days, helping with the irrigation of the corn field, before he decided to return to school. (Deyhle & LeCompte, 1999, p. 128)

On the surface, Jack's parents appeared unconcerned that Jack had neither come home nor attended school. But in fact, most parents, including Jack's, care deeply about their children's safety and welfare. What alternative explanations might there be for the parents' delay in looking for Jack?

■ **group differences** Consistently observed differences (on average) among diverse groups of students (e.g., students of different genders or ethnic backgrounds).

KEEPING GROUP DIFFERENCES IN PERSPECTIVE

It would be very easy to think that neither Jack nor his parents cared much about Jack's education. But to truly understand this situation, we need to know a few things about Navajo culture. Navajos place high value on individual autonomy: People must respect others' right (even children's right) to make their own decisions (Deyhle & LeCompte, 1999). From this perspective, good parenting does not mean demanding that children do certain things or behave in certain ways; thus, Jack's parents did not insist that Jack come home after going to see a movie. Instead, Navajo parents offer suggestions and guidance, perhaps in the form of gentle teasing ("Now maybe school will look easy!"), that nudge children toward productive choices. When children make poor choices, they often learn a great deal from the consequences.

In addition, Navajos value cooperation and interdependence: People should work together for the common good. Even though Jack enjoyed school, when he returned home his highest priority was helping his family. In the Navajo view, people must cooperate of their own free will; being forced to help others is not true cooperation at all (Chisholm, 1996). Such respect for both individual autonomy and cooperative interdependence is seen in certain other Native American communities as well (Rogoff, 2003).

Notice how Jack and his parents waited in the car when they stopped to visit Donna Deyhle. Although this behavior might be unusual in mainstream Western culture, it is quite appropriate in Navajo communities. If the family had knocked on Donna's door, they would have been imposing their own desires (to talk with Donna) on their potential host. By waiting in the car, they gave Donna the choice of either accepting or rejecting their visit and so preserved her autonomy. Had she found the visit undesirable or inconvenient, she could have ignored their presence outside. Eventually they would have left, with everyone's dignity still intact (Deyhle & LeCompte, 1999).

When students and their families act in accordance with beliefs, values, and social conventions very different from our own, it is all too easy to write them off as being "odd," "unmotivated," or "negligent." Such conclusions are usually both incorrect and counterproductive. As teachers, we can best help students learn, develop, and thrive when we understand the fundamental assumptions and conventions that underlie their behavior.

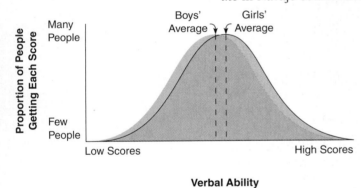

FIGURE 4.1 Typical "difference" between boys and girls on tests of verbal ability

As we consider group differences in the upcoming sections, we must keep in mind two very important points. First, *there is a great deal of individual variability within any group.* I will be describing how students of different groups behave *on average,* yet some students may be very different from that "average" description. Second, *there is almost always a great deal of overlap between two groups.* Consider gender differences in verbal ability as an example. Research studies often find that girls demonstrate slightly higher verbal performance than boys (Halpern & LaMay, 2000). This difference is sometimes statistically significant; in other words, it probably doesn't happen just by chance in one particular study. Yet the average difference between girls and boys in verbal ability is quite small, with a great deal of overlap between the two groups. Figure 4.1 shows the typical overlap between boys and girls on measures of verbal ability: Notice how many of the boys are *better* than some of the girls despite the average advantage for girls.

If we are to maximize the learning and development of all of our students, we must be aware of group differences that may influence their learning and classroom performance. Our challenge is to keep these differences in mind without assuming that all students from a particular group fit typical group patterns. Teachers' preconceived notions about how students will behave may actually *increase* differences among those students—a phenomenon we'll look at more closely in Chapter 12.

■ For more information on the effects of teachers' erroneous assumptions, see the section "Teacher Expectations and Attributions" in Chapter 12.

CULTURAL AND ETHNIC DIFFERENCES

When we use the term **culture**, we are referring to the behaviors and belief systems that chara-terize a long-standing social group. One's cultural background influences the perspectives and values one acquires, the skills one masters and finds important, and the adult roles to which one aspires. It also guides the development of language and communication skills, expression and regulation of emotions, and formation of a sense of self. Cultures are not static entities; they continue to change over time as they incorporate new ideas, innovations, and ways of thinking, and especially as they come into contact with other cultures (O. Lee, 1999; Rogoff, 2003). Fur-thermore, we see considerable variation in attitudes and behaviors within a particular culture; individuals may adopt some cultural values and practices but reject others (Tudge et al., 1999).

An **ethnic group** is a group of individuals with a common culture and the following char-acteristics:

- Its roots either precede the creation of or are external to the country in which it resides; for example, it may be comprised of people of the same race, national origin, or religious background.
- Its members share a sense of interdependence—a sense that their lives are intertwined. (NCSS Task Force on Ethnic Studies Curriculum Guidelines, 1992)

We cannot determine students' ethnicity strictly on the basis of physical characteristics (e.g., race) or birthplace (Wlodkowski & Ginsberg, 1995). For instance, my daughter Tina, although she was born in Colombia and has Hispanic and Native American ancestors, was raised by two European American parents; ethnically, Tina is probably more "White" than anything else.

In general, we can get the best sense of students' cultural backgrounds and ethnic group memberships by learning the extent to which they've participated and continue to participate in various cultural and ethnic-group activities (Gutiérrez & Rogoff, 2003). For instance, some Mex-ican American students live in small, close-knit communities where Spanish is spoken and tra-ditional Mexican practices and beliefs permeate everyday life; others live in more culturally heterogeneous communities in which Mexican traditions are often cast aside. In some instances students may participate actively in two or more cultures, perhaps because their parents come from distinctly different ethnic or racial backgrounds (A. M. Lopez, 2003; Root, 1999). All in all, *membership in a particular cultural or ethnic group is not an either-or situation; rather, it is a more-or-less phenomenon.*

Navigating Different Cultures at Home and at School

You may recall from Chapter 3 that many children entering school for the first time experience some culture shock. This culture shock is more intense for some students than for others (Casanova, 1987; Ramsey, 1987). Most schools in North America and western Europe are based largely on European American, middle-class, "mainstream" culture, so students with this cultural background often adjust quickly to the classroom environment. But students who come from other cultural backgrounds, sometimes with very different norms regarding acceptable behavior, may initially find school a confusing and incomprehensible place. For example, recent immigrants may not know what to expect from others or what behaviors others expect of them (C. R. Harris, 1991; Igoa, 1995). Children raised in a society where gender roles are clearly differentiated—where males and females are expected to behave very differently—may have difficulty adjusting to a school in which similar expectations are held for boys and girls (Kirschenbaum, 1989; Vasquez, 1988). Any such **cultural mismatch** between home and school cultures can interfere with students' adjustment to the school setting and ultimately with their academic achievement as well (García, 1995; C. D. Lee & Slaughter-Defoe, 1995; Ogbu, 1992; Phelan et al., 1994).

Cultural mismatch is compounded when teachers misinterpret the behaviors of students from ethnic minority groups. The following exercise provides an example.

Experiencing FIRSTHAND ·Ruckus in the Lunchroom

In the following passage, a young adolescent named Sam is describing an incident in the school cafeteria to his friend Joe:

> I got in line behind Bubba. As usual the line was moving pretty slow and we were all getting pretty restless. For a little action Bubba turned around and said, "Hey Sam! What you doin' man? You so

Holiday Family Traditions

Ever year I do a gringer bread makeing party with all of my friends at and with my cousins too.

Considerable diversity exists even in a single culture. For example, different families may celebrate the same religious holiday quite differently. Making a gingerbread house is an annual holiday tradition at 7-year-old Emma's house.

■ **culture** Behaviors and belief systems of a long-standing social group.

■ **ethnic group** People who have common historical roots, values, beliefs, and behaviors and who share a sense of interdependence.

■ **cultural mismatch** Situation in which a child's home culture and the school culture hold conflicting expectations for the child's behavior.

ugly that when the doctor delivered you he slapped your face!" Everyone laughed, but they laughed even harder when I shot back, "Oh yeah? Well, you so ugly the doctor turned around and slapped your momma!" It got even wilder when Bubba said, "Well, man; at least my daddy ain't no girl scout!" We really got into it then. After a while more people got involved—4, 5, then 6. It was a riot! People helping out anyone who seemed to be getting the worst of the deal. All of a sudden Mr. Reynolds the gym teacher came over to try to quiet things down. The next thing we knew we were all in the office. The principal made us stay after school for a week; he's so straight! On top of that, he sent word home that he wanted to talk to our folks in his office Monday afternoon. Boy! Did I get it when I got home. That's the third notice I've gotten this semester. As we were leaving the principal's office, I ran into Bubba again. We decided we'd finish where we left off, but this time we would wait until we were off the school grounds (R. E. Reynolds, Taylor, Steffensen, Shirey, & Anderson, 1982, p. 358)

Exactly what happened in the school cafeteria? Were the boys fighting? Or were they simply having a good time?

· · · · · · ·

The story you just read is actually about "playing the dozens,"[1] a friendly exchange of insults common among male youth in some African American communities (e.g., DeLain, Pearson, & Anderson, 1985; R. E. Reynolds et al., 1982). Some boys engage in such exchanges to achieve status among their peers—those thinking up the biggest insults are the winners—whereas others do it simply for amusement. If you interpreted the cafeteria incident as a knock-down-drag-out fight, you're hardly alone; many eighth graders in a research study did likewise (R. E. Reynolds et al., 1982).

When we don't understand the cultural traditions of the community in which students have been raised, we will inevitably misinterpret some of their behaviors. For example, people in certain Native American communities find it unnecessary to say hello or good-bye (Sisk, 1989), yet a teacher from another culture may misunderstand when he or she isn't greeted in the morning. In other Native American communities, people rarely express their feelings through facial expressions (Montgomery, 1989), giving some teachers the mistaken impression that students are inattentive or bored.

As students gain experience with the culture of their school, they become increasingly aware of their teachers' and peers' expectations for behavior and ways of thinking, and many eventually become adept at switching their cultural vantage point as they move from home to school and back again (Hong, Morris, Chiu, & Benet-Martínez, 2000; LaFromboise, Coleman, & Gerton, 1993; Phelan et al., 1994). One Mexican American student's recollection provides an example:

> At home with my parents and grandparents the only acceptable language was Spanish; actually that's all they really understood. Everything was really Mexican, but at the same time they wanted me to speak good English. . . . But at school, I felt really different because everyone was American, including me. Then I would go home in the afternoon and be Mexican again. (Padilla, 1994, p. 30)

Not all students make an easy adjustment, however. Some students actively resist adapting to the school culture, perhaps because they view it as being inconsistent with—even contradictory to—their own cultural background and identity (W. E. Cross et al., 1999; Ogbu, 1999; Phelan et al., 1994). Still others try desperately to fit in at school yet find the inconsistencies between home and school difficult to resolve, as a teacher who has worked with immigrant Muslim children from Pakistan and Afghanistan reports:

> During the days of preparation for Ramadan Feast, the children fasted with the adults. They were awakened by their parents before dawn. They had breakfast and then went back to sleep until it was time to get themselves ready for school. In school they refrained from food or drink—even a drop of water—until sunset. By noon, especially on warm days, they were a bit listless. I had observed that they refrained from praying in a public school even though prayer was a part of their cultural attitude. They spoke about their obligation to pray five times daily. In their writing they expressed the conflict within:
>
> > *I always think about my country. I think about going there one day, seeing it and practicing my religion with no problems. Here we don't have enough priests. We call them mullah. Here we have only the mosque. The mullah is important because we learn the Koran from him. I can't practice my religion. Before sunrise, I can pray with my family. But at school we can't say to my teacher, "Please, teacher, I need to pray." (Igoa, 1995, p. 135)*

■ Can you think of ways in which your own school environment was mismatched with the culture in which you were raised?

---

[1] You may also see the terms *joaning, sounding, signifying,* or *snapping.*

As teachers, we must do our part by learning as much as we can about the ways in which students from various cultural and ethnic backgrounds are apt to be different from one another and from ourselves. Armed with such knowledge, we can make reasonable accommodations to help students from all walks of life adjust to and thrive in our classrooms.

Examples of Cultural and Ethnic Diversity

Tremendous cultural variation exists within African American, Asian American, Hispanic, Native American, and European American groups. Thus, we must be careful not to form stereotypes about *any* group. At the same time, knowledge of frequently observed cultural differences can sometimes help us better understand why students behave as they do.

Psychologists and educators have identified many ways in which students from diverse backgrounds may think and act differently. In the following sections, we consider a variety of differences in language, interpersonal behaviors, and belief systems.

Language and dialect.   One obvious cultural difference is in language. In the United States more than 6 million students speak a language other than English at home, and in some large city school systems, more than a hundred different languages are spoken (McKeon, 1994; National Association of Bilingual Education, 1993; U.S. Bureau of the Census, 1994). Children who have not encountered English before they begin school will naturally have difficulty with schoolwork and classroom assessments in an English-based classroom.

Even when children speak English at home, they may use a form of English different from the **Standard English** that is typically considered acceptable at school. More specifically, they may speak in a different **dialect**, a form of English that includes some unique pronunciations and grammatical structures. For example, consider the following sentences:

> It would take you to get there early.
> I'm just after my dinner. (Milroy, 1994, p. 157)

If you have been raised in North America, you may not be able to make much sense of these statements, because they reflect a dialect of English spoken in Northern Ireland. (The two sentences mean, "It's advisable to arrive early" and "I've just finished my dinner," respectively.)

Some dialects are associated with particular ethnic and cultural groups. Perhaps the most widely studied ethnic dialect is **African American English**.[2] This dialect, which is actually a group of similar dialects, is used in many African American communities throughout the United States and is characterized by sentences such as these:

> He got ten dollar.
> Momma she mad.
> Nobody don't never like me.
> I be going to dance tonight. (R. E. Owens, 1995, p. A–8)

At one time researchers believed that an African American dialect represented a less complex form of speech than Standard English and urged educators to teach students to speak "properly" as quickly as possible. But they now realize that African American dialects are, in fact, very complex language systems with their own predictable grammatical rules and their own unique idioms and proverbs. In addition, these dialects promote communication and complex thought as readily as Standard English (DeLain et al., 1985; Fairchild & Edwards-Evans, 1990; Owens, 1996).

When a local dialect is the language most preferred by residents of a community, it is often the means through which people can most effectively connect with one another in day-to-day interactions. Furthermore, many children and adolescents view their native dialect as an integral part of their ethnic identity (Garrison, 1989; McAlpine, 1992; Ogbu, 1999). The following incident among rural Native American students at a boarding school in Alaska is an example:

> Many of the students at the school spoke English with a native dialect and seemed unable to utter certain essential sounds in the English language. A new group of speech teachers was sent in to correct the problem. The teachers worked consistently with the students in an attempt to improve speech patterns and intonation, but found that their efforts were in vain.
>
> One night, the boys in the dormitory were seeming to have too much fun, and peals of laughter were rolling out from under the door. An investigating counselor approached cautiously, and

■ In Chapter 16 we'll look at the effects that language and other cultural differences may have on assessments of students' achievement and abilities.

■ **Standard English**   Form of English generally considered acceptable at school, as reflected in textbooks and grammar instruction.

■ **dialect**   Form of a language characteristic of a particular region or ethnic group.

■ **African American English**   Dialect of some African American communities that includes some pronunciations, grammatical constructions, and idioms different from those of Standard English.

---

[2] African American English is also known as *Black English*, *Black English vernacular*, and *Ebonics*.

listened quietly outside the door to see if he could discover the source of the laughter. From be-hind the door he heard a voice, speaking in perfect English, giving instructions to the rest of the crowd. The others were finding the situation very amusing. When the counselor entered the room he found that one of the students was speaking. "Joseph," he said, "You've been cured! Your Eng-lish is perfect." "No," said Joseph returning to his familiar dialect, "I was just doing an imitation of you." "But if you can speak in standard English, why don't you do it all of the time?" the coun-selor queried. "I can," responded Joseph, "but it sounds funny, and I feel dumb doing it." (Garri-son, 1989, p. 121)

Many people in mainstream Western culture associate higher social status with people who speak Standard English, and they perceive speakers of other dialects in a lesser light (Gollnick & Chinn, 2002; Purcell-Gates, 1995; H. L. Smith, 1998). For this reason, most experts recommend that all students develop proficiency in Standard English because success in mainstream adult so-ciety will be difficult to achieve without it (Casanova, 1987; Craft, 1984; Ogbu, 1999).

Ideally, children and adolescents from diverse backgrounds probably function most effec-tively when they can use both their local dialect and Standard English in appropriate settings (Gollnick & Chinn, 2002; Ogbu, 1999; Warren & McCloskey, 1993). For example, although we may wish to encourage Standard English in most written work or in formal oral presentations, we might find other dialects quite appropriate in creative writing or informal classroom discus-sions (Smitherman, 1994). One teacher of African American students explains to her classes that facility with two dialects is a form of bilingualism:

> I don't want them to be ashamed of what they know but I also want them to know and be com-fortable with what school and the rest of the society requires. When I put it in the context of "translation" they get excited. They see it is possible to go from one to the other. It's not that they are not familiar with Standard English. . . . They hear Standard English all the time on TV. It's cer-tainly what I use in the classroom. But there is rarely any connection made between the way they speak and Standard English. I think that when they can see the connections and know that they can make the shifts, they become better at both. They're bilingual! (Ladson-Billings, 1994a, p. 84)

Views about talking versus remaining silent. Relatively speaking, mainstream Western culture is a chatty one. People often say things to one another even when they have very little to com-municate; they make small talk as a way of maintaining interpersonal relationships and filling awkward silences (Irujo, 1988; Trawick-Smith, 2003). In some African American communities as well, people speak frequently; for instance, in church services they may spontaneously shout out or move about (Lein, 1975).

In certain other cultures, however, silence is golden. Brazilians and Peruvians often greet their guests silently, Arabs stop talking to indicate they want privacy, and many Native American communities value silence in general (Basso, 1972; Menyuk & Menyuk, 1988; Trawick-Smith, 2003). Among many Japanese and the Inuit people of northern Quebec, talking a lot can be in-terpreted as a sign of immaturity or low intelligence (Crago, 1988; Minami & McCabe, 1996). For example, when working at an Inuit school, one researcher asked a teacher about a boy whose language seemed unusually advanced for his age. The teacher replied:

> "Do you think he might have a learning problem? Some of these children who don't have such high intelligence have trouble stopping themselves. They don't know when to stop talking." (Crago, 1988, p. 219)

Different cultural and ethnic groups also have diverse views about when it is appropriate for children to speak to adults. In most Western communities the expectation is that children will speak up whenever they have comments or questions. Yet many children raised in rural Mexico and in the Yup'ik culture of Alaska are expected to learn primarily by close, quiet observation of adults; they rarely ask questions or otherwise interrupt what adults are doing (E. E. García, 1994; Gutiérrez & Rogoff, 2003). In many other cultures children learn very early that they should en-gage in conversation with adults only when their participation has been directly solicited; this is the case in many Mexican American and Southeast Asian communities, as well as in some African American communities in the southeastern United States (Delgado-Gaitan, 1994; Grant & Gomez, 2001; Ochs, 1982). In fact, children from some backgrounds, including many Puerto Ri-cans, Mexican Americans, and Native Americans, have been taught that speaking directly and as-sertively to adults is rude, perhaps even rebellious (Delgado-Gaitan, 1994; Hidalgo, Siu, Bright, Swap, & Epstein, 1995; Lomawaima, 1995).

■ Notice how the counselor tells Joseph that he's been "cured." What assumption does this statement reveal?

Eye contact. For many of us, looking someone in the eye is a way to show that we are trying to communicate or are listening intently to what the person is saying. But in many Native American, African American, Mexican American, and Puerto Rican communities, a child who looks an adult in the eye is showing disrespect. In these communities children are taught to look down in the presence of adults (Gilliland, 1988; Irujo, 1988; Torres-Guzmán, 1998). The following anecdote shows how a teacher's recognition of this culturally learned behavior can make a difference:

> A teacher [described a Native American] student who would never say a word, nor even answer when she greeted him. Then one day when he came in she looked in the other direction and said, "Hello, Jimmy." He answered enthusiastically, "Why hello Miss Jacobs." She found that he would always talk if she looked at a book or at the wall, but when she looked at him, he appeared frightened. (Gilliland, 1988, p. 26)

Personal space. In some cultures, such as in some African American and Hispanic communities, people stand close together when they talk and may touch one another frequently (Hale-Benson, 1986; Slonim, 1991; D. W. Sue, 1990). In contrast, European Americans and Japanese Americans tend to keep a fair distance from one another—they maintain some **personal space**—especially if they don't know one another very well (Irujo, 1988; Trawick-Smith, 2003). As teachers, we must be sensitive to the personal space that students from various cultural backgrounds need in order to feel comfortable in interactions with us and with classmates.

Questions. A common interaction pattern in many Western classrooms is the **IRE cycle:** A teacher *initiates* an interaction by asking a question, a student *responds* to the question, and the teacher *evaluates* the response (Mehan, 1979). Similar interactions are often found in parent-child interactions in middle-class European American homes. For instance, when my own children were toddlers and preschoolers, I often asked them questions such as "How old are you?" and "What does a cow say?" and praised them when they answered correctly. But children raised in other environments—for instance, many of those raised in lower-income homes, as well as those raised in some Mexican American, Native American, and Hawaiian communities—are unfamiliar with such question-and-answer sessions when they first come to school (Losey, 1995; Rogoff, 2003). Furthermore, some children may be quite puzzled when a teacher asks questions to which the teacher already knows the answer (Crago, Annahatak, & Ningiuruvik, 1993; Heath, 1989; Rogoff, 2003).

It's not that children are unaccustomed to questions; it's only that they have little experience with certain *kinds* of questions. For example, parents in African American communities in parts of the southeastern United States are more likely to ask questions involving comparisons and analogies; rather than asking "What's that?" they may instead ask "What's that like?" (Heath, 1989). In addition, children in these communities are specifically taught *not* to answer questions from strangers about personal and home life—questions such as "What's your name?" and "Where do you live?" The complaints of parents in these communities illustrate how much of a cultural mismatch there can be between the children and their European American teachers:

- "My kid, he too scared to talk, 'cause nobody play by the rules he know. At home I can't shut him up."
- "Miss Davis, she complain 'bout Ned not answerin' back. He says she asks dumb questions she already know about." (Heath, 1980, p. 107)

Teachers' comments about these children reflect their own lack of understanding about the culture from which the children come:

- "I would almost think some of them have a hearing problem; it is as though they don't hear me ask a question. I get blank stares to my questions. Yet when I am making statements or telling stories which interest them, they always seem to hear me."
- "The simplest questions are the ones they can't answer in the classroom; yet on the playground, they can explain a rule for a ballgame or describe a particular kind of bait with no problem. Therefore, I know they can't be as dumb as they seem in my class." (Heath, 1980, pp. 107–108)

Waiting versus interrupting. Teachers frequently ask their students questions and then wait for an answer. But exactly how long do they wait? The typical **wait time** for many teachers is a second or even less; at that point, they either answer a question themselves or call on another

In some cultures (e.g., in many Native American communities), children are taught to look down as a sign of respect to an adult who speaks to them.

■ **personal space** Personally or culturally preferred distance between two people during social interaction.

■ **IRE cycle** Adult-child interaction marked by adult initiation (e.g., a question), child response, and adult evaluation.

■ **wait time** Length of time a teacher pauses, either after asking a question or hearing a student's comment, before saying something.

student (M. B. Rowe, 1974, 1987). Yet people from some cultures leave lengthy pauses before responding as a way of indicating respect, as this statement by a Northern Cheyenne illustrates:

> Even if I had a quick answer to your question, I would never answer immediately. That would be saying that your question was not worth thinking about. (Gilliland, 1988, p. 27)

Students from such cultures are more likely to participate in class and answer questions when given several seconds to respond (Grant & Gomez, 2001; Mohatt & Erickson, 1981; Tharp, 1989). Not only does such an extended wait time allow students to show respect, but it also gives those with limited English proficiency some mental "translation" time (Gilliland, 1988). And in general, increasing wait time enhances cognitive processing, as we'll discover in Chapter 6.

Rather than pausing as a way to show respect, children from certain other backgrounds may interrupt adults or peers who haven't finished speaking—behavior that many of us might interpret as rudeness. For instance, in some African American, Puerto Rican, and Jewish families, adults and children alike sometimes speak spontaneously and simultaneously; in such settings, waiting for one's turn may mean being excluded from the conversation altogether (Condon & Yousef, 1975; Farber, Mindel, & Lazerwitz, 1988; Hale-Benson, 1986; Slonim, 1991). And in some Hawaiian communities, an interruption is taken as a sign of personal involvement in the conversation (Tharp, 1989).

Private versus public performance. In many classrooms learning is a very public enterprise. Individual students are often asked to answer questions or demonstrate skills in full view of their classmates, and they are encouraged to ask questions themselves when they don't understand. Such practices, which many teachers take for granted, may confuse or even alienate the students of some ethnic groups (Eriks-Brophy & Crago, 1994; García, 1994; Lomawaima, 1995). Many Native American children are accustomed to practicing a skill privately at first, performing in front of a group only after they have attained a reasonable level of mastery (García, 1994; S. Sanders, 1987; Suina & Smolkin, 1994). And children in some Native American and Hawaiian communities may feel more comfortable responding to adults' questions as a group rather than interacting with adults one-on-one (K. H. Au, 1980; L. S. Miller, 1995).

Such preferences have obvious implications for classroom assessment practices. One strategy is to let students practice new skills away from the limelight and show us their progress in private, one-on-one sessions. Another is to ask students to respond to simple questions (e.g., those requiring single-word responses) in chorus.

Views about teasing. Although some people think of teasing as being mean-spirited and inappropriate, it is a common form of social interaction in some cultures. For example, in the "Ruckus in the Lunchroom" exercise presented earlier, two African American boys engaged in one-upmanship, flinging increasingly outlandish insults at each other. And in the opening case study, Jack's mother teased Jack by suggesting that "Now maybe school will look easy!" When taken in the right spirit, teasing serves a variety of functions for particular cultural groups, perhaps providing a source of amusement and an outlet for verbal creativity, perhaps exerting gentle pressure to engage in more productive behavior, or perhaps helping children learn how to take criticism in stride (Rogoff, 2003).

Cooperation versus competition. In a traditional classroom, school learning is often a solitary, individual endeavor: Students receive praise, stickers, and good grades when they perform at high levels, regardless of how their classmates perform. Sometimes, instead, school achievement is quite competitive: A student's performance is evaluated in comparison with the performance of classmates. Some teachers may identify the "best" papers or drawings in the class; others may grade "on a curve," with some students doing quite well and others inevitably failing.

■ Why do you think some teachers encourage competition among students?

Yet in some cultures (e.g., in many Native American, Mexican American, Southeast Asian, and Pacific Island communities), it is neither individual achievement nor competitive achievement that is recognized, but rather *group* achievement: The success of the village or community is valued over individual success. Students from such cultures are more accustomed to working cooperatively than competitively and for the benefit of the community rather than for themselves (Garcia, 1992; Lomawaima, 1995; Tharp, 1994). We saw this situation in the opening case study when Jack stayed home from school to help the family herd sheep in preparation for the spring shearing.

Students from cooperative cultures may resist when asked to compete against their classmates, as 16-year-old Maria explains:

I love sports, but not competitive sports. [My brother is] the same way. I think we learned that from our folks. They both try to set things up so that everyone wins in our family and no one is competing for anything. (Pipher, 1994, p. 280)

They may also be confused when teachers scold them for helping one another on assignments or for "sharing" answers, and they may feel uncomfortable when their individual achievements are publicly acknowledged (Deyhle & Margonis, 1995; Lipka, 1998; Rogoff, 2003). Group work, with an emphasis on cooperation rather than competition, often facilitates the school achievement of these students (García, 1995; Losey, 1995; McAlpine & Taylor, 1993; L. S. Miller, 1995).

In many Mexican American and Native American communities, group achievement is valued over individual or competitive achievement, and cooperation is commonplace.

Family relationships and expectations. In some groups—for example, in many Hispanic, Native American, and Asian communities, as well as in rural communities in the Appalachian Mountains—family bonds and relationships are especially important, and extended family members often live nearby. Students raised in these cultures are likely to feel responsibility for their family's well-being and a strong sense of loyalty to other family members; they may also go to great efforts to please their parents. It is not unusual for students in such communities to leave school when their help is needed at home (Abi-Nader, 1993; Banks & Banks, 1995; Fuligni, 1998; Timm & Borman, 1997).

In most cultures school achievement is valued highly, and parents encourage their children to do well in school (Duran & Weffer, 1992; Goldenberg, Gallimore, Reese, & Garnier, 2001; Hossler & Stage, 1992; A. H. Yee, 1992). But in a few cases classroom achievement may be less valued than achievement in other areas. For example, in some very traditional Native American and Polynesian communities, children are expected to excel in art, dance, and other aspects of their culture rather than in more academic pursuits such as reading or mathematics (Kirschenbaum, 1989; Reid, 1989). And in some African American and Native American families, early pregnancies are cause for joy even if the mothers-to-be have not yet completed high school (Deyhle & Margonis, 1995; Stack & Burton, 1993).

We must certainly be sensitive to situations in which the achievements that *we* think are important are not those valued by students' families. Whenever possible, we must show our students how the school curriculum and classroom activities relate to their cultural environment and their own life goals. We must also maintain open lines of communication with students' parents. Because some parents, especially parents of minority children, may be intimidated by school personnel, teachers often need to take the first step in establishing productive parent-teacher relationships. When teachers and parents realize that both groups want students to succeed in the classroom, they are more apt to work cooperatively to promote student achievement (Banks & Banks, 1995; Salend & Taylor, 1993; R. L. Warren, 1988). Chapter 14 identifies some specific strategies for working effectively with parents.

Conceptions of time. Many people regulate their lives by the clock: Being on time to appointments, social engagements, and the dinner table is important. This emphasis on punctuality is not characteristic of all cultures, however; for example, many Hispanic and Native American communities don't observe strict schedules and time lines (H. G. Burger, 1973; Garrison, 1989; Gilliland, 1988). Not surprisingly, children from these communities may often be late for school and may have trouble understanding the need to complete school tasks within a certain time frame.

To succeed in mainstream Western society, students eventually need to learn punctuality. At the same time, we must recognize that not all of our students will be especially concerned about clock time when they first enter our classrooms. Certainly we should expect students to arrive at class on time and to turn in assignments when they are due. But we must be patient and understanding when, for cultural reasons, students do not develop such habits immediately.

World views. The cultural and ethnic differences we've identified so far reveal themselves, in one way or another, in students' behaviors. Yet recall our earlier definition of culture: the behaviors and *belief systems* that characterize a social group. Our beliefs and assumptions about the world are often so integral to our everyday thinking that we take them for granted and aren't consciously aware of them. Some beliefs that permeate the curriculum in traditional Western schools are not universally shared, however. Consider the following examples:

- After a major hurricane ripped through southern Florida in the summer of 1992, many fourth and fifth graders attributed the hurricane to natural causes, but some children from minority backgrounds, because of explanations heard from family members, neighbors, or church groups, believed that people's actions or supernatural forces also played a role in the hurricane's origins and destructiveness (O. Lee, 1999).

- When American high school students talk about American history, European Americans are likely to depict historical events as leading up to increasing freedom, equality, and democracy for its citizens. In contrast, some African Americans are apt to depict historical events as contributing to or maintaining racist and oppressive attitudes and practices (T. Epstein, 2000).
- Whereas most students of European descent think of "progress" as comprising techno-logical advancements and a higher standard of living, Navajo students are more likely to think of progress as comprising spiritual advancement (Nelson-Barber & Estrin, 1995).

Such beliefs and perspectives will invariably color how students interpret what they learn in history, science, and other subject areas, for reasons you'll discover in Chapters 6 and 7.

People of all ages become more aware of cultural and ethnic differences when they come into contact with cultural practices different from their own. In the following exercise, we look at what one 8-year-old learned when he and his family lived in another country for a short time.

Interpreting Student Artifacts and Behaviors

Australia

When his father's career brought the family to Australia for several months, 8-year-old Tony attended an Australian school. In communicating with his class back home in New Hampshire, Tony created a list of differences between Australia and the United States. Following are excerpts from his list. As you read the list:

- Look for patterns in the things Tony has noticed about his new cultural environment
- Identify one or more cultural differences Tony has *not* noticed, and speculate about possible reasons for his oversight(s)

Did you know that in Australia . . .?

sprinkles here are called hundreds and thousands.

cookies are called biscuits and they come in unique flavors like, Pigs in Mud, Hokey Pokey, and Banana Split.

at school on Fridays is Sport Day and in the afternoon the whole school does different things like swimming, running, and soccer.

money here is made out of plastic with a little window that you can see through. There are also no pennies.

the native people here are called aboriginals, and started living in Australia 40,000 years ago. People think they are the oldest group of humans.

cars drive on the left side of the road and the steering wheel is on the right side of the car.

houses here are mostly one story, many have verandas (porches) and some are even on stilts to help them be cooler.

the game of netball, it's like basketball but you can't dribble the ball, is played by the most people. Cricket and Rugby are the favorite sports that people watch.

some children live hundreds of miles away from other people and the children listen to school and have girl and boy meetings on the radio. They get their work from their teacher by the mail that reaches them by planes and helicoptors.

nurses are called sisters.

a popular sandwich made with vegemite and butter is like peanutbutter and jelly in America. It's salty and is something you have to get use to eating. We don't like it.

there are many animals which were brought here from people moving to Australia many years ago. Some of these animals were let loose and are now called feral. Feral animals are a problem because they eat the food that animals from Australia are suppose to eat. Some feral animals are pigs, camels, rabbits, and foxes.

just like you can tell which direction is north from the Big Dipper in the sky we can tell the direction south is by looking at the Southern Cross. This constellation is also on the Australian flag.

One of the most obvious aspects of any culture is its language, and Tony has readily picked up on differences in labels used in America and Australia. He has also noticed differences in common objects (e.g., currency, cars, houses, food) and activities (e.g., school, sports). He has learned that some Australian practices that differ from those back home are the result of the environment (houses are built on stilts to make them cooler, some children are schooled through radio and mail because they live in remote locations, orientation is different because different constellations are visible). And he has learned some facts about Australia's unique qualities (e.g., its aboriginal people and feral animals). As far as we can tell, however, any differences in people's belief systems and world views have eluded him.

In general, Tony has focused on concrete differences. Many of these are readily apparent in his day-to-day experiences, although a few (e.g., his knowledge of rural education, aboriginal peoples, and feral animals) are probably the result of explicit instruction either at school or at home. Tony would have difficulty thinking about and understanding the culture's belief systems and world views, probably because they tend to be abstract (8-year-olds have difficulty with abstract ideas; see Chapter 2) and are unlikely to be topics of discussions for children his age.

Creating a More Multicultural Classroom Environment

Clearly, we must be sensitive to the ways in which students of various ethnic groups are likely to act and think differently from one another. It is equally important that we help *students* develop such sensitivity: When they reach adulthood, they will almost certainly have to work effectively with people from diverse backgrounds. It is in students' best interests, then, that we promote awareness and understanding of numerous cultures in our classrooms. We can foster greater multicultural understanding through strategies such as the following:

- Coming to grips with our own cultural lenses
- Incorporating the values, beliefs, and traditions of many cultures into the curriculum
- Working to break down ethnic stereotypes
- Acknowledging that students may have multiple cultural affiliations
- Promoting productive interactions among students from diverse racial and ethnic groups
- Fostering democratic ideals

Coming to Grips with Our Own Cultural Lenses   In the opening case study, Jack's English teacher complained that "his parents don't care!" and that, in general, the parents of Navajo students "just don't support their [children's] education" (Deyhle & LeCompte, 1999, p. 127). This teacher was jumping to a conclusion based on a couple of assumptions common in mainstream Western culture: (a) School should take priority over needs at home and elsewhere, and (b) responsible parents insist that their children attend school. Yet as we have seen, many Native Americans, while appreciating the value of a formal education, also believe that all family members must contribute to the family's well-being; in rural farming families, this may often mean helping out with the crops and livestock. We have seen, too, that members of Navajo communities tend not to place demands on children; instead, they make suggestions, and they acknowledge that children can learn valuable lessons by occasionally making poor choices.

The assumptions and world views we have acquired in our own culture—perhaps including an assumption that good parents "control" their children—are often so pervasive in our lives that we tend to treat them as common sense, or even as facts, rather than as the beliefs they really are. These beliefs become a *cultural lens* through which we view events, and they may lead us to conclude that other cultures' practices are somehow irrational and inferior to our own. One prominent sociocultural theorist, Barbara Rogoff, has put it this way: "Like the fish that is unaware of water until it has left the water, people often take their own community's ways of doing things for granted" (2003, p. 13). Only when we find ourselves in a very different cultural environment can we truly begin to understand how we, too, are very much a product of our own culture.

We can work most effectively with students from diverse cultural backgrounds when we try to understand *why* they think and act as they do. Until we achieve such understanding, we should resist making value judgments about the behaviors of students and their families (Rogoff, 2003).

Incorporating the Values, Beliefs, and Traditions of Many Cultures into the Curriculum   True **multicultural education** is not limited to cooking ethnic foods, celebrating Cinco de Mayo, or studying famous African Americans during Black History Month. Rather, it integrates the perspectives and experiences of numerous cultural groups throughout the curriculum and gives all students reason for pride in their own cultural heritage (Banks, 1995; García, 1995; Hollins, 1996; NCSS Task Force on Ethnic Studies Curriculum Guidelines, 1992).

■ This tendency to view the world from our own cultural lens may also lead us to use *culturally biased* assessment instruments. We'll look at *cultural bias* in Chapter 16.

■ **multicultural education** Instruction that integrates perspectives and experiences of numerous cultural groups throughout the curriculum.

In his high school Spanish class, Ben created this burlap-and-yarn eagle inspired by Mexican designs. A culture's art should be only a small part of a multicultural education that also looks at the culture's beliefs, values, and world views.

As teachers, we can incorporate content from diverse cultures into many aspects of the school curriculum. Following are some examples:

- In literature, read the work of authors and poets from a variety of ethnic groups.
- In art, consider the creations and techniques of artists from around the world.
- In physical education, learn games from other countries.
- In mathematics, use mathematical principles to address multicultural tasks and problems (e.g., using graph paper to design a Navajo rug).
- In history, look at wars and other major events from diverse perspectives (e.g., the Spanish perspective of the Spanish-American War, the Japanese perspective of World War II, the Native American perspective of the pioneers' westward migration in North America).
- In social studies, look at different religious beliefs and their effects on people's behaviors (e.g., see Figure 4.2).
- In current events, consider such issues as discrimination and oppression.

As we explore various cultures, we should help students recognize that diverse cultural groups have much to learn from one another. For example, students may be surprised to discover that several key practices underlying many democratic governments in Western nations—for instance, sending delegates to represent particular groups, allowing only one person in a governing council to speak at a time, keeping government and military bodies separate—were adopted from governing practices of the Iroquois League in North America in the 1700s (Rogoff, 2003; Weatherford, 1988).

In our exploration of diverse cultures, we should look for commonalities as well as differences. For example, we might study how various cultural groups celebrate the beginning of a new year, discovering that "out with the old and in with the new" is a common theme among many such celebrations (Ramsey, 1987). At the secondary level it can be beneficial to explore issues that adolescents of all cultures face: gaining the respect of elders, forming trusting relationships with peers, and finding a meaningful place in society (Ulichny, 1994). One important goal of multicultural education should be to communicate that, underneath it all, people are more alike than different.

FIGURE 4.2   Thirteen-year-old Melinda wrote about the Shinto religion of Japan for her language arts and social studies classes. Students were required to go beyond the facts to draw their own conclusions and relate what they have learned to their personal lives. These excerpts from Melinda's paper show her efforts to do so.

Shinto has some neat mythology. In the 700's A.D. many myths and legends were written. Mythology says Japan and Japanese people were created by deities. The creator god was said to have created the world and established customs and laws. The legend of how the Japanese islands were created is told like this: Two gods, Izanagi and Izanami, looked down from the "bridge of heaven," and wondered what was below. Izanagi took a jeweled spear and lowered the point. As Izanagi moved it around it splashed into the ocean. Izanagi raised the jeweled spear and the salt water dried into "pearly drops." The pearly drops fell off into the ocean and formed the islands of Japan. Izanagi and Izanami decided to live on the islands. After many years they had three children. One was the sun goddess, whose grandson was the first emperor of Japan. Her two brothers were the moon god and the wind god.

Shinto gods are called Kami. It is believed that these spirits are found in the basic forces of fire, wind, and water.

Most influence agriculture and this of course was how the earliest people survived. They relied on what they grew to live. So the gods had to help them grow their crops or they died. It seems natural for people to worship things that will help them survive, and worshiping forces that affect what you grow was the common practice in early history. These basic forces even affect the survival of modern people. We all still need agriculture to live and forces of nature really determine whether crops grow or not.

Shintoists never developed strong doctrines, such as the belief in life after death that many other religions have. However they have developed some moral standards such as devotion, sincerity, and purity. . . .

All Shintoists have a very good and simple set of rules or practice. They want to be honorable, have feelings for others, support the government, and keep their families safe and healthy. I think these are good principles for all people, whether they practice a religion or not. . . .

Breaking Down Ethnic Stereotypes

Experiencing FIRSTHAND ·Picture This #1

Form a picture in your mind of someone from each of the following three places. Focus on the *first* image that comes to mind in each case.

The Netherlands (Holland)
Mexico
Hawaii

Now answer yes or no to each of these questions:

- Was the person from the Netherlands wearing wooden shoes?
- Was the person from Mexico wearing a sombrero?
- Was the person from Hawaii wearing a hula skirt or flower lei?

· · · · · · ·

If you answered yes to any of the three questions, then one or more of your images reflected an ethnic stereotype. Most people in the Netherlands, Mexico, and Hawaii do *not* routinely wear wooden shoes, sombreros, or hula skirts and leis.

Although we and our students should certainly be aware of true differences among various ethnic groups, it is counterproductive to hold a **stereotype**—a rigid, simplistic, and inevitably inaccurate caricature—of any particular group. As teachers, we must make a concerted effort to develop and select curriculum materials that represent all cultural groups in a positive and competent light; for example, we should choose textbooks, works of fiction, and videotapes that portray people of diverse ethnic backgrounds as legitimate participants in mainstream society, rather than as exotic "curiosities" who live in a separate world. And we must definitely avoid or modify curriculum materials that portray members of minority groups in an overly simplified, romanticized, exaggerated, or otherwise stereotypical fashion (Banks, 1994; Boutte & McCormick, 1992; Ladson-Billings, 1994b; Pang, 1995).

Stereotypes don't exist only in curriculum materials, however. They may also exist in the minds of students' family members and neighbors. In some instances family members communicate stereotypes through prejudicial remarks and practices (Branch, 1999; F. H. Davidson & Davidson, 1994). In other cases a history of conflict and animosity between two groups may lead children to conclude that people in the opposing group have undesirable qualities (Pitner, Astor, Benbenishty, Haj-Yahia, & Zeira, 2003).

We can help break down ethnic stereotypes in several simple yet effective ways. For one thing, we can arrange opportunities for students to interact with people from diverse groups (and ideally to create a sense that "we are all in this together"), perhaps through cooperative group activities or community service projects (Oskamp, 2000; Ramsey, 1995). We might explore the historical roots of cultural differences—for example, by explaining that such differences sometimes reflect the various economic and social circumstances in which particular groups have historically found themselves. And finally, we must emphasize that individual members of any single group are often very different from one another—for instance, that not all members of a particular ethnic group share the same cultural behaviors, beliefs, and values (Gutiérrez & Rogoff, 2003; O. Lee, 1999).

Acknowledging That Students May Have Multiple Cultural Affiliations   In their efforts to be multiculturally sensitive, some well-meaning educators make the mistake of thinking of their students as belonging exclusively to particular categories: African American, Asian American, European American, Hispanic, and so on. Although it is helpful to know how students from different cultural and ethnic backgrounds may behave and think differently, we must be careful that we don't routinely assume—perhaps based on skin color, surname, or country of origin—that students belong to any particular group. As noted earlier, many students participate actively in two or more cultural groups. Perhaps they do so because they have a mixed ethnic or racial heritage, or perhaps, as recent immigrants, they want to interact effectively both in their local immigrant neighborhood and in mainstream Western society (C. R. Cooper, Jackson, Azmitia, Lopez, & Dunbar, 1995; Harter, 1999).

In its 2000 census the United States began to allow respondents to categorize themselves as having mixed heritage rather than belonging to one particular racial group. As teachers, we, too, would be smart to acknowledge, both to ourselves and to our students, that in this age of

■ **stereotype** Rigid, simplistic, and erroneous caricature of a particular group of people.

■ Hear Crystal's concerns about racism in the "Emotions: Early Adolescence" clip on Video CD 1.

increasing multiracial and multicultural interaction, many people cannot easily be pigeonholed (A. M. Lopez, 2003; Root, 1999).

Promoting Productive Interactions Among Students from Diverse Racial and Ethnic Groups

For a variety of reasons, some students treat peers from other racial or ethnic groups poorly. For example, in the "Emotions: Early Adolescence" clip on Video CD 1, 13-year-old Crystal mentions racism, saying that "people go after [others] for things that they didn't do." But when students from diverse groups interact regularly—and especially when they come together as equals, work toward a common goal, and see themselves as members of the same "team"—they are more apt to accept and possibly even *value* one another's differences (Dovidio & Gaertner, 1999; Oskamp, 2000; Ramsey, 1995). Such interactions can sometimes occur within the context of planned classroom activities; for example, we can hold classroom discussions in which students describe the traditions, conventions, and perceptions of their own ethnic or racial groups (K. Schultz, Buck, & Niesz, 2000). We can also promote friendships among students of diverse ethinic backgrounds by using some of the strategies identified in Chapter 3—for instance, by using cooperative learning activities, teaching the rudiments of one another's native languages, and encouraging schoolwide participation in extracurricular activities. By learning to appreciate the multicultural differences within a single classroom, students take an important first step toward appreciating the multicultural nature of the world at large (Casanova, 1987; Craft, 1984; Pettigrew & Pajonas, 1973).

Not all schools have a culturally diverse population, of course. In such situations we may have to take students, either physically or vicariously, beyond school boundaries. For example, we can engage them in community action projects that provide services to particular ethnic groups—perhaps in preschools, nursing homes, or city cultural centers. Or we can initiate a "sister schools program" in which students from two ethnically different communities regularly communicate through the mail or the Internet, possibly exchanging news, stories, photographs, art projects, and various artifacts from the local environment (Koeppel & Mulrooney, 1992).

FIGURE 4.3
In an essay for his American history class, 16-year-old Randy reveals his appreciation for cultural differences.

> To me, diversity is not only a fact of life, but it is life. To be different and unique is what allows people to live a fulfilling life. To learn and admire other people's differences is perhaps one of the keys to life and without that key, there will be too many doors that will be locked, keeping you out and not allowing you to succeed. To learn that a majority of one kind in one place may be a minority of another kind in another place can help to initiate an outlook on life that promotes perspective and reason of any situation.

Fostering Democratic Ideals

Ultimately, any multicultural education program must include such democratic ideals as human dignity, equality, justice, and appreciation of diverse viewpoints (NCSS Task Force on Ethnic Studies Curriculum Guidelines, 1992; Sleeter & Grant, 1999). We better prepare students to function effectively in a democratic society when we help them understand that virtually any nation includes numerous cultures and that such diversity provides a richness of ideas and perspectives that will inevitably yield a more creative, productive society overall. The student writing sample presented in Figure 4.3 illustrates such understanding.

Teaching respect for diverse perspectives does not necessarily mean that we accept all beliefs as equally acceptable; for instance, we should certainly not embrace a culture that blatantly violates some people's basic human rights. It does mean, however, that we and our students should try to understand another cultural group's behaviors within the context of that culture's beliefs and assumptions.

A democracy involves **equity**—freedom from bias or favoritism—as well as equality. To help students achieve maximal classroom success, we must be equitable in our treatment of them; in other words, we must tailor instruction to meet the unique characteristics of each and every one. The Into the Classroom feature "Creating a Multicultural Classroom" illustrates some ways of doing so.

The notion of equitable treatment applies not only to students of diverse ethnic backgrounds but also to both boys and girls. We now consider how boys and girls are apt to be different and how we can help students of both genders work and learn effectively in the classroom.

GENDER DIFFERENCES

What gender differences[3] did you notice among your classmates when you were in elementary school? when you were in high school? What differences do you see now that you are taking college classes?

■ **equity (in instruction)** Instruction without favoritism or bias toward particular individuals or groups of students.

_____

[3] Some theorists suggest that we use the term *sex differences* for those differences based on biology (e.g., Halpern, 1992). However, *gender differences* is becoming increasingly common as a generic term for all male-female differences, hence my use of it throughout the discussion.

Creating a Multicultural Classroom

 Educate yourself about the cultures in which students have been raised.

A teacher accepts an invitation to have dinner with several of his students and their families, all of whom are dining together one evening at one family's home on the Navajo Nation in western New Mexico. During his visit the teacher discovers why his students are always interrupting one another and completing one another's sentences: Their parents converse with one another in a similar manner (Jackson & Ormrod, 1998).

 Build on students' background experiences.

A language arts teacher asks a classroom of inner-city African American students to vote on their favorite rap song. She puts the words to the song on an overhead transparency and asks students to translate each line for her. In doing so, she shows students how their local dialect and Standard English are interrelated, and she gives them a sense of pride in being bilingual (Ladson-Billings, 1994a).

 Use curriculum materials that represent all ethnic groups in a positive and competent light.

A history teacher peruses a history textbook to make sure that it portrays members of all ethnic groups in a nonstereotypical manner. He supplements the text with readings that highlight the important roles that members of various ethnic groups have played in history.

 Expose students to successful models from various ethnic backgrounds.

A teacher invites several successful professionals from minority groups to speak with her class about their careers. When some students seem especially interested in one or more of these careers, she arranges for the students to spend time with the professionals in their workplaces.

 Provide opportunities for students of different backgrounds to get to know one another better.

For a cooperative learning activity, a teacher forms groups that integrate students from various neighborhoods and ethnic groups.

In their academic abilities, boys and girls are probably more similar than you think. But in other respects they may be more different than you realize. In the following sections, we examine similarities and differences in physical activity and motor skills, cognitive and academic abilities, achievement motivation, sense of self, interpersonal behavior and relationships, classroom behavior, and career aspirations.

Physical activity and motor skills. Boys are temperamentally predisposed to be more active than girls. Thus, they have more trouble sitting still for long periods, are less likely to enjoy reading (a decidedly sedentary activity), and are more apt to pose classroom discipline problems (W. D. Eaton & Enns, 1986; B. A. Freedman, 2003; J. D. Nichols, Ludwin, & Iadicola, 1999; Sadker & Sadker, 1994). Before puberty boys and girls seem to have similar *potential* for physical and motor growth, although girls have a slight edge in fine motor skills (e.g., writing numbers and letters). Overall, boys develop their physical and motor skills more, perhaps through participation in organized sports. After puberty boys have a biological advantage in height (they're taller) and muscular strength (because of increased testosterone levels, they're stronger) (M. C. Linn & Hyde, 1989; J. R. Thomas & French, 1985).

Such differences are hardly justification for favoring either gender when enhancing students' physical fitness, of course. Physical education curricula and sports programs should provide equal opportunities for boys and girls to maximize their physical well-being and athletic skills.

Cognitive and academic abilities. On average, boys and girls perform similarly on tests of general intelligence, in part because people who construct the tests eliminate items that favor one group or the other (Halpern & LaMay, 2000). Researchers do find differences in more specific cognitive abilities, with girls showing slightly higher verbal ability and boys showing slightly higher visual-spatial ability (Halpern & LaMay, 2000; Lippa, 2002). As previously noted, such differences tend to be quite small, with considerable overlap between the two groups (e.g., see Figure 4.1). At the same time, boys often show greater *variability* in cognitive abilities than girls, such that more boys than girls appear at the extreme upper and lower ends of the population (Feingold, 1992; Halpern & LaMay, 2000; Hedges & Nowell, 1995).

Although ability levels may be similar, girls consistently earn higher grades in school (Halpern & LaMay, 2000; Wigfield et al., 1996). If achievement is measured by achievement tests rather than grades, research findings are inconsistent. When differences are found, boys typically have an advantage in mathematical problem solving (after puberty) and girls tend to have the upper hand in reading and writing (Halpern & LaMay, 2000; Hedges & Nowell, 1995; Penner, 2003).

Boys tend to develop their physical skills more than girls, often through organized sports. When a second-grade teacher asked her students to create self-portraits, 8-year-old Andrew "dressed" himself as a basketball player.

We must assure girls that they have just as much potential for mastering such subjects as mathematics and science as boys do.

We should note here that not only are gender differences in verbal, visual-spatial, and mathematical performance quite small, but some researchers have found them to be getting *smaller* in recent years. In other words, boys and girls are becoming increasingly similar in their academic performance (Eisenberg et al., 1996; Gustafsson & Undheim, 1996). For all intents and purposes, we should expect boys and girls to have similar academic aptitudes for different subject areas.

Achievement motivation. On average, girls are more concerned about doing well in school: They are more engaged in classroom activities, work harder on school assignments, and are more likely to graduate from high school (Halpern, 1992; H. M. Marks, 2000; McCall, 1994). Furthermore, girls are more interested in getting a college education than boys are (Binns, Steinberg, Amorosi, & Cuevas, 1997). Yet girls' eagerness to achieve academically leads them to prefer tasks at which they know they can succeed, and some find failure devastating. Boys are more willing to take on academic challenges and risks, and they typically take their failures in stride (Dweck, 2000; Yu, Elder, & Urdan, 1995). In Chapter 12 we'll identify strategies for encouraging students to take on challenges and risks in academic subject matter.

By the time students reach high school, course selection patterns reveal gender differences in preferences for academic subject areas. Especially when choosing advanced classes, boys are more likely to enroll in mathematics and physical science classes, whereas girls choose language and literature (Davenport et al., 1998; Wigfield et al., 1996). To some degree, such preferences probably reflect gender differences in students' sense of self, the gender difference we consider next.

Sense of self. Beginning in the upper elementary or middle school grades, boys have a higher overall sense of self-worth than girls. This gender difference appears to be due to boys' tendency to *over*estimate their abilities and possibly also to girls' tendency to *under*estimate theirs (Bornholt, Goodnow, & Cooney, 1994; D. A. Cole, Martin, Peeke, Seroczynski, & Fier, 1999; Harter, 1999; Pajares & Valiante, 1999).

Additional gender differences exist in the specific areas of strength and weakness that students perceive in themselves (Binns et al., 1997; Block, 1983; D. A. Cole et al., 2001). On average, boys see themselves as being better athletes, and they have greater self-confidence in their ability to control the world and solve problems. Girls are more apt to judge themselves as being well behaved in school and competent in social relationships: They tend to perceive themselves as considerate and sensitive individuals who work well with others. Beginning at puberty, girls rate their physical appearance less favorably than boys do, and they are more preoccupied with how they look (reflecting the *imaginary audience* phenomenon described in Chapter 3) (D. A. Cole et al., 2001; Harter, 1999; R. M. Ryan & Kuczkowski, 1994).

Both boys and girls tend to rate themselves higher in academic areas that are stereotypically "appropriate" for their gender (Eccles et al., 1998; Herbert, et al., 2003; Marsh, 1989). Especially in mathematics and science—stereotypically masculine domains—boys evaluate themselves more highly than girls do, even when no true differences in achievement exist (Eccles, 1989; Herbert et al., 2003; E. Rowe, 1999).

Girls' relative lack of self-confidence in math and science is probably one reason that girls ultimately take fewer advanced classes in these subjects than boys do (Fennema, 1987; Kahle & Lakes, 1983; M. C. Linn & Hyde, 1989). Unfortunately, by not choosing to enroll in such courses, girls are eliminating many options for themselves. Careers in engineering, computer science, and business management all require skills in mathematics. If we want to help girls keep their options open, we must convince them that they have considerable potential for mastering math and science. But as we discovered in Chapter 3, we are most likely to raise their self-confidence if we also help them achieve continuing success in these subjects.

Interpersonal behavior and relationships. Boys and girls interact with peers in distinctly different ways. One of the most consistently observed gender differences involves aggression. Boys are more physically aggressive than girls in early childhood and throughout the elementary and secondary school years (Lippa, 2002; Loeber & Stouthamer-Loeber, 1998). This gender difference is especially large for *unprovoked* aggression; for example, boys are more apt to bully their peers for no apparent reason (Lippa, 2002; Pellegrini, 2002).

Boys' more aggressive nature often shows up in their fantasy play and fiction, as in this story by 7-year-old Grant. (His teacher has corrected some of his misspellings.)

However, girls can be equally aggressive in a nonphysical way. As noted in Chapter 3, they are more apt to engage in *relational aggression*, behavior that adversely affects interpersonal relationships, such as spreading rumors or snubbing peers (Crick et al., 2002; D. C. French et al., 2002).

Boys' and girls' playgroups and friendships are different as well. Boys tend to hang out in relatively large groups that engage in rough-and-tumble play, organized group games, and physical risk-taking activities (Maccoby, 2002; Pellegrini, Kato, Blatchford, & Baines, 2002). They enjoy competition and can be fairly assertive in their efforts to achieve individual and group goals (Benenson et al., 2002; Eisenberg et al., 1996; Maccoby, 2002). Especially as they get older, they prefer keeping some personal space between themselves and their friends (in some cases as a way of affirming their heterosexuality), and they may often try to hide their true emotions in social situations (Eisenberg et al., 1996; Lippa, 2002; K. M. Williams, 2001a). For instance, in the "Emotions: Late Adolescence" clip on Video CD 1, 15-year-old Greg responds to the question, "What are some things that kids do when they're sad?" by saying, "Cry . . . if you're a guy, you don't show it."

Whereas boys tend to be competitive, girls are more affiliative and cooperative. Girls seem to be more attuned to others' mental states and more sensitive to the subtle, nonverbal messages—the body language—that others communicate (Bosacki, 2000; Deaux, 1984). They spend much of their leisure time with one or two close friends, with whom they may share their innermost thoughts and feelings (Block, 1983; Eisenberg et al., 1996; A. J. Rose, 2002). They tend to be concerned about maintaining group harmony, and so they may subordinate their own wishes to those of others (Benenson et al., 2002; Maccoby, 2002). In the three "Friendships" clips on Video CD 1, notice how 8-year-old Kate talks about compromise and working out conflicts with friends, whereas 13-year-old Ryan and 17-year-old Paul are more apt to deal with conflict by "just forget[ting] about it." In fact, Paul specifically mentions a gender difference in conflict resolution strategies:

> Normally with, like, my guy friends, we just get over it. There's no working it out, you just sit . . . like, "Fine, whatever," you know? And we get over it. Girlfriends, you gotta talk to them and work it out slowly. Apologize for doing whatever you did wrong. There's a whole process.

To accommodate girls' affiliative nature, we should provide numerous opportunities for cooperative group work and frequent interaction with classmates. And most girls will achieve at higher levels if we minimize, and ideally eliminate, competitive activities (Inglehart, Brown, & Vida, 1994).

Classroom behavior. On average, boys are more active participants in class (Altermatt, Jovanovic, & Perry, 1998; Sadker & Sadker, 1994). They talk more and ask more questions, sometimes without waiting to be called on. They also tend to dominate small-group discussions and work sessions. Girls are more reticent classroom participants. They are less likely to publicly volunteer ideas and ask questions, perhaps for fear of looking stupid or perhaps because they worry that looking too smart will reduce their popularity (Jovanovic & King, 1998; Sadker & Sadker, 1994; Théberge, 1994). If they do have something to say, they typically wait until they are called on (Sadker & Sadker, 1994).

When boys and girls are asked to work together, boys take a more active role than girls, and they often ignore girls' ideas and requests (Eccles, 1989; Harter, 1999; Jovanovic & King, 1998; Kahle & Lakes, 1983). When paired in a science lab, boys handle the equipment and perform experiments while girls watch or take notes. When paired in a computer lab, boys work on the computers while girls sit back and observe (Arenz & Lee, 1990). Thus, it may sometimes be beneficial to group girls with girls, and boys with boys, to ensure that girls participate actively in classroom activities (Kahle & Lakes, 1983; MacLean, Sasse, Keating, Stewart, & Miller, 1995). Girls are more likely to express their opinions in small-group discussions (Théberge, 1994). They are also more apt to assume the role of leader in same-sex groups and, in the process, to develop valuable leadership skills (Fennema, 1987).

Career aspirations. Even preschoolers are aware that men and women tend to hold different kinds of jobs (e.g., doctors and police officers are usually men, nurses and secretaries are usually women). By the time they begin elementary school, children have formed definite stereotypes about the careers that are appropriate for males and females, and these gender stereotypes influence their own career aspirations (Deaux, 1984; A. Kelly & Smail, 1986; Liben, Bigler, & Krogh, 2002). As they move into the high school grades, students are more likely to recognize that both

■ Observe Greg's belief that boys hide their emotions in the "Emotions: Late Adolescence" clip on Video CD 1.

■ Observe gender differences in conflict resolution strategies in the three "Friendships" clips on Video CD 1.

TABLE 4.1

Gender-Related Characteristics at Different Grade Levels

GRADE LEVEL	AGE-TYPICAL CHARACTERISTICS	SUGGESTED STRATEGIES
K–2	• Physical abilities, general intelligence, and more specific cognitive abilities roughly equivalent for boys and girls • Recognition that gender remains constant despite changes in dress, hairstyle, and so on • Rigid stereotypes about "gender-appropriate" behavior; eagerness to conform to these stereotypes • Play groups largely segregated by gender • Different themes in fantasy play (e.g., boys depict heroism, girls depict romance) • Play activities more active and forceful for boys than for girls; less awareness in boys that some activities are potentially dangerous	• Foster athletic skills equally in boys and girls. • Expect and encourage equal achievement in all areas of the academic curriculum. • Provide materials for a wide range of play activities (e.g., household items, dress-up clothes, toy trucks, building blocks, balls). • Monitor students' play activities for potentially dangerous behaviors; provide guidance about what actions are and are not safe.
3–5	• Emergence of gender differences in self-evaluations of math ability, with boys rating themselves more highly than girls despite equal math achievement • Play groups largely segregated by gender • Organized group games more common for boys than for girls • More competition, aggression, and risk taking in boys than in girls • Onset of puberty earlier for girls (average age 10)	• Assure students that boys and girls have equal potential in all areas of the academic curriculum. • Provide materials for group games (balls, bats, soccer goal nets, etc.). • Set and enforce reasonable limits on play behaviors so that students' physical safety is ensured. • Be especially sensitive and supportive as girls show signs of puberty (e.g., allow trips to the restroom as needed).
6–8	• Onset of puberty later for boys (average age 11½) • Greater physical ability, as well as more participation in sports, for boys than for girls; participation in sports more prestigious for boys • Emergence of gender differences in visual-spatial ability, with boys being higher • Emergence of gender differences in overall self-esteem and assessments of physical attractiveness and athletic competence, with boys' self-ratings higher than girls'; preoccupation with appearance greater in girls • Increasing flexibility about what behaviors are "gender-appropriate," especially for girls • Tendency for boys' social groups to be larger and less intimate than girls' • Increasing social interaction between boys and girls	• Respect students' modesty and need for privacy when they must change clothes or take a shower in physical education or after-school sports. • Encourage both boys and girls to pursue extracurricular sports activities; encourage attendance at both boys' and girls' games. • Use concrete objects to facilitate visual-spatial understandings in math and science. • Compliment students (especially girls) when they have performed well or taken great pains to enhance their physical appearance.
9–12	• Gradual improvement in girls' self-assessments of physical attractiveness • Gender differences in course selection, with boys more likely to enroll in advanced math and science and girls more likely to enroll in language and literature • Greater interest in a college education for girls than for boys • Tendency for boys to aspire more to "hands-on" professions (e.g., work with tools and machines) and for girls to aspire more to social or artistic occupations (e.g., teaching, counseling, writing) • Prosocial behavior seen more frequently in girls than in boys, despite equal ability to act prosocially • More positive attitudes about casual sexual intercourse, as well as earlier sexual experiences, for boys than for girls • More substance abuse (alcohol, drugs) for boys than girls • Depression and eating disorders more common in girls than in boys	• Encourage students to cross stereotypical "boundaries" in course selection (e.g., encourage girls to take advanced math, encourage boys to take creative writing). • Provide information about the benefits of a college education (e.g., ask school alumni to come talk with students about their college experiences). • Expose students to diverse occupations and professions (through guest lectures, trips to community businesses and agencies, etc.). • Encourage and acknowledge prosocial behavior in both boys and girls. • Work with colleagues and parents to vigorously address unhealthful and risky out-of-school behaviors. • Alert the school counselor when you suspect substance abuse, serious depression, an eating disorder, or some other potentially life-threatening condition.

Sources: Benenson & Christakos, 2003; Binns et al., 1997; Bussey & Bandura, 1992; D. A. Cole et al., 2001; Davenport et al., 1998; Eisenberg et al., 1996; Fabes, Martin, & Hanish, 2003; M. E. Ford, 1996; Hardy, 2002; J. R. Harris, 1995; Harter, 1999; Hegarty & Kozhevnikov; 1999; Herbert et al., 2003; Liben & Bigler, 2002; Lippa, 2002; Maccoby, 2002; McDevitt & Ormrod, 2004; Rogoff, 2003; R. M. Ryan & Kuczkowski, 1994; Sadker & Sadker, 1994; Stein & Reichert, 1990; J. R. Thomas & French, 1985; Trautner, 1992; Wigfield et al., 1996.

males and females can hold virtually any job; nevertheless, most continue to aspire to careers consistent with gender stereotypes (Bandura, Barbaranelli, Caprara, & Pastorelli, 2001; Lippa, 2002).

Some gender differences are especially prevalent for particular age-groups. Table 4.1 identifies differences you are apt to see at various grade levels and offers relevant classroom strategies.

Origins of Gender Differences

Theorists speculate that several factors contribute to gender differences. Inherited characteristics and tendencies play a substantial role in some differences, whereas environmental factors are probably more responsible for others. In many cases biology (heredity) and experience (environment) interact and build on one another, thereby amplifying each other's effects (Lippa, 2002). Let's take a simple example. As we discovered earlier, adolescent boys tend to be stronger than adolescent girls, courtesy of biology and, in particular, higher testosterone levels. As a result, boys are better able to play certain sports (e.g., American football) and to carry out certain kinds of manual labor (e.g., auto repair). As they engage in such activities, they increase their strength; thus, practice enhances their biological advantage. Furthermore, as members of society see boys more often engaging in these activities, they begin to think of the activities as being "for males." Society conveys these stereotypes to successive generations in a variety of ways—through household chore assignments, career advice, roles played by males and females in television and film, and so on—and such environmental factors further entice boys into, and encourage girls to steer clear of, the activities.

In the next few pages, we'll look at specific ways in which biology and socialization experiences seem to influence the development of gender differences. We'll then focus in on two specific school-related factors that play a role—peer behaviors and teacher behaviors—and also see how children themselves contribute to gender differences through self-socialization.

Role of Biology   Obviously, heredity determines physiological differences (some present at birth, some emerging at puberty) between males and females. Because of heredity, too, girls reach puberty earlier and boys eventually become taller and stronger. Underlying such differences are different levels of gender-related hormones, especially estrogen for girls and testosterone for boys.

Hormones may account for some nonphysiological gender differences as well. The gender difference in physical aggression almost certainly has a biological basis: It is seen across cultures and across species, and in humans it appears to be related to testosterone levels (Lippa, 2002). Furthermore, hormones may play a role in the small differences observed in visual-spatial and verbal abilities, possibly by affecting neurological development in different areas of the brain (Lippa, 2002; O'Boyle & Gill, 1998; H. Thomas & Kail, 1991). Hormones even influence children's preferences for male-stereotypical and female-stereotypical behaviors; for instance, girls who were exposed to unusually high levels of testosterone during their mothers' pregnancies tend to prefer "boy" toys and activities (Hines et al., 2002; Lippa, 2002).

Socialization   On the environmental side of the equation, virtually every culture teaches children that some behaviors are more appropriate for males and others more appropriate for females (Fuller, 2001). As an example, try the following exercise.

Experiencing FIRSTHAND ·Picture This #2

Form a picture in your mind of each of the following individuals. Focus on the *first* image that comes to mind in each case.

Secretary	Scientist
Bank president	Fashion model
Elementary school teacher	Building contractor

Now answer this question: Which individuals did you picture as male, and which did you picture as female?

· · · · · · ·

If you are like most people, your bank president, scientist, and building contractor were males, and your secretary, teacher, and fashion model were females. Gender stereotypes—rigid ideas about how males and females "typically" behave—persist throughout our society, and even preschool children are aware of them (Bornholt et al., 1994; Eisenberg et al., 1996).

■ Are the gender differences just described consistent with your own observations? If not, can you resolve the discrepancies?

■ What environmental factors are different for boys and girls? Before you read on, generate a list based on your own experiences.

Many aspects of society conspire to teach growing children to conform to gender stereotypes. For example, research consistently indicates that parents treat their sons and daughters differently. Parents keep a more watchful eye on their daughters and respond more frequently to their daughters' requests for help; they allow their sons to wander farther from home and expect them to solve problems independently (Rogoff, 2003; Ruble, 1988; Sprafkin et al., 1983). Many parents encourage gender-typical play activities, which may foster some skills over others (Frost, Shin, & Jacobs, 1998; Liss, 1983; Lytton & Romney, 1991). For instance, girls get dolls and stuffed animals, and they play "house" and board games—toys and activities that foster the development of verbal and social skills. Boys get blocks, model airplanes, and science equipment, and they play football, basketball, and video games—toys and activities that foster greater development of visual-spatial skills. Boys are often reinforced for aggressive behavior and athletic accomplishments, whereas girls are reinforced for being nurturant and ladylike (Block, 1983; Erdley, Qualey, & Pietrucha, 1996; Fagot, Hagan, Leinbach, & Kronsberg, 1985; J. R. Thomas & French, 1985). Even parents who try hard to treat their sons and daughters equally are susceptible to gender stereotypes, as the following autobiographical essay from one of my students reveals:

> My parents have always made an extra effort to expose their three children to both male and female gender characteristics, hoping to break the familiar "male" and "female" molds cast on society. In fact, my sister Lisa and I received trucks and footballs and were expected to mow the lawn and take out the garbage. Likewise, my brother Craig received dolls and fingernail polish and was expected to wash the dishes and clean the house. But Lisa's and my trucks were pink and our footballs were purple, and when Craig was old enough we did not do any more lawn work. Likewise, my brother was discouraged from taking his doll outside the house and was told to take his fingernail polish off when we went out. Mom always had Lisa and me do the dishes and clean the house because we were faster. (courtesy of Kim Sandman)

In addition, many parents believe that their sons and daughters have different strengths, and these beliefs can influence what children believe about themselves. Consistent with common stereotypes, many parents believe that boys are "naturally" better at math and girls are "naturally" better at reading, even in cases where no gender differences in achievement exist (Eccles et al., 1993; Herbert et al., 2003).

Society at large, including the media, also influences the development of stereotypes, in part by providing adult models who demonstrate very different behaviors for males and females. Children more often see women, rather than men, reading (B. A. Freedman, 2003). Males appear far more often than females in history and science textbooks (Eisenberg et al., 1996; Sadker, Sadker, & Klein, 1991). Movies, television programs, and books often portray males and females in gender-stereotypical ways: Males are aggressive leaders and successful problem solvers, whereas females are domestic, demure, and obedient followers (Furnham & Mak, 1999; Huston et al., 1992; Sadker & Sadker, 1994; T. L. Thompson & Zerbinos, 1995). With such consistent messages, many children must easily conclude that males are the true "movers and shakers" that have an impact on the world.

As teachers, we must make a concerted effort to develop and select curriculum materials that represent both genders in a positive and competent light. Nonsexist materials reduce gender stereotypes when students are exposed to them on a continual and consistent basis (Fennema, 1987; Horgan, 1995; Sadker & Miller, 1982).

Peer Behaviors   Children's playmates and classmates frequently encourage adherence to traditional gender stereotypes. Peers tend to respond more positively to children who play in "gender-appropriate" ways and more negatively to those who do not, with such responses being especially common in boys (Bussey & Bandura, 1992; Eisenberg et al., 1996; Fagot, 1985). Peers may also ridicule or avoid age-mates who enroll and excel in "gender-inappropriate" subjects, such as high school girls who excel in science and mathematics (Casserly, 1980; Sadker & Sadker, 1994; Schubert, 1986). As a result, many students engage in counterstereotypical activities only when success in such activities can be hidden from their classmates (Eccles, 1989; Huston, 1983; Ruble, 1988). As teachers, we can do a great deal to keep student achievement out of the public eye—for example, by keeping grades confidential and perhaps by allowing

■ There are also legal reasons for keeping grades confidential (see Chapter 16).

[handwritten margin note: That's why "Star Trek" & like "Star Trek" they don't.]

students to demonstrate their achievement through written assignments rather than through oral responses to in-class questions.

Boys and girls may also acquire different behaviors depending on the types of groups in which they interact and play (Benenson et al., 2002; Maccoby, 2002). As previously noted, boys tend to congregate in larger groups than girls do. In large groups children must be fairly assertive and possibly more competitive ("boy" traits) to satisfy their goals and desires. In pairs and threesomes, however, children can often meet their own needs through collaboration and compromise ("girl" traits).

Teacher Behaviors   A greater awareness of gender differences in recent years has led to concern among many teachers about treating their male and female students equitably. Even so, subtle differences in the treatment of boys and girls continue (Altermatt et al., 1998; Eisenberg et al., 1996; Sadker & Sadker, 1994). For instance, teachers tend to give more attention to boys, partly because boys ask more questions and present more discipline problems. Teachers also give boys more feedback (praise and criticism alike) than they give girls.

In most cases teachers are probably unaware that they discriminate between boys and girls as much as they do. The first step toward ensuring more equitable treatment of males and females is to become aware of existing inequities. Then we can try to correct those inequities—for example, by interacting frequently with *all* of our students, giving them the kinds of feedback they need to improve their performance, and having equivalent expectations for achievement in stereotypically male and female subject areas.

Self-Socialization   As young children become increasingly aware of the typical characteristics and behaviors of boys, girls, men, and women, they begin to pull their knowledge together into self-constructed understandings, or **gender schemas**, of "what males are like" and "what females are like." These gender schemas, in turn, become part of their sense of self and provide guidance for how they themselves should behave—how they should dress, what toys they should play with, what interests and academic subject areas they should pursue, and so on. By the time they reach school age, some of the pressure to act "appropriately" for their gender comes from within rather than from others (Bem, 1981; Bussey & Bandura, 1992; C. L. Martin, 2000; C. Martin & Halverson, 1987). For instance, when teachers actively encourage children to engage in nongender-stereotypical activities, the children may do so for a short time, but they soon revert to their former, gender-typical ways (Lippa, 2002). And when researchers tell female students that a particular math test is something on which men usually outscore women, the students perform at lower levels than they would otherwise—a phenomenon known as *stereotype threat* (Spencer, Steele, & Quinn, 1999).

■ We'll learn more about stereotype threat in Chapter 11.

Because gender schemas are self-constructed, their contents may vary considerably from one individual to another (Liben & Bigler, 2002). In adolescence, for example, some girls incorporate into their "female" schema the unrealistic standards for beauty presented in popular media (films, fashion magazines, etc.). As they compare themselves to these standards, they almost invariably come up short and so, as we discovered earlier, their self-assessments of their physical attractiveness decline. In an effort to achieve the super-thin body they believe to be ideal, they may fall victim to eating disorders (Attie, Brooks-Gunn, & Petersen, 1990). Likewise, some teenage boys go out of their way to meet self-constructed "macho" standards for male behavior by putting on a tough-guy act at school and bragging (perhaps accurately, but more often not) about their many sexual conquests (K. M. Williams, 2001a).

Not all students have rigid stereotypes of what their gender should be like, and those with more flexible views are more apt to pursue counterstereotypical interests and career paths (Liben & Bigler, 2002). In the following exercise, we look at one middle school student's beliefs about what it means to be female.

■ **gender schema** Self-constructed, organized body of beliefs about the traits and behaviors of males or females.

Interpreting Student Artifacts and Behaviors

Which Is Easier—Being a Girl or a Boy?
In her language arts class, 13-year-old Trish wrote a response to the statement "It's easier to be a girl than boy." As you read her composition at the top of the following page, consider

■ What types of gender differences she focuses on
■ Whether her gender schema incorporates rigid stereotypes about girls

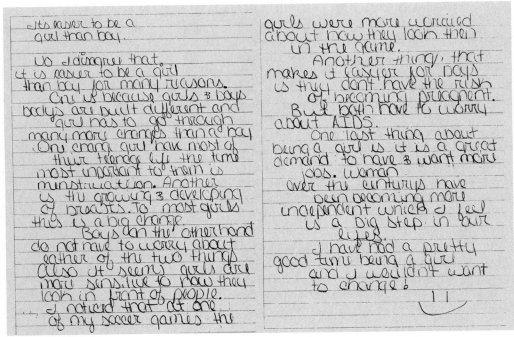

It's easier to be a girl than boy.

I disagree that, it is easier to be a girl than boy. for many reasons. One is because girls & boys bodys are built different and a girl has to go through many more changes than a boy. One change girl have most of their teenage life the time most important to them is menstruation. Another is the growing & developing of breasts. To most girls this is a big change. Boys on the otherhand do not have to worry about eather of the two things. Also it seems girls are more sensitive to how they look in front of people. I noticed that at one of my soccer games the

girls were more worried about how they look then in the game.
Another thing, that makes it easier for boys is they don't have the risk of becoming pregnent. But both have to worry about AIDS.
One last thing about being a girl is it is a great demand to have & want more jobs. Woman over the centurys have been becoming more independent which I feel is a big step in our lifes.
I have had a pretty good time being a girl and I wouldn't want to change.

A good deal of Trish's discussion focuses on physical differences, especially those differences that appear at puberty. She has recently gone through puberty herself, and she is certain that girls undergo more changes than boys (male readers would almost certainly disagree!). Trish has also picked up on something we noted earlier: Girls are more concerned about their appearance than boys are. (This insight shows *perspective taking*, an important ingredient for successful social relationships; see Chapter 3.) Her comment about jobs ("it is a great demand to have & want more jobs") is difficult to interpret, but her approval of women's increasing independence suggests that she does not hold rigidly to stereotypical female roles.

Ultimately, we must help all of our students recognize that gender stereotypes are just that—*stereotypes*—and do not necessarily reflect most people's expectations for what males and females can or should be. We can do this in a variety of ways, including the following:

- Expose students to many adults who exhibit counterstereotypical behaviors.
- Talk with students about the importance of all academic content areas for their future success.
- Help students understand that knowledge of stereotypes does not require *endorsement* of them.
- Explain the historical roots of stereotypes—for instance, that different expectations for males and females are a holdover from days when cooking and housework were quite time-consuming.
- Engage students in discussion about the negative consequences of rigid stereotypes for society as a whole, noting, for instance, that adhering to such roles causes a great deal of talent to go to waste. (Bem, 1983, 1984; Fennema, 1987; A. Kelly & Smail, 1986)

In the preceding sections we have considered numerous strategies for treating male and female students equitably; the Into the Classroom feature "Promoting Gender Equity" offers additional ideas. Yet equity must be extended to students of different socioeconomic circumstances as well. We now look at characteristics that students from lower-income families, including those growing up in true poverty, may have, as well as at strategies for helping these students achieve classroom success.

SOCIOECONOMIC DIFFERENCES

The concept of **socioeconomic status** (often abbreviated as **SES**) encompasses a number of variables, including family income, parents' occupations, and parents' education levels. A family's socioeconomic status—whether high-SES, middle-SES, or low-SES—gives us a sense of their standing in the community: how much flexibility they have in where they live and what they buy, how much influence they have on political decision making, what educational opportunities they can offer their children, and so on. When I have spoken of "low-income" or "middle-income" students and families in previous chapters, I have essentially been talking about socioeconomic status.

Students' school performance is correlated with their socioeconomic status: Higher-SES students tend to have higher academic achievement, and lower-SES students tend to be at greater risk for dropping out of school (McLoyd, 1998; L. S. Miller, 1995; Portes, 1996; H. W. Stevenson, Chen, & Uttal, 1990). As students from lower-SES families move through the grade levels, they fall further and further behind their higher-SES peers (Jimerson, Egeland, & Teo, 1999).

■ **socioeconomic status (SES)** One's general social and economic standing in society (encompasses family income, occupation, and educational level).

Promoting Gender Equity

 Use your knowledge of typical gender differences to create greater equity for males and females, *not* to form expectations about how well males and females are apt to perform in various activities.

A physical education teacher realizes that most of the girls in her class have probably not had as much experience throwing overhand as the boys have, so she gives them basic instruction and extra practice in the overhand throw.

 Be on the lookout for gender stereotypes in textbooks. Counteract such biases with instructional materials that portray both genders in a counterstereotypical fashion.

An English teacher assigns Harper Lee's *To Kill a Mockingbird*, in which an attorney named Atticus Finch is portrayed as a gentle, affectionate, and compassionate man, and his daughter Scout is portrayed as a courageous and adventuresome 8-year-old. The teacher also assigns Zora Neale Hurston's *Their Eyes Were*

Watching God, in which an African American woman grows from a teenager dependent entirely on others to meet her needs into a self-sufficient woman who can easily fend for herself.

 Occasionally ask students to work together in single-sex pairs or groups.

A science teacher has students work in groups of three boys or three girls to conduct an assigned laboratory activity.

 Monitor yourself to see if you are unintentionally treating boys and girls differently.

A French teacher decides to count the number of times he calls on boys and girls during class. He finds that he calls on boys more than three times as frequently as girls, partly because the boys raise their hands more often. To combat his bad habit, he institutes a new procedure: He alternates between boys and girls when he calls on students, and he sometimes calls on students who are not raising their hands.

When researchers find achievement differences among students from different ethnic groups, the differences in the students' socioeconomic status, *not* their cultural differences per se, seem to be largely to blame (Byrnes, 2003; N. E. Hill, Bush, & Roosa, 2003; Murdock, 2000).

For some children, poverty is a short-term situation, brought on by divorce, temporary unemployment, fire or flood, or other unfortunate circumstances. For other children, it's an ongoing way of life. All in all, poverty is more common than you might think: In 1995 an alarming number of children in the United States, *one in every five*, were classified as poor (Hernandez, 1997; Lewit, Terman, & Behrman, 1997).

Low-SES students are a diverse group (Sidel, 1996). Many live in inner-city neighborhoods, others live in rural areas, and some live in modest apartments or homes in wealthy suburban towns. Some come from families who can meet life's basic necessities (e.g., food, warm clothes, and adequate shelter) but have little money left over for luxuries. Many others live in extreme poverty, and these are the ones most at risk for academic failure and so most in need of our attention and support.

In the following sections, we will look at risk factors associated with poverty and identify particular challenges that homeless students face. We will then discover that many students successfully rise above their impoverished circumstances and will find out how, as teachers, we can foster such *resilience*. We will also identify strengths we can build on when working with students from low-SES backgrounds.

Risk Factors Associated with Poverty

Several factors probably contribute to the generally lower school achievement of low-SES students. Students who face only one or two of the challenges listed here often do quite well in school, but those who face most or all of them are at high risk for academic failure (Grissmer, Williamson, Kirby, & Berends, 1998).

Poor nutrition. Some low-income families cannot afford regular, nutritional meals for their children. Poor nutrition in the early years of life is associated with lower IQ scores (see Chapter 5); it is also associated with poorer attention and memory and impaired learning ability (D' Amato, Chitooran, & Whitten, 1992; L. S. Miller, 1995). Poor nutrition can influence school achievement both directly—for instance, by hampering early brain development—and indirectly—for instance, by leaving children listless and inattentive in class (Byrnes, 2001; Sigman & Whaley, 1998; R. A. Thompson & Nelson, 2001). As teachers, we must take any necessary steps to ensure that our students are adequately fed; for instance, we can make sure that all eligible children have access to free and reduced-cost meal programs offered by our school districts.

Inadequate housing. Many poor children live in tight quarters, perhaps sharing only one or two rooms with other family members (Hawkins, 1997). In old, poorly maintained apartment buildings, they may be exposed to lead in the dust from deteriorating paint; ingesting lead can cause brain damage (Byrnes, 2001). In addition, if children move frequently from one rental apartment to another, they must often change schools as well. In the process, they lose existing social support networks and may miss lessons on important academic skills (J. R. Harris, 1998; Knutson & Mantzicopoulos, 1999).

Emotional stress. For reasons we will discover in Chapter 11, students learn and perform less effectively when they are highly anxious. Even wealthy students can experience considerable emotional stress, especially in adolescence (Luthar & Becker, 2002). But in general, students from poor families have more than their share (McLoyd, 1998). Perhaps as a result, students from low-SES families show higher-than-average rates of depression and other emotional problems (Caspi, Taylor, Moffitt, & Plomin, 2000; G. W. Evans & English, 2002; Seaton et al., 1999).

Obviously, economic difficulties are a source of stress; children may wonder where their next meal is coming from or how long it will be before the landlord evicts them for not paying the rent. The preponderance of single-parent homes among low-SES families is another source of anxiety; a single parent may be overwhelmed with worries about supporting the family (Scott-Jones, 1984). Not all poor children live in chronically stressful conditions, however, and those whose families provide consistent support, guidance, and discipline generally enjoy good mental health (N. E. Hill et al., 2003).

We must continually be on the lookout for signs that our students are undergoing unusual stress at home and provide whatever support we can for these students. In some instances such support may involve nothing more than being a willing listener. In other cases we may want to consult with a school district counselor or social worker about possible support systems at school and resources in the local community.

Gaps in background knowledge. Some students from low-SES families lack basic knowledge and skills (e.g., familiarity with letters and numbers) on which successful school learning so often depends (Case & Okamoto, 1996; Hauser-Cram, Sirin, & Stipek, 2003; McLoyd, 1998). Access to early educational opportunities that might develop such skills—books, educational toys, trips to zoos and museums, and so on—is always somewhat dependent on a family's financial resources. Furthermore, if parents are preoccupied with providing basic necessities such as food and clothing, they may have little time or energy to consider how they might promote their children's intellectual development. In addition, some parents have few literacy skills to share with their children (Portes, 1996). We must be careful not to overgeneralize, however: Some low-income parents have considerable education (sometimes college degrees) and are in other ways well-equipped to read to their children and provide other enriching educational experiences (Goldenberg, 2001; Sidel, 1996).

As teachers, it is essential that we identify and teach any missing basic skills in our students from low-income families. When we do so, we are likely to see significant improvements in students' classroom performance (S. A. Griffin, Case, & Capodilupo, 1995; McLoyd, 1998; G. Phillips, McNaughton, & MacDonald, 2004).

Less parental involvement in school activities and homework. The great majority of parents at all income levels want their children to get a good education (H. W. Stevenson et al., 1990). Some parents in lower-SES households are actively invested in their children's learning and education, and their children achieve at higher levels as a result (Jimerson et al., 1999). But others are less involved, for a variety of reasons. Economic factors may prevent some parents from attending meetings and activities at school; they may have difficulty getting off work, finding suitable child care, or arranging transportation (Finders & Lewis, 1994; Heymann & Earle, 2000; Salend & Taylor, 1993). Other parents may suffer from chronic depression or other mental illness, limiting their ability to support their children academically or otherwise (Brooks-Gunn, 2003; Mistry, Vandewater, Huston, & McLoyd, 2002; Petterson & Albers, 2001). Still others, because they have had only limited education themselves, may not be capable of helping their children with assigned schoolwork (Finders & Lewis, 1994). And a few parents may have had such bad experi-

■ You can learn more about the effects of early literacy experiences in the chapter "Learning in the Content Areas" in the *Study Guide and Reader.*

ences when they themselves were students that they feel uncomfortable in a school building (Finders & Lewis, 1994).

As teachers, we should be especially flexible about when and where we meet with the parents of lower-income students; we should also be especially conscientious about establishing comfortable, trusting relationships with them (Finders & Lewis, 1994; Salend & Taylor, 1993). Furthermore, we must realize that not all parents are in a position to support their children's academic progress, and in such instances we must work with colleagues and community agencies to find alternative support mechanisms. One effective strategy is to offer a structured after-school homework assistance program in which students get help on their assignments and acquire skills for keeping themselves on task and monitoring their own progress (Belfiore & Hornyak, 1998; Cosden, Morrison, Albanese, & Macias, 2001).

Visits to museums, zoos, aquariums, and other community resources provide firsthand experiences on which classroom instruction can build. Such trips may be especially beneficial for students from low-income families, who often don't have the financial resources to make such visits or their own.

Lower-quality schools. Unfortunately, students who are in most need of a good education are those least likely to have access to it. Schools in low-income neighborhoods and communities tend to receive less funding and, as a result, are often poorly equipped and in disrepair. Teacher turnover rates are high. Furthermore, some teachers at these schools have lower expectations for students—and so offer a less-challenging curriculum, assign less homework, and provide fewer opportunities to develop advanced thinking skills—than tends to be true for teachers in wealthier school districts (Becker & Luthar, 2002; Eccles et al., 1998; McLoyd, 1998; Portes, 1996).

Neighborhood influences. The neighborhoods in which children live can have a significant impact on their academic achievement and emotional well-being. Higher frequencies of community violence, greater prevalence of alcoholism and drug abuse, greater numbers of antisocial peers, less access to educational and social resources (libraries, recreation centers, etc.), fewer successful and prosocial adult models—all of these make growing up all the more challenging for children and adolescents in low-income neighborhoods (T. D. Cook, Herman, Phillips, & Settersten, 2002; J. R. Harris, 1998; Leventhal & Brooks-Gunn, 2000; R. J. Rose et al., 2003).

Public attitudes. Adults from economically advantaged backgrounds (including many teachers) often have mixed feelings toward students from low-SES families (K. L. Alexander, Entwisle, & Thompson, 1987; Chafel, 1997; McLoyd, 1998). Especially if these adults have limited knowledge of students' home circumstances, they may feel some empathy yet simultaneously believe that the students' families have only themselves to blame for their impoverished circumstances. Furthermore, in schools that serve economically diverse populations, students from low-income families are often rejected by their middle- and upper-SES classmates and so may have few opportunities to assume leadership roles or in other ways participate meaningfully in group activities (Knapp & Woolverton, 1995). Strategies described in Chapter 3 in the sections "Fostering Social Skills" and "Promoting Social Interaction Among Diverse Groups" should prove useful in helping students from low-income backgrounds forge new friendships and enhance their status at school.

Fewer resources to achieve long-term success. Students from low-SES backgrounds, especially girls, typically have lower aspirations for educational and career achievement (Knapp & Woolverton, 1995; S. M. Taylor, 1994). Their parents and teachers, too, may have low expectations for their long-term achievement (Bandura et al., 2001; McLoyd, 1998; Portes, 1996). As we will discover in Chapter 12, low teacher expectations can lead to a self-fulfilling prophecy: What teachers expect is what they actually see, in part because their expectations affect how they teach, interact with, and support students.

Even when students have high aspirations, they may have few resources—either external or internal—to achieve their goals. Not only are their financial resources limited, but they may also lack the knowledge and skills to keep themselves on track toward successful academic achievement. In one recent study (B. L. Wilson & Corbett, 2001), researchers interviewed middle school students in a low-income neighborhood in inner-city Philadelphia. Many of these students aspired to a professional career (doctor, lawyer, teacher, etc.) but were hardly on track toward their goal: They misbehaved in class, inconsistently completed homework, and often skipped school. They had an overly simplistic notion of what it would take to turn their lives around, as this interview with one boy reveals:

Student: I'm going to high school and college.
Adult: Think you will finish both?
Student: Yep.
Adult: What will it take?
Student: Good grades.
Adult: How are your grades now?
Student: They're bad, but I'm trying to pull them up.
Adult: Is that hard to do?
Student: I just haven't felt like doing it. (dialogue from B. L. Wilson & Corbett, 2001, p. 23)

Such naivete may be due, in part, to the fact that the student sees few academically diligent models (either adults or peers) at home or in the neighborhood. Yet it may also be partly the result of his inability to regulate his own behavior and motivation. Such *self-regulation* requires a number of skills that, even under the best of circumstances, develop only slowly over the course of childhood and adolescence.

Certainly we must encourage *all* of our students to aim high in their educational and professional goals. Yet we must also provide the extra support they need to achieve such goals; offering help sessions for challenging classroom material, finding low-cost academic enrichment programs available during the summer, and helping students fill out applications for college scholarships are just a few of the forms that such support might take. In addition, we can teach students many skills, both cognitive and motivational, that will enable them to take charge of their lives; we will discover ways of doing so in our discussions of self-regulation in Chapter 10.

Working with Homeless Students

Children of homeless families typically face far greater challenges than other students from low-SES families. Many have health problems, low self-esteem, a short attention span, poor language skills, and inappropriate behaviors (Coe, Salamon, & Molnar, 1991; McLoyd, 1998; Pawlas, 1994). Some may be reluctant to come to school because they lack bathing facilities and appropriate clothing (Gollnick & Chinn, 2002). And some may have moved so frequently from one school to another that there are large gaps in their academic skills (Pawlas, 1994).

As teachers, we, too, will face unusual challenges when teaching students who live in homeless shelters. Following are several suggestions for giving them the extra support they may need to achieve both academic and social success at school (Pawlas, 1994):

- Pair new students with classmates who can "show them the ropes"—for example, by explaining school procedures and making introductions to other students.
- Provide a notebook, clipboard, or other portable "desk" on which students can do their homework at the shelter.
- Find adult or teenage volunteers to serve as tutors at the shelter.
- Enlist the help of civic organizations to collect clothing and school supplies for the students.
- Meet with parents at the shelter rather than at school.
- Share copies of homework assignments, school calendars, and newsletters with shelter officials.

When we use such strategies, however, we must keep in mind that students and their families are apt to feel embarrassed about their homeless status. Accordingly, respect for their privacy must be a high priority.

Fostering Resilience

Fortunately, many students of low-income families succeed in school despite exceptional hardships (Humphreys, 1992; Nieto, 1995; B. Williams & Newcombe, 1994). Some are **resilient students:** They develop characteristics and coping skills that help them rise above their adverse circumstances. As a group, resilient students have likable personalities, positive self-concepts, strong motivation to succeed, and high yet realistic goals. They believe that success comes with

■ **resilient students** Students who succeed in school and in life despite exceptional hardships at home.

hard work, and their bad experiences serve as constant reminders of the importance of getting a good education (Masten & Coatsworth, 1998; McMillan & Reed, 1994; Werner, 1995; Werner & Smith, 2001).

Resilient students usually have one or more individuals in their lives whom they trust and can turn to in difficult times (Masten, 2001; McLoyd, 1998; Werner, 1995). Such individuals may be family members, neighbors, or school personnel; for example, resilient students often mention teachers who have taken a personal interest in them and have been instrumental in their school success (R. M. Clark, 1983; McMillan & Reed, 1994; D. A. O'Donnell, Schwab-Stone, & Muyeed, 2002). As teachers, we are most likely to promote resilience in low-SES students when we show that we like and respect them, are available and willing to listen to their views and concerns, hold high expectations for their performance, and provide the encouragement and support they need to succeed both inside and outside of the classroom (Masten & Coatsworth, 1998; McMillan & Reed, 1994; Werner, 1995).

Building on Students' Strengths

Although some students from lower-SES backgrounds lag behind their classmates in such basic academic skills as reading, writing, and computation, they bring other strengths to the classroom. For example, they are often more clever at improvising with everday objects (Torrance, 1995). If they work part-time to help their families make ends meet, they may have a good understanding of the working world. If they are children of single, working parents, they may know far more than their classmates about cooking, cleaning house, and taking care of younger siblings. If financial resources have been particularly scarce, they may know firsthand what it is like to be hungry for days at a time or to live in an unheated apartment in the winter; they may therefore have a special appreciation for basic human needs and true empathy for victims of war or famine around the world.

As teachers, then, we must remember that students who have grown up in poverty may, in some respects, have more knowledge and skills than their more economically advantaged peers. Such knowledge and skills can often provide a basis for teaching classroom subject matter. Furthermore, students who are willing to talk about the challenges they've faced can sensitize their classmates to the serious inequities that currently exist in our society. And in general, research gives us cause for optimism that our students from low-income backgrounds can achieve at high levels if we ourselves are committed to helping them do so and give them a strong academic program that supports their learning efforts (Becker & Luthar, 2002; Goldenberg, 2001; G. Phillips et al., 2004).

STUDENTS AT RISK

Do you remember classmates in elementary school who never seemed to complete in-class assignments or get their homework done? Do you remember classmates in high school who did poorly in most of their classes and rarely participated in extracurricular activities? How many of those students eventually graduated from high school? What are they doing now?

Students at risk are students with a high probability of failing to acquire the minimum academic skills necessary for success in the adult world. Many of them drop out before high school graduation; many others graduate without basic skills in reading or mathematics (Slavin, 1989). Such individuals are often ill equipped to make productive contributions to their families, communities, or society at large.

In the United States the percentage of high school graduates who go on to college has risen dramatically since 1970. Unfortunately, the percentage of students who drop out before earning high school diplomas has also risen considerably—from 24 percent in 1970 to 29 percent in 2000 (Carnoy, Elmore, & Siskin, 2003) Clearly, then, although many students are currently achieving at high levels in American schools, a great many others are falling by the wayside.

A common assumption is that the reasons for high dropout rates lie largely in students themselves (V. E. Lee & Burkam, 2003; U.S. Dept. of Education, 1992). But as we shall see, characteristics of *schools* also play a significant role. In the next few pages, we will discover reasons why so many students fail to thrive at school and identify strategies that can increase their chances for high school success and graduation.

■ **students at risk** Students who have a high probability of failing to acquire minimal academic skills necessary for success in the adult world.

Characteristics of Students at Risk

Some students at risk are those with identified special educational needs; for example, they may have learning disabilities or emotional and behavioral problems that interfere with learning and achievement. Others may be students whose cultural backgrounds don't mesh easily with the dominant culture at school. Still others may be students from home environments in which academic success is neither supported nor encouraged.

Students at risk come from all socioeconomic levels, but children of poor, single-parent families are especially likely to leave school before high school graduation. Boys are more likely to drop out than girls. African Americans, Hispanics, and Native Americans are more likely to drop out than European American and Asian American students. Students in large cities and rural areas are more likely to drop out than students in the suburbs. Students at greatest risk for dropping out are those whose families speak little or no English and whose own knowledge of English is also quite limited (Hardre & Reeve, 2003; L. S. Miller, 1995; Roderick & Camburn, 1999; Rumberger, 1995; L. Steinberg, Blinde, & Chan, 1984; U.S. Dept. of Education, 1997).

In addition, students at risk, especially those who eventually drop out, typically have some or all of the following characteristics:

- *A history of academic failure.* High school dropouts often have a history of poor academic achievement going back as far as third grade (K. L. Alexander, Entwisle, & Dauber, 1995; Garnier, Stein, & Jacobs, 1997). On average, they have less effective reading and study skills, earn lower grades, obtain lower achievement test scores, and are more likely to have repeated a grade level than their classmates who graduate (Battin-Pearson et al., 2000; Jozefowicz, Arbreton, Eccles, Barber, & Colarossi, 1994; Raber, 1990; L. Steinberg et al., 1984; Wilkinson & Frazer, 1990).

- *Older age in comparison with classmates.* Because low achievers are more likely to have repeated a grade level, they are often older than their classmates (Raber, 1990; Wilkinson & Frazer, 1990). Some (but not all) research studies find that students who are overage in comparison with classmates are those most likely to drop out of school (D. C. Gottfredson, Fink, & Graham, 1994; Roderick, 1994; Rumberger, 1995). Quite possibly, school becomes less attractive when students find they must attend class with peers they consider to be less physically and socially mature.

- *Emotional and behavioral problems.* Potential dropouts tend to have lower self-esteem than their more successful classmates. They also are more apt to create discipline problems in class, to use drugs, and to engage in criminal activities (Finn, 1991; Garnier et al., 1997; Jozefowicz et al., 1994; Rumberger, 1995; U.S. Dept. of Education, 1992).

- *Lack of psychological attachment to school.* Students who are at risk for academic failure are less likely to identify with their school or to perceive themselves as a vital part of the school community; for example, they engage in fewer extracurricular activities and are more apt to express dissatisfaction with school in general (Christenson & Thurlow, 2004; Hymel, Comfort, Schonert-Reichl, & McDougall, 1996; Rumberger, 1995).

- *Regular interaction with low-achieving peers.* Students who drop out tend to associate with low-achieving, and in some cases antisocial, peers (Battin-Pearson et al., 2000; Hymel et al., 1996). Such peers may argue that school is not worthwhile, and they are likely to distract students' attention away from academic pursuits.

- *Increasing disinvolvement with school.* Dropping out is not necessarily an all-or-none thing. In fact, many high school dropouts show lesser forms of "dropping out" many years before they officially leave school. Future dropouts are absent from school more frequently than their peers, even in the early elementary grades (Finn, 1989; G. A. Hess, Lyons, & Corsino, 1990; Jozefowicz et al., 1994). They are more likely to have been suspended from school, and they are more likely to show a long-term pattern of dropping out, returning to school, and dropping out again (Raber, 1990). Over time, then, we see decreasing involvement—physical, academic, and social—in school activities.

The characteristics just listed are by no means surefire indicators of which students will drop out, however. For instance, some dropouts come from two-parent, middle-income homes, and some are actively involved in school activities almost until the time they drop out (Hymel et al., 1996; Janosz, Le Blanc, Boulerice, & Tremblay, 2000).

■ What are possible reasons why some students don't participate in their school's extracurricular activities?

Why Students Drop Out

Students drop out for a variety of reasons. Some have little family and peer encouragement and support for school success. Others have extenuating life circumstances; for example, they may have medical problems, take an outside job to help support the family, or get pregnant. Many simply become dissatisfied with school: They don't do well in their classes, have trouble getting along with classmates, find the school environment too dangerous or restrictive, or perceive the curriculum to be boring and irrelevant to their needs (Hardre & Reeve, 2003; Portes, 1996; Raber, 1990; Rumberger, 1995; L. Steinberg et al., 1984). Sadly, teacher behaviors can enter into the picture as well, as the following dialogue between an interviewer (Ron) and two at-risk high school students (George and Rasheed) reveals:

Many students who drop out find the school curriculum boring and irrelevant to their needs.

Ron: Why do you think someone drops out of school?

George: I think people drop out of school cuz of the pressure that school brings them. Like, sometimes the teacher might get on the back of a student so much that the student doesn't want to do the work. . . . And then that passes and he says, "I'm gonna start doing good. . . . " Then he's not doing as good as he's supposed to and when he sees his grade, he's, "you mean I'm doin' all that for nothin'? I'd rather not come to school." . . .

Rasheed: I think kids drop out of school because they gettin' too old to be in high school. And I think they got, like, they think it's time to get a responsibility and to get a job and stuff. And, like George says, sometimes the teachers, you know, tell you to drop out, knowing that you might not graduate anyway.

Ron: How does a teacher tell you to drop out?

Rasheed: No, they recommend you take the GED program sometimes.[4] Like, some kids just say, "Why don't you just take the GED. Just get it over with." Then, job or something.

Ron: You talked about a kid being too old. Why is a kid too old?

Rasheed: Cuz he got left back too many times. (Farrell, 1990, p. 91)

Supporting Students at Risk

Students who are at risk for academic failure are a diverse group of individuals with a diverse set of needs, and so there is probably no single strategy that can keep all of them in school until high school graduation (Finn, 1991; Janosz et al., 2000). However, a combination of strategies can help many students at risk succeed and stay in school:

◎ *Identify students at risk as early as possible.* We begin to see indicators of "dropping out," such as low school achievement and high absenteeism, as early as elementary school. And such other signs as low self-esteem, disruptive behavior, and lack of involvement in school activities often appear years before students officially withdraw from school. So it is quite possible to identify at-risk students early in their school careers and to take steps to prevent or remediate academic difficulties before they become insurmountable. Research indicates clearly that for students at risk, prevention, early intervention, and long-term support are more effective than later, short-term efforts (Brooks-Gunn, 2003; Christenson & Thurlow, 2004; McCall & Plemons, 2001; Ramey & Ramey, 1998).

◎ *Create a warm, supportive school and classroom atmosphere.* Teachers and schools that have high success rates with students at risk tend to be those that communicate a sense of caring, concern, and high regard for students (L. W. Anderson & Pellicer, 1998; Christenson & Thurlow, 2004; Pianta, 1999). The Creating a Productive Classroom Environment feature "Encouraging and Supporting Students at Risk" offers several suggestions. Chapter 14 presents additional strategies in its section "Creating an Effective Classroom Climate."

◎ *Make the curriculum relevant to students' lives and needs.* Students are more apt to stay in school, and also more apt to learn and achieve at high levels, if they find the curriculum relevant to their own cultural values, life experiences, and personal needs (Knapp, Turnbull, & Shields, 1990;

---

[4] Rasheed is referring to a general equivalency diploma, obtained by taking a series of achievement tests rather than completing the requirements for high school graduation.

CREATING A PRODUCTIVE CLASSROOM ENVIRONMENT

Encouraging and Supporting Students at Risk

 Engage students' interest with stimulating activities.

As a way of introducing basic principles of physics, a fourth-grade teacher has small groups of students design miniature bridges and build them using Popsicle sticks and glue. The groups place a series of increasingly heavy objects on the completed bridges to test their strength.

 Use students' strengths to promote high self-esteem.

A low-income, inner-city elementary school forms a singing group (the "Jazz Cats") for which students must try out. The group performs at a variety of community events, and the students enjoy considerable visibility for their talent. Group members exhibit increased self-esteem, improvement in other school subjects, and greater teamwork and leadership skills (Jenlink, 1994).

 Provide extra support for academic success.

A middle school homework program meets every day after school in Room 103, where students find their homework assignments on a shelf. Students follow a particular sequence of steps to do each assignment (assembling materials, having someone check their work, etc.) and use a checklist to make sure no step is missed. Initially, a supervising teacher closely monitors what they do, but with time and practice the students are able to complete their homework with only minimal help and guidance (Belfiore & Hornyak, 1998).

Communicate high expectations for students' performance.

Jaime Escalante, a mathematics teacher at a low-income inner-city high school, recruits students to participate in an intensive math program. The teacher and students work on evenings, Saturdays, and vacations, and many of them eventually pass the Advanced Placement calculus exam (Menéndez, 1988).

 Show students that they are personally responsible for their successes.

A teacher says to a student, "Your essay about recent hate crimes in the community is very powerful. You've given the topic considerable thought, and you've clearly mastered some of the techniques of persuasive writing that we've talked about this semester. I'd like you to think seriously about submitting your essay to the local paper for its editorial page. Can we spend some time during lunch tomorrow fine-tuning the grammer and spelling?"

 Get students involved in extracurricular activities.

A teacher encourages a student with a strong throwing arm to go out for the school baseball team and introduces the student to the baseball coach. The coach, in turn, expresses his enthusiasm for having the student join the team and asks several current team members to help him feel at home during team practices.

Involve students in school policy and management decisions.

At an inner-city high school, students and teachers hold regular "town meetings" to discuss issues of fairness and justice and establish rules for appropriate behavior. Meetings are democratic, with students and teachers alike having one vote apiece, and the will of the majority is binding (Higgins, 1995).

Lee-Pearce, Plowman, & Touchstone, 1998; Ramey & Ramey, 1998). To increase the relevance of school for students at risk, we should place academic skills within the context of real-world tasks and particularly within the context of students' local environments. As an example, a mathematics teacher at an inner-city middle school consistently encouraged her students to identify problems in their community and work to solve them (Tate, 1995). One of her classes expressed concern about the thirteen liquor stores located within 1,000 feet of the school and about the inebriated customers and shady drug dealers the stores attracted. The students used yardsticks and maps to calculate the distance of each store from the school, gathered information about zoning restrictions and other city government regulations, identified potential violations, met with a local newspaper editor (who published an editorial describing the situation), and eventually met with state legislators and the city council. As a result of the students' efforts, city police monitored the liquor stores more closely, major violations were identified (leading to the closing of two stores), and the city council made it illegal to consume alcohol within 600 feet of the school (Tate, 1995).

■ Such a project might enhance students' *collective self-efficacy*, the belief that, working together, they can make a difference (see Chapter 10).

◎ *Communicate high expectations for academic success.* Although many students at risk have a history of academic failure, under *no* circumstances should we write these students off. On the contrary, we should communicate to them that school success is both possible and expected and, furthermore, that they are capable of achieving at high levels (L. W. Anderson & Pellicer, 1998; Garcia, 1994; Garibaldi, 1993; Ladson-Billings, 1994a). We can acknowledge past learning problems but let students know that there are ways to overcome those problems and that we will help them acquire the knowledge and skills they need for classroom success (Alderman, 1990). And we should focus their attention on how effectively they are mastering important topics and skills rather than on how their achievement compares to that of their classmates (Maehr & Anderman, 1993). In fact, this focus on *mastery goals* is beneficial for all students, for reasons we will discover in Chapter 12.

◎ *Provide extra academic support.* Because students at risk often have a history of academic failure and may have little support for academic achievement at home, these students may need more than the usual amount of assistance from teachers and other school personnel to succeed. Following are some specific ways to facilitate their academic success:

- Help them develop better reading and learning strategies and more effective study skills.
- Adapt instruction to their current skills and knowledge.
- Give them relatively structured tasks, and tell them exactly what is expected.
- Develop mastery of one skill before moving to a more difficult one.
- Assess their progress frequently, and give them specific criteria for measuring their own success.
- Increase one-on-one teacher-student interactions.
- Deliver as much instruction as possible within the context of general education classrooms; make any necessary instruction in self-contained settings as brief as possible.
- Provide structured after-school assistance with homework.
- Identify community agencies that can provide academic support after school. (Alderman, 1990; Belfiore & Hornyak, 1998; Cosden et al., 2001; Covington & Beery, 1976; Eilam, 2001; Garibaldi, 1993; Slavin, Karweit, & Madden, 1989)

As you may have noticed, these recommendations would be helpful for *any* student. Research indicates that the most effective programs for students at risk are those that incorporate common, educationally sound teaching practices (Slavin et al., 1989).

◎ *Show students that they are the ones who have made success possible.* When we help students at risk improve academically, we must also help them recognize that *they themselves* are responsible for their success (Alderman, 1990). For example, we might give messages such as these:

- "Wow, look how much you've improved! That extra practice really helped."
- "You certainly deserved this A. You are writing in complete sentences now, and you are checking your work for spelling and punctuation errors."

With such messages, we increase students' *self-efficacy* through the *attributions* we give for their success. We will discuss these concepts in Chapters 10 and 12, respectively.

◎ *Encourage and facilitate identification with school.* Students at risk may need extra encouragement to become involved in academic and social activities at school. To help them become more involved in, and feel more psychologically attached to, the school community, we can do the following:

- Establish close working relationships with students.
- Include instructional techniques that promote active class involvement (e.g., class discussions, cooperative learning).
- Encourage participation in athletic programs, extracurricular activities, and student government. (This is especially important when students are having academic difficulties, because it provides an alternative way of experiencing school success.)
- Involve students in school policy and management decisions.
- Give students positions of responsibility in managing school activities.
- Provide rewards (e.g., trips to a local amusement park) for good attendance records. (Finn, 1989; Garibaldi, 1992; Newmann, 1981; M. G. Sanders, 1996)

Students are more likely to stay in school when they feel as if they truly belong there.

Students are far more likely to stay in school and try to succeed at school activities when they feel as if they truly belong there.

REMEMBERING WITHIN-GROUP DIVERSITY

Before we wrap up our discussion of group differences, let's return to two points made at the beginning of the chapter: *There is always a great deal of variability within any group, and there is always a great deal of overlap between any two groups.* We must never—and I do mean *never*—form expectations for individual students on the basis of group averages alone. As we tailor our curriculum and instructional strategies for each of our students, what we know about them as *individuals* should be our primary guides. At the same time, what we know about their group membership—their cultural and ethnic heritage, their gender, their socioeconomic background—can help us immeasurably in understanding why they behave as they do and how we can better foster their cognitive and social development.

Group Differences and Special Needs

Group differences also have implications for students with special educational needs. For example, students from lower socioeconomic backgrounds are more likely to be identified as having either cognitive or behavioral difficulties that require special educational services (Caspi et al., 2000; G. W. Evans & English, 2002; U.S. Dept. of Education, 1997). Some cultures discourage females, even those with high IQ scores and considerable academic promise, from pursuing advanced educational opportunities; as a result, some female students are reluctant to make the most of their advanced cognitive abilities (M. L. Nichols & Ganschow, 1992). Other gender differences exist as well; for example, we will more often identify specific cognitive or

TABLE 4.2   STUDENTS IN INCLUSIVE SETTINGS

Considering Group Differences in Students with Special Educational Needs

CATEGORY	CHARACTERISTICS YOU MIGHT OBSERVE	SUGGESTED CLASSROOM STRATEGIES
Students with specific cognitive or academic difficulties	• Greater frequency in males than females (for learning disabilities and attention-deficit hyperactivity disorder) • Higher than average dropout rate (for students with learning disabilities)	• Remember that students with difficulties in one area (e.g., those with specific learning disabilities) may nevertheless be capable of average or above-average performance in other areas.
Students with social or behavioral problems	• Gender differences in types of problems exhibited, with males more apt to exhibit overt misbehaviors (e.g., aggression, antisocial behavior) and females more apt to exhibit internal problems (e.g., depression, social withdrawal, excessive anxiety) • Greater frequency of occurrence in low-SES students • Higher dropout rate than for any other category of special needs (for students with emotional or behavioral disorders)	• Be on the lookout for possible emotional problems when students (especially girls) are exceptionally quiet or withdrawn. • Take steps to decrease the likelihood of students dropping out (e.g., make the curriculum relevant, provide extra support for academic success).
Students with general delays in cognitive and social functioning	• Delays more common in males than females • Delays more common in students from low-SES backgrounds, sometimes as a result of increased exposure to environment toxins (e.g., lead-based paint) • Higher-than-average dropout rate	• To maximize cognitive and academic growth, identify delays as early as possible and tailor instruction to students' unique abilities and needs. • Remember that the great majority of students from low-SES backgrounds have average or above-average intelligence.
Students with physical or sensory challenges	• Chronic illness more common in students from lower-SES families, in part due to more limited access to adequate health care	• Consult with a school nurse or social worker to identify appropriate health-care services in students' neighborhoods.
Students with advanced cognitive development	• Giftedness possibly manifested in different ways in different cultures (e.g., richness of oral language among African American students, exceptional sensitivity to others' perspectives among Native American students) • Less self-confidence about abilities in females than males • Tendency for many girls to hide their giftedness to maintain good relations with peers • In some cultures, discouragement of females from acting too "intelligently" or pursuing advanced education • Little exposure to female and ethnically diverse high-ability role models	• Recognize that giftedness may reveal itself differently in students from diverse backgrounds. • Help students accurately appraise their own abilities. • Encourage females as well as males to achieve at high levels; identify avenues whereby students can demonstrate their talents in ways that their families and cultures value. • Expose students to talented female and minority role models.

Sources: Alderman, 1990; American Psychiatric Association, 1994; Barga, 1996; Barkley, 1998; Beirne-Smith et al., 2002; L. A. Bell, 1989; Byrnes, 2001; *Center for the Future of Children,* 1997; G. A. Davis & Rimm, 1998; Eisenberg et al., 1996; Finn, 1989; Garibaldi, 1993; Halpern, 1997b; Knapp et al., 1990; Lippa, 2002; Maker & Schiever, 1989; McLoyd, 1998; Nolen-Hoeksema, 2001; Piirto, 1999; Sadker & Sadker, 1994; R. Turnbull et al., 2004; U.S. Dept. of Education, 1992, 1997.

academic difficulties (e.g., learning disabilities) in boys than girls, and we are likely to see different kinds of problems in boys and girls with emotional and behavioral disorders (Caseau, Luckasson, & Kroth, 1994; Halpern, 1997b; U.S. Dept. of Education, 1992). Table 4.2 presents numerous examples of group differences among students with special needs, along with classroom strategies specifically related to such differences.

All students have strengths and talents on which they can build, and all students have considerable potential to develop new skills and abilities. Furthermore, the unique characteristics and backgrounds that different students bring to class—for example, many minority-group students' preference to be cooperative rather than competitive, many girls' concern about maintaining group harmony, and some students' firsthand knowledge about such social issues as poverty and homelessness—together create a situation in which we and our students have much to learn from one another.

THE BIG PICTURE

All human beings draw on their own prior knowledge and beliefs when trying to make sense of new situations. This general principle applies not only to the learning of academic subject matter (more on this point in Chapters 6 and 7) but also to the interpretation of social interactions, including those between teachers and students. We all tend to use our own cultural lenses when interacting with others; that is, we interpret others' behaviors in accordance with what such behaviors typically mean in *our* culture and ethnic group. We may be further biased in thinking that our own culturally based ways of doing things are unquestionably the *best* ways of doing them.

As teachers, if we want to work effectively with students from diverse backgrounds, we must work hard to overcome such biases. Specific behaviors and messages mean different things for different cultural and ethnic groups, and in some cases for different genders and socioeconomic groups as well. For instance, when children look adults in the eye, that communicates respect in some cultural and ethnic groups but *dis*respect in others. When children ask questions of adults who are demonstrating new skills, adults in some communities might see the children as intelligent and interested, but adults in other communities might view them as being cognitively immature and out of line. When students are asked to compete with one another, many boys may delight in the challenge, but many girls may wilt at the potential for alienating peers. For most students from middle-income homes, a homework assignment is, at worst, a chore they would rather not do, but for some students from low-income homes, even finding a time and quiet place to complete it may be a challenge.

We must remember, too, that there are often many effective ways of doing things. The people of a teacher's own culture don't always know what's best, and in many cases there is no "best." Asking questions of a teacher is one good way to learn a new skill, but watching quietly and reflectively can be equally valuable. Competition might prepare students for working as adults in a capitalistic society, but cooperative activities offer a very different set of advantages: fostering social skills, enabling students to build on one another's strengths, and ultimately also enabling them to accomplish more complex tasks than they could complete on their own. Growing up in a wealthy family increases the odds that children have good health care and enriching educational opportunities, yet many children who grow up in poverty do quite well in school and in life despite (and in some cases probably *because of*) the challenges they have faced.

Ultimately, our knowledge about group differences is useful only when (a) we use it to understand why different students behave and perform as they do and then (b) modify our instructional practices in light of our understandings. The final case study provides some practice in thinking about such matters.

CASE STUDY: *The Active and the Passive*

Ms. Stewart has noticed that only a few students actively participate in her junior high school science classes. When she asks a question, especially one that requires students to draw inferences from information presented in class, the same hands always shoot up. She gives the matter some thought and realizes that all of the active participants are Caucasian and that most of them are boys.

She sees the same pattern in students' involvement in lab activities. When she forms small groups for particular lab assignments, the same students (notably the Caucasian males) always take charge. The females and minority males take more passive roles, either providing assistance to the group "leaders" or else just sitting back and watching.

Ms. Stewart is a firm believer that students learn much more about science when they participate in class and when they engage in hands-on activities. She is concerned about the lack of involvement of many of her students. She wonders whether they really even care about science.

- What are some possible reasons why the girls and minority students are not participating in classroom activities?

- What strategies might Ms. Stewart use to increase their participation?

Once you have answered these questions, compare your responses with those presented in Appendix B.

KEY CONCEPTS

group differences (p. 103)
culture (p. 105)
ethnic group (p. 105)
cultural mismatch (p. 105)
Standard English (p. 107)
dialect (p. 107)

African American English (p. 107)
personal space (p. 109)
IRE cycle (p. 109)
wait time (p. 109)
multicultural education (p. 113)
stereotype (p. 115)

equity (in instruction) (p. 116)
gender schema (p. 123)
socioeconomic status (SES) (p. 124)
resilient students (p. 128)
students at risk (p. 129)

PRAXIS Turn to Appendix C, "Matching Book and Ancillary Content to the Praxis Principles of Learning and Teaching Tests," to discover sections of this chapter that may be especially applicable to the Praxis tests.

Companion Website

Now go to our Companion Website at **www.prenhall. com/ormrod** to assess your understanding of chapter content with "Multiple-Choice Questions," apply comprehension in "Essay Questions," broaden your knowledge of educational psychology with related "Web Links," gain greater insight about classroom learning in "Learning in the Content Areas," and analyze and assess classroom work in the "Student Artifact Library."

Chapter 5

Individual Differences and Special Educational Needs

In what ways do you think you fall short in comparison with your fellow students? Perhaps you have more difficulty remembering course material than other students seem to, or perhaps you are so shy that you rarely talk to your classmates. But can you also identify ways in which you surpass many others? Perhaps you are someone for whom learning a foreign language comes easily, or perhaps you have the stick-to-itiveness that enables you to meet the challenges that many of your peers abandon in frustration.

In Chapter 4 we considered many ways in which students of different ethnic groups, genders, and socioeconomic backgrounds tend to be different from one another. Yet we noted, too, that considerable **individual differences** exist within any group. All learners are individuals with unique patterns of strengths and weaknesses. They differ greatly in cognitive abilities; for instance, some learn complex classroom material quickly and easily, whereas others struggle to master basic concepts and skills. Students also show a wide variety of social and behavioral characteristics; for example, some may be friendlier and more outgoing than others, and some may be easily distracted or exceptionally fidgety. Most of the time we can accommodate students' individual differences within general education practices and activities. Once in a while, however, students have characteristics that require specially adapted instructional materials or practices; in other words, they are **students with special needs**.

In this chapter we will explore two important sources of individual differences: intelligence and temperament. We will then look more closely at the categories of special needs introduced in Chapter 1. As we examine these topics, we will address questions such as the following:

- What does *intelligence* encompass? How can we foster its development in children and adolescents?
- How are students' individual *temperaments* likely to affect their classroom performance? How can we accommodate temperamental diversity?
- Why are most students with special educational needs enrolled in general education classrooms rather than in "special" classes or schools?
- How do educators typically categorize students with special needs, and what characteristics are associated with each category?
- How can we help students with cognitive deficits, behavioral problems, and physical disabilities be successful in general education classrooms?
- What can we do to maximize the growth of students who show exceptional gifts and talents?

CASE STUDY: *Tim*

At age 17, Tim is a quiet and reserved young man. He is not very outgoing and rarely joins organized clubs or athletic teams, but he has several close friends who clearly enjoy his company.

In elementary school Tim was well behaved and earned reasonable grades. Nonetheless, he was often "in a daze" during classroom activities, and he had poor reading comprehension despite good word recognition skills. Yet a diagnostic evaluation in third grade found no cognitive or physical disability that would make him eligible for special educational services.

In middle school Tim's grades began to decline, and teachers complained of his "spaciness" and tendency to daydream. He had trouble completing in-class assignments and was so disorganized that he seldom finished his work at home. As teachers expected increasing independence in later years, Tim's school performance continued to drop. He failed several classes in the ninth and tenth grades and had to retake them in summer school.

Now, midway through his eleventh-grade year, Tim's mother takes him for an in-depth psychological evaluation at a university diagnostic clinic. An IQ test yields a score of 96 (reflecting average intelligence), and measures of social and emotional adjustment are within an average range, but measures of attention consistently show this to be an area of weakness. Tim explains to clinic staff that he has trouble ignoring distractions and must find a very quiet place to do his schoolwork; even then, he often has to reread something several times to grasp its meaning. (based on a case described by Hathaway, Dooling-Litfin, & Edwards, 1998, pp. 329–333)

■ **individual differences** Variability in abilities and characteristics (intelligence, personality, etc.) among students at a particular age.

■ **students with special needs** Students different enough from their peers that they require specially adapted instructional materials and practices.

In previous chapters we've talked about five general categories of special needs: specific cognitive and academic deficits, social and behavioral problems, general delays in cognitive and social functioning, physical and sensory challenges, and advanced cognitive development. In which of these categories does Tim fall? Can you guess the specific diagnosis that the clinic reached?

As a teacher, what strategies might you use to accommodate Tim's unique needs?

KEEPING INDIVIDUAL DIFFERENCES IN PERSPECTIVE

Tim's difficulty is primarily a cognitive one: He seems to have good social skills (his friends enjoy his company) and appropriate classroom behaviors (his teachers complain of "spaciness" rather than disciplinary problems). Thus we would put him in the general category of *specific cognitive and academic deficits*. The clinic evaluation team's final diagnosis is that Tim has attention-deficit hyperactivity disorder (ADHD). The team suspects that a subtle learning disability might be at the root of the problem; however, currently available diagnostic techniques are too imprecise for the team to determine this with certainty.

"Tim isn't hyperactive," you might be thinking, "so how can he have ADHD?" As we will see later in the chapter, the labels used for various disabilities almost always refer to a *group* of disabling conditions rather than to specific, well-defined disabilities. For example, some children with ADHD exhibit attention problems *without* hyperactivity (Barkley, 1998), and in fact Tim's actual diagnosis is "ADHD, Predominantly Inattentive Type" (Hathaway, Dooling-Litfin, & Edwards, 1998, p. 332).

Virtually any label we apply to students—whether it be a category of special needs (e.g., *ADHD* or *autism*) or a more general description of cognitive ability or temperament (e.g., *above-average intelligence* or *shy temperament*)—inevitably encompasses students who are probably as different as they are alike. Nevertheless, such labels can often help us choose appropriate instructional strategies for particular students. For instance, researchers and practitioners have identified many effective strategies for students with ADHD—including locating a quiet place to read and study, teaching organizational skills, and breaking complex tasks into several shorter, simpler ones—and such strategies are apt to help 17-year-old Tim stay on task and complete assignments (Barkley, 1998).

As we explore individual differences in this chapter, we will find that such differences are typically the result of heredity and environment working in concert to create distinctly unique human beings. Heredity provides a general blueprint that guides physical and neurological development, determines levels of various hormones, and so on, and this blueprint predisposes children to exhibit somewhat different abilities and behaviors. Yet as we will see, environmental conditions (including those in the classroom) also have a significant influence on children's abilities and behaviors. As we examine intelligence, temperament, and special needs in the pages that follow, we will identify a great many ways in which we, as teachers, can accommodate students' individual differences and maximize each student's long-term cognitive development and interpersonal success.

INTELLIGENCE

What kinds of behaviors lead you to believe that someone is "intelligent"? Do you think of intelligence as a general ability that contributes to success in many different areas? Or is it possible for an individual to be intelligent in one area yet not in another? What exactly *is* intelligence?

Unfortunately, psychologists have not yet reached consensus on the answers to these questions. But here are several components of what many theorists construe **intelligence** to be:

- It is *adaptive*. It involves modifying and adjusting one's behaviors to accomplish new tasks successfully.
- It is related to *learning ability*. Intelligent people learn information more quickly and easily than less intelligent people.
- It involves the *use of prior knowledge* to analyze and understand new situations effectively.
- It involves the complex interaction and coordination of *many different mental processes*.
- It may be seen in *different arenas*—for example, on academic tasks or in social situations.
- It is *culture-specific*. What is "intelligent" behavior in one culture is not necessarily intelligent behavior in another culture. (Laboratory of Human Cognition, 1982; Neisser et al., 1996; Sternberg, 1997; Sternberg & Detterman, 1986)

■ Think of someone you think is intelligent. Does that individual's behavior fit these criteria?

■ **intelligence** Ability to modify and adjust behaviors to accomplish new tasks successfully; involves many different mental processes and may vary in nature depending on one's culture.

For most theorists, intelligence is somewhat distinct from what a person has actually learned (e.g., as reflected in school achievement). At the same time, intelligent thinking and intelligent behavior *depend* on prior learning. The more students know about their environment and about the tasks they need to perform, the more intelligently they can behave. Intelligence, then, is not necessarily a permanent, unchanging characteristic. As you will soon discover, it can be modified through experience and learning.

Measuring Intelligence

Curiously, although psychologists cannot pin down exactly what intelligence is, they have been trying to measure it for more than a century. In 1904 government officials in France asked Alfred Binet to develop a method of identifying students unlikely to benefit from regular school instruction and therefore in need of special educational services. To accomplish the task, Binet devised a test that measured general knowledge, vocabulary, perception, memory, and abstract thought. In doing so, he designed the earliest version of what we now call an **intelligence test**. To get a feel for what intelligence tests are like, try the following exercise.

One component of intelligence is the ability to use prior knowledge to analyze new situations. These students are trying to calculate the volume of the large pyramid by applying geometric principles they've learned in their math class.

Experiencing FIRSTHAND ·Mock Intelligence Test

Answer each of these questions:

1. What does the word *quarrel* mean?
2. How are a goat and a beetle alike?
3. What should you do if you get separated from your family in a large department store?
4. Three kinds of people live on the planet Zircox: bims, gubs, and lops. All bims are lops. Some gubs are lops. Which one of the following must also be true?

    a. All bims are gubs.   c. Some gubs are bims.

    b. All lops are bims.   d. Some lops are bims.

5. Complete the following analogy:

    a.   b.   c.   d.

    · · · · · · ·

These test items are modeled after items on many modern-day intelligence tests. Think, for a moment, about the capabilities you needed to answer them successfully. Does general knowledge about the world play a role? Is knowledge of vocabulary important? Is abstract thought involved? The answer to all three questions is yes. Although intelligence tests have evolved considerably since Binet's time, they continue to measure many of the same abilities that Binet's original test did.

IQ Scores   Scores on intelligence tests were originally calculated using a formula that involves division; hence, they were called "intelligence quotient," or **IQ**, scores. Even though we still use the term IQ, intelligence test scores are no longer based on the old formula. Instead, they are determined by comparing a student's performance on the test with the performance of others in the same age-group. A score of 100 indicates average performance: Students with this score have performed better than half of their age-mates on the test and not as well as the other half. Scores below 100 indicate below-average performance on the test; scores above 100 indicate above-average performance.

Figure 5.1 shows the percentage of students getting scores at different points along the scale (e.g., 12.9% get scores between 100 and 105). Notice how the curve is high in the middle and low at both ends. This tells us that we have many more students obtaining scores close to 100 than we have students scoring very much higher or lower than 100. For example, if we add up the percentages in different parts of Figure 5.1, we find that approximately two-thirds (68%) of students score within 15 points of 100 (i.e., between 85 and 115). In contrast, only 2 percent of students score as low as 70, and only 2 percent score as high as 130. This symmetric and predictable distribution of scores happens by design rather than by chance; psychologists have created a method of scoring intelligence test performance that intentionally yields such a distribution.

■ **intelligence test** General measure of current cognitive functioning, used primarily to predict academic achievement over the short run.

■ **IQ score** Score on an intelligence test; determined by comparing a person's performance with that of others in the same age-group.

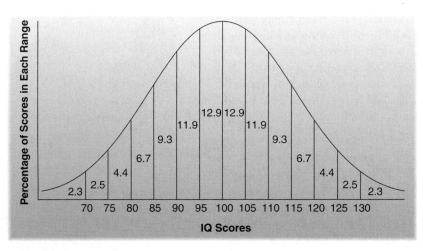

FIGURE 5.1 Percentage of IQ scores in different ranges

■ When might it be appropriate for a teacher to use intelligence test results? What potential dangers are there in relying solely on IQ scores as a measure of students' abilities?

■ Observe developmental differences in interpreting proverbs in the middle childhood and late adolescence "Cognitive Development" clips on Video CD 1.

In the opening case study, Tim's performance on an intelligence test yields an IQ score of 96. We are now in a better position to interpret this score. As you can see in Figure 5.1, a score of 96 is so close to 100 that we should consider it to be well within an "average" range. We will look more closely at the nature of IQ scores in our discussion of *standard scores* in Chapter 16.

IQ and School Achievement   Modern intelligence tests have been designed with Binet's original purpose in mind: to predict how well individual students are likely to perform in the classroom and similar situations. Studies repeatedly show that performance on intelligence tests is correlated with school achievement (N. Brody, 1997; Gustafsson & Undheim, 1996; Sattler, 2001). On average, children with higher IQ scores do better on standardized achievement tests, have higher school grades, and complete more years of education. In other words, IQ scores often *do* predict school achievement, albeit imprecisely. As a result, intelligence tests are frequently used by school psychologists and other specialists in their efforts to identify students with special educational needs.

While recognizing the relationship between intelligence test scores and school achievement, we must also keep three points in mind about this relationship. First, intelligence does not necessarily *cause* achievement; it is simply correlated with it. Even though students with high IQs typically perform well in school, we cannot say conclusively that their high achievement is actually the result of their intelligence. Intelligence probably does play an important role in school achievement, but many other factors are also involved—factors such as motivation, quality of instruction, family resources, parental support, and peer group norms.

Second, the relationship between IQ scores and achievement is not a perfect one; there are exceptions to the rule. For a variety of reasons, some students with high IQ scores do not perform well in the classroom. And other students achieve at higher levels than we would predict from their IQ scores alone. Therefore, we should never base our expectations for students' achievement solely on intelligence test scores.

Third and most important, we must remember that IQ scores simply reflect a student's performance on a particular test at a particular time and that some change is to be expected over the years. In fact, the very nature of what intelligence is changes somewhat as students get older—and so how it is measured must also change—as Table 5.1 reveals. (One ability listed in the table, interpreting proverbs, is depicted in the "Cognitive Development: Middle Childhood" and "Cognitive Development: Late Adolescence" clips on Video CD 1.) The longer the time interval between two measures of intelligence, the greater the fluctuation in IQ we are likely to see, especially when young children are involved (Hayslip, 1994; Sattler, 2001). IQ scores and other measures of cognitive ability often increase over time when children are highly motivated and independent learners and when adults provide stimulating activities and a variety of reading materials (Echols, West, Stanovich, & Kehr, 1996; Sameroff, Seifer, Baldwin, & Baldwin, 1993; Stanovich, West, & Harrison, 1995).

Limitations of Intelligence Tests   Intelligence tests are nothing more than collections of questions and tasks that psychologists have developed and continue to revise over the years to get a handle on how well children and adolescents think, reason, and learn. They are hardly magical instruments that can mysteriously determine a person's true intelligence—if, in fact, such a thing as "true" intelligence even exists.

Nevertheless, on some occasions we might find ourselves considering IQ scores along with other information as we make instructional decisions about some of our students—for example, as we meet with colleagues and parents to identify the most appropriate instructional program for a student with special educational needs. It is critical, then, to be aware of the following limitations of traditional intelligence tests:

- Different kinds of intelligence tests may yield somewhat different scores.
- A student's performance on any test is inevitably affected by many temporary factors present at the time the test is taken, including general health, mood, fatigue, time of day,

TABLE 5.1 DEVELOPMENTAL TRENDS

Intelligence and Its Measurement at Different Grade Levels

GRADE LEVEL	AGE-TYPICAL CHARACTERISTICS	SUGGESTED STRATEGIES
K–2	• Success on test items that involve defining concrete words, copying geometric figures (e.g., squares, diamonds), remembering short lists, identifying similarities and differences • Tendency to define words in an overly simplistic manner • Short attention span, influencing test performance • Variability in test scores from one occasion to the next	• Use IQ tests primarily to identify significant delays in cognitive development; follow up by seeking appropriate interventions for students with such delays. • Do *not* use test scores to make long-term predictions about students' ability to learn and achieve.
3–5	• Success on test items that involve defining concrete words, remembering sentences and short sequences of digits, recognizing concrete analogies, and identifying absurdities in illogical statements • Emerging ability to define common abstract words • Some consistency in overall test scores from one occasion to the next • Tendency for some cognitive abilities to be more developed than others	• Individualize instruction to accommodate students' varying abilities to learn classroom topics. • Do *not* assume that poor performance in some domains necessarily indicates limited ability to learn in other areas. • When students show dramatic differences in performance in different domains (e.g., when fourth graders understand fractions but cannot read simple words), consult with specialists about possible learning disabilities.
6–8	• Success on test items that involve defining commonly used abstract words, drawing logical inferences from verbal descriptions, and identifying similarities across dissimilar concepts • Considerable individual differences in the ability to understand abstract material • Tendency for some students from minority backgrounds to hide their high ability, perhaps for fear of "acting White"	• Expect considerable diversity in students' ability to master abstract classroom material, and individualize instruction accordingly. • Recognize that intelligence may take different forms in different cultures; for instance, it may be reflected in exceptional communication and "people" skills or in originality and resourcefulness in problem solving.
9–12	• Success on test items that involve defining infrequently encountered vocabulary, identifying differences between similar abstract words, interpreting proverbs, and breaking down complex geometric figures into component parts • Relative stability in most students' IQ scores from one occasion to the next • Continuing tendency for some students to hide high ability levels to maintain popularity with peers • Increasing independence (e.g., obtaining drivers' licenses), enabling students to seek out opportunities that enhance talents in particular areas	• Remember that all students can think more "intelligently" when they have appropriate physical and social support (see the discussion of *distributed intelligence*). • Provide challenging activities for students who show exceptional ability in particular areas. • Encourage bright adolescents from lower-income families to pursue postsecondary education, and help them with the logistics of college applications (e.g., applying for financial aid).

Sources: N. Brody, 1992; G. A. Davis & Rimm, 1998; Maker & Schiever, 1989; McLoyd, 1998; Neisser et al., 1996; Ogbu, 1994; Roid, 2003; Salomon, 1993; Sattler, 2001; Terman & Merrill, 1972; Thorndike, Hagen, & Sattler, 1986; Wechsler, 2003.

and the number of distracting stimuli. (Such temporary factors affect a test's *reliability*, a concept we will consider in Chapter 15.)

- Test items typically focus on skills that are important in mainstream Western culture, and particularly in school settings; they do not necessarily tap into skills that may be more highly valued in other contexts or other societies.
- Some students may be unfamiliar with the content or types of tasks involved in particular test items and so perform poorly on those items.
- Students with limited English proficiency (LEP) are at an obvious disadvantage when an intelligence test is administered in English.
- Some students (e.g., minority students who want to avoid "acting White") may not be motivated to perform at their best and so may obtain scores that underestimate their capabilities. (Dirks, 1982; Heath, 1989; Neisser et al., 1996; Ogbu, 1994; Perkins, 1995; Sternberg, 1996b; Zigler & Finn-Stevenson, 1992)

■ Are any of your prior beliefs about intelligence tests inconsistent with what you've just read? If so, can you resolve the inconsistencies?

Used within the context of other information, IQ scores can, in many cases, give a general idea of a student's current cognitive functioning. But as you can see from the limitations just listed, we should always maintain a healthy degree of skepticism about the accuracy of IQ scores, especially when students come from diverse cultural backgrounds or have acquired only limited proficiency in English.

How Theorists Conceptualize Intelligence

Up to this point, we have been talking about intelligence as it is represented by a single IQ score. Yet not all theorists believe that intelligence is a single entity that people "have" in varying degrees; some theorists instead propose that people may behave more or less intelligently in different situations and on different kinds of tasks. Here we will look at four very different perspectives on the nature of intelligence. We'll first consider the traditional idea that intelligence is a single, generalized trait—a concept often referred to as the g factor. We will then examine two theories, developed by Howard Gardner and Robert Sternberg, that portray intelligence as multidimensional and context-dependent. Finally, we will address the concept of "distributed" intelligence.

Spearman's Concept of g   Whenever we use an IQ score as an estimate of a person's cognitive ability, we are, to some extent, buying into the notion that intelligence is a single entity. Historically, considerable evidence has supported this idea (McGrew, Flanagan, Zeith, & Vanderwood, 1997; Neisser et al., 1996; Spearman, 1927). Although various intelligence tests yield somewhat different scores, people who score high on one test tend to score high on others as well. Charles Spearman (1904, 1927) called this single entity a *general factor*, or *g*. Some contemporary information processing theorists believe that *g* is a reflection of the speed and efficiency with which people can process information, learning tasks, and problems (N. Brody, 1992; Demetriou, Christou, Spanoudis, & Platsidou, 2002; Dempster & Corkill, 1999; Vernon, 1993).

Close attentioin to detail in 10-year-old Luther's drawing of a plant suggests some talent in what Gardner calls *naturalist* intelligence.

Gardner's Theory of Multiple Intelligences   In addition to a general factor in intelligence, many researchers (including Spearman) have found evidence for more specific abilities, and measures of these abilities can sometimes predict performance on particular school tasks more accurately than general intelligence tests do (McGrew et al., 1997; Neisser et al., 1996; Spearman, 1927; Thurstone, 1938). Howard Gardner (1983, 1998, 1999; Gardner & Hatch, 1990) suggests that there are at least eight different abilities, or *intelligences*, that are relatively independent of one another (see Table 5.2).[1] Gardner's perspective presents the possibility that most, and quite possibly all, of our students may be quite intelligent in one way or another. Some students may show exceptional promise in language, others may be talented in music, and still others may be able to learn mathematics more easily than their classmates.

Gardner proposes that the various intelligences manifest themselves somewhat differently in different cultures. For example, in mainstream Western culture, spatial intelligence might be reflected in painting, sculpture, or geometry. But among the Gikwe bushmen of the Kalahari Desert, it might be reflected in one's ability to recognize and remember many specific locations over a large area (perhaps over several hundred square miles), identifying each location by its rocks, bushes, and other landmarks (Gardner, 1983).

Gardner presents some evidence to support the existence of multiple intelligences. For example, he describes people who are quite skilled in one area (perhaps in composing music) and yet have seemingly average abilities in other areas. He also points out that people who suffer brain damage sometimes lose abilities that are restricted primarily to one intelligence; for instance, one person might show deficits primarily in language, whereas another might have difficulty with tasks that require spatial skills.

Among psychologists, reviews of Gardner's theory are mixed. Some theorists do not believe that Gardner's evidence is sufficiently compelling to support the notion of eight distinctly different abilities (Berk, 2003; N. Brody, 1992; Corno et al., 2002; Kail, 1998). Others disagree that

■ *g* Theoretical general factor in intelligence that influences one's ability to learn in a wide variety of contexts.

---

[1] Gardner (1999) suggests that there may also be a ninth, *existential* intelligence. However, he acknowledges that evidence for it is weaker than that for the other eight intelligences, hence its exclusion from Table 5.2.

TABLE 5.2

Gardner's Multiple Intelligences

TYPE OF INTELLIGENCE	EXAMPLES OF RELEVANT BEHAVIORS
Linguistic Intelligence Ability to use language effectively	• Making persuasive arguments • Writing poetry • Noticing subtle nuances in word meanings
Logical-Mathematical Intelligence Ability to reason logically, especially in mathematics and science	• Solving mathematical problems quickly • Generating mathematical proofs • Formulating and testing hypotheses about observed phenomena[a]
Spatial Intelligence Ability to notice details of what one sees and to imagine and manipulate visual objects in one's mind	• Conjuring up mental images • Drawing a visual likeness of an object • Making fine discriminations among visually very similar objects
Musical Intelligence Ability to create, comprehend, and appreciate music	• Playing a musical instrument • Composing a musical work • Having a keen awareness of the underlying structure of music
Bodily-Kinesthetic Intelligence Ability to use one's body skillfully	• Dancing • Playing basketball • Performing pantomime
Interpersonal Intelligence Ability to notice subtle aspects of other people's behaviors	• Reading another's mood • Detecting another's underlying intentions and desires • Using knowledge of others to influence their thoughts and behaviors
Intrapersonal Intelligence Awareness of one's own feelings, motives, and desires	• Discriminating among such similar emotions as sadness and regret • Identifying the motives guiding one's own behavior • Using self-knowledge to relate more effectively with others
Naturalist Intelligence Ability to recognize patterns in nature and differences among various life-forms and natural objects	• Identifying members of particular plant or animal species • Classifying natural forms (e.g., rocks, types of mountains) • Applying one's knowledge of nature in such activities as farming, landscaping, or animal training

[a]This example may remind you of Piaget's theory of cognitive development. Many of the stage-specific characteristics that Piaget described fall within the realm of logical-mathematical intelligence.

abilities in specific domains, such as in music or bodily movement, are really "intelligence" per se (Bracken, McCallum, & Shaughnessy, 1999; Sattler, 2001). Still others are simply taking a wait-and-see attitude about Gardner's theory until more research is conducted.

Despite such a lukewarm reception in psychological circles, many educators have whole-heartedly embraced Gardner's theory of multiple intelligences because of its optimistic view of human potential. Gardner's perspective encourages us to use many different teaching methods so that we may capitalize on students' diverse abilities (Armstrong, 1994; L. Campbell, Campbell, & Dickinson, 1998; Gardner, 1995, 2000). For example, when my son Jeff took high school biology, he had to write a short story that included at least four examples of living things (either plants or animals) changing energy from one form into another—an assignment in which both linguistic and logical-mathematical intelligence played substantial roles. Consider, too, how an eighth-grade teacher took advantage of two girls' musical intelligence to teach spelling:

> [B]oth [girls] enjoyed playing the piano. [I] asked the girls to label the piano keys with the letters of the alphabet, so that the girls could "play" the words on their keyboards. Later, on spelling tests, the students were asked to recall the tones and sounds of each word and write its corresponding letters. Not only did spelling scores improve, but the two pianists began thinking of other "sound" texts to set to music. Soon, they performed each classmate's name and transcribed entire sentences. (L. Campbell et al., 1998, p. 142)

Whether or not human beings have eight or more distinctly different intelligences, they certainly benefit when they are encouraged to think about a particular topic in several ways—perhaps with words, pictures, bodily movements, and so on. We'll look at such multiple forms of *encoding* in Chapter 6.

■ In which of Gardner's intelligences are you most "intelligent"?

Environmental Context

- Adapts behavior to fit the environment
- Adapts the environment to fit one's needs
- Selects an environment conducive to success

Prior Experience

- Deals with a new situation by drawing on past experience
- Deals with a familiar situation quickly and efficiently

Cognitive Processes

- Interprets new situations in useful ways
- Separates important information from irrelevant details
- Identifies effective problem-solving strategies
- Finds relationships among seemingly different ideas
- Makes effective use of feedback
- Applies other cognitive processes as well

FIGURE 5.2 Sternberg's three dimensions of intelligence

Sternberg's Triarchic Theory   Whereas Gardner focuses on different kinds of intelligence, Robert Sternberg focuses more on the nature of intelligence itself. Sternberg (1984, 1985, 1998) suggests that intelligent behavior involves an interplay of three factors, all of which may vary from one occasion to the next: (1) the *environmental context* in which the behavior occurs, (2) the way in which one's *prior experience* is brought to bear on a task, and (3) the *cognitive processes* required by that task. These three dimensions are summarized in Figure 5.2. Let's look at each one in more detail.

Role of environmental context.   Earlier in the chapter we noted that intelligence is both *adaptive* and *culture-specific*. Sternberg proposes that intelligent behavior involves adaptation: Individuals must adapt their behaviors to deal successfully with specific environmental conditions, modify the environment to better fit their own needs, or select an alternative environment more conducive to success. He also proposes that behavior may be more or less intelligent in different cultural contexts. For example, learning to read is an adaptive response in some cultures yet may be irrelevant in others.

Sternberg has identified three general skills that may be particularly adaptive in mainstream Western culture. One is *verbal ability*—for example, one's ability to speak and write clearly, to develop and use a large vocabulary, and to understand and learn from what one reads. A second skill is *social competence*—for example, one's ability to interact effectively with other human beings, to be sensitive to others' needs and wishes, and to provide leadership. A third skill is *practical problem-solving ability*—for example, one's ability to correctly identify the problem in a particular situation, to reason logically (both deductively and inductively), and to generate a multitude of possible problem solutions (e.g., see Sternberg et al., 2000).

Role of prior experience.   Sternberg proposes that intelligent behavior sometimes involves dealing successfully with a brand-new task or activity. When people find themselves in a new situation, they must draw on their past experiences and consider the kinds of responses that have been effective in similar contexts. An ability to *generalize* appropriately from past learning experiences increases their ability to adapt quickly and conquer new challenges.

On other occasions intelligence involves dealing with familiar tasks and situations in a rapid and efficient manner. As an example, try the following exercise.

Experiencing FIRSTHAND ·Solving for *x*

How quickly can you solve for *x* in this problem?

$$\frac{4}{5} = \frac{x}{30}$$

· · · · · · ·

If you were able to identify the correct answer (24) quickly and easily, then your ability to solve problems involving proportions shows **automaticity**, an ability to respond quickly, efficiently, and with minimal mental effort. Automaticity results from performing certain tasks over and over again—that is, it results from experience—and in most instances greatly enhances performance. We'll look at the nature of automaticity in more depth in Chapter 6.

Role of cognitive processes.   In addition to considering how context and prior experience affect behavior, we must also consider how an individual thinks about (mentally processes) a particular task. Sternberg proposes that numerous cognitive processes are involved in intelligent behavior: interpreting new situations in ways that promote successful adaptation, separating important and relevant information from unimportant and irrelevant details, identifying possible strategies for solving a problem, finding relationships among seemingly different ideas, making effective use of external feedback about one's performance, and so on. Different cognitive processes may

■ **automaticity** Ability to respond quickly and efficiently while mentally processing or physically performing a task.

be more or less important in different situations, and an individual may behave more or less "intelligently" depending on the specific abilities needed at the time.

To date, research neither supports nor refutes Sternberg's belief that intelligence has this "triarchic" nature, and in fact the vagueness of Sternberg's theory makes it difficult to test empirically (Sattler, 2001; Siegler, 1998). At the same time, the theory reminds us that students' ability to behave "intelligently" may vary considerably depending on the specific knowledge, skills, and cognitive processes that a task requires. We won't always want to teach to students' strengths, however. In some instances we should present tasks that encourage students to address, and thereby strengthen, their areas of weakness (Sternberg, 2002).

Another useful aspect of Sternberg's theory is the importance it places on environmental context: What's "intelligent" in one context is not necessarily intelligent in another. As an example, let's revisit an anecdote I presented in Chapter 4. When a researcher seemed especially impressed with a talkative Inuit boy with advanced language skills, his Native American teacher replied, "Some of these children who don't have such high intelligence have trouble stopping themselves. They don't know when to stop talking." (Crago, 1988, p. 219). In the teacher's culture, silence, rather than verbal ability, was the mark of maturity.

Some theorists believe that context makes all the difference in the world. This belief is clearly evident in the concept of *distributed intelligence*.

Distributed Intelligence   Implicit in our discussion so far has been the assumption that intelligent behavior is something that people engage in with little if any help from the objects or people around them. But some theorists point out that people are far more likely to think and behave intelligently when they have the support of their physical and social environments (Barab & Plucker, 2002; Pea, 1993; Perkins, 1995; Salomon, 1993; Sternberg & Wagner, 1994). For instance, it's easier for many people to solve for x in $4/5 \times x/30$ if they have pencil and paper, or perhaps even a calculator, with which to work out the problem. It should be easier to solve a complex problem in science or social studies if people can debate the pros and cons of various strategies with a few peers. As noted in Chapter 2, virtually anyone can perform more difficult tasks when he or she has the support structure, or *scaffolding*, to do so.

This idea that intelligent behavior depends on people's physical and social support systems is sometimes referred to as **distributed intelligence**. People can "distribute" their thinking (and therefore think more intelligently) in at least three ways (Perkins, 1992, 1995). First, they can use physical objects, and especially technology (e.g., calculators, computers), to handle and manipulate large amounts of information. Second, they can represent and think about the situations they encounter using the various symbolic systems their culture provides; for instance, they can use diagrams, charts, mathematical equations, and so on to help them simplify or summarize complex topics and problems. And third, they can work with other people to explore ideas and solve problems; after all, two heads are usually better than one. In fact, when students work together on complex, challenging tasks and problems, they teach one another strategies and ways of thinking that can help each of them think even *more* intelligently on future occasions (Salomon, 1993).

Ultimately, intelligence depends *both* on students' own thought processes and on the supportive contexts within which students work (Salomon, 1993; Sfard, 1998). As teachers, rather than asking the question, "How intelligent are our students?" we should instead be asking, "How can we help our students think as intelligently as possible? What tools, social networks, and symbolic systems can we provide?"

Furthermore, we should think of intelligence as something we can *nurture*, perhaps by ensuring that students frequently work on tasks and problems they can accomplish only with physical and social support. (In Lev Vygotsky's lingo, we foster students' cognitive development by having them work in their individual *zones of proximal development*). We turn now to a closer look at the effects of nurture, as well as those of its "partner" nature, in the development of intelligence.

Nature, Nurture, and Group Differences in Intelligence

Research tells us that heredity probably does play some role in intelligence. For instance, identical twins tend to have more similar IQ scores than fraternal twins do, even when the twins are raised in different homes (Bouchard, 1997; Plomin, 1994). And in many respects, the intellectual abilities of adopted children more closely correlate with those of their biological parents than those of their

The concept of *distributed intelligence* suggests that students can often think more intelligently by using technology to manipulate large bodies of data, brainstorming possible problem solutions with classmates, and using symbolic systems (words, mathematical symbols, charts, diagrams, etc.) to simplify complex ideas and processes.

■ **distributed intelligence** Idea that people act more "intelligently" when they have physical, symbolic, or social support.

adoptive parents, especially as the children grow older (McGue, Bouchard, Iacono, & Lykken, 1993; Plomin, Fulker, Corley, & DeFries, 1997). This is not to say, however, that children inherit a single "IQ gene" that determines their intellectual ability. Rather, they probably inherit a variety of characteristics that in one way or another affect particular cognitive abilities and talents (Simonton, 2001).

The environment clearly has an effect on intelligence as well. For instance, poor nutrition in the early years of development (including the nine months before birth) leads to lower IQ scores, as does a mother's excessive use of alcohol during pregnancy (D'Amato et al., 1992; Neisser et al., 1996; Ricciuti, 1993). Attending school has a consistently positive effect on IQ scores (Ceci, 2003; Ramey, 1992). Changing a child's environment from an impoverished one to a more stimulating one (e.g., through adoption) can result in IQ gains of 15 points or more (Capron & Duyme, 1989; Scarr & Weinberg, 1976; Zigler & Seitz, 1982). Furthermore, researchers are finding that, worldwide, there is a slow but steady increase in people's IQ scores—a trend that is probably due to better nutrition, smaller family sizes, better schooling, increasing cognitive stimulation (through increased access to television, reading materials, etc.), and other improvements in people's environments (Daley, Whaley, Sigman, Espinosa, & Neumann, 2003; Flynn, 1987, 2003; Neisser, 1998b).

But how *much* of a role do nature and nurture each play in the development of intelligence? This question has been a source of considerable controversy over the years, especially when group differences are considered. One fairly consistent research finding is that, on average, African American students have lower IQ scores than European American students (McLoyd, 1998; Neisser, 1998a). In their widely publicized book *The Bell Curve*, Herrnstein and Murray (1994) proposed that these differences are due largely to heredity—in other words, that, genetically speaking, European Americans have a biological advantage over African Americans. As you might guess, the book's proposal that there are racial differences in intelligence has generated much controversy and a great deal of outrage.

Scholars have poked so many holes in *The Bell Curve*'s arguments that they don't seem to hold water (Jacoby & Glauberman, 1995; J. Marks, 1995; Montagu, 1999). For instance, experts find numerous weaknesses in the research studies and statistical analyses that Herrnstein and Murray described; as one simple example, they remind us that we can ultimately never draw conclusions about causation by looking only at correlational studies. They argue that any innate intelligence differences among races have not had sufficient time to evolve, nor does it seem logical that some groups would evolve to be less adaptive (i.e., less intelligent) than others. They point out, too, that the very concept of *race*, though widely used to categorize people in our society, actually has no basis in biology: It is virtually impossible to identify a person's "race" by analyzing his or her DNA.

Many psychologists believe that it may ultimately be impossible to separate the effects of heredity and environment—that the two interact to influence children's cognitive development and measured IQ in ways that cannot be disentangled (Bidell & Fischer, 1997; Petrill & Wilkerson, 2000; Simonton, 2001; Wahlsten & Gottlieb, 1997). Yet we have considerable evidence that IQ differences between African American and European American children are due largely to *differences in environment*—more specifically, to economic circumstances that affect the quality of prenatal and postnatal nutrition, availability of stimulating books and toys, access to educational opportunities, and so on (Brooks-Gunn, Klebanov, & Duncan, 1996; Byrnes, 2003; McLoyd, 1998). We find, too, that African American and European American children have, in recent years, become increasingly *similar*; this trend can be attributed only to more equitable environmental conditions for the two groups (Neisser et al., 1996). Furthermore, we must remember that IQ scores are, at best, imperfect measures of intelligence. In general, then, we should assume that African American and European American children (and presumably other racial and ethnic groups as well) have equivalent potential to develop intelligence and various cognitive abilities.

Being Optimistic About Students' Potential

Contemporary views of intelligence give us reason to be optimistic about students' abilities, especially when we actively nurture and support students' cognitive growth. If intelligence is as multifaceted as theorists such as Gardner and Sternberg believe, then scores from any single IQ test cannot possibly give a complete picture of students' "intelligence" (Neisser et al., 1996). In fact, we are likely to see intelligent behavior in many of our students—perhaps in *all* of them— in one way or another. One student may show promise in mathematics, another may be an exceptionally gifted writer, a third may be skillful in interpersonal relationships, and a fourth may show talent in art, music, or sports. Furthermore, as Sternberg's triarchic theory points out, intelligent behavior draws on a variety of cognitive processes that can clearly improve over time with experience and practice (Sternberg et al., 2000). And the notion of distributed intelligence suggests that intelligent behavior should be relatively commonplace when students have the right tools, symbolic systems, and social groups with which to work.

For optimal intellectual development, students need a variety of stimulating experiences throughout childhood, including age-appropriate toys and books, frequent verbal interactions with adults and other children, and numerous opportunities to observe and practice important behavioral and cognitive skills (R. H. Bradley & Caldwell, 1984; Brooks-Gunn et al., 1996; Ericsson & Chalmers, 1994; R. D. Hess & Holloway, 1984; McGowan & Johnson, 1984). When parents and other caregivers cannot provide such experiences, most welcome the availability of enriching preschool and after-school programs. Regularly attending such programs can enhance a student's cognitive development and potential to lead a productive life, especially if these programs continue to offer support throughout childhood (Brooks-Gunn, 2003; F. A. Campbell & Ramey, 1994, 1995; McCall & Plemons, 2001; Slaughter-Defoe, 2001).

We must remember, too, that to the extent that intelligence is culture-dependent, intelligent behavior is apt to take different forms in children from different backgrounds (Gardner, 1995; Neisser et al., 1996; Perkins, 1995; Sternberg, 1985). In mainstream Western culture, children's intelligence may be reflected in their ability to deal with complex problems and abstract ideas. Among students who have been raised in predominently African American communities, it may be reflected in oral language, such as in colorful speech, creative storytelling, or humor (Torrance, 1989). In Native American cultures it may be reflected in interpersonal skills or exceptional craftsmanship (Kirschenbaum, 1989; Maker & Schiever, 1989). We must be careful not to limit our conception of intelligence only to students' ability to succeed at traditional academic tasks.

Finally, intelligence—no matter how we define it—is hardly the only characteristic that affects students' academic achievement. Factors such as prior knowledge, learning strategies, self-regulation, motivation, self-perceptions, and temperament also play important roles (Corno et al., 2002; B. K. Keogh, 2003). It is to the last of these, temperament, that we turn now.

TEMPERAMENT

Let's return to Tim in our opening case study. Tim is on the "quiet" side both physically and socially: He's well behaved in class, rarely participates in team sports, and is not terribly outgoing. At the same time, his mind easily wanders, and so he has trouble focusing on classroom tasks and activities. From what we can see, Tim has had this subdued yet distractible temperament throughout his childhood and adolescence.

In general, **temperament** is one's typical style of responding to environmental stimuli and events. Children seem to have distinct temperaments almost from birth. For instance, some are cheerful and easy to care for; others are fussy and demanding. Researchers have identified many temperamental styles that emerge early in life and are relatively enduring, including general activity level, adaptability, persistence, adventurousness, shyness, inhibitedness, irritability, and distractibility. Most psychologists agree that such temperamental differences are biologically based and have genetic origins (Caspi & Silva, 1995; B. K. Keogh, 2003; Pfeifer, Goldsmith, Davidson, & Rickman, 2002; Plomin, 1989; A. Thomas & Chess, 1977).

Keep in mind, however, that genetic differences in temperament are only *predispositions* to behave in certain ways, and environmental factors may point different children with the same predisposition in somewhat different directions (B. K. Keogh, 2003; R. A. Thompson, 1998). The *personalities* that children eventually acquire are the result of environmental circumstances as well as built-in temperaments. For instance, in mainstream Western culture, shyness and inhibitedness are viewed as more acceptable for girls than for boys, and high activity levels and impulsivity are more often tolerated for boys than for girls. Thus adults may prod shy boys to be more outgoing and adventuresome yet chastise girls who appear overly energetic.

Furthermore, different cultural groups encourage different behavioral styles. For example, many children in China are raised to be shy, whereas many in Zambia are raised to smile and be outgoing (X. Chen et al. 1992; Hale-Benson, 1986; D. Y. F. Ho, 1986, 1994). European American families often encourage assertiveness and independence, but families from many other countries (e.g., Mexico, China, Japan, India) encourage restraint, obedience, and deference to elders (Chao, 1994; Goodnow, 1992; Joshi & MacLean, 1994; Rothbaum, Weisz, Pott, Miyake, & Morelli, 2000).

■ **temperament** Genetic predisposition to respond in particular ways to one's physical and social environments.

Nature and nurture interact in various ways to shape children's personalities (N. A. Fox, Henderson, Rubin, Calkins, & Schmidt, 2001; B. K. Keogh, 2003). Children who are naturally vivacious and outgoing will have more opportunities to learn social skills and establish rewarding interpersonal relationships. Children who are energetic and adventuresome will seek out a wider variety of experiences than those who, like Tim, are quiet and restrained. When children have temperaments that clash with cultural expectations—for instance, when an exuberant child grows up in a "restrained" culture—they may often be punished for their "troublesome" behavior. And some temperaments—for instance, tendencies to be adaptable, persistent, and outgoing—help children be resilient and succeed in the face of difficult family circumstances or challenging environmental conditions (D. Hart, Atkins, & Fegley, 2003; B. K. Keogh, 2003).

Temperament in the Classroom

Many temperamental variables affect how students engage in and respond to classroom activities and so also affect students' academic achievement (B. K. Keogh, 2003). For instance, students are more likely to achieve at high levels if they are persistent, reasonably (but not overly) energetic, and able to ignore minor distractions. They can also achieve greater academic success if their behaviors lead to friendly, productive relationships with teachers and peers—people who can bolster their sense of self and support their efforts to learn.

Yet there is no single "best" temperament that maximizes classroom achievement. Instead, children are more likely to succeed in the classroom when their behaviors are a good fit, rather than a mismatch, with classroom expectations (B. K. Keogh, 2003). Highly energetic, outgoing children are apt to shine—but quieter students might feel anxious or intimidated—when teachers want students to participate actively in group discussions and projects. Quieter children do better—and some energetic children may be viewed as disruptive—when teachers require a lot of independent seatwork.

CREATING A PRODUCTIVE CLASSROOM ENVIRONMENT

Accommodating Students' Diverse Temperaments

 For students with high energy levels, minimize downtime between activities.

A third-grade boy seems unable to sit still for more than a couple of minutes. As a way of letting him release pent-up energy throughout the school day, his teacher gives him small chores to do (erasing the board, sharpening pencils, cleaning art supplies, etc.) and shows him how to complete the chores quietly so as not to disturb his classmates.

 Be especially warm and attentive with very shy students.

A ninth-grade teacher notices that a new girl in his language arts class comes to class alone each day and doesn't join in conversations with peers before or after class. One day, he sees this student eating lunch by herself in the cafeteria. He sits down beside her with his own lunch and engages her in conversation about her previous school and community. The following day in class, he assigns a small-group, cooperative learning project that students will work on periodically over the next two weeks. He forms cooperative groups of three or four students each, making sure that he partners the new girl with two students who he knows will be friendly and take her under their wing.

 When students have trouble adapting to new circumstances, give them advance notice of unusual activities and provide extra structure and reassurance.

A kindergarten teacher has discovered that two children in his class do well when the school day is orderly and predictable, but they often become anxious or upset whenever the class departs from its usual routine. To prepare the children for a field trip to the fire station on Friday, he begins to talk about the trip at the beginning of the week, explaining what the class will do and see during the visit. He also recruits the father of one of the children to serve as a parent assistant that day.

 If students seem overwhelmed by noisy or chaotic situations, find or create a more calm and peaceful environment for them.

Several middle school students find the school cafeteria overwhelming and unsettling. Their math teacher offers her classroom as a place where they can occasionally eat instead. On some days she eats with them. At other times she sits at her desk and grades papers, but they know that she will gladly stop to talk if they have a question or concern.

Teach self-regulation strategies to students who act impulsively.

A high school student often shouts out comments and opinions in her history class. The student's teacher takes her aside after school one day and gently explains that her lack of restraint is interfering with her classmates' ability to participate in discussions. To sensitize the student to the extent of the problem, the teacher asks her to keep a daily tally of how many times she talks without first raising her hand. A week later, the two meet again, and the teacher suggests a "self-talk" strategy that can help the student participate actively without dominating discussion. (We will look more closely at self-regulation strategies in Chapter 10).

Some strategies based on suggestions by B. K. Keogh, 2003.

As teachers, we must recognize that to a considerable degree, students' ways of behaving in the classroom—their energy levels, their sociability, their impulse control, and so on—reflect temperamental differences that are not entirely within their control. If we keep this fact in mind, we are apt to be more tolerant of their behavioral idiosyncrasies and more willing to adapt our instruction and classroom management strategies to accommodate their individual behavioral styles (B. K. Keogh, 2003). The feature "Accommodating Students' Diverse Temperaments" presents several examples of strategies we might use.

In some instances students have temperaments or cognitive abilities so very different from what is typical for their age-group that they require special educational services. We now look more closely at such students.

EDUCATING STUDENTS WITH SPECIAL NEEDS IN GENERAL EDUCATION CLASSROOMS

In the United States more than two-thirds of students with special educational needs are in general education classrooms for part or all of the school day (U.S. Dept. of Education, 1996). In fact, federal legislation mandates a practice known as **inclusion**: School districts must educate students with special needs, including those with severe and multiple disabilities, in regular classrooms in neighborhood schools to the greatest extent possible. Let's briefly consider one landmark piece of legislation—Public Law 94-142—and research findings that shed light on the practice of inclusion.

Public Law 94-142: Individuals with Disabilities Education Act (IDEA)

In 1975 the U.S. Congress passed Public Law 94-142, which is now known as the **Individuals with Disabilities Education Act (IDEA)**. IDEA has been amended several times, in 1983 (PL 98-199), 1986 (PL 99-457), and 1990 (PL 101-476), and it was reauthorized in 1997 (PL 105-17). IDEA now grants educational rights to people with cognitive, emotional, or physical disabilities from birth until age 21, and it guarantees several rights for students with disabilities: a free and appropriate education, fair and nondiscriminatory evaluation, education in the least restrictive environment, an individualized education program, and due process.

A free and appropriate education. All students with disabilities are entitled to a free educational program designed specifically to meet their unique educational needs. For example, a student with a learning disability who has unusual difficulty with reading is entitled to a special educational program (perhaps including one-on-one instruction, different instructional strategies, and tailor-made reading materials) designed to promote reading skills. A student in a wheelchair may not be able to participate physically in the school's traditional unit on basketball but can possibly benefit from practice in dribbling and shooting baskets and from certain modifications of the sport (e.g., playing in wheelchair basketball games).

Fair and nondiscriminatory evaluation. A multidisciplinary team conducts an in-depth evaluation of any student who may be eligible for special services. This team typically consists of the student's parents or guardians, at least one general education teacher, at least one special education teacher, and often one or more specialists who can appropriately administer evaluation instruments and interpret the results. If the student is at least 18 years old, he or she is also a member of the evaluation team; in some instances students younger than 18 are included in decision making. The exact makeup of the team depends on the needs of the student and varies somewhat from state to state.

School personnel use tests and other evaluation tools that can provide an accurate, meaningful, and complete assessment of potential disabling conditions; thus, they may evaluate general intelligence, specific academic abilities, social and emotional functioning, communication skills, vision, hearing, health, and motor skills. Evaluation instruments must be administered by individuals trained in their use, and evaluation procedures must take students' backgrounds and any suspected physical or communication difficulties into account. Tests must be administered in students' primary language; for example, if a student is learning English but has been raised in a Spanish-speaking home, tests are given in Spanish. As a final safeguard, students must be evaluated on the basis of multiple assessment methods, *never* on the basis of a single test score.

Education in the least restrictive environment. To the greatest extent possible, students with disabilities should be included in the same academic environment, extracurricular activities, and

■ Chapter 14 offers numerous strategies for communicating and working effectively with parents.

■ **inclusion** Practice of educating all students, including those with severe and multiple disabilities, in neighborhood schools and general education classrooms.

■ **Individuals with Disabilities Education Act (IDEA)** U.S. legislation granting educational rights to people with cognitive, emotional, or physical disabilities from birth until age 21.

FIGURE 5.3 Typical components of an individualized education program (IEP)

The IEP is a written statement for a child or student, age 3 to 21, who has been identified as having a special educational need. Any IEP that is developed or revised should contain the following:

- Present levels of educational performance, including:
  - How the disability affects involvement and progress in the general education curriculum (for students 6–21 years old), *or*
  - How the disability affects participation in appropriate activities (for children 3–5 years old)
- Measurable annual goals, including "benchmarks" or short-term objectives, related to:
  - Meeting needs resulting from the disability, to ensure that the student is involved in and can progress through a general education curriculum
  - Meeting each of the individual's other disability-related needs
- The special education, related services, supplementary aids, program modifications, and supports that will be provided so that the student can:
  - Advance appropriately toward annual goals
  - Be involved in and progress through the general curriculum
  - Participate in extracurricular and other nonacademic activities
  - Participate in general education with other students with disabilities and with students who do not have disabilities
- The extent, if any, to which the student will *not* participate with nondisabled students in general education classes and in extracurricular and other nonacademic activities of the general curriculum

- Any modifications in the administration of state- or district-wide assessments of achievement so that the student can participate in those assessments; or, if the IEP determines that the student will not participate in part or all of an assessment, why the assessment is inappropriate and how the student will alternatively be assessed
- The projected date for beginning service and program modifications and the anticipated frequency, location, and duration of each
- Transition plans, including:
  - Beginning at age 14 and each year thereafter, a statement of the student's needs related to transition services, including those that focus on courses of study (e.g., participation in advanced-placement courses or in a vocational education program)
  - Beginning at age 16 (or sooner, if the IEP team decides it is appropriate), a statement of needed transition services, including (when appropriate) a statement of the interagency responsibilities or any other needed linkages
  - Beginning at least one year before the student reaches the age of majority under state law (usually at age 18), a statement that the student has been informed of those rights under IDEA that will transfer from parents to student when the student becomes of age
- How the student's progress toward annual goals will be assessed and how the student's parents will be regularly informed of the student's progress toward those goals

Note: Adapted from EXCEPTIONAL LIVES 4/E by Turnbull et al., 2004, Upper Saddle River, NJ: Merrill/Prentice Hall. Adapted by permission of Pearson Education, Inc., Upper Saddle River, NJ.

social interactions as their nondisabled peers. In other words, they must have the **least restrictive environment**, the most typical and standard educational environment that can reasonably meet their needs. The general rule here is that educators must begin by assuming that a student *will* be educated within a regular classroom context and given sufficient supplementary aids and support services to make success in that context possible. Exclusion from general education is warranted only when teachers or other students are clearly jeopardized (e.g., when a student with an emotional or behavioral disorder is extremely violent) or when, even with proper support and assistance, the student cannot make appreciable progress in a general education setting.

Individualized education program (IEP). An instructional program tailored to the student's strengths and weaknesses, called an **individualized education program (IEP)**, must be developed and described in written form for each student identified as having a special educational need. The same multidisciplinary team that has evaluated the student typically develops this IEP and includes in it the components listed in Figure 5.3. All team members agree to and sign it and then continue to review and (if appropriate) revise it at least once a year—more frequently if conditions warrant doing so or if a parent or teacher requests a review. A bit later in the chapter, we will examine excerpts from one student's IEP.

Due process Implicit in IDEA is the assumption that a student with disabilities has the same rights as any other U.S. citizen. IDEA mandates several practices that ensure that the student's rights, as well as those of parents acting on behalf of their child, are preserved throughout the decision-making process:

- Parents must be notified in writing before the school takes any action (e.g., testing, change in educational placement) that may change their child's educational program.
- Parents can give or withhold permission to have their child evaluated for special education services.

■ **least restrictive environment** Most typical and standard educational environment that can reasonably meet a student's needs.

■ *individualized education program (IEP)* Written description of an appropriate instructional program for a student with special needs.

- At their request, parents can see all school records about their child.
- If parents and the school system disagree on the most appropriate placement for a child, mediation or a hearing before an impartial individual (someone who is not an employee of the school district) can be used in an attempt to resolve the differences.

In the early years of IDEA, particularly in the late 1970s and throughout the 1980s, many classroom teachers continued to use their regular curriculum and methods for their nondisabled students and adapted the curriculum and methods as necessary to accommodate students with special needs. One or more special education teachers would visit the classroom periodically to give guidance and support or perhaps to provide individualized instruction to students with special needs. But within the past decade or so, two notable changes in thinking have occurred (R. Turnbull et al., 2004). First, special education experts have begun to argue that truly inclusive practices require individualization of instruction for *all* students, not just those with identified needs. Such individualization must necessarily entail a major overhaul of traditional curriculum materials and instructional practices, rather than just occasional modifications or "add-ons" for students who have disabilities. Second, experts now see effective teaching as involving an equal, collaborative partnership between regular classroom teachers and special educators who jointly teach all students—both those with disabilities and those without—throughout the school day (e.g., Thousand, Villa, & Nevin, 1994).

Is Inclusion in the Best Interest of Students?

Despite the clear mandates of IDEA, inclusion is a controversial and hotly debated practice among both theorists and practitioners (Brantlinger, 1997; B. K. Keogh & MacMillan, 1996; W. Stainback & Stainback, 1992). Some argue that all students, including those with severe and multiple disabilities, have the right to be educated in neighborhood schools and general education classrooms with their nondisabled peers (e.g., Kunc, 1984; S. Stainback & Stainback, 1985, 1990). They further argue that students are most likely to develop normal peer relationships and social skills when they participate as fully as possible in the overall "life" of their school (e.g., Hahn, 1989; Will, 1986). Yet other experts worry that when students with special needs are in a regular classroom for the entire school day, they cannot possibly get the intense specialized instruction that many need to achieve essential basic skills in reading, mathematics, and so on (Manset & Semmel, 1997; Zigmond et al., 1995).

In fact, many research studies indicate that placement in general education classrooms can have several benefits over educating students in self-contained "special education" classrooms:

- Academic achievement equivalent to (and sometimes higher than) what it would be in a self-contained classroom
- More positive self-concept and greater self-esteem
- More frequent interaction with nondisabled peers
- Better social skills
- More appropriate classroom behavior

■ Why do you think students placed in regular classrooms often have more appropriate classroom behavior?

We are especially likely to see such benefits when regular classroom materials and instruction are tailored to students' specific educational needs and academic levels (Halvorsen & Sailor, 1990; Hunt & Goetz, 1997; Scruggs & Mastropieri, 1994; Slavin, 1987; S. Stainback & Stainback, 1992). It is important to note, however, that many studies comparing the effectiveness of regular class versus special class placement are correlational rather than experimental studies, making it difficult to draw firm conclusions about causal relationships (Madden & Slavin, 1983; D. M. Murphy, 1996). Furthermore, research has focused more on students with mild disabilities than severe disabilities and more on students in the elementary grades rather than those in the secondary grades (B. K. Keogh & MacMillan, 1996).

Students with special needs are probably not the only ones who benefit from inclusive practices. Nondisabled students often benefit as well: They develop an increasing awareness of the very heterogeneous nature of the human race and discover that individuals with special needs, apart from some obvious disabilities, are in many respects very much like themselves (Hunt & Goetz, 1997; D. Staub, 1998). As an example, I think of my son Jeff's friendship with classmate Evan during their third-grade year. Evan had

Inclusion has benefits for students both with and without disabilities.

severe physical and cognitive disabilities, and a teacher aide was by his side throughout the day to tend to his health needs. The only recognizable word in Evan's oral vocabulary was *hi*; more often, he communicated simply by making the sound "aaaahhh." Early in the school year, the teacher asked Jeff to be a "special friend" to Evan, interacting with him at lunch and whenever else the class schedule allowed time. Evan always made it clear through gestures and facial expressions that he was delighted to spend time with his friend, giving Jeff—who, as a child, was quite shy—a considerable boost in social self-confidence. Several years later Jeff reflected on his friendship with Evan:

> It made me realize that Evan was a person too. It made me realize that I could have a friendship with a boy with disabilities. Doing things that made Evan happy made me happy as well. I knew that *Evan* knew that we were friends.

Classifying Students with Special Needs

The practice of classifying students with special needs has some inherent difficulties. Experts often disagree about how to define categories of special needs; categories that cannot be described in terms of a readily observable physical condition (e.g., learning disabilities, emotional and behavioral problems, giftedness) are especially difficult to pin down with precise definitions. Experts also disagree about the best ways to identify members of those categories, yet different identification methods sometimes lead to different conclusions as to which students have special needs. Even when experts do agree on such issues, any category of students with special needs includes individuals who are often as different as they are similar and so require different types of support and services (Adelman, 1996; MacMillan & Meyers, 1979). A final concern is that labels such as "mental retardation" or "learning disability" may unintentionally communicate the message that students with special needs are somehow inferior; thus, these labels can adversely affect self-esteem.

■ Why do you think it is so difficult to define some categories of special needs?

It is important to note, however, that some students with special needs develop low self-esteem as a result of their disabilities (perhaps because they consistently experience failure or because other people treat them as "different") *before* any label is ever applied to them at school (M. C. Reynolds, 1984). In such instances, discovering that their failures are due to a previously undiagnosed disability can actually help repair some of the damage (e.g., Zambo, 2003). An essay written by 17-year-old Colin, presented in Figure 5.4, reveals some of the mixed effects a label can have on students' self-perceptions.

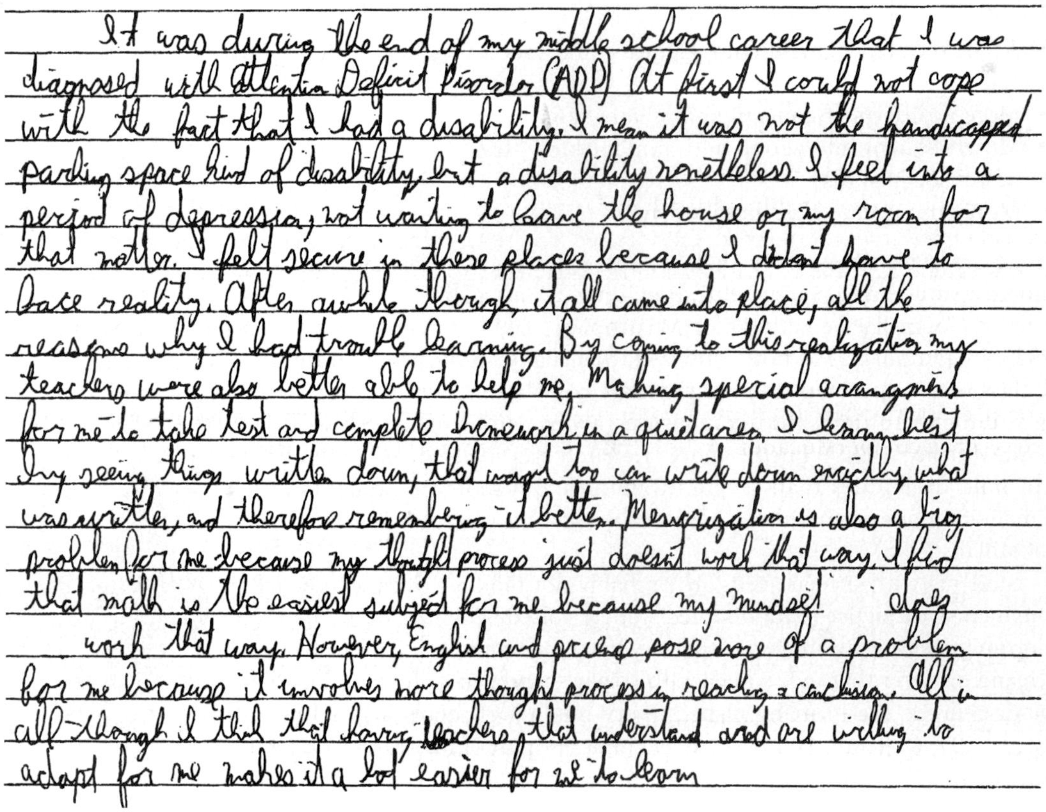
It was during the end of my middle school career that I was diagnosed with Attention Deficit Disorder (ADD). At first I could not cope with the fact that I had a disability. I mean it was not the handicapped parking space kind of disability, but a disability nonetheless. I feel into a period of depression, not wanting to leave the house or my room for that matter. I felt secure in these places because I didn't have to face reality. After awhile though, it all came into place, all the reasons why I had trouble learning. By coming to this realization my teachers were also better able to help me, making special arangments for me to take test and complete homework in a quiet area. I learn best by seeing things written down, that way I too can write down exactly what was written, and therefore remembering it better. Memorization is also a big problem for me because my thought process just doesn't work that way. I find that math is the easiest subject for me because my mindset does work that way. However, English and science pose more of a problem for me because it involves more thought process in reading & cachion. All in all though I think that having teachers that understand and are willing to adapt for me makes it a lot easier for me to learn

FIGURE 5.4 Labeling students with special needs has both advantages and disadvantages, as 17-year-old Colin reveals.

Classifying students with special needs has other advantages as well. Although members of the same category are in some respects very different from one another, they also tend to have characteristics in common; these similarities allow educators to make certain generalizations about how to foster the academic and social development of students in any given category. In addition, categories provide a rallying point around which social and political forces can promote the interests of these students. For example, over the years such organizations as the American Association on Mental Retardation and the Autism Society of America, and such journals as the *Journal of Learning Disabilities* and *Gifted Child Quarterly*, have emerged. Special interest groups are often instrumental in collecting information, supporting and publishing research, and campaigning for federal and state legislation to help students with special needs (Hobbs, 1980).[2] But probably the most influential factor affecting educators' use of categories and labels, at least in the United States, is that federal funds, available to support special educational services for up to 12 percent of the student population, are provided only when students have been formally identified as having a disabling condition.

For such reasons, the great majority of educators continue to use categories and labels when identifying and working with students who have special educational needs. They worry, however, that labels may focus others' attention on students' weaknesses rather than on their many strengths and age-typical characteristics. To minimize such an effect, special educators urge us all to use **people-first language** whenever we refer to students with disabilities—in other words, to mention the person *before* the disability. For instance, we might say *students with mental retardation* rather than *mentally retarded students* or *student who is blind* rather than *blind student*. Placing the person before the disability when we speak and write can help us remind both ourselves and others that a disability is only one of many characteristics that a particular student has.

I have organized the upcoming discussion of students with special needs using the five general categories that appear in the "Inclusion" tables throughout the book. Table 5.3 lists the specific kinds of special needs that fall within each category. Note that giftedness is listed as a special need in the table but is not specifically covered by IDEA.[3] In the United States the Jacob K. Javits Gifted and Talented Student Education Act (PL 103-382, reauthorized in 1994 by PL 103-382, XIV) encourages, but does not necessarily mandate, special educational services for students who are gifted. In addition, many state governments either encourage or mandate such services (Council for Exceptional Children, 1995). Most students with exceptional gifts and talents are unlikely to reach their full potential within the context of regular classroom assignments and activities; for this reason, many school districts *do* provide special programs for these students.

STUDENTS WITH SPECIFIC COGNITIVE OR ACADEMIC DIFFICULTIES

Some students with special educational needs may show few if any outward signs of physical disability yet have cognitive difficulties that interfere with their ability to learn academic material or perform typical classroom tasks. This section describes three categories of special needs that involve specific cognitive or academic difficulties: learning disabilities, attention-deficit hyperactivity disorder, and speech and communication disorders.

Learning Disabilities

Students with **learning disabilities** comprise the largest single category of students with special needs (U.S. Dept. of Education, 1996). Experts have not reached complete agreement about how

---

[2] Most of these organizations offer a wealth of information through their Web sites. You may want to visit www.aamr.org (American Association on Mental Retardation), www.asha.org (American Speech-Language-Hearing Association), www.autism-society.org (Autism Society of America), www.ccbd.net (Council for Children with Behavioral Disorders), www.cec.sped.org (Council for Exceptional Children), www.ldanatl.org (Learning Disabilities Association of America), www.nagc.org (National Association for Gifted Children), or other sites located through a Web search.

[3] IDEA does not specifically identify attention-deficit hyperactivity disorder as a qualifying condition, but students with ADHD are often eligible for services under the category "other health impaired" (Barkley, 1998).

■ **people-first language** Language in which a student's disability is identified *after* the student is named.

■ **learning disabilities** Deficiencies in one or more specific cognitive processes rather than in overall cognitive functioning.

TABLE 5.3   S T U D E N T S   I N   I N C L U S I V E   S E T T I N G S

General and Specific Categories of Students with Special Needs

GENERAL CATEGORY	SPECIFIC CATEGORIES	DESCRIPTION
Students with specific cognitive or academic difficulties	Learning disabilities	Difficulties in specific cognitive processes (e.g., in perception, language, memory, or metacognition) that cannot be attributed to such other disabilities as mental retardation, emotional or behavioral disorders, or sensory impairments
	Attention-deficit hyperactivity disorder (ADHD)	Disorder marked by either or both of these characteristics: (a) difficulty focusing and maintaining attention and (b) frequent hyperactive and impulsive behavior
	Speech and communication disorders	Impairments in spoken language (e.g., mispronunciations of certain sounds, stuttering, or abnormal syntactical patterns) or language comprehension that significantly interfere with classroom performance
Students with social or behavioral problems	Emotional and behavioral disorders	Emotional states and behaviors that are present over a substantial period of time and significantly disrupt academic learning and performance
	Autism	Condition marked by varying degrees of impaired social interaction and communication, repetitive behaviors, and restricted interests; a strong need for a predictable environment also commonly observed
Students with general delays in cognitive and social functioning	Mental retardation	Condition marked by significantly below-average general intelligence and deficits in adaptive behavior (i.e., in practical and social intelligence)
Students with physical or sensory challenges	Physical and health impairments	Physical or medical conditions (usually long-term) marked by one or more of three characteristics: limited energy and strength, reduced mental alertness, or little muscle control
	Visual impairments	Malfunctions of the eyes or optic nerves that prevent normal vision even with corrective lenses
	Hearing loss	Malfunctions of the ear or associated nerves that interfere with the perception of sounds within the frequency range of normal speech
	Severe and multiple disabilities	Presence of two or more disabilities, the combination of which requires significant adaptations and highly specialized educational services
Students with advanced cognitive development	Giftedness	Unusually high ability or aptitude in one or more of these areas: general intellectual ability, aptitude in a specific academic field, creativity, visual or performing arts, or leadership

best to define this category, but the following criteria are typically used (Mercer, Jordan, Allsopp, & Mercer, 1996; National Joint Committee on Learning Disabilities, 1994):

- *The student has significant difficulties in one or more specific cognitive processes.*   Such difficulties are often present throughout a person's life and are assumed to result from a specific, possibly inherited dysfunction of the brain (J. G. Light & Defries, 1995; Manis, 1996). Figure 5.5 lists some forms that a learning disability might take.
- *The student's difficulties cannot be attributed to other disabilities, such as mental retardation, an emotional or behavioral disorder, hearing loss, or a visual impairment.*   Many students with learning disabilities have average or above-average intelligence. For example, they may obtain average scores on an intelligence test, or at least on some of its subtests.
- *The student's difficulties interfere with academic achievement to such a degree that special educational services are warranted.*   Students with learning disabilities invariably show poor performance in one or more specific areas of the academic curriculum. At the same time, they may exhibit average or above-average achievement in other subjects.

Common Characteristics   Students identified as having a learning disability are a particularly heterogeneous group: They are probably far more different than they are similar (Bassett et al., 1996;

FIGURE 5.5 Examples of cognitive processing deficiencies in students with learning disabilities

Perceptual difficulty. Students may have difficulty understanding or remembering the information they receive through a particular sensory modality. For example, they may have trouble perceiving subtle differences between similar sounds in speech (a difficulty in auditory discrimination), retaining a clear image of letters they have seen (a difficulty in visual-spatial perception), or remembering the correct order of letters in a word (a difficulty in memory for a visual sequence).

Memory difficulty. Students may have less capacity for remembering the information they receive, over either the short or long run; more specifically, they may have problems with either *working memory* or *long-term memory* (see Chapter 6).

Metacognitive difficulty. Students may have difficulty using effective learning strategies, monitoring progress toward learning goals, and in other ways directing their own learning.

Difficulty processing oral language. Students may have trouble understanding spoken language or remembering what they have been told.

Reading difficulty. Students may have trouble recognizing printed words or comprehending what they read. An extreme form of this condition is known as *dyslexia.*

Written language difficulty. Students may have problems in handwriting, spelling, or expressing themselves coherently on paper. An extreme form of this condition is known as *dysgraphia.*

Mathematical difficulty. Students may have trouble thinking about or remembering information involving numbers. For example, they may have a poor sense of time or direction or they may have difficulty learning basic number facts. An extreme form of this condition is known as *dyscalculia.*

Difficulty with social perception. Students may have trouble interpreting the social cues and signals that others give them (e.g., they may have difficulty perceiving another person's feelings or reactions to a situation) and therefore may respond inappropriately in social situations.

Sources: Conte, 1991; Eden, Stein, & Wood, 1995; Hanich, Jordan, Kaplan, & Dick, 2001; Landau & McAninch, 1993; Lerner, 1985; H. L. Swanson, 1993; H. L. Swanson, Cooney, & O'Shaughnessy, 1998; R. Turnbull et al., 2004; Wong, 1991a, 1991b.

Chalfant, 1989; National Joint Committee on Learning Disabilities, 1994). Students with learning disabilities typically have many strengths; however, they may face such challenges as these:

- Difficulty sustaining attention when confronted with competing stimuli
- Poor reading skills
- Ineffective learning and memory strategies
- Difficulty with tasks involving abstract reasoning
- Poor self-concept and low motivation for academic tasks (especially if they receive no remedial assistance in areas of difficulty)
- Poor motor skills
- Poor social skills
  (Chapman, 1988; Gresham & MacMillan, 1997; Mastropieri & Scruggs, 2000; Mercer, 1997; H. L. Swanson, 1993; Wong, 1991b.)

Such characteristics are typical of many students with learning disabilities, but they certainly do not describe *all* of these students. For instance, some students with learning disabilities are attentive in class and work diligently on assignments, and some are socially skillful and popular with their peers (Heward, 2003).

Learning disabilities may also manifest themselves somewhat differently in elementary and secondary school students (Lerner, 1985). At the elementary level, students with learning disabilities are apt to exhibit poor attention and motor skills and often have trouble acquiring one or more basic skills. As these students reach the upper elementary grades, they may also begin to show emotional problems, due at least partly to frustration about their repeated academic failures.

At the secondary school level, difficulties with attention and motor skills may diminish. But at this level, students with learning disabilities may be particularly susceptible to emotional problems. On top of dealing with the usual emotional issues of adolescence (e.g., dating, peer pressure), they must also deal with the more stringent demands of the junior high and high school curriculum. Learning in secondary schools is highly dependent on reading and learning from relatively sophisticated textbooks, yet the average high school student with a learning disability reads at a third- to fifth-grade level and has acquired few if any effective study strategies (Alley & Deshler, 1979; E. S. Ellis & Friend, 1991). To get a sense of how these students may feel under such circumstances, try the following exercise.

Students with learning disabilities often have less effective learning and memory skills, lower self-esteem, and less motivation to succeed at academic tasks.

Experiencing FIRSTHAND ·A Reading Assignment

Read the following passage carefully. I will be testing you on its contents later in the chapter.

> Personality research needs to refocus on global traits because such traits are an important part of every-day social discourse, because they embody a good deal of folk wisdom and common sense, because understanding and evaluating trait judgments can provide an important route toward the improvement of social judgment, and because global traits offer legitimate, if necessarily incomplete, explanations of behavior. A substantial body of evidence supporting the existence of global traits includes personality correlates of behavior, interjudge agreement in personality ratings, and the longitudinal stability of personality over time. Future research should clarify the origins of global traits, the dynamic mechanisms through which they influence behavior, and the behavioral cues through which they can most accurately be judged. (Funder, 1991, p. 31)

How well do you think you are likely to perform on the upcoming test over the passage?

· · · · · · ·

You probably found the passage more challenging to read than the rest of the chapter. In fact, this passage is a fairly typical one from *Psychological Science*, a professional journal written for people with advanced education in psychology; many of its readers hold doctoral degrees. Essentially, I was asking you to read something that was written well above the typical college student's reading level. (If it's any consolation; I won't *really* be testing you on its contents.)

I hope that during the exercise you experienced just a little bit of the frustration that high school students with learning disabilities probably experience each day. Yet secondary school teachers rarely teach reading or study skills as a part of their course content. For many students with learning disabilities, school success may constantly seem like an uphill battle. Perhaps for this reason, students with learning disabilities are among those students most at risk for dropping out of school (Barga, 1996).

Adapting Instruction   As we have seen, students with learning disabilities are a heterogeneous group, and instructional strategies must be tailored to specific strengths and weaknesses. Nevertheless, several strategies should benefit a broad range of students:

◎   *Minimize potentially distracting stimuli.* Because many students with learning disabilities are easily distracted, we should minimize the presence of other stimuli likely to compete for their attention. For example, we might make sure that the classroom is fairly quiet during seatwork time. We might pull down window shades if students in other classes are working or playing outside. And we might ask students to keep their desks clear of all objects and materials except those with which they are presently working (Buchoff, 1990).

◎   *Use multiple modalities to present information.* Some students with learning disabilities have trouble learning through a particular modality—for example, through seeing or listening. We therefore need to be flexible in the modalities we use to communicate information to these students. In different situations we might want to use visual, auditory, tactile (touch), or even kinesthetic (movement) approaches (J. W. Wood, 1998). For example, when teaching a student how to read and spell a particular word, we might write the word for the student (visual input), say its letters aloud (auditory input), have the student feel the word spelled with sandpaper letters (tactile input), have the student trace or write the word (kinesthetic), and have the student repeat the word's letters (both kinesthetic and auditory). In our lectures to secondary students, we may want to incorporate videos, graphics, and other visual materials; we might also encourage students to audiotape the lectures (J. W. Wood & Rosbe, 1985).

◎   *Analyze students' errors for clues about processing difficulties.* Like anyone else, students with learning disabilities are apt to make errors in responding to questions, problems, and other academic tasks. Rather than thinking of certain responses simply as being wrong, we can examine them for clues about specific difficulties students are having (Lerner, 1985). For example, a student who solves a subtraction problem this way:

$$\begin{array}{r} 85 \\ -29 \\ \hline 64 \end{array}$$

may be applying an inappropriate rule (*always subtract the smaller number from the larger one*) to subtraction. A student who reads the sentence *I drove the car* as "I drove the *cat*" may be having trouble using context clues in reading words and sentences. The following exercise can give you a taste of what error analysis might involve.

Interpreting Student Artifacts and Behaviors

Policeman
Daniel, age 7, wrote and illustrated the sentence to the right. In small print, his first-grade teacher clarified what he intended to say: "I trust a policeman." As you look at Daniel's sentence:

- Identify one or more patterns of errors in his word spellings
- Speculate about cognitive processing difficulties that such errors might reflect

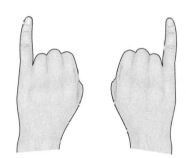

I trust a policeman.

In spelling the words, Daniel captured several sounds correctly, including the "s" and final "t" sounds in *trust* and all of the consonant sounds in *policeman*. However, he misrepresented the first two consonant sounds in *trust*, replacing the *T* and *R* with an *N*. He also neglected to represent most of the vowel sounds in both *trust* and *policeman*, and two of the three vowels he did include (I for the article *a* and the *E* near the end of *policeman*) are incorrect. We might suspect that Daniel has difficulty hearing all the distinct sounds in spoken words and matching them with the letters he sees in written words. Such difficulties are quite common in young elementary school students who have significant reading disabilities (Hulme & Joshi, 1998; Stanovich, 2000; H. L. Swanson, Mink, & Bocian, 1999).

◎ *Teach learning and memory strategies.* Many students with learning disabilities benefit from being taught specific strategies for performing tasks and remembering classroom subject matter. For example, we might teach students to give themselves mental "instructions" that help them follow the appropriate steps in a task (Graham & Harris, 1996; Meichenbaum, 1985). We might teach them to identify the underlying themes of stories by asking themselves such questions as "What was the main character's problem?" and "Was what happened good or bad? Why?" (Wilder & Williams, 2001). We might teach them concrete strategies for taking notes and organizing their homework assignments (Eilam, 2001; J. W. Wood & Rosbe, 1985). We might also teach them certain **mnemonics,** or memory tricks, to help them remember particular facts (Mastropieri & Scruggs, 1992). (Figure 5.6 presents one simple mnemonic as an illustration.) Additional strategies for helping students study and learn more effectively are described in Chapters 6 and 8.

◎ *Provide study aids.* In addition to teaching more effective study strategies, we can provide scaffolding to support the sometimes overwhelming task of studying classroom material. For instance, we might provide study guides that help students identify important ideas (Mastropieri & Scruggs, 1992). We might show how material is organized, perhaps with outlines that enumerate major and subordinate ideas or with graphics that show how key concepts are interrelated (Brigham & Scruggs, 1995; J. W. Wood & Rosbe, 1985). And we might let students copy (or receive a duplicate of) the notes of a classmate who is a particularly good note taker.

These teaching strategies are helpful not only for students with learning disabilities, but also for students with attention-deficit hyperactivity disorder, the category we turn to now.

Young children with learning disabilities often confuse lowercase *b* and *d*. By clenching their fists as shown here and "reading" their hands in the normal left-to-right direction, they can more easily remember the difference: *b* comes first in both the alphabet and the fists.

FIGURE 5.6 A mnemonic for remembering the letters *b* and *d*

Attention-Deficit Hyperactivity Disorder (ADHD)

Almost all children and adolescents can be inattentive, hyperactive, and impulsive at one time or another. But students with **attention-deficit hyperactivity disorder (ADHD)** typically have marked deficits in these areas, as follows (American Psychiatric Association, 1994; Barkley, 1998):

- *Inattention.*   Students may have considerable difficulty focusing and maintaining attention on assigned tasks. For instance, they often have trouble listening to and following directions, make frequent and careless mistakes, are easily distracted by highly appealing alternatives, and may fail to persist at tasks that require sustained mental effort.

■ **mnemonic** Memory aid or trick designed to help students learn and remember a specific piece of information.

■ **attention-deficit hyperactivity disorder (ADHD)** Disorder marked by inattention, hyperactivity, impulsive behavior, or some combination of these.

- *Hyeractivity.*   Students may seem to have an excess amount of energy. For instance, they are apt to be fidgety, move around the classroom at inappropriate times, talk excessively, have difficulty working or playing quietly, and perhaps act as if they are "driven by a motor."
- *Impulsivity.*   Students almost invariably have trouble inhibiting inappropriate behaviors. They may blurt out answers, interrupt others, begin an assignment without waiting for instructions, or engage in risky or destructive behavior without thinking about potential consequences.

Students with ADHD do not always show all three of these characteristics. For instance, some are inattentive without also being hyperactive, as is true for Tim in the opening case study. But all students with ADHD appear to have one characteristic in common: an *inability to inhibit inappropriate thoughts, inappropriate actions, or both* (Barkley, 1998; Casey, 2001). Tim, for example, is easily distracted by his thoughts and daydreams when he should be focusing on a classroom lesson.

ADHD is assumed to have a biological and possibly genetic origin; it seems to run in families and is far more common in boys than in girls (Barkley, 1998; Purdie, Hattie, & Carroll, 2002). But once identified as having ADHD, many students can be helped through medication (e.g., Ritalin) in combination with behaviorist techniques (see Chapter 9) and remediation of cognitive difficulties (DuPaul, Barkley, & Connor, 1998; Gulley et al., 2003; Purdie et al., 2002).

Common Characteristics   In addition to inattentiveness, hyperactivity, and impulsivity, students identified as having ADHD may have characteristics such as these:

- Cognitive processing difficulties (e.g., see Figure 5.7)
- Poor school achievement
- Exceptional imagination and creativity
- Classroom behavior problems (e.g., disruptiveness, noncompliance with classroom rules)
- Difficulty interpreting and reasoning about social situations
- Greater emotional reactivity (e.g., excitability, hostility) in interactions with peers
- Few friendships; in some instances, outright rejection by peers
- Increased probability of using tobacco and alcohol in adolescence
  (Barkley, 1998; Gresham & MacMillan, 1997; Grodzinsky & Diamond, 1992; Hallowell, 1996; Lahey & Carlson, 1991; Landau & McAninch, 1993; E. P. Lorch et al., 1999; Milch-Reich et al., 1999; Whalen, Jamner, Henker, Delfino, & Lozano, 2002)

Some students with ADHD may also be identified as having a learning disability or an emotional or behavior disorder, while others may be gifted (Barkley, 1998; Conte, 1991; R. E. Reeve, 1990). The symptoms associated with ADHD may diminish in adolescence, but to some degree they persist throughout the school years, making it difficult for students to handle the increasing demands for independence and responsible behavior that come in high school (Barkley, 1998; Claude & Firestone, 1995; E. L. Hart, Lahey, Loeber, Applegate, & Frick, 1995). Accordingly, students with ADHD are at greater risk than average for dropping out of school (Barkley, 1998).

I am just doce with book. I really like ths book that I chose and id was a good chose. She dose not go back to San Fransico and find her peo pal She stay io the Artic. . I would be sared too and cold. Mya X has survied there. About done.

FIGURE 5.7 Like many students with ADHD, 10-year-old Joshua has specific cognitive processing difficulties. Although he has the math skills of a typical fifth grader, the book report shown here reflects his delayed reading comprehension and writing skills. Josh can more easily express his thoughts orally.

Adapting Instruction   Researchers and practitioners have offered several suggestions for helping students with ADHD:

◎   *Modify students' schedules and work environments.* The symptoms of ADHD tend to get progressively worse as the day goes on; ideally, then, students should have most academic subjects and challenging tasks in the morning rather than in the afternoon. Furthermore, students with ADHD often are distracted by what they see and hear in the classroom and have difficulty working in group situations. Moving their desks away from distractions (e.g., away from the door and window, not too close to classmates) and close to the teacher (where both independent and group work can be monitored) can enhance their attention and achievement (Barkley, 1998).

◎   *Teach attention-maintaining strategies.* As is true for students with learning disabilities, we can certainly remove stimuli that are likely to compete for students' attention. But in addition, we can teach students concrete strategies for keeping their attention on an assigned task

(Buchoff, 1990). For instance, we can ask them to keep their eyes on us when we're giving directions or providing new information. We can also tell them what specifically to listen for; for instance, we might say, "Listen carefully while I explain the things you should include in your essay." And we can encourage them to move to a new location if the current one presents too many distracting sights or sounds.

◎ *Provide outlets for excess energy.* To help students control excess energy, we should intersperse quiet academic work with frequent opportunities for physical exercise (Pfiffner & Barkley, 1998). We might also give students a "settling-in" time after recess or lunch before we ask them to engage in any activity that involves quiet concentration (Pellegrini & Horvat, 1995). For example, when students return from lunch, many elementary teachers begin the afternoon class session by reading a chapter from a high-interest storybook.

◎ *Help students organize and use their time effectively.* Because of their inattentiveness and hyperactivity, students with ADHD (like Tim in the opening case) often have difficulty completing daily classroom tasks. Several strategies can help these students organize themselves and use class time more effectively. We can show them how to establish a daily routine (including times to sharpen pencils, gather work materials together, etc.) and post that routine on their desks (Buchoff, 1990). We can break large tasks into smaller ones and set a short time limit for each subtask (Pfiffner & Barkley, 1998). We can provide daily or weekly "to do" lists on which students check off completed assignments (Buchoff, 1990; J. W. Wood & Rosbe, 1985). And we can provide a folder in which students can transport homework assignments to and from school (Buchoff, 1990).

◎ *Teach and encourage appropriate classroom behaviors.* A structured environment with clear expectations for behavior and definite consequences for appropriate and inappropriate actions is often effective for students with ADHD (Buchoff, 1990; Landau & McAninch, 1993; N. Nussbaum & Bigler, 1990; Pfiffner & Barkley, 1998). Our discussion of behaviorist techniques in Chapter 9 will provide many useful strategies for creating such an environment.

Speech and Communication Disorders

If you have studied a foreign language, think back to your early attempts to speak the language. Did you feel awkward, knowing that your pronunciation and grammar were almost certainly flawed? Did you sometimes worry that your imperfect speech might make you look foolish to your teacher or classmates? If you had such feelings, then you perhaps have an inkling of how some students with speech and communication disorders feel when they are asked to speak in class.

Speech and communication disorders are impairments in spoken language or in language comprehension that significantly interfere with students' classroom performance. Examples include persistent articulation problems (mispronunciations of certain sounds and words), stuttering, abnormal syntactical patterns, and difficulty understanding the speech of others. Speech and communication disorders are also suspected when students fail to demonstrate age-appropriate language (e.g., a kindergartner who communicates only by pointing and gesturing, or a third grader who says, "Him go," instead of, "He's gone"). In many cases the exact causes of these disorders are unknown (Wang & Baron, 1997).

The great majority of students with speech and communication disorders are in general education classrooms for most or all of the school day (U.S. Dept. of Education, 1996). Some of these students may have other disabilities as well, such as hearing loss or mental retardation (R. Turnbull et al., 2004). But many others are, in all other respects, just typical students.

Common Characteristics   Several characteristics are sometimes, although not always, observed in students with speech and communication disorders:

- Reluctance to speak
- Embarrassment and self-consciousness when speaking
- Difficulties in reading and writing
  (Fey, Catts, & Larrivee, 1995; LaBlance, Steckol, & Smith, 1994; Rice, Hadley, & Alexander, 1993)

■ **speech and communication disorders** Impairments in spoken language or language comprehension that significantly interfere with classroom performance.

We clied (climbed) up the pley gonds (playground) hist (highest) prot (part) of it and we wavd (waved) ane (our) roms (arms) the ick (ice) crem (cream) trok (truck) did not stop. Boom! iT is a thundr (thunder) said Mac.

We saw a big bolt rit (right) in frot of (front) us. Connor shoted (shouted) Lats (let's) get oot of (out) here! so we got o of (out) cyce. (quick) We Whent (went) in the ick (ice) creme (cream) shop anstead. (instead) we bot (bought)

ick (ice) creme. (cream) They gef us (gave) a Free mape (map) we stred to (started) go back. We went oll (all) ofer (over) tone. (town) but ven (then) fond (found) ot (out) the (that) was connors hoes (house) ocenst (across) the stert. (street)

Seven-year-old Issac receives speech therapy at school to address his consistent mispronunciation of certain sounds (e.g., he says "th" as "v"). In his writing, he sometimes spells words as he says them rather than as he hears them (e.g., he writes "ven" for *then*).

Adapting Instruction   Typically, a trained specialist will work with students, either in the regular classroom or in a separate setting, to help them improve or overcome their speech and communication difficulties. Nevertheless, general education teachers can assist in several ways:

◎ *Encourage regular oral communication.* Because students with speech and communication disorders need as much practice in classroom-based "public" speaking as their classmates, we can encourage them to talk in class, provided that doing so does not create exceptional stress for them (Patton, Blackbourn, & Fad, 1996).

◎ *Listen patiently.* When students have difficulty expressing themselves, we may be tempted to assist them—for example, by finishing their sentences. But we better help them when we allow them to complete their own thoughts, no matter how long it takes them to do so. We must learn to listen attentively and politely to students with speech problems without criticizing or ridiculing them, and we must encourage their peers to do likewise (R. B. Lewis & Doorlag, 1991; Patton et al., 1996).

◎ *Ask for clarification when a message is unclear.* On occasions when we haven't understood what students are saying, we should explain the things we *did* understand and ask them to clarify the rest. Honest feedback helps students learn how well they are communicating (Patton et al., 1996).

General Recommendations for Students with Specific Cognitive or Academic Difficulties

In addition to the instructional strategies described in the preceding pages, there are several more general strategies we can use to help students with specific cognitive or academic difficulties:

◎ *Promote success on academic tasks.* Many of the students just described, especially those with learning disabilities or ADHD, perform poorly on academic tasks and assignments. They may lack some of the basic concepts and skills that their nondisabled peers have already acquired and so need individualized instruction and practice to fill in the gaps. Many theorists suggest that one or another form of *direct instruction*, whereby students are specifically taught the things they need to learn, can be especially effective (E. S. Ellis & Friend, 1991; Tarver, 1992; R. Turnbull et al., 2004). Other theorists recommend that we also teach students specific ways of *thinking* about

■ See Chapter 13 for more details about direct instruction.

classroom tasks. For example, when we teach students how to write stories or essays, we should give them extensive instruction and practice in each phase of the writing process: planning, drafting, editing, and revising (Hallenbeck, 1996).

◎ *Clearly describe expectations for academic performance.* Students will have an easier time performing classroom tasks successfully when they know exactly what we expect them to do. We may sometimes need to explain in very concrete and precise terms what an assigned task entails. For instance, before students begin a science lab activity, we might remind them to carefully follow the steps described on the lab sheet, review the safety precautions they should take while using the equipment, and repeat the details they should be sure to include in their lab reports.

◎ *Address students' reading difficulties, and take their skill levels into account when assigning reading materials.* Many students with specific cognitive or academic difficulties have poor reading skills. Certainly we must take active steps to remediate their reading difficulties; students who receive intervention for reading problems *early* in their school careers have fewer learning problems later on (Pitoniak & Royer, 2001). Yet reading difficulties often persist, and so we may sometimes need to identify alternatives to standard grade-level textbooks to present academic content. For example, we might reduce the amount of reading required of these students, substitute materials written at a simpler (yet not "babyish") level, or present information through some medium other than written text (E. S. Ellis & Friend, 1991; R. B. Lewis & Doorlag, 1991).

◎ *Take steps to enhance self-confidence and motivation.* Because students with specific cognitive or academic difficulties typically have a history of failure at certain kinds of tasks—including many tasks that seem to come easily to their peers—they may have little self-confidence or motivation to perform those tasks. In such situations we can help students see that they are making progress and that they do some things very well (Buchoff, 1990). For example, we can give them daily or weekly goals that we know they can attain. We can have them keep journals in which they describe the successes they have achieved each day. And we can give them opportunities to do tasks that they enjoy and usually perform successfully (Buchoff, 1990).

■ Chapters 10 and 12 describe the nature of self-confidence (more specifically, *self-efficacy*) and its role in motivation.

Our focus so far has been on cognitive and academic difficulties. For some students, however, social and behavioral problems predominate over academic concerns. It is to such students that we turn now.

STUDENTS WITH SOCIAL OR BEHAVIORAL PROBLEMS

Many students have minor social, emotional, or behavioral difficulties at one time or another, particularly during times of unusual stress or major life changes. Often these problems are temporary, especially when students have the support of caring adults. At other times the problems are more enduring but do *not* reflect a disability. Perhaps there is a mismatch between a student's temperament and a teacher's expectations for classroom behavior (see the earlier section "Temperament in the Classroom"), or perhaps a teacher has simply not made expectations and rules for classroom behavior clear (B. K. Keogh, 2003; Mehan, 1979). In such situations students' "problems" may decrease or disappear with a change in instructional practices or classroom management strategies.

Yet a few students show a pattern of behavioral problems that consistently interfere with their learning and performance *regardless* of the teacher and classroom environment, and thus indicate a need for special educational services. This section looks at two groups of students who fall into this category: those with emotional and behavioral disorders and those with autism.

Emotional and Behavioral Disorders

Students with **emotional and behavioral disorders** become identified as students with special needs—and therefore as students who qualify for special educational services—when their problems have a substantial negative impact on classroom success and achievement. As is true for students with learning disabilities, students with emotional and behavioral disorders exhibit a wide variety of problems and are often more different from one another than they are similar. Examples of such problems include an inability to establish and maintain satisfactory interpersonal relationships with adults and peers, excessive and long-term depression or anxiety, exaggerated mood swings, and exceptionally aggressive or antisocial behavior.

■ **emotional and behavioral disorders** Emotional states and behaviors that consistently and significantly disrupt academic learning and performance.

■ Can you recall former classmates who had emotional or behavioral problems severe enough to interfere with their academic achievement?

The symptoms of emotional and behavioral disorders are often divided into two broad categories. **Externalizing behaviors** have direct or indirect effects on other people; examples are aggression, defiance, disobedience, lying, stealing, and lack of self-control. **Internalizing behaviors** primarily affect the student with the disorder; examples are anxiety, depression, withdrawal from social interaction, eating disorders, and suicidal tendencies. Although teachers are more likely to refer students with externalizing behaviors for evaluation and possible special services (M. M. Kerr & Nelson, 1989), students with internalizing behaviors can be at just as much risk for school failure.

Some emotional and behavioral disorders are believed to result from environmental factors, such as child abuse, inconsistent parenting practices, stressful living conditions, exposure to violence, and family alcohol or drug abuse (D. Glaser, 2000; H. C. Johnson & Friesen, 1993; Maughan & Cicchetti, 2002; G. R. Patterson, DeBaryshe, & Ramsey, 1989). But biological causes, such as inherited predispositions, chemical imbalances, brain injuries, and illnesses, may also contribute to emotional and behavioral problems (Hallowell, 1996; H. C. Johnson & Friesen, 1993). Some students with a genetic predisposition for an emotional or behavioral disorder exhibit few if any signs of a problem until adolescence, as the following case illustrates:

> As a high school freshman, Kirk was a well-behaved, likable student who was earning As and Bs and showing particular promise in science and mathematics. During his sophomore year, however, his grades began to slip, and he occasionally exhibited mildly hostile or defiant behaviors. Concerned, Kirk's parents and teachers imposed stricter limits on his behavior, but Kirk increasingly resisted any attempts to keep him in line. By the end of his junior year, Kirk was hanging out regularly with high school dropouts who engaged in minor criminal activities, and his grades had fallen to Cs and Ds.
>
> When Kirk failed three classes during the fall of his senior year, the school principal called him, his parents, and his faculty advisor to a meeting to determine how to help Kirk get back on track. At the meeting the principal described several occasions on which Kirk had acted disoriented, belligerent, and seemingly "high" on marijuana or some other illegal substance. At this point, an appropriate and constructive response on Kirk's part would have been to appear contrite and willing to change his behavior so that he could graduate—an essential goal given his strong desire to attend college the following year. Instead, Kirk sat at the meeting smirking (seemingly gleeful about his predicament) and focusing his attention on picking the peanuts out of a bowl of trail mix on the conference room table. By the end of the meeting, the principal was so infuriated by his behavior that she expelled him from school.
>
> A few days after his expulsion, Kirk was arrested for carrying an illegal weapon (a knife) on school property. Over the next two weeks, as he waited in the juvenile detention facility for his court hearing, his mental condition deteriorated rapidly, and a judge ordered his hospitalization in the state mental institution.

Kirk was eventually diagnosed with *bipolar disorder*, a condition (usually inherited) characterized by excessive mood swings (hence, the disorder is sometimes called manic depression) and in some cases (including Kirk's) by distorted thought processes. Bipolar disorder often does not appear until adolescence, even though its biological underpinnings have been present since birth (Griswold & Pessar, 2000).

Factors at school may exacerbate the challenges that students with emotional and behavioral problems already face. Their inappropriate behaviors interfere not only with academic achievement but also with peer relationships, thus leading to social as well as academic failure. Many students, especially those with externalizing behaviors, may eventually seek the companionship of the few peers who will accept them—peers who typically behave in similarly inappropriate ways. Antisocial students often provide mutual support for one another's antisocial behavior and may introduce one another to drugs, alcohol, or criminal activity (Dishion et al., 1999; G. R. Patterson et al., 1989). Such factors undoubtedly contribute to the high dropout rate of students with emotional and behavioral disorders: Fewer than 50 percent of these students graduate from high school (Bassett et al., 1996; Koyanagi & Gaines, 1993).

Common Characteristics   Although students with emotional and behavioral disorders are a very heterogeneous group indeed, many of them exhibit characteristics such as the following:

- Difficulty interacting with others in socially acceptable ways
- Difficulty establishing and maintaining satisfactory interpersonal relationships

■ **externalizing behavior** Symptom of an emotional or behavioral disorder that has direct or indirect effects on other people.

■ **internalizing behavior** Symptom of an emotional or behavioral disorder that primarily affects the student with the disorder, with little or no effect on others.

- Low self-esteem
- Frequent absences from school
- Deteriorating academic performance with increasing age
- Lack of awareness of the severity of their problems
  (DuPaul & Eckert, 1994; Grinberg & McLean-Heywood, 1999; Harter, 1999; Leiter & Johnsen, 1997; McGlynn, 1998; Morgan & Jenson, 1988; Richards, Symons, Greene, & Szuszkiewicz, 1995; R. Turnbull et al., 2004)

Some students with emotional and behavioral disorders have other special needs as well, including learning disabilities, mental retardation, or giftedness (Fessler, Rosenberg, & Rosenberg, 1991; R. Turnbull et al., 2004).

Adapting Instruction   Effective educational programs for students with emotional and behavioral disorders are usually tailored to each student's unique needs. Nevertheless, several strategies can benefit many of these students:

◎   *Show an interest in students' well-being.* Many students with emotional and behavioral disorders have few positive and productive relationships with individuals outside school; we can often help these students simply by showing them that we care about their welfare (Diamond, 1991). For example, we can greet them warmly when we see them in the hallway. We can express concern when they seem upset, worried, or overly stressed. We can lend a ready and supportive ear when they want to share their ideas, opinions, feelings, or frustrations. And we can let them know that such sharing is welcome by revealing aspects of our own personal lives (Diamond, 1991).

◎   *Make classroom activities relevant to students' interests.* Students with emotional and behavioral disorders are more likely to get involved in their schoolwork when teachers take their personal interests into account (Clarke et al., 1995; McWhiter & Bloom, 1994). Chapter 12 identifies several ways we can meet important instructional objectives while also addressing students' interests.

◎   *Give students a sense that they have some control over their circumstances.* Some students— especially those who exhibit defiance toward authority figures—often respond to efforts to control them by behaving even *less* appropriately. With such students, it is important to avoid power struggles—situations where only one person "wins" and the other inevitably loses. Instead, we must create situations in which we ensure that the students conform to classroom expectations and yet feel as if they have some control over what happens to them. For instance, we can teach them techniques for observing and monitoring their own actions, with the goal of developing more productive classroom behavior (Kern, Dunlap, Childs, & Clark, 1994). We can also give them choices (within reasonable limits) about how to proceed in particular situations (Knowlton, 1995). We will examine such approaches in more depth in our discussions of *self-regulation* in Chapter 10 and *self-determination* in Chapter 12.

To create "win-win" situations with students who misbehave frequently, teach them strategies for controlling their own behavior and give them choices when appropriate.

◎   *Be alert for signs of possible child abuse or neglect.* Possible indicators of abuse or neglect are frequent or serious physical injuries (e.g., bruises, burns, broken bones), untreated medical needs, obvious hunger, lack of warm clothing in cold weather, and exceptional knowledge about sexual matters (R. Turnbull et al., 2004). As teachers, we are both morally and legally obligated to report any cases of suspected child abuse to the proper authorities. You should consult with your principal about the specific policy in your own school district.

◎   *Be alert for signs that a student may be contemplating suicide.* Seriously depressed students often exhibit behaviors indicating that they may be thinking about taking their own lives. Warning signs include

- Sudden withdrawal from social relationships
- Increasing disregard for personal appearance
- Dramatic personality change
- Sudden elevation in mood
- Preoccupation with death and morbid themes
- Overt or veiled threats (e.g., "I won't be around much longer")
- Actions that indicate "putting one's affairs in order" (e.g., giving away prized possessions)
  (Kerns & Lieberman, 1993; Wiles & Bondi, 2001)

As teachers, we must take any of these warning signs seriously. We must show potentially suicidal students that we care very much about what happens to them, and we should seek help from trained professionals, such as a school psychologist or counselor, immediately (K. McCoy, 1994).

It is also essential that we help students with emotional and behavioral disorders acquire more appropriate behaviors—both those important for interacting effectively with others and those essential for maintaining a classroom environment conducive to learning. Strategies to improve behavior are likely to help students with autism as well; accordingly, I will describe such strategies after we discuss autism in the section that follows.

Autism

Autism is a condition that is almost certainly caused by a brain abnormality (Gillberg & Coleman, 1996). Perhaps its most central characteristic is a marked impairment in social interaction: Many students with autism prefer to be alone and form weak if any emotional attachments to other people (Denkla, 1986; Schreibman, 1988). Several other characteristics are also frequently observed: communication impairments (e.g., absent or delayed speech), repetitive behaviors (e.g., continually rocking or waving fingers in front of one's face), narrowly focused and odd interests (e.g., an unusual fascination with watches), aggression toward self or others, and a strong need for a predictable environment (American Psychiatric Association, 1994; E. G. Carr et al., 1994; Dalrymple, 1995; R. Turnbull et al., 2004). Some theorists have speculated that underlying autism is either an undersensitivity or oversensitivity to sensory stimulation and that the abnormal behaviors so commonly observed reflect various attempts to make the environment more tolerable (R. C. Sullivan, 1994; D. Williams, 1996). Temple Grandin, a woman who has gained international prominence as a desinger of livestock facilities, recalls what it was like to be a child with autism:

> From as far back as I can remember, I always hated to be hugged. I wanted to experience the good feeling of being hugged, but it was just too overwhelming. It was like a great, all-engulfing tidal wave of stimulation, and I reacted like a wild animal. . . .
>
> When I was little, loud noises were also a problem, often feeling like a dentist's drill hitting a nerve. They actually caused pain. I was scared to death of balloons popping, because the sound was like an explosion in my ear. Minor noises that most people can tune out drove me to distraction. (Grandin, 1995, pp. 63, 67)

Although the majority of students with autism are educated in self-contained classrooms or special schools, approximately one-fifth of them are enrolled in general education classrooms for part or all of the school day (U.S. Dept. of Education, 1996).[4]

Common Characteristics   In addition to the traits just listed, students with autism often have these characteristics:

- Strong visual-spatial thinking skills
- A lack of basic social skills (e.g., in making eye contact or seeking comfort from others when hurt or upset)
- Impaired social cognition (e.g., with regard to interpreting social situations or inferring others' thoughts and intentions)
- Echolalia (i.e., continually repeating a portion of what someone has just said)
- Strong attachments to certain inanimate objects
- Abnormal movements (e.g., an awkward gait, repetitive gestures)
  (Baron-Cohen, Tager-Flusberg, & Cohen, 1993; Denkla, 1986; Grandin, 1995; Koegel, 1995; Leary & Hill, 1996; C. C. Peterson, 2002; Schreibman, 1988; D. Williams, 1996)

Although some students with autism have average or above-average intelligence, others have varying degrees of mental retardation (Ritvo & Freeman, 1978). Individuals with autism often show great variability in their specific abilities. In a few instances students with autism may

■ **autism** Disability characterized by impaired social interaction and communication, repetitive behaviors, restricted interests, and a strong need for a predictable environment.

[4] For children with *Asperger syndrome*, a condition that shares some features with autism, the proportion enrolled in general education classes is considerably higher (Little, 2002). Students with Asperger syndrome exhibit major difficulties in social cognition and social functioning despite average or above-average intelligence.

exhibit *savant syndrome*, in that they possess an extraordinary ability (such as exceptional artistic or musical talent) that is quite remarkable in contrast to other aspects of their mental functioning (Treffert & Wallace, 2002; Winner, 2000b).

Adapting Instruction   Many of the classroom strategies described throughout this chapter are applicable for students with autism. In addition, the following strategies can be quite useful:

◎ *Minimize changes in the arrangement of the classroom.* Many students with autism feel more comfortable and secure in a predictable environment (Dalrymple, 1995) and become quite upset when objects or pieces of furniture in a familiar environment are rearranged. If we anticipate having a student with autism in class, we should identify a physical layout for the classroom that will be serviceable throughout the school year and change it later only if absolutely necessary.

◎ *Follow a regular daily or weekly schedule.* To the extent possible, we should schedule certain activities at the same time each day or on a particular day of each week. When the schedule changes (perhaps because of a fire drill or school assembly), we should prepare the student well in advance of the change and indicate when the schedule will be back to normal again (Dalrymple, 1995).

◎ *Use visual approaches to instruction.* Because students with autism often have strong visual-spatial skills but deficits in oral communication, a heavy emphasis on visual materials can be beneficial (Hogdon, 1995; C. C. Peterson, 2002; Quill, 1995). For instance, we might use objects, pictures, and photographs to convey ideas about academic topics. We might also provide a visual depiction of a student's daily schedule and give some sort of visual cue to indicate the start of a new activity.

General Recommendations for Students with Social or Behavioral Problems

Although the causes of emotional and behavioral disorders and those of autism are probably quite different, students with these disabilities may nevertheless benefit from some of the same teaching strategies. Certainly we want to promote success on academic tasks, perhaps by using some of the instructional strategies recommended earlier for students with specific cognitive or academic difficulties. In addition, students with social or behavioral problems may need extra assistance in learning appropriate and productive classroom behaviors. Several specific examples are presented in the Creating a Productive Classroom Environment feature "Helping Students with Social or Behavioral Problems." More general strategies include the following:

◎ *Teach interpersonal skills.* Many students with social or behavioral problems have never learned appropriate ways of relating to others and have trouble interpreting the nonverbal social cues (e.g., body language) that guide effective social interaction. Some students lack even the most basic social skills, and many others have difficulty cooperating, communicating, or resolving interpersonal conflicts. Directly teaching these students how to interact effectively with others is one obvious approach (see the section "Fostering Social Skills" in Chapter 3). The behaviorist techniques described in Chapter 9 can also be quite powerful (E. G. Carr et al., 1994; Koegel, Koegel, & Dunlap, 1996; Landau & McAninch, 1993; Morgan & Jenson, 1988). In addition, students with autism or emotional and behavioral disorders benefit from explicit training in social perspective taking (Hudley & Graham, 1993; LeBlanc et al., 2003). And, of course, students need opportunities to *practice* their new skills, perhaps through structured interactions in the classroom or through "partner" programs with young adults in the community (Slavin, 1990; Themann & Goldstein, 2001; R. Turnbull et al., 2004).

◎ *Communicate clear expectations for behavior.* When students exhibit serious behavior problems, it is especially important to specify exactly which behaviors are acceptable and unacceptable in precise and concrete language. For example, we can provide specific guidelines about when students can speak in class and when they are free to move about the classroom. Students are more likely to behave appropriately when they are given reasonable limits for their behavior.

◎ *Try to anticipate problems and then nip them in the bud.* After we have gotten to know students fairly well, we can in some cases predict the circumstances that are likely to precede and possibly trigger undesirable behaviors. For instance, I think of Ben, a 9-year-old boy who, although usually mild-mannered, had occasional unpredictable temper tantrums that would

■ Have you seen the movie *Rain Man*? Dustin Hoffman plays a man with autism and mental retardation who is especially adept at calculating probabilities.

Students with social or behavioral problems may need considerable guidance on how to interact appropriately with peers.

CREATING A PRODUCTIVE CLASSROOM ENVIRONMENT

Helping Students with Social or Behavioral Problems

Show an interest in students' well-being.

A teacher who sees a girl weeping quietly every day in class takes her aside when the other students have gone to lunch. As the student describes the nasty divorce proceedings in which her parents are involved, the teacher empathizes, explaining that his own parents divorced in an equally unpleasant fashion. He also connects her with a weekly support group that the school psychologist has formed for students whose parents are going through divorce.

Teach interpersonal skills.

When a student speaks to classmates only to insult them, her teacher meets with her after school to demonstrate more appropriate ways of initiating interaction. Together, they practice the new strategies through various role-playing situations.

Make expectations for classroom behavior clear and specific.

A teacher reminds a student, "You cannot borrow Mary's bottle of glue without asking. Check with Mary first to make sure it's all right for you to use her things. If Mary says no, ask another student."

Specify and follow through on consequences for appropriate and inappropriate behaviors.

A teacher tells a student, "Sam, you know that certain four-letter words, such as the two you just used, are unacceptable in this classroom. You also know the consequence for such behavior, so please go to the time-out corner for ten minutes."

Give feedback about specific behaviors rather than general areas of performance.

A teacher tells a student, "You did a good job in study hall today. You focused your attention on your homework, and you didn't retaliate when Jerome accidentally brushed past you on his way to my desk."

Expect gradual improvement rather than immediate perfection.

A teacher is pleased that a student who once refused to participate in classroom activities now gets involved in activities once or twice a week, even though that student still has some days when little is accomplished.

disrupt the entire class. Eventually his teacher discovered that his ears always turned red just before an outburst; this knowledge allowed her to divert Ben's tantrums to a punching bag, where he could unleash his feelings with only minimal distraction to the rest of the class (Jackson & Ormrod, 1998).

◎ *Specify and follow through on consequences.* When working with students with social or behavioral problems, it is especially important to describe the consequences—either reinforcing or punishing—to which various behaviors will lead; it is equally critical to follow through with those consequences (Knowlton, 1995; Pfiffner & Barkley, 1998). Furthermore, we should give students explicit feedback about their behavior. When praising desirable behavior, rather than saying "Well done" or "Nice job," we should describe exactly what behaviors we are praising. When imposing punishment for inappropriate behavior, we should tell students exactly what they have done wrong. For example, we might say, "You borrowed Austin's book without asking him first. You know that taking other students' possessions without their permission is against class rules."

① Tell what they have done wrong
② OR get them to tell you the consequence

You should be aware that the job of helping students with social or behavioral problems is often a challenging one. Many of these students will at first resist any efforts to help them. It may only be when they themselves observe the natural consequences of their changing behavior—for example, when they start to make new friends or when they get along better with their teachers—that they begin to recognize the value of your guidance and support.

STUDENTS WITH GENERAL DELAYS IN COGNITIVE AND SOCIAL FUNCTIONING

One of the categories in the "Students in Inclusive Settings" tables located throughout the book is *students with general delays in cognitive and social functioning*. I have intentionally used this term so that it might include any student with a pattern of developmental delays in all areas, whether the student is specifically identified as having a disability or not. For instance, educators sometimes use the term *slow learner* to describe a student who obtains intelligence test scores in the 70s and has difficulties with virtually all aspects of the academic curriculum yet does not qualify for special educational services. A student with more pronounced developmental delays may be specifically identified as having *mental retardation*, a diagnosis that does fall under the auspices of IDEA.

Mental Retardation

Students with **mental retardation** show developmental delays in most aspects of their academic and social functioning. More specifically, they exhibit *both* of the following characteristics (Luckasson et al., 2002):

- *Significantly below-average general intelligence.* Intelligence test scores of students with mental retardation are quite low—usually no higher than 65 or 70, reflecting performance in the bottom 2 percent of their age-group (B. K. Keogh & MacMillan, 1996; R. Turnbull et al., 2004). These students show other signs of below-average intelligence as well; for instance, they learn slowly and perform quite poorly on school tasks in comparison with their age-mates. And they show consistently poor achievement across virtually all academic subject areas.
- *Deficits in adaptive behavior.* In addition to showing low intelligence and achievement, students with mental retardation typically behave in ways that we would expect of much younger children. Their deficits in **adaptive behavior** include limitations in *practical intelligence*—managing the ordinary activities of daily living—and *social intelligence*—conducting themselves appropriately in social situations.

Mental retardation is often caused by genetic conditions; for example, most children with Down syndrome have delayed cognitive development. Other cases are due to biological but non-inherited causes, such as severe malnutrition or excessive alcohol consumption during the mother's pregnancy or oxygen deprivation during a difficult birth (Dorris, 1989; B. K. Keogh & MacMillan, 1996). In still other situations, environmental factors, such as parental neglect or an extremely impoverished and unstimulating home environment, may be at fault (Batshaw & Shapiro, 1997; A. A. Baumeister, 1989). Although usually a long-term condition, mental retardation is not necessarily a lifelong disability, especially when the presumed cause is environmental rather than genetic (Jackson & Ormrod, 1998; Landesman & Ramey, 1989).

Common Characteristics Although most students with mental retardation are educated in self-contained classrooms, separate schools, or other facilities, a small proportion of them attend general education classes for part or all of the school day (U.S. Dept. of Education, 1996). Students with mental retardation are likely to display many or all of the following characteristics:

- A desire to "belong" and fit in at school
- Less general knowledge about the world
- Poor reading and language skills
- Lack of metacognitive awareness and few, if any, effective learning and memory strategies
- Difficulty with abstract ideas
- Difficulty generalizing something learned in one situation to a new situation
- Difficulty filling in details when instructions are incomplete or ambiguous
- Poor motor skills
- Immature play behaviors and interpersonal skills
  (Beirne-Smith et al., 2002: Butterfield & Ferretti, 1987; Gresham & MacMillan, 1997; F. P. Hughes, 1998; Kail, 1990; Patton et al., 1996; R. Turnbull et al., 2004)

Adapting Instruction Many of the strategies I've previously described in this chapter can be useful for students with mental retardation. Here are some additional strategies to keep in mind:

◎ *Pace instruction slowly enough to ensure a high rate of success.* When working with a student who has mental retardation, we should move through topics and assign new tasks slowly enough that the student experiences a high degree of success. Students with mental retardation typically have a long history of failure at academic tasks; hence they need frequent success experiences to learn that they *can* succeed in school.

◎ *Explain tasks concretely, specifically, and completely.* As noted earlier, students with mental retardation have difficulty filling in details correctly when instructions are ambiguous or incomplete. If we tell a student only to "Take this absentee sheet to the principal's office," it may not occur to the student to return to the classroom after completing the errand. Instead, we should provide concrete, specific, and complete instructions; for example, we might say, "John, go to the principal's office, give Mrs. Smith the absentee sheet, and come back here" (Patton et al., 1996, p. 105).

■ For more information on adaptive behavior, see the supplementary reading "Adaptive Behavior and Mental Retardation" in the *Study Guide and Reader* that accompanies this book.

■ **mental retardation** Disability characterized by significantly below-average general intelligence and deficits in adaptive behavior.

■ **adaptive behavior** Behavior related to daily living skills and appropriate conduct in social situations; used as a criterion for identifying students with mental retardation.

When instruction is appropriately paced and provides sufficient scaffolding, students with mental retardation can succeed in a wide variety of domains.

◎ *Provide considerable scaffolding to foster effective cognitive processing.* Students with mental retardation often have little awareness of how to direct and regulate their own learning. So it is often helpful to provide extra guidance to assist cognitive processing. For instance, we can help students focus their attention by using such phrases as "get ready," "look," or "listen." We can teach them a few simple, concrete memory strategies, such as repeating instructions to themselves or physically rearranging a group of items they need to remember (Fletcher & Bray, 1995; A. P. Turnbull, 1974). We can also provide simple, structured study guides that quite specifically tell students what to focus on when they study (Mastropieri & Scruggs, 1992).

◎ *Include vocational and general life skills in the curriculum.* After high school most students with mental retardation join the adult workforce rather than go on to higher education. Accordingly, an important part of their high school curriculum is training in general life and work skills. Because of students' limited ability to generalize what they have learned from one situation to another, it is especially important to teach life and work skills in realistic settings that closely resemble those in which students will find themselves once they leave school (R. Turnbull et al., 2004).

At this point, we turn our attention to a very different group of students—those with physical and sensory challenges. Some (but by no means all) of these students may also have some of the cognitive or social difficulties that characterize other students with special needs.

STUDENTS WITH PHYSICAL AND SENSORY CHALLENGES

Some students with special needs have obvious physical disabilities caused by medically detectable physiological conditions. These include physical and health impairments, visual impairments, hearing loss, and severe and multiple disabilities.

Physical and Health Impairments

Physical and health impairments are general physical or medical conditions (usually long-term) that interfere with school performance to such an extent that special instruction, curricular materials, equipment, or facilities are necessary. Students in this category may have limited energy and strength, reduced mental alertness, or little muscle control. Examples of specific conditions that may qualify students for special services include traumatic brain injury, spinal cord injury, cerebral palsy, muscular dystrophy, epilepsy, cystic fibrosis, asthma, heart problems, arthritis, cancer, and AIDS. The majority of students with physical and health impairments attend general education classrooms for part or all of the school day (U.S. Dept. of Education, 1996).

Common Characteristics   It is difficult to generalize about students with physical and health impairments because their conditions are so very different from one another. Nevertheless, several noteworthy characteristics are commonly seen:

- Learning ability similar to that of nondisabled students
- Fewer opportunities to experience and interact with the outside world in educationally important ways (e.g., less use of public transportation, fewer visits to museums and zoos, fewer family trips)
- Low stamina and a tendency to tire easily
- Possible low self-esteem, insecurity, embarrassment, or overdependence (depending partly on how parents and others have responded to their impairments) (Patton et al., 1996; J. W. Wood, 1998)

Adapting Instruction   To get a glimpse of the kinds of challenges that many students with physical disabilities face each day, try the following exercise.

Experiencing FIRSTHAND ·Stiffen Up

Stand up, and then make your arms and legs totally straight and stiff. Also stiffen your wrists, fingers, and neck. While keeping all of these body parts totally stiff, try the following activities:

- Skip around the room.
- Bend over and touch your toes.
- Find a tissue or handkerchief and blow your nose.

■ **physical and health impairments** General physical or medical conditions that interfere with school performance to such an extent that special instruction, materials, equipment, or facilities are needed.

- Go back to your chair and sit down.
- Take a piece of scrap paper, and use it to mark this page. Turn back to the beginning of the chapter, read the first paragraph, and then return to this page.
- While continuing to keep your elbows, wrists, and fingers completely stiff, try "cutting" an imaginary sheet of paper using an imaginary pair of scissors. Then "glue" two pieces of paper together using an imaginary bottle of rubber cement. Remember to "unscrew" the top off the bottle before you use it.

Now return your body to its usual, more relaxed state.

· · · · · · ·

What kinds of difficulties did you encounter in your stiffness? You were probably able to skip around the room, although not as quickly and gracefully as you would otherwise. You may have been able to touch your toes, but did you find that your stiff neck made the task more difficult? And how did you blow your nose? I myself found that I couldn't do it in any way that would be presentable in a public place. You may have experienced varying degrees of difficulty with the last three activities as well. Can you think of special equipment that might help you perform these activities more successfully? Would a different kind of chair be more comfortable? Would a metal book holder help you keep the textbook open while you read it? Might specially shaped scissors better fit your stiff fingers?

Although we will not always need to modify the class curriculum for students with physical and health impairments, we will definitely want to make other accommodations:

◎ *Be sensitive to specific needs and disabilities, and accommodate them flexibly.* Despite normal learning capabilities, students with physical and health impairments may not be able to perform certain tasks as easily as classmates. One student may require extra time with a writing assignment and perhaps should not be held to the same standards of neatness and legibility. Another may need to respond to test questions orally rather than on paper. Still another may tire easily and need to take frequent breaks from school tasks. In your previously "stiffened" condition, you may have needed all of these accommodations.

◎ *Know what to do in emergencies.* Some students have conditions that may occasionally bring on health-threatening situations. For example, a student with diabetes may go into insulin shock, a student with asthma may have trouble breathing, or a student with epilepsy may have a *grand mal* seizure. We should consult with school medical personnel ahead of time so that we are prepared to respond appropriately to such emergencies.

◎ *If the student and parents give their permission, educate classmates about the nature of the disability.* Although many classmates are apt to treat a student with a physical or health impairment with kindness and respect, others may be less considerate and tolerant. In some situations such mistreatment may be due to ignorance about the nature of the disability, and accurate information must be made available. In one widely publicized case, Ryan White, a student with AIDS, was initially barred from his neighborhood school because of classmates' and parents' unwarranted fear that other children would be infected (R. White & Cunningham, 1991). Ryan returned to school only after the public was convinced that AIDS could not be contracted through breathing or normal bodily contact. Even so, his reception was hardly a warm one, as Ryan himself revealed:

> [K]ids backed up against their lockers when they saw me coming, or they threw themselves against the hallway walls, shouting, "Watch out! Watch out! There he is!" (R. White & Cunningham, 1991, p. 118)

Only when his family moved to a different school district—one that went to great lengths to inform parents and students about the true nature of AIDS—did Ryan find teachers and peers who were happy to have him at their school.

Visual Impairments

Students with **visual impairments** have malfunctions of their eyes or optic nerves that prevent normal vision even with corrective lenses, to the point where classroom performance is adversely affected. Some students are totally blind. Others have limited sensitivity to light, perhaps seeing fuzzy patterns of light and dark. Still others have a restricted visual field (sometimes called *tunnel vision*) that allows them to see only a very small area at a given time. Visual impairments are caused by congenital abnormalities in, or later damage to, either the eye or the visual pathway to the brain.

■ **visual impairment** Malfunction of the eyes or optic nerves that prevents normal vision even with corrective lenses.

Common Characteristics   Students with visual impairments are apt to have many or all of these characteristics:

- Normal functioning of other senses (hearing, touch, etc.)
- General learning ability similar to that of nondisabled students
- Fewer opportunities to experience and interact with the outside world in educationally important ways (for example, less exposure to maps, films, and other visual material); as a result, a more limited vocabulary and less general knowledge about the world
- Reduced capability to imitate the behaviors of others
- Inability to observe the body language and other nonverbal cues often present in human interactions, leading to occasional misperceptions of intended meanings
- Occasional uncertainty and anxiety (especially in chaotic environments, such as the lunchroom or playground) as a result of having no visual knowledge of ongoing events
- In the primary grades, less knowledge about the conventions of written language (direction of print, punctuation, etc.)
(M. Harris, 1992; Patton et al., 1996; M. C. Reynolds & Birch, 1988; Tompkins & McGee, 1986; R. Turnbull et al., 2004; Tuttle & Tuttle, 1996)

Adapting Instruction   Specialists will typically give students the training they need in Braille, orientation and mobility, and specially adapted computer technology. Apart from such additions to the curriculum, regular classroom content and objectives are usually appropriate for these students.

At the same time, we can help students with visual impairments learn and achieve more successfully with strategies such as the following:

◎   *Orient students ahead of time to the physical layout of the classroom.* Students with serious visual impairments should have a chance to explore the classroom before other students arrive—ideally, well before the first day of class. During such a session we can help students locate various objects in the classroom (wastebasket, pencil sharpener, etc.) and can point out special sounds (such as the buzzing of a clock on the wall) so that students can get their bearings (J. W. Wood, 1998).

Students with visual impairments can often keep pace with their sighted classmates if instructional materials are adapted to meet their individual needs.

◎   *Use visual materials with sharp contrast.* Some students with partial sight can use printed materials with clearly distinguishable features, such as the large-print books available at most public libraries. Students' eyes will tend to tire quickly, however, so we should limit any use of visual materials to short time periods (Patton et al., 1996).

◎   *Depend heavily on other modalities.* For students who are blind, we must find nonvisual mechanisms for presenting classroom subject matter. We can obtain Braille copies of required books and assignments or audiotapes of novels and other literature. We can engage students in hands-on activities involving objects they can feel and manipulate. Plastic relief maps that portray mountains, valleys, and coastlines three-dimensionally can be embellished by making pin pricks along borders or placing small dabs of nail polish on major cities. When exclusively visual material must be used for large-group instruction, it should be described in considerable detail, perhaps by a teacher aide, parent volunteer, or classmate.

◎   *Allow extra time for learning and performance.* Learning by hearing often takes more time than learning by seeing: When students *look* at something, they can perceive a great deal of information all at once, but when they *listen* to it, they receive it just one piece at a time. Hence we may often need to give students with visual impairments extra time to learn classroom material and complete assignments (M. B. Rowe, 1978).

Hearing Loss

Students with **hearing loss** have a malfunction of the ears or associated nerves that interferes with the perception of sounds within the frequency range of normal human speech. Students who are completely *deaf* have insufficient sensation to understand any spoken language, even with the help of a hearing aid. Students who are *hard of hearing* understand some speech but experience exceptional difficulty in doing so. Approximately half of the students identified as having hearing loss are in general education classrooms for part or all of the school day (U.S. Dept. of Education, 1995).

■ **hearing loss** Malfunction of the ears or associated nerves that interferes with perception of sounds within the frequency range of normal human speech.

Common Characteristics   Most students with hearing loss have normal intellectual abilities (Braden, 1992; Schirmer, 1994). However, they may have characteristics such as the following:

- Delayed language development, especially if the hearing impairment was present at birth or occurred early in life, because of reduced exposure to spoken language
- Less oral language than hearing classmates; speech may have a monotonous, "hollow" quality to it (e.g., listen to the boy with the green shirt about two minutes into the "Bilingual Classroom" clip on Video CD 2)
- Some ability to read lips (*speechreading*)
- Proficiency in sign language, such as American Sign Language (ASL) or finger spelling
- Less developed reading skills, especially if language development has been delayed
- Less general knowledge about the world than peers, due to reduced exposure to verbal information
- In some cases, social isolation, more limited social skills, and reduced perspective-taking ability as a result of a reduced ability to communicate
(Bassett et al, 1996; Chall, 1996; Gearheart, Weishahn, & Gearheart, 1992; C. C. Peterson, 2002; M. C. Reynolds & Birch, 1988; M. B. Rowe, 1978; R. Turnbull et al., 2004)

■ Hear the speech of a child with hearing loss in the "Bilingual Classroom" clip on Video CD 2.

■ Think about struggling to hear conversation at a noisy party. Might the frustration you feel be similar to how a student with hearing loss feels?

Adapting Instruction   Specialists typically provide training in such communication skills as American Sign Language, finger spelling, and speechreading. Aside from the addition of these topics, the regular school curriculum is appropriate for most students with hearing loss. Several accommodations can help these students be successful in general education classrooms:

◎ *Minimize irrelevant noise.* Even when students use hearing aids, what they hear is often diminished or distorted. For students who have some hearing ability, then, it is helpful to minimize irrelevant and potentially distracting sounds. Carpet on the floor and multiple bulletin boards on the walls can absorb some extraneous noise. And noisy devices such as fans and pencil sharpeners should be as far away as possible.

◎ *Supplement auditory presentations with visual information and hands-on experiences.* For obvious reasons, we should supplement any auditory presentations (such as directions, lectures, or classroom discussions) with information provided through other (especially visual) modalities. For example, we can write important points on the chalkboard. We can illustrate key ideas with pictures and other graphics. We can offer reading materials that duplicate lectures. We can ask a classroom aide or student volunteer to take notes on in-class discussions. And we can use concrete activities (e.g., role playing, experiments, field trips) to make abstract ideas more obvious.

◎ *Provide conditions that help students hear and speechread.* Students who are hard of hearing are most likely to understand words spoken in a normal tone of voice (not overly loud) and with a distinct but otherwise normal pronunciation of words (Gearheart et al., 1992; J. W. Wood, 1998). They should sit in places where they can clearly see the speaker's face. As teachers, we should speak only while facing students and never while sitting in a dark corner or standing in front of a window or bright light.

◎ *Occasionally check for understanding.* Even the most skillful speechreaders won't always get our messages exactly as we've transmitted them. To make sure students correctly understand what we are telling them, we can occasionally ask them to repeat what we've said. By doing so, we can identify and correct misunderstandings (Gearheart et al., 1992; Patton et al., 1996).

◎ *Address deficiencies in reading and other language skills.* We must be sure to address any language and reading deficiencies that students may have (Bassett et al., 1996). In some cases a special educator or other specialist can give us guidance and assistance in this regard. Many of the strategies in Chapter 2 (see the section on language development) and the chapter "Learning in the Content Areas" in the *Study Guide and Reader* (see the sections on reading and writing) may also be helpful.

◎ *Teach American Sign Language and finger spelling to other class members.* To facilitate communication with students who have hearing loss, other class members—ourselves included—should gain some competence in American Sign Language and finger spelling. For instance, I once taught at a school where *every* student—those with hearing loss and those without—received some instruction in signing. One girl in my class was totally deaf yet quite

Many students with hearing loss have proficiency in American Sign Language. ASL is not a word-for-word representation of English; it has its own unique vocabulary and syntax.

popular with her classmates; she and her friends communicated freely and easily both before and after (and, unfortunately, sometimes at inappropriate times *during*) class.

Severe and Multiple Disabilities

Students with **severe and multiple disabilities** have two or more of the disabilities already described and require significant adaptations and highly specialized services in their educational program. These disabilities are almost always due to organic causes, such as genetic abnormalities or serious complications before or during birth. Despite extensive need for special services, some students with severe and multiple disabilities may be in general education classrooms for part of the school day.

Common Characteristics   Students with severe and multiple disabilities often have these characteristics:

- Varying degrees of intellectual functioning (some students may have average intelligence hidden beneath a limited ability to communicate)
- Limited awareness of surrounding stimuli and events; periods of alertness and responsiveness for some students
- Limited communication skills (often consisting of gestures, facial expressions, or other nonverbal means)
- Limited adaptive behaviors (e.g., social skills, self-care skills)
- Significant delays in motor development
- Mild or severe sensory impairments
- Extensive medical needs (e.g., medications, intravenous tubes) (Guess, Roberts, Siegel-Causey, & Rues, 1995; R. Turnbull et al., 2004)

Adapting Instruction   If we have students with severe and multiple disabilities in our classrooms, we will almost certainly work with one or more specialists or teacher aides who assist us in their education. Even so, the following strategies can enhance their successful integration into the classroom community:

◎   *Teach behaviors and skills essential for a student's general welfare and successful inclusion in the classroom.* Virtually all students with disabilities have some capacity to adapt to new environments. We should identify those behaviors that will enhance learning and performance for the time we will have a student with us—behaviors that may include more effective ways of communicating, rudimentary word recognition or arithmetic skills, or the use of special-needs technological devices. In teaching a basic skill, we may find it useful to guide the student slowly through the skill one step at a time, verbally or manually scaffolding his or her actions, and then gradually remove such assistance as the student gains competence and self-confidence.

◎   *Pair students with and without disabilities in the same activity.* In some cases student pairs might work toward different objectives within the same content area; for example, when two students conduct a science experiment, one might be learning methods of scientific experimentation while the other is mastering basic scientific concepts. In other cases a pair might work toward objectives in two completely different areas; for example, while one is learning experimentation techniques, the other can practice communication skills (Giangreco, 1997).

◎   *Keep the mind-set that all students can and should participate in classroom activities to the fullest extent possible.* Many teachers have found that when they keep open minds about what their students can accomplish, and especially when they think creatively and collaboratively about how they can adapt regular classroom activities to accommodate students with special needs, all students can participate in some meaningful way in virtually any classroom activity (Logan, Alberto, Kana, & Waylor-Bowen, 1994; Salisbury, Evans, & Palombaro, 1997).

General Recommendations for Students with Physical and Sensory Challenges

In addition to the strategies we've identified for specific physical disabilities, several more general strategies apply to all students with physical and sensory challenges:

◎   *Ensure that all students have access to important educational resources and opportunities.* Sometimes such access involves modifying instructional materials, such as providing Braille versions of books or written versions of classroom lectures. In other instances it involves modifying a classroom's physical arrangement, such as widening aisles and placing bulletin boards at eye

■ **severe and multiple disabilities**
Combination of two or more disabilities that, taken together, require significant classroom adaptations and highly specialized educational services.

level to accommodate students in wheelchairs (Stephens, Blackhurst, & Magliocca, 1988). In still other cases it may involve advance planning and creative thinking so that students can participate in sports activities, go on field trips, and the like.

◎ *Provide assistance only when students really need it.* In their eagerness to help students with physical and sensory challenges, many adults inadvertently perform tasks and solve problems that these students are perfectly capable of handling on their own. Yet one of our goals for these students is to promote their independence, not their dependence on others. So if we see students having difficulty with a task, we should ask if they need assistance before we try to help them.

◎ *Use technology to facilitate learning and performance.* Many technological aids can help students with physical and sensory challenges in daily school activities. For example, some calculators "talk" as buttons are pushed and answers are displayed, some software "tells" a student what appears on the computer screen or converts scanned text into an audio message, and some printers print in Braille. Specially adapted joysticks and voice recognition systems can help students with limited muscle control use a computer. Machines known as augmentative communication devices can provide synthesized speech to facilitate the communication of individuals incapable of normal speech (Roblyer, 2003; Stephens et al., 1988; R. Turnbull et al., 2004).

As noted earlier, all students with identified disabilities should have individualized education programs (IEPs) that guide instruction. Now that we've considered various kinds of disabilities, let's apply what we've learned while examining an IEP for a boy named Harry.

Interpreting Student Artifacts and Behaviors

Looking at an IEP

Eight-year-old Harry (a pseudonym) has been identified as having special educational needs, and a team consisting of Harry's classroom teacher, the "resource room" teacher, the school psychologist, the school counselor, and Harry's father has developed an IEP for him. The following excerpts represent only a small portion of Harry's complete IEP. As you read the excerpts, think about

- The particular disability that Harry may have
- How helpful the IEP is likely to be in guiding instruction

Strengths: Intelligent, creative, good visual memory, enjoys working on the computer, likes structured activities, persists at difficult tasks when motivated

Needs: To follow classroom expectations, to be productive, to be more socially appropriate and less anxious in social situations, to be less impulsive

Strategies
- Establish eye contact before giving directions.
- Encourage Harry to repeat directions to make sure he understands.
- Provide structure to help Harry meet written expectations and organize himself.
- Use one-on-one coaching to ward off potential outbursts and encourage Harry to be productive.
- Use behavioral techniques to help Harry control excess verbiage, begin tasks on time, and meet classroom expectations.
- Break tasks down into smaller units that Harry can follow sequentially.
- Encourage Harry to increase his positive self-talk.
- Provide positive reinforcement when Harry takes responsibility for his own work.
- Give advance notice about transitions and the end of activities.
- Communicate frequently with home to share positive accomplishments.

Accommodations
- Support in the areas of written language, behavior management, productivity, and meeting classroom expectations.

- Counseling to support emotional control, appropriate and courteous language, and social skills.
- Accommodations for the length of assignments and amount of written work.

Instructional Objectives
Written Language
- Harry will sustain his independent writing for a specified period of time, writing first and then drawing.
- Harry will commit basic sight, phonetic, and content area words to memory for spelling with 80 percent accuracy on weekly tests.
- Harry will be able to identify and apply correct punctuation to the end of a sentence.

Study/Organizational/Behavioral Skills
- Harry will follow his teacher's directions and begin a task within a given amount of time.
- Harry will complete a task within a reasonable amount of time.
- Given advance warning, Harry will make successful transitions to new activities.
- With teacher guidance, Harry will work cooperatively in a small group and contribute positively.

Social/Emotional Functioning
- Harry will increase his awareness of the emotions of others, as demonstrated by their facial expressions.
- Harry will increase his understanding that others may have a legitimate point of view.
- Harry will increase his understanding that his behaviors may upset other people (i.e., when he talks too loudly or behaves disrespectfully).

To what category of special needs do you think Harry belongs? As you read the IEP, you may have formed several hypotheses: perhaps a learning disability, ADHD, or an emotional or behavioral disorder. In reality, school personnel have identified Harry as having an *emotional handicap*, the school district's terminology for what we have been calling an emotional or behavioral disorder. As you can see, categorizing students as having particular disabilities is not always a clear-cut process, especially when, like Harry, a student has deficits in several areas. Ultimately, the most important goal is not so much to give Harry a specific "diagnosis" as it is to modify instructional materials and practices to best meet his individual needs and help him develop both academically and socially.

How helpful will this IEP be in guiding instruction? Certainly the strategies identified provide some useful ideas for working with Harry, and the instructional objectives listed provide some goals to shoot for. But several critical things are missing from the excerpts presented here. For instance, what is Harry's *present level of performance* in each of these areas? How will Harry's progress on each goal be *objectively measured*? Which team members (e.g., classroom teacher, resource room teacher, counselor) are responsible for which objectives, and in which settings? Ideally, an IEP should include such information (see Figure 5.3). (Harry's complete IEP addresses some but not all of these issues.)

We have considered many ways of helping students with a variety of disabilities adapt successfully to a general education environment. Yet an additional group of students—those who show exceptional ability in one or more areas—may also have special educational needs. The next section addresses the specific needs of these students.

STUDENTS WITH ADVANCED COGNITIVE DEVELOPMENT

Many students are apt to have advanced abilities, either in specific subject areas or across the board, that warrant our attention and encouragement. You should think of *students with advanced cognitive development* as being on a continuum of abilities rather than being a distinct category, and in fact, we will want to nurture the specific gifts and talents that *all* students bring to the classroom. Yet some students—those who are *gifted*—are so far above the norm that special educational services are appropriate.

Giftedness

In the United States **giftedness** is defined as unusually high ability or aptitude in one or more of the following areas:

Students identified as gifted show exceptional achievement or promise in general intellectual ability, aptitude in a specific academic field, creativity, leadership, or visual and performing arts.

- General intellectual ability
- Aptitude in a specific academic field
- Creativity
- Visual or performing arts
- Leadership
  (Jacob K. Javits Gifted and Talented Students Education Act of 1988 [PL 100-297, IV(B); PL 103-382, XIV]; U.S. Dept. of Education, 1993)

When we try to pin it down more precisely, we find considerable disagreement among experts (Carter, 1991; B. K. Keogh & MacMillan, 1996). Compounding the problem is the fact that giftedness may take somewhat different forms in different cultures and ethnic groups (recall our earlier discussion of how intelligence is culture-dependent). Whatever its nature, giftedness is probably the result of both genetic predispositions and environmental nurturance (Simonton, 2001; Winner, 2000b).

How to identify students who are gifted (they are sometimes called *gifted and talented*) is an equally controversial issue. The traditional approach, one seen in many school districts over the years, is to identify students based on overall IQ scores, perhaps using 125 or 130 as a cutoff point (B. K. Keogh & MacMillan, 1996; J. T. Webb, Meckstroth, & Tolan, 1982). Yet as we learned earlier, intelligence tests focus primarily on skills valued in mainstream Western culture, and they will not necessarily reveal students who show exceptional promise in specific academic fields, creativity, the arts, or leadership. Furthermore, many students, especially girls, try to hide their talents, perhaps because they fear classmates' ridicule or perhaps because their cultures do not value high achievement in females (Covington, 1992; G. A. Davis & Rimm, 1998; DeLisle, 1984). With such concerns in mind, some experts urge us to use multiple criteria (perhaps including creativity, motivation, or personality variables) when identifying students who warrant special

■ **giftedness** Unusually high ability in one or more areas, to the point where students require special educational services to help them meet their full potential.

educational services (e.g., Renzulli, 2002; Sternberg & Zhang, 1995). However, they have yet to agree on what those criteria should be.

Common Characteristics   Students who are gifted tend to be quite different from one another in their unique strengths and talents, and students who show exceptional talent in one area may show only average ability in another (Winner, 2000b). Nevertheless, many students who are gifted have characteristics such as these:

- More advanced vocabulary, language, and reading skills
- More general knowledge about the world
- Ability to learn more quickly, easily, and independently than peers
- More advanced and efficient cognitive processes and metacognitive skills
- Greater flexibility in ideas and approaches to tasks
- High standards for performance (sometimes to the point of unhealthy perfectionism)
- High motivation to accomplish challenging tasks; feelings of boredom about easy tasks
- Positive self-concept, especially with regard to academic endeavors
- Above-average social development and emotional adjustment (although a few extremely gifted students may have difficulties because they are so *very* different from their peers) (Candler-Lotven, Tallent-Runnels, Olivárez, & Hildreth, 1994; Carter & Ormrod, 1982; B. Clark, 1997; Cornell et al., 1990; A. W. Gottfried et al., 1994; Hoge & Renzulli, 1993; Janos & Robinson, 1985; Lupart, 1995; Parker, 1997; Rabinowitz & Glaser, 1985; Steiner & Carr, 2003; Winner, 2000a, 2000b)

We should note here that students can be gifted and also have a disability, perhaps a learning disability, ADHD, or an emotional or behavioral disorder (Brown-Mizuno, 1990; Hettinger & Knapp, 2001). In planning instruction for such students, we must address their disabilities as well as their unique gifts.

Adapting Instruction   Critics of gifted education argue that students with high abilities can certainly achieve normal school objectives without assistance. Yet many students with special gifts and talents become bored or frustrated when their school experiences don't provide tasks and assignments that challenge them and help them develop their unique abilities (Feldhusen, Van Winkel, & Ehle, 1996; Winner, 2000b). In the "Motivation: Middle Childhood" clip on Video CD 1, 9-year-old Elena reveals her desire for challenge in her description of PEAK, a program at her school for students who are gifted:

■ Observe Elena's desire for challenge in the "Motivation: Middle Childhood" clip on Video CD 1.

Adult: What do you like best about school?
Elena: I like PEAK. . . . It's for smart kids who have, like, good ideas for stuff you could do. And so they make it more challenging for you in school. So instead of third-grade math, you get fourth-grade math.

Recalling Lev Vygotsky's view of cognitive development from Chapter 2, we could say that gifted students are unlikely to be working within their zone of proximal development if we limit them to the tasks we assign to other students; thus, they are unlikely to develop new cognitive skills. In fact, gifted students are among our schools' greatest underachievers; when required to progress at the same rate as their nongifted peers, they achieve at levels far short of their capabilities (Carter, 1991; Gallagher, 1991; Reis, 1989).

We can foster the special abilities and talents of gifted students in numerous ways, including the following:

◎   *Provide individualized tasks and assignments.* No single curriculum can meet the specific needs of each and every student. Different students may need special services in very different areas—for example, in mathematics, creative writing, or studio art. Some students who are gifted, especially those with limited English background, may even need training in certain basic skills (C. R. Harris, 1991; Udall, 1989).

◎   *Form study groups of students with similar interests and abilities.* When several students have common interests and abilities, it may be helpful to pull them together into study groups in which they can cooperatively pursue a particular topic or task (Fiedler, Lange, & Winebrenner, 1993; Stanley, 1980). In some cases a study group may explore a topic with greater depth and more sophisticated analysis than other students (an *enrichment* approach). In other instances it may simply move through the standard school curriculum at a more rapid pace (an *acceleration* approach). Students appear to benefit both academically and socially from increased contact with peers who have similar interests (J. A. Kulik & Kulik, 1997; McGinn, Viernstein, & Hogan, 1980). Furthermore, they are less likely to hide their abilities and enthusiasm for the subject matter when their classmates are equally talented and motivated (Feldhusen, 1989).

◎ *Teach complex cognitive skills within the context of specific subject areas.* Some programs for the gifted have tried to teach complex thought processes such as creativity and critical thinking as skills totally separate from school subject matter. But this approach tends to have minimal impact on students' cognitive development; in fact, it often focuses on skills that many students have already acquired. Instead, we are better advised to teach complex thinking skills within the context of specific topics—for example, reasoning and problem-solving skills in science, or creativity in writing (M. C. Linn et al., 1989; Moon, Feldhusen, & Dillon, 1994; Pulos & Linn, 1981; Stanley, 1980).

◎ *Provide opportunities for independent study.* Because many students who are gifted are highly motivated and have advanced learning and metacognitive skills, independent study in topics of interest may be quite appropriate (Candler-Lotven et al., 1994; Lupart, 1995). If we provide such opportunities, we must be sure students have the study habits and research skills they will need to use their time and resources effectively.

◎ *Encourage students to set high goals.* Because gifted students are capable of exceptionally high performance in certain areas, we should encourage them to aim high in those areas (Patton et al., 1996; Sanborn, 1979). At the same time, we must caution them not to expect perfection: Making missteps and mistakes is an inevitable part of tackling the challenging tasks that can best enhance their cognitive growth.

◎ *Seek outside resources.* When students have high abilities in domains outside our own areas of expertise, it is often helpful to identify suitable *mentors* elsewhere in the school district or in the community at large. For example, local universities, government offices, private businesses, and volunteer community groups all provide arenas in which students may be able to develop their unique talents (Ambrose, Allen, & Huntley, 1994; Piirto, 1999; Seeley, 1989).

CONSIDERING DIVERSITY WHEN IDENTIFYING AND ADDRESSING SPECIAL NEEDS

Sadly, a disproportionately large number of students identified as having disabilities are from ethnic minority groups and low-income neighborhoods (McLoyd, 1998; U.S. Dept. of Education, 1996, 1997). And members of some minority groups, especially African Americans and Hispanic Americans, are underrepresented in gifted programs (U.S. Dept. of Education, office of Civil Rights, 1993).

Most theorists believe that differences in environment account for the disproportionate numbers of students from various backgrounds found in special education programs (McLoyd, 1998; H. W. Stevenson et al., 1990). For instance, students from some ethnic minority groups are more likely than their classmates to grow up in lower-income neighborhoods, where lack of adequate medical care, increased exposure to environmental toxins, more stressful living conditions, and less access to early educational resources can contribute to lower intellectual functioning and more serious behavior problems (Conlon, 1992; McLoyd, 1998).

The inequitable representation of particular groups in various categories of disabilities poses a dilemma for educators. On the one hand, we don't want to use categories such as *mental retardation* or *emotional and behavioral disorders* for students whose classroom performance and behavior may be due primarily to the adverse environmental conditions in which they have been raised. On the other hand, we also don't want to deprive these students of special educational services that might very well help them learn and achieve more successfully over the long run. In such situations we need to conduct fair and nondiscriminatory evaluations of students' needs and, if students qualify under a special needs category, create individualized education programs (IEPs) to meet those needs. We should consider these categories of special needs as *temporary* classifications that may no longer be applicable as students' classroom performance improves. It's important to remember that students are placed within a special education category because they need specialized services; all students, with and without disability classifications, have changing needs that evolve over time.

■ For suggestions on promoting library research skills, see the supplementary reading "Promoting Information Literacy Skills" in the *Study Guide and Reader.*

We must remember, too, that many students from minority groups may not be identified as gifted when traditional intelligence tests and other standardized measures of ability are used. Students raised in some cultures may have had little experience with some of the tasks commonly used in intelligence tests, such as reasoning about self-contained logical problems or finding patterns in geometric figures (see items 4 and 5 in the "Mock Intelligence Test" on page 141; Rogoff, 2003). It is critical, then, that we be on the lookout for students who show other signs of special abilities and talents and so may benefit from enriched educational experiences. Following are examples of traits we might look for:

- Ability to learn quickly from experiences
- Exceptional communication skills (e.g., articulateness, richness of language)
- Originality and resourcefulness in thinking and problem solving
- Ability to generalize concepts and ideas to new, seemingly unrelated situations
- Unusual sensitivity to the needs and feelings of others
  (Maker & Schiever, 1989)

For the growth of our society over the long run, it is imperative that we nurture the many gifted and talented students that we find in *all* cultural and ethnic groups.

THE BIG PICTURE

In our discussions of intelligence, temperament, and special needs in this chapter, we have discovered many ways in which students in any single classroom may be different from one another. As a beginning teacher, you may initially find such differences a bit overwhelming, but with time and experience you will begin to take them in stride and grow increasingly appreciative of the many benefits that diversity brings to a classroom community. Following are several strategies for accommodating students' differing abilities and disabilities within a general education classroom:

◎ *Obtain as much information as possible about each student.* Whether or not students have been identified as having special educational needs, they are *individuals* first, each with a unique set of strengths and weaknesses. The more we know about students' specific characteristics and needs—whether academic, social, behavioral, or medical—the better our position to help each and every student succeed at classroom tasks and activities (e.g., B. A. Keogh & Becker, 1973; Stephens et al., 1988). Test results, performance on assignments, informal observations of students' behavior, insights from colleagues who have previously worked with students, discussions with parents and other family members—all of these can enhance our understanding of how we can best help every student learn and achieve.

◎ *Individualize instruction for nondisabled students as well as for those with disabilities.* Students are less likely to compare their own performance to that of others, and students with special needs can more easily blend in with their classmates, when all students receive instructional materials and assignments tailored to their unique characteristics. To the extent that our time and resources allow us to do so, then, we should try to individualize instruction for everyone (T. Bryan, 1991; Madden & Slavin, 1983; M. C. Reynolds & Birch, 1988).

◎ *Be flexible in approaches to instruction.* Some instructional methods may work better than others for teaching students with diverse abilities and needs, and we cannot always predict which methods will be most effective for a given student. If we don't succeed with a particular approach, we should try again. But each time, we might want to try *differently*.

◎ *Unless there is reason to do otherwise, hold the same expectations for students with disabilities as for other students.* Sometimes disabilities make it difficult or impossible for students to accomplish certain school tasks, and we will have to modify our expectations and assessment practices accordingly (see Chapters 15 and 16 for possible ways to modify assessments). Aside from such situations, we should generally have the same expectations for students with special needs that we have for other students. Rather than think of reasons why a student *cannot* do something, we should instead think about how we can help the student *do* it. Many people have achieved great success despite major disabilities (Armstrong, 1994). For example, Albert Einstein had delayed speech development and may have had dyslexia, Vincent Van Gogh had emotional problems, Ludwig von Beethoven composed symphonies even after becoming totally deaf, and the world-renowned astrophysicist Stephen Hawking cannot walk, talk, or use pencil and paper.

◎ *Identify and teach the prerequisite knowledge and skills a student may not have acquired because of a disability.* Some students lack knowledge and skills essential for their school success, perhaps because of inexperience or perhaps as a direct result of a disability. For instance, students with reduced physical mobility may have had few opportunities to manipulate objects in their environment. Students with visual impairments have not been able to observe many of the cause-effect relationships that form a foundation for learning science—for instance, the changes in wood's appearance when it is burned (M. B. Rowe, 1978). And students whose medical conditions have limited their contact with other children may have poorly developed interpersonal skills.

◎ *Consult and collaborate with specialists.* School districts usually employ a variety of educational specialists, including special educators, counselors, school psychologists, nurses, speech pathologists, and physical and occupational therapists. Some students leave the classroom for part of the day to work with such individuals. Nevertheless, in today's inclusive schools many special services are provided within a regular classroom context by teachers and specialists working in close collaboration (B. L. Driver, 1996; Scruggs & Mastropieri, 1994).

◎ *Include students in planning and decision making.* So far, we have been working on the assumption that we, as teachers, will decide what goals to set and what instructional strategies to use. Although gifted programs often give students a fair amount of autonomy to choose topics and methods of study, educational programs for most students with special needs are highly structured, to the point where students have little say regarding what and how they learn. But increasingly, educators are recognizing the importance of letting all students, including those with disabilities, make some choices about academic goals and curriculum (Algozzine, Browder, Karvonen, Test, & Wood, 2001; Mithaug & Mithaug, 2003; Sands & Wehmeyer, 1996). Student decision making can ultimately promote greater *self-regulation*—increasing independence from, and less need for, the guidance of other people (see Chapter 10). It can also lead to a greater feeling of *self-determination*—a sense of being able to set one's own life course, which many theorists believe is essential for intrinsic motivation (see Chapter 12).

◎ *Promote interaction between students with special needs and their nondisabled peers.* Students with special needs are more likely to thrive in general education settings if they interact frequently with their classmates (Scruggs & Mastropieri, 1994). Yet productive social interaction does not necessarily happen on its own (Hymel, 1986; Juvonen & Hiner, 1991; Yuker, 1988). Nondis-abled students may willingly accept students with obvious physical or sensory disabilities yet reject or victimize students who behave differently without an obvious physical reason for doing so (B. Cook & Semmel, 1999; Morrison et al., 1994; Yuker, 1988). Furthermore, nondisabled students may feel resentment or anger about inappropriate behaviors that they think a classmate should be able to control (Juvonen, 1991).

To create a truly cohesive, mutually supportive classroom community, we must often take active steps to promote appropriate social interactions between students with disabilities and their nondisabled peers. Following are examples of things we might do:

- Explicitly teach effective social skills.
- Explicitly point out a student's strengths.
- Ask students with and without disabilities to assist others in their particular areas of strength.
- Plan academic and recreational activities that require cooperation.
- Encourage students with special needs to participate in extracurricular activities and community events. (Bassett et al., 1996; DuPaul, Ervin, Hook, & McGoey, 1998; Madden & Slavin, 1983; A. P. Turnbull et al., 2000; S. Vaughn, 1991)

◎ *Keep your eyes open for students who may qualify for special services.* As we gain experience as teachers, we become better aware of what abilities and behaviors are typical for a particular age-group, and so we are often in an excellent position to identify children who are atypical in one way or another. Although we will usually need to depend on specialists to conduct the in-depth assessments necessary to identify a particular disability or area of giftedness, the job of referring students for such assessments—and thereby gaining them access to the special services they may need—will ultimately be up to us. The final case study illustrates this very important role.

CASE STUDY: *Quiet Amy*

Mr. Mahoney has been teaching kindergarten for fifteen years, and he has learned through experience that many kindergartners have some temporary difficulty adjusting to the school environment, especially if they haven't previously attended daycare or preschool. But Amy is giving him cause for concern: After being in his class for several weeks, her behavior has changed very little from what it was on the first day of school. Amy never speaks, either to him or to the other children, even when she is directly spoken to. On the infrequent occasions when she wants to communicate—perhaps to express her desire for an object or her distress about something that's happened—she does so primarily by looking and pointing at something or someone in the room. She has trouble following simple directions, almost as if she hasn't heard what she's been asked to do. And she seems distracted during daily storybook readings and science lessons. The only activities that give her pleasure are arts and crafts; she enjoys working with construction paper, crayons, scissors, and glue, and her creations are often among the most inventive in the class.

To see if he can identify the root of Amy's difficulties, Mr. Mahoney visits her mother, a single woman raising five other children as well. "Amy doesn't talk at home either," the mother admits. "I work two jobs to make ends meet, and I haven't been able to spend as much time with her as I'd like. Her brothers and sisters take good care of her, though. They always seem to know what she wants, and they make sure she gets it."

"My conversation with Mom didn't give me any ideas about how to help Amy," Mr. Mahoney thinks as he drives home after his visit. "It does seem, though, that Amy's primary caretakers are her brothers and sisters, who probably mean well by always responding to her nonverbal behaviors but are doing nothing to encourage her to speak. When I get to school tomorrow morning, my first order of business will be to refer Amy for an in-depth evaluation."

Mr. Mahoney suspects that Amy may qualify for special educational services. If she does, in what category of special needs might she fall? Can you develop at least three different hypotheses as to where her difficulties may lie?

Amy's evaluation will undoubtedly take several weeks to complete. In the meantime, what strategies might Mr. Mahoney try to improve Amy's classroom performance?

Once you have answered these questions, compare your responses with those presented in Appendix B.

KEY CONCEPTS

individual differences (p. 139)
students with special needs (p. 139)
intelligence (p. 140)
intelligence test (p. 141)
IQ score (p. 141)
g (general factor in intelligence) (p. 144)
automaticity (p. 146)
distributed intelligence (p. 147)
temperament (p. 149)
inclusion (p. 151)
Individuals with Disabilities Education
   Act (IDEA) (p. 151)

least restrictive environment (p. 152)
individualized education program
   (IEP) (p. 152)
people-first language (p. 155)
learning disabilities (p. 155)
mnemonic (p. 159)
attention-deficit hyperactivity disorder
   (ADHD) (p. 159)
speech and communication disorders
   (p. 161)
emotional and behavioral disorders (p. 163)

externalizing behavior (p. 164)
internalizing behavior (p. 164)
autism (p. 166)
mental retardation (p. 169)
adaptive behavior (p. 169)
physical and health impairments (p. 170)
visual impairment (p. 171)
hearing loss (p. 172)
severe and multiple disabilities (p. 174)
giftedness (p. 176)

PRAXIS Turn to Appendix C, "Matching Book and Ancillary Content to the Praxis Principles of Learning and Teaching Tests," to discover sections of this chapter that may be especially applicable to the Praxis tests.

Companion Website

Now go to our Companion Website at www.prenhall. com.ormrod to assess your understanding of chapter content with "Multiple-Choice Questions," apply comprehension in "Essay Questions," broaden your knowledge of educational psychology with related "Web Links," gain greater insight about classroom learning in "Learning in the Content Areas," and analyze and assess classroom work in the "Student Artifact Library."

Learning and Cognitive Processes

We human beings are extremely adaptable creatures:
We can adjust to and thrive in a wide variety of physical, social, and cultural environments. Much of our adaptability results from our ability to learn. For us, learning begins at birth, perhaps even *before* birth (e.g., DeCasper & Spence, 1986). As children, we learn many motor skills, such as eating with a fork, using scissors, and riding a bicycle. We also learn a great deal of information, such as how *cat* is spelled, what *atom* means, and where the Panama Canal is located. Furthermore, we learn patterns and relationships among pieces of information, such as the "at" pattern found in words like *cat* and *sat,* the relationship between atoms and molecules, and the role of the Panama Canal in world trade. And we learn that certain situations call for certain behaviors; for instance, we raise our hands when we want to speak in class, turn in an assignment on the day it is due, and apologize when we've hurt someone else's feelings.

We've touched on learning in previous chapters, especially in our discussion of cognitive development in Chapter 2. For example, Piaget's concepts of *assimilation* and *accommodation,* Vygotsky's process of *internalization,* and information processing theorists' descriptions of *rehearsal, organization,* and *elaboration* all have given us glimpses into how children and adolescents learn.

In this and the next four chapters, we will look at learning more closely. Here and in Chapters 7 and 8, we'll focus on cognitive processes involved in learning and in such complex thinking skills as problem solving and creativity. In Chapters 9 and 10, we'll look at how behavior often changes as people learn and at how environmental conditions can bring about such changes. As we begin our exploration of learning in this chapter, we'll address the following questions:

■ To learn about the specific forms that thinking and learning may take in reading, writing, mathematics, science, and social studies, read the supplementary reading "Learning in the Content Areas" in the *Study Guide and Reader* that accompanies this book.

- What is *learning,* and what general theoretical perspectives can we use to describe and explain it?
- What have researchers discovered about the brain and how it functions?
- What basic assumptions and concepts are central to cognitive psychologists' beliefs about learning?
- What is the nature of human memory?
- What cognitive processes are involved in learning (*storing*) something new, and how can teachers best help students use these processes?
- What factors influence students' ability to remember (*retrieve*) information over the long run, and why do students sometimes forget what they've learned?

CASE STUDY: *Darren's Day at School*

At the dinner table one night, Darren's mother asks him, "How was your day at school?"
Darren shrugs, thinks for a moment, and says, "OK, I guess."
"What did you learn?" his father asks.
"Nothing much," Darren replies.
Nothing much, indeed! Let's look at several slices of Darren's school day and see how much he actually did learn.

- During his daily math lesson, Darren and his classmates study and practice multiplication facts for the number 9 by solving a variety of word problems (e.g., "A Girl Scout troop is selling cookies. If each of the troop's 9 members sells 8 boxes, how many boxes will the troop sell altogether?"). Darren finds that some multiplication facts are easy to learn and remember because he can relate them to things he already knows; for example, $9 \times 2 = 18$ is like adding 9 plus 9, and $9 \times 5 = 45$ can be derived from counting by fives. Others, such as $9 \times 4 = 36$ and $9 \times 8 = 72$, are more difficult because he can't connect them to any number facts he has learned before. When Ms. Caffarella finds Darren and a few of his classmates struggling, she teaches the class two tricks for learning the nines multiplication table:

  1. The first digit in the product is 1 less than the number by which 9 is being multiplied. For 9×6, the first digit in the product must be $6 - 1$, or 5.
  2. The two digits of the product, when added together, equal 9. Because 5 plus 4 equal 9, the product of 9×6 must be 54.

With these two tricks, Darren discovers a pattern in the nines table that helps him recite the table correctly.

- During a geography lesson Ms. Caffarella describes the trip she took to Greece last summer. She holds up a picture postcard of the Parthenon and explains that the building is constructed entirely of marble. Darren is sitting near the back of the room and can't see the picture very clearly; he envisions a building made entirely of *marbles* and silently wonders how the ancient Greeks managed to glue them all together.
- In physical education Darren's class has begun a unit on soccer. Darren has never played soccer before, and his first attempts to move and control the ball are clumsy and inept. His teacher watches his footwork closely, praising him when he moves his feet appropriately, and eventually Darren can dribble and pass the ball with some proficiency.
- In the afternoon's art lesson, Darren's class is making papier-mâché masks. His friend Carla gives her mask a very large nose by adding a crumpled wad of paper below the eye holes and then covering and shaping the wad with several pieces of glue-covered paper. Darren watches Carla closely throughout the process and then makes a nose for his mask in a similar way.

What has Darren learned during his math, geography, physical education, and art lessons? Can you identify one or more principles of learning that might describe what has happened in each situation?

LOOKING AT LEARNING FROM DIFFERENT PERSPECTIVES

Despite his apparent amnesia at the dinner table, Darren has clearly learned a number of things at school today, including the nines table in multiplication, the "fact" that the Parthenon was made with marbles, some rudimentary techniques for moving a soccer ball, and a strategy for sculpting with papier-mâché.

Exactly what do we mean by the word **learning**? One early definition was this one:

Definition 1: Learning is a relatively permanent change in behavior due to experience.

Over the past few decades, however, psychologists have increasingly begun to define learning in a way similar to this definition:

Definition 2: Learning is a relatively permanent change in mental representations or associations due to experience.

■ In general, I will use the term *learning* when talking about the *process* of acquiring new behaviors, representations, or associations. I will use the term *achievement* when talking about *outcomes* of the learning process.

The definitions are similar in two ways. First, both describe learning as a *relatively permanent change*—something that lasts for a period of time. Second, the change is due to an *experience* of some sort—perhaps a lesson in multiplication, a teacher's description of the Parthenon, soccer instruction, or an opportunity to watch a classmate work with papier-mâché. Changes due to something other than experience—perhaps to physiological maturation, brain injury, illness, or fatigue—fall outside the realm of learning.

Now let's look at how the two definitions differ. The first describes learning as a change in *behavior*; the second one describes it as a change in *mental representations or associations*. In Darren's day at school, we see several examples of learning as a change in behavior: Darren recites the nines table correctly for the first time, shows improvement in his ability to dribble a soccer ball, and tries a new way of shaping papier-mâché. We also see several examples of learning as a change in mental representations or associations: Darren relates $9 \times 2 = 18$ to $9 + 9 = 18$, acquires tricks for recalling the nines table, relates the marble in the Parthenon to the marbles he has at home, and remembers the steps his friend has used to sculpt a nose.

■ From a teacher's perspective, what are the potential advantages of defining learning as a change in behavior? as a change in mental representations and associations?

Some learning theories focus largely on how people's behaviors change over time and on how environmental conditions bring such changes about. Other theories focus more on internal mental processes—on thinking—than on observable behaviors. Let's look briefly at each of these approaches.

Learning as a Change in Behavior

■ **learning** Relatively permanent change, due to experience, either in behavior or in mental representations or associations.

A problem we encounter when we study thinking is that we can never actually *see* thought processes such as "remembering," "paying attention," or "studying." All we can really observe is behavior:

what people do and say. For example, we cannot directly observe Karl "remember"; we can only hear him say, "Oh, yes, now I remember . . . the capital of Spain is Madrid." We cannot truly determine whether Karen is "paying attention"; we can only see whether she is directing her eyes toward the teacher. Nor do we know that Keith is "studying" simply because we see him looking at his textbook.

When psychologists began to study the nature of learning and cognition in the late 1800s, they often asked people to "look" inside their own minds and describe what they were thinking (i.e., to engage in *introspection*). But beginning in the early 1900s, some psychologists criticized this approach for its subjectivity and lack of scientific rigor. To study learning in an objective and scientific manner, they proposed, researchers must focus on two things that can be observed: people's behaviors (**responses**) and the environmental events (**stimuli**) that precede and follow those responses. Since then, many psychologists have attempted to describe and understand learning primarily through identifying stimulus-response relationships that bring about changes in behavior. Such psychologists are called *behaviorists,* and their theories of learning are collectively known as **behaviorism.**

We see an example of the behaviorist perspective in Darren's physical education class. The teacher watches Darren's *footwork* (his responses) and gives him *praise* (a stimulus) when he makes the right moves. Rather than worry about what Darren might be thinking about soccer, the teacher focuses exclusively on Darren's behavior and provides a desirable consequence when it shows improvement. The teacher is applying a simple behaviorist principle: *A response that is followed by a desired (reinforcing) stimulus is more likely to occur again.*

Learning as a Change in Mental Representations or Associations

During the first half of the twentieth century, many psychologists adhered to the behaviorist perspective, especially in North America. As the years went by, however, it became increasingly clear that looking at stimuli and responses alone could not yield a complete picture of learning. For example, early behaviorists believed that learning can occur only when learners actually behave in some way—perhaps when they make a response and experience the consequences of that response. But in the 1940s, some psychologists proposed that people can also learn a new behavior simply by watching what *other* people do (N. E. Miller & Dollard, 1941). This idea of *modeling* provided the impetus for an alternative perspective that considers how people learn from observing those around them. Originally called *social learning theory,* this perspective has increasingly incorporated cognitive processes into its explanations of learning; it is now more commonly called **social cognitive theory.**

We find an example of modeling in Darren's experience with the papier-mâché masks. Darren watches Carla as she makes a nose for her mask; after she finishes, he follows the same steps. Notice that Darren imitates what Carla has done only after she has already completed her nose; hence, he makes his nose by using his *memory* of what he has previously seen Carla do. According to social cognitive theorists, learning itself occurs at the time that observation takes place; a behavior change as a result of that learning may or may not occur. For example, Darren might possibly watch Carla and remember what she has done, yet choose *not* to make his nose in the same way.

By the 1960s, many learning theorists were beginning to realize that they could not completely understand learning unless they considered thinking as well as behavior, and they began to conceptualize learning as a mental rather than a behavioral change. These psychologists shifted their attention away from a detailed analysis of stimulus-response relationships and focused more on the thought processes involved in learning new knowledge and skills. The perspective that emerged, **cognitive psychology,** addressed such mental phenomena as memory, attention, concept learning, problem solving, and reasoning (e.g., Neisser, 1967). Some cognitive psychologists have incorporated the ideas of such early theorists as Jean Piaget and Lev Vygotsky into their explanations of how people learn. (The evolution of learning theories is depicted graphically in Figure 6.1.)

What about behaviorists' early concern that thinking cannot be studied objectively? Cognitive and social cognitive theorists (and some behaviorists as well) propose that by observing people's responses to various stimuli, it is possible to draw *inferences*—to make educated guesses—about the internal mental events that probably underlie those responses. As an example of how we might learn about thought processes by observing people's behaviors, turn back to "Mental Maneuver," an Experiencing Firsthand exercise in Chapter 2 (p. 44). If you have not already done the exercise, do it now.

Social cognitive theory proposes that people can learn a new behavior simply by watching and imitating what other people do.

■ **response (R)** Specific behavior that an individual exhibits.

■ **stimulus (S)** Specific object or event that influences an individual's learning or behavior.

■ **behaviorism** Theoretical perspective in which learning and behavior are described and explained in terms of stimulus-response relationships.

■ **social cognitive theory** Theoretical perspective in which learning by observing others is the focus of study.

■ **cognitive psychology** Theoretical perspective that focuses on the mental processes underlying learning and behavior.

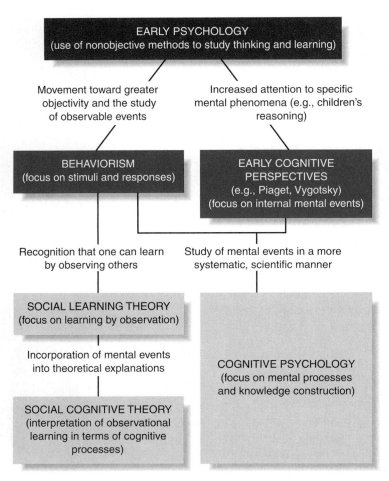

FIGURE 6.1 The evolution of learning theories

Did you write down the words in the order in which you read them? Probably not. If you are like most people, you recalled the words by category—perhaps clothing first, then vegetables, then furniture. From the order in which you wrote the words (from your *behavior*), we can draw an inference about an internal cognitive process that occurred as you learned the words: You mentally *organized* them into categories.

Researchers are certainly not the only ones who can draw inferences about cognitive processes from observable behaviors; we, as teachers, can do likewise. By observing what our students say and write, by asking them to explain their reasoning, by looking closely at their mistakes, and so on, we can make some educated guesses about what and how they are thinking about classroom topics.

Learning and the Brain

Regardless of the perspective we take to understand learning, we can reasonably assume that learning has a biological basis in the brain. The neuropsychology of learning is a very young science and, to date, gives us only the most general picture of how and where learning occurs. As noted in Chapter 2, many experts believe that learning results in an increase in both the size and number of interconnections (**synapses**) between brain cells (**neurons**). A second phenomenon may be involved as well. Until recently, it was common "knowledge" that all the neurons a person would ever have are produced in the first few weeks after conception. Researchers are finding, however, that some formation of neurons continues throughout life in the *hippocampus,* a small structure in the middle of the brain, and possibly also in certain areas of the cortex (Gould, Beylin, Tanapat, Reeves, & Shors, 1999; Sapolsky, 1999; R. A. Thompson & Nelson, 2001). Neuron formation appears to be stimulated by new learning experiences, but the precise role it plays in the learning process is still unknown.

From a physiological standpoint, the brain's ability to adapt to changing circumstances—that is, its ability to *learn*—continues throughout the lifespan (Kolb, Gibb, & Robinson, 2003). As noted in Chapter 2, students have considerable learning "brainpower" throughout the school years, and in fact their brains continue to mature even in early adulthood.

Different parts of the brain appear to serve somewhat different functions. The area of the cortex near the forehead is the center for much of our "conscious" thinking, including our reasoning, planning, and decision making. Other parts of the brain are actively involved in perception, movement, emotion, and such basic physiological processes as breathing and sleeping. To some degree, the left and right halves, or *hemispheres,* of the cortex have different specialties, with the left hemisphere having primary responsibility for language and logical thinking and the right hemisphere being more dominant in visual and spatial tasks (Byrnes, 2001; Ornstein, 1997; T. Roberts & Kraft, 1987).

Yet contrary to popular beliefs, people rarely if ever think exclusively in one part of the brain, or even in one hemisphere. There is no such thing as "left-brain" or "right-brain" thinking: The two hemispheres constantly collaborate in day-to-day tasks. In fact, the various parts of the brain *all* communicate continually with one another. Any single neuron may have synapses with hundreds or thousands of other neurons (Damasio, 1994; Goodman & Tessier-Lavigne, 1997; Lichtman, 2001). As information travels through the brain, messages go across areas that handle very different sensory modalities and tasks. In essence, learning or thinking about virtually anything tends to be *distributed* across many parts of the brain. A task as seemingly simple as identifying a particular word in speech or print activates numerous areas of the cortex (Bressler, 2002; Byrnes, 2001; Rayner, Foorman, Perfetti, Pesetsky, & Seidenberg, 2001; Thelen & Smith, 1998).

Figure 6.2 shows a computer-generated "average" of brain activation patterns measured in six adults who were asked to look at various photographs of single objects (Haxby et al., 2001).

■ **synapse** Junction between two neurons that allows transmission of messages from one to the other.

■ **neuron** Cell in the brain or another part of the nervous system that transmits information to other cells.

The figure shows two horizontal "slices" of the brain from the perspective of someone looking at the brain from above. Although the specific activation patterns differed somewhat depending on the kind of object being viewed (faces, cats, houses, or shoes, for instance), multiple parts of both the left and right hemispheres were activated for each of the objects.

I occasionally hear educators talking about applying "brain research" in the classroom. When I listen closely to what they are saying, they are typically talking about what we have learned from studies of *behavior* rather than from studies of brain anatomy and physiology. Although our current knowledge of the brain gives us optimism that students of all ages and ability levels can benefit in significant ways from their experiences, it provides little if any guidance about how *best* to help them learn. Nor can we can boil down specific psychological phenomena—thoughts, knowledge, beliefs, interpretations, and so on—into strictly neurological entities. Fortunately, as you will discover in the upcoming pages, psychological theories of learning—derived from more than a century of research on human behavior—have a great deal to offer as we strive to understand the nature of learning and to identify instructional strategies that maximize learning in the classroom.

Keeping an Open Mind About Theories of Learning

The three theoretical perspectives of learning we'll consider in this and the next four chapters—cognitive psychology, behaviorism, and social cognitive theory—encompass different views on several fundamental issues and will take us in somewhat different directions as we explore the multifaceted nature of human learning. Yet all three perspectives provide valuable insights for helping students learn, achieve, and be successful in the classroom.

In terms of the number of articles published in professional journals and the number of presentations given at professional conferences, cognitive psychology's view of learning is the one most in vogue at present (e.g., Robins, Gosling, & Craik, 1999). Hence, this is the perspective we will take as we begin our exploration of how we can help students learn effectively in classroom settings, and we will rely on it almost exclusively in Chapters 6 through 8. When we shift our attention to behaviorism in Chapter 9, we will find that we can help students learn more appropriate and productive behaviors if we identify environmental stimuli that promote such behaviors. I have saved social cognitive theory for Chapter 10 because it integrates elements of both cognitive psychology and behaviorism; at that point, we will consider several topics that have implications for classroom practice, including modeling, self-efficacy, and self-regulation. As we discuss motivation in Chapters 11 and 12, we will find that all three perspectives provide useful strategies for helping students *want* to learn.

BASIC ASSUMPTIONS OF COGNITIVE PSYCHOLOGY

Underlying cognitive psychology are several basic assumptions about how people learn. These assumptions, summarized in Table 6.1, are as follows:

◎ *Cognitive processes influence the nature of what is learned.* Cognitive psychologists have offered numerous explanations for how people mentally process information; many of these theories are collectively known as **information processing theory**, a perspective we first encountered in Chapter 2. As an illustration of the role that cognitive processes play, consider how, in the opening case, Darren relates $9 \times 2 = 18$ to $9 + 9 = 18$ and relates $9 \times 5 = 45$ to counting by fives. Consider, too, how the teacher's description of a pattern in the nines table helps Darren remember more difficult facts such as $9 \times 8 = 72$. These two examples illustrate two principles from cognitive psychology: (1) *People learn new information more easily when they can relate it to something they already know,* and (2) *people learn several pieces of new information more easily when they can relate the pieces to an overall organizational structure.*

This focus on the nature of cognitive processes can be extremely helpful to us as teachers. We must consider not only *what* we want our students to learn but also *how* they can most effectively learn it.

◎ *People are selective about what they process and learn.* Consider the various stimuli you are encountering at this very moment. How many separate stimuli appear on these two open pages of your textbook? How many objects do you see right now *in addition to* your textbook? How many sounds are reaching your ears? How many objects—perhaps on your fingertips, on your toes, at your back, or around your waist—do you feel? I suspect that you had been ignoring most of these stimuli until just now; you were not processing them until I asked you to do

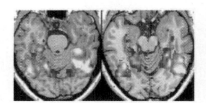

FIGURE 6.2 Computer-generated pattern of typical brain activation in two different horizontal "slices" of the brain when people look at photographs of single objects. Areas in red, orange, and yellow indicate higher-than-normal activation, and areas in blue indicate lower-than-normal activation (as compared to a "non-looking" baseline).

From "Distributed and Overlapping Representations of Faces and Objects in Ventral Temporal Cortex," by J. V. Haxby, M. I. Gobbini, M. L. Furey, A. Ishai, J. L. Schouten, and P. Pietrini, 2001, *Science, 293*, p. 2427. Reprinted by permission of the American Association for the Advancement of Science.

■ What concepts and principles can you recall from the discussion of information processing theory in Chapter 2?

■ **information processing theory** Theoretical perspective focusing on the specific ways in which learners mentally think about ("process") new information and events.

TABLE 6.1   PRINCIPLES/ASSUMPTIONS

Basic Assumptions of Cognitive Psychology and Their Educational Implications

ASSUMPTION	EDUCATIONAL IMPLICATION	EXAMPLE
Influence of cognitive processes	Encourage students to think about class material in ways that will help them remember it.	When introducing the concept *mammal*, ask students to identify numerous examples.
Selectivity about what is learned	Help students identify the most important things for them to learn. Also help them understand why these things are important.	Give students questions that they should try to answer as they read their textbooks. Include questions that ask them to apply what they read to their own lives.
Construction of meaning	Provide experiences that will help students make sense of the topics they are studying.	When studying Nathaniel Hawthorne's *The Scarlet Letter*, have small groups of students discuss possible reasons why Reverend Arthur Dimmesdale refuses to acknowledge that he is the father of Hester Prynne's baby.
Role of prior knowledge and beliefs	Relate new ideas to what students already know and believe about the world.	When introducing the vocabulary word *debut* to Mexican American students, relate it to *quinceañera*, a "coming-out" party that many Mexican American families hold for their 15-year-old daughters.
Active involvement in learning	Plan classroom activities that get students actively thinking about and using classroom subject matter.	To help students understand latitude and longitude, ask them to track the path of a hurricane using a series of latitude-longitude coordinates obtained on the Internet.

■ It is useful to distinguish between *sensation*—one's ability to sense stimuli in the environment—and *perception*—one's interpretation of stimuli. What the body senses is not always perceived (interpreted).

so. People are constantly bombarded with information, and they can typically handle only a small fraction of it at a given time. Thus, they must be selective, focusing on what they think is important and ignoring everything else.

As an analogy, consider the hundreds of items a typical household receives in the mail each year, including all the packages, letters, bills, brochures, catalogs, fliers, advertisements, requests for donations, and sweepstakes announcements. Do you open, examine, and respond to every piece of mail? Probably not. If you're like me, then you "process" only a few key items (e.g., packages, letters, bills, and some miscellaneous things that catch your eye). You may inspect other items long enough to know that you don't need them; you may even discard some items without opening them at all.

In much the same way, students will encounter a great deal of new information every day—information delivered by way of teacher instruction, textbooks, bulletin boards, classmates' behaviors, and so on. They will inevitably make choices as to which pieces of information are most important. They will select a few stimuli to examine and respond to in depth, give other stimuli only a cursory glance, and ignore other stimuli altogether. As teachers, we must help students make wise decisions about the pieces of information they choose to attend to, process, and save.

◎ *Meaning is constructed by the learner, rather than being derived directly from the environment.* The process of **construction** lies at the core of many cognitive theories of learning: People take many separate pieces of information and use them to create an understanding or interpretation of the world around them (e.g., Bransford & Franks, 1971; Hegland & Andre, 1992; Marshall, 1992; Neisser, 1967). To experience the process of construction firsthand, try the following exercise.

Experiencing FIRSTHAND ·Three Faces

Figure 6.3 contains three pictures. What do you see in each one? Most people perceive the picture on the left as being that of a woman, even though many of her features are missing. Enough pieces are visible—an eye, parts of the nose, mouth, chin, and hair—that you can construct a meaningful perception from them. Is enough information available in the other two figures for you to construct two more faces? Construction of a face from the figure on the right may take a while, but it can be done.

■ **construction** Mental process in which a learner takes many separate pieces of information and uses them to build an overall understanding or interpretation.

· · · · · · ·

Objectively speaking, the three configurations of black splotches in Figure 6.3, and especially the two rightmost ones, leave a lot to the imagination. The woman in the middle is missing half of her face, and the man on the right is missing the top of his head. Yet knowing how human faces typically appear may have been enough to enable you to add the missing features (mentally) and perceive a complete picture. Curiously, once you have constructed faces from the figures, they then seem obvious. If you were to close this book now and not pick it up again for a week or more, you would probably see the faces almost immediately, even if you had had considerable difficulty perceiving them originally.

FIGURE 6.3 Can you construct a person from each of these pictures?

From "Age in the Development of Closure Ability in Children," by C. M. Mooney, 1957, *Canadian Journal of Psychology, 11*, p. 220. Copyright 1957 by the Canadian Psychological Association. Reprinted with permission.

We see the process of construction in our case study as well. When Ms. Caffarella describes the Parthenon's marble construction, Darren envisions a building made of marbles similar to the ones he has at home (such a misconception has been described by Sosniak & Stodolsky, 1994). He combines new information with what he already knows to make sense of Ms. Caffarella's description.

Some cognitive theories focus primarily on the ways that learners construct knowledge; many of these theories are collectively known as **constructivism**. We first encountered the constructivist perspective in Chapter 2: As early as the 1920s, Jean Piaget proposed that children construct their own understandings of the world based on their experiences with their physical and social environments.

As teachers, we must remember that students won't necessarily learn information exactly as we present it to them; in fact, they will each interpret classroom subject matter in their own, idiosyncratic ways. In some cases students may construct *mis*information, as Darren did. Accordingly, we should frequently monitor students' understanding by asking questions, encouraging dialogue, and listening carefully to students' ideas and explanations.

◎ *Prior knowledge and beliefs play a major role in the meanings that people construct.* One major reason that different students in the same classroom learn different things is that they have different bodies of knowledge and beliefs from which to draw as they interpret new information and events. Students all have their own personal histories, and they are likely to come from a wide variety of neighborhoods and cultural backgrounds. Most cognitive psychologists believe that existing understandings of the world have a major influence on what and how effectively people can learn from their experiences. We will repeatedly see the effects of prior knowledge and beliefs in this and the next two chapters.

◎ *People are actively involved in their own learning.* As should be clear by now, cognitive psychologists do not believe that people simply "absorb" knowledge from their surroundings. Instead, people are, and in fact *must be,* active participants in their own learning. Cognitive processing and knowledge construction require a certain amount of mental "work." In our discussion of memory in the pages ahead, we will begin to find out what this work involves—in other words, what our students must do (mentally) to learn effectively.

BASIC TERMINOLOGY IN COGNITIVE PSYCHOLOGY

Four concepts—memory, storage, encoding, and retrieval—will be important in our upcoming discussions of the cognitive processes involved in learning.

Memory. The term **memory** refers to learners' ability to "save" things (mentally) they have previously learned. In some instances we will use the term to refer to the actual process of saving previously learned knowledge or skills over a period of time. In other instances it will refer to a "location"—perhaps *working* memory or *long-term* memory—where learners "put" what they learn.

Storage. The term **storage** refers to the acquisition of new knowledge—the process of putting what is learned into memory in the first place. For example, you have, I hope, been *storing* the ideas you have been reading in this chapter. And each time you go to class, you undoubtedly store some of the ideas presented in a lecture or class discussion. You may store other information from class as well—perhaps the name of the person sitting next to you (George), the shape and size of

■ **constructivism** Theoretical perspective proposing that learners construct (rather than absorb) a body of knowledge from their experiences.

■ **memory** Ability to save something (mentally) that has been previously learned, *or* the mental "location" where such information is saved.

■ **storage** Process of "putting" new information into memory.

the classroom (rectangular, about 15 by 30 meters), or the pattern of the instructor's shirt (a ghastly combination of orange and purple horizontal stripes).

Encoding. We rarely store information exactly as we receive it. We usually modify it in some way; that is, we **encode** it. For example, when you listen to a story, you may picture some of the story's events in your mind. When you see that orange and purple striped shirt, you may think, "Hmmm, my instructor really needs a wardrobe makeover."

People frequently store information in a different way from how it was presented to them. For example, they may change information from auditory to visual form, as when they form a mental picture of a story they are listening to. Or they may change information from visual to auditory form, as when they read aloud a passage from a textbook. Furthermore, encoding often involves assigning specific *meanings* and *interpretations* to stimuli and events. As an illustration, try this exercise.

This student might have more prior knowledge about shellfish and other sea creatures than her classmates because of her recent family trip to Florida.

Experiencing FIRSTHAND · · · · · · · · · · · ·The Old Sea Dog at the Admiral Benbow Inn

Read the following passage *one time only:*

> He was a very silent man by custom. All day he hung round the cove, or upon the cliffs, with a brass telescope; all evening he sat in a corner of the parlour next the fire, and drank rum and water very strong. Mostly he would not speak when spoken to; only look up sudden and fierce, and blow through his nose like a fog-horn; and we and the people who came about our house soon learned to let him be. Every day, when he came back from his stroll, he would ask if any seafaring men had gone by along the road. At first we thought it was the want of company of his own kind that made him ask this question; but at last we began to see he was desirous to avoid them. When a seaman put up at the "Admiral Benbow" (as now and then some did, making by the coast road for Bristol), he would look in at him through the curtained door before he entered the parlour; and he was always sure to be as silent as a mouse when any such was present. For me, at least, there was no secret about the matter; for I was, in a way, a sharer in his alarms. He had taken me aside one day, and promised me a silver fourpenny on the first of every month if I would only keep my "weather-eye open for a seafaring man with one leg," and let him know the moment he appeared. Often enough, when the first of the month came round, and I applied to him for my wage, he would only blow through his nose at me, and stare me down; but before the week was out he was sure to think better of it, bring me my fourpenny piece, and repeat his orders to look out for "the seafaring man with one leg." (from Robert Louis Stevenson's *Treasure Island*)

Now that you have finished the passage, take a few minutes to write down as much of the passage as you can remember.

· · · · · · ·

As you reflected on the passage, you probably remembered that the man was afraid of a one-legged seafarer. You may also have recalled that the man paid the story's narrator some money to keep an eye out for such an individual. But could you remember *each and every detail* about the events that took place? Could you recall the *exact words* the author used to describe the man's behavior? If you are like most people, you stored the gist of the passage (its general meaning) without necessarily storing the specific words. This tendency to encode gist rather than verbatim information increases as children get older (Brainerd, Reyna, Howe, & Kingma, 1990).

Retrieval. Once you have stored information in your memory, you may later discover that you need to use the information. The process of remembering previously stored information—that is, "finding" it in memory—is called **retrieval**. The following exercise illustrates this process.

■ Think of an exam you have taken recently. Which student would have done better on that exam: one who had encoded course information verbatim or one who had encoded its meanings?

Experiencing FIRSTHAND ·Retrieval Practice

See how quickly you can answer each of the following questions:

1. What is your name?
2. In what year did World War II end?
3. What is the capital of Spain?
4. What did you have for dinner three years ago today?
5. When talking about serving appetizers at a party, we sometimes use a French term instead of the word *appetizer*. What is that French term, and how is it spelled?

· · · · · · ·

■ **encoding** Changing the format of new information as it is being stored in memory.

■ **retrieval** Process of "finding" information previously stored in memory.

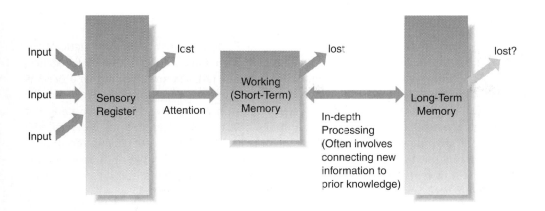

FIGURE 6.4 A model of the human memory system

As you probably just noticed when you tried to answer these questions, retrieving information from memory is sometimes an easy, effortless process; for example, you undoubtedly had little difficulty remembering your name. But other things stored in memory can be retrieved only after some thought and effort; for example, it may have taken you some time to remember that World War II ended in 1945 and that the capital of Spain is Madrid. Still other things, even though they may have been stored in memory at one time, may never be retrieved at all; perhaps a dinner menu three years ago and the correct spelling of *hors d'oeuvre* fall into this category.

How is information stored and encoded in memory? And what factors influence the ease with which we can retrieve it later? We now look at a model of how human memory might work.

A MODEL OF HUMAN MEMORY

Cognitive psychologists do not agree about the exact nature of human memory. However, many of them believe that memory may have three key components: a sensory register, a working (short-term) memory, and a long-term memory. A three-component model of human memory, based loosely on one proposed by Atkinson and Shiffrin in 1968 but modified to reflect more recent research findings, is presented in Figure 6.4. The model oversimplifies the nature of memory to some degree (more about this point later), but it provides a good way to organize much of what we know about how memory works.

Please note that in referring to three components of memory, I am *not* necessarily referring to three separate parts of the brain. The model of memory that I describe has been derived from studies of human behavior, not from studies of the brain. In the pages that follow, we will look at the characteristics of each component of memory and at how information is moved from one component to the next.

The Nature of the Sensory Register

If you have ever played with a lighted sparkler at night, then you've undoubtedly noticed the tail of light that follows a sparkler as you wave it about. If you have ever daydreamed in class, then you may have noticed that when you tune back in to the lecture, you can still "hear" three or four words spoken just *before* you started paying attention to your instructor again. The sparkler's tail and the words that linger after they have already been spoken are not "out there" in the environment—they are recorded in your sensory register.

The **sensory register** is the component of memory that holds the information you receive—*input*—in more or less its original, *unencoded* form. Probably everything your body is capable of seeing, hearing, and otherwise sensing is stored in the sensory register. In other words, the sensory register has a *large capacity*; it can hold a great deal of information at one time.

That's the good news. The bad news is that information stored in the sensory register doesn't last very long (Cowan, 1995; Wingfield & Byrnes, 1981). Visual information (what you *see*) probably lasts for less than a second. As a child, I never could spell out my entire first name (Jeanne) with a sparkler; the *J* had always faded before I got to the first *N*, no matter how quickly I wrote. Auditory information (what you *hear*) might last slightly longer, but probably not for more than a couple of seconds. To keep information for any time at all, then, we need to move it to *working memory*. Whatever information isn't moved is probably lost, or forgotten.

■ **sensory register** Component of memory that holds incoming information in an unanalyzed form for a very brief period of time (perhaps a second or less).

Moving Information to Working Memory: The Role of Attention

Sensory information, such as the light cast by a sparkler, doesn't last very long no matter what we do. But we can preserve a memory of it by encoding it in some minimal way—for instance, by perceiving the letters *Jea* written in the sparkler's curlicue tail. The first step in this process is **attention**: *Whatever people pay attention to (mentally) moves into working memory.* Anything in the sensory register that does not get a person's attention disappears from the memory system. For example, imagine yourself reading a textbook for one of your classes. Your eyes are moving down each page, but meanwhile you are thinking about something altogether different—a recent fight with a friend, a high-paying job advertised in the newspaper, or your growling stomach. What will you remember from the textbook? Little or nothing. Even though your eyes were focused on the words in your book, you weren't really paying attention to those words.

■ Observe how David's lack of attention affects learning in the "Memory and Metacognition: Middle Childhood" clip on Video CD 1.

Children, too, often have trouble keeping their attention on a task at hand. We find an example in the "Memory and Metacognition: Middle Childhood" clip on Video CD 1. Ten-year-old David remembers only 3 of the 12 words that an interviewer reads to him. When he says, "My brain was turned off right now," he really means that his *attention* was turned off, or at least directed to something other than what the interviewer was saying.

Unfortunately, people can attend to only a very small amount of information at any one time. In other words, attention has a *limited capacity*. For example, if you are in a room where several conversations are occurring at once, you can usually attend to—and therefore can learn from—only one of those conversations; this phenomenon is sometimes called the *cocktail party phenomenon* (Cherry, 1953; Norman, 1969). If you are sitting in front of the television with your textbook open in your lap, you can attend to the *Friends* rerun *or* to your book, but not to both simultaneously. If you are preoccupied in class with your instructor's need for a fashion makeover, you are unlikely to be paying attention to the content of the lecture.

Exactly *how* limited is the limited capacity of human attention? People can often perform two or three well-learned, automatic tasks at once; for example, you can walk and chew gum simultaneously, and you can probably drive a car and drink a Coke at the same time. But when a stimulus or event is detailed and complex (as is true for both textbooks and *Friends* reruns) or when a task requires considerable thought (understanding a lecture and driving a car on an icy mountain road are examples of tasks requiring one's utmost concentration), then people can usually attend to only one thing at a time (J. R. Anderson, 1990; Reisberg, 1997).

■ Do you talk on a mobile (cellular) phone while driving? Thanks to attention's limited capacity, doing so significantly impairs your driving performance (Just et al., 2001; Strayer & Johnston, 2001).

Because of the limited capacity of human attention, only a very small amount of information stored in one's sensory register ever moves on to working memory. The vast majority of information the body initially receives is quickly lost from the memory system, much as we might quickly discard all that junk mail we receive every day.

Attention in the Classroom   Obviously, it is critical that students pay attention to what we want them to learn. To some extent, we can tell which students are paying attention by their overt behaviors (Grabe, 1986; Piontkowski & Calfee, 1979). But appearances can be deceiving. For example, you can probably think of times when, as a student, you looked at a teacher without really hearing anything the teacher said. You can probably also think of times when you looked at a textbook without a single word on the page sinking in. Attention is not just a behavior, it is also a mental process. It is not enough that students' eyes and ears are directed toward their classroom material. Their minds must be directed toward it as well.

How can we be sure students are really paying attention? For one thing, we can ask questions that test their understanding of new ideas; students are more likely to keep their minds on a lecture or reading assignment if they know that they will be immediately accountable for it (Grabe, 1986; Piontkowski & Calfee, 1979). We can also ask students to put classroom material to use—for example, by having them draw an inference or solve a problem using new information. A third strategy is to encourage students to take notes; research tells us that note taking usually helps students learn information, partly because it makes them pay attention to what they are hearing or reading (Di Vesta & Gray, 1972; Kiewra, 1989).

Every classroom has students who have trouble keeping their minds on school subject matter. Such students are more likely to pay attention when they are seated near their teacher and perhaps at a comfortable distance from classmates (Pfiffner & Barkley, 1998; Schwebel & Cherlin, 1972). We can also help these students by providing a stimulating classroom environment in which everyone *wants* to pay attention. Children and adolescents are more likely to be attentive when we present exciting and personally relevant topics, use a variety of instructional

■ **attention** Focusing of mental processes on particular stimuli.

methods, and are lively and enthusiastic about the subject matter. They are less likely to keep their minds on their work when they study the same topics and follow the same routine day after day and when, as teachers, we seem to be as bored with the subject matter as they are (Berlyne, 1960; Good & Brophy, 1994; Klinger, 1996; Zirin, 1974). In the "Motivation: Early Adolescence" clip on Video CD 1, 12-year-old Claudia describes some of the things that teachers do to keep her attention:

> They kind of sound enthusiastic. They don't just teach everything. They have a little fun with it, too.

She also describes occasions in which they quickly lose her attention:

> If the teacher's not sure what they're doing, or they just keep playing movies over and over.

Yet even the most attentive students cannot keep their minds on any particular topic forever. They need occasional breaks from intensive mental activity (Pellegrini & Bjorklund, 1997). Some breaks are built into the daily school schedule in such forms as recess, passing periods, and lunch. But we may want to give students additional mental breathers as well—perhaps by asking them to perform a physical task related to the topic at hand or perhaps, after an intensive work session, by giving them a chance to take a one-minute stretch.

The Nature of Working (Short-Term) Memory

Working memory is the component of memory where new information stays while it is mentally processed. Initially, theorists conceived of it only as a temporary holding bin for new information and so called it *short-term memory*. But increasingly they have realized that this component also does most of the mental work of the memory system; for instance, it is where we try to make sense of a lecture, understand a textbook passage, or solve a problem.

Rather that being a single entity, working memory probably has several components for holding and working with different kinds of information—for example, for handling visual information, auditory information, and meanings—as well as a component that integrates multiple kinds of information (Baddeley, 2001; E. E. Smith, 2000; D. T. Willingham, 2004). It may also include a *central executive* that focuses attention, oversees the flow of information throughout the memory system, selects and controls complex voluntary behaviors, and inhibits inappropriate thoughts and actions (Baddeley, 2001; Carlson & Moses, 2001; Kimberg et al., 1997; G. R. Lyon & Krasnegor, 1996).[1] Furthermore, working memory, especially its central executive component, enables people to control and reflect on their own thought processes (Borkowski & Burke, 1996; Eslinger, 1996); we'll explore the nature of this *metacognition* in Chapter 8.

Working memory has two characteristics that are particularly worth noting: a short duration and a limited capacity.

Short duration. Imagine that you need to call a friend, so you look up the friend's number in the telephone book. Once you have the number in your head, you discover that someone else is using the only available telephone. You have no paper and pencil handy. What do you do to remember the number until you can use the phone?

Because you've paid attention to the number, it is presumably in your working memory. But working memory, as its alternative name "short-term memory" implies, is *short*. Unless you do something further with the telephone number, it will last for less than half a minute, and perhaps for only a few seconds (Baddeley, 1999; L. R. Peterson & Peterson, 1959). To keep it in your head until the phone is available, you might simply repeat it to yourself over and over. This process, known as **maintenance rehearsal**, keeps information in working memory for as long as you're willing to continue talking to yourself. But once you stop, the number quickly disappears. In general, you must *actively think* about information if you want to keep it in your working memory.

I sometimes hear students talking about putting class material in "short-term memory" so they can do well on an upcoming exam. Such a statement reflects the common misconception that this component of memory lasts for several days, weeks, or even months. Now you know

---

[1] As you may have guessed, working memory functions are located in the front part of the cortex, which we identified earlier as the center for much of our "conscious" thinking. Certain other parts of the brain (e.g., the hippocampus) are involved as well (Byrnes, 2001).

■ In the "Motivation: Early Adolescence" clip on Video CD 1, hear Claudia describe things her teachers do that capture or lose her attention.

■ The discussion of motivation in Chapters 11 and 12 offers additional ideas for capturing and keeping students' attention.

■ **working memory** Component of memory that holds and actively thinks about and processes a limited amount of information.

■ **maintenance rehearsal** Repetition of information over and over to keep it "fresh" in working memory.

■ Did you have this misconception about short-term memory before you read this section?

otherwise. Working memory is obviously *not* the "place" to leave information you need for an exam later in the week, or even for information you'll need for a class later today.

Limited capacity. Let's put your working memory to work for a moment.

Experiencing FIRSTHAND ·A Divisive Situation

Try computing the answer to this division problem in your head:

$$59\overline{)49{,}383}$$

· · · · · · ·

THE FAR SIDE® BY GARY LARSON

"Mr. Osborne, may I be excused? My brain is full."

Working memory is a bottleneck in the human memory system, in that it has a very limited capacity. In contrast, long-term memory probably has as much room as we would ever need.

THE FAR SIDE® By Gary Larson © 1986 FARWORKS, INC. All rights reserved. Used with permission.

Did you find yourself having trouble remembering some parts of the problem while you were dealing with other parts? Did you ever arrive at the correct answer of 837? Most people cannot solve a division problem with this many digits unless they can write the problem on paper. The fact is, working memory just doesn't have room to hold all that information at once—it has a *limited capacity* (Baddeley, 2001; Luck & Vogel, 1997; G. A. Miller, 1956; Simon, 1974).

Just like other human beings, students have limited space in their working memories, so they can learn only so much so fast. We must keep this in mind as we plan classroom lessons and activities. A mistake many new teachers make is to present too much information too quickly, and their students' working memories simply can't keep up. Instead, we should pace the presentation of new information so that students have time to process it all. In addition to slowing our pace, we might repeat the same idea several times (perhaps rewording it each time), stop to write important points on the chalkboard, and provide numerous examples and illustrations.

Even when the pace of instruction is appropriate, students can probably never learn *everything* presented to them in a lecture, activity, or textbook. Most teachers and textbooks present much more information than students can possibly store (Calfee, 1981). One psychologist (E. D. Gagné, 1985) has estimated that students are likely to learn only about one to six new ideas from each minute of a lecture—a small fraction of the ideas typically presented during that time! Although they must continually make choices about what to learn and what *not* to learn, students aren't always the best judges of what is important (Garner, Alexander, Gillingham, Kulikowich, & Brown, 1991; Mayer, 1984; R. E. Reynolds & Shirey, 1988). We can help them make the right choices if we tell them what information is most important, give them guidelines on how and what to study, and omit unnecessary details from lessons.

Moving Information to Long-Term Memory: Connecting New Information with Prior Knowledge

In the memory model depicted in Figure 6.4, you will notice that the arrow between working memory and long-term memory points in both directions. The process of storing new information in long-term memory usually involves drawing on "old" information already stored there; in other words, it necessitates using prior knowledge. Here are some examples:

- When Patrick reads about the feuding between the Montagues and the Capulets in *Romeo and Juliet*, he thinks, "Hmmm . . . sounds a lot like the relationship my family has with our next-door neighbors."
- Paolo discovers that the initial letters of each of the five Great Lakes—Huron, Ontario, Michigan, Erie, and Superior—spell the word *HOMES*.
- Like many young children, Priscilla believes the world is flat. When her teacher tells her the world is round, Priscilla pictures a flat, circular disk (which is, of course, round *and* flat).

Each student is connecting new information with something he or she already knows or believes. Patrick finds a similarity between *Romeo and Juliet* and his own neighborhood. Paolo connects the five Great Lakes with a common, everyday word. And Priscilla relates the idea that the world is round to her previous conception of a flat world and to the many flat, circular objects (e.g., coins, pizzas) she has encountered over the years.

Later in the chapter we will look more specifically at the processes through which information is stored in long-term memory. For now, let's focus on the characteristics of long-term memory and the nature of that "old" information stored within it.

The Nature of Long-Term Memory

Long-term memory holds information for a relatively long time—perhaps a day, week, month, year, or lifetime. Your own long-term memory is where you've stored such pieces of information as your name, a few frequently used telephone numbers, your general knowledge about the world, and the things you've learned in school (perhaps the year in which World War II ended, the capital of Spain, or the correct spelling of *hors d'oeuvre*). It is also where you've stored your knowledge about how to perform various behaviors, such as how to ride a bicycle, swing a baseball bat, or write a cursive letter *J*.

Long-term memory has three characteristics especially worth noting: a long duration, an essentially unlimited capacity, and a rich network of interconnections.

(Indefinitely) long duration. As you might guess, information stored in long-term memory lasts much longer than that in working memory. But exactly *how* long is long-term memory? As you well know, people often forget things they have known for a day, a week, or even longer. Some psychologists believe that information may slowly "weaken" and possibly disappear from long-term memory, especially if it is not used regularly (J. R. Anderson, 1990; Reisberg, 1997; D. L. Schacter, 1999). Others instead believe that once information is stored in long-term memory, it remains there permanently but may in some cases be extremely difficult to retrieve (Loftus & Loftus, 1980). The exact duration of long-term memory has not been determined and perhaps never can be (Eysenck & Keane, 1990).

Unlimited capacity. Long-term memory seems to be capable of holding as much information as a learner needs to store there—there is probably no such thing as "running out of room." In fact, for reasons you will discover shortly, the more information already stored in long-term memory, the easier it is to learn new things.

Interconnectedness. Theorists have discovered that much of the information stored in long-term memory is organized and interrelated. To see what I mean, try the following exercise.

■ Can you summarize the model of memory described in the last few pages?

Experiencing FIRSTHAND ·Horse #1

What is the first word that comes to your mind when you hear the word *horse*? And what word does that second word remind you of? And what does that third word remind you of? Beginning with the word *horse*, follow your train of thought, letting each word remind you of another one, for a sequence of at least eight words or phrases. Write down your sequence of words as each word comes to mind.

· · · · · · ·

You probably found yourself easily following a train of thought from the word *horse*, perhaps something like the route I followed:

horse → cowboy → lasso → rope → knot → Girl Scouts → cookies → chocolate

The last word in your sequence may be one with little or no obvious relationship to horses. Yet you can probably see a logical connection between each pair of words in the sequence. Cognitive psychologists believe that related pieces of information in long-term memory are often connected with one another, perhaps in a network similar to the one depicted in Figure 6.5.

Critiquing the Three-Component Model

In the last few pages, we have considered the sensory register, working memory, and long-term memory. But as I mentioned earlier, the three-component model presented in Figure 6.4 oversimplifies—and perhaps overcompartmentalizes—the nature of human memory. For example, working memory (in particular, its central executive aspect) influences what we pay attention to; thus, the flow of information from sensory register to working memory is not as simple as the

■ **long-term memory** Component of memory that holds knowledge and skills for a relatively long time.

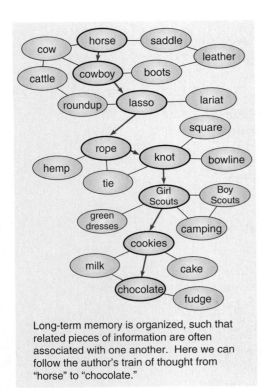

Long-term memory is organized, such that related pieces of information are often associated with one another. Here we can follow the author's train of thought from "horse" to "chocolate."

FIGURE 6.5 Interconnectedness in long-term memory

one-way arrow in the figure suggests (Demetriou et al., 2002; Sergeant, 1996). In fact, attention may be a *part* of working memory, rather than the separate entity I depict in Figure 6.4 (Engle, 2002; R. K. Wagner, 1996). Furthermore, research yields mixed results about whether working memory and long-term memory are distinctly different entities (Baddeley, 2001; Cowan, 1995; Crowder, 1993; Woltz, 2003).

Some psychologists (e.g., J. R. Anderson, 1995; Cowan, 1995; Sadoski & Paivio, 2001) have proposed that working and long-term memory simply reflect different **activation** states of a single memory. According to this view, all information stored in memory is in either an active or inactive state. Active information, which may include both incoming information and information previously stored in memory, is what people are paying attention to and processing—information I have previously described as being in working memory. As attention shifts, other pieces of information in memory become activated, and the previously activated information gradually becomes inactive. The bulk of information stored in memory is in an inactive state, so that we are not consciously aware of it; this is information I have previously described as being in long-term memory.

The three-component model, though not perfect, is similar to how many cognitive psychologists conceptualize human memory. This model also emphasizes aspects of memory we should keep in mind as we teach. For example, it highlights the importance of *attention* in learning, the *limited capacity* of attention and working memory, the *interconnectedness* of the knowledge learners acquire, and the importance of *relating* new information to things learned on previous occasions.

Regardless of whether there are three truly distinct components of memory, some aspects of memory are definitely "long-term." Certainly we remember many things for a considerable length of time, and in this sense, at least, these things are in long-term memory. We now look more closely at the nature of long-term memory storage.

LONG-TERM MEMORY STORAGE

What forms does "knowledge" take in long-term memory? How do people think about and process new information and skills so they can remember them later? As teachers, what can we do to help students engage in effective long-term memory storage processes? These are issues we turn to now.

The Various Forms of Knowledge

Some theorists suggest that information stored in long-term memory may be encoded in several different forms (e.g., J. R. Anderson, 1995; E. D. Gagné, 1985; Sadoski & Paivio, 2001). Some information may be encoded in a *verbal* form, perhaps as actual words. Things you remember word for word—for example, your name, your address, the nursery rhyme "Jack and Jill," Hamlet's soliloquy—are all verbally encoded. Other information may be encoded as *imagery*, or how that information appears perceptually. For instance, if, in your mind, you can "see" the face of a relative, "hear" that person's voice, or conjure up a mental "whiff" of that person's favorite perfume or aftershave lotion, you are retrieving images. Finally, a great deal of information in long-term memory is probably encoded *semantically*, as underlying meanings. For example, when you listen to a lecture or read a textbook, you probably store the gist of the message more frequently than you store the words themselves. All of these examples are instances of **declarative knowledge**, knowledge that relates to the nature of *how things are*.

Sometimes declarative information is encoded in more than one form, and such information is more easily remembered. For example, students more readily learn and remember information they receive in both a verbal form (e.g., a lecture or textbook passage) and a graphic form (e.g., a picture, map, or diagram) (Kulhavy, Lee, & Caterino, 1985; Sadoski & Paivio, 2001; Winn, 1991). Thus, by presenting information to students in multiple modalities, or perhaps by explicitly asking them to represent it in at least two different ways (e.g., see Figure 6.6), we increase the likelihood that they will be able to remember it over the long run.

Not everything in long-term is declarative in nature, however. People also acquire **procedural knowledge**; that is, they learn *how to do things* (e.g., J. R. Anderson, 1983; Phye, 1997;

■ **activation** Degree to which something in memory is being actively attended to and mentally processed.

■ **declarative knowledge** Knowledge related to "what is"—that is, to the nature of how things are, were, or will be.

■ **procedural knowledge** Knowledge concerning how to do something (e.g., a skill).

Tulving, 1983). For example, you probably know how to ride a bicycle, wrap a birth-day present, and multiply a three-digit number by a two-digit number. To perform such actions successfully, you must adapt your behavior to changing conditions; for example, when you ride a bicycle, you must be able to turn left or right when an object blocks your path, and you must be able to come to a complete stop when you reach your destination. Accordingly, procedural knowledge must often include information about how to respond under different circumstances; in such instances, it's also known as *conditional knowledge*.

Most of declarative knowledge is *explicit knowledge*: Once we recall it, we are quite conscious of what it is we know. But a good deal of procedural knowledge is *implicit knowledge*: We cannot consciously recall or explain it, but it affects our behavior nevertheless (J. R. Anderson, 1990; Bachevalier, Malkova, & Beauregard, 1996). In addition, declarative knowledge can sometimes be learned very quickly, perhaps after a single presentation of information. In contrast, procedural knowledge is often learned slowly and with considerable practice (Corno et al., 2002; Tulving, 1983). Let's look more closely at how declarative and procedural knowledge are learned.

How Declarative Knowledge Is Learned

Consider this situation:

> In biology class Kanesha has been struggling to learn the names of the bones in the human body, from head (cranium) to toe (metatarsus). She has learned a few bones quickly and easily; for example, it makes sense that the *nasal bone* is near the nose, and she remembers the *humerus* (upper arm bone) by thinking of it as being just above one's funny (humorous?) bone. But she is still confused about a few bones; for example, the *tibia* and *fibula* have similar-sounding names and are located in the same place (the lower leg). And she keeps thinking that the *sternum* (at the front of the chest) is in back just like the stern of a boat. She has trouble remembering many of the other bones—the coccyx, ulna, sacrum, clavicle, patella—because she's never encountered these words before and can't relate them to anything she knows.
>
> To prepare for her upcoming biology quiz, Kanesha looks at a diagram of the human skeleton and whispers the name of each bone to herself several times. She also writes each name on a sheet of paper. "These terms should certainly sink in if I repeat them enough times," she tells herself.
>
> Kanesha scores only 70 percent on the biology quiz. As she looks over her incorrect answers, she sees that she confused the tibia and the fibula, labeled the ulna as "clavicle," put the sternum in the wrong place, and completely forgot about the coccyx, sacrum, and patella.

Kanesha is thinking about different bones in different ways. She makes some kind of logical sense of the nasal bone and humerus; she also tries to make sense of the sternum, but her strategy backfires when she relates this bone to the stern of a boat. Kanesha gives little if any thought to why the other bones have the names they do. The extent to which Kanesha mentally processes the material she needs to learn and the *ways* in which she processes it affect her performance on the biology quiz.

The specific cognitive processes a learner uses when trying to learn new information affect the learner's ability to remember and use the information later. Here we'll consider five processes (summarized in Table 6.2) that people use in storing declarative information in long-term memory: rehearsal, meaningful learning, organization, elaboration, and visual imagery.

Rehearsal   Earlier I described how maintenance rehearsal—repeating something over and over verbally—helps us keep information in working memory indefinitely. Early theorists (e.g., R. C. Atkinson & Shiffrin, 1968) believed that **rehearsal** is also a means through which information is stored in long-term memory. In other words, if we repeat something often enough, it might eventually sink in.

The main disadvantage in using rehearsal is that we make few if any connections between new information and the knowledge already stored in long-term memory. Thus, we are engaging

Seasons
Fall... Jump in the leaves
Winter... Play in the snow
Spring... Watch flowers grow
Sumer... Swim in pools and at the beach

FIGURE 6.6 Students learn and remember information more effectively if they encode it in more than one way. Here 6-year-old Nadia illustrates the four seasons in both verbal and visual form.

■ **rehearsal** Cognitive process in which information is repeated over and over as a possible way of learning and remembering it.

TABLE 6.2

Five Possible Ways of Learning Declarative Knowledge

PROCESS	DEFINITION	EXAMPLE	EFFECTIVENESS	EDUCATIONAL IMPLICATION
Rehearsal	Repeating information verbatim, either mentally or aloud	Repeating a word-for-word definition of *inertia*	Relatively ineffective: Storage is slow, and later retrieval is difficult	Suggest that students use rehearsal only as a last resort.
Meaningful learning	Making connections between new information and prior knowledge	Putting a definition of *inertia* into one's own words or identifying examples of inertia in one's own life experiences	Effective if associations made with prior knowledge are appropriate ones	Help students connect new information to things they already know.
Organization	Making connections among various pieces of new information	Studying how one's lines in a play relate to the play's overall story line	Effective if organizational structure is legitimate and consists of more than just a listing of separate facts	Present material in an organized way, and point out the organizational structure and interrelationships in the material.
Elaboration	Adding additional ideas to new information based on what one already knows	Thinking about possible reasons why historical figures behaved as they did	Effective if the ideas added are appropriate inferences	Encourage students to go beyond the information itself—for example, to draw inferences and speculate about possible implications.
Visual imagery	Forming a mental picture of information	Imagining how various characters and events in *Ivanhoe* might have looked	Individual differences in effectiveness; especially beneficial when used to supplement meaningful learning, organization, or elaboration	Illustrate verbal instruction with visual materials (e.g., pictures, maps, diagrams).

in **rote learning**: We are studying information in a relatively uninterpreted form, without making much sense of it or attaching much meaning to it. Contrary to what many students think, rote learning is a slow and relatively ineffective way of storing declarative information in long-term memory (J. R. Anderson, 1995; Craik & Watkins, 1973; Nickerson & Adams, 1979). Furthermore, for reasons you'll discover later, information stored in a rote manner is often difficult to retrieve later on.

If you have already read the discussion of cognitive development in Chapter 2, then you may recall that rehearsal is one of the first learning strategies children develop (usually in the early elementary school years). Verbally rehearsing information is probably better than not processing it at all, and in cases where students have little if any prior knowledge to draw on to help them understand new material (as when Kanesha was trying to learn *tibia*, *fibula*, *coccyx*, *ulna*, etc.), rehearsal may be one of the few strategies they can use (E. Wood, Willoughby, Reilley, Elliott, & DuCharme, 1994). But regardless of students' age or experience, we should encourage them to use other, more effective methods—meaningful learning, organization, elaboration, and visual imagery—whenever possible.

Meaningful Learning　The process of **meaningful learning** involves recognizing a relationship between new information and something else already stored in long-term memory. When we use such words as *comprehension* or *understanding*, we are talking about meaningful learning. Here are some examples:

- When Jane reads that World War II ended on August 10, 1945, she thinks, "Hey, August tenth is my birthday!"
- Students in a German class notice that the word *Buch* is pronounced like its English equivalent, *book*.

■ **rote learning** Learning information in a relatively uninterpreted form, without making sense of it or attaching much meaning to it.

■ **meaningful learning** Cognitive process in which learners relate new information to things they already know.

• When Julian reads J. D. Salinger's *Catcher in the Rye*, he sees similarities between Holden Caulfield's emotional struggles and his own adolescent concerns.

We find other examples in the "Memory and Metacognition: Late Adolescence" clip on Video CD 1. Sixteen-year-old Hilary explains how she makes some connections on her own and how her teacher helps her make additional ones:

> When I'm trying to study for a test, I try to associate the things that I'm trying to learn with familiar things. Like if I have a Spanish vocabulary test, I'll try to . . . with the Spanish words, I'll try to think of the English word that it sounds like, because sometimes it does sound like the English word. And then our Government teacher is teaching us the amendments and we're trying to memorize them. He taught us one trick for memorizing Amendment 2, which is the right to bear arms. He said, "Bears have two arms, so that's Amendment 2."

Research clearly indicates that meaningful learning is more effective than rote learning (Ausubel, Novak, & Hanesian, 1978; Bransford & Johnson, 1972; Mayer, 1996). It is especially effective when learners relate new ideas not only to the things they already know but also to *themselves* (e.g., Rogers, Kuiper, & Kirker, 1977). For instance, in Figure 6.6 Nadia explains the four seasons in terms of the things *she* does during each season.

As illustrations of the effectiveness of meaningful learning, try the following two exercises.

Experiencing FIRSTHAND ·Two Letter Strings, Two Pictures

1. Study each of the following strings of letters until you can remember them perfectly:

   AIIRODFMLAWRS   FAMILIARWORDS

2. Study each of the two pictures to the right until you can reproduce them accurately from memory.

· · · · · · ·

No doubt the second letter string was easier to learn because you could relate it to something you already knew: "familiar words." How easily were you able to learn the two pictures? Do you think you could draw them from memory a week from now? Do you think you would be able to remember them more easily if they had meaningful titles such as "a midget playing a trombone in a telephone booth" and "an early bird who caught a very strong worm"? The answer to the latter question is a very definite yes: Meaningful labels enhance people's memory for simple line drawings (Bower, Karlin, & Dueck, 1975).

Some students approach school assignments with meaningful learning in mind: They turn to what they already know to make sense of new information. These students are apt to be the high achievers in the classroom. Other students instead use rote learning strategies, such as repeating something over and over to themselves without really thinking about what they are saying. As you might guess, these students learn less successfully (Britton, Stimson, Stennett, & Gülgöz, 1998; Novak, 1998; Van Rossum & Schenk, 1984).

Yet we cannot always blame students when they take a relatively meaning*less* learning approach to their studies. Inadvertently, many teaching practices encourage students to learn school subjects by rote. Think back to your own experiences in school. How many times were you allowed to define a word by repeating a dictionary definition, rather than being expected to explain it in your own words? In fact, how many times were you *required* to learn something word for word? And how many times did an exam test your knowledge of facts or principles without ever testing your ability to relate those facts and principles to everyday life or to things learned in previous courses? Perhaps you had assignments and quizzes similar to the fill-in-the-blank questions shown in Figure 6.7. When students discover that assignments and assessments focus on recall of unrelated facts—rather than on understanding and application of an integrated body of knowledge—many rely on rote learning, believing that this approach will yield a higher score and that meaningful learning would be counterproductive (Crooks, 1988). It is little wonder, then, that meaningful learning is the exception rather than the rule in many classrooms (J. B. Cooney, 1991; McCaslin & Good, 1996; Novak & Musonda, 1991; Schoenfeld, 1985).

■ Observe how Hilary engages in meaningful learning in the "Memory and Metacognition: Late Adolescence" clip on Video CD 1.

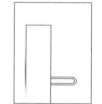 

Figures are from "Comprehension and Memory for Pictures" by G. H. Bower, M. B. Karlin, and A. Dueck, 1975, *Memory and Cognition, 3*, p. 217. Reprinted by permission of Psychonomic Society, Inc.

■ Meaningful learning is similar to Piaget's concept of *assimilation* (see Chapter 2).

1) One of the coolest things about dinosaurs is that of all the millions there were, we only know about a few _thousand_ of them.
2) The word "fossil" comes from the Latin word meaning _dug up_.
3) What four things can fossils tell us about dinosaurs?
   1 _ate_   3 _what they did wi young_
   2 _look like_   4 _size/weight_
4) Two steps in the process of fossilization are:
   -need to die   -then are covered in layers of sediment
5) One of the processes which forms a fossil is _pre-mineralized_ This means that minerals replace the bones of the dinosaur.
6) The evidence that dinosaurs once lived is found in discovering _fossils_.
7) Scientists can learn about dinosaurs by observing _where_ their fossils are buried, how _deep_ the fossils are, and what is buried _nearby_ the dinosaur fossils.
8) Dinosaurs lived on earth for about _1160_ _million_ years.
9) Dinosaurs died out about _65_ _million_ years ago.
10) One reason dinosaurs may have become extinct is _a meteorite_.

FIGURE 6.7 Seventh-grade science students complete these and other fill-in-the-blank questions as they watch a video about dinosaurs. Although the questions probably help students pay attention to the video, they encourage rote rather than meaningful learning.

■ A *meaningful learning set* is an example of a *disposition*, a concept we will consider in Chapter 12.

■ Observe a teacher promote meaningful learning in the "Civil War" clip on Video CD 2.

■ **meaningful learning set** Attitude that one can make sense of the information one is studying.

■ **knowledge base** One's knowledge about specific topics and the world in general.

Why do some students learn things meaningfully, whereas others persist in their attempts at rote memorization? At least three conditions probably facilitate meaningful learning (Ausubel et al., 1978):

◎ *The learner has a meaningful learning set.* When students approach a learning task believing they can make sense of the information—that is, when they have a **meaningful learning set**—they are more likely to learn that information meaningfully. For example, students who recognize that chemical reactions occur in accordance with familiar mathematical principles are more likely to make sense of those reactions. Students who realize that historical events can often be explained in terms of human personality are more likely to understand why World War II occurred.

My daughter Tina once came home from middle school with an assignment to learn twelve of the gods and goddesses of ancient Greece (e.g., Zeus was the king of gods; Athena, the goddess of the city and civilization; Apollo, the god of light; Aphrodite, the goddess of love). Unfortunately, there had been little discussion in school of the relevance of these gods and goddesses to anything else Tina knew—for example, to the city of Athens or to the Apollo space flights. And given Tina's age, I was reluctant to introduce the word *aphrodisiac* simply to help her remember Aphrodite. As a result, Tina had no meaningful learning set for the twelve gods and goddesses—no expectation of connecting them with their domains in any meaningful way. Refusing my motherly offers to help, yet determined to do well on an upcoming quiz, Tina confined herself to her room and rehearsed those gods and goddesses over and over until she could recite all twelve. A month later, I asked her how many she could still recall. She remembered only Zeus.

Do we present information merely as "something to be learned" or instead as something that can help students better understand their world? Do we ask students to define new terminology by using the exact definitions presented in the textbook or instead require them to define terms in their own words? When asking students to give examples of a concept, do we expect examples already presented in the textbook or instead request that students generate new ones? How we present a learning task clearly affects the likelihood that students will adopt a meaningful learning set (Ausubel et al., 1978). Ideally, we must communicate our belief that students *can* and *should* make sense of the things they study. In the "Civil War" clip on Video CD 2, you can find many examples of how a teacher tries to make events preceding the American Civil War meaningful for fifth graders. Following are two examples:

If you think of the way people lived then and what we didn't have in terms of stores, what's something that everybody did for his family in this time? . . . What do you think they would all have *had* to do [to make a living]? (A student responds, "Farm.") Good for you. They would have to have farmed, wouldn't they because . . . they had to eat.

We've talked about slavery. Now I want you to pretend inside your head that *you* are a slave. . . . One of the problems that the slaves had was that they wanted to be free. So they did things . . . and they were angry at their masters very many times, because they were beaten and they were not cared for as they should have been. If you were a slave, what are some things that you might have done [to] get back at a master? (A student responds, "Put rocks in the machines.") They broke the equipment; I think that's a little bit of what Jesse was saying. Yes, they would break the tools. Makes sense, doesn't it?

◎ *The learner has previous knowledge to which the new information can be related.* Meaningful learning can occur only when long-term memory contains a relevant **knowledge base**, information to which a new idea can be connected. Students will better understand scientific principles if they have already seen those principles in action, either in their own lives or in the laboratory. They will more easily learn the events of an important battle if they have visited the battlefield. They will better understand how large some dinosaurs were if they have seen life-size dinosaur skeletons at a museum of natural history. The more information students have already stored in long-term memory, the easier it is for them to learn new information, because there are more things with which it can be associated.

Calvin and Hobbes   by Bill Watterson

◎   *The learner is aware that previously learned information is related to new information.* Even when they have relevant prior knowledge, students don't necessarily retrieve it when learning something new, and so they resort to rote learning unnecessarily. Oftentimes we can promote meaningful learning by reminding students of things they know that bear directly on a topic of classroom study—a teaching strategy known as **prior knowledge activation** (Machiels-Bongaerts, Schmidt, & Boshuizen, 1991; L. B. Resnick, 1989; Spires & Donley, 1998). For example, we can relate works of literature to students' own thoughts, feelings, and experiences. We can point out instances when foreign language vocabulary is similar to words in English. We can tie science to students' day-to-day observations and experiences. And we can relate mathematics to such commonplace activities as cooking, building a treehouse, or throwing a ball.

As teachers, we should not only encourage meaningful learning through classroom activities and assessments, but we should also look for evidence of it in students' comments, questions, and written work. The following exercise gives you a chance to do just that.

Interpreting Student Artifacts and Behaviors

Matter and Space

In a science activity in his third-grade class, 9-year-old Nicholas copied the scientific principle "No two pieces of matter can occupy the same space at the same time" onto a sheet of paper. He and a lab partner then filled a cup with water and dropped, one at a time, more than a dozen small metal cubes into the cup. In the artifact on the right, he recorded his observations with both words and a drawing. Nick has difficulties with written language that qualify him for special educational services, but you can probably decipher his meaning. As you look at the artifact, think about

- Whether Nick engaged in meaningful learning during the activity
- Why Nick might have written his description of what he observed ("We por so mene QUBS . . . ") by beginning at the bottom of the cup and writing *up*, rather than in the conventional top-down manner

[Handwritten student artifact:] no two pieces of matter cwh occupy the same space at the same time.

ourflod the BlOlTS
tok up all the room
Kup the QUBS mene so por We

Copying something from the chalkboard, by itself, involves nothing more than rote learning. But we see evidence of meaningful learning in Nick's description of what he observed. Omitting punctuation and using his own words (as well as several invented spellings), Nick said: "We poured so many cubes [that] the cup overflowed. The blocks took up all the room." His explanation reflects an understanding that the cubes and water could not occupy the same space at the same time.

We can only speculate about why, as Nick described and interpreted his observations, he wrote *up*, across the top of the glass, and then down the other side. One possible explanation is that, with his limited language skills, Nick had not yet mastered the conventional direction of written English; this hypothesis seems unlikely, however, as other samples of Nick's writing (not shown here) typically begin at the top of the page and work downward. Another possibility is

■ **prior knowledge activation** Process of reminding students of things they have already learned relative to a new topic.

that he was thinking about the direction of the water flow (up and out) as he wrote and either intentionally or unintentionally "followed" the water in his writing. His limited working memory capacity may have been a factor here: Perhaps he had insufficient "room" in working memory to think simultaneously about his observations, word spellings, and conventions of written English.

The two storage processes discussed next—organization and elaboration—also involve relating new information to prior knowledge; hence, both of these processes incorporate meaningful learning. Yet each one has an additional twist as well.

Organization   Have you ever had an instructor who came to class and spoke aimlessly for an hour, flitting from one idea to another in an unpredictable sequence? Have you ever read a textbook that did the same thing, so that you never knew how ideas related to one another? In general, how easily can you learn in a situation where information is disorganized?

The fact is, we learn and remember a body of new information more easily when we organize it in some way (e.g., Bjorklund et al., 1994; Mandler & Pearlstone, 1966; Tulving, 1962). Such **organization** invariably involves making connections among various pieces of new information; it often involves making connections with existing knowledge as well. Consider the following examples of how students might organize school learning tasks:

- Giorgio is trying to remember a list of eleven events leading up to the American Revolution: the Navigation Acts, the Sugar Act, the Stamp Act, the Tea Act, the Boston Massacre, the Boston Tea Party, the attack of the *Gaspee*, the Battle of Lexington, the Battle of Concord, the Battle of Bunker Hill, and the signing of the Declaration of Independence. He puts them into three groups: British legislation, acts of colonial defiance, and pre-war battles.
- Genevieve's ten spelling words end with a "long e" sound. She decides to group the words based on their endings (*v*, *ev*, or *ie*), like this:

body	key	movie
family	donkey	cookie
party	monkey	calorie
gravy		

Learners are more likely to organize information if the material fits an organizational structure with which they are already familiar—for example, if the material can be placed into discrete categories or into a hierarchical arrangement (Bousfield, 1953; Bransford & Franks, 1971; DuBois, Kiewra, & Fraley, 1988; Gauntt, 1991). (Notice how 6-year-old Brent, 12-year-old Colin, and 16-year-old Hilary organize words by categories in three of the four "Memory and Metacognition" clips on Video CD 1.) Learners are also more likely to organize new material if it is presented with its organizational structure laid out and if interrelationships among ideas are made clear (Bower, Clark, Lesgold, & Winzenz, 1969; deLeeuw & Chi, 2003). As an illustration, let's consider the results of a classic experiment (Bower et al., 1969). College students were given four study trials in which to learn 112 words falling into four categories (e.g., minerals, plants). For some students, the words were arranged in an organized fashion (Figure 6.8 is an example). For other students, the words were arranged randomly. Look at the average number of words that each group remembered after one study period (about four minutes) and again after three additional study periods:

■ Observe organization in long-term memory storage in the early childhood, early adolescence, and late adolescence "Memory and Metacogniton" clips on Video CD 1.

Number of Study Periods	Organized Words	Unorganized Words
1	73 (65%)	21 (19%)
4	112 (100%)	70 (63%)

Notice that, after studying the words one time, students with organized words remembered more than three times as many words as students who received them in mixed-up order. After four study periods, students with the organized words remembered the entire list of 112!

Unfortunately, many students tend to "organize" the things they study merely as a list of separate facts, rather than as a set of interrelated ideas (Kletzien, 1988; B. J. F. Meyer, Brandt, & Bluth, 1980). As teachers, how can we help our students organize class material more effectively? Obviously, we should organize new material in a logical way before we present it. We can then draw students' attention to this organizational structure. For example, we might point out

■ **organization** Cognitive process in which learners find connections (e.g., by forming categories, identifying hierarchies, determining cause-effect relationships) among the various pieces of information they need to learn.

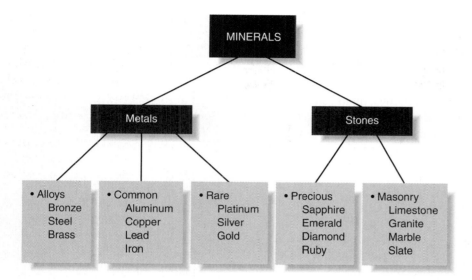

FIGURE 6.8 We can remember information more easily when it is organized in some way.

Figure from "Hierarchical Retrieval Schemes in Recall of Categorized Word Lists," by G. H. Bower, M. C. Clark, A. M. Lesgold, and D. Winzenz, 1969, *Journal of Verbal Learning and Verbal Behavior, 8*, pp. 323–345, copyright 1969, Elsevier Science (USA), reproduced by permission of the publisher.

the categories in which facts can be grouped, the hierarchical nature of concepts, or important interrelations (e.g., cause and effect) among various ideas. We can also present related pieces of information close together in time; students are more likely to associate related ideas when they encounter those ideas together (Glanzer & Nolan, 1986; Hayes-Roth & Thorndyke, 1979). And we can give students specific structures they can use to organize information themselves; the artifact in Figure 6.9 is an example.

■ Additional organizational strategies are *concept mapping* (Chapter 8) and *advance organizers* (Chapter 13).

Elaboration   People sometimes use their prior knowledge to expand on a new idea, thereby storing *more* information than was actually presented. This process of adding to newly acquired information in some way is called **elaboration**. Following are some examples:

- Maria learns that an allosaur had powerful jaws and sharp, pointed teeth. "Allosaurs must have been meat eaters," she deduces.
- When you read Nick's run-on sentence, "We por so mene QUBS the KUP ovrflod the Bloks tok up all the room," you were probably able to translate it into two meaningful sentences: "We poured so many cubes [that] the cup overflowed. The blocks took up all the room."
- When I took a course in Mandarin Chinese in high school, I learned that the Chinese word *wŏmen* means "we." "Aha," I thought to myself, "the sign on the restroom that *we* girls use says *women*."

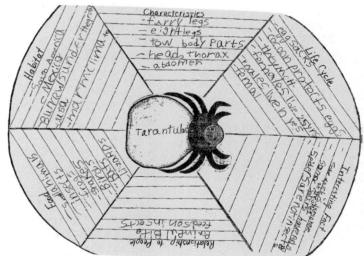

FIGURE 6.9 Using a form his second-grade teacher has provided, 7-year-old Tony organizes what he has learned about tarantulas.

In most cases, the more students elaborate on new material—the more they use what they already know to help them understand and interpret the material—the more effectively they will store and remember it (J. R. Anderson, 1995; Paxton, 1999). I remember very little of the Chinese I learned in high school (unfortunately, I relied mostly on rote memorization when I studied it), but the meaning of the word *wŏmen* remains indelibly stored in my long-term memory. Students who elaborate on the things they learn in school are usually better students than those who simply take information at face value (McDaniel & Einstein, 1989; Pressley, 1982; Waters, 1982).

As teachers, we will often want our students to go beyond the information actually presented to them. We can help them to elaborate in numerous ways. For example, we can ask frequent questions along these lines:

- Why do you think this happens?
- Can you think of some examples of this concept?
- How could we use this idea in our everyday lives?
- What things can you conclude from this information?

■ **elaboration** Cognitive process in which learners expand on new information based on what they already know.

The following assessment activity illustrates yet another strategy.

Interpreting Student Artifacts and Behaviors

Moving to Ohio

In a unit on westward migration in the United States during the 1800s, a third-grade teacher asks her students to imagine traveling west with their families by covered wagon and to write several journal entries describing their trip. Following is an excerpt from one of 8-year-old Shea's entries. (It will help you to know that Noah and Drew are Shea's younger brother and sister; Kevin is her father.) As you read the excerpt, consider these questions:

For a moment we all just looked at each other. I am scared. What will Ohio be like? My dad quietly took his and my mom's stuff and put it in the back of the wagon. Drew started to cry and my mom held her. It was 8 o'clock. With all of us dressed in our warmest things and holding our things. Noah, Drew, and

I climbed into the back of the wagon. 3 beds made from the quilts and pillows off our bed were on the wagon floor. Right a way Drew and Noah fell a sleep. I climbed to the back of the and looked at the firmilyar town. We soon would be leaving. Half an hour later we were out of North

Carolina. At 9. o'clock well be at the Appalachian Mountains," said my dad. "Thats where we'll stop for to night." "Oh, Kevin," said my mom. "Are you sure its safe? Maybe we should turn back." "No," my dad said firmly "were not turning back."

- What long-term memory storage processes does the assignment promote?
- What things does Shea write that suggest that she is, in fact, engaging in these processes?

By giving such an assignment, the teacher presumably wants students to relate the westward migration to their own experiences traveling to unknown places (i.e., to learn meaningfully) and, in the process, to draw inferences about the thoughts and feelings people may have had about the trip (i.e., to elaborate). In the excerpt we see evidence of both meaningful learning and elaboration. For instance, from her own experience, Shea knows that leaving familiar ("firmilyar") territory can be unsettling and assumes that the travelers are afraid ("I'm scared") and uncertain ("are you sure it's safe?") yet also determined ("were [we're] not turning back"). At the same time, some of Shea's knowledge about modern-day travel is not applicable to travel in the 1800s. For instance, she thinks that leaving North Carolina would take only half an hour (unlikely unless the family lived near the state line) and that the family can travel until 9:00 P.M. (which would mean traveling at dusk or after dark). When we encourage students to relate new material to what they already know, we must also monitor their thinking for any inappropriate connections.

Visual Imagery   Earlier in the chapter I mentioned imagery as one possible way in which information might be encoded in long-term memory. Numerous research studies indicate that **visual imagery**—forming mental pictures of objects or ideas—can be a particularly effective method of storing information (Dewhurst & Conway, 1994; Johnson-Glenberg, 2000; Sadoski, Goetz, & Fritz, 1993; Sadoski & Paivio, 2001). To show you how effective visual imagery can be, let me teach you a few of the Mandarin Chinese words I studied in high school.

Experiencing FIRSTHAND ·Five Chinese Words

Try learning these five Chinese words by forming the visual images I describe (don't worry about learning the marks over the words):

Chinese Word	English Meaning	Image
fáng	house	Picture a *house* with large teeth (*fangs*) growing out of its walls.
mén	door	Picture a restroom *door* with the word *MEN* painted on it.
ké	guest	Picture someone giving someone else (the *guest*) a *key* to the house.
fàn	food	Picture a plate of *food* being cooled by a *fan*.
shū	book	Picture a *shoe* with a *book* sticking out of it.

■ **visual imagery** Process of forming mental pictures of objects or ideas.

At this point, find something else to do for a couple of minutes. Stand up and stretch, get a glass of water, or use the bathroom. But be sure to come back to your reading in just a minute or two. . . .

Now that you're back, cover the list of Chinese words, English meanings, and visual images. Try to remember what each word means:

ké   fàn   mén   fáng   shū

. . . .

Did the Chinese words remind you of the visual images you stored? Did the images, in turn, help you remember the English meanings of the Chinese words?

You may have remembered all five words easily, or you may have remembered only one or two. People differ in their ability to use visual imagery: Some form images quickly and easily, whereas others form them only slowly and with difficulty (Behrmann, 2000; J. M. Clark & Paivio, 1991; Kosslyn, 1985). For those in the former category, imagery can be a powerful means of storing information in long-term memory.

As teachers, we can promote the use of visual imagery in several ways. We can ask students to imagine how certain events in literature or history might have looked (Sadoski & Paivio, 2001). (As an example, notice how students envision the character Hester Prynne in the "Scarlet Letter" clip on Video CD 2.) We can provide visual materials (pictures, charts, graphs, etc.) that illustrate important, but possibly abstract, ideas (R. K. Atkinson et al., 1999; R. Carlson, Chandler, & Sweller, 2003; Verdi, Kulhavy, Stock, Rittschof, & Johnson, 1996). And we can ask students to draw their *own* illustrations or diagrams of the things they are studying (Edens & Potter, 2001; Van Meter, 2001); Figure 6.10 presents an example.

■ Observe students' depictions of Hester Prynne in the "Scarlet Letter" clip on Video CD 2.

The last three storage processes—organization, elaboration, and visual imagery—are clearly *constructive* in nature: They all involve combining several pieces of information into a meaningful whole. When we organize information, we rearrange the specific items we need to learn so that they fit within a familiar framework (categories, a hierarchy, or the like). When we elaborate on new information, we use what we already know to help us make better sense of it. And when we use visual imagery, we construct mental pictures (perhaps a house with fangs, or a restroom door labeled *MEN*) based on how certain objects typically look. In Chapter 7 we will examine the constructive nature of long-term memory storage more closely.

Developmental Trends in Storage Processes for Declarative Information

Development psychologists have found that at least three of the storage processes we've just examined increase and improve with age. In Chapter 2 we briefly looked at developmental changes in rehearsal, organization, and elaboration. Table 6.3 expands on the nature of these changes.

The tendency to relate new information to things already known—meaningful learning—is probably a more universal phenomenon across all age levels. We see this idea reflected in Piaget's concept of *assimilation*: Even in infancy, children try to respond to objects and events using existing schemes (see Chapter 2). Nevertheless, children's expanding knowledge bases will, over the years, increasingly enable them to make sense of new information and ideas (e.g., Kintsch, 1998).

To my knowledge, researchers have not systematically investigated how visual imagery as a learning strategy changes with age. My own conversations with children and adolescents suggest that they infrequently use imagery as an intentional strategy. Some evidence indicates that youngsters who live in rural areas—where they must travel large distances to get from one place to another—can better remember images and spatial arrangements than urban and suburban children, perhaps because knowing how various landmarks in the countryside look helps them find their way around (Gauvain, 1999; Kearins, 1981). Visual imagery, then, may be something that children develop in part because their circumstances require it.

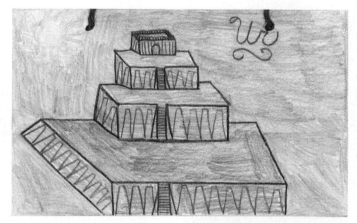

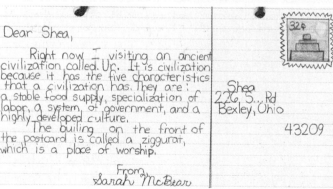

FIGURE 6.10 In a sixth-grade social studies unit, students create postcards that an imaginary friend might send them from ancient cultures. Here 11-year-old Shea depicts and describes ancient Ur.

TABLE 6.3

Typical Learning Strategies at Different Grade Levels

GRADE LEVEL	AGE-TYPICAL CHARACTERISTICS	SUGGESTED STRATEGIES
K–2	• Organization of physical objects as a way to remember them • Appearance of rehearsal to remember verbal material; used infrequently and relatively ineffectively • In general, few intentional efforts to learn and remember verbal material; learning and memory are a by-product of other things children do (creating things, talking about events, listening to stories, etc.)	• Get students actively involved in topics, perhaps through hands-on activities, engaging reading materials, or fantasy play. • Relate new topics to students' prior experiences. • Model rehearsal as a strategy for remembering things over the short run.
3–5	• Spontaneous, intentional, and increasingly effective use of rehearsal to remember things for a short time period • Increasing use of organization as an intentional learning strategy for verbal information	• Emphasize the importance of making sense of, rather than memorizing, information. • Encourage students to organize what they are learning; suggest possible organizational structures for topics.
6–8	• Predominance of rehearsal as a learning strategy • Greater abstractness and flexibility in categories used to organize information • Appearance of elaboration as an intentional learning strategy	• Suggest questions that students might ask themselves as they study; emphasize questions that promote elaboration (e.g., "Why would _____ do that?" "How is _____ different from _____?"). • Assess true understanding rather than rote memorization in assignments and quizzes.
9–12	• Continuing reliance on rehearsal as an intentional learning strategy, especially by low-achieving adolescents • Increasing use of organization and elaboration to learn, especially by high-achieving adolescents	• Ask thought-provoking questions that engage students' interest and help students see the relevance of topics for their own lives. • Have students work in mixed-ability cooperative groups, in which high-achieving students can model effective learning strategies for low-achieving students.

Sources: Bjorklund & Coyle, 1995; Bjorklund & Jacobs, 1985; Bjorklund et al., 1994; DeLoache & Todd, 1988; Flavell et al., 1993; Gathercole & Hitch, 1993; Kunzinger, 1985; Lucariello, Kyratzis, & Nelson, 1992; L. S. Newman, 1990; Plumert, 1994; Pressley, 1982; W. Schneider & Pressley, 1989.

How Procedural Knowledge Is Learned

Some of the procedures people learn—for example, baking a cake, serving a volleyball, driving a car with a stick shift—consist primarily of overt behaviors. Many others—for instance, writing a persuasive essay, surfing the Internet, solving for *x* in an algebraic equation—are more mental than physical in nature. Most procedures obviously involve a combination of physical behaviors and mental activities.

Procedural knowledge ranges from relatively simple actions (e.g., using scissors or holding a pencil correctly) to far more complex ones. Complex procedures are usually not learned in one fell swoop. In part because they consist of many smaller skills, they are acquired slowly over time, often only with a great deal of practice (J. R. Anderson, 1983; Ericsson & Chalmers, 1994; Proctor & Dutta, 1995; D. B. Willingham, 1998).

Helping Students Acquire New Procedures

 Help students understand the logic behind the procedures they are learning.

As a teacher demonstrates the correct way to swing a tennis racket, she asks her students, "Why is it important to have your feet apart rather than together? Why is it important to hold your arm straight as you swing?"

 When skills are especially complex, break them into simpler tasks that students can practice one at a time.

Knowing how overwhelming the task of driving a car can initially be, a driver education teacher begins behind-the-wheel instruction by having students practice steering and braking in an empty school parking lot. Only later, after students have mastered these skills, does he have them drive in traffic on city streets.

 Provide mnemonics that can help students remember a sequence of steps.

In a unit on basketball, a teacher coaches her students on an effective approach to making a free throw. "Just remember BEEF," she says. "*B*alance the ball, put your *e*lbows in, *e*levate your arms, and *f*ollow through."

 Give students many opportunities to practice new skills, and provide the feedback they need to help them improve.

A science teacher asks his students to write lab reports after each week's lab activity. Many of his students have had little or no previous experience in scientific writing, so when he grades the reports, he writes numerous comments as well. Some comments describe the strengths that he sees, and others provide suggestions for making the reports more objective, precise, or clear.

Researchers are just beginning to identify the cognitive processes involved in storing procedural knowledge. To some extent, of course, learners store procedures as actual behaviors. Yet many procedures, especially complex ones, may begin largely as explicit, declarative knowledge—in other words, as *information* about how to execute a procedure rather than as the actual *ability* to execute it (J. R. Anderson, 1983, 1987). When learners use declarative knowledge to guide them as they carry out a new procedure, their performance is slow and laborious, the activity consumes a great deal of mental effort, and they often talk themselves through their actions. As they continue to perform the activity, however, their declarative knowledge gradually evolves into procedural knowledge. This knowledge becomes fine-tuned over time and eventually allows learners to perform an activity quickly, efficiently, and effortlessly—that is, with *automaticity* (J. R. Anderson, 1983, 1987). (We'll look at automaticity more closely later in the chapter.)

Theorists have suggested several teaching strategies that seem to help students learn and remember procedures more effectively. For instance, we can demonstrate a procedure or show pictures of its specific steps (R. M. Gagné, 1985). We can verbalize our thoughts, thereby demonstrating *mental* procedures, as we engage in a complex task (Schunk, 1981). We can encourage students to use verbal rehearsal as they learn a new skill—in other words, to repeat the required steps over and over to themselves (Weiss & Klint, 1987). And as you might guess, students will be more likely to remember a procedure when we give them a chance to carry it out themselves and when we provide regular feedback about how they are doing (R. L. Cohen, 1989; Heindel & Kose, 1990; Kladopoulos & McComas, 2001; Proctor & Dutta, 1995). When procedures are fairly complicated, we may want to break them down into smaller tasks and have students practice each one separately at first (J. R. Anderson, Reder, & Simon, 1996). The Into the Classroom feature "Helping Students Acquire New Procedures" illustrates these and other strategies. Chapter 8 describes additional ones within the context of such complex cognitive processes as metacognition and problem solving.

■ Which of these strategies remind you of Vygotsky's theory of cognitive development (described in Chapter 2)?

Prior Knowledge and Working Memory in Long-Term Memory Storage

Occasionally students' prior knowledge interferes with something they need to learn; as examples, recall Darren's confusion about the marble Parthenon, Kanesha's difficulty remembering where the sternum is located, and Shea's assumption that people moving by covered wagon would travel after dark. In general, however, a relevant knowledge base helps students encode and store classroom subject matter more effectively (P. A. Alexander, Kulikowich, & Schulze, 1994; Hamman et al., 1995; Schneider, 1993). Students' prior knowledge contributes to their learning in several ways:

- It helps them determine what is most important to learn; thus, it helps them direct their *attention* appropriately.

- It enables them to understand something—that is, to engage in *meaningful learning*—instead of learning it by rote.
- It provides a framework for *organizing* new information.
- It helps them *elaborate* on information—for example, by filling in missing details, clarifying ambiguities, or drawing inferences. (Ausubel et al., 1978; Bjorklund, Muir-Broaddus, & Schneider, 1990; Carpenter & Just, 1986; Lindberg, 1991; Rumelhart & Ortony, 1977; West, Farmer, & Wolff, 1991; P. T. Wilson & Anderson, 1986)

■ Do you now see why Kanesha had such difficulty remembering the coccyx, ulna, sacrum, clavicle, and patella?

Yet as we noted in our discussion of meaningful learning, it is not enough that students have the knowledge they need to interpret new material; they must also be *aware* that the knowledge is relevant. They must then retrieve it from their long-term memories while thinking about the new material, such that they have both the "old" and the "new" in working memory simultaneously and can make the appropriate connections (Bellezza, 1986; Glanzer & Nolan, 1986).

As teachers, we should keep students' existing knowledge in mind and use it as a starting point whenever we introduce a new topic. For example, we might begin a first-grade unit on plants by asking students to describe what their parents do to keep flowers or vegetable gardens growing. Or, in a secondary English literature class, we might introduce Sir Walter Scott's *Ivanhoe* (in which Robin Hood is a major character) by asking students to tell the tale of Robin Hood as they know it. We should also remember that students from diverse cultural backgrounds may have somewhat different knowledge bases and modify our starting points accordingly.

Using Mnemonics in the Absence of Relevant Prior Knowledge

When you were in elementary and secondary school, there were probably many times when you had difficulty making sense of classroom subject matter. Perhaps you had trouble learning the symbols for some of the chemical elements because those symbols seemed unrelated to the elements' names (e.g., why is *Au* the symbol for gold?). Perhaps you couldn't remember words in a foreign language because those words were very different from their English equivalents. Or perhaps you couldn't remember lists of things (e.g., four things you should do when treating a victim of shock, eleven events leading up to the American Revolution) because they always contained several seemingly unrelated items and one item didn't help you remember any of the others.

■ Hear David describe his mnemonic for the Hebrew letter *pay* in the "Memory and Metacognition: Middle Childhood" clip on Video CD 1.

When students are apt to have trouble finding relationships between new material and their prior knowledge, or when a body of information has an organizational structure with no apparent logic behind it (e.g., as is true for many lists), special memory tricks known as **mnemonics** can help them learn classroom material more effectively. For example, in the "Memory and Metacognition: Middle Childhood" clip on Video CD 1, 10-year-old David describes a mnemonic he uses to remember the Hebrew letter *pay* (פ):

Pay, it kind of goes like this, then this, then this, then this, then this, and then there's a little person right there. Well, not a little person, but a dot right there. . . . We pretend that in front of the dot is a counter and then the dot is a head, and then the head is "paying." So that's how we remember *pay*.

Three commonly used mnemonics are verbal mediation, the keyword method, and superimposed meaningful structures.

Verbal Mediation   A **verbal mediator** is a word or phrase that creates a logical connection, or "bridge," between two pieces of information. Verbal mediators can be used for such paired pieces of information as foreign language words and their English meanings, countries and their capitals, chemical elements and their symbols, and words and their spellings. Following are examples:

■ **mnemonic** Memory aid or trick designed to help students learn and remember a specific piece of information.

■ **verbal mediator** Word or phrase that forms a logical connection or "bridge" between two pieces of information.

Information to Be Learned	Verbal Mediator
Handschuh is German for "glove."	A glove is a *shoe* for the *hand*.
Quito is the capital of Ecuador.	Mosqui*to*s at the equator.
Au is the symbol for gold.	'*Ay, you* stole my gold watch!
The word *principal* ends in *pal* (not *ple*).	The principal is my *pal*.
The second amendment to the U.S. Constitution is the right to bear arms.	A *bear* has *two arms*.

In our earlier case study, Kanesha uses a verbal mediator to help her remember one of the bones: She thinks of the humerus as being just above the funny (*humorous*) bone.

Keyword Method   Like verbal mediation, the **keyword method** aids memory by making a connection between two things. This technique is especially helpful when there is no logical verbal mediator to fill the gap—for example, when there is no obvious sentence or phrase to relate a foreign language word to its English meaning. The keyword method involves two steps, which I will illustrate using the Spanish word *amor* and its English meaning *love*:

1. Identify a concrete object to represent each piece of information. The object may be either a commonly used symbol (e.g., a heart to symbolize *love*) or a soundalike word (e.g., a suit of armor to represent *amor*). Such objects are *keywords*.
2. Form a mental picture of the two objects together. To remember that *amor* means *love*, you might picture a knight in a suit of armor with a huge red heart painted on his chest.

You used the keyword method when you did the "Five Chinese Words" exercise earlier. Following are additional examples:

Information to Be Learned	Visual Image
Das Pferd is German for "horse."	Picture a *horse* driving a *Ford*.
Augusta is the capital of the state of Maine.	Picture *a gust of* wind blowing through a horse's *mane*.
Tchaikovsky composed "Swan Lake."	Picture a *swan* swimming on a *lake* wearing a *tie* and *cough*ing.

Superimposed Meaningful Structure   A larger body of information (e.g., a list of items) can often be learned by superimposing a meaningful organization—a familiar shape, word, sentence, rhythm, poem, or story—on it. Following are examples of such **superimposed meaningful structures:**

Information to Be Learned	Superimposed Meaningful Structure
The shape of Italy	A "boot"
The shape of France	A "bearskin rug"
The Great Lakes (Huron, Ontario, Michigan, Erie, Superior)	HOMES
Lines on the treble clef (EGBDF)	Elvis's guitar broke down Friday, *or* every good boy does fine.
The distinction between stalagmites and stalactites	When the "mites" go up, the "tites" come down.
The number of days in each month	Thirty days has September . . .

In the second scenario in the "Group Work" clip on Video CD 2, you can watch a junior high school science teacher using a small-group activity to teach students how to develop a superimposed meaningful structure—in particular, a story—to help them remember the life cycle of a sheep liver fluke.

Superimposed meaningful structures can be used to remember procedures as well as declarative information. Following are three examples that my students have shared with me:

■ Observe a teacher helping students develop superimposed meaningful structures in the "Group Work" clip on Video CD 2.

Procedure to Be Learned	Superimposed Meaningful Structure
Turning a screw (clockwise to tighten it, counterclockwise to loosen it)	Righty, tighty. Lefty, loosey.
Throwing a free throw in basketball	BEEF: *b*alance the ball, *e*lbows in, *e*levate the arms, *f*ollow through.
Multiplying a mathematical expression of the form $(ax + b)(cx + d)$	FOIL: multiply the *f*irst terms within each set of parentheses, then the two *o*uter terms, then the two *i*nner terms, and finally the *l*ast terms.

■ **keyword method** Mnemonic technique in which an association is made between two ideas by forming a visual image of one or more concrete objects (*keywords*) that either sound similar to, or symbolically represent, those ideas.

■ **superimposed meaningful structure** Familiar shape, word, sentence, poem, or story imposed on information in order to facilitate recall

Research consistently supports the effectiveness of mnemonics in student learning (e.g., Bower & Clark, 1969; Bulgren, Schumaker, & Deshler, 1994; M. S. Jones, Levin, Levin, & Beitzel, 2000; Pressley, Levin, & Delaney, 1982; Rummel, Levin, & Woodward, 2003; Scruggs & Mastropieri, 1989). In addition to helping students store information and procedures in long-term memory, mnemonics also appear to help students retrieve what they stored at an earlier time. We turn to the topic of retrieval now.

LONG-TERM MEMORY RETRIEVAL

As you learned earlier in the chapter, some information is easily retrieved from long-term memory. But it may take you considerable time to "find" some of the other information you have stored there. Try the following exercise as an example.

Experiencing FIRSTHAND ·More Retrieval Practice

The answer to each of the following questions has appeared earlier in this chapter. See how many answers you can retrieve from your long-term memory and how quickly you can retrieve each one.

1. What are the five Great Lakes?
2. What is the German word for "book"?
3. In what year did World War II end?
4. Who wrote *Catcher in the Rye*?
5. How do you spell the French term for "appetizer"?

· · · · · · ·

Did you find yourself unable to remember one or more of the answers even though you know you "processed" the information at the time you read it? If so, then you have just discovered first-hand that, in some cases, information is retrieved from long-term memory only with great difficulty, or perhaps not at all.

The Nature of Long-Term Memory Retrieval

■ Can you still remember what the Mandarin Chinese words *ké*, *fà*, *mén*, *fáng*, and *shū* mean? How helpful were the visual images you stored in the "Five Chinese Words" exercise?

Retrieving information from long-term memory appears to be a process of following a "pathway" of associations. One idea reminds us of another idea, which reminds us of still another, and so on, just as we saw in the "Horse #1" exercise earlier in the chapter. Retrieval is successful only when we eventually stumble on the information we are looking for. We are most likely to do so if we have connected the desired information to something else—presumably something logically related to it—in long-term memory.

To illustrate this idea, I return once again to all those letters, bills, advertisements, and so on that arrive in your mailbox throughout each year. Imagine that, on average, you receive five important items—things you really need to save—every day. At six postal deliveries a week and 52 weeks a year (minus a dozen or so holidays), you have been saving about 1,500 pieces of mail every year. If you have been saving your mail for the last 15 years, then you have more than 22,000 really important things stashed somewhere in your home.

One day you hear that stock in a clothing company (Mod Bod Jeans, Inc.) has tripled in value. You remember that your wealthy Aunt Agnes sent you some Mod Bod stock certificates for your birthday several years ago, and you presumably decided they were important enough to save. But where in the world did you put them? How long will it take you to find them among all those important letters, bills, brochures, catalogs, fliers, and sweepstakes announcements?

How easily you find the certificates and, in fact, whether you find them at all depend on how you have been storing your mail as you've accumulated it. If you've stored it in a logical, organized fashion—for example, by putting all paid bills on a closet shelf, all mail-order catalogs on the floor under your bedside table, and all items from relatives in a file cabinet (in alphabetical order by last name)—then you should quickly retrieve Aunt Agnes's gift. But if you simply tossed each day's mail randomly around the house, you will be searching your home for a long, long time, possibly without ever finding a trace of that Mod Bod stock.

Like a home with fifteen years' worth of mail, long-term memory contains a great deal of information. And like finding the Mod Bod certificates, the ease with which information is retrieved from long-term memory depends somewhat on whether that information is stored in a logical "place"—that is, whether it is connected with related pieces of information. By making those important connections with existing knowledge, we will know where to "find" the information when we need it later on. In contrast, learning something by rote is like throwing Aunt Agnes's gift randomly among thousands of pieces of unorganized mail: We may never retrieve it again.

Factors Affecting Retrieval

Even when we connect new information to our existing knowledge base, we can't always find it when we need it. At least four factors promote our ability to retrieve information from long-term memory: making multiple connections with existing knowledge, learning information to mastery and beyond, using knowledge frequently, and having a relevant retrieval cue.

If this student has been studying classroom subject matter by relating it to what he already knows about the world, then he should be able to retrieve it easily as he works on this writing assignment.

Making Multiple Connections with Existing Knowledge   If retrieving information from long-term memory is a process of following a pathway of associations, what happens if we take the wrong "route" and go in an inappropriate "direction"? In such a situation we may never find what we are looking for.

We are more likely to retrieve information when we have many possible pathways to it—in other words, when we have associated the information with many other things in our existing knowledge base. Making multiple connections is like using cross-references in your mail storage system. You may have filed the Mod Bod stock in the "items from relatives" file drawer, but you've also written the stock's location on notes left in many other places—perhaps with your birth certificate (after all, you received the stock on your birthday), with your income tax receipts, or in your safe-deposit box. By looking in any one of these logical places, you will discover where to find your valuable stock.

As teachers, we can help students more effectively remember classroom subject matter over the long run if we help them connect it to numerous pieces of information in their existing knowledge base. For example, we can show them how new material relates to

- Concepts and ideas within the same subject area (e.g., showing them how multiplication is related to addition)
- Concepts and ideas in other subject areas (e.g., talking about how scientific discoveries have affected historical events)
- Students' general knowledge of the world (e.g., drawing parallels between the "Black Death" of the fourteenth century and the modern-day AIDS epidemic)
- Students' personal experiences (e.g., finding similarities between the family feud in *Romeo and Juliet* and students' own interpersonal conflicts)
- Students' current activities and needs outside of the classroom (e.g., showing how persuasive writing skills might be used to craft a powerful essay for a college application)

The more interrelationships students form among pieces of information in long-term memory, the more easily they can retrieve those pieces later on.

Learning Things to Mastery and Beyond   Is it enough for students to demonstrate mastery of information or skills—for example, to write all their spelling words correctly—on just one occasion? Probably not. Research tells us that people are far more likely to retrieve what they have learned if they continue to study and practice it, ideally in a variety of contexts (Graham, Harris, & Fink, 2000; Semb & Ellis, 1994; L. A. Shepard, 2000; Underwood, 1954).

When students continue to practice things they have already mastered, they eventually achieve **automaticity**: They can retrieve what they've learned quickly and effortlessly and can use it almost without thinking (J. R. Anderson, 1983; P. W. Cheng, 1985; Proctor & Dutta, 1995). As an example, think of driving a car, a complicated skill that you can probably perform easily. Your first attempts at driving many years ago may have required a great deal of mental effort. But now you can drive without having to pay much attention to what you are doing—you execute the skill automatically.

Remember, working memory has a limited capacity: It can do only so much at one time. When much of its capacity must be used for retrieving single facts or executing simple procedures, little room is left for understanding more complex situations or dealing with more difficult tasks. One key reason for learning some facts and procedures to automaticity, then, is to free up enough working memory capacity for students to tackle the complex tasks that require those facts and procedures (D. Jones & Christensen, 1999; Proctor & Dutta, 1995; L. B. Resnick, 1989; Stanovich, 2000). For example, second graders reading a story can better focus

■ If you have already read Chapter 5, then you may recall that automaticity plays a role in Robert Sternberg's theory of intelligence.

■ **automaticity** Ability to respond quickly and efficiently while mentally processing or physically performing a task.

their efforts on understanding it if they don't have to sound out common words like *before* and *after*. Fourth graders faced with the multiplication problem

$$\begin{array}{r} 87 \\ \times\ 59 \\ \hline \end{array}$$

can solve it more easily if they can quickly retrieve such basic facts as $9 \times 8 = 72$ and $5 \times 7 = 35$. High school chemistry students can more easily interpret Na_2CO_3 (sodium carbonate) if they don't have to stop to think about what the symbols Na, C, and O represent.

Unfortunately, automaticity is achieved in only one way: practice, practice, and more practice. This is not to say, however, that we must continually assign drill-and-practice exercises involving isolated facts and procedures (e.g., see Figure 6.11). Such activities promote rote rather than meaningful learning, are often boring, and are unlikely to convince students of the value of the subject matter (Mac Iver, Reuman, & Main, 1995). A more effective approach is to routinely incorporate basic knowledge and skills into a variety of meaningful and enjoyable activities, such as problem-solving tasks, group projects, games, brainteasers, and so on.

It is important to note, too, that although automaticity of basic knowledge and skills is essential for effective problem solving, it can become a nuisance if assigned tasks require students to solve problems in creative, *non*automatic ways. We'll explore this idea further in our discussion of *mental set* in Chapter 8.

Using Knowledge Frequently   Frequently used knowledge is retrieved more easily than knowledge that is used rarely or not at all (R. Brown & McNeill, 1966; Yarmey, 1973). It is easier to remember your own birthday than the birthday of a friend or relative. It is easier to remember the current year than the year in which World War II ended. And it is definitely easier to remember the spelling of *information* than the spelling of *hors d'oeuvre*, even though both terms have the same number of letters.

As teachers, we should occasionally have classroom activities that require students to review what they have learned earlier in the year or in previous years. For example, we might have refresher discussions of "old" material, or we might ask students to use the material to understand new topics or solve new problems. Research is clear on this point: Occasional review enhances students' memory for information over the long run, especially when review sessions are spaced out over several months or years (Bahrick, Bahrick, Bahrick, & Bahrick, 1993; Dempster, 1991; Di Vesta & Smith, 1979; McDaniel & Masson, 1985).

Having a Relevant Retrieval Cue   If you were educated in North America, then you probably learned the names of the five Great Lakes at one time or another. Yet you may have trouble retrieving all five names, even though they are all still stored in your long-term memory. Perhaps Lake Michigan doesn't come to mind when you retrieve the other four. The *HOMES* mnemonic presented earlier provides a **retrieval cue**, or hint about where to "look" in long-term memory. The mnemonic tells you that one lake begins with the letter *M*, and so you search among the *M* words in your long-term memory until (we hope) you find "Michigan." Learners are more likely to retrieve information when relevant retrieval cues are present to start their search of long-term memory in the right direction (e.g., Morris, Bransford, & Franks, 1977; Tulving & Thomson, 1973).

For another example of how retrieval cues can aid retrieval, try the following exercise.

Experiencing FIRSTHAND ·Recall Versus Recognition

Earlier in the chapter I described a process that can keep information in working memory indefinitely. Can you retrieve the name of that process from your long-term memory? See if you can before you read any further.

If you can't remember the term, then try answering the same question posed in a multiple-choice format:

What do we call the process that keeps information in working memory for as long as you need it?

    a. Facilitative construction

    b. Internal organization

    c. Short-term memorization

    d. Maintenance rehearsal

· · · · · · ·

FIGURE 6.11 Although occasional rote practice of numerals and letters can be helpful in promoting automaticity, too much conveys the message that learning basic skills is boring and tedious. Here 5-year-old Gunnar practices writing numerals in his kindergarten class. Notice, however, that he gets practice in writing 9 *backward*!

■ **retrieval cue** Hint about where to "look" for a piece of information in long-term memory.

Did you experience an "Aha, now I remember" feeling? The correct answer is *d*. Perhaps the multiple-choice format provided a retrieval cue for you, directing you to the correct answer you had stored in long-term memory. Generally, it is easier to remember something in a **recognition task** (in which you simply need to recognize correct information among irrelevant information or incorrect statements) than in a **recall task** (in which the correct information must be retrieved in its entirety from long-term memory) (Semb, Ellis, & Araujo, 1993).

Ultimately, students must learn to develop their own retrieval cues. This student has written notes to himself on his hands.

As teachers, we won't always want to help students retrieve information by putting that information right in front of them. Nevertheless, there will be occasions when providing hints is certainly appropriate. For example, if a student asks what the symbol *Au* stands for, we might respond by saying, "In class we talked about how *Au* comes from the Latin word *aurum*. Can you remember what aurum means?" Another example comes from one of my former teacher interns, Jess Jensen. A student in her eighth-grade history class had been writing about the Battle of New Orleans, which was a decisive victory for the United States in the War of 1812. The following exchange took place:

Student: Why was the Battle of New Orleans important?
Jess: Look at the map. Where is New Orleans?

(The student locates New Orleans.)

Jess: Why is it important?
Student: Oh! It's near the mouth of the Mississippi. It was important for controlling transportation up and down the river.

In the early grades, teachers typically provide many retrieval cues for their students: They remind students about the tasks they need to do and when they need to do them ("I hear the fire alarm. Remember, we all walk quietly during a fire drill"; or "It's time to go home. Do you all have the field trip permission slip to take to your parents?"). But as students grow older, they must develop greater independence, relying more on themselves and less on their teachers for the things they need to remember. At all grade levels, we can teach students ways of providing retrieval cues for *themselves*. For example, if we expect first graders to get permission slips signed, we might ask them to write a reminder on a piece of masking tape that they put on their jackets or lunch boxes. If we give junior high school students a major assignment due in several weeks, we might suggest that they tape a note with the due date to the bedside table or mark the date on the kitchen calendar.

Now that you know something about retrieval and the factors that affect it, try the following activity.

■ **recognition task** Memory task in which one must identify correct information among irrelevant information or incorrect statements.

■ **recall task** Memory task in which one must retrieve information in its entirety from long-term memory.

Analyzing Teacher Strategies

Moving to Canada
Another of my former teacher interns, Gerry Holly, was teaching a unit on Canada to his eighth-grade geography students. The class had already reviewed information about the topography (mountain ranges, rivers, etc.) and climate of various regions in the country. They had also studied social, political, and cultural issues (e.g., the separatist movement and use of French in Quebec). As you read the classroom dialogue at the bottom of this activity, consider

- How Gerry hoped his students would respond when he asked his question
- What the students' responses revealed about their ability to retrieve and use what they had learned
- What Gerry might do differently next time

Gerry: Imagine that you're moving to Canada. Where would you go, and why? How would your life be different?
Student: I'd go to Cambridge, Ontario, because I have relatives there.
Student: Toronto, to see the Raptors [a basketball team] play!
Student: I'd move to northern Quebec so I could swim in Hudson Bay.

Gerry was trying to help his students relate what they had learned about the physical and social environment of Canada to their own lives and needs. For instance, he hoped that they might retrieve what they had learned about the scenery, typical weather, or social milieu of various parts of Canada in making their decision. Unfortunately, the first two students retrieved none of that information in making their choices, and the third retrieved one piece of information (Hudson Bay) without retrieving another, equally important piece (Hudson Bay is *much* too cold for swimming). An excellent intern, Gerry learned very quickly that he would occasionally need to provide retrieval cues to get his students to use what they had learned. To do so, he might ask, "*Given what you now know about Canada's topography, climate, and social conditions*, where would you go, and why?"

Even so, a retrieval cue would not necessarily have enabled all of Gerry's students to recall what they learned about Canada. And perhaps when you did the "Recall Versus Recognition" exercise a few minutes ago, you couldn't remember *maintenance rehearsal* even when it was staring you in the face. Let's now look at some reasons why learners forget.

Why Learners Sometimes Forget

Fortunately, we don't need to remember everything. For example, we probably have no reason to remember the phone number of a florist we called yesterday, the plot of last week's episode of *Friends*, or the due date of an assignment we turned in last semester. Much of the information we encounter is—like our junk mail—not worth keeping, and forgetting enables us to get rid of the needless clutter (D. L. Schacter, 1999).

But as we have just seen, we sometimes have trouble recalling what we *do* need. Psychologists have numerous explanations for why people seem to forget. Here we consider five of them: failure to retrieve, reconstruction error, interference, decay, and failure to store.

Failure to Retrieve   A man at the supermarket looks familiar, but you can't remember who he is or when you met him. He smiles at you and says, "Hi there, nice to see you again." Gulp. You desperately search your long-term memory for his name, but you have clearly forgotten who he is.

A few days later, you have a bowl of chili for dinner. The chili reminds you of the "Chili for Charity" supper at which you worked a few months back. Of course! You and the man at the supermarket had stood side by side serving chili to hundreds of people that night. Oh yes, you now recall, his name is Melville Herman.

One reason we forget is an **inability to retrieve**: We can't locate information stored in long-term memory (e.g., D. L. Schacter, 1999). Sometimes we stumble on the information later, while "looking" for something else. But sometimes we never do retrieve the information, perhaps because we learned it by rote or for some other reason don't have sufficient retrieval cues to guide our search in long-term memory.

Reconstruction Error   Retrieval isn't necessarily an all-or-nothing phenomenon. Sometimes we retrieve part of the information we are seeking from long-term memory but cannot recall the rest. In such situations we may fill in the gaps using our general knowledge and assumptions about the world (Kolodner, 1985; Roediger & McDermott, 2000; P. T. Wilson & Anderson, 1986). Even though the gaps are filled in "logically," they aren't always filled in correctly—a form of forgetting called **reconstruction error**. Chapter 7 looks at the reconstructive nature of retrieval in greater detail.

Interference

Experiencing FIRSTHAND ·Six Chinese Words

Here are six more Mandarin Chinese words and their English meanings (for simplicity, I've omitted the "tone" marks on the words). Read them two or three times, and try to store them in your long-term memory. But don't do anything special to learn the words; for example, don't intentionally develop mnemonics to help you remember them.

Chinese	English
jung	middle
ting	listen
sung	deliver
peng	friend
ching	please
deng	wait

■ **inability to retrieve** Failure to locate information that currently exists in long-term memory.

■ **reconstruction error** Construction of a logical but incorrect "memory" by using information retrieved from long-term memory plus one's general knowledge and beliefs about the world.

Maximizing Retrieval and Minimizing Forgetting

 Where important information is concerned, never assume that once is enough.

A language arts teacher introduces the parts of speech (e.g., nouns, verbs, adjectives) early in the school year. Because these concepts will be important for students to know when they study a foreign language in later grades, he continues to review them throughout the year—for example, by frequently incorporating them into classroom activities.

 When information must be retrieved rapidly, assign practice exercises that enable students to learn it to automaticity.

An elementary school teacher gives frequent practice in the addition and subtraction facts until each student can add and subtract single digits quickly and accurately. She does several things to make such practice motivating and enjoyable. Sometimes she poses problems related to children or objects in the classroom (e.g., "There are 3 erasers on this chalkboard and 4 more on that one. How many erasers do we have altogether?") Sometimes she has pairs of students quiz each other on their facts. Once every two weeks, she has students time their performance on "Math Facts Sheets" and chart their continuing improvement on graph paper.

 Teach students to develop their own retrieval cues for things they need to remember.

A middle school teacher shows students how to create and use "Daily Organizer" folders that help them keep track of assignments and due dates.

 When important details are difficult to fill in logically, make sure students learn them well.

A teacher gives students extra practice in troublesome spelling words, such as those that are spelled differently than they are pronounced (e.g., *people*, *February*).

 Provide retrieval cues when appropriate.

When a high school student puzzles over how to compute the area of a circle, her math teacher says, "We studied this last week. Do you remember the formula?" The student shakes her head, and so the teacher continues, "Because the problem involves a circle, the formula probably includes *pi*, doesn't it?"

Now cover up the list of words and test yourself. What was the word for *friend*? *please*? *listen*? *wait*?

· · · · · · ·

Did you find yourself getting confused, perhaps forgetting which English meaning went with each Chinese word? If you did, then you were the victim of **interference**. The various pieces of information you stored in memory were interfering with one another; in a sense, the pieces were getting "mixed up." Notice that I told you *not* to use mnemonics to learn the Chinese words. Interference is especially likely to occur when pieces of information are similar to one another and when they are learned in a rote rather than meaningful fashion (e.g., Dempster, 1985; Lustig & Hasher, 2001; Postman & Underwood, 1973).

Decay   As noted earlier, some psychologists believe that information remains in long-term memory forever. But others propose that information may weaken over time and perhaps disappear altogether, especially if it is not used frequently (Altmann & Gray, 2002; J. R. Anderson, 1995; D. L. Schacter, 1999). Theorists often use the word **decay** when describing this gradual fading process.

Failure to Store   Last on my list of reasons for forgetting is **failure to store**: Information never reached long-term memory to begin with. Perhaps a person receiving a piece of information didn't pay attention to it, so it never went beyond the sensory register. Or perhaps the learner, after attending to it, didn't continue to process it, so it went no further in the memory system than working memory. Obviously, failure to store is not an explanation of information loss; however, it is one possible reason why students who *think* they have learned something cannot recall it later on (D. L. Schacter, 1999). Failure to store is less likely to occur when students engage in *comprehension monitoring*, a process we'll consider in Chapter 8.

All five explanations for forgetting underscore the importance of instructional strategies we've identified earlier: We must make sure students are paying attention, help them relate new material to things they already know, and give them opportunities to review, practice, and apply the material frequently. The Into the Classroom feature "Maximizing Retrieval and Minimizing Forgetting" presents examples of what we might do.

Yet even when we encourage effective storage processes, and even when we provide helpful retrieval cues, long-term memory storage and retrieval processes don't necessarily happen in a split second. For example, it may take time for students to relate new material to their existing knowledge and, at some later date, to retrieve all the "pieces" of what they have learned. What happens when teachers give students more time to process and retrieve information? The results can be quite dramatic, as we shall see now.

■ Recall the earlier case involving Kanesha. The similarity between *tibia* and *fibula* is one reason she confuses the names of the two bones.

■ **interference** Phenomenon whereby something stored in long-term memory inhibits one's ability to remember something else correctly.

■ **decay** Weakening over time of information stored in long-term memory, especially if the information is used infrequently.

■ **failure to store** Failure to mentally process information in ways that promote its storage in long-term memory.

GIVING STUDENTS TIME TO PROCESS: EFFECTS OF INCREASING WAIT TIME

Consider the following situation.

Mr. Smith likes to ask questions in his classroom. He also likes to keep class sessions going at a rapid pace. A typical day goes something like this:

Mr. Smith: Why is it warmer in summer than in winter?

Amelia: Because the sun is hotter.

Mr. Smith: Well, yes, the sun *feels* hotter. What changes in the earth make it feel hotter?

Arnold: The earth is closer to the sun in the summer.

Mr. Smith: That's a possibility, Arnold. But there's something we need to consider here. When it's summer in the Northern Hemisphere, it's winter in the Southern Hemisphere. When North America is having its warmest days, Australia is having its coldest days. Can we use the earth's distance from the sun to explain that?

Arnold: Uh . . . I guess not.

Mr. Smith: So . . . why is it warmer in summer than in winter? (No one responds.) Do you know, Angela? (She shakes her head.) How about you, Andrew?

Andrew: Nope.

Mr. Smith: Can you think of anything we discussed yesterday that might help us with an explanation? (No one responds.) Remember, yesterday we talked about how the earth changes its tilt in relation to the sun throughout the year. This change in the earth's tilt explains why the days get longer throughout the winter and spring and why they get shorter during the summer and fall. (Mr. Smith continues with an explanation of how the angle of the sun's rays affects temperature on earth.)

Mr. Smith is hoping that his students will draw a connection between information they learned yesterday (changes in the earth's tilt relative to the sun) and today's topic (the seasons). Unfortunately, Mr. Smith is moving too quickly from one question to the next and from one student to another. His students don't make the connection he expects because he simply doesn't give them enough time to do so.

■ How much wait time do your own instructors exhibit? Is it long enough to promote good classroom discussions?

The problem with Mr. Smith's lesson is one seen in many classrooms: too short a **wait time**. When teachers ask students a question, they typically wait one second or less for a response. If students don't respond in that short time interval, teachers tend to speak again—sometimes by asking different students the same question, sometimes by rephrasing the question, sometimes even by answering the question themselves. Teachers are equally reluctant to let much time lapse after students answer questions or make comments in class; once again, they typically allow *one second or less* of silence before responding to a statement or asking another question (M. B. Rowe, 1974, 1987).

If we consider basic principles of cognitive psychology—for example, the importance of relating new information to prior knowledge and the difficulty often associated with retrieving information from long-term memory—then we realize that one second is a very short time indeed for students to develop their responses. When teachers instead allow at least *three seconds* to elapse after their own questions and after students' comments, dramatic changes can occur in both students' and teachers' behaviors:

Changes in students' behaviors:

- *More class participation.* More students participate in class; this is especially true for females and students from ethnic minority groups. Students are more likely to answer questions correctly and to contribute spontaneously to a class discussion, perhaps by asking their own questions, presenting their own perspectives, and responding to one another's comments.

- *Better quality of responses.* Students give a greater variety of responses to the same question, and their responses are longer and more sophisticated. They are more likely to support their reasoning with evidence or logic and more likely to speculate when they don't know an answer.

■ **wait time** Length of time a teacher pauses, either after asking a question or hearing a student's comment, before saying something.

- *Better overall classroom performance.* Students are more likely to feel confident that they can master the material and more motivated to learn it. Academic achievement increases, and discipline problems decrease.

Changes in teachers' behaviors:

- *Different kinds of questions.* Teachers ask fewer "simple" questions (e.g., those requiring recall of facts) and a greater number of complex questions (e.g., those requiring students to elaborate or develop alternative explanations).
- *Increased flexibility in teaching.* Teachers modify the direction of discussion to accommodate students' comments and questions, and they allow their classes to pursue a topic in greater depth than they had originally anticipated.
- *Higher expectations.* Teachers' expectations for many students, especially previously low-achieving students, begin to improve. (Mohatt & Erickson, 1981; M. B. Rowe, 1974, 1987; Tharp, 1989; Tobin, 1987)

From the perspective of cognitive psychology, increasing wait time appears to have two benefits for student learning (Tobin, 1987). First, it allows students more time to process classroom subject matter. Second, it can change the very nature of teacher-student discussions; for example, teachers are more likely to ask challenging, thought-provoking questions. In fact, the nature of the questions that teachers ask is probably as important as—and perhaps even more important than—the amount of wait time per se (Giaconia, 1988).

When teachers increase wait time to three seconds or longer, students participate more actively and give more complex responses to questions.

When our objective is simple recall—when students need to retrieve classroom material very quickly, to "know it cold"—then wait time should be short. Students may sometimes benefit from rapid-fire drill and practice to learn information and skills to automaticity. But when our instructional goals include more complex processing of ideas and issues, longer wait time may give both us and our students the time needed to think things through.

ACCOMMODATING DIVERSITY IN COGNITIVE PROCESSES

As we've explored basic principles of cognitive psychology in this chapter, we've considered many factors—attention, working memory capacity, long-term memory storage processes, prior knowledge, retrieval cues, and so on—that influence what and how well children and adolescents are likely to learn and remember in the classroom. Naturally, students will differ considerably with regard to these factors. For example, on average, girls will have a slight edge over boys in keeping their attention focused on classroom activities and in performing certain kinds of memory tasks, such as remembering lists or specific life events (Das, Naglieri, & Kirby, 1994; Halpern & LaMay, 2000). On average, too, children from low-income homes may have fewer literacy and mathematical skills when they begin school, but they will bring a wealth of knowledge about other topics on which we can build (see Chapter 4).

Students from different cultural backgrounds may have had varying experiences with different kinds of learning tasks. For instance, students from North American and Asian schools are apt to have had experience learning lists of things, whereas students from certain cultures in Africa, Australia, and Central America may have instead been encouraged to remember oral histories or spatial locations (Flavell et al., 1993; Purdie & Hattie, 1996; Rogoff, 2001, 2003). Also as a result of diverse experiences, students from different cultures may rely more heavily on one modality than another (Kirk, 1972; Trawick-Smith, 2003). For example, if oral histories have been a significant part of their cultural heritage, students might be accustomed to learning from information presented auditorily rather than visually.

The importance of wait time partly depends on students' cultures as well. As we discovered in Chapter 4, some Native American students may wait several seconds before responding as a way of showing respect for an adult. Furthermore, students with limited proficiency in English may require some "mental translation" time.

Yet group differences hardly account for all of the diversity we will see in our students. We will also notice significant individual differences *within* any group. For instance, students will differ considerably in how quickly they can think about, encode, and respond to new events and ideas (Demetriou et al., 2002; Kail, 2000). Furthermore, even students from very similar backgrounds will have unique knowledge bases on which to draw, and so they will elaborate differently on the ideas we present (e.g., Cothern, Konopak, & Willis, 1990; Grant & Gomez, 2001; R. E. Reynolds et al., 1982).

TABLE 6.4

Facilitating Cognitive Processing in Students with Special Educational Needs

CATEGORY	CHARACTERISTICS YOU MIGHT OBSERVE	SUGGESTED CLASSROOM STRATEGIES
Students with specific cognitive or academic difficulties	• Deficiencies in one or more specific cognitive processes (e.g., perception, encoding) • Distractibility, inability to sustain attention (in some students) • Difficulty screening out irrelevant stimuli • Less working memory capacity, or less efficient use of working memory • Impulsivity in responding	• Analyze students' errors as a way of identifying possible processing difficulties. • Identify weaknesses in specific cognitive processes, and provide instruction that enables students to compensate for these weaknesses. • Present information in an organized fashion, and make frequent connections to students' prior knowledge as ways of promoting more effective long-term memory storage. • Teach mnemonics to aid long-term memory storage and retrieval. • Encourage greater reflection before responding—for instance, by reinforcing accuracy rather than speed, or by teaching self-instructions (see Chapter 10). • Intersperse activities requiring sustained attention with opportunities for physical exercise.
Students with social or behavioral problems	• Lack of attention because of off-task thoughts and behaviors • Difficulty shifting attention quickly (for students with autism) • Impulsivity; less ability to inhibit inappropriate social behaviors (sometimes due to neurological deficits) • Possible difficulties in other cognitive processes (e.g., undiagnosed learning disabilities)	• Make sure you have students' attention before giving instructions or presenting information. • Refer students to a school psychologist for evaluation and diagnosis of possible learning disabilities.
Students with general delays in cognitive and social functioning	• Slower cognitive processing • Difficulty with attention to task-relevant information • Reduced working memory capacity, or less efficient use of working memory • Less intentional control of cognitive processes • Smaller knowledge base on which to build new learning	• Keep instructional materials simple, emphasizing relevant stimuli and minimizing irrelevant stimuli. • Provide clear instructions that focus students' attention on desired behaviors (e.g., "Listen," "Write," "Stop"). • Pace instruction to allow students enough time to think about and process information adequately (e.g., provide ample wait time after questions). • Assume little prior knowledge about new topics (i.e., "begin at the beginning").
Students with physical or sensory challenges	• Normal cognitive processing ability in most students • Less general knowledge due to limited experiences in the outside world	• Assume equal ability for learning and understanding new information and skills, but consider how students' physical and sensory challenges may interfere with some learning processes. • Expose students to life experiences they may have missed due to their disabilities.
Students with advanced cognitive development	• More rapid cognitive processing • Greater intentional control of cognitive processes • Larger knowledge base (the nature of which will vary, depending on students' cultural backgrounds) • More interconnections among ideas in long-term memory • More rapid retrieval of information from long-term memory	• Proceed through topics more quickly or in greater depth. • Create interdisciplinary lessons to foster integration of material in long-term memory.

Sources: Barkley, 1998; Beirne-Smith et al., 2002; Bulgren et al., 1994; Butterfield & Ferretti, 1987; B. Clark, 1997; Courchesne et al., 1994; Heward, 2003; Landau & McAninch, 1993; E. P. Lorch et al., 1999; G. R. Lyon & Krasnegor, 1996; Mercer, 1997; Morgan & Jenson, 1988; Piirto, 1999; Pressley, 1995; Rabinowitz & Glaser, 1985; H. L. Swanson et al., 1998; R. Turnbull et al., 2004.

To maximize each student's learning and achievement in the classroom, we must, of course, take such individual and group differences into account. For example, we should be especially careful to engage the interest of, and minimize distractions for, those students whose attention wanders easily. In our attempts to promote meaningful learning and other effective storage processes, we should relate classroom subject matter to the diverse background experiences that students have had. We should provide practice in a variety of learning and memory tasks (including those involving different sensory modalities) and help students acquire effective learning strategies for these varying situations (we'll explore this point more fully in Chapter 8). And we must allow sufficient wait time after questions and comments (both our own and those of students) that students can actively think about and elaborate on topics of discussion.

Facilitating Cognitive Processing in Students with Special Needs

Some of our students with special educational needs may have particular trouble attending to and processing classroom subject matter in an effective manner. This will certainly be true for students with learning disabilities (by definition, they have deficits in certain cognitive processes), and it will often be true for students with ADHD as well (Barkley, 1998; E. P. Lorch et al., 1999; Mercer, 1997). Furthermore, students with mental retardation will typically process information more slowly than their classmates, and students with emotional and behavioral disorders may have trouble keeping their attention on the task at hand (Courchesne et al., 1994; R. Turnbull et al., 2004). In contrast, gifted students are likely to process new ideas more rapidly and in a more complex manner than many of their classmates (B. Clark, 1997; Heward, 2003). Table 6.4 identifies cognitive processing differences we are likely to see in students with special educational needs.

Virtually all students, including those without any identified special needs, will occasionally have difficulty learning or remembering class material. Accordingly, many of the instructional strategies in Table 6.4—getting students' attention, analyzing their errors, teaching them mnemonics, and so on—need not be limited to use with students with special needs. *All* of our students can benefit from help in processing information more effectively.

THE BIG PICTURE

Long-term memory appears to have as much capacity as we could ever need; in fact, the more information we have already stored there, the more easily we can learn new material. Yet attention and working memory have a limited capacity (we can attend to and think about only a small amount of information at any one time), creating a major bottleneck in the memory system. No matter how fascinating a topic may be, we can learn only so much so fast.

To learn and remember something effectively, we must, first and foremost, give it our undivided attention; that is, we must mentally focus on it and, for at least a brief time, make it the center of our cognitive world. We must then actively try to make it more meaningful, organized, logical, and vivid for ourselves—for instance, by identifying ways in which it is similar to things we already know, finding interconnections among its various pieces, drawing inferences from it, or forming a visual image that helps us understand it better. To ensure that we master the execution of certain procedures, and to ensure that we can recall basic knowledge and skills quickly and efficiently, we must practice using these things over and over at regular intervals and in different contexts.

Basic principles of effective cognitive processing apply not only to ourselves but also, of course, to the children and adolescents in our classrooms. We must always consider not only what students are doing but also what they are *thinking*. The specific ways that students interpret and make sense of classroom material, and in fact the extent to which they interpret and make sense of it *at all*, influence how quickly and easily they learn it, how success-

fully they retrieve it, and (as we will discover in Chapter 8) how likely they are to apply it to real-world situations and problems.

As teachers, we must continually emphasize the importance of *understanding* classroom subject matter—making sense of it, drawing inferences from it, seeing how it all ties together, and so on—rather than simply memorizing it in a relatively "thoughtless" manner. This emphasis must be reflected not only in our words but also in our instructional activities, classroom assignments, and assessment practices. For instance, rather than just presenting important ideas in classroom lectures and asking students to take notes, we might also ask thought-provoking questions that require students to evaluate, synthesize, or apply what they are learning. As an alternative to asking students to memorize procedures for adding two two-digit numbers, we might ask them to suggest at least three *different* ways they might solve problems such as 15 + 45 or 29 + 68 and to justify their reasoning. Rather than assessing their knowledge of history by asking them to recite names, places, and dates, we might ask them to explain why certain historical events happened and how those events altered the course of subsequent history. Such approaches will not only make students' learning more meaningful and effective but will also enhance their belief that classroom topics are interesting, enjoyable, and in some way relevant to their own lives.

In Chapter 7 we'll look more closely at what students learn, as well as at why they don't always learn what we think they are learning. In the meantime, let's apply what we've already learned about learning as we look at how one new teacher approaches her first year of teaching high school history.

CASE STUDY: *How Time Flies*

Ms. Llewellyn is a first-year social studies teacher at an American high school; she recently completed her degree in United States history and knows her subject matter well. Her history classes begin in September with a study of early explorers of the Western Hemisphere. By early October, students are reading about the colonial settlements of the 1600s. By December, they have covered the French and Indian War, the Revolutionary War, and the Declaration of Independence. The winter months are spent studying the nineteenth century (e.g., the Industrial Revolution, the Civil War), and the spring is spent studying the twentieth century (including both world wars, the Korean War, the Vietnam War, the Persian Gulf crisis, and modern-day terrorism).

Ms. Llewellyn has high expectations for her students. In her daily class lectures, she describes historical events in detail, hoping to give her students a sense of how complex many of these events really were. In addition to having students read the usual high school textbook, she also assigns articles in the historical journals that she herself reads.

Occasionally, Ms. Llewellyn stops a lecture a few minutes before the bell rings to ask questions that check her students' recall of the day's topics. Although her students can usually remember the gist of her lecture, they have difficulty with the details, either mixing them up or forgetting them altogether. A few students remember so little that she can hardly believe they were in class that day. Her students perform even more poorly on monthly essay exams; it's obvious from their written responses that they can remember little of what Ms. Llewellyn has taught them.

"I explained things so clearly to them," she tells herself. "Perhaps these kids just don't want to learn."

Why might Ms. Llewellyn's students be having difficulty learning and remembering the things she is trying to teach them? Can you think of possible reasons related to the class curriculum? to Ms. Llewellyn's style of teaching? to Ms. Llewellyn's reading assignments?

From the perspective of cognitive psychology, what would you do differently than Ms. Llewellyn?

Once you have answered these questions, compare your responses with those presented in Appendix B.

KEY CONCEPTS

PRAXIS Turn to Appendix C, "Matching Book and Ancillary Content to the Praxis Principles of Learning and Teaching Tests," to discover sections of this chapter that may be especially applicable to the Praxis tests.

Now go to our Companion Website at **www.prenhall. com/ormrod** to assess your understanding of chapter content with "Multiple-Choice Questions," apply comprehension in "Essay Questions," broaden your knowledge of educational psychology with related "Web Links," gain greater insight about classroom learning in "Learning in the Content Areas," and analyze and assess classroom work in the "Student Artifact Library."

Knowledge Construction

*T**hink back to a time* when you tried to carry on a conversation with someone in a noisy room—maybe at a party, in a bar where a band was playing, or in a workshop with
loud machinery operating nearby. You probably couldn't hear everything the other person was
saying, but perhaps you were able to get the gist of the message by combining what you *did* hear
with things you could see (e.g., gestures and facial expressions) and with things you already knew
about the topic under discussion. We often construct meanings from the stimuli around us—
meanings that aren't necessarily obvious from the stimuli themselves, and meanings that may or
may not be accurate.

As we discovered in the preceding chapter, many cognitive psychologists do not believe that
learning is a simple process of absorbing information from the environment. Instead, learning
involves constructing one's own knowledge from one's experiences. This chapter focuses on constructive processes in learning and memory. More specifically, we will address these questions:

- How are both storage and retrieval constructive in nature?
- How do people sometimes work together in their efforts to construct meaning?
- What forms might constructed knowledge take?
- Why do students acquire misconceptions about the world, and how do such beliefs affect
  their later learning?
- What strategies can we use to help students construct accurate and useful knowledge
  about classroom topics?
- What strategies can we use to encourage students to correct their misconceptions about
  the world? In other words, how can we promote *conceptual change*?

CASE STUDY: *Pulling It All Together*

Rita attends fourth grade at a school in Michigan. Her class has recently had a unit on
Michigan's state history. Rita still knows little about U.S. history; she will study that subject
as a fifth grader next year. Despite her limited background in history, Rita willingly
responds to an interviewer's questions about the New World.

Interviewer: Our country is in the part of the world called America. At one time,
America was called the New World. Do you know why it was called
the New World?

Rita: Yeah. We learned this in social studies.

Interviewer: What did you learn?

Rita: Because they used to live in England, the British, and they didn't know
about . . . they wanted to get to China 'cause China had some things
they wanted. They had some cups or whatever—no, they had furs.
They had fur and stuff like that and they wanted to have a shorter way
to get to China so they took it and they landed in Michigan, but it
wasn't called Michigan. I think it was the British that landed in
Michigan and they were there first and so they tried to claim that land,
but it didn't work out for some reason so they took some furs and
brought them back to Britain and they sold them, but they mostly
wanted it for the furs. So then the English landed there and they
claimed the land and they wanted to make it a state, and so they got it
signed by the government or whoever, the big boss, then they were
just starting to make it a state so the British just went up to the Upper
Peninsula and they thought they could stay there for a little while.
Then they had to fight a war, then the farmers, they were just
volunteers, so the farmers went right back and tried to get their family
put together back again.

Interviewer: Did you learn all this in state history this year?

Rita: Um hum. (VanSledright & Brophy, 1992, p. 849; reprinted by
permission)

Which parts of Rita's response accurately describe the history of the New World? Which parts are clearly *inaccurate*?

Michigan's Upper Peninsula is separated from the rest of the state by the Straits of Mackinac, which connect Lake Michigan and Lake Huron. Why might Rita think that making Michigan a state caused the British to move to the Upper Peninsula?

At the time that British colonists were first settling in Michigan, merchants back in England were seeking a new trade route to the Far East so they could more easily secure the tea, spices, and silk available there. Why might Rita initially suggest that the British wanted to get cups from China? Why might she then say they wanted to get furs?

CONSTRUCTIVE PROCESSES IN LEARNING AND MEMORY

Rita has certainly learned some facts about her state and its history. For example, she is aware of a region called the Upper Peninsula, and she knows that many of the state's early European settlers were British. Using what she's learned, she creates a scenario that makes sense to her but might give a historian heart failure.

To some extent, Rita's lack of knowledge about certain things is limiting her understanding of Michigan's history. For instance, Rita doesn't know that the British and the English were the *same people*. Thinking of them as two different groups, she assumes that the arrival of one group drove the other group to the Upper Peninsula.

Yet occasionally what Rita *does* know also gets in her way. For instance, she associates *China* with dinnerware (including cups), and she has learned that some early European explorers were seeking furs to send back to their homeland. She uses such information to draw logical but incorrect inferences about why the British were so eager to find a new route to China.

Rita may have constructed her unique view of history at the time she learned it—that is, during storage. Alternatively, she may have constructed it while the adult was interviewing her—in other words, while she was retrieving what she'd previously learned. As we will see now, knowledge construction can occur during both storage and retrieval.

Construction in Storage

Experiencing FIRSTHAND ·Rocky

Read the following passage *one time only*:

> Rocky slowly got up from the mat, planning his escape. He hesitated a moment and thought. Things were not going well. What bothered him most was being held, especially since the charge against him had been weak. He considered his present situation. The lock that held him was strong but he thought he could break it. He knew, however, that his timing would have to be perfect. Rocky was aware that it was because of his early roughness that he had been penalized so severely—much too severely from his point of view. The situation was becoming frustrating; the pressure had been grinding on him for too long. He was being ridden unmercifully. Rocky was getting angry now. He felt he was ready to make his move. He knew that his success or failure would depend on what he did in the next few seconds. (R. C. Anderson, Reynolds, Schallert, & Goetz, 1977, p. 372)

Now summarize what you've just read in two or three sentences.

· · · · · · ·

Were you able to make sense of the passage? What did you think it was about? A prison escape? A wrestling match? Or perhaps something else altogether? The passage about Rocky includes a number of facts but leaves a lot unsaid; for example, it tells us nothing about where Rocky was, what kind of "lock" was holding him, or why timing was of the utmost importance. Yet you were probably able to use the information you were given to construct an overall understanding of Rocky's situation. Most people do find meaning of one sort or another in the passage (R. C. Anderson et al., 1977).

Different people often construct different meanings from the same stimuli or events, in part because they each bring unique prior experiences and knowledge to the situation. For example, when the Rocky passage was used in an experiment with college students, physical education

■ Skillful readers often skip some of the words on the page and yet understand what they read quite accurately. How is this possible?

majors frequently interpreted it as a wrestling match, but music education majors (most of whom had little or no knowledge of wrestling) were more likely to think it was about a prison break (R. C. Anderson et al., 1977).

Furthermore, people often interpret what they see and hear based on what they *expect* to see and hear. As an example, try the following exercise.

Experiencing FIRSTHAND ·Nursery Rhymes

Here are three well-known nursery rhymes. Read them *as quickly as you can*, and read them *one time only*:

1   **Hey Diddle Diddle**

2   Hey diddle diddle,
3   The cat and the fiddle.
4   The cow jumped over the moon.
5   The little dog laughed to see such sport,
6   And tha dish ran away with the spoon.

7   **This Little Piggy**

8   This little piggy want to market
9   This little piggy stayed home
10   This little piggy had roost beef
11   This little piggy had none
12   This little piggy went wee, wee, wee all the way home.

13   **Little Bo Peep**

14   Little Bo Peep
15   Has lost her sheep
16   And dosn't know where to find them.
17   Leave them alone
18   And they'll come home,
19   Waggng their tails behind them.

· · · · · · ·

You may have noticed one or two typographical errors in the rhymes. But did you catch them all? Altogether, five words were misspelled: *the* (line 6), *went* (line 8), *roast* (line 10), *doesn't* (line 16), and *wagging* (line 19). If you didn't notice all the errors—and many people don't—then your perception of the nursery rhymes was influenced by what words you *expected* to see in them.

Prior knowledge and expectations are especially likely to influence learning when new information is ambiguous (e.g., Eysenck & Keane, 1990). To see what I mean, try another exercise.

Experiencing FIRSTHAND ·A Pen-and-Ink Sketch

Take a look at Figure 7.1. Look at the details carefully. Notice the shape of the head, the facial features, and the relative proportion of one part to another. But what exactly *do* you see?

· · · · · · ·

Did you see a picture of a rat or mouse, or did you see a bald-headed man? In fact, the drawing isn't a very good picture of *anything*; too many details have been left out. Despite the missing pieces, people can usually make sense of the figure. Whether they see a man or a rodent depends, in large part, on whether they expect to see a human being or a nonhuman creature (Bugelski & Alampay, 1961). Interpretations of ambiguous information are particularly susceptible to biases and expectations because so much of the information necessary for an "accurate" perception (if such is possible) is simply not available.

As teachers, we will find our students constructing their own idiosyncratic meanings and interpretations in virtually every area of the classroom curriculum. For example, as the Rocky exercise illustrates, the activity of reading is often very constructive in nature: Students combine the ideas they read with their prior knowledge and then draw logical conclusions about what the text is trying to communicate (Dole, Duffy, Roehler, & Pearson, 1991; Otero & Kintsch, 1992).

Even though these students are working together on a science activity, their prior knowledge and beliefs may lead each one to derive a different understanding from the experience.

FIGURE 7.1 What do you see in this picture?

From "The Role of Frequency in Developing Perceptual Sets" by B. R. Bugelski and D. A. Alampay, 1961, *Canadian Journal of Psychology, 15*, p. 206. Copyright 1961. Canadian Psychological Association. Reprinted with permission.

FIGURE 7.2 As you can see from her journal entries, 8-year-old Darcy initially interpreted a casual remark to the school nurse in a way very different from the teacher's intended meaning. Fortunately, the teacher corrected the misunderstanding a few days later.

October 22nd, 2001
I went to a new school today. My teacher's name is Mrs. Whaley. I accidentally cracked an egg on my head. Mrs. Whaley told the nurse that I was a showoff and a nuisance. I got really sad and wanted to run away from school, but I didn't leave.

· · ·

October 27th, 2001
We presented our book reports today. I was the last one to present my book report. Whenever I did my book report, they laughed at me, but the teacher said they were laughing with me. I asked the teacher why she had called me a nuisance the first day. And she said, "Darcy, I didn't call you a nuisance. I was saying to Mrs. Larson that it was a nuisance to try to wash egg out of your hair." I was so happy. I decided to like Mrs. Whaley again.

So, too, will we find constructive processes in such subject areas as mathematics, science, and social studies (R. Driver, Asoko, Leach, Mortimer, & Scott, 1994; L. B. Resnick, 1989; VanSledright & Brophy, 1992). When we want our students to interpret classroom subject matter in particular ways, we must be sure to communicate clearly and unambiguously, so that there is little room for misinterpretation. We must also leave little room for doubt in the messages we communicate about nonacademic matters, as Figure 7.2 illustrates.

Construction in Retrieval

Have you ever remembered an event very differently than someone else did? Were you and the other person both equally convinced of the accuracy of your memories? How might constructive processes explain this difference of opinion?

As noted in Chapter 6, retrieval isn't always an all-or-nothing phenomenon. Sometimes we retrieve only certain parts of whatever information we are looking for in long-term memory. In such situations we may construct our "memory" of an event by combining the tidbits we can retrieve with our general knowledge and assumptions about the world (Kolodner, 1985; Loftus, 1991; Rumelhart & Ortony, 1977). As an example of how retrieval of a specific event or idea often involves drawing on our knowledge about other things as well, try the following exercise.

Experiencing FIRSTHAND ·Missing Letters

Can you fill in the missing letters of these five words?

1. sep - rate
2. exist - nce
3. adole - - - nce
4. perc - - ve
5. hors d'o - - - - -

· · · · · · ·

Were you able to retrieve the missing letters from your long-term memory? If not, then you may have found yourself making reasonable guesses, using either your knowledge of how the words are pronounced or your knowledge of how words in the English language are typically spelled. For example, perhaps you used the "i before e except after c" rule for word 4; if so, then you reconstructed the correct spelling of *perceive*. Perhaps you used your knowledge that *ance* is a common word ending. Unfortunately, if you used this knowledge for word 2, then you spelled *existence* incorrectly. Neither pronunciation nor typical English spelling patterns would have helped you with *hors d'oeuvre*, a term borrowed from the French. (The correct spellings for words 1 and 3 are *separate* and *adolescence*.)

■ What implications does the notion of reconstruction error have for the credibility of eyewitness testimony?

When people fill in the gaps in what they've retrieved based on what seems "logical," they often make mistakes—a phenomenon known as **reconstruction error**. Rita's version of Michigan history is a prime example: She retrieves certain facts from her history lessons and integrates them into what is, for her, a logical sequence of events. So, too, will our own students sometimes fall victim to reconstruction error, pulling together what they can recall in ways we may hardly recognize (Leichtman & Ceci, 1995; Roediger & McDermott, 2000). If important details are difficult to fill in logically, we must make sure students learn them well enough to retrieve them easily from long-term memory.

■ **reconstruction error** Construction of a logical but incorrect "memory" by using information retrieved from long-term memory plus one's general knowledge and beliefs about the world.

■ **individual constructivism** Theoretical perspective that focuses on how people, as individuals, construct meaning from the events around them.

Up to this point, we have been talking about construction as a process that occurs within a single learner. Theories that focus on how people, as individuals, construct meaning from events are collectively known as **individual constructivism**. Views about storage processes such as organization, elaboration, and visual imagery (see Chapter 6) have an element of individual constructivism, as do Piaget's theory of cognitive development and many explanations of language development (see Chapter 2). Yet sometimes people work *together* to construct meaning and knowledge, as we shall see now.

KNOWLEDGE CONSTRUCTION AS A SOCIAL PROCESS

Think about times when you've been confused about material in one of your high school or college classes. In such situations, did you ever work cooperatively with classmates (who perhaps were just as confused as you were) to make sense of the material *together*? Quite possibly, by sharing your various interpretations, you jointly constructed a better understanding of the subject matter than any of you could have constructed on your own. Unlike individually constructed knowledge, which may differ considerably from one individual to another, socially constructed knowledge is shared by two or more people simultaneously. A perspective known as **social constructivism**, which we first encountered in Chapter 2, focuses on such collective efforts to impose meaning on the world.

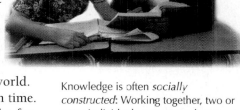

Knowledge is often *socially constructed*: Working together, two or more individuals construct a better understanding of a topic than they could have constructed on their own.

Sometimes meaning is jointly constructed by two or more people at a single point in time. For example, this would be the case if, by working together in a study group, you and a few classmates made sense of puzzling course material. At other times, social construction of meaning may take weeks, years, or even centuries, as is seen in the evolution of such academic disciplines as mathematics, science, history, economics, and psychology. Through these disciplines, people have developed concepts (e.g., *pi* [π], *molecule*, and *revolution*) and principles (e.g., *Pythagorean theorem*, *supply and demand*, and the *limited capacity of working memory*) to simplify, organize, and explain the very diverse nature of the world. Literature, music, and fine arts help us to impose meaning on the world as well—for instance, by trying to portray the thoughts and feelings that characterize human experience. Here we see the very critical role that *culture* plays in knowledge construction: To the extent that different groups of people use different concepts and principles to explain their physical experiences, and to the extent that they have unique bodies of literature, music, and art to capture their psychological experiences, they will inevitably see the world in diverse ways (Hong, Morris, Chiu, & Benet-Martínez, 2000; O. Lee, 1999; Tomasello, 2000).

In many instances the social construction of knowledge involves students and their teacher working actively together to make better sense of information and events (e.g., recall our discussion of a *mediated learning experience* in Chapter 2). In other cases, although the teacher may initiate and monitor a learning activity, students work primarily with one another to understand academic topics.

Benefits of Joint Meaning-Making with Peers

Increasingly, psychologists and educators are recognizing the value of having students work together to construct meaning about classroom subject matter—for instance, to explore, explain, discuss, and debate certain topics either in small groups or as an entire class. When learners work together in such a manner, they are, in essence, engaging in **distributed cognition**: They spread the learning task across many minds and can draw on multiple knowledge bases and ideas (Hewitt & Scardamalia, 1998; Kuhn, 2001b; Palincsar & Herrenkohl, 1999; Salomon, 1993). (This concept may remind you of, and in fact overlaps with, the concept of *distributed intelligence*, which we examined in Chapter 5.)

By having students share their ideas and perspectives with one another, we can enhance their understanding of a topic in several ways:

- We encourage students to clarify and organize their ideas well enough to explain and justify them to others.
- We provide opportunities for students to *elaborate* on what they have learned—for example, by drawing inferences, generating hypotheses, and asking questions.
- We expose students to the views of others, who may have a more accurate understanding of a topic.
- We enable students to discover flaws and inconsistencies in their own thinking, thereby helping them identify gaps in their understanding.
- We help students discover how people from different cultural and ethnic backgrounds may interpret the topic in different, yet perhaps equally valid, ways. (L. M. Anderson, 1993; Banks, 1991; Barnes, 1976; M. Carr & Biddlecomb, 1998; Fosnot, 1996; Hatano & Inagaki, 1993, 2003; E. H. Hiebert & Raphael, 1996; K. Hogan, Nastasi, & Pressley, 2000; A. King, 1999; Schwarz, Neuman, & Biezuner, 2000; N. M. Webb & Palincsar, 1996)

■ **social constructivism** Theoretical perspective that focuses on people's collective efforts to impose meaning on the world.

■ **distributed cognition** Process whereby learners think about an issue or problem together, sharing ideas and working collaboratively to draw conclusions or develop solutions.

Yet as we have seen in earlier chapters, and will continue to see in later chapters, the benefits of student interaction are not restricted to a better understanding of the particular topic under discussion. Consider these additional advantages:

- Disagreements among peers are likely to promote progress to higher stages of cognitive and moral development (see the discussion of Piaget's and Kohlberg's theories in Chapters 2 and 3, respectively).
- By discussing and debating issues with one another, children begin to internalize the concepts, thought processes, and lines of reasoning they use in their social interactions. They may also internalize the "arguing" process and so acquire the ability to look at a single issue from multiple perspectives (see the discussion of Vygotsky's theory in Chapter 2).
- Students can develop more effective interpersonal skills (see Chapter 3).
- Students can model effective ways of thinking about and studying academic subject matter for one another (see the discussion of *metacognition* in Chapter 8).
- In the process of debating controversial material, students have firsthand experience with the processes that experts in a discipline use to advance the frontiers of knowledge—for instance, presenting evidence in support of one's conclusions and examining the strengths and weaknesses of various explanations (P. Bell & Linn, 2002). They may also gain a more sophisticated view of the nature of knowledge and learning; for example, they may begin to realize that acquiring "knowledge" involves acquiring an integrated set of ideas about a topic and that such knowledge is likely to evolve gradually over time (see the discussion of *epistemological beliefs* in Chapter 8).
- Students may acquire greater self-confidence for performing a task when they see their peers accomplishing the same task successfully (see the discussion of *self-efficacy* in Chapter 10).
- Students may be more motivated to participate in learning activities in which they can satisfy social needs (see the discussion of *relatedness* in Chapter 11).

Clearly, then, students have a great deal to gain—not only cognitively, but also personally, socially, and motivationally—from conversing with one another regularly about classroom subject matter. Later in the chapter we'll discuss several strategies for promoting the social construction of meaning. In the meantime, however, let's look at the forms that constructed knowledge—whether derived individually or socially—might take.

When students must explain their thinking to someone else, they usually organize and elaborate on what they've learned. These processes help them develop a more integrated and thorough understanding of the material.

ORGANIZING KNOWLEDGE

In the process of constructing knowledge, people also organize it in a variety of ways, thereby creating the interconnected long-term memory described in Chapter 6. This section introduces several ways in which people appear to organize the things they learn: *concepts*, *schemas*, *scripts*, and *theories*. Of these, we will spend the most time looking at concepts, in part because they reflect simpler and more basic forms of organization and in part because researchers have been studying them for a longer time and so have a better understanding of them.

Concepts

A **concept** is a way of mentally grouping or categorizing objects or events that are similar in some way. For instance, the concept *furniture* encompasses such objects as chairs, tables, beds, and desks. The concept *swim* encompasses a variety of actions—breast stroke, crawl, dog paddle—that all involve propelling onself through water.

Concepts are at the very core of our thinking, and some theorists consider them to be our "smallest units of thought" (Ferrari & Elik, 2003, p. 25). Many concepts (e.g., *dog*, *walk*, *hot*) are shared by people around the world. Others (e.g., *tortilla*, *burka*, *spreadsheet*) are specific to certain cultures. And as noted in our earlier discussion of social constructivism, people in various academic disciplines have developed numerous concepts (e.g., *pi*, *molecule*) to help them make better sense of the phenomena they study.

Human beings seem to have a natural tendency to organize their world, and they begin to do so as early as 3 months old (Quinn, 2002). As children begin to speak, their concept development is to some extent reflected in the size of their vocabulary. By the time they reach school age, they typically understand 8,000 to 14,000 words (S. Carey, 1978).

■ **concept** Mental grouping of objects or events that have something in common.

Students learn thousands of additional concepts during the school years. They acquire some concepts quickly and easily. They acquire others more gradually and continue to modify them over time; in the meantime, they may have an "almost-but-not-quite" understanding of what the concepts are. Following are several examples of such partial understanding:

- Lonnigan thinks of an *animal* as something with four legs and fur. He is quite surprised when his teacher says that fish, birds, and insects are also animals.
- Lisa correctly defines a *rectangle* as a geometric figure composed of two sets of parallel lines that are joined by right angles; this definition appropriately includes squares as examples of rectangles. Yet when she is shown a variety of shapes and asked to pick out all the rectangles, she doesn't identify the squares as being rectangles (P. S. Wilson, 1988).
- Luis learns that a *noun* is "a person, place, or thing." Using this definition, he classifies words like *you* and *me* as nouns because they refer to people. Only later, when Luis learns about other parts of speech, does he realize that *you* and *me* are pronouns rather than nouns.

Students continually encounter new concepts as they study classroom subject matter, and such concepts often help them make better sense of their physical and social worlds.

In some cases students **undergeneralize** a concept: They have too narrow a view about which objects or events the concept includes. Lonnigan undergeneralizes when he excludes fish, birds, and insects from his concept of *animal*. And Lisa's current conception of a *rectangle* is an undergeneralization because she doesn't realize that squares are also rectangles. On other occasions students may **overgeneralize** a concept, inappropriately including objects and events that aren't true members of the category. For instance, Luis overgeneralizes when he identifies *you* and *me* as nouns. Students don't fully understand a concept until they can identify both examples (**positive instances**) and nonexamples (**negative instances**) of the concept with complete accuracy.

As Piaget and other researchers have found, children become increasingly able to think about abstract ideas as they get older (see Chapter 2). This developmental trend is reflected in their concept development (e.g., R. M. Gagné, 1985; Liu, Golinkoff, & Sak, 2001). For instance, they may initially think of various family members (cousins, uncles, etc.) in terms of things they can actually see (e.g., an *uncle* is any man who is nice and brings presents), rather than in terms of the nature of the relationship (Keil, 1989). Similarly, they may first develop a concrete understanding of *circle* (i.e., a "roundish" thing); later, perhaps in a high school geometry class, they may develop an abstract concept of a circle (i.e., all points on a plane equidistant from another single point). And they may first think of *summer* as a time when it's hot and there's no school; only later do they discover that, to scientists, it's the earth's tilt in relation to the sun that determines the seasons. As is true for the concepts *circle* and *summer*, formal instruction is one key means through which children acquire abstract understandings of concepts.

Interconnectedness of Concepts   In Chapter 6 we discovered that much of the information in long-term memory is interconnected. An important part of learning concepts, then, is learning how they are related to one another. For example, in the elementary grades, students learn that a *complete sentence* includes, at a minimum, both a *subject* (including either a *noun* or *pronoun*) and a *verb*. In a middle school music class, they might learn that a *waltz* is a melody in *three-quarters time*. In high school physics, they might learn that *velocity* equals *acceleration* times *time*.

In some instances concepts are nested within one another in a hierarchical fashion. For instance, as a student, you learned that *dogs* and *cats* are both *mammals*, that *mammals* and *birds* are both *vertebrates*, and that *vertebrates* and *invertebrates* are both *animals*. The more general, all-encompassing concepts (those near the top of the hierarchy) tend to be relatively abstract, whereas the more specific ones (those near the bottom of the hierarchy) tend to be fairly concrete (Flavell et al., 1993; Rosch, Mervis, Gray, Johnson, & Boyes-Braem, 1976).

As you discovered in Chapter 2, Piaget described young children as being unable to view objects as belonging to two or more categories at the same time—a phenomenon known as *single classification*. As children reach the concrete operations stage, they become capable of *multiple classification* (see Table 2.1). From the perspective of contemporary cognitive psychology, however, multiple classification is not necessarily an ability that children either have or don't have. Instead, children become able to categorize objects in two or more ways simultaneously when they learn how various concepts are interrelated—knowledge that is apt to evolve, at least in part, as a result of formal education (Flavell et al., 1993).

■ **undergeneralization** Overly narrow view of what objects or events a concept includes.

■ **overgeneralization** Overly broad view of what objects or events a concept includes.

■ **positive instance** Specific example of a concept.

■ **negative instance** Nonexample of a concept.

The Nature of Concepts Theorists have differing opinions about what people actually learn when they acquire a new concept. For instance, they've suggested that a concept might be learned as a *feature list*, a *prototype*, or a set of *exemplars*.

Concepts as feature lists. Some theorists have proposed that learning a concept involves learning the specific attributes, or *features*, that characterize positive instances of the concept (e.g., Bourne, Dominowski, Loftus, & Healy, 1986; Bruner, Goodnow, & Austin, 1956; Ward, Vela, & Haas, 1990). **Defining features** are characteristics present in *all* positive instances. For example, a *square* must have four equal sides connected at 90° angles, and an *animal* must be a consumer of food (rather than a producer of food through photosynthesis). In Figure 7.3, 8-year-old Noah shows his understanding of one of the defining features of the concept *insect*.

Discovering a concept's defining features is not always easy. Consider this situation:

> A father goes to work. On the way home from work in the evening he stops at a bar to have a drink. His friends there are drunkards and he becomes a drunkard too. Is he still a father? (Saltz, 1971, p. 28)

Many 8-year-olds deny that a drunkard can also be a father (Saltz, 1971). Their response reflects their ignorance of the defining features of the concept *father*. Rather than recognize that fatherhood is defined simply in terms of a biological or adoptive relationship, many young children believe that a defining feature of fatherhood is "goodness," so a "bad" drunkard is automatically disqualified. "Goodness" is a **correlational feature** of fatherhood—a feature present in many positive instances of the concept but not essential for concept membership.

A concept is most easily learned when its defining features are concrete and obvious—in other words, when they are *salient*—rather than when they are abstract or difficult to pin down. The concept *red* has a single defining feature—a particular range of light wavelengths—that is easily seen by anyone who isn't color-blind. But what about the defining feature of *plant*? The process of photosynthesis is not readily observable. Instead, we are more apt to notice other characteristics of plants (e.g., that they have leaves or that they grow in gardens) that are correlational rather than defining features.

When children first encounter concepts, they are sometimes led astray by correlational features, especially if those features are more salient than the defining ones (Anglin, 1977; Keil, 1989; Mervis, 1987). Thus, we should not be surprised to find Lisa omitting squares from her concept of *rectangle*. Most of the figures her teachers have specifically labeled as "rectangle" have probably had noticeably different widths and lengths. Nor is it surprising that Lonnigan excludes fish and birds from his concept of *animal*. Two very obvious correlational features—fur and four legs—have undoubtedly characterized many of the critters that people in Lonnigan's life have specifically referred to as "animal" (S. Carey, 1985).

As teachers, we can do several things to help students discover what features are essential for concept membership. We can provide a definition, which is especially helpful when a concept's defining features are abstract or not easily noticed (R. M. Gagné, 1985; Tennyson & Cocchiarella, 1986). We can illustrate a concept (perhaps with a line drawing) in a way that highlights defining features while downplaying correlational or irrelevant ones. We can provide a variety of examples and contrast positive instances with negative ones (e.g., ants and butterflies are insects; spiders are not). And we might assess students' understanding by having them identify or generate their *own* examples of concepts (R. M. Gagné, 1985; H. C. Ellis & Hunt, 1983; M. D. Merrill & Tennyson, 1977; Tennyson & Cocchiarella, 1986).

Concepts as prototypes. For many concepts, learners seem to construct a mental **prototype**: an idea (perhaps a visual image) of a "typical" example (Rosch, 1973a, 1973b, 1977; Tennyson & Cocchiarella, 1986). To see what I mean, try the following exercise.

Experiencing FIRSTHAND ·Visual Images

1. Close your eyes and picture a *bird*. Take a good look at the visual image you create.
2. Now close your eyes again and picture a *vehicle*. Once again, look closely at your image.

· · · · · · ·

a dut ter fly is an in seck t beckese it hase six leags

FIGURE 7.3 Eight-year-old Noah has learned one of the defining features of an *insect*: six legs.

■ Are definitions likely to be effective when students memorize them word for word? Why or why not?

■ **defining feature** Characteristic that must be present in all positive instances of a concept.

■ **correlational feature** Characteristic present in many positive instances of a concept but not essential for concept membership.

■ **prototype** Mental representation of a "typical" positive instance of a concept.

What came to mind when I asked you to picture a bird and a vehicle? If you are like most people, you probably visualized a relatively small bird, perhaps one about the size of a robin or sparrow, rather than a penguin or an ostrich. Likewise, your image of a vehicle probably resembled a car or a truck, rather than a skateboard or an elevator. Prototypes are usually based on the positive instances that learners encounter most frequently. For instance, people see small birds, cars, and trucks more frequently than they see large birds, skateboards, and elevators.

Once learners have formed a prototype for a particular concept, they may compare new objects and events against the prototype. Objects or events similar to the prototype are easily identified as positive instances. Objects or events very different from the prototype are apt to be identified (perhaps mistakenly) as negative instances. As an illustration, let's say that your prototype of an *animal* looks something like a small dog, perhaps similar to Figure 7.4. How quickly are you likely to recognize that the following critters are also animals?

FIGURE 7.4 A possible prototype for the concept *animal*

Horse	Whale
Grizzly bear	Earthworm
Frog	Snail
Person	Sponge

The more different the critter is from your doglike prototype, the more difficulty you will have identifying it as an animal.

Concepts as sets of exemplars. We probably cannot explain all concept learning strictly in terms of feature lists and prototypes. For one thing, how we categorize an object depends on the context in which we find it. If a cuplike object contains flowers, we might identify it as a *vase* rather than a *cup*; if it contains mashed potatoes, we might instead identify it as a *bowl* (Labov, 1973; B. Schwartz & Reisberg, 1991). Furthermore, not all concepts lend themselves readily to a specific set of defining features or a single prototype (Eysenck & Keane, 1990; Hampton, 1981; McCloskey & Glucksberg, 1978). For instance, I myself have a difficult time identifying the defining features or a typical example of *music*: Classical, rock, jazz, country-western, rap, and Asian music are all quite different from one another.

In some cases, knowing a concept may depend largely on knowing numerous examples, or **exemplars**, of the concept (Carmichael & Hayes, 2001; Reisberg, 1997; B. H. Ross & Spalding, 1994). Exemplars give learners a sense of the variability they are apt to see in any category of objects or events. For instance, the concept *fruit* may bring to mind many different things: Apples, bananas, raspberries, pineapples, and coconuts are all possibilities. If you encounter a new instance of fruit—a blackberry, let's say—you could compare it to the variety of exemplars you have already stored and find one (a raspberry, perhaps) that is relatively similar.

Students typically learn concepts more effectively when they are given many examples rather than only one or two. The examples we provide should illustrate the full range of the concept so that students do not undergeneralize (E. V. Clark, 1971; M. D. Merrill & Tennyson, 1978; Tennyson & Cocchiarella, 1986). For instance, we might illustrate the concept *mammal* with whales and platypuses as well as with cats and dogs.

It is possible that prototypes or exemplars are used to identify positive instances in clear-cut situations, whereas defining features are used in other, more ambiguous ones—for instance, when deciding whether a sponge is an *animal* (Andre, 1986; Glass & Holyoak, 1975; Glass, Holyoak, & Santa, 1979). It may also be that children rely on prototypes or exemplars in the early years and then discover defining features later on. As a preschooler, my son Jeff adamantly denied that the concept *animal* includes people, fish, and insects. When he began studying the animal kingdom in school, he learned a biology-based definition of *animal* that incorporates some of its major features: a form of life that derives its food from other organisms, responds immediately to its environment, and can move its body. Jeff then acknowledged that people, fish, and creepy-crawlies are legitimate animals. (Someday, however, he may learn that biologists do not completely agree on a definition of *animal* and that true defining features of the concept are difficult to identify.)

The Into the Classroom feature "Teaching Concepts" offers suggestions for fostering concept learning in a variety of academic disciplines. In the following exercise, you will find a strategy that one teacher has used.

■ **exemplar** Specific example that is part of a learner's general knowledge and understanding of a concept.

Analyzing Teacher Strategies

Quadrilaterals

A middle school mathematics teacher designed the following worksheet to teach her students the concept *quadrilateral*. As you examine it, think about

- The defining features of a quadrilateral
- The strategies the teacher is using to teach the concept
- Additional strategies the teacher might use to enhance students' understanding of the concept

Worksheet courtesy of Dinah Jackson.

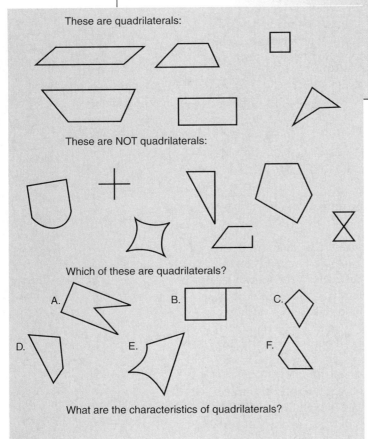

These are quadrilaterals:

These are NOT quadrilaterals:

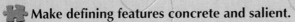

Which of these are quadrilaterals?

A.   B.   C.   D.   E.   F.

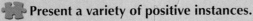

What are the characteristics of quadrilaterals?

If you could not recall what a quadrilateral was from your own schooling, the exercise probably enabled you to discover that a quadrilateral is a closed figure made up of four straight line segments that connect at their end points but do not otherwise intersect. To teach the concept, the teacher presents both positive and negative instances; in the process, she illustrates the variability that quadrilaterals can have and includes some almost-but-not-quite nonexamples ("near misses"). Furthermore, the teacher assesses students' understanding by asking them to identify new positive and negative instances and to identify a quadrilateral's defining features. One weakness of the activity is that it does not encourage students to relate the concept to real-world objects; for instance, the teacher might ask students to identify examples of quadrilaterals among two-dimensional items in the classroom. A second weakness is that the activity does not encourage students to relate the concept *quadrilateral* to other geometric figures; for instance, the teacher might ask students to list the kinds of shapes that quadrilaterals include (squares, rectangles, parallelograms, and rhombi are all possibilities). The forms of knowledge we consider next—schemas, scripts, and (later) personal theories—typically incorporate at least two, and often many, concepts and their interrelationships.

INTO THE CLASSROOM

Teaching Concepts

Give a definition.

A geometry teacher defines a *sphere* as "the set of points in three-dimensional space that are equidistant from a single point."

Make defining features concrete and salient.

A teacher illustrates the concept *insect* with a line drawing that emphasizes its defining features, such as three body parts and three pairs of legs, in bold black lines. The drawing downplays other, irrelevant characteristics that students might see, such as the insect's color or the presence of wings.

Present a "best example," or prototype.

To illustrate the concept *democracy*, a social studies teacher describes a hypothetical, "ideal" government.

Present a variety of positive instances.

A music teacher plays a *primary chord* in several keys.

Present negative instances—especially "near misses"—to show what the concept is not.

When a teacher describes what a *mammal* is, he explains why frogs and lizards do not fall in this category.

Ask students to identify positive and negative instances from among numerous possibilities.

A language arts teacher gives students a list of sentences and asks them to identify the sentences containing a *dangling participle*.

Ask students to generate their own positive instances of the concept.

A teacher asks students to think of examples of *adjectives* that they use frequently in their own speech.

Show students how various concepts are related to one another.

A science teacher explains that the concepts *velocity* and *acceleration* have somewhat different meanings, even though they both involve speed.

Schemas and Scripts

Experiencing FIRSTHAND ·Horse #2

Take a moment to think about what you know about horses. For instance, what do they look like? How do they spend their time? Where are you most likely to see them? Write down as many things about a horse as you can think of.

· · · · · · ·

You probably had little difficulty retrieving many different things about horses, perhaps including their manes and elongated heads, their fondness for running and eating oats, and their frequent appearance in pastures and at racetracks. The various things you know about horses are closely interrelated in your long-term memory in the form of a "horse" schema.

More generally, a **schema** is a tightly organized set of facts related to a particular object or phenomenon (e.g., Rumelhart & Ortony, 1977; Willingham, 2004).[1] Schemas give us an idea of what is typically true about an object or event. For instance, horses are usually seen in pastures, at racetracks, and in a few other locations, although it would certainly be possible to see one in a city park or at a shopping mall.

Not only do schemas provide a means for organizing information, they also help us interpret new situations; for instance, they enable us to fill in gaps and draw inferences. As an example, try the following exercise.

Experiencing FIRSTHAND ·John

Read the following passage *one time only*:

> John was feeling bad today so he decided to go see the family doctor. He checked in with the doctor's receptionist, and then looked through several medical magazines that were on the table by his chair. Finally the nurse came and asked him to take off his clothes. The doctor was very nice to him. He eventually prescribed some pills for John. Then John left the doctor's office and headed home. (Bower, Black, & Turner, 1979, p. 190)

· · · · · · ·

You probably had no trouble understanding the passage because you have been to a doctor's office yourself and have a schema for how those visits usually go. You can therefore fill in a number of details that the passage doesn't tell you. For example, you probably inferred that John must have *gone* to the doctor's office, although the story omits this essential step. Likewise, you probably concluded that John took his clothes off in the examination room, *not* in the waiting room, even though the story never makes it clear where John did his striptease. When a schema involves a predictable sequence of events related to a particular activity, as is the case with a visit to the doctor's office, it is sometimes called a **script**.

Many schemas and scripts are unique to particular cultures. As an illustration, try the next exercise.

Experiencing FIRSTHAND ·The War of the Ghosts

Read the following story *one time only*:

> One night two young men from Egulac went down to the river to hunt seals, and while they were there it became foggy and calm. Then they heard war-cries, and they thought, "Maybe this is a war-party." They escaped to the shore, and hid behind a log. Now canoes came up, and they heard the noise of paddles, and saw one canoe coming up to them. There were five men in the canoe, and they said:
>
> "What do you think? We wish to take you along. We are going up the river to make war on the people."
>
> One of the young men said: "I have no arrows."
>
> "Arrows are in the canoe," they said.

■ What is a typical script for a trip to the grocery store? to the movies? to a fast-food restaurant?

■ **schema** Organized body of knowledge about a specific topic.

■ **script** Schema that involves a predictable sequence of events related to a common activity.

---

[1] Different theorists have somewhat different conceptions of the term *schema* (and many can be frustratingly vague in their use of the term). Some theorists use the term as a rough equivalent to the term *concept*. Others think of a schema as being a larger body of knowledge that may involve several concepts; this is the meaning I use here.

"I will not go along. I might be killed. My relatives do not know where I have gone. But you," he said, turning to the other, "may go with them."

So one of the young men went, but the other returned home.

And the warriors went on up the river to a town on the other side of Kalama. The people came down to the water, and they began to fight, and many were killed. But presently the young man heard one of the warriors say, "Quick, let us go home: that Indian has been hit." Now he thought: "Oh, they are ghosts." He did not feel sick, but they said he had been shot.

So the canoes went back to Egulac, and the young man went ashore to his house, and made a fire. And he told everybody and said, "Behold I accompanied the ghosts, and we went to fight. Many of our fellows were killed, and many of those who attacked us were killed. They said I was hit, and I did not feel sick."

He told it all, and then he became quiet. When the sun rose he fell down. Something black came out of his mouth. His face became contorted. The people jumped up and cried.

He was dead. (Bartlett, 1932, p. 65)

Now cover the story, and write down as much of it as you can remember.

· · · · · · ·

Compare your own rendition of the story with the original. What differences do you notice? Your version is almost certainly the shorter of the two, and you probably left out a number of details. But did you also find yourself distorting certain parts of the story so that it made more sense to you?

A Native American ghost story, "The War of the Ghosts" is probably not totally consistent with the schemas and scripts you've learned if you were raised in another culture. In an early study of long-term memory (Bartlett, 1932), students at England's Cambridge University were asked to read the story twice and then to recall it at various times later on. The students' recollections of the story often included additions and distortions that made the story more consistent with English culture. For example, people in England rarely go "to the river to hunt seals" because seals are saltwater animals and most rivers have fresh water. Students might therefore say that the men went to the river to *fish*. Similarly, the ghostly element of the story did not fit comfortably with the religious beliefs of most Cambridge students and so was often modified. For example, one student was asked to recall the story six months after he had read it; notice how the version he remembers leaves out many of the story's more puzzling aspects (puzzling, at least, from the perspective of the student):

Four men came down to the water. They were told to get into a boat and to take arms with them. They inquired, "What arms?" and were answered "Arms for battle." When they came to the battle-field they heard a great noise and shouting, and a voice said: "The black man is dead." And he was brought to the place where they were, and laid on the ground. And he foamed at the mouth. (Bartlett, 1932, pp. 71–72)

Students from diverse cultural backgrounds typically come to school with somewhat different schemas and scripts (Lipson, 1983; R. E. Reynolds et al., 1982; Steffensen, Joag-Dev, & Anderson, 1979). As a result, they may interpret the same classroom materials or activities differently, and in some cases they may have trouble making sense of a particular lesson or reading assignment. As teachers, we need to find out whether students have the appropriate schemas and scripts to understand the subject matter we are teaching. When our students *don't* have such knowledge, we may sometimes need to back up and help them develop it before we forge full-steam ahead with new material.

Theories

Experiencing FIRSTHAND ·Coffeepots and Raccoons

Consider each of the following situations:

1. People took the coffeepot shown in drawing A. They removed the handle, sealed the top, took off the top knob, sealed the opening to the spout, and removed the spout. They also sliced off the base and attached a flat piece of metal. They attached a little stick, cut a

A

window in it, and filled the metal container with birdseed. When they were done, it looked like drawing B.

After these changes, was this a coffeepot or a bird feeder?

2. Doctors took the raccoon shown in drawing C and shaved away some of its fur. They dyed what was left black. Then they bleached a single stripe all white down the center of the animal's back. Then, with surgery, they put in its body a sac of super smelly odor, just as a skunk has.

    After they were all done, the animal looked like drawing D. After the operation, was this a skunk or a raccoon?

Both scenarios based on Keil, 1989, p. 184.

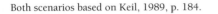

Chances are, you concluded that the coffeepot had been transformed into a bird feeder but that the raccoon was still a raccoon despite its cosmetic makeover and major surgery; even fourth graders come to these conclusions (Keil, 1986, 1989). Now how is it possible that the coffeepot could be made into something entirely different, whereas the raccoon could not?

Long before they start school, children begin to construct general belief systems—**theories**—about how the world operates (Keil, 1989, 1994; Kuhn, 2001b; Wellman & Gelman, 1998). These theories include many concepts and the relationships (e.g., correlational and cause-effect relations) among them. For example, even children as young as 8 or 9 seem to make a basic distinction between human-made objects (e.g., coffeepots, bird feeders) and biological entities (e.g., raccoons, skunks). Furthermore, they seem to conceptualize the two categories in fundamentally different ways: Human-made objects are defined largely by the *functions* they serve (e.g., keeping coffee warm, feeding birds), whereas biological entities are defined primarily by their origins (e.g., the parents who brought them into being, their DNA). Thus, when a coffeepot begins to hold birdseed rather than coffee, it becomes a bird feeder because its function has changed. But when a raccoon is cosmetically and surgically altered to look and smell like a skunk, it still has raccoon parents and raccoon DNA and so cannot possibly *be* a skunk (Keil, 1987, 1989). Thinking along similar lines, even preschoolers will tell you that you can't change a yellow finch into a bluebird by giving it a coat of blue paint or dressing it in a "bluebird" costume (Keil, 1989).

Students' theories about the world seem to guide them as they identify potential defining features of the concepts they are learning (Keil, 1987). For example, if you were trying to learn what a *horse* is, knowing that it's an animal would lead you to conclude that its location (in a stable, a pasture, a shopping mall, or whatever) is irrelevant. In contrast, if you were trying to learn what the *equator* is, knowing that it's something on a map of the world should lead you to suspect that location is of the utmost importance.

By the time children reach school age, they have developed some preliminary theories about their physical, biological, social, and mental worlds; for instance, recall our discussion of *theory of mind* in Chapter 3 (Delval, 1994; Hofer, 2001; Wellman & Gelman, 1998). Not only do such theories facilitate concept learning, they also help children organize and make sense of personal experiences, classroom subject matter, and other new information (Reiner, Slotta, Chi, & Resnick, 2000; Wellman & Gelman, 1998). Yet children's early theories typically evolve with little or no guidance from other, more knowledgeable individuals—hence, they are often called **naive theories**—and so often include erroneous beliefs, or **misconceptions** (e.g., Vosniadou, 2003). We now look at the origins and effects of misconceptions.

WHEN KNOWLEDGE CONSTRUCTION GOES AWRY: ORIGINS AND EFFECTS OF MISCONCEPTIONS

When learners construct their own understandings, there is, of course, no guarantee that they will construct accurate ones. For example, recall how, in the opening case study, Rita thinks that

■ **theory** Integrated set of concepts and principles developed to explain a particular phenomenon.

■ **naive theory** Early (and possibly inaccurate) theory developed by a child who has limited knowledge about the phenomenon involved.

■ **misconception** Belief inconsistent with commonly accepted scientific explanations.

One day I wondered, "Why is the world round?" So I went to my Dad to ask him why the world was round. He said, "Well, the world used to be flat, but a long time ago some space rangers accidentally threw a gigantic bomb at the world and it got inside. That's why the world is round." I said, " Well I don't really understand, but I'll tell Mom." So that's just what I did. I told Mom what Dad said, about how the world was round. Mom said, "What Dad said was wrong. The real story is that more than a hundred years ago your greatest greatest great great great greatest great grandfather said, "I'm tired of the world being flat, you can just walk right off into nowhere." So he decided to change the world to round.

He stole a changing spell from the wizard of winter. Then he threw the bottle so high that it touched the heavens and broke and the spell smeared everywhere. That's why the world is round. I still didn't understand. The next day I asked my teacher. She said "No, no, no. Your parents are absolutely wrong. The world was round right from the start." After school I told my mom and dad about the world being round. They said, "I know. We were just fooling around. You don't need to worry anymore." So boys and girls, that is how come the world is round.

Many 7-year-olds have the misconception that the world is flat or perhaps round in the same way as a pancake. In this story, however, 7-year-old Charlotte shows she understands that the world is spherical; for instance, her father gets tired of a world from which "you can just walk right off into nowhere."

the British wanted to go to China to get furs and that they moved to the Upper Peninsula after the English arrived. And consider how 7-year-old Rob thinks mountains are formed:

Interviewer:	How were the mountains made?
Rob:	Some dirt was taken from outside and it was put on the mountain and then mountains were made with it.
Interviewer:	Who did that?
Rob:	It takes a lot of men to make mountains, there must have been at least four. They gave them the dirt and then they made themselves all alone.
Interviewer:	But if they wanted to make another mountain?
Rob:	They pull one mountain down and then they could make a prettier one. (dialogue from Piaget, 1929, p. 348)

Construction workers and professional landscapers apparently play a major role in Rob's personal theory about the physical world.

Research tells us that children and adolescents have a variety of misconceptions about the world around them. Table 7.1 lists some common ones that researchers have observed at various grade levels. Its focus is on students' understandings of their physical, biological, and social worlds. (We'll consider the rightmost column of the table, "Suggested Strategies," a bit later.) Students are also likely to have misconceptions about psychological phenomena—for instance, about the nature of thinking and learning. We saw one example in Chapter 2: Children in the elementary grades tend to overestimate how much they can reasonably remember. We'll encounter additional examples in our discussion of epistemological beliefs in Chapter 8.

Students' misconceptions probably have a variety of sources. In many instances they arise out of students' own well-intended efforts to make sense of what they see (Vosniadou, 2003). Consider this teacher's anecdote about a young boy's interpretation of evaporating water:

Wesley and I had become friends over a forlorn empty fish tank. It *did* contain big rocks and enough water to cover them. He had recounted to me that they had to put water in the tank almost every week, and I had asked him where he thought that water went. Wesley had answered, "Into the rocks." (Hawkins, 1997, p. 337)

Like Wesley, students sometimes draw erroneous conclusions from how things *appear* to be (diSessa, 1996; Duit, 1991; Reiner et al., 2000). For instance, they may occasionally infer incorrect cause-effect relationships between two objects or events simply because the two things occur at the same time (Keil, 1991; Kuhn, 2001b).

Society and culture may foster misconceptions as well. Common expressions in language sometimes misrepresent the true nature of physical events (Duit, 1991; Mintzes, Trowbridge, Arnaudin, & Wandersee, 1991). For instance, when we talk about the sun "rising" and "setting," children may easily conclude that the sun revolves around the earth, rather than vice versa. Fairy tales and television cartoon programs may play a role in promoting misconceptions (Glynn, Yeany, & Britton, 1991); as an example, think of cartoon bad guys who run off a cliff and remain suspended in air until they realize there's nothing holding them up. Unfortunately, students may also acquire erroneous ideas from other people, including, in some instances, teachers and textbook authors (Begg, Anas, & Farinacci, 1992; Duit, 1991).

Regardless of their origins, students' existing misconceptions can wreak havoc on new learning (Kuhn, 2001b; Reiner et al., 2000; K. J. Roth & Anderson, 1988). Thanks to the processes of meaningful learning and elaboration—processes that usually facilitate learning—students may change or distort new information to fit their existing misbeliefs. As a result, they can spend a great deal of time learning the wrong thing! Consider the case of Barry, an eleventh grader whose physics class was studying the idea that an object's mass and weight do *not* affect the speed at which it falls. Students were asked to design and build an egg container that would keep an egg from breaking when dropped from a third-floor window. The students were told that on the day of the egg drop, they would record the time it took for the eggs to reach the ground. Convinced that heavier objects fall faster, Barry added several nails to his egg's container. Yet when he dropped it, classmates timed its fall at 1.49 seconds, a time very similar to that for other students' lighter egg containers. Barry explained this result to his teacher (and presumably to himself as well) by rationalizing that "the people weren't timing real good" (Hynd, 1998a, p. 34).

TABLE 7.1

D E V E L O P M E N T A L   T R E N D S

Common Misunderstandings at Different Grade Levels

GRADE LEVEL	EXAMPLES OF AGE-TYPICAL BELIEFS	SUGGESTED STRATEGIES[a]
K–2	• Undergeneralization of the concept *animal* (e.g., using the term only for mammals) • Belief that natural features (e.g., lakes, mountains) are manmade and that natural objects exist for a particular purpose (e.g., rocks are pointy so that animals can scratch themselves) • Belief that the world is flat or that it's both round and flat (i.e., pancake-shaped) • Belief that features on maps depict physical entities (e.g., lines separating states and countries are painted on the earth)	• Use the word *animal* in diverse contexts (e.g., use it in reference to fish or insects). • Describe physical causes of natural phenomenon in a simple, concrete manner (e.g., "lakes form when a lot of rain falls in a low part of the ground"). • Use globes to find various countries; talk about the earth as being a ball rather than a pancake. • Provide practice in using maps of the local neighborhood and community, showing how some map features are different from physical reality.
3–5	• Belief that space has an absolute "up" and "down"; people standing at the South Pole will fall off the earth • Belief that plants "eat" soil and fertilizer in much the same way that people eat meat and vegetables • Belief that in vision, something travels from the eye (rather than light traveling *to* the eye) • Belief that the problem of poverty can be easily solved by giving poor people a small amount of money	• Explain that gravity draws people to the center of the earth; show videos of people living in the southern hemisphere. • Explore the process of photosynthesis, contrasting the idea of plants making their own food with that of plants simply absorbing food as people do. • Ask students to draw a line depicting the direction that light travels when a person sees an object (see the case study "In the Eye of the Beholder" at the end of Chapter 2); have them explain why they drew the line in the direction they did. • Have students explore multiple reasons why some people are so poor; brainstorm more enduring solutions to poverty.
6–8	• Failure to identify squares as being rectangles • Belief that more digits always means a larger number (e.g., 2.34 > 2.8) • Assumption that in algebraic equations, $(x + y)^2 = x^2 + y^2$; $\sqrt{a + b} = \sqrt{a} + \sqrt{b}$; and the like	• Explore hierarchical relationships among geometric figures (e.g., squares are rectangles, rectangles are parallelograms, parallelograms are polygons). • Provide practice with more-less relationships among decimals and fractions; embed some practice within the context of hands-on problems involving real objects. • Study the appropriate order of calculations in an algebraic expression; contrast correct results with the results one might obtain when following an inappropriate sequence.
9–12	• Belief that any moving object has a force acting on it (force is actually needed only to *change* the direction or speed of movement) • Belief that the process of division always leads to a smaller number—for instance, that 5 ÷ 0.65 yields an answer less than 5 (actual solution is about 7.69) • Beliefs that Christopher Columbus was Spanish, was the first person to assert that the world was round, and landed on the mainland of North America	• Introduce the concept of *inertia*; show how it explains movement of planets and spaceships in outer space; explore explanations for apparent violations of this concept on the earth (e.g., friction slows an object's speed as it travels along a surface). • Provide practice with mathematical problems that yield counterintuitive results; ask students to explain why these results are correct. • When describing historical events, explicitly contrast students' beliefs with more accurate information (e.g., Columbus was Italian and landed on islands in the Caribbean; Aristotle suggested that the world was round more than 1,500 years before Columbus's birth).

[a] These strategies merely provide a starting point. Some misconceptions are such an integral part of students' belief systems that they may require multiple strategies over a lengthy period. (See the section "The Challenge of Conceptual Change.")

Sources: Behr & Harel, 1988; S. Carey, 1985; Delval, 1994; diSessa, 1996; J. F. Eaton, Anderson, & Smith, 1984; Gardner, Torff, & Hatch, 1996; Hynd, 2003; Kelemen, 1999; Liben & Downs, 1989; Piaget, 1929; K. J. Roth & Anderson, 1988; Sneider & Pulos, 1983; Tirosh & Graeber, 1990; Vosniadou, 1994; P. S. Wilson, 1988.

As teachers, our job is twofold: Not only must we help students construct accurate understandings of the world around them, but we must also encourage them to discard any erroneous beliefs they have previously constructed. As we consider how to promote knowledge construction and conceptual change in the next two sections, we'll identify strategies for accomplishing both of these goals.

PROMOTING EFFECTIVE KNOWLEDGE CONSTRUCTION

Knowing that learning is a constructive process does not necessarily tell us how we can most effectively promote such learning (K. R. Harris & Alexander, 1998; Hirsch, 1996; Nuthall, 1996). In fact, cognitive psychologists believe there are many ways to help students construct a richer and more sophisticated knowledge base. A few possibilities are (a) providing opportunities for experimentation, (b) presenting the ideas of others, (c) emphasizing conceptual understanding, (d) promoting dialogue, (e) using authentic activities, and (f) creating a community of learners. These strategies are illustrated in the Into the Classroom feature "Promoting Knowledge Construction." Let's look at each one more closely.

Providing Opportunities for Experimentation

■ Observe an in-class demonstration in the "Charles's Law" clip on Video CD 2.

By interacting and experimenting with the objects around them, students can discover some characteristics and principles of the world firsthand (e.g., Fosnot, 1996). As teachers, we can create numerous hands-on opportunities for students to touch, manipulate, modify, combine, and recombine concrete objects. For example, at the elementary school level, we might use beads or pennies to help students discover basic addition and subtraction facts, or we might use two balls of clay and a scale to promote the realization that an object's weight remains the same despite changes in its shape (Piaget's notion of *conservation*). At the secondary level, such activities as science labs, computer simulations, and in-class demonstrations can also help students construct knowledge about the world around them (e.g., see the demonstration in the "Charles's Law" clip on Video CD 2). Some kinds of opportunities for exploration and experimentation are more effective than others, as we'll find out in our discussion of *discovery learning* in Chapter 13.

Teachers often teach students clearly delineated, step-by-step procedures for accomplishing certain tasks. Yet on some occasions it might be more helpful to let students develop such procedures *on their own* through experimentation. For example, when teaching cooking, it may sometimes be more productive to cast aside recipes and instead let students try different combinations and proportions of ingredients (Hatano & Inagaki, 1993). As another example, let's consider a

---

INTO THE CLASSROOM

Promoting Knowledge Construction

 Provide opportunities for experimentation.

A teacher has students experiment with clay and water to discover the principle that a certain quantity of a solid displaces the same amount of water regardless of the shape of the solid.

 Expose students to others' interpretations of the world.

A teacher has students read poetry from a variety of countries and cultures.

 Focus on an in-depth understanding of a few key ideas instead of covering many topics superficially.

A teacher tells his class, "As we study the geography of South America, we aren't going to worry about memorizing a lot of place names. Instead, we will look at how topography and climate have influenced the economic and cultural development of different regions of the continent."

 Create opportunities for small-group or whole-class discussions in which students can freely exchange their views.

A teacher asks students to speculate on how the Japanese people must have felt after the atomic bomb was dropped over Hiroshima.

 Include authentic activities in the curriculum.

A social studies teacher asks students to develop a "Student Bill of Rights" that reflects the typical views and preferences of the school's student body. To create this document, students must survey their peers throughout the school and then summarize their data using percentages and graphs (Barab & Landa, 1997).

 Have students work in groups to research certain topics and then teach one another what they have learned.

In a unit on zoology, different groups of students "major" in different classes of vertebrates (e.g., mollusks, segmented worms, sponges) and then prepare illustrated "textbooks" to share with classmates in other groups.

study in which kindergarten students had one of two different experiences raising animals (Hatano & Inagaki, 1993). Some students had pet rabbits in their classrooms; they took turns feeding and taking care of the rabbits by using procedures their teacher had carefully prescribed for them. Other students were raising goldfish at home; these students had to make their own decisions about how best to care for their pets and, in doing so, could experiment with feeding schedules, water purity, and other variables that might affect the fish's welfare. The children who raised the goldfish appeared to develop a better understanding of animals in general—for example, learning that baby animals grow bigger over time—and were able to apply what they learned from their own pets to other species. One goldfish owner, when asked whether one could keep a baby frog the same size forever, said, "No, we can't, because the frog will grow bigger as the goldfish grew bigger. My goldfish were small before, but now they are big" (Hatano & Inagaki, 1993, p. 121).

Presenting the Ideas of Others

As noted earlier, knowledge is constructed not only by people working independently but also by people working together over the course of years or centuries to make sense of complex phenomena. Although it may sometimes be beneficial to have students discover basic principles for themselves (as the goldfish owners did), we should also provide opportunities for them to hear and read about the ideas of others—the concepts, principles, theories, and so on, that society has developed to explain both the physical and psychological aspects of human experience (R. Driver, 1995; Vygotsky, 1962). Students are most likely to construct a productive view of the world when they have the benefit of experiencing the world firsthand *and* the benefit of learning how those before them have interpreted human experience.

We needn't present others' ideas in a didactic, this-is-how-it-is manner, however. For instance, we might apply Vygotsky's notion that in informal discussions with children, we can help them impose meaning on the objects and events around them by attaching labels, identifying underlying principles, or imposing certain interpretations (Eacott, 1999; Feuerstein et al., 1991; John-Steiner & Mahn, 1996). Teacher Katherine Maria took this approach in a series of conversations with 6½-year-old Jennifer about the nature of gravity. Katherine had been trying to help Jennifer understand that people and objects in the southern hemisphere don't fall off the earth just because, from the standpoint of someone looking at a globe, they are located on the earth's "bottom" side. Katherine reported the following discussion between herself (K) and Jennifer (J) to show the progress Jennifer was making in her understanding of gravity:

Students can more effectively construct meaningful interpretations of events when they examine how others have interpreted similar events. For example, by reading classic works of literature, they view daily life from the perspectives of numerous authors.

> I used [an] inflatable globe and a figure stuck to the lower part of South America to explain to Jennifer that I had visited this place and had not fallen off the earth. We then had [this] discussion . . . :
>
> K: What would happen if there was a hole in the earth and this person (the figure stuck to South America) dropped a ball through it?
> J: People might think that if you dropped a rock into the hole it might go back out.
> K: Why would they think that?
> J: Because it's at the bottom of the earth. . . . They think that maybe the gravity did that.
> K: But what does gravity pull you toward?
> J: Down.
> K: (sticking the figure on the top of the inflatable globe) : If you're standing here, where is down?
>
> Jennifer points her finger in a downward direction. I move the figure to the South Pole.
>
> K: But suppose this was you. If you were here, where is down? Jennifer points to a spot in the middle of the globe.
> K: Yeah, so it's pulling toward the?
> J: Middle
> K: Right. So where would the rock end up then?
> J: In the middle. (Maria, 1998, p. 13)

Emphasizing Conceptual Understanding

Let's look again at the chapter's opening case study. Rita has acquired a few miscellaneous facts in her history lessons, but she clearly has no idea about how those facts are interconnected. Unfortunately, such learning of isolated facts, without any sense of how they fit together, is all

■ Unfortunately, the researchers in the animal-raising study didn't eliminate other possible explanations for their results. Besides teacher-prescribed versus self-chosen procedures, what other differences between the groups might account for the study's results?

too common at both the elementary and secondary grade levels (J. Hiebert & Lefevre, 1986; Hollon, Roth, & Anderson, 1991; Lesgold, 2001; McRobbie & Tobin, 1995; Paxton, 1999).

Without a doubt, students benefit more from acquiring facts, concepts, and ideas in an integrated, interrelated, and meaningful fashion; in other words, they benefit from developing a **conceptual understanding** of academic subject matter (L. M. Anderson, 1993; Bédard & Chi, 1992; J. J. White & Rumsey, 1994). For example, rather than simply memorize basic mathematical computation procedures, students should learn how those procedures reflect underlying principles of mathematics. Rather than learn historical facts as a list of unrelated people, places, and dates, students should place those facts within the context of major social and religious trends, migration patterns, economic considerations, human personality characteristics, and so on.

Construction of an integrated understanding of any complex topic will inevitably take time. Accordingly, many educators advocate the principle, "Less is more": *Less* material studied thoroughly (rather than superficially) is learned *more* completely and with greater understanding (Brophy & Alleman, 1992; Kyle & Shymansky, 1989; Marshall, 1992; Sizer, 1992).

Following are several ways in which we might help students develop a conceptual understanding of classroom subject matter:

- Organize units around a few core ideas and themes, always relating specific content back to this core.
- Explore each topic in depth—for example, by considering many examples, examining cause-effect relationships, and discovering how specific details relate to more general principles.
- Explain how new ideas relate to students' own experiences and to things they have previously learned.
- Show students—through the things we say, the assignments we give, and the criteria we use to evaluate learning—that conceptual understanding of classroom subject matter is far more important than knowledge of isolated facts.
- Ask students to teach what they have learned to others. This task encourages them to focus on and pull together main ideas in a way that makes sense. (L. M. Anderson, 1993; Brophy & Alleman, 1992; Hatano & Inagaki, 1993; Prawat, 1993; VanSledright & Brophy, 1992; J. J. White & Rumsey, 1994)

■ **conceptual understanding**
Knowledge acquired in an integrated and meaningful fashion.

The last two of these suggestions—emphasizing conceptual understanding in assignments and evaluation criteria, and asking students to teach what they have learned to others—are reflected in the assignment described in the following exercise.

Interpreting Student Artifacts and Behaviors

What Is Multiplication?

A third-grade teacher gives her class this assignment:

Imagine that a representative from a distant planet has just landed in your backyard. He knows how to count and add but does not know anything about multiplication. Explain how you might teach him the *concept* of multiplication. Then describe a strategy you might teach him to remember a set of multiplication facts.

Eight-year-old Tony writes the response shown in this exercise. As you read it, consider

■ Whether Tony understands the nature of multiplication
■ Whether Tony's "circles and dots" strategy will yield correct solutions to multiplication problems

You may need to read Tony's response two or three times to determine his meaning; getting a handle on students' reasoning often takes effort and persistence on a teacher's part.

Multiplication is sorta like addition. You can answer the question by using dots. to represent the number of sets and how many dots are in each set.

When you multiply you can come up with the answer by making as many sets as the first number says. And then putt the second number of dots inside each set next you count how many dots ther are altogether and that is called the answer.

First you look at the first number of the problem and make that number of sets (circles).①

①. 2 × 2 =   Then you take the second number and put that number of dots in each set.② Then count that number of dots in the circles and that is your answer.

When Tony says that multiplication is "sorta" like addition, we know he has at least some understanding of the process. His second sentence is confusing, and so we must read further. He soon explains that we should create as many circles (representing "sets") as the first number in a multiplication problem indicates. Inside each circle, we should put as many dots as the second number indicates. Using his example, we would depict the problem 2×2 as follows:

If we count all the dots, we get a correct answer of 4. Unfortunately, our picture might illustrate how 2 and 2 could be *added* rather than multiplied, so let's use his strategy with another problem, say 3×4. We make 3 circles and put 4 dots in each one, like so:

This time there is no mistaking that Tony's strategy works for multiplication but not for addition ($3 \times 4 = 12$, but $3 + 4 = 7$).

As it turns out, Tony is describing the strategy his teacher has taught the class for figuring out multiplication problems. Does he truly understand the nature of multiplication? We probably need to get more information to find out for sure. For one thing, we might ask Tony to apply his strategy to a problem with larger numbers (e.g., 3×4, 7×9). Even better, we might ask him to devise a *new* strategy for solving multiplication problems. Such a task might be difficult for him to do on his own but quite possible if he exchanges ideas with his peers. Accordingly, our next strategy involves having students dialogue about complex tasks and topics.

Promoting Dialogue

We have already identified numerous advantages to having students talk with one another about classroom topics. And in fact, students *do* seem to remember new ideas and experiences more effectively and accurately when they talk about these things with others (Hacker, 1998b; Schank & Abelson, 1995; Tessler & Nelson, 1994; Wasik, Karweit, Burns, & Brodsky, 1998). Accordingly, many theorists recommend that classroom dialogues be a regular feature of classroom instruction (J. Hiebert et al., 1997; Marshall, 1992; Paris & Cunningham, 1996; Sosniak & Stodolsky, 1994). For example, in the "Scarlet Letter" clip on Video CD 2, you can see how a high school English teacher encourages students to construct a better understanding of the character Arthur Dimmesdale in Nathaniel Hawthorne's *The Scarlet Letter*. After reading a paragraph describing Dimmesdale, she tells her students:

> In your logs, jot down some of the important characteristics of that description. What's the diction that strikes you as being essential to understanding Dimmesdale's character? How do you see him? If you were going to draw a portrait of him, what would you make sure he had? Just write some things, or draw a picture if you'd like.

She then solicits diverse opinions ("well-dressed," "unsure of himself," "sweating really bad," "a nerd-type guy") that can help students construct a complex, multifaceted understanding of Dimmesdale.

As another example of how students might work together to construct meaning, let's look in on Ms. Lombard's fourth-grade class, which has been studying fractions. Ms. Lombard has never taught her students how to divide a number by a fraction. Nevertheless, she gives them the following problem, which can be solved by dividing 20 by ¾:[2]

> Mom makes small apple tarts, using three-quarters of an apple for each small tart. She has 20 apples. How many small apple tarts can she make? (J. Hiebert et al., 1997, p. 118)

Ms. Lombard asks the students to work in small groups to figure out how they might solve the problem. One group of four girls—Jeanette, Liz, Kerri, and Nina—has been working on the

■ Observe a teacher encourage knowledge construction in the "Scarlet Letter" clip on Video CD 2.

---

[2] In case your memory of how to divide by a fraction is rusty, you can approach the problem $20 \div \frac{3}{4}$ by inverting the fraction and multiplying, like so: $20 \times \frac{4}{3} = \frac{80}{3} = 26\frac{2}{3}$. Thus, Mom can make 26 tarts and have enough apple to make two-thirds of another tart. If she has two-thirds of the three-fourths of an apple she needs to make another whole tart, then she has half an apple left over ($\frac{2}{3} \times \frac{3}{4} = \frac{1}{2}$).

problem for some time and so far has arrived at such answers as 15, 38, and 23. We join them midway through their discussion, when they've already agreed that they can use three-fourths of each apple to make a total of 20 tarts:

Jeanette: In each apple there is a quarter left. In each apple there is a quarter left, so you've used, you've made twenty tarts already and you've got a quarter of twenty see—

Liz: So you've got twenty quarters *left.*

Jeanette: Yes, . . . and twenty quarters is equal to five apples, . . . so five apples divided by—

Liz: Six, seven, eight.

Jeanette: But three-quarters equals three.

Kerri: But she can't make only three apple tarts!

Jeanette: No, you've still got twenty.

Liz: But you've got twenty quarters, if you've got twenty quarters you might be right.

Jeanette: I'll show you.

Liz: No, I've drawn them all here.

Kerri: How many quarters have you got? Twenty?

Liz: Yes, one quarter makes five apples and out of five apples she can make five tarts which will make that twenty-five tarts and then she will have, wait, one, two, three, four, five quarters, she'll have one, two, three, four, five quarters. . . .

Nina: I've got a better . . .

Kerri: Yes?

Liz: Twenty-six quarters and a remainder of one quarter left. (J. Hiebert et al., 1997, p. 121)

The discussion and occasional disagreements continue, and the girls eventually arrive at the correct answer: Mom can make 26 tarts and then will have half an apple left over.

As the preceding conversation illustrates, classroom dialogues can help students achieve a conceptual understanding of classroom subject matter—for instance, a conceptual understanding of what it means to divide by a fraction (J. Hiebert et al., 1997; Lampert, Rittenhouse, & Crumbaugh, 1996). Yet classroom dialogues have an important benefit for teachers as well: By carefully monitoring students' comments and questions, we can identify and address any misconceptions that might interfere with their ability to acquire further knowledge and skills (Presseisen & Beyer, 1994; Sosniak & Stodolsky, 1994).

■ Chapter 13 describes strategies for promoting student dialogue through class discussion, reciprocal teaching, computer technology, and cooperative learning.

Using Authentic Activities

In my description of Vygotsky's theory in Chapter 2, I mentioned that children typically learn a great deal by interacting with adults and other knowledgeable individuals within the context of everyday cultural activities. Picking up on this idea, many contemporary cognitive theorists suggest that students can construct a more useful, productive, and integrated knowledge base if they learn classroom subject matter within the context of **authentic activities**, activities similar to those they might encounter in the outside world. For example, rather than have students practice writing skills through short, artificial writing exercises, we might ask them to write stories or essays or to send letters to real people (e.g., see Figure 7.5). Students' writing improves in both quality and quantity when they engage in such authentic writing tasks (E. H. Hiebert & Fisher, 1992). Likewise, rather than have students develop map interpretation skills (e.g., interpreting symbols, scale, and latitude and longitude) by answering a series of unrelated questions in a workbook, we might instead have them construct their own maps, asking them to choose appropriate symbols and scale and to integrate information about latitude and longitude.

FIGURE 7.5 One "authentic" way to work on writing skills is to write letters to real people. For an assignment in her fourth-grade class, 9-year-old Cindy wrote a letter to her town's city council.

Dear Bexley City Council,
   I suggest that a law should be passed that say littering is not allowed. The law would help keep Bexley looking nice.
   Everyday when I go outside to walk to school or to a friend's house, I find at least two pieces of litter someone else put in our yard.
   No one in my family ever litters. I think it is because we feel so strongly about protecting the environment. This why I am writing this letter.
   I always see signs on the lamp posts saying, "Keep Bexley Beautiful," and I think this would be the first step to keep Bexley beautiful.
   I know I am only a fourth grade student, but I would like you to consider my idea. Thank you for your time.

                          Sincerely,
                          Cindy M.

■ **authentic activity** Classroom activity similar to one students are apt to encounter in the outside world.

Although students may sometimes feel a bit overwhelmed by the complexity of such map-making activities, they are apt to gain a more complete understanding of how to use and interpret maps effectively than do students who simply engage in workbook exercises (Gregg & Leinhardt, 1994).

Authentic activities can be identified for virtually any area of the curriculum. For example, we might ask students to

- Give an oral report
- Write an editorial
- Participate in a debate
- Find information in the library
- Conduct an experiment
- Graph data
- Construct a chart or model
- Create and distribute a class newsletter
- Converse in a foreign language

- Play in an athletic event
- Complete an art project
- Perform in a concert
- Tutor a classmate
- Make a videotape
- Perform a workplace routine
- Develop classroom Web pages to showcase special projects

In many cases these activities may require considerable support (scaffolding) to ensure that students carry them out successfully. As such, they may remind you of the *guided participation* I described in Chapter 2.

By placing classroom activities in real-world contexts, we help students discover the reasons why they are learning academic subject matter. We also increase the likelihood that, later on, they will actually use the information and skills we have taught them (A. Collins et al., 1989; De Corte et al., 1996). And, of course, we gain insights into students' knowledge and skills, as the following exercise reveals.

■ Authentic activities may be especially important for students at risk (see Chapter 12).

Interpreting Student Artifacts and Behaviors

Mapping the Neighborhood

For an assignment in her middle school social studies class, 12-year-old Mary Lynn constructed this map of the area between her home and school. As you look at the map, keep in mind that Mary Lynn has never actually seen her neighborhood from the air. Now consider

- ■ What cognitive abilities the map-making task requires
- ■ What things Mary Lynn has learned about maps and map making

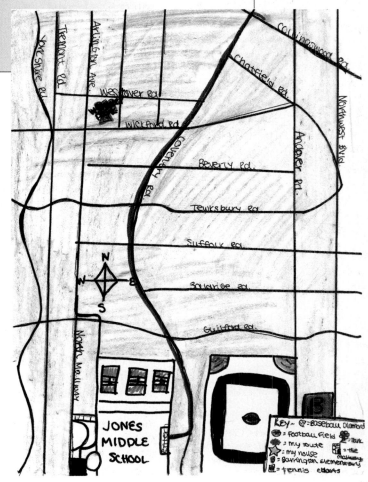

To depict her neighborhood with a map, Mary Lynn must represent concrete physical features (e.g., roads, buildings, tennis courts) with abstract symbols. She must also mentally translate the spatial arrangement she sees on the ground into a bird's-eye view. And while "shrinking" her neighborhood so that it fits on a single page, she must preserve relative distances among features (that is, she must create the map to scale). Judging from her completed map, Mary Lynn is able to do all of these things. Furthermore, Mary Lynn has learned several conventions used in map making; for instance, she labels streets and the school building, provides a key to explain symbols she's used, and includes a compass rose to indicate cardinal directions (north, east, etc.).

Educators are becoming increasingly convinced of the effectiveness of authentic activities for promoting learning. We will revisit their importance when we discuss *transfer* in Chapter 8, *values* in Chapter 12, and *instructional strategies* in Chapter 13, and we will consider a related topic, *authentic assessment*, in Chapter 15.

Creating a Community of Learners

With the benefits of dialogue and other forms of student interaction in mind, and with the goal of promoting the social construction of meaning, some psychologists and educators suggest that we create a **community of learners**, a classroom in which we and students consistently work to help one another learn (A. L. Brown & Campione, 1994; Prawat, 1992; Rogoff, Matusov, & White, 1996). A classroom that operates as a community of learners is likely to have characteristics such as the following:

- All students are active participants in classroom activities.
- Discussion and collaboration among two or more students are common occurrences and play a key role in learning.
- Diversity in students' interests and rates of progress is expected and respected.
- Students and teacher coordinate their efforts at helping one another learn; no one has exclusive responsibility for teaching others.
- Everyone is a potential resource for the others; different individuals are likely to serve as resources on different occasions, depending on the topics and tasks at hand. (In some cases students may "major" in a particular topic and become local "experts" on it.)
- The teacher provides some guidance and direction for classroom activities, but students may also contribute to such guidance and direction.
- Students regularly critique one another's work.
- The process of learning is emphasized as much as, and sometimes more than, the finished product. (A. L. Brown & Campione, 1994, 1996; Campione, Shapiro, & Brown, 1995; Rogoff, 1994; Rogoff et al., 1996)

As one example of how a community of learners might be structured (A. L. Brown & Campione, 1994), students are divided into small groups to study different subtopics falling within a general theme; for instance, subtopics for the theme *changing populations* might be *extinct, endangered, artificial, assisted,* and *urbanized.* Each group conducts research and prepares teaching materials related to its subtopic. The class then reassembles into new groups that include at least one representative from each of the previous groups; within these groups, the students teach one another the things they have learned.

Another approach is to use a computer network to promote a community of learners (Hewitt & Scardamalia, 1998). For instance, we might have all students store their classwork (short stories, essays, problem solutions, etc.) as computer files that their classmates can read and respond to. We can also create computer-based "chat rooms" in which students present questions or issues to which others respond. As an example, consider three students' online responses to another student's question, "How does heat affect solids?"; note that they use the headings "My theory" and "I need to understand" to structure their discussion:

JA: *My theory*: I think that heat makes solids burn or melt. I think that my prediction is right because I've seen solids melt and burn.

AR: *My theory*: I think that if a solid comes in contact with heat, it becomes hot. I also think it might change colour. Generally if any solid comes in contact with heat then it becomes hot. I think that the solid would become hot faster if it could conduct energy well. If an object didn't conduct energy well then it would heat up, but take a longer time than an object that conducts energy well. It might change colour because we think that if something is very hot it is white or red and sort of hot it is orange or yellow. There might be some truth to this.

AD: *My theory*: I think that it depends on how much heat there is. I also think that it depends on what sort of solid it is. For instance, the heat that might melt rubber might not melt metal. (This last sentence might be wrong, I'm just using it as an example.)

I need to understand: What makes wood burn instead of melt?

My theory: I think that it might have something to do with wood being organic, because I can't think of anything that is organic, and would melt. (dialogue from Hewitt & Scardamalia, 1998, p. 85)

Such online discussions may be especially valuable for students who are shy or for other reasons feel uncomfortable communicating with their classmates in a more public fashion (Hewitt & Scardamalia, 1998).

A community of learners incorporates several instructional strategies that we'll consider in more detail in Chapter 13, including discovery learning, class discussions, cooperative learning, and peer tutoring. It also is, in many respects, similar to the approach that scientists and other scholars take when they advance the frontiers of knowledge: They conduct individual and collaborative research, share ideas, build on one another's findings, and so on. Hence, this

■ This approach illustrates the *jigsaw technique,* described in Chapter 13.

■ The use of electronic dialogue is discussed in greater depth in the section "Technology-Based Discussions" in Chapter 13.

■ **community of learners** Class in which teacher and students actively and collaboratively work to help one another learn.

approach may help students acquire some rather sophisticated and adultlike knowledge-building skills (A. L. Brown & Campione, 1996; Hewitt & Scardamalia, 1998; Karpov & Haywood, 1998).

Researchers have not yet systematically compared the academic achievement of communities of learners to the achievement of more traditional classrooms. Case studies do indicate that classes structured as communities of learners have some positive effects, however. For one thing, these classes appear to promote fairly complex thinking processes for extended periods of time (A. L. Brown & Campione, 1994). They are also highly motivating for students; for instance, students often insist on going to school even when they are ill, and they are disappointed when summer vacation begins (Rogoff, 1994). To illustrate, one eighth-grade English teacher described her experiences with a community of learners this way:

> The classroom became . . . like a dining-room table, where people could converse easily about books and poems and ideas. I would watch my students leave the classroom carrying on animated conversations about which book was truly Robert Cormier's best, why sequels are often disappointing, which books they planned to reread or pack into their trunks for summer camp. Books became valuable currency, changing hands after careful negotiation: "Okay, you can borrow Adams's *So Long and Thanks for All the Fish* (Pocket), but you have to lend me the first two books in the Xanth series." The shelves neatly lined with class sets of books gradually gave way to a paperback library, stocked with books donated by students and their families, bonus copies from book clubs, and books I ordered with my budgeted allotment each year. (S. Moran, 1991, p. 439)

In addition to its cognitive and motivational benefits, a community of learners can foster effective peer relationships and social skills. It can also help create a *sense of community* in the classroom—a sense that we and our students have shared goals, are mutually respectful and supportive of one another's efforts, and believe that everyone makes an important contribution to classroom learning. We will look at this idea more closely in Chapter 14.

Yet we should note a couple of potential weaknesses that communities of learners, and group discussions more generally, may have (A. L. Brown & Campione, 1994; Hynd, 1998b). For one thing, what students learn will inevitably be limited to the knowledge that they themselves acquire and share with one another. Second, students may occasionally pass on their own misconceptions to their classmates. Obviously, then, when we conduct classroom discussions or structure our classrooms as communities of learners, we must carefully monitor student interactions to make sure that students ultimately acquire thorough and accurate understandings of the subject matter they are studying. If they do not, we may need to take active steps to encourage conceptual change. We look at strategies for doing so now.

THE CHALLENGE OF CONCEPTUAL CHANGE

Teachers often present new information in class with the expectation that such information will replace any erroneous beliefs that students currently have. Yet research indicates that students of all ages often hold quite stubbornly to their misconceptions, even after considerable instruction that explicitly contradicts the misconceptions (S. Carey, 1986; Chambliss, 1994; Chinn & Brewer, 1993; Shuell, 1996). Consider the following situation (described by J. F. Eaton et al., 1984):

> A class of fifth graders was about to study a unit on light and vision. A pretest revealed that most students believed incorrectly that vision occurs simply as the result of light shining on an object and making it bright. During the unit the teacher presented the correct explanation of human vision: Light must be reflected off an object *and then travel to the eye* before the object can be seen. Even though students both read and heard the correct explanation of how people see objects, most of them "learned" what they already believed: that an object can be seen as soon as light hits it. Posttest results indicated that only 24 percent of the class had learned the correct explanation. (This study is depicted in the case study "In the Eye of the Beholder" at the end of Chapter 2.)

Why are students' misconceptions often so resistant to change? Theorists have offered several possible explanations:

◎   *Students' existing beliefs affect their interpretations of new information.* Thanks to the processes of meaningful learning and elaboration—processes that usually facilitate learning—learners are apt to interpret new information in ways consistent with what they already "know" about the world. The result is that they continue to believe what they have always believed. In

As teachers, we must remember that students' misconceptions often arise out of their well-intended efforts to make sense of what they see.

general, maintaining existing perspectives, rather than considering alternative and possibly conflicting ones, is the "default" mode in human cognition (De Lisi & Golbeck, 1999).

■ Observe confirmation bias in the "Designing Experiments" clip on Video CD 2.

◎ *Most children and adolescents have a confirmation bias.* Students of all ages (even college students) tend to look for information that confirms their existing beliefs and to ignore or discredit contradictory evidence—a phenomenon known as **confirmation bias** (Hynd, 1998b; Kuhn, Amsel, & O'Loughlin, 1988; Schauble, 1990). For example, when students in a high school science lab observe results that contradict what they expected to happen, they might complain that "our equipment isn't working right" or "I can never do science anyway" (Minstrell & Stimpson, 1996). (Recall how, in the earlier anecdote about the egg-drop project, Barry insisted that his classmates "weren't timing real good" when his heavy egg container fell at the same rate as other, lighter containers.) You can see another example of confirmation bias in the "Designing Experiments" clip on Video CD 2. Even though the four seventh graders simultaneously vary both weight and length in their experiments with a pendulum—thereby making a clear-cut conclusion impossible—at least two of them incorrectly conclude that weight affects a pendulum's oscillation rate.

◎ *Students' misconceptions may be consistent with their everyday experiences.* Viable scientific theories are often fairly abstract and may seemingly contradict everyday reality (P. A. Alexander, 1997; R. Driver et al., 1994; M. C. Linn, Songer, & Eylon, 1996). For example, although the law of inertia tells us that force is needed to *start* an object in motion but not to *keep* it in motion, we know from experience that if we want to move a heavy object across the floor, we must keep pushing it until we get it where we want it (R. Driver et al., 1994).

Students often have erroneous beliefs about how the earth, sun, and moon move in relation to one another. These students are trying to get a better understanding of the solar system through computer simulations and a multimedia presentation.

◎ *Some beliefs are integrated into cohesive theories, with many interrelationships existing among various ideas.* In such circumstances, changing misconceptions involves changing an organized body of knowledge rather than a single belief (Derry, 1996; Sinatra & Pintrich, 2003a; C. L. Smith, Maclin, Grosslight, & Davis, 1997). For example, the misconception that the sun revolves around the earth may be part of a more general "earth-centered" view of things, perhaps one that includes the moon, stars, and other heavenly bodies revolving around the earth as well. In reality, of course, the moon revolves around the earth, the earth revolves around the sun, and other stars are not directly involved with the earth one way or the other. Yet the earth-centered view is a much easier one to understand and accept (on the surface, at least), and everything fits so nicely together.

◎ *Students may fail to notice an inconsistency between new information and their existing beliefs.* Sometimes this happens because students learn the new information in a rote manner, without relating it to things they already know and believe (Chambliss, 1994; Strike & Posner, 1992). In other cases it occurs because existing misconceptions take the form of *implicit knowledge*—knowledge that students are not consciously aware of (Keil & Silberstein, 1996; Strike & Posner, 1992). In either situation students do not realize that the new things they have learned contradict what they already believe, and they may continue to apply their misconceptions when interpreting new situations (Champagne, Klopfer, & Gunstone, 1982; Hynd, 2003; Luque, 2003).

◎ *Students have a personal or emotional investment in their existing beliefs.* For one reason or another, students may be especially committed to certain beliefs, perhaps insisting, "This theory is what I believe in! Nobody can make me change it!" (Mason, 2003, p. 228). In some instances their beliefs may be an integral part of their religion or culture (Hatano & Inagaki, 1996; Southerland & Sinatra, 2003). In other cases students may interpret challenges to their belief systems as threats to their overall self-esteem (Linnenbrink & Pintrich, 2003; Minstrell & Stimpson, 1996; Sherman & Cohen, 2002).

When students have few prior misunderstandings about a particular phenomenon, helping them acquire more sophisticated theories about the phenomenon is relatively easy. When they have many naive beliefs and misconceptions about a topic, however, helping them acquire more advanced understandings can be quite challenging. Not only must we help students learn new things, but we must also help them *unlearn*, or at least *inhibit*, existing misconceptions (Hynd, 2003). In other words, we must help them undergo **conceptual change**. Let's look at some strategies for doing so.

■ **confirmation bias** Tendency to seek information that confirms rather than discredits current beliefs.

■ **conceptual change** Revision of one's understanding of a topic in response to new information.

Promoting Conceptual Change   In the rightmost column of Table 7.1 on page 237, you learned strategies for addressing common misconceptions at various grade levels. These strategies are specific to the misconceptions listed in the table, and as I indicate in a footnote to the table, *multiple* strategies may be necessary to address misconceptions that are integral to students' overall theories about the world.

Table 7.2 identifies and illustrates several general principles for promoting conceptual change. The following strategies are derived from these principles:

◎   *Identify existing misconceptions before instruction begins.* As teachers, we can more easily address students' misconceptions when we know what they are (Kyle & Shymansky, 1989; Putnam, 1992; K. J. Roth & Anderson, 1988). Thus we should probably begin any new topic by assessing students' current beliefs about the topic—perhaps simply by asking a few informal questions. The following conversation illustrates the kinds of misconceptions that questioning may reveal:

■ The term *conceptual change* may or may not involve changes in specific concepts, but it invariably involves revision in how those concepts are interrelated in memory.

Adult: What is rain?
Child: It's water that falls out of a cloud when the clouds evaporate.
Adult: What do you mean, "clouds evaporate"?
Child: That means water goes up in the air and then it makes clouds and then, when it gets too heavy up there, then the water comes and they call it rain.
Adult: Does the water stay in the sky?
Child: Yes, and then it comes down when it rains. It gets too heavy.
Adult: Why does it get too heavy?
Child: 'Cause there's too much water up there.
Adult: Why does it rain?
Child: 'Cause the water gets too heavy and then it comes down.
Adult: Why doesn't the whole thing come down?
Child: Well, 'cause it comes down at little times like a salt shaker when you turn it upside down. It doesn't all come down at once 'cause there's little holes and it just comes out.
Adult: What are the little holes in the sky?
Child: Umm, holes in the clouds, letting the water out. (dialogue from Stepans, 1991, p. 94)

TABLE 7.2   PRINCIPLES/ASSUMPTIONS

Principles for Promoting Conceptual Change

PRINCIPLE	EDUCATIONAL IMPLICATION	EXAMPLE
Conceptual change is more likely when teachers are aware of and so can directly address students' misconceptions.	Probe students' understanding of a topic through a short pretest or series of discussion questions.	When beginning a lesson on what it means to be *warm-blooded*, ask students why sweaters and jackets keep them warm on a cold day. (Many erroneously believe that clothing generates heat; Gardner, 2000.)
Students are most likely to revise erroneous beliefs when they recognize that their beliefs are inadequate.	Show students how new information contradicts the things they currently believe.	When students express the stereotypical belief that new immigrants are "lazy," their teacher invites several recent immigrants to visit the class and describe their efforts and experiences in adapting to a new culture.
Students are more likely to undergo conceptual change when they are motivated to learn correct explanations.	Show students how correct explanations relate to their own personal interests.	Demonstrate how the laws of physics relate to auto mechanics and, indirectly, to auto repair.
Students are more apt to change their beliefs if they feel emotionally "comfortable" about doing so.	Communicate that students of all ability levels have misconceptions and that revising beliefs is an important part of learning.	When a student expresses a misconception, the teacher says, "You know, many of my students come to class thinking exactly that. It's a very logical thing to think. But the truth of the matter is. . . ."
Some misconceptions may persist despite instruction designed to contradict them.	Carefully scrutinize what students say and write, not only during a lesson but after the lesson as well, for signs of partial or total misunderstanding.	When a student refers to a spider as an *insect*, respond: "A spider is actually an *arachnid*, not an insect. Think back to what we learned about insects. Why don't spiders fit in that category?"

As you well know, this conception of a cloud as a "salt shaker" is hardly consistent with the scientifically accepted view of how and why rain comes about.

Informal pretesting will be especially important in your first few years of teaching. As you gain experience teaching a particular topic year after year, you may eventually find that you can anticipate students' existing beliefs and misbeliefs about the topic.

◎   *Convince students that their existing beliefs are inadequate.* As teachers, we can more effectively promote conceptual change when we show students how new information contradicts what they currently believe and when we demonstrate why their existing conceptions are inadequate. In Piaget's terminology, we need to create *disequilibrium.* To do so, we might use strategies such as these:

- Ask questions that challenge students' current beliefs.
- Present phenomena that students cannot adequately explain using their existing beliefs.
- Ask students to make predictions (i.e., about what will happen in various circumstances) that, given their present beliefs, are apt to be wrong.
- Encourage students to conduct experiments to test various hypotheses.
- Ask students to provide possible explanations for puzzling phenomena.
- Engage students in discussions of the pros and cons of various explanations.
- Show how one explanation of an event or phenomenon is more plausible (i.e., makes more sense) than others. (Andre & Windschitl, 2003; Chinn & Brewer, 1993; Chinn & Malhotra, 2002; Guzzetti, Snyder, Glass, & Gamas, 1993; Hatano & Inagaki, 2003; Howe, Tolmie, Greer, & Mackenzie, 1995; Pine & Messer, 2000; Posner, Strike, Hewson, & Gertzog, 1982; K. J. Roth, 1990; Slusher & Anderson, 1996; Vosniadou & Brewer, 1987)

Such strategies may encompass a wide variety of instructional methods, including demonstrations, hands-on experiments, teacher explanations, and student discussions. In the "Properties of Air" clip on Video CD 2, a first-grade teacher uses several strategies—probing students' existing beliefs, asking the children to make predictions, and presenting a phenomenon that some of them have difficulty explaining—to teach her class, in a very concrete way, that air has substance and occupies space.

In general, students will notice inconsistencies between new information and their existing beliefs only if they try to make connections between the "new" and the "old"—in other words, if they engage in meaningful learning. In Chapter 6 we found that students who engage in meaningful rather than rote learning acquire new information more quickly and retrieve it more easily. Here we see an additional reason to encourage meaningful learning: It helps unravel existing misconceptions.

◎   *Motivate students to learn correct explanations.* Students are most likely to engage in meaningful learning and undergo conceptual change when they are motivated to do so (Pintrich, Marx, & Boyle, 1993; Sinatra & Pintrich, 2003a). At a minimum, they must be interested in the subject matter, see it as helping them achieve their personal goals, set their sights on mastering it, and have sufficient self-confidence to believe they *can* master it (Andre & Windschitl, 2003; Hynd, 2003; Pintrich et al., 1993). As we consider motivation in Chapters 11 and 12, we'll identify strategies for accomplishing these things.

◎   *When pointing out errors or weaknesses in students' reasoning or beliefs, preserve their self-esteem.* Students must not interpret the uncovering of new, contradictory information as threatening to their self-esteem (Minstrell & Stimpson, 1996; Sherman & Cohen, 2002). And ideally, the classroom should be socially and emotionally *supportive* of conceptual change (Hatano & Inagaki, 2003). For instance, students must feel confident that their teacher and classmates will not ridicule them for expressing logical but incorrect ideas and that the ultimate goal of a lesson is understanding the subject matter rather than simply performing well on a quiz or assignment.

◎   *Monitor what students say and write for persistent misconceptions.* Because of students' natural tendency to reinterpret new information within the context of what they already know and believe, some misconceptions may persist despite our best efforts. These misconceptions are sometimes blatantly incorrect; at other times, they may be sort-of-but-not-quite correct. As an example of the latter situation, students sometimes describe a transparent object as "something you can see through" (K. J. Roth & Anderson, 1988). Although such a description is consistent

■ Observe a teacher encourage conceptual change in the "Properties of Air" clip on Video CD 2.

■ Here we are distinguishing between a mastery goal (understanding a topic) versus a performance goal (getting a good grade). We'll explore this distinction in Chapter 12.

with how we ordinarily speak about *transparency*, it may nevertheless reflect the erroneous belief that sight originates with the eye and goes outward to and through the transparent object. Describing the object as "something light passes through" indicates a more accurate understanding of *transparency*.

Throughout each lesson we should continue to check students' beliefs about the topic at hand, looking for subtle signs that their understanding is not quite accurate and giving corrective feedback when necessary. As an example, consider the following classroom discussion about vision and opaque objects. Using an overhead projector, Ms. Ramsey is showing her fifth graders a picture of a girl standing in front of her house; there is an 8-foot wall between the girl and the family car:

Ms. Ramsey:	Why can't the girl see around the wall?
Annie:	The girl can't see around the wall because the wall is opaque.
Ms. Ramsey:	What do you mean when you say the wall is opaque?
Annie:	*You can't see through it. It is solid.*
Brian:	(calling out) The rays are what can't go through the wall.
Ms. Ramsey:	I like that answer better. Why is it better?
Brian:	The rays of light bounce off the car and go to the wall. They can't go through the wall.
Ms. Ramsey:	Where are the light rays coming from originally?
Students:	The sun.
Annie:	*The girl can't see the car because she is not far enough out.*
Ms. Ramsey:	So you think her position is what is keeping her from seeing it. (She flips down the overlay with the answer.) Who was better?
Students:	Brian.
Ms. Ramsey:	(to Annie) Would she be able to see if she moved out beyond the wall?
Annie:	Yes.
Ms. Ramsey:	Why?
Annie:	*The wall is blocking her view.*
Ms. Ramsey:	It is blocking her view? What is it blocking?
Student:	Light rays.
Ms. Ramsey:	Light rays that are doing what?
Annie:	If the girl moves out beyond the wall, then the light rays that bounce off the car are not being blocked. (K. J. Roth & Anderson, 1988, pp. 129–130)

Notice how Ms. Ramsey is not satisfied with Annie's original answer that the wall is opaque. With further questioning, it becomes clear that Annie's understanding of opaqueness is off target: She talks about the girl being unable to "see through" the wall, rather than about light's inability to pass through the wall. With Ms. Ramsey's continuing insistence on precise language, Annie eventually begins to bring light rays into her explanation (K. J. Roth & Anderson, 1988).

Assessment of students' comprehension is important *after* a lesson as well. We are more likely to detect and correct misconceptions when we ask students to *use* and *apply* what they have learned (as Ms. Ramsey does in the preceding class discussion), rather than just to spit back memorized facts, definitions. and formulas (Pine & Messer, 2000; K. J. Roth, 1990; K. J. Roth & Anderson, 1988). For example, if we want students in a social studies class to understand that there are often valid and compelling perspectives on both sides of a controversial issue, rather than to believe that controversy is always a matter of the "good guys" versus the "bad guys," we might ask them to engage in a debate in which they must convincingly present a perspective contrary to their own beliefs. If students in a creative writing class have previously learned that complete sentences are always essential in good writing and we want to convince them otherwise, we might ask them to find examples of how incomplete sentences are sometimes used quite effectively in short stories and novels.

As teachers, then. we can do a variety of things to nudge students toward conceptual change. But ultimately, students themselves are in control of the cognitive processes (meaningful learning, organization, elaboration, etc.) that will enable them to make sense of new ideas and acquire more accurate understandings. Their proficiency in directing their own learning efforts and their understanding of what it actually *means* to learn something are key elements in their ability to revise their thinking about classroom subject matter. We will look more at these issues in our discussions of metacognition and epistemological beliefs in Chapter 8 and in our discussions of self-regulated learning in Chapter 10.

CONSIDERING DIVERSITY IN CONSTRUCTIVE PROCESSES

We have explored a number of reasons why students will inevitably interpret classroom subject matter in unique, idiosyncratic ways. Different students will have different knowledge bases—different concepts, schemas, scripts, theories, and so on—that they will use to make sense of any new situation. For instance, as noted in Chapter 4, students from diverse backgrounds may come to us with a variety of belief systems—*world views*—derived from their cultural, ethnic, and religious heritages (O. Lee, 1999; Southerland & Sinatra, 2003). Students whose cultures attribute natural events (such as hurricanes or earthquakes) to supernatural causes may have trouble buying into more scientific, "earthly" explanations. And students whose religions espouse the divine creation of humankind may readily dismiss the idea that the human race has evolved over a long time period. In such situations a more achievable goal may be to help students *understand* (rather than *accept*) scientific explanations and lines of reasoning (Southerland & Sinatra, 2003).

As we help students construct a meaningful understanding of the world around them, we can increase their multicultural awareness by promoting *multiple constructions* of the same situation. For example, we might present the western migration across North America during the 1700s and 1800s from two different perspectives: that of the European settlers and that of the Native Americans already residing on the land. One simple way to do this is to point out that migrating peoples are referred to as *pioneers* or *settlers* in most United States history books but might instead have been called *foreigners* or *invaders* by Native Americans (Banks, 1991). Ultimately, we must help students to understand the very complex nature of human "knowledge" and to appreciate the fact that there may be several possible interpretations of any single event.

A community of learners may be especially valuable when we have a diverse classroom of students (García, 1994; Ladson-Billings, 1995). Such a community values the contributions of all students, using everyone's individual backgrounds, cultural perspectives, and unique abilities to enhance the overall performance of the class. It also provides a context in which students can

■ How might you introduce multiple perspectives into the subject matter you will be teaching?

TABLE 7.3 STUDENTS IN INCLUSIVE SETTINGS

Promoting Knowledge Construction in Students with Special Educational Needs

CATEGORY	CHARACTERISTICS YOU MIGHT OBSERVE	SUGGESTED CLASSROOM STRATEGIES
Students with specific cognitive or academic difficulties	• Possible holes in students' knowledge base that may limit meaningful understanding of some classroom topics • Occasional unusual or inappropriate interpretations of prose • Occasional misinterpretations of social situations	• Determine students' prior knowledge about a new topic; remind them of what they already know about the topic. • Monitor students' comprehension of prose; correct misinterpretations. • Encourage alternative interpretations of others' behaviors.
Students with social or behavioral problems	• Frequent misinterpretations of social situations • Overly literal interpretations of things heard and read (for students with autism)	• Encourage alternative interpretations of others' behaviors, and identify suitable courses of action based on the most reasonable interpretation of a given situation. • Monitor students' understandings of implied meanings, figurative language, and the like.
Students with general delays in cognitive and social functioning	• Smaller knowledge base from which to draw • Difficulty constructing an accurate interpretation when information is ambiguous or incomplete	• Assume little if any prior knowledge about topics unless you have evidence to the contrary; remind students of what they *do* know about a topic. • Present information clearly and unambiguously.
Students with physical or sensory challenges	• Limited knowledge base to which students can relate new information, due to fewer opportunities to interact with the outside world	• Provide the background experiences (e.g., field trips) that students need to make sense of classroom subject matter.
Students with advanced cognitive development	• Larger knowledge base from which to draw • Rapid concept learning • Greater conceptual understanding of classroom material (e.g., greater understanding of cause-effect relationships) • Greater ability to draw inferences	• Assign challenging tasks that enable students to develop and use their advanced understanding of topics. • Ask thought-provoking questions that encourage inference drawing.

Sources: Butterfield & Ferretti, 1987; Graham & Hudley, 1994; J. N. Hughes, 1988; Klin, Volkmar, & Sparrow, 2000; Lochman & Dodge, 1994; Patton et al., 1996; Piirto, 1999; Pressley, 1995; Schumaker & Hazel, 1984; R. Turnbull et al., 2004; J. P. Williams, 1991.

form friendships across the lines of ethnicity, gender, socioeconomic status, and disability. Such friendships are, as noted in Chapters 3 and 4, critical for students' social development and multicultural understanding.

Accommodating Students with Special Needs

We will see evidence of diversity in constructive processes in our students with special educational needs. For example, students with learning disabilities may construct inappropriate meanings from stories they hear and read (Pressley, 1995; J. P. Williams, 1991). Students with emotional and behavioral disorders may construct counterproductive interpretations of social situations; for example, they might "see" an act of aggression in an innocent gesture or "hear" an insult when none was intended (recall our discussion of *hostile attributional bias* in Chapter 3). Table 7.3 identifies patterns that researchers have found in the constructive processes of students with special needs. It also presents suggestions for helping these students acquire appropriate meanings from academic and social situations.

THE BIG PICTURE

Through their many learning experiences—both formal instruction and informal encounters—students continually add to and modify their understanding of their physical and social worlds. To some degree, this knowledge construction is an individual enterprise, in that students must ultimately create their own views of physical and social phenomena. Yet students' knowledge and beliefs are also shaped considerably by their social and cultural environments. For example, students draw on explanations that previous generations have developed—perhaps the concepts and theories of various academic disciplines, or perhaps the folk wisdom of their local communities—to understand current situations and events. They work in partnership with parents and teachers to make better sense of puzzling phenomena. And they frequently discuss classroom subject matter and other topics with peers and, as a group, may reach different understandings than they might reach on their own.

Regardless of the extent to which our students acquire their understandings on their own or with the help of others, they will all construct somewhat unique interpretations of the ideas and events they encounter both in and outside of the classroom. Such constructions will affect their understandings not only of academic subject matter but also of themselves, their interpersonal relationships, and their views about morality (see Chapter 3) Many of their interpretations, though perhaps different from those of other people, may be equally valid and appropriate. But others—for example, beliefs that the earth is flat, that rote learning is more effective than meaningful learning, or that a classmate is trying to pick a fight—may interfere with their future success in the outside world. As teachers, we must help our students interpret the world around them in ways that will be productive over the long run.

CASE STUDY: *Earth-Shaking Summaries*

Ms. Jewell spends the first half hour of her seventh-grade geography class describing how earthquakes occur. She introduces the theory of *plate tectonics*—the notion that the earth's crust is made up of many separate pieces (*plates*) that rest upon a layer of hot, molten rock (the *mantle*). She explains that plates occasionally shift and rub against each other, making the immediate area shake and leaving *faults* in the earth's surface.

Her students listen attentively throughout her explanation. When she finishes, she asks whether there are any questions. Finding that there are none, she says, "Great! I'm glad you all understand. What I'd like you to do now is to take out a piece of paper and write a paragraph answering this question: *Why do we have earthquakes?*" She's recently read in a professional journal that asking students to summarize what they've learned often helps them remember it better later on, and she figures her assignment is an excellent way to encourage summarization.

As students leave for their next class, Ms. Jewell collects their papers. Glancing quickly through the stack, she is distressed by what she sees. Some of her students have provided a relatively complete and accurate description of plate tectonics. But the responses of others are vague enough to make her uneasy about how thoroughly they understood her explanation; here are two examples:

Frank: The earth's crust shifts around and shakes us up.
Mitchell: Earthquakes happen when really big plates on the earth move around.

And three of her students clearly have made little sense of the lesson:

Adrienne: Scientists use technology to understand how earthquakes happen. They use computers and stuff.
Toni: When there are earthquakes, people's plates move around the house.
Jonathan: Earthquakes aren't anybody's fault. They just happen.

Ms. Jewell sighs, clearly discouraged by the feedback she's just gotten about her lesson. "I guess I still have a lot to learn about teaching this stuff," she concludes.

Why is Ms. Jewell not convinced that Frank and Mitchell have mastered the material? What critical aspects of the lesson did each boy omit in his response?

What pieces of information from the lesson did Adrienne, Toni, and Jonathan apparently use when answering Ms. Jewell's question? Can you explain their responses using the concept of knowledge construction?

What instructional strategies might Ms. Jewell have used to help her students gain a better understanding of plate tectonics?

Once you have answered these questions, compare your responses with those presented in Appendix B.

KEY CONCEPTS

reconstruction error (p. 226)
individual constructivism (p. 226)
social constructivism (p. 227)
distributed cognition (p. 227)
concept (p. 228)
undergeneralization (p. 229)
overgeneralization (p. 229)
positive instance (p. 229)
negative instance (p. 229)

defining feature (p. 230)
correlational feature (p. 230)
prototype (p. 230)
exemplar (p. 231)
schema (p. 233)
script (p. 233)
theory (p. 235)
naive theory (p. 235)
misconception (p. 235)

conceptual understanding (p. 240)
authentic activity (p. 242)
community of learners (p. 244)
confirmation bias (p. 246)
conceptual change (p. 246)

PRAXIS   Turn to Appendix C, "Matching Book and Ancillary Content to the Praxis Principles of Learning and Teaching Tests," to discover sections of this chapter that may be especially applicable to the Praxis tests.

Companion Website

Now go to our Companion Website at **www.prenhall. com/ormrod** to assess your understanding of chapter content with "Multiple-Choice Questions," apply comprehension in "Essay Questions," broaden your knowledge of educational psychology with related "Web Links," gain greater insight about classroom learning in "Learning in the Content Areas," and analyze and assess classroom work in the "Student Artifact Library."

Chapter 8

Higher-Level Thinking Processes

In Chapters 6 and 7, we learned a great deal about learning. For example, in our discussion of long-term memory storage in Chapter 6, we discovered that people store new information more effectively when they relate it to things they have previously learned—that is, when they engage in meaningful learning. From our discussion of knowledge construction in Chapter 7, we discovered that learning is often a process of creating one's own, idiosyncratic understandings by combining both new and old information into something that makes some sort of "sense." In this chapter we'll look at cognitive processes in which learners go far beyond the specific information they have acquired—perhaps so that they can better remember it, apply it to a new situation, use it to solve a problem or create a product, or critically evaluate it. Such processes are collectively known as **higher-level thinking**.

As we consider various forms of higher-level thinking in the upcoming pages, we'll address the following questions:

- How do students' knowledge and beliefs about their own cognitive processes—that is, their metacognition—influence their ability to learn?
- What study strategies seem to facilitate academic achievement, and how can we help students acquire them?
- Under what circumstances are students most likely to apply—that is, transfer—what they've learned to new situations?
- What cognitive processes are involved in effective problem solving, and how can we help students solve problems more successfully?
- How can we foster creativity in the classroom?
- What is critical thinking, and how can we promote it?

As we address these questions, I hope that you, too, will learn more effective ways of studying, applying, and evaluating the subject matter you encounter in your *own* classes.

CASE STUDY: *A Question of Speed*

Mary is studying for tomorrow's exam in her physics class. As she looks over her class notes, she finds the following statement in her notebook:

Velocity equals acceleration times time.

She also finds a formula expressing this idea:

$$v = a \times t$$

Mary repeats the statement and formula over and over until she knows both by heart. The following day, she encounters this problem on her exam:

An automotive engineer has designed a car that can reach a speed of 50 miles per hour within 5 seconds. What is the car's rate of acceleration?

She puzzles over the problem for several minutes. She thinks about a car reaching 50 miles per hour: Is this the car's acceleration, its velocity, or something else altogether? She realizes that she doesn't know the difference between acceleration and velocity. She finally turns in her exam with this and several similar questions unanswered.

She later confides to a classmate, "I really blew that test today, but I don't know why. I mean, I really studied *hard*!"

- How does Mary study for her physics exam? What things does she *not* do as she studies—things that might have led to better performance?

- If you were Mary's physics teacher, how might you help Mary study more effectively for the next exam?

■ **higher-level thinking** Thinking that involves going well beyond information specifically learned (e.g., analyzing, applying, or evaluating it).

THE NATURE OF HIGHER-LEVEL THINKING

One critical mistake Mary makes is to use only rote learning as she studies for her exam. Although she memorizes "velocity equals acceleration times time," she never really learns what velocity and acceleration *are*. (*Velocity* is the speed at which an object travels in a particular direction. *Acceleration* is the rate at which an object's velocity changes.) As a result, she is unable to apply her knowledge in any meaningful way.

Let's now put *you* in the role of learner. In the following exercise, you'll study a topic we haven't addressed before: the world's diminishing rain forests.

Experiencing FIRSTHAND ·Rain Forests

Read this passage, then answer the questions that follow.

> Almost half of the world's plants and animals live in its rain forests. From tropical plants we get a variety of foods (e.g., fruits, nuts, coffee, chocolate) and ingredients for many household products (e.g., toothpaste, fabric dyes, pesticides). Furthermore, plants that grow only in rain forests produce substances used in treatments for Hodgkin's disease, multiple sclerosis, and Parkinson's disease. One researcher studying the rain forest of Costa Rica estimated that 15 percent of its plants had potential for treating cancer.
>
> Valuable as they are, rain forests are diminishing at an alarming rate every year. Millions of people in developing countries rely on rain forest land for farming. They clear large areas to grow their crops, slashing and burning the existing vegetation. Within a few years, they deplete the soil of its nutrients, and so they must move farther into the rain forest to find new farmland. Oftentimes cattle ranchers occupy the land that peasant farmers have left behind, but soon the soil cannot even support grasses to feed cattle.
>
> Each day we lose 75,000 acres of rain forest to such short-sighted practices—a rate that translates into about 27 million acres (an area the size of Austria) annually. (based on Hosmer, 1987, p. 6)

> 1. What are three illnesses that can be treated by using rain forest plants?
> 2. How does peasant farming change the nature of rain forest land?
> 3. Why do peasants continue to farm more and more rain forest land despite the environmental consequences of doing so?
> 4. What things might be done to halt the destruction of rain forests?
> 5. What are the most useful ideas to be gained from the passage?

· · · · · · ·

Which of the five questions were the easiest ones to answer? Which questions were the most *important* ones to answer? You may have found questions 1 and 2 relatively easy because the answers were clearly stated in the passage. These two **lower-level questions** asked you to recall information you were specifically given. You may have found the last three questions more difficult because you couldn't find the answers in the passage itself. To answer question 3, you had to apply something that you know about people in general—the fact that people usually do whatever they can to make a living—to your understanding of the peasant farmers' plight. To answer question 4, you had to combine your prior knowledge with information in the passage to generate possible solutions to a difficult problem. And to answer question 5, you needed to make a judgment about what information was most likely to be useful to you at a later time. Such **higher-level questions**, which ask you to go *beyond* the information actually presented, are usually more difficult than lower-level questions. Yet these higher-level questions are often the most important ones for learners to address.

Mastering basic facts and skills is important, to be sure. But students gain little if they cannot also make *use* of what they've learned—for instance, by applying, analyzing, or evaluating it. The ideal classroom is one that regularly addresses *both* lower-level and higher-level forms of thinking and learning (B. S. Bloom, Englehart, Furst, Hill, & Krathwohl, 1956; N. S. Cole, 1990; Onosko & Newmann, 1994; Paxton, 1999). Such a classroom encourages students to think about and use academic subject matter in new, productive, and otherwise "intelligent" ways.

■ **lower-level question** Question that requires students to express what they've learned in essentially the same way they learned it.

■ **higher-level question** Question that requires students to engage in higher-level thinking.

One essential strategy for promoting higher-level thinking is to help students understand what effective learning involves—in other words, to enhance students' metacognition and study strategies. We look at ways of doing so now.

METACOGNITION AND STUDY STRATEGIES

What specific study strategies do you use? For example, do you take notes? Do you try to relate certain concepts and principles to your own life and experiences? Do you occasionally test yourself on class material to see how well you've learned it? What does your current grade point average tell you about the effectiveness of your study strategies?

Students vary considerably in the study strategies they use. Consider these three students:

- Kate is studying for a geography exam that will include multiple-choice, short-answer, and essay questions. She moves her eyes down each of the assigned pages in the textbook, but all the while she is thinking about the upcoming school dance. Kate seems to think that as long as her eyes are looking at the page, the information printed on it will somehow sink in.
- Ling is studying for the same exam. She spends most of her time memorizing terms and definitions in her textbook. Eventually, she can recite many of them word for word.
- Sarah, too, is studying for the geography exam. She focuses her efforts on trying to understand basic geographical principles and on generating new examples of those principles.

Ideally, students should not only master academic subject matter but also *use* it in meaningful ways.

Which student will probably perform best on the geography exam? Considering what we know about learning and memory, we can predict that Sarah will get the highest score of the three girls. Unfortunately, Ling has not yet discovered that she learns better when she relates new ideas to her prior knowledge than when she memorizes things without trying to make sense of them. Poor Kate knows even less about learning: She's not even paying attention to what she thinks she is reading!

The concept **metacognition** includes learners' knowledge and beliefs about their own cognitive processes, as well as their attempts to regulate their cognitive processes to maximize learning and memory. For example, it includes

- Reflecting on the nature of thinking and learning
- Knowing the limits of one's own learning and memory capabilities
- Knowing what learning tasks one can realistically accomplish within a certain time period
- Knowing which learning strategies are effective and which are not
- Planning a reasonable approach to a learning task
- Using effective strategies to learn and remember new material
- Monitoring one's own knowledge and comprehension—in other words, knowing when information has been successfully learned and when it has not

To illustrate, you have undoubtedly learned by now that you can acquire only so much information so fast; you cannot possibly absorb the contents of an entire textbook in an hour. You have also discovered that you can learn information more quickly and recall it more easily when you put it into some sort of organizational framework. And perhaps you have discovered the advantage of checking yourself as you read a textbook, stopping every so often to make sure that you've understood what you've just read. In other words, you are metacognitively aware of some things you can do (mentally) to learn new information effectively. Notice how aware 9-year-old Eamon is of what he does when he encounters new ideas in science:

■ Metacognition takes somewhat different forms in different subject areas. For more details, see the chapter "Learning in the Content Areas" in the *Study Guide and Reader*.

> I try to look for a fit. Like if it doesn't fit with any . . . of the ideas that I have in my head I just leave it and wait for other ideas to come in so that I can try to fit them together with my ideas. Maybe they will go with my ideas and then another idea will come in and I can fit it together with that idea and my understanding just keeps on enlarging. An idea usually does fit. (M. G. Hennessey, 2003, p. 123)

The more students know about effective learning strategies—the greater their metacognitive awareness—the more likely they are to *use* such strategies and the higher their classroom achievement will be (L. Baker, 1989; Perkins, 1995; P. L. Peterson, 1988). Furthermore, students who have a more sophisticated understanding of learning and thinking are more likely to

■ **metacognition** One's knowledge and beliefs about one's own cognitive processes and one's resulting attempts to regulate those cognitive processes to maximize learning and memory.

undergo conceptual change when such change is warranted (Gunstone, 1994; Sinatra & Pintrich, 2003a; Wittrock, 1994).

Unfortunately, many students know little about how they can best learn and remember information. As we discovered in Chapter 2, younger children are especially naive about effective learning strategies. Yet older students are also prone to misconceptions about how they can best learn and remember. For example, many students at all grade levels (even many college students!) erroneously believe that rote learning is an effective way to study (Barnett, 2001; Pintrich & De Groot, 1990; Prawat, 1989; Schommer, 1994a).

Table 8.1 summarizes the typical nature of metacognition at various grade levels. You can also get a general sense of how metacognitive awareness changes with age by listening to 6-year-old Brent, 10-year-old David, 12-year-old Colin, and 16-year-old Hilary talk about learning,

■ Did you have misconceptions about how best to study before you read this book?

TABLE 8.1

DEVELOPMENTAL TRENDS

Metacognition at Different Grade Levels

GRADE LEVEL	AGE-TYPICAL CHARACTERISTICS	SUGGESTED STRATEGIES
K–2	• Awareness of thought in oneself and others, albeit in a simplistic form; limited ability to reflect on the specific nature of one's own thought processes • Considerable overestimation of what has been learned and how much can be remembered in the future • Belief that learning is a relatively passive activity • Belief that the absolute truth about any topic is "out there" somewhere, waiting to be discovered	• Talk often about thinking processes (e.g., "I *wonder* if . . . " "Do you *remember* when . . . ?"). • Provide opportunities for students to "experiment" with their memories (e.g., playing "I'm going on a trip and am going to pack _____," in which each student repeats items previously mentioned and then adds another item to the list). • Introduce simple learning strategies (e.g., rehearsal of spelling words, repeated practice of motor skills).
3–5	• Increasing ability to reflect on the nature of one's own thought processes • Some overestimation of memory capabilities • Emerging realization that learning is an active, constructive process and that people may misinterpret what they observe • Continuing belief in an absolute truth "out there"	• Provide simple techniques (e.g., self-test questions) that enable students to monitor learning progress. • Examine scientific phenomena through hands-on activities and experimentation; have students make predictions for what will happen and debate competing explanations for what they observe.
6–8	• Increasing flexibility in the use of learning strategies (e.g., rehearsal, organization) • Few and relatively ineffective study strategies (e.g., poor note-taking skills, little if any comprehension monitoring) • Belief that "knowledge" about a topic consists largely of a collection of discrete facts • Increasing realization that knowledge can be subjective and that conflicting perspectives may each have some validity (e.g., "people have a right to have their own opinions")	• Teach and model effective strategies within the context of various subject areas. • Scaffold students' studying efforts (e.g., provide a structure for note taking, give students questions to answer as they read a textbook). • Provide in-class time for structured small-group study sessions (e.g., *elaborative interrogation*; see later discussion). • Introduce multiple perspectives about topics (e.g., asking whether Christopher Columbus was a brave scientist in search of new knowledge or, instead, an entrepreneur in search of personal wealth).
9–12	• Growing (but incomplete) knowledge of which cognitive strategies are effective in different situations • Persistent use of rehearsal by some students • Increasing recognition that knowledge involves understanding interrelationships among ideas • Increasing recognition that mastering a topic or skill takes time and practice (rather than happening quickly as a result of innate ability) • Emerging understanding that conflicting perspectives should be evaluated on the basis of evidence and logic (seen in a small minority of high school students)	• Continue to teach and model effective learning strategies. • Design classroom assessments that emphasize understanding, integration, and application, rather than recall of discrete facts. • Present various subject areas as dynamic entities that continue to evolve with new discoveries and theories. • Have students weigh pros and cons of various explanations using objective criteria (e.g., hard evidence, logical reasoning processes).

Sources: Andre & Windschitl, 2003; Astington & Pelletier, 1996; Barnett, 2001; Chandler, Hallett, & Sokol, 2002; Elder, 2002; Flavell et al., 1970, 1993; Hatano & Inagaki, 2003; P. M. King & Kitchener, 2002; Kuhn et al., 1995; Kuhn & Weinstock, 2002; Lovett & Flavell, 1990; Markman, 1977; Schommer, 1994a, 1997; Short et al., 1993; J. W. Thomas, 1993a; Wellman, 1985, 1990.

memory, and studying in the "Memory and Metacognition" clips on Video CD 1. For instance, to explain his performance on a task involving memory of twelve words, 6-year-old Brent says only "Think" and "Hold it in my brain." In contrast, 16-year-old Hilary is much more introspective about why she's done well on the task: "Just 'cause they're things that I have in the house and that we use every day . . . and just thinking it over, I guess. It helps when I picture things, too."

With each transition to a higher educational level (from elementary to middle school, from middle school to high school, and from high school to college), teachers expect students to learn more material and think about it in more sophisticated ways. Thus the simple learning strategies that students develop in grade school (e.g., rehearsal) become less and less effective with each passing year (e.g., Hacker, 1998a). All too often, however, teachers teach academic content areas—history, biology, mathematics, and so on—without also teaching students how to *learn* in those content areas (Hamman, Berthelot, Saia, & Crowley, 2000; Pressley et al., 1990; E. Wood et al., 1997). When left to their own devices, most students develop effective strategies very slowly (if at all) and so over the years encounter increasing difficulty in their attempts to master classroom subject matter. And when they *don't* master it, they may not know why they have failed, nor may they know how to improve their chances of succeeding the next time around (Hacker et al., 2000; Loranger, 1994; O'Sullivan & Joy, 1990).

In the upcoming sections we'll review research findings on a variety of study strategies. We'll then consider factors that influence students' use of such strategies, as well as ways in which we can help our own students study and learn more effectively.

■ Listen to Brent, David, Colin, and Hilary reflect on their thought processes in the four "Memory and Metacognition" clips on Video CD 1.

■ Are teachers' expectations for your learning more demanding at the college level than they were in high school? If so, have you been able to adapt your study strategies accordingly?

Effective Study Strategies

Earlier we saw Kate "study" for a geography test by moving her eyes down the pages of her textbook while thinking about a school dance. And in the opening case study, Mary "studies" for her physics test simply by rehearsing a statement and formula relating velocity, acceleration, and time. But truly *effective* study strategies require thinking actively about and elaborating on classroom material. Researchers have identified a number of effective study strategies, including (a) identifying important information, (b) retrieving relevant prior knowledge, (c) taking notes, (d) organizing information (e) intentional elaboration, (f) creating summaries, and (g) monitoring comprehension. As we examine these strategies, you'll undoubtedly find some that you yourself use as you study.

Identifying Important Information   What cues do you use to identify important ideas in your textbooks? Are you more likely to believe that something is important if it's printed in italics or boldface type? Do you look for important points in headings, introductions, concluding paragraphs, or summaries? Do you focus on definitions, formulas, or lists of items?

As we discovered in Chapter 6, students can rarely learn everything they read in a textbook or remember everything they hear in class, and so they must be selective when studying classroom material. The things they choose to study—whether main ideas and critical pieces of information, or isolated facts and trivial details—inevitably affect their learning and school achievement (Dee-Lucas & Larkin, 1991; Dole et al., 1991; R. E. Reynolds & Shirey, 1988).

Students often have trouble separating central and important information from the trivial and unimportant. In the following excerpts from interviews conducted by students in my own educational psychology classes, Damon (an eighth grader) and Annie (a fifth grader) reveal their naivete about how to identify the most important things to learn in a lesson:

Adult: What do you think are the important things to remember when your teacher is talking?
Damon: The beginning sentences of their speech or if there's a formula or definition.

Adult: When you read, how do you know what the important things are?
Annie: Most of my books have words that are written darker than all of the other words. Most of the time the "vocab" words are important. In my science books there are questions on the side of the page. You can tell that stuff is important because it is written twice. (excerpts courtesy of Jenny Bressler and an anonymous student)

In general, students are apt to focus on

- The first sentence of a lesson or paragraph
- Items that look different (e.g., definitions, formulas, print in *italics* or **boldface**)

Students often need help distinguishing important ideas from more trivial information, especially when they first begin to study a topic.

- Items presented in more than one way (e.g., both verbally and visually)
- Items that are intrinsically interesting
  (P. A. Alexander & Jetton, 1996; Garner, Brown, Sanders, & Menke, 1992; Harp & Mayer, 1998; Kiewra, 1989; Mayer, 1984)

Thus, when important ideas are presented within the middle of a lesson or paragraph, without any obvious cues to make them stand out, and especially when those ideas do not grab students' immediate interest, students may often overlook them.

As teachers, we can help students learn more effectively by letting them know what ideas are most important in lectures and reading materials. We could, of course, simply tell them exactly what to study. But we can also get the same message across through more subtle means:

- Provide a list of objectives for a lesson.
- Write key concepts and major ideas on the chalkboard.
- Ask questions that focus students' attention on important ideas.

Students (especially low-achieving ones) are more likely to learn the important points of a lesson when such "prompts" (scaffolding) are provided for them (Kiewra, 1989; R. E. Reynolds & Shirey, 1988; Schraw & Wade, 1991). As our students become better able to distinguish important from unimportant information on their own, we can gradually phase out our guidance.

Retrieving Relevant Prior Knowledge   As we discovered in Chapter 6, students can engage in meaningful learning only when they have previous knowledge to which they can relate new information and are also *aware* of the potential relationship. How can we encourage students to think about the things they already know as they encounter new information? One approach is to model this strategy for students. For example, we might read aloud a portion of a textbook, stopping occasionally to tie an idea in the text to something previously studied in class or to something in our own personal experiences. We can then encourage students to do likewise, giving suggestions and guiding their efforts as they proceed (Spires, Donley, & Penrose, 1990). Especially when working in the elementary grades, we might want to provide specific questions that remind students to think about what they already know as they read and study:

- What do you already know about your topic?
- What do you hope to learn about your topic?
- Do you think what you learn by reading your books will change what you already know about your topic? (questions from H. Thompson & Carr, 1995, p. 9)

■ Does this approach remind you of the concept of *scaffolding*?

With time and practice, our students should eventually get in the habit of retrieving relevant prior knowledge with little or no assistance from us (Spires et al., 1990).

Taking Notes   No doubt you have at one time or another missed a class and therefore had to rely on a fellow student's notes from the class lecture. And no doubt you discovered that the classmate's notes were different (perhaps *very* different) from the notes that you yourself usually take. For twenty students in the same classroom, we will find twenty different sets of notes. Each student makes unique assumptions about what is important, what is useful, and what is likely to be on an upcoming exam, and these assumptions influence the amount and type of notes that the student takes.

In general, note taking is associated with more successful classroom learning; in fact, when students have *no* opportunity either to take or review notes, they may recall very little of what they hear in a lecture (Hale, 1983; Kiewra, 1989). The process of note taking seems to serve two very important functions (Di Vesta & Gray, 1972; Katayama & Robinson, 2000; Kiewra, 1989). First, it helps learners pay attention to and *encode* information, thus facilitating effective storage in memory. Second, it provides a means of *external storage* for the information. Long-term memory is often unreliable (recall our discussion of forgetting in Chapter 6), whereas notebooks are fairly dependable and allow students to review the material on one or more later occasions.

The extent to which note taking helps students learn and achieve naturally depends on the quantity and quality of the notes taken, as the exercise on the following page reveals.

Interpreting Student Artifacts and Behaviors

King Midas

To help her students learn how to take notes in class, seventh-grade language arts teacher Barbara Dee gives them a note-taking form to fill in during a unit on Greek mythology. At the end of the unit, the students can use their notes—but *only* their notes—as they take a test about the myths they have studied. Following are two students' notes on the story "King Midas and the Golden Touch." As you look at the notes, consider

- Which set of notes you'd rather have as you study for and take the test
- How much the form scaffolds students' note-taking efforts

Story Note taking Form

Title: King Midas and the golden touch
Author:

I. Characters (write a few notes after each character's name to describe them, make a abbreviation after the character's name for further notes)
a. King Midas - King of Phrygia
b. Silenus - a demigod
c. Dionysus - god of wine
d. Daughter of King Midas
e.
f.
g.
h.
i.

II. Setting (write a few notes after the place to describe it, try to discover the time period)
a.
b.
c.

III. Events
a. Silenus was someone tearing up km's rosebushs
b. Silenus tutored dionysus, dionysus watches over silenus
c. silenus got a feast from km, silenus stayed for a while
d. Dionysus wants to pay km for being nice to silenus, Dionysus gives him a wish
e. Km picks gold now everything he touches turns to gold
f. Km Turns daughter to gold km washes everything in the Pactolus & loses gold touch.

IV. Conflict (what is the problem, who is involved)
a.
b.

V. Solution (how did the problem work itself out, was there a lesson to learn)
a.
b.

Story Note taking Form

Title: King midas and the golden touch
Author:

I. Characters (write a few notes after each character's name to describe them, make a abbreviation after the character's name for further notes)
a. King Midas
b. first guard
c. second guard
d. silenus
e. Dionysus
f. Daughter of the king
g.
h.
i.

II. Setting (write a few notes after the place to describe it, try to discover the time period)
a. Castle
b.
c.

III. Events
a. Sylinus destroys roses
b. King gets him
c.
d.
e.
f.

IV. Conflict (what is the problem, who is involved)
a. every thing he touches turns to gold
b.

V. Solution (how did the problem work itself out, was there a lesson to learn)
a.
b.

You probably preferred the notes on the left, which give a relatively complete synopsis of the King Midas story: Had you attended the class yourself, these notes might provide enough retrieval cues to help you remember the story fairly accurately. In contrast, the notes on the right are too brief and disjointed to make much sense. Quantity of notes is positively correlated with achievement: Students who take more notes do better (Kiewra, 1989). But the quality of notes is equally critical: Notes must reflect the main ideas of a lesson or reading assignment (A. L. Brown, Campione, & Day, 1981; Kiewra, 1985; Peverly, Brobst, Graham, & Shaw, 2003). Good notes seem to be particularly important for students who have little prior knowledge about the subject matter they are studying (Shrager & Mayer, 1989).

Especially when students are first starting to take notes in class (typically in the middle school or junior high grades), we should scaffold their efforts by giving them an idea about what things are most important to include (Pressley, Yokoi, van Meter, Van Etten, & Freebern, 1997; Yokoi, 1997). One approach is to provide a specific structure to use, much as Barbara Dee does in her unit on Greek mythology. The two students whose notes are depicted here don't follow the structure to the letter (one neglects to address the setting and conflict, and neither addresses the solution), but they at least have some guidance about the things they should be thinking about as they listen in class. Another strategy to consider, especially if students are novice note takers, is to occasionally check their notebooks for accuracy and appropriate emphasis and then give constructive feedback.

Organizing Information   As we discovered in Chapter 6, organized information is stored and retrieved more easily than unorganized information. When students engage in activities that help them organize what they are studying, they learn more effectively (DuBois et al., 1988; M. A. McDaniel & Einstein, 1989; Mintzes, Wandersee, & Novak, 1997). One useful way of organizing information is *outlining* the material—a strategy that may be especially helpful to low-achieving students (L. Baker, 1989; M. A. McDaniel & Einstein, 1989; Wade, 1992). Another approach is to make a **concept map**, a diagram that depicts the concepts of a unit and their interrelationships (Novak, 1998; Novak & Gowin, 1984). Figure 8.1 shows concept maps constructed by two fifth graders after they watched a slide lecture on Australia. The concepts themselves are in circles; their interrelationships are designated by lines and phrases that link pairs of concepts. The map on the right shows many more interconnections among concepts than does the map on the left, and we can reasonably assume that the student who drew the right-hand map learned the subject matter more effectively.

■ **concept map** Diagram of concepts and their interrelationships.

FIGURE 8.1 Concept maps constructed by two fifth-grade students after watching a slide lecture on Australia

From *Learning How to Learn* (pp. 100–101) by J. D. Novak and D. B. Gowin, 1984, Cambridge, England: Cambridge University Press. Copyright 1984 by Cambridge University Press. Reprinted with the permission of Cambridge University Press.

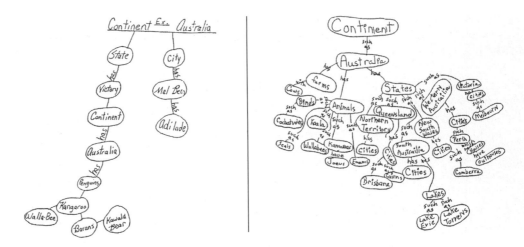

You can gain a better understanding of the advantages of concept maps by creating one yourself, as you will in the following exercise.

Experiencing FIRSTHAND · · · · · · · · · · · · · · · · · Mapping Concepts About Concepts

Quickly review the beginning of the "Concepts" section in Chapter 7 (pp. 228–230). These pages contain numerous concepts and ideas concerning the topic of concept learning:

Undergeneralization   Defining features
Overgeneralization   Correlational features
Positive instances   Salient features
Negative instances

The text talks about how these concepts are related to one another; for example, *overgeneralization* is a case of incorrectly identifying *negative instances* as examples of a concept, and a concept is easier to learn when its *defining features* are *salient*.

On a separate sheet of paper, make a concept map with the seven "concepts about concepts" just listed. Write the concepts in an arrangement that makes sense to you, circle each one, and then add lines and phrases to describe the interrelationships between pairs of concepts.

· · · · · · ·

There is certainly more than one "correct" way to map the seven concepts; Figure 8.2 (see p. 264) shows just one of many possibilities. I hope the exercise helped you organize some of the things you learned about concepts in the preceding chapter. I hope it also gave you a better understanding of the process of concept mapping itself.

Students benefit in numerous ways from constructing their own concept maps for classroom material. By focusing on how key concepts relate to one another, students organize material better. They are also more likely to notice how new concepts are related to concepts they already know: thus, they are more likely to learn the material meaningfully. Furthermore, when students construct a concept map from verbal material (e.g., from a lecture or a textbook), they can encode the material visually as well as verbally. And the very process of concept mapping may promote a more sophisticated perspective of what learning *is*; more specifically, students may begin to realize that learning is not just a process of "absorbing" information but instead involves actively making connections among ideas (Holley & Dansereau, 1984; Mintzes et al., 1997; Novak, 1998; Novak & Gowin, 1984). Such awareness is an example of an *epistemological belief*, a concept we'll look at more closely a bit later in the chapter.

Not only do concept maps help students, they can also help teachers. When we develop a concept map for a lesson, the organizational scheme of the lesson becomes clearer, and we have a better idea about how to sequence the presentation of ideas. And when we examine the concept maps our students have constructed, their understanding of a topic becomes readily apparent, as do their misconceptions about it (Novak, 1998; Novak & Gowin, 1984; Novak & Musonda, 1991). The two concept maps in Figure 8.1 reveal considerable differences in depth and organization of knowledge about Australia. Furthermore, the map on the left has a few errors.

For example, Adelaide is *not* part of Melbourne; it is a different city altogether. If geographic knowledge about Australia is an important instructional goal, then this student clearly needs further instruction to correct such misconceptions.

Intentional Elaboration   As we discovered in Chapters 2 and 6, students typically learn and remember academic subject matter better when they elaborate on it—for instance, when they draw inferences, generate new examples, or consider implications. However, most students don't *intentionally* elaborate as a way to learn and remember information until sometime around puberty. Even in the high school grades, only high-achieving students elaborate regularly as they read and study (see Chapter 2).

There are a variety of things we can do to teach students—even those in the elementary grades—to elaborate on classroom topics. For one thing, when we model retrieval of relevant prior knowledge, we can model elaboration as well. For example, we can identify our own examples of a new concept, consider the implications of a new principle, and so on. We can also give students specific questions to consider as they listen to a lecture or read a textbook; for example:

- Explain why . . .
- How would you use . . . to . . . ?
- What is a new example of . . . ?
- What do you think would happen if . . . ?
- What is the difference between . . . and . . . ? (questions from A. King, 1992, p. 309)

Yet another approach is to have students work in pairs or small groups to formulate and answer their *own* elaborative questions; such group questioning is known as *elaborative interrogation* or *guided peer questioning* (Kahl & Woloshyn, 1994; A. King, 1994, 1999; Rosenshine, Meister, & Chapman, 1996; E. Wood et al., 1999). In the following dialogue, fifth graders Katie and Janelle are working together to study class material about tide pools. Katie's job is to ask Janelle questions that encourage elaboration:

Katie: How are the upper tide zone and the lower tide zone different?
Janelle: They have different animals in them. Animals in the upper tide zone and splash zone can handle being exposed—have to be able to use the rain and sand and wind and sun—and they don't need that much water and the lower tide animals do.
Katie: And they can be softer 'cause they don't have to get hit on the rocks.
Janelle: Also predators. In the spray zone it's because there's predators like us people and all different kinds of stuff that can kill the animals and they won't survive, but the lower tide zone has not as many predators.
Katie: But wait! Why do the animals in the splash zone have to survive? (A. King, 1999, p. 97)

Notice how the two girls are continually relating the animals' characteristics to survival in different tide zones, and eventually Katie asks why animals in the splash zone even *need* to survive. Such analyses are quite sophisticated for fifth graders. Imagine what high school students, with their increasing capacity for abstract thought, might be able to do!

Creating Summaries   Another effective study strategy is summarizing the material being studied (Dole et al., 1991; Hidi & Anderson, 1986; A. King, 1992). Effective summarizing usually entails at least three processes (Hidi & Anderson, 1986; Spivey, 1997):

- Separating important from unimportant information
- Condensing details into more general ideas
- Identifying important relationships among general ideas

Many students have trouble summarizing material even at the high school level (V. Anderson & Hidi, 1988/1989). Probably the best way of helping students develop this strategy is to

Frog and and Toad are friends.
Toad is very silly. One of silliest things
that Toad does is when he sings songs
to his seeds and reads poems to his seed
and plays music for his seeds. He also reads
books to his seeds.

In this book report, 7-year-old Ashton shows some elaboration when he says that Toad's habit of singing and reading to his seeds is "very silly." However, most children don't *intentionally* elaborate as a way to learn and remember information until sometime around puberty.

■ *Reciprocal teaching,* an approach to teaching reading described in Chapter 13, is another effective means of encouraging elaboration.

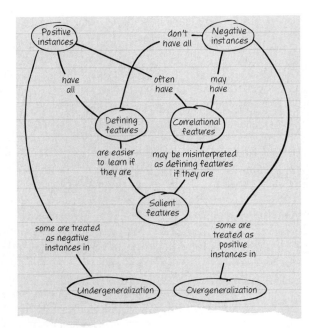

FIGURE 8.2 One possible concept map for concepts related to concept learning. Connections in the map are correctly interpreted by starting at the top and following the lines downward.

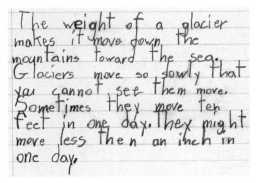

FIGURE 8.3 Eight-year-old Neville summarizes a lesson about glaciers.

■ As you read a textbook, when is the information in working memory? in long-term memory? With your answers in mind, explain why students should monitor their comprehension both as they read and also at a later time.

■ **comprehension monitoring** Process of checking oneself to be sure one understands information being read or heard.

■ **illusion of knowing** Thinking that one knows something that one actually does *not* know.

■ **self-explanation** Process of occasionally stopping to verbalize to oneself (and hence to better understand) material being read or studied.

■ **self-questioning** Process of asking oneself questions as a way of checking one's understanding of a topic.

ask them to summarize what they hear and read on a regular basis (e.g., see Figure 8.3). For example, we might occasionally give homework assignments asking students to write a summary of a textbook chapter. Or we might ask them to work in cooperative groups to develop a brief oral presentation that condenses information they've learned about a topic. At first we should restrict summarizing assignments to short, simple, and well-organized passages involving material with which students are familiar; we can assign more challenging material as students become more proficient summarizers (V. Anderson & Hidi, 1988/1989).

Monitoring Comprehension

Experiencing FIRSTHAND ·Looking Back

Stop for a minute and ask yourself this question:

What have I learned from the last five pages of this textbook?

Write your answer on a sheet of scrap paper.

· · · · · · ·

Now go back and look at the five pages just before this one. Does your answer include all the major points covered in these pages? Is there something you thought you understood but realize now that you didn't? Is there something you never learned at all—perhaps something you were "reading" when your mind was someplace altogether different?

Successful students engage in **comprehension monitoring**: They periodically check themselves to make sure they understand what they are reading or hearing. Furthermore, they take steps to correct the situation when they *don't* comprehend, perhaps by rereading a section of a textbook or asking a question in class (Hacker, 1998b; Haller, Child, & Walberg, 1988; Stone, 2000). In contrast, low achievers rarely check themselves or take appropriate action when they don't comprehend. Poor readers, for instance, seldom reread paragraphs they haven't completely understood the first time around (L. Baker & Brown, 1984).

Many students engage in little if any comprehension monitoring (Dole et al., 1991; Markman, 1979; J. W. Thomas, 1993a). When they don't monitor their learning, they don't know what they know and what they don't know: They may think they have mastered something when they really haven't (D. L. Butler & Winne, 1995; Hacker, 1998b; Stone, 2000). This **illusion of knowing** is seen in students at all levels, even college students (L. Baker, 1989; Horgan, Hacker, & Huffman, 1997). Our case study at the beginning of the chapter provides an example: When Mary studies, she fails to realize that she doesn't understand the difference between *velocity* and *acceleration*, so she is later quite surprised to find herself doing poorly on her physics test.

To be successful learners—and more specifically, to *know what they know*—students should monitor their comprehension both *while* they study and *after* they study (Hacker et al., 2000; T. O. Nelson & Dunlosky, 1991; Weaver & Kelemen, 1997). Comprehension monitoring does not have to be a solitary activity, of course. If students work in small study groups, their comprehension monitoring might easily take the form of elaborative interrogation. In a small-group study session, peers may detect gaps in understanding or misconceptions of which students themselves have previously been unaware (Hacker, 1998b).

Yet to be truly effectively learners, students must ultimately learn how to test *themselves* as well. One effective strategy is **self-explanation**, in which students frequently stop to explain to themselves what they have learned (deLeeuw & Chi, 2003). Another, similar approach is **self-questioning**, in which students periodically stop and ask themselves questions—essentially internalizing the mutual question-asking process they have learned from small-group study sessions (Wong, 1985). Their self-questions should, of course, include not only simple, fact-based questions but also the elaborative questions described earlier.

Experiencing FIRSTHAND ·Self-Reflection

Which of the study strategies we've just discussed do you use frequently? Which do you use seldom or not at all? Take a minute to fill in the empty boxes in Table 8.2.

· · · · · · ·

TABLE 8.2

Which Study Strategies Do You Use, and When?

STUDY STRATEGY	IN WHICH CLASSES OR SUBJECTS DO YOU USE THIS STRATEGY FREQUENTLY?	IN WHICH CLASSES OR SUBJECTS MIGHT YOU USE THIS STRATEGY MORE OFTEN?	WHAT FACTORS AFFECT YOUR ABILITY TO USE THIS STRATEGY SUCCESSFULLY?
Identifying important information			
Retrieving relevant prior knowledge			
Taking notes			
Organizing information			
Intentionally elaborating			
Creating summaries			
Monitoring comprehension			

Judging from the entries you have made in Table 8.2, do you think you are using effective study strategies? Do you see areas for improvement? Study strategies are complex metacognitive skills that are not easily acquired; your own strategies will undoubtedly continue to improve over time as you study increasingly challenging material in your college courses.

Some of the study strategies just described, such as taking notes and making outlines, are behaviors we can actually see. Others, such as retrieving relevant prior knowledge and monitoring comprehension, are internal mental processes that we *can't* see. It is probably the latter set of strategies—internal mental processes—that ultimately affect students' learning (Kardash & Amlund, 1991). As we help students develop study strategies, we must remember that behavioral strategies (e.g., taking notes) will be useful only to the extent that they promote more effective cognitive processing.

Factors Affecting Strategy Use

Several factors appear to influence students' choice and use of strategies: (a) the nature of assigned tasks, (b) students' knowledge base relative to the subject matter, (c) previous comprehension monitoring, (d) beliefs about the nature of knowledge and learning, (e) motivation, and (f) instruction in effective study strategies.

Nature of assigned tasks. In some situations teachers may assign tasks for which effective strategies are either counterproductive or impossible. If we assign simple tasks that involve lower-level skills (e.g., if we insist that facts and definitions be learned verbatim), students are unlikely to engage in such processes as meaningful learning and elaboration (J. C. Turner, 1995; Van Meter, Yokoi, & Pressley, 1994). If we expect students to master a great deal of material for an exam, students may have to devote the limited time they have to getting a general "impression" of everything rather than to developing an in-depth understanding and integration of the subject matter (J. W. Thomas, 1993b).

Knowledge base. Students are more likely to use effective strategies when they have a fair amount of prior knowledge about a topic (Greene, 1994; Schneider, 1993; E. Wood et al., 1994). Considering what you've learned about long-term memory storage processes, this point should hardly surprise you. Such processes as meaningful learning, organization, and elaboration all involve making connections between new material and things already stored in long-term memory—connections that are possible only when long-term memory contains information relevant to the topic at hand.

Previous comprehension monitoring. Students are apt to acquire and use new, more effective strategies only if they realize that their prior strategies have been *in*effective. And they will come to such a conclusion only if they monitor their comprehension regularly and so are aware that they are not learning and understanding classroom subject matter as well as they would like (Kuhn et al., 1995; Lodico, Ghatala, Levin, Pressley, & Bell, 1983; Loranger, 1994). Comprehension monitoring, then, does not just affect students' understanding of classroom subject matter. It also plays a pivotal role in the development of *other* metacognitive strategies.

Beliefs about the nature of knowledge and learning. In Chapter 7 we considered children's self-constructed theories about their physical, biological, and social worlds. Yet children also construct theories about their psychological world (recall our discussion of *theory of mind* in Chapter 2), and such theories include ideas about the nature of knowledge, academic subject matter, and knowledge acquisition. For example, I once had a conversation with my son Jeff, then an eleventh grader, about the Canadian Studies program that a local university had just added to its curriculum. Jeff's comments revealed a very simplistic view of what "history" is:

Jeff: The Canadians don't have as much history as we [Americans] do.
Me: Of course they do.
Jeff: No, they don't. They haven't had as many wars.
Me: History's more than wars.
Jeff: Yeah, but the rest of that stuff is really boring.

As I write the fifth edition of this book, Jeff is a college junior majoring in history. Obviously, he's discovered that history is a lot more than wars and other, "really boring" stuff. But I'm frustrated that he had to wait so long to find out.

Students' beliefs about knowledge and learning—collectively known as **epistemological beliefs**—often influence how they study and learn (Hofer & Pintrich, 1997; Purdie, Hattie, & Douglas, 1996; Schommer, 1997). For example, many students believe that knowledge is black and white (ideas are indisputably either right or wrong) and that you either have that knowledge or you don't. But other students recognize that there may be different, equally valid viewpoints on the same topic that could all be called "knowledge" (Schommer, 1994b). The former students are more likely to believe that learning should be a relatively rapid process, and so they will give up quickly if they find themselves struggling to understand classroom material. The latter students are more apt to persist in their learning efforts (Schommer, 1994b).

As another example, some students believe that when they read a textbook, they are passively absorbing information directly from the page to themselves; they may also believe that learning from a textbook requires studying isolated facts (recall Mary's approach to studying physics in the opening case study). In contrast, other students believe that learning from reading requires them to construct their own meanings by actively interpreting, organizing, and applying the information presented in the textbook. Students who think of reading as a constructive process are those most likely to process what they read in a meaningful and effective fashion (Paxton, 1999; Purdie et al., 1996; Schommer, 1994b; Schommer-Aikins, 2001).

Students' epistemological beliefs tend to evolve as they grow older. Students in the elementary grades typically believe in the certainty of knowledge; they think that for any topic there is an absolute truth "out there" somewhere (Astington & Pelletier, 1996; Kuhn & Weinstock, 2002). As they reach high school, some students (but by no means all of them) begin to realize that knowledge is a subjective entity and that different perspectives on a topic may be equally valid (Kuhn & Weinstock, 2002; Schommer, 1997). Other changes may also occur at the high school level. For example, students in twelfth grade are more likely than ninth graders to believe that knowledge consists of complex interrelationships (rather than discrete facts), that learning happens slowly (rather than quickly), and that one's ability to learn something can improve with practice (rather than depending solely on inherited intelligence) (Schommer, 1997). Such developmental trends are reflected in some of the entries in Table 8.1.

As teachers, we must communicate to students—both in what we *say* and in what we *do* (e.g., what activities we assign, how we assess students' learning)—what we ourselves have already learned about knowledge and learning (Hofer & Pintrich, 1997; P. M. King & Kitchener, 2002; Schommer, 1994b):

- Knowledge does not always mean having clear-cut answers to difficult, complex issues.
- Knowledge involves not only knowing facts, concepts, and ideas but also understanding interrelationships among these things.
- Learning involves active construction of knowledge, rather than just a passive "reception" of it.
- Mastering a body of information or a complex skill sometimes requires persistence and hard work.

■ **epistemological beliefs** Beliefs about the nature of knowledge and knowledge acquisition.

In communicating such messages, we increase the likelihood that our students will apply effective study strategies, critically evaluate classroom subject matter, and undergo conceptual change when they encounter explanations that contradict their current beliefs (Hofer & Pintrich, 1997; P. M. King & Kitchener, 2002; Purdie et al., 1996; Schommer, 1994b; Sinatra & Pintrich, 2003a).

Motivation. Motivational factors also influence the extent to which students use effective strategies to learn and study. Some students may be more interested in "getting by" with a passing grade than in truly mastering the subject matter (P. A. Alexander et al., 1998; Nolen, 1996; Palmer & Goetz, 1988). Others may think that meaningful learning and other effective strategies involve too much time and effort to be worthwhile. Still others may have so little faith in their ability to learn that they believe they will do poorly regardless of the strategy they use. In our discussions of cognitive factors underlying motivation in Chapter 12, we'll identify many things we can do to overcome such impediments to successful learning and achievement.

Instruction in effective study strategies. Can students be taught to study more effectively? Research studies answer this question with a firm yes (see the reference list at the bottom of Table 8.3). Effective study skills training programs often include components such as these:

- Time management (e.g., planning when and how long to study)
- Effective learning and reading strategies
- Note-taking strategies
- Specific memory techniques (e.g., mnemonics)
- Comprehension-monitoring strategies
- Test-taking strategies

In general, graduates of study skills training programs are more confident about their ability to succeed in the classroom and, in fact, do achieve at higher levels (e.g., Paris, 1988; Pressley, El-Dinary, Marks, Brown, & Stein, 1992; J. E. Wilson, 1988).

How can we help students *learn how to learn?* Researchers have identified several principles that describe the conditions under which students are most likely to acquire and use effective study skills. Table 8.3 presents these principles, along with their implications for classroom practice.

As teachers, we should not only teach our students to learn and study more effectively but should also monitor how they typically *do* learn and study. Let's look at what one high school student does when she studies.

Interpreting Student Artifacts and Behaviors

Emily's Strategies

For an assignment in my educational psychology class, Melissa Tillman interviewed an 18-year-old high school senior whom I'll call "Emily." In her early high school years, Emily was earning mostly Cs and Ds, but by the end of eleventh grade she had started to work more diligently on her schoolwork, and at the time of this interview, she was earning As and Bs. As you read the interview, consider

- What strategies Emily uses when she studies
- How effective these strategies are
- What Emily believes about the nature of learning and academic subject matter (i.e., her epistemological beliefs)

Melissa:	How did you learn to study for a test?
Emily:	I'm not really sure. I never learned the correct way to study for a test. I use my own methods, and they seem to be working because I'm now receiving the grades I want.
Melissa:	How did you go about studying for a test when you were younger?
Emily:	Honestly, I never really studied too hard. I never studied for math tests because I didn't know how to. For other subjects like history, I'd just skim over the text. Skimming the text never made the material stick in my head. I guess I never really had a strategy for studying.
Melissa:	Now that you're receiving good grades, how do you study for a test?
Emily:	Well, it's different for every subject. Now when I study for a math test, I do many practice problems. When I'm studying for a history or science test, I first review my notes. My favorite thing to do is make flash cards with the important facts. I then go through the flash cards many times and try to learn the facts on them.
Melissa:	What do you mean, "learn" the facts on them?

Emily:	I guess I try to memorize the facts. I'll go through the flash cards many times and say them over and over in my head until I remember them.
Melissa:	How do you know when a fact is memorized?
Emily:	I'll repeat a fact over and over in my head until I think I've memorized it. Then I'll leave and do something else, like get a snack. I know I've memorized something if I still remember it after taking my break.
Melissa:	Do you consider yourself a good textbook reader?
Emily:	Not really. Textbooks are pretty boring. I'll try to read everything in the textbook, but at times I find myself looking for boldface print. Phrases in bold print are important.
Melissa:	What are some good methods for studying for a test?
Emily:	I really like the flash card method because it helps me to memorize facts. I also like to reread the text and my notes. Another good method is outlining the text, but this method takes too long so I rarely use it.

TABLE 8.3   PRINCIPLES/ASSUMPTIONS

Promoting More Effective Study Strategies

PRINCIPLE	EDUCATIONAL IMPLICATION	EXAMPLE
Study strategies are most effectively learned within the context of particular subject areas.	When presenting academic content through lectures, reading assignments, and so on, simultaneously teach students how to study that content.	Give students specific questions to ask themselves (thereby facilitating comprehension monitoring) as they read their textbooks.
Group learning situations often promote the development of effective strategies, perhaps because students verbalize and model various ways to think about classroom subject matter.	Occasionally ask students to study instructional material in pairs or small cooperative learning groups.	Have students work in pairs to develop and answer questions that require them to elaborate on textbook content.
Students are more likely to acquire sophisticated study strategies when their initial efforts are scaffolded to promote success.	Scaffold students' attempts to use new strategies—for instance, by modeling the strategies, giving clues about when to use them, and providing feedback on appropriate and inappropriate strategy use.	To encourage students to organize material in a particular way, provide an organizational chart that cooperative learning groups fill out.
Students learn more effectively when their study strategies are numerous and varied.	As opportunities arise, continue to introduce new strategies—note taking, elaboration, self-questioning, mnemonics, and so on—throughout the school year.	Suggest that students use such mnemonics as verbal mediation and the keyword method to learn the capitals of South American countries or the meanings of Japanese vocabulary words.
Students are more likely to use effective study strategies when they understand why those strategies are useful.	Explain the usefulness of various strategies in ways that students understand.	Show students how note taking helps them keep their minds from wandering during class and how comprehension monitoring enables them to identify gaps in their knowledge.
Students use strategies more effectively if they know when each one is most appropriate.	Point out occasions in which particular strategies are apt to be helpful.	Encourage students to elaborate on material—by drawing implications, generating new examples, and so on—when they know they will need to apply it to new situations later on.
Students are most likely to master effective strategies when they can practice them regularly across a wide variety of tasks.	Give students opportunities to apply each strategy in numerous contexts.	Ask students' previous teachers what strategies they have taught, and then explain how such strategies are applicable for current learning tasks as well.
Students are likely to use effective strategies only when they believe such strategies can ultimately help them achieve at higher levels.	When teaching study strategies, make sure each student is eventually able to apply them successfully. Also, expose students to peers who model effective use of the strategies.	After a lecture, have small groups of students look at one another's notes and then combine them into a single, comprehensive set.

Sources: P. A. Alexander et al., 1998; R. C. Anderson et al., 2001; Barnett, Di Vesta, & Rogozinski, 1981; Borkowski, Carr, Rellinger, & Pressley, 1990; D. L. Butler & Winne, 1995; A. Collins et al., 1989; Hacker, 1998b; Hattie, Biggs, & Purdie, 1996; Kahl & Woloshyn, 1994; A. King, 1992, 1994; Kucan & Beck, 1997; Kuhn et al., 1995; Mayer & Wittrock, 1996; Meloth & Deering, 1994; Nist, Simpson, Olejnik, & Mealey, 1991; Palincsar & Brown, 1984; Paris, 1988; Paris & Winograd, 1990; Pintrich, Garcia, & De Groot, 1994; Pressley, Borkowski, & Schneider, 1987; Pressley, El-Dinary, et al., 1992; Pressley, Harris, & Marks, 1992; Rosenshine & Meister, 1992; Rosenshine et al., 1996; Starr & Lovett, 2000; J. W. Thomas, 1993a; Vygotsky, 1978; C. E. Weinstein, Goetz, & Alexander, 1988; West et al., 1991; Winne, 1995; E. Wood et al., 1999, 1994.

Emily uses several strategies: solving practice problems (for math), taking and reviewing notes, making flash cards and repeating what's on them, and (rarely) outlining a reading assignment. Although she makes some attempt to impose meaning on what she is studying (e.g., she identifies "important facts"), her heavy reliance on flash cards and rehearsal and her view that "phrases in bold print are important" indicate that she engages primarily in rote learning and reads her textbooks only superficially. (From what she says, we can't tell what she does when she works on the math problems.) One good sign is that she monitors her comprehension after a delay ("I know I've memorized something if I still remember it after taking my break"); nevertheless she is concerned primarily about learning things verbatim. Apparently, Emily believes that, with the exception of math (which involves solving problems), most school subjects consist of isolated facts that must be committed to memory.

How students learn and study school subject matter has implications not only for how effectively they can remember it but also for how likely they are to *use* it on later occasions, as we shall see in our upcoming exploration of transfer.

TRANSFER

Consider these three students:

- Elena is bilingual: She speaks both English and Spanish fluently. She begins a French course in high school and immediately recognizes many similarities between French and Spanish. "Aha," she thinks, "what I know about Spanish will help me learn French."
- In her middle school history class, Stella discovers that she does better on exams when she takes more notes. She decides to take more notes in her geography class as well, and once again the strategy pays off.
- Ted's fifth-grade class has been working with decimals for several weeks. His teacher asks, "Which number is larger, 4.4 or 4.14?" Ted recalls something that he knows about whole numbers: Numbers with three digits are larger than numbers with only two digits. "The larger number is 4.14," he mistakenly concludes.

People often use something they have learned in one situation to help them in another situation. What students learn in school and at home can potentially help them later on—perhaps in more advanced classwork, in their personal lives, or in their later careers. But occasionally students (like Ted) learn something at one time that, rather than helping, actually *interferes* with something they must learn or do later.

When something students have previously learned affects how they learn or perform in another situation, **transfer** is occurring. Ideally, transfer should be a major objective for classrooms at all grade levels. When people cannot use their basic arithmetic skills to compute correct change or balance a checkbook, when they cannot use their knowledge of English grammar in a job application or business report, and when they cannot apply their knowledge of science to an understanding of personal health or environmental problems, then we have to wonder whether the time spent learning the arithmetic, the grammar, and the science might have been better spent doing something else. As we explore the nature of transfer in this section, we will identify numerous ways to help students apply classroom subject matter to new situations, both in their future academic studies and in the outside world.

Basic Concepts in Transfer

We begin our discussion by distinguishing between various kinds of transfer—in particular, between positive and negative transfer, and between specific and general transfer.

Positive Versus Negative Transfer **Positive transfer** occurs when something a person has learned in one situation *helps* the person learn or perform in another situation. Positive transfer took place when Elena's Spanish helped her learn French and when Stella's experiences with note taking in history class improved her performance in geography. In contrast, **negative transfer** occurs when prior knowledge *hinders* a person's learning or performance at a later time. This was the situation for poor Ted: He transferred a principle related to whole numbers (one number is always larger than another if it has more digits) to a situation where it didn't apply: the comparison of decimals. We also see negative transfer at work when students erroneously apply rules of pronunciation and grammar in their native language as they study a different language

■ **transfer** Phenomenon in which something a student has learned at one time affects how the student learns or performs in a later situation.

■ **positive transfer** Phenomenon in which something learned at one time facilitates learning or performance at a later time.

■ **negative transfer** Phenomenon in which something learned at one time interferes with learning or performance at a later time.

■ Can you think of a recent situation in which you exhibited positive transfer? negative transfer?

(Littlewood, 1984). We see it, too, in some students' tendency to confuse the various wars they've studied in history, perhaps "recalling" that the American Revolution was a battle between the English and the French (as was true for the French and Indian War) or between the Northern and Southern states (as was true for the American Civil War) (McKeown & Beck, 1990).

In Chapter 7 we discovered that previously acquired misconceptions can have a negative impact on learning. Here we see that *correct* ideas and information sometimes have a negative impact as well, in that students may apply them inappropriately in new situations.

Specific Versus General Transfer   Transfer from one situation to another often occurs when the two situations overlap in content. Consider Elena, the student fluent in Spanish who is now taking French. Elena should have an easy time learning to count in French because the numbers (*un, deux, trois, quatre, cinq*) are very similar to the Spanish she already knows (*uno, dos, tres, cuatro, cinco*). When transfer occurs because the original learning task and the transfer task overlap in content, we have **specific transfer**.

Now consider Stella's strategy of taking more notes in geography because note taking was beneficial in her history class. History and geography don't necessarily overlap in content, but a strategy that she developed in one class has been effectively applied in the other. Here is an instance of **general transfer**: Learning in one situation affects learning and performance in a somewhat dissimilar situation.

Historically, research studies have indicated that specific transfer occurs far more often than general transfer (W. D. Gray & Orasanu, 1987). In fact, the question of whether general transfer occurs at all has been the subject of considerable debate. Many early educators believed that certain subjects (e.g., Latin, Greek, mathematics, logic) had great potential for general transfer: Because these subjects required considerable attention to precision and detail, they would "strengthen" students' minds and thereby enable students to tackle other, unrelated tasks more easily. This **formal discipline** perspective of transfer persisted throughout the first several decades of the twentieth century. For instance, when I was in high school in the mid-1960s, most college-bound students were encouraged to take both French and Latin, the only two languages my school offered. Taking French made a great deal of sense: Growing up in Massachusetts, we were within a day's drive of French-speaking Quebec. "But why should I take Latin?" I asked my guidance counselor. "I can use it only if I attend Catholic mass or run across phrases like 'caveat emptor' or 'in Deo speramus.' Hardly anyone speaks the language anymore." The counselor pursed her thin red lips and gave me a look that told me that she knew best. "Latin will discipline your mind," she told me. "It will help you learn better."

■ Does this discussion contradict what you previously believed about the value of general mental exercise? If so, have you undergone *conceptual change*?

Research has generally discredited this "mind as muscle" notion of transfer (Perkins & Salomon, 1989; E. L. Thorndike, 1924). For example, practice in memorizing poems does not necessarily make one a faster poem memorizer (James, 1890). And studying computer programming, though often a worthwhile activity in its own right, does not necessarily help a person with dissimilar kinds of logical tasks (Mayer & Wittrock, 1996; Perkins & Salomon, 1989). Such results have led some theorists to suggest that general transfer is a rare animal indeed—that, in fact, knowledge and thinking skills acquired in specific contexts are unlikely to be used outside those contexts (Hirschfeld & Gelman, 1994; Lave & Wenger, 1991; P. Light & Butterworth, 1993; Singley & Anderson, 1989). This principle is often referred to as **situated cognition**: Knowledge and thinking skills are *situated* within the context in which they develop (e.g., J. S. Brown et al., 1989).

If you have read the discussion of cognitive development in Chapter 2, then you have already seen examples of situated cognition. As you may recall, Piaget proposed that such thinking abilities as abstract thought, proportional reasoning, and separation and control of variables emerge at about age 11 or 12 (at the onset of the formal operations stage) and are then used in a wide variety of tasks. Yet we reviewed evidence in Chapter 2 to indicate that students do not acquire formal operational abilities in one fell swoop and then apply them equally across all subject domains. Instead, students are more likely to exhibit formal operational reasoning in some domains than in others, and they are especially likely to exhibit them in contexts where they have the most experience.

■ **specific transfer** Instance of transfer in which the original learning task and the transfer task overlap in content.

■ **general transfer** Instance of transfer in which the original learning task and the transfer task are different in content.

■ **formal discipline** View of transfer suggesting that the study of rigorous subjects enhances one's ability to learn other, unrelated things.

■ **situated cognition** Knowledge and *thinking skills acquired and used primarily within certain contexts, with limited if any transfer to other contexts.*

Certainly some of the basic skills that students learn in school—reading and arithmetic, for example—*do* transfer to out-of-school tasks and situations (J. R. Anderson, Greeno, Reder, & Simon, 2000). Furthermore, if we broaden our view of *what* might transfer, we become more optimistic about the extent to which general transfer can occur. We frequently see general transfer of learning and study strategies: When students acquire effective learning and study strategies within the context of one academic discipline, they often apply them in a very different discipline (Brooks & Dansereau, 1987; Perkins, 1995; Pressley, Snyder, & Cariglia-Bull, 1987). In addition, the general beliefs and attitudes that students acquire about learning and thinking—for instance, confidence in their ability to master school subject matter, recognition that learning often takes hard work, and willingness to consider multiple viewpoints on controversial issues—can have a profound impact on later learning and achievement across multiple domains (see Chapters 10 and 12) and so clearly illustrate general transfer at work (De Corte, 2003; Pugh, Bergin, & Rocks, 2003; Volet, 1999).

Factors Affecting Transfer

Although both specific and general transfer do occur, students often *don't* transfer the knowledge and skills they learn in school on occasions when such knowledge and skills are clearly applicable (Mayer & Wittrock, 1996; Perkins, 1992; Renkl, Mandl, & Gruber, 1996). A number of factors influence the extent to which transfer occurs: (a) amount of instructional time, (b) meaningful learning, (c) learning of general principles, (d) examples and practice opportunities, (e) similarity, (f) time between instruction and application, and (g) perception of information as context-free. Let's look more closely at each of these.

Brain aerobics

The formal discipline view of transfer portrays the mind as a muscle that benefits from general mental exercise.

Amount of instructional time. Instructional time is clearly an important variable affecting transfer: The more time students spend studying a single topic, the more likely they are to transfer what they learn to a new situation (Gick & Holyoak, 1987; Schmidt & Bjork, 1992; Voss, 1987). Conversely, when students study a great many topics without learning very much about any one of them, they are unlikely to apply what they have learned at a later date. Here we see another instance of the *less is more* principle introduced in Chapter 7: Students are more likely to transfer their school learning to new situations, including those beyond the classroom, when we have them study a few things in depth and learn them *well*, rather than study many topics superficially (Brophy, 1992b; Porter, 1989).

Meaningful learning. In Chapter 6 we identified two advantages of meaningful learning over rote learning: Information is stored more quickly and is retrieved more easily. An additional advantage is that information learned in a meaningful fashion is more likely to be transferred or applied to a new situation (Bereiter, 1995; Brooks & Dansereau, 1987; Mayer & Wittrock, 1996).

Remember, meaningful learning involves connecting information with what one already knows. The more associations students make between new information and the various other things in their long-term memories, the more likely it is that they will "find" (retrieve) that information at a time when it will be useful.

Learning of general principles. Learners can transfer general (and perhaps somewhat abstract) principles more easily than specific, concrete facts (J. R. Anderson et al., 1996; Judd, 1932; Perkins & Salomon, 1987). The following exercise illustrates this idea.

Experiencing FIRSTHAND ·Central Business Districts

Consider these two ideas from geography:

- Boston's central business district is located near Boston Harbor.
- The central business districts of most older cities, which were settled before the development of modern transportation, are found in close proximity to a navigable body of water, such as an ocean or a river.

Which statement would be more helpful to you if you were trying to find your way around Liverpool, Toronto, or Pittsburgh?

· · · · · · ·

No doubt the second statement would prove more useful to you. The first one is a fact about a particular city, whereas the second one reflects a general principle applicable to many different cities.

■ Think about the subject matter you will be teaching. What general principles should have wide applicability for students?

Specific facts have an important place in the classroom; for example, students should know what two plus three equal, what the Berlin Wall signified, and where to find Africa on a globe. Yet facts themselves have limited utility in new situations. The more we can instead emphasize general principles—for example, that two positive whole numbers added together always equal a larger number, that a country's citizens sometimes revolt when their government officials act unjustly, and that the cultures of various nations are influenced by their location and climate—the more we facilitate students' ability to transfer what they learn.

Examples and practice opportunities. Students are much more likely to transfer what they learn if, within the course of instruction, they are given many examples and have numerous opportunities to practice in different situations (Cox, 1997; Reimann & Schult, 1996; J. A. Ross, 1988; Schmidt & Bjork, 1992). For example, students will be more apt to apply their knowledge of fractions and ratios to real-world tasks if they practice using it in such activities as cooking, converting dollars to a foreign currency, and drawing objects to scale. By using knowledge in many contexts, students store it in association with each of those contexts and so are more likely to retrieve the information on a future occasion (Perkins & Salomon, 1987; Voss, 1987).

Similarity. Let's return to the problem that Mary encounters in our opening case study:

> An automotive engineer has designed a car that can reach a speed of 50 miles per hour within 5 seconds. What is the car's rate of acceleration?

Imagine that Mary eventually learns how to solve this problem using the formula $v = a \times t$. Because the velocity (v) is 50 miles per hour and the time (t) is 5 seconds, the rate of acceleration (a) must be 10 miles per hour per second.

Now Mary encounters two additional problems:

> A car salesperson tells a customer that a particular model of car can reach a speed of 40 miles per hour within 8 seconds. What is the car's rate of acceleration?

> A biologist reports that a cheetah she has been observing can attain a speed of 60 kilometers per hour within a 10-second period. How quickly can the cheetah increase its speed?

Which problem do you think Mary will find easier to solve?

Transfer is more likely to occur when a new situation appears to be similar to a previous situation (Bassok, 1990; Blake & Clark, 1990; Di Vesta & Peverly, 1984). Mary will probably have an easier time solving the problem involving the car salesperson because it superficially resembles the problem about the automotive engineer: Both problems involve cars, and both use miles as the unit of measure. The cheetah problem, even though it can be solved using the same approach as the other two, involves a different domain (animals) and a different unit of measure (kilometers).

Here we see the value of *authentic activities* in the curriculum. Of the many examples and opportunities for practice that we give our students, at least some should be very similar to the situations that students are likely to encounter in future studies or in the outside world. The more that school tasks resemble students' later life experiences, the more likely it is that students will put their school learning to use (Perkins, 1992).

Yet we should note that the similarity of two situations, although usually promoting positive transfer, can sometimes promote negative transfer instead. To see what I mean, try the following exercise.

Experiencing FIRSTHAND ·A Division Problem

Quickly estimate an answer to this division problem:

$$20 \div 0.38$$

Is your answer larger or smaller than 20?

· · · · · · ·

If you applied your knowledge of division by whole numbers here, you undoubtedly concluded that the answer is smaller than 20. In fact, the answer is approximately 52.63, a number *larger* than 20. Has this exercise reminded you of Ted's erroneous conclusion—4.14 is larger than 4.4—based on his knowledge of how whole numbers can be compared? Many students, even at the university level, show negative transfer of whole-number principles to situations involving decimals (Tirosh & Graeber, 1990). Working with decimals appears, on the surface, to be similar to working with whole numbers; the only difference—a very important one, as it turns out—is a tiny decimal point.

To prevent negative transfer, we, as teachers, must be sure to point out differences between two superficially similar topics. For example, Ted's teacher could have identified some of the specific ways in which decimals are *not* like whole numbers. As another example, I find that students in my educational psychology classes often have trouble using the term *maturation* correctly in our discussions of child development because the term has a different meaning in everyday conversation. So when I first introduce the concept of maturation, I take great pains to show students how psychology's meaning of the word (the unfolding of genetically controlled developmental changes) differs from other meanings they may have for the word (e.g., possession of effective, "mature" social skills).

Time between instruction and application. Learners are most apt to apply new information soon after they have learned it. They are less likely to use it as time goes on (Gick & Holyoak, 1987). Whenever possible, then, we should try to present topics close in time to when students will need to use them.

To illustrate, consider again the physics principle that Mary learns in the opening case study: $v = a \times t$ (velocity equals acceleration times time). The formula tells Mary how to calculate velocity when she knows both the acceleration and the time. But let's say that she instead wants to calculate the rate of acceleration, as she needs to do for the "car" and "cheetah" problems. If Mary is studying algebra concurrently with her physics class, or else has studied it very recently, she is more likely to see the usefulness of algebra in rearranging the formula like so: $a = \frac{v}{t}$.

Children are more apt to transfer their knowledge of fractions and ratios to future situations if they perceive it to be context-free and if they practice using it in a variety of real-world contexts.

Perception of information as context-free. On many occasions we may hope that students transfer their knowledge in one content domain to a different domain. For example, we'd like them to transfer math to physics, grammar to creative writing, history to current events, and health to personal eating habits. Yet many students tend to think of academic subject areas as being distinct, unrelated disciplines; they also tend to think of their school learning as being separate from real-world concerns (Perkins & Simmons, 1988; Rakow, 1984). When students see what they learn in school as being related only to a particular topic or discipline, or *context-bound*, they are unlikely to transfer it to situations outside that context (P. A. Alexander & Judy, 1988; J. R. Anderson et al., 1996; Bassok, 1997; Renkl et al., 1996).

When we teach material within a particular academic discipline, then, we should relate the material to other disciplines and to the outside world as often as possible (Blake & Clark, 1990; Perkins, 1992). For example, we might show students how human digestion provides a justification for categorizing food into several basic food groups or how economic issues affect tropical rain forests. Ideally, we should have students use what they learn in many different contexts, including a variety of authentic activities, so that eventually their knowledge and skills become *context-free* (A. Collins et al., 1989).

■ What implications does this idea have for classroom assessment practices?

Importance of Retrieval in Transfer

The factors we've just examined point to a key principle in transfer: From a cognitive perspective, information learned in one situation helps in another situation only if the information is *retrieved* within the context of the second situation (Cormier, 1987; Gick & Holyoak, 1987; Halpern, 1998). Several factors—in-depth study, meaningful learning, focus on general principles, variety of examples and practice opportunities, and perception of a domain as context-free—are likely to encourage students to make numerous connections between class material and other aspects of their world, and such multiple connections will invariably enhance the likelihood of retrieving the material on occasions where it is potentially relevant. Students are *un*likely to apply information they have not previously connected to other things (information they have acquired through rote learning), partly because they probably won't retrieve it when they need it and partly because they won't see its relevance if they *do* retrieve it.

Another factor—similarity between the learning situation and transfer situation—is related to retrieval as well. Students are more likely to transfer what they learn in one situation to a similar (rather than dissimilar) situation because a similar situation provides *retrieval cues* that remind students of specific, relevant things they have already learned (Gick & Holyoak, 1987; Perkins & Salomon, 1989; Sternberg & Frensch, 1993). Yet another factor—the time elapsed between initial learning and later transfer situation—probably affects retrieval indirectly. As we discovered in our discussion of forgetting in Chapter 6, information stored in long-term memory may weaken (decay) over time, especially if it is not used regularly.

At this point, let's take a look at one student's attempts to transfer classroom subject matter to real-world tasks and problems.

Interpreting Student Artifacts and Behaviors

Applying Math

A fourth-grade teacher gives her students the following assignment:

> In what ways do you see your parents and other adults using math in their daily activities? List lots of ways in which math is used every day. The person with the most examples will win a small prize. Good luck!

In the artifact at the left, 9-year-old Peyton brainstorms real-world contexts in which math is used. As you look at his list:

- Speculate about the extent to which Peyton is aware of real-world applications of mathematics
- Evaluate the quality of his responses
- Identify possible reasons why some of Peyton's responses are better than others
- Speculate about the probable effectiveness of the assignment for promoting transfer

1. cooking.
2. putting lego's together.
3. Building
4. counting
5. Measuring height
6. Fractions (how mouch drink you can have).
7. shopping
8. sorting
9. Baseball
10. pencils
11. counting
12. forks
13. spoons
14. Knives
15. plates
16. cups
17. cups
18. TV channels
19. Time
19. radio channels
20. Work book for math.

Peyton identifies a variety of contexts in which math is used (e.g., cooking, building, shopping, measuring, counting, telling time), suggesting that he sees math as a context-free discipline with many potential applications. Unfortunately, the brevity of Peyton's responses makes it difficult to predict how much he might actually *use* math in such activities as cooking and shopping. In fact, some responses (e.g., "forks," "spoons," "knives") are so brief that we really don't know what he means. Perhaps Peyton is simply listing items that can be counted; in essence, he might be "padding" his list.

Several possible reasons might account for the varying quality of Peyton's responses. As a fourth grader, his writing skills are, of course, somewhat limited, and so he may simply not know how to explain how he might, say, use math to put Lego blocks together. Furthermore, the assignment doesn't *ask* him to be specific. In fact, it encourages him to do quite the opposite: to generate as many different examples as he can (the student with the most will win a prize). We'll return to this point when we discuss reinforcement in Chapter 9.

Asking students to brainstorm possible applications of classroom subject matter can certainly encourage them to connect the subject matter with a variety of real-world contexts (J. R. Anderson et al., 1996). Without doubt, however, such connections will be stronger and more enduring if students actually *use* the subject matter in those contexts on a regular basis. Three activities in which students regularly transfer what they have learned are problem solving, creativity, and critical thinking. In the next three sections, we will look at each of these higher-level processes in turn.

PROBLEM SOLVING

Experiencing FIRSTHAND ·Four Problems

How many of these problems can you solve?

1. You buy two apples for 25¢ each and one pear for 40¢. How much change will you get back from a dollar bill?

2. You are building a treehouse with the shape and dimensions illustrated in Figure 8.4. You need to buy planks for a slanted roof. How long must the roof planks be to reach from one side of the treehouse to the other?

3. As a teacher, you want to illustrate the idea that metal battleships float even though metal is denser (and so heavier) than water. You don't have any toy boats made of

metal. What can you use instead to show students that a metal object with a hollow interior can float on water?

4. Every day almost 75,000 acres of tropical rain forest disappear. What steps might be taken to curtail this alarming rate of deforestation?

· · · · · · ·

Sometimes problems are straightforward and relatively easy to solve. For example, problem 1 requires only simple addition and subtraction procedures; you probably had little difficulty finding the correct solution, 10¢. Problem 2 (Figure 8.4) is more difficult, partly because you don't encounter such problems very often. But if you have studied geometry, then you probably learned the Pythagorean theorem: In any right triangle, the square of the hypotenuse equals the sum of the squares of the other two sides. Looking at the top part of the treehouse (from the dotted line upward) as a triangle, we can find the length for the roof planks (x) this way:

$$(\text{slanted side})^2 = (\text{horzontal side})^2 + (\text{vertical side})^2$$
$$x^2 = 4^2 + (5-2)^2$$
$$x^2 = 16 + 9$$
$$x^2 = 25$$
$$x = 5$$

How long do the roof planks of this treehouse need to be?

FIGURE 8.4 Building a treehouse

Problems don't always have a single correct solution, of course. If you are looking for a metal object with a hollow interior to float on water (problem 3), you might use a variety of objects to solve your problem—possibly a pie pan, bucket, or thimble. And you might identify several possible ways of addressing rain forest deforestation (problem 4), but you probably wouldn't know which of these (if any) are correct solutions (i.e., which ones would successfully help preserve tropical rain forests) until you actually implemented them.

We most commonly associate problem solving with mathematics and science. Yet problems can occur in virtually any content domain—for instance, in social studies, language arts, or sports. The "rain forest" problem may require knowledge of economics, political science, and psychology. To write a persuasive essay, a writer must identify evidence and arguments that will be convincing to readers. To win a game against a challenging competitor, a basketball team may need to develop new strategies to keep the other team's star shooter away from the basket.

In the upcoming pages we will explore the multifaceted nature of human problem solving. After defining several basic concepts, we will examine cognitive factors that help or hinder successful problem solving; in the process, we will also identify strategies for helping students become more successful problem solvers. As we go along, you should find places where you can apply (*transfer!*) what you have previously learned about transfer.

Basic Concepts in Problem Solving

As we have just seen, the problems people encounter differ widely in content and scope; for instance, one problem may involve a backyard treehouse, and another may involve the devastation of tropical rain forests. Furthermore, different problems may call for different strategies; for instance, one might be solved by using the Pythagorean theorem, whereas another might require a world summit conference. Yet virtually all problems can be considered either *well-defined* or *ill-defined* (or perhaps somewhere in between), and virtually all problem-solving strategies can be categorized as either *algorithms* or *heuristics*.

Well-Defined and Ill-Defined Problems   Problems differ in the extent to which they are clearly specified and structured. A **well-defined problem** is one in which the goal is clearly stated, all information needed to solve the problem is present, and only one correct answer exists. Calculating change from a dollar after a purchase (problem 1) and determining the length of planks needed for a treehouse roof (problem 2) are examples of well-defined problems.

In contrast, an **ill-defined problem** is one in which the desired goal is unclear, information needed to solve the problem is missing, or several possible solutions exist. To some extent, finding a suitable substitute for a metal ship (problem 3) is an ill-defined problem: Many objects might serve as a ship substitute, and some might work better than others. The rain forest

■ **well-defined problem** Problem in which the goal is clearly stated, all information needed to solve the problem is present, and only one correct answer exists.

■ **ill-defined problem** Problem in which the desired goal is unclear, information needed to solve the problem is missing. and/or several possible solutions to the problem exist.

■ The distinction between well-defined and ill-defined problems is better conceptualized as a continuum than an "either-or" situation.

deforestation problem (problem 4) is even less defined. First, the goal—curtailing deforestation—is ambiguous. Do we want to stop deforestation altogether or just slow it down a bit? If we just want to decrease the rate, what rate is acceptable? Second, we need more information to solve the problem. For instance, it would be helpful to determine whether previously cleared and farmed lands can be reclaimed and rejuvenated, and to identify economically reasonable alternatives to slash-and-burn farming practices. Some of this needed information may require extensive research. Finally, there is no single "correct" solution for problem 4: Curtailing deforestation will undoubtedly require a number of steps taken more or less simultaneously. Ill-defined problems, then, are usually more difficult to solve than well-defined ones.

Most problems presented in school are well defined: A question clearly specifies a goal, all needed information is present, and only one answer is correct. Consider this typical mathematics word problem as an example:

> Old MacDonald has planted potatoes in a field 100 yards long and 50 yards wide. If the field yields an average of 5 pounds of potatoes in each square yard, how many pounds of potatoes can MacDonald expect to harvest from his field?

In this problem, the goal is clear: Determine how many pounds of potatoes the field will yield. We also have all the information needed to solve the problem, with no irrelevant information to distract us. And there is only one correct answer, with no room for debate.

But the real world presents ill-defined problems far more often than well-defined ones, and students need practice in dealing with them (L. B. Resnick, 1988; Sternberg et al., 2000). Consider this problem as an example:

> Old MacDonald's son wants to go to a small, coeducational college 200 miles away. MacDonald doesn't know whether he can afford the college tuition; it all depends on how well his potato crop does this summer. What should MacDonald tell his son?

Notice how the problem has a rather vaguely stated goal: determining what MacDonald should say to his son. It does not identify the specific questions he needs to address before he gives an answer. Nor does it give us all the information we need to solve the problem, such as the size of MacDonald's potato field, the predicted size of his crop, the probable value of the potatoes, the family's day-to-day living expenses, or the cost of college tuition. Finally, there may be no single correct answer: Whether MacDonald encourages his son to go to college depends not only on finances but also on his beliefs about the value of a college education and on his need to have his son stay at home to help with farm chores.

One way of helping students learn to solve problems is to teach them techniques for better defining ill-defined problems. For example, we can teach them how to break large problems into smaller, well-defined ones (e.g., determining the probable size of the potato crop, calculating the farmer's daily living expenses). We can also teach them to distinguish information they need (e.g., the size of the farmer's potato field) from information they may *not* need (e.g., the fact that the college is coeducational). And we can teach techniques for finding missing information (e.g., how to measure distance, how to use the library or Internet to find the market price of potatoes, how to obtain information about tuition rates at different colleges).

Problem-Solving Strategies: Algorithms and Heuristics   Some problems can be successfully solved by following specific, step-by-step instructions—that is, by using an **algorithm**. We can correctly assemble the pieces of a new bookcase by following the "Directions for Assembly" that come with the package. We can calculate the length of a slanted roof by using the Pythagorean theorem. When we follow an algorithm faithfully, we invariably arrive at a correct solution.

Yet not all problems come equipped with directions for assembly. There are no rules we can follow to identify a substitute metal ship, no list of instructions to help us solve the deforestation problem. When there is no algorithm for solving a problem, people must instead use a **heuristic**, a general problem-solving strategy that may or may not yield a workable solution. For example, one heuristic that we might use in solving the deforestation problem is this: Identify a new behavior that adequately replaces the problem behavior (in particular, *identify another way that* peasant farmers can meet their survival needs). As another example of a heuristic, consider the addition problem in the exercise that follows.

■ **algorithm** Prescribed sequence of steps that guarantees a correct problem solution.

■ **heuristic** General strategy that facilitates problem solving but does not always yield a problem solution.

Calvin and Hobbes

by Bill Watterson

Experiencing FIRSTHAND ·Grocery Shopping

Solve this addition problem *as quickly as you possibly can*:

You are purchasing three items at the store, at these prices:

$19.95
$39.98
$29.97

About how much money are you spending? (Don't worry about a possible sales tax.)

· · · · · · ·

The fastest way to solve the problem is to round off and approximate. The first item costs about $20, the second about $40, and the third about $30; therefore, you are spending about $90 on your shopping spree. Rounding is often an excellent heuristic for arriving quickly at approximate answers to mathematical problems.

At school, students typically get far more practice solving well-defined problems than ill-defined ones, and they are taught many more algorithms than heuristics. For example, they are likely to spend more school time learning problem-solving strategies useful in determining the length of planks needed for a treehouse roof than strategies applicable to the problem of defor-estation. And they are apt to spend more time using laws of physics to make predictions about when battleships will float than wrestling with ways of preventing the conflicts that require those battleships in the first place. Yet many real-world problems—problems that students will en-counter after graduation—probably cannot be solved with cut-and-dried algorithms. Further-more, few algorithms exist for solving problems outside the domains of mathematics and science.

Problem-solving strategies, algorithms and heuristics alike, are often specific to a particular content domain. But here are three general problem-solving heuristics that students may find helpful in a variety of contexts:

- *Identify subgoals.* Break a problem into two or more subproblems that can be better defined and more easily solved.
  Example: Students addressing the problem of diminishing rain forests identify several smaller problems: poor economic circumstances of local residents, lack of good agricultural land, and lack of government regulation of deforestation practices. They then discuss possible ways to solve each problem.
- *Work backward.* Begin at the problem goal (the solution needed) and work backward, one step at a time, toward the initial problem statement.
  Example: A student is given the problem to the right. To prove this statement, the student decides to start with the idea that the two lines are, in fact, parallel and then work backward, step by step, to show that $a + b$ must equal c.
- *Draw an analogy.* Identify a situation analogous to the problem situation, and derive potential problem solutions from that analogy.
  Example: A student who needs to calculate the volume of an irregularly shaped object recognizes that, just as she herself displaces water when she steps into the bathtub, the object will displace its volume when immersed in water. She places the object into a container filled to the brim with water, collects the water that sloshes out, and measures the amount.

■ Using the subject matter you will be teaching, develop two problems, one well defined and one ill defined. Do your problems require algorithms or heuristics to be solved?

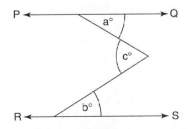

Prove that, if $a + b = c$, then lines PQ and RS must be parallel.

We all desided our jobs. Mrs. Pemperkin filled up our gar with a half of a galkn of water. We sent up our supllies person and he got stirerafomb, clay, rubber bands, tacks, coubs and serandrap. First we tried a block with clay on it it sunk. then we trayed serandrap. coubs and a tack it floted. We then tride clay and stairrafomb, it floted. Then gust thumb tacks sunk. Clay, stirofom and ru bber bands, It floted. Petter said every time he made something "This will bring us to wictory". Then we tried to make one with clay, stirerafomb, tacks, and rubber bands. Then we tried tacks and stirerafomb, it floted. Petter tried seramrap with clay, it flooted. Then we tride clay, tacks and wrood, it floted. Then we tried paper towals, it floted. It was time to cleen up. we did not have a good time

FIGURE 8.5 In a third-grade activity, cooperative groups try to design an object that "flinks"—that is, one that neither floats to the top nor sinks to the bottom of a jar of water. Here 8-year-old Tony describes his group's trial-and-error approach to the problem.

■ Observe group problem solving in the "Group Work" clip on Video CD 2.

Teaching problem-solving strategies. Occasionally students develop problem-solving strategies on their own; for instance, many children invent simple addition and subtraction strategies long before they encounter arithmetic at school (Carpenter & Moser, 1984). Yet without some formal instruction in effective strategies, even the most inventive of students may occasionally resort to unproductive trial and error to solve problems (e.g., see Figure 8.5).

To be truly effective problem solvers, students must have a solid grounding in—that is, a conceptual understanding of—the subject matter in question (more about this point shortly). But they also benefit from explicit instruction in the use of both algorithms and heuristics. Following are some strategies we might use:

For teaching algorithms:

- Describe and demonstrate specific algorithms and the situations in which each can be used.
- Provide worked-out examples of algorithms being applied, and ask students to explain what is happening in each step.
- Help students understand why particular algorithms are relevant and effective in certain situations.
- When a student's application of an algorithm yields an incorrect answer, look closely at what the student has done and locate the trouble spot (e.g., see Figure 8.6).

For teaching heuristics:

- Give students practice in making ill-defined problems more specific and well defined.
- Teach heuristics that students can use in situations where no specific algorithms apply; for example, encourage rounding, identifying subgoals, working backward, and drawing analogies.

For teaching both algorithms and heuristics:

- Teach problem-solving strategies within the context of specific subject areas (*not* as a topic separate from academic content) and, ideally, within the context of authentic activities.
- Engage in joint problem-solving activities with students, modeling effective strategies and guiding students' initial efforts.
- Provide scaffolding for difficult problems (e.g., break them into smaller and simpler problems, give hints about possible strategies, or provide partial solutions).
- Ask students to explain what they are doing as they work through a problem.
- Have students solve problems in small groups, sharing ideas about problem-solving strategies, modeling various approaches for one another, and discussing the merits of each approach. (R. K. Atkinson, Derry, Renkl, & Wortham, 2000; Barron, 2000; Crowley & Siegler, 1999; Gauvain, 2001; Heller & Hungate, 1985; Mayer, 1985, 1992; Noddings, 1985; Reimann & Schult, 1996; Renkl & Atkinson, 2003; L. B. Resnick, 1983; Rogoff, 2003)

As an example of the last strategy, the final part of the "Group-Work" clip on Video CD 2 shows student groups using what they've learned about the life cycle of a sheep liver fluke to identify strategies to keep this parasite from proliferating.

Cognitive Factors Affecting Problem Solving

As we have seen, well-defined problems are usually more easily solved than ill-defined ones, and problems that can be solved with algorithms are generally easier than those requiring heuristics. Factors we previously identified as affecting transfer (amount of instructional time, meaningful learning, etc.) affect problem solving as well. Cognitive psychologists have identified several additional factors that influence problem-solving success, including (a) working memory capacity, (b) problem encoding, (c) depth and integration of relevant knowledge, (d) long-term memory retrieval, and (e) metacognitive processes. As we consider each of these factors, we'll continue to identify ways to help students become more effective problem solvers.

Working Memory Capacity You may recall from an exercise in Chapter 6 just how difficult it is to solve a long division problem in your head. Remember, working memory has a limited capacity: It can hold only a few pieces of information and can accommodate only so much cognitive processing at any one time. If a problem requires a student to deal with too much information at once or to manipulate that information in a very complex way, working memory capacity may be insufficient for effective problem processing. Once working memory capacity is exceeded, the problem cannot be solved (Johnstone & El-Banna, 1986; Perkins, 1995).

Students can overcome the limits of working memory in at least two ways. One obvious way is to create an external record of needed information—for example, by writing it on a piece of paper. (This is typically our strategy when we do long division problems, so that we don't have to hold all the numbers in working memory at once.) Another approach is to learn some skills to automaticity—in other words, to learn them to a point where they can be retrieved quickly and easily (N. Frederiksen, 1984a; Mayer & Wittrock, 1996). Yet in the case of automaticity, it's possible to have too much of a good thing, as we'll see in a moment.

Problem Encoding When we discussed cognitive processes in Chapter 6, we talked about *encoding*, changing the form of new information while storing it in memory. Encoding is clearly a factor that affects problem-solving ability. Sometimes students have trouble encoding a problem in a way that allows them to begin working to solve it. As an example, see whether you can solve the problem in the following exercise.

Experiencing FIRSTHAND ·Pigs and Chickens

> Old MacDonald has a barnyard full of pigs and chickens. Altogether there are 21 heads and 60 legs in the barnyard (not counting MacDonald's own head and legs). How many pigs and how many chickens are running around the barnyard?

Can you figure out the answer? If you are having difficulty, try thinking about the problem this way:

> Imagine that the pigs are standing in an upright position on only their two hind legs; their front two legs are raised over their heads. Therefore, all the animals—pigs and chickens alike—are standing on two legs. Figure out how many legs are on the ground and how many must be in the air. From this, can you determine the number of pigs and chickens MacDonald has?

· · · · · · ·

In case you are still having difficulty with the problem, follow this logic:

- Obviously, because there are 21 heads, the total number of animals must be 21.
- Because each animal has 2 legs on the ground and because there must be twice as many legs on the ground as there are number of heads, there are 42 (21×2) legs on the ground.
- Because there are 42 legs on the ground, there must be 18 ($60 - 42$) pigs' legs in the air.
- Because each pig has 2 front legs, there must be 9 ($18 \div 2$) pigs.
- Because there are 9 pigs, there must be 12 ($21 - 9$) chickens.

If you initially had trouble solving the pigs-and-chickens problem, you may have been struggling to encode the problem in a way that allowed you to solve it. Students often have trouble solving mathematical word problems because they don't know how to translate the problems into procedures or operations with which they are familiar (Mayer, 1992; L. B. Resnick, 1989; Reusser, 1990).

At other times students may encode a problem in a seemingly logical way that nevertheless fails to yield a correct problem solution. As an example, take a stab at the problem in the following exercise.

$$6(2x+y)+2(x+4y)$$
$$12x+6y+2x+4y$$
$$14x+10y$$

FIGURE 8.6 Thirteen-year-old Malika incorrectly simplifies the expression $6(2x + y) + 2(x + 4y)$ as $14x + 10y$. The correct answer is $14x + 14y$. Where did Malika go wrong?

Some ways of encoding a problem promote more successful problem solving than others.

■ How might you use algebra to solve the pigs and chickens problem?

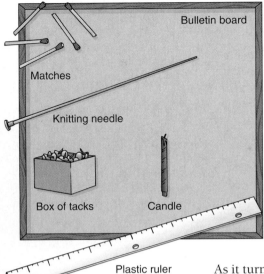

Bulletin board

Matches

Knitting needle

Box of tacks

Candle

Plastic ruler

You are in a room with a bulletin board firmly affixed to the wall about 4 feet above the floor. You task is to *stand a candle upright* in front of the bulletin board. You do not want the candle touching the bulletin board, because the candle's flame must not singe the board. Instead, you need to place the candle about a centimeter away. How can you accomplish the task with the following materials?

> Small candle
> Metal knitting needle
> Matches
> Box of thumbtacks
> 12-inch plastic ruler

See whether you can solve the problem before you read further.

Based on Duncker, 1945.

· · · · · · ·

As it turns out, the ruler and knitting needle are useless in solving the candle problem (if you try to pierce the candle with the knitting needle, you will probably break the candle; if you try to balance the ruler on a few tacks, it will probably fall down). The easiest solution is to fasten the thumbtack box to the bulletin board with tacks and then attach the candle to the top of the box with either a tack or some melted wax. Many people don't consider this solution, however, because they encode the box only as a *container of tacks*, thereby overlooking its potential use as a candle stand. When we encode a problem in a way that excludes potential solutions, we are the victims of a **mental set**.

Mental sets in problem solving sometimes emerge when students practice solving a particular kind of problem (e.g., doing subtraction problems in math; or calculating velocity, given time and acceleration, in physics) without also practicing other kinds of problems at the same time (E. J. Langer, 2000; Luchins, 1942). Such repetitive practice can lead students to encode problems in a particular way without really thinking about the problems; that is, it can lead to automaticity in encoding. Although automaticity in the basic information and skills needed for problem solving is often an advantage (it frees up working memory capacity), automaticity in *encoding* problems may lead students to solve them incorrectly (E. J. Langer, 2000).

Following are several strategies that can help students encode problems more effectively yet not fall victim to counterproductive mental sets:

- Present problems in a concrete way; for example, provide real objects that students can manipulate, or present an illustration of a problem's components (Luchins & Luchins, 1950; Mayer, 1992).
- Encourage students to make problems concrete *for themselves*; for example, encourage them to draw a picture or diagram (Anzai, 1991; Mayer, 1986; Prawat, 1989; K. Schultz & Lochhead, 1991).
- Point out any features of problems that students *can* solve, and when those features appear again in a different problem, indicate that the same information can be applied or the same approach to problem solution can be used (Prawat, 1989).
- Give problems that look different on the surface yet require the same or similar problem-solving procedures (Z. Chen, 1999; L. S. Fuchs et al., 2003).
- Mix the kinds of problems that students tackle in any single practice session (E. J. Langer, 2000; Mayfield & Chase, 2002).
- Have students work in cooperative groups to identify several ways of representing a single problem—perhaps as a formula, a table, and a graph (Brenner et al., 1997; J. C. Turner, Meyer, et al., 1998).

Depth and Integration of Relevant Knowledge

Let's return once again to Mary in our opening case study. Mary has learned a principle of physics (velocity equals acceleration multiplied by time) by rote, without really comprehending what she's been studying. As a result, she is unable to use her knowledge to solve a problem about a car's acceleration rate.

Research consistently indicates that when people have a thorough *conceptual understanding* of a topic—when they have stored a great deal of information about it, with various pieces of in-

■ The candle problem illustrates a particular kind of mental set—*functional fixedness*—in which an individual thinks of an object as having only one possible function and so overlooks other functions the object might serve.

■ **mental set** Inclination to encode a problem in a way that excludes potential problem solutions.

formation appropriately organized and interrelated in long-term memory—they can more easily use their knowledge to solve problems (P. A. Alexander & Judy, 1988; Heller & Hungate, 1985; Voss, Greene, Post, & Penner, 1983). For instance, students are more likely to apply a principle of physics to a specific situation if they understand the concepts underlying the principle and the situations to which it relates. Students are more likely to apply the Pythagorean theorem to the calculation of a diagonal roof if they have learned the theorem in a meaningful way and have associated it with such ideas as "diagonal" and "measurement." And when proposing possible solutions to the problem of rain forest destruction, they are more likely to draw from their knowledge of several disciplines (e.g., from ecology, economics, and psychology) if they have stored ideas from those disciplines in an interrelated, cross-disciplinary fashion. In the "Charles's Law" clip on Video CD 2, a high school science teacher uses several strategies to promote a conceptual understanding of Charles's law: She activates students' prior knowledge relevant to the law, demonstrates the law "in action" with balloons and water of various temperatures, and presents examples of how students can use the law to make predictions and solve problems. (In a later part of the class not depicted in the video clip, she gives students additional problems to solve on their own and monitors their progress and understanding.)

■ Observe a teacher promote conceptual understanding in the "Charles's Law" clip on Video CD 2.

In contrast, when students have limited knowledge about a topic, and particularly when they don't have a conceptual understanding of it, they are apt to encode problems on the basis of superficial problem characteristics (Chi, Feltovich, & Glaser, 1981; Schoenfeld & Hermann, 1982). For example, when I was in elementary school, I recall that some of my classmates were having trouble deciding how to attack word problems. Our teacher told us that the word *left* in a problem indicates that subtraction is called for. Encoding a "left" problem as a subtraction problem works well in some instances, such as this one:

■ In what content areas do you have the depth of knowledge necessary for solving problems successfully? In what areas has your relative lack of knowledge been a handicap?

Tim has 7 apples. He gives 3 apples to Emily. How many apples does he have left?

But it is inappropriate in other instances, such as this one:

Ana went shopping. She spent $3.50 and then counted her money when she got home. She had $2.35 left. How much did Ana have when she started out? (L. B. Resnick, 1989, p. 165)

The latter problem requires addition, not subtraction. Obviously, words alone can be deceiving.

The fact that conceptual understanding facilitates problem solving is yet another reason for teaching a few topics thoroughly, rather than many topics superficially (the *less is more* notion once again). It also suggests that, as is true for transfer more generally, we should provide a wide variety of examples of, and opportunities to apply, important principles and procedures. By doing so, we foster associations between those principles and procedures, and the contexts and problems to which they are applicable. For instance, students can study arithmetic operations by working on such diverse problems as calculating change, balancing a checkbook, or estimating profits and necessary supplies for a lemonade stand. They can apply the concept of *scale* in cartography by estimating distances on a variety of local, state, and country maps.

Variety in applications should characterize assessment as well as instruction (Bransford, Franks, Vye, & Sherwood, 1989; Sternberg & Frensch, 1993). Figure 8.7 presents an assessment task that asks students to apply their knowledge of geographic principles to several new problems. By consistently incorporating application of classroom topics into assessment tasks and problems, we clearly communicate that the subject matter can be used in many different contexts. We will revisit the importance of assessing higher-level thinking skills in our discussion of classroom assessment in Chapter 15.

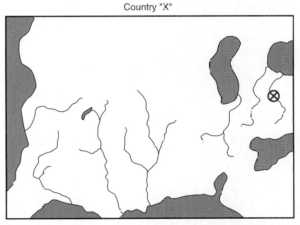

Country "X"

0 250 500
Scale (miles)

Major Rivers———   Bodies of Water (Seas) ▧

• If people living at the point marked 'X' on the map began to migrate *or* expand, where would they go and what direction might they take?
• What would be the distribution of population in country "X"; that is, where would many people live, few, and so on?
• Where would large cities develop in country "X"?
• How would you judge the country's economic potential; that is, what areas might be best for development, which worst, and so on?

FIGURE 8.7 Example of an assessment activity that asks students to apply what they've learned in geography to new problems

Problems and figure are from *Teaching Creatively: Learning Through Discovery* by B. G. Massialas and J. Zevin, 1983, pp. 121, 127, Malabar, FL: Krieger. Reprinted by permission.

Long-Term Memory Retrieval   Obviously, students cannot solve a problem unless they retrieve from long-term memory the information and procedures necessary to solve it. But as we discovered in Chapter 6, long-term memory contains a great deal of information, and students cannot possibly retrieve it all in a given situation. Successful problem solving, then, requires that students search the right "places" in long-term memory at the right time.

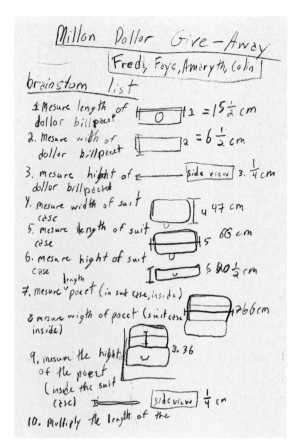

FIGURE 8.8 In a small-group project, four fifth graders brainstormed strategies for determining how many one-dollar bills can fit in a suitcase their teacher has brought to class. Here we see 10-year-old Amaryth's notes of the group's discussion (she didn't complete her thought in item 10).

Where a student "looks" in long-term memory depends, in part, on how the student initially encodes the problem. For instance, if Robert sees the word *left* in a word problem and thinks "subtraction," he will retrieve rules of subtraction even if addition is required. An inappropriate mental set can interfere with retrieval in that it sends students in the wrong "direction" in their long-term memory search. In other instances students may be victims of situated cognition: They may associate a problem-solving strategy with a particular context and so do not retrieve and apply it when they find themselves in a different context (Lave, 1993; Saljo & Wyndhamn, 1992; Schliemann & Carraher, 1993). As an example, let's consider a study with 15- and 16-year-old high school students (Saljo & Wyndhamn, 1992). The students were asked to figure out how much postage they should put on an envelope of a particular weight, and they were given a table of postage rates with which to determine the correct amount. When students were given the task in a social studies class, most used the postage table and correctly determined the necessary postage. As a former social studies teacher myself, I suspect that these students were well accustomed to finding information in tables and charts in that class. In contrast, when students were given the task in a *math* class, most ignored the table and tried to *calculate* the postage—sometimes figuring it to several decimal places—and often obtained an incorrect amount.

Some of the instructional strategies we've already identified—for instance, giving hints about possible approaches to a problem, having students use concepts and procedures in a wide variety of contexts—should facilitate retrieval in problem solving. In addition, if students are struggling with an especially difficult problem, we might have them put it aside for a while (e.g., have them "sleep on it") and return to it later when they aren't so locked in to a particular line of reasoning (J. E. Davidson & Sternberg, 1998). And we might have them work on complex problems in small groups: Different group members are apt to bring different ideas to the table, increasing the odds of retrieving helpful concepts and principles (e.g., see Figure 8.8).

Metacognitive Processes   Earlier in the chapter we discovered the importance of metacognition for effective learning and studying. Metacognitive processes play an important role in problem solving as well. For instance, effective problem solvers tend to

- Identify one or more goals that represent problem solution
- Break a complex problem into two or more subproblems
- Plan a systematic, sequential approach to solving the problem and any subproblems
- Continually monitor and evaluate their progress toward their goal(s)
- Identify any obstacles that may be impeding their progress
- Change to a new strategy if the current one is not working

Such metacognitive processes enable students to use problem-solving strategies flexibly, to apply them to more complex problem situations, and to know when particular strategies are and are not appropriate (J. E. Davidson & Sternberg, 1998; Dominowski, 1998). In contrast, *in*effective problem solvers tend to apply problem-solving procedures mindlessly, without any real understanding of what they are doing or why they are doing it (M. Carr & Biddlecomb, 1998; J. E. Davidson & Sternberg, 1998).

To some extent, students' metacognitive problem-solving processes depend on their conceptual understanding of the subject matter (M. Carr & Biddlecomb, 1998; J. E. Davidson & Sternberg, 1998). Yet students can also be taught more effective metacognitive processes. For instance, we can enhance students' metacognitive awareness when we ask them to explain what they are doing, and why they are doing it, as they work on a problem (Dominowski, 1998; Johanning, D'Agostino, Steele, & Shumow, 1999). We can give them questions they can ask *themselves* as they work on a problem—questions such as "Are we getting closer to our goal?" and "Why is this strategy most appropriate?" (A. King, 1999, p. 101; Kramarski & Mevarech, 2003, p. 286). Such approaches are especially effective when students work in pairs or small groups on challenging problems and must explain and defend their reasoning to one another (Johanning et al., 1999; A. King, 1999; Kramarski & Mevarech, 2003).

In the past few pages, we've identified numerous instructional strategies for facilitating problem solving and other forms of transfer; some of the most important ones are reviewed and

■ Such instructional strategies are more likely to be helpful for average-ability rather than high-ability students (J. E. Davidson & Sternberg, 1998). Why might this be so?

Promoting Successful Transfer and Problem Solving

 Teach important topics in depth and be sure students learn them thoroughly.

A teacher of a second-year Spanish class teaches only two new verb tenses (preterit and imperfect) during fall semester, saving other tenses (e.g., near past, near future) for later instruction.

 Tie class material to what students already know.

After teaching that water expands when it freezes, a science teacher explains that many of the bumps seen in country roads are frost heaves caused by freezing water.

Give students practice in dealing with ill-defined problems, and show them how to better define such problems.

A teacher asks students in an interdisciplinary class to work in small groups to wrestle with the problem of diminishing rain forests. He starts them off by asking, "What should be the final goal of preservation efforts?" and "What are some of the biological, social, and political factors you need to consider as you try to solve this problem?"

 Teach the basic information and skills needed in problem solving to a level of automaticity.

An elementary school teacher makes sure that students have thoroughly mastered basic multiplication and division facts before teaching them long division.

 Provide opportunities for students to apply what they've learned to new situations and problems.

A geography teacher asks students to apply their knowledge of human settlement patterns in explaining why the populations of various countries are distributed as they are.

Make school tasks similar to the tasks that students are likely to encounter in the outside world.

An English teacher teaches persuasive writing skills by having students write editorials for the school newspaper.

 Ask students to apply what they know in tests and other assessments.

A science teacher asks students to use principles of physics to describe how they might single-handedly move a 500-pound object to a location twenty feet away.

---

illustrated in the Into the Classroom feature "Promoting Successful Transfer and Problem Solving." The strategies we've considered thus far (e.g., using paper and pencil, meeting in cooperative groups) have all been "low tech" in nature. Yet we can also capitalize on computer technology to foster problem solving, as we shall see now.

Using Computer Technology to Promote Problem Solving

Researchers and educators have identified a variety of ways in which we might use computer technology to promote problem solving and other higher-level skills, including the following:

- Use computer-based tutoring programs to promote mathematical and scientific reasoning and problem solving.
- Show students how to use spreadsheets to analyze complex sets of data.
- Use computer simulations that allow students to formulate hypotheses, design experiments to test those hypotheses, and interpret the virtual results.
- Present complex real-world problems (i.e., authentic activities) that students must solve. (Cognition and Technology Group at Vanderbilt, 1990, 1996; Vye et al., 1998)

We find an example of the last of these—presenting authentic activities—in the Adventures of Jasper Woodbury series,[1] a videodisc program in which middle school students encounter a number of real-life problem situations. In one episode, "Journey to Cedar Creek," Jasper has just purchased an old boat that he is hoping to pilot home the same day. Because the boat has no running lights, he must figure out whether he can get home by sunset, and because he has spent all his cash and used his last check, he must figure out whether he has enough gas to make the trip. Throughout the video, all the information students need to answer these questions is embedded in authentic contexts (e.g., a marine radio announces time of sunset, and mileage markers are posted at various landmarks along the river), but students must sift through a lot of irrelevant information to find it. In another episode, "The Right Angle," teenager Paige Littlefield searches for a cave in which her Native American grandfather left her a special gift before he died. Her

---

[1] For online information about the series, visit http://peabody.vanderbilt.edu and enter "Jasper Woodbury" in the search box.

The Adventures of Jasper Woodbury series uses videodisc technology to present authentic problem-solving tasks. To assist Jasper in his decision making in "Journey to Cedar Creek," students must use information presented in real-world contexts to determine distance, speed, and gas mileage.

grandfather gave her directions to the cave that require knowledge and use of geometric principles (e.g., "From the easternmost point of Black Hawk Bluff, travel at a bearing of 25 degrees until you are almost surrounded by rock towers. Go to Flat Top Tower . . . . You will know Flat Top Tower because at a distance of 250 feet from the northern side of its base, the angle of elevation of its top is 45 degrees"). Using the directions and a map of the region, students must locate the cave. There are numerous ways to approach each Jasper problem, and students work in small groups to brainstorm and carry out possible problem solutions. Students of all ability levels find the Jasper series highly motivating. Furthermore, they acquire new problem-solving skills and often transfer these skills to new problems (Cognition and Technology Group at Vanderbilt, 1990, 1997; Hickey, Moore, & Pellegrino, 2001; Learning Technology Center at Vanderbilt, 1996).

In the Jasper series we again see the value of authentic activities. When students use certain principles and skills to solve problems in authentic contexts, they will be more likely to retrieve those principles and skills later on when they encounter similar problems in the adult world. Authentic activities can be time-consuming, of course, and in some cases (such as with the Jasper series) they require equipment or computer software that we don't necessarily have. Accordingly, teachers sometimes look for easier ways to help students make real-world connections. The following exercise presents one teacher's approach. See what you think.

Analyzing Teacher Strategies

Dogs, Cats, Hamsters, Penguins, and Ladybugs

A third-grade teacher asks her students to write and then solve their own subtraction problems. An example, created by 8-year-old Morris, appears to the left. As you look at Morris's work, consider

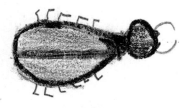

■ What benefits this approach might have
■ Whether this activity engages students in an authentic activity

Undoubtedly the teacher hopes that the activity will encourage students to apply mathematics to their own lives and, perhaps, to look around for situations in which subtraction might be appropriate and useful. As you can see, however, Morris writes a problem that seems highly artificial: The probability that he would have that many hamsters, penguins, and ladybugs is quite small. In essence, Morris writes a traditional mathematical word problem that has little relevance to his own life circumstances; thus, the activity is, at least for Morris, not a truly authentic one.

Bugs are big,

Bugs are small.

Bugs are black,

Bugs are all...

NEAT!

CREATIVITY

As a second grader, my critter-happy son Alex wrote and illustrated the problem on the left. His teacher thought the poem reflected a certain degree of creativity; so did his not-so-objective mother. What do *you* think?

Creativity, like problem solving, is a form of transfer, in that it involves applying previously learned knowledge or skills to a new situation. But what exactly do we mean by the term **creativity**? Different theorists define it somewhat differently, but most definitions include two components (Ripple, 1989; Runco & Chand, 1995):

- *New and original behavior:* Behavior not specifically learned from someone else
- *An appropriate and productive result:* A useful product or effective problem solution

Both criteria must be met before we identify behavior as creative.

To illustrate these two components, let's say I am giving a lecture on creativity and want a creative way of keeping my students' attention. One possible solution would be to come to class stark naked. This solution certainly meets the first criterion for creativity: It is new and original behavior, and I did not learn it from any other teacher. It does not, however, meet the second criterion: It isn't appropriate or productive within the context of our culture. A second possible solution might be to give my students several challenging problems that require creative thinking.

■ **creativity** New and original behavior that yields an appropriate and productive result.

This approach is more likely to meet both criteria. Not only is it a relatively original way of teaching, but it is also appropriate and productive for students to learn about creativity by exploring the process firsthand.

Although a certain degree of intelligence is probably necessary for creative thinking, intelligence and creativity are somewhat independent abilities (Sternberg, 1985; I. A. Taylor, 1976; Torrance, 1976). In other words, highly intelligent students are not always the most creative ones. Many theorists believe that the cognitive processes involved in intelligence and creativity may be somewhat different (e.g., see Kogan, 1983). Tasks on intelligence tests often involve **convergent thinking**—pulling several pieces of information together to draw a conclusion or to solve a problem. In contrast, creativity often involves **divergent thinking**—starting with one idea and taking it in many different directions. To see the difference firsthand, try the following exercise.

Experiencing FIRSTHAND · · · · · · · · · · · · · · · · · · · Convergent and Divergent Thinking

On a sheet of paper, write your responses to each of the following:

- Why are houses more often built with bricks than with stones?
- What are some possible uses of a brick? Try to think of as many different and unusual uses as you can.
- Add improvements to the wagon drawing so that the object will be more fun to play with.

Modeled after Torrance, 1970.

· · · · · · ·

To answer the first question, you must use convergent thinking to pull together the things you know about bricks, stones, and houses. But the other two items require divergent thinking about a single object: You consider how a brick might be used in many different contexts and how a child's wagon might be embellished in a variety of ways.

Contrary to a popular belief, creativity is probably *not* a single entity that people either have or don't have (e.g., Hocevar & Bachelor, 1989). Rather, it is probably a combination of many specific thinking processes, characteristics, and behaviors. Among other things, creative individuals tend to

- Interpret problems and situations in a flexible manner
- Have a great deal of information relevant to a task
- Combine existing information and ideas in new ways
- Evaluate their accomplishments in accordance with high standards
- Have a passion for—and therefore invest much time and effort in—what they are doing (Csikszentmihalyi, 1996; Glover, Ronning, & Reynolds, 1989; Runco & Chand, 1995; Russ, 1993; Simonton, 2000; Weisberg, 1993)

Furthermore, creativity is probably somewhat specific to different situations and different content areas (R. T. Brown, 1989; Feldhusen & Treffinger, 1980; Ripple, 1989). Students may show creativity in art, writing, or science, but they aren't necessarily creative in all these areas.

Fostering Creativity

Certain components of creative thinking may have their roots in hereditary factors, but environmental factors play an equally important role in creativity's development (Esquivel, 1995; Ripple, 1989; Simonton, 2000; Torrance, 1976). Research studies suggest several strategies for promoting creativity in the classroom:

◎ *Show students that creativity is valued.* We are more likely to foster creativity when we show students that we value creative thoughts and behaviors. One way to do this is to encourage and reward unusual ideas and responses. For example, we can teach strategies that allow students to break out of their traditional ways of thinking about and doing things (e.g., see Figure 8.9). We can express excitement when students complete a project in a unique and unusual manner. As we evaluate students' performance on classroom assessments, we should acknowledge

■ **convergent thinking** Process of pulling several pieces of information together to draw a conclusion or solve a problem.

■ **divergent thinking** Process of proceeding in a variety of directions from a single idea.

A full moon is watching all sleep.
Lime green hills drink pink lemonade slowly and steadily.
Pitch brown covers hilly hills.
The moon is hidden in a turquoise sky.
It is night.

FIGURE 8.9 Creativity involves using information and ideas in new ways, as in this piece by 7-year-old Andrew. Andrew's second-grade teacher showed students how to create interesting designs with watercolor paints; she then asked them to interpret and describe their designs using colorful language.

responses that, though not what we were expecting, are legitimately correct. Engaging in creative activities ourselves also shows that we value creativity (Feldhusen & Treffinger, 1980; B. A. Hennessey & Amabile, 1987; Parnes, 1967; Torrance & Myers, 1970).

◎   *Focus students' attention on internal rather than external rewards.* Students are more creative when they engage in activities they enjoy and can take pride in what they are doing (B. A. Hennessey, 1995; Lubart, 1994). To foster creativity, then, we should occasionally give students opportunities to explore their own interests—interests they will gladly pursue without having to be prodded. We can also foster creativity by downplaying the importance of grades, instead focusing students' attention on the internal satisfaction that their creative efforts bring (B. A. Hennessey, 1995; B. A. Hennessey & Amabile, 1987; Perkins, 1990). For example, we might tell students in an art class:

> Please don't worry too much about grades. As long as you use the materials appropriately and give each assignment your best shot, you will do well in this class. The important thing is to find an art form that you enjoy and through which you can express yourself.

Essentially, I am suggesting that we encourage *intrinsic* rather than *extrinsic* motivation; we'll address this distinction in Chapter 12.

◎   *Promote mastery of a subject area.* Creativity in a particular subject area is more likely to occur when students have considerable mastery of a topic; it is unlikely to occur when students have only minimal understanding (Simonton, 2000). One important way of fostering creativity, then, is to help students master course content (Amabile & Hennessey, 1992; Perkins, 1990; Sternberg, 1985). For example, if we want students to apply scientific principles in a creative manner—perhaps as they complete a science fair experiment or develop a solution to an environmental problem—we should make sure that they first have those principles down pat.

◎   *Ask thought-provoking questions.* Students are more apt to think creatively when we ask higher-level questions that require them to use previously learned information in new ways. Questions that require divergent thinking may be especially helpful (Feldhusen & Treffinger, 1980; Feldhusen, Treffinger, & Bahlke, 1970; Perkins, 1990; Torrance & Myers, 1970). For example, during a unit on the Pony Express, we might ask:

- What are all the ways mail might have been transported across the United States at that time?
- Can you think of some very unusual way that no one else has thought of to transport mail today? (Feldhusen & Treffinger, 1980, p. 36)

◎   *Give students the freedom and security they need to take risks.* To be creative, students must be willing to take risks—something they are unlikely to do if they are afraid of failing (Houtz, 1990). To encourage risk taking, we can allow students to engage in certain activities without evaluating their performance. We can also urge them to think of their mistakes and failures as an inevitable—but usually temporary—aspect of the creative process (Feldhusen & Treffinger, 1980; B. A. Hennessey & Amabile, 1987; Pruitt, 1989). For example, when students are writing a creative short story, we might give them several opportunities to get our feedback, and perhaps the feedback of their peers, before they turn in a final product.

◎   *Provide the time that creativity requires.* Students need time to experiment with new materials and ideas, to think in divergent directions, and occasionally to make mistakes. A critical aspect of promoting creativity, then, is to give them that time (Feldhusen & Treffinger, 1980; Pruitt, 1989). For example, when teaching a foreign language, we might ask small groups of students to write and videotape a television commercial spoken entirely in that language. This is hardly a project that students can do in a day; they may need several weeks to brainstorm various ideas, write and revise a script, find or develop the props they need, and rehearse their lines. Creative ideas and projects seldom emerge overnight.

Using what you have learned about the nature of creativity and about strategies for promoting it, try the following exercise.

The activity requires divergent thinking, a key component of creative thinking. By assigning the activity, the teacher is showing her students that she values creative ideas. However, creativity is not a single entity we can easily "train" with simple exercises such as this one. Instead, it may take different forms in different content areas, and students are more apt to be creative in a particular area when they have considerable mastery of that area. Thus, the activity is unlikely to promote creativity over the long run.

CRITICAL THINKING

Experiencing FIRSTHAND · · · · · Happiness Is a Well-Behaved Classroom

Here is a research finding presented at the annual conference of the American Educational Research Association in 1994:

> Teachers who feel happy when they teach are more likely to have well-behaved students (Emmer, 1994).

If you want to have well-behaved students, then, should you try to feel happy when you enter the classroom each morning?

· · · · · · ·

If you answered yes to my question, then you made a mistake that I warned you about in Chapter 1: You drew a conclusion about a cause-effect relationship (i.e., teacher happiness causes good behavior in students) on the basis of a correlational research study. Although Dr. Emmer found that teacher happiness and student behavior are *associated* with each other, he did not necessarily find that teacher happiness *causes* good behavior (nor did he say that he did). In fact, there are other possible explanations for the correlation. For instance, perhaps good student behavior makes teachers feel happy (rather than vice versa), or perhaps teachers who use effective teaching techniques feel happy *and* keep students on task as the result of using those techniques (Emmer, 1994).

Evaluating research findings is an example of critical thinking. More generally, **critical thinking** involves evaluating the accuracy and worth of information and lines of reasoning (Beyer, 1985). Critical thinking can take a variety of forms, depending on the context. For instance, it may involve any one or more of the following (Halpern, 1997a, 1998):

• *Verbal reasoning:* Understanding and evaluating persuasive techniques found in oral and written language (e.g., deductive and inductive logic). For example, consider this:

> Aren't you tired of sniffles and runny noses all winter? Tired of always feeling less than your best? Get through a whole winter without colds. Take Eradicold Pills as directed. (R. J. Harris, 1977, p. 605)

Do Eradicold Pills reduce cold symptoms? The passage provides no proof that they do. Instead, it simply includes the suggestion to "Take Eradicold Pills as directed" within the context of a discussion of undesirable symptoms—a common ploy in persuasive advertising.

■ **critical thinking** Process of evaluating the accuracy and worth of information and lines of reasoning.

- *Argument analysis:* Discriminating between reasons that do and do not support a conclusion. For example, imagine this situation:

  > You have a beat-up old car and have invested several thousand dollars to get the car in working order. You can sell the car in its present condition for $1,500, or you can invest a couple of thousand dollars more on repairs and then sell it for $3,000. What should you do? (modeled after Halpern, 1998)

  Obviously, it makes more sense to sell the car now: If you sell the car for $3,000 after making $2,000 worth of repairs, you make $500 less than you would otherwise. Yet many people mistakenly believe that their *past* investments justify making additional ones, when in fact past investments are irrelevant to the present state of affairs (Halpern, 1998).

- *Probabilistic reasoning:* Determining the likelihood and uncertainties associated with various events. As an example, consider the following situation:

  > You have been rolling a typical six-sided die (i.e., one member of a pair of dice). You know for a fact that the die is not "loaded" (it's not heavier on one side than another), and yet in the past 30 rolls you have not rolled a number 4 even once. What are the odds that you will get a 4 in the next roll?

  ■ Such reasoning is known as the *gambler's fallacy.*

  Many people mistakenly believe that a roll of 4 is long overdue and so is more likely in the next roll than it would be otherwise. In fact, on any roll of an unloaded (fair) die, the probability is 1 in 6 that its outcome will be a 4, *regardless* of the outcomes of any previous rolls.

- *Hypothesis testing:* Judging the value of data and research results in terms of the methods used to obtain them and their potential relevance to certain conclusions. When hypothesis testing includes critical thinking, it involves considering questions such as these:

  > Was an appropriate method used to measure a particular outcome?
  > Have other possible explanations or conclusions been eliminated?
  > Can the results obtained in one situation be reasonably generalized to other situations?

  The "Happiness" exercise you did earlier illustrates this form of critical thinking.

- *Decision making:* Identifying several alternatives and selecting the best alternative. For example, when, as teachers, we choose a particular approach to teaching a topic by considering several possible strategies and weighing the pros and cons of each one, we are engaging in critical thinking.

Critical thinking takes different forms in different content domains.

The nature of critical thinking is, of course, different in various content domains. In writing, critical thinking may involve reading the first draft of a persuasive essay to look for errors in logical reasoning or for situations in which opinions have not been sufficiently justified. In science, it may involve revising existing theories or beliefs to account for new evidence; in other words, it may involve conceptual change. In history, it may involve drawing inferences from historical documents, attempting to determine whether things *definitely* happened a particular way or only *maybe* happened that way.

As you might guess, critical thinking abilities emerge gradually over the course of childhood and adolescence (P. M. King & Kitchener, 2002; Pillow, 2002). Yet all too often, students at all grade levels (even college students) take the information they see in textbooks, advertisements, media reports, and elsewhere at face value; in other words, they engage in little or no critical thinking as they consider its accuracy and worth. Students are more likely to look analytically and critically at new information if they believe that even experts' understanding of any single topic continues to evolve as new evidence accumulates; they are less likely to engage in critical thinking if they believe that "knowledge" is an absolute, unchanging entity (Kardash & Scholes, 1996; Kuhn, 2001a; Schommer-Aikins, 2001). In other words, students' *epistemological beliefs* enter into the critical thinking process.

Fostering Critical Thinking

Perhaps because critical thinking encompasses such a variety of skills, research about how to promote it in the classroom is sketchy at best. Nevertheless, theorists have offered a few suggestions:

- Teach fewer topics, but in greater depth—the *less is more* principle yet again (Onosko, 1989; Onosko & Newmann, 1994).
- Encourage some intellectual skepticism—for instance, by urging students to question and challenge the ideas they read and hear—and communicate the message that our knowledge and understanding of any single topic will continue to change over time (Kardash & Scholes, 1996; Kuhn, 2001a; Onosko, 1989).
- Model critical thinking—for instance, by thinking aloud while analyzing a persuasive argument or scientific report (Onosko & Newmann, 1994).
- Show students that critical thinking involves considerable mental effort but that its benefits make the effort worthwhile (Halpern, 1998).
- Give students many and varied opportunities to practice critical thinking—for instance, by identifying flaws in the arguments of persuasive essays, evaluating the quality and usefulness of scientific findings, and using evidence and logic to support their viewpoints (Halpern, 1998; Kuhn & Weinstock, 2002).
- Ask questions such as these to encourage critical thinking:

> What additional information do I need?
>
> What information is relevant to this situation? What information is irrelevant?
>
> What persuasive technique is the author using? Is it valid, or is it designed to mislead the reader?
>
> What reasons support the conclusion? What reasons do *not* support the conclusion?
>
> What actions might I take to improve the design of this study? (based on Halpern, 1998, p. 454)

■ Might such questions also be useful in your own studying?

- Have students debate controversial issues from several perspectives, occasionally asking them to take a perspective quite different from their own (Reiter, 1994).
- Embed critical thinking skills within the context of authentic activities as a way of helping students retrieve those skills later on, both in the workplace and in other aspects of adult life (Derry, Levin, Osana, & Jones, 1998; Halpern, 1998).

The Into the Classroom feature "Fostering Critical Thinking" presents examples of what teachers in might do in language arts, social studies, and science.

As we've examined metacognition, transfer, problem solving, creativity, and critical thinking in this chapter, you have, I hope, discovered that all of these processes involve knowledge and strategies that most students can acquire with time, appropriate educational experiences, and practice. Yet even when students have the capability to engage in higher-level thinking processes, they do not always do so. Motivational factors—especially students' achievement goals and dispositions—also come into play. We'll look at these factors more closely in Chapter 12.

INTO THE CLASSROOM

Fostering Critical Thinking

 Teach elements of critical thinking.

In a unit on persuasion and argumentation, a junior high school language arts teacher explains that a sound argument meets three criteria (Halpern, 1997a): (1) The evidence presented to justify the argument is accurate and consistent; (2) the evidence is relevant to, and provides sufficient support for, the conclusion; and (3) there is little or no missing information that, if present, would lead to a contradictory conclusion. The teacher then has students practice applying these criteria to a variety of persuasive and argumentative essays.

 Foster epistemological beliefs that encourage critical thinking.

Rather than teach history as a collection of facts to be memorized, a high school history teacher portrays the discipline as an attempt by informed but inevitably biased scholars to interpret and make sense of historical events. On several occasions he asks his students to read two or three different historians' accounts of the same incident and to look for evidence of personal bias in each one (Paxton, 1999).

 Embed critical thinking skills within the context of authentic activities.

In a unit on statistical and scientific reasoning, an eighth-grade science class studies concepts related to probability, correlation, and experimental control. Then, as part of a simulated "legislative hearing," the students work in small groups to develop arguments for or against a legislative bill concerning the marketing and use of vitamins and other dietary supplements. To find evidence to support their arguments, the students apply what they've learned about statistics and experimentation as they read and analyze journal articles and government reports about the possible benefits and drawbacks of nutritional supplements (Derry et al., 1998).

CONSIDERING DIVERSITY IN HIGHER-LEVEL THINKING PROCESSES

We have noted the importance of a solid knowledge base—the *less is more* idea—for effective study strategies, successful transfer and problem solving, and creative and critical thinking. Students with different backgrounds will, of course, have different knowledge bases, and such diversity will naturally affect their ability to accomplish higher-level thinking tasks. For instance, students will use more effective study strategies when they read textbook materials consistent with their own cultural experiences (Pritchard, 1990).

Furthermore, students' previous experiences may have influenced the particular thinking skills they've developed. For example, thanks to the phenomenon of situated cognition, some students may have developed effective problem-solving strategies within the contexts of their own home and neighborhood environments (e.g., easily performing complex mathematical cal-

TABLE 8.4   STUDENTS IN INCLUSIVE SETTINGS

Promoting Higher-Level Thinking Skills in Students with Special Educational Needs

CATEGORY	CHARACTERISTICS YOU MIGHT OBSERVE	SUGGESTED CLASSROOM STRATEGIES
Students with specific cognitive or academic difficulties	• Less metacognitive awareness or control of learning • Use of few and relatively inefficient learning strategies • Increased strategy use after explicit instruction in strategies • Difficulty in transferring learned information to new situations • Difficulties in problem solving, perhaps because of limited working memory capacity, inability to identify important aspects of a problem, inability to retrieve appropriate problem-solving strategies, or limited metacognitive problem-solving skills	• Teach more effective learning strategies (e.g., taking notes, using mnemonics, finding general themes in reading material), and identify occasions when each strategy can be useful. • Scaffold students' use of new learning strategies (e.g., provide outlines to guide note taking, ask questions that encourage retrieval of prior knowledge). • Present simple problems at first, then gradually move to more difficult ones as students gain proficiency and self-confidence. • Teach techniques for minimizing the load on working memory during problem solving (e.g., writing parts of a problem on paper, drawing a diagram of the problem).
Students with social or behavioral problems	• Limited metacognitive awareness of one's own processing difficulties (for some students) • Few effective learning strategies (for some students) • Deficiencies in social problem-solving skills	• Provide guidance in using effective learning and study strategies (e.g., model strategies, give outlines that guide note taking, ask questions that encourage retrieval of prior knowledge). • Teach social problem-solving skills (see Chapter 10 for ideas).
Students with general delays in cognitive and social functioning	• Lack of metacognitive awareness or control of learning • Lack of learning strategies, especially in the absence of strategies training • Difficulty in transferring information and skills to new situations • Few effective problem-solving strategies	• Teach relatively simple learning strategies (e.g., rehearsal, specific mnemonics), and give students ample practice in using them. • Teach new information and skills in the specific contexts and situations in which you want students to use them. • Present simple problems and guide students through each step of the solutions.
Students with physical or sensory challenges	• No consistent deficits in higher-level thinking processes; any deficits observed may be due to students' limited experiences with tasks that require higher-level thinking	• Address any deficits in higher-level thinking skills using strategies that you would use with nondisabled students, making appropriate accommodations for physical and sensory limitations.
Students with advanced cognitive development	• Use of relatively sophisticated learning strategies • Greater transfer of learning to new situations • Greater effectiveness in problem solving, more sophisticated problem-solving strategies, greater flexibility in strategy use, less susceptibility to mental sets • Divergent thinking (e.g., asking unusual questions, giving novel responses) • Greater potential for critical thinking	• Place greater emphasis on higher-level thinking skills (e.g., transfer, problem solving) within the curriculum. • Teach higher-level thinking skills within the context of specific classroom topics rather than in isolation from academic content. • Accept and encourage divergent thinking, including responses that you haven't anticipated. • Encourage critical analysis of ideas, opinions, and evidence.

Sources: Beirne-Smith et al., 2002; Brownell, Mellard, & Deshler, 1993; Candler-Lotven et al., 1994; Campione et al., 1985; B. Clark, 1997; DuPaul & Eckert, 1994; N. R. Ellis, 1979; Frasier, 1989; Graham & Harris, 1996; Grodzinsky & Diamond, 1992; K. R. Harris, 1982; Heward, 2003; M. C. Linn et al., 1989; Maker, 1993; Mastropieri & Scruggs, 2000; McGlynn, 1998; Meichenbaum, 1977; Mercer, 1997; Piirto, 1999; Porath, 1988; Pressley, 1995; Pulos & Linn, 1981; Scruggs & Mastropieri, 1992; Slife, Weiss, & Bell, 1985; Stanley, 1980; H. L. Swanson, 1993; Torrance, 1989; R. Turnbull et al., 2004; Wilder & Williams, 2001; Wong, 1991a.

culations while selling gum and candy to neighbors) yet have difficulty transferring what they've learned to more formal classroom tasks (Carraher, Carraher, & Schliemann, 1985; Gay & Cole, 1967). In some cultures the high value placed on respecting one's elders may foster the epistemological belief that knowledge is a fact-based, cut-and-dried entity that is best gained from authority figures; such a belief can discourage critical thinking. (Delgado-Gaitan, 1994; Qian & Pan, 2002). And students whose previous educational experiences have focused on drills and rote memorization—as is true in some schools in Asia and in many low-income, inner-city school districts in the United States—may have learned to rely heavily on rehearsal as a study strategy (Eccles et al., 1998; D. Y. F. Ho, 1994; Purdie & Hattie, 1996). For such reasons, some students may need more time and scaffolding than others to develop the higher-level thinking skills that will serve them well in the years to come.

Accommodating Students with Special Needs

We are especially apt to find diversity in the higher-level thinking skills of our students with special needs. Table 8.4 presents characteristics common in these students. Particularly noteworthy is the diversity in students' metacognitive awareness and use of study strategies. Many of our students with learning disabilities, and some with emotional and behavioral disorders as well, will demonstrate little knowledge or use of effective strategies (McGlynn, 1998; H. L. Swanson, 1993; Wong, 1991a). Students with mental retardation are likely to show even greater deficits in metacognitive skills; in addition, they will often have difficulty transferring any strategies they learn to new situations (Campione, Brown, & Bryant, 1985). In contrast, students who are gifted will typically have more sophisticated study strategies than their classmates (Candler-Lotven et al., 1994).

For many students with special needs, we may have to teach complex cognitive skills explicitly and with considerable scaffolding—that is, with close guidance and assistance in the use of specific learning strategies. For example, we might provide partially filled-in outlines to guide students' note taking (e.g., see Figure 8.10). We might also tell students when particular strategies (e.g., elaboration, comprehension monitoring) are appropriate and model the use of such strategies with specific classroom subject matter (E. S. Ellis & Friend, 1991; Graham & Harris, 1996). Finally, we must give students opportunities to practice their newly acquired strategies, along with feedback about how effectively they are using each one (E. S. Ellis & Friend, 1991).

FIGURE 8.10 Example of a partially filled-in outline that can guide students' note taking

MUSCLES

A. *Number of Muscles*
   1. There are approximately _____ muscles in the human body.
B. *How Muscles Work*
   1. Muscles work in two ways:
      a. They _____ , or shorten.
      b. They _____, or lengthen.
C. *Kinds of Muscles*
   1. _____ muscles are attached to the bones by _____ .
      a. These muscles are _____ (voluntary/involuntary).
      b. The purpose of these muscles is to _____
         _____ .
   2. _____ muscles line some of the body's _____ .
      a. These muscles are _____ (voluntary/involuntary).
      b. The purpose of these muscles is to _____
         _____ .
   3. The _____ muscle is the only one of its kind.
      a. This muscle is _____ (voluntary/involuntary).
      b. The purpose of this muscle is to _____
         _____ .

THE BIG PICTURE

If you have already read the discussion of individual differences in Chapter 5, then you are familiar with Robert Sternberg's theory of intelligence. Sternberg proposes that specific cognitive processes are one critical aspect of human intelligence. To the extent that students are able to process information in sophisticated ways—to separate important information from irrelevant details, find relationships among seemingly different ideas, apply what they've learned to new situations and problems, critically analyze and evaluate what they read, and so on—they all become more "intelligent" human beings.

If we focus classroom activities on the learning of isolated facts, and if we also use assessment techniques that emphasize students' knowledge of those facts, our students will naturally begin to believe that school learning is a process of absorbing information in a rote fashion and regurgitating it later on. But if we instead focus class time and activities on *doing things with* information—for instance, understanding, organizing, elaborating, applying, analyzing, and critically evaluating it—then our students should acquire the cognitive processes and skills that will serve them well in the world beyond the classroom.

Throughout the chapter we've identified numerous strategies for fostering effective study strategies, transfer, problem solving, creativity, and critical thinking. Let's briefly revisit those strategies that are likely to foster a wide variety of higher-level thinking skills:

◎ *Emphasize meaningful learning and conceptual understanding over rote memorization.* Students can better apply and critique classroom subject matter when they acquire an integrated, cohesive, and thorough understanding of it. Thus, we have repeatedly encountered the *less is more* principle: Teaching a few topics in depth is almost invariably more effective than skimming over the surface of a great many.

◎ *Teach higher-level thinking skills within the context of specific topics.* As teachers, we will occasionally run across packaged curricular programs designed to teach complex mental processes such as study strategies, problem solving, or critical thinking. But as a general rule, we are better advised to teach higher-level thinking skills within the context of specific topics—for example, teaching critical thinking and problem-solving skills as we study science or teaching creative thinking as we study writing

(M. C. Linn et al., 1989; Porath, 1988; Pulos & Linn, 1981; Stanley, 1980).

◎ *Communicate that much of what we "know" about the world is subject to change as new evidence comes in.* Learners' epistemological beliefs about a particular academic discipline, as well as about knowledge and learning more generally, have a significant impact on how learners study, what they learn, how readily they apply classroom subject matter, and how often they critically evaluate it. Some classroom topics are cut-and-dried, to be sure; 2 + 2 will always equal 4 (as long as we're working with a base-10 number system), mammals definitely have backbones (they are vertebrates), and Columbus's first trip across the Atlantic is well documented as having occurred in 1492. Yet many other things—how the brain works, why historical figures made the decisions they did, how best to curb deforestation, and so on—are still a source of considerable debate, and we should say so.

◎ *Encourage higher-level thinking through group discussions and projects.* When students talk with one another, they must verbalize (and therefore become more metacognitively aware of) what and how they themselves are thinking. They also hear other (possibly better) ideas, interpretations, problem-solving strategies, and critical analyses. Invariably, too, they scaffold one another's attempts at higher-level tasks that might be too difficult for any one of them to accomplish individually.

◎ *Use authentic activities to promote transfer of thinking skills to real-life settings.* We do not necessarily want to make the school day just one authentic activity after another, as students may need the time and opportunity to practice certain things (basic math facts, grammatical rules, the symbols for various elements in chemistry, etc.) without too much distraction (J. R. Anderson et al., 1996). Yet unless authentic activities are a regular part of the school curriculum, students may find that higher-level thinking skills have little relevance to their own lives.

◎ *Incorporate higher-level thinking into assessment activities.* As you will discover in Chapter 15, it is fairly easy to construct assignments and tests that assess knowledge of basic facts and procedures. But it is ultimately more important that we assess what students can *do* with that knowledge. In Chapter 15 we will identify a variety of strategies for assessing higher-level thinking skills.

CASE STUDY: *Checks and Balances*

In his middle school social studies class, Mr. Chen has just finished a unit on the three branches of the United States government: executive, legislative, and judicial. He is appalled at some of his students' responses to an essay question he gives. Following are examples of students' responses to this question:

How do the three branches of government provide a system of "checks and balances"? Use an example to illustrate how one branch might serve as a check and balance for another branch. Do *not* use an example that was presented in class.

Debra: The judicial branch finds out if people are innocent or guilty. The executive branch executes the sentences that guilty people get.

Mark: The system of checks and balances is when one branch of government makes sure another branch doesn't do something wrong. I can't think of any examples.

Seth: I don't have anything about this in my notes. Checks and balances have something to do with the way the government spends money.

Karen: I did all the reading, honest I did! But now I can't remember anything about this.

How thoroughly have these students learned the material that Mr. Chen was trying to teach them? Why are they apparently unable to identify new examples of checks and balances?

What evidence do you see that Mr. Chen's students have poor study skills? If you were teaching Mr. Chen's class, what might you do to help the students study and learn more effectively?

Once you have answered these questions, compare your responses with those presented in Appendix B.

KEY CONCEPTS

higher-level thinking (p. 255)
lower-level question (p. 256)
higher-level question (p. 256)
metacognition (p. 257)
concept map (p. 261)
comprehension monitoring (p. 264)
illusion of knowing (p. 264)
self-explanation (p. 264)
self-questioning (p. 264)

epistemological beliefs (p. 266)
transfer (p. 269)
positive transfer (p. 269)
negative transfer (p. 269)
specific transfer (p. 270)
general transfer (p. 270)
formal discipline (p. 270)
situated cognition (p. 270)
well-defined problem (p. 275)

ll-defined problem (p. 275)
algorithm (p. 276)
heuristic (p. 276)
mental set (p. 280)
creativity (p. 284)
convergent thinking (p. 285)
divergent thinking (p. 285)
critical thinking (p. 287)

PRAXIS Turn to Appendix C, "Matching Book and Ancillary Content to the Praxis Principles of Learning and Teaching Tests," to discover sections of this chapter that may be especially applicable to the Praxis tests.

Companion Website

Now go to our Companion Website at **www.prenhall. com/ormrod** to assess your understanding of chapter content with "Multiple-Choice Questions," apply comprehension in "Essay Questions," broaden your knowledge of educational psychology with related "Web Links," gain greater insight about classroom learning in "Learning in the Content Areas," and analyze and assess classroom work in the "Student Artifact Library."

Behaviorist Views of Learning

Chapter 9

As we grow from young infants into mature adults, we learn thousands of new behaviors. As toddlers, we learn to walk, feed ourselves, and ask for what we want. As preschoolers, we learn to brush our teeth, ride a tricycle, and use scissors. During the elementary school years, we begin to use a calculator, write in cursive letters, and play team sports. As adolescents, we may learn how to drive a car, ask someone for a date, or perform in a marching band. In many cases we develop such behaviors because our environment encourages us to do so.

Chapter 6 briefly introduced a theoretical perspective known as **behaviorism**, which focuses on how environmental stimuli bring about changes in people's behaviors. In this chapter we will look more closely at this perspective and use behaviorist theories to understand how, as teachers, we can help students acquire behaviors that are perhaps more complex, productive, or prosocial than the ones they exhibit when they first enter our classrooms. In particular, we will address these questions:

- What basic assumptions are central to behaviorists' beliefs about learning?
- How can we explain students' emotional responses to classroom events using the behaviorist notion of classical conditioning?
- What strategies can we use to encourage desirable behaviors in the classroom?
- What behaviorist principles can assist us in our efforts to reduce inappropriate classroom behaviors?
- How can we apply behaviorist principles systematically to address especially difficult classroom behaviors?

CASE STUDY: *The Attention Getter*

James is the sixth child in a family of nine children. He likes many things; for example, he likes rock music, comic books, basketball, and strawberry ice cream. But more than anything else, James likes attention.

James is a skillful attention getter. He gets his teacher's attention by blurting out answers in class, throwing paper clips and erasers in the teacher's direction, and refusing to turn in classroom assignments. He gets the attention of classmates by teasing them, poking them, or writing obscenities on the restroom walls. By the middle of the school year, James is getting an extra bonus as well: His antics send him to the main office often enough that he has the assistant principal's attention at least once a week.

It's true that the attention James gets is often in the form of a teacher's scolding, a classmate's angry retort, or the assistant principal's admonishment, "We can't have any more of this behavior, young man." But after all—attention is attention.

Why do you think James chooses such inappropriate behaviors (rather than more appropriate ones) as a way of getting the attention of others? Can you speculate on possible reasons?

Exactly what has James learned? Can you derive a principle of learning from James's attention-getting behavior?

BASIC ASSUMPTIONS OF BEHAVIORISM

As you consider James's situation, think back to your own experiences as a student in elementary and secondary school. Which students received the most attention, those who behaved well or those who behaved poorly? Chances are, it was the *mis*behaving students to whom your teachers and classmates paid the most attention (e.g., J. C. Taylor & Romanczyk, 1994). James has undoubtedly learned that if he wants to be noticed—if he wants to stand out in a crowd—then he must behave differently than other students.

Our case study illustrates a basic assumption of behaviorism: People's behaviors are largely the result of their experiences with environmental stimuli. This and other key assumptions underlying behaviorist views of learning (summarized in Table 9.1) are as follows:

◎ *People's behaviors are largely the result of their experiences with environmental stimuli.* Many behaviorists believe that, with the exception of a few simple reflexes, a person is born as a "blank

■ **behaviorism** Theoretical perspective in which learning and behavior are described and explained in terms of stimulus-response relationships.

295

TABLE 9.1   PRINCIPLES/ASSUMPTIONS

Basic Assumptions of Behaviorism and Their Educational Implications

ASSUMPTION	EDUCATIONAL IMPLICATION	EXAMPLE
Influence of the environment	Develop a classroom environment that fosters desirable student behaviors.	When a student often has trouble working independently, inconspicuously praise her every time she completes an assignment without having to be prompted.
Focus on observable events (stimuli and responses)	Identify specific stimuli (including your own actions as a teacher) that may be influencing students' behaviors.	If a student frequently engages in disruptive classroom behavior, consider whether you might be encouraging such behavior by giving him attention every time he misbehaves.
Learning as a behavior change	Don't assume that learning has occurred unless students exhibit a change in classroom performance.	Regularly assess students' learning, and look for ongoing progress in what they know and can do.
Contiguity of events	If you want students to associate two events (stimuli, responses, or stimulus and response) with each other, make sure those events occur close together in time.	Include enjoyable yet educational activities in each day's schedule as a way of helping students associate school subject matter with pleasurable feelings.
Similarity of learning principles across species	Remember that research with nonhuman species often has relevance for classroom practice.	Reinforce a hyperactive student for sitting quietly for successively longer periods of time—a *shaping* process based on early research studies with rats and pigeons.

■ Is this "blank slate" assumption inconsistent with anything you've read in earlier chapters?

slate" (sometimes referred to by the Latin term *tabula rasa*), with no inherited tendency to behave one way or another. Over the years, the environment "writes" on this slate, slowly molding, or **conditioning**, the person into someone who has unique characteristics and ways of behaving.

As teachers, we must keep in mind the very significant effect that students' past and present environments are likely to have on their behaviors. We can use this basic principle to our advantage: By changing the classroom environment, we may also be able to change how students behave.

◎   *Learning can be described in terms of relationships among observable events—that is, relationships among stimuli and responses.* As mentioned in Chapter 6, behaviorists have traditionally believed that phenomena occurring inside a person (thoughts, beliefs, feelings, etc.) cannot be observed and so cannot be studied scientifically. Some behaviorists describe a person as a "black box" that cannot be opened for inspection. They suggest that psychological inquiry should instead focus on things that can be observed and studied objectively; more specifically, it should focus on the **responses** that learners make (symbolized as *R*s) and the environmental **stimuli** (*S*s) that bring those responses about (e.g., Kimble, 2000).

Not all behaviorists hold firmly to this black box assumption. In recent years, many have begun to incorporate cognitive processes and other internal phenomena into their theoretical explanations (DeGrandpre, 2000; Forsyth & Eifert, 1998; Rachlin, 1991; Rescorla, 1988; B. Schwartz & Reisberg, 1991). It is becoming increasingly evident, even to behaviorists, just how difficult it is to omit thinking from explanations of learning and behavior. As you read the chapter, you will find that I occasionally allude to internal phenomena in my discussion of behaviorist principles; in doing so, I reveal my own biases as a cognitive psychologist, and "pure" behaviorists might object.

◎   *Learning involves a behavior change.* From a behaviorist perspective, learning itself should be defined as something that can be observed and documented; in other words, it should be defined as a change in behavior. This definition can be especially useful for us as teachers. To illustrate, consider this scenario:

> Your students look at you attentively as you explain a difficult concept. When you finish, you ask, "Any questions?" You look around the room, and not a single hand is raised. "Good," you think, "they all understand."

■ **conditioning** Term for learning commonly used by behaviorists.

■ **response (R)** Specific behavior that an individual exhibits.

■ **stimulus (S)** Specific object or event that influences an individual's learning or behavior.

But *do* your students understand? On the basis of what you've just observed, you really have no idea whether they do or not. Only observable behavior changes—perhaps an improvement in test scores, a greater frequency of independent reading, or a reduction in hitting and kicking—can ultimately tell us that learning has occurred. Accordingly, this idea will resurface as we begin our discussion of assessment in Chapter 15.

◎ *Learning is most likely to take place when stimuli and responses occur close together in time.* For stimulus-response relationships to develop, certain events must occur in conjunction with other events. When two events occur at more or less the same time, we say that there is **contiguity** between them. The following two examples illustrate contiguity:

- One of your instructors (Professor X) scowls at you as she hands back an exam she has just corrected. You discover that you have gotten a D− on the exam, and you get an uncomfortable feeling in the pit of your stomach. The next time Professor X scowls at you, that same uncomfortable feeling returns.
- Another instructor (Professor Y) smiles and calls on you every time you raise your hand. Although you are fairly quiet in your other classes, you find yourself raising your hand and speaking up more and more frequently in this one.

In the first situation Professor X's scowl and the D− on your exam are presented more or less simultaneously; here we see contiguity between two stimuli. In the second situation your response of raising your hand is followed immediately by Professor Y's smile and his calling on you; in this case we see contiguity between a response and two stimuli (although smiling and calling on you are responses that Professor Y makes, they are *stimuli* for *you*). In both situations your behavior has changed: You've learned to respond with an unpleasant feeling in your stomach every time one instructor scowls, and you've learned to raise your hand and speak up more frequently in another instructor's class.

◎ *Many species of animals, including humans, learn in similar ways.* Behaviorists are well known for their experiments with such animals as rats and pigeons. They assume that many species share similar learning processes; hence, they apply learning principles derived from observing one species to an understanding of how many other species (including humans) learn.

Students in my own educational psychology classes sometimes resent having their own learning compared to the learning of rats and pigeons. But the fact is that behaviorist theories developed from the study of nonhuman animals often *do* explain human behavior. In the upcoming pages we will focus on two behaviorist theories—classical conditioning and operant conditioning—that have been derived largely from animal research yet can help us understand many aspects of human learning and behavior. Before we explore these two forms of conditioning, however, let's apply what we've learned so far in the following assessment exercise.

THE FAR SIDE® BY GARY LARSON

"Stimulus, response! Stimulus, response! Don't you ever *think*?"

■ **contiguity** Occurrence of two or more events at the same time.

Interpreting Student Artifacts and Behaviors

Listening
In a unit on interpersonal skills, a ninth-grade teacher presents a lecture on effective listening skills. One of his students, 15-year-old Geoff, takes extensive notes during the lecture; an excerpt is shown to the right.

As you examine the notes:

■ Identify things Geoff appears to have learned
■ Identify things he has *not* necessarily learned

We know a couple of things about Geoff by looking at his notes. We know that he has, at some point, learned to take thorough, well-organized notes from a lecture. We also know that he has learned some suggestions about how to be a good listener. We can reasonably assume that Geoff hasn't always been able to take good notes, but the lecture did not address note taking (he probably learned this skill at an earlier time). We can also assume that he hasn't always known the ideas he has written in his notes. His behavior change—his communication of the ideas from the lecture—tells us that learning has occurred.

What we *don't* know, however, is whether Geoff would actually put the suggestions he has learned into practice—whether, as a result of the lesson, he would practice better listening skills. We have not, in fact, specifically seen a change in his interpersonal behaviors. From a behaviorist perspective, Geoff is more likely to acquire productive interpersonal skills by actually *practicing* them, perhaps in role-playing activities or perhaps in normal, everyday interactions with classmates.

CLASSICAL CONDITIONING

Consider this situation:

> Alan has always loved baseball. But in a game last year, he was badly hurt by a wild pitch while he was up at bat. Now, although he still plays baseball, he gets anxious whenever it is his turn at bat, to the point where his heart rate increases and he often backs away from the ball instead of swinging at it.

One possible explanation of Alan's learning is **classical conditioning**, a theory that explains how we sometimes learn new responses as a result of two stimuli (in this case, the sight of an oncoming baseball and the ball's painful impact) being present at approximately the same time. Alan's current responses to a pitched ball—his physiological feelings of anxiety and his backing away—are ones he didn't exhibit before his painful experience with a baseball; thus, learning has occurred.

Classical conditioning was first described by Ivan Pavlov (e.g., 1927), a Russian physiologist who was conducting research about salivation. Pavlov often used dogs in his research projects and presented meat to get them to salivate. He noticed that the dogs frequently began to salivate as soon as they heard the lab assistant coming down the hall, even though they could not yet smell the meat the assistant was carrying. Curious about this phenomenon, Pavlov conducted an experiment to examine more systematically how a dog learns to salivate to a new stimulus. His experiment went something like this:

1. Pavlov flashes a light. The dog does not salivate to the light stimulus. Using S for stimulus and R for response, we can symbolize Pavlov's first observation like so:

$$S \text{ (light)} \quad \rightarrow \quad R \text{ (none)}$$

2. Pavlov flashes the light again and presents meat immediately afterward. He repeats this procedure several times, and the dog salivates every time. The dog is demonstrating something it already knows how to do—salivate to meat—so it has not yet learned anything new. We can symbolize Pavlov's second observation like so:

$$\left.\begin{array}{l} S \text{ (light)} \\ S \text{ (meat)} \end{array}\right\} \rightarrow \quad R \text{ (salivation)}$$

3. Pavlov flashes the light once more, but this time without any meat. The dog salivates; in other words, it has learned a new response to the light stimulus. We can symbolize Pavlov's third observation this way:

$$S \text{ (light)} \quad \rightarrow \quad R \text{ (salivation)}$$

In more general terms, classical conditioning proceeds as follows:

1. It begins with a stimulus-response association that already exists—in other words, with an *unconditioned* stimulus-response association. For example, Pavlov's dog salivates automatically whenever it smells meat, and Alan becomes anxious and backs away whenever he encounters a painful stimulus; no learning is involved in either case. When a stimulus leads to a particular response without prior learning, we say that an **unconditioned stimulus (UCS)** elicits an **unconditioned response (UCR)**. The unconditioned response is typically an automatic, involuntary one—one over which the learner has little or no control.

2. Conditioning occurs when a **neutral stimulus**— one that doesn't elicit any particular response—is presented immediately before the unconditioned stimulus. In the case of Pavlov's dog, a light is presented immediately before the meat; in the case of Alan, a

Classical conditioning often helps us understand students' feelings about various school activities. This boy's feelings about soccer will be influenced both by his success at the sport and by the quality of his interactions with teammates.

■ **classical conditioning** Form of learning in which a new, involuntary response is acquired as a result of two stimuli being presented at the same time.

■ **unconditioned stimulus (UCS)** Stimulus that, without prior learning, elicits a particular response.

■ **unconditioned response (UCR)** Response that, without prior learning, is elicited by a particular (unconditioned) stimulus.

■ **neutral stimulus** Stimulus that does not elicit any particular response.

baseball is pitched immediately before the painful hit. Conditioning is especially likely to occur when both stimuli are presented together on several occasions and when the neutral stimulus occurs *only* when the unconditioned stimulus is about to follow (R. R. Miller & Barnet, 1993; Rachlin, 1991; Rescorla, 1967).

3. Before long, the new stimulus also elicits a response, usually one very similar to the unconditioned response. The neutral stimulus has become a **conditioned stimulus (CS)**, and the response to it has become a **conditioned response (CR)**. For example, Pavlov's dog acquires a conditioned response of salivation to a new, conditioned stimulus—the light. Likewise, Alan acquires conditioned responses of anxiety and backing away to a pitched baseball. Like the unconditioned response, the conditioned response is an involuntary one; it occurs automatically every time the conditioned stimulus is presented.

■ The word *elicit,* meaning "draw forth or bring out," is frequently used in descriptions of classical conditioning.

Classical Conditioning of Emotional Responses

Experiencing FIRSTHAND ·"Classical" Music

Some songs make people feel certain ways. For example, Handel's "Water Music" always elicits especially happy feelings in me, perhaps because it's the music that was played at my wedding. The theme from the old television show *Dragnet* still elicits tinges of anxiety in me because the show frightened me when I was a young child. Take a minute to think about particular songs you might listen to if you wanted to experience each of the following feelings:

Feeling	Song
Happiness	_____
Relaxation	_____
Anxiety	_____
Sadness	_____

Why do the songs bring out such feelings? Can you trace those feelings to significant occasions in your life when each song was playing?

· · · · · · ·

In some cases your emotional reactions to a song may be attributable simply to the mood that the song conveys. But in other cases a song may make you feel the way you do because you associate it with particular events. Consider the case of Brenda:

At the school dance, Brenda has one dance with Joe, a boy she has a tremendous crush on. They dance to "Michelle," an old Beatles song. Later, whenever Brenda hears "Michelle," she feels happy.

In this situation Joe is initially the source of Brenda's good feelings. A second stimulus—"Michelle"—is associated with Joe, and so the song begins to elicit those same feelings. From a classical conditioning perspective, we can analyze the situation this way:

UCS: Joe   →   UCR: happy reaction to Joe

CS: "Michelle" →   CR: happy reaction to "Michelle"

Following are additional examples of how emotional responses might be learned through classical conditioning. Notice that in each case two stimuli are presented together. One stimulus already elicits a response, and as a result of the pairing, the second stimulus begins to elicit a similar response.

• Bernard falls into a swimming pool and almost drowns. A year later, when his mother takes him to the local recreation center for a swimming lesson, he cries hysterically as she tries to drag him to the side of the pool.

UCS: inability to breathe   →   UCR: fear of being unable to breathe

CS: swimming pool   →   CR: fear of the swimming pool

• Bobby misses a month of school because of illness. When he returns to school, he does not know how to do his long division assignments. After a number of frustrating experiences

■ **conditioned stimulus (CS)** Stimulus that, through classical conditioning, begins to elicit a particular response.

■ **conditioned response (CR)** Response that, through classical conditioning, begins to be elicited by a particular (conditioned) stimulus.

The best part of third grade was

division
algebra
multiplication
math
reading

In a personal "yearbook," Ashton identifies math and reading as being the best part of his third-grade year. He clearly associated these subjects with pleasure rather than anxiety.

■ Recall the earlier example of Professor X's scowl, and use classical conditioning to explain why her scowl might elicit discomfort.

in which he cannot solve long division problems, he begins to feel anxious whenever he encounters a division task.

UCS: failure/frustration   →   UCR: anxiety about failure

CS: long division   →   CR: anxiety about long division

- Beth's teacher catches Beth writing a letter to one of her classmates during class. The teacher reads the note to the entire class, revealing some very personal and private information about Beth. Beth now feels embarrassed whenever she goes into that teacher's classroom.

UCS: humiliation   →   UCR: embarrassment in response to humiliation

CS: teacher/classroom   →   CR: embarrassment in response to teacher/classroom

Classical conditioning is frequently used to explain why people sometimes respond emotionally to what might otherwise be fairly "neutral" stimuli. When a particular stimulus is associated with something that makes us happy or relaxed, it may begin to elicit those same feelings of happiness or relaxation. When a stimulus is associated with something that makes us fearful or anxious, it, too, may begin to elicit feelings of fear and anxiety.

As teachers, we must create a classroom environment in which stimuli (including our own behaviors) are likely to elicit such responses as enjoyment or relaxation, *not* fear or anxiety, in students. When students associate school with pleasant stimuli—positive feedback, enjoyable activities, and so on—they soon learn that school is a place where they want to be. But when they instead encounter unpleasant stimuli in school—negative comments, public humiliation, or constant frustration and failure—they may eventually learn to fear or dislike a particular activity, subject area, teacher, or (perhaps) school in general.

Common Phenomena in Classical Conditioning

Behaviorists have described a number of phenomena related to conditioning processes. At least two of them, generalization and extinction, have been observed in both classical and operant conditioning. For now we'll look only at generalization and extinction in classical conditioning; later in the chapter we'll examine the forms they take in operant conditioning.

Generalization. When people learn a conditioned response to a new stimulus, they may respond in the same way to similar stimuli—a phenomenon known as **generalization.** For example, a boy who learns to feel anxious about long division tasks may generalize that anxiety to other aspects of mathematics. And a girl who experiences humiliation in one classroom may generalize her embarrassment to other classrooms as well. In behaviorist theory, generalization is the primary means through which learners *transfer* what they have learned in one setting to new situations. Here we see one more reason why students should associate pleasant feelings with classroom subject matter. Students' reactions to a paticular topic, activity, or context may generalize (transfer) to similar topics, activities, or contexts.

Extinction. Pavlov discovered that conditioned responses don't necessarily last forever. By pairing a light with meat, he conditioned a dog to salivate to the light alone. But later, when he flashed the light repeatedly without ever again following it with meat, the dog salivated less and less. Eventually, the dog no longer salivated when it saw the light flash. When a conditioned stimulus occurs repeatedly *in the absence of* the unconditioned stimulus—for example, when a light is never again associated with meat, when mathematics is never again associated with failure, or when a teacher is never again associated with humiliation—the conditioned response may decrease and eventually disappear. In other words, **extinction** occurs.

Many conditioned responses fade over time. Unfortunately, many others do not; a child's fear of water or anxiety about mathematics may persist for years. One reason that fears and anxieties may persist over time is that people tend to avoid situations that cause such emotional reactions. If they stay away from a stimulus that makes them fearful, they never have a chance to experience the stimulus in the absence of the unconditioned stimulus with which it was originally paired. As a result, they have no opportunity to learn to be *un*afraid; in other words, they have no opportunity for the response to undergo extinction.

As teachers, how can we reduce the counterproductive conditioned responses that students may exhibit—for example, their fear of water or their math anxiety? Psychologists have learned that one way to extinguish a negative emotional reaction to a particular conditioned stimulus is

■ **generalization** Phenomenon in which a person learns a response to a particular stimulus and then makes the same response to similar stimuli; in classical conditioning, involves making a conditioned response to stimuli similar to a conditioned stimulus.

■ **extinction** Gradual disappearance of an acquired response; in classical conditioning, results from repeated presentation of a conditioned stimulus in the absence of the unconditioned stimulus.

to introduce the stimulus *slowly and gradually* while the student is happy or relaxed (M. C. Jones, 1924; Wolpe, 1969). For example, if Bernard is afraid of water, we might begin his swimming lessons someplace where he feels at ease—perhaps on dry land or in the baby pool—and move to deeper water only as he begins to feel more comfortable. If Bobby gets overly anxious every time he encounters a math problem, we might revert back to very easy problems—those he can readily solve—and gradually increase the difficulty of his assignments only as he demonstrates greater competence and self-confidence. (We will consider the nature and effects of anxiety in more detail in Chapter 11.)

There is nothing like success to help students feel good about being in the classroom. One thing we can do to promote student success is structure the classroom environment so that appropriate behaviors are reinforced and inapppropriate behaviors are not. It is to the role that reinforcement plays in learning—to operant conditioning—that we turn now.

OPERANT CONDITIONING

Mark is a student in Ms. Ferguson's geography class. This is what happens to Mark during the first week in October:

- *Monday.* Ms. Ferguson asks the class to locate Colombia on the globe. Mark knows where Colombia is, and he sits smiling, with his hands in his lap, hoping that Ms. Ferguson will call on him. Instead, Ms. Ferguson calls on another student.
- *Tuesday.* Ms. Ferguson asks the class where Colombia got its name. Mark knows that Colombia is named after Christopher Columbus, so he raises his hand a few inches. Ms. Ferguson calls on another student.
- *Wednesday.* Ms. Ferguson asks the class why people in Colombia speak Spanish rather than English or French. Mark knows that Colombians speak Spanish because many of the country's early European settlers came from Spain. He raises his hand high in the air. Ms. Ferguson calls on another student.
- *Thursday.* Ms. Ferguson asks the class why Colombia grows coffee but Canada does not. Mark knows that coffee can be grown only in certain climates. He raises his hand high and waves it wildly back and forth. Ms. Ferguson calls on him.
- *Friday.* Whenever Ms. Ferguson asks a question that Mark can answer, Mark raises his hand high and waves it wildly about.

Notice how several of Mark's behaviors in geography class, such as sitting quietly, smiling, and raising his hand politely, bring no results. Waving his hand wildly brings Mark the result that he wants: his teacher's attention. The response that has attracted Ms. Ferguson's attention continues. Other responses disappear.

The change in Mark's behavior illustrates **operant conditioning**, a form of learning described by many behaviorists and most notably by B. F. Skinner (e.g., 1953, 1954, 1968). The basic principle of operant conditioning is a simple one:

A response that is followed by a reinforcing stimulus (a reinforcer) is more likely to occur again.

When behaviors are followed by desirable consequences, they tend to increase in frequency. When behaviors don't produce results, they typically decrease and may disappear altogether.

Students often learn and demonstrate new behaviors for the consequences those behaviors bring. Following are examples:

- Samirah studies hard for her French vocabulary quiz. She gets an A on the quiz.
- Sharon copies her answers to the French quiz from Samirah's paper. She, too, gets an A.
- Julian changes how he holds a basketball before shooting it toward the basket. He now gets more baskets than he used to.
- James throws paper clips at the girl beside him and discovers that this is one way he can get her attention.

Many appropriate and productive behaviors—such as studying for a French quiz or holding a basketball in a particular way—are acquired because of the desirable consequences to which they lead. Many less desirable behaviors—such as cheating on a quiz or throwing paper clips at a classmate—may be acquired for the same reason.

When students associate school with pleasant stimuli, they learn that school is a place where they want to be.

■ **operant conditioning** Form of learning in which a response increases in frequency as a result of its being followed by reinforcement.

Operant conditioning can occur only under two conditions. First, of course, the learner must make a response; that is, the learner must *do* something. Behaviorists believe that little is accomplished by having students sit quietly and listen passively to their teacher; instead, students are more likely to learn when they are making active, overt responses in the classroom (e.g., Drevno et al., 1994). Second, the reinforcer should be **contingent** on the learner's response; that is, it should occur when, and *only* when, the desired response has occurred. A teacher who praises students only when they behave appropriately is making reinforcement contingent on desired behavior. In contrast, the teacher who laughs at the antics of a chronically misbehaving student is providing reinforcement even when an acceptable response hasn't occurred, so the student's behavior is unlikely to improve.

As teachers, we should be sure to reinforce the behaviors we want students to acquire. If we want students to read frequently, volunteer in class, demonstrate good form in basketball, or work cooperatively with their classmates, we should reinforce such behaviors as they occur. At the same time, we should be careful *not* to reinforce any inappropriate and counterproductive behaviors that students exhibit. If we repeatedly allow Carol to turn in assignments late because she says she forgot her homework and if we often let Colin get his way by bullying his classmates on the playground, then we are reinforcing (and hence increasing) Carol's excuse making and Colin's aggressiveness.

Contrasting Classical and Operant Conditioning

Like classical conditioning, operant conditioning involves both a stimulus and a response. But operant conditioning is different from classical conditioning in two important ways:

- *The way in which conditioning comes about.* Classical conditioning results from the *pairing of two stimuli*, one (the UCS) that initially elicits a response and another (the CS) that begins to elicit the same or a similar response. In contrast, operant conditioning occurs when *a response is followed by a stimulus (in particular, a reinforcer).*
- *The nature of the response.* In classical conditioning, the response is involuntary: When a particular (conditioned) stimulus is present, the response follows almost automatically. For example, Alan doesn't *choose* to be anxious about a baseball pitched in his direction; he simply *is* anxious. In operant conditioning, however, the response is usually a voluntary one: The learner can control whether or not it occurs. For example, when, in the opening case study, James blurts out answers, throws erasers across the room, or teases classmates, he is willingly behaving in these ways. No particular stimulus is forcing him to do so.

Reinforcement in the Classroom

Experiencing FIRSTHAND ·What Would It Take?

Imagine this scenario:

> You are currently enrolled in my educational psychology class. As your instructor, I ask you if you would be willing to spend an hour after class tutoring two classmates who are having difficulty understanding the course material. You have no other commitments for that hour, but you'd really rather spend the time at a nearby coffee shop where several friends are having lunch. What would it take for you to spend the hour tutoring your classmates instead of joining your friends? Would you do it to gain my approval? Would you do it for a candy bar? How about if I gave you five dollars? Would you do it simply because it made you feel good inside to be helping someone else? Write down a reward—perhaps one I have listed or perhaps a different one altogether—that would persuade you to help your classmates instead of meeting your friends.

Now imagine this second scenario:

> A few weeks later I ask you to spend the weekend (eight hours a day on both Saturday and Sunday) tutoring the same two struggling classmates. What would it take this time to convince you to do the job? Would my approval do the trick? A candy bar? Five dollars? Five *hundred* dollars? Or would your internal sense of satisfaction be enough? Once again, write down what it would take for you to agree to help your classmates.

· · · · · · ·

■ How is the concept of *contingency* different from *contiguity*?

■ **contingency** Situation in which one event happens only after another event has already occurred (one event is *contingent* on the other's occurrence).

GARFIELD / Jim Davis

Obviously, there are no right answers to the exercise you just completed. Different people would agree to tutor classmates for different reasons. But you were probably able to identify at least one consequence in each situation that would entice you to give up your own personal time to help others.

We often talk about giving students rewards for academic achievement and appropriate classroom behavior. But as you may have noticed, I have not used the term *reward* in my description of operant conditioning, and for a very important reason. The word *reward* brings to mind things we would all agree are pleasant and desirable—perhaps praise, money, trophies, or special privileges. But some individuals increase their behavior for consequences that others would not find so appealing. A **reinforcer** is *any consequence that increases the frequency of a particular behavior*, whether or not other people find that consequence pleasant. The act of following a particular response with a reinforcer is called **reinforcement**.

Let's return once again to our opening case study. James has learned that he can get his teacher's attention by blurting out answers in class, throwing objects around the room, and refusing to turn in classroom assignments. We can assume that James's teacher is not smiling or praising him for such behavior. Probably the teacher is frowning, scolding, or even yelling. We don't usually think of frowning, scolding, and yelling as rewards. Yet those consequences are leading to an increase in James's misbehaviors, so they are apparently reinforcing for him. Attention from others, regardless of the form it might take, can be highly reinforcing for some students and often serves to maintain counterproductive classroom behaviors (e.g., Flood, Wilder, Flood, & Masuda, 2002; McComas, Thompson, & Johnson, 2003).

Reinforcement comes in all shapes and sizes. In the following sections, we will look at two basic distinctions—primary versus secondary reinforcers, and positive versus negative reinforcement—and, in the process, identify potentially effective reinforcers in classroom settings. We will then consider how both timing and motivation influence a reinforcer's effectiveness.

Primary Versus Secondary Reinforcers   A **primary reinforcer** satisfies a basic biological need; food, water, warmth, and oxygen are all examples. To some extent, physical affection and cuddling may address built-in biological needs as well (Harlow & Zimmerman, 1959; Vollmer & Hackenberg, 2001). And for an adolescent addicted to an illegal substance, the next "fix" is a primary reinforcer (Lejuez, Schaal, & O'Donnell, 1998).

A **secondary reinforcer** does not satisfy any physiological need; instead, it becomes reinforcing over time through its association with another reinforcer. For example, perhaps praise was once associated with a special candy treat from mother, or a good grade was associated with a hug from father. Through such associations, consequences such as praise, good grades, money, feelings of success, and perhaps even scolding become reinforcing in their own right: They become secondary reinforcers.

Secondary reinforcers are far more common in classrooms than primary reinforcers. But we must remember that secondary reinforcers are *learned* reinforcers, and not everyone has come to appreciate them. Although most students respond positively to such consequences as praise or a good grade, a few students may not.

Positive Versus Negative Reinforcement   Up to this point, we have been speaking of reinforcement as the *presentation* of a particular reinforcing stimulus. But in some cases we can also reinforce a behavior through the *removal* of a stimulus. Operant conditioning theorists use the terms *positive reinforcement* and *negative reinforcement*, respectively, for these two situations.

■ **reinforcer** Consequence (stimulus) of a response that leads to increased frequency of that response.

■ **reinforcement** Act of following a response with a reinforcer.

■ **primary reinforcer** Consequence that satisfies a biologically built-in need.

■ **secondary reinforcer** Consequence that becomes reinforcing over time through its association with another reinforcer.

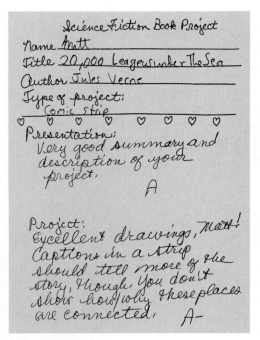

Science Fiction Book Project

Name Matt

Title 20,000 Leagues under The Sea

Author Jules Verne

Type of project:
 Comic strip

♡   ♡   ♡   ♡   ♡   ♡   ♡

Presentation:
 Very good summary and
 description of your
 project.
                    A

Project:
 Excellent drawings, Matt!
 Captions in a strip
 should tell more of the
 story, though. You don't
 show how/why these places
 are connected.   A-

FIGURE 9.1 In commenting on Matt's book project, the teacher is explicit about what he can do to improve but vague about what he has done well. Knowing what *specific* things made his summary and project description "very good" would help Matt repeat these things in the future.

■ **positive reinforcement** Consequence that brings about the increase of a behavior through the presentation (rather than removal) of a stimulus.

■ **concrete reinforcer** Reinforcer that can be touched.

■ **social reinforcer** Gesture or sign that one person gives another, often to communicate positive regard.

■ **activity reinforcer** Opportunity to engage in a favorite activity.

■ **Premack principle** Phenomenon in which students do less-preferred activities in order to engage in more-preferred activities.

■ **positive feedback** Message that an answer is correct or a task has been well done.

■ **extrinsic reinforcer** Reinforcer that comes from the outside environment, rather than from within the learner.

■ **intrinsic reinforcer** Reinforcer provided by oneself or inherent in the task being performed.

Positive reinforcement. Whenever a particular stimulus is *presented* after a behavior, and the behavior increases as a result, **positive reinforcement** has occurred. This is the case whether or not the presented stimulus is one that others would agree is pleasant and desirable. For instance, some students will make a response to get a teacher's praise, but others (like James in the opening case study) may behave to get themselves a scolding. Most students will work for As, but a few may actually prefer Cs or even Fs. Depending on the individual, any one of these stimuli—the praise, the scolding, the A, or the F—can be a positive reinforcer. Following are examples of the forms that positive reinforcement might take:

- A **concrete reinforcer** is an actual object—something that can be touched (e.g., a snack, a sticker, or a toy).
- A **social reinforcer** is a gesture or sign (e.g., a smile, attention, praise, or "thank you") that one person gives another, often to communicate positive regard.
- An **activity reinforcer** is an opportunity to engage in a favorite activity. Students will often do one thing, even something they don't like to do, if doing so enables them to do something they do enjoy; this phenomenon is sometimes called the **Premack principle** (Premack, 1959, 1963).
- Sometimes the simple message that an answer is correct or that a task has been done well—**positive feedback**—is reinforcement enough. Positive feedback is most effective when it tells students in explicit terms what they are doing well and what they can do to improve their performance even further (Bangert-Drowns, Kulik, Kulik, & Morgan, 1991; D. L. Butler & Winne, 1995; Feltz, Chase, Moritz, & Sullivan, 1999). As an example, see Figure 9.1.

The reinforcers just listed are **extrinsic reinforcers**, those provided by the external environment (often by other people). Yet some positive reinforces are **intrinsic reinforcers**, those supplied by learners themselves or inherent in the tasks being performed. Students engage in some activities simply because they enjoy those activities or because they like to feel competent and successful. When students perform certain behaviors in the absence of any observable reinforcers—when they read an entire book without putting it down, do extra classwork without being asked, practice on their electric guitars into the wee hours of the morning—they are probably working for the intrinsic reinforcement that such behaviors yield. Intrinsic reinforcers are *not* observable events; as such, they do not fit comfortably within traditional behaviorist theory. Yet students clearly do engage in some behaviors solely for the intrinsic satisfaction those behaviors bring. We will talk more about such *intrinsic motivation* in Chapters 11 and 12.

Children's preferences for various kinds of reinforcers tend to change as they grow older. For example, concrete reinforcers (e.g., candy, small trinkets) can be effective with young children, but teenagers are more likely to appreciate opportunities to converse with friends. Table 9.2 presents forms of reinforcement that may be especially effective at various grade levels.

From our perspective as teachers, positive feedback (an extrinsic reinforcer) and the feelings of pleasure and satisfaction that such feedback can bring (intrinsic reinforcers) are probably the most desirable forms of classroom reinforcement. Yet we must remember that the classroom successes that yield such forms of reinforcement can occur only when classroom instruction has been carefully tailored to individual skill levels and abilities, and only when students have learned to value academic achievement. When students are not motivated to achieve academic success (for whatever reasons), then social reinforcers, activity reinforcers, and (if necessary) even concrete reinforcers can be used to increase desired classroom behaviors.

Experiencing FIRSTHAND · · · · · · · · · · · · · · · Take Two on "What Would It Take?"

In a preceding exercise you identified consequences that would entice you to spend time tutoring classmates when you'd really rather join your friends at the local coffee shop. For each one of the following consequences for tutoring your classmates, determine the kind of reinforcer it reflects:

Consequence	Kind of Reinforcer
You gain my approval.	_____
You get a candy bar.	_____
You get five dollars.	_____
You feel good about helping someone else.	_____

TABLE 9.2   DEVELOPMENTAL TRENDS

Effective Reinforcers at Different Grade Levels

GRADE LEVEL	AGE-TYPICAL CHARACTERISTICS	SUGGESTED STRATEGIES

K–2	• Preference for small, immediate rewards over larger, delayed ones
	• Examples of effective reinforcers:
	  Concrete reinforcers (e.g., stickers, crayons, small trinkets)
	  Teacher approval (e.g., smiles, praise)
	  Privileges (e.g., going to lunch first)
	  "Grown-up" responsibilities (e.g., taking absentee forms to the office)
		• Give immediate praise for appropriate behavior.
		• Describe enjoyable consequences that may come later as a result of students' present behaviors.
		• Use colorful stickers to indicate a job well done; choose stickers that match students' interests (e.g., use favorite cartoon characters).
		• Have students line up for recess, lunch, or dismissal based on desired behaviors (e.g., "Table 2 is the quietest and can line up first").
		• Rotate opportunities to perform classroom duties (e.g., feeding the goldfish, watering plants) among all students; make such duties contingent on appropriate behavior.

3–5	• Increasing ability to delay gratification (i.e., to put off small reinforcers in order to gain larger ones later on)
	• Examples of effective reinforcers:
	  Concrete reinforcers (e.g., candy, pencils)
	  Teacher approval and positive feedback
	  "Good citizen" certificates
	  Free time (e.g., to draw or play games)
		• Use concrete reinforcers only occasionally, perhaps to add novelty to a classroom activity.
		• Award a certificate to a "citizen of the week," identifying things the recipient has done especially well; be sure that every student gets at least one certificate during the school year.
		• Plan a trip to a local amusement park for students with good attendance records (especially useful for students at risk).

6–8	• Increasing desire to have social time with peers
	• Examples of effective reinforcers:
	  Free time with friends
	  Acceptance and approval from peers
	  Teacher approval and support (becomes especially critical after the transition to middle school)
	• Specific positive feedback about academic performance (preferably given in private)
		• Make short periods of free time (e.g., five minutes) with peers contingent on accomplishing assigned tasks.
		• Spend one-on-one time with students, especially those who seem socially isolated.
		• Provide explicit feedback about what things students have done well (e.g., pointing out their use of colorful language in an essay or commending them for prosocial behaviors).

9–12	• Considerable ability to postpone immediate pleasures in order to gain long-term rewards
	• Concern about getting good grades (for students who are applying to selective colleges)
	• Examples of effective reinforcers:
	  Opportunities to interact with friends
	  Specific positive feedback about academic performance
	  Public recognition for group performance (e.g., newspaper articles about a club's public service work)
	  Positions of responsibility (e.g., being student representative to Faculty Senate)
		• Acknowledge students' concern about earning good grades, but focus their attention on the value of learning school subject matter for its own sake (see Chapter 12).
		• Be sure that good grades are contingent on students' own work; do not reinforce cheating or plagiarism.
		• Publicize accomplishments of extracurricular groups and athletic teams in local news media.
		• Provide opportunities for independent decision making and responsibility, especially when students show that they can make wise decisions.

Sources: L. H. Anderman, Patrick, Hruda, & Linnenbrink, 2002; Cizek, 2003; Fowler & Baer, 1981; Green, Fry, & Myerson, 1994; Hine & Fraser, 2002; Krumboltz & Krumboltz, 1972; Rimm & Masters, 1974; Rotenberg & Mayer, 1990; M. G. Sanders, 1996.

You can find the correct answers below—but no peeking until you've made your own decisions!

· · · · · · ·

Answer key: My approval is a social reinforcer, the candy bar and money are concrete reinforcers, and feeling good about what you have done is an intrinsic reinforcer. Of these, only the candy bar is a primary reinforcer; the other three are secondary reinforcers.

Negative reinforcement. As we have just seen, positive reinforcement involves the presentation of a stimulus. In contrast, **negative reinforcement** brings about the increase of a behavior through the *removal* of a stimulus (typically an unpleasant one). The word *negative* here is not a value

■ **negative reinforcement**
Consequence that brings about the increase of a behavior through the removal (rather than presentation) of a stimulus.

■ Table 9.3 on page 316 contrasts positive and negative reinforcement with each other and with punishment.

■ What stimulus is being removed in each example? What response is being reinforced as a result?

judgment; it simply refers to the act of taking away a stimulus.[1] When people make a response to get rid of something, they are being negatively reinforced. Consider the following examples:

- Reuben must read *Ivanhoe* for his English literature class before the end of the month. He doesn't like having this assignment hanging over his head, so he finishes it early. When he's done, he no longer has to worry about it.
- Rhonda is in the same literature class. Each time she sits down at home to read *Ivanhoe*, she finds the novel confusing and difficult to understand. She quickly ends her study sessions by finding other things she "needs" to do instead—washing her hair, folding her laundry, playing basketball with the neighbors, and so on.
- Ms. Randolph yells at her rowdy seventh graders. They quiet down. By yelling, Ms. Randolph terminates a noisy and unpleasant situation, even if only temporarily.

We see another example of negative reinforcement in our opening case study. When James misbehaves, he is often sent to the assistant principal's office; this negatively reinforces his behavior because it enables him to *get out of class*, thereby removing a stimulus—some aspect of the class environment—that may be aversive for him. (If James likes spending time with the assistant principal he is receiving positive reinforcement as well.) Whereas some students misbehave in class to get attention (a positive reinforcer), many others misbehave to escape something they do not want to do—for instance, to complete a difficult assignment—and such escape behavior is negatively reinforced (e.g., McComas et al., 2003).

In the examples just considered, notice how negative reinforcement sometimes promotes desirable behaviors (such as completing an assignment early) and at other times promotes undesirable behaviors (such as procrastination). Notice, as well, how students are not the only ones who respond to reinforcement in the classroom. After all, teachers are human beings too!

As teachers, we will use negative reinforcement rarely if at all; ideally, we want to create a classroom environment in which there are few stimuli that students want to be rid of. Nevertheless, we should recognize that negative reinforcement *does* have an effect on behavior. Some students may finish an assignment more to "get it out of the way" than for any intrinsic satisfaction the assignment brings. Others may engage in inappropriate classroom behavior as a way of avoiding the assignment altogether. When certain responses enable students to remove unpleasant stimuli—perhaps classroom assignments or perhaps even the classroom itself—those responses will increase in frequency.

Importance of Timing   In B. F. Skinner's original conception of operant conditioning, reinforcement is likely to be effective only if it occurs *immediately* after a desired response has occurred; in other words, the response and the reinforcing stimulus should occur in close contiguity. Considerable research indicates that timing does make a difference: The more closely a reinforcer follows a response, the more effective it is apt to be (J. A. Kulik & Kulik, 1988; Rachlin, 1991).

■ Can you use the concept of *working memory* (Chapter 6) to explain why immediate reinforcement might be better than delayed reinforcement?

Yet as children get older, they become better able to **delay gratification:** They can forego small, immediate reinforcers for the larger reinforcers that their long-term efforts may bring down the road (Green et al. 1994; Rotenberg & Mayer, 1990). Whereas a preschooler is apt to choose a small reinforcer she can have *now* over a larger and more attractive reinforcer she cannot get until tomorrow, an 8-year-old may be willing to wait a day or two for the more appealing item. Many adolescents can delay gratification for weeks at a time. For instance, as a 16-year-old, my son Jeff worked long hours stocking shelves at the local grocery store (hardly an intrinsically reinforcing activity!) to earn enough money to pay half the cost of a $400-a-night limousine for his high school prom.

Some children and adolescents are better able to delay gratification than others, and those who can are less likely to yield to temptation, more carefully plan their future actions, and achieve at higher levels in academic settings (Durkin, 1995; Shoda, Mischel, & Peake, 1990; Veroff, McClelland, & Ruhland, 1975). However, even 4- and 5-year olds can learn to delay gratification for

---

■ **delay of gratification**   Ability to forego small, immediate reinforcers to obtain larger ones later on.

[1] You might draw an analogy between positive and negative reinforcement and positive and negative numbers. Positive numbers and positive reinforcement both *add* something to a situation. Negative numbers and negative reinforcement both *subtract* something from a situation.

a few hours if their teachers tell them that rewards for desired behaviors (such as sharing toys with other children) will be coming later in the day (Fowler & Baer, 1981). Teaching children effective "waiting" strategies—for example, encouraging them to focus their attention on something else during the duration, or teaching them such self-talk as "If I wait a little longer, I will get a better one"—enhances their ability to delay gratification as well (Binder, Dixon, & Ghezzi, 2000).

Role of Motivation   In the opening case study, James engages in a variety of inappropriate behaviors to gain the attention of his teacher, his classmates, and sometimes the assistant principal. Students are far more likely to misbehave if they have very little social contact with others *unless* they misbehave (McGill, 1999). We might reasonably guess that James would prefer more appropriate interactions with adults and peers, yet for whatever reasons (perhaps because his academic performance rarely gains his teacher's praise, perhaps because he lacks the social skills to make and maintain friendships), he seldom has such interactions.

We will look at motivation in more detail in Chapters 11 and 12, but for now we should note that motivation plays a significant role in determining the consequences that students find reinforcing (McGill, 1999; Michael, 2000). For example, some students (like James) may thrive on teacher scoldings even though others dislike them. Some students may respond well to praise, but others (perhaps those who don't want to be labeled "teacher's pet" by peers) may view a teacher's praise as a fate worse than death (e.g., Pfiffner, Rosen, & O'Leary, 1985). Some students may work at academic tasks simply for the feelings of success and accomplishment that such activities bring, but others may work diligently at the same tasks only if doing so leads to social benefits—perhaps the respect of classmates or the opportunity to spend time with friends. Some students like getting As, but others (perhaps those afraid of being labeled a "nerd") may actually prefer Cs. An important principle of operant conditioning, then, is that *different stimuli are reinforcing for different individuals*. We must never make assumptions about what specific events are reinforcing for particular students.

At this point, let's stop for a moment to examine one teacher's use of reinforcement to encourage desired classroom behavior.

Analyzing Teacher Strategies

Paper Trophy
At the end of the school year, a kindergarten teacher awards paper "trophies" to each of her students. Five-year-old Katie receives the trophy depicted here. As you look at the trophy, consider

- What kind of reinforcement it represents
- How effective the reinforcement is likely to be

The trophy is a secondary, positive reinforcer. If it were an *actual* trophy, it would be a concrete reinforcer, but in its paper version, it is probably better classified as positive feedback. Although the teacher's intentions are good, the trophy is likely to have limited impact on Katie's future behavior. For one thing, it is awarded at the end of the school year, so it is neither immediate nor contingent on a particular behavior. Second, because Katie is only 5 years old, she thinks about the world in a concrete rather than abstract fashion (see Chapter 2) and so may have difficulty understanding what an "excellent attitude" is or how it relates to her own behavior (McMillan et al., 1994).

Using Reinforcement Effectively

As teachers, we may often want to use reinforcement to help students behave more productively. Several strategies will increase the likelihood that we do so effectively:

◎ *Specify the desired behavior at the beginning.* Behaviorists recommend that we describe, up front, the behavior we want students to learn and demonstrate. They further urge us to describe this end result—the **terminal behavior**—in specific, concrete, observable terms. Rather than talk about the need for students to "learn world history," we might instead talk about students being able to describe the antecedents and consequences of World War I. Rather than say

■ **terminal behavior** Form and frequency of a desired response that a teacher is hoping to foster through operant conditioning.

that students should "learn responsibility," we might instead talk about their need to follow instructions, bring the necessary books and supplies to class every day, and turn in assignments by the due date. By specifying the terminal behavior at the very beginning, we give both ourselves and our students a target to shoot for (see the discussion of *instructional goals* in Chapter 13), and we can better determine whether we are, in fact, making progress toward that target.

◎   *Identify consequences that are truly reinforcing for each student.* The use of reinforcement is far more effective when reinforcers are tailored to individual students than when the same consequences are used for everyone (e.g., Pfiffner et al., 1985). How can we determine which reinforcers are likely to be effective with particular students? One approach is to ask students themselves (or perhaps their parents) about the consequences they find especially appealing. If we do so, however, we must keep in mind that children do not always have a good sense of which consequences are truly reinforcing for them (Northup, 2000). Another approach is to observe students' behaviors, keeping a lookout for consequences that students seem to appreciate. Still another is to draw inferences from the things students say, as will be evident in the following exercise.

Interpreting Student Artifacts and Behaviors

Soccer Game

Today I had a soccer game to see who would go to the state finals. Unfortunly we lost. I was very dis apontated, not because we lost, but because my coach only put me in for 10 mins. I feel that the coach was ignoring me and was just focused on winning. I wish the coach would take notice of me on the side lines and not just focuse on winning.

At home one night, 11-year-old Amie writes an entry in the class journal that she and her teacher regularly use to communicate. As you read Amie's journal entry, speculate about the things that Amie does and does not find reinforcing.

Amie obviously enjoys playing soccer; in other words, soccer is intrinsically reinforcing for her. It appears, too, that Amie appreciates attention from her coach—perhaps in part because it might allow her to gain entry onto the playing field and in part because she would like feedback about what she is doing well and how she might improve her skills. Although Amie might appreciate winning and advancing to the state finals under other circumstances, these things have little appeal when she sits on the sidelines for most of a game.

In some cases we can let students choose their own reinforcers and perhaps even choose different reinforcers on different occasions (L. G. Bowman, Piazza, Fisher, Hagopian, & Kogan, 1997; Fisher & Mazur, 1997). One mechanism through which we can do this is a **token economy**, in which students who exhibit desired behaviors receive *tokens* (poker chips, specially marked pieces of colored paper, etc.) that they can later use to "purchase" a variety of **backup reinforcers**—perhaps small treats, free time in the reading center, or a prime position in the lunch line.

By and large, however, we should stay away from concrete reinforcers such as toys and candy. Such reinforcers can be expensive and distract students' attention away from their schoolwork. Fortunately, many nontangible reinforcers—for instance, positive feedback, special privileges, favorite activities, and parental reinforcement at home for school behaviors—can be quite effective with school-age children and adolescents (e.g., Feltz et al., 1999; Homme, deBaca, Devine, Steinhorst, & Rickert, 1963; Kelley & Carper, 1988).

◎   *When trying to encourage the same behavior in a group of students, consider using a group contingency.* Up to this point, we have been talking about reinforcing students for their own, individual behaviors. But positive reinforcement can also take the form of a **group contingency**: Students are reinforced only when *everyone* in a particular group (perhaps a cooperative learning group, perhaps an entire class) achieves at a certain level or behaves appropriately. Following are two examples:

- A class of 32 fourth graders was not doing very well on weekly spelling tests. On average, only 12 students (38%) had perfect spelling tests in any given week. Hoping for improvement, their teacher announced that any student with a perfect test score would get free time later in the week. The new reinforcement program had a noticeable effect: The average number of perfect spelling tests rose to 25 a week (80%). But then the teacher added a group contingency: Whenever the entire class achieved perfect spelling tests by

■ **token economy** Technique in which desired behaviors are reinforced by tokens that learners can use to "purchase" a variety of other reinforcers.

■ **backup reinforcer** Reinforcer that a student can "purchase" with one or more tokens earned in a token economy.

■ **group contingency** Situation in which everyone in a group must make a particular response before reinforcement occurs.

Friday, the class could listen to the radio for 15 minutes. The group contingency produced an average of 30 perfect spelling tests (94%) a week (Lovitt, Guppy, & Blattner, 1969).

- Another fourth-grade teacher was dealing with an unusually unruly class: In any given minute, chances were that one or more students would be talking out of turn or getting out of their seats. In a desperate move, the teacher divided the class into two teams that competed in a "good behavior game." Each time a student was observed talking out of turn or getting out of his or her seat, the student's team received a chalk mark on the chalkboard. The team that received fewer marks during a lesson won special privileges— for example, being first in the lunch line or having free time at the end of the day. When both teams had five marks or fewer, everyone won privileges. Misbehaviors in the class dropped almost immediately to less than 20 percent of their initial frequency (Barrish, Saunders, & Wolf, 1969).

■ Observe a group contingency in the "Cooperative Learning" clip on Video CD 2.

You can find another example of a group contingency in the "Cooperative Learning" clip on Video CD 2: If the average test score for a cooperative learning group is high enough, all group members get certificates with which they can buy free time during class.

Group contingencies are clearly effective in improving academic achievement and classroom behavior, provided that everyone in the group is capable of making the desired responses (Barbetta, 1990; Heck, Collins, & Peterson, 2001; Lentz, 1988). One probable reason for their effectiveness is peer pressure: Students encourage one another to achieve and behave appropriately and then reinforce one another to achieve and behave appropriately and then reinforce one another for doing so (O'Leary & O'Leary, 1972). Furthermore, when students' own success is riding on the success of their classmates, students who have mastered a topic begin to tutor those who are struggling with it (e.g., Pigott, Fantuzzo, & Clement, 1986). Group contingencies play an important role in *cooperative learning*, an instructional strategy we will discuss in Chapter 13.

Playing a team sport is an example of a behavior reinforced by a group contingency: The team wins together or loses together.

◎ *Make response-consequence contingencies explicit.* Reinforcement is typically more effective when students know exactly what consequences will follow various behaviors. For example, kindergarten students are more likely to respond appropriately when they are told, "The quietest group will be first to get in line for recess." High school students are more likely to complete their Spanish assignments if they know that by doing so they will be able to take a field trip to a local Cinco de Mayo festival.

One explicit way of communicating expectations and contingencies is through a **contingency contract**. To develop such a contract, the teacher meets with a student to discuss a problem behavior (e.g., talking to friends during independent seatwork or making rude comments to classmates). The teacher and student then identify and agree on desired behaviors that the student will demonstrate (e.g., completing seatwork assignments within a certain time frame or speaking with classmates in a friendly, respectful manner). The two also agree on one or more reinforcers for those behaviors (e.g., a certain amount of free time, or points earned toward a particular privilege or prize) that the student values. Together the teacher and the student write and sign a contract that describes the behaviors the student will perform and the reinforcers that will result. Contingency contracts can be a highly effective strategy for improving a wide variety of academic and social behaviors (Brooke & Ruthren, 1984; D. L. Miller & Kelley, 1994; Rueger & Liberman, 1984; Welch, 1985).

We should also make contingencies clear at the time we administer reinforcement. In the "Reading Group" clip on Video CD 2, a second-grade teacher is quite explicit in the behaviors she praises; for example, she says, "I like the way you're working quietly" and "You should see Ricky being so polite. Thank you, Ricky, for not disturbing the rest of the class."

■ Observe explicit praise in the "Reading Group" clip on Video CD 2.

◎ *When giving reinforcement publicly, make sure that all students have an opportunity to earn it.* In our attempts to improve the behavior of some students, we may unintentionally slight other, equally deserving students. Furthermore, some students may be unable to exhibit particular behaviors through little fault of their own. Consider the case of a young immigrant girl who had to adjust very quickly from a 10:00–5:00 school day in Vietnam to a 7:45–3:45 school day in the United States:

> [E]very week on Friday after school, the teacher would give little presents to kids that were good during the week. And if you were tardy, you wouldn't get a present. . . . I would never get one

■ **contingency contract** Formal agreement between teacher and student that identifies behaviors the student will exhibit and the reinforcers that will follow.

As teachers, we must consider how our own actions affect students' behavior. This teacher is reinforcing one student's diligence at the plant center with attention and affection.

because I would always come to school late, and that hurt at first. I had a terrible time. I didn't look forward to going to school. (Igoa, 1995, p. 95)

Ultimately, school should be a place where *all* students can, in one way or another, earn reinforcement and in other ways be successful. Classrooms are busy places, however, and it may be all too easy to overlook a few students who desperately want and need our attention. In such cases we can explicitly *teach* them appropriate ways of seeking out and getting reinforcement—for instance, by raising their hands or walking quietly to our desks at an appropriate time, asking questions (e.g., "How am I doing?" "What do I do next?"), and keeping us informed of their progress ("Look, I'm all finished!") (Craft, Alberg, & Heward, 1998; K. A. Meyer, 1999).

◎*Administer reinforcement consistently.* As you might guess, responses increase more quickly when they are reinforced every time they occur—that is, when they lead to **continuous reinforcement**. As teachers, we will see more rapid improvements in students' behavior if we reinforce desired responses whenever we observe them. Continuous reinforcement, then, is most important when students are first *learning* a behavior. Once they have mastered it and exhibit it frequently, we may want to reinforce it less often (we'll look more closely at such *intermittent reinforcement* later in the chapter).

◎*Monitor students' progress.* When we use reinforcement in the classroom, behaviorists urge us to determine, as objectively as possible, whether our efforts are bringing about the desired results. More specifically, they urge us to assess the frequency of the terminal behavior both before and during our attempts to increase it through operant conditioning. The frequency of a behavior *before* we intentionally begin reinforcement is called the **baseline** level of that behavior. Some behaviors occur frequently even when they are not being explicitly reinforced, whereas other behaviors occur rarely or not at all.

By comparing the baseline frequency of a response with its frequency after we begin reinforcing it, we can determine whether our reinforcement procedure is actually bringing about a behavior change. As an example, let's look once again at James in the opening case study. James rarely turns in classroom assignments; this is a behavior with a low baseline. An obvious reinforcer to use with James is attention, a consequence that, until now, has effectively reinforced such counterproductive behaviors as blurting out answers in class and throwing objects across the room. When we make our attention contingent on James's turning in assignments, rather than on his refusals to do so, we might see an almost immediate increase in the number of assignments we receive from James. If we see no significant change in James's behavior, we may need to consider alternative reinforcers; we should also consider and address possible reasons (e.g., poor reading skills) that may make it difficult for him to do his assignments.

But what if a desired behavior has a baseline level of *zero*? How can we encourage behaviors that students never exhibit at all? Operant conditioning theorists provide one possible solution to this problem: the process of shaping.

SHAPING NEW BEHAVIORS

Consider this situation:

> Donald is very shy and withdrawn. He rarely interacts with other students, either in class or on the playground. When he is in a situation where he must interact with a classmate, he doesn't seem to know how to behave.

Donald has apparently not learned how to interact effectively with his classmates. How might we help Donald develop appropriate social behaviors when the baseline level for such behaviors is essentially zero?

When a desired behavior occurs rarely or not at all, we can use a procedure called **shaping**. Shaping is a process of reinforcing a series of responses that increasingly resemble the desired terminal behavior; that is, it involves reinforcing successively closer and closer approximations to that behavior. To shape a new response, we

1. First reinforce any response that in some way resembles the terminal behavior
2. Then reinforce a response that more closely approximates the terminal behavior (no longer reinforcing the previously reinforced response)
3. Then reinforce a response that resembles the terminal behavior even more closely

■ **continuous reinforcement** Reinforcement of a response every time it occurs.

■ **baseline** Frequency of a response before operant conditioning begins.

■ **shaping** Process of reinforcing successively closer and closer approximations to a desired terminal behavior.

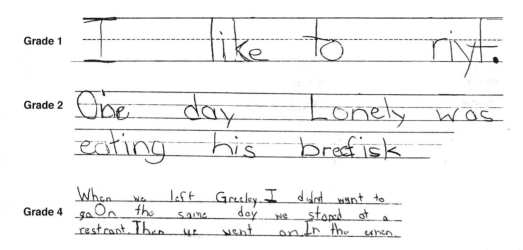

Grade 1 I like to riyt.

Grade 2 One day Lonely was eating his brecfisk

Grade 4 When we left Greeley I didnt want to go On the same day we stoped at a restrant. Then we went on In the ernen

FIGURE 9.2 As Jeff moved through the elementary grades, gradual changes in his writing paper required him to write smaller and, eventually, with only a single line to guide him.

4. Continue reinforcing closer and closer approximations to the terminal behavior
5. Finally reinforce only the terminal behavior

Each response in the sequence is reinforced every time it occurs until we see it regularly. Only at that point do we begin reinforcing a behavior that more closely approaches the terminal behavior.

To illustrate this process, let's consider how we might shape Donald's social behavior. We might first reinforce him for something that he occasionally does, such as smiling at a classmate. After we begin to see him smiling frequently (perhaps after a few days), we might reinforce him only when he makes a verbal response to the comments or questions of a classmate. When that behavior occurs frequently, we might reinforce him only when he initiates a conversation. Later steps to take would be reinforcing Donald for approaching a group of peers, for suggesting a group activity, and so on.

Through shaping, we can help students gain a variety of complex academic skills and classroom behaviors over time. For example, kindergartners and first graders are taught to print their letters on wide-lined paper; they are praised for well-formed letters and for letters whose bottoms rest on one line and whose tops touch another line. As children progress through the grade levels, the spaces between the lines become smaller, and teachers become fussier about how well letters are formed. Most children begin to write consistently sized and carefully shaped letters with the benefit of only a lower line, and eventually they need no line at all. In Figure 9.2 we see how Jeff's handwriting was gradually shaped from first to fourth grade.

When complex skills are involved, it's unreasonable to expect students to make dramatic changes overnight. If we want them to exhibit behavior radically different from what they are doing now, we may need to shape their behavior by first reinforcing one small step in the right direction, then by reinforcing another small step, and then yet another, until eventually the desired terminal behavior is achieved. Imagine, for example, that we have a student, Bernadette, who can't seem to sit still long enough to get much of anything done. We would ultimately like her to sit still for 20-minute periods, but we may first have to reinforce her for staying in her seat for just *two* minutes, gradually increasing the "sitting" time required for reinforcement as she makes progress. In much the same way, we can (and often do) use shaping to teach students to work independently on classroom assignments. We begin by giving first graders structured tasks that may take only five to ten minutes to complete. As students move through the elementary school years, we expect them to work independently for longer periods, and we also give them short assignments to do at home. By the time they reach high school, students have extended study halls and complete lengthy assignments at home. In the college years, student assignments require a great deal of independence and self-direction.

EFFECTS OF ANTECEDENT STIMULI AND RESPONSES

In our discussion of operant conditioning so far, we've focused on the *consequences* of desired behaviors. Yet stimuli and responses that *precede* a desired behavior (i.e., **antecedent stimuli** and **antecedent responses**) can also have an effect. Here we will look at several phenomena—cueing, setting events, generalization, and discrimination—that involve antecedent stimuli, as well as one phenomenon—behavioral momentum—that involves antecedent responses.

■ **antecedent stimulus** Stimulus that increases the likelihood that a particular response will follow.

■ **antecedent response** Response that increases the likelihood that a certain other response will follow.

■ Observe cueing in the "Reading Group" clip on Video CD 2.

■ How are the concepts of *cueing* and *retrieval cue* (Chapter 6) similar? How are they different?

Cueing. Students are more likely to behave appropriately when they are given reminders (often called *cues* or *prompts*) that certain behaviors are expected (e.g., Northup et al., 1995; Shabani et al., 2002; B. A. Taylor & Levin, 1998). Such **cueing** sometimes involves a nonverbal signal, such as ringing a bell or flicking overhead lights off and on to remind students to talk quietly rather than loudly. At other times it involves a verbal reminder, either direct or indirect, about what students should be doing. In the "Reading Group" clip on Video CD 2, a second-grade teacher provides many cues about appropriate behavior, including the following:

- "I called the Tigers. Someone wasn't listening."
- "It's not time to open our books yet."
- "Back on task, Chris. Remember Your English work. . . . "

When students are dispersed over a large area, such as on the playground during physical education, we might even use a microphone and loudspeaker to remind them about appropriate behavior; we should, of course, turn the mike off when working with an individual student (S. Ryan, Ormond, Imwold, & Rotunda, 2002).

Setting events. In cueing, we use specific stimuli to prompt students to behave in particular ways. An alternative approach is to create an overall environment—a **setting event**—that is apt to foster desired behaviors. For example, young children are more likely to interact with peers during free-play time if they have a relatively small area in which to play and if the toys available to them (balls, puppets, toy housekeeping materials) encourage cooperation and group activity (W. H. Brown, Fox, & Brady, 1987; Frost et al., 1998; S. S. Martin, Brady, & Williams, 1991). Similarly, the nature of the games children are asked to play influences the behaviors they exhibit: Cooperative games promote cooperative behavior, whereas competitive games promote aggressive behavior (Bay-Hinitz et al., 1994).

Generalization. Once children have learned that a response is likely to be reinforced in one set of circumstances (i.e., in the presence of one antecedent stimulus), they are apt to make the same response in a similar situation; in other words, they show **generalization**. For example, after Bernadette has learned to sit quietly and attentively in her kindergarten class, she may generalize that behavior to her first-grade class. After Donald has learned how to make friends at school, he may begin to apply the same skills in his out-of-school activities.

This process of generalization should remind you of the generalization that occurs in classical conditioning: In both cases an individual learns a response to one stimulus and then responds in the same way to a similar stimulus. The major difference is one of learner control: Generalization involves an automatic, involuntary response in classical conditioning but a voluntary response in operant conditioning.

Discrimination. Sometimes people learn that responses are reinforced only when certain stimuli (certain environmental conditions) are present. For example, Bernadette might learn that she can get up and leave the classroom when, and only when, her teacher has given her permission to do so. Donald might discover that a classmate who smiles at him is more likely to reinforce his attempts at being friendly than a classmate who scowls. When people learn that responses are reinforced in the presence of one stimulus but not in the presence of another (perhaps very similar) stimulus, they have learned **discrimination** between the two stimuli.

Occasionally students may overgeneralize, exhibiting responses they have learned in situations where such responses are unproductive or inappropriate. In such cases we must teach them to discriminate between suitable and unsuitable stimulus conditions. For instance, we should describe in very concrete terms the circumstances in which certain behaviors are and are not productive and acceptable. We then must be sure to reinforce students for exhibiting behaviors *only* when the behaviors are appropriate.

Behavioral momentum. In many cases students are more apt to make desired responses if they are already making similar responses—a phenomenon known as **behavioral momentum** (Ardoin, Martens, & Wolfe, 1999; Belfiore, Lee, Vargas, & Skinner, 1997; Mace et al., 1988; Nevin, Mandell, & Atak, 1983). Consider this situation as an example:

Two high school students, Allison and Roberta, have a history of refusing to do academic assignments. A researcher finds that the girls more willingly attempt difficult three-digit multiplication problems after they have first worked on a few simple one-digit problems (Belfiore et al., 1997).

■ **cueing** Use of signals to indicate that a certain behavior is desired or that a certain behavior should stop.

■ **setting event** Complex environmental condition in which a particular behavior is most likely to occur.

■ **generalization** In operant conditioning, involves making a voluntary response to stimuli similar to a stimulus antecedent to a response-reinforcement contingency.

■ **discrimination** Phenomenon in which a student learns that a response is reinforced in the presence of one stimulus but not in the presence of another, similar stimulus.

■ **behavioral momentum** Increased tendency for a learner to make a particular response immediately after making similar responses.

CREATING A PRODUCTIVE CLASSROOM ENVIRONMENT

Encouraging Productive Behaviors

 Reinforce desired behaviors.

To a student who has just completed an excellent oral book report, a teacher says, "Nice job, Monica. You made the book sound so interesting. *I* certainly want to read it now, and I suspect that many of your classmates do as well."

 Remember that different things are reinforcing to different students.

A teacher allows students to engage in favorite activities during the free time they earn each day. Some students work on the classroom computer, others work on art projects, and still others converse with friends.

 Give feedback about specific behaviors rather than general areas of performance.

As his kindergartners are cleaning up after a class art project, a teacher says, "I like how everyone is remembering to pick up the scraps of paper around their desks. And look at how LaMarr and Julia are collecting every group's boxes of markers and bottles of glue without my even having to ask them!"

 Provide opportunities for students to practice correct behaviors.

In a unit on basketball, a physical education teacher makes sure that every student has several successful shots at the basket.

 When the baseline level of a desired behavior is low, gradually shape the behavior over time by reinforcing closer and closer approximations.

A teacher praises a shy and withdrawn boy for smiling or making eye contact with peers. After such behaviors become more frequent, the teacher begins praising him when he responds to classmates' questions or comments. As the latter behavior also increases, the teacher praises the boy only when he initiates a conversation with someone else.

 Cue appropriate behaviors.

As students are busily working on cooperative group projects, their teacher sees that one group's discussion is being dominated by a single student. She announces to the class, "Please remember a point I made earlier: You are more likely to create a good product when *all* group members contribute their ideas."

Similarly, we might ask students to tidy up a messy classroom after they have already cleaned their own desktops, or to try a backward roll after they have already executed a forward roll successfully. In general, we can promote behavioral momentum by assigning relatively easy or enjoyable tasks that lead naturally into more complex and potentially frustrating ones.

I hope that in our discussion of operant conditioning, you've discovered a variety of ways in which you might apply operant conditioning in your own classroom. The Creating a Productive Classroom Environment feature "Encouraging Productive Behaviors" reviews and illustrates some of the strategies we've identified. Let's now look at how one teacher applies operant conditioning in her classroom.

Analyzing Teacher Strategies

Auction

How might we encourage students to read independently? One third-grade teacher's approach is described below. As you read about it, consider

- What behaviorist strategy it reflects
- What advantages and disadvantages it might have

The teacher gives her students a token each time they read 25 pages in a chapter book appropriate for their reading level. She gives them two additional tokens when they finish a book and another one for writing a reaction to it. Once every couple of months, the teacher holds a class auction where the students can use their tokens to bid on and buy various inexpensive items she has purchased (pencils, erasers, combs, etc.). She arranges the process so that each student gets something in the first round of the auction; after that, children with more tokens have more purchasing power.

The teacher is using a token economy to reinforce reading behavior. The reinforcement will probably lead students to read more than they would otherwise, and her use of tokens allows flexibility in how different students are reinforced: If the array of backup reinforcers is broad enough, presumably all students will be able to purchase something they want. Potential downsides to this strategy are that (a) students might choose books based on brevity rather than intrinsic appeal (they get two extra tokens each time they finish a book) and (b) students might "read" so quickly that they don't really think about the content (recall our discussion of attention in Chapter 6). In essence, the students may become more interested in the extrinsic reinforcers they get for reading than in any intrinsic pleasure reading brings them (more about this point near the end of the chapter). The teacher will need to monitor her students' independent reading activities—for instance, by occasionally asking them questions about what they are reading—to make sure that the benefits outweigh any possible drawbacks.

REDUCING AND ELIMINATING UNDESIRABLE BEHAVIORS

Our focus so far has been on promoting desirable behaviors. Yet we will also need to address *un*desirable behaviors—those that interfere with students' own learning and achievement and possibly with the learning and achievement of their classmates as well. How do we decrease, perhaps even eliminate, such behaviors? Behaviorists offer several possible strategies, including extinction, cueing inappropriate behaviors, reinforcing incompatible behaviors, and punishment.

Extinction

What happens when a response is no longer reinforced? As you might guess, a nonreinforced response decreases in frequency and usually returns to its baseline level. Like the decrease of a conditioned response in classical conditioning, the decrease of a nonreinforced response in operant conditioning is known as **extinction**. For example, the class clown whose jokes are ignored may stop telling jokes. The aggressive child who never gets what she wants by hitting or shoving others may become less aggressive. One way of reducing the frequency of an inappropriate behavior, then, is simply to make sure it is never reinforced.

There are several points to keep in mind about extinction, however. First of all, once reinforcement stops, a previously reinforced response doesn't always decrease immediately. Sometimes the behavior initially *increases* for a short time (Lerman & Iwata, 1995; McGill, 1999). To illustrate how this might occur, imagine you have a cantankerous television set that gives you a clear picture only when you bang its side once or twice. Eventually, something changes in the inner workings of your set, so that banging is no longer an effective remedy. As you desperately try to get a clear picture, you may bang your TV a number of times in succession (more times than you usually do) before giving up that response. In much the same way, the class clown who is now being ignored may tell more jokes at first and the aggressive child may act out more frequently before learning that such behaviors no longer produce the desired results.

Second, we may sometimes find situations in which a response never decreases when we remove a reinforcer. In such situations—when extinction doesn't occur—chances are that we haven't been able to remove *all* reinforcers of the response. Perhaps the behavior is leading to a naturally reinforcing consequence; for example, a class clown's peers may continue to snicker even if the teacher ignores his jokes. Or perhaps the response is intrinsically reinforcing; for example, a student's physically aggressive behavior may release pent-up energy (and so may "feel good") even if it doesn't otherwise get her what she wants. Only when all reinforcers are removed will extinction occur.

Finally, we must remember that extinction can occur with desirable behaviors as easily as with undesirable ones. The student who is never called on in class may stop raising his hand. The student who never passes classroom quizzes no matter how hard she studies may eventually stop studying. As teachers, we must be very sure that while counterproductive classroom behaviors are not being reinforced, productive responses *are* being reinforced, either through such extrinsic reinforcers as attention, praise, or favorite activities or through the intrinsic satisfaction that classroom accomplishments bring.

Cueing Inappropriate Behaviors

Just as we can use cueing to remind students about what they should be doing, we can also cue them about what they should *not* be doing. For example, we might use *body language*—perhaps making eye contact, raising an eyebrow, or frowning—to let students know that we disapprove

■ How is extinction similar in classical and operant conditioning? How is it different?

■ **extinction** Gradual disappearance of an acquired response; in operant conditioning, results from repeated lack of reinforcement for the response.

of their behavior and would like it to cease (Emmer, 1987; Shrigley, 1979; Wool-folk & Brooks, 1985). When body language doesn't get the attention of a misbehaving student, a more obvious cue is *physical proximity*: moving closer to the student and standing there until the problem behavior stops (Emmer, 1987; Woolfolk & Brooks, 1985). Particularly if we are walking around the room anyway during a classroom activity, this strategy can attract the attention of the guilty party without also drawing undue attention from classmates.

Yet sometimes subtlety doesn't work and we have to be more explicit. In such cases a brief *verbal cue*—stating a student's name, reminding a student about correct behavior, or (if necessary) pointing out an inappropriate behavior—may be in order (G. A. Davis & Thomas, 1989; Emmer, 1987; Northup et al., 1995). For example, we might say something as simple as "Please keep your eyes on your own work" or "Lucy, put the magazine away."

Simple body language is often an effective cue. While this teacher is temporarily preoccupied, her hand on a student's shoulder provides a subtle reminder about what he should and should not be doing.

Reinforcing Incompatible Behaviors

Experiencing FIRSTHAND ·Asleep on Your Feet

Have you ever tried to sleep while standing up? Horses can do it, but most of us humans really can't. In fact, there are many pairs of responses that we can't possibly perform simultaneously. Take a minute to identify something you cannot possibly do when you perform each of these activities:

When you:	You cannot simultaneously:
Sit down	_____
Eat crackers	_____
Take a walk	_____

· · · · · · ·

Two behaviors are **incompatible** when they cannot be performed simultaneously. For example, sitting is incompatible with standing. Eating crackers is incompatible with singing, or at least with singing *well*. Taking a walk is incompatible with taking a nap. In each case it is physically impossible to perform both activities at exactly the same time.

When our attempts at extinction or cueing are unsuccessful, another way to reduce an inappropriate behavior is to reinforce an incompatible (and presumably more desirable) one; the inappropriate response must inevitably decrease as the incompatible one increases (Lerman, Kelley, Vorndran, Kuhn, & LaRue, 2002; Zirpoli & Melloy, 2001). This is the approach we are taking when we reinforce a hyperactive student for sitting down: Sitting is incompatible with getting-out-of-seat and roaming-around-the-room behaviors. It is also an approach we might use to deal with forgetfulness (we reinforce students when they remember to do what they were supposed to do), being off task (we reinforce on-task behavior), and verbal abusiveness (we reinforce prosocial statements). And consider how we might deal with a chronic litterbug:

> Walt is a junior high school student who consistently leaves garbage (banana peels, sunflower seed shells, etc.) on the lunchroom floor, in school corridors, and on the playground. When the school faculty establishes an "anti-litter" committee, it decides to put Walt on the committee, and the committee eventually elects Walt as its chairman. Under Walt's leadership, the committee institutes a massive anti-litter campaign, complete with posters and lunchroom monitors, and Walt receives considerable recognition for the campaign's success. Curiously (or perhaps not), school personnel no longer find Walt's garbage littering the school grounds. (Krumboltz & Krumboltz, 1972)

Punishment

Some misbehaviors require an immediate remedy—they interfere significantly with classroom learning, or they put students' physical safety or psychological well-being in jeopardy—

■ **incompatible behaviors** Two or more behaviors that cannot be performed simultaneously.

TABLE 9.3   COMPARE/CONTRAST

Distinguishing Among Positive Reinforcement, Negative Reinforcement, and Punishment

CONSEQUENCE	EFFECT	EXAMPLE
Positive reinforcement	Response *increases* when a new stimulus (presumably one the person finds desirable) is *presented*.	• A student *is praised* for writing an assignment in cursive. She begins to write other assignments in cursive as well. • A student *gets lunch money* by bullying a girl into surrendering hers. He begins bullying his classmates more frequently.
Negative reinforcement	Response *increases* when a previously existing stimulus (presumably one the person finds undesirable) is *removed*.	• A student *no longer has to worry* about a research paper he has completed several days before the due date. He begins to do his assignments ahead of time whenever possible. • A student *escapes the principal's wrath* by lying about her role in a recent incident of school vandalism. After this incident, she begins lying to school faculty whenever she finds herself in an uncomfortable situation.
Presentation punishment	Response *decreases* when a new stimulus (presumably one the person finds undesirable) is *presented*.	• A student *is scolded* for taunting other students. She taunts others less frequently after that. • A student *is ridiculed by classmates* for asking a "stupid" question during a lecture. He stops asking questions in class.
Removal punishment	Response *decreases* when a previously existing stimulus (presumably one the person finds desirable) is *removed*.	• A student *is removed from the softball team for a week* for showing poor sportsmanship. She rarely shows poor sportsmanship in future games. • A student *loses points on a test* for answering a question in a creative but unusual way. He takes fewer risks on future tests.

and so we cannot simply wait for gradual improvements over time. Consider this student as an example:

> Bonnie doesn't handle frustration very well. Whenever she encounters an obstacle she cannot immediately overcome, she responds by hitting, kicking, or breaking something. Over the course of the school year, she has knocked over several pieces of furniture, smashed two windows, made several dents in the wall, and broken innumerable pencils. Not only is Bonnie's behavior hindering her academic progress, but it's also getting very expensive.

Bonnie's inappropriate behaviors are difficult to extinguish because they aren't really being reinforced to begin with (not extrinsically, at least). They are also behaviors with no obvious incompatible responses that can be reinforced. And we can reasonably assume that Bonnie's teacher has already cued her about her inappropriate behavior on many occasions. When other strategies are inapplicable or ineffective, punishment may be a useful alternative.

Earlier in the chapter we defined a reinforcer as a consequence that increases the frequency of a particular behavior. In contrast, **punishment** is a consequence that *decreases* the frequency of the response it follows.

All punishing consequences fall into one of two groups. **Presentation punishment** involves presenting a new stimulus, presumably something a student finds unpleasant and doesn't want. Scoldings and teacher scowls, if they lead to a reduction in the behavior they follow, are instances of presentation punishment. **Removal punishment** involves removing a previously existing stimulus, presumably one a student finds desirable and doesn't want to lose. The loss of a privilege, a fine (involving the loss of money or previously earned points), and "grounding" (when certain pleasurable outside activities are missed) are all possible examples of removal punishment.

Over the years, I have observed many occasions when people have used the term *negative reinforcement* when they were really talking about punishment. Remember, negative reinforcement increases a response, whereas punishment has the *opposite effect*. Table 9.3 should help you understand how negative reinforcement, presentation punishment, and removal punishment are all very different concepts.

■ **punishment** Consequence that decreases the frequency of the response it follows.

■ **presentation punishment** Punishment involving presentation of a new stimulus, presumably one a learner finds unpleasant.

■ **removal punishment** Punishment involving removal of an existing stimulus, presumably one a learner doesn't want to lose.

Strictly speaking, punishment is not a part of operant conditioning. Many early behaviorists believed that punishment was a relatively *ineffective* means of changing behavior—that it may temporarily suppress a response but can never eliminate it—and suggested that teachers focus their efforts on reinforcing desirable behaviors rather than on punishing undesirable ones. More recently, however, behaviorists have found that some forms of punishment can be quite effective in reducing problem behaviors.

Effective Forms of Punishment   As a general rule, we should use only mild forms of punishment in the classroom; severe consequences can lead to such unwanted side effects as resentment, hostility, or truancy. Researchers and educators have identified several forms of mild punishment that can be effective in reducing classroom misbehaviors: reprimands, response cost, logical consequences, time-out, and in-school suspension.

Verbal reprimands (scolding). Although some students seem to thrive on teacher scolding because of the attention it brings, most students, especially if they are scolded relatively infrequently, find **verbal reprimands** to be unpleasant and punishing (Pfiffner & O'Leary, 1993; Van Houten, Nau, MacKenzie-Keating, Sameoto, & Colavecchia, 1982). In general, reprimands are more effective when they are immediate, brief, and unemotional; they also work better when they are given in a soft voice and in close proximity to the student, perhaps because they are less likely to be noticed and so less likely to draw the attention of classmates (O'Leary, Kaufman, Kass, & Drabman, 1970; Pfiffner & O'Leary, 1993). Reprimands should be given in private whenever possible: When scolded in front of classmates, some students may relish the peer attention, and others (e.g., many Native American and Hispanic students) may feel totally humiliated (Fuller, 2001).

Response cost. Because it involves the loss either of a previously earned reinforcer or of an opportunity to obtain reinforcement, **response cost** is an instance of removal punishment. Teachers of students with chronic behavior problems sometimes incorporate response cost into a point system or token economy: They award points, check marks, plastic chips, or the like for good behavior (reinforcement) and take away these things for inappropriate behavior (response cost). Students who accumulate a sufficient number of points or tokens can use them to "buy" objects, privileges, or enjoyable activities that are otherwise not available. Response cost is especially effective when coupled with reinforcement of appropriate behavior (Iwata & Bailey, 1974; Lentz, 1988; Rapport, Murphy, & Bailey, 1982).

Logical consequences. Something that follows naturally or logically from a student's misbehavior, a **logical consequence** is a punishment that fits the crime. For example, if a student destroys a classmate's possession, a reasonable consequence is for the student to replace it or pay for a new one. If two close friends talk so much that they aren't completing assignments, a reasonable consequence is for them to be separated. If a student intentionally makes a mess in the cafeteria, an appropriate consequence is to clean it up. The use of logical consequences makes "logical" sense, and numerous research studies and case studies vouch for its effectiveness (Dreikurs, 1998; Lyon, 1984; Schloss & Smith, 1994; L. S. Wright, 1982).

Time-out. A misbehaving student given a **time-out** is placed in a dull, boring (but not scary) situation—perhaps a separate room designed especially for time-outs, a little-used office, or a remote corner of the classroom. A student in time-out has no opportunity to interact with classmates and no opportunity to obtain reinforcement. The length of the time-out is typically quite short (perhaps two to ten minutes, depending on the student's age), but the student is not released until inappropriate behavior (e.g., screaming, kicking) has stopped. Time-outs have been used successfully to reduce a variety of noncompliant, disruptive, and aggressive behaviors (e.g., Pfiffner & Barkley, 1998; Rortvedt & Miltenberger, 1994; A. G. White & Bailey, 1990). Keep in mind, however, that a time-out is apt to be effective only if ongoing classroom activities are a source of enjoyment and reinforcement for a student. If, instead, it allows a student to escape difficult tasks or an overwhelming amount of noise and stimulation, it might actually be reinforcing and so *increase* undesirable behavior (Alberto & Troutman, 2003; McClowry, 1998; Pfiffner & Barkley, 1998).

In-school suspension. Like time-out, **in-school suspension** involves placing a student in a quiet, boring room within the school building; however, it often lasts one or more school days and involves close adult supervision. Students receiving in-school suspension spend the day working on the same assignments that their nonsuspended peers do and so are able to keep up with their

■ **verbal reprimand** Scolding for inappropriate behavior.

■ **response cost** Loss either of a previously earned reinforcer or of an opportunity to obtain reinforcement.

■ **logical consequence** Consequence that follows naturally or logically from a student's misbehavior.

■ **time-out** Form of punishment in which student is placed in a dull, boring situation with no opportunity for reinforcement or social interaction.

■ **in-school suspension** Form of punishment in which a student is placed in a quiet, boring room within the school building, typically to do schoolwork under close adult supervision.

Some mild forms of punishment, such as brief time-outs, can reduce counter-productive behaviors, but we must monitor their effectiveness for different students. Can you explain how *release from a time-out situation* is *negative reinforcement?*

schoolwork. But they have no opportunity for interaction with peers—an aspect of school that is reinforcing to most students. Although in-school suspension programs have not been systematically investigated through controlled research studies, practitioners report that these programs are often effective in reducing chronic misbehaviors, particularly when part of the suspension session is devoted to teaching appropriate behaviors and tutoring academic skills and when the supervising teacher acts as a supportive resource rather than as a punisher (Gootman, 1998; Huff, 1988; Pfiffner & Barkley, 1998; J. S. Sullivan, 1989).

Just as we must use different reinforcers for different students, ideally we should also individualize our use of punishment. For example, some students enjoy the attention that verbal reprimands bring (remember James in the opening case study), and others appreciate the peace and quiet of an occasional time-out. If we find that a certain form of punishment has no noticeable effect on a student's behavior, we should conclude that it isn't really punishing for the student and consider other alternatives.

Ineffective Forms of Punishment   Several forms of punishment are typically *not* recommended: physical punishment, psychological punishment, extra classwork, and out-of-school suspension.

Physical punishment.   Most experts advise against physical punishment for school-age children (W. Doyle, 1990; Zirpoli & Melloy, 2001); furthermore, its use in the classroom is *illegal* in many places. Even mild physical punishment, such as a spank or slap with a ruler, can lead to such undesirable behaviors as resentment of the teacher, inattention to school tasks, lying, aggression, vandalism, avoidance of school tasks, and truancy. When carried to extremes, physical punishment constitutes child abuse and may cause long-term or possibly even permanent physical damage.

Psychological punishment.   Any consequence that seriously threatens a student's self-esteem is **psychological punishment** and is not recommended (G. A. Davis & Thomas, 1989; J. E. Walker & Shea, 1995). Embarrassing remarks and public humiliation can lead to some of the same side effects as physical punishment (e.g., resentment of the teacher, inattention to school tasks, truancy from school) and have the potential to inflict long-term psychological harm. By deflating students' sense of self, psychological punishment can also lower their expectations for future performance and their motivation to learn and achieve (more on this point in the discussion of *self-efficacy* in Chapters 10 and 12).

Extra classwork.   Asking a student to complete makeup work for time missed in school is a reasonable and justifiable request. But assigning extra classwork or homework beyond that required for other students is inappropriate if it is assigned simply to punish a student's wrongdoing (H. Cooper, 1989; Corno, 1996). In this case we have a very different side effect: We inadvertently communicate the message that "schoolwork is unpleasant."

Out-of-school suspension.   Teachers and administrators are negatively reinforced when they suspend a problem student. After all, they get rid of something they don't want—a problem! But out-of-school suspension is usually *not* an effective means of changing a student's behavior (Moles, 1990; J. D. Nichols, Ludwin, & Iadicola, 1999; Pfiffner & Barkley, 1998). In the first place, being suspended from school may be exactly what the student wants, in which case inappropriate behaviors are being reinforced rather than punished. Second, because many students with chronic behavior problems also tend to do poorly in their schoolwork, suspension involves a loss of valuable instructional time and interferes with any psychological "attachment" to school, thereby decreasing even further the students' chances for academic and social success (J. D. Nichols et al., 1999; Skiba & Raison, 1990).

An additional form of punishment—missing recess—gets mixed reviews regarding its effectiveness. In some situations missing recess may be a logical consequence for students who fail to complete their schoolwork during regular class time due to off-task behavior. Yet research tells us that, at least at the elementary level, students can more effectively concentrate on school tasks when they have occasional breaks from academic activities (Maxmell et al., 1998; Pellegrini, Huberty, & Jones, 1995). Perhaps the best piece of advice is to withdraw recess privileges infrequently, if at all, and to monitor the effectiveness of such a consequence on students' classroom behavior over the long run.

■ **psychological punishment**
Consequence that seriously threatens self-esteem.

Using Punishment Humanely   A frequent criticism of using punishment is that it is "inhumane," or somehow cruel and barbaric. Indeed, certain forms of punishment, such as physical abuse or public humiliation, do constitute inhumane treatment. We must be *extremely careful* in our use of punishment in the classroom. When administered judiciously, however, some forms of mild punishment can lead to a rapid reduction in misbehavior without causing physical or psychological harm. And when we can decrease counterproductive classroom behaviors quickly and effectively—especially when those behaviors are harmful to self or others—then punishment may, in fact, be one of the most humane approaches we can take (Lerman & Vorndran, 2002). Following are several guidelines for using punishment effectively and humanely:

◎   *Inform students ahead of time that certain behaviors will be punished, and explain how those behaviors will be punished.* When students are informed of response-punishment contingencies ahead of time, they are less apt to engage in forbidden behaviors; they are also less apt to be surprised or resentful if punishment must be administered (G. D. Gottfredson & Gottfredson, 1985; Moles, 1990). Ultimately, students should learn that their behaviors influence the consequences they experience—that they have some control over what happens to them. We will consider this idea of control more closely when we look at *attribution theory* in Chapter 12.

◎   *Follow through with specified consequences.* One mistake some teachers make is to continually threaten punishment without ever following through. One warning is desirable, but repeated warnings are not. The teacher who says, "If you bring that rubber snake to class one more time, Tommy, I'm going to take it away, " but never does take the snake away, is giving the message that no response-punishment contingency really exists.

For this reason, after-school detentions can be problematic: Some students simply cannot stay after school hours (J. D. Nichols et al., 1999). Perhaps they have transportation issues, perhaps they are reluctant to walk through certain neighborhoods after dark, or perhaps they must take care of younger siblings until parents get home from work. Unless we can address such concerns, imposing after-school detention is unrealistic.

◎   *Administer punishment privately.* By administering punishment in private, we protect students from public embarrassment or humiliation. We also eliminate the possibility that the punishment will draw the attention of classmates—a potential reinforcer for the very behavior we are trying to eliminate.

◎   *Explain why the punished behavior is unacceptable.* We must explain exactly why a certain behavior cannot be tolerated in the classroom (perhaps because it interferes with learning, threatens the safety or self-esteem of other students, or damages school property). Punishment is far more effective when accompanied by one or more reasons why the punished behavior is unacceptable (Cheyne & Walters, 1970; Parke, 1974; D. G. Perry & Perry, 1983). (Recall our discussion of *induction* in Chapter 3.)

◎   *Emphasize that it is the behavior that is undesirable, not the student.* As teachers, we must emphasize that certain behaviors interfere with students' success in learning—that students are preventing themselves from becoming the very best they can be.

◎   *Simultaneously teach and reinforce desirable alternative behaviors.* Punishment of misbehavior is almost always more effective when appropriate behaviors are being reinforced at the same time (Lerman & Vorndran, 2002; Pfiffner & Barkley, 1998). Furthermore, by reinforcing desirable responses as well as punishing undesirable ones, we give students the positive, optimistic message that, yes, behavior can and will improve. Ultimately, the overall classroom atmosphere we create must be a positive one that highlights the good things students do and de-emphasizes the "bad" (e.g., R. E. Smith & Smoll, 1997).

The Creating a Productive Classroom Environment feature "Decreasing and Eliminating Undesirable Behaviors" reviews and illustrates some of the strategies we've identified in the last few pages.

MAINTAINING DESIRABLE BEHAVIORS OVER THE LONG RUN

As noted in our discussion of extinction, responses that are no longer reinforced decrease in frequency and often return to their baseline level; in some cases the responses disappear altogether. Yet we cannot continue to reinforce every student each time he or she engages in appropriate

CREATING A PRODUCTIVE CLASSROOM ENVIRONMENT

Decreasing and Eliminating Undesirable Behaviors

 Don't inadvertently reinforce undesirable behaviors.

A teacher realizes that a particular "problem" student, a girl who often makes inappropriate remarks in class, seems to thrive on any kind of attention. He also realizes that the girl's behavior has gotten worse instead of better. Rather than continue to reinforce the girl by scolding her publicly, he meets with her after school, and together they develop a contingency contract designed to improve her behavior.

 Cue students when you see them behaving inappropriately.

As she describes the morning's assignment, a teacher notices that two boys on the other side of the classroom are whispering, giggling, and obviously not paying attention. While continuing her description of the assignment, she walks slowly across the room and stands next to the boys.

Reinforce behaviors that are incompatible with undesirable behaviors.

A student is out of her seat so frequently that she gets little of her work done and often distracts her classmates from doing theirs. Her teacher discusses the problem behavior with her, and together they decide that she will earn points for staying in her seat and keeping on task; she may use the points to "buy" time with her friends at the end of the day.

 When a misbehavior must be suppressed quickly, choose a mild punishment, yet one that is likely to deter the behavior in the future.

When members of the school soccer team have an unexcused absence from team practice, they are not allowed to play in that week's soccer game.

 Describe both appropriate and inappropriate behaviors, as well as their consequences, in concrete and explicit terms.

The soccer coach reminds students that those who miss practice will sit out at the next game and that all students who *do* make practice each day will play at least part of the game.

 When misbehaviors continue despite all reasonable efforts to correct them, seek the advice of experts.

A teacher consults with the school psychologist about three students who are often physically aggressive in their interactions with classmates. Together they identify several strategies to help these students.

---

behavior. And we won't be able to reinforce students at all after they leave our classrooms at the end of the school year. So how can we ensure that students will continue to behave in productive ways over the long run? Two viable strategies are promoting intrinsic reinforcement and using intermittent reinforcement.

Promoting Intrinsic Reinforcement

The advantage of intrinsic reinforcers is that they come from students themselves, rather than from some outside source. Students will often engage in activities that are enjoyable or satisfy their curiosity. They will also exhibit behaviors that lead to success and to feelings of mastery, accomplishment, and pride. Ideally, it is such internal consequences that are most effective in sustaining productive behaviors both in the classroom and in the outside world.

Yet success is not always achieved easily and effortlessly. Many of the tasks that students tackle in school—reading, writing, solving mathematical problems, reasoning scientifically, understanding historical and social events, participating skillfully in team sports, learning to play a musical instrument—are complex, challenging, and often frustrating, especially at first. When students struggle with a challenging task and encounter frequent failure, we should probably provide extrinsic reinforcement for the little improvements they make. And when we find that we must break down a complex task into smaller pieces that, though easier to accomplish, are less fulfilling in their own right (e.g., if we assign drill-and-practice activities to foster automaticity in basic reading or math skills), we will probably need to reinforce students' many seemingly "meaningless" successes. Once students have mastered tasks and skills to a level that brings them frequent successes and feelings of mastery, however, extrinsic reinforcers should no longer be necessary (Covington, 1992; Lepper, 1981). In fact, as you will discover later in the chapter, it may actually be counterproductive to provide extrinsic reinforcers when students are already finding intrinsic reinforcement in the things they are doing.

Using Intermittent Reinforcement

Earlier in the chapter I mentioned that desired responses increase more quickly if they are reinforced every time they occur. Yet once those responses are occurring regularly, such *continuous*

■ One statement in this paragraph is based on the concept of *shaping*. Another reflects the concept of *scaffolding* (Chapter 2). Can you identify each of these statements?

reinforcement may not be optimal. We may instead want to switch to **intermittent reinforcement**, reinforcing desired behavior on some occasions and not on others.

■ Which of your behaviors are reinforced only intermittently?

To show you what I mean, let's consider Molly and Maria, two students with low baseline levels for volunteering in class. Their teacher, Mr. Oliver, decides to reinforce the girls for raising their hands. Every time Molly raises her hand, Mr. Oliver calls on her and praises her response; she is receiving continuous reinforcement. But when Maria raises her hand, Mr. Oliver doesn't always notice her. He calls on Maria whenever he sees her hand in the air, but he doesn't often look in her direction; she is therefore receiving intermittent reinforcement. As you've already learned, Molly's volunteering behavior should increase more rapidly than Maria's.

But let's move ahead in time a few months. Thanks to Mr. Oliver's attentiveness to Molly and Maria, both girls are now volunteering frequently in class. Mr. Oliver turns his attention to several other students who have been failing to participate. Foolishly, he no longer reinforces either Molly or Maria for raising her hand. As you might expect, the girls begin to participate less; in other words, we see signs of extinction. But for which girl will class participation extinguish more rapidly?

If you predicted that Molly's volunteering will decrease more rapidly than Maria's, you are correct. Responses that have previously been reinforced continuously tend to extinguish relatively quickly once reinforcement stops. But because Maria has been receiving intermittent reinforcement, she is accustomed to being occasionally ignored. It may take her longer to realize that she is no longer going to be called on when she raises her hand. Behaviors that have previously been reinforced intermittently decrease slowly (if at all) once reinforcement stops; in other words, they are more *resistant to extinction* (e.g., Freeland & Noell, 1999).

Once students have acquired a desired terminal behavior, we should continue to reinforce the behavior only intermittently, especially if it does not otherwise lead to intrinsic reinforcement. Mr. Oliver doesn't need to call on Molly and Maria every time they raise their hands, but he should certainly call on them once in a while. In a similar manner, we might occasionally reinforce diligent study habits, completed homework assignments, prosocial behaviors, and so on, even for the best of students, as a way of encouraging these responses to continue.

■ Which form of reinforcement, continuous or intermittent, would you use to teach students to persist at difficult tasks?

ADDRESSING ESPECIALLY DIFFICULT CLASSROOM BEHAVIORS

Educators and other practitioners sometimes apply behaviorism in a very systematic way, especially when they want to address difficult and chronic behavior problems. Here we consider three systematic approaches for modifying especially challenging behaviors: applied behavior analysis, functional analysis, and positive behavioral support.

Applied Behavior Analysis

A group of procedures that systematically apply behaviorist principles are collectively known as **applied behavior analysis** (also called *behavior modification*, *behavior therapy*, or *contingency management*). Applied behavior analysis, or **ABA**, is based on the assumptions that behavior problems result from past and present environmental circumstances and that modifying a student's present environment will promote more productive responses. When teachers and therapists use ABA to help a student acquire more appropriate classroom behavior, they typically use strategies such as these:

- Describe both the present behaviors and the desired terminal behaviors in observable, measurable terms.
- Identify one or more effective reinforcers.
- Develop a specific intervention or treatment plan. The plan may involve reinforcement of desired behaviors, shaping, extinction, reinforcement of incompatible behaviors, punishment, or some combination of these.
- Measure the frequency of desired and undesired behaviors both before treatment (i.e., at baseline level) and during treatment.
- Monitor the treatment program for effectiveness by observing how various behaviors change over time, and modify the program if necessary.
- Take steps to promote generalization of newly acquired behaviors (e.g., by having the student practice the behaviors in a variety of realistic situations).
- Gradually phase out the treatment (e.g., through intermittent reinforcement) after the desired behaviors are acquired.

■ **intermittent reinforcement** Reinforcement of a response only occasionally, with some occurrences of the response going unreinforced.

■ **applied behavior analysis (ABA)** Systematic application of behaviorist principles in educational and therapeutic settings.

Consistent use of reinforcement for appropriate responses gives a clear message about which behaviors are acceptable and which are not.

Hundreds of research studies tell us that the systematic use of behaviorist principles can lead to significant improvements in academic performance and classroom behavior. For example, when we reinforce students for successful achievement, we find improvements in such subjects as mathematics, reading, spelling, and creative writing (Piersel, 1987). When we reinforce appropriate classroom behaviors—paying attention, interacting cooperatively and prosocially with classmates, and so on—misbehaviors decrease (S. N. Elliott & Busse, 1991; E. McNamara, 1987; Ormrod, 2004). In many situations ABA is effective when other approaches have not been (Emmer & Evertson, 1981; O'Leary & O'Leary, 1972; Piersel, 1987).

One probable reason ABA often works so well is that students know exactly what is expected of them. Consistent use of reinforcement for appropriate responses gives a clear message about which behaviors are acceptable and which are not. Another likely reason is that through the gradual process of *shaping*, students begin to learn new behaviors only when they are truly ready to acquire them, and so their probability of achieving success and reinforcement is quite high.

Functional Analysis and Positive Behavioral Support

Traditional ABA focuses on changing response-reinforcement contingencies to bring about more appropriate behavior. In recent years some theorists have suggested that we also consider the purposes, or *functions*, that students' inappropriate behaviors may serve. In particular, they recommend identifying the specific conditions (i.e., antecedent stimuli) present when students tend to misbehave and also the consequences (reinforcers, punishments, or both) that typically follow such misbehaviors, like so:

$$\text{Antecedent} \rightarrow \text{Behavior} \rightarrow \text{Consequence}$$

Such an approach is known as **functional analysis** (you may also see the term *functional behavioral assessment*). For example, we have speculated that James, in our opening case study, misbehaves to get the attention he apparently cannot get in any other way. Functional analyses have shown that students with chronic classroom behavior problems often misbehave when they are asked to do difficult or unpleasant tasks (this is the *antecedent*) and that their misbehavior either (a) allows them to avoid having to do such tasks or (b) gains the attention of their teacher or peers (these are possible *consequences*) (K. M. Jones, Drew, & Weber, 2000; McComas et al., 2003; K. A. Meyer, 1999; Van Camp et al., 2000).

Positive behavioral support takes the process a step further: After identifying the purposes that inappropriate behaviors may serve, a teacher or, more often, a team of teachers and other professionals develops and carries out a plan to encourage appropriate behaviors. In particular, positive behavioral support involves strategies such as these (Crone & Horner, 2003; Koegel et al., 1996; Ruef, Higgins, Glaeser, & Patnode, 1998):

- Teach behaviors that can serve the same purpose as—and can therefore replace—inappropriate behaviors.
- Modify the classroom environment to minimize conditions that might trigger inappropriate behaviors.
- Establish a predictable daily routine as a way of minimizing anxiety and making the student feel more comfortable and secure.
- Give the student opportunities to make choices; in this way, the student can often gain desired outcomes without having to resort to inappropriate behavior.
- Make adaptations in the curriculum, instruction, or both to maximize the likelihood of academic success (e.g., build on the student's interests, present material at a slower pace, or intersperse challenging tasks among easier and more enjoyable ones).
- Monitor the frequency of various behaviors to determine whether the intervention is working or, instead, requires modification.

As an illustration of how positive behavioral support might work, let's consider a 9-year-old named Samantha:

Samantha had been identified as having autism and moderate speech disabilities. She frequently ran out of her third-grade classroom, damaging school property and other students' belongings in her flight. When a teacher or other adult tried to intervene, she would fight back by biting, hitting, kicking, or pulling hair. On such occasions school personnel would often call her parents and ask that they come to take her home.

■ **functional analysis** Examination of inappropriate behavior and its antecedents and consequences to determine functions that the behavior might serve for the learner.

■ **positive behavioral support** Variation of traditional ABA that involves identifying the purposes of undesirable behaviors and providing alternative behaviors that more appropriately accomplish those purposes.

A multidisciplinary team discovered that Samantha's destructive and aggressive behaviors typically occurred when she was given a difficult assignment or was expecting such an assignment. Departures from the routine schedule or the absences of favorite teachers further increased the probability of inappropriate responses.

The team hypothesized that Samantha's undesirable behaviors served two purposes: They (1) helped her avoid unpleasant academic tasks and (2) enabled her to gain the attention of valued adults. The team suspected, too, that Samantha felt as if she had little or no control over classroom activities and that she yearned for social interaction with her teachers and classmates. (DeVault, Krug, & Fake, 1996)

Armed with this information, the team took several steps to address the roots of Samantha's inappropriate behaviors and help her acquire more productive ones (DeVault et al., 1996):

- Samantha was given a consistent and predictable daily schedule that included frequent breaks from potentially challenging academic tasks and numerous opportunities to interact with others.
- Samantha was given "goal sheets" from which she could choose the academic tasks she would work on, the length of time she would work on them, and the reinforcer she would receive for achieving each goal.
- Samantha was taught how to ask for assistance when she needed it—a strategy that she could use instead of fleeing from the classroom when she encountered a challenging task.
- When Samantha felt she needed a break from academic tasks, she could ask to spend some time in the "relaxation room," a quiet and private space where she could sit in a beanbag chair and listen to soothing audiotapes.
- If Samantha attempted to leave the classroom, an adult would place her immediately in the relaxation room, where she could calm down without a great deal of adult attention.
- Samantha was given explicit instruction in how to interact appropriately with classmates. Initially, she earned points for appropriate social behaviors and could trade them for special treats (e.g., a family trip to Dairy Queen or a video store). Eventually, her new social skills led to natural consequences—friendly interactions with peers—that made extrinsic reinforcers unnecessary.

Samantha's behavior changed dramatically within the course of a few months. By the time she was 12 years old and in sixth grade, her grades consistently earned her a place on the honor roll, and she had a group of friends with whom she participated in several extracurricular activities. Her teachers described her as sociable, inquisitive, and creative; her principal called her a "model student" (DeVault et al., 1996).

Positive behavioral support clearly has elements of behaviorist theory, including its focus on structuring an environment that reinforces desired behaviors and extinguishes undesirable ones. At the same time, it also incorporates contemporary theories of motivation, as reflected in its attempts to minimize anxiety, provide opportunities for choice making, and promote mastery of classroom tasks. The importance of doing all of these things will become clearer when we discuss motivation in Chapters 11 and 12.

CONSIDERING DIVERSITY IN STUDENT BEHAVIORS

When we take a behaviorist perspective, we realize that our students will each bring a unique set of previous environments and experiences to the classroom, and such diversity will undoubtedly be a key reason for the different behavior patterns we are apt to see. For one thing, students will have been reinforced and punished—by their parents, siblings, previous teachers, peers, and so on—for different kinds of behaviors. Some students may have been reinforced for completing tasks in a careful and thorough manner, whereas others may have been reinforced for completing tasks quickly but sloppily. Some students may have been reinforced for initiating interactions with age-mates; others may have been punished (perhaps in the form of peer rejection) for similar outgoing behavior. Some diversity in students' classroom responses will also be due to the different behaviors that various cultures encourage (reinforce) and discourage (punish) in their children.

We will see differences, too, in the consequences that students find reinforcing and punishing. In some cultures (e.g., in Haiti) reprimands are often used to communicate concern and affection. For example, on one occasion, a teacher was reprimanding her Haitian students for proceeding across a parking lot without her. The following conversation ensued:

Teacher:	Did I tell you to go?
Children:	No.
Teacher:	Can you cross this parking lot by yourselves?
Children:	No.
Teacher:	That's right. There are cars here. They're dangerous. I don't want you to go alone. Why do I want you to wait for me, do you know?
Claudette:	Yes . . . because you like us. (dialogue from Ballenger, 1992, p. 205)

Students from certain other cultures may be unaccustomed to direct praise for their successes, perhaps because adults in their culture express their approval in other ways—for instance, by telling other people how skillful a child is (Rogoff, 2003). Many Native American students may feel uncomfortable when praised for their work as individuals yet feel quite proud when they receive praise for group success (Fuller, 2001). Such preference for group praise is consistent with the cooperative spirit in which these students have been raised (see the discussion of ethnic differences in Chapter 4).

With such diversity in mind, we will inevitably need to tailor our strategies to the particular students with whom we are working. Responses to particular stimuli, effective reinforcers, and baseline rates of desired behaviors will be different for every student.

Accommodating Students with Special Needs

A behaviorist approach allows us to consider characteristics of students with special needs from a somewhat different angle than we have in previous chapters. Table 9.4 illustrates how responses, reinforcement, generalization, and discrimination might be different in some of our students with special needs.

STRENGTHS AND POTENTIAL LIMITATIONS OF BEHAVIORAL APPROACHES

Behaviorist techniques are especially helpful when we need to address chronic classroom behavior problems. Although such approaches as applied behavior analysis, functional analysis, and positive behavioral support can be quite time-consuming (J. N. Hughes, 1988), they are often effective when other approaches have failed.

Psychologists have had mixed feelings about the value of behaviorist techniques in addressing *academic* problems, however. Reinforcement and other behaviorist strategies often do lead to improved academic performance, but we should keep the following drawbacks in mind:

◎   *Attempts at changing behaviors ignore cognitive factors that are potentially interfering with learning.* When students are simply not motivated to learn a new behavior, systematic use of reinforcement may be all that is needed to bring about effective learning. But when cognitive deficiencies hinder students' ability to acquire certain skills (e.g., perhaps a student has little background knowledge, poor reading skills, or ineffective study strategies), reinforcement alone may be insufficient to bring about significant improvement. For instance, if James in our opening case study has poor reading skills that he wants to hide from his teacher and classmates, he may sometimes misbehave to escape tasks that, to him, seem impossible. For those students who have significant weaknesses in their knowledge or cognitive abilities, teaching strategies based on cognitive theories (e.g., see Chapters 6 through 8) may be more effective.

◎   *Reinforcement for accomplishing academic tasks may encourage students to do things quickly rather than well.* In the "Applying Math" exercise in Chapter 8 (page 274), we saw 9-year-old Peyton "padding" his list of applications of mathematics with such responses as "forks," "spoons," and "knives." By promising to reinforce quantity but not quality (the student with the most responses would win a prize), Peyton's teacher unintentionally encouraged him to do the assignment quickly and with little thought. In general, reinforcement only for accomplishing a particular task focuses students' attention and effort more on getting the task done quickly, perhaps at a minimally acceptable level, than on *learning* from the activity. Especially if we want students to engage in complex, higher-level thinking—for example, to think flexibly and creatively

■ In a number of places throughout the chapter, I have sneaked unobservable phenomena (thoughts, feelings, etc.) into my description of behaviorist principles. Can you find some places where I have done so?

TABLE 9.4   STUDENTS IN INCLUSIVE SETTINGS

Encouraging Appropriate Behaviors in Students with Special Educational Needs

CATEGORY	CHARACTERISTICS YOU MIGHT OBSERVE	SUGGESTED CLASSROOM STRATEGIES
Students with specific cognitive or academic difficulties	• Inappropriate classroom behaviors (in some students) • Difficulty discriminating among similar stimuli, especially when perceptual deficits exist • Difficulty generalizing responses from one situation to another	• Be explicit about, and consistently reinforce, desired classroom behaviors. • Emphasize differences among similar stimuli (e.g., the letters *b*, *d*, *p*, and *q*), and provide opportunities to practice making subtle discriminations. • Promote generalization of new responses (e.g., by pointing out similarities among different situations and by teaching skills in real-world contexts).
Students with social or behavioral problems	• Inappropriate responses, especially in social situations; difficulty determining when and where particular responses are appropriate • A history of inappropriate behaviors being reinforced (e.g., intrinsically or by teacher attention) • Responsiveness to teacher praise if given in private (for students with emotional and behavioral disorders) • Difficulty generalizing appropriate responses to new situations	• Describe desired behaviors clearly. • Give precise feedback regarding students' behavior. • Reinforce desired behaviors using teacher attention, private praise, activity reinforcers, and group contingencies (for students with emotional and behavioral disorders). • Reinforce accomplishments immediately using concrete reinforcers, activity reinforcers, or praise (especially for students with autism). • Shape desired behaviors over time; expect gradual improvement rather than immediate perfection. • Punish inappropriate behaviors (e.g., using time-out or response cost); consider applied behavior analysis or positive behavioral support for persistently challenging behaviors. • Promote generalization of new responses to appropriate situations (e.g., by teaching skills in real-world contexts and providing opportunities to role-play new responses).
Students with general delays in cognitive and social functioning	• High reinforcing value of extrinsic reinforcers • Behavior more likely to improve when reinforcement is immediate rather than delayed • Inappropriate responses in social situations • Difficulty discriminating between important and unimportant stimuli • Difficulty generalizing responses from one situation to another	• Cue students regarding appropriate behaviors. • Reinforce accomplishments immediately (e.g., using concrete reinforcers, activity reinforcers, praise). • Use continuous reinforcement during the acquisition of new responses. • Shape desired behaviors over time; expect gradual improvement rather than immediate perfection. • Reprimand minor misbehaviors; use time-out or response cost for more serious and chronic misbehaviors. • Emphasize the stimuli to which you want students to attend. • Promote generalization of new responses (e.g., by teaching skills in real-world contexts and by reinforcing generalization).
Students with physical or sensory challenges	• Loss of some previously learned behaviors if students have had traumatic brain injury	• Shape desired behaviors over time; expect gradual improvement rather than immediate perfection.
Students with advanced cognitive development	• Unusual and sometimes creative responses to classroom tasks	• Keep an open mind about acceptable responses to classroom assignments. • Encourage and reinforce creative responses.

Sources: Barbetta, 1990; Barbetta, Heward, Bradley, & Miller, 1994; Beirne-Smith et al., 2002; Buchoff, 1990; E. S. Ellis & Friend, 1991; Gearheart et al., 1992; Heward, 2003; Landau & McAninch, 1993; Mercer, 1997; Morgan & Jenson, 1988; Patton et al., 1996; Pfiffner & Barkley, 1998; Piirto, 1999; Pressley, 1995; R. Turnbull et al., 2004.

about the subject matter—then extrinsic reinforcement simply for task accomplishment may be counterproductive (Clifford, 1990; Deci & Ryan, 1985; B. A. Hennessey & Amabile, 1987; Mc-Caslin & Good, 1996).

◎   *Extrinsic reinforcement of an activity that students already find intrinsically reinforcing may undermine students' enjoyment of the activity.* Students often engage in behaviors because of the intrinsic reinforcers (e.g., feelings of success or sheer enjoyment) that those behaviors bring. Some research studies indicate that enjoyable activities can be increased through extrinsic reinforcement but will then *decrease* to a below-baseline frequency once the reinforcers are removed. Extrinsic reinforcers are most likely to have this adverse effect when students perceive them as controlling or manipulating them, rather than as providing information about their progress (Deci, Koestner, & Ryan, 2001; B. A. Hennessey, 1995; Lepper & Hodell, 1989). In such cases extrinsic reinforcers are essentially undermining students' sense of *self-determination*, a concept we'll examine in Chapter 12.

Before using extrinsic reinforcers to increase certain behaviors, then, we should be sure that such reinforcers are truly necessary—that students show no intrinsic motivation to develop the academic skills essential for their school success. Extrinsic reinforcement can be quite useful when students otherwise have no desire to acquire appropriate desirable behaviors. Students may initially find a new activity boring, difficult, or frustrating and need external encouragement to continue (Cameron, 2001; Deci et al., 2001; Hidi & Harackiewicz, 2000). With continuing practice, their competence and skills should improve, and they may eventually begin to find the activity worth doing for its own sake.

THE BIG PICTURE

Clearly, we can understand a great deal about human learning and behavior by looking at stimulus-response principles. Conditions already present in a learner's environment—antecedent stimuli—tend to evoke certain kinds of responses either involuntarily (in classical conditioning) or voluntarily (in operant conditioning). Those responses may, in turn, lead to changes in the learner's environment; for instance, they may lead to reinforcement or punishment. If we think of reinforcing and punishing consequences as *stimuli* (because indeed they are), then we see a continuing interaction between a learner and his or her environment, like so:

$$S \rightarrow R \rightarrow S \rightarrow R \rightarrow S \rightarrow R \rightarrow \ldots$$

By changing any part of this chain of events—whether by altering the classroom environment (the stimulus conditions) or by teaching students a more effective way of responding to that environment—we can help students acquire more productive classroom behaviors. For instance, we can increase students' on-task behavior and simultaneously decrease their off-task behavior by giving them attention (reinforcement) only when they are on task. And we can help them gain the attention (reinforcement) of their peers by teaching and shaping increasingly effective social skills.

Helpful as they may be, however, stimulus-response principles alone do not give us a complete picture of human learning. For example, although reinforcement may increase the amount of time that students study, it does not necessarily increase the effectiveness of that study time; cognitive psychology provides more guidance as to how we can help students learn information more effectively, remember it longer, and apply it to new situations more readily. Furthermore, it appears that people learn not only the behaviors that they themselves are reinforced for but also the behaviors they see *others* being reinforced for; social cognitive theory, which we will consider in the next chapter, provides more guidance on helping students learn through their observations of others. In addition, as I've mentioned on several occasions, motivational factors play a key role in determining what consequences are likely to be reinforcing at any given time; we will explore the nature of motivation in Chapters 11 and 12.

CASE STUDY: *Hostile Helen*

Mr. Washington has a close-knit group of friends in one of his high school vocational education classes. He is concerned about one particular student in this group, a girl named Helen. Helen uses obscene language in class. She is rude and disrespectful to Mr. Washington. She taunts and insults classmates outside her own circle of friends. And she is physically aggressive toward school property—she defaces furniture, kicks equipment, punches walls, and so on.

At first, Mr. Washington tries to ignore Helen's hostile and aggressive behaviors, but this strategy doesn't lead to any improvement in her behavior. He then tries praising Helen on those rare occasions when she does behave appropriately, but this strategy doesn't seem to work either.

In behaviorist terminology, what is Mr. Washington trying to do when he ignores Helen's inappropriate behavior? What are some possible reasons this approach isn't working?

In behaviorist terminology, what is Mr. Washington trying to do when he praises Helen's appropriate behavior? What are some possible reasons this approach isn't working either?

How might *you* use behaviorist learning principles to bring about a behavior change in Helen?

Once you have answered these questions, compare your responses with those presented in Appendix B.

KEY CONCEPTS

behaviorism (p. 295)
conditioning (p. 296)
response (p. 296)
stimulus (p. 296)
contiguity (p. 297)
classical conditioning (p. 298)
unconditioned stimulus (UCS) (p. 298)
unconditioned response (UCR) (p. 298)
neutral stimulus (p. 298)
conditioned stimulus (CS) (p. 299)
conditioned response (CR) (p. 299)
generalization in classical conditioning (p. 300)
extinction in classical conditioning (p. 300)
operant conditioning (p. 301)
contingency (p. 302)
reinforcer (p. 303)
reinforcement (p. 303)
primary reinforcer (p. 303)
secondary reinforcer (p. 303)

positive reinforcement (p. 304)
concrete reinforcer (p. 304)
social reinforcer (p. 304)
activity reinforcer (p. 304)
Premack principle (p. 304)
positive feedback (p. 304)
extrinsic reinforcer (p. 304)
intrinsic reinforcer (p. 304)
negative reinforcement (p. 305)
delay of gratification (p. 306)
terminal behavior (p. 307)
token economy (p. 308)
backup reinforcer (p. 308)
group contingency (p. 308)
contingency contract (p. 309)
continuous reinforcement (p. 310)
baseline (p. 310)
shaping (p. 310)
antecedent stimulus (p. 311)
antecedent response (p. 311)

cueing (p. 312)
setting event (p. 312)
generalization in operant conditioning (p. 312)
discrimination (p. 312)
behavioral momentum (p. 312)
extinction in operant conditioning (p. 314)
incompatible behaviors (p. 315)
punishment (p. 316)
presentation punishment (p. 316)
removal punishment (p. 316)
verbal reprimand (p. 317)
response cost (p. 317)
logical consequence (p. 317)
time-out (p. 317)
in-school suspension (p. 317)
psychological punishment (p. 318)
intermittent reinforcement (p. 321)
applied behavior analysis (ABA) (p. 321)
functional analysis (p. 322)
positive behavioral support (p. 322)

PRAXIS Turn to Appendix C, "Matching Book and Ancillary Content to the Praxis Principles of Learning and Teaching Tests," to discover sections of this chapter that may be especially applicable to the Praxis tests.

Now go to our Companion Website at **www.prenhall.com/ormrod** to assess your understanding of chapter content with "Multiple-Choice Questions," apply comprehension in "Essay Questions," broaden your knowledge of educational psychology with related "Web Links," gain greater insight about classroom learning in "Learning in the Content Areas," and analyze and assess classroom work in the "Student Artifact Library."

Chapter 10 Social Cognitive Views of Learning

What behaviors have you learned by observing other people do them first? Can you think of academic skills you've learned by watching or listening to someone else? Perhaps you learned a mathematical procedure or the correct conjugation of *estudiar*. What about social skills? Perhaps you observed how to answer the telephone politely or how to apologize to someone whose feelings you've hurt. And what about motor skills? Perhaps you discovered how to swing a softball bat or write letters in cursive. We learn a wide variety of behaviors by observing the people around us and those in the media. We also learn which behaviors are likely to get us ahead—and which behaviors are not—by seeing their consequences for others. In part by watching what others do, we develop a sense of what our own capabilities are likely to be, and we begin to direct our behavior toward goals we think we can achieve.

In this chapter we will explore **social cognitive theory**, a perspective that can help us understand what and how people learn by observing others and how, in the process, people begin to assume control over their own behavior. More specifically, we will address questions such as these:

- What basic assumptions are central to the social cognitive perspective of learning?
- How do cognitive processes influence the effects of reinforcement and punishment?
- How can we effectively use modeling to facilitate students' learning?
- What role does *self-efficacy* play in learning, and how can we enhance it in children and adolescents?
- How can we help students take control of their own behavior and learning? In other words, how can we promote *self-regulation*?

CASE STUDY: *Parlez-Vous Français?*

Nathan isn't taking French because he wants to; he has enrolled in French I only because his mother insisted. Although he does well in his other high school courses, he's convinced he'll be a failure in French. After all, three friends who took French last year got mostly Ds and Fs on quizzes and homework, and two of them dropped the class after the first semester.

On the first day of French class, Nathan notices that most of his classmates are girls; the few boys are students he doesn't know very well. He sits sullenly in the back row, convinced he'll do no better in French than his friends did. "I do OK in math and science, but I'm just no good at learning languages," he tells himself. "Besides, learning French is a 'girl' thing."

Although Nathan comes to class every day, his mind usually wanders to other topics as his teacher explains simple syntactical structures and demonstrates the correct pronunciation of new vocabulary words. He makes feeble attempts at homework assignments but quickly puts them aside whenever he encounters something he doesn't immediately understand.

Sure enough, Nathan is right: He can't do French. He gets a D— on his first exam.

- What has Nathan learned about French by observing other people?
- Why do Nathan's beliefs lead to a self-fulfilling prophecy?

BASIC ASSUMPTIONS OF SOCIAL COGNITIVE THEORY

You might initially think that Nathan has learned nothing from observing others because he has apparently not benefited from his teacher's explanations and demonstrations. Yet at second glance, you might realize that Nathan *has* learned something through observation after all: He has seen what happened to his three friends and concluded that *he* probably won't succeed in French class either. As we proceed through the chapter, you will discover some reasons why Nathan seems to have learned more from his friends than from his teacher.

Social cognitive theory has its roots in behaviorism but over the past few decades has increasingly incorporated cognitive processes into its explanations of learning; it now includes a blend of ideas from behaviorism and cognitive psychology. Yet it addresses *motivation* to a greater degree than either the cognitive or behaviorist perspective; accordingly, it provides a good transition to our discussion of motivation in Chapters 11 and 12. Social cognitive theory

■ As you read the chapter, look for references to motivation in the sections on modeling, self-efficacy, and self-regulation.

■ **social cognitive theory** Theoretical perspective in which learning by observing others is the focus of study.

TABLE 10.1   PRINCIPLES/ASSUMPTIONS

Basic Assumptions of Social Cognitive Theory and Their Educational Implications

ASSUMPTION	EDUCATIONAL IMPLICATION	EXAMPLE
Learning by observation	Help students acquire new behaviors more quickly by demonstrating those behaviors yourself.	Demonstrate appropriate ways to deal with and resolve interpersonal conflicts. Then ask students to role-play conflict resolution in small groups, and compliment those who use prosocial strategies.
Learning as an internal process that may or may not be reflected in behavior	Remember that learning does not always appear immediately, but may instead be reflected in students' later behaviors.	When one student engages in disruptive classroom behavior, take appropriate steps to discourage it. Otherwise, classmates who have witnessed the misbehavior may be similarly disruptive in the future.
Goal-directed behavior	Encourage students to set goals for themselves, especially goals that are challenging yet achievable.	When teaching American Sign Language to help students communicate with a classmate who is deaf, ask them to predict how many new words and phrases they can learn each week.
Self-regulation of behavior	Teach students strategies for helping themselves learn effectively and behave appropriately.	Give students concrete suggestions about how they can remind themselves to bring needed supplies to school each day.
Indirect effects of reinforcement and punishment	Ensure that the consequences of students' behaviors communicate the right messages about which actions are and are not acceptable in the classroom.	To encourage students to speak in German, respond to questions only if students make a reasonable attempt to ask the questions in German.

has developed in large part through the research efforts of Albert Bandura at Stanford University. You will find references to Bandura and others who build on his ideas (e.g., Dale Schunk, Barry Zimmerman) throughout the chapter.

In our case study of Nathan, we can see one basic assumption underlying social cognitive theory: People can learn from observing others. This and several other assumptions are summarized in Table 10.1. Let's look at them more closely:

Social cognitive theorists propose that people can sometimes learn more quickly and easily by watching how others behave and noticing which behaviors lead to reinforcement and which lead to punishment.

◎   *People can learn by observing others.* From the perspective of operant conditioning (Chapter 9), learning is often a process of trial and error: People try many different responses, increasing those that bring about desirable consequences and eliminating unproductive ones. Social cognitive theorists argue that learners don't necessarily have to "experiment" in this way; instead, they can acquire many new responses simply by observing the behaviors of other individuals (**models**). For example, a student might learn how to solve a long division problem, spell the word *synonym* correctly, or mouth off at the teacher simply by watching someone else do these things first.

◎   *Learning is an internal process that may or may not lead to a behavior change.* Some of the things people learn appear in their behavior immediately, other things affect their behavior at a later time, and still others never influence their behavior at all. For example, you might attempt to swing a tennis racket as soon as you learn the correct form. But you probably won't demonstrate that you've learned how to apologize tactfully until a later time when an apology is necessary. And you might *never* walk barefoot over hot coals, no matter how many times you see someone else do it. Social cognitive theory, like cognitive psychology, defines learning as an internal mental process that may or may not be reflected in the learner's behavior.

◎   *Behavior is directed toward particular goals.* Because you are reading this book, you probably want to become a teacher or enter some related profession, and you are taking an educational psychology class to help you attain that goal. Social cognitive theorists propose that people often set goals for themselves and direct their behavior accordingly; in essence, they are *motivated* to accomplish their goals. Students are apt to have a variety of goals—perhaps a high grade point average, a college scholarship, popularity with classmates, athletic prowess, or a

■ **model** Person who demonstrates a behavior for someone else.

reputation as the class clown. Throughout the chapter we will see the relevance of such goals for learning and behavior.

◎   *Behavior eventually becomes self-regulated.* From a behaviorist perspective, people's behaviors are governed largely by the things that happen *to* them—the stimuli they encounter, the reinforcers that follow their behaviors, and so on. In contrast, social cognitive theorists believe that people eventually begin to regulate their *own* learning and behavior. As an example, let's consider Shih-tai, a third grader who is learning to write in cursive. A traditional behaviorist might say that Shih-tai can best learn cursive if her teacher reinforces her for increasingly more appropriate responses, thereby shaping skillful penmanship over a period of several weeks or months. But a social cognitive theorist would suggest that Shih-tai can learn to write cursive letters more effectively by looking carefully at the examples her teacher has written on the chalkboard, copying those letters as closely as possible, and then comparing the letters she has written with those on the board. If she is happy with her work, she will give herself a mental pat on the back; if she is not, she may continue to practice until her letters are comparable to those of her teacher. From the social cognitive perspective, people often set their own standards for acceptable and unacceptable behavior and then strive to behave in accordance with those standards.

◎   *Reinforcement and punishment have indirect (rather than direct) effects on learning and behavior.* Operant conditioning theorists believe that reinforcement is essential for learning, in that responses increase only when they are reinforced. Some behaviorists have also argued that punishment is a counterpart to reinforcement, decreasing the frequency of a behavior it follows. Implied in the behaviorist perspective is the idea that reinforcement and punishment are directly responsible for behavior change and learning.

Reinforcement and punishment are less critical in social cognitive theory, but they have several indirect effects on learning and behavior. In the next section we will find out exactly how reinforcement and punishment fit into the social cognitive perspective.

■ Do you think your own behaviors are regulated more by the environment or by your own standards for what is acceptable and what is not?

THE SOCIAL COGNITIVE VIEW OF REINFORCEMENT AND PUNISHMENT

According to social cognitive theorists (e.g., Bandura, 1977, 1986; T. L. Rosenthal & Zimmerman, 1978), both reinforcement and punishment influence learning and behavior in several ways:

- People form *expectations* about the likely consequences of future responses based on how current responses are reinforced or punished.
- People's expectations are also influenced by their observations of the consequences that follow other people's behaviors—in other words, by *vicarious experiences*.
- Expectations about probable future consequences affect how people *cognitively process* new information.
- Expectations also influence people's *decisions about how to behave*.
- The *nonoccurrence of an expected consequence* may have a reinforcing or punishing effect in and of itself.

As we explore these points, we'll see some of the ways in which both environmental and cognitive factors enter into the learning process.

Expectations

Perhaps you have taken a course in which all exam questions were based on the textbook, without a single question coming from class lectures. After the first exam, did you find yourself reading the textbook carefully but skipping class frequently? Perhaps you have also taken a course in which exams were based almost *entirely* on class lectures and activities. In that situation, did you go to class regularly but rarely open your textbook?

According to social cognitive theory, people form expectations about the consequences that are likely to result from various behaviors. When a particular response is reinforced every time we make it, we typically expect to be reinforced for behaving that way in future situations, and when a response frequently leads to punishment, we expect that response to be punished on later occasions as well. For example, you use your own experiences with classroom tests to form expectations as to what specific behaviors (e.g., reading your textbook, going to class) are apt to be reinforced on future tests.

■ Can you think of an occasion when you chose not to do something because of the ridicule you thought it might bring you?

Students sometimes form expectations about what things will be reinforced and punished on the basis of very little hard data. For example, one student might believe (perhaps erroneously) that by bragging about his high test scores, he will gain the admiration of his classmates (a reinforcer). Another student might believe that her classmates will ridicule and reject (i.e., punish) her for being smart, regardless of whether they would actually do so.

From the social cognitive perspective, reinforcement increases the frequency of a behavior only when students think or know that the behavior is being reinforced—that is, when they are *aware* of a response-reinforcement contingency (Bandura, 1986). As teachers, then, we should be very clear about what we are reinforcing, so that students know the real response-reinforcement contingencies operating in the classroom. For example, if Sam gets an A on an essay but we don't let him know *why* he's earned that grade, he won't necessarily know how to get an A the next time. To improve Sam's performance, we might tell him that the essay earned an A because he supported his opinion with a logical train of thought. Similarly, if we praise Sandra for her "good game" at the basketball tournament even though she scored only one basket, she may understandably be a bit confused. We might instead tell her that we were pleased with her high energy level and cooperation with other team members throughout the game.

Vicarious Experiences

When I was in third grade, I entered a Halloween costume contest dressed as "Happy Tooth," a character in several toothpaste commercials at the time. I didn't win the contest; a "witch" won first prize. So the following year, I entered the same contest dressed as a witch, figuring I was a shoo-in for first place. Our expectations about the consequences of certain responses come not only from making those responses ourselves but also from observing what happens when others make them. In other words, we sometimes experience reinforcement and punishment *vicariously.*

People who observe someone else being reinforced for a particular behavior tend to exhibit that behavior more frequently themselves—a phenomenon known as **vicarious reinforcement**. For example, by watching the consequences their classmates experience, students might learn that studying hard leads to good grades, that being elected to class office brings status and popularity, or that neatness counts.

Conversely, when we see someone else get punished for a certain behavior, we are *less* likely to behave that way ourselves—a phenomenon known as **vicarious punishment**. For example, when a coach benches a football player for poor sportsmanlike conduct, other players are unlikely to mimic such behavior. But unfortunately, vicarious punishment may suppress desirable behaviors as well. For example, when a teacher belittles a student for asking a "silly" question, other students may be reluctant to ask questions of their own.

As teachers, we must be extremely careful that we don't vicariously reinforce undesirable behaviors or vicariously punish desirable ones. If we give too much attention to a misbehaving student, others who want our attention may misbehave as well. If we ridicule a student who unwittingly volunteers an incorrect answer or erroneous belief, classmates will hardly be eager to voice their opinions.

Cognitive Processing

Experiencing FIRSTHAND ·Planning Ahead

Quickly skim the contents of Chapter 11 to get a general sense of the topics it includes. Once you have done so, imagine yourself in each of these situations:

1. Your instructor announces, "Chapter 11 won't be on your test, but please read it anyway." How thoroughly and carefully will you read the chapter? Jot down a brief answer to this question.
2. The following day, your instructor announces, "I misled you yesterday. In reality, half of next week's test will be based on the ideas presented in Chapter 11." *Now* how thoroughly and carefully will you read the chapter? Once again, jot down a brief answer.

· · · · · · ·

If you don't expect to be reinforced for reading Chapter 11, you may very well *not* read it too carefully (perhaps you'll read it later, you think to yourself, but you have many other things to

■ **vicarious reinforcement**
Phenomenon in which a response increases in frequency when another (observed) person is reinforced for that response.

■ **vicarious punishment** Phenomenon in which a response decreases in frequency when another (observed) person is punished for that response.

do right now). If, instead, you discover that getting an A in your educational psychology class depends on knowing the material in Chapter 11 like the back of your hand, you are apt to read it slowly and carefully, possibly trying to learn and remember each and every detail.

When we believe we will be reinforced for learning something, we are more likely to pay attention to it and mentally process it in an effective fashion. When we *don't* expect to be reinforced for learning it, we are far less likely to think about or process it in any significant way. As an example of the latter situation, let's return to Nathan in our opening case study. Already convinced that he can't learn French, Nathan pays little attention to what his teacher says in class, and he makes only halfhearted efforts to complete his homework assignments.

Decisions About How to Behave

People learn many things that they never demonstrate because there is no reinforcement for doing so. To see what I mean, try the following exercise.

Students make decisions about how to behave based, in part, on the responses for which their peers are reinforced and punished.

Experiencing FIRSTHAND ·Dr. X

How many of the following questions can you answer about your educational psychology instructor? For lack of a better name, I'm going to call your instructor "Dr. X."

1. Is Dr. X right-handed or left-handed?
2. Is Dr. X a flashy dresser or a more conservative one?
3. What kind of shoes does Dr. X wear to class?
4. Does Dr. X wear a wedding ring?
5. Does Dr. X bring a briefcase to class each day?

· · · · · · ·

If you've been going to class regularly, you probably know the answers to at least two of the questions, and possibly you can answer all five, even though you never thought you'd have a reason to know such information. Every time I teach educational psychology, I take a minute sometime during the semester to hide my feet behind the podium; I then ask my students to tell me what my shoes look like. My students first look at me as if I have two heads; information about my shoes is something that many of them have learned, but until now they have had absolutely no reason to demonstrate their knowledge. After a few seconds of awkward silence, at least a half dozen students (usually those sitting in the first two rows) begin to describe my shoes, right down to the rippled soles, scuffed leather, and beige stitching.

Students learn many things in the classroom. They learn facts and figures, they learn ways of getting their teacher's attention, and they may even learn such tiny details as which classmate stores Twinkies in his desk and what kind of shoes the teacher wears to school. Of all the things they learn, students will be most likely to demonstrate the ones they think will bring them reinforcement. The things they think will *not* be reinforced may remain hidden forever.

When students choose to behave in a way that may bring them reinforcement in the future, they are working for an **incentive**. Incentives are never guaranteed: Students never know that they are going to get an A on a test when they study for it or that they are going to win a Halloween costume contest when they enter it. An incentive is an expected or hoped-for consequence, one that may or may not actually occur.

Students don't work for incentives they don't believe they can achieve. For example, in a classroom of thirty children, a class competition in which one prize will be awarded for the highest test score provides an incentive to just a handful of top achievers. An incentive is effective only if it is obtainable and if a student perceives it as such. Therefore, when we provide incentives for high achievement, we should make sure that students believe they can actually achieve at that level. We'll return to this point later in our discussion of *self-efficacy*.

Nonoccurrence of Expected Consequences

When, as a fourth grader, I entered the Halloween costume contest as a witch, I lost once again. (First prize went to a girl with a metal colander over her head. She was dressed as *Sputnik*, the first satellite launched into space by what was then the Soviet Union.) That was the last time I entered a Halloween contest. I had expected reinforcement and felt cheated because I didn't get it. Social

■ incentive Hoped-for, but not guaranteed, consequence of behavior.

Administering Consequences from a Social Cognitive Perspective

 Describe the specific behaviors you are reinforcing, so that students are aware of the response-reinforcement contingencies operating in the classroom.

A teacher tells his class, "Because everyone remained on task throughout the cooperative group activity this morning, we'll have ten minutes of free time just before lunch."

 Make sure students believe they can achieve the incentives offered in the classroom.

A teacher realizes that if she were to grade her students' science projects on a curve, only a few students could possibly get As. Instead, she gives her students a checklist of the specific criteria she will use to grade the science projects; she tells her class that any project meeting all the criteria will get an A.

 Tell students what behaviors are unacceptable in the classroom, and describe the consequences that will result when those behaviors occur.

A teacher reminds students that anyone seen pushing in the lunch line will go to the end of the line.

 Follow through with the reinforcements you have promised for desirable student behaviors; also follow through with the adverse consequences students expect for undesirable behaviors.

When announcing tryouts for an upcoming holiday play, a teacher tells students that only those who sign up ahead of time may try out. Although she later regrets making this statement—some of the most talented students don't sign up in time—she sticks to her word during tryout sessions and turns away anyone whose name does not appear on her sign-up sheet.

Remember that the consequences you administer for a particular student's behavior have a potential effect on any students who observe those consequences.

The student council president, even though she is well liked and highly respected by both students and teachers, is nevertheless punished in accordance with school policy when she is caught cheating on an exam.

---

cognitive theorists propose that the nonoccurrence of expected reinforcement is a form of punishment (e.g., Bandura, 1986). When people think that a certain response is going to be reinforced, yet the response is *not* reinforced, they are less likely to exhibit that response in the future.

Perhaps you can think of a time when you broke a rule, expecting to be punished, but got away with your crime. Or perhaps you can remember seeing someone else break a rule without being caught. When nothing bad happens after a forbidden behavior, people may actually feel as if they have been reinforced for the behavior. Just as the nonoccurrence of reinforcement is a form of punishment, the nonoccurrence of punishment is a form of reinforcement (Bandura, 1986).

When students work hard to achieve a desired end result—perhaps a compliment, high grade, or special privilege—and the anticipated result doesn't materialize, they will be unlikely to work as hard the next time. And when students break school rules yet are not punished for doing so, they are more likely to break those rules again. As teachers, it is important that we follow through with promised reinforcements for desirable student behaviors. It is equally important that we impose the consequences students have come to expect for undesirable behaviors. The Creating a Productive Classroom Environment feature "Administering Consequences from a Social Cognitive Perspective" illustrates this idea, along with several others I've presented in the preceding discussion.

As we have seen, students learn a great deal from observing those around them. But they don't necessarily copy everything they see other people do. What kinds of people are they most likely to imitate? And how can we help them acquire the behaviors and skills we demonstrate? We turn to such questions now.

MODELING

■ **live model** Individual whose behavior is observed "in the flesh."

■ **symbolic model** Real or fictional character portrayed in the media that influences an observer's behavior.

■ **modeling** Demonstrating a behavior for another, *or* observing and imitating another's behavior.

As human beings, we have some ability to imitate others almost from birth (Collie & Hayne, 1999; T. F. Field, Woodson, Greenberg, & Cohen, 1982). Many of the models from whom we learn are **live models**—real people that we observe doing something. But we are also influenced by **symbolic models**—real or fictional characters portrayed in books, in films, on television, and through various other media. For instance, students can learn valuable lessons from studying the behaviors of important figures in history or reading stories about people who accomplish great things in the face of adversity. Social cognitive theorists sometimes use the term **modeling** to describe what a model does (i.e., demonstrate a behavior) and at other times to describe what the observer does (i.e., imitate that behavior).

Potential models are everywhere, and research indicates that they can have a significant impact on the behaviors that children and adolescents acquire. Let's look at some examples.

Behaviors That Can Be Learned Through Modeling

Many behaviors are learned, at least in part, through modeling. For example, students

- Are better readers when their parents read often at home (R. D. Hess & McDevitt, 1989)
- Master new athletic skills more effectively when shown specific techniques for improving their performance (Kitsantas, Zimmerman, & Clearly, 2000; Zimmerman & Kitsantas, 1997)
- Better resist the enticements of a stranger when a peer has modeled resistance strategies (Poche, Yoder, & Miltenberger, 1988)
- Are less likely to tolerate racist statements when people around them refuse to tolerate such statements (Blanchard, Lilly, & Vaughn, 1991)
- Are more likely to violate traditional gender stereotypes—that is, to behave without regard to what is "appropriate" behavior for males and females—when they see others behaving in a nonstereotypical manner (B. E. Carlson, 1984; Hoffman, 1984; Ruble & Ruble, 1982; Selkow, 1984)

Considerable research has been conducted concerning the impact of models in three areas: academic skills, aggression, and morality.

Academic skills. Students learn many academic skills by seeing other people demonstrate them. For instance, they may learn how to solve long-division problems or write a cohesive composition partly by observing how their teachers and peers do these things (Braaksma, Rijlaarsdam, & van den Bergh, 2002; Sawyer, Graham, & Harris, 1992; Schunk & Hanson, 1985; Schunk & Swartz, 1993). In small groups with classmates, they may adopt one another's strategies for conducting discussions about literature, perhaps learning how to solicit one another's opinions ("What do you think, Jalisha?"), express agreement or disagreement ("I agree with Kordell because . . . "), and justify a point of view ("I think it shouldn't be allowed, because . . . ") (R. C. Anderson et al., 2001, pp. 14, 16, 25).

Often students learn academic skills more effectively when others demonstrate not only how to do something but also how to *think about* something—in other words, when others engage in **cognitive modeling** (Sawyer et al., 1992; Schunk, 1981, 1998; Schunk & Swartz, 1993). As an example, consider how a teacher might model the thinking processes involved in the long division problem in the margin:

> "First I have to decide what number to divide 4 into. I take 276, start on the left and move toward the right until I have a number the same as or larger than 4. Is 2 larger than 4? No. Is 27 larger than 4? Yes. So my first division will be 4 into 27. Now I need to multiply 4 by a number that will give an answer the same as or slightly smaller than 27. How about 5? $5 \times 4 = 20$. No, too small. Let's try 6. $6 \times 4 = 24$. Maybe. Let's try 7. $7 \times 4 = 28$. No, too large. So 6 is correct." (Schunk, 1998, p. 146)

$$4\overline{)276}$$

Cognitive modeling is one component of a *cognitive apprenticeship,* a strategy we considered in Chapter 2.

Aggression. Numerous research studies have indicated that children become more aggressive when they observe aggressive or violent models (Bandura, 1965; Goldstein, Arnold, Rosenberg, Stowe, & Ortiz, 2001; Guerra, Huesmann, & Spindler, 2003). Children learn aggression not only from live models but also from the symbolic models they see in films, on television, or in video games (C. A. Anderson et al., 2003). In fact, their imitations tend to take the same *forms* as the aggression they see (Bandura, Ross, & Ross, 1963; Mischel & Grusec, 1966). Boys in particular are apt to copy other people's aggressive behaviors (Bandura et al., 1963; Bushman & Anderson, 2001; Lowry, Sleet, Duncan, Powell, & Kolbe, 1995).

Morality. In Chapter 3, I suggested that exposing students to people who model moral and prosocial behavior can promote students' moral development. Many aspects of moral thinking and moral behavior—for example, more advanced moral judgments, sympathy, sharing, and generosity—are apparently influenced by observation and modeling (Friedrich and Stein, 1973; Huston, Watkins, & Kunkel, 1989; Prentice, 1972; Radke-Yarrow, Zahn-Waxler, & Chapman, 1983; Rushton, 1982). In one study (Rushton, 1980), children observed an adult playing a bowling game and reinforcing himself with tokens for high performance. Some children saw the

In the Bleachers
by Steve Moore

Not all the people in children's lives model desirable behaviors. A child is most apt to imitate undesirable behaviors that appear to have no adverse consequences and that seem to lead to reinforcement.

■ **cognitive modeling** Demonstrating how to think about as well as how to do a task.

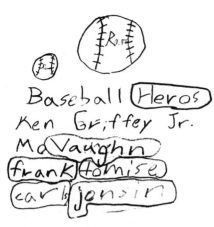

Professional athletes can be powerful role models. Here 8-year-old Tony identifies his "baseball heros."

adult donate half of his earned tokens to a poor boy named Bobby pictured on a poster in the room; other children observed the adult keep all of his winnings for himself despite the poster. The children then had the opportunity to play the game and reward themselves with tokens. The more tokens they earned, the better the prize they could puchase (thus, donating to Bobby meant that they would have to purchase a lesser prize for themselves). Children who had watched generous models were more likely to donate some of their own tokens to Bobby than were children who had watched selfish models. This difference was true not only in the initial experimental session but also in a follow-up session two months later.

What about situations in which a model preaches one set of moral values and practices another? Modeling clearly wins out over lecturing: When children hear a model say one thing and do something else, they are more likely to imitate what the model *does* than what the model *says* (J. H. Bryan, 1975). To be truly effective, then, models must practice what they preach.

How Modeling Affects Behavior

Social cognitive theorists (e.g., Bandura, 1977, 1986; T. L. Rosenthal & Zimmerman, 1978) propose that modeling has several possible effects on human behavior: observational learning, response facilitation, response inhibition, and response disinhibition.

The **observational learning effect** occurs when *the observer acquires a new behavior demonstrated by the model.* By seeing and hearing models, students learn how to dissect an earthworm, swim the elementary backstroke, and pronounce *¿Estudia usted español?* correctly. They may also acquire the political and religious beliefs they hear their parents advocate. And they may adopt the attitudes of their teachers—perhaps enthusiasm about baseball, curiosity about puzzling scientific phenomena, or fear of mathematics (e.g., Rushton, 1980).

The **response facilitation effect** occurs when *the observer displays a previously learned behavior more frequently after seeing a model being reinforced for the behavior* (i.e., after receiving vicarious reinforcement). As an example, consider this situation:

> Billy returns to school in September to discover that his expensive new jeans are no longer in style. All his classmates are now wearing old, well-worn jeans; those with holes in the knees are especially fashionable. When he arrives home after his first day of school, Billy digs through his dresser drawers and the family rag bag, looking for old jeans. The next day, much to his parents' dismay, Billy goes to school wearing a pair of jeans with one large hole in the left knee and a three-inch rip running up the right thigh. The brand new jeans that Billy's mother has purchased for him are relegated to the top shelf of his closet, where they remain for the rest of the school year.

Students are more likely to wear ragged old jeans if their classmates appear to be winning popularity with this attire. Similarly, they are more likely to complete reading assignments on time and to work cooperatively rather than competitively with classmates—behaviors they may have learned long ago—if they see others being reinforced for doing so.

The **response inhibition effect** occurs when *the observer displays a previously learned behavior less frequently after seeing a model being punished for that behavior* (i.e., after receiving vicarious punishment). Students tend to inhibit (*not* engage in) behaviors that result in adverse consequences for those around them. For example, students are less likely to be aggressive on the playground if they see their friends being punished for aggression. They are less likely to cheat on assignments if their peers are caught in the act. And they are less likely to volunteer to answer questions in class when classmates' incorrect answers are ridiculed.

The **response disinhibition effect** occurs when *the observer displays a previously forbidden or punished behavior more frequently after seeing a model exhibit the behavior without adverse consequences.* Although students will inhibit behaviors leading to punishment, they may begin to engage in behaviors they have previously inhibited if they observe those behaviors going unpunished for other people. For example, students are more likely to chew gum, copy homework from classmates, or fight in the corridors if they see other students getting away with such behaviors. Remember, the nonoccurrence of expected punishment is reinforcing, so naturally any forbidden activities that seem to have no adverse effects for others may easily increase.

Yet students don't always imitate the people around them. What factors determine when students are most likely to adopt the behaviors they see? A look at characteristics of effective models will help us with the answer.

■ **observational learning effect** Occurs when an observer acquires a new behavior after watching someone else do it.

■ **response facilitation effect** Occurs when an observer displays a previously learned behavior more frequently after seeing someone else reinforced for it.

■ **response inhibition effect** Occurs when an observer displays a previously learned behavior less frequently after seeing someone else punished for it.

■ **response disinhibition effect** Occurs when an observer displays a previously forbidden or punished behavior more frequently after seeing someone else do it without adverse consequences.

Characteristics of Effective Models

Experiencing FIRSTHAND ·Five People

Write down the names of five people whose behaviors you would like to imitate in some way. Then, beside each name, write one or more reasons why you admire these people.

· · · · · · ·

Social cognitive theorists have found some consistency in the types of models that others are likely to imitate (Bandura, 1986; T. L. Rosenthal & Bandura, 1978; Schunk, 1987). Effective models typically exhibit one or more of the following characteristics—characteristics that you probably see reflected in the list you just created.

Competence. Students will typically try to imitate people who do something well, not those who do it poorly. They will try to imitate the basketball skills of a professional basketball player, rather than those of the class klutz. They will copy the fashions of a popular classmate, rather than those of a social isolate. They will adopt the mathematical problem-solving procedures of teachers who clearly know what they are doing, rather than the procedures of teachers who make frequent mistakes at the chalkboard. Even preschoolers have some ability to discriminate between competent and incompetent models (Want & Harris, 2001). Figure 10.1 illustrates how one teacher effectively uses competent models to teach creative writing.

Prestige and power. Children and adolescents often imitate people who are famous or powerful. Some effective models—a world leader, a renowned athlete, a popular rock star—are famous at a national or international level. The prestige and power of other models—a head cheerleader, the captain of the high school hockey team, a gang leader—may be limited to a more local environment. For example, children are more likely to interact with students who have disabilities when they see popular classmates initiating such interactions (Sasso & Rude, 1987).

In addition to modeling desired behaviors ourselves, then, we should expose students to a variety of models that they are likely to view as prestigious and powerful. For example, we might invite respected professionals (e.g., police officer, nurse, newspaper reporter) to come to class and talk with students about topics within their areas of expertise. We might also have students read and learn about appropriate models through such media as books and films; for example, students might read Helen Keller's autobiography or watch news clips of Martin Luther King, Jr.

"Gender-appropriate" behavior. Remember Nathan's belief that French is a "girl" thing? Students are most likely to adopt behaviors they believe are appropriate for their gender. (Different students are, of course, apt to define *gender-appropriate* somewhat differently.) For example, many girls and boys limit their academic choices and career aspirations to the subjects and professions they believe are "for women" and "for men," respectively. Some girls may shy away from careers in mathematics as being too "masculine." Some boys may not take typing because they perceive it to be a secretarial skill, and most secretaries are women. Yet mathematics and keyboarding are useful skills for both genders. Exposure to numerous examples of people in so-called nontraditional careers—female mathematicians and engineers, male secretaries and nurses—can help broaden students' perceptions as to what behaviors are gender appropriate. In the process, such models can also broaden students' academic choices and possibly enhance their career aspirations.

Behavior relevant to the learner's own situation. Students are most likely to adopt behaviors they believe will help them in their own circumstances. A boy may wear the torn jeans that his popular classmates wear if he thinks he can become popular with such attire; however, he will have less reason to dress this way if he thinks his thick glasses and adolescent acne will prevent him from ever being popular regardless of his clothing. A teenage girl may be tempted to join her friends in drinking beer if she thinks that doing so will help her win their acceptance; she is less likely to indulge if she is the "designated driver" and knows that her friends are depending on her to stay sober.

FIGURE 10.1 Students in Barbara Dee's seventh-grade language arts class chose these examples of effective figurative writing from books they were reading. Such examples could then serve as models for students' own writing efforts.

"The blackness of the night came in, like snakes around the ankles."
—Caroline Cooney, *Wanted,* p. 176

"Flirtatious waves made passes at the primly pebbled beach."
—Lilian Jackson Braun, *The Cat Who Saw Stars,* p. 120

"Water boiled up white and frothy, like a milkshake."
—Lurlene McDaniel, *For Better, for Worse, Forever,* p. 60

"Solid rocket boosters suddenly belched forty-four million horsepower."
—Ben Mikaelsen, *Countdown,* p. 148

"I try to swallow the snowball in my throat."
—Laurie Halse Anderson, *Speak,* p. 72

**IN THE BLEACHERS
by Steve Moore**

"Don't cry, Megan. Remember, it's not whether Daddy wins the brawl in the stands that's important. It's how you played the game."

When we work with children, our actions will often speak louder than our words.

IN THE BLEACHERS © 2001 Steve Moore. Reprinted with permission of UNIVERSAL PRESS SYNDICATE. All rights reserved.

■ Is this point consistent with what you learned about human memory in Chapter 6? Why or why not?

In the classroom we will model a variety of behaviors throughout the day. But students will imitate what we do only if they believe that such behaviors will truly be useful and productive for them. Therefore, we must show them how the problem-solving methods we teach, the writing skills we demonstrate, and the physical fitness regimen we advocate are all applicable to their own situations.

Students are less likely to perceive the relevance of modeled behaviors when the model is different from them in some obvious way. For instance, students from cultures other than our own may think that some of the things we try to teach them don't apply to their own cultural circumstances. Similarly, students with disabilities may believe that they are incapable of accomplishing the things a nondisabled teacher demonstrates. So it is important that we include individuals from minority cultures and individuals with disabilities in the models we present to students. Minority students benefit from observing successful minority adults, and students with disabilities become more optimistic about their own futures when they meet adults successfully coping with and overcoming their own disabilities (Pang, 1995; L. E. Powers, Sowers, & Stevens, 1995).

You can probably think of teachers you've admired and wanted to be like. Most teachers have one or more characteristics of an effective model; for example, students typically view their teachers as being competent and having power, at least within the school environment. So as teachers, we "teach" not only by what we say but also by what we do. It is critical that we model appropriate behaviors and *not* model inappropriate ones. Do we model fairness to all students or favoritism to a small few? Do we model enthusiasm and excitement about the subject matter or merely tolerance for a dreary topic the class must muddle through? Do we expound on the virtues of innovation and creativity yet use the same curriculum materials year after year? Our actions often speak louder than our words.

Yet even when models are competent and prestigious and even when they exhibit behaviors that students think are appropriate for themselves as well, successful learning from models does not necessarily occur. What must students do to learn modeled behavior effectively? Let's find out.

Helping Students Learn from Models

According to social cognitive theorists (e.g., Bandura, 1986), four conditions are necessary before a student can successfully learn from observing modeled behavior: attention, retention, motor reproduction, and motivation.

Attention. In the opening case study, Nathan paid little attention to his French teacher. Yet to learn effectively, *the learner must pay attention to the model* and, in particular, to critical aspects of the modeled behavior. Before imitation is possible, our students must observe carefully as we show proper procedures in the science lab, watch closely as we demonstrate the elementary backstroke, or listen attentively as we pronounce *Comment allez-vous?*

Retention. After paying attention, *the learner must remember what the model does*. If you have already read the discussion of cognitive processes in Chapter 6, you know that students are more likely to remember information they have encoded in memory in more than one way—perhaps as both a visual image and a verbal representation. As teachers, then, we may often want to describe what we're doing as we demonstrate behaviors. We may also want to give descriptive labels to complex behaviors that might otherwise be difficult to remember (Gerst, 1971; T. L. Rosenthal, Alford, & Rasp, 1972). To illustrate, when teaching swimming, an easy way to help students remember the sequence of arm positions in the elementary backstroke is to teach them the labels *chicken*, *airplane*, and *soldier* (see Figure 10.2). It may be especially helpful for students to repeat such labels aloud as they copy a model's actions (R. L. Cohen, 1989; Mace, Belfiore, & Shea, 1989; Schunk, 1989c). As an example, consider the following set of self-instructions taught to students who are first learning a basic tennis stroke:

1. Say *ball* to remind yourself to look at the ball.
2. Say *bounce* to remind yourself to follow the ball with your eyes as it approaches you.
3. Say *hit* to remind yourself to focus on contacting the ball with the racket.
4. Say *ready* to get yourself into position for the next ball to come your way. (Ziegler, 1987)

Tennis students taught to give themselves these simple instructions—*ball*, *bounce*, *hit*, and *ready*—improve the accuracy of their returns more quickly than students not taught to do so (Ziegler, 1987).

Motor reproduction. In addition to attending and remembering, *the learner must be physically capable of reproducing the modeled behavior.* When a student lacks the ability to reproduce an observed behavior, motor reproduction obviously cannot occur. For example, first graders who watch a high school student throw a softball do not possess the muscular coordination to mimic the throw. High school students who haven't yet learned to roll their *R*s will have trouble repeating the Spanish teacher's tongue twister:

> Erre con erre cigarro, erre con erre barril.
> Rápido corren los carros del ferrocarril.

It will often be useful to have students imitate a desired behavior immediately after they watch us demonstrate it. When they do so, we can give them the feedback they need to improve their performance. Modeling accompanied by verbal guidance and frequent feedback—a technique sometimes known as *coaching*—is often more effective than modeling alone (S. N. Elliott & Busse, 1991; Kitsantas et al., 2000; Schunk & Swartz, 1993). When considering this approach, we must keep in mind a point made in Chapter 4: Students from some ethnic groups (e.g., many Native Americans) may prefer to practice new behaviors in private at first, showing us what they have learned only after they have achieved sufficient mastery.

Motivation. Finally, *the learner must be motivated to demonstrate the modeled behavior.* Some students may be eager to show what they have observed and remembered; for example, they may have seen the model reinforced for a certain behavior and so have already been vicariously reinforced. But other students may not have any motivation to demonstrate something they have seen a model do, perhaps because the model was punished or perhaps because they don't see the model's actions as being appropriate for themselves. In Chapters 11 and 12, we will identify numerous strategies for increasing students' motivation to exhibit desired behaviors.

When all four factors—attention, retention, motor reproduction, and motivation—are present, modeling can be an extremely powerful teaching technique (e.g., Kitsantas et al., 2000; Schloss & Smith, 1994; Schunk & Hanson, 1985). As an example, consider the following lesson.

"Chicken"   "Airplane"   "Soldier"

FIGURE 10.2 Students can often more easily remember a complex behavior, such as the arm movements for the elementary backstroke, when those behaviors have verbal labels.

Analyzing Teacher Strategies

Fielding a Ground Ball
In a recent educational psychology class, I asked my students to apply what they'd learned about learning to teach a topic or skill to an elementary or high school student. One student, Ryan Francoeur, then a starting player on the university's baseball team, taught his 8-year-old cousin Collin how to field a ground ball (i.e., one traveling low to the ground) in baseball. As you read the following excerpts from Ryan's report, think about

- Principles of social cognitive theory that Ryan put into practice
- Principles of other theories that Ryan applied

I began by . . . videotaping Collin fielding a series of ground balls hit by me. This was done before Collin had any instruction. . . . I videotaped an episode of "Baseball Tonight," which is on every night during the major league baseball season. I then edited the video and showed Collin parts of the video that I felt were good examples of how to properly field a ground ball. . . .

Next I modeled the steps to Collin on how to form the correct base for fielding the ground ball and the steps on receiving the hit ball. I slowly explained each and every step to Collin, and had him do each one for me and tell me why he was doing it after he did it. Collin did very well at this, and I think [his] telling me why he was doing each step helped him remember the steps. . . .

I found that my next step . . . worked very well with Collin, and definitely increased his performance. . . . I was presenting him with harder tasks, and he too felt that he was accomplishing something by me making each task harder . . . . First I allowed Collin to use his baseball glove while fielding the ball. . . . Next, I told Collin to take away his glove and just use his bare hands for fielding the ball. Not only did Collin do well at this step, but also I watched him as he fielded the ball with soft hands like he was catching an egg; this was encouraging because this is one of the steps I had explained to him earlier. The final task was for Collin to field the ball with a flat wooden board attached to his hand; this is extremely difficult even for good players since you cannot squeeze a glove or hand around the ball. Collin had some difficulty in getting used to this step, but with more practice he continued to improve. After doing all of these tasks, I then videotaped Collin taking another series of ground balls.

I finished my lesson by showing Collin three videotapes. First was the original videotape of Collin fielding ground balls, followed by the videotape of him fielding the balls after the lesson. We were both amazed at his improvement. . . . The final video I showed Collin was the video of "Baseball Tonight," which was the same one he had watched earlier. I pointed out to Collin the similarities in techniques between himself and the pro players, and he thought that this was very neat. I made sure that Collin also understood that he still had things he needed to work on, and that he could only improve with lots of practice. . . .

[Collin] liked it when I gave him analogies that he could relate to. He really liked the analogies of thinking of his arms, hands, and fingers as the jaw, mouth, and teeth of an alligator. . . . Also he liked the analogy of thinking of his belly button as a vacuum cleaner sucking up the ball and glove. . . . He especially liked it when I was comparing what he was doing with the pros; you could tell by his giggling that he thought it was pretty cool.

As you may have noticed, Ryan used competent and prestigious models (one live model—himself—and several symbolic models on the videotapes) to teach Collin how to field a ground ball. Furthermore, he made sure that all four conditions for successful modeling were met. First, he engaged Collin's *attention* with videotapes and one-on-one instruction on how to field a ground ball. Second, he helped Collin *retain* what he was learning by using vivid analogies (catching an egg, alligator jaws, vacuum cleaner) and asking Collin to explain why he was doing each step. Third, Ryan encouraged *motor reproduction* by adapting tasks to Collin's ability level and then gradually asking him to perform increasingly difficult tasks. Fourth, Ryan *motivated* Collin by making the lesson enjoyable and showing him how his skills were becoming more like those of professional players.

In teaching the lesson, Ryan borrowed from other theoretical perspectives as well. He borrowed from Vygotsky and other cognitive developmentalists when he gave Collin a challenging task (a task presumably within Collin's zone of proximal development) and gradually increased its difficulty as Collin became more proficient. He borrowed from cognitive psychology when he asked Collin to relate certain actions to things Collin already knew—for instance, "thinking of his belly button as a vacuum cleaner sucking up the ball and glove." And he borrowed from behaviorism when he gave Collin positive feedback—for instance, by showing Collin how much he had improved and pointing out ways in which his technique had become similar to that of the pros. As teachers, we are more likely to be effective when we apply a variety of theoretical perspectives in the classroom (recall our discussion about "Keeping an Open Mind About Theories of Learning" in Chapter 6).

As Ryan's lesson so aptly demonstrates, modeling doesn't just enhance students' performance. It can also boost their self-confidence that they can accomplish the things they observe skilled models accomplishing. For example, when a student from a low-income neighborhood meets someone from the same neighborhood who has succeeded at becoming a physician, and when a student with a physical disability meets an individual with cerebral palsy who is a top executive at the local bank, these students may begin to believe that they, too, are capable of such achievements. Students who believe in their own ability to succeed have high *self-efficacy*. We turn to this concept now.

SELF-EFFICACY

Experiencing FIRSTHAND ·Self-Appraisal

Take a moment to answer the following questions:

1. Do you believe you'll be able to understand and apply educational psychology by reading this textbook and thinking carefully about its content? Or do you believe you're going to have trouble with the material regardless of how much you study?

2. Do you think you could learn to execute a reasonable swan dive from a high diving board if you were shown how to do it and given time to practice? Or do you think you're such a klutz that no amount of training and practice would help?

3. Do you think you could walk barefoot over hot coals unscathed? Or do you think the soles of your feet would be burned to a crisp?

· · · · · · ·

People are more likely to engage in certain behaviors when they believe they will be able to execute those behaviors successfully—that is, when they have high self-efficacy (e.g., Bandura, 1997). For example, I hope you believe that with careful thought about what you read, you will be able to understand the ideas in this textbook; in other words, I hope you have high self-efficacy for learning educational psychology. You may or may not believe that with instruction and practice, you will eventually be able to perform a passable swan dive; in other words, you may have high or low self-efficacy about learning to dive. You are probably quite skeptical that you could ever walk barefoot over hot coals, so my guess is that you have low self-efficacy regarding this activity.

In general, **self-efficacy** is a person's self-constructed judgment about his or her ability to execute certain behaviors or reach certain goals. Self-efficacy is obviously a part of the *sense of self* described in Chapter 3. It may seem similar to the concept of *self-concept*, but important qualities distinguish the two (Bong & Skaalvik, 2003; Pajares & Schunk, 2002; Pietsch, Walker, & Chapman, 2003). When theorists talk about self-concept, they are typically describing a fairly general self-view that may include both judgments and feelings (e.g., "Am I a good student?" "Do I feel good about my academic achievements?"). In contrast, self-efficacy is more situation-specific and involves judgments (rather than feelings) almost exclusively (e.g., "Can I master long division?"). Quite possibly, children's self-efficacy for various tasks and subject areas contributes to the development of their overall self-concept over time (Bong & Skaalvik, 2003).

Most 4- to 6-year-olds are quite confident about their ability to perform various tasks; in fact, they often overestimate what they are capable of doing (Butler, 1990; Eccles et al., 1998; Nicholls, 1979). As they move through the elementary grades, however, they can better recall their past successes and failures, and they become increasingly aware of how their performance compares with that of their peers (Eccles et al., 1998; Feld, Ruhland, & Gold, 1979). Presumably as a result of these changes, they become less confident, though usually more realistic, about what they can and cannot do (Bandura, 1986).

Ideally, it is probably best for students to slightly *over*rate their competence; by doing so, they are more likely to try challenging tasks that help them develop new skills and abilities (Assor & Connell, 1992; Bandura, 1997). But sometimes students (girls especially) *under*estimate their chances of success, perhaps because of a few bad experiences (D. A. Cole et al., 1999; D. Phillips & Zimmerman, 1990). For example, a girl who gets a C in science from a teacher with exceptionally strict grading criteria may erroneously believe that she is "no good" in science. A new boy at school whose attempts at being friendly are rejected by two or three thoughtless classmates may erroneously believe that "no one likes me."

A student must believe that she has the ability to make friends before she will actually try to make them (e.g., Patrick, Anderman, & Ryan, 2002).

How Self-Efficacy Affects Behavior and Cognition

Students' sense of self-efficacy affects their choice of activities, their goals, and their effort and persistence in classroom activities. Ultimately, then, it also affects their learning and achievement (Bandura, 1982, 2000; Schunk, 1989c; Zimmerman, Bandura, & Martinez-Pons, 1992).

Choice of activities. Imagine yourself on registration day, perusing the hundreds of courses in the semester schedule. You fill most of your schedule with required courses, but you have room for an elective. Only two courses are offered at the time slot you have open. Do you sign up for Advanced Psychoceramics, a challenging seminar taught by the famous Dr. Josiah S. Carberry? Or do you sign up for an English literature course known across campus as being an "easy A"? Perhaps you find the term *psychoceramics* a bit intimidating, and you think you can't possibly pass such a course, especially if Dr. Carberry is as grouchy and demanding as everyone claims. So you settle for the literature course, knowing it is one in which you can succeed.

People tend to choose tasks and activities at which they believe they can succeed and to avoid those at which they think they will fail. Students who believe they can win a role in the school musical are more likely to try out than students with little faith in their acting or singing ability.

■ **self-efficacy** Belief that one is capable of executing certain behaviors or reaching certain goals.

■ Observe Claudia's high self-efficacy for math in the "Motivation: Early Adolescence" clip on Video CD 1.

■ Such effort and persistence reflect the *intrinsic motivation* of students with high self-efficacy (more about this concept in Chapters 11 and 12).

Students who believe they can succeed at mathematics are more likely to take math courses than students who believe they are mathematically incompetent. In the "Motivation: Early Adolescence" clip on Video CD 1, 12-year-old Claudia offers a simple yet powerful reason why she likes math: "I'm good at it."

Goals. People set higher goals for themselves when they have high self-efficacy in a particular domain. For instance, adolescents' choices of careers and occupational levels reflect subject areas in which they have high rather than low self-efficacy (Bandura et al., 2001). Their choices are often consistent with traditional gender stereotypes: Boys are more likely to have high self-efficacy for, and so aspire to careers in, science and technology, whereas girls are more likely to have high self-efficacy for, and so choose, careers in education, health, and social services (Bandura et al., 2001).

Effort and persistence. Think back once again to our case study of Nathan. As you may recall, Nathan was convinced he couldn't learn French. Because of his low self-efficacy, he gave up quickly on French homework assignments whenever he encountered something he didn't understand.

Students with a high sense of self-efficacy are more likely to exert effort when attempting a new task. They are also more likely to persist (to "try, try again") when they confront obstacles to their success. In contrast, students with low self-efficacy about a task will put in little effort and give up quickly in the face of difficulty.

Learning and achievement. Students with high self-efficacy tend to learn and achieve more than students with low self-efficacy even when actual ability levels are the same (Bandura, 1986; Eccles, Wigfield, et al., 1989; Klassen, 2002). In other words, when several students have equal ability, those students who *believe* they can do a task are more likely to accomplish it successfully than those who believe they are incapable of success. Students with high self-efficacy may achieve at superior levels partly because they engage in cognitive processes that promote learning—paying attention, organizing, elaborating, and so on (Bong & Skaalvik, 2003; Pintrich & Schunk, 2002). As teachers, then, we should do whatever we can to enhance our students' beliefs that they can succeed at school tasks.

Factors in the Development of Self-Efficacy

According to social cognitive theorists (e.g., Bandura, 1986, 1997; Schunk, 1989a; Schunk, Hanson, & Cox, 1987), several factors affect the development of self-efficacy, including a person's previous successes and failures, the messages that other people communicate, the successes and failures of others, and the successes and failures of the group as a whole.

Previous Successes and Failures   Students feel more confident that they can succeed at a task—that is, they have higher self-efficacy—when they have succeeded at that task or similar ones in the past (Bandura, 1986; Valentine et al., 2002). For example, Edward is more likely to believe he can learn to divide fractions if he has already mastered the process of multiplying fractions. Elena will be more confident about her ability to play field hockey if she has already developed skills in soccer. One important strategy for promoting students' self-efficacy, then, is to help them be successful in various content domains—for instance, by teaching important basic skills to mastery and by providing the necessary instructional support that enables students to make noticeable progress on difficult and complex tasks.

We find developmental differences in *how far back* students look when they consider their prior successes and failures. Perhaps because of more limited cognitive abilities, children in the early elementary grades typically recall only their most recent experiences when judging their competence to perform a particular activity; in contrast, older children and adolescents are apt to consider a long-term pattern of successes and failures (Eccles et al., 1998). We can help students of all ages develop high self-efficacy by showing them in a concrete way—for instance, by comparing earlier work samples with their current efforts—just how much they've improved over time (R. Butler, 1998a). We can also show them how their successes are the result of their own hard work and so hardly a fluke (Pintrich & Schunk, 2002).

Once students have developed a high sense of self-efficacy, an occasional failure is unlikely to dampen their optimism much. In fact, when these students encounter small setbacks on the way to achieving success, they learn that sustained effort and perseverance are key ingredients of that success; in other words, they develop **resilient self-efficacy** (Bandura, 1989). When students *consistently* fail at an activity, however, they tend to have little confidence about their ability to succeed at the activity in the future. For instance, students with learning disabilities, who may

■ **resilient self-efficacy** Belief that one can perform a task successfully even after experiencing setbacks.

have encountered failure after failure in classroom activities, often have low self-efficacy for mastering school subject matter (Schunk, 1989c).

Messages from Others   We can certainly enhance students' self-efficacy by pointing out their previous successes in a content domain. The certificate in Figure 10.3 reminds 5-year-old Anthony about the swimming skills he has mastered. Similarly, in the "Author's Chair" clip on Video CD 2, a second-grade teacher points out particular strengths in a short story written by a student named Liz. For instance, she says, "I could just *see* Liz hitting that pie thing in her face. Very well said."

We may also be able to boost students' self-efficacy by giving them reasons to believe they can be successful in the future (e.g. Zeldin & Pajares, 2000). Statements such as "You can do this problem if you work at it" or "I bet Judy will play with you if you just ask her" do give students a slight boost in self-confidence. The effects of our optimistic messages will be short-lived, however, unless students' efforts at a task ultimately meet with success (Schunk, 1989a).

Sometimes the messages we give students are implied rather than directly stated, yet such messages can have just as much of an effect on self-efficacy. For example, by giving constructive criticism about how to improve a poorly written research paper—criticism that indirectly communicates the message that "I know that you can do better, and here are some suggestions how"—we can enhance students' self-confidence about writing such research papers (Parsons, Kaczala, & Meece, 1982; Pintrich & Schunk, 2002). In some cases we communicate our beliefs about students' competence through our actions rather than our words. For example, if we give struggling students more assistance than they really need, we may inadvertently communicate the message that "I don't think you can do this on your own" (Schunk, 1989b).

Successes and Failures of Others   We often form opinions about our own abilities by observing the successes and failures of other people, especially those similar to ourselves (Eccles et al., 1998; Zeldin & Pajares, 2000). For example, you are more likely to enroll in Dr. Carberry's Advanced Psychoceramics class if several of your friends have done well in the course. After all, if they can do it, so can you. But if your friends in the course have been dropping like flies, then (like Nathan in the opening case study) you may suspect that your own chances of succeeding are pretty slim.

In much the same way, students often consider the successes and failures of their classmates, especially those of similar ability, when appraising their own chances of success. So we can enhance students' self-efficacy—and so enhance their willingness to attempt challenging classroom material—by pointing out that others like themselves have mastered it (Schunk, 1983b, 1989c). For example, a class of chemistry students horrified about the number of chemical symbols they must learn can perhaps be reassured with a statement such as this: "I know it seems like a lot to learn in such a short amount of time. My students last year thought so too, but they found that they could learn the symbols within three weeks if they studied a few new symbols each day."

When students actually *see* others of similar age and ability successfully reaching a goal, they are especially likely to believe that they, too, can achieve that goal. Hence, students sometimes develop greater self-efficacy when they see a fellow student model a behavior than when they see their teacher model the behavior. For example, in one study (Schunk & Hanson, 1985), elementary school children having trouble with subtraction were given 25 subtraction problems to complete. Children who had seen another student successfully complete the problems got an average of 19 correct, whereas those who saw a teacher complete the problems got only 13 correct, and those who saw no model at all solved only 8!

So another way to enhance students' self-efficacy for academic tasks is to have them observe their peers—ideally, peers similar to themselves in ability—successfully accomplishing those tasks. It may be especially beneficial for students to see one or more peers struggling with a task or problem at first (as they themselves are likely to do) and then eventually mastering it (Braaksma et al., 2002; Kitsantas et al., 2000; Schunk et al., 1987; Schunk & Zimmerman, 1997).

Successes and Failures of the Group as a Whole   In Chapter 5 we noted that students can often think more intelligently when they work together rather than alone (recall our discussion of

■ Observe efficacy-enhancing feedback in the "Author's Chair" clip on Video CD 2.

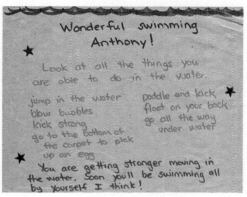

FIGURE 10.3 In this "certificate," a swimming teacher reminds 5-year-old Anthony of the skills he has recently mastered and gives him cause for optimism about swimming by himself.

■ What factors in Nathan's situation may have contributed to his low self-efficacy for learning French?

Enhancing Students' Self-Efficacy

 Teach basic knowledge and skills to mastery.

A biology teacher makes sure all students clearly understand the basic structure of DNA before moving to mitosis and meiosis, two topics that require a knowledge of DNA's structure.

 Help students make noticeable progress on complex skills.

In November a creative writing teacher shows students samples of their work from September and points out ways in which each student has improved over the two-month period.

Present some tasks at which students can succeed only with effort and perseverance.

A physical education teacher tells her students, "Today we've determined how far each of you can go in the broad jump. We will continue to practice the broad jump a little bit every week. Let's see if each one of you can jump at least two inches farther when I test you again at the end of the month."

 Assure students that they can be successful, and remind them that others like themselves have succeeded before them.

Students in beginning band express frustration about learning to play their instruments. Their teacher reminds them that students in last year's beginning band—like themselves—started out with little knowledge but eventually mastered their instruments.

 Have students see successful peer models.

The students in beginning band class hear the school's advanced band (last year's beginning band class) play a medley from the Broadway musical *Cats*.

 Assign large, complex tasks as small-group activities.

A fifth-grade teacher has students work in groups of three or four to write research papers about early colonial life in North America. The teacher makes sure that the students in each group collectively have the skills in library research, writing, word processing, and art necessary to complete the task. She also makes sure that every student has some unique skills to contribute to the group effort.

■ Think of a recent situation in which you had especially high or low self-efficacy. Which of the four factors just described affected your self-confidence in that situation?

distributed intelligence), and in Chapter 7 we noted that students who participate in group discussions often gain a more complex understanding of a topic than they might otherwise acquire (recall our discussion of joint meaning-making). Cooperation and collaboration have another benefit as well: Students may have greater self-efficacy when they work in a group than when they work alone. Such **collective self-efficacy** depends not only on students' perceptions of their own and others' capabilities but also on their perceptions of how effectively they can work together and coordinate their roles and responsibilities (Bandura, 1997, 2000).

The concept of collective self-efficacy is fairly new, and research to date has focused largely on adults (Bandura, 1997; Goddard, 2001; Tschannen-Moran, Woolfolk Hoy, & Hoy, 1998). Yet we can reasonably assume that students are apt to have higher self-efficacy when they work in groups, provided that those groups function smoothly and effectively. We will consider strategies for fostering effective group work in our discussion of cooperative learning in Chapter 13.

Fostering High Self-Efficacy

In the preceding discussion of factors affecting self-efficacy, we identified a number of strategies for bolstering students' beliefs about their capabilities. The Into the Classroom feature "Enhancing Students' Self-Efficacy" illustrates each of these strategies. Following are additional strategies to keep in mind:

◎ *Provide competence-promoting feedback.* As we noted in Chapter 9, positive feedback is often an effective reinforcer for students. Positive feedback tends to be most effective when it conveys the message that students have the ability to perform a task successfully and so enhances their self-efficacy. In fact, even negative feedback can promote high self-efficacy if it tells students how they can improve their performance and communicates confidence that improvement is likely (Deci & Ryan, 1985; Pintrich & Schunk, 2002). Following are examples of negative feedback that might positively influence student motivation:

- "I can see from the past few homework assignments that you're having trouble with long division. I think I know what the problem is. Here, let me show you what you need to do differently."

- "In the first draft of your research paper, many of your paragraphs don't lead logically to the ones that follow. A few headings and transitional sentences would make a world of difference. Let's find a time to discuss how you might use these techniques to improve the flow of your paper."

■ **collective self-efficacy** People's beliefs about their ability to be successful when they work together on a task.

- "Your time in the 100-meter dash was not as fast as it could be. It's early in the season, though, and if you work on your endurance, I know you'll improve. Also, I think you might get a faster start if you stay low when you first come out of the starting blocks."

◎ *Promote mastery on challenging tasks.* In Chapter 2 we discovered that challenging activities promote cognitive development, in part by encouraging students to stretch their existing abilities. But in addition, mastering challenges can greatly enhance students' self-efficacy. We must, of course, tailor the level of challenge to students' current self-efficacy levels: Students who have little or no confidence in their ability to perform in a particular domain may initially respond more favorably when we give them tasks at which they will probably do well (Stipek, 1996). Furthermore, the school day shouldn't necessarily be one challenge after another. Such a state of affairs would be absolutely exhausting, and probably quite discouraging as well. Instead, we should strike a balance between easy tasks, which will boost students' self-confidence over the short run, and the challenging tasks so critical for a long-term sense of high self-efficacy (Spaulding, 1992; Stipek, 1993, 1996).

◎ *Define success in terms of improvement or task accomplishment, rather than in terms of performance relative to others.* When students see classmates who are similar to themselves being successful, they have reason to be optimistic about their own success. But *defining* success in comparative terms—for instance, identifying the "best" writer, science student, or oboe player—is another matter altogether. Doing so sets up a competitive situation in which most students must inevitably lose (Deci & Ryan, 1992; Shih & Alexander, 2000; Stipek, 1996). Furthermore, some students (e.g., those from some Native American communities) may resist competitive activities if they believe their own successes will contribute to their classmates' failures (Grant & Gomez, 2001).

Most students will have higher self-efficacy and achieve at higher levels if we encourage them to define success in terms of task accomplishment or improvement over time, rather than in terms of how they stack up against others (Covington, 1992; Graham & Golen, 1991). One way to help them focus on their own progress is to minimize their awareness of classmates' performance levels. For example, we can use absolute rather than comparative criteria to assess their work (awarding high grades to all students who meet those criteria rather than grading on a curve), keep performance on assignments confidential, and give feedback in private. Second, we can provide opportunities for students to assess their own performance and monitor their improvement over time. For example, in the "Portfolio" clip on Video CD 1, 8-year-old Keenan and her teacher identify several ways in which Keenan's writing has improved over the past year.

As we focus students' attention on their improving knowledge and skills, we must remember that they may sometimes expect overnight success in areas that realistically require hard work over the course of several months or years. In such instances we may need to provide concrete mechanisms that highlight smaller, day-to-day improvements—for example, by giving students progress charts they can fill in themselves (e.g., see Figure 10.4) and providing frequent verbal or written feedback about the "little things" students are doing well. Veteran teacher Frances Hawkins recalls an incident in which she had been helping 7-year-old Dorothy and her classmates learn to weave on small, circular looms. Dorothy was distressed about all the mistakes she had made at the beginning of the project, but Hawkins helped her put the mistakes in perspective:

> [S]he was in tears, holding her now-finished small round weaving. Sorrow poured out: "Look," she said, tears falling, pointing to the pink and blue and yellow weaving, "It's so bad where I began. I didn't know how. Can I take it out and do it right like the last part?"
> In spite of early mistakes, the weaving was quite lovely. These circular looms absorb mistakes. . . . I had an idea: "Look, Dorothy, this is the history, your own history, of learning to weave. You can look at this and say, 'Why, I can see how I began, here I didn't know how very well, I went over two instead of one; but I learned, and then—it is perfect all the way to the end!' Now turn it over and do another." Dorothy thought about this. The tears stopped, and slowly she walked back to her group of weavers, still properly intent on her first weaving. The next visit she brought me an elegant and flawless circle in different shades of pink, with novelty yarns—some nubby, some plain—all done without consulting me! (Hawkins, 1997, p. 332)

◎ *Be sure errors occur within an overall context of success.* At one time, many educators argued that students should never be allowed to fail. But whether we like it or not, occasional

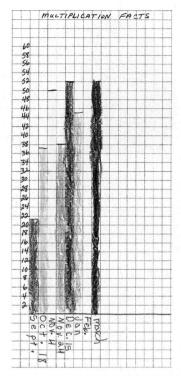

FIGURE 10.4 Nine-year-old Sophie has been charting her monthly progress in remembering multiplication facts. Although she has had minor setbacks, her general progress is upward. (She was absent for February's assessment.)

■ Observe the focus on improvement in the "Portfolio" clip on Video CD 1.

As students master difficult tasks, their self-efficacy increases, and they may become eager to take on additional challenges.

failures are a normal, inevitable, and often beneficial part of the learning process, and students need to learn to take them in stride. When students never make mistakes, we can reasonably assume they are not being challenged by the tasks we are assigning. Furthermore, students unaccustomed to failure in their school curriculum have difficulty coping with failure when they eventually do encounter it (Dweck, 2000).

Yet when students encounter failure *too* frequently, they develop low self-efficacy, believing that nothing they do will produce positive results. Ideally, then, students should experience occasional failure within the context of overall success. This way, they learn that they *can* succeed if they try, and they also develop a realistic attitude about failure—that it at worst is a temporary setback and at best can give them useful information about how to improve their performance.

An additional way to enhance students' self-efficacy is to have high self-efficacy *ourselves.* Let's take a minute to consider why teacher self-efficacy makes a difference.

Teacher Self-Efficacy

Not only should our students have high self-efficacy about their ability to succeed in the classroom, but so, too, should we, as teachers, have high self-efficacy about our ability to *help* them succeed. As noted in Chapter 1, students are more likely to achieve at high levels when their teachers have confidence that they can help students master classroom topics (Ashton, 1985; J. A. Langer, 2000; Tschannen-Moran et al., 1998). Some of this teacher confidence may take the form of *collective* self-efficacy: When teachers at a school believe that, as a group, they can make a significant difference in the lives of their students, students have higher self-efficacy themselves and achieve at higher levels (Goddard, 2001; Goddard, Hoy, & Woolfolk Hoy, 2000; Tschannen-Moran et al., 1998).

When teachers have high self-efficacy about their effectiveness in the classroom, they influence students' achievement in several ways:

- They are more willing to experiment with new ideas and teaching strategies that can better help students learn.
- They have higher expectations regarding, and set higher goals for, students' performance.
- They put more effort into their teaching and are more persistent in helping students learn. (Bandura, 1997; Roeser, Marachi, & Gehlbach, 2002; Tschannen-Moran et al., 1998)

These effects should look familiar: Just as self-efficacy affects students' choice of activities, goals, effort, and persistence, so, too, does it affect *teachers'* choices, goals, effort, and persistence.

Teachers' self-efficacy and expectations for students are, in part, the result of the explanations, or *attributions,* teachers have for students' successes and failures. We'll look at the nature of such attributions in Chapter 12.

Up to this point we've been assuming that teachers call most of the shots in the classroom. Certainly teachers play a critical role in helping students learn—for instance, by teaching, modeling, and reinforcing desired behaviors. But to be truly effective learners over the long run, students must eventually learn to direct and regulate their *own* learning and behavior. We turn to this process of self-regulation now.

SELF-REGULATION

Experiencing FIRSTHAND · · · · · · · · · · · · · · · · · ·Self-Reflection About Self-Regulation

In each of the following situations, choose the alternative that most accurately describes your attitudes and behavior as a college student. No one will see your answers except you, so be honest!

1. In terms of my final course grades, I am trying very hard to:
   a. Earn all As.
   b. Earn all As and Bs.
   c. Keep my overall grade point average at or above the minimally acceptable level at my college.
2. As I am reading or studying a textbook:
   a. I often notice when my attention is wandering, and I immediately get my mind back on my work.
   b. I sometimes notice when my attention is wandering, but not always.
   c. I often get so lost in daydreams that I waste a lot of time.

3. Whenever I finish a study session:
   a. I write down how much time I have spent on my schoolwork.
   b. I make a mental note of how much time I have spent on my schoolwork.
   c. I don't really think much about the time I have spent.
4. When I turn in an assignment:
   a. I usually have a good idea of the grade I will get on it.
   b. I am often surprised by the grade I get.
   c. I don't think much about the quality of what I have done.
5. When I do exceptionally well on an assignment:
   a. I feel good about my performance and might reward myself in some way.
   b. I feel good about my performance but don't do anything special for myself afterward.
   c. I don't feel much differently than I had before I received my grade.

. . . .

The standards we set for ourselves, the ways in which we monitor and evaluate our own cognitive processes and behaviors, and the consequences we impose on ourselves for our successes and failures are all aspects of **self-regulation**. If our thoughts and actions are under our *own* control, rather than being controlled by the people and circumstances around us, we are self-regulating individuals (Zimmerman, 1998).

Ideally, students should become increasingly self-regulating as they grow older, and in fact many of them do (see Table 10.2). Through both direct and vicarious reinforcement and punishment, growing children gradually learn which behaviors are and are not acceptable to the people around them. Eventually, they develop their *own* ideas about appropriate and inappropriate behavior, and they choose their actions accordingly. Once they reach adulthood and leave the relatively structured and protective environments of home and school, they will make most of their own decisions about what they should accomplish and how they should behave. Ultimately, we want them to make wise choices that enable them to achieve their goals and make productive contributions to society.

In the pages that follow, we will identify some of the things learners do when they engage in *self-regulated behavior*. We will then use what we have learned to consider how we might promote *self-regulated learning* and *self-regulated problem solving*.

Self-Regulated Behavior

By observing how our environment reacts when we behave in particular ways—by discovering that some behaviors are reinforced and others are punished or otherwise discouraged—we begin to distinguish between desirable and undesirable responses. As we develop an understanding about which responses are appropriate (for ourselves, at least) and which are not, we begin to control and monitor our own behavior (Bandura, 1986). We find several examples of such **self-regulated behavior** in the three "Emotions" clips on Video CD 1. Ten-year-old Daniel, 13-year-old Crystal, and 15-year-old Greg describe several strategies—reading a book, playing a video game, venting frustrations on someone who will listen without being judgmental, or just sitting down for a while—that they might use to help themselves calm down when they get overly excited, angry, or sad.

Five aspects of self-regulated behavior are presented in Figure 10.5. Let's look at the nature and potential implications of each one.

Self-Determined Standards and Goals As human beings, we tend to set standards for our own behavior; in other words, we determine criteria for evaluating our performance. We also establish certain goals that we value and toward which we direct many of our behaviors. Meeting our standards and reaching our goals give us considerable self-satisfaction, enhancing our self-efficacy and spurring us on to greater heights (Bandura, 1986, 1989).

Different students will inevitably adopt different standards and goals for themselves. For example, Robert may be striving for a report card with straight As, whereas Richard is content with Cs. Rebecca may be seeking out many friends of both sexes, whereas Rachel believes that a single, steady boyfriend is the best companion. To some extent, students' standards and goals are modeled after those they see other people adopt (Bandura, 1986; Locke & Latham, 1990). For

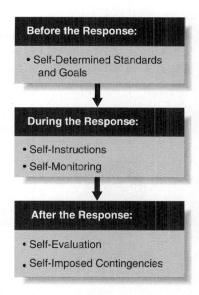

Before the Response:
- Self-Determined Standards and Goals

During the Response:
- Self-Instructions
- Self-Monitoring

After the Response:
- Self-Evaluation
- Self-Imposed Contingencies

FIGURE 10.5 Components of self-regulated behavior

■ Observe self-regulation strategies in the three "Emotions" clips on Video CD 1.

■ **self-regulation** Process of setting goals for oneself and engaging in behaviors and cognitive processes that lead to goal completion.

■ **self-regulated behavior** Self-chosen behavior that leads to the fulfillment of personally chosen standards and goals.

TABLE 10.2

Self-Regulation at Different Grade Levels

GRADE LEVEL	AGE-TYPICAL CHARACTERISTICS	SUGGESTED STRATEGIES
K–2	• Internalization of adults' standards for behavior • Emerging ability to set self-chosen goals for learning and achievement • Use of self-talk to guide behavior • Some self-evaluation of effectiveness and appropriateness of actions; feelings of guilt about wrongdoings • Individual differences in self-control of impulses, emotions, and attention; amount of self-control in these areas affects peer relationships and classroom performance	• Discuss rationales for classroom rules. • Show students how some behaviors can help them reach their goals and how other behaviors interfere with goal attainment. • Organize the classroom so that students can carry out some activities on their own (e.g., have reading centers where children can listen to storybooks on tape). • Give students some leeway to solve minor interpersonal problems on their own; intervene if problems escalate. • When students show impulsiveness or poor emotional control, provide consistent guidelines and consequences for behavior.
3–5	• Improving ability to assess own performance and progress • Guilt and shame about unsatisfactory performance and moral transgressions • Emerging self-regulated learning strategies (e.g., conscious attempts to focus attention, ability to do short assignments independently at home) • Difficulties with self-control for some students with cognitive or behavioral disabilities	• Encourage students to assess their own performance; provide criteria they can use to evaluate their work. • Ask students to engage in simple, self-regulated learning tasks (e.g., small-group learning activities, homework assignments); give suggestions about how to accomplish these tasks successfully. • Encourage students to use their peers as resources. • If students have continuing difficulty with self-control, teach self-instructions that can help them control their behavior.
6–8	• Increasing ability to plan future actions, due in part to increased capacity for abstract thought • Increasing mastery of some self-regulated learning strategies, especially those that involve overt behaviors (e.g., keeping a calendar of assignments and due dates) • Self-motivational strategies (e.g., minimizing distractions, devising ways to make a boring task more interesting and enjoyable, reminding oneself about the importance of doing well)	• Assign homework and other tasks that require independent learning. • Provide concrete strategies for keeping track of learning tasks and assignments (e.g., provide monthly calendars in which students can write due dates). • Provide concrete guidance about how to learn and study effectively (e.g., give students questions that they should answer as they complete reading assignments at home). • Give students frequent opportunities to assess their own learning; have them compare your evaluations with their own.
9–12	• More long-range goal setting • Increasing mastery of internal (cognitive) learning strategies (e.g., intentional elaboration, comprehension monitoring) • Wide variation in ability to self-regulate learning (many low-achieving high school students have few if any self-regulatory learning strategies)	• Relate classroom learning tasks to students' long-range personal and professional goals. • Don't assume that all students are metacognitively sophisticated; describe and model effective cognitive strategies for reading, learning, and studying. • Assign complex independent learning tasks, providing the necessary structure and guidance for students who are not yet self-regulated learners.

Sources: Blair, 2002; Bronson, 2000; Damon, 1988; Eccles, et al., 1998; Kochanska et al., 2002; Meichenbaum & Goodman, 1971; S. D. Miller, Heafner, Massey, & Strahan, 2003; Paris & Paris, 2001; Wolters & Rosenthal, 2000.

■ Students from low-income families typically set low goals for themselves in terms of career aspirations (Durkin, 1995). Can you explain this fact in light of the discussion here?

example, at the high school I attended, many students wanted to go to the best college or university they possibly could; in such an environment, others began to share the same academic aspirations. But at a different high school, getting a job after graduation (or perhaps *instead* of graduation) might be the aspiration more commonly modeled by a student's classmates.

Students are typically more motivated to work toward goals—and thus more likely to accomplish them—when they have set those goals for themselves, rather than when others have imposed goals on them (M. E. Ford, 1992; Spaulding, 1992). So one way we can help students develop self-regulation is to provide situations in which they set their own goals. For example, we might ask them to decide how many addition facts they are going to learn by Friday, determine the topic they wish to study for a research project, or identify the particular gymnastic skills they would like to master.

Ideally, we should encourage students to establish standards and goals that are challenging yet realistic. When students have standards and goals that are too low—for instance, when intelligent students are content getting Cs on classroom assignments—then they will not achieve at maximal levels. In contrast, when students' standards are too high—for example, when they are satisfied only if every grade is 100 percent—then they are doomed to frequent failure and equally frequent self-recrimination. Such students may become excessively anxious or depressed when they can't achieve the impossible goals they have set for themselves (Bandura, 1986; Covington, 1992).

To promote productive goal setting, we can show our students that challenging goals are attainable, perhaps by describing individuals of similar ability who have attained them with reasonable effort. In some situations we might even want to provide incentives that encourage students to set and achieve challenging goals (Stipek, 1996). At the same time, we must help any overly ambitious students understand and accept the fact that no one is perfect and that an occasional failure is nothing to be ashamed of.

■ Self-selected goals promote a greater sense of *self-determination*, a topic we will consider in Chapter 12.

Self-Instructions   Consider the formerly "forgetful" student who, before leaving the house each morning, now asks herself, "Do I have everything I need for my classes? I have my math homework for period 1, my history book for period 2, my change of clothes for gym during period 3. . . ." And consider the once impulsive student who now pauses before beginning a new assignment and says to himself, "OK, what am I supposed to do? Let's see . . . I need to read the directions first. What do the directions tell me to do?" And consider, as well, the formerly aggressive student who has learned to count to ten every time she gets angry—an action that gives her a chance to cool off.

Sometimes students simply need a reminder about how to respond in particular situations. By teaching students how to talk themselves through these situations using **self-instructions**, we provide them with a means through which *they remind themselves* about appropriate actions, thereby helping them to control their own behavior. Such a strategy is often effective for students who otherwise seem to behave without thinking (Casey & Burton, 1982; Meichenbaum, 1985).

One effective way of teaching students to give themselves instructions involves five steps (Meichenbaum, 1977):

1. *Cognitive modeling.* The teacher models self-instruction by repeating instructions aloud while simultaneously performing the activity.
2. *Overt, external guidance.* The teacher repeats the instructions aloud while the student performs the activity.
3. *Overt self-guidance.* The student repeats the instructions aloud while performing the activity.
4. *Faded, overt self-guidance.* The student whispers the instructions while performing the activity.
5. *Covert self-instruction.* The student silently thinks about the instructions while performing the activity.

■ Can you relate steps 3, 4, and 5 to Vygotsky's notions of *self-talk* and *inner speech* (Chapter 2)?

As you can see, the teacher initially serves as a model not only for the behavior itself but also for self-instructions. Responsibility for performing the activity *and* for guidance about how to perform the task is gradually turned over to the student.

Through these five steps, impulsive elementary school children can effectively learn to slow themselves down and think through what they are doing (Meichenbaum & Goodman, 1971). For example, notice how one formerly impulsive student was able to talk his way through a matching task in which he needed to find two identical pictures among several very similar ones:

> I have to remember to go slowly to get it right. Look carefully at this one, now look at these carefully. Is this one different? Yes, it has an extra leaf. Good, I can eliminate this one. Now, let's look at this one. I think it's this one, but let me first check the others. Good, I'm going slow and carefully. Okay, I think it's this one. (Meichenbaum & Goodman, 1971, p. 121)

Self-Monitoring   An important part of self-regulation is to observe oneself in action—a process known as **self-monitoring** (also known as *self-observation*). To make progress toward important goals, we must be aware of how well we are currently doing; we must know which aspects of our performance are working well and which need improvement. Furthermore, when we see ourselves making progress toward our goals, we are more likely to continue with our efforts (Schunk & Zimmerman, 1997).

■ **self-instructions** Instructions that one gives oneself while performing a complex behavior.

■ **self-monitoring** Observing and recording one's own behavior.

FIGURE 10.6 Example of a self-monitoring sheet for staying on task

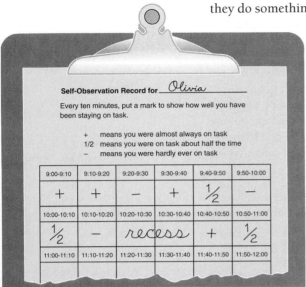

Self-Observation Record for *Olivia*

Every ten minutes, put a mark to show how well you have been staying on task.

+   means you were almost always on task
1/2   means you were on task about half the time
−   means you were hardly ever on task

9:00-9:10	9:10-9:20	9:20-9:30	9:30-9:40	9:40-9:50	9:50-10:00
+	+	−	+	1/2	−
10:00-10:10	10:10-10:20	10:20-10:30	10:30-10:40	10:40-10:50	10:50-11:00
1/2	−	*recess*	+	1/2	
11:00-11:10	11:10-11:20	11:20-11:30	11:30-11:40	11:40-11:50	11:50-12:00

Yet students aren't necessarily accurate observers of their own behavior; they aren't always aware of how frequently they do something incorrectly or ineffectively or of how *infrequently* they do something well. To help students attend to the things they do and don't do, we can have them observe and record their own behavior. If Raymond is speaking out of turn too often, we can bring the seriousness of the problem to his attention by asking him to make a check mark on a sheet of paper every time he catches himself speaking out of turn. If Olivia has trouble staying on task during assigned activities, we can ask her to stop and reflect on her behavior every few minutes (perhaps with the aid of an egg timer or electronic beeper) to determine whether she was staying on task during each interval. Figure 10.6 provides an example of the type of form we might give Olivia to record her observations.

Research indicates clearly that such self-focused observation and recording can bring about changes (sometimes dramatic ones) in student behavior. For example, self-monitoring can be used to increase students' attention to their work (their *time on task*) and the number of assignments they complete. It is also effective in reducing aggression and such disruptive behaviors as talking out of turn and getting out of one's seat (K. D. Allen, 1998; Belfiore & Hornyak, 1998; K. R. Harris, 1986; Mace & Kratochwill, 1988; Webber, Scheuermann, McCall, & Coleman, 1993).

FIGURE 10.7 After a cooperative group activity with three classmates, Rochelle and her teacher use the same criteria to rate Rochelle's performance and that of her group. With the two sets of ratings side by side, Rochelle can evaluate the accuracy of her self-assessments.

Project description ___*Travel Guide*___

Evaluate with a 1 for weak, a 2 for fair, a 3 for good, a 4 for very good, and a 5 for excellent.

Student	Teacher	
4	4	1. The task was a major amount of work in keeping with a whole month of effort.
5	4	2. We used class time quite well.
4	5	3. The workload was quite evenly divided. I did a fair proportion.
4	5	4. I showed commitment to the group and to a quality project.
5	4	5. My report went into depth; it didn't just give the obvious, commonly known information.
5	5	6. The project made a point: a reader (or viewer) could figure out how all of the details fitted together to help form a conclusion.
5	5	7. The project was neat, attractive, well assembled. I was proud of the outcome.
4	5	8. We kept our work organized; we made copies; we didn't lose things or end up having to redo work that was lost.
5	4	9. The work had a lot of original thinking or other creative work.
4	4	10. The project demonstrated mastery of basic language skills—composition, planning, oral communication, writing.
45	45	Total

Comments:

46 group average   (A)^G   (A)^I

Self-Evaluation   Both at home and in school, students' behaviors are frequently judged by others—their parents, teachers, classmates, and so on. To become self-regulating, however, students must begin to judge their *own* behavior; in other words, they must engage in **self-evaluation**. Their ability to evaluate themselves with some degree of objectivity and accuracy will be critical for their long-term success in the adult world (Vye et al., 1998).

Once students have developed appropriate standards and goals, and once they have developed some objective techniques for observing their own behavior, there are many ways we can help them evaluate their own performance. For example, we can have them

- Write in daily or weekly journals in which they address the strengths and weaknesses of their performance
- Participate in peer conferences in which several students discuss their reactions to one another's work
- Assemble portfolios of what they think is their best work, with self-evaluations of each entry (see Chapter 16 for details) (Paris & Ayres, 1994; Paris & Paris, 2001)

In addition, we can provide self-assessment instruments that show students what to look for as they evaluate their work, and we might have them compare their self-assessments with our own, independent judgments of their performance (Paris & Ayres, 1994; D. J. Smith, Young, West, Morgan, & Rhode, 1988). Figure 10.7 presents a form one teacher has used to help her students learn to evaluate their performance in a cooperative group activity.

In the following "Interpreting Student Artifacts and Behaviors" activity, let's use what we have learned about self-regulation so far to examine one student's efforts to regulate her own behavior.

Interpreting Student Artifacts and Behaviors

Goals Project

As part of a middle school "life skills" course, a teacher asks students to identify at least one goal for themselves in each of three areas—physical, mental/emotional, and social—and then keep records of whether they are achieving their goals each day. Twelve-year-old Laticia sets several goals, including increasing her physical activity, telling herself to try again if she misses a shot in a tennis game, smiling at her teachers at least twice a day, giving others at least seven compliments a day, taking out the trash at home, and going to bed each night without arguing. In the essay shown here, she reflects on the success of the project after a five-week period. Following the essay is an example of the tables she has created to record her behavior. As you look at the artifacts, consider

- How well Laticia achieves her goals
- How useful Laticia's goals appear to be for her physical and personal development
- What self-regulation skills Laticia acquires during the goals project

I learned a lot from doing the goals project. I realized that it was hard to do all of the sports things, especially after I broke my toe, because I usually didn't have a whole bunch of time. It was very difficult to find time to run 3 times a week at night but I ran in gym, which was good. Taking out the trash was also hard because the trashcans weren't always full. (However, I did pick up trash when I saw it.) The easiest was going to bed without arguing and 7 nice complements per day. I have to go to bed sometime so I might as well be happy about it. I felt so good after I complemented someone else because I not only made them feel better, but I also felt good.

This project, I shortly found out, was so habit forming! Once I started following these goals, like smiling at my teachers at least twice a day, I did that all the time. It carried over into other areas, too, such as my social life. I'll just smile as I'm walking down the hall with my friends. In tennis my serves are becoming better and better because I aim and practice. Also, it is a habit to practice and I am more willing to do so.

Following through with goals was fairly easy, as I have mentioned before, there are some hard parts, mostly because I am crunched for time. There is only one goal I haven't told you about before and that is "if I miss a shot in tennis, I will say to myself TRY AGAIN." This is probably a lot like life: if something goes wrong that's ok, just try again! That is probably the goal I will remember the most.

Goal

If I miss a shot in tennis I will tell myself TRY AGAIN

Sun	Mon	Tues	Wed	Thurs	Fri	Sat	
yes	yes	no	yes	no	no	yes	WEEK 1
no	no	yes	no	yes	yes	no	WEEK 2
yes	yes	no	yes	yes	yes	no	WEEK 3
no	yes	no	yes	yes	yes	yes	WEEK 4
yes	yes	yes	yes	yes	yes	yes	WEEK 5

As you can see, Laticia doesn't achieve all of her goals, in part because she breaks her toe, has limited time, and sometimes finds the trashcans empty. Nevertheless, her goals seem to be guiding her in productive directions; for instance, her tennis improves, and her increased tendency to smile at teachers generalizes to how she behaves toward peers. Probably more important, however, is the fact that Laticia acquires two essential self-regulation strategies: setting attainable goals and monitoring her own behavior.

Self-Imposed Contingencies   How do you feel when you accomplish a difficult task—for instance, when you earn an A in a challenging course, get elected president of an organization, or make a three-point basket in a basketball game? How do you feel when you fail in your endeavors—for instance, when you get a D on an exam because you forgot to study, thoughtlessly hurt a friend's feelings, or miss an easy goal in a soccer game?

When you accomplish something you've set out to do, especially if the task is complex and challenging, you probably feel quite proud of yourself and give yourself a mental pat on the back. In contrast, when you fail to accomplish a task, you are probably unhappy with your performance; you may also feel guilty, regretful, or ashamed (e.g., Harter, 1999). Likewise, as our students become increasingly self-regulating, they will begin to reinforce themselves (perhaps by feeling proud or telling themselves they did a good job) when they accomplish their goals. And they may punish themselves (perhaps by feeling sorry, guilty, or ashamed) when they do something that does not meet their own performance standards. As an example, see 16-year-old Melinda's poem about horseback riding in Figure 10.8.

■ **self-evaluation** Judgment of one's own performance or behavior.

FIGURE 10.8 Sixteen-year-old Melinda expresses guilt and pride—two examples of self-imposed contingencies—in this piece about horseback riding.

"Sit up,
    shoulders back,
        drop your right shoulder."
Now I feel guilty because I'm making the horse work harder.
"Heels down,
    elbows at your sides,
        lower leg back,
            drop your right shoulder down and back."
Now I feel like I have no talent and like I'm hurting the horse.
"More impulsion from the left hind leg!
    Send him into the rein more!"
Now I'm thinking, "This is so complicated!"
"Good job!
    Walk when you're ready and give him the rein.
        Did you feel that?"
"Yeah!"
"Good! That was really good!
    You've accomplished so much with him and your position."
Now I feel warm inside and proud. All this time has paid off
    and I realize that's why I love horseback riding so much!

Yet such **self-imposed contingencies** are not necessarily confined to emotional reactions. Many self-regulating individuals reinforce themselves in far more concrete ways when they do something successfully. For example, I have a colleague who goes shopping every time she completes a research article or report (she has one of the best wardrobes in town). I myself am more frugal: When I finish each major section of a chapter, I either help myself to a piece of chocolate or take a half hour to watch one of my favorite quiz shows (as a result, I am chubbier than my colleague, but I have a wealth of knowledge of game-show trivia and would almost certainly beat her in a game of Trivial Pursuit).

Thus an additional way to help students become more self-regulating is to teach them self-reinforcement. When students begin to reinforce themselves for appropriate responses—perhaps by giving themselves some free time, allowing themselves to engage in a favorite activity, or simply praising themselves—their study habits and classroom behavior often improve significantly (K. R. Harris, 1986; Hayes et al., 1985; H. C. Stevenson & Fantuzzo, 1986). For example, in one research study, students who were performing poorly in arithmetic were taught to give themselves points when they did well on their assignments; they could later use these points to "buy" a variety of items and privileges. Within a few weeks, these students were doing as well as their classmates on both in-class assignments and homework (H. C. Stevenson & Fantuzzo, 1986). In some instances self-reinforcement is as effective as reinforcement administered by a teacher (Bandura, 1977).

We should note here that techniques designed to promote self-regulation work only when students are motivated to change their behavior. In such circumstances these techniques can help students discover that they have some control, not only over their behavior, but over their environment as well. We must keep three things in mind, however. First, to be successful self-regulators, students must be capable of achieving the goals they are shooting for; for example, students who want to improve their study habits will achieve higher grades only if they have adequate academic skills to ensure success. Second, students must *believe* that they can make the necessary behavior changes; in other words, they must have high self-efficacy (Schunk, 1998). And third, we must caution students not to expect too much of themselves too quickly. Many students would prefer overnight success, but acquiring effective self-regulation skills is often a slow, gradual process. For students to stick with their newly acquired self-regulation skills, their expectations for themselves must be practical and realistic.

Experiencing FIRSTHAND ·More Self-Reflection

Return to the exercise "Self-Reflection About Self-Regulation" at the beginning of this section. Consider what you have just learned about effective self-regulation to evaluate your responses to each question.

· · · · · · ·

Self-Regulated Learning

Social learning theorists and cognitive psychologists alike are beginning to realize that to be truly effective learners, students must engage in some of the self-regulating activities just described. In fact, not only must students regulate their own behaviors, but they must also regulate their own cognitive processes. In particular, **self-regulated learning** includes the following processes, many of which are metacognitive in nature:

■ **self-imposed contingency** Self-reinforcement or self-punishment that follows a behavior.

■ **self-regulated learning** Regulation of one's own cognitive processes in order to learn successfully.

- *Goal setting.* Self-regulated learners know what they want to accomplish when they read or study. For instance, they may want to learn specific facts, get an overall understanding of the ideas being presented, or simply acquire enough knowledge to do well on a classroom exam (Nolen, 1996; Winne & Hadwin, 1998; Wolters, 1998; Zimmerman, 1998). Typically, they tie their goals for a particular learning activity to longer-term goals and aspirations (Zimmerman, 1998).

- *Planning.* Self-regulated learners determine ahead of time how best to use the time and resources they have available for learning tasks (Zimmerman, 1998; Zimmerman & Risemberg, 1997).

- *Attention control.* Self-regulated learners try to focus their attention on the subject matter at hand and to clear their minds of potentially distracting thoughts and emotions (Harnishfeger, 1995; Kuhl, 1985; Winne, 1995).

- *Self-motivation.* Self-regulated learners typically have high self-efficacy regarding their ability to accomplish a learning task successfully (Schunk & Zimmerman, 1997; Zimmerman & Risemberg, 1997). They use a variety of strategies to keep themselves on task—perhaps embellishing on the task to make it more fun, reminding themselves of the importance of doing well, or promising themselves a reward when they are finished (Corno, 1993; Wolters, 2003).

- *Flexible use of learning strategies.* Self-regulated learners choose different learning strategies depending on the specific goal they hope to accomplish. For example, how they read a magazine article depends on whether they are reading it for entertainment or studying for an exam (Linderholm, Gustafson, van den Broek, & Lorch, 1997; Winne, 1995).

- *Self-monitoring.* Self-regulated learners continually monitor their progress toward their goals, and they change their learning strategies or modify their goals if necessary (D. L. Butler & Winne, 1995; Carver & Scheier, 1990; Zimmerman & Risemberg, 1997). *Comprehension monitoring* (described in Chapter 8) is an example of such self-monitoring.

- *Solicitation of outside help when needed.* Truly self-regulated learners don't necessarily try to do everything on their own. On the contrary, they recognize when they need other people's help and seek out such assistance; they are especially likely to ask for the kind of help that will enable them to work more independently in the future (R. Butler, 1998b; A. M. Ryan, Pintrich, & Midgley, 2001).

- *Self-evaluation.* Self-regulated learners determine whether what they have learned fulfills the goals they have set for themselves (D. L. Butler & Winne, 1995; Schraw & Moshman, 1995; Zimmerman & Risemberg, 1997). Ideally, they also use their self-evaluations to modify their selection and use of various learning strategies on future occasions (Winne & Hadwin, 1998).

Self-regulated learners seek assistance when they need it and are especially likely to ask for help with skills that will make them more independent.

As you saw in Table 10.2, a few elements of self-regulated learning (conscious attempts to focus attention, ability to complete short learning tasks at home) emerge in the upper elementary grades, and additional ones (e.g., planning, self-motivation) appear in the middle school and high school years. To some extent, self-regulated learning probably develops from opportunities to engage in independent, self-directed learning activities appropriate for the age-group (Paris & Paris, 2001; Vye et al., 1998; Zimmerman, 1998). But if we take Vygotsky's perspective for a moment, we might reasonably suspect that self-regulated learning also has roots in socially regulated learning (Stright, Neitzel, Sears, & Hoke-Sinex, 2001; Vygotsky, 1962; Zimmerman, 1998). At first, other people (e.g., teachers, parents) might help students learn by setting goals for a learning activity, keeping students' attention focused on the learning task, suggesting effective learning strategies, monitoring learning progress, and so on. Over time, students assume increasing responsibility for these processes; that is, they begin to set their *own* learning goals, stay on task with little prodding from others, identify potentially effective strategies, and evaluate their own learning.

Developmentally speaking, a reasonable bridge between other-regulated learning and self-regulated learning is **co-regulated learning,** in which an adult and one or more children share responsibility for directing the various aspects of the learning process (McCaslin & Good, 1996). For instance, a teacher and students might mutually agree on the specific goals of a learning endeavor, or the teacher might describe the criteria that indicate successful learning and then have students evaluate their own performance in light of those criteria. Initially, the teacher might provide considerable structure, or scaffolding, for the students' learning efforts; in a true Vygotskian fashion, such scaffolding is gradually removed as students become more effectively self-regulating.

Now that we've considered the general nature of self-regulated learning, let's look at how it might be reflected in a particular student's approach to studying.

■ **co-regulated learning** Process through which an adult and child share responsibility for directing various aspects of the child's learning.

Interpreting Student Artifacts and Behaviors

Different Ways of Learning

As an assignment for my educational psychology class, one of my students, Shelly Lamb, interviewed her 17-year-old sister Becky about study habits. As you read the conversation, think about

- The specific metacognitive and self-regulatory strategies Becky uses
- Becky's metacognitive awareness of what she does as she studies

Shelly: What are the different ways that you learn?

Becky: By doing it myself, not just watching. I can pick up random facts by reading, they are easy to make sense of. When I read a textbook, I have to stop and think about it, then I get the concept. I learn some from lectures, but it is harder to stop and think about the material, so I learn less. When a teacher does an example out on the board, I have to do it myself to get it and see where it comes from.

Shelly: When you have a test, how do you study for it and when?

Becky: I don't usually study; I just look over the notes. If I have to memorize something, I repeat it over and over or write it down, which is like repeating it. I sometimes use [word association], patterns and oversimplification to remember. I will also look it over at night and then again in the morning. I derive math formulas, those I don't memorize. . . .

Shelly: What types of study skills do you practice on a regular basis?

Becky: Organize homework. I rewrite my assignments. I do smaller tasks first, then put the bigger ones in a pile. I do the easier ones first, then writing and studying I do last. Long-term projects I do last, or first if I want to force myself to do them. . . .

Shelly: If you have a lot of work for one subject and a few things in other subjects, in what kind of order do you attack the tasks?

Becky: I do the little ones first and then leave the big task till the end. I get more of a sense of accomplishment that way.

Shelly: At what time of day do you learn best? [At what time do you] best study on your own?

Becky: I learn better early in the day. I am in a better mood and I am not sick of school yet. At the end of the day, my brain is full. I study best in the morning; that's when I edit my essays from the night before.

Now that you've read Becky's description of how she studies and learns, it may not surprise you to learn that she is a high-achieving high school senior. Becky uses a wide variety of strategies to regulate her learning and studying: She prioritizes her assignments and plans the best times for doing each one (e.g., "I do the easier ones first, then writing and studying I do last"), chooses certain strategies that have proven to be effective for her (e.g., "I will . . . look it over at night and then again in the morning"), motivates herself to take on challenges (e.g., "Long-term projects I do last, or first if I want to force myself to do them"), and knows how to reinforce herself when she completes her work (e.g., "I get more of a sense of accomplishment that way"). Becky describes exactly what she does *behaviorally* as she studies, and she sometimes knows what she does *cognitively* as well—for example, using "patterns" (reflecting organization) and deriving formulas (reflecting elaboration). Yet she is not always totally aware of her mental processes: A great deal is undoubtedly going on inside her head when she has "to stop and think" or when she "just look[s] over the notes."

When students are self-regulated learners, they set more ambitious academic goals for themselves, learn more effectively, and achieve at higher levels in the classroom (Corno et al., 2002; D. L. Butler & Winne, 1995; Zimmerman & Risemberg, 1997). Furthermore, a great deal of adolescent and adult learning—doing homework, reading, surfing the Internet, and so on—occurs in isolation from other people and so requires considerable self-regulation (Winne, 1995). Unfortunately, however, few students develop a high level of self-regulated learning, perhaps in part because traditional instructional practices do little to encourage it (Paris & Ayres, 1994; Zimmerman & Risemberg, 1997).

Promoting Self-Regulated Learning   To promote self-regulated learning, we must, of course, teach students the kinds of cognitive processes that facilitate learning and memory (see the discussion of metacognition in Chapter 8). In addition, theorists have suggested the following strategies:

- Encourage students to set some of their own goals for learning, and then to monitor their progress toward those goals.
- Give students opportunities to learn and achieve without teacher direction or assistance, including both independent learning activities in which students study by themselves (e.g., seatwork assignments, homework) and group activities in which students help one another learn (e.g., peer tutoring, cooperative learning).
- Occasionally assign activities (e.g., research papers, creative projects) in which students have considerable leeway regarding goals, use of time, and so on.
- Provide scaffolding as needed to help students acquire self-regulating strategies (e.g., show them how to use checklists to identify what they need to do each day and to determine when they have completed all assigned work).
- Model self-regulating cognitive processes by "thinking aloud" about such processes, and then give students constructive feedback as they engage in similar processes.
- Consistently ask students to evaluate their own performance, and have them compare their self-assessments to teacher assessments. (Belfiore & Hornyak, 1998; Bronson, 2000; A. King, 1997; McCaslin & Good, 1996; Paris & Paris, 2001; N. E. Perry, 1998; N. E. Perry, VandeKamp, Mercer, & Nordby, 2002; Schunk & Zimmerman, 1997; J. W. Thomas, 1993b; Winne & Hadwin, 1998; Zimmerman & Risemberg, 1997)

Self-Regulated Problem Solving

We can sometimes use self-regulation techniques to help students independently handle problems; that is, we can teach strategies for **self-regulated problem solving**. For example, to elicit greater creativity in problem solutions, we might encourage students to give themselves instructions such as these:

> I want to think of something no one else will think of, something unique. Be free-wheeling, no hangups. I don't care what anyone thinks; just suspend judgment. I'm not sure what I'll come up with; it will be a surprise. The ideas can just flow through me. (Meichenbaum, 1977, p. 62)

We might also give them a general structure to follow as they approach problems. When one fifth-grade teacher asked her class to design inventions to solve everyday problems, she suggested several questions (including "How can I make this appealing?" and "Who might have trouble using this?") that could guide students' thinking. Figure 10.9 shows how 10-year-old Amaryth used these questions as she designed an invention for turning off a bedroom light.

Self-regulated problem solving is important not only for solving academic problems but for solving social ones as well. For instance, to help students deal more effectively with interpersonal conflicts, we might teach them to take steps such as these:

1. Define the problem.
2. Identify several possible solutions.
3. Predict the likely consequences of each solution.
4. Choose the best solution.
5. Identify the steps required to carry out the solution.
6. Carry out the steps.
7. Evaluate the results. (S. N. Elliott & Busse, 1991; Meichenbaum, 1977; Weissburg, 1985; Yell, Robinson, & Drasgow, 2001)

Such steps often help students who have interpersonal problems (e.g., students who are either socially withdrawn or overly aggressive) to develop more effective social skills (K. R. Harris, 1982; Meichenbaum, 1977; Yell et al., 2001).

Another approach is to provide training in **peer mediation**, in which students *help one another* solve interpersonal problems. More specifically, we teach students how to mediate conflicts

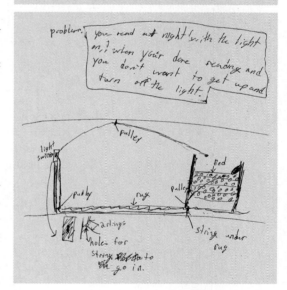

FIGURE 10.9 In these journal pages, 10-year-old Amaryth describes how she followed a teacher-provided structure to design an invention that would enable someone to turn off a bedroom light while lying in bed.

■ **self-regulated problem solving** Employment of self-directing strategies to address one's own problems.

■ **peer mediation** Approach to conflict resolution in which a student (mediator) asks peers in conflict to express their differing viewpoints and then work together to identify an appropriate compromise.

Fostering Self-Regulation

 Help students set challenging yet realistic goals and standards.

A teacher encourages a pregnant student to stay in school until she graduates. Together they discuss strategies for juggling motherhood and schoolwork.

 Have students observe and record their own behavior.

A student with attention-deficit hyperactivity disorder frequently tips his chair back to the point where he is likely to topple over. Concerned for the student's safety, his teacher asks him to record each instance of such behavior on a sheet of graph paper. Both student and teacher notice how quickly the behavior disappears once the student has become aware of his bad habit.

 Teach students instructions they can give themselves to remind them of what they need to do.

To help a student control her impulsive behavior on multiple-choice tests, her teacher has her mentally say this to herself as she reads each question: "Read the entire question. Then look at each answer carefully, and decide whether it is correct or incorrect. Then choose the answer that seems most correct of all."

 Encourage students to evaluate their own performance.

A science teacher gives students a list of criteria to evaluate the lab reports they have written. In assigning grades, she considers how accurately students have evaluated their own reports.

 Teach students to reinforce themselves for appropriate behavior.

A teacher helps students develop more regular study habits by encouraging them to make a favorite activity—for example, shooting baskets, watching television, or calling a friend on the telephone—contingent on completing their homework first.

 Give students opportunities to practice learning with little or no help from their teacher.

A middle school social studies teacher distributes various magazine articles related to current events in the Middle East, making sure that each student receives an article appropriate for his or her reading level. He asks students to read their articles over the weekend and prepare a one-paragraph summary to share with other class members. He also provides guidelines about what information students should include in their summaries.

 Provide strategies that students can use to solve interpersonal problems.

A teacher teaches her students a sequence to follow when they find themselves in a conflict with a classmate: *Identify* the source of the conflict, *listen* to each other's perspectives, *verbalize* each other's perspectives, and *develop* a solution that provides a reasonable compromise.

among classmates by asking opposing sides to express their differing points of view and then work together to devise a reasonable resolution (M. Deutsch, 1993; D. W. Johnson & Johnson, 1996, 2001; Stevahn, Oberle, Johnson, & Johnson, 2001). For example, in a study involving several classrooms at the second through fifth grade levels (D. W. Johnson, Johnson, Dudley, Ward, & Magnuson, 1995), students were trained to help peers resolve interpersonal conflicts by asking the opposing sides to do the following:

1. Define the conflict (the problem)
2. Explain their own perspectives and needs
3. Explain the *other* person's perspectives and needs
4. Identify at least three possible solutions to the conflict
5. Reach an agreement that addressed the needs of both parties

Students took turns serving as mediator for their classmates, such that everyone had experience resolving the conflicts of others. In comparison to students in an untrained control group, students who completed the training more frequently resolved their *own* interpersonal conflicts in ways that addressed the needs of both parties, and they were less likely to ask for adult intervention. Similarly, in a case study involving adolescent gang members (Sanchez & Anderson, 1990), students were given mediation training and asked to be responsible for mediating gang-related disputes. After only one month of training, rival gang members were exchanging friendly greetings in the corridors, giving one another the "high five" sign, and interacting at lunch; meanwhile, gang-related fights virtually disappeared from the scene.

In peer mediation we see yet another example of Vygotsky's notion that effective cognitive processes often have their roots in social interactions. In a peer mediation session, students model effective conflict resolution skills for one another, and they may eventually internalize the skills they use in solving others' problems to solve their *own* problems.

Peer mediation is most effective when students of diverse ethnic backgrounds, socioeconomic groups, and achievement levels serve as mediators (Casella, 2001a; K. M. Williams, 2001b). Furthermore, it is typically most useful for relatively small, short-term interpersonal problems (hurt feelings, conflicts over use of limited academic resources, etc.). Even the most proficient of peer mediators may be ill prepared to handle conflicts that reflect deep-seated and emotionally charged attitudes and behaviors—for instance, conflicts that involve sexual harassment or homophobia (Casella, 2001a). In such cases the intervention and guidance of teachers and other school personnel may be necessary.

The right-hand column of Table 10.2 suggests strategies for promoting self-regulation at various grade levels. The Into the Classroom feature "Fostering Self-Regulation" presents several more specific ideas.

When students set challenging goals for themselves and achieve those self-chosen goals through their own efforts, their self-efficacy is enhanced and their motivation to undertake new challenges increases (Bandura, 1989; Bandura & Schunk, 1981). And when students have a high sense of self-efficacy and engage in self-regulating activities, they are more likely to believe that they control their environment, rather than that their environment controls them. In fact, social cognitive theorists assert that people, their behaviors, and the environment all have a somewhat "controlling" influence on one another, as we shall see now.

RECIPROCAL CAUSATION

Throughout the chapter we've discussed aspects of learners' environments and the behaviors that result from various environmental conditions. We've also talked about personal variables (e.g., expectations and self-efficacy) that learners bring with them to a task. Now which one of these three factors—environment, behavior, or person—lays the foundation for learning? According to social cognitive theorists, all three are essential ingredients, and each one influences the other two (see Figure 10.10). This interdependence among environment, behavior, and person is known as **reciprocal causation** (Bandura, 1989). Examples of how each factor affects the other two are presented in Table 10.3.

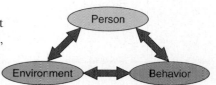

FIGURE 10.10 In social cognitive theory, personal, behavioral, and environmental variables mutually influence one another.

As a concrete illustration of how environment, behavior, and personal factors can mutually influence one another, let's consider "Scene One" in the case of Lorraine:

Scene One

Lorraine, a student in Mr. Broderick's seventh-grade social studies class, often comes to class late and ill prepared for the day's activities. In class she spends more time interacting with her friends (e.g., whispering, passing notes) than getting involved in classroom activities. Lorraine's performance on most exams and assignments (when she turns the latter in at all) is unsatisfactory.

One day in mid-October, Mr. Broderick takes Lorraine aside to express his concern about her lack of classroom effort. He suggests that Lorraine could do better if she paid more attention in class; he also offers to work with her twice a week after school to help her understand class material. Lorraine is less optimistic, describing herself as "not smart enough to learn this stuff."

For a week or so after her meeting with Mr. Broderick, Lorraine seems to buckle down and exert more effort, but she never does stay after school for extra help. And before long, Lorraine is back to her old habits. Mr. Broderick eventually concludes that she is a lost cause and decides to devote his time and effort to helping more motivated students.

Lorraine's low self-efficacy (a *person* factor) is probably one reason she spends so much class time engaged in task-irrelevant activities (*behaviors*). The fact that she devotes her attention (another *person* factor) to her classmates, rather than to her teacher, affects the particular stimuli she experiences (her *environment*). Lorraine's poor performance on assignments and exams (*behaviors*) affects both her self-efficacy (*person*) and Mr. Broderick's treatment of her (*environment*). By eventually concluding that Lorraine is a lost cause, Mr. Broderick begins to ignore Lorraine (*environment*), contributing to her further failure (*behavior*) and even lower self-efficacy (*person*). (See Table 10.3 for examples of such interactive effects under the column marked "Scene One.") Clearly, Lorraine is showing signs of being at risk for long-term academic failure.

■ Can you think of occasions when you, like Lorraine, might have doomed yourself to failure through your own behaviors?

■ **reciprocal causation**
Interdependence of environment, behavior, and personal variables as these three factors influence learning and development.

TABLE 10.3

Mutual Influences (Reciprocal Causation) Among Environment, Behavior, and Person

		A GENERAL EXAMPLE	AN EXAMPLE IN LORRAINE'S CASE (SCENE ONE)	AN EXAMPLE IN LORRAINE'S CASE (SCENE TWO)
Effect of Environment	**On Behavior**	Reinforcement and punishment affect future behavior.	Teacher's ignoring Lorraine leads to future classroom failure.	New instructional methods lead to improved academic performance.
	On Person	Feedback from others affects sense of self-efficacy.	Teacher's ignoring Lorraine perpetuates low self-efficacy.	New instructional methods capture Lorraine's interest and attention.
Effect of Behavior	**On Environment**	Specific behaviors affect the amount of reinforcement and punishment received.	Poor classroom performance leads the teacher to meet privately with Lorraine, then eventually to ignore her.	Better academic performance leads to more reinforcement from the teacher.
	On Person	Success and failure affect expectations for future performance.	Poor classroom performance leads to low self-efficacy.	Better academic performance leads to higher self-efficacy.
Effect of Person	**On Environment**	Self-efficacy affects choices of activities and therefore the specific environment encountered.	Attention to classmates rather than classroom activities affects environment experienced.	Attention to classroom activities leads to greater influence of teacher's instruction.
	On Behavior	Attention, retention, motor reproduction, and motivation affect degree to which a learner imitates modeled behavior.	Attention to classmates rather than classroom activities leads to academic failure.	Greater self-efficacy and increased motivation lead to more persistent study habits.

But now imagine that after reading several research articles about how to work with students at risk, Mr. Broderick develops greater optimism that he can break the vicious cycle of environment/behavior/person for students such as Lorraine. Midway through the school year, he makes the following changes in his classroom:

- He communicates clearly and consistently that he expects all students to succeed in his classroom.
- He incorporates students' personal experiences and interests into the study of social studies.
- He identifies specific, concrete tasks that students will accomplish each week.
- He provides guidance and structure for how each task should be accomplished.
- After consulting with the school's reading specialist and school psychologist, he helps students develop more effective reading and learning strategies.
- He gives a quiz every Friday so that students can assess their own progress.
- When students perform well on weekly quizzes, he reminds them that they themselves are responsible for their performance.

Let's see what happens next, as we consider "Scene Two":

Teachers' actions are an important part of the environment in the three-way interaction among *environment, behavior,* and *person.*

Scene Two

By incorporating students' personal experiences and interests into his daily lesson plans, Mr. Broderick begins to capture Lorraine's interest and attention. She begins to realize that social studies has implications for her own life and becomes more involved in classroom activities. With the more structured assignments, better guidance about how to study class material, and frequent quizzes, Lorraine finds herself succeeding in a subject at which she has previously experienced only failure. Mr. Broderick is equally pleased with her performance, something he tells her frequently through his facial expressions, his verbal feedback, and his willingness to provide help whenever she needs it.

By the end of the school year, Lorraine is studying course material more effectively and completing her assignments regularly. She is eagerly looking forward to next year's social studies class, confident that she will continue to do well.

Once again, we see the interplay among environment, behavior, and person. Mr. Broderick's new instructional methods (*environment*) engage Lorraine's attention (*person*) and facilitate her academic performance (*behavior*). Lorraine's improved academic performance, in turn, influences Mr. Broderick's treatment of her (*environment*) and her own self-efficacy (*person*). And her improved self-efficacy, her greater attention to classroom activities, and her increased motivation to succeed (all *person* variables) affect her ability to benefit from Mr. Broderick's instruction (*environment*) and her classroom success (*behavior*). (See the column marked "Scene Two" in Table 10.3 for examples of such interactive effects.)

As you can see, then, the things we do in the classroom—the *environment* we create—affect both the behaviors that students exhibit and the personal factors that influence their learning. Students' behaviors and personal factors, in turn, influence the future classroom environment they experience. As teachers, we must create and maintain a classroom environment that helps students develop the behaviors (e.g., academic and social skills) and personal characteristics (e.g., high self-efficacy and the expectation that their efforts will be rewarded) that are likely to bring them academic and personal success.

■ Can you explain reciprocal causation in your own words? Can you provide an example from your own experience?

CONSIDERING DIVERSITY FROM A SOCIAL COGNITIVE PERSPECTIVE

Social cognitive theory provides several insights into how we can adapt our classroom practices to serve students with diverse backgrounds, characteristics, and needs. The concepts of *modeling*, *self-efficacy*, and *self-regulation* can be especially useful in this context.

Using Diverse Models to Promote Success and Self-Efficacy

Two principles identified earlier in the chapter are particularly pertinent when discussing diversity in the classroom:

- Students are most likely to adopt behaviors they believe are relevant to their own situation.
- Students develop greater self-efficacy for a task when they see others like themselves performing the task successfully.

Both principles lead to the same conclusion: *Students need models who are similar to themselves in race, cultural background, socioeconomic status, gender, and (if applicable) disability.* Such models may be especially important for minorities, for girls, and for students from lower-income families, as the majority of professionally successful adults that most children see, especially in male-stereotypical occupations, are middle-income and upper-income White men (e.g., Eccles [Parsons], 1984; Howe, 1994; Torrance, 1995).

As teachers, we cannot possibly be all things to all students. We must therefore expose our students to as wide a variety of successful models—child and adolescent models as well as adults—as possible. In some cases we may be able to find such models within the school building itself. In other cases we might invite people from the local community or region to visit the classroom. Occasionally, as Ryan discovered when he taught his cousin Collin how to field a ground ball (see "Fielding a Ground Ball" on pp. 339–340), we may even find it effective to videotape students performing desired behaviors and then have them watch *themselves* being successful (Kehle, Clark, & Jenson, 1996).

Symbolic models—like the professional ballplayers Collin watched on videotape—can teach students a great deal as well. For instance, we might ask students to read biographies or autobiographies about such successful individuals as Maya Angelou (who, as an African American growing up in Arkansas in the 1930s, was raised in an environment of poverty and racial intolerance), Franklin D. Roosevelt (who had polio and was wheelchair-bound), and Stephen Hawking (who has a degenerative nerve disorder and "talks" through computer technology). Or we might have students watch the video *Stand and Deliver*, the story of eighteen Mexican American high school students from a lower-income neighborhood in East Los Angeles who, through hard work and perseverance, earned college credit by passing the national Advanced Placement calculus exam.

Although we may differ from our students in many ways, we are likely to be powerful models for them nonetheless. Regardless of our own heritage, we must *always* model acceptance and respect for people with diverse backgrounds and characteristics.

Promoting Self-Regulation in Students at Risk

Some students have few outside role models for effective study habits—few people in their out-of-school lives who can show them the self-regulated learning skills they will need to succeed in high school and postsecondary education. As a result, although they may hope to graduate, go on to college, and eventually become successful professionals, they may have little idea about how to accomplish these things (Belfiore & Hornyak, 1998; B. L. Wilson & Corbett, 2001). The following interview with a middle school student illustrates the problem:

Adult: Are you on track to meet your goals?
Student: No. I need to study more.
Adult: How do you know that?
Student: I just know by some of my grades. [mostly Cs]
Adult: Why do you think you will be more inclined to do it in high school?
Student: I don't want to get let back. I want to go to college.
Adult: What will you need to do to get better grades?
Student: Just do more and more work. I can rest when the school year is over. (dialogue from B. L. Wilson & Corbett, 2001, p. 23)

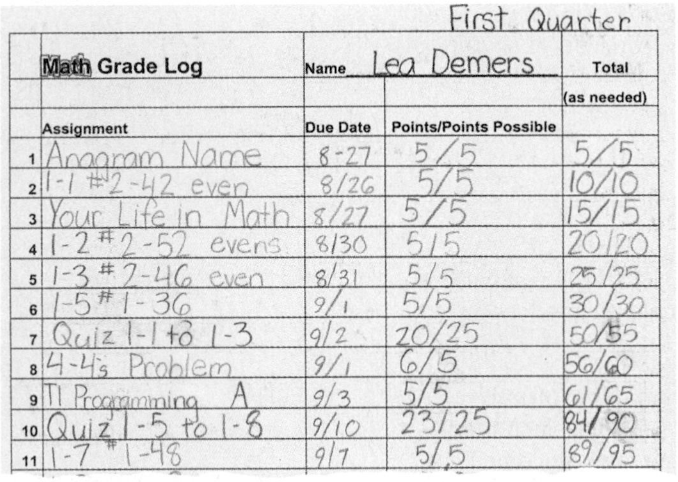
First Quarter

Math Grade Log — Name Lea Demers

	Assignment	Due Date	Points/Points Possible	Total (as needed)
1	Anagram Name	8-27	5/5	5/5
2	1-1 #2-42 even	8/26	5/5	10/10
3	Your Life in Math	8/27	5/5	15/15
4	1-2 #2-52 evens	8/30	5/5	20/20
5	1-3 #2-46 even	8/31	5/5	25/25
6	1-5 #1-36	9/1	5/5	30/30
7	Quiz 1-1 to 1-3	9/2	20/25	50/55
8	4-4's Problem	9/1	6/5	56/60
9	TI Programming A	9/3	5/5	61/65
10	Quiz 1-5 to 1-8	9/10	23/25	84/90
11	1-7 #1-48	9/7	5/5	89/95

FIGURE 10.11 In this daily log sheet, 13-year-old Lea has kept track of her math assignments, their due dates, and her performance on them.

Motivation and effort are important, to be sure, but so are planning and time management, effective learning strategies, and other self-regulatory strategies—things that many students at risk seem to have little awareness of (B. L. Wilson & Corbett, 2001).

Fortunately, explicit instruction in self-regulatory strategies can help students at risk begin to acquire more effective study habits (Cosden et al., 2001; Eilam, 2001; Graham & Harris, 1996; S. D. Miller et al., 2003). Sometimes instruction takes place in structured after-school homework programs, where students have considerable scaffolding in acquiring such basic skills as keeping track of homework assignments and due dates, identifying the specific tasks involved in each assignment, developing a plan to complete all assignments in a timely manner, and locating helpful resources. Yet we can also provide some scaffolding for self-regulated activities during regular school hours—for instance, by distributing forms that students can use to keep track of what they have done and need to do. As an example, the daily log sheet presented in Figure 10.11 can help middle school students keep track of their math assignments and monitor their performance. The form has its limits, in that it focuses students' attention entirely on the number of problems they are getting right; it provides no place for students to record the types of problems they get wrong, the kinds of errors they make, or any other information that might help them improve. For students with few if any self-regulatory strategies, however, such a form can get them on the road to self-monitoring.

Supporting Students with Special Needs

Most of our students will undoubtedly stand to gain from teaching strategies that promote greater self-regulation. But students with special educational needs will often be among those in greatest need of becoming more self-regulating (Sands & Wehmeyer, 1996). Such students are especially likely to benefit when we encourage them to set and strive for their own goals, particularly when those goals are concrete, specific, and accomplishable within a short time period. They will also be well served when we teach them self-monitoring, self-reinforcement techniques, and self-regulated problem-solving skills (Abery & Zajac, 1996; C. E. Cunningham & Cunningham, 1998; E. S. Ellis & Friend, 1991; Mithaug & Mithaug, 2003; L. E. Powers et al., 1996; Schunk, 1991; Yell et al., 2001).

Table 10.4 presents a social cognitive perspective of characteristics commonly seen in students with special needs; it also presents a number of strategies for promoting the academic and social success of these students. As you can see, the concepts *modeling*, *self-efficacy*, and *self-regulation* appear repeatedly throughout the table.

TABLE 10.4

Applying Social Cognitive Theory with Students Who Have Special Educational Needs

CATEGORY	CHARACTERISTICS YOU MIGHT OBSERVE	SUGGESTED CLASSROOM STRATEGIES
Students with specific cognitive or academic difficulties	• Difficulty predicting the consequences of specific behaviors • Low self-efficacy for academic tasks in areas where there has been a history of failure • Less self-regulation of learning and behavior	• Help students form more realistic expectations about the consequences of their behaviors. • Scaffold students' efforts on academic tasks to increase the probability of success. • Identify students' areas of strength, and give students opportunities to tutor peers in those areas. • Promote self-regulation (e.g., by teaching self-monitoring, self-instructions, self-reinforcement).
Students with social or behavioral problems	• Unusual difficulty in learning from the social environment (for students with autism) • Difficulties predicting the consequences of specific behaviors • Friendships with peers who are poor models of effective social skills and prosocial behavior (for some students with emotional and behavioral disorders) • Little self-regulation of behavior • Deficits in social problem solving	• Help students recognize and interpret social cues and nonverbal language. • Discuss possible consequences of various courses of action in social conflict situations. • Model appropriate classroom behaviors; combine modeling with explicit verbal instruction, and use visual aids to communicate desired behaviors. • Provide opportunities for students to interact with peers who model effective social and prosocial behaviors. • Videotape students as they exhibit appropriate behaviors, and then have them view themselves as models for such behavior. • Teach self-regulation (e.g., self-monitoring, self-instructions, self-regulated problem-solving strategies).
Students with general delays in cognitive and social functioning	• Low self-efficacy for academic tasks • Tendency to watch others for guidance about how to behave • Low goals for achievement (possibly as a way of avoiding failure) • Little if any self-regulation of learning and behavior	• Scaffold students' efforts on academic tasks to increase the probability of success. • Model desired behaviors; identify peers who can also serve as appropriate models. • Encourage students to set high yet realistic goals for achievement. • Promote self-regulation (e.g., by teaching self-monitoring, self-instructions, self-reinforcement).
Students with physical or sensory challenges	• Few opportunities to develop self-regulation skills due to health limitations, a tightly controlled environment, or both	• Teach skills that promote self-sufficiency and independence. • Teach students to make positive self-statements (e.g., "I can do it!") to enhance their self-efficacy for acting independently.
Students with advanced cognitive development	• High self-efficacy for academic tasks • High goals for performance • More effective self-regulated learning • For some students, a history of easy successes and, hence, little experience dealing with failure effectively	• Provide the academic support that students need to reach high goals. • Provide opportunities for independent study. • Provide challenging tasks at which students may sometimes fail; teach constructive strategies for dealing with failure (e.g., persistence, using errors to guide future practice efforts).

Sources: Balla & Zigler, 1979; Bandura, 1989; Beirne-Smith et al., 2002; Biemiller, Shany, Inglis, & Meichenbaum, 1998; C. E. Cunningham & Cunningham, 1998; E. S. Ellis & Friend, 1991; Graham & Harris, 1996; J. N. Hughes, 1988; Kehle, Clark, Jenson, & Wampold, 1986; Lupart, 1995; Mercer, 1997; Mithaug & Mithaug, 2003; Morgan & Jenson, 1988; J. R. Nelson, Smith, Young, & Dodd, 1991; Piirto, 1999; Sands & Wehmeyer, 1996; Schumaker & Hazel, 1984; Schunk et al., 1987; R. Turnbull et al., 2004 Yell et al., 2001.

THE BIG PICTURE

As you've read about social cognitive theory in this chapter, perhaps you've noticed that certain ideas have kept popping up over and over again. Let's look at some of the central concepts that tie social cognitive theory together. After that, we'll consider how the social cognitive perspective compares to the theories of learning we've considered in previous chapters.

UNIFYING IDEAS IN SOCIAL COGNITIVE THEORY

As you look back at our preceding discussions of underlying assumptions, reinforcement and punishment, modeling, self-efficacy, or self-regulation, you should find three general ideas permeating much of social cognitive theory:

The power of observation.   As noted early on, social cognitive theory focuses on how people learn by watching others. The process of learning new behaviors from models is the most obvious example, but observation has other effects as well. For instance, people learn what behaviors are most likely to lead to reinforcement and punishment by watching what happens to others (i.e., through vicarious experiences). They develop beliefs about what tasks they are and are not capable of doing (i.e., they develop high or low self-efficacy) in part by watching their peers either succeed or fail at those tasks. As they become increasingly self-regulating, the standards that they set for their own behavior are often modeled after those they see others adopt.

The role of control.   The environment, personal variables, and behavior all influence one another (this is the idea of *reciprocal causation*). Yet much of social cognitive theory focuses on how people can clearly be masters of their environments. For instance, they can often choose the activities in which they participate, thereby controlling the particular experiences they have. When they observe models demonstrating certain behaviors, they control what and if they learn by paying attention (or not) and by encoding what they see (or not) in particular ways. When they self-regulate, they take charge of their own behavior and learning—for instance, by setting their own goals, monitoring their own progress, and evaluating their own performance. And their self-efficacy for various tasks encompasses their beliefs about *how well* they can master and control their environment.

The importance of motivation.   As we examined the assumptions that underlie social cognitive theory, we noted that people's behavior is often goal-directed. Furthermore, people form expectations about the probable future consequences of various behaviors by observing the typical outcomes of the behaviors, and they are likely to exhibit the behaviors that others model only if they think that doing so is apt to benefit themselves. To be truly motivated—to consciously choose certain activities, work hard at them, and persist in the face of failure—people must have high self-efficacy and believe they will eventually achieve success. Ultimately, many people take charge of their own motivation—for instance, by imposing their own response-reinforcement contingencies and by using a variety of strategies for staying on task during self-regulated learning activities.

COMPARING THE THREE PERSPECTIVES OF LEARNING

If you have been reading the chapters of Part 2 of the text in sequence, then you have now examined three different theoretical perspectives of learning: cognitive psychology, behaviorism, and social cognitive theory. At the beginning of Chapter 6, I briefly identified some ways in which these perspectives differ from one another. Now that you have studied each perspective in depth, it might be helpful to make additional comparisons. Table 10.5 identifies some of the major ways in which the three theories are similar and different.

It is important to reiterate a point made in Chapter 6: *No single theoretical orientation can give us a complete picture of how people learn.* All three perspectives provide valuable lessons about how to help students achieve in the classroom. For example, principles from cognitive psychology give us ideas about how we can help students remember information and apply it to new situations and problems. Principles from behaviorism yield strategies for helping students develop and maintain more productive classroom behaviors. Principles from social cognitive theory show us how we can effectively model the skills we want students to acquire and how we can promote greater self-regulation. And principles from all three perspectives are useful for motivating students to succeed in the classroom, as you will discover in the next two chapters.

TABLE 10.5   COMPARE/CONTRAST

Comparing the Three Perspectives of Learning

ISSUE	COGNITIVE PSYCHOLOGY	BEHAVIORISM	SOCIAL COGNITIVE THEORY
Learning is defined as . . .	an internal mental phenomenon that may or may not be reflected in behavior.	a behavior change.	an internal mental phenomenon that may or may not be reflected in behavior
The focus of investigation is on . . .	cognitive processes.	stimuli and responses that can be readily observed.	both behavior and cognitive processes.
Principles of learning describe how . . .	people mentally process the information they receive and construct knowledge from their experiences.	people's behaviors are affected by environmental stimuli.	people's observations of those around them affect behavior and cognitive processes.
Consequences of behavior . . .	are not a major focus of consideration.	must be experienced directly if they are to affect learning.	can be experienced either directly or vicariously.
Learning and behavior are controlled . . .	primarily by cognitive processes within the individual.	primarily by environmental circumstances.	partly by the environment and partly by cognitive processes; people become increasingly self-regulating (and therefore less controlled by the environment) over time.
Educational implications focus on how we can help students . . .	process information in effective ways and construct accurate and complete knowledge about classroom topics.	acquire more productive classroom behaviors.	learn effectively by observing others.

CASE STUDY: *Teacher's Lament*

"Sometimes a teacher just can't win," complains Mr. Adams, a sixth-grade teacher. "At the beginning of the year, I told my students that homework assignments would count for 20 percent of their grades. Yet some students hardly ever turned in any homework, even though I continually reminded them about their assignments. After reconsidering the situation, I decided that I probably shouldn't use homework as a criterion for grading. After all, in this poor, inner-city neighborhood, many kids don't have a quiet place to study at home.

"So in November I told my class that I wouldn't be counting homework assignments when I calculated grades for the first report card. Naturally, some students—the ones who hadn't been doing their homework—seemed relieved. But the students who *had* been doing it were absolutely furious! And now hardly anyone seems to turn in homework anymore."

- Why were students who had regularly been doing their homework so upset? Can you explain their reaction using social cognitive theory?

- From a social cognitive perspective, Mr. Adams inadvertently punished some students and reinforced others. Which students in the class were reinforced, and how? Which students were punished, and how?

- What might Mr. Adams do to encourage and help all students to complete homework assignments?

Once you have answered these questions, compare your responses with those presented in Appendix B.

KEY CONCEPTS

social cognitive theory (p. 329)
model (p. 330)
vicarious reinforcement (p. 332)
vicarious punishment (p. 332)
incentive (p. 333)
live model (p. 334)
symbolic model (p. 334)
modeling (p. 334)
cognitive modeling (p. 335)

observational learning effect (p. 336)
response facilitation effect (p. 336)
response inhibition effect (p. 336)
response disinhibition effect (p. 336)
self-efficacy (p. 341)
resilient self-efficacy (p. 342)
collective self-efficacy (p. 344)
self-regulation (p. 347)
self-regulated behavior (p. 347)

self-instructions (p. 349)
self-monitoring (p. 349)
self-evaluation (p. 350)
self-imposed contingency (p. 352)
self-regulated learning (p. 352)
co-regulated learning (p. 353)
self-regulated problem solving (p. 355)
peer mediation (p. 355)
reciprocal causation (p. 357)

PRAXIS Turn to Appendix C, "Matching Book and Ancillary Content to the Praxis Principles of Learning and Teaching Tests," to discover sections of this chapter that may be especially applicable to the Praxis tests.

Now go to our Companion Website at **www.prenhall. com/ormrod** to assess your understanding of chapter content with "Multiple-Choice Questions," apply comprehension in "Essay Questions," broaden your knowledge of educational psychology with related "Web Links," gain greater insight about classroom learning in "Learning in the Content Areas," and analyze and assess classroom work in the "Student Artifact Library."

*W*hat motivated you to open your textbook and start reading this chapter just now? Perhaps you have an upcoming exam on the topic of motivation. Perhaps you want to show that you've done the assigned reading when you go to class. Or perhaps you're simply curious about the nature of human motivation and want to know how you might foster it in the classroom.

We have already touched on motivation in previous chapters. For instance, in our discussion of conceptual change in Chapter 7, we found that students are more likely to revise incorrect beliefs when they are motivated to do so. In our discussion of metacognition in Chapter 8, we discovered that motivational factors influence the extent to which students use effective learning strategies as they study. In our exploration of behaviorism in Chapter 9, we learned that certain consequences may be reinforcing to some students but not others, presumably because of students' differing motives. And motivational issues pervaded much of our discussion of social cognitive theory—modeling, self-efficacy, self-regulation, and so on—in Chapter 10.

In this chapter we'll look more closely at motivation and its close companion, emotion (we'll use the more general term *affect*). As we proceed through the chapter, we'll address questions such as these:

- In what ways does motivation affect learning?
- What theoretical approaches have psychologists used to study and explain motivation?
- What basic needs do human beings have? How can we address such needs in the classroom?
- What roles do emotions play in learning? How can we maximize productive ones while minimizing unproductive ones?
- To what extent are students from different backgrounds apt to have diverse needs and motives?

We will continue our exploration of motivation in Chapter 12, where our focus will be on the cognitive factors that influence students' motivation to study, learn, and achieve in the classroom.

CASE STUDY: *Quick Draw*

Unlike her more socially oriented classmates, Anya is a quiet student who usually prefers to be alone. Whenever she has free time in class, she grabs some paper and a pencil and begins to sketch. Her love of drawing appears at other times as well. For example, she decorates her notebooks with elaborate doodles. She embellishes stories and essays with illustrations. She even draws pictures of some of the words on each week's spelling list.

Not surprisingly, Anya looks forward to her art class, paying particularly close attention on those days when her art teacher describes or demonstrates a new drawing technique. She buries herself in every drawing assignment, seemingly oblivious to the classroom around her. Anya's art teacher notes with pride how much Anya's skill in drawing has improved over the course of the school year.

Anya makes no bones about her interest. "When I grow up, I want to be a professional artist," she states emphatically. "In the meantime, I'm going to practice, practice, practice."

Which of Anya's behaviors reflect her interest in art? Are these behaviors likely to enhance her performance in art class? If so, how?

THE NATURE OF MOTIVATION

When it comes to art, Anya is highly motivated. We can reasonably draw this conclusion based on her close attention in class, her eagerness to draw whenever she can, and her career goal. **Motivation** is something that energizes, directs, and sustains behavior; it gets students moving, points them in a particular direction, and keeps them going. We often see students' motivation reflected in *personal investment* and *cognitive engagement* in an activity (Maehr & Meyer, 1997; Paris & Paris, 2001; L. Steinberg, 1996).

Virtually all students are motivated in one way or another. One student may be keenly interested in classroom subject matter and so may seek out challenging coursework, participate

■ **motivation** State that energizes, directs, and sustains behavior.

actively in class discussions, and earn high marks on assigned projects. Another student may be more concerned with the social side of school, interacting with classmates frequently, attending extracurricular activities almost every day, and perhaps running for a student government office. Still another may be focused on athletics, excelling in physical education classes, playing or watching sports most afternoons and weekends, and faithfully following a physical fitness regimen. And yet another student, perhaps because of an undetected learning disability, a shy temperament, or a seemingly uncoordinated body, may be interested primarily in *avoiding* academics, social situations, or athletic activities.

■ How is *situated motivation* similar to *situated cognition* (Chapter 8)?

Anya brings her strong interest in art with her when she enters the classroom. Yet motivation is not always something that people "carry around" inside of them; it can also be influenced by environmental conditions. When we talk about how the environment can enhance a person's motivation to learn particular things or behave in particular ways, we are talking about **situated motivation** (Paris & Turner, 1994; Rueda & Moll, 1994). As we proceed through this chapter and the next, we will find that, as teachers, we can do many things to create a classroom environment that motivates students to learn and behave in ways that promote their long-term success.

How Motivation Affects Learning and Behavior

Motivation has several effects on students' learning and behavior, which I've summarized in Figure 11.1:

■ Can you find each of these effects in the case study of Anya?

◎   *It directs behavior toward particular goals.* As we discovered in Chapter 10, social cognitive theorists propose that individuals set goals for themselves and direct their behavior toward those goals. Motivation determines the specific goals toward which people strive (Maehr & Meyer, 1997; Pintrich et al., 1993). Thus, it affects the choices students make—whether to enroll in trigonometry or studio art, whether to attend a school basketball game or write an assigned research paper, whether to try out for the school play or instead rush home after school to catch a favorite television show.

◎   *It leads to increased effort and energy.* Motivation increases the amount of effort and energy that students expend in activities directly related to their needs and goals (Csikszentmihalyi & Nakamura, 1989; Maehr, 1984; Pintrich et al., 1993). It determines whether students pursue a task enthusiastically and wholeheartedly, on the one hand, or apathetically and lackadaisically, on the other.

◎   *It increases initiation of, and persistence in, activities.* Students are more likely to begin a task they actually *want* to do. They are also more likely to continue the task until they've completed it, even if they are occasionally interrupted or frustrated in the process (Larson, 2000; Maehr, 1984; Wigfield, 1994). In general, then, motivation increases students' **time on task**, an important factor affecting their learning and achievement (Brophy, 1988; G. A. Davis & Thomas, 1989).

◎   *It enhances cognitive processing.* Motivation affects what and how information is processed (Eccles & Wigfield, 1985; Pintrich & Schunk, 2002; Voss & Schauble, 1992). For one thing, motivated students are more likely to pay attention, and as we have seen, attention is critical for getting information into working memory. They also try to understand material—to learn it meaningfully—rather than simply "go through the motions" of learning in a superficial, rote manner.

◎   *It determines what consequences are reinforcing and punishing.* The more students are motivated to achieve academic success, the more proud they will be of an A and the more upset they will be by an F or perhaps even a B (recall our discussion of self-imposed contingencies in Chapter 10). The more students want to be accepted and respected by peers, the more meaningful membership in the "in group" will be, and the more painful the ridicule of classmates will seem. To a student uninterested in athletics, making or not making the school football team is no big deal, but to a student whose life revolves around football, making or not making the team may be a consequence of monumental importance.

■ **situated motivation** Phenomenon in which aspects of the immediate environment enhance motivation to learn particular things or behave in particular ways.

■ **time on task** Amount of time that students are actively engaged in a learning activity.

◎   *It leads to improved performance.* Because of these other effects—goal-directed behavior, energy and effort, initiation, persistence, cognitive processing, and impact of consequences—motivation often leads to improved performance. As you might guess, then, students who are most motivated to learn and excel in classroom activities will tend to be our highest achievers (A. E. Gottfried, 1990; Schiefele, Krapp, & Winteler, 1992; Walberg & Uguroglu, 1980). Conversely, students who are least motivated are at high risk for dropping out before they graduate from high school (Hardre & Reeve, 2003; Hymel et al., 1996; Vallerand, Fortier, & Guay, 1997).

Not all forms of motivation have exactly the same effects on human learning and performance. For instance, extrinsic motivation and intrinsic motivation lead to somewhat different outcomes, as we shall see now.

Extrinsic Versus Intrinsic Motivation

Consider these two students in a trigonometry class:

- Sheryl detests mathematics and is taking the class for only one reason: Earning a C or better in trigonometry is a requirement for admission to State University, where she desperately wants to go to college.
- Shannon has always liked math. Trigonometry will help her gain admission to State University, but in addition, Shannon truly wants to understand how to use trigonometry. She sees its usefulness for her future profession as an architect. Besides, she's discovering that trigonometry is actually a lot of fun.

Sheryl exhibits **extrinsic motivation:** She is motivated by factors external to herself and unrelated to the task she is performing. Students who are extrinsically motivated may want the good grades, money, or recognition that particular activities and accomplishments bring. Essentially, they are motivated to perform a task as a means to an end, not as an end in and of itself. In contrast, Shannon exhibits **intrinsic motivation:** She is motivated by factors within herself and inherent in the task she is performing. Students who are intrinsically motivated may engage in an activity because it gives them pleasure, helps them develop a skill they think is important, or is the ethically and morally right thing to do. Some students with high levels of intrinsic motivation become so focused on and absorbed in an activity that they lose track of time and completely ignore other tasks—a phenomenon known as **flow** (Csikszentmihalyi, 1990, 1996).

Students are most likely to show the beneficial effects of motivation when they are *intrinsically* motivated to engage in classroom activities. Intrinsically motivated students tackle assigned tasks willingly and are eager to learn classroom material, are more likely to process information in effective ways (e.g., by engaging in meaningful learning, elaboration, and visual imagery), and are more likely to achieve at high levels. In contrast, extrinsically motivated students may have to be enticed or prodded, may process information only superficially, and are often interested in performing only easy tasks and meeting minimal classroom requirements (A. E. Gottfried, Fleming, & Gottfried, 2001; Larson, 2000; Schiefele, 1991; Spaulding, 1992; Tobias, 1994; Voss & Schauble, 1992).

In the second-grade class depicted in the "Author's Chair" clip on Video CD 2, we see numerous indications that the students are intrinsically motivated to learn and achieve. Several students are eager to read their stories to the class, and most others seem genuinely interested in listening. Furthermore, the story authors don't seem to mind having their work critiqued; their willingness to hear constructive criticism reflects a *mastery goal*, a concept we'll examine in Chapter 12.

Unfortunately, students' intrinsic motivation for learning school subject matter tends to decline during the school years. In the early elementary grades, children are often eager and excited to learn new things at school. But sometime between grades 3 and 9, children become less intrinsically motivated, and more *extrinsically* motivated, to learn and master school subject matter (Covington & Müeller, 2001; Harter, 1992; J. M. T. Walker, 2001). Their intrinsic motivation may be especially low when they make the transition from elementary to secondary school (more about this transition later in the chapter).

The decline in intrinsic motivation for academic subject matter is probably the result of several factors. As students get older, they are increasingly reminded of the importance of good grades (extrinsic motivators) for promotion, graduation, and college admission, and many begin to realize that they are not necessarily "at the top of the heap" in comparison with their peers (Covington & Müeller, 2001; Harter, 1992). Furthermore, they become more cognitively able to set and strive for long-term goals, and they begin to evaluate school subjects in terms of their relevance to such goals, rather than in terms of any intrinsic appeal. And they may grow increasingly impatient with the overly structured, repetitive, and boring activities that they often encounter at school (Battistich, Solomon, Kim, Watson, & Schaps, 1995; Larson, 2000).

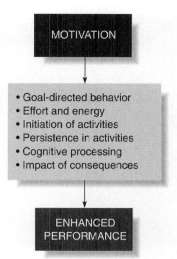

FIGURE 11.1 How motivation affects learning and behavior

■ Observe numerous examples of intrinsic motivation in the "Author's Chair" clip on Video CD 2.

■ **extrinsic motivation** Motivation promoted by factors external to the individual and unrelated to the task being performed.

■ **intrinsic motivation** Internal desire to perform a particular task.

■ **flow** Intense form of intrinsic motivation, involving complete absorption in and concentration on a challenging activity.

Students learn more and are more likely to engage in meaningful learning and elaboration when they are genuinely interested in what they are learning.

This is not to say, however, that extrinsic motivation is necessarily a bad thing. Oftentimes students are motivated by both intrinsic and extrinsic factors simultaneously (Cameron & Pierce, 1994; Covington, 2000; Deci, 1998; Hidi & Harackiewicz, 2000). For example, although Shannon enjoys studying trigonometry, she also knows that a good grade in her trigonometry course will help her gain admission to State U. Furthermore, good grades and other external rewards for high achievements may confirm for Shannon that she is, in fact, mastering school subject matter (Hynd, 2003). And as we noted in Chapter 9, extrinsic motivation, perhaps in the form of extrinsic reinforcers for academic achievement or productive behavior, may be essential for getting some students on the road to successful classroom learning and productivity. Yet intrinsic motivation is ultimately what will sustain students over the long run: It will encourage them to make sense of and apply what they are studying, and it will increase the odds that they continue to read and learn about science, history, and other academic subject matter long after they have graduated and ventured out into the adult world.

The origins of both extrinsic and intrinsic motivation have been the source of considerable debate for many years. Let's look at how various researchers have studied and tried to explain the nature and sources of motivation.

THEORETICAL PERSPECTIVES OF MOTIVATION

Researchers and theorists have approached the study of motivation from four major angles: the trait, behaviorist, social cognitive, and cognitive perspectives. Each of these approaches can better help us understand the complex nature of human motivation, and so each has implications for classroom practice.

The Trait Perspective

Trait theorists propose that motivation takes the form of relatively enduring personality characteristics that people have to a greater or lesser degree. For example, children and adolescents differ in their tendency to forge friendly relationships with others and in their desire to gain other people's regard and respect (more about such needs for *affiliation* and *approval* shortly). They may also differ in the extent to which they seek out new, exciting, and possibly dangerous experiences—that is, in the extent to which they are *sensation seekers* (R. E. Snow, Corno, & Jackson, 1996).

Of the various needs that people might have, the majority of research has focused on the need for achievement, more often called **achievement motivation**. Achievement motivation is the need for excellence for its own sake, without regard for any external rewards that one's accomplishments might bring (e.g., J. W. Atkinson & Feather, 1966; McClelland, Atkinson, Clark, & Lowell, 1953; Veroff et al., 1975). Students with high achievement motivation seek out challenging tasks that they know they can accomplish with effort and persistence. They rarely rest on their laurels; instead, they set increasingly higher standards for excellence as their current standards are met (Eccles et al., 1998; Veroff et al., 1975). And they are willing and able to delay gratification: They put off small, immediate rewards for the larger rewards that long-term efforts will yield.

In its earliest conceptualization, achievement motivation was thought to be a general trait that students exhibit consistently in a variety of tasks and across many domains. More recently, however, many theorists have proposed that achievement motivation may instead be somewhat specific to particular tasks and occasions (e.g., Dweck & Elliott, 1983; Stipek, 1996; Wigfield, 1997). Theorists are also beginning to explain achievement motivation in terms of specific cognitive factors that influence the choices learners make and the tasks they pursue. Thus, explanations of achievement motivation have shifted away from a "trait" approach to a more cognitive approach.

Although the trait approach to achievement motivation is losing prominence in contemporary theory and research, personality characteristics clearly *do* influence the motives students exhibit in the classroom (e.g., Covington & Omelich, 1991; Harter & Jackson, 1992). We'll see examples of enduring individual differences in motivation in our upcoming discussion of *relatedness* in this chapter and in our discussions of *personal interests*, *dispositions*, and *learned helplessness* in Chapter 12. The following exercise illustrates some of the motivational traits we might see.

■ **trait theory** Theoretical perspective portraying motivation as involving enduring personality characteristics that learners have to a greater or lesser degree.

■ **achievement motivation** Need for excellence for its own sake, without regard for external rewards that accomplishments might bring.

Interpreting Student Artifacts and Behaviors

There's Nothing to Do in Greeley

When my daughter Tina was in ninth grade, she took part in a school district writing assessment. For the assessment, she was asked to write an essay in response to the statement "There is nothing to do in Greeley" (her hometown). As you read her essay, speculate about

- What traits guided Tina's choices for leisure-time activity
- What Tina most enjoyed about school

There is nothing to do in Greeley! I know every parent has heard that line before!

I am going to disagree with this quote. I think that it depends on who the person is who's saying this. The person who is proposing this is really remarking that they do not choose to do anything, not that there is little or nothing to do.

From my experiences with nothing to do, I have always been successful with curing that awful plague of boredom. When caught with this disease I usually call my friends who may also be suffering. Our phone conversations typically consist of at least two remedies and finally a cure. I myself often suggest a few good ideas to our problem, but if the case is really nasty my cronies and I work together to find the solution. Anybody can find entertainment if they really choose to.

Greeley isn't half as bad as people see it to be. I guess we Greeley folk are lucky we aren't living somewhere like Ordway, Colorado. Or better yet, how about Black Pebble, North Dakota? I'll bet you have never even heard of Black

Pebble! Probably not, since it is in the middle of nothing. I heard about it from a book I have called <u>Places Never Even Dreamed of in the U.S.</u> The person who wrote that book must have been homesick with boredom.

Luckily, if you are ever caught in an uninviting situation one can find many thrills. For example, if you are forced to go see a movie (with the gang) that you have already seen five times, then why not bring a needle and thread? While everyone else is engulfed in the movie you can be busily sewing their sleeves together! See what I mean? If not, read on. If two people are sitting next to each other, there is a little bit of space between them because of the arm slot. Simply grasp the clothing you can get without them noticing and go at it! That will probably take up part of the show. The other half will go by quickly as you try to refrain from blowing up with laughter. If this isn't your fancy, then try to think of something else. You can do it!

All in all, remember, there is always something to do no matter what the situation is if you have a creative mind that's ready to run wild!

Tina's essay is as informative in what it *doesn't* say as in what it does say. Notice how her solution to finding something to do rests entirely on other people; she doesn't mention any form of solitary entertainment. From the time she was a toddler, Tina was happy only when she was with others, and by the time she was 10, those "others" had to be her friends. Thus Tina had a high need for affiliation, which made hanging out with friends her highest priority both in and outside of school. Furthermore, her thoughts about provoking others (e.g., by sewing their clothes together) suggest that she was a bit of a sensation seeker; as her mother, I can tell you that she sought enough thrills in her adolescent years that I was quite relieved that she lived to see her high school graduation.

The Behaviorist Perspective

From a behaviorist perspective, people behave primarily to obtain reinforcing outcomes (or perhaps to avoid punishing ones), and many of their behaviors are those that have been reinforced in the past. For instance, students might study hard if their teacher praises them for their efforts, and they might misbehave in class if doing so gains them the attention of their teacher and classmates.

Early behaviorists proposed that specific consequences are reinforcing only if they address a particular **drive**, an internal state in which something necessary for optimal functioning (food, water, warmth, etc.) is missing. For example, a hungry person finds food reinforcing, and a thirsty person enjoys water. In recent years, however, motivation theorists have largely left drive reduction theory by the wayside (Bolles, 1975; Graham & Weiner, 1996). For one thing, learning sometimes occurs without satisfying, or reducing, any apparent drive (e.g., Sheffield, Wulff, & Backer, 1951). And a great deal of human behavior seems to be aimed at accomplishing long-term goals rather than fulfilling short-term needs (Pintrich & Schunk, 2002). Furthermore, people sometimes behave in ways that actually *increase* drive (Rachlin, 1991), perhaps by going to scary movies, riding roller coasters, or (like Tina) annoying companions by sewing their clothes together.

Rather than focusing on physiological needs and drives, many behaviorists now look more generally at the purposes that particular behaviors may serve for people (see the discussion of *functional analysis* in Chapter 9). Other theorists, whether or not they take a behaviorist approach to learning and motivation, nevertheless recognize that the consequences of behaviors can

drive Motivational state in which something necessary for optimal functioning is missing.

certainly affect students' motivation to exhibit those behaviors. For instance, psychologists of a variety of theoretical persuasions have studied the circumstances under which *feedback* is likely to be effective. In general, feedback is most effective when it provides information that students cannot get on their own, identifies specific strengths that students have and specific weaknesses that can be addressed, and maintains students' self-efficacy and self-esteem (Kluger & DeNisi, 1998; Pintrich & Schunk, 2002; Tunstall & Gipps, 1996).

The Social Cognitive Perspective

As we noted in Chapter 10, social cognitive theory has contributed in several important ways to our understanding of motivation. For instance, this perspective places heavy emphasis on the *goals* people strive for, as reflected in the choices they make and the behaviors they exhibit. It also acknowledges that the reinforcers and punishments that follow various behaviors affect people's *expectations* for the consequences of future behaviors. And it points out that people's *self-efficacy*—their beliefs about their own capability to perform a particular activity—is a key factor in their decisions to engage in and persist at the activity. All three of these concepts—goals, expectations, and self-efficacy—have emerged as important cognitive factors in motivation, and so we will revisit them in Chapter 12.

The Cognitive Perspective

To motivate students in the classroom, a cognitive psychologist might propose capitalizing on their natural curiosity by presenting new and puzzling situations.

As you might guess, cognitive psychologists focus on how mental processes affect motivation. They propose that human beings are naturally inclined to make sense of their world, that their curiosity is often piqued by new and puzzling events, and that they are especially motivated by perceived discrepancies between new information and their existing beliefs (e.g., recall Piaget's concept of *disequilibrium*, described in Chapter 2). People also try to make sense of the things that happen to them—for instance, by identifying possible causes of (*attributions* for) their successes and failures ("I got an A on my report because I'm smart," "I didn't get to start in Saturday's game because the coach doesn't like me," etc.). This need to make sense of one's environment and experiences is undoubtedly a primary source of intrinsic motivation, but it is probably not the only source. For instance, some cognitive theorists propose that two essential conditions for intrinsic motivation are *self-efficacy* and a *sense of self-determination*—a belief that one has some control over the direction one's life is taking. We'll return to these ideas in Chapter 12.

Within the last two or three decades, the cognitive and social cognitive perspectives have dominated theory and research in motivation (A. M. Ryan, 2000; Winne & Marx, 1989), and so you will see their influence throughout this chapter and the next. Yet we must keep in mind that no single theory gives us a complete picture of human motivation. Each of the perspectives just summarized provides pieces of the motivation "puzzle," and so each offers useful ideas about how we can motivate students in classroom settings. Table 11.1 contrasts the four perspectives and describes general educational implications of each one.

WHAT BASIC NEEDS DO PEOPLE HAVE?

■ For an early yet influential perspective of how people prioritize needs, see the supplementary reading "Maslow's Hierarchy of Needs" in the *Study Guide and Reader* that accompanies this book.

As I described the four perspectives of motivation in the preceding section, I occasionally talked about *needs*; for instance, I mentioned the needs for affiliation and approval, the need for achievement, and the need to make sense of the world. Over the years, psychologists have speculated that people have a wide variety of needs. Some needs—for oxygen, food, water, warmth, and so on—are related to physical well-being, and these needs undoubtedly take high priority when physical survival is in jeopardy (e.g., Maslow, 1973, 1987). Other needs are more closely related to *psychological* well-being—that is, to feeling comfortable and content in one's day-to-day activities. Although psychologists have not pinned down a list of specific needs essential for psychological well-being, many agree that most or all human beings have a basic need to believe that they can effectively deal with their environment—that is, a need for *self-worth*—as well as a basic need to interact with other people—that is, a need for *relatedness*.

Self-Worth

Some theorists have proposed that people have a basic need to feel *competent*: They want to believe that they can deal effectively with the objects and events they encounter (R. M. Ryan & Deci, 2000; R. White, 1959). To achieve this sense of competence, children spend a great deal of time

TABLE 11.1

Comparing Theoretical Perspectives of Motivation

ISSUE	TRAIT THEORIES	BEHAVIORISM	SOCIAL COGNITIVE THEORY	COGNITIVE PSYCHOLOGY
Sources of motivation are . . .	relatively enduring characteristics and personality traits.	the consequences of various behaviors.	personal goals, beliefs about one's ability to perform tasks successfully, and expectations regarding the probable outcomes of future efforts.	inconsistencies between current beliefs and new experiences, interpretations of past successes and failures, and perceptions of personal competence and control.
Examples of motivational concepts are . . .	achievement motivation, need for affiliation, need for approval.	drive, reinforcement, punishment, functional analysis, feedback.	goals, self-efficacy, expectations.	curiosity, interest, disequilibrium, attributions, sense of competence, sense of self-determination.
Educational implications focus on . . .	identifying motivational traits and using instructional strategies that address students' individual needs.	administering consequences that increase desirable behaviors and decrease nonproductive ones.	encouraging efforts toward self-chosen goals and facilitating success through instruction, modeling, and ongoing guidance and support.	pointing out how new information contradicts students' existing beliefs, showing students how their successes and failures are due to factors within their control (e.g., effort, learning strategies), and providing opportunities for choice and self-direction.

engaged in exploring and attempting to gain mastery over various aspects of their world. The need for competence may have evolutionary significance: It pushes growing children to develop ways of dealing more effectively with a variety of circumstances and thus increases their chances of survival (R. White, 1959).

One recent theorist has proposed that *protecting* one's sense of competence—something he calls **self-worth**—is one of people's highest priorities (Covington, 1992). Occasionally, people seem more concerned about maintaining *consistent* self-perceptions, even if those self-perceptions are negative ones (Cassidy, Ziv, Mehta, & Feeney, 2003; Hay, Ashman, van Kraayenoord, & Stewart, 1999). By and large, however, positive self-perceptions do appear to be a high priority.

Other people's judgments and approval play a key role in the development of self-worth, especially in the early years (Harter, 1999). Achieving success on a regular basis is, of course, another important way of maintaining, perhaps even enhancing, self-worth. But consistent success isn't always possible, especially when people must tackle challenging tasks. In the face of a difficult task, an alternative way to maintain self-worth is to *avoid failure*, because failure gives the impression of low ability (Covington, 1992; Covington & Müeller, 2001; Urdan & Midgley, 2001). Failure avoidance manifests itself in a variety of ways. Students might refuse to engage in a task, minimize the task's importance, or set exceedingly low expectations for their performance (Covington, 1992; Harter, 1990; A. J. Martin, Marsh, & Debus, 2001). They might also hold tightly to their current beliefs despite considerable evidence to the contrary (Sherman & Cohen, 2002). The need to protect self-worth, then, may be one reason why students are reluctant to undergo conceptual change.

When students can't avoid tasks at which they think they will do poorly, they have alternative strategies at their disposal. Occasionally they make excuses that seemingly justify their poor performance (Covington, 1992; Urdan & Midgley, 2001). They may also do things that actually *undermine* their chances of success—a phenomenon known as **self-handicapping**. One self-handicapping strategy is simply to expend very little effort in an assigned activity. In the following interview, a student named Christine explains why she sometimes doesn't work very hard on her assignments:

Interviewer: What if you don't do so well?

Christine: Then you've got an excuse. . . . It's just easier to cope with if you think you haven't put as much work into it.

Interviewer: What's easier to cope with?

Christine: From feeling like a failure because you're not good at it. It's easier to say, "I failed because I didn't put enough work into it" than "I failed because I'm not good at it." (A. J. Martin, Marsh, Williamson, & Debus, 2003, p. 621)

■ **self-worth** Beliefs about one's own general ability to deal effectively with the environment.

■ **self-handicapping** Undermining one's own success as a way of protecting self-worth during difficult tasks.

Self-handicapping takes a variety of forms, including the following:

- *Reducing effort.* Putting forth an obviously insufficient amount of effort to succeed
- *Setting unattainably high goals.* Working toward goals that even the most able students couldn't achieve
- *Taking on too much.* Assuming so many responsibilities that no one could possibly accomplish them all successfully
- *Procrastinating.* Putting off a task until success is virtually impossible
- *Cheating.*   Presenting others' work as one's own
- *Using alcohol or drugs.* Taking substances that will inevitably reduce performance (E. M. Anderman, Griesinger, & Westerfield, 1998; Covington, 1992; D. Y. Ford, 1996; E. E. Jones & Berglas, 1978; Riggs, 1992; Urdan, Ryan, Anderman, & Gheen, 2002)

Self-handicapping behaviors have been observed in students as early as fifth grade, and those who frequently self-handicap achieve at lower levels than those who rarely do (Urdan & Midgley, 2001). As we learned in Chapter 3, young children (e.g., kindergartners and first graders) are generally fairly optimistic about their chances of future success; hence they would have little reason to self-handicap.

It might seem paradoxical that students who want to be successful would actually try to undermine their own success. But if they believe they are unlikely to succeed no matter what they do—and especially if failure will reflect poorly on their intelligence and ability—they increase their chances of *justifying* the failure and thereby protecting their self-worth (Covington, 1992; Riggs, 1992; Urdan et al., 2002). Curiously, some students are more likely to perform at their best, and less likely to display self-handicapping behaviors, when outside circumstances indicate that their chances of success are slim; in such cases, failure doesn't indicate low ability and so doesn't threaten their sense of self-worth (Covington, 1992).

Ideally, students' sense of self-worth should be based on a reasonably accurate appraisal of what they can and cannot accomplish. Students who underestimate their abilities will set unnecessarily low goals for themselves and give up easily after only minor setbacks. Those who overestimate their abilities (perhaps because they have been lavished with praise by parents or teachers, or perhaps because school assignments have been consistently easy and nonchallenging) may set themselves up for failure by forming unrealistically high expectations, exerting insufficient effort, or not addressing their weaknesses (Lockhart et al., 2002; Paris & Cunningham, 1996; H. W. Stevenson et al., 1990). The strategies for enhancing students' self-concept, self-esteem, and self-efficacy that we've previously identified in Chapters 3 and 10—for instance, scaffolding students' efforts at challenging tasks—can help them maintain a healthy sense of self-worth.

To date, most research on self-worth theory and self-handicapping has focused on academic tasks and accomplishments. We must keep in mind, however, that academic achievement isn't necessarily the most important thing affecting students' sense of self-worth. For many students, such factors as social success or physical appearance may be more influential (Eccles et al., 1998). To the extent that we can, then, we should support their successes in the nonacademic as well as academic aspects of their lives.

Relatedness

How much time do you spend with other people? Do you enjoy being with others for a good part of each day? Or, like Anya, are you content spending much of your time alone? And how much do you care about what others think of you? Do you continually worry about how others might judge your words and actions? Or do you have such confidence in your convictions that you do what you think is best regardless of any social repercussions?

To some extent, we are all social creatures: We live, work, and play with our fellow human beings. Some theorists have proposed that people of all ages have a fundamental need to feel socially connected and to secure the love and respect of others; in other words, they have a **need for relatedness** (Connell & Wellborn, 1991; R. M. Ryan & Deci, 2000). As is true for the need for competence, the need for relatedness may be important from an evolutionary standpoint, in that people who live in cohesive, cooperative social groups are more likely to survive and reproduce than people who go it alone (R. Wright, 1994).

In the classroom a student's need for relatedness may manifest itself in a wide variety of behaviors. Many children and adolescents place high priority on interacting with friends, often at

■ **need for relatedness** Need to feel socially connected to others and to secure others' love and respect.

the expense of getting their schoolwork done (Dowson & McInerney, 2001; W. Doyle, 1986a; Wigfield, Eccles, Mac Iver, Reuman, & Midgley, 1991). They may also be concerned about projecting a favorable public image—that is, by looking smart, popular, athletic, or cool; in doing so, they can enhance their sense of self-worth as well as satisfy their need for relatedness (Harter, 1999; Juvonen, 2000). Prosocial behaviors can address students' need for relatedness as well; for instance, students might show concern for other people's welfare or help peers who are struggling with classroom assignments (Dowson & McInerney, 2001; M. E. Ford, 1996).

The need for relatedness seems to be especially high in early adolescence (B. B. Brown et al., 1986; Juvonen, 2000; A. M. Ryan & Patrick, 2001). (As an example, see 11-year-old Ben's description of his class trip to Gettysburg in Figure 11.2.) Young adolescents tend to be overly concerned about what others think, prefer to hang out in tight-knit groups, and are especially susceptible to peer influence (recall our discussions of the *imaginary audience*, *cliques*, and *peer pressure* in Chapter 3).

As teachers, we must remember that social relationships will be among most students' highest priorities (Dowson & McInerney, 2001; Geary, 1998). Students are more likely to be academically motivated and successful—and more likely to stay in school rather than drop out—when they believe that their teachers and peers like and respect them and when they feel that they belong to the classroom community (Goodenow, 1993; Furrer & Skinner, 2003; Hymel et al., 1996; A. M. Ryan & Patrick, 2001). In our discussions of *classroom climate*, *teacher-student relationships*, and *sense of community* in Chapter 14, we will consider how we can foster such beliefs and feelings.

Individual Differences in the Need for Relatedness Although the need for relatedness may be universal, some children and adolescents seem to have a greater need for interpersonal relationships than others (Kupersmidt, Buchele, Voegler, & Sedikides, 1996). Let's briefly take a "trait" approach to motivation as we consider research related to needs for affiliation and approval.

Need for affiliation. Students differ in the extent to which they desire and actively seek out friendly relationships with others; in other words, they differ in their **need for affiliation**. For example, as I mentioned earlier, my daughter Tina has always been a very social creature; the thought of spending more than a couple of hours alone horrifies her. In contrast, my youngest child, Jeff, has always been able to work or play alone quite happily for hours at a time.

Students' needs for affiliation will be reflected in the choices they make at school (Boyatzis, 1973; E. G. French, 1956; Wigfield et al., 1996). For instance, students with a low need for affiliation may prefer to work alone, whereas students with a high need for affiliation more often prefer to work in small groups. When choosing work partners, students with a low affiliation need are apt to choose classmates whom they believe will be competent at an assigned task; students with a high affiliation need are apt to choose their friends even if these friends are relatively incompetent. In high school, students with a low need for affiliation are likely to choose a class schedule that meets their own interests and ambitions, whereas students with a high need for affiliation tend to choose one that enables them to be with their friends. As you can see, then, a high need for affiliation can sometimes interfere with maximal classroom learning and achievement (Urdan & Maehr, 1995; Wentzel & Wigfield, 1998).

As teachers, we cannot ignore the high need for affiliation that many students bring to the classroom. On the contrary, as we plan daily lessons and classroom activities, we must provide opportunities for students to interact with one another. Ideally, we should find ways to help students learn academic subject matter *and* meet their affiliation needs simultaneously (Wentzel & Wigfield, 1998). Although some instructional goals can best be accomplished when students work independently, others can be accomplished just as easily (perhaps even more so) when students work together. Group-based activities, such as discussions, debates,

FIGURE 11.2 In this personal narrative, 11-year-old Ben describes a school field trip to a Civil War battlefield. In the last paragraph he reveals what was, from his perspective, the *most* valuable part of the trip: the chance to be with his friends for the entire day.

My Trip to Gettysburg

"Honk!" sounded the bus. We had just left for one of the best times of my life. My friends, mom, teachers, and I were all going.

Last spring was my trip to Gettysburg. We had to wake up at 5:00 a.m. When we got there, I said "Hi!" to everyone in my group. We were at Gettysburg on time even though the bus was late.

When we got there, we went to the tour center and watched an informational video about Gettysburg. Now we were ready for a tour of the real battlefield the union and confederate soldiers fought on. Our guide tried to convince us that Lee was a great general. He told us the book and movie were a lie based on Longstreet's autobiography.

Then we went to the Wax Museum. It was cool! They looked so real. I liked the battlefield scene most.

We went to the Stonehenge for dinner. After that we went to the Jennie Wade house. While we where there we had a wax person talk to us. Finally we left. We watched three movies on the way home.

There were a lot of cool things I did at Gettysburg, but most of all I got closer to my friends because we spent all 18 hours together. We ate together, sat with each other on the bus, and went to every activity together. That's why I call it the best time of my life!!

■ **need for affiliation** Tendency to seek out friendly relationships with others.

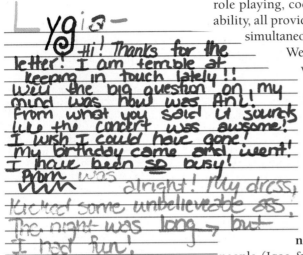

Passing notes in class is one way that some students regularly address their need for affiliation.

role playing, cooperative learning tasks, and competitions among two or more teams of equal ability, all provide the means through which students can satisfy their need for affiliation while simultaneously acquiring new knowledge and skills (Brophy, 1987; Urdan & Maehr, 1995). We must remember, too, that many of our students will want to affiliate not only with their classmates but with their teachers as well. Therefore, we should show students that we like them, enjoy being with them, and are concerned about their well-being (Patrick et al., 2002; Stipek, 1996). We can communicate our fondness for students in numerous ways; for example, we can express an interest in their outside activities and accomplishments, provide extra help or support when they need it, or lend a sympathetic ear. These "caring" messages may be especially important for students from culturally different backgrounds: Such students are more likely to succeed at school if we show interest in their lives and concern for their individual needs (Phelan, Davidson, & Cao, 1991).

Need for approval. Another need in which we see individual differences is the **need for approval**, a desire to gain the acceptance and positive judgments of other people (Igoe & Sullivan, 1991; Juvonen & Weiner, 1993; Urdan & Maehr, 1995). Many elementary school students have a strong desire to attain the approval of their teacher; at the secondary level, students are more apt to seek the approval of peers (Harter, 1999; Juvonen & Weiner, 1993; Urdan & Maehr, 1995). Cultural background may also influence whether children and adolescents prefer adult or peer approval; for instance, many teenagers from Asian cultures highly value the approval of adult authority figures (e.g., Dien, 1998).

Students with a high need for approval are often those with low self-esteem (Crowne & Marlowe, 1964). They may go out of their way to behave in ways they think will please others, sometimes compromising their own standards for acceptable behavior (Berndt & Keefe, 1996; Crowne & Marlowe, 1964). They are apt to engage in and persist at school tasks primarily to gain their teacher's praise, and they may self-handicap in activities at which they expect to do poorly (H. A. Davis, 2003; Harter, 1975; S. C. Rose & Thornburg, 1984). Especially in adolescence, students with a high need for approval give in easily to peer pressure, for fear that they might otherwise be rejected (Crowne & Marlowe, 1964; Wentzel & Wigfield, 1998). Such efforts are often counterproductive, however: Perhaps because they are trying *too* hard to be liked, students with a high need for approval tend to be relatively unpopular with peers (Boyatzis, 1973; Crowne & Marlowe, 1964).

When students have a high need for approval, we can promote their classroom achievement by praising them frequently for the things they do well. We must keep in mind, however, that some students (especially in the secondary grades) may be concerned about gaining the approval of peers who disapprove of high academic achievement (Juvonen & Weiner, 1993; L. Steinberg, 1996; Wigfield et al., 1996). If being a high achiever is not the socially acceptable thing to do, many students will prefer that their accomplishments be praised privately rather than publicly. Ultimately, how well our students are accomplishing instructional goals is no one's business but theirs, their parents', and ours. The Creating a Productive Classroom Environment feature "Addressing Students' Social Needs" presents several examples of how we might address students' need for relatedness—and in particular, their needs for affiliation and approval—in the classroom.

Relationships with peers and teachers are, for many students, a source of considerable pleasure and enjoyment. Conversely, difficulties in interpersonal interactions, which may impede students' ability to satisfy their need for relatedness, are often a source of sadness and anxiety. Pleasure, enjoyment, and anxiety are all examples of what psychologists call *affect*, our next topic of discussion.

AFFECT AND ITS EFFECTS

A close partner of motivation is **affect**—the feelings, emotions, and general moods that a learner brings to bear on a task.[1] For example, earlier in the chapter we noted that intrinsically motivated individuals typically find pleasure in what they are doing. Yet too much motivation—perhaps

■ **need for approval** Desire to gain acceptance and positive judgments from others.

■ **affect** Feelings, emotions, and moods that a learner brings to bear on a task.

---

[1] Some psychologists use the terms *affect* and *emotion* interchangeably. But others suggest that we use *emotion* to refer only to short-term states and that we use *affect* in a broader sense to include both short-term emotions and longer-term moods and temperaments (Forgas, 2000; Linnenbrink & Pintrich, 2002; Rosenberg, 1998).

CREATING A PRODUCTIVE CLASSROOM ENVIRONMENT

Addressing Students' Social Needs

 Have students work together on some learning tasks.

A high school history teacher incorporates classroom debates, small-group discussions, and cooperative learning tasks into every month's activities.

 Continually communicate the message that you like and respect your students.

A middle school teacher tells one of his students that he saw her dancing troupe's performance at the local mall over the weekend. "I had no idea you were so talented," he says. "How many years have you been studying dance?"

Create a classroom culture in which respect for *everyone's* needs and well-being is paramount.

When a fourth-grade teacher overhears two boys making fun of a fellow student who stutters, she discretely pulls them aside, explains that the classmate is extremely self-conscious about his speech and is working hard to improve it, and she reminds the boys that they, too, have imperfections as well as strengths.

Give frequent praise to students who have a high need for approval.

Several students in a second-grade class have difficulty staying on task during independent assignments. Their teacher seats them near her desk, where she can frequently commend them for their work.

Praise students privately when being a high achiever is not sanctioned by their peer group.

While reading a stack of short stories his students have written, a high school English teacher discovers that one student—a young woman who, he knows, is quite concerned about looking cool in front of her classmates—has written a particularly creative story. On the second page of her story (where the student's classmates won't be likely to see his comment), he writes, "This is great work, Brigitta! I think it's good enough to enter into the state writing contest. I'd like to meet with you before or after school some day this week to talk more about the contest."

---

wanting something too much—may lead to an intense sense of anxiety. In the following sections, we will examine numerous ways in which affect is interrelated not only with motivation but also with learning and cognition. We will then look at the causes and effects of anxiety in the classroom and at developmental changes in anxiety and other forms of affect during childhood and adolescence.

How Affect Is Related to Motivation

How children and adolescents feel depends, to a considerable degree, on whether their needs are being met and their goals are being accomplished. You can find numerous examples of this relationship in the three "Emotions" clips on Video CD 1. For example, 10-year-old Daniel explains that one common source of anger is "not getting what you want." For 13-year-old Crystal, people will be happy if they "have a boyfriend or girlfriend or if they get one." For 15-year-old Greg, friends and good grades are a source of happiness, and disrupted peer relationships can be a source of anger or sadness.

Affect and motivation are interconnected in other ways as well. As students make plans and set goals for themselves, they will be more optimistic about what they can accomplish if they feel cheerful rather than depressed (Harter, 1988). And they will consider how they are apt to feel later on—in particular, they'll think about feeling good (e.g., happy or proud) if they succeed and about feeling bad (e.g., sad or ashamed) if they fail (Mellers & McGraw, 2001).

Affect also comes into play after students complete an activity. They will, of course, react emotionally to their successes and failures. But they are more likely to feel excited about their successes if they didn't expect to be successful, and they will experience more intense negative emotions about their failures—and often about the activity in question—if they didn't expect to fail (Bower & Forgas, 2001; Shepperd & McNulty, 2002). Furthermore, their specific reactions will depend on how they *interpret* the outcomes of events—in particular, whether they hold themselves, other people, environmental circumstances, or something else responsible for what has happened (Hareli & Weiner, 2002; Harter, 1999; J. E. Turner, Husman, & Schallert, 2002). For example, if they believe they themselves are responsible for a failure, they may feel guilty or ashamed, and such feelings may spur them to address their shortcomings. If they instead think that someone else was to blame, they are more apt to be angry, an emotion that's less likely to lead to productive behaviors. Here I'm giving you a brief glimpse into the emotional repercussions of students' *attributions*; we'll take up this topic in more detail in Chapter 12.

■ Observe how affect and motivation are related in the three "Emotions" clips on Video CD 1.

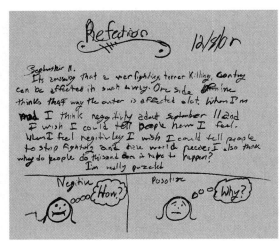

Information and events that evoke strong emotional reactions often remain vivid in memory for quite some time. In this reflection in her class journal, written more than a year after terrorists' attacks on the World Trade Center and Pentagon, 12-year-old Amaryth still has strong feelings about the attacks.

How Affect Is Related to Learning and Cognition

Affect is often an integral part of human learning and cognition (Damasio, 1994; D. K. Meyer & Turner, 2002; Ochsner & Lieberman, 2001). For example, while learning how to perform a task, students simultaneously learn whether or not they like doing it (Zajonc, 1980). Problem solving is easier when students enjoy what they're doing, and successful attempts at learning and problem solving often bring on feelings of excitement, pleasure, and pride (McLeod & Adams, 1989; R. E. Snow et al., 1996). In contrast, students may feel frustrated and anxious when they must struggle to master new material, and they may develop a dislike for the subject matter (Carver & Scheier, 1990; Stodolsky, Salk, & Glaessner, 1991). An exchange between one of my educational psychology students (Brian) and his 16-year-old sister Megan illustrates the effects of mastery and nonmastery on students' feelings for what they are studying:

Brian: How do you know when you have learned something?

Megan: I know that I have learned something when I get really excited about that topic while I am talking to a person about it. When I haven't learned something I tend to say that I hate it, because I don't understand it. When I am excited and can have a discussion about something is when I know that I fully understand and have studied enough on that topic. (courtesy of Brian Zottoli)

In addition, specific facts and ideas can occasionally evoke emotional reactions, as you will discover in the following exercise.

Experiencing FIRSTHAND ·Flying High

As you read each of the following statements, decide whether it evokes positive feelings (e.g., happiness, excitement), negative feelings (e.g., sadness, anger), or no feelings whatsoever. Check the appropriate blank in each case.

	Positive Feelings	Negative Feelings	No Feelings
1. The city of Denver opened a new international airport in 1995.	_____	_____	_____
2. In a recent commercial airline crash, ninety passengers and eight crew members lost their lives.	_____	_____	_____
3. A dozen people survived that crash, including a 3-month-old infant found in the rear of the plane.	_____	_____	_____
4. The area of an airplane in which food is prepared is called the *galley*.	_____	_____	_____
5. Several major airlines are offering $69 round-trip fares to Acapulco, Mexico.	_____	_____	_____
6. Those $69 fares apply only to flights leaving at 5:30 in the morning.	_____	_____	_____
7. Some flights between North America and Europe now include two full-course meals.	_____	_____	_____

· · · · · · ·

You probably had little if any emotional reaction to statements 1 (the new airport) and 4 (the definition of *galley*). In contrast, you may have had pleasant feelings when you read statements 3 (the surviving infant) and 5 (the low fares to Acapulco) and unpleasant feelings when you read statements 2 (the high number of deaths) and 6 (the dreadful departure time for those Acapulco flights). Your response to statement 7 (the two full-course meals) may have been positive, negative, or neutral, depending on your previous experiences with airline cuisine.

As people think about, learn, or retrieve something, their very thoughts and memories may be emotionally charged—a phenomenon known as **hot cognition** (e.g., Hoffman, 1991; P. H. Miller, 1993). For example, students might get excited when they read about advances in science that could lead to effective treatments for spinal cord injuries, cancer, AIDS, or mental

■ **hot cognition** Learning or cognitive processing that is emotionally charged.

illness. They may feel sad when they read about the living conditions in certain parts of the world. They will, we hope, get angry when they learn about the atrocities committed against African American slaves in the pre-Civil War days of the United States or against millions of Jewish people and members of other minority groups in Europe during World War II.

When information is emotionally charged, students are more apt to pay attention to it, continue to think about it over a period of time, and repeatedly elaborate on it (Bower, 1994; Heuer & Reisberg, 1992; D. L. Schacter, 1999). Encountering information that conflicts with what they currently know or believe can cause considerable mental discomfort, something that Piaget called *disequilibrium* but that many contemporary theorists call **cognitive dissonance**. (As an example of how a teacher might create dissonance, watch the "Properties of Air" clip on Video CD 2.) Such dissonance typically leads learners to try to resolve the inconsistency in some way, perhaps undergoing *conceptual change* or perhaps ignoring or discrediting the new information (Buehl & Alexander, 2001; Harmon-Jones, 2001; Sinatra & Pintrich, 2003b). Later on, students can usually retrieve material with high emotional content more easily than they can recall relatively nonemotional information (Barkley, 1996; LaBar & Phelps, 1998; Reisberg & Heuer, 1992).[2] It appears that students' affective reactions to classroom subject matter become integral parts of their network of associations in long-term memory (Bower & Forgas, 2001).

■ Observe a teacher creating cognitive dissonance on the "Properties of Air" clip on Video CD 2.

Academic subject matter certainly doesn't need to be dry and emotionless. On the contrary, students will probably remember more if they have strong feelings about the things they study, perhaps getting very excited about a scientific discovery or quite angry about social injustices. In addition to presenting subject matter that evokes emotional reactions, we can promote hot cognition by revealing our own feelings about a topic—perhaps by bringing in newspaper articles and other outside materials about which we are excited, presenting material in an enthusiastic or impassioned fashion, and sharing the particular questions and issues about which we ourselves are concerned (Brophy, 2004; R. P. Perry, 1985). And although we don't necessarily want to give the impression that schoolwork is all fun and games, we can occasionally incorporate a few gamelike features into classroom tasks and activities (Brophy, 2004)—perhaps by assigning simple crossword puzzles to introduce new spelling words or by using a television game show format for a class history review (the latter strategy also addresses students' need for relatedness).

Not all forms of affect contribute productively to learning and cognition, of course. For instance, students usually learn less effectively when they are sad or depressed (Bower, 1994; Hertel, 1994; R. E. Snow et al., 1996). Another emotion—anxiety—can have either positive or negative effects, depending on the circumstances. Because so many students experience anxiety at school and because instructional practices and the classroom environment can contribute significantly to students' anxiety levels, we will now look at this particular form of affect more closely.

One way to promote positive affect about a classroom topic is to model our own enthusiasm for it.

Anxiety

Imagine you are enrolled in Professor Josiah S. Carberry's course in advanced psychoceramics. Today is your day to give a half-hour presentation on the topic of psychoceramic califractions. You have read several books and numerous articles on your topic and undoubtedly know more about psychoceramic califractions than anyone else in the room. Furthermore, you have meticulously prepared a set of note cards to refer to during your presentation. As you sit in class waiting for your turn to speak, you should be feeling calm and confident. But instead you're a nervous wreck: Your heart is pounding wildly, your palms are sweaty, and your stomach is in a knot. When Professor Carberry calls you to the front of the room and you begin to speak, you have trouble remembering what you wanted to say, and you can't read your note cards because your hands are shaking so much.

It's not as if you *want* to be nervous about speaking in front of your psychoceramics class. Furthermore, you can't think of a single reason why you *should* be nervous. After all, you are an expert on your topic, you know your underwear isn't showing (you double-checked), and your

---

[2] Occasionally people may have trouble retrieving highly anxiety-arousing memories. This phenomenon, known as *repression*, is most likely to occur with very traumatic personal events (Erdelyi, 1985; Pezdek & Banks, 1996). It is unlikely to be a factor in the retrieval of classroom subject matter.

■ **cognitive dissonance** Feeling of mental discomfort caused by new information that conflicts with current knowledge or beliefs.

Nervousness:

Nervousness has very little patience, and absolutely no Confidence. Nervousness and Fear often go together. One senses Nervousness' presence right before you do something you've never done before or when you're afraid about what will happen next. I felt nervous when I was on my way to camp.

FIGURE 11.3 Laurel (age 11) tries to put her finger on what "nervousness" (anxiety) feels like.

classmates are not the type to giggle or throw rotten tomatoes if you make a mistake. So what's the big deal? What happened to the self-assured student who stood practicing in front of the mirror last night?

You are a victim of **anxiety**: You have a feeling of uneasiness and apprehension about an event because you're not sure what its outcome will be. This feeling is accompanied by a variety of physiological symptoms, including a rapid heartbeat, increased perspiration, and muscular tension (e.g., a "knot" or "butterflies" in the stomach). Anxiety is similar to fear but is different in one important respect: Although we are usually *afraid* of something in particular (a roaring lion, an intense electrical storm, or the bogeyman under the bed), we usually don't know exactly why we're *anxious* (Lazarus, 1991). And it's difficult to deal with anxiety when we can't pinpoint its cause. In Figure 11.3, 11-year-old Laurel describes what she thinks anxiety, or "nervousness," is.

Almost everyone is anxious at one time or another. Many students become anxious just before a test they know is going to be difficult, and most get nervous when they have to give a prepared speech in front of their peers. Such temporary feelings of anxiety are instances of **state anxiety**. Yet some students are anxious a good part of the time, even when the situation is not especially dangerous or threatening. For example, some students may get excessively nervous even before very easy exams, and others may be so anxious about mathematics that they can't concentrate on the simplest math assignment. When a learner shows a pattern of responding with anxiety even in nonthreatening situations, we have a case of **trait anxiety**. It is our trait-anxious students whose performance is most hampered by anxiety and for whom we may have to go the extra mile to convince them that they can succeed at classroom tasks.

How Anxiety Affects Learning and Performance   Imagine, for a moment, that you are not at all anxious—not even the teeniest bit—about your grade in Professor Carberry's psychoceramics class. Without any anxiety at all, will you study for Carberry's tests? Will you turn in the assigned research papers? If you have no anxiety whatsoever, you might not even buy the textbook or go to class. And you probably won't get a very good grade in your psychoceramics class.

A small amount of anxiety often improves performance: It is **facilitating anxiety**. A little anxiety spurs students into action; for instance, it makes them go to class, read the textbook, do assignments, and study for exams (see Figure 11.4). It also leads students to approach their classwork carefully and to reflect before making a response (Shipman & Shipman, 1985). Yet too much anxiety usually interferes with effective performance: It is **debilitating anxiety**. Excessive anxiety distracts people and interferes with their attention to the task at hand.

At what point does anxiety stop facilitating and begin debilitating performance? In general, very easy tasks—things that students can do almost without thinking (e.g., running)—are facilitated by high levels of anxiety. But more difficult tasks—those that require considerable thought and mental effort—are best performed with only a small or moderate level of anxiety (Kirkland, 1971; Yerkes & Dodson, 1908). An excessive level of anxiety in difficult situations can interfere with several processes critical for successful learning and performance:

■ Did you previously believe that *any* amount of anxiety is detrimental? If so, have you now revised your thinking about anxiety's effects?

- Paying attention to what needs to be learned
- Processing information effectively (e.g., engaging in meaningful learning, organization, or elaboration)
- Retrieving information and demonstrating skills that have previously been learned (Cassady, 2002; Covington, 1992; Eysenck, 1992; Hagtvet & Johnsen, 1992; I. G. Sarason, 1980)

Anxiety is especially likely to interfere with such processes when a task places heavy demands on working memory or long-term memory—for instance, when a task involves creativity or problem solving (Eysenck, 1992; McLeod & Adams, 1989; Mueller, 1980; Tobias, 1985; J. C. Turner, Thorpe, & Meyer, 1998).

As you might expect, highly anxious students tend to achieve at levels below their potential; in other words, they are underachievers (K. T. Hill, 1984; Tobias, 1980; Zeidner. 1998). Highly anxious students are often so preoccupied about doing poorly that they simply can't get their minds on what they need to accomplish (Eccles & Wigfield, 1985; Wine, 1980).

Sources of Anxiety   Under what circumstances are students apt to experience debilitating anxiety? Students sometimes develop feelings of anxiety about particular stimuli through the

■ **anxiety** Feeling of uneasiness and apprehension concerning a situation with an uncertain outcome.

■ **state anxiety** Temporary feeling of anxiety elicited by a threatening situation.

■ **trait anxiety** Pattern of responding with anxiety even in nonthreatening situations.

■ **facilitating anxiety** Level of anxiety (usually relatively low) that enhances performance.

■ **debilitating anxiety** Anxiety of sufficient intensity that it interferes with performance.

process of classical conditioning (see Chapter 9). Students are also more likely to experience debilitating anxiety when they face a **threat**—a situation in which they believe they have little or no chance of succeeding—than when they face a **challenge**—a situation in which they believe they can probably achieve success with a significant yet reasonable amount of effort (Combs, Richards, & Richards, 1976; Csikszentmihalyi & Nakamura, 1989; Deci & Ryan, 1992). Furthermore, many school-age children and adolescents experience a certain amount of anxiety about the following:

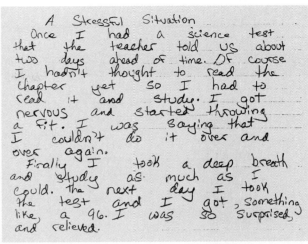

- *Physical appearance.* For example, students may be concerned about being too fat or thin or about reaching puberty either earlier or later than peers.
- *A new situation.* For example, students may experience uncertainty when moving to a new school district.
- *Judgment or evaluation by others.* For example, students may worry about being liked and accepted by classmates or about receiving a low grade from a teacher.
- *Frustrating subject matter.* For example, some students have considerable anxiety about mathematics, often because they've had difficulty tackling mathematical concepts and problems in the past.
- *Excessive classroom demands.* For example, students are apt to feel anxious when teachers expect them to learn a great deal of material in a very short time.
- *Classroom tests.* For example, some students panic at the mere thought of having to take a test, and many students are exceedingly anxious about exams that affect their chances for promotion or graduation (more about such *high-stakes* tests in Chapter 16).
- *Any situation in which physical safety may be at risk.* For example, students understandably feel anxious if violence is common in their school or neighborhood.
- *Any situation in which self-worth is threatened.* For example, students may feel anxious when they perform a task awkwardly or incorrectly in front of others.
- *The future.* For example, adolescents may worry about how they will make a living after they graduate from high school. (Ashcraft, 2002; Cassady, 2002; Chabrán, 2003; Covington, 1992; Harter, 1992; Hembree, 1988; N. J. King & Ollendick, 1989; Phelan et al., 1994; I. G. Sarason, 1980; S. B. Sarason, 1972; Stipek, 1993; Stodolsky et al., 1991; Wigfield & Meece, 1988; K. M. Williams, 2001a)

Students' particular concerns change somewhat as they grow older; Table 11.2 describes developmental trends in anxiety, as well as in affect more generally, across childhood and adolescence. But developmentally speaking, probably the most anxiety-arousing period is the transition from elementary school to middle school or high school, as we shall see now.

Making the Transition from Elementary School to Middle School or High School: A Multiple Whammy   Elementary school classrooms are often very warm, nurturing ones in which teachers get to know twenty or thirty students very well. Students in elementary classrooms also get to know *one another* quite well: They often work together on academic tasks and may even see themselves as members of a classroom "family." But somewhere around fifth to seventh grade, many students move from elementary school to a middle school or junior high school. As they do so, they simultaneously encounter numerous changes in the nature of their schooling:

- The school is larger and has more students.
- Students have several teachers at a time, and each teacher has many students. Teacher-student relationships are therefore more superficial and less personal than in elementary school, and teachers have less awareness of how well individual students are understanding and mastering classroom subject matter.
- There is more whole-class instruction, with less individualized instruction that takes into account each student's academic needs.
- Classes are less socially cohesive; students may not know their classmates very well and may be reluctant to ask peers for assistance.

FIGURE 11.4 This writing sample, by 14-year-old Loretta, illustrates how anxiety can sometimes improve learning and achievement.

■ **threat** Situation in which a learner believes there is little or no chance of success.

■ **challenge** Situation in which a learner believes that success is possible with sufficient effort.

TABLE 11.2　　　　　　　　　　　　　　　　　　　　　D E V E L O P M E N T A L   T R E N D S

Anxiety and Other Forms of Affect at Different Grade Levels

GRADE LEVEL	AGE-TYPICAL CHARACTERISTICS	SUGGESTED STRATEGIES
K–2	• Potential culture shock upon beginning school, especially if students have had few or no preschool experiences • Possible separation anxiety when parents first leave the classroom (especially in the first few days of kindergarten) • Reduced anxiety when teachers are warm and supportive • Only limited control of overt emotional behaviors (e.g., may cry easily if distressed or act impulsively if frustrated)	• Ask parents about routines and procedures followed at home; when appropriate, incorporate them into classroom procedures. • If possible, provide an opportunity for students to meet you a few days or weeks before school begins. • Be warm, caring, and supportive with all students (but check school policies about hugs and other forms of physical affection). • Address inappropriate behaviors gently but firmly (see suggestions in Chapters 9 and 14).
3–5	• Increasing control of overt emotional behaviors • Emergence of math anxiety for some students, especially if they are given little support or assistance with math tasks • Tendency for close friends (especially girls) to talk about and dwell on negative emotional events; continues into adolescence • Possible stress as a result of others' racist and sexist behaviors (e.g., racial slurs, unkind remarks about emerging sexual characteristics); continues into adolescence	• Monitor students' behaviors for subtle signs of serious anxiety or depression; talk with students privately if they are anxious or upset, and consult with the school counselor if necessary. • Ensure that students master basic concepts and procedures before proceeding to more complex material that depends on those concepts and procedures (especially important in teaching math, a subject area in which advanced knowledge and skills build on more basic ones). • Insist on respect for all class members' characteristics, feelings, and backgrounds; do not tolerate racist or sexist actions.
6–8	• General decline in positive emotions; extreme mood swings, partly as a result of hormonal changes accompanying puberty • Increased anxiety and potential depression accompanying the transition to middle school or junior high school • Decrease in enjoyment of school (especially for boys) • Increasing concern and anxiety about how one appears to others (*imaginary audience*; see Chapter 3)	• Expect mood swings, but monitor students' behavior for signs of long-term depression. • Make a personal connection with every student; express confidence that students can succeed with effort, and offer support to facilitate success. • Design activities that capture students' interest in the subject matter; relate topics to students' personal lives and goals (see Chapter 12). • Provide opportunities for students to form friendships with classmates (e.g., cooperative group projects).
9–12	• Continuing emotional volatility (especially in grades 9 and 10) • Considerable anxiety if transition to a secondary school format has been delayed until high school • Susceptibility to serious depression in the face of significant stress • Increasing prevalence of debilitating anxiety regarding tests, especially high-stakes tests • Feelings of uncertainty about life after graduation	• Be especially supportive if students have just made the transition from elementary school (e.g., show personal interest in students' welfare, teach effective study skills). • Be on the lookout for signs that a student may be planning suicide (see the warning signs in Chapter 5). • Give frequent classroom assessments so that no single test score is a "fatal" one; help students prepare for high-stakes tests. • Present multiple options for post-graduation career paths.

Sources: Arnett, 1999; Ashcraft, 2002; Chabrán, 2003; DuBois et al., 2002; Eccles & Midgley, 1989; Elkind, 1981; Gentry, Gable, & Rizza, 2002; K. T. Hill & Sarason, 1966; Hine & Fraser, 2002; Kuhl & Kraska, 1989; Lapsley, 1993; Larson, Moneta, Richards, & Wilson, 2002; Midgley, Middleton, Gheen, & Kumar, 2002; Roderick & Camburn, 1999; A. J. Rose, 2002; Rudolph, Lambert, Clark, & Kurlakowsky, 2001; R. E. Snow et al., 1996; Spear, 2000.

• Students have fewer opportunities to make choices about the topics they pursue and the tasks they complete. At the same time, they have more independence and responsibility regarding their learning; for instance, they sometimes have relatively unstructured assignments to be accomplished over a two- or three-week period, and they must take the initiative to seek help when they are struggling.
• Teachers place greater emphasis on demonstrating (rather than acquiring) competence; for instance, mistakes are more costly for students. (This change reflects a shift from *mastery goals* to *performance goals*, a distinction we'll consider in Chapter 12.)

- Standards for assigning grades are more rigorous, so students may earn lower grades than they did in elementary school. Grades are often assigned on a comparative and competitive basis, with only the highest-achieving students getting As and Bs.
- High-stakes tests—tests that affect promotion to the next grade level—become increasingly common. (H. A. Davis, 2003; Eccles & Midgley, 1989; Harter, 1996; Hine & Fraser, 2002; Midgley et al., 2002; Wentzel & Wigfield, 1998; Wigfield et al., 1996)

Furthermore, previously formed friendships can be disrupted as students move to new (and sometimes different) schools (Pellegrini & Bartini, 2000; Wentzel, 1999). And, of course, students are also dealing with the physiological changes that accompany puberty and adolescence.

For many students, all these changes lead to decreased confidence, lower self-esteem, and considerable anxiety. Students develop less positive attitudes about school and academic subjects and show less intrinsic motivation to learn. Focus on social relationships increases, academic achievement drops, and some students become emotionally disengaged from the school environment—a disengagement that may eventually result in dropping out of school (Eccles & Midgley, 1989; Gentry et al., 2002; Urdan & Maehr, 1995; Wigfield et al., 1996).

If students remain in an elementary school in early adolescence, rather than moving to a middle school or junior high environment, their attitudes and motivation are more apt to remain positive, and they are less apt to experience anxiety or depression (Midgley et al., 2002; Rudolph et al., 2001). By the time they reach ninth grade, however, they inevitably make the transition to a secondary school format, where they will experience many of the changes that their peers in other school districts experienced a few grades earlier—more demanding expectations, increased emphasis on demonstrating competence, less supportive teacher-student relationships, lack of class cohesiveness, and so on (Hine & Fraser, 2002; Midgley et al., 2002; Roderick & Camburn, 1999). Students in lower-income, inner-city school districts (especially males and minorities) are especially at risk for making a rough transition from elementary to high school. For instance, in one recent study, 42 percent of students in the Chicago public schools had failed at least one major course in the first semester of ninth grade. By tenth grade, 50 percent had failed at least one course (Roderick & Camburn, 1999).

In theory, *middle schools* were developed to ease the transition to a secondary school format (e.g., Kohut, 1988; Lounsbury, 1984). Ideally, middle schools are designed to accommodate the unique needs of preadolescents and early adolescents, including their anxieties about more demanding academic expectations, the changing nature of peer relationships, and their own rapidly maturing bodies. Effective middle schools give attention to students' personal, emotional, and social development as well as to academic achievement, and they are attuned to students' individual differences and unique academic needs. They teach learning and study skills that help students move toward increasing independence as learners. At many middle schools, teams of four or five teachers work with a subset of the student population (perhaps 75 to 125 students per team), coordinating activities and exchanging information about how particular students are progressing. Such strategies can ease the transition to a secondary school setting (Hine & Fraser, 2002; Midgley et al., 2002).

Students who make a smooth transition to a secondary school format are more likely to be successful there and, as a result, are more likely to graduate from high school (Roderick & Camburn, 1999; Wigfield et al., 1996). The Into the Classroom feature "Easing the Transition to Middle and Secondary School" suggests several strategies for teachers at the middle school and high school levels.

Keeping Students' Anxiety at a Facilitative Level   Even when students aren't making a significant transition from one educational setting to another, they may have many reasons to be anxious at school. We can address their concerns about social matters—for instance, their worries about peer acceptance and respect—by teaching social skills and planning activities that foster frequent and productive student interactions (see Chapter 3). We can address their concerns about an uncertain future through career counseling and assistance with college applications. But

Students entering the middle school grades face new challenges—more stringent evaluation criteria, less individualized instruction, greater competition in classes and sports—while also undergoing the unsettling physiological changes of puberty.

Easing the Transition to Middle and Secondary School

 Provide a means through which every student can feel part of a small, close-knit group.

During the first week of school, a ninth-grade math teacher establishes *base groups* of three or four students who provide support and assistance for one another throughout the school year. At the beginning or end of every class period, the teacher gives group members five minutes to help one another with questions and concerns about daily lessons and homework assignments.

 Find time to meet one-on-one with every student.

Early in the school year, while his classes are working on a variety of cooperative learning activities, a middle school social studies teacher schedules individual appointments with each of his students. In these meetings he searches for common interests that he and his students share and encourages the students to seek him out whenever they need help with academic or personal problems. Throughout the semester he continues to touch base with individual students (often during lunch or before or after school) to see how they are doing.

 Teach students the skills they need to be successful independent learners.

After discovering that many of her students have little idea of how to take effective notes in class, a high school science teacher distributes a daily "notes skeleton" that guides them through the note-taking process that day; it might include such headings as "Topic of the Lesson," "Definitions," "Important Ideas," and "Examples." As students' class notes improve over the course of the school year, she gradually reduces the amount of structure she provides.

 Assign grades on the basis of mastery (not on comparisons with peers), and provide reasonable opportunities for improvement.

A junior high school language arts teacher requires students to submit two drafts of every essay and short story he assigns; he gives students the option of submitting additional drafts as well. He judges the compositions on four criteria: cohesiveness, word usage, grammar, and spelling. He explains and illustrates each of these criteria and gives ample feedback on every draft that students turn in.

---

perhaps most importantly, we must take steps to ensure that students don't become overly anxious about classroom tasks and subject matter. For instance, we can reduce the uncertainty of the classroom environment by communicating clear, concrete expectations for students' performance. Highly trait-anxious students perform better in a well-structured classroom in which expectations for academic achievement and social behavior are explicitly laid out (Hembree, 1988; Stipek, 1993; Tobias, 1977).

In addition, we must make sure students have a good chance of achieving academic success and give them reasons to believe they can succeed with effort; in other words, we must make sure they have high self-efficacy about classroom tasks. Thus we are more likely to keep students' anxiety at a facilitative level when we

- Set realistic expectations for performance, taking students' prior performance and current abilities into account
- Match instruction to students' cognitive levels and capabilities—for example, by using concrete materials to teach mathematics to students not yet capable of abstract thought
- Provide supplementary sources of support for learning subject matter (e.g., additional practice, individual tutoring, a structure for taking notes) until mastery is attained
- Teach strategies (e.g., effective study skills) that enhance learning and performance
- Assess students' performance independently of how well their peers are doing, and encourage students to assess their own performance in a similar manner
- Provide feedback about specific behaviors, rather than global evaluations of students' performance
- Allow students to correct errors, so that no single mistake is ever a "fatal" one (Brophy, 1986; K. T. Hill & Wigfield, 1984; L. P. McCoy, 1990; I. G. Sarason, 1980; Stipek, 1993; Tryon, 1980; Zeidner, 1998)

We'll identify additional strategies—those for keeping students' anxiety at reasonable levels during tests and other classroom assessments—in Chapter 15.

As teachers, we must continually be on the lookout for how students' feelings of anxiety and other emotions may be affecting their classroom learning and achievement. Sometimes students will actually tell us how they feel; for instance, they may express apprehensiveness about an upcoming exam. On other occasions their body language—energy, enthusiasm, facial expressions, and so on—may reveal their feelings. In still other cases their writing will be a good source of information, as the following exercise illustrates.

Interpreting Student Artifacts and Behaviors

James Dean and Walt Disney

Students in an eleventh-grade history class have been giving oral reports about prominent individuals and institutions in twentieth-century American culture. In the following reaction paper, 16-year-old Shelby describes her reactions to several reports and assesses her own presentation on Walt Disney. As you read the paper, look for examples of

- Facilitating or debilitating anxiety
- Hot cognition

The first oral that we listened to was Paula's talk about J. Edgar Hoover. Hoover was one of our presidents. He was racist and a very narrow-minded man. Allison gave her report on NASA. She had many facts and talked about different missions.

Another oral that the class listened to was Kevin's on James Dean. He was an actor and supposedly a heart throb of the 50's. He was in movies like "Rebel Without A Cause." I remember my mom saying awhile ago that she thought that he was pretty good looking. Kevin brought in some clips from "Rebel Without A Cause" and "East of Eden." They were interesting to watch. It seemed as though he was in many movies where he played a rebel or a slacker. I remember thinking that James Dean played characters that were good fighters and I remember people saying that he was a good fighter. After seeing these clips Mr. M. asked if any of the girls thought that James Dean was hot. Paula said that he was a hotty and Nicole and I were mumbling to each other that we thought he was pretty attractive, but we were too shy to say anything.

I think that it's amazing how people can be influenced so easily by movie stars. Back then it seemed that people were influenced very easily by movie stars because they were so new and they seemed so cool and interesting. For example, many people started to smoke because James Dean smoked. I think that people also started to wear leather jackets because of James Dean.

Kevin said that he found out that James Dean might have been bisexual and he said that if this had gotten out back then his image might not have been so big. I agree with Kevin. I think that people back then weren't as open to homosexuals and bisexuals as they are now. I think that there is no way that he would have been such a heart throb back then if people knew. I also think that if the public knew there might have been a big decrease in smoking because people wouldn't want to be so much like him.

Before Kevin presented his oral I did mine on Walt Disney. I think that it went pretty well and I'm happy with the grade that I got. I was very nervous, although I don't know if you could tell. Nicole said that she couldn't. I think that it went well. I wish that I had had some more visuals and that I had some more information about him being racist and more about how he came up with the idea for the amusement parks. I also wish that I had more information about how and why Michael Eisner got the Disney company, because he's not related to Walt at all. I had a good time doing my oral though because it made me think of one of my favorite places and it also made me think of when I was younger.

One other oral that we heard this week was Kolo's on Malcolm X. I didn't really know anything about Malcolm X until Kolo's report. I learned that he did a lot with the Civil Rights Movement and many other things.

Shelby was anxious during her own presentation ("I was very nervous . . . "), but her anxiety appears to have been facilitative rather than debilitative (" . . . I don't know if you could tell. Nicole said that she couldn't. I think that it went well"). She knows that she could have done some things more effectively, but all in all she enjoyed her time in front of the class.

We see several signs that Shelby engaged in hot cognition as she listened to Kevin's presentation on James Dean. She thinks that Dean was attractive ("hot"). She is amazed (perhaps appalled) that many people began smoking because Dean was a smoker, and she wonders how Dean's image and popularity might have been different if his sexual orientation had been made public. Finally, notice how much Shelby focuses her paper on James Dean: She clearly remembers quite a bit of what Kevin had to say. In contrast, she seems to recall very little of the presentations on J. Edgar Hoover, NASA, and Malcolm X (in fact, she "recalls" that Hoover was president, thus confusing him with *Herbert* Hoover). We can reasonably guess that these presentations had little of the emotional impact that Kevin's report did.

ADDRESSING DIVERSITY IN MOTIVATION AND AFFECT

In our discussion thus far, we've identified several sources of diversity in students' motivation and affect. For instance, we've learned that although all students probably have the need to maintain a sense of self-worth, some students may paradoxically try to protect their self-worth by engaging in self-handicapping and thereby undermining their chances of success. Furthermore, although all students probably have some need for relatedness, some have higher needs for affiliation or approval than others. And a few students exhibit high trait anxiety, making them more vulnerable to debilitating anxiety on occasions when their classmates might successfully rise to a challenge.

Researchers have observed some consistent differences in the motivation and affect of students from different cultural and ethnic backgrounds, genders, and socioeconomic levels. Let's look at group differences that have particular relevance for students' classroom behavior and performance.

Cultural and Ethnic Differences

Regardless of their cultural and ethnic background, children around the world have some basic needs in common, including their needs for self-worth and relatedness. How they *satisfy* those needs may vary, however. For example, researchers have found cultural differences in how students address their need for relatedness. In comparison to other groups, Asian students tend to spend less time socializing with peers and place greater importance on gaining teachers' attention and approval (Dien, 1998; L. Steinberg, 1996). Furthermore, whereas Asian students are likely to have friends who encourage academic achievement, students from certain other ethnic groups (boys especially) may be subject to considerable peer pressure *not* to achieve at high levels (e.g., recall our discussion of "acting White" in Chapter 3) (B. B. Brown, 1993; Graham, 1997; L. Steinberg, 1996). An additional factor in how students address their need for relatedness is their family ties: Students from many cultural and ethnic groups (e.g., those from many Native American, Hispanic, and Asian communities, as well as in rural communities in the Appalachian Mountains) have especially strong loyalties to family and may have been raised to achieve for their respective communities, rather than just for themselves as individuals (see Chapter 4). Motivating statements such as "Think how proud your family will be!" and "If you go to college and get a good education, you can really help your community!" are likely to be especially effective for such students (Abi-Nader, 1993; Dien, 1998; Suina & Smolkin, 1994).

Ethnicity and gender can be important factors influencing students' motivation, yet all students have certain basic motives, such as the need for self-worth and relatedness.

Degrees of emotional control may differ among different cultures as well. Mainstream Western culture encourages children to act and speak up if someone infringes on their rights and needs, and expressing anger in a nonviolent way is considered quite appropriate. In many Southeast Asian cultures, however, any expression of anger is viewed as potentially undermining adults' authority or disrupting social harmony (P. M. Cole, Bruschi, & Tamang, 2002). Children brought up in some Buddhist communities are encouraged to not even *feel* anger. For instance, if unfairly embarrassed or accused, a child who has grown up in the Tamang culture of Nepal might respond, "Tilda bomo khaba?" ("Why be angry?"), because the event has already occurred and being angry about it serves no purpose (P. M. Cole et al., 2002, p. 992).

Students from various ethnic backgrounds may have somewhat different sources of anxiety. For instance, some students from Asian American families may feel so much family pressure to perform well in school that they experience debilitating test anxiety (Pang, 1995). And students who are recent immigrants are frequently anxious about a variety of things in their new country—how to behave, how to interpret others' behaviors, how to make friends and, more generally, how to make sense of the strange new culture in which they now find themselves (Dien, 1998; Igoa, 1995).

■ **stereotype threat** Awareness of a negative stereotype about one's own group and accompanying uneasiness that low performance will confirm the stereotype; leads (often unintentionally) to a reduction in performance.

Anxiety may be at the root of a phenomenon known as **stereotype threat**, in which students from stereotypically low-achieving groups perform more poorly on classroom assessments than they otherwise would simply because they are aware that their group traditionally *does* do poorly (Steele, 1997). When students are aware of the unflattering stereotype, and especially when they know that the task they are performing reflects their ability in an important domain, their heart rate and other physiological correlates of anxiety go up and their performance goes down (J. Aronson et al., 1999; McKown & Weinstein, 2003; Osborne & Simmons, 2002). We are less likely to see the negative effects of stereotype threat when students don't interpret their performance on a task as an evaluation of their competence (McKown & Weinstein, 2003).

Gender Differences

Researchers have found some consistent gender differences in motivation. Girls are more concerned about doing well in school: They work harder on assignments, earn higher grades, engage in less self-handicapping, and more often graduate from high school (Urdan & Midgley, 2001; also see Chapter 4). We will typically find more boys than girls achieving at levels far below their potential (Eccles et al., 1998; McCall, 1994). Despite such differences, boys tend to have greater confidence in their academic ability and higher expectations for future success (D. A. Cole et al., 1999; Deaux, 1984; Eccles et al., 1998).

Girls are more likely than boys to have a high need for affiliation. Perhaps for this reason, they achieve at higher levels when their teachers encourage cooperation rather than competition (Block, 1983; Eccles, 1989; Inglehart et al., 1994). And perhaps because girls are more likely to seek out friendly relationships with others, more girls than boys have a good sense of relatedness with teachers and peers, at least at the middle school level (Furrer & Skinner, 2003). Students' feelings of relatedness with others are correlated with their motivation and performance in the classroom; the correlation is particularly strong for boys, and especially for boys' feelings of connectedness with teachers (Furrer & Skinner, 2003).

Researchers have observed gender differences in affect as well. In general, girls express their emotions more openly than boys do. However, girls sometimes hide their feelings in order to preserve social harmony with others, whereas boys are often quite willing to show their anger (Eisenberg et al., 1996; Lippa, 2002; Sadker & Sadker, 1994). Girls are also more anxious about their classroom performance (this may partly explain their higher achievement) and have greater difficulty coping with stressful circumstances (Frydenberg & Lewis, 2000; Pomerantz, Altermatt, & Saxon, 2002). Clearly, then, boys and girls alike will need our social and emotional support, but for somewhat different reasons.

Socioeconomic Differences

Many students from low socioeconomic backgrounds want to do well in school (Shernoff, Schneider, & Csikszentmihalyi, 2001; Wilson & Corbett, 2001). However, they are apt to have significant sources of stress in their lives (see Chapter 4), and they may have few effective learning strategies and self-regulation skills (see Chapter 10). They are most likely to thrive in school settings when they have our social and emotional support, but they will need considerable academic support as well (L. W. Anderson & Pellicer, 1998; Becker & Luthar, 2002). Many of the motivational strategies presented in Chapter 12 will have particular relevance to students from low-income families.

Accommodating Students with Special Needs

Our students with special educational needs will typically be among those who show the greatest diversity in motivation. For example, students with learning disabilities may be easily discouraged by challenging tasks, yet students who are gifted may become easily bored if classroom activities *don't* challenge their abilities (Mercer, 1997; Winner, 2000b). Furthermore, although some students with special needs are quite adept at social relationships, others will have greater-than-average difficulty satisfying their need for relatedness, perhaps as a result of few opportunities to interact with age-mates (true for many students with physical disabilities), poor social skills (true for many students with emotional and behavioral disorders), or interests and ability levels that are significantly different from those of classmates (true for some students who are highly gifted). Table 11.3 identifies additional ways in which students with exceptionalities are likely to show different motivational characteristics and behaviors than their peers; it also offers suggestions for addressing these students' unique needs.

TABLE 11.3   STUDENTS IN INCLUSIVE SETTINGS

Enhancing Motivation in Students with Special Educational Needs

CATEGORY	CHARACTERISTICS YOU MIGHT OBSERVE	SUGGESTED CLASSROOM STRATEGIES
Students with specific cognitive or academic difficulties	• Less intrinsic motivation to succeed at academic tasks • High test anxiety • Reluctance to ask questions or seek assistance, especially at the secondary level	• Use extrinsic reinforcers to encourage students' classroom effort and achievement; gradually phase out reinforcers as students show signs of intrinsic motivation. • Minimize anxiety-arousing statements and procedures during testing situations (see Chapter 15 for ideas). • Offer assistance when you think students may really need it, but refrain from offering help when you know students are capable of succeeding on their own.
Students with social or behavioral problems	• Desire to succeed in the classroom, despite behaviors that may indicate a lack of motivation • Stronger desire for power over classmates than for affiliation with them (for some students with emotional and behavioral disorders) • Need for predictability; debilitating anxiety in new or unpredictable situations (for students with autism) • Excessive anxiety and uneasiness (for students with *anxiety disorders*)	• Provide the guidance and support that students need to succeed at classroom tasks. • Help students discover the benefits of equitable and prosocial (rather than domineering) interactions with peers. • Create a structured and predictable classroom environment, especially for students with autism.
Students with general delays in cognitive and social functioning	• Less intrinsic motivation than age-mates; responsiveness to extrinsic motivators • Tendency to give up easily in the face of difficulty	• Use extrinsic reinforcers to encourage productive behaviors; gradually phase out reinforcers as students show signs of intrinsic motivation. • Reinforce persistence as well as success.
Students with physical or sensory challenges	• Fewer opportunities to satisfy affiliation needs • Anxiety in chaotic environments as a result of being unable to see what is happening (for students who are blind)	• Assign "buddies" who can help students with assigned tasks or provide companionship at lunch and on the playground. • Collaborate with parents to promote interaction with classmates outside of school.
Students with advanced cognitive development	• High intrinsic motivation (e.g., curiosity about how things work) • Strong commitment to certain (especially self-chosen) tasks • Persistence in the face of failure (although some may give up easily if they aren't accustomed to failure) • Social isolation (for some students who are exceptionally gifted) • Possible self-handicapping if there is a strong desire to affiliate with low-achieving peers	• Provide opportunities for students to pursue complex tasks and activities over an extended time. • Give assignments that students find stimulating and challenging. • Form special-interest groups for students who might otherwise be socially isolated. • Keep students' exceptional achievements confidential if their friends don't value high achievement.

Sources: Beirne-Smith et al., 2002; B. Clark, 1997; Covington, 1992; Friedel, 1993; Good & Brophy, 1994; A. W. Gottfried et al., 1994; Heward, 2003; Mercer, 1997; Morgan & Jenson, 1988; Patrick, 1997; Patton et al., 1996; B. N. Phillips, Pitcher, Worsham, & Miller, 1980; Piirto, 1999; S. Powell & Nelson, 1997; Renzulli, 1978; Sanborn, 1979; G. F. Schultz & Switzky, 1990; R. Turnbull et al., 2004; Winner, 1997, 2000b.

THE BIG PICTURE

In our discussions of development and learning in earlier chapters, we've focused primarily on the question "What can our students do and learn?" Now that we've turned to the topic of motivation, we've begun to focus on a very different question: "How *likely* are they to do what they're capable of doing and to learn what they're capable of learning?" Even when students have the capabilities and prior experiences necessary to do something, their *motivation* will determine whether they actually do it.

Occasionally I hear teachers, administrators, and policy makers talking about "unmotivated" students. In reality, all students

(and in fact, all human beings) have needs and desires they are motivated to satisfy. For instance, virtually all students want to feel physically safe in their environment, want to believe they are competent human beings, and want to "connect" with other people in some way. Some students may perceive school to be a place in which they can satisfy such needs, but others may find that one or more of their needs—perhaps their need for physical well-being, self-worth, or relatedness—is actually thwarted in the classroom.

As teachers, we are more likely to motivate children and adolescents if our instructional strategies take their existing motives into account. Ideally, of course, we would like for them to find school subject matter intrinsically fascinating, enjoyable, and satisfying. If they do not initially have such intrinsic motivation, we can promote it in a variety of ways—for example, by relating classroom topics to their personal interests, showing them how academic skills will help them achieve their long-term goals, giving them choices about how to meet instructional objectives, and so on (more about such strategies in Chapter 12). On occasion we may need to rely on extrinsic motivation, perhaps by praising or in some other way reinforcing students for learning the skills that will be essential for their long-term success in and outside of the classroom.

Students' emotions (affect) will play a role in their learning and achievement as well. If they repeatedly discover that classroom topics are exciting and offer answers to some of life's puzzling mysteries, they will be eager to pursue those topics further. But if they instead find that assigned tasks more often lead to frustration and anxiety than to pleasure, they will avoid the tasks as often as possible.

GENERAL GUIDING PRINCIPLES

If I could offer you only one piece of advice for motivating students, it would be this: Think not about how you can coerce students but instead about how you can *entice* them into learning and achieving in the classroom. Following are three additional guiding principles (M. E. Ford, 1992):

◎ *Remember that different students will respond to different motivational strategies.* When it comes to motivation, diversity may be more typical than uniformity: Although our students may share certain basic needs, they are likely to have widely varying abilities, interests, goals, and expectations, and such things will inevitably affect the approaches that are likely to be effective in enticing them to engage in classroom activities.

◎ *Show students that they can be successful.* Throughout the book we have repeatedly talked about the importance of success for students' learning and achievement, but success is ultimately *most* important for students' motivation. As we have seen in this chapter, successes are critical for maintaining a sense of self-worth. As we shall discover in the following chapter, successes are also important for fostering "motivating" cognitions; for instance, they help students find value in, and set and achieve goals related to, mastering school subject matter.

◎ *Above all, communicate respect for all students.* As teachers, we must remember that each and every student is a human being with legitimate thoughts, beliefs, perspectives, strengths, needs, and goals. When we focus on students' strong points rather than on their weaknesses (and every student has many strengths), we are more likely to give them the confidence they need to do their best; we are also more likely to identify ways to *help* them do their best.

CASE STUDY: *When "Perfect" Isn't Good Enough*

Mrs. Gaskill's second graders are just beginning to learn how to write the letters of the alphabet in cursive. Every day Mrs. Gaskill introduces a new cursive letter and shows her students how to write it correctly. She also shows them some common errors in writing the letter—for instance, claiming that she's going to make the "perfect *f*" and then making it much too short and crossing the lines in the wrong place—and the children delight in finding her mistakes. After the class explores each letter's shape, Mrs. Gaskill asks her students to practice it, first by writing it in the air using large arm movements and then by writing it numerous times on lined paper.

Meanwhile, Mrs. Gaskill has decided to compare the effects of two different kinds of feedback on the children's performance. She has placed a small sticker on each child's desk, with one color indicating membership in the control group and another indicating membership in the treatment group. When children in the control group write a letter with good form, she gives them a "happy face" token, says "Great" or "Perfect!," and either smiles at them or gives them a pat on the back. When children in the treatment group write a letter with good form at least once, she gives them a happy face token and says something along the lines of "You sure are working hard," "You can write beautifully in cursive," or "You are a natural at this." When children in either group fail to meet her standards for cursive writing, she gives them whatever corrective feedback they need.

Thus the only way in which Mrs. Gaskill treats the two groups differently is in what she says to them when they do well, either giving them fairly cryptic feedback (for the control group) or telling them that they are trying hard or have high ability (for the treatment group). Despite such a seemingly minor difference, Mrs. Gaskill finds that the children in the treatment group say they enjoy cursive writing more, and they use it more frequently in their spelling tests and other writing tasks. Curiously, too, the children in the control group often seem disappointed when they receive their "positive" feedback. For instance, on one occasion a girl who writes beautifully but has the misfortune of being in the control group asks, "Am *I* a natural at this?" Although the girl consistently gets a grade of " + " for her cursive writing, she never writes in cursive voluntarily throughout the three-week period in which Mrs. Gaskill conducts her experiment. (Gaskill, 2001)

Why might feedback such as "You sure are working hard" or "You can write beautifully in cursive" be more effective than feedback such as "Great" or "Perfect"? Use what you have learned about motivation to speculate.

Might the control group's feedback be more effective if Mrs. Gaskill used it for *all*, rather than just some, of her students? Explain your reasoning. (For help in answering this question, return to the section "Factors Influencing the Development of Self-Views" in Chapter 3.)

Once you have answered these questions, compare your responses with those presented in Appendix B.

KEY CONCEPTS

motivation (p. 365)
situated motivation (p. 366)
time on task (p. 366)
extrinsic motivation (p.367)
intrinsic motivation (p. 367)
flow (p. 367)
trait theory of motivation (p. 368)
achievement motivation (p. 368)
drive (p. 369)

self-worth (p. 371)
self-handicapping (p. 371)
need for relatedness (p. 372)
need for affiliation (p. 373)
need for approval (p. 374)
affect (p. 374)
hot cognition (p. 376)
cognitive dissonance (p. 377)
anxiety (p. 378)

state anxiety (p. 378)
trait anxiety (p. 378)
facilitating anxiety (p. 378)
debilitating anxiety (p. 378)
threat (p. 379)
challenge (p. 379)
stereotype threat (p. 384)

PRAXIS Turn to Appendix C, "Matching Book and Ancillary Content to the Praxis Principles of Learning and Teaching Tests," to discover sections of this chapter that may be especially applicable to the Praxis tests.

Companion Website

Now go to our Companion Website at **www.prenhall. com/ormrod** to assess your understanding of chapter content with "Multiple-Choice Questions," apply comprehension in "Essay Questions," broaden your knowledge of educational psychology with related "Web Links," gain greater insight about classroom learning in "Learning in the Content Areas," and analyze and assess classroom work in the "Student Artifact Library."

Chapter 12 Cognitive Factors in Motivation

Think about the college courses you've taken in recent years. In which courses were you more interested in the grade you received than in anything you might learn in class? In which courses did you truly want to learn the subject matter, and why? Did you perceive some topics to be relevant to your own needs and goals? Were other topics so fascinating that you simply had to find out more about them? Did your instructors do anything in particular that made certain topics intriguing, thought-provoking, or just plain fun?

In this chapter we will look at how students' perceptions, beliefs, expectations, values, interests, goals, dispositions, and attributions influence their motivation; in other words, we will focus on "cognitions that motivate." We will also examine the effects that *teacher* cognition—especially teachers' expectations and attributions regarding students' behaviors and accomplishments—have on students' performance and achievement. As we explore these issues, we'll address questions such as these:

* How do students' beliefs about themselves affect their motivation to learn and succeed in the classroom?
* Under what conditions are students most likely to find school subject matter valuable, interesting, or in some other way desirable to learn?
* What kinds of goals do children and adolescents set for themselves, and how do these goals affect their learning?
* What general dispositions do students have regarding how they approach academic subject matter?
* How do students' explanations for success and failure (their *attributions*) influence their thoughts and behaviors?
* How do teachers' beliefs about students affect their teaching practices and thereby affect students' classroom achievement? As teachers, what precautions can we take to make sure that our beliefs boost rather than hinder students' progress?

CASE STUDY: *Passing Algebra*

Fourteen-year-old Michael has been getting failing grades in his eighth-grade algebra class, and so his family asks graduate student Valerie Tucker to tutor him. In their initial tutoring session, Michael tells Ms. Tucker that he has no hope of passing algebra because he has little aptitude for math and his teacher doesn't teach the subject matter very well. In his mind, he is powerless to change either his own ability or his teacher's instructional strategies, and so continuing failure is inevitable.

As Ms. Tucker works with Michael over the next several weeks, she encourages him to think more about what *he* can do to master algebra and less about what his teacher may or may not be doing to help him. She points out that he has done well in math in earlier years and so he clearly does have the ability to learn algebra if he puts his mind to it. She also teaches him a number of strategies for understanding and applying algebraic principles.

Michael takes a first giant step forward when he finally realizes that his own efforts play a role in his classroom success:

> [M]aybe I can try a little harder. . . . The teacher is still bad, but maybe some of this other stuff can work. (Tucker & Anderman, 1999, p. 5)

When Michael sees gradual improvement on his algebra assignments and quizzes, he becomes increasingly aware that the specific *strategies* he uses are just as important as his effort:

> I learned that I need to understand information before I can hold it in my mind. . . . Now I do things in math step by step and listen to each step. I realize now that even if I don't like the teacher or don't think he is a good teacher, it is my responsibility to listen. I listen better now and ask questions more. (Tucker & Anderman, 1999, p. 5)

As Michael's performance in algebra continues to improve in later weeks, he gains greater confidence that he *can* master algebra after all, and he comes to realize that his classroom success is ultimately up to him:

[T]he teacher does most of his part, but it's no use to me unless I do my part. . . . [N]ow I try and comprehend, ask questions and figure out how he got the answer. . . . I used to just listen and not even take notes. I always told myself I would remember but I always seemed to forget. Now I take notes and I study at home every day except Friday, even if I don't have homework. Now I study so that I know that I have it. I don't just hope I'll remember. (Tucker & Anderman, 1999, p. 6)

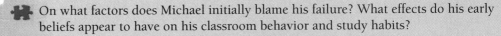 On what factors does Michael initially blame his failure? What effects do his early beliefs appear to have on his classroom behavior and study habits?

To what factors does Michael later attribute his success? How have his changing beliefs affected his learning strategies?

THE INTERPLAY OF COGNITION AND MOTIVATION

Michael initially believes he is failing algebra because of two things he cannot control—his own low ability and his teacher's poor instruction—and so he doesn't listen very attentively or take notes in class. With Ms. Tucker's guidance, however, Michael acquires a better understanding of algebra and learns how to use it to solve mathematical problems. He also discovers that increased effort and better strategies (taking notes, asking questions when he doesn't understand, studying regularly, etc.) *do* affect his classroom performance. Suddenly Michael himself—not his teacher and not some genetically predetermined inability that lurks within him—is in control of the situation, and his confidence skyrockets.

Michael's dramatic turnaround illustrates a point made in Chapter 11: *Motivation affects cognitive processing.* Like Michael, motivated students are more likely to pay attention, engage in meaningful learning, and seek help when they don't understand. Yet the case illustrates the reverse as well: *Cognitive processes affect motivation.* Michael's initial beliefs about his own ability (his self-efficacy) and his explanations for poor performance (low ability and poor instruction) contribute to a lackadaisical attitude: He simply *hopes* that he'll remember (but usually forgets) his teacher's explanations. Later, when Michael's appraisal of the situation changes (when his self-efficacy increases and he attributes success to effort and better strategies), he is a much more engaged and proactive learner.

Just as affective reactions to classroom subject matter are integral parts of what students store in long-term memory (see Chapter 11), so, too, are cognitive aspects of motivation—including self-perceptions, expectancies, values, interests, goals, dispositions, and attributions—closely connected with what students know and learn (Mischel & Shoda, 1995). As we explore these topics in the pages that follow, we will frequently see how cognition and motivation interact in their effects on learning and behavior. We'll begin by looking at two self-perceptions that play key roles in intrinsic motivation: self-efficacy and self-determination.

SELF-PERCEPTIONS AND INTRINSIC MOTIVATION

Experiencing FIRSTHAND · Enjoyable Activities

1. Make a list of five different things you like to do. You might list hobbies, favorite sports, or other activities in which you are intrinsically motivated to engage.
2. Using the following scale, rate each of the activities you've just listed in terms of *how successfully you usually perform it:*

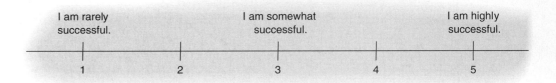

I am rarely successful.		I am somewhat successful.		I am highly successful.
1	2	3	4	5

3. Using the following scale, rate each of your activities in terms of *how much choice you have regarding whether you engage in the activity*:

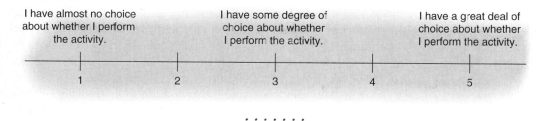

I have almost no choice about whether I perform the activity.		I have some degree of choice about whether I perform the activity.		I have a great deal of choice about whether I perform the activity.
1	2	3	4	5

· · · · · · ·

Take a close look at the numerical ratings you've just assigned to your favorite activities. Chances are, your ratings were almost exclusively 3 or higher on both scales. A number of theorists have proposed that people are most likely to be intrinsically motivated to do something (to perform a particular task or engage in a particular activity) when two conditions exist:

1. They have high **self-efficacy**: They believe they can successfully accomplish the task or activity.
2. They have a sense of **self-determination**: They believe they are in control of their own destinies and can make choices about the directions their lives will take. (Boggiano & Pittman, 1992; Corno & Rohrkemper, 1985; Deci & Ryan, 1985, 1992; R. M. Ryan & Deci, 2000; Spaulding, 1992)

Self-Efficacy

In Chapter 11 we noted that protecting one's general sense of competence and self-worth may be a basic human need. When people feel competent in a *particular activity*—that is, when they have high self-efficacy for the activity—they are more likely to pursue the activity largely for the pleasure it brings. In the opening case, Michael's self-efficacy for passing his algebra class is initially rock-bottom: In his mind, he doesn't have the ability to succeed, and his teacher does little to help the situation. But as he sees himself improve with effort and new strategies, he gains confidence and begins to show signs of intrinsic motivation to master algebra; for instance, he says, "I study at home every day except Friday, even if I don't have homework."

In our discussion of social cognitive theory in Chapter 10, we identified numerous strategies for enhancing students' self-efficacy for classroom subject matter:

- Teach basic skills to mastery.
- Help students make noticeable progress on complex skills.
- Present some tasks at which students can succeed only with effort and perseverance.
- Assure students that they can be successful, and remind them that others like themselves have succeeded before them.
- Have students see successful peer models.
- Assign large tasks as small-group activities.
- Provide competence-promoting feedback.
- Promote mastery on challenging tasks.
- Define success in terms of improvement or task accomplishment, rather than in terms of performance relative to others.
- Be sure errors occur within an overall context of success.

Among the most effective of these strategies for promoting self-efficacy and, indirectly, intrinsic motivation is this one: *Promote mastery on challenging tasks.* Students who take on and master challenges experience considerable pleasure, satisfaction, and pride in their accomplishments (Csikszentmihalyi & Nakamura, 1989; Shernoff, Knauth, & Makris, 2000; A. G. Thompson & Thompson, 1989; J. C. Turner, 1995). The artifact in Figure 12.1 reveals 8-year-old Anthony's pride about finishing a 100-page book. The "Motivation: Middle Childhood" and "Motivation: Late Adolescence" clips on Video CD 1 also reveal a desire for challenge at school. When 9-year-old Elena is asked what she likes best about school, she responds:

> I like PEAK [a program for students identified as gifted]. . . . It's for smart kids who have, like, good ideas for stuff you could do. And so they make it more challenging for you in school. So instead of third-grade math, you get fourth-grade math.

■ Observe Elena's and Greg's desire for challenge in the middle childhood and late adolescence "Motivation" clips on Video CD 1.

■ **self-efficacy** Belief that one is capable of executing certain behaviors or reaching certain goals.

■ **self-determination** Sense that one has some choice and control regarding the future course of one's life.

A Book That canged me

The Book that canged me was At The Plat With Ken Jriffey Jr. This Book canged me becouse it was my first book that had over onehondred pagis after that I read On The Cort With Mikeol Jorden. I asow liked it becouse it was by Matt Crister the Frst spotswiter for Kids.

FIGURE 12.1 In writing about "A Book That Changed Me," 8-year-old Anthony expresses pride in reading his first book of more than a hundred pages. Also notice Anthony's emerging interest in sports: One book (*At the Plate*) involves baseball, the other (*On the Court*) basketball.

Similarly, when 15-year-old Greg is asked what things encourage him to do well at school, he says, "The challenge. If it's a really hard class, then I . . . I will usually try harder in harder classes."

Once students are intrinsically motivated, they often pursue further challenges of their own accord. They also exhibit considerable persistence in the face of difficulty, and they continue to remain interested in an activity even when they make frequent errors (Covington, 1992; Deci, 1992; Harter, 1992). As you can see, then, challenges and intrinsic motivation mutually enhance one another, leading to a "vicious" cycle of the most desirable sort.

As teachers, we are more likely to encourage students to tackle challenging tasks when, through the feedback we give and the criteria we use for evaluation, we create an environment in which students feel free to take risks and make mistakes (Clifford, 1990). We can also provide greater rewards for succeeding at challenging tasks than for achieving easy successes; for example, we might give students a choice between doing an easy task or a more difficult one but give them more points for accomplishing the difficult one (Clifford, 1990; Lan, Repman, Bradley, & Weller, 1994).

Self-Determination

Experiencing FIRSTHAND · Painting Between the Lines

Imagine that I give you a set of watercolor paints, a paintbrush, two sheets of paper (a fairly small one glued on top of a larger one), and some paper towels. I ask you to paint a picture of your house, apartment building, or dormitory and then give you the following instructions:

> Before you begin, I want to tell you some things you will have to do. They are rules that I have about painting. You have to keep the paints clean. You can paint only on this small sheet of paper, so don't spill any paint on the big sheet. And you must wash out your brush and wipe it with a paper towel before you switch to a new color of paint, so that you don't get the colors all mixed up. In general, I want you to be a good art student and not make a mess with the paints. (based on Koestner, Ryan, Bernieri, & Holt, 1984, p. 239)

How much fun do you think your task would be? After reading my rules, how eager are you to begin painting?

· · · · · · ·

My rules about painting are somewhat restrictive, aren't they? In fact, they are quite *controlling*: They make it clear that I am in charge of the situation and that you, as the artist, have little choice about how to go about your task. Chances are, you have little intrinsic motivation to paint the picture I've asked you to make (Deci, 1992; Koestner et al., 1984). Furthermore, you would probably be less creative in your painting than if I had not been so controlling (Amabile & Hennessey, 1992).

Students are more likely to be intrinsically motivated when they have a sense of self-determination—in other words, when they have some feeling of *autonomy* regarding the things they do and the directions their lives take (Boggiano & Pittman, 1992; deCharms, 1972; Deci, 1992; Deci & Ryan, 1992; Spaulding, 1992; J. C. Turner, 1995). For instance, when they think "I *want* to do this" or "I would *find it valuable* to do that," they have a high sense of self-determination. In contrast, when they think "I *have to*" or "I *should*," they are telling themselves that someone or something else is making the decisions for them.

A sense of self-determination increases the likelihood that students will become actively engaged in in-class and extracurricular activities, use skills acquired at school in out-of-school settings, and stay in school until graduation (Hardre & Reeve, 2003; E. J. Langer, 1997; J. Reeve, Bolt, & Cai, 1999; Shernoff et al., 2000). For example, students who learn new athletic skills in physical education classes that enhance their sense of autonomy (e.g., by offering choices about the sports they might learn) are more likely to spend leisure time engaging in healthful physical activities (Hagger, Chatzisarantis, Culverhouse, & Biddle, 2003; Standage, Duda, & Ntoumanis, 2003).

Even kindergartners seem to value classroom activities of their own choosing, and students' perceptions of autonomy versus control are often seen in their notions of "play" or "work" (E. J. Langer, 1997; Paley, 1984). Kindergarten teacher Vivian Gussin Paley recounts a conversation she once had with some of the girls in her class:

Mary Ann:	The boys don't like to work.
Ms. Paley:	They're making a huge train setup right now.
Mary Ann:	That's not work. It's just playing.
Ms. Paley:	When do girls play?
Charlotte:	In the doll corner.
Ms. Paley:	How about at the painting table?
Mary Ann:	That's work. You could call it play sometimes, but it's really schoolwork.
Ms. Paley:	When is it work and when is it play?
Clarice:	If you paint a real picture, it's work, but if you splatter or pour into an egg carton, then it's play.
Charlotte:	It's mostly work, because that's where the teacher tells you how to do stuff. (dialogue from Paley, 1984, pp. 30–31)

The boys in Ms. Paley's class had a similar perspective:

Ms. Paley:	The girls think the block area is for play and not for work. Is that what you think?
Jonathan:	It *is* for play. But you could be a work person.
Ms. Paley:	If you're a work person, then what do you do in the blocks?
Andrew:	Build very neatly and don't knock it down and don't play.
Ms. Paley:	How can you tell if you're working or playing?
Andrew:	No Star Wars or superheroes. None of that stuff.
Paul:	No shooting. And no robbers.
Jonathan:	And no running.
Ms. Paley:	What else is work in this room?
Andrew:	If you color or put your name on a thing. On a paper.
Paul:	It has to be work if *you* tell us to do something. (dialogue from Paley, 1984, p. 31)

Students are more likely to be intrinsically motivated when they have a sense of self-determination about classroom activities.

Naturally, we can't always give students total freedom about what they will and will not do in the classroom. Nor can we always convince them that classroom activities are really play rather than work. Nevertheless, we *can* do several things to enhance students' sense of self-determination about school-related tasks and assignments:

◎   *Present rules and instructions in an informational rather than controlling manner.* Virtually any classroom needs a few rules and procedures to ensure that students act appropriately and activities run smoothly. Furthermore, we must sometimes impose guidelines and restrictions related to how students carry out their assignments. The challenge is to present these rules, procedures, guidelines, and restrictions without communicating a message of *control* (like that in the "Painting Between the Lines" exercise). Instead, we can present them as *information*—for instance, as conditions that can help students accomplish classroom objectives (Deci, 1992; Koestner et al., 1984). Here are three examples of rules or instructions presented in an informational rather than controlling manner:

- "We can make sure everyone has an equal chance to speak and be heard if we listen without interrupting and if we raise our hands when we want to contribute to the discussion."
- "I'm giving you a particular format to follow when you do your math homework. If you use this format, it will be easier for me to find your answers and to figure out how I can help you improve."
- "Let's remember that other students will be using the same paints and brushes later today, so as we work, we need to make sure everything we use now is still in tip-top shape when we're done. It's important, then, that we rinse the brushes in water and wipe them on a paper towel before we switch to a new color. We should also clean the brushes thoroughly when we're done painting."

■ You can find additional examples in Figure 14.2 of Chapter 14.

Whether rules and instructions are presented in an informational or controlling manner is sometimes in the eye of the beholder. For example, when I have shown my own classes the "Reading Group" and "Classroom Rules" clips on Video CD 2, some students perceive the teacher to be providing helpful information and guidance about classroom behavior, whereas others find her overly controlling.

◎   *Give students opportunities to make choices.* Sometimes there is only one way to accomplish a particular instructional objective. But more often, a variety of routes will lead to the same

■ Observe the teacher in the "Classroom Rules" and "Reading Group" clips on Video CD 2. Would you characterize this teacher's style as "informational" or "controlling"?

Students are more likely to be intrinsically motivated when they have a sense of self-determination (e.g., when they can choose some of their activities) and when they have high self-efficacy (e.g., when they are successful in those activities). Experiences that promote self-determination and self-efficacy can be especially important for students with disabilities.

destination. In such cases, why not let students choose how to get there? For example, we might allow them to make decisions, either individually or as a group, about some or all of the following:

- Rules and procedures to make the class run more smoothly
- Ways of achieving mastery of an instructional objective (e.g., which of several possible procedures to use, whether to work individually or in small groups)
- Specific topics for research or writing projects
- Specific works of literature to be read
- Due dates for some assignments
- The order in which specific tasks are done during the school day
- Ways of demonstrating that an instructional objective has been mastered (e.g., see Figure 12.2)
- Criteria by which some assignments will be evaluated (Kohn, 1993; Meece, 1994; Stipek, 1993)

When students can make choices such as these, they are more likely to be interested in what they are doing, to work diligently, to complete assignments quickly and efficiently, and to take pride in their work (Deci & Ryan, 1992; Lepper & Hodell, 1989; J. A. Ross, 1988; J. C. Turner, 1995). Furthermore, students who are given choices—even students with serious behavior problems—are less likely to misbehave in class (Dunlap et al., 1994; S. Powell & Nelson, 1997; B. J. Vaughn & Horner, 1997).

In some situations students' choices can be almost limitless; for example, in a unit on expository writing, a wide variety of student-selected research topics might be equally appropriate. In other situations we may need to impose certain limits on the choices students make; for example, if we allow a class to set its own due dates for certain assignments, we might insist that the schedule provides enough time for us to grade each assignment. In still other situations we may want to provide a handful of options from which students can choose; for instance, we might allow them to choose from among several works of literature, specialize in one of several art media (e.g., watercolors, pastels, clay), or select a piece of equipment (e.g., parallel bars, rings, floor mats) on which to develop gymnastic skills.

◎   *Give students considerable autonomy within their organized extracurricular activities.* Ideally, students' extracurricular activities (clubs, theater groups, community service projects,

FIGURE 12.2 We can enhance students' sense of self-determination by giving them choices about how to accomplish instructional objectives. Here a sixth-grade language arts teacher gives her students several options for demonstrating their understanding of a science fiction book.

Choose One!

SCIENCE FICTION BOOK PROJECTS

_____ Write a "Dear Abby" letter from one of the main characters, in which he or she asks for advice on solving his or her main problem. Then answer the letter.

_____ Draw a time line of the main events of the book.

_____ Create a comic book or a comic strip page that features a major scene from the book in each box.

_____ Make a collage of objects and printed words from newspapers and magazines that give the viewer a feeling for the mood of the book.

_____ Your book probably takes place in an unusual or exotic setting, so illustrate and write a travel brochure describing that location.

_____ Imagine yourself as a scientist who has been asked to explain the unusual events in the book. Write up a report in scientific style.

_____ With other students who have read the same book, plan a bulletin board display. Write a plot summary; character and setting descriptions; discussions of special passages. Each group member must contribute one artistic piece—for example, new book cover, bookmark, poster, banner, some of the ideas listed above. Arrange the writing and artwork under a colorful heading announcing the book.

etc.) can provide both the challenges that enhance students' self-efficacy and the autonomy that enhances their sense of self-determination (Larson, 2000). When we supervise such activities, then, we can foster intrinsic motivation—not to mention the development of initiative and skills in planning and negotiation—by giving students considerable freedom and responsibility in determining the direction the activities take (Larson, 2000). At the same time, we will often need to provide the guidance students may need to tackle challenges; for instance, we might help them think through the likely outcomes of various courses of action (Larson, 2000).

◎ *Evaluate students' performance in a noncontrolling way.* As teachers, we will inevitably need to evaluate students' accomplishments. But we must keep in mind that external evaluations may undermine students' intrinsic motivation, especially if communicated in a controlling manner (Deci & Ryan, 1992; Harter, Whitesell, & Kowalski, 1992). Ideally, we should present our evaluations of students' work not as "judgments" to remind students of how they *should* perform but as information that can help them improve their knowledge and skills (Stipek, 1996). Furthermore, we can give students criteria by which they can evaluate *themselves* (see Chapters 10 and 15). In the "Author's Chair" clip on Video CD 2, a second-grade teacher creates an environment in which evaluation is an important part of helping students improve. For example, in preparing her class for an activity in which some children will read their stories aloud, she tells the class, "As you listen to a friend, you may want to give them a compliment, or you may want to tell them something that will help them become a better writer."

■ Observe examples of noncontrolling evaluation in the "Author's Chair" clip on Video CD 2.

◎ *Be selective about when and how you use extrinsic reinforcers.* Our discussion of behaviorism in Chapter 9 emphasized the importance of relying on intrinsic reinforcers—such as students' own feelings of pride and satisfaction about their accomplishments—as often as possible. A problem with using *extrinsic* reinforcers (praise, stickers, favorite activities, and so on) is that they may undermine intrinsic motivation, especially if students perceive them as controlling behavior and limiting choices (Deci, 1992; A. E. Gottfried, Fleming, & Gottfried, 1994; Lepper & Hodell, 1989). Extrinsic reinforcers may also communicate the message that classroom tasks are unpleasant "chores" (why else would a reinforcer be necessary?), rather than activities to be carried out and enjoyed for their own sake (B. A. Hennessey, 1995; Stipek, 1993).

Extrinsic reinforcers appear to have no adverse effects when they're unexpected—for instance, when students get special recognition for a public service project in the local community—or when they're not contingent on specific behaviors—for instance, when they're used simply to make an activity more enjoyable (Cameron, 2001; Deci et al., 2001). They can even be beneficial if used to encourage students not only to do something but also to do it *well* (Cameron, 2001). And if they communicate that students *have* done something well (as a high grade might) or have made considerable improvement, they can enhance students' sense of self-efficacy and focus students' attention on mastering the subject matter (L. H. Anderman, personal communication, February 9, 2004; Hynd, 2003).

Intrinsic motivation and extrinsic motivation are not necessarily incompatible. As noted in Chapter 11, students may be simultaneously motivated by both extrinsic reinforcers and the intrinsic feelings of pleasure their actions bring. Furthermore, students may initially find a new topic or skill boring or frustrating and therefore need external encouragement to continue (Cameron, 2001; Deci et al., 2001; Hidi & Harackiewicz, 2000). With continuing practice, their competence should improve, and they may eventually begin to find the subject matter intrinsically rewarding.

So how can we use extrinsic reinforcers without diminishing students' sense of self-determination? For one thing, we can use reinforcers such as praise to communicate information rather than to control behavior (Deci, 1992; R. M. Ryan, Mims, & Koestner, 1983); consider these statements as examples:

- "Your description of the main character in your short story makes her come alive."
- "I think you have finally mastered the rolling *R* sound in Spanish."
- "This poster clearly states the hypothesis, method, results, and conclusions of your science project. Your use of a bar graph makes the differences between your treatment and control groups easy to see and interpret."

Furthermore, as noted in the discussion of self-regulation in Chapter 10, we may want to encourage *self*-reinforcement, a practice that clearly keeps control in students' hands.

◎   *Help students keep externally imposed constraints in perspective.* Students will often encounter circumstances that cast a "controlling" light on school activities: Competitions, extrinsic rewards, and external evaluation are frequent events in most schools. For example, students often compete in athletic contests, spelling bees, and science fairs. They may make the honor roll, win a first-place ribbon at an art exhibit, or receive a free pizza coupon for reading a certain number of books each month. And they will almost inevitably receive grades, in one form or another, that reflect teachers' evaluations of their achievement.

To help students keep such external constraints in perspective as they engage in a learning task, we should remind them that although competition, extrinsic rewards, or evaluation may be present, the most important thing is for them to focus on the inherent value of the task itself (Amabile & Hennessey, 1992; B. A. Hennessey, 1995). For example, we might encourage them to tell themselves something along this line:

> I like to get good grades, and when I bring home a good report card, my parents always give me money. But that's not what's really important. I like to learn a lot. There are a lot of things that interest me, and I want to learn about them, so I work hard because I enjoy it. (Amabile & Hennessey, 1992, p. 68)

Self-efficacy and self-determination are not the only factors involved in intrinsic motivation. Students' expectations and values are also important, as we shall see now.

EXPECTANCIES AND VALUES

Some theorists (e.g., Eccles [Parsons], 1983; Feather, 1982; Weiner, 2000; Wigfield & Eccles, 2000, 2002) have proposed that motivation for performing a particular task depends on two variables, both of which are fairly subjective. First, students must have a high expectation, or **expectancy**, that they will be successful. Certainly their prior history of success and failure at a particular task— and thus their self-efficacy—has a strong influence (e.g., Dweck, Goetz, & Strauss, 1980). But other factors affect expectancy level as well: the perceived difficulty of a task, the availability of resources and support, the quality of instruction (remember Michael's concerns about his algebra teacher), and the amount of effort that will be necessary (Dweck & Elliott, 1983; Wigfield & Eccles, 1992; Zimmerman et al., 1992). From such factors, students come to a conclusion— perhaps correct, perhaps not—about their chances of success.

Equally important, and equally subjective, is **value**: Students must believe there are direct or indirect benefits in performing a task. Theorists have suggested four possible reasons why value might be high or low: importance, utility, interest, and cost (Eccles [Parsons], 1983; Wigfield & Eccles, 1992, 2000). Some activities are valued because they are associated with desirable personal qualities; that is, they are viewed as *important*. For example, a boy who wants to be smart and thinks that smart people do well in school will place a premium on academic success. Other activities have high value because they are seen as means to a desired goal; that is, they have *utility*. For example, much as she found mathematics confusing and frustrating, my daughter Tina struggled through four years of high school math classes because many colleges require that much math. Still other activities are valued because they bring pleasure and enjoyment; in other words, they are *interesting*. For example, you may recall Anya's passion for art in the preceding chapter's opening case study.

We can also anticipate the circumstances in which students will probably not value an activity very much. Some activities may require a lot more effort than they are worth; this is the *cost* factor. For example, you could probably become an expert on some little-known topic (e.g., the nature of rats' dreams, animal-eating plants of Borneo), but I'm guessing that you have more important things to which to devote your time and energy right now. Other activities may be associated with too many bad feelings; for example, if students become frustrated often enough in their efforts to understand mathematics, they may eventually begin to steer clear of the subject whenever possible. And of course, anything likely to threaten a student's sense of self-worth is a "must" to avoid.

Expectancies and values are related to different aspects of students' behavior and performance (Mac Iver, Stipek, & Daniels, 1991; Wigfield & Eccles, 2002). Values affect the choices students make (e.g., their high school course selections). In contrast, expectancies are related to students' effort and achievement (e.g., their grade point average). Yet as you may have inferred from the preceding discussion, expectancies and values are somewhat interdependent (Eccles et al., 1998). More specifically, students who don't expect to do well in a particular activity may

These girls may be motivated in their math class because they *expect* to be successful in it and because they find *value* in the problem-solving skills they are learning.

■ **expectancy** Belief that as a result of both personal ability and external circumstances, one will be successful in accomplishing a task or achieving a goal.

■ **value** Belief that an activity has direct or indirect benefits.

find reasons to devalue it. And students who don't value an activity are less likely to work hard at it and so have lower expectancies about their performance.

In the early elementary years, students often pursue activities they find interesting and enjoyable, regardless of their expectancies for success (Wigfield, 1994). As they get older, however, they increasingly attach value to activities for which they have high expectancy for success and to activities they think will help them meet long-term goals; meanwhile, they begin to *devalue* the things they do poorly (Jacobs, Lanza, Osgood, Eccles, & Wigfield, 2002; Wigfield, 1994). Sadly, the value students find in many school subjects (e.g., math, English, music, and sports) declines markedly over the school years (Eccles et al., 1998; Jacobs et al., 2002; Wigfield et al., 1991). As one 16-year-old put it, "School's fun because you can hang out with your friends, but I know I won't use much of this stuff when I leave here" (Valente, 2001).

Internalizing the Values of Others

Earlier we identified four factors affecting the extent to which students value particular tasks and activities: importance, utility, interest, and cost. Yet the social and cultural environment also plays a role: As children grow older, they tend to adopt many of the priorities and values of the people around them. Such **internalized motivation** typically develops gradually over the course of development, perhaps in the following sequence (Deci & Ryan, 1995; R. M. Ryan & Deci, 2000):

1. *External regulation.* Learners are motivated to engage in certain activities based primarily on the external consequences that will result from various behaviors; in other words, they are extrinsically motivated. For instance, students may do schoolwork mostly to avoid being punished for poor grades, and they are likely to need a lot of prodding and reinforcement to complete assigned tasks.

2. *Introjection.* Learners engage in activities to gain the approval of others; for example, they may willingly complete an easy, boring assignment as a means of gaining their teacher's praise. At this point, they feel some internal pressure to adopt certain behaviors; for instance, they may feel guilty when they violate certain standards or rules for behavior. However, they do not fully understand the rationale behind these standards and rules. Instead, their primary motives appear to be avoiding a negative self-evaluation and protecting their sense of self-worth.

3. *Identification.* Learners now see some activities as being personally important and valuable for themselves. For instance, they may value academic success for its own sake, perceive assigned classroom tasks as essential for helping them learn, and so need little prodding to get their work done. Their acceptance of certain values as their own reflects the fact that they identify with a social or cultural group that has these values.

4. *Integration.* Learners have fully accepted the desirability of certain behaviors and integrated them into an overall system of motives and values. For example, a student might have acquired a keen interest in art as a career goal; if so, we are likely to see that interest reflected in many things the student does regularly (recall Anya in the opening case study in Chapter 11).

As you can see, then, extrinsic and intrinsic motivation are not necessarily either/or phenomena; in some situations extrinsic motivation gradually evolves into internalized values.

The more that students have internalized the importance of academic success, the more cognitively engaged they become in school subject matter and the better their overall learning and classroom success is likely to be (R. M. Ryan & Deci, 2000). Internalized motivation is also an important aspect of self-regulated learning; it fosters a general work ethic in which students spontaneously engage in activities that, although not always fun or immediately gratifying, are essential for reaching long-term goals (Harter, 1992; McCombs, 1996; R. M. Ryan, Connell, & Grolnick, 1992; Stipek, 1993).

Theorists have suggested that three conditions promote the development of internalized motivation (R. M. Ryan et al., 1992). First, growing children need a *warm, responsive, and supportive environment* in which they gain a feeling of relatedness to important individuals (e.g., parents and teachers) in their lives. Second, they need *some degree of autonomy*, so that they have a sense of self-determination as they make choices and decisions. Finally, they need *appropriate guidance and structure*, including information about expected behaviors and why they're important, as well as clear consequences for inappropriate behaviors. Fostering the development of internalized motivation, then, involves striking a delicate balance between giving students enough

■ **internalized motivation** Adoption of others' priorities and values as one's own.

opportunities to experience self-determination and providing some guidance about appropriate behavior. In a sense, we need to "scaffold" desired behaviors at first, gradually reducing such scaffolding as students exhibit those behaviors more easily and frequently.

Fostering Expectancies and Values in the Classroom

As teachers, we must certainly give students reasons why they should expect to succeed at classroom tasks—for instance, by providing the necessary resources, support, and strategies that will enable them to do so (recall how Ms. Tucker taught Michael strategies for mastering algebra). We must also help them find value in school activities. In the following assessment exercise, we consider how one teacher tried to foster value for classroom subject matter and what one of her students wrote in response.

Interpreting Student Artifacts and Behaviors

Why We Study History

After a fifth-grade class discussed the importance of studying history, the teacher asked her students to write an essay summarizing and reacting to the discussion. As you read 10-year-old Renata's essay:

- Identify the primary reason Renata gives for studying history
- Speculate about the likelihood that Renata will actually pursue history with the enthusiasm she describes

Why We Study History

One reason we study history is to prevent us from making mistakes that were made in the past. As an old saying goes; if you do not know your history, then you are dumed to repet it. Just about that saying makes me want to jump up grab a 1,000 paged history book and read the whole thing because I would hate to make the same mistakes that were made in the past. You are supost to learn from the past, not repet it.

But the there are something you do want to repet such as the kindness of Teodore Roosevelt and Abraham Lincon, the determenation of Benjaman Franklin, and the courage of Harriet Tubman.

Renata focuses on the same reason for studying history that I heard as a student many years ago (perhaps you heard it as well): History allows us to avoid making the same mistakes as our predecessors. I suspect that for most students, such a reason is too abstract and vague to cultivate a genuine desire to learn about historical events. Although Renata initially shows considerable enthusiasm—she wants to jump up and read a 1,000-page history book—we can reasonably guess that she never follows up by actually reading such a book. *Showing* that you value something is a lot more convincing than merely *saying* that you do.

Theorists and practitioners have offered several suggestions for fostering value for academic subject matter. For instance, we can identify the specific knowledge and skills that students will acquire from an instructional unit (Keller, 1987). We can show students how the things they learn will help them address their present concerns and long-term goals (C. Ames, 1992; Brophy & Alleman, 1991; Ferrari & Elik, 2003). We can embed the use of many basic skills within the context of meaningful, real-world (authentic) tasks (Newmann & Wehlage, 1993). We can convey how classroom subject matter, even when it doesn't relate to students' career goals, can help them make better sense of the world around them (Finke & Bettle, 1996). We can demonstrate how we ourselves value academic activities—for example, by sharing our fascination with certain topics and describing how we apply the things we've learned in school (Brophy, 2004; Brophy & Alleman, 1991). And by all means we must refrain from asking students to engage in activities with little long-term benefit—memorizing trivial facts for no good reason, reading material that is clearly beyond students' comprehension levels, and so on (Brophy, 2004).

One common reason that learners value something is that they find it interesting. Let's learn more about what theorists have to say about the role of interest in human motivation.

INTEREST

When we say that people have **interest** in a particular topic or activity, we mean that they find the topic or activity intriguing and engaging. Interest, then, is a form of intrinsic motivation. Positive affect accompanies interest; for example, people pursuing a task in which they are interested experience such feelings as pleasure, excitement, and liking (Hidi & Anderson, 1992; Schiefele, 1998).

Take a minute to consider your own interests in the following exercise.

■ **interest** Feeling that a topic is intriguing or enticing.

Experiencing FIRSTHAND · The Doctor's Office

You have just arrived at the doctor's office for your annual checkup. The receptionist tells you the doctor is running late and you will probably have to wait an hour before you can be seen. As you sit down in the waiting room, you notice six magazines on the coffee table: *Better Homes and Gardens*, *National Geographic*, *Newsweek*, *People*, *Popular Mechanics*, and *Sports Illustrated*.

1. Rate each of these magazines in terms of how *interesting* you think its articles would be to you:

	Not at All Interesting	Somewhat Interesting	Very Interesting
Better Homes and Gardens	_____	_____	_____
National Geographic	_____	_____	_____
Newsweek	_____	_____	_____
People	_____	_____	_____
Popular Mechanics	_____	_____	_____
Sports Illustrated	_____	_____	_____

2. Even though you think some of the magazines will be more interesting than others, you decide to spend ten minutes reading each one. Estimate how much you think you might *remember* from what you read in each of the six magazines:

	Hardly Anything	A Moderate Amount	Quite a Bit
Better Homes and Gardens	_____	_____	_____
National Geographic	_____	_____	_____
Newsweek	_____	_____	_____
People	_____	_____	_____
Popular Mechanics	_____	_____	_____
Sports Illustrated	_____	_____	_____

· · · · · · ·

Now compare your two sets of ratings. Chances are, the magazines that you rated highest in interest to you are also the magazines from which you would learn and remember the most.

Learners who are interested in a particular topic devote more attention to it and become more cognitively engaged in it (M. A. McDaniel, Waddill, Finstad, & Bourg, 2000; Schiefele & Wild, 1994; Wigfield, 1994). They are also apt to learn it in a more meaningful, organized, and elaborative fashion—for instance, by relating it to prior knowledge, interrelating ideas, drawing inferences, forming visual images, generating examples, and identifying potential applications (Pintrich & Schrauben, 1992; Renninger, Hidi, & Krapp, 1992; Schraw & Lehman, 2001; Tobias, 1994). And unless they are emotionally attached to their current beliefs, they are more likely to undergo conceptual change when they encounter information that contradicts their existing understandings (Andre & Windschitl, 2003; Linnenbrink & Pintrich, 2003). As you might guess, then, students who are interested in what they study show higher academic achievement and are more likely to remember the subject matter over the long run (Garner et al., 1992; Hidi & Harackiewicz, 2000; Renninger et al., 1992).

Situational Versus Personal Interest

Theorists distinguish between two general types of interest (Hidi & Harackiewicz, 2000; Renninger et al., 1992; Schraw & Lehman, 2001). **Situational interest** is evoked by something in the immediate environment. Things that are new, different, unexpected, or especially vivid often generate situational interest, as do things that involve a high activity level or intense emotions (Hidi, 1990; Mitchell, 1993; Renninger et al., 1992; Schank, 1979). (As examples, notice 6-year-old Joey's interest in physical activities and 9-year-old Elena's curiosity about new words in the "Motivation: Early Childhood" and "Motivation: Middle Childhood" clips on Video CD 1.) Students also tend to be intrigued by topics related to people and culture (e.g., disease, violence, holidays), nature (e.g., dinosaurs, weather, the sea), and current events (e.g., television shows, popular music, substance abuse, gangs) (Zahorik, 1994). Works of fiction (novels, short stories, movies, and so on) are more interesting and engaging when they include themes and characters with which students can personally identify (Hidi & Harackiewicz, 2000; Schank, 1979; Wade,

■ Observe examples of situational interest in the early childhood and middle childhood "Motivation" clips on Video CD 1.

■ **situational interest** Interest evoked temporarily by something in the environment.

FIGURE 12.3 Many students have personal interests that pervade much of what they do. Here we see two examples of Matt's passion for soccer in high school: (1) an excerpt from an essay assigned in writing class and (2) artwork created two years earlier for a language arts class portfolio. Matt's interest in soccer actually dates back to first grade; you will see evidence of his early interest in "A Two-Way Journal," an assessment exercise in Chapter 14.

Soccer, the Pride and Passion

The sharp light blinds all onlookers from the reflection off the newly polished cast iron gauntlets of the twenty-two men of steel. Helms lowered, bodies bent in preparation for the battle Royal. Weapons drawn, shields raised, minds focused, focused on their enemy, their foe, their fellow competitor. Small colored flags wave in the stands, color coded with their respective prides and passions. Noises rumble through the stadium as random as the droplets of sweat flowing down the warriors' faces; teeth gritted, fists clenched, hearts pounding, pounding in anticipation of the things to come, the ultimate challenge of wills, the will to win for your fans, for your teammates, for yourself.

Fussebol, calcio, football, soccer; hundreds of names, one sport. Soccer is the most popular and most played game in the world, but that is not why I play the "Beautiful Game." Twenty-two players on a 120 by 90-yard battlefield scraping, fighting over one ball; that is not why I play it. Millions of players striving to be on their country's roster to play in the world's tournament that occurs only once every four years; that is not why I play it. The dream of playing in front of thousands of roaring fans and scoring the game-winning goal; that is not why I play it. For the emotion and passion of being able to walk out of my door every day to play the game I love, to give my all to the game, while taking everything I can from it, and not just progressing as a player, but a person; that is why I play it. That is why I play the "world's game." That is why I play soccer. . . .

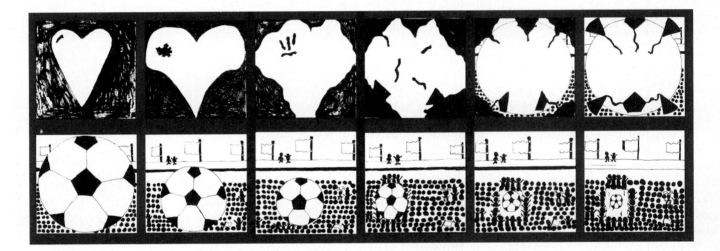

1992). Nonfiction is more interesting when it is easy to understand and relationships among ideas are clear (Schraw & Lehman, 2001; Wade, 1992). And challenging tasks are often more interesting and engaging than easy ones (Danner & Lonky, 1981; Harter, 1978).

Other interests lie within: Students tend to have personal preferences about the topics they pursue and the activities in which they engage. Because such **personal interests** are relatively stable over time, we see a consistent pattern in the choices students make (e.g., see Figure 12.3). Some personal interests probably come from students' prior experiences with various activities and topics; for example, events and subject matter that initially invoke situational interest may provide the seeds from which a personal interest eventually grows (Hidi & Harackiewicz, 2000). Students may also find that acquiring more knowledge and skill in a particular area enhances their sense of self-efficacy, thereby enhancing intrinsic motivation. Often, interest and knowledge seem to perpetuate each other: Personal interest in a topic fuels a quest to learn more about the topic, and the increased knowledge gained, in turn, promotes greater interest (P. A. Alexander, 1997; Hidi & McLaren, 1990; Tobias, 1994).

In the early grades, interests are mostly situational: Young children are readily attracted to novel, attention-getting events and stimuli. By the middle to upper elementary grades, however, children acquire specific interests—perhaps in reptiles, ballet, or outer space—that persist over a period of time (Eccles et al., 1998). By and large, students form interests in activities that they can do well and that are stereotypically appropriate for their gender and socioeconomic group (L. S. Gottfredson 1981; Wigfield, 1994). Personal interests are ultimately more beneficial than situational interest: Whereas the latter may temporarily capture a student's attention, personal interest is the force that ultimately sustains involvement in an activity over the long run (P. A. Alexander et al., 1994).

■ **personal interest** Long-term, relatively stable interest in a particular topic or activity.

Promoting Interest in Classroom Subject Matter

Almost all students learn more when a topic is interesting; students with little background knowledge in the topic are especially likely to benefit (P. A. Alexander, 1997; Garner et al., 1991). Yet students often report that they find little of interest in classroom subject matter, especially after they reach the middle school and high school grades (Gentry et al., 2002; Larson, 2000).

As teachers, we can certainly capitalize on students' personal interests by allowing some flexibility in the topics about which they read, learn, write, and study (e.g., see Figure 12.4). On other occasions we can temporarily pique students' interest, and in the process perhaps stimulate the beginnings of more enduring personal interests, by the activities we develop and the ways we present information. Following are several strategies that often evoke interest in classroom topics:

◎ *Include occasional novelty, variety, and mystery in classroom materials and procedures.* Students are often interested in things that are new and different and in events that are surprising and puzzling (Brophy, 1987; Lepper & Hodell, 1989; Sheveland, 1994; Stipek, 1993).

◎ *Relate information and ideas to students' own lives.* Students typically enjoy subject matter to which they can relate on a personal level—for instance, math lessons that involve students' favorite foods, works of literature that feature characters with whom students can readily identify, or history textbooks that portray historical figures as real people with distinctly human qualities (Anand & Ross, 1987; Levstik, 1994).

◎ *Provide opportunities to respond actively to the subject matter.* Students typically enjoy engaging in a topic in an active way, perhaps by manipulating and experimenting with physical objects, creating new products, discussing controversial issues, or teaching something they've learned to peers (Andre & Windschitl, 2003; Certo et al., 2002; Hidi, Weiss, Berndorff, & Nolan, 1998; Zahorik, 1994). In the "Motivation: Early Adolescence" clip on Video CD 1, 12-year-old Claudia explains how much she enjoys interacting with school subject matter in some way:

Adult: What do you like best about school?
Claudia: I like to do projects. Like creative ones where you get to . . . make models of things. And if you are in a group, then you get to get more ideas. Sometimes the teacher will start you out a little, but then you get to do most of it.
Adult: What kinds of things interest you in school?
Claudia: Um . . . like math and science. . . . You get to interact with them a little bit. That's always fun.

◎ *Encourage occasional fantasy and make-believe.* Many students enjoy fantasy and make-believe—for example, playing out the roles of key figures in historical events or imagining what it must be like to be weightless in space (Brophy, 1987, 2004; Lepper & Hodell, 1989).

Figure 12.5 presents examples of how such strategies might be implemented in different content domains. Yet another strategy for generating interest is to relate classroom subject matter to students' short-term and long-term goals (Brophy, 2004; Parsons et al., 1982). We now look at the kinds of goals students are likely to have.

GOALS

As we discovered in Chapters 10 and 11, much of human behavior is directed toward particular goals. Children and adolescents typically have a wide variety of goals: Being happy and healthy, doing well in school, being popular with classmates, gaining recognition for accomplishments, defeating others in competitive events, earning money, and finding a long-term mate are just a few of the many possibilities (M. E. Ford, 1996; Schutz, 1994). Some goals (e.g., "I want to finish reading my dinosaur book") are short-term and transitory; others (e.g., "I want to be a paleontologist") are long-term and relatively enduring. Yet among students' many goals are certain **core goals** that drive much of what they do (Schutz, 1994). For instance, students who attain high levels of academic achievement typically make classroom learning a high priority; students who achieve at lower levels are often more concerned with social relationships (Wentzel & Wigfield, 1998; Wigfield et al., 1996).

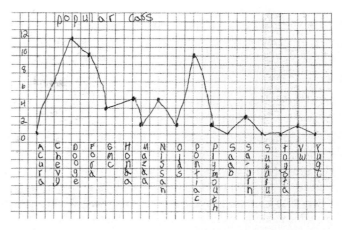

FIGURE 12.4 We can capitalize on students' personal interests by allowing flexibility in the topics students explore as they work on basic skills. Twelve-year-old Connor gained practice in basic research and graphing skills by surveying fellow students about a favorite topic: cars. His results are shown here.

■ Observe Claudia's eagerness for hands-on activities and social interaction in the "Motivation: Early Adolescence" clip on Video CD 1.

■ **core goal** Long-term goal that drives much of what a person does.

FIGURE 12.5 Examples of how teachers might generate interest in various content domains

Music: In a unit on musical instruments, let students experiment with a variety of simple instruments.

Health education: In a lesson about alcoholic beverages, have students role-play being at a party and being tempted to have a beer or wine cooler.

Reading: Turn a short story into a play, with each student taking a part.

Biology: Have a classroom debate about the ethical implications of conducting medical research on animals.

Spelling: Occasionally depart from standard word lists, instead asking students to learn how to spell the names of favorite television shows or classmates' surnames.

Physical education: Incorporate steps from hip-hop, swing, or country line dancing into an aerobics workout.

Art: Have students make a mosaic from items they've found on a scavenger hunt around the school building.

Physical science: Have each student make several paper airplanes and then fly them to see which design travels farthest.

Mathematics: Have students play computer games to improve their automaticity for number facts.

History: Have students read children's perspectives of historical events (e.g., Anne Frank's diary during World War II, Zlata Filipovic's diary during the Bosnian War).

Geography: Present household objects not found locally, and ask students to guess where they might be from.

Sources: Some ideas derived from Brophy, 1986; Lepper & Hodell, 1989; Spaulding, 1992; Stipek, 1993; Wlodkowski, 1978.

In the upcoming sections we'll look at research findings related to several kinds of goals: achievement goals, work-avoidance goals, social goals, and career goals. We'll also identify strategies for fostering productive goals and helping students address multiple goals simultaneously.

Achievement Goals

As I mentioned in Chapter 11, motivation theorists originally conceptualized achievement motivation as a general characteristic that people exhibit consistently in a variety of areas. However, most contemporary theorists believe that achievement motivation can take different forms, depending on people's specific goals. To illustrate, let's consider what three different boys might be thinking during the first day of a basketball unit in Mr. Wesolowski's physical education class:

Tim: This is my chance to show all the guys what a great basketball player I am. If I stay near the basket, Travis and Tony will keep passing to me, and I'll score a lot of points. I can really impress Wesolowski and my friends.

Travis: Boy, I hope I don't screw this up. If I shoot at the basket and miss, I'll look like a real jerk. Maybe I should just stay outside the three-point line and keep passing to Tim and Tony.

Tony: I'd really like to become a better basketball player. I can't figure out why I don't get more of my shots into the basket. I'll ask Wesolowski to give me feedback about how I can improve my game. Maybe some of my friends will have suggestions, too.

All three boys want to play basketball well; that is, they all have *achievement goals*. But they have different reasons for wanting to play well. Tim is concerned mostly about looking good in front of his teacher and classmates and so wants to maximize opportunities to demonstrate his skill on the court. Travis, too, is concerned about the impression he'll make, but he just wants to make sure he *doesn't* look *bad*. Unlike Tim and Travis, Tony isn't thinking about how his performance will appear to others. Instead, he is interested mainly in developing his basketball skills and doesn't expect immediate success. For Tony, making mistakes is an inevitable part of learning a new skill, not a source of embarrassment or humiliation.

Tony's approach to basketball illustrates a **mastery goal**, a desire to acquire additional knowledge or master new skills. Tim and Travis each have a **performance goal**, a desire to present themselves as competent in the eyes of others. More specifically, Tim has a **performance-approach goal**: He wants to look good and receive favorable judgments from others. In contrast, Travis has a **performance-avoidance goal**: He wants to *avoid* looking bad and receiving unfavorable judgments. In some cases performance goals have an element of social comparison, in that students are concerned about how their accomplishments compare to those of their peers (Elliot & McGregor, 2000; Elliot & Thrash, 2001; Midgley et al., 1998).

■ **mastery goal** Desire to acquire additional knowledge or master new skills.

■ **performance goal** Desire to demonstrate high ability and make a good impression.

■ **performance-approach goal** Desire to look good and receive favorable judgments from others.

■ **performance-avoidance goal** Desire not to look bad or receive unfavorable judgments from others.

Mastery goals, performance-approach goals, and performance-avoidance goals are not necessarily mutually exclusive; students may simultaneously have two kinds, or even all three (Covington & Müeller, 2001; Hidi & Harackiewicz, 2000; Meece & Holt, 1993). For example, returning to our basketball example, we could imagine another boy, Trey, who wants to improve his basketball skills *and* look good in front of his classmates *and* not come across as a klutz.

Effects of Mastery and Performance Goals   A considerable body of research indicates that mastery goals are the optimal situation. As Table 12.1 illustrates, students with mastery goals tend to engage in the very activities that will help them learn: They pay attention in class, process information in ways that promote effective long-term memory storage, and learn from their mistakes. Furthermore, students with mastery goals have a healthy perspective about learning,

■ In which of these goal(s) do you see intrinsic motivation? In which do you see extrinsic motivation?

TABLE 12.1   COMPARE/CONTRAST

Students with Mastery Versus Performance Goals

STUDENTS WITH MASTERY GOALS	STUDENTS WITH PERFORMANCE GOALS (ESPECIALLY THOSE WITH PERFORMANCE-AVOIDANCE GOALS)
Are more likely to be interested in and intrinsically motivated to learn course material	Are more likely to be extrinsically motivated (i.e., motivated by expectations of external reinforcement and punishment) and more likely to cheat to obtain good grades
Believe that competence develops over time through practice and effort	Believe that competence is a stable characteristic (people either have talent or they don't); think that competent people shouldn't have to try very hard
Exhibit more self-regulated learning and behavior	Exhibit less self-regulation
Use learning strategies that promote true comprehension (e.g., meaningful learning, elaboration, comprehension monitoring)	Use learning strategies that promote only rote learning (e.g., repetition, copying, word-for-word memorization); may procrastinate on assignments
Choose tasks that maximize opportunities for learning; seek out challenges	Choose tasks that maximize opportunities for demonstrating competence; avoid tasks and actions (e.g., asking for help) that make them look incompetent
Are more likely to undergo conceptual change when confronted with convincing evidence that contradicts current beliefs	Are less likely to undergo conceptual change, in part because they are less likely to notice the discrepancy between new information and existing beliefs
React to easy tasks with feelings of boredom or disappointment	React to success on easy tasks with feelings of pride or relief
Seek feedback that accurately describes their ability and helps them improve	Seek feedback that flatters them
Willingly collaborate with peers when doing so is apt to enhance learning	Collaborate with peers primarily when doing so can help them look competent or enhance their social status
Evaluate their own performance in terms of the progress they make	Evaluate their own performance in terms of how they compare with others
Interpret failure as a sign that they need to exert more effort	Interpret failure as a sign of low ability and therefore predictive of future failures
View errors as a normal and useful part of the learning process; use errors to improve performance	View errors as a sign of failure and incompetence; engage in self-handicapping to provide apparent justification for errors and failures
Are satisfied with their performance if they try hard and make progress	Are satisfied with their performance only if they succeed
View a teacher as a resource and guide to help them learn	View a teacher as a judge and as a rewarder or punisher
Remain relatively calm during tests and classroom assignments	Are often quite anxious about tests and other assessments
Are more likely to be enthusiastic about, and become actively involved in, school activities	Are more likely to distance themselves from the school environment

Sources: Ablard & Lipschultz, 1998; C. Ames & Archer, 1988; R. Ames, 1983; E. M. Anderman et al., 1998; E. M. Anderman & Maehr, 1994; Dweck, 1986; Dweck & Elliott, 1983; Entwisle & Ramsden, 1983; L. S. Fuchs et al., 1997; Gabriele & Boody, 2001; Graham & Weiner, 1996; Jagacinski & Nicholls, 1984, 1987; Kaplan, 1998; Kaplan & Midgley, 1999; Levy, Kaplan, & Patrick, 2000; Linnenbrink & Pintrich, 2002, 2003; McCombs, 1988; McGregor & Elliot, 2002; Meece, 1994; Middleton & Midgley, 1997; P. K. Murphy & Alexander, 2000; Newman & Schwager, 1995; Nolen, 1996; B. M. Powell, 1990; Rawsthorne & Elliot, 1999; A. M. Ryan et al., 2001; Schiefele, 1991, 1992; Shernoff & Hoogstra, 2001; Skaalvik, 1997; Southerland & Sinatra, 2003; Stipek, 1993; Turner, Thorpe, & Meyer, 1998; Urdan & Midgley, 2001; Urdan, Midgley, & Anderman, 1998.

effort, and failure: They realize that learning is a process of trying hard and continuing to persevere even in the face of temporary setbacks. Consequently, it is usually these students who are most likely to stay on task and who benefit the most from their classroom experiences (Gabriele & Montecinos, 2001; Kumar et al., 2002; Wentzel & Wigfield, 1998).

In contrast, students with performance goals—especially those with performance-*avoidance* goals—may stay away from some of the very tasks that, because of their challenging nature, would do the most to help them master new skills. Furthermore, these students often experience debilitating anxiety about tests and other classroom tasks. Performance-*approach* goals are a mixed bag: They sometimes have very positive effects, spurring students on to achieve at high levels, especially in the secondary grades and especially in combination with mastery goals (Hidi & Harackiewicz, 2000; McNeil & Alibali, 2000; Pintrich, 2000; Rawsthorne & Elliot, 1999; Urdan, 1997). Yet by themselves, performance-approach goals may be less beneficial than mastery goals: To achieve them, students may use relatively superficial learning strategies (e.g., rote memorization), exert only the minimal effort necessary to achieve desired outcomes, engage in self-handicapping, and perhaps cheat (E. A. Anderman et al., 1998; Brophy, 1987; Midgley, Kaplan, & Middleton, 2001). Performance-approach goals appear to be most detrimental when students are younger (e.g., in the elementary grades) and have low self-efficacy for classroom tasks (Hidi & Harackiewicz, 2000; Kaplan, 1998; Kaplan & Midgley, 1997; Midgley et al., 2001).

In the "Portfolio" clip on Video CD 1, 8-year-old Keenan says several things that reflect mastery goals related to writing. She acknowledges her errors and doesn't seem embarrassed by them. And when she doesn't know how to spell a word, she is quite willing to ask a friend or teacher for help. Mastery goals are also evident in the "Author's Chair" clip, in which students willingly accept constructive suggestions from their classmates.

Developmental Trends in Achievement Goals   Before children reach school age, they seem to focus primarily on mastery goals. For instance, infants and toddlers seek out experiences that will increase their competence and mastery of the environment, and they derive genuine pleasure from new accomplishments (Dweck & Elliott, 1983). But performance goals become increasingly prevalent as children progress through the elementary and secondary school grades (Blumenfeld, 1992; W. Doyle, 1986b; Elliot & McGregor, 2000; Harter, 1992). Most high school students, if they are motivated to succeed in their schoolwork, are primarily concerned about getting good grades, and they prefer short, easy tasks to lengthier, more challenging ones. Performance goals are also common in team sports, where the focus is often more on winning and gaining public recognition than on developing new skills and seeing improvement over time (G. C. Roberts, Treasure, & Kavussanu, 1997).

When children begin school at age 5 or 6, several things happen that orient them more toward performance goals (Dweck & Elliott, 1983). First, they suddenly have many peers with whom they can compare their own behavior; as a result, they may begin to define success more in terms of doing better than classmates than in terms of task mastery. Second, whereas they have previously dealt primarily with physical tasks (e.g., learning to fasten buttons and ride a tricycle), they are now being asked to master tasks of a more cognitive, abstract, and multifaceted nature (e.g., learning to read, write, and perform mathematical computations). The inherent value of such activities is not always obvious to them (especially as they move beyond basic skills), and they must often rely on others (e.g., teachers) to make judgments about their competence and progress. As children approach adolescence, yet another factor kicks in: They are far more likely to worry about what others think of them than they were in their early years (Juvonen, 2000; Midgley, 1993). (Recall our discussion of the *imaginary audience* in Chapter 3.)

In many instances students adopt performance goals that can help them maintain their sense of self-worth and—especially if their need for relatedness is high—enhance status and popularity with peers (L. H. Anderman & Anderman, 1999; Covington, 1992). Furthermore, they may realize that performing at high levels—in particular, getting good grades—is critical for their future educational and professional opportunities (Covington & Müeller, 2001).

Many common teaching and coaching practices also contribute to the development of performance goals (Midgley, 2002). Although undoubtedly well-intentioned, such strategies as reinforcing students only for correct answers, posting only "best" work on a bulletin board, scoring tests on a curve, displaying grades for everyone to see, reminding students that they need good grades to get into college, and striving to surpass other schools and athletic teams all encourage

■ In what areas do you have mastery goals? In what areas are you interested only in how you appear to others? How is your learning affected by the particular goals you have?

■ Observe mastery goals in the "Portfolio" and "Author's Chair" clips on Video CD 1.

students to focus their attention more on "looking good" than on learning. Some of these practices promote competition among students, and competitive situations typically promote performance goals—and in some cases promote self-handicapping as a way to maintain a sense of competence and self-worth—rather than mastery goals (C. Ames, 1984; A. J. Martin et al., 2003; Stipek, 1996).

Fostering Productive Achievement Goals   To some degree, performance goals are inevitable in today's schools and in society at large (R. Butler, 1989; Elliot & McGregor, 2000). Children and adolescents will often look to their peers' performance as a means of evaluating their own performance, universities and colleges will continue to use high grades and test scores when screening applicants, and many aspects of the adult world (seeking employment, working in private industry, playing professional sports, etc.) are inherently competitive in nature. Ultimately, however, mastery goals are the ones most likely to lead to effective learning and performance over the long run.

Sometimes mastery goals come from within, especially when students have high interest in, and high self-efficacy for, learning something (Bandura, 1997; P. K. Murphy & Alexander, 2000; Schiefele, 1992). Yet our classroom practices can also encourage mastery goals (Church, Elliot, & Gable, 2001; Newman, 1998; Wentzel, 1999). For instance, we can

Students with mastery goals recognize that competence comes only from effort and practice.

- Present subject matter that students find valuable in and of itself
- Show how topics and skills are relevant to students' future personal and professional goals
- Insist that students *understand*, rather than simply memorize, classroom material
- Show students that they are making significant progress
- Communicate the belief that effective learning requires exerting effort and making mistakes
- Give specific feedback about how students can improve
- Encourage students to use their peers *not* as a reference point for their own progress, but rather as a source of ideas and help
(C. Ames, 1992; E. M. Anderman & Maehr, 1994; Bong, 2001; Brophy, 2004; Graham & Weiner, 1996; Meece, 1994; Middleton & Midgley, 2002; J. C. Turner, Meyer, et al., 1998; Urdan et al., 2002)

Focusing attention on mastery goals, especially when these goals relate to students' own lives, may especially benefit students from diverse ethnic backgrounds and students at risk for academic failure (Alderman, 1990; García, 1992; Wlodkowski & Ginsberg, 1995).

Students typically work harder toward *self-chosen* goals than toward those others have chosen for them (Wentzel, 1999), possibly because self-chosen goals help them maintain a sense of self-determination. Although we should certainly encourage students to develop long-term goals (e.g., going to college, becoming an environmental scientist), such goals are sometimes too general and abstract to guide immediate behavior (Bandura, 1997; Husman & Freeman, 1999). (For examples, look once again at the dialogue in the section "Promoting Self-Regulation in Students at Risk" in Chapter 10.) Self-chosen goals are especially motivating when they are specific ("I want to learn how to do a cartwheel"), challenging ("Writing a limerick looks difficult, but I'm sure I can do it"), and short-term ("I'm going to learn to count to 100 in French by the end of the month") (Alderman, 1990; Brophy, 2004). By setting and working for a series of short-term, concrete goals—sometimes called **proximal goals**—students get regular feedback about the progress they are making, develop a greater sense of self-efficacy that they can master school subject matter, and achieve at higher levels (Bandura, 1997; Locke & Latham, 2002; Page-Voth & Graham, 1999; Schunk, 1996).

Different kinds of mastery goals may be more useful at different points in learning, especially when students are trying to learn a skill of some sort (Schunk & Swartz, 1993; Schunk & Zimmerman, 1997; Zimmerman & Kitsantas, 1997). Initially, students may want to focus on a **process goal**, perfecting the form or procedure that a skill involves without regard for the final outcome. As the desired form or procedure becomes more automatic, they may then want to shift their attention to a **product goal**, striving for a certain standard of performance—for instance, solving a certain number of math problems correctly or getting a certain percentage of balls through a basketball hoop. On the surface, a product goal may look like a performance goal rather than a mastery goal. However, even when focusing on a final product, the student continues to be concerned primarily about *mastering* the skill rather than about making a good impression on others.

■ For such reasons, goal setting is an important part of self-regulated learning (see Chapter 10).

■ **proximal goal** Concrete goal that one can accomplish within a short time period; may be a stepping stone toward a longer-range goal.

■ **process goal** Desire to perfect the form or procedure that a skill involves.

■ **product goal** Desire to attain a certain, concrete standard of excellence.

Work-Avoidance Goals

As we have just seen, students sometimes want to avoid looking bad as they perform classroom tasks. On other occasions they may want to avoid having to do classroom tasks *at all*, or at least they will try to put as little effort as possible into those tasks. In other words, they may have a **work-avoidance goal** (Dowson & McInerney, 2001; Gallini, 2000; Nicholls, Cobb, Yackel, Wood, & Wheatley, 1990).

To date, research on work-avoidance goals has focused on the middle school grades, where such goals seem to be fairly common (Dowson & McInerney, 2001; Gallini, 2000; J. E. Turner et al., 2002). Students with work-avoidance goals use a variety of strategies to minimize their workload; for instance, they may engage in off-task behavior, ask for help on easy tasks and problems, pretend they don't understand something even when they do, complain loudly about challenging assignments, and select the least taxing alternatives whenever choices are given (Dowson & McInerney, 2001). They rarely use effective learning strategies or pull their weight in small-group activities (Dowson & McInerney, 2001; Gallini, 2000).

A couple of conditions seem to foster work-avoidance goals. First, students are apt to have low self-efficacy for success; by avoiding assigned tasks, they can hide their low ability (Urdan et al., 2002). Second, they may see no payoffs for mastering the subject matter (Garner, 1998). In other words, students are most likely to have work-avoidance goals when they have neither intrinsic nor extrinsic motivation to achieve instructional goals. Students with work-avoidance goals may thus be our biggest challenges, and we will have to use a variety of motivational strategies—probably including extrinsic reinforcement—to get them truly engaged in, and eventually committed to mastering, academic subject matter.

Social Goals

■ To refresh your memory about the benefits of interacting with peers, you may want to reread the section "Peer Relationships" in Chapter 3.

In Chapter 11 we noted that most students make social relationships a high priority, and in fact all students probably have some need for relatedness. Peer relationships can be a source of considerable emotional support and thereby enhance students' psychological well-being (see Chapter 3). Many students seek good relationships with teachers as well, not only for the academic assistance that teachers can give but also for the emotional support and positive feedback that can enhance their sense of self-worth.

Students may hope to accomplish a variety of goals in their interactions with others, typically including some or all of the following:

- Forming and maintaining friendly or intimate social relationships
- Becoming part of a cohesive, mutually supportive group; gaining a sense of "belonging" in the classroom
- Gaining other people's approval
- Adhering to the rules and conventions of the group (e.g., being a "good citizen")
- Achieving status, popularity, and prestige among peers
- Meeting social obligations and keeping interpersonal commitments
- Assisting and supporting others, and ensuring their welfare
(H. A. Davis, 2003; Dowson & McInerney, 2001; M. E. Ford, 1996; Hicks, 1997; Hinkley, McInerney, & Marsh, 2001; Patrick et al., 2002; Schutz, 1994)

Interacting with peers is a high priority for many young adolescents.

■ **work-avoidance goal** Desire either to avoid classroom tasks or to complete them with only minimal effort.

The specific nature of students' social goals affects their classroom behavior and academic performance. If students want to gain their teacher's attention and approval, they are apt to strive for good grades and in other ways shoot for performance goals (Hinkley et al., 2001). If they are seeking friendly relationships with classmates or are concerned about others' welfare, they may eagerly engage in such activities as cooperative learning and peer tutoring; concern for others' welfare also fosters mastery goals (L. H. Anderman & Anderman, 1999; Dowson & McInerney, 2001). If students want to develop or maintain close relationships with peers, they may ask their peers for help, but if they are more interested in impressing peers with their high ability, they probably will *not* ask for help (A. M. Ryan, Hicks, & Midgley, 1997). If they want to gain the approval of *low-achieving* peers, they may exert little effort in their studies (see Chapter 3) and possibly even adopt work-avoidance goals (B. Brown, 1990; M. E. Ford & Nichols, 1991).

As teachers, we must continually consider how we can help students achieve their social goals at the same time that they work toward more academically oriented ones. For example, we can make ample use of small-group activities, enlist students' assistance in schoolwide and community service projects, and provide opportunities for all students to "shine" in some way and thereby gain the admiration of their peers. We should also attend to the quality of our own relationships with students; we'll identify strategies for doing so in Chapter 14.

Career Goals

Many students include career goals among their long-term goals. Young children set such goals with little thought and change them frequently; for instance, a 6-year-old may want to be a firefighter one week and a professional baseball player the next. By late adolescence, some (though by no means all) have reached some tentative and relatively stable decisions about the career paths they want to pursue (e.g., Marcia, 1980).

In earlier decades boys set higher aspirations for themselves than girls did, especially in domains that were stereotypically masculine (Deaux, 1984; Durkin, 1995; Lueptow. 1984). Perhaps things are changing, however: One recent study found *girls* to have higher career aspirations (Lapan, Tucker, Kim, & Kosciulek, 2003). Even in poor, inner-city neighborhoods, many students aspire to professional careers, perhaps in medicine, law, teaching, or computer science (B. L. Wilson & Corbett, 2001). (How equipped they are to *achieve* their aspirations is another matter; see the section "Promoting Self-Regulation in Students at Risk" in Chapter 10.)

Despite high aspirations, many students, especially those raised in fairly traditional cultures, tend to limit themselves to gender-stereotypical careers (Lippa, 2002; Olneck, 1995; S. M. Taylor, 1994). Even as traditional boundaries between what professions are "appropriate" for men and women are slowly melting away, the majority of college students enrolled in engineering programs continue to be males, and the majority of education majors continue to be females. Certainly gender stereotypes are not the only things affecting students' career goals; students' self-efficacy, expectations for success, and values are also involved. As teachers, we best serve our students when we open their eyes to the many rewarding careers they might consider, expose them to adults of both genders and numerous ethnic groups successfully pursuing those careers, and help them achieve the successes they need to convince them that they, too, have what it takes to do well in a variety of professions.

needels

Surgeon
I want to be a surgeon
because I can help people
if the get sick and can
treat the so they will feel better.
And can save ther lives. I will
study hard for lots of years.

Many children begin thinking about careers in the preschool and early elementary years. Here 7-year-old Ashton explains why he wants to be a surgeon.

Coordinating Multiple Goals

Most students have numerous goals at any one time and use a variety of strategies to juggle them (Covington, 2000; Dodge, Asher, & Parkhurst, 1989; Urdan & Maehr, 1995). Sometimes they find activities that allow them to address two or more goals simultaneously; for instance, they can address both achievement goals and social goals by forming a study group to prepare for a test. Sometimes they pursue one goal while temporarily putting others on the "back burner"; for instance, they might complete a required reading assignment while bypassing more interesting but unassigned material. Occasionally they may modify their idea of what it means to achieve a particular goal; for instance, an ambitious high school student who initially hopes to earn all As in three advanced classes may eventually realize that earning Bs in two of them may be more realistic.

In other situations students may believe they must abandon one goal to satisfy another (McCaslin & Good, 1996; Phelan et al., 1994). For example, as we have seen, students who want to do well in school may choose *not* to perform at their best in order to maintain relationships with peers who don't value academic achievement. And students with mastery goals in particular subject areas may find that the multiple demands of school coerce them into focusing on performance goals (e.g., getting good grades) rather than studying the subject matter as thoroughly as they'd like. Brian, a junior high school student, expresses his concern about leaving his mastery goals in the dust as he strives for performance goals:

> I sit here and I say, "Hey, I did this assignment in five minutes and I still got an A+ on it." I still have a feeling that I could do better, and it was kind of cheap that I didn't do my best and I still got this A. . . . I think probably it might lower my standards eventually, which I'm not looking forward to at all. . . . I'll always know, though, that I have it in me. It's just that I won't express it that much. (S. Thomas & Oldfather, 1997, p. 119)

Our students will, of course, be most successful when their multiple goals all lead them in the same direction (M. E. Ford, 1992; Wentzel, 1999). For example, students might work toward mastery goals by learning and practicing new skills within the context of group projects (thus meeting their social goals) and with evaluation criteria that allow for risk taking and mistakes (thus also meeting their performance goals). Students are *unlikely* to strive for mastery goals when assignments ask little of them (consider Brian's concern about low standards), when we insist that they compete with one another for resources or high test scores (thereby interfering with their social goals), and when any single failure has a significant impact on their final grades (thereby thwarting their progress toward performance goals).

Now that we've looked at the variety of goals that students might have, let's consider one student's goals and their potential impact on his classroom achievement.

Interpreting Student Artifacts and Behaviors

Goals for the Quarter

At his teacher's request, 12-year-old Kelvin reflected on goals he had previously set for himself and identified a new set of goals. As you read Kelvin's self-evaluation, presented to the left, think about

goals and self evaluation on this quarter

I hope to improve more on reading and become a more advanced speller. I have improved on writing, but I think I could be a lot better at writing. I should put more on my portfolio and come up with better ideas to write about. Over all I think I've done pretty well, but I hope to appriciate writing and reading more.

■ What kinds of goals Kelvin is describing

■ How useful his goals are likely to be in helping him evaluate his academic progress and focus his future efforts

Kelvin's goals are mastery goals: improving his skills in reading, spelling, and writing. Unfortunately, his goals are so vague and general that they will be essentially useless in helping him direct his efforts and monitor his progress. For instance, how will he know when he is a "more advanced speller" or "a lot better at writing"? We cannot necessarily blame Kelvin for his imprecision; as a 12-year-old, he probably hasn't had much practice with either goal setting or self-monitoring. When we ask students to set goals for their learning, we should give them examples of concrete criteria toward which they might strive. For instance, rather than become "better at writing," Kelvin might work toward "greater variety in sentence structure." And rather than "more advanced speller," he might shoot for "a maximum of two misspellings per page." We can often incorporate such suggestions into the feedback we give students about their work.

The topics we've explored so far have given us numerous ideas about how we can enhance students' intrinsic motivation to learn academic subject matter. The Creating a Productive Classroom Environment feature "Promoting Intrinsic Motivation" lists and illustrates several key strategies. We turn now to individual differences in motivation—dispositions—that reflect students' general approaches to thinking about and learning classroom material.

DISPOSITIONS

By **disposition**, I mean a general inclination to approach learning and problem-solving situations in a particular way—perhaps in a thoughtful, analytical, evaluative manner, on the one hand, or in a thought*less*, unquestioning manner, on the other. For example, while I was observing one of my teacher interns present a unit on Canada, a boy in his class asked whether the province of Quebec was bigger than Texas. The map of Canada at the front of the room did not show Texas, but it did show Alaska, which was clearly smaller than Quebec. Another boy answered his classmate's question by reasoning: "If Alaska's the largest state, then Quebec *must* be bigger than Texas." His response showed a disposition to reason logically from the information he had, rather than always to seek answers from an authority figure.

We encountered an example of a disposition in Chapter 6: We learned that students are more apt to engage in meaningful learning—to try to make sense of what they are studying—when they have a *meaningful learning set*. Researchers have identified several other dispositions that predispose students to think about and learn classroom topics in effective ways:

■ **disposition** General inclination to approach and think about a task in a particular way.

- *Stimulation seeking.* Eagerly interacting with one's physical and social environment
- *Need for cognition.* Regularly seeking and engaging in challenging cognitive tasks

CREATING A PRODUCTIVE CLASSROOM ENVIRONMENT

Promoting Intrinsic Motivation

 Define success as eventual, rather than immediate, mastery of class material, and acknowledge that occasional mistakes are to be expected.

When a middle school student is disappointed in her mediocre performance on a difficult assignment, her teacher consoles her by saying, "You're a very talented student, and you're probably used to having your schoolwork come easily. But remember, as you move into the upper grades, your assignments will become more challenging. They *have* to challenge you, or else you wouldn't grow. With a little more study and practice, I know you'll improve quite a bit."

Encourage self-comparison, rather than comparison with other students.

In January an elementary school teacher asks his students to write a short story. After reading students' stories and writing feedback in the margins, he returns the stories to the authors; he also returns stories that the students wrote in early September. "Do you see how much your writing has improved over the past four months?" he asks. "The stories you wrote this week are longer and better developed, and you made fewer spelling and grammatical errors."

Enhance students' sense of self-determination regarding classroom assignments and activities.

A high school science teacher tells her students, "I know you can't always complete your lab reports the same day that you did a lab in class. Let's see whether we can set some reasonable due dates for your reports so that *you* have time to write them and *I* have sufficient time to read them and give you feedback before the next lab activity."

Model your own interest in, and enthusiasm for, the subject matter.

A junior high school history teacher introduces a reading assignment this way: "The chapter I've assigned for tonight is an exciting one. As the chapter unfolds, you'll see how the American colonists became increasingly discontented with British rule. You'll also learn how the colonists eventually managed to break free and form the United States of America. It's a story I never get tired of reading!"

Communicate the belief that students *want* to learn.

Early in the school year, a social studies teacher explains that her class will help students become "social scientists." She frequently refers back to this idea—for example, by saying, "Since you are social scientists, you will recognize that the description of this area as a tropical rain forest has implications about what kinds of crops will grow there," or "Thinking as social scientists, what conclusions might we draw from this information?" (Brophy, 2004, p. 272)

Relate classroom material to students' personal lives and interests.

An elementary school teacher asks students to bring in objects they use to celebrate holidays at home. He incorporates these objects into a lesson on how holiday traditions differ not only from religion to religion but also from family to family.

Grab students' attention and pique their interest by occasionally introducing variety and novelty into classroom activities.

After clearing her strategy with the school principal, a high school psychology teacher brings Taffy, her mild-mannered cocker spaniel, to class for the day. She uses Taffy to demonstrate the various ways in which reinforcement (in this case, dog biscuits) can influence behavior.

Encourage students to set mastery goals.

A high school Spanish teacher often reminds his students, "The important thing in this class is to learn how to speak Spanish comfortably and with correct pronunciation. We'll all work together until we can communicate easily with one another in Spanish."

- *Critical thinking.* Consistently evaluating information or arguments in terms of their accuracy, logic, and credibility, rather than accepting them at face value
- *Open-mindedness.* Being willing to consider alternative perspectives and multiple sources of evidence and to suspend judgment rather than leap to an immediate conclusion
- *Future time perspective.* Predicting and considering the long-term consequences of various courses of action
  (Cacioppo, Petty, Feinstein, & Jarvis, 1996; Halpern, 1997a; Husman & Freeman, 1999; Kardash & Scholes, 1996; P. M. King & Kitchener, 2002; Raine, Reynolds, & Venables, 2002; Southerland & Sinatra, 2003; Stanovich, 1999)

Dispositions often have a significant effect on students' motivation, learning, and achievement. For instance, children who, as preschoolers, eagerly seek out physical and social stimulation are, at age 11, better readers and earn higher grades at school (Raine et al., 2002). Students with a high need for cognition learn more from what they read and are more likely to base conclusions on sound evidence and logical reasoning (Cacioppo et al., 1996). Students who critically evaluate new evidence and are receptive to and open-minded about diverse perspectives show more advanced reasoning capabilities; they are also more likely to undergo conceptual change when it's warranted (Southerland & Sinatra, 2003; Stanovich, 1999). Students who have a strong future time perspective are more motivated to engage in activities that will help them achieve their future goals (Husman & Freeman, 1999; Raynor, 1931).

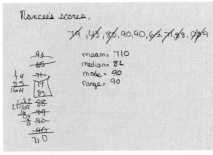

FIGURE 12.6 Computing a mean (average) of 710 for a group of scores that range from 0 to 90, this sixth grader shows little disposition to check her work to make sure it makes sense. Can you identify the two errors in the student's calculations?

Courtesy of Dinah Jackson.

Unfortunately, many students *don't* have the dispositions to approach classroom subject matter in a thoughtful, analytical manner. As an example, a sixth-grader learning how to compute the mean, median, mode, and range of a data set was practicing with a hypothetical set of test scores (79, 43, 85, 90, 90, 65, 71, 88, 0, 89). As you can see in Figure 12.6, the student calculated a mean (average) of 710, a number that cannot possibly be correct, yet she failed to notice her error or take steps to correct it.

Researchers do not yet have a good understanding of where various dispositions come from. Perhaps inherited temperamental differences (e.g., in stimulation seeking) and parental encouragement of critical thinking are involved (Kuhn, Daniels, & Krishnan, 2003; Raine et al., 2002). Epistemological beliefs—for instance, the belief that knowledge is fixed and unchanging, on the one hand, or dynamic and continually evolving, on the other—may also play a role (P. M. King & Kitchener, 2002; Mason, 2003; also see Chapter 8). And quite possibly, teachers' instructional strategies make a difference. In the following classroom interaction, a teacher actually seems to *discourage* any disposition to think analytically and critically about classroom material:

Teacher: Write this on your paper . . . it's simply memorizing this pattern. We have meters, centimeters, and millimeters. Let's say . . . write millimeters, centimeters, and meters. We want to make sure that our metric measurement is the same. If I gave you this decimal, let's say .234 m (yes, write that). In order to come up with .234 m in centimeters, the only thing that is necessary is that you move the decimal. How do we move the decimal? You move it to the right two places. (Jason, sit up please.) If I move it to the right two places, what should .234 m look like, Daniel, in centimeters? What does it look like, Ashley?

Ashley: 23.4 cm.

Teacher: Twenty-three point four. Simple stuff. In order to find meters, we're still moving that decimal to the right, but this time, boys and girls, we're only going to move it one place. So, if I move this decimal one place, what is my answer for millimeters? (dialogue from J. C. Turner, Meyer, et al., 1998, p. 741)

Undoubtedly, this teacher means well: She wants her students to understand how to convert from one unit of measurement to another. But notice the attitude she engenders: "Write this . . . it's simply memorizing this pattern."

To date, researchers have focused more on how students differ in their dispositions than on how to *promote* certain dispositions. But we can reasonably assume that encouraging and modeling productive dispositions—for example, by asking students to evaluate the quality of scientific evidence, insisting that students defend opinions about social issues with sound rationales, teaching strategies for constructing persuasive arguments, and consistently exhibiting our own open-mindedness about diverse perspectives—we will get students off to a good start (e.g., Baron, 1987; Derry et al., 1998; Halpern, 1998; Kuhn, 2001b).

Although we have identified numerous cognitive factors in motivation, we have largely ignored a very important one: the extent to which students make a mental connection between what they do and what happens to them. Certainly students are more eager to pursue an activity when they think their behaviors will lead to desired outcomes. But some students fail to recognize existing contingencies between the behaviors they exhibit and the consequences that result. We'll look at these ideas more closely as we explore attributions in the next section.

ATTRIBUTIONS: PERCEIVED CAUSES OF SUCCESS AND FAILURE

Experiencing FIRSTHAND · Carberry and Seville #1

1. Professor Josiah S. Carberry has just returned the first set of exams, scored and graded, in your advanced psychoceramics class. You discover that you've gotten one of the few high test scores in the class: an A−. Why did you do so well when most of your classmates did poorly? On a sheet of paper, jot down several possible explanations as to why you might have received a high grade in Carberry's class.

2. An hour later, you get the results of the first test in Professor Barbara F. Seville's sociocosmetology class, and you learn that you *failed* it! Why did you do so poorly? Jot down several possible reasons for your F on Seville's test.

3. You will be taking second exams in both psychoceramics and sociocosmetology in about three weeks' time. How much will you study for each exam?

. . . .

Here are some possible explanations for your A— in Carberry's class:

- You studied hard.
- You're smart.
- Psychoceramics just comes naturally to you.
- You were lucky. Carberry asked the right questions; if he'd asked different questions, you might not have done so well.
- Carberry likes you, so he gave you a good grade even though you didn't know what you were talking about.
- All those hours you spent in Carberry's office, asking questions about psychoceramics and requesting copies of the articles he's written (which you never actually read), really paid off.

In contrast, here are some possible reasons you failed the exam in Seville's class:

- You didn't study enough.
- You didn't study the right things.
- You didn't feel well when you took the test.
- The student next to you was sick, and the constant wheezing and coughing distracted you.
- You were unlucky. Seville asked the wrong questions; if she'd asked different questions, you would have done better.
- You're stupid.
- You've never been very good at sociocosmetology.
- It was a bad test: The questions were ambiguous and tested knowledge of trivial facts.
- Seville hates you and gave you a poor grade out of spite.

The amount of time you spend studying for your upcoming exams will, to some extent, depend on how you've interpreted your earlier performances (i.e., your success on Carberry's exam and your failure on Seville's exam). Let's first consider your A— on Professor Carberry's exam. If you think you did well because you studied hard, you will probably spend a lot of time studying for the second test as well. If you think you did well because you're smart or because you're a whiz at psychoceramics, you may not study quite as much. If you believe that your success was a matter of luck, you may not study much at all, but you might wear your lucky sweater when you take the next exam. And if you think the A— reflects how much Carberry likes you, you may decide that time spent flattering him is more important than time spent studying.

Now let's consider your failing grade on Professor Seville's exam. Once again, the reasons you identify for your failure will influence the ways in which you prepare for her second exam—if, in fact, you prepare at all. If you believe that you didn't study enough or didn't study the right things, you may spend more time studying the next time. If you think your poor grade was due to a temporary situation—you were ill, the student sitting next to you distracted you, or Seville asked the wrong questions—then you may study in much the same way as you did before, hoping and praying you'll do better on the second try. And if you believe that your failure was due to your stupidity, your ineptitude in sociocosmetology, Seville's dislike of you, or the fact that she writes lousy tests, then you may study even less than you did the first time. After all, what good will it do to study when your poor test performance is beyond your control?

Students' beliefs about what behaviors lead to what outcomes are **attributions** (e.g., Dweck, 1986; Weiner, 1984, 1986, 1994, 2000). Attributions are an excellent example of knowledge construction in action: Students interpret new events in light of existing knowledge and beliefs about themselves and the world and then develop what is, for them at least, a reasonable explanation of what has happened. Because attributions are self-constructed, they may or may not reflect the true state of affairs. For instance, a student may blame a low test grade on a "tricky" test or an "unfair" teacher when the cause is really the student's own lack of effort or poor study skills.

Students form a variety of attributions about the causes of classroom events; they have beliefs about why they do well or poorly on tests and assignments, why they are popular with their classmates or have trouble making friends, why they are skilled athletes or total klutzes, and so on. They may attribute their school successes and failures to such factors as aptitude or

■ **attribution** Personally constructed causal explanation for success or failure.

ability (how smart or proficient they are), effort (how hard they tried), other people (how well the teacher taught or how much their classmates like them), task difficulty (how easy or hard something is), luck, mood, illness, fatigue, or physical appearance. These various attributions differ from one another in three primary ways: locus, stability, and controllability (Weiner, 1986, 2000).

Locus ("place"): Internal versus external.[1] Students sometimes attribute the causes of events to *internal* things—to factors within themselves. Thinking that a good grade is due to your own hard work and believing that a poor grade is due to your lack of ability are examples of internal attributions. At other times students attribute events to *external* things—to factors outside themselves. Concluding that you received a scholarship because you "lucked out" and interpreting a classmate's scowl as a sign of her bad mood (rather than to anything you might have done to deserve it) are examples of external attributions. In general, students tend to attribute their successes to internal causes (e.g., high ability, hard work) and their failures to external causes (e.g., luck, behaviors of others) (Marsh, 1990a; Whitley & Frieze, 1985). By patting themselves on the back for the things they do well and putting the blame elsewhere for poor performance, they are able to maintain their sense of self-worth (Clifford, 1990; Paris & Byrnes, 1989).

IN THE BLEACHERS
by Steve Moore

"And remember, kids: If you play to the best of your ability and still lose the game, just blame it all on the umpire."

By blaming the umpire for a loss, children can more easily maintain a sense of self-worth. However, such external attributions are counterproductive when the true causes for success and failure are actually internal and within children's control.

Stability: Stable versus unstable. Sometimes students believe that events are due to *stable* factors—to things that probably won't change much in the near future. For example, if you believe that you do well in science because of your innate intelligence or that you have trouble making friends because you're overweight, then you are attributing events to stable, relatively long-term causes. But sometimes students instead believe that events result from *unstable* factors—things that can change from one time to the next. Thinking that winning a tennis game was just a matter of luck and believing that you got a bad test grade because you were tired when you took the test are examples of attributions involving unstable factors.[2]

Controllability: Controllable versus uncontrollable. On some occasions students attribute events to *controllable* factors—to things they can influence and change. For example, if you think a classmate invited you to his birthday party because you always smile and say nice things to him, and if you think that you probably failed a test simply because you didn't study the right things, then you are attributing these events to controllable factors. On other occasions students attribute events to *uncontrollable* factors—to things over which they themselves have no influence. For example, if you think that you were chosen for the lead in the school play only because the drama teacher thinks you look "right" for the part or that you played a lousy game of basketball because you were sick, then you are attributing these events to uncontrollable factors.

With these three factors in mind, let's return to Michael in the opening case study. Notice how Michael initially attributes his failure in algebra to two stable and uncontrollable factors: low aptitude (an internal attribution) and poor instruction (an external attribution). As his tutor helps him understand algebraic principles and procedures, however, Michael begins to attribute his performance to two factors that are internal, unstable, and controllable: effort and better strategies.

How Attributions Influence Affect, Cognition, and Behavior

As Michael's attributions change, his expectations for success change as well. Students' attributions for their successes and failures have numerous effects, including the following:

Emotional reactions to success and failure. Naturally, students will be happy when they succeed. But they will also have feelings of pride and satisfaction when they attribute their successes to internal causes—that is, to something they themselves have done. When they instead credit their successes to the actions of another person or to some other external force, they are apt to

---

[1] This dimension is sometimes referred to as *locus of control*; however, Weiner (1986, 2000) has pointed out that *locus* and *control* are probably two somewhat different dimensions.

[2] People occasionally think of *effort* and *luck* as being relatively stable, long-term characteristics (Weiner, 1986). To be consistent with much of the literature in attribution theory, however, we will use both terms to refer to a temporary state of affairs.

feel grateful rather than proud. Along a similar vein, students will usually feel a certain amount of sadness after a failure. They will also feel guilty or ashamed when they blame their failures on internal causes, such as their own lack of ability or effort. But when they blame their failures on external causes—on events and people outside of themselves—they are apt to be angry (Hareli & Weiner, 2002; Weiner, Russell, & Lerman, 1978).

Expectations for future success or failure. When students attribute their successes and failures to stable factors, they expect their future performance to be similar to their current performance. In other words, successful students anticipate that they will continue to succeed, and failing students believe that they will always be failures. In contrast, when students attribute their successes and failures to *unstable* factors such as effort or luck, then their current success rate will have less influence on their expectation for future success, and a few failures won't put much of a dent in their self-efficacy (Dweck, 2000; Schunk, 1990; Weiner, 1986). The most optimistic students— those with the highest expectations for future success—are the ones who attribute their successes to stable, dependable (and usually internal) factors such as innate ability and their failures to unstable factors such as lack of effort or inappropriate strategies (Fennema, 1987; Pomerantz & Saxon, 2001; Weiner, 1984).

Effort and persistence. When students believe that their failures result from their own lack of effort, they are apt to try harder and persist in the face of difficulty (Dweck, 2000; Feather, 1982; Weiner, 1984). But when they instead attribute failure to a lack of innate ability (they couldn't do it even if they tried), they give up easily and sometimes can't even perform tasks they have previously accomplished successfully (Dweck, 1978, 2000; Eccles [Parsons], 1983).

Learning strategies and classroom performance. Students who expect to succeed in the classroom and believe that academic success is a result of their own doing are more likely to apply effective study strategies (especially when they are *taught* these strategies) and more apt to approach problem-solving tasks in a logical, systematic, and meaningful way (Palmer & Goetz, 1988; Pressley, Borkowski, & Schneider, 1987; Tyler, 1958). These students are also more likely to be self-regulating learners and to seek help when they need it (R. Ames, 1983; Zimmerman, 1998). In contrast, students who expect failure and believe that their academic performance is largely out of their hands often reject effective learning and problem-solving strategies in favor of rote-learning approaches. It should not surprise you to learn, then, that students with internal, controllable attributions for classroom success (rather than external, uncontrollable ones) are more likely to achieve at high levels and graduate from high school (L. E. Davis, Ajzen, Saunders, & Williams, 2002; Pintrich, 2003).

Future choices. As you might expect, students whose attributions lead them to expect success in a particular subject area are more likely to pursue that area— for example, by enrolling in more courses in the same discipline (Eccles [Parsons], 1984; Stipek & Gralinski, 1990; Weiner, 1986). Students who believe that their chances for future success in an activity are slim will avoid the activity whenever they can. Naturally, when students don't continue to pursue an activity, they can't possibly get better at it.

Developmental Trends in Attributions

Students become increasingly able to distinguish among various attributions as they get older. In the preschool years children don't have a clear understanding of the differences among the possible causes—effort, ability, luck, task difficulty, and so on—of their successes and failures (Eccles et al., 1998; Nicholls, 1990). Especially troublesome is the distinction between effort and ability, which they gradually get a better handle on over time (Nicholls, 1990). At about age 6, they begin to recognize that effort and ability are separate qualities but see them as positively correlated: People who try hardest have the greatest ability, and effort is the primary determiner of success. Sometime around age 9, they begin to understand that effort and ability often compensate for one another and that people with less ability may need to exert greater effort to achieve the same outcome as their more able peers. By age 13 or so, they make a clear distinction between effort and ability: They realize that people differ both in inherent ability to perform a task and in the amount of effort exerted on a task. They also know that ability and effort can compensate for each other but that a lack of ability sometimes precludes success no matter *how* much effort a person puts forth.

Students are usually happy when they succeed at classroom tasks. But whether they also feel proud and satisfied, or instead feel relieved and grateful, depends on whether they attribute their success to internal or external causes. (self-portrait by Corey, age 9)

Asking For Extra Help
① Clear Time
② State ambition, not ignorance
③ have specific questions
④ ask for help
⑤ go to extra help w/ the right tools

Despite his teacher's suggestions about how to ask for extra help, 14-year-old Geoff will actually *seek* help only if he thinks his efforts will pay off—that is, only if he has internal attributions about his academic performance.

A related trend is an increasing tendency to attribute success and failure to ability rather than to effort (Covington, 1992; Dweck & Elliott, 1983; Nicholls, 1990). In the early elementary grades, students tend to attribute their successes to hard work and practice; therefore, they are usually fairly optimistic about their chances for success and so may try harder when they fail. As students get older, many begin to attribute successes and failures to an inherited ability (e.g., to "intelligence") that they perceive to be fairly stable and beyond their control. If these students are usually successful at school tasks, then they will have high self-efficacy about such tasks; if failures are frequent, their self-efficacy may plummet (Dweck, 1986; Eccles [Parsons], 1983; Schunk, 1990). Table 12.2 summarizes developmental trends in attributions and other aspects of students' motivation.

TABLE 12.2   DEVELOPMENTAL TRENDS

Motivation at Different Grade Levels

GRADE LEVEL	AGE-TYPICAL CHARACTERISTICS	SUGGESTED STRATEGIES
K–2	• Tendency to define teacher-chosen activities as "work" and self-chosen activities as "play" • Rapidly changing interests • Pursuit of interesting and enjoyable activities regardless of expectancy for success • Emerging tendency to distinguish between effort and ability as causes for success and failure; belief that high effort is a sign of high ability • Tendency to attribute success to hard work and practice, yielding optimism about what can be accomplished	• Engage students' interest in important topics through hands-on, playlike activities. • Entice students into reading, writing, and other basic skills through high-interest books and subject matter (e.g., animals, superheroes, princes and princesses). • Show students how they've improved over time; point out how their effort and practice have contributed to their improvement.
3–5	• Emergence of fairly stable interests • Increasing tendency to observe peers' performance as a criterion for judging one's own performance • Increasing focus on performance goals • Recognition that effort and ability compensate for each other, that people with lower ability must work harder to succeed • Increasing belief in innate ability as a significant and uncontrollable factor affecting learning and achievement • Increasing awareness of the kinds of attributions that will elicit positive reactions from others (e.g., "I didn't feel well during the test")	• Allow students to pursue personal interests in independent reading and writing tasks. • Teach students strategies for tracking their own progress over time. • Demonstrate your own fascination and enthusiasm about classroom topics; communicate that many topics are worth learning about for their own sake. • Identify strengths in every student; provide sufficient support to enable students to gain proficiency in areas of weakness.
6–8	• Noticeable decline in motivation to master academic subject matter • Increasing focus on social goals (e.g., interacting with peers, making a good impression) • Increasing tendency to value activities associated with long-term goals and high expectancies for success • Decline in perceived value of many content domains (e.g., English, math, music, sports) • Emerging realization that high effort cannot totally make up for low ability, that some tasks may be impossible regardless of effort	• Promote interest in classroom topics by presenting puzzling phenomena and building on students' personal interests. • Provide opportunities for students to interact as they study and learn (e.g., through role-playing activities, classroom debates, cooperative learning projects). • Relate classroom subject matter to students' long-term goals (e.g., through authentic activities). • Focus students' attention on their improvement; minimize opportunities for them to compare their own performance to that of classmates.
9–12	• Increasing integration of certain values and behaviors into one's overall sense of self • Prevalence of performance goals (e.g., getting good grades) rather than mastery goals for most students • Increase in cheating as a means of accomplishing performance goals • Increasing focus on postgraduation goals (e.g., college, careers); some students have insufficient self-regulation strategies to achieve these goals	• Provide opportunities to pursue interests and values through out-of-class projects and extracurricular activities (e.g., community service work). • Make it possible for students to attain high grades through reasonable effort and effective strategies (e.g., minimize competitive grading practices, such as grading on a curve). • Discourage cheating (see Chapter 15 for specific strategies). • Teach self-regulation strategies that can help students reach their long-term goals (see Chapter 10 for specific strategies).

Sources: Cizek, 2003; Covington, 1992; Dweck & Elliott, 1983; Eccles et al., 1998; Jacobs et al., 2002; Juvonen, 2000; Nicholls, 1990; Nicholls et al., 1990; Paley, 1984; Patrick et al., 2002; Wigfield, 1994; Wigfield et al., 1991; B. L. Wilson & Corbett, 2001; Youniss & Yates, 1999.

   The degree to which intelligence is actually a stable or unstable characteristic is a matter of some controversy among psychologists (see Chapter 5), and even children and adolescents have differing opinions on the matter. Students with an **entity view** believe that intelligence is a "thing" that is fairly permanent and unchangeable. Students with an **incremental view** believe that intelligence can and does improve with effort and practice. As you might guess, students who have an incremental view of intelligence and other abilities are more likely to attribute their failures to a temporary and unstable, rather than permanent, state of affairs (Dweck & Leggett, 1988; Weiner, 1994). In contrast, students with an entity view may continually try to assess their "natural" ability by comparing their own performance with that of others, and they are apt to adopt performance goals rather than mastery goals (Dweck, 2000).

Factors Influencing the Development of Attributions

Why does one student see a failure as a temporary setback due to her own insufficient effort, whereas another thinks it reveals a lack of ability and so signals more failures to come, and still another blames the failure on the teacher's capricious and unpredictable actions? Researchers have identified several factors that influence students' attributions: past successes and failures, situational cues, reinforcement and punishment, messages from others, and image management.

Past successes and failures. Students' attributions are partly the result of their previous success and failure experiences (Covington, 1987; Hong, Chiu, & Dweck, 1995; Klein, 1990). Students who usually succeed when they give a task their best shot are likely to credit success to internal factors such as effort or high ability. Those who frequently fail despite their best efforts are apt to attribute success to something beyond their control—perhaps to an ability they don't possess or to such external factors as luck or a teacher's arbitrary judgment.

   Metacognition plays a role here as well. In Chapter 8 we discovered that students often think they have learned something they actually have *not* learned; that is, they have an *illusion of knowing*. When these students do poorly on an exam, they cannot attribute their performance to internal factors; after all, they may have studied hard and so seemingly "know" the material. Instead, they are apt to attribute it to such external factors as bad luck, exam difficulty, or teacher capriciousness (Horgan, 1990).

   Here we find yet another reason both to promote student success on a regular basis and to teach students how to evaluate their learning progress: In doing so, we also promote more internal, and thus more productive, attributions. When we know that students have high self-efficacy about the subject matter in question, we may occasionally want to give them a series of tasks that they can perform successfully only if they exert considerable time and mental effort. In doing so, we can promote **learned industriousness**: Students will begin to realize that they can succeed at some tasks only with effort, persistence, and well-chosen strategies (Eisenberger, 1992; Winne, 1995).

■ How might learned industriousness be related to students' *epistemological beliefs* (described in Chapter 8)?

Situational cues. Characteristics specific to a particular situation often influence students' attributions. Obvious features of a task are taken into account; for example, complex math problems (e.g., those with many numbers) are perceived as more difficult, and so failure to solve them can readily be attributed to task difficulty rather than to internal causes (Schunk, 1990). Peers' performance provides another cue; for example, students are apt to attribute a failure to task difficulty if everyone else is also struggling with it, whereas they're likely to attribute failure to lack of ability if others are succeeding (Schunk, 1990; Weiner, 1984).

Reinforcement and punishment. In general, children are more likely to attribute events to internal, controllable causes when adults reinforce their successes but don't punish their failures. Conversely, they are more likely to make external attributions when adults punish failures and ignore successes (Katkovsky, Crandall, & Good, 1967). It appears that our students will be more apt to accept responsibility for their failures if, as teachers, we don't make a big deal out of them.

   As noted in Chapter 9, however, mild punishment is sometimes necessary to discourage behaviors that seriously interfere with classroom learning. On such occasions we must make response-consequence contingencies clear—for example, by describing unacceptable behaviors in advance and by using punishment in a consistent, predictable way. In the process, we help students learn that their *own behaviors* lead to desirable and undesirable consequences and that they can therefore influence the events that occur by changing how they behave. Thus, we help them

■ **entity view of intelligence** Belief that intelligence is a "thing" that is relatively permanent and unchangeable.

■ **incremental view of intelligence** Belief that intelligence can improve with effort and practice.

■ **learned industriousness** Recognition that one can succeed at some tasks only with effort, persistence, and well-chosen strategies.

develop internal attributions regarding the consequences they experience and a greater sense of control over classroom events.

Messages from others. Let's return to the case study "When 'Perfect' Isn't Good Enough" at the end of Chapter 11. For students in the treatment group, Mrs. Gaskill attributes good writing to either ability ("You are a natural at this") or effort ("You sure are working hard"). Curiously, the students in Mrs. Gaskill's control group appear to be frustrated that they're aren't getting such information ("Am *I* a natural at this?"). Children don't always know why they are or are not doing well, and in such cases they may eagerly seek out information to help them explain their successes and failures (Weiner, 2000).

Parents, teachers, and other important individuals in students' lives often communicate their beliefs about students' strengths and weaknesses and about possible explanations for students' successes and failures. Sometimes their messages are explicit, as Mrs. Gaskill's comments often are. At other times they are more subtle, as we will discover in the upcoming section "Teacher Expectations and Attributions." Regardless of *how* adults transmit their messages, when they communicate the belief that students are incapable of mastering a task, students are apt to attribute their failures to low ability and may therefore conclude that they will gain little by trying harder (R. Butler, 1994; Weiner, 2000; D. K. Yee & Eccles, 1988).

Image management. The attributions that students *express* don't always reflect their true beliefs about reasons for their successes and failures. As children get older, they discover that different attributions elicit different reactions from others. To maintain positive interpersonal relationships (and thereby satisfy their need for relatedness), they begin to modify their attributions for the particular audience at hand (Juvonen, 2000). We might call this phenomenon *image management*.

Teachers, parents, and other adults are often sympathetic and forgiving when students fail because of something beyond their control (illness, lack of ability, etc.) but frequently get angry when students fail simply because they didn't try very hard. By the time students reach fourth grade, most of them realize this and so may verbalize attributions that will elicit a favorable reaction (Juvonen, 1996, 2000; Weiner, 1995). To illustrate, a student who knows very well that she did poorly on an assignment because she didn't put forth her best effort may distort the truth, telling her teacher that she "can't seem to make sense of this stuff" or "wasn't feeling well."

Students become equally adept at tailoring their attributions for the ears of their peers. Fourth graders generally believe that their peers value diligence and hard work, and so they are likely to tell classmates that they did well on an assignment because they worked hard. By eighth grade, however, many students believe that their peers will disapprove of those who exert much effort on academic tasks, and so they often prefer to convey the impression that they *aren't* working very hard—for instance, that they "didn't study very much" for an important exam or "just lucked out" when they have performed at a high level (Howie, 2002; Juvonen, 1996, 2000).

For reasons we've just identified, different students may interpret the same events in very different ways. As they grow older, students gradually develop predictable patterns of attributions and expectations for their future performance, as we shall see now.

Mastery Orientation Versus Learned Helplessness

Consider these two students, keeping in mind that *their actual academic ability is the same*:

- Jared is an enthusiastic, energetic learner. He seems to enjoy working hard at school activities and takes obvious pleasure in doing well. He likes challenges and especially likes to solve the "brain teaser" problems that his teacher assigns as extra credit work each day. He can't always solve the problems, but he takes failure in stride and is eager for more problems the following day.
- Jerry is an anxious, fidgety student. He doesn't seem to have much confidence in his ability to accomplish school tasks successfully. In fact, he is always underestimating what he can do: Even when he has succeeded, he doubts that he can do it again. He seems to prefer filling out drill-and-practice worksheets that help him practice skills he's already mastered, rather than attempting new tasks and problems. As for those daily brain teasers Jared likes so much, Jerry sometimes takes a stab at them, but he gives up quickly if the answer isn't obvious.

Over time, some students, like Jared, develop a general sense of optimism that they can master new tasks and succeed in a variety of endeavors. They attribute their accomplishments to their own ability and effort and have an *I can do it* attitude known as a **mastery orientation**. Other students, like Jerry, who are either unsure of their chances for success or else convinced that they can*not* succeed, display a growing sense of futility about their chances for future success. They have an *I can't do it* attitude known as **learned helplessness**.

Even though students with a mastery orientation and those with learned helplessness may have equal ability initially, those with a mastery orientation behave in ways that lead to higher achievement over the long run: They set ambitious goals, seek challenging situations, and persist in the face of failure. Students with learned helplessness behave very differently: Because they underestimate their own ability, they set goals they can easily accomplish, avoid the challenges likely to maximize their learning and growth, and respond to failure in counterproductive ways (e.g., giving up quickly) that almost guarantee future failure (Dweck, 2000; Graham, 1989; C. Peterson, 1990; Seligman, 1991).

Even preschoolers can develop learned helplessness about a particular task if they consistently encounter failure when attempting it (Burhans & Dweck, 1995). By age 5 or 6, some children begin to show a consistent tendency either to persist at a task and express confidence that they can master it, on the one hand, or to abandon a task quickly and say they don't have the ability to do it, on the other (Ziegert, Kistner, Castro, & Robertson, 2001). As a general rule, however, children younger than 8 rarely exhibit extreme forms of learned helplessness, perhaps because they still believe that success is due largely to their own efforts (Eccles et al., 1998; Lockhart et al. 2002; Paris & Cunningham, 1996). By early adolescence, feelings of helplessness are more common: Some middle schoolers believe they cannot control the things that happen to them and are at a loss for strategies about how to avert future failures (Paris & Cunningham, 1996; C. Peterson, Maier, & Seligman, 1993).

Many of the strategies we've previously identified for enhancing self-efficacy—giving competence-promoting feedback, promoting mastery on challenging tasks, defining success in terms of improvement or task accomplishment, and so on—should promote a mastery orientation as well. Nevertheless, even when students are highly motivated to learn, they cannot always do so on their own. They should have a variety of resources to which they can turn in times of difficulty. These include their teacher, of course, and possibly such additional resources as supplementary readings, extra practice sheets, self-instructional computer programs, or outside tutoring (perhaps by classmates, older students, or community volunteers). In general, students must have sufficient academic support to believe that *I can do this if I really want to.*

As mentioned earlier, the messages that teachers and other adults give students can have a significant influence on the attributions that students form. We now look more closely at the effects of teachers' expectations and attributions. As we do so, we'll identify additional strategies for promoting productive attributions in students.

TEACHER EXPECTATIONS AND ATTRIBUTIONS

Teachers typically draw conclusions about their students relatively early in the school year, forming opinions about each one's strengths, weaknesses, and potential for academic success. In many instances teachers size up their students fairly accurately: They know which ones need help with reading skills, which ones have short attention spans, which ones have trouble working together in a cooperative group, and so on, and they can adapt their instruction and assistance accordingly (Goldenberg, 1992; Good & Brophy, 1994; Good & Nichols, 2001).

Yet even the best teachers inevitably make errors in their judgments. For example, teachers often underestimate the abilities of students who

- Are physically unattractive
- Frequently misbehave in class
- Speak in dialects other than Standard English
- Are members of ethnic minority groups
- Are recent immigrants
- Come from low-income backgrounds
  (Banks & Banks, 1995; R. E. Bennett, Gottesman, Rock, & Cerullo, 1993; Knapp & Woolverton, 1995; McLoyd, 1998; Oakes & Guiton, 1995; Ritts, Patterson, & Tubbs, 1992)

■ Think of the distinction between a mastery orientation and learned helplessness as a continuum of individual differences rather than a complete dichotomy. You might also look at it as a difference between *optimists* and *pessimists* (C. Peterson, 1990; Seligman, 1991).

■ **mastery orientation** General belief that one is capable of accomplishing challenging tasks.

■ **learned helplessness** General belief that one is incapable of accomplishing tasks and has little or no control of the environment.

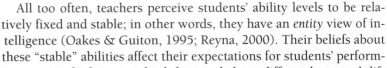

All too often, teachers perceive students' ability levels to be relatively fixed and stable; in other words, they have an *entity* view of intelligence (Oakes & Guiton, 1995; Reyna, 2000). Their beliefs about these "stable" abilities affect their expectations for students' performance, which in turn lead them to behave differently toward different students. For example, when teachers have high expectations for students, they create a warmer classroom climate, interact with students more frequently, provide more opportunities for students to respond, and give more positive feedback; they also present more course material and more challenging topics. In contrast, when teachers have low expectations for certain students, they offer fewer opportunities for speaking in class, ask easier questions, give less feedback about students' responses, and present few if any challenging assignments (Babad, 1993; Good & Brophy, 1994; Graham, 1990; R. Rosenthal, 1994). Minority students with a history of academic failure are especially likely to be the recipients of such low-ability signals (Graham, 1990).

Teachers who hold high expectations for their students are more likely to give specific feedback about the strengths and weaknesses of students' responses.

Teachers' beliefs about students' abilities also affect their attributions for students' successes and failures (Weiner, 2000). Consider the following interpretations of a student's success:

- "You did it! You're so smart!"
- "That's wonderful. Your hard work has really paid off, hasn't it?"
- "You've done very well. It's clear that you really know how to study."
- "Terrific! This is certainly your lucky day!"

And now consider these interpretations of a student's failure:

- "Hmmm, maybe this just isn't something you're good at. Perhaps we should try a different activity."
- "Why don't you practice a little more and then try again?"
- "Let's see whether we can come up with some study strategies that might work better for you."
- "Maybe you're just having a bad day."

All of these comments are presumably intended to make a student feel good. But notice the different attributions they imply. The student's success or failure is attributed in some cases to uncontrollable abilities (being smart or not "good at" something); in other cases to controllable—and therefore changeable—student behaviors (hard work, lack of practice, effective or ineffective study strategies); and in still other cases to external, uncontrollable causes (a lucky break, a bad day). In the "Author's Chair" clip on Video CD 2, a second-grade teacher clearly communicates that acquiring good writing skills is within students' control; for instance, she tells her students, "Our job is to help [Lindsey] become a better writer. Give her, maybe, a compliment and something she can do to be a better writer."

■ Observe teacher messages about internal attributions in the "Author's Chair" clip on Video CD 2.

Teachers communicate their attributions for students' successes and failures in more subtle ways as well—for instance, through the emotions they convey (Reyna & Weiner, 2001; Weiner, 2000). As an example, let's return to the opening case study of Michael, who is initially doing poorly in his eighth-grade algebra class. Imagine that you are Michael's teacher. Imagine, too, that you believe Michael has low mathematical ability: He just doesn't have a "gift" for math. When you see him get Ds and Fs consistently on assignments and quizzes, you might reasonably conclude that such poor performance is beyond his control, and so you frequently communicate pity and sympathy. But now imagine, instead, that you believe Michael has *high* math ability: He definitely has what it takes to do well in your class. When you see his poor marks on assignments and quizzes, you naturally assume he isn't trying very hard. In your eyes, Michael has complete control over the amount of effort he exerts, and so you might express anger or annoyance when he doesn't do well. Some teachers might even punish him for his poor performance (Reyna & Weiner, 2001).

How Expectations and Attributions Affect Classroom Performance

Most children and adolescents are well aware of their teachers' differential treatment of individual students and use such treatment to draw logical inferences about their own and others' abilities

(R. Butler, 1994; Good & Nichols, 2001; R. S. Weinstein, 1993). When their teachers repeatedly give them low-ability messages, they may begin to see themselves as their teachers see them. Furthermore, their behavior may mirror their self-perceptions; for example, they may exert little effort on academic tasks, or they may frequently misbehave in class (Marachi, Friedel, & Midgley, 2001; Murdock, 1999). In some cases, then, teachers' expectations and attributions may lead to a **self-fulfilling prophecy**: What teachers expect students to achieve becomes what students actually *do* achieve.

We find a good example of a self-fulfilling prophecy in a classic early study by Rosenthal and Jacobson (1968). In May of 1964, researchers administered the "Harvard Test of Inflected Acquisition" to kindergartners through fifth graders at an elementary school in a low-income neighborhood. Just before school resumed the following fall, the researchers gave teachers the names of students who, according to the test results, would probably show dramatic achievement gains during the school year. In fact, the researchers had chosen these academic "spurters" entirely at random—essentially pulling their names out of a hat. Despite the researchers' bogus predictions, the chosen children made greater achievement gains during the school year than their nonchosen classmates, and teachers rated these children in more favorable terms (e.g., as being more "intellectually curious"). The results were especially dramatic for children in grades 1 and 2.

Certainly teacher expectations don't always lead to self-fulfilling prophecies. In some cases teachers follow up on low expectations by offering the kinds of instruction and assistance that students need to improve, and so students *do* improve (Goldenberg, 1992). In other cases students may develop an "I'll show *you*" attitude that spurs them on to greater effort and achievement than a teacher anticipated (Good & Nichols, 2001). In still other cases assertive parents may step in and offer evidence that their children are more capable than a teacher initially thought (Good & Nichols, 2001).

So how prevalent are self-fulfilling prophecies? In other words, to what extent do teacher expectations affect students' classroom performance and overall academic growth? Research on this topic yields mixed results (Eccles et al., 1998; Goldenberg, 1992; R. Rosenthal, 1994, 2002). Some research indicates that girls, students from low-income families, and students from ethnic minority groups are more susceptible to teacher expectations than boys from European American backgrounds (Graham, 1990; Jussim, Eccles, & Madon, 1996). Teacher expectations also appear to have a greater influence in the early elementary school years (grades 1 and 2), in the first year of secondary school and, more generally, within the first few weeks of school—in other words, at times when students are entering new and unfamiliar school environments (Jussim et al., 1996; Kuklinski & Weinstein, 2001; Raudenbush, 1984).

Forming Productive Expectations and Attributions for Student Performance

Sometimes teacher expectations are based on completely erroneous information. More often, however, teachers' initial impressions of students are reasonably accurate. In the latter case, a problem emerges when teachers don't *change* their expectations in light of new data (H. M. Cooper & Good, 1983; Good & Brophy, 1994). The constructive nature of learning and memory often gets in the way here: People's prior beliefs and expectations influence how they interpret new information (see Chapter 7). For example, if you have read Chapter 1, then you may recall the opening case study involving 6-year-old Lupita, the daughter of migrant workers who has been raised in Mexico by her grandmother (Carrasco, 1981). Lupita's kindergarten teacher, Ms. Padilla, quickly jumps to the conclusion that Lupita has few academic skills and probably needs a second year of kindergarten. She is quite surprised to see a very different, and very competent, side of Lupita captured by a researcher's video camera. Ms. Padilla readily admits that her early expectations have colored her assessment of Lupita: "I had written her off . . . her and three others. They had met my expectations and I just wasn't looking for anything else." Just as Ms. Padilla does, teachers often look for evidence that confirms and perpetuates their own previously formed beliefs and expectations, and they may turn a blind eye and deaf ear to any evidence to the contrary—an example of the *confirmation bias* I spoke of in Chapter 7.

Unfortunately, teachers' beliefs about students' ability, as well as their attributions for students' performance, are sometimes affected by gender and ethnic stereotypes (Deaux, 1984; C. B. Murray & Jackson, 1982/1983; Reyna, 2000). For instance, a high school math teacher who believes that "girls aren't good in math" is apt to convey pity for low-achieving girls and perhaps give them less challenging problems. A fourth-grade teacher who believes that a particular ethnic group is "lazy"

■ self-fulfilling prophecy Situation in which expectations for an outcome either directly or indirectly lead to the expected result.

and "doesn't care about education" is apt to blame members of that group for their own failures and, as a result, give them little emotional support or assistance. Even the most fair-minded of us can be influenced by deep-seated biases and stereotypes of which we are not consciously aware (Dovidio, Kawakami, & Gaertner, 2000). For instance, Michael, in the chapter's opening case study, is African American. Had I given you this information at the beginning of the chapter, do you think it would have influenced your own explanations (attributions) for Michael's initially poor math achievement?

As teachers, we are most likely to facilitate our students' learning and to motivate them to achieve at high levels if we have optimistic expectations for their performance (within realistic limits, of course) and if we attribute their successes and failures to things over which either they or we have control (*their* effort, *our* instructional methods, etc.). Several strategies can help us form productive expectations and attributions:

◎ *Remember that teachers can definitely make a difference.* We are more likely to have high expectations for our students—and they are more likely to have high expectations as well—when we have high self-efficacy about our ability to help them achieve academic and social success (Ashton, 1985; Roeser et al., 2002; R. S. Weinstein, Madison, & Kuklinski, 1995). We must keep in mind an important point from Chapter 5 about intelligence: Ability can and does change over time, especially when environmental conditions are conducive to such change. For this reason, we should take an *incremental view* of students' intelligence and other abilities (Pintrich & Schunk, 2002). Accordingly, we must continually reassess our expectations and attributions for individual students, modifying them as new evidence presents itself.

◎ *Look for strengths in every student.* Sometimes students' weaknesses are all too evident. It is essential that we also look for the many unique qualities and strengths that students will inevitably have. For example, many African American students show considerable creativity when they converse; they joke, tease, and tell lively stories (Hale-Benson, 1986). We can certainly take advantage of such playfulness in students' speech—perhaps by having students create songs, jokes, or short stories that relate to classroom subject matter.

◎ *Consider multiple possible explanations for students' low achievement and misbehavior.* Low achievement can be due to a variety of factors, many of which we might be able to address; for example, students may have insufficient background knowledge about a topic, poor study skills and self-regulatory behaviors, or undiagnosed medical problems. Classroom misbehaviors, too, can stem from a variety of sources; for instance, students may have unusually high energy levels or may never have been taught appropriate classroom behavior (Darch & Kame'enui, 2004; B. K. Keogh, 2003). If we keep an open mind about the source of a student's problem (recall that *open-minded* disposition I spoke of earlier), we are more likely to *solve* the problem successfully.

◎ *Communicate optimistic and controllable attributions.* As teachers, we must be careful about the attributions we make regarding student performance. Probably the best strategy is to attribute success partly to a relatively stable ability (thus promoting optimism about future success) and partly to such controllable factors as effort and learning strategies (thus emphasizing that continued success will come only with hard work). When considering possible causes for failure, however, we should focus primarily on factors that are internal, unstable, and controllable; thus, attributions for failures should focus on effort and learning strategies, rather than on low ability (which students are likely to believe is stable and uncontrollable) or external factors (Pressley, Borkowski, & Schneider, 1987; Schunk, 1983a; C. E. Weinstein, Hagen, & Meyer, 1991).

We can communicate optimistic attributions and expectations for student performance through statements such as these:

- "You've done very well. Obviously you're good at this, and you've been trying very hard to get better."
- "Your project shows a lot of talent and a lot of hard work."
- "The more you practice, the better you will get."
- "Perhaps you need to study a little bit more next time. And let me give you some suggestions on how you might study a little differently, too."

Studies have shown that when students' failures are consistently attributed to ineffective learning strategies or a lack of effort, rather than to low ability or uncontrollable external factors, and when new strategies or increased effort *do* produce success, then students work harder, persist longer in the face of failure, and seek help when they need it (Dweck & Elliott, 1983; Eccles & Wigfield, 1985; Graham, 1991; Paris & Paris, 2001).

All students have their strengths; for instance, some are good readers, others are inquisitive scientists, and still others are creative storytellers. As teachers, we are more likely to have high expectations for students when we look for things they do *well* rather than focus entirely on their weaknesses.

We must be careful when we attribute either success or failure to effort, however. There are at least two occasions when such attributions can backfire. To see what I mean, try the next exercise.

Experiencing FIRSTHAND · Carberry and Seville #2

1. Imagine that Professor Carberry wants you to learn to spell the word *psychoceramics* correctly. He gives you ten minutes of intensive training in the spelling of the word. He then praises you profusely when you are able to spell it correctly. In which of the following ways would you be most likely to respond?
    a. You are delighted that he approves of your performance.
    b. You proudly show him that you've also learned how to spell *sociocosmetology*.
    c. You wonder, "Hey, is this all he thinks I can do?"
2. Now imagine that you drop by Professor Seville's office to find out why you did so poorly on her sociocosmetology exam. Professor Seville is warm and supportive, suggesting that you simply try harder next time. But the fact is, you tried as hard as you could the *first* time. Which one of the following conclusions would you be most likely to draw?
    a. You need to try even harder next time.
    b. You need to exert the same amount of effort the next time and just keep your fingers crossed that you'll make some lucky guesses.
    c. Perhaps you just weren't meant to be a sociocosmetologist.

· · · · · · ·

Chances are that you answered *c* to both questions. Let's first consider the situation in which Carberry spent ten minutes teaching you how to spell *psychoceramics*. When students succeed at a very easy task and are then praised for their effort, they may get the unintended message that their teacher doesn't have much confidence in their ability (Graham, 1991; Stipek, 1996). Attributing students' successes to effort is apt to be beneficial only when students have, in fact, exerted a great deal of effort.

Now consider the second scenario, in which Seville encouraged you to try harder even though you had already studied as hard as you could for the first exam. When students fail at a task at which they've expended a great deal of effort and are then told that they didn't try hard enough, they are likely to conclude that they simply don't have the ability to perform the task successfully (Curtis & Graham, 1991; Robertson, 2000; Stipek, 1996). Attributing students' failures to a lack of effort is apt to be helpful only when they really haven't given classroom tasks their best shot.

When students have worked hard but still failed, we should probably attribute their failure to a lack of effective strategies (Curtis & Graham, 1991; Pressley, Borkowski, & Schneider, 1987). As we discovered in our discussion of metacognition in Chapter 8, students can and do acquire more effective learning and study strategies over time, especially when they are specifically trained to use these strategies. By teaching effective strategies, not only do we promote students' academic success, but we also promote their beliefs that they can *control* their success (C. E. Weinstein et al., 1991).

◎   *Learn more about students' backgrounds and home environments.* Teachers are most likely to have low expectations and pessimistic attributions for students' achievement when they have formed rigid stereotypes about students from certain ethnic or socioeconomic groups (McLoyd, 1998; Reyna, 2000; R. E. Snow et al., 1996). Such stereotypes often result from ignorance about students' cultures and home environments (K. L. Alexander et al., 1987). Even without rigid stereotypes, most of us have a natural tendency to view other cultural groups less favorably than our own (see the section "Coming to Grips with Our Own Cultural Lenses" on p. 113 in Chapter 4). Education is the key here: We must learn as much as we can about our students' backgrounds and local communities. When we have a clear picture of their activities, habits, values, and families, we are far more likely to think of them as individuals who bring a unique set of individual and cultural strengths to the classroom.

◎   *Assess students' progress regularly and objectively.* Because our expectations for students' performance are likely to color our informal evaluations of what they actually accomplish, we need to identify objective ways of assessing learning and achievement. Furthermore, we should assess students' progress frequently, so that we have ongoing and reasonably accurate information with which to make instructional decisions (Goldenberg, 1992). Chapter 15 offers several suggestions for assessing students' work objectively.

Promoting Productive Attributions

 Communicate optimism about what students can accomplish.

In September a high school teacher tells his class, "Next spring, I will ask you to write a fifteen-page research paper. Fifteen pages may seem like a lot now, but in the next few months we will work on the various skills you will need to research and write your paper. By April, fifteen pages won't seem like a big deal at all!"

Attribute students' successes to a combination of high ability and such controllable factors as effort and learning strategies.

In a unit on basketball, a physical education teacher tells students, "From what I've seen so far, you all have the capability to play a good game of basketball. And it appears that many of you have been practicing after school."

Attribute students' successes to effort only when they have actually exerted considerable effort.

A teacher observes that his students complete a particular assignment more quickly and easily than he expected. He briefly acknowledges their success and then moves on to a more challenging task.

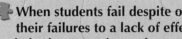 **Attribute students' failures to factors that are controllable and easily changed.**

A high school student seeks his teacher's advice about how he might improve his performance in her class. "I know you can do better than you have been, Frank," she replies. "I'm wondering if part of the problem might be that, with your part-time job and all your extracurricular activities, you just don't have enough time to study. Let's sit down before school tomorrow and look at what and how much you're doing to prepare for class."

When students fail despite obvious effort, attribute their failures to a lack of effective strategies and then help them acquire such strategies.

A student in an advanced science class is having difficulty on the teacher's challenging weekly quizzes. The student works diligently on her science every night and attends the after-school help sessions her teacher offers on Thursdays, yet to no avail. Her teacher observes that the student is trying to learn the material by rote—an ineffective strategy for answering the higher-level questions typically on the quizzes—and helps the student develop strategies that promote more meaningful learning.

The Into the Classroom feature "Promoting Productive Attributions" illustrates some of the strategies we've just identified. We look now at sources of diversity in the cognitive aspects of motivation.

CONSIDERING DIVERSITY IN THE COGNITIVE ASPECTS OF MOTIVATION

In earlier sections of the chapter, we've seen several examples of diversity in motivation. For instance, we've learned that students have widely varying personal interests and may find greater or lesser value in particular subject areas. Furthermore, the degree to which students have high self-efficacy, mastery goals, productive attributions, and a mastery orientation influences the degree to which they enjoy challenges, persist at difficult tasks, and take failure in stride. We now look at the diversity we are likely to see in students of various ethnic backgrounds, genders, and income levels, as well as in students with special educational needs.

Ethnic Differences

Children and adolescents around the world want some autonomy and self-determination, but the amount and forms that autonomy and self-determination take may differ considerably from group to group (d'Ailly, 2003; Deyhle & LeCompte, 1999; Rogoff, 2003). For example, as we saw in the opening case study in Chapter 4, adults in the Navajo culture of the southwestern United States give children more autonomy and control over decision making, and do so at an earlier age, than do many adults in mainstream Western culture. In contrast, many African American parents give children *less* autonomy than the "average" American parent, apparently as a way of ensuring children's safety in potentially hostile environments (Hale-Benson, 1986; McLoyd, 1998).

Children and adolescents from most ethnic groups place high value on getting a good education, but those from some minority groups have lower expectancies for academic and professional success. To some extent, these low expectations may be the result of discriminative practices encountered in society (Eccles et al., 1998; Fordham & Ogbu, 1986). Teachers' expectations and attributions may also be a factor, for reasons we considered earlier in the chapter.

Furthermore, students from different ethnic backgrounds may define academic success differently and so set different goals for themselves. For instance, Asian American students, on average, shoot for higher grades than students in other ethnic groups, in part because they believe their parents would be angry if they got grades lower than A— (Steinberg, 1996). Even so, Asian American students—and African American students as well—may be more focused on mastery goals (i.e., on truly learning and understanding what they are studying) than European American students (Freeman, Gutman, & Midgley, 2002; Qian & Pan, 2002). Students raised in cultures that value group achievement over individual achievement (e.g., many Native American, Mexican American, Southeast Asian, and Pacific Islander cultures; see Chapter 4) tend to focus their mastery goals not on how much they alone can improve, but instead on how much they *and their classmates* can improve (Kaplan, 1998). And students from some ethnic backgrounds (e.g., those from some native American and rural Appalachian communities) may place higher priority on helping their families and communities than on graduating from high school (Deyhle & Margonis, 1995; Timm & Borman, 1997).

Students' ethnic backgrounds influence their attributions as well. For instance, students from Asian cultures are more likely to attribute classroom success and failure to unstable factors—effort in the case of academic achievement, and temporary situational factors in the case of appropriate or inappropriate behaviors—than students brought up in mainstream Western culture (R. D. Hess, Chih-Mei, & McDevitt, 1987; Lillard, 1997; Steinberg, 1996). Also, some studies indicate a greater tendency for African American students to develop a sense of learned helplessness about their ability to achieve academic success (Graham, 1989; Holliday, 1985). To some extent, racial prejudice may contribute to their learned helplessness: Some students may begin to believe that because of the color of their skin, they have little chance of success no matter what they do (S. Sue & Chin, 1983; van Laar, 2000).

Gender Differences

Boys and girls tend to find greater or lesser value in various academic domains depending on whether they view these domains as being stereotypically appropriate for boys or girls. Many (but by no means all) students perceive some domains (e.g., writing, instrumental music) to be for girls and others (e.g., math, science) to be for boys (Eccles et al., 1998; Kahle, 1983; Pajares & Valiante, 1999), and such perceptions invariably influence their effort and course selection. Boys' and girls' *self-efficacy* for various content domains—self-perceptions that are undoubtedly affected by gender stereotypes, exposure to same-gender models, and so on—will also influence the extent to which they value different domains (Bandura et al., 2001; Jacobs et al., 2002).

As we discovered in our earlier discussion of career goals, girls are catching up to boys in their long-term aspirations. If we look more closely at students' *confidence* to achieve ambitious goals, however, we sometimes find a gender difference: Despite the higher grades for girls than for boys, girls tend to *under*estimate their competence, whereas boys tend to *over*estimate it (D. A. Cole et al., 1999; Eccles et al., 1998; Middleton, 1999). In addition, girls (including many high-achieving girls) are more easily discouraged by failure than boys (Dweck, 1986, 2000). We can explain this difference, at least in part, by looking at gender differences in attributions. Some research studies indicate that boys tend to attribute their successes to a fairly stable ability and their failures to lack of effort, thus having an *I know I can do this* attitude. Girls show the reverse pattern: They attribute their successes to effort and their failures to lack of ability, believing that *I don't know whether I can keep on doing it, because I'm not very good at this type of thing*. Such differences, which can appear even when boys' and girls' previous levels of achievement are equivalent, are more frequently observed in stereotypically male domains such as mathematics and sports (Eccles & Jacobs, 1986; Fennema, 1987; Stipek, 1984; Vermeer, Boekaerts, & Seegers, 2000).

As we work to encourage high levels of motivation in all of our students, we may want to focus our efforts in somewhat different directions for males and females. For boys, who have less concern about doing well in school (see Chapter 11), we may need to stress the imprtance of high classroom achievement for their own long-term goals. For girls, we may need to encourage open-mindedness about a wide variety of career options (including traditionally masculine ones) and show them how these options are, with effort and appropriate strategies, well within their grasp.

■ Have you observed this difference in the males and females you know? Can you think of individuals who are exceptions to the pattern?

Socioeconomic Differences

As we noted in Chapter 11, many students from lower socioeconomic backgrounds would ultimately like to do well in school. However, teachers' attitudes, instructional practices, and relationships with students have a significant influence on these students' motivation to achieve academic success; this is especially true for students at high risk for academic failure (L. W.

Anderson & Pellicer, 1998; Kumar et al., 2002; Maehr & Anderman, 1993; Murdock, 1999). Schools at which students from low-income families flourish are those in which teachers have high expectations, engage students in high-interest activities and subject matter, emphasize mastery goals more than performance goals, and make students feel that they are bona fide members of the classroom community (more on this *sense of community* in Chapter 14).

When working with students from lower socioeconomic backgrounds, we should remember that two conditions—self-efficacy and self-determination—are essential for intrinsic motivation. We are most likely to enhance students' self-efficacy if we communicate high (yet realistic) expectations for their performance and if we provide the academic support through which they can meet those expectations. And when we give them a sense of self-determination and control over their lives—for instance, when we involve them in classroom decision making and teach them effective ways of bringing about change in their local communities—they will attend school more regularly and achieve at higher levels (deCharms, 1972; NCSS Task Force on Ethnic Studies Curriculum Guidelines, 1992).

In addition, we can increase the perceived value of school activities by making them relevant to students' own lives and experiences (P. A. Alexander et al., 1994; Knapp et al., 1990; Wlodkowski & Ginsberg, 1995). All too often, students at schools in low-income neighborhoods encounter instruction that focuses on rote learning and lower-level skills (e.g., memorization of facts)—instruction that is unlikely to entice even the most motivated of them (Becker & Luthar, 2002; Portes, 1996). The following interviews with middle school students in an inner-city Philadelphia school illustrate the problem:

Adult: What do you do in science? . . .
Student: We outline the chapter.
Adult: Who creates the outline?
Student: The teacher do it and we copy it. Sometimes we do it on our own.
Adult: What else do you do?
Student: We answer questions from the end of the chapter.
Adult: Do you do experiments?
Student: No, not many. We did some at the beginning of the year. (dialogue from B. L. Wilson & Corbett, 2001, pp. 43, 46)

_____

Adult: How often do you write in English class?
Student: Every day.
Adult: What kinds of things are you writing?
Student: We copy notes from the board and we do dictionary work.
          We also answer questions from our workbook.
Adult: Do you ever write your own stories?
Student: No. (dialogue from B. L. Wilson & Corbett, 2001, p. 52)

Not only is such instruction unengaging, but it is also unlikely to prepare students for the demands of a college curriculum (e. g., Suskind, 1998).

As we introduce new topics, we should, of course, relate them to the knowledge that the students are apt to have, thereby increasing the likelihood of meaningful learning. We should also relate classroom tasks and activities to students' specific, day-to-day needs and interests; for example, by teaching academic subject matter within the context of *authentic activities* as often as we can, we enhance the value that students attach to the subject matter. And we can occasionally solicit students' ideas about issues and questions they'd like to study in class.

It is essential, too, that we help students acquire the skills and strategies they will need to achieve their long-term goals for higher education and careers. Students are unlikely to achieve ambitious academic and professional goals unless they master higher-level thinking skills and self-regulation strategies. In addition, we must promote a realistic understanding of what college achievement and professional success involve to students who may have had little direct contact with college life or high-income professions. Once, when speaking with a group of middle school boys who hoped to go to college, one researcher encountered considerable naivete about college life:

They got a dazed look in their eyes when I talked about the reality of actually getting into college: filling out an application, the importance of getting good grades, and so on. So, I asked them what they thought college was like. The response was nearly unanimous—it was all about partying—drinking, smoking weed, and hanging out. Never did it come up that they would attend classes or do homework. College meant partying, and that was why they wanted to go. They thought, also, that college would help them get a job at which they could make a lot of money. This explained to me why students who say they hate school still wish to attend college. (K. M. Williams, 2001a, p. 106)

Such misconceptions are perhaps not surprising if we consider how college life is often portrayed in television and films. College parties certainly yield more interesting plot lines for adolescent viewers than going to class and studying at the library.

Accommodating Students with Special Needs

Students with specific or general academic difficulties (e.g., those with learning disabilities, those with mental retardation) may show signs of learned helplessness with regard to classroom tasks, especially if their past efforts have repeatedly met with failure (Deshler & Schumaker, 1988; Jacobsen, Lowery, & DuCette, 1986; Seligman, 1975). Students who have difficulty getting along with their classmates (e.g., those with emotional and behavioral disorders) may inappropriately attribute their social failures to factors beyond their control (e.g., see the discussion of *hostile attributional bias* in Chapter 3). Table 12.3 presents these and other motivational tendencies in students with special needs.

In recent years special educators have become especially concerned about the need for students with disabilities to develop a sense of self-determination—to believe that they have some control over the direction their lives take (Algozzine et al., 2001; Sands & Wehmeyer, 1996).

TABLE 12.3   STUDENTS IN INCLUSIVE SETTINGS

Promoting "Cognitions That Motivate" in Students with Special Educational Needs

CATEGORY	CHARACTERISTICS YOU MIGHT OBSERVE	SUGGESTED CLASSROOM STRATEGIES
Students with specific cognitive or academic difficulties	• Low self-efficacy for many classroom tasks • Tendency to attribute poor achievement to low ability rather than to more controllable factors; tendency to attribute successes to external causes (e.g., luck) • Tendency to give up easily; learned helplessness regarding performance on some classroom tasks	• Establish challenging yet realistic goals for achievement. • Teach effective learning strategies, and encourage students to attribute their successes to such strategies. • Encourage students to develop more productive attributions regarding their achievement difficulties (e.g., attributing failures to insufficient effort or ineffective strategies).
Students with social or behavioral problems	• Tendency to interpret praise as an attempt to control them (when students exhibit defiance or oppositional behavior) • Perception of classroom tasks as having little relevance to personal needs and goals • Tendency to attribute negative consequences to uncontrollable factors (things just "happen")	• When students are concerned about control issues, use subtle reinforcers (e.g., leave notes describing productive behaviors) rather than more obvious and seemingly "controlling" ones. • Provide choices about academic activities as a way of increasing a sense of self-determination. • Relate the curriculum to students' specific needs and interests. • Teach behaviors that lead to desired consequences; stress cause-effect relationships between actions and outcomes.
Students with general delays in cognitive and social functioning	• Limited (if any) ability to conceptualize long-term goals • Tendency to attribute poor achievement to low ability or to external sources rather than to more controllable factors; in some situations, a sense of learned helplessness	• Set specific, short-term goals for performance. • Help students see the relationship between their own actions and the resulting consequences.
Students with physical or sensory challenges	• Low sense of self-determination about the course that their lives are taking	• Give students some choices within the curriculum. • Teach self-regulating behaviors and independence skills.
Students with advanced cognitive development	• High self-efficacy • Boredom when classroom tasks don't challenge their abilities • May seek out challenges on their own • Variety of interests, sometimes pursued with a passion • Higher-than-average goal-directedness	• Encourage students to set high goals, but without expecting perfection. • Promote learned industriousness by assigning a series of tasks that require considerable effort and persistence.

Sources: Beirne-Smith et al., 2002; M. Carr & Borkowski, 1989; B. Clark, 1997; Duchardt, Deshler, & Schumaker, 1995; Dunlap et al., 1994; Foster-Johnson, Ferro, & Dunlap, 1994; A. E. Gottfried et al., 1994; Heward, 2003; Hoge & Renzulli, 1993; Jacobsen et al., 1986; Knowlton, 1995; Morgan & Jenson, 1988; Piirto, 1999; S. Powell & Nelson, 1997; Sands & Wehmeyer, 1996; R. Turnbull et al., 2004; U. S. Dept. of Education, 1992; Winner, 1997, 2000a, 2000b; Wong, 1991a.

Many of these students, especially those with physical or sensory challenges, may live in sheltered environments in which other people are calling most of the shots (Wehmeyer, 1996). We can do many simple things to enhance the self-determination that these students feel; for instance, we can let them make choices and set some of their own goals, help them develop skills that enable them to gain increasing independence, and teach the many self-regulation strategies that we identified in Chapter 10 (Abery & Zajac, 1996; L. E. Powers et al., 1996).

THE BIG PICTURE

In Chapters 11 and 12, we've found that motivation aids learning and achievement in a variety of ways; for example, effectively motivated students pay attention, process information meaningfully, persist in the face of failure, use their errors to help them improve their skills, and seek out ever more challenging tasks. We have also seen how learning and achievement can foster the development of productive motivational patterns: When students discover that they can usually accomplish academic tasks successfully, they bring a sense of self-confidence and a desire to learn when they come to class. So motivation and learning go hand in hand, with each playing a crucial role in the development of the other.

The best-case scenario is that students are *intrinsically* motivated to learn and master classroom subject matter. They are most likely to be intrinsically motivated when they believe that

- They have the ability to succeed, especially if they apply reasonable effort and appropriate strategies
- Sufficient resources and support in the classroom are available to *help* them succeed
- They find the subject matter interesting and relevant to their goals
- They are voluntarily choosing to pursue classroom activities

In some situations, however, students may not be intrinsically motivated to learn important building blocks for more complex and interesting material. In such situations we can foster extrinsic motivation, and possibly some degree of intrinsic motivation, in a variety of ways. For instance, we can have students set short-term goals with which they can monitor their progress, embed skills practice within enjoyable small-group activities, and reinforce students' achievements.

As teachers, we will invariably find that each student has unique strengths and weaknesses. Yet we must remember that our own behaviors toward students—how challenging our assignments are, how often we call on students in class, how we interpret their successes and failures, and so on—provide regular messages about how we have sized up each student's potential for learning and classroom success. Our early assessments of students' abilities should guide us in our choice of instructional strategies; they should *not* give students reason to question their ability and thereby undermine their confidence about mastering classroom subject matter.

GENERAL PRINCIPLES OF MOTIVATION

Many of the classroom strategies we've considered for enhancing students' motivation can be summed up in six words: task, auton- omy, recognition, grouping, evaluation, and time (J. L. Epstein, 1989; Maehr & Anderman, 1993). This multifaceted "TARGET" approach to motivation is presented in Table 12.4. If you look closely at the entries in the table, you'll find that they reflect many of the concepts we've addressed in Chapters 11 and 12, including needs for self-worth and relatedness, hot cognition, self-efficacy, self-determination, expectancies, values, interests, goals, and attributions.

REVISITING THE FOUR THEORETICAL PERSPECTIVES

As we've discussed motivation, we've drawn ideas from each of the theoretical perspectives identified in Chapter 11; we've also drawn from what we've learned about learning in earlier chapters. Following are some examples of how the trait, behaviorist, social cognitive, and cognitive perspectives have each entered into our discussion:

Trait perspective:
- Students differ in their *need for affiliation* with others and in their *need for approval* from others.
- Students' *personal interests* tend to be relatively stable over time.

Behaviorist perspective:
- Motivation determines what particular things are *reinforcing* to different students.
- Students are more likely to attribute success to internal factors when they are *reinforced* (e.g., praised) for success.

Social cognitive perspective:
- Students are more likely to be intrinsically motivated to engage in and persist at classroom tasks when they have high *self-efficacy* about performing those tasks.
- We can foster intrinsic motivation to learn classroom subject matter when we *model* our own interest and enthusiasm about school subject matter.
- Students' *expectations* (expectancies) for future success and failure—expectations derived from their beliefs about their ability, their perceptions of classroom support for their efforts, and their attributions for previous successes and failures—influence their choices and actions.

Cognitive perspective:
- Students who have mastery goals rather than performance goals are more likely to engage in *meaningful learning* and *elaboration*.

TABLE 12.4

Six "TARGET" Principles of Motivation

PRINCIPLE	EDUCATIONAL IMPLICATIONS	EXAMPLE
Classroom **tasks** affect motivation.	• Present new topics through tasks that students find interesting, engaging, and perhaps emotionally charged. • Encourage meaningful rather than rote learning. • Relate activities to students' lives and goals. • Provide sufficient support that students can be successful.	Ask students to conduct a scientific investigation about an issue that concerns them.
The amount of **autonomy** students have affects motivation, especially intrinsic motivation.	• Give students some choice about what and how they learn. • Teach self-regulation strategies. • Solicit students' opinions about classroom practices and policies. • Have students take leadership roles in some activities.	Let students choose among several ways of accomplishing an instructional objective, being sure that each choice offers sufficient scaffolding to make success likely.
The amount and nature of the **recognition** students receive affect motivation.	• Acknowledge not only academic successes but also personal and social successes. • Commend students for improvement as well as for mastery. • Provide concrete reinforcers for achievement only when students are not intrinsically motivated to learn. • Show students how their own efforts and strategies are directly responsible for their successes.	Commend students for a successful community service project.
The **grouping** procedures in the classroom affect motivation.	• Provide frequent opportunities for students to interact (e.g., cooperative learning activities, peer tutoring). • Plan activities to which all students can make valuable contributions. • Teach the social skills that students need to interact effectively with peers. • Create an atmosphere of mutual caring, respect, and support.	Have students work in small groups to tackle a challenging issue or problem for which there is no single "right" answer.
The forms of **evaluation** in the classroom affect motivation.	• Make evaluation criteria clear; specify them in advance. • Minimize or eliminate competition for grades (e.g., don't grade "on a curve"). • Give specific feedback about what students are doing well. • Give concrete suggestions for how students can improve. • Teach students how to evaluate their own work.	Give students concrete criteria with which they can evaluate their writing (e.g., see Figure 2.7).
How teachers schedule **time** affects motivation.	• Give students enough time to gain mastery of important topics and skills. • Let students' interests dictate some activities. • Include variety in the school day (e.g., intersperse high-energy activities among more sedentary ones). • Provide opportunities for independent learning.	After explaining a new concept, present a hands-on activity that lets students see the concept in action.

Sources: J. L. Epstein, 1989; Maehr & Anderman, 1993.

• Students' attributions regarding events—their *constructed interpretations* of the causes of successes and failures—influence how they respond to those events.

• Students are more optimistic about future success when they attribute failure to ineffective *study strategies* rather than to a general and relatively permanent lack of ability.

The principles and theories of learning and motivation that we've examined in Chapters 6 through 12 have yielded innumerable strategies for helping students learn and achieve more successfully in the classroom. In the chapters to come, we will translate the same principles and theories more directly into classroom practice as we consider instruction, classroom management, and assessment.

CASE STUDY: *Writer's Block*

On the first day of school, Mr. Grunwald tells students in his English composition class, "I expect you all to be proficient writers by the end of the school year. In fact, you won't get a passing grade unless you can write a decent essay by May."

Mr. Grunwald's statement raises anxious thoughts in many of his students. After all, a passing grade in English composition is a requirement for high school graduation. Furthermore, the colleges and universities to which some students are applying prefer As and Bs in composition. A few students are beginning to worry that their straight A averages will be destroyed.

Mr. Grunwald is far less concerned than his students; he firmly believes that all students should be able to develop writing proficiency before the year is out. He gives his students a new writing assignment every Monday, making each one more challenging than those preceding it. When he finds poorly written work among the papers he grades at the end of the week, he tries to motivate his students with such comments as "Below average work this time—you can do better" or "Try harder next week."

The writing skills of some students improve as the year progresses. But those of other students seem almost to be deteriorating. He questions Janis, one of his low-achieving students, about the problem and is startled to hear her response.

"No matter what I do, I seem to get poor grades in your class, " Janis laments. "I've pretty much given up trying. I guess I just wasn't meant to be a writer."

- How is Mr. Grunwald defining success in his English composition class? How are his students defining success? Are they focusing their attention on mastery goals or performance goals?

- To what does Janis attribute her writing failure? What effect has her attribution had on her behavior?

- What strategies might Mr. Grunwald use to help his students become more intrinsically motivated to develop proficient writing skills?

Once you have answered these questions, compare your responses with those presented in Appendix B.

KEY CONCEPTS

self-efficacy (p. 393)	mastery goal (p. 404)	disposition (p. 410)
self-determination (p. 393)	performance goal (p. 404)	attribution (p. 413)
expectancy (p. 398)	performance-approach goal (p. 404)	entity view of intelligence (p. 417)
value (p. 398)	performance-avoidance goal (p. 404)	incremental view of intelligence (p. 417)
internalized motivation (p. 399)	proximal goal (p. 407)	learned industriousness (p. 417)
interest (p. 400)	process goal (p. 407)	mastery orientation (p. 419)
situational interest (p. 401)	product goal (p. 407)	learned helplessness (p. 419)
personal interest (p. 402)	work-avoidance goal (p. 408)	self-fulfilling prophecy (p. 421)
core goal (p. 403)		

PRAXIS Turn to Appendix C, "Matching Book and Ancillary Content to the Praxis Principles of Learning and Teaching Tests," to discover sections of this chapter that may be especially applicable to the Praxis tests.

Now go to our Companion Website at **www.prenhall.com/ormrod** to assess your understanding of chapter content with "Multiple-Choice Questions," apply comprehension in "Essay Questions," broaden your knowledge of educational psychology with related "Web Links," gain greater insight about classroom learning in "Learning in the Content Areas," and analyze and assess classroom work in the "Student Artifact Library."

Chapter 13

Instructional Strategies

*U*nder what conditions do you best learn and achieve in your college classes? Do you learn more when your instructors have clearly described what they hope you will learn and have planned their lessons accordingly? What kinds of instructional methods—lectures, hands-on activities, class discussions, cooperative learning groups, and so on—effectively help you understand and remember classroom material? Does the general "climate" in the classroom—for instance, whether the instructor is friendly or aloof, whether the atmosphere is businesslike or laid-back—make a difference for you? And how do your instructors' assessment practices (tests, papers, group projects, etc.) influence what you study and learn?

Such issues are the focus of the final four chapters of the book, where we will consider how to plan and carry out instruction (Chapter 13), create a productive classroom environment (Chapter 14), and assess students' performance (Chapters 15 and 16). All of these activities are essential aspects of effective teaching and have an impact on what students ultimately learn and achieve. Yet as we make decisions in these areas, we must also keep in mind what we know about individual students. As we proceed through this and the next three chapters, we will repeatedly see examples of how planning, instruction, the classroom environment, and assessment practices affect one another and how, in addition, they both influence and are influenced by student characteristics and behaviors (see Figure 13.1). And we will often revisit principles and concepts of development, learning, cognition, and motivation introduced in Chapters 1 through 12.

Our focus in this chapter will be on questions such as these:

- How can we best plan for instruction, both on a daily basis and over the course of the school year?
- How can we effectively teach new material through expository instruction—that is, by directly presenting the information we want our students to know, understand, and apply?
- How can we also help students acquire new knowledge and skills through various hands-on and practice activities?
- What strategies can maximize students' ability to learn from one another as well as from us?
- What general guiding principles can help us identify appropriate instructional strategies for different situations?

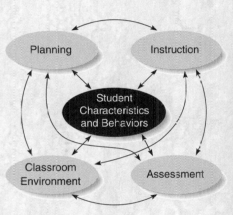

FIGURE 13.1 Planning, instruction, the classroom environment, assessment, and student characteristics and behaviors are not independent; each one influences the others.

CASE STUDY: *Oregon Trail*

Fifth-grade teacher Michele Minichiello has recently begun a unit about American settlers traveling west on the Oregon Trail during the 1840s. Today's lesson focuses on how families prepared for the long, arduous trip.[1]

"The covered wagons were about 4 feet by 10 feet," Ms. Minichiello tells her class. She has students move their desks to clear the middle of the classroom and then instructs two students to mark a 4-by-10-foot rectangle on the carpet with masking tape. "These are the dimensions of a typical covered wagon. How much room would that give you for your family and supplies?" The students agree that the wagon is smaller than they had realized and that it would not provide much room for an entire family.

"So they would have to be pretty choosy about what they brought on their trip," Ms. Minichiello observes. "Let's brainstorm some of the things the settlers might have packed." The students volunteer many possibilities—food, spare wagon parts, pots and pans, blankets, extra clothes, rifles, bullets, barrels of water, medicine—and Ms. Minichiello writes them on the chalkboard. She has the class get more specific about the list (e.g., what kinds of food? how much of each kind?) and then passes out reading materials that describe the supplies a typical family would actually pack for the journey. As the students read the materials in their cooperative groups, Ms. Minichiello circulates among them to show photographs of how the inside of a covered wagon looked when occupied by a family and its possessions.

■ As Figure 13.1 illustrates, the classroom environment both influences and is influenced by student characteristics and behaviors. Of what concept in social cognitive theory (Chapter 10) does this statement remind you?

---

[1] I observed Michele's lesson when I was supervising her teaching internship at the end of her master's program, and I'm delighted that she gave me permission to describe it here. The students' names are pseudonyms.

Once the students have finished their reading, Ms. Minichiello directs their attention to their own supply list on the chalkboard, and the following discussion ensues with the students and Ms. Berry, a special education teacher who is also in the room.

Ms. M:	Do you think our list was accurate? Is there anything you want to change?
Lacy:	We need much more flour.
Janie:	(referring to an item listed in the reading materials) I don't think they should bring 100 pounds of coffee.
Curt:	(also referring to the reading materials) I don't think they need 50 pounds of lard.
Ms. M:	Does anyone know what lard is?
Tom:	It's a kind of animal fat.
Ms. B:	They used it for cooking, but they used it for lots of other things, too.
Ms. M:	Do you think they used it for water-proofing?
Ms. B:	Maybe so.
Ms. M:	What were some of the things that pioneers had to be prepared for? (Here she is asking students to recall information they have just learned from the reading materials.)
Mark:	Mountain travel.
René:	Crossing rivers.
Ms. B:	How about if you were going across the desert?
Lacy:	You'd need a lot of water.
Tom:	Food for the oxen.
Ms. M:	If *you* were taking such a trip now—if you were moving far away from where you live now—what things would you bring with you?
Misha:	Computer.
Lou:	Cell phone.
Dana:	Refrigerator.
Cerise:	My dog.
Ms. M:	Where would pioneers go now?
Curt:	North or south pole.
Tom:	Space.
Ms. M:	Imagine that your family isn't doing well, and so you decide to travel to a distant planet. It's very expensive to travel there. You can only take *one* item, so pick the one item you would bring. Assume there will be food and a place to sleep. Take five minutes to pick one item, and explain why you would take it.

Ms. Minichiello distributes index cards on which the students can write their responses. She gives them a few minutes to do so and then asks, "Who found that it was hard to pick just one item?" Almost all of the students raise their hands. "What I wanted you to realize is that if you were a child back then, it would be really hard to leave most of your things behind."

Are the students engaged in the lesson? What evidence do you see to indicate that they are learning?

What specific instructional strategies is Ms. Minichiello using to engage and motivate her students? What strategies is she using to help them understand the nature of travel in the mid-1800s?

OVERVIEW OF INSTRUCTIONAL STRATEGIES

The students in Ms. Minichiello's class are clearly engaged in the lesson (e.g., they are actively responding to her questions), and they have definitely learned some things (e.g., they notice differences between the supply list in their reading and the list they've generated themselves, and they can recall some of the difficulties the settlers faced). To engage and motivate her students, Ms. Minichiello uses several strategies identified in Chapters 11 and 12: She gets the students physically active (they move their desks and make a "wagon" on the floor), creates cognitive dissonance (the list in the reading materials doesn't entirely match the one the class has generated), poses a challenging question ("You can only take *one* item. . . ."), and makes the lesson a very social, interactive one. Furthermore, Ms. Minichiello promotes learning and understanding by encouraging visual imagery, meaningful learning, organization, and elaboration—for instance, by making the subject matter concrete and vivid (through the masking-tape wagon and the photographs), having the class consider cause-effect relationships that justify the supply list ("What were some of the things that pioneers had to be prepared for?"), and asking students to relate the settlers' situation to one they themselves might face.

In this chapter we'll explore a wide variety of instructional strategies. The first step any teacher must take, of course, is *planning*—deciding in advance both what needs to be accomplished and how best to accomplish it. We'll then look at three general categories of instructional methods: *expository approaches* (directly presenting the information to be learned), *hands-on and practice activities* (involving students actively in the subject matter, perhaps by having them discover a phenomenon for themselves, practice a new procedure, or apply a concept to a new situation), and *interactive and collaborative approaches* (having students discuss topics and in other ways help one another learn).

When students are actively involved in designing and carrying out classroom projects, they can develop important self-regulatory skills.

Keep in mind that the four sets of strategies just listed—planning, expository approaches, hands-on and practice activities, and interactive and collaborative approaches—can intermingle considerably. For instance, planning does not take place *only* before instruction begins; as teachers, we will continue to revise our plans (mentally, if not on paper) as a lesson or instructional unit proceeds (recall Figure 13.1). Expository approaches sometimes have a hands-on element (the Experiencing Firsthand exercises in this book are an example), often involve some teacher-student interaction, and may involve student-student interaction as well. And some hands-on activities are very collaborative in nature; for instance, students may work on challenging problems or authentic activities in small, cooperative groups. Furthermore, as teachers, we will frequently find that the best way to accomplish our instructional goals is to combine two or more strategies. For example, in the opening case study, Ms. Minichiello employs expository instruction (e.g., the reading materials) as well as a hands-on activity (e.g., the masking-tape wagon) and student interaction (e.g., the discussion of needed supplies).

We can subdivide instructional strategies in another way as well: teacher-directed or learner-directed.[2] In **teacher-directed instruction**, the teacher calls most of the shots, choosing what topics will be addressed, directing the course of the lesson, and so on; most forms of expository instruction fall into this category. In **learner-directed instruction**, students have considerable say in the issues they address and how to address them; most hands-on, interactive, and collaborative approaches fall into this category. Increasingly, educators are recognizing the value of learner-directed activities not only for fostering classroom learning and achievement but also for promoting the metacognitive and self-regulatory skills essential for lifelong success (e.g., De Lisi & Golbeck, 1999; Vye et al., 1998). But ultimately, we should choose teacher-directed or student-directed strategies based on our goals for instruction and on the knowledge and skills that our students bring to the situation.

■ The American Psychological Association's fourteen *Learner-Centered Psychological Principles* encompass many of the concepts and principles identified in Chapters 2–12. You can find these principles at APA's Web site at http://www.apa.org.

As you read the chapter, then, don't think about choosing a single "best" approach or two. Instead, think about how different strategies may be more or less suitable in different situations. Think, too, about how you might effectively use many or all of them over the course of the school year.

PLANNING FOR INSTRUCTION

Effective teaching begins long before students enter the classroom. Good teachers engage in considerable advance planning: They identify the knowledge and skills they want students to acquire, determine an appropriate sequence in which to teach such knowledge and skills, and develop classroom activities that will promote maximal learning and keep students continually motivated and on task. Ideally, teachers also coordinate their plans with one another—for example, by identifying common goals toward which they will all strive or by developing interdisciplinary units that involve two or more classes and subject areas.

■ **teacher-directed instruction**
Approach to instruction in which the teacher is largely in control of the course of the lesson.

■ **learner-directed instruction**
Approach to instruction in which students have considerable say in the issues they address and how to address them.

─────────────

[2] Some theorists instead use the terms *teacher-centered* and *learner-centered*. In my mind, these terms misrepresent the distinction. Virtually all instructional strategies focus (center) on the *student's* learning; the essential difference lies in who has control of the instructional activity.

Here we consider three aspects of instructional planning: identifying the goals of instruction, conducting a task analysis, and developing lesson plans.

Identifying the Goals of Instruction

An essential part of planning is identifying the specific things we want students to learn during a lesson or unit, as well as the things we want them to accomplish over the course of the semester or school year. Educators use a variety of terms for such **instructional goals**; for instance, they might talk about *objectives*, *outcomes*, *proficiencies*, *targets*, *benchmarks*, or *standards*. Here I'll typically use the term *instructional goals* when referring to general, long-term outcomes of instruction; I'll use the term **instructional objectives** when referring to more specific outcomes of a particular lesson or unit. Regardless of what term we use, however, the desired end results of instruction will—and *should*—influence what we teach, how we teach it, and how we assess students' learning and achievement. For example, if our objective for a unit on addition is *knowledge* of number facts, then we may want to use drill and practice (perhaps flash cards, perhaps game-like computer software) to enhance students' automaticity for these facts, and we may want to use a timed test to measure students' ability to recall them quickly and easily. But if our objective is *application* of number facts, then we may want to focus our instruction and assessment methods on word problems or on activities involving real objects and hands-on measurements.

Students, too, benefit from knowing the objectives of a lesson or unit. When they know what we hope they'll accomplish, they can make more informed decisions about how to focus their efforts and allocate their study time, and they can more effectively monitor their comprehension as they read and study (Gronlund, 2004; McAshan, 1979). For example, if we tell students that we expect them to "apply mathematics procedures to everyday situations," they will probably think about and study mathematics very differently than if we were to tell them to "know definitions by heart." In the "Civil War" clip on Video CD 2, the teacher tells students exactly what she hopes they will gain from the lesson; she also explains that the lesson will be only a first step toward gaining an understanding of the American Civil War:

> When this lesson is over, this is what I hope you will understand more about. The geography of the Civil War is our topic. I want you to understand better the meaning of these words, and you will. And I want you to have an understanding of the dynamics of the war—why it was fought, how it was fought, and why it ended the way it did. . . . I would like for you to have some good questions in your head that we don't answer today. This is like meeting somebody for the first time. You're going to meet the Civil War again in junior high and in high school and in college. So this is just a little introduction to the Civil War.

■ Hear a teacher describe instructional objectives in the "Civil War" clip on Video CD 2.

Aligning Instructional Goals with State and National Standards   In the United States many state governments and state departments of education—and some local school districts as well—have established comprehensive lists of content area **standards** that guide instruction and assessment from kindergarten or first grade through high school.[3] Such standards identify specific goals for different grade levels in reading, writing, mathematics, science, social studies, and sometimes also in such domains as art, music, foreign languages, and physical education. As an illustration, the middle column of Table 13.1 presents examples of California's state standards for reading comprehension at grades 1, 4, 7, and 11–12. In the rightmost column I present examples of teaching strategies that might address one or more of those standards. We'll revisit California's standards again in Chapter 15, when we consider how we might assess students' achievement relative to these standards.

An additional source of guidance comes from national (and in some cases international) standards created by professional organizations that represent various academic disciplines. Such standards typically reflect the combined thinking of many experts in a discipline and so almost certainly reflect much of the best of what the discipline has to offer. Examples are presented in Table 13.2.

As we'll discover in Chapter 16, the use of standards to evaluate student achievement, especially in *high-stakes tests*, is somewhat controversial. Furthermore, no data exist to indicate

■ **instructional goal** Desired long-term outcome of instruction.

■ **instructional objective** Desired outcome of a lesson or unit.

■ **standards** General statements regarding the knowledge and skills that students should gain and the characteristics that their accomplishments should reflect.

---

[3] As I write the fifth edition of this book, the Web site *Developing Educational Standards* provides links to standards in all fifty states and the District of Columbia. You can find this site at http://edstandards.org/Standards.html.

TABLE 13.1   DEVELOPMENTAL TRENDS

Examples of California State Standards for Reading Comprehension at Different Grade Levels

GRADE LEVEL	EXAMPLES OF GRADE-SPECIFIC STANDARDS	EXAMPLES OF STRATEGIES THAT ADDRESS ONE OR MORE STANDARDS
Grade 1	• Respond to who, what, when, where, and how questions. • Use context to resolve ambiguities about word and sentence meanings. • Relate prior knowledge to textual information. • Retell the central ideas of simple expository or narrative passages.	• Read high-interest stories, stopping frequently to ask questions that require students to go beyond the text itself; for instance, ask them to speculate about what a character might be feeling or to predict the consequences of a character's actions. • As students in a reading group read a story, occasionally ask them to summarize what has happened so far.
Grade 4	• Use appropriate strategies when reading for different purposes (e.g., full comprehension, location of information, personal enjoyment). • Make and confirm predictions about text by using prior knowledge and ideas presented in the text itself, including illustrations, titles, topic sentences, important words, and foreshadowing clues. • Evaluate new information and hypotheses by testing them against known information and ideas. • Distinguish between cause and effect and between fact and opinion in expository text.	• As students seek information in the school library, describe effective strategies for locating needed information in reference books. • As a reading group discusses an age-appropriate novel, ask students to speculate about how the plot might progress and to identify clues in the text that support their predictions. • As students read a passage in a history book, have them identify cause-effect relationships (stated or implied) among events.
Grade 7	• Understand and analyze the differences in structure and purpose between various categories of informational materials (e.g., textbooks, newspapers, instructional materials, signs). • Identify and trace the development of an author's argument, point of view, or perspective in text. • Understand and explain the use of a simple mechanical device by following technical directions. • Assess the adequacy, accuracy, and appropriateness of the author's evidence to support claims and assertions, noting instances of bias and stereotyping.	• Have students identify ways in which they might use the headings and organizational structure of a textbook to help them organize and study its content. • Present examples of persuasive essays, and ask students to identify the main idea and supporting arguments. • After demonstrating how to use a microscope and prepare slides of water taken from a local frog pond, have students repeat the process by following a set of written instructions.
Grades 11–12	• Analyze the way in which clarity of meaning is affected by the patterns of organization, hierarchical structures, repetition of the main ideas, syntax, and word choice in the text. • Verify and clarify facts presented in other types of expository texts by using a variety of consumer, workplace, and public documents. • Analyze an author's implicit and explicit philosophical assumptions and beliefs about a subject. • Critique the power, validity, and truthfulness of arguments set forth in public documents; their appeal to both friendly and hostile audiences; and the text to which the arguments anticipate and address reader concerns and counterclaims (e.g., appeal to reason, to authority, to pathos and emotion).	• When studying poetry, have students find words and phrases with multiple possible meanings; ask them to consider how the poetic meter affects the mood a poem conveys. • Ask students to identify the unstated assumptions (e.g., that one group is "good" or "right" and another is "bad" or "wrong") underlying a history textbook's depiction of events. • Have students read several editorials on the same issue and evaluate the effectiveness of each author's persuasive strategies.

Source: Standards (middle column) are from a Web site maintained by California State University Northridge: *California Academic Content Standards Site: English and Language Arts* (n.d.). Retrieved February 18, 2004, from http://www.csun.edu/~hcbio027/k12standards/standards/ela.html

that the explicit use of standards actually improves students' overall achievement or enhances their later performance in the workforce (Amrein & Berliner, 2002b, 2002c; Levin, 1998; Wolf, 1998). An additional problem is that teachers, parents, taxpayers, and even experts often disagree on the specific goals that students at various grade levels should achieve. For example, some constituencies ask us to increase students' factual knowledge—a perspective sometimes referred to as "back to the basics" or "cultural literacy" (e.g., Hirsch, 1996). Others, meanwhile, encourage us to foster higher-level thinking skills such as problem solving and critical thinking and to help students develop the "habits of mind" (e.g., scientific reasoning, drawing inferences

TABLE 13.2

Web Sites with Standards for Various Academic Disciplines

CONTENT DOMAIN	ORGANIZATION	INTERNET ADDRESS	ONCE YOU GET THERE . . . [a]
Civics and government	Center for Civic Education	http://www.civiced.org	Go to *Curricular Materials*.
English and language arts	National Council of Teachers of English	http://www.ncte.org	Select *Standards* from the *Quick Links* menu.
Foreign language	American Council on the Teaching of Foreign Languages	http://www.actfl.org	Go to *Publications*.
Geography	National Council for Geographic Education	http://www.ncge.org	Select *National Geography Standards* from the *Jump to page* menu.
Health, physical education, and dance	National Association for Sport and Physical Education	http://www.aahperd.org/NASPE	Select *Standards* from the *Professional Development* menu.
History	National Center for History in the Schools	http://www.sscnet.ucla.edu/nchs	Click on *Standards*.
Information literacy	American Association of School Librarians	http://www.ala.org/aasl	Type "information literacy standards" in the *Search* box.
Mathematics	National Council of Teachers of Mathematics	http://www.nctm.org	Click on *NCTM Standards*.
Music	National Association for Music Education	http://www.menc.org	Select *Music Standards* from the *Resources* menu.
Science	National Academy of Sciences	http://www.nap.edu	Type "science, education, standards" in the *Find* box.
Visual arts	National Art Education Association	http://www.getty.edu/artsednet/ resources/Scope/Standards/index.html[b]	

[a]These steps worked for me when this book was in production in August 2004. Given the dynamic nature of many Web sites, you may find that you have to do something different when you get to the site in question.
[b]The NAEA site does not list the standards; however, you can find them here.

from historical documents) central to various academic disciplines (P. A. Alexander, 1997; Berliner, 1997; L. S. Shulman & Quinlan, 1996).

Existing standards are certainly useful in helping us focus our instruction on important educational goals—including problem solving, critical thinking, and other higher-level processes—in various content domains. If we rely on content area standards exclusively, however, we are apt to neglect other, equally important goals, such as helping students acquire effective learning strategies, self-regulation techniques, and social skills. In addition to any existing standards we may use, then, we will also want to formulate some of our *own* goals and objectives. We look at some strategies for doing so now.

Formulating Useful Goals and Objectives

Experiencing FIRSTHAND · Being a Good Citizen

Consider this instructional goal:

Students will learn and practice principles of good citizenship.

Write down at least three implications of this statement for your own classroom practices.

· · · · · · ·

Certainly good citizenship is a goal toward which all students should strive. But did you find yourself having trouble translating the statement into specific things you might do in the classroom? Did you also find yourself struggling with what the term *good citizenship* means (honesty? empathy? involvement in school activities? all of the above?)? The "good citizenship" goal is nothing more than *word magic*: It looks great at first glance but really doesn't give us specific information about what we want students to achieve (Dyer, 1967).

Ideally, we should identify goals and objectives that can give us concrete guidance as we plan instructional activities and assessment procedures. Following are several strategies for developing useful ones:

◎ *Include goals at varying degrees of complexity and sophistication.* Notice how the standards presented in Table 13.1 focus largely on higher-level skills, such as identifying main ideas, making predictions, and evaluating information. Even as we identify more specific objectives for a lesson or unit, we typically won't want to limit them to simple learning of facts. One tool that can help us broaden our view of what students should learn and be able to do is a recent revision of **Bloom's taxonomy**, a list of six general cognitive processes that vary from simple to complex:

1. *Remember:* Recognizing or recalling information learned at an earlier time and stored in long-term memory
2. *Understand:* Constructing meaning from instructional materials and messages (e.g., drawing inferences, identifying new examples, summarizing)
3. *Apply:* Using knowledge in a familiar or new situation
4. *Analyze:* Breaking information into its constituent parts, and perhaps identifying interrelationships among the parts
5. *Evaluate:* Making judgments about information using certain criteria or standards
6. *Create:* Putting together knowledge, procedures, or both to form a coherent, structured, and possibly original whole
   (L. W. Anderson et al., 2001)

This list is hardly an exhaustive list of what students should be able to do while learning classroom subject matter—for instance, it doesn't include psychomotor skills, attitudes, or general dispositions—but it can certainly remind us that there is much more to school learning and academic achievement than learning and recalling facts.

◎ *Focus on what students should do, not on what teachers should do.* Consider these objectives for a unit on soccer:

- Describe the rules of the game.
- Show students how to kick, dribble, and pass the ball.

The problem with these statements is that they tell us only what the teacher will do during instruction; they tell us nothing about what students should be able to do as a result. Useful goals and objectives focus on what students will do rather than on what the teacher will do (Gronlund, 2004). With this point in mind, let's consider some alternative objectives for our soccer unit:

- Students will describe the basic rules of the game and identify the procedures to be followed in various situations (e.g., when a player touches the ball with an arm or hand, when the ball goes out of bounds).
- Students will demonstrate effective ways of kicking, dribbling, and passing the ball.

Here we have refocused our objectives on student accomplishments; in other words, we have described the knowledge and skills we want students to acquire during their unit on soccer.

◎ *Describe the ultimate outcomes of instruction.* Consider these goals for a French class:

- Students will practice pronouncing French words.
- Students will learn how to conjugate French verbs.

These goals describe what students will do during French class; in other words, they describe learning *processes*. Yet goals and objectives are usually more helpful when they tell us what students should be able to do *at the end* of instruction (Gronlund, 2004). Accordingly, we might revise our French class goals as follows:

- Students will pronounce French words correctly.
- Students will correctly conjugate common French verbs in the present and past tenses.

■ You can find additional taxonomies, including Bloom's original taxonomy and an expanded version of the revision shown here, in the supplementary reading "Using Taxonomies to Formulate Instructional Goals and Objectives" in the *Study Guide and Reader.*

We will usually want to include higher-level skills, such as application and analysis, among our instructional objectives.

■ **Bloom's taxonomy** Taxonomy of six cognitive processes, varying in complexity, that lessons might be designed to foster.

In past years many behaviorists recommended that we describe desired objectives using specific, observable behaviors (e.g., *recite*, *define*, *perform*); essentially, they were suggesting that we apply the concept of *terminal behavior* (see Chapter 9) when we develop objectives. Such objectives can often be quite helpful for a single unit or lesson; for instance, the objectives for a soccer unit presented earlier are fairly specific and might help us keep our focus. But particularly when we look at what we want to accomplish over a lengthy time period—perhaps a month, a semester, or the school year—too much emphasis on specific behaviors can lead to very long lists of relatively trivial outcomes (R. L. Linn & Miller 2005; Newmann, 1997; Popham, 1995).

Ultimately, we must adjust our level of specificity to the time frame in question. If we are developing general goals to guide us over the long run, we may want to omit reference to specific knowledge or skills. One workable approach is to describe a few general and relatively abstract goals (perhaps three to ten items) and then list examples of behaviors that reflect each one (Gronlund, 2004). Following is an example:

> [The student] prepares a plan for an experiment:
> • Identifies the problem to be solved.
> • Formulates questions relevant to the problem.
> • Formulates hypotheses in appropriate verbal or mathematical form.
> • Describes controls for variables.
> • Formulates experimental procedures.
> • Formulates observation and measurement procedures.
> • Describes the methods of data analysis.
> • Describes how the results will be presented. (goal and examples from Gronlund, 2004, p. 68)

Obviously, not all aspects of planning an experiment are identified, but the examples listed give both us and our students a good idea of the kinds of behaviors that reflect achievement of this goal.

◎ *Identify both short-term and long-term goals.* Ideally, our instructional goals should include both *short-term goals*—those that can be accomplished within a limited period of time (perhaps within a single lesson or unit, and certainly within a single school year)—and *long-term goals*—those that require years of instruction and practice before they are achieved (Brophy & Alleman, 1991; N. S. Cole, 1990; Gronlund, 2000). When we want students to use effective learning strategies as they study, read critically rather than take everything at face value, and apply scientific methods as they try to understand and explain the world around them, we are setting long-term goals.

Some short-term objectives and goals are "minimum essentials": Students *must* accomplish them before proceeding to the next unit, course, or grade level (Gronlund, 2000). For example, elementary school students can more easily master multiplication if they already know how to add, and high school students must know the symbols for the chemical elements before they learn how to symbolize chemical reactions. In contrast, many long-term goals can be thought of as "developmental" in nature: They include skills and abilities that continue to evolve and improve throughout the school years and perhaps into adulthood as well (Gronlund, 2000). Yet even when long-term goals cannot be completely accomplished within the course of students' formal education, they are often among the most important ones for us to set for students and must therefore have a prominent place in our list of goals.

◎ *Provide opportunities for students to identify their own goals and objectives.* For example, different students might choose different gymnastic skills to master, different art media to use, or different historical events to study in depth. By allowing students to identify some of their own goals and objectives, we are encouraging the *goal setting* that, from the perspective of social cognitive theory, is an important aspect of self-regulation. We are also fostering the sense of *self-determination* that many theorists believe is so critical for intrinsic motivation.

How do we break down a large instructional task—for example, a course in government, a unit on basketball, or a driver education class—into specific goals? Several procedures known collectively as *task analysis* can help us analyze the components of a complex topic or skill.

Conducting a Task Analysis

Consider these five teachers:

• Ms. Begay plans to teach her third graders how to solve arithmetic word problems. She also wants to help them learn more effectively from the things they read.

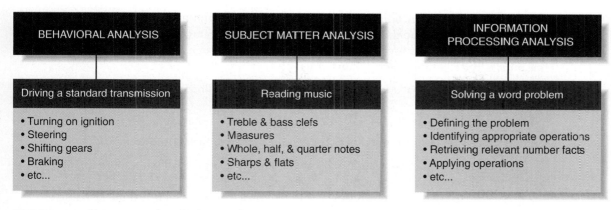

FIGURE 13.2 Three ways of analyzing a task

- Mr. Marzano, a middle school physical education teacher, is beginning a unit on basketball. He wants his students to develop enough proficiency in the sport to feel comfortable playing both on organized school basketball teams and in less formal games with friends and neighbors.
- Ms. Flores, an eighth-grade social studies teacher, is going to introduce the intricacies of the federal judicial system to her classes.
- Mr. Wu, a junior high school music teacher, needs to teach his new trumpet students how to play a recognizable version of "Seventy-Six Trombones" in time for the New Year's Day parade.
- Mr. McKenzie must teach the students in his high school driver education class how to drive a car safely on city streets.

These teachers have something in common: They want to teach complex topics or skills. All five should probably conduct a **task analysis**: They should identify the specific knowledge and behaviors necessary to master the subject matter in question. Such a task analysis can then guide them as they select the most appropriate methods and sequence in which to teach that subject matter.

Figure 13.2 illustrates three general approaches to task analysis (Jonassen, Hannum, & Tessmer, 1989):

◎ *Behavioral analysis.* One way of analyzing a complex task is to identify the specific behaviors required to perform it (much as a behaviorist might do). For example, Mr. Marzano can identify the specific physical movements involved in dribbling, passing, and shooting a basketball. Mr. McKenzie can identify the actions required in driving an automobile with a standard transmission: turning on the ignition, steering, accelerating, stepping on the clutch, shifting gears, releasing the clutch, and braking. And Mr. Wu can identify the behaviors that students must master to play a trumpet successfully: holding the instrument with the fingers placed appropriately on the valves, blowing correctly into the mouthpiece, and so on.

◎ *Subject matter analysis.* Another approach is to break down the subject matter into the specific topics, concepts, and principles that it includes. For example, Ms. Flores can identify various aspects of the judicial system (concepts such as "innocent until proven guilty" and "reasonable doubt," the roles that judges and juries play, etc.) and their interrelationships. Mr. Wu, who needs to teach his new trumpet students how to read music as well as how to play the instrument, can identify the basic elements of written music that students must know to interpret written music: the difference between the treble and bass clefs, the number of beats associated with different kinds of notes, and so on.

Subject matter analysis is especially important when the subject matter being taught includes many interrelated ideas and concepts. From the perspective of cognitive psychology, we can help students learn class material more meaningfully, organize it better in their long-term memories, and remember it more effectively if we teach them the interconnections among various ideas and concepts along with the ideas and concepts themselves.

◎ *Information processing analysis.* A third approach, using a cognitive perspective once again, is to specify the cognitive processes involved in a task. To illustrate, Ms. Begay can identify the mental processes involved in successfully solving an arithmetic word problem, such as

■ **task analysis** Process of identifying the specific knowledge, behaviors, or cognitive processes necessary to master a particular subject area or skill.

correct classification (encoding) of the problem (e.g., determining whether it requires addition, subtraction, etc.) and rapid retrieval of basic number facts. Similarly, she can identify some specific cognitive strategies useful in reading comprehension, such as finding main ideas, learning meaningfully, elaborating, and summarizing.

To get a taste of what a task analysis involves, try the following exercise.

Experiencing FIRSTHAND · · · · · · · · · · · · · · · · · · · Making a Peanut Butter Sandwich

Conduct a task analysis for the process of making a peanut butter sandwich:

1. Decide whether your approach should be a behavioral analysis, a subject matter analysis, or an information processing analysis.
2. Now, using the approach you've selected, break the sandwich-making task into a number of small, "teachable" steps.

· · · · · · ·

Chances are, you chose a behavioral analysis. Making a peanut butter sandwich is largely a behavioral rather than mental task; for instance, you must know how to unscrew the peanut butter jar lid, get an appropriate amount of peanut butter on your knife, spread the peanut butter gently enough that you don't tear the bread, and so on.

Conducting task analyses for complex skills and topics has at least two advantages (Desberg & Taylor, 1986; Jonassen et al., 1989). First, when we identify a task's specific components—whether those components are behaviors, concepts and ideas, or cognitive processes—we have a better sense of what things students need to learn and the order in which they can most effectively learn them. For example, Mr. McKenzie must teach his driver education students how to control the clutch before he can teach them how to shift gears, and Mr. Wu must teach his trumpet students how to blow into the mouthpiece before he can teach them how to play different notes. In the process, we may find that certain skills or topics we thought were important are actually *not* important. For example, a science teacher may realize that learning the history of science, though possibly having value in its own right, has little to do with how well students can apply scientific principles.

A second advantage in conducting a task analysis is that it helps us choose appropriate instructional strategies. Different tasks—and perhaps even different components of a single task—may require different approaches to instruction. For example, if one necessary component of solving arithmetic word problems is the rapid retrieval of math facts from memory, then repeated practice of these facts may be critical for developing automaticity. If another component of solving these problems is identifying the appropriate operation to apply in various situations, then promoting a true understanding of mathematical concepts and principles (perhaps by using concrete manipulatives or authentic activities) is essential.

A task analysis of a topic or skill can help us identify the specific things we should teach and appropriate strategies for teaching them.

Sometimes a task analysis will lead us to conclude that we can most effectively teach a complex task by teaching some or all of its components separately from one another. For instance, Mr. Wu may ask his beginning trumpet students to practice blowing into the mouthpiece correctly without worrying about the specific notes they produce. On other occasions, however, it may be more appropriate to teach the desired knowledge and behaviors entirely within the context of the overall task; by doing so, we make the subject matter more meaningful for students. For instance, Ms. Begay should almost certainly teach her students the processes involved in learning effectively from reading materials—elaborating, summarizing, and so on—primarily within the context of authentic reading tasks.

Developing a Lesson Plan

Once they have identified their goals for instruction, and perhaps conducted a task analysis as well, effective teachers develop a lesson plan to guide them during instruction. A lesson plan typically includes the following:

- The goal(s) or objective(s) of the lesson
- Instructional strategies and the sequence in which they'll be used
- Instructional materials (e.g., textbooks, handouts) and equipment required
- Assessment method(s) planned

Any lesson plan should, of course, take into account the students who will be learning—their developmental levels, prior knowledge, cultural backgrounds, and so on.

As a beginning teacher, you will probably want to develop fairly detailed lesson plans that describe how you are going to help your students learn the subject matter in question (Calderhead, 1996; Sternberg & Horvath, 1995). For instance, when I began teaching middle school geography, I spent many hours each week writing down the information, examples, questions, and student activities I wanted to use during the following week (one of my early lessons appears in the *Study Guide and Reader* that accompanies this book). But as you gain experience teaching certain topics, you will learn which strategies work effectively and which do not, and you may use some of the effective ones frequently enough that you can retrieve them quickly and easily from long-term memory. As time goes on, you will find that planning lessons becomes far less time-consuming and that you can do a lot of your planning in your head rather than on paper (Calderhead, 1996).

We should think of lesson plans more as guides than as recipes—in other words, as a general plan of attack that we can and should adjust as events unfold (Calderhead, 1996). For instance, during the course of a lesson, we may find that students have less prior knowledge than we realized, and so we may need to "back up" and teach material we thought they had already mastered. Or, if students express curiosity or have intriguing insights about a particular topic, we may want to spend more time exploring the topic than we had originally intended.

As we proceed through the school year, our long-range plans will also change somewhat. For instance, we may find that our task analyses of desired knowledge and skills were overly simplistic. Or we may discover that the expectations we have for students' achievement, as reflected in the instructional goals we've identified, are either unrealistically high or unnecessarily low. We must continually revise our plans as instruction proceeds and as classroom assessments reveal how well our students are learning and achieving.

In planning our lessons, we must, of course, choose instructional strategies that are suitable for our goals and objectives. As we examine various strategies in the pages that follow, we will identify the circumstances in which each one might be most appropriate and effective.

EXPOSITORY APPROACHES

Without a doubt, the most widely used approach to teaching is **expository instruction**: Information is presented (*exposed*) in essentially the same form that students are expected to learn it. Ms. Minichiello's lesson on the Oregon Trail has elements of expository instruction: She gives her students reading materials about how the settlers packed for the long trip west, and she shows photographs depicting the inside of a typical covered wagon. Some forms of expository instruction are largely "one-way" in nature, in that information goes primarily from teacher to student; textbooks are the best example of such one-way communication. Other forms are more interactive, in that they incorporate an exchange of information between teacher (or perhaps a "virtual" teacher, such as a computer) and student. In this section we consider several expository instructional formats and methods: lectures and textbooks, mastery learning, direct instruction, computer-based instruction, and online research.[4]

■ Educational videos and field trips are two additional forms of expository instruction. What particular benefits might these forms of instruction have?

Lectures and Textbooks

Some theorists have criticized lectures and textbooks for putting students in a passive role. From a behaviorist perspective, students learn only when they are actively making responses (and perhaps getting reinforced for those responses), and students make very few observable responses when they sit quietly listening to a lecture or reading a textbook (Skinner, 1968). However, many cognitivists argue that students are often *mentally* active during such seemingly passive activities (Ausubel et al., 1978; Mayer, 2004; Weinert & Helmke, 1995). From the perspective of cognitive psychology, the degree to which students learn from expository instruction depends on how they process information—that is, on the particular cognitive

■ **expository instruction** Approach to instruction in which information is presented in more or less the same form in which students are expected to learn it.

---

[4] Many theorists use the term *expository instruction* only in reference to lectures and textbooks. I am using the term more broadly to refer to any approach that centers around the *transmission* of information from expert (e.g., classroom teacher, textbook writer, computer software designer) to student.

TABLE 13.3   PRINCIPLES/ASSUMPTIONS

Principles of Expository Instruction

PRINCIPLE	EDUCATIONAL IMPLICATION	EXAMPLE
An **advance organizer**—a verbal or graphic introduction that lays out the general organizational framework of the material—helps students organize and interrelate the things they learn.	Introduce a new unit by describing the major ideas and concepts to be discussed and showing how they are interrelated.	Introduce a unit on vertebrates by saying something like this: "Vertebrates all have backbones. We will be talking about five phyla of vertebrates—mammals, birds, reptiles, amphibians, and fish—that differ from one another in several ways, including whether their members are warm-blooded or cold-blooded; whether they have hair, scales, or feathers; and whether they lay eggs or bear live young."
Connections to prior knowlege help students learn classroom material more meaningfully, provided that their prior "knowledge" is accurate. (See the discussion of *prior knowledge activation* in Chapter 6.)	Remind students of something they already know—that is, activate students' prior knowledge—and point out how a new idea is related.	Draw an analogy between *peristalsis* (muscular contractions that push food through the digestive tract) and the process of squeezing ketchup from a packet: "You squeeze the packet near one corner and run your fingers along the length of the packet toward an opening at the other corner. When you do this, you push the ketchup through the packet, in one direction, ahead of your fingers, until it comes out of the opening" (Newby, Ertmer, & Stepich, 1994, p. 4).
An **organized presentation** of material helps students make appropriate interconnections among ideas.	Help students organize material in a particular way by presenting the information using that same organizational structure.	Use a *concept map* to depict the main concepts and ideas of a topic and their interrelationships (see the section "Organizing Information" on p. 261 in Chapter 8.)
Various **signals** built into a presentation (e.g., italicized print, interspersed questions) can draw students' attention to important points.	Stress important points—for instance, by writing them on the chalkboard, asking questions about them, or simply telling students what things are most important to learn.	When assigning a textbook chapter for homework, identify several questions that students should try to answer as they read the chapter.
Visual aids help students encode material visually as well as verbally.	Illustrate new material through pictures, photographs, diagrams, maps, physical models, and demonstrations.	When describing major battles of the American Civil War, present a map illustrating where each battle took place and point out that some battles were fought in especially strategic locations.
Appropriate **pacing** gives students adequate time to process information.	Pace a presentation slowly enough that students can engage in meaningful learning, elaboration, and other effective storage processes.	Intersperse lengthy explanations with demonstrations or hands-on activities that illustrate some of the principles you are describing.
Summaries help students review and organize material and identify main ideas.	After a lecture or reading assignment, summarize the key points of the lesson.	At the end of a unit on Emily Dickinson, summarize her work by describing the characteristics that made her poetry so unique and influential.

Sources: Ausubel et al., 1978; Bulgren, Deshler, Schumaker, & Lenz, 2000; Carney & Levin, 2002; Corkill, 1992; Dansereau, 1995; Donnelly & McDaniel, 1993; E. L. Ferguson & Hegarty, 1995; Hall & O'Donnell, 1994; Hansen & Pearson, 1983; Hartley & Trueman, 1982; Krajcik, 1991; J. R. Levin & Mayer, 1993; M. C. Linn et al., 1996; R. F. Lorch, Lorch, & Inman, 1993; Mayer, 1989; Mayer & Gallini, 1990; M. A. McDaniel & Einstein, 1989; Newby, Ertmer, & Stepich, 1994; Pittman & Beth-Halachmy, 1997; R. E. Reynolds & Shirey, 1988; Sadoski & Paivio, 2001; Scevak, Moore, & Kirby, 1993; M. Y. Small, Lovett, & Scher, 1993; Tennyson & Cocchiarella, 1986; Verdi & Kulhavy, 2002; Wade, 1992; P. T. Wilson & Anderson, 1986; Winn, 1991; Zook, 1991; Zook & Di Vesta, 1991.

responses they make. The more students pay attention, and the more they engage in meaningful learning, organization, elaboration, and so on, the more they will benefit from the lectures they hear and the textbooks they read.

Unfortunately, lectures and textbooks don't always present information in ways that promote learning. For instance, you can undoubtedly think of high school or college instructors whose lectures were dry, disorganized, confusing, or in some other way *non*motivating and *non*informative. And analyses of school textbooks in such diverse disciplines as history, geography, and science have found that the focus of most texts is on teaching specific facts, with little attention to helping students learn the facts in a meaningful way (Alleman & Brophy, 1992; Beck & McKeown, 1994; Chambliss, Calfee, & Wong, 1990).

■ **advance organizer** Introduction to a lesson that provides an overall organizational scheme for the lesson.

What specific techniques can we use to help students learn from classroom lectures and reading assignments? The following exercise might give you a few ideas about techniques that work for *you* as a student.

Experiencing FIRSTHAND · Finding Pedagogy in the Book

1. Look back at two or three of the chapters you've already read in this book. Find several places where specific things that I've done have helped you learn and remember the material more effectively. What specific techniques did I use to facilitate your cognitive processing?

2. In those same chapters, can you find places where you had difficulty processing the material presented? What might I have done differently in such instances?

· · · · · · ·

I'm hoping that the Experiencing Firsthand exercises and some of the questions in the margins have helped you relate new topics to your own knowledge and experiences. Perhaps some of the graphics, tables, and summaries have helped you organize concepts and principles. Perhaps the Interpreting Student Artifacts and Behaviors features and the Analyzing Teacher Strategies features have encouraged you to elaborate on and apply what you were reading. If you've found certain parts of the books particularly troublesome, I encourage you to let me know.[5]

Researchers have identified several factors that improve the effectiveness of expository instruction. Table 13.3 presents these factors as general principles we should keep in mind whenever we need to present information in a largely "one-way" fashion. You can see most of these principles in action in the "Civil War" clip (a fifth-grade class) and "Charles's Law" clip (a high school class) on Video CD 2. (Notice how much more abstract the Charles's law lecture is, consistent with high school students' greater capacity for abstract thought.) After looking at the table and videos, apply what you've learned in the discussion thus far in the following exercise.

■ Observe effective lectures in the "Civil War" and "Charles's Law" clips on Video CD 2.

Interpreting Student Artifacts and Behaviors

Apartheid

A middle school social studies class has just completed two reading assignments about segregation practices in South Africa and the United States during the latter half of the twentieth century. To help students compare events in the two countries during this time period, the teacher distributes a handout with two vertical timelines and asks students to use it to list significant events in each country related to segregation and civil rights. By completing the activity, he hopes, students will be better able to see similarities and differences in events in the two nations.

Martina's timelines appear to the right. As you look at the artifact, think about

■ How effectively Martina uses the timelines to organize what she's learning
■ What cognitive process(es) the activity facilitates
■ What cognitive process(es) the activity does *not* necessarily facilitate

As far as we know, Martina lists all the major events her social studies lesson has included. She appropriately lists events in South Africa on one timeline and events in the United States on the other, and she puts the events in chronological order. However, she misses one essential point of the activity: to align the two "histories" so that she can see what was happening in the two countries *at the same time*. Martina starts off well—she puts 1948 events side by side at the tops of the two lines—but then uses more vertical space to depict a 38-year time span in South

---

[5] I'm always eager to hear my readers' suggestions for improving the book (e-mail address: jormrod@alumni. brown.edu).

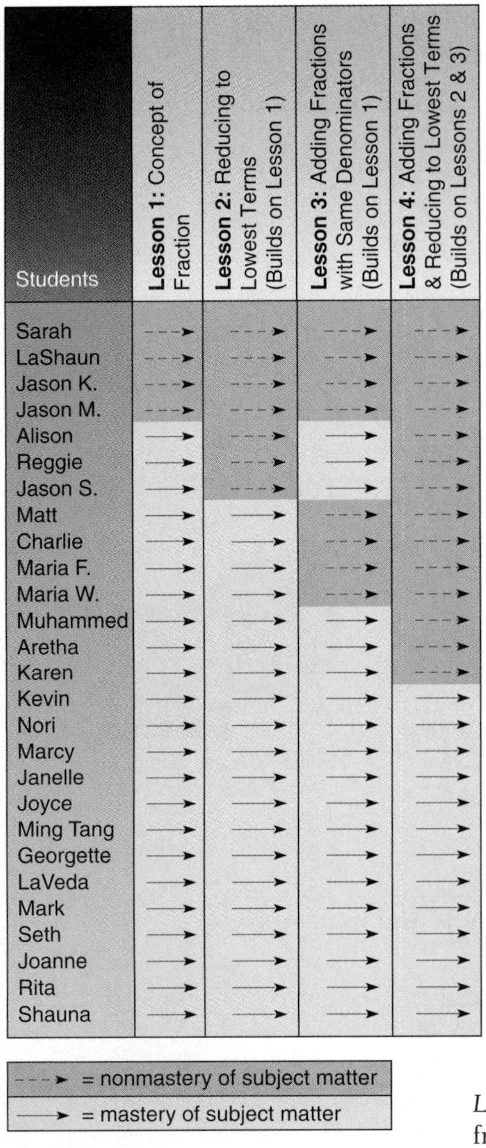

Students	Lesson 1: Concept of Fraction	Lesson 2: Reducing to Lowest Terms (Builds on Lesson 1)	Lesson 3: Adding Fractions with Same Denominators (Builds on Lesson 1)	Lesson 4: Adding Fractions & Reducing to Lowest Terms (Builds on Lessons 2 & 3)
Sarah	- - →	- - →	- - →	- - →
LaShaun	- - →	- - →	- - →	- - →
Jason K.	- - →	- - →	- - →	- - →
Jason M.	- - →	- - →	- - →	- - →
Alison	──→	- - →	──→	- - →
Reggie	──→	- - →	──→	- - →
Jason S.	──→	- - →	──→	- - →
Matt	──→	──→	- - →	- - →
Charlie	──→	──→	- - →	- - →
Maria F.	──→	──→	- - →	- - →
Maria W.	──→	──→	- - →	- - →
Muhammed	──→	──→	──→	- - →
Aretha	──→	──→	──→	- - →
Karen	──→	──→	──→	- - →
Kevin	──→	──→	──→	──→
Nori	──→	──→	──→	──→
Marcy	──→	──→	──→	──→
Janelle	──→	──→	──→	──→
Joyce	──→	──→	──→	──→
Ming Tang	──→	──→	──→	──→
Georgette	──→	──→	──→	──→
LaVeda	──→	──→	──→	──→
Mark	──→	──→	──→	──→
Seth	──→	──→	──→	──→
Joanne	──→	──→	──→	──→
Rita	──→	──→	──→	──→
Shauna	──→	──→	──→	──→

- - → = nonmastery of subject matter
──→ = mastery of subject matter

FIGURE 13.3 Sequential and hierarchical nature of mastery learning

Africa than to depict a 43-year time span in America. Thus, it appears as if "Bush lifts sactions [sanctions]" (1991) occurred at about the same time as "police found blamless [blameless]" (1977).

If completed appropriately, the timeline activity can help students organize events in the two countries in chronological order; it may also promote visual imagery by making verbal information more graphic. The activity does little more than these things, however. To promote maximal understanding of apartheid in South Africa, the civil rights movement in the United States, and their possible parallels and interrelationships—that is, to promote meaningful learning and elaboration about the events, as well as greater organization and visual imagery—the teacher might supplement the activity with verbal explanations of why certain events were critical, old magazine articles and newspaper editorials about injustices in the two countries, videotapes of Nelson Mandela and Martin Luther King, Jr., and so on.

Lectures, textbooks, and other one-way forms of instruction have a distinct advantage: They enable us to present information quickly and efficiently. A major *disadvantage* is that, by themselves, they do not allow us to assess students' progress in learning the subject matter. When we need to make sure that students master information and skills that are prerequisites for later lessons, mastery learning may be a better approach.

Mastery Learning

Imagine that a class of 27 students, listed in Figure 13.3, is beginning a unit on fractions. The class progresses through several lessons as follows:

Lesson 1: The class studies the basic idea that a fraction represents parts of a whole: The denominator indicates the number of pieces into which the whole has been divided, and the numerator indicates how many of those pieces are present. By the end of the lesson, 23 children understand what a fraction is. But Sarah, LaShaun, Jason K., and Jason M. are either partly or totally confused.

Lesson 2: The class studies the process of reducing fractions to lowest terms (e.g., ²⁄₄ can be reduced to ½, ¹²⁄₂₀ can be reduced to ⅗). By the end of the lesson, 20 children understand this process. But Alison, Reggie, and Jason S. haven't mastered the idea that they need to divide both the numerator and denominator by the same number. Sarah, LaShaun, and the other two Jasons still don't understand what fractions *are* and so have trouble with this lesson as well.

Lesson 3: The class studies the process of adding two fractions, for now looking only at fractions with equal denominators (e.g., ⅖ + ⅖ = ⅘, ¹⁄₂₀ + ¹¹⁄₂₀ = ¹²⁄₂₀). By the end of the lesson, 19 children can add fractions with the same denominator. Matt, Charlie, Maria F., and Maria W. keep adding the denominators together as well as the numerators (e.g., figuring that ⅖ + ⅖ = ⁴⁄₁₀). And Sarah, LaShaun, Jason K., and Jason M. still don't know what fractions actually are.

Lesson 4: The class combines the processes of adding fractions and reducing fractions to lowest terms. They must first add two fractions together and then, if necessary, reduce the sum to its lowest terms (e.g., after adding ¹⁄₂₀ + ¹¹⁄₂₀, they must reduce the sum of ¹²⁄₂₀ to ⅗). Here we lose Muhammed, Aretha, and Karen because they keep forgetting to reduce the sum to lowest terms. And of course, we've already lost Sarah, LaShaun, Alison, Reggie, Matt, Charlie, the two Marias, and the three Jasons on prerequisite skills. *We now have 13 of our original 27 students understanding what they are doing—less than half the class!* (See Figure 13.3.)

When we move through lessons without making sure that all students master the content of each one, we may lose more and more students as we go along, especially if early lessons provide the foundation for later ones. **Mastery learning**, in which students demonstrate mastery of one topic before proceeding to the next, minimizes the likelihood that we leave students in the dust as we proceed to increasingly challenging material (e.g., B. S. Bloom, 1981; Guskey, 1985; Hunter, 1982; J. F. Lee & Pruitt, 1984). This approach is based on three underlying assumptions:

- Almost every student can learn a particular topic to mastery.
- Some students need more time to master a topic than others.
- Some students need more assistance than others.

■ **mastery learning** Approach to instruction in which students learn one topic thoroughly before moving to a subsequent one.

As you can see, mastery learning represents a very optimistic approach to instruction: It assumes that most children *can* learn school subject matter if they are given sufficient time and instruction to do so.

Mastery learning usually includes the following components:

1. *Small, discrete units.* The subject matter is broken up into numerous lessons, with each one covering a small amount of material and aimed at accomplishing a small number (perhaps one to three) of instructional objectives.
2. *A logical sequence.* Units are sequenced such that basic, foundational concepts and procedures are studied before more complex ones.
3. *Demonstration of mastery at the end of each unit.* Students move to a new unit only after they show mastery of the preceding one (e.g., by taking a test). Mastery is defined in specific, concrete terms (e.g., answering at least 90 percent of test items correctly). (Here we see an example of how instruction and assessment often work hand in hand.)
4. *Additional activities for students needing extra help or practice to attain mastery.* Support and resources are tailored to individual needs and might include alternative approaches to instruction, different materials, workbooks, study groups, or individual tutoring.

Students engaged in mastery learning often proceed through the various units at their own speed; hence, different students may be studying different units at any given time. But it is also possible for an entire class to proceed through a sequence at the same time: Students who master a unit earlier than their classmates can pursue various enrichment activities, or they can serve as tutors for those still working on the unit (Block, 1980; Guskey, 1985).

We find justification for mastery learning in several theoretical perspectives. Operant conditioning theorists tell us that complex behaviors are often more easily learned through *shaping,* whereby a simple response is reinforced until it occurs frequently (i.e., until it is mastered), then a slightly more difficult response is reinforced, and so on. Cognitive psychologists point out that information and skills that need to be retrieved rapidly or used in complex problem-solving situations must be practiced and learned thoroughly so that *automaticity* is attained. Finally, as social cognitive theorists have noted, the ability to perform a particular task successfully and easily is likely to enhance students' sense of self-efficacy for performing similar tasks.

Research indicates that mastery learning has several advantages over nonmastery approaches. In particular, students tend to

- Learn more and perform better on classroom assessments
- Maintain better study habits, studying regularly rather than procrastinating and cramming
- Enjoy their classes and teachers more
- Have greater interest in the subject
- Have more self-confidence about their ability to learn the subject
- (Block & Burns, 1976; Born & Davis, 1974; C. C. Kulik, Kulik, & Bangert-Drowns, 1990; J. A. Kulik, Kulik, & Cohen, 1979; Shuell, 1996)

Mastery learning is most appropriate when the subject matter is hierarchical in nature—that is, when certain concepts and skills provide the foundation for future learning. When instructional goals deal with such basics as word recognition, rules of grammar, arithmetic, or key scientific concepts, instruction designed to promote mastery learning may be in order. Nevertheless, the very notion of mastery may be *in*appropriate for some of our long-term instructional goals. As noted earlier, skills such as critical reading, scientific reasoning, and creative writing may continue to improve over the years without ever being completely mastered.

Direct Instruction

An approach incorporating elements of both expository instruction and mastery learning is **direct instruction**, which uses a variety of techniques to keep students continually and actively engaged in learning and applying classroom subject matter (Englemann & Carnine, 1982; R. M. Gangné, 1985; Rosenshine & Stevens, 1986; Tarver, 1992; Weinert & Helmke, 1995). To some extent, direct instruction is based on behaviorist ideas; for instance, it requires learners to make frequent overt responses and provides immediate reinforcement of correct responses through teacher feedback. But it also considers principles from cognitive psychology, including the importance of

■ Don't confuse mastery *learning* with mastery *goals.* Here we're talking about an instructional strategy. In contrast, mastery goals reflect students' focus on gaining competence in the subject matter rather than on, say, simply getting a good grade (see Chapter 12).

■ **direct instruction** Approach to instruction that uses a variety of techniques (e.g., explanations, questions, guided and independent practice) to promote learning of basic skills.

attention and long-term memory storage processes in learning, the limited capacity of working memory, and the value of learning basic skills to automaticity (Rosenshine & Stevens, 1986).

Different theorists describe and implement direct instruction somewhat differently. But in general, this approach involves small and carefully sequenced steps, fast pacing, and a great deal of teacher-student interaction. Each lesson typically involves most or all of the following components (Rosenshine & Stevens, 1986):

1. *Review of previously learned material.* The teacher reviews relevant content from previous lessons, checks homework assignments involving that content, and reteaches any information or skills that students have apparently not yet mastered.

2. *Statement of the objectives of the lesson.* The teacher describes one or more concepts or skills that students should master in the new lesson.

3. *Presentation of new material in small, carefully sequenced steps.* The teacher presents a small amount of information or a specific skill, perhaps through a verbal explanation, modeling, and one or more examples. The teacher may also provide an advance organizer, ask questions, or in other ways scaffold students' efforts to process and remember the material.

4. *Guided student practice and assessment after each step.* Students have frequent opportunities to practice what they are learning, perhaps by answering questions, solving problems, or performing modeled procedures. The teacher gives hints during students' early responses, provides immediate feedback about their performance, makes suggestions about how to improve, and provides remedial instruction as needed.

5. *Assessment of student progress.* After students have completed guided practice, the teacher checks to be sure they have mastered the information or skill in question, perhaps by having them summarize what they've learned or answer a series of follow-up questions.

6. *Independent practice.* Once students have acquired some mastery (e.g., by correctly answering 80 percent of questions), they engage in further practice either independently or in small, cooperative groups. By doing so, they work toward achieving automaticity for the material in question.

7. *Frequent follow-up reviews.* The teacher provides many opportunities for students to review previously learned material over the course of the school year—perhaps through homework assignments, writing tasks, or paper-pencil quizzes.

Direct instruction typically involves many opportunities to practice new skills, often with considerable teacher guidance in the early stages.

The teacher moves back and forth among these steps as necessary to ensure that all students are truly mastering the subject matter.

Like mastery learning, direct instruction is most suitable for teaching information and skills that are well defined and should be taught in a step-by-step sequence (Rosenshine & Stevens, 1986). Because of the high degree of teacher-student interaction, it is often implemented more easily with small groups rather than with an entire classroom. Under such circumstances, research indicates that it can be a highly effective technique, leading to substantial gains in achievement of both basic skills and higher-level thinking processes, high student interest and self-efficacy for the subject matter in question, and low rates of student misbehavior (Rosenshine & Stevens, 1986; Tarver, 1992; Weinert & Helmke, 1995). Using direct instruction *exclusively* may be too much of a good thing, however, especially if we don't vary instructional methods to maintain students' interest and engagement (Mac Iver et al., 1995; Wasley, Hampel, & Clark, 1997). A teenager named Tommy shows disgust about the rut one of his high school teachers has gotten into:

> [W]e just get one ditto after the next. My math teacher doesn't like the textbook, so he works up his own work sheets, and he gives us a million of them every day. If we get through all of them, we can pretty much get a good grade. (From *Kids and School Reform*, p. 117, by P. A. Wasley, R. L. Hample, & R. W. Clark, 1997, San Francisco: Jossey-Bass. Copyright 1997 by Jossey-Bass. This material is used by permission of John Wiley & Sons, Inc.)

Even in direct instruction, then, variety is the spice of—and an important source of motivation in—life.

One advantage of both mastery learning and direct instruction approaches is that because students must demonstrate mastery at the completion of each unit, they receive frequent feedback about the progress they are making. Yet another approach—computer-based instruction—can provide even *more* frequent feedback, as we shall see now.

Computer-Based Instruction

As we have seen, behaviorists argue that students learn effectively only when they are actively and physically involved in a learning activity. In behaviorism's heyday in the middle decades of the twentieth century, B. F. Skinner (1954, 1968) suggested an approach known as *programmed instruction*, which incorporates three principles of operant conditioning as it presents new material:

1. *Active responding.* The learner is continually making responses—for instance, by answering questions.
2. *Shaping.* Instruction begins with information the learner already knows and then slowly presents new information. As the learner acquires more knowledge and answers questions of increasing difficulty, the desired terminal behavior (mastery of the subject matter) is gradually shaped.
3. *Immediate reinforcement.* Because instruction involves such a gradual progression through material, mastery of each new piece is almost guaranteed. Thus, the learner almost always answers questions correctly and gets immediate positive feedback.

In the 1950s and 1960s, programmed instruction was typically presented through books and other printed materials. But with the increasing availability and affordability of computers in the 1970s and 1980s, most programmed instruction was presented through computer software and so became known as *computer-assisted instruction (CAI)*.

Contemporary educational computer programs often incorporate cognitivist principles as well as those of behaviorism (R. M. Gagné, Briggs, & Wager, 1992; P. F. Merrill et al., 1996; Morena, Mayer, Spires, & Lester, 2001). For example, effective programs often take steps to capture and hold students' *attention*, elicit students' *prior knowledge* about a topic, and encourage long-term retention and transfer. Some programs provide drill and practice of basic knowledge and skills (e.g., math facts, typing, fundamentals of music), helping students develop automaticity in these areas. Others serve as "intelligent tutors" that skillfully guide students through complex subject matter and can anticipate and address a wide variety of learning difficulties (Lajoie & Derry, 1993; Roblyer, 2003). The term **computer-based instruction (CBI)** encompasses recent innovations in computer-delivered instruction as well as the more traditional CAI.

Although some computer-based instructional programs provide a fairly lockstep sequence of instruction, most do not. Perhaps, as a student, you have had experience with computer software that allowed you to jump around from one topic to related topics, thereby enabling you to decide what things to study and in what order. If so, then you have had experience with either hypertext or hypermedia (e.g., Jonassen, 1996; P. F. Merrill et al., 1996). **Hypertext** is a collection of computer-based verbal material that allows students to read about one topic and then proceed to related topics at will; for example, you might read a short, introductory passage about airplanes and then decide whether to proceed to more specific information about aerodynamics, the history of air travel, or military aircraft. **Hypermedia** include such other media as pictures, sound, animations, and videos as well as text; for example, some computer-based encyclopedias enable students to bounce from text to a voice message and then to a video about a particular topic. The use of hypertext and hypermedia for instructional purposes is based on the assumption that students benefit from imposing their own organization on a subject area and selecting topics that are most personally relevant (Jonassen, 1996; R. V. Small & Grabowski, 1992). Keep in mind, however, that not all students can make wise choices about what to study and in what sequence to study it. They may be overwhelmed by the many directions in which they can go, may have trouble identifying important information, or may lack the self-regulatory skills to use a program effectively and determine when they have mastered the material (Garhart & Hannafin, 1986; Hartley & Bendixen, 2001; Lanza & Roselli, 1991; E. R. Steinberg, 1989).

Numerous research studies have documented the effectiveness of CBI: Students often have higher academic achievement and better attitudes toward their schoolwork than is true for students taught with more traditional methods (e.g., J. A. Kulik, Kulik, & Cohen, 1980; Lepper & Gurtner, 1989; Wise & Olson, 1998). Furthermore, students studying academic subject matter on a computer may gain an increased sense that they can control their own learning, thereby developing more intrinsic motivation to learn (Swan, Mitrani, Guerrero, Cheung, & Schoener, 1990).

Achievement differences for computer-based versus more traditional instructional methods are usually fairly small; using computers for expository instruction doesn't make a *huge* difference in how effectively students learn (Blok, Oostdam, Otter, & Overmaat, 2002; Christmann,

■ You can find an example of paper-pencil programmed instruction in the supplementary reading "A Shocking Lesson" in the *Study Guide and Reader*.

■ **computer-based instruction (CBI)** Instruction provided via computer technology.

■ **hypertext** Collection of computer-based reading material that allows students to proceed from one topic to another, related one in a self-chosen sequence.

■ **hypermedia** Collection of multimedia, computer-based instructional material (e.g., text, pictures, sound, animations) that students can examine in a sequence of their own choosing.

Badgett, & Lucking, 1997; Dillon & Gabbard, 1998). Furthermore, CBI gives students few opportunities for social interaction (Winn, 2002). Nevertheless, computers offer several advantages that we often do not have with other media. For one thing, instructional programs can include animations, video clips, and spoken messages—components that are, of course, not possible with traditional printed materials. Second, a computer can record and maintain ongoing data for every student, including such information as how far students have progressed in a program, how often they are right and wrong, how quickly they respond, and so on. With such data, we can monitor each student's progress and identify students who appear to be struggling with the material. Finally, a computer can be used to provide instruction when flesh-and-blood teachers are not available; for example, CBI is often used in **distance learning,** a situation in which learners receive technology-based instruction at a location physically separate from that of their instructor.

In later sections of the chapter, we will explore additional uses of computer technology. Yet keep in mind that using a computer is not, *in and of itself,* necessarily the key to better instruction (R. E. Clark, 1983; Roblyer, 2003). A computer can help students achieve at higher levels only when it provides instruction that we cannot offer as easily or effectively by other means. There is little to be gained when a student merely reads information on a computer screen rather than in a textbook.

Online Research

Students' access to new information through computer technology is not necessarily limited to computer programs in our own schools and classrooms. Through telephone and cable lines, students at many schools now have access to the Internet and *World Wide Web*, a network of computers, software programs, and computer databases that can be accessed from any microcomputer with the appropriate hardware and software. For example, my middle school geography students and I once used the U.S. Geological Survey Web site to track the path of a hurricane as it made its way through the Caribbean and up the Atlantic coast. A wide variety of government offices, public institutions, private associations, and individual educators provide information, lesson plans, and links to other relevant Web sites. Following are a few examples you might want to explore:

Website
- What is sucrose? _____
- What percent of sap is sucrose? _____
- How many gallons of sap does it take to make ONE gallon of syrup? _____
- Name one of the types of maple tree that yields the best syrup. _____
- How many links are on this website? _____

FIGURE 13.4 Students may need some scaffolding—for instance, specific questions to answer as they look at a Web site about maple sugaring—to develop their information literacy skills. (Artifact courtesy of Carol Lincoln)

U.S. Geological Survey: http://www.usgs.gov
U.S. Census bureau: http://www.census.gov
National Aeronautic and Space Administration: http://www. nasa.gov
National Museum of Natural History: http://www.mnh.si.edu
The Knowledge Loom: http://knowledgeloom.org
Discovery Channel: http://school.discovery.com

In addition, Internet *search engines,* such as Google (http://www.google.com) and Yahoo! (http://www.yahoo.com) allow students and teachers to find Web sites on virtually any topic.

Students may initially need considerable scaffolding in their use of the Internet to acquire information. For instance, elementary school librarian Carol Lincoln gives students precise, step-by-step directions on how to use EBSCO Information Services's "Searchasaurus" search engine, telling them what icons to click on, what words to type in a search box, and so on. When students reach the Web site she has in mind, she provides specific questions that guide their learning (e.g., see Figure 13.4). In such an activity, she enhances their information literacy skills as well as their knowledge about a particular topic.

Educators are just beginning to capitalize on the Internet's potential for students' learning, and we still await systematic research on its potential benefits and liabilities. Considerable anecdotal evidence indicates that students often use it in productive ways—for instance, finding useful information for research papers and oral presentations. However, there is no quality-control mechanism to ensure that information is accurate, especially when posted by individuals rather than government agencies and professional organizations. Furthermore, students may sometimes venture into unproductive domains, perhaps finding prewritten research papers they can pass off as their own (plagiarism) or perhaps stumbling upon sites that preach racist attitudes or offer pornographic images. Clearly, then, the Internet offers a mixed bag of resources, and we must carefully monitor its use in the classroom.

■ For more information about information literacy, see the supplementary reading "Promoting Information Literacy Skills" in the *Study Guide and Reader.*

■ **distance learning** Technology-based instruction in which students are at a location physically separate from their instructor.

HANDS-ON AND PRACTICE ACTIVITIES

In the opening case study, Ms. Minichiello doesn't just describe the dimensions of a covered wagon; she has students measure the dimensions for themselves and get a firsthand view of a family's living space. More generally, when we talk about hands-on and practice activities, we are talking about having students actually *do* something rather than just hearing or reading about it. Here we look at several such activities: discovery learning, in-class activities, computer simulations and applications, homework, and authentic activities.

Discovery Learning

Think about something you've learned through your own research or experimentation. How thoroughly did you learn the information or skill? Do you think you learned it more thoroughly and understood it better than you would have if you had simply read about it in a book or heard about it from another person?

Unlike expository instruction, where information is presented in its final form, **discovery learning** is a process through which students interact with their environment—for example, by exploring and manipulating objects or by performing experiments—and derive information for themselves. Common examples of discovery learning are laboratory experiments and opportunities for students to learn by trial and error (e.g., as they "fiddle" with computer software, a soccer ball, or watercolor paints). Discovery learning can sometimes be incorporated into other forms of instruction; for example, the Experiencing Firsthand exercises in this very "expository" book have, I hope, helped you discover a number of important principles on your own.

Learners often remember and transfer information more effectively when they construct it for themselves rather than simply reading or hearing about it (de Jong & van Joolingen, 1998; M. A. McDaniel & Schlager, 1990; D. S. McNamara & Healy, 1995). We can easily explain this finding using principles of cognitive psychology (Bruner, 1961, 1966; M. A. McDaniel, Waddill, & Einstein, 1988; B. Y. White & Frederiksen, 1998). When learners discover something on their own, they typically give more thought to the information or skill than they might otherwise, and so they are more likely to engage in meaningful learning. In addition, when learners *see* something happen as well as reading or hearing about it, they can encode it in long-term memory visually as well as verbally. And from a developmental perspective, many students, especially those in the elementary grades, understand concrete experiences more easily than abstract ideas (see Chapter 2).

How effective is discovery learning in the classroom? Unfortunately, research does not give us a clear answer. Ideally, to determine whether discovery learning works better than other approaches, we would need to compare two groups of students who differ on only *one* variable: the extent to which discovery learning is a part of their instructional experience. Yet few research studies have made this crucial comparison, and the studies that have been conducted yield inconsistent results. Nevertheless, some general conclusions about discovery learning can be gleaned from research findings:

- When we consider *overall academic achievement*, discovery learning is not necessarily better or worse than "traditional" (e.g., more expository) approaches to instruction; research yields mixed findings on this issue.
- When we consider *higher-level thinking skills*, discovery learning is often preferable for fostering transfer, problem solving, creativity, and self-regulated learning.
- When we consider *motivational and affective benefits*, discovery learning often promotes a more positive attitude toward teachers and schoolwork than does traditional instruction; in other words, students like school better. (E. L. Ferguson & Hegarty, 1995; Giaconia & Hedges, 1982; Marshall, 1981; Mayer, 1974, 1987; P. L. Peterson, 1979; Roughead & Scandura, 1968; Shymansky, Hedges, & Woodworth, 1990; B. Y. White & Frederiksen, 1998)

We should also note two potential problems with discovery learning (Hammer, 1997; Schauble, 1990). First, students sometimes construct incorrect understandings from discovery activities; for instance, they may misinterpret or distort the evidence they gather in an experiment, possibly "confirming" existing misconceptions (recall our discussion of *confirmation bias* in Chapter 7). Second, discovery learning activities often take considerably more time than expository instruction, and teachers may feel torn between providing discovery experiences and

Students may better understand scientific principles when they actually observe those principles in action.

■ **discovery learning** Approach to instruction in which students develop an understanding of a topic through firsthand interaction with the environment.

Promoting Discovery Learning

 Identify a concept or principle about which students can learn through interaction with their physical or social environment.

A fifth-grade teacher realizes that rather than tell students how to calculate the area of a triangle, she can help them discover the procedure for themselves.

 Make sure students have the necessary prior knowledge for discovering new ideas and principles.

A first-grade teacher asks students what they already know about air (e.g., people breathe it, wind involves its movement). After activating students' prior knowledge about air, she and her class conduct an experiment in which a glass containing a crumpled paper towel is turned upside-down and immersed in a bowl of water. The teacher eventually removes the glass from the water and asks students to explain why the paper towel didn't get wet. (A portion of this lesson is depicted in the "Properties of Air" clip on Video CD 2.)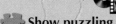

 Show puzzling results to arouse curiosity.

A science teacher shows her class two glasses of water. In one glass an egg floats at the water's surface; in the other glass an egg rests on the bottom. The students give a simple and logical explanation for the difference: One egg has more air inside and so must be lighter. But then the teacher switches the eggs into opposite glasses. The egg that the students believe to be "heavier" now floats, and the "lighter"

egg sinks to the bottom. The students are quite surprised and demand to know what is going on. (Ordinarily, water is less dense than an egg, so an egg placed in it will quickly sink. But in this situation one glass contains salt water—a mixture denser than an egg and so capable of keeping it afloat.) (based on E. L. Palmer, 1965)

 Structure the experience so that students proceed logically toward discoveries you want them to make.

To demonstrate the effects of prejudice, a middle school social studies teacher creates a situation in which some students, because of an arbitrarily chosen physical characteristic they possess, experience the prejudice of classmates. After 15 minutes—long enough for students to feel the sting of prejudice but not so long as to damage peer relationships—she stops the activity and asks students to share their reactions to the experience.

 Have students record their findings.

A biology teacher has students make sketches of the specific organs they observe as they dissect an earthworm.

 Help students relate their findings to concepts and principles in the academic discipline they are studying.

After students in a social studies class have collected data on average incomes and voting patterns in different counties within their state, their teacher asks, "How can we interpret these data given what we've learned about the relative wealth of members of the two major political parties?"

"covering" mandated topics for the year. In my own experience I've found that students typically remember what they learn in hands-on discovery activities so much more effectively than what they learn through expository instruction that the extra time I devote to these activities is time well spent (another instance of the *less is more* principle).

Psychologists and educators have offered numerous suggestions for making discovery learning effective (e.g., see the Into the Classroom feature "Promoting Discovery Learning"). The following two guidelines are probably most critical:

◎ *Make sure students have the knowledge they need to interpret their findings appropriately.* Students are most apt to benefit from a discovery learning activity when they can draw on prior knowledge to interpret their observations (Bruner, 1966; de Jong & van Joolingen, 1998; N. Frederiksen, 1984a). For example, having students conduct experiments to determine the influence of gravity on the velocity of a falling object will typically be more beneficial if students are already familiar with the concepts *gravity* and *velocity*. As cognitive psychologists tell us, meaningful learning can occur only when students have appropriate knowledge to which they can relate new experiences. And from Vygotsky's perspective, students must ultimately tie their observations to the ways in which their culture interprets the world. The central concepts and principles of various academic disciplines are, indeed, a very important part of that culture.

◎ *Provide some structure to guide students' discovery activities.* Young children often learn from random exploration of their environment—for example, by experimenting with, and thereby discovering the properties of, dry sand, wet sand, and water (Hutt, Tyler, Hutt, & Christopherson, 1989). By and large, however, students benefit more from carefully planned and structured activities that help them construct appropriate interpretations (Hickey, 1997; Mayer, 2004; Minstrell & Stimpson, 1996; B. Y. White & Frederiksen, 1998). In science, for example, such structure (*scaffolding*) might take the form of questions that guide students' thinking; here are three examples:

- In what ways has the culture in this petri dish changed since yesterday?
- How can we measure an object's rate of acceleration in an objective way?

- When we add these two chemicals together and then heat them, how can we be sure the *heat*, rather than some other variable, is bringing about the change that we see?

The extent to which a discovery session needs to be structured depends somewhat on the reasoning and problem-solving skills of the students (de Jong & van Joolingen, 1998; B. Y. White & Frederiksen, 1998). Some students may have difficulty tackling vague, ill-defined problems (see Chapter 8). And others—perhaps those who have not yet acquired formal operational thinking capabilities—may have trouble formulating and testing hypotheses or separating and controlling variables (see Chapter 2). Such students will probably work more effectively when they are given problems and questions that are concrete and well defined and when they are given specific suggestions about how to proceed.

With what you have learned about discovery learning in mind, try the following exercise.

Interpreting Student Artifacts and Behaviors

Pig Lungs

A fifth-grade class works in small groups to dissect the lungs of a pig. Afterward the students write individual lab reports describing what they have observed and learned. As you read 10-year-old Berlinda's report, consider

- What Berlinda has learned from the activity
- What Berlinda may *not* have learned from the activity

Pig Lungs Dissection

It was 10:40a.m. on Friday, November 1, 1996. We were going to dissect a set of lungs which had belonged to a pig. I could read just about everyones minds. Ew. Grose. Its bloody. This thing stinks!

Our table was given an esophogus with felt wet and smooth. The main blood vessel which felt hard, almost as though someone had stuck a toothpick inside of it. The trachea which felt felt wet and slitely textured. The heart which, well you couldn't tell. Two lungs which felt a little bit like silly pudy. As 11:30 rolled around most of us had changed our thoughts. It was now cool, neat, and still bloody.

Berlinda has clearly learned what some of a pig's internal organs look and feel like. She has responded to the activity emotionally as well as cognitively (e.g., "grose" [gross], "cool, neat"), and this *hot cognition* will undoubtedly help her remember what she has experienced (see Chapter 11). However, there is no evidence that Berlinda has related her observations to her previous knowledge and beliefs about anatomy or tied them to an understanding of respiration in mammals. To help her students make such connections, the teacher might have asked them to respond to questions that would guide their exploration and writing (e.g., "Do the lungs look and feel the way you thought they would?" "How do the lungs help the pig get oxygen into its body?").

In-Class Activities

Students are typically asked to accomplish a wide variety of tasks and assignments in class during the school year. For example, they might be asked to complete worksheets, solve problems, write short stories, practice basketball skills, play musical instruments, or perhaps (as in the opening case study) imagine trying to pack for a trip to a distant planet. Naturally, students can do only so many things in any single school year. How do we decide which activities will be most beneficial to their long-term learning and achievement?

As teachers, we should, first and foremost, assign in-class activities that will help students accomplish our instructional goals. Some of these goals may be at a "knowledge" level; for instance, we may want students to conjugate the French verb *être* ("to be"), know members of different biological classes and orders, and be familiar with current events around the globe. Other goals will be higher-level ones; for instance, we may want students to write a persuasive essay, use scientific principles to interpret physical phenomena, or apply arithmetic operations to real-world problems. Particularly when such higher-level objectives are involved, we should assign activities that help students learn classroom material in a meaningful, integrated way.

In addition to choosing activities that help students accomplish instructional goals, we are more likely to facilitate students' learning and achievement when we assign activities that

- Clearly define each task and its purpose
- Capture students' attention and interest
- Accommodate diversity in student's abilities and needs

■ How might Ms. Minichiello's "distant planet" activity in the opening case study help students learn?

- Begin at an appropriate difficulty level—ideally, involving tasks that challenge students to "stretch" existing knowledge and skills (i.e., tasks within each student's zone of proximal development)
- Provide sufficient scaffolding to promote success
- Progress in difficulty and complexity as students gain proficiency
- Provide opportunities for frequent teacher monitoring and feedback
- Encourage students to reflect on and evaluate their work
(Brophy & Alleman, 1991, 1992; Brophy & Good, 1986)

The ways in which we *assess* students' performance will also have an impact on what class activities actually accomplish (W. Doyle, 1983). For example, if we give full credit for completing an assignment without regard to the *quality* of responses, students may focus more on "getting the work done" than on acquiring a conceptual understanding of what they are studying. But if our criteria for acceptable performance are overly strict, we may discourage students from taking risks and making errors—risks and errors that are inevitable when students tackle the challenges that can best promote their cognitive growth.

Computer Simulations and Applications

Earlier we talked about computer-based instruction as a means of introducing new material. Yet we can also use computer technology to give students valuable hands-on experiences with a variety of academic topics and skills—for instance, by using simulations and such computer tools as word processing programs, databases, and spreadsheets. Often the tasks involved are sufficiently complex and challenging that students must work on them in small groups rather than as individuals, and many students find such small-group work especially motivating (Lou, Abrami, & d'Apollonia, 2001).

Simulations   Some computer programs promote higher-level thinking skills (e.g., problem solving) within the context of gamelike or authentic tasks. One popular software program, Where in the World Is Carmen Sandiego?, teaches geography while students act as detectives. Other programs provide simulations of such events as running a lemonade stand, dissecting a frog, growing plants under varying environmental conditions, or exploring the effects of various business practices. Still others present authentic problem-solving tasks; as an example, see the description of the Adventures of Jasper Woodbury series in the section "Cognitive Factors Affecting Problem Solving" in Chapter 8. Computer simulations are often both motivating and challenging (thereby keeping students on task for extended periods) and can significantly enhance students' problem-solving and scientific reasoning skills (Cognition and Technology Group at Vanderbilt, 1996; de Jong & van Joolingen, 1998; Vye et al., 1998; B. Y. White & Frederiksen, 1998). In some cases, simulated "hands-on" activities are just as effective as those in which students manipulate actual physical objects (e.g., Triona & Klahr, 2003).

Computer Tool Applications   Basic computer skills are essential in today's society. For instance, many professions require expertise in such *computer tools* as word processing, desktop publishing, databases, and spreadsheets. Hence, our instructional objectives may often include computer skills as well as skills in traditional academic areas. But we can often kill two birds with one stone, simultaneously addressing instructional goals in both computer literacy and traditional content domains. For instance, word processing programs can enhance the quality of students' writing *if* students are sufficiently competent in keyboarding and other basic computer skills (Guinee, 2003; Sitko, 1998). Concept mapping and brainstorming software can help students generate and organize ideas, perhaps to facilitate studying for a test or writing a research paper. Database programs can help students organize information about trees or planets. Spreadsheets enable students to predict changes in weather patterns or declines in endangered species populations. Tools known as *music editors* let students create musical compositions and experiment with different notes, keys, instrumental sounds, and time signatures (P. F. Merrill et al., 1996). And hypermedia programs (e.g., HyperCard) can help students develop engaging multimedia presentations (Lehrer, 1993).

The popular software program Where in the World Is Carmen Sandiego? promotes knowledge of geography and higher-level thinking skills by asking students to act as detectives in international mysteries.

Courtesy of The Learning Company.

When I was young it was almost impossible to read. One of my teachers told me I could learn to read if I worked hard. Learning to read was like climbing Mount Rushmore. It took a very long time but I finally got it. My Mom said she was vary proud. Reading was hard for me. It took five years for me to learn to read. Every day I would go to the learning center to learn my 400 site words. It was hard for me to learn these words but I did it. Reading is one of the most important things I have learned so far in my life.

Daniel, a fifth grader who struggles with reading and writing, wrote this very cohesive paragraph with the help of a word processing program. A spell checker enabled him to spell most, but not all, of the words correctly (he meant to use *very* and *sight*, not *vary* and *site*).

Homework

Students can accomplish only so much during class time, and homework provides a means through which we can, in essence, extend the school day. On some occasions we may want to use homework to give students extra practice with familiar information and procedures (perhaps as a way of promoting review and automaticity) or to introduce them to new yet simple material (H. Cooper, 1989). In other situations we can give homework assignments that ask students to apply classroom material to their outside lives (Alleman & Brophy, 1998). For example, in a unit on lifestyle patterns, we might ask second graders to

- Compare their own home or apartment with homes of different time periods (e.g., caves, stone huts, log cabins)
- Tour their homes (perhaps with a parent) and identify the modern conveniences that make their lives easier and more comfortable (e.g., sinks, electrical outlets, thermostats)
- Ask parents to explain why they made the choices they did about where they live (e.g., considering the tradeoffs of renting versus purchasing a residence) (Alleman & Brophy, 1998)

On still other occasions we might encourage students to bring items and ideas from home (e.g., tadpoles from the local pond, events that occurred over the weekend) and use them as the basis for in-class activities (Corno, 1996; C. Hill, 1994). When we ask students to make connections between classroom material and the outside world through homework assignments, we are, of course, promoting transfer.

Unfortunately, researchers have conducted few carefully controlled studies on the importance of homework for learning and achievement (Trautwein & Köller, 2003). Existing data indicate that doing homework probably has a small effect on achievement in the middle school and high school grades but little if any effect at the elementary level (H. Cooper, 1989; H. Cooper, Lindsay, Nye, & Greathouse, 1998; H. Cooper & Valentine, 2001). Although homework in the elementary grades may not enhance achievement very much, it may help students develop some of the study strategies and self-regulatory skills they will need in later years (H. Cooper & Valentine, 2001; Zimmerman, 1998). We can reasonably guess that the *quality* of assignments (e.g., whether they encourage rote memorization, on the one hand, or meaningful learning and elaboration, on the other) probably makes an appreciable difference both in what and how much students learn and in what kinds of learning and self-regulatory strategies they develop.

Students report that their motivation to do homework is largely extrinsic; for instance, they are more likely to do it to please their teacher and stay out of trouble than because they enjoy a subject and want to master it (J. M. T. Walker, 2001). Yet even when they are motivated to do their homework, many students have neither the self-regulatory skills nor sufficient parent support to complete assignments on a regular basis (e.g., Eilam, 2001). In such cases, in-school and after-school homework programs are an effective alternative (Belfiore & Hornyak, 1998; Cosden et al., 2001; B. L. Wilson & Corbett, 2001).

When we assign homework, we must remember that students differ considerably in the time and resources (reference books, computers, etc.) they have available to them and in the amount and kind of assistance they can get from parents and other family members (H. Cooper, 1989; Hoover-Dempsey et al., 2001). Furthermore, we should assign tasks that will truly help them achieve important educational goals; we should *never* assign homework simply because we think students should have it every night or, worse still, because we want to punish them for misbehavior.

We can maximize the benefits of homework by following a few simple guidelines (H. Cooper, 1989):

- Use assignments primarily for instructional and diagnostic purposes; minimize the degree to which homework is used to assess learning and determine final class grades.
- Provide the information and structure students need to complete assignments without assistance from others.
- Give a mixture of required and voluntary assignments (voluntary ones should help to give students a sense of self-determination and control, hence enhancing intrinsic motivation).

Let's consider how one teacher's homework assignment measures up in terms of the preceding discussion.

i HAVL HOMWRK Andrew

Dear Parents:

   Tomorrow we will be working on the letter T . Could you please help your child find an object that begins with the letter T for show and tell tomorrow. Thank you!

T +

Young children don't always have the self-regulatory skills they need to complete homework on their own. Six-year-old Andrew and his teacher jointly constructed the homework reminder shown here.

Book Report

Name Katie

Title of Book: Me Too Iguana
Author: Jacquelyn Reingch
Main Characters: Iguana and her friends

Write 3 or more sentences telling about the book.

Iguana had lovely things but she wasn't satisfied. She wanted to look like every one else. When she dressed like her friends they got worried. They had an iguana party to show her that being herself was better.

Draw and color a picture about your book.

Clearly, Katie's mother can scaffold Katie's efforts at what, for most first graders, would be a fairly challenging task. Furthermore, with her mother's assistance, Katie might develop her writing and spelling skills. Not all of Katie's classmates will have the expert guidance that Katie does, however. Some well-meaning parents may provide the wrong kind of help, perhaps using confusing instructional methods, focusing on rote-level drill and practice, or providing so much direction that their children lose any sense of autonomy about the task (H. Cooper & Valentine, 2001; Gallimore & Goldenberg, 2001). Some parents may not have the basic skills they need to assist their children; this increasingly becomes an issue as students get older and encounter more challenging schoolwork (J. L. Epstein & Van Voorhis, 2001). And, of course, some parents may be so overwhelmed with other issues and responsibilities that they have neither the time nor energy to help.

Authentic Activities

In our discussion of knowledge construction in Chapter 7, and again in our discussion of transfer and situated cognition in Chapter 8, we noted the importance of assigning activities similar to those that students are likely to encounter in the outside world. Such **authentic activities** help students form meaningful connections between classroom subject matter and real-world contexts; thus, when we use authentic activities regularly, we are more likely to find students applying what they learn in school to their own personal and professional lives. In addition, we may increase the *value* that students attach to academic subject matter (see Chapter 12). Figure 13.5 presents examples of authentic activities in different academic disciplines.

It may occasionally be possible to assign authentic activities as homework; for example, we might ask students to write an editorial, design an electrical circuit, or plan a family budget while working at home in the evening (if we do so, we should keep in mind the earlier guidelines about assigning homework). But many authentic activities may require considerable interaction, with students asking one another questions, sharing ideas, and offering explanations of their thinking (Hickey, 1997; Newmann & Wehlage, 1993; Paris & Turner, 1994). Furthermore, because authentic activities are typically less structured and more complex than traditional classroom tasks, they may require considerable teacher scaffolding (Brophy, 1992a; van Merriënboer, Kirschner, & Kester, 2003). For such reasons, many authentic activities can be accomplished more effectively in class than at home, or perhaps through a combination of group work during class and independent work after school hours.

Researchers have only begun to study the effects of authentic activities on students' learning and achievement, but preliminary results are encouraging. For example, students' writing skills may show greater improvement in both quality and quantity when students write stories, essays, and letters to real people, rather than when they complete short, artificial writing exercises (E. H. Hiebert & Fisher, 1992). Students gain a more complete understanding of how to use and interpret maps effectively when they construct their own maps than when they engage in workbook exercises involving map interpretation (Gregg & Leinhardt, 1994). Students are more apt to check their solutions to mathematics problems—in particular, to make sure their solutions make logical sense—when they use math for real-life tasks (Cognition and Technology Group at Vanderbilt, 1993; Rogoff, 2003). And the motivational benefits of authentic activities can be considerable, as one high school student explains:

■ **authentic activity** Classroom activity similar to one students are apt to encounter in the outside world.

In ninth grade, we did this moon-tracking activity. It was the first time I can remember in school doing something that wasn't in the textbook, that was real, like we were real scientists or something. We had to keep data sheets, measure the time and angle of the moonrise every day for a month. It drove my mom nuts because sometimes we'd be eating dinner, and I'd look at my watch and race out the door! We had to measure the river near us to see how it was affected by the moon. I spent a lot of time outside while I was doing that, and I went down to the river more than I have in my whole life, I think. Then we had to do the calculations, that was another step, and we had to chart our findings. The test was to analyze your findings and tell what they meant about the relationship of the tides and the moon. It was hard, and you had to know what you were talking about or you didn't get credit for it. . . . I felt that I did something real, and I could see the benefit of it. (From *Kids and School Reform*, p. 117–118, by P. A. Wasley, R. L. Hample, & R. W. Clark, 1997, San Francisco: Jossey-Bass. Copyright 1997 by Jossey-Bass. This material is used by permission of John Wiley & Sons, Inc.)

Theorists have suggested that an authentic activity is most likely to be effective when:

- It requires a fair amount of background knowledge about a particular topic; in other words, students must know the subject matter thoroughly and have learned it in a meaningful fashion.
- It promotes higher-level thinking skills; for example, it may involve synthesizing information, forming and testing hypotheses, solving problems, and drawing conclusions.
- It requires students to seek out information in a variety of contexts and perhaps from a variety of academic disciplines.
- It conveys high expectations for students' performance yet also encourages students to take risks and experiment with new strategies.
- Its final outcome is complex and somewhat unpredictable; there may be no single "right" response or answer. (Newmann & Wehlage, 1993; Paris & Turner, 1994)

It is not necessarily desirable to fill the entire school day with complex, authentic tasks, however. For one thing, students can often master basic skills more effectively when they practice them in relative isolation from other activities; for example, when learning to play the violin, they need to master their fingering before they join an orchestra, and when learning to play soccer, they need to practice dribbling and passing before they play in a game (J. R. Anderson et al., 1996). Second, some authentic tasks may be too expensive and time-consuming to warrant regular use in the classroom (M. M. Griffin & Griffin, 1994). It is probably more important that classroom tasks encourage students to engage in such cognitive processes as meaningful learning, organization, and elaboration—processes that promote long-term retention and transfer of classroom subject matter—than that tasks always be authentic (J. R. Anderson et al., 1996).

Experiencing FIRSTHAND · Thinking Authentically

Take a few minutes to think about and answer these questions:

- In what ways will the subject matter you teach help your students succeed in their personal or professional lives? In other words, how would you like your students to use and apply school subject matter outside the classroom?
- How might you translate those long-term, real-world applications into activities your students can do in the classroom?

With your answers in mind, develop several authentic activities appropriate for the subject matter and age range of students you will be teaching.

· · · · · · ·

INTERACTIVE AND COLLABORATIVE APPROACHES

In the opening case study, we see a lesson with considerable interaction: Ms. Minichiello asks several questions that get her students thinking about and then discussing westward migration in the 1840s. In Chapter 7 we identified numerous advantages of social interaction in the classroom; for instance, when students talk about and exchange ideas, they must organize and elaborate on their own thoughts, may discover gaps and inconsistencies in their understandings,

Authentic Tasks in Writing
- Write a letter to a penpal.
- Write an editorial for the local newspaper.
- Write a short story for the school literary magazine.
- Write a resumé.

Authentic Tasks in Mathematics
- Balance a checkbook.
- Compare the pound-for-pound costs of different brands of the same product.
- Plan a family budget.
- Compute the amount of cement needed to build a "half-pipe" for a skate park.

Authentic Tasks in Science
- Locate Mars on a clear night.
- Identify various food chains in a nearby forest.
- Conduct a chemical analysis of the community drinking water.
- Construct a device that can easily lift a heavy object.

Authentic Tasks in Social Studies
- Construct a map of the school neighborhood.
- Create a poster that encourages people to vote.
- Give an oral presentation about an event in local history.
- Compare different newspaper accounts of a current event to identify possible biases in reporting.

FIGURE 13.5 Examples of authentic tasks in different disciplines

■ Before you read further, you may want to reread the section "Knowledge Construction as a Social Process" in Chapter 7.

and may encounter explanations that are more accurate and useful than their own. Clearly, then, students have a great deal to gain from interacting frequently not only with us but also with *one another*.

In this section we examine six interactive and collaborative strategies: teacher questions, class discussions, reciprocal teaching, technology-based discussions, cooperative learning, and peer tutoring. Of these, the last five are largely learner-directed. Only the first—teacher questions—is teacher-directed, and it often provides the impetus for learner-directed class discussions.

Teacher Questions

■ Observe the wide variety of teacher questions, as well as the many purposes they serve, in the clips on Video CD 2.

In the classroom lessons depicted in the clips on Video CD 2, the teachers ask many questions, and their questions serve a variety of purposes. Teacher questioning is a widely used teaching strategy (e.g., Mehan, 1979). Some teacher questions are **lower-level questions** that ask students to retrieve information they've already acquired. Such questions have several benefits (Airasian, 1994; F. W. Connolly & Eisenberg, 1990; P. W. Fox & LeCount, 1991; Wixson, 1984). First, they give us a good idea of students' prior knowledge and misconceptions about a topic (see Chapter 7). Second, they tend to keep students' attention on the lesson in progress (see Chapter 6). Third, they help us assess whether students are learning class material successfully or are confused about particular points; even very experienced teachers sometimes overestimate what students are actually learning during expository instruction. Fourth, they give students the opportunity to monitor their *own* comprehension—to determine whether they understand the information being presented or whether they should ask for help or clarification. Finally, when questions ask students about material they've studied earlier, they encourage review of the material, which should promote greater recall later on. Following is an example of how one eighth-grade teacher (we'll call her Teacher A) promoted review of a lesson on ancient Egypt by asking questions.

Teacher:	The Egyptians believed the body had to be preserved. What did they do to preserve the body in the earliest times?
Student:	They dried them and stuffed them.
Teacher:	I am talking about from the earliest times. What did they do? Carey.
Carey:	They buried them in the hot sands.
Teacher:	Right. They buried them in the hot sands. The sand was very dry, and the body was naturally preserved for many years. It would deteriorate more slowly, at least compared with here. What did they do later on after this time?
Student:	They started taking out the vital organs.
Teacher:	Right. What did they call the vital organs then?
Norm:	Everything but the heart and brain.
Teacher:	Right, the organs in the visceral cavity. The intestines, liver, and so on which were the easiest parts to get at.
Teacher:	Question?
Student:	How far away from the Nile River was the burial of most kings? (Aulls, 1998, p. 62)

At the end of the dialogue, a *student* asks a question—one that requests information not previously presented. The student is apparently trying to elaborate on the material; perhaps he or she is thinking that only land that was far from the Nile would be dry enough to preserve bodies for a lengthy period. We can encourage such elaboration, and therefore also encourage new knowledge construction, by asking **higher-level questions**—those that require students to go beyond the information they have learned (Meece, 1994; Minstrell & Stimpson, 1996). For instance, a higher-level question might ask students to think of their own examples of a concept, use a new principle to solve a problem, or speculate about possible explanations for a cause-effect relationship. As an illustration, consider these questions from a lesson on the telegraph:

> Was the need for a rapid communications system [in North America] greater during the first part of the nineteenth century than it had been during the latter part of the eighteenth century? Why do you think so? (Torrance & Myers, 1970, p. 214)

■ **lower-level question** Question that requires students to express what they've learned in essentially the same way they learned it.

■ **higher-level question** Question that requires students to engage in higher-level thinking.

To answer these questions, students must recall what they know about the eighteenth and nineteenth centuries (including the increasing movement of settlers to distant western territories) and pull that knowledge together in a way they have perhaps never done before.

When we ask questions during a group lesson or provide follow-up questions to an independent reading assignment, we will often enhance students' learning (Allington & Weber, 1993; Liu, 1990; Redfield & Rousseau, 1981). This is especially likely when we ask higher-level questions that call for inferences, applications, justifications, or solutions to problems. Yet we must give students adequate time to respond to the questions we ask. Just as students need time to process the information they are hearing or reading, they also need time to consider questions and retrieve information relevant to possible answers. As we discovered in our discussion of *wait time* in Chapter 6, when teachers allow at least three seconds to elapse after asking a question, a greater number of students volunteer answers, and their responses tend to be longer, more complex, and more accurate. Furthermore, even when students can retrieve an answer almost immediately, those from some ethnic backgrounds may allow several seconds to elapse before responding as a way of showing courtesy and respect (see Chapter 4).

Given what you now know about teacher questioning, as well as about effective learning and motivation, try the following exercise.

Analyzing Teacher Strategies

Round Robin

An eighth-grade social studies teacher (we'll call him Teacher B) is conducting a review session for a unit on ancient Egypt, using a technique that he calls a "round robin." Each row of students comprises a team, and the teams compete to see which one remembers the most about ancient Egyptian society. He presents a definition of a concept or a description of a certain location and calls on a student to give the term or place to which he is referring. A student who fails to respond correctly must stand up beside his or her desk, indicating a "strike" for the team. After three strikes, the team is out of the competition. The following dialogue illustrates his approach. As you read it, be aware that the class has two students named Scott, and consider

■ What objectives the teacher appears to have for his students
■ How his lesson compares to Teacher A's review session (presented earlier) on the same topic

Teacher:	. . . Scott, "a society at an advanced stage of culture."
Scott:	Pass. [Strike one]
Teacher:	Stand up, please. . . . Robert?
Robert:	*Civilization.*
Teacher:	. . . "Shortage of food," Helen.
Helen:	That is a *drought.*
Teacher:	Marcy, "a substance used for making paper."
Marcy:	*Parchment.*
Teacher:	Fred, "a water-raising device."
Fred:	(No response) [Strike two]
Teacher:	Stand up, please. . . . Remember the definitions you were given. . . . Scott Parker.
Scott:	*Shadoof.*
Teacher:	Rula, "a city along the rapids."
Rula:	Not sure. [Strike three]
Teacher:	The right side row has three strikes. OK, next row. (Aulls, 1998, p. 61; punctuation and italics added)

Teacher B apparently wants his students to learn basic information about ancient Egypt (especially terminology and place names), perhaps to a level of automaticity (note his apparent lack of wait time). His focus, then, is on lower-level skills. Unfortunately, the activity promotes rote learning (memorization of word-for-word definitions) and discourages meaningful learning. Teacher A's question-and-answer session (about Egyptian burials, on the previous page) also focuses on lower-level skills, but it is more likely to facilitate learning and achievement for at least three reasons. First, it fosters meaningful learning and integration of ideas rather than verbatim recall of isolated facts. Second, it gives students the opportunity to ask questions. And third, it focuses less on evaluating students; thus, it is less likely to arouse anxiety and more likely to promote intrinsic motivation.

Teacher questions, especially higher-level questions, often get the ball rolling in class discussions. By asking thought-provoking questions, we can encourage students to think about what they have already learned and begin to elaborate on it with their peers (Aulls, 1998; Pogrow & Londer, 1994). We now look at additional strategies for conducting effective discussions.

Class Discussions

What knowledge and skills have you learned primarily through discussions with your classmates? Does a fellow student sometimes explain confusing course material more clearly than an instructor has? Do you sometimes understand course material better after *you* have explained it to someone else? Do classroom debates about controversial issues help you clarify your own thinking about those issues?

As you know from reading Chapter 7, social constructivists propose that learners often work together to construct meaningful interpretations of their world. Class discussions in which students feel they can speak freely, asking questions and presenting their ideas and opinions in either a whole-class or small-group context, obviously provide an important mechanism for promoting such socially constructed understandings (Haseman, 1999; G. J. Kelly & Chen, 1998; Marshall, 1992).

Class discussions lend themselves readily to a variety of academic disciplines. For example, students may discuss various interpretations of classic works of literature, addressing questions that have no easy or "right" answers; when they do so, they are more likely to relate what they are reading to their personal lives and so can understand it better (Eeds & Wells, 1989; E. H. Hiebert & Raphael, 1996; L. M. McGee, 1992). In history classes, students may study and discuss various documents related to a single historical event and so begin to recognize that history is not necessarily as cut-and-dried as traditional textbooks portray it (Leinhardt, 1994). In science, discussions of various and conflicting explanations of observed phenomena can enhance scientific reasoning skills, promote conceptual change, and help students begin to understand that science is not a collection of "facts" as much as it is a dynamic and continually evolving set of understandings (P. Bell & Linn, 2002; K. Hogan et al., 2000; Schwarz et al., 2000). And in mathematics, discussions that focus on alternative approaches to solving the same problem can promote more complete understanding and better transfer to new situations and problems (Cobb et al., 1991; J. Hiebert & Wearne, 1996; Lampert, 1990). You can find examples of whole-class or small-group discussions in each of these domains—literature, history, science, and math—in several clips on Video CD 2; in particular, see "Scarlet Letter," "Civil War," "Designing Experiments," "Properties of Air," "Group Work," and "Cooperative Learning."

Although students typically do most of the talking in class discussions, teachers nevertheless play a critical role. Theorists have offered several guidelines for promoting effective discussions:

■ Observe examples of whole-class and small-group discussions in several content domains in the clips on Video CD 2.

◎ *Focus on topics that lend themselves to multiple perspectives, explanations, or approaches* (L. M. Anderson, 1993; E. H. Hiebert & Raphael, 1996; Lampert, 1990). Controversial topics appear to have several benefits: Students are more likely to express their views to their classmates, seek out new information that resolves seemingly contradictory data, reevaluate their own positions on issues, and develop a meaningful and well-integrated understanding of the subject matter (E. G. Cohen, 1994; D. W. Johnson & Johnson, 1985; Kuhn, Shaw, & Felton, 1997; K. Smith, Johnson, & Johnson, 1981).

◎ *Make sure students have enough prior knowledge about a topic to discuss it intelligently.* Such knowledge may come either from previous class sessions or from students' personal experiences (Bruning, Schraw, & Ronning, 1995). In many cases it has come from studying a particular topic in depth (Onosko, 1996).

◎ *Create a classroom atmosphere conducive to open debate and the constructive evaluation of ideas.* Students are more likely to share their ideas and opinions if their teacher is supportive of multiple viewpoints and if disagreeing with classmates is socially acceptable (A.-M. Clark et al., 2003; Cobb & Yackel, 1996; Lampert et al., 1996). To promote such an atmosphere, we might

- Communicate the message that understanding a topic at the end of a discussion is more important than having the "correct" answer at the beginning of the discussion
- Communicate the beliefs that asking questions reflects curiosity, that differing perspectives on a controversial topic are both inevitable and healthy, and that changing one's opinion on a topic is a sign of thoughtful reflection
- Encourage students to explain their reasoning and to try to understand one another's explanations

- Suggest that students build on one another's ideas whenever possible
- Encourage students to be open in their agreement or disagreement with their classmates—that is, to "agree to disagree"
- Depersonalize challenges to a student's line of reasoning by framing questions in a third-person voice—for example, by saying, "What if someone were to respond to your claim by saying . . . ?"
- Occasionally ask students to defend a position that is in direct opposition to what they actually believe
- Require students to develop compromise solutions that take into account opposing perspectives

(Cobb & Yackel, 1996; Hatano & Inagaki, 1993, 2003; Herrenkohl & Guerra, 1998; K. Hogan et al., 2000; Lampert et al., 1996; Onosko, 1996; Reiter, 1994)

When students become comfortable with disagreeing in a congenial way, they often find the interactions highly motivating (A.-M. Clark et al., 2003). One fourth grader, whose class regularly had small-group discussions about literature, put it this way:

> I like it when we get to argue, because I have a big mouth sometimes, and I like to talk out in class, and I get really tired of holding my hand up in the air. Besides, we only get to talk to each other when we go outside at recess, and this gives us a chance to argue in a nice way. (A.-M. Clark et al., 2003, p. 194)

◎ *Use small-group discussions as a way of encouraging all students to participate.* Students gain more from a class discussion when they participate actively in the discussion (e.g., O'Donnell, 1999; Webb, 1989). And they are more likely to speak openly when their audience is a handful of classmates rather than the class as a whole; the difference is especially noticeable for girls and for students with special needs (A.-M. Clark et al., 2003; Théberge, 1994). On some occasions, then, we may want to have students discuss an issue in small groups first, thereby giving them the chance to test and possibly gain support for their ideas in a relatively private context; we can then bring them together for a whole-class discussion (Minstrell & Stimpson, 1996; Onosko, 1996).

Many students feel more comfortable discussing issues in a small group than in front of the entire class.

◎ *Provide a structure to guide the discussion.* Providing a structure for a discussion—perhaps setting a particular goal toward which students should work or assigning different roles to different class members (e.g., some evaluate the quality of evidence presented, others evaluate the validity of conclusions, etc.)—often increases the productivity of the conversation (Calfee, Dunlap, & Wat, 1994; Herrenkohl & Guerra, 1998; Palincsar & Herrenkohl, 1999). For example, before students conduct an experiment, we might ask them to make predictions about what will happen and to explain and defend their predictions; later, after students have observed the outcome of the experiment, we might ask them to explain what happened and why (Hatano & Inagaki, 1991; B. Y. White & Frederiksen, 1998). Another strategy, useful when the topic under discussion is especially controversial, is to follow a sequence such as this one:

1. The class is divided into groups of four students apiece. Each group of four subdivides into two pairs.
2. Within a group, each pair of students studies a particular position on the issue and presents its position to the other two students.
3. The group of four has an open discussion of the issue, giving each student an opportunity to argue persuasively for his or her own position.
4. Each pair presents the perspective of the *opposing* side as sincerely and persuasively as possible.
5. The group strives for consensus on a position that incorporates all the evidence presented. (M. Deutsch, 1993)

By following such a procedure, and in particular by asking students to argue both sides of an issue, we encourage them to think critically about various viewpoints and to begin to recognize that opposing perspectives may *both* have some validity (Reiter, 1994).

At the same time, we must recognize that the most effective group discussions are often ones in which students have some control over the direction of discourse—perhaps by asking their own questions, initiating new issues related to the topic, or going out on a risky but creative "limb" (Aulls, 1998; K. Hogan et al., 2000; Onosko, 1996). Learner-directed discussions (rather than teacher-directed ones) are also more likely to encourage effective group interaction skills (R. C. Anderson et al., 2001). For instance, when fourth graders meet in small, self-directed groups to discuss children's literature, they may develop and model such skills as expressing agreement ("I agree with Kordell because . . . "), disagreeing tactfully ("Yeah, but they could see the fox sneak in"), justifying an opinion ("I think it shouldn't be allowed, because if he got to be king, who knows what he would do to the kingdom"), and seeking everyone's participation ("Ssshhh! Be quiet! Let Zeke talk!") (R. C. Anderson et al., 2001, pp. 16, 25; A.-M. Clark et al., 2003). Ultimately, the amount of structure we impose must depend on how much scaffolding students need to have a productive discussion; for instance, we may want to be more directive with a small discussion group that seems to be unfocused and floundering than with one that is effectively articulating, critiquing, and building on one another's ideas (K. Hogan et al., 2000).

◎   *Give students guidance about how to behave.* Students will have more productive discussions when we describe appropriate behaviors for discussion sessions. We must take steps to ensure that students' reactions to one another's ideas are not disparaging or mean-spirited (Onosko, 1996). And we may find it helpful to provide guidelines such as these for small-group discussions:

- Encourage everyone to participate, and listen to everyone's ideas.
- Restate what someone else has said if you don't understand.
- Be critical of ideas rather than people.
- Try to pull ideas from both sides together in a way that makes sense.
- Focus not on winning, but on resolving the issue in the best possible way.
- Change your mind if the arguments and evidence presented indicate that you should do so. (based on M. Deutsch, 1993)

◎   *Provide closure at the end of the discussion.* Although students may sometimes come to consensus about a topic at the end of a class discussion, this will certainly not always be the case. Nevertheless, a class discussion should have some form of closure that helps students tie various ideas together. For instance, when I conduct discussions about controversial topics in my own classes, I spend a few minutes at the end of class identifying and summarizing the key issues that students have raised. Another strategy is to have students explain how a particular discussion has helped them understand a topic more fully (Onosko, 1996).

Whole-class and small-group discussions are not necessarily stand-alone instructional strategies; for instance, we may often want to incorporate them into expository instruction or discovery learning sessions. Student dialogues not only encourage students to think about and process classroom subject matter more completely, but they can also promote more effective learning strategies during reading and listening activities (A. L. Brown & Reeve, 1987; D. R. Cross & Paris, 1988; Paris & Winograd, 1990). One particular form of discussion, *reciprocal teaching*, is especially effective for this purpose.

Reciprocal Teaching

As you may recall from our discussion of metacognition in Chapter 8, students typically know very little about how they can best learn information. As illustrations, here are three high school students' descriptions of how they study a textbook (A. L. Brown & Palincsar, 1987, p. 83):

- " . . . I stare real hard at the page, blink my eyes and then open them—and cross my fingers that it will be right here." (Student points at head).
- "It's easy, if [the teacher] says study, I read it twice. If she says read, it's just once through."
- "I just read the first line in each paragraph—it's usually all there."

None of these students mentions any attempt to understand the information, relate it to prior knowledge, or otherwise think about it in any way, so we might guess that they are *not* engaging in meaningful learning, organization, or elaboration. In other words, they are not using cognitive processes that should help them store and retain information in long-term memory.

One important instructional goal, of course, is that students learn to read. But an equally important goal is that students *read to learn*—in other words, that they acquire new information from what they read. When we examine the cognitive processes that good readers (successful learners) often use, especially when reading challenging material, we find strategies such as these (A. L. Brown & Palincsar, 1987):

- *Summarizing.* Good readers identify the gist and main ideas of what they read.
- *Questioning.* Good readers ask themselves questions to make sure they understand what they're reading; in other words, they monitor their comprehension.
- *Clarifying.* Good readers take steps to clarify confusing or ambiguous parts of the text, perhaps by rereading or making logical inferences.
- *Predicting.* Good readers anticipate what they are apt to read next based on cues in the text (e.g., headings) and ideas that have already been presented.

In contrast, poor readers—those who learn little from textbooks and other reading materials—rarely summarize, question, clarify, or predict. For example, many students cannot adequately summarize a typical *fifth*-grade textbook until high school or even junior college (A. L. Brown & Palincsar, 1987; Palincsar & Brown, 1984). Clearly, many students do not easily acquire the ability to read for learning.

Reciprocal teaching (A. L. Brown & Palincsar, 1987; Palincsar & Brown, 1984, 1989; Palincsar & Herrenkohl, 1999) is an approach to teaching reading through which students learn effective reading-to-learn strategies by observing and imitating what their teacher and fellow students do. The teacher and several students meet in a group to read a piece of text, occasionally stopping to discuss and process the text aloud. Initially, the teacher leads the discussion, asking questions about the text to promote summarizing, questioning, clarifying, and predicting. But gradually, he or she turns the role of "teacher" over to different students, who then take charge of the discussion and ask one another the kinds of questions their teacher has modeled. Eventually, students can read and discuss a text almost independently of their teacher: They work together to construct meaning and check one another for comprehension and possible misunderstandings, and they become increasingly flexible in how they apply their newly acquired strategies.

As an illustration, let's look at a reciprocal teaching session for a group of six first graders reading a passage about snowshoe rabbits. In this particular case the classroom teacher reads the text in small segments (at higher grade levels, students take turns reading). After each segment, the teacher pauses while students discuss and process the segment. As you read the dialogue, look for examples of summarizing, questioning, clarifying, and predicting (there is at least one instance of each).

The children were reading about the snowshoe rabbit, and it was the sixteenth day of dialogue. The teacher had just read a segment of text describing the season in which baby rabbits are born and the ways in which the mother rabbit cares for her babies. A student named Kam is the dialogue leader.

Kam: When was the babies born?
Teacher: That's a good question to ask. Call on someone to answer that question.
Kam: Robby? Milly?
Milly: Summer.
Teacher: What would happen if the babies were born in the winter? Let's think.

Several children make a number of responses, including: "The baby would be very cold." "They would need food." "They don't have no fur when they are just born."

Kam: I have another question. How does she get the babies safe?
Kris: She hides them.
Kam: That's right but something else. . . .
Teacher: There is something very unusual about how she hides them that surprised me. I didn't know this.
Travis: They are all in a different place.
Teacher: Why do you think she does this?
Milly: Probably because I heard another story, and when they're babies they usually eat each other or fight with each other.
Teacher: That could be. And what about when that lynx comes?

Several children comment that that would be the end of all the babies.

Travis: If I was the mother, I would hide mine, I would keep them all together.
Kris: If the babies are hidden and the mom wants to go and look at them, how can she remember where they are?

■ How often do *you* engage in these processes when you read? Can you explain the value of each one by relating it to effective memory storage processes?

■ **reciprocal teaching** Approach to teaching reading and listening comprehension in which students take turns asking teacher-like questions of classmates.

Teacher:	Good question. Because she does have to find them again. Why? What does she bring them?
Milly:	She needs to bring food. She probably leaves a twig or something.
Teacher:	Do you think she puts out a twig like we mark a trail?

Several children disagree and suggest that she uses her sense of smell. One child, recalling that the snowshoe rabbit is not all white in the winter, suggests that the mother might be able to tell her babies apart by their coloring.

Teacher:	So we agree that the mother rabbit uses her senses to find her babies after she hides them. Kam, can you summarize for us now?
Kam:	The babies are born in the summer. . . .
Teacher:	The mother . . .
Kam:	The mother hides the babies in different places.
Teacher:	And she visits them . . .
Kam:	To bring them food.
Travis:	She keeps them safe.
Teacher:	Any predictions?
Milly:	What she teaches her babies . . . like how to hop.
Kris:	They know how to hop already.
Teacher:	Well, let's read and see. (dialogue courtesy of A. Palincsar)

■ Can you find at least one example each of summarizing, questioning, clarifying, and predicting in this reciprocal teaching session?

Reciprocal teaching provides a mechanism through which both the teacher and students can model effective reading and learning strategies; hence, this approach has an element of social cognitive theory. But when we consider that we are encouraging effective cognitive processes by first having students practice them aloud in group sessions, we realize that Vygotsky's theory of cognitive development is also at work here: Students should eventually *internalize* the processes that they first use in their discussions with others. Furthermore, the structured nature of a reciprocal teaching session scaffolds students' efforts to make sense of the things they read and hear. For example, in the preceding dialogue the teacher models elaborative questions and connections to prior knowledge ("What would happen if the babies were born in the winter?" "Do you think she puts out a twig like we mark a trail?") and provides general guidance and occasional hints about how students should process the passage about snowshoe rabbits ("Kam, can you summarize for us now?" "And she visits them . . . "). Also notice in the dialogue how students support one another in their efforts to process what they are reading; consider this exchange as an example:

■ In what way does reciprocal teaching reflect a *cognitive apprenticeship* (see Chapter 2)?

Kam:	I have another question. How does she get the babies safe?
Kris:	She hides them.
Kam:	That's right but something else. . . .

Reciprocal teaching has been used successfully with a wide variety of students, ranging from first graders to college students, to teach effective reading and listening comprehension skills (Alfassi, 1998; E. R. Hart & Speece, 1998; Johnson-Glenberg, 2000; K. D. McGee, Knight, & Boudah, 2001; Palincsar & Brown, 1989; Rosenshine & Meister, 1994). In an early study of reciprocal teaching (Palincsar & Brown, 1984), six seventh-grade students with a history of poor reading comprehension participated in twenty reciprocal teaching sessions, each lasting about thirty minutes. Despite this relatively short intervention, students showed remarkable improvement in their reading comprehension skills. They became increasingly able to process reading material in an effective manner and to do so independently of their classroom teacher. Furthermore, they generalized their new reading strategies to other classes, sometimes even surpassing the achievement of their classmates (A. L. Brown & Palincsar, 1987; Palincsar & Brown, 1984).

Reciprocal teaching can be employed with an entire classroom of students almost as easily as in a small group. Although teachers are often very skeptical of such a radically different approach to teaching and learning, their enthusiasm grows once they've tried it themselves (A. L. Brown & Palincsar, 1987; Palincsar & Brown, 1989). Using it effectively may take some practice, however, as well as a concerted effort to make sure that students formulate higher-level questions as well as lower-level ones (e.g., Hacker & Tenent, 2002).

Technology-Based Discussions

Effective student discussions don't necessarily have to be face to face. Through such mechanisms as electronic mail (e-mail), Web-based chat rooms, and electronic bulletin boards, computer technology enables students to communicate with peers (either in their own classroom or elsewhere), exchange perspectives, and build on one another's ideas (Fabos & Young, 1999; Hewitt & Scardamalia, 1996; J. Schacter, 2000). Technology also allows subject matter experts to be pulled occasionally into the conversation (A. L. Brown & Campione, 1996; Winn, 2002).

Researchers do not yet have a good handle on the specific benefits that cross-school and cross-cultural discussions may have (Fabos & Young, 1999), but at least one form of within-class electronic "discussion" shows considerable promise. Researchers at the University of Toronto have developed software that allows students to communicate regularly using a classwide database and essentially creates a computer-based community of learners (Hewitt & Scardamalia, 1996; Lamon, Chan, Scardamalia, Burtis, & Brett, 1993).[6] Students use the database to share their questions, ideas, notes, writing products, and graphic constructions. Their classmates (and sometimes a subject matter expert as well) respond regularly, perhaps by giving feedback, building on ideas, offering alternative perspectives, or summarizing what has been learned. As an example, in an anthropology unit on "Prehistory of the New World" in a fifth- and sixth-grade classroom, students worked in groups of three or four to study particular topics and then shared their findings through their computer database (Hewitt, Brett, Scardamalia, Frecker, & Webb, 1995). One group, which studied various theories about how human beings first migrated from Asia to the Americas, reported the following:

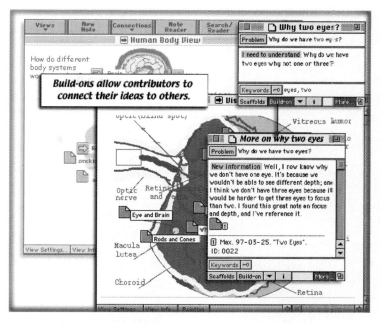

Build-ons allow contributors to connect their ideas to others.

This Knowledge Forum® software allows students to exchange and interconnect ideas not only with their classmates but also with peers and adults at other institutions.

Knowledge Forum® www.KnowledgeForum.com was designed by Marlene Scardamalia, Carl Bereiter, and the CSILE/Knowledge-Building Team at the Ontario Institute of Studies in Education at the University of Toronto (OISE-UT) and is published by Learning in Motion, Inc.

> **What we have learned**: We know that we have learned lots on this project, but the more that we learn the more we get confused about which is fact and which is fiction. The problem within this problem is that there isn't any real proof to say when they came or how. The theory that is most believed is the Bering Strait theory in which people from Asia walked over a land bridge. Another theory is they kayaked the distance between the two continents. We have also unfortunately found racist theories done by people who hate people unlike their own saying that the people of the New World are these people because of human sacrifices and only this race of people would do that.
>
> We have made are [our] own theories using information we found and trying to make sense of it. We have heard some people say they come from outer space but this theory is pretty much out of the question. I don't think the Native peoples or the Inuit would like to hear that theory either. How they came isn't easily answered for some of the theories but it does make since [sense] with the Bering Strait theory. (Hewitt et al., 1995, p. 7)

■ Judging from the students' summary, what can we say about their *epistemological beliefs* (Chapter 8) related to anthropology?

Studies of the interactive software's effects have been encouraging: Students are concerned about truly understanding classroom subject matter rather than simply "getting things done" (i.e., they adopt mastery goals rather than performance goals), actively try to relate new material to what they already know (i.e., they engage in meaningful learning), and can better remember and apply classroom subject matter (e.g., Lamon et al., 1993). Also, as you can see, the software enables the classroom to become a *community of learners* in which students regularly collaborate and contribute to one another's learning and achievement.

■ You can find another example of a technology-based discussion in the section "Creating a Community of Learners" in Chapter 7.

Cooperative Learning

Experiencing FIRSTHAND · Purple Satin

Imagine yourself as a student in each of the three classrooms described here. How would you behave in each situation?

---

[6] An early version of this software was known as Computer Supported Intentional Learning Environment, or CSILE (pronounced like the name *Cecil*). A second generation of CSILE, called Knowledge Forum (available commercially from Learning in Motion, Inc.), allows collaboration across schools and other institutions (e.g., see http://www.KnowledgeForum.com).

1. Mr. Alexander tells your class, "Let's find out which students can learn the most in this week's unit on the human digestive system. The three students getting the highest scores on Friday's test will get free tickets to the Purple Satin concert." Purple Satin is a popular musical group; you would give your eyeteeth to hear them perform, but the concert has been sold out for months.

2. Ms. Bernstein introduces her lesson this way: "Let's see whether each of you can learn all about the digestive system this week. If you can get a score of at least 90 percent on this Friday's test, I'll give you a free ticket to the Purple Satin concert."

3. Mr. Camacho begins the same lesson like this: "Today we begin studying the human digestive system. Let's see how many students can get scores of 90 percent or better on Friday's test. I want you to work in groups of three to help one another learn the material. If all three members of a group score at least 90 percent on the test, then that group will get free tickets to the Purple Satin concert."

In which class(es) are you likely to work hard to get free tickets to Purple Satin? How might you work *differently* in the different situations?

· · · · · · ·

The first classroom (Mr. Alexander's) is obviously a very competitive one: Only the three best students are getting tickets to the concert. Will you try to earn one of those tickets? It all depends on what you think your chances are of being a top scorer on Friday's test. If you've been doing well on tests all year, then you will undoubtedly study harder than ever during this week's unit. If, instead, you have been doing poorly in class despite your best efforts, then you probably won't work for something you're unlikely to get. But in either case, will you help your fellow students learn about the digestive system? Not if you want to go to the concert yourself!

In Ms. Bernstein's classroom there's no competition for concert tickets. As long as you get a score of 90 percent or higher on the test, you get a ticket. Even if you think half the students in class are smarter than you are, you know that you have a good chance of going to the concert, and so you will probably study diligently for Friday's test. But will you help your classmates understand what the pancreas does or learn the difference between the large and small intestines? Maybe . . . *if* you have the time and are in a good mood.

Now consider Mr. Camacho's classroom. Whether or not you get a concert ticket depends on how well you *and two other students* score on Friday's test. Are you going to help those two students learn about salivation and digestive enzymes? And can you expect them, in turn, to help you understand where the liver fits into the whole system? Absolutely!

In **cooperative learning**,[7] students work in small groups to achieve a common goal. Unlike an individualistic classroom such as Ms. Bernstein's (where one student's success is unrelated to peers' achievement) or a competitive classroom such as Mr. Alexander's (where one student's success actually depends on the *failure* of others), students in a cooperative learning environment such as Mr. Camacho's work together to achieve common successes. In other words, they *sink or swim together* (D. W. Johnson & Johnson, 1991).

On some occasions groups are formed on a short-term basis to accomplish specific tasks—perhaps to study new material, solve a problem, or complete an assigned project. In other instances groups are formed to work toward long-term classroom goals. For example, **base groups** are cooperative groups that work together an entire semester or school year; they provide a means through which students can clarify assignments for one another, help one another with class notes, and give one another a general sense of support and belonging in the classroom (D. W. Johnson & Johnson, 1991).

■ **cooperative learning** Approach to instruction in which students work with a small group of peers to achieve a common goal and help one another learn.

■ **base group** Cooperative learning group in which students work together for an entire semester or school year to provide mutual support for one another's learning.

---

[7] Some theorists distinguish between *cooperative* learning and *collaborative* learning, although different theorists draw the line somewhat differently (e.g., see Palincsar & Herrenkohl, 1999; B. L. Smith & MacGregor, 1992; Teasley & Roschelle, 1993). Part of their reasoning, I suspect, is that the term *cooperative learning* has historically been associated with particular theorists and particular instructional strategies (e.g., D. W. Johnson & Johnson, 1991; Slavin, 1983, 1990). Here I am using *cooperative learning* more broadly to refer to any instructional method in which students work together in a somewhat structured format to achieve a shared learning goal.

We find justification for cooperative learning in several theoretical frameworks. From the perspective of cognitive psychology, cooperative learning yields the same benefits that emerge from class discussions: greater comprehension and integration of the subject matter, recognition of inadequacies or misconceptions in understanding, and increased perspective taking. Furthermore, when students help one another learn, they provide scaffolding for one another's efforts, and they may jointly construct more sophisticated ideas and strategies than any single group member might be able to construct alone (Good et al., 1992; Hatano & Inagaki, 1991; A. M. O'Donnell & O'Kelly, 1994; N. M. Webb & Palincsar, 1996). From a behaviorist point of view, reinforcing group success is consistent with the operant conditioning notion of a *group contingency*. From a social cognitive perspective, students should have higher self-efficacy for performing a task when they know they will have the help of several peers; furthermore, students can model effective learning and problem-solving strategies for one another (A. L. Brown & Palincsar, 1989; Good et al., 1992). And theorists of various theoretical persuasions point out that cooperative ventures are important elements of scientific inquiry and adult work environments (Greeno, 1997; D. W. Johnson & Johnson, 1991).

Numerous research studies indicate that cooperative learning activities, when designed and structured appropriately, are effective in many ways. Students of all ability levels show higher academic achievement; females, members of minority groups, and students at risk for academic failure are especially likely to show higher achievement (Lou et al., 1996, 2001; J. D. Nichols, 1996; Qin, Johnson, & Johnson, 1995; Rohrbeck, Ginsburg-Block, Fantuzzo, & Miller, 2003).

The benefits of well-designed cooperative learning activities are not limited to gains in learning and achievement. Students have higher self-efficacy about their chances of success, express more intrinsic motivation to learn school subject matter, participate more actively in classroom activities, and exhibit more self-regulated learning. They better understand the perspectives of others and more frequently engage in prosocial behavior, making decisions about how to divide a task fairly and equitably, resolving interpersonal conflicts, and encouraging and supporting one another's learning. Furthermore, they are more likely to believe they are liked and accepted by their classmates, and friendships across racial and ethnic groups and between students with and without disabilities are apt to form (Lou et al., 1996, 2001; Marsh & Craven, 1997; J. D. Nichols, 1996; R. J. Stevens & Slavin, 1995; N. M. Webb & Palincsar, 1996).

Cooperative learning has several potential pitfalls, however. Some students may be less interested in mastering the material than they are in meeting social and performance goals (e.g., making friends, creating a good impression, getting the right answer quickly), and their willingness to assist one another or ask for help may be compromised as a result (Levy et al., 2000; M. C. Linn et al., 1996; Moje & Shepardson, 1998). Students who do most of the work and most of the talking are likely to learn more than other group members (Blumenfeld, 1992; Gayford, 1992; N. M. Webb, 1989). Students may occasionally agree to use an incorrect strategy or method that a particular group member has suggested, or they may share misconceptions about the topic they are studying (Good et al., 1992; Stacey, 1992). In some cases students may simply not have the skills to help one another learn (D. M. Hogan & Tudge, 1999; A. M. O'Donnell & O'Kelly, 1994). Clearly, then, we must keep a close eye on group discussions, providing additional structure and guidance when necessary to promote maximal learning and achievement.

Cooperative learning has personal and social benefits as well as academic ones. For instance, it often promotes self-efficacy, intrinsic motivation, social skills, and cross-cultural friendships.

As you can see, cooperative learning is not simply a process of putting students in groups and setting them loose to work on an assignment together. Oftentimes, students will be more accustomed to competitive and individualistic classroom situations than they are to working cooperatively with their peers. For a cooperative learning activity to be successful, we must structure the activity in such a way that cooperation is not only helpful for academic success but in fact even necessary for it (D. W. Johnson & Johnson, 1991). Following are several strategies that enhance the effectivenes of cooperative groups:

◎ *Form groups based on which students are likely to work effectively with one another.* Cooperative groups are typically comprised of two to six members; groups of three to four students are especially effective (Hatano & Inagaki, 1991; Lou et al., 1996). In most cases *we* should form the groups, identifying combinations of students that will be productive (D. W. Johnson & Johnson, 1991).

Many advocates of cooperative learning suggest that each group be relatively heterogeneous—that each group include high achievers and low achievers, boys and girls, and children of various ethnic backgrounds (D. W. Johnson & Johnson, 1991; Shachar & Sharan, 1994; R. J. Stevens & Slavin, 1995; N. M. Webb, Nemer, Chizhik, & Sugrue, 1998). In recent years, however, some theorists have begun to question the practice of combining students of widely differing achievement levels, arguing that such a practice makes ability differences among students more obvious than they would otherwise be. High-ability students may dominate discussions and discourage low-ability students from fully participating. Low-ability students may be reluctant to ask for help when they don't understand, or they may simply sit back and let other group members do most or all of the work. And if a group fails to achieve its goals, high performers in the group may resent and blame those who contributed little or nothing to the group's efforts (E. G. Cohen & Lotan, 1995; Kumar et al., 2002; Moje & Shepardson, 1998; A. M. O'Donnell & O'Kelly, 1994; S. E. Peterson, 1993; N. M. Webb, Nemer, & Zuniga, 2002).

Research regarding the effects of heterogeneous cooperative groups has yielded mixed results. Some studies indicate that heterogeneous groups benefit both high-achieving students (who can sharpen their knowledge by explaining it to peers) and low-achieving students (who benefit from hearing such explanations) (Lou et al., 1996; R. J. Stevens & Slavin, 1995; N. M. Webb et al., 1998; N. M. Webb & Palincsar, 1996). Yet other studies indicate that high-achieving students do not always gain from working with their low-achieving classmates; in fact, these students occasionally even lose ground (D. M. Hogan & Tudge, 1999; Lou et al., 1996; N. M. Webb et al., 2002). Furthermore, students of similar ability levels may sometimes be able to work more collaboratively than students of widely differing abilities (L. S. Fuchs, Fuchs, Hamlett, & Karns, 1998). Given such mixed messages from research, our best bet is probably to experiment with varying degrees of heterogeneity in our cooperative groups and to determine which approach works best in our own circumstances.

◎   *Give group members one or more common goals toward which to work.* At the beginning of a cooperative group activity, we should specify clearly and concretely what each group should accomplish (Crook, 1995; D. W. Johnson & Johnson, 1991). For instance, when my daughter Tina was enrolled in high school Spanish, the goal of one cooperative activity was to write and videotape an episode of a television soap opera spoken entirely in Spanish. The students knew that these *telenovelas* would eventually be shown at an "Academy Awards" banquet for the students and parents, and "Oscars" would be presented for best picture, best screenplay, best leading and supporting actors and actresses, and so on. (Tina won for best actress, no surprise to me given her frequent emotional tirades on the home front.) Another example, this one used in an eighth-grade social studies class, is presented in Figure 13.6.

◎   *Provide clear guidelines about how to behave.* Without instruction about appropriate group behaviors, students may act in a decidedly uncooperative manner; for example, they may try to dominate discussions, ridicule one another's ideas, or exert pressure to complete a task in a particular way (Blumenfeld, Marx, Soloway, & Krajcik, 1996; N. M. Webb & Palincsar, 1996). Instruction on such group skills as the following seems to increase cooperative and productive group behaviors:

- Listening to others politely and attentively
- Making sure that everyone has an equal chance to participate and that everyone eventually understands the material
- Asking clear, precise questions when one doesn't understand
- Giving encouragement to others and offering assistance as needed
- Addressing differences of opinion amiably and constructively
  (E. G. Cohen, 1994; M. Deutsch, 1993; Gillies & Ashman, 1998; Lou et al., 1996; A. M. O'Donnell & O'Kelly, 1994; N. M. Webb & Farivar, 1999)

■ Observe a math class's discussion of appropriate group behavior in the "Cooperative Learning" clip on Video CD 2.

In the "Cooperative Learning" clip on Video CD 2, a seventh-grade math class identifies several ground rules (e.g., "help others," "be patient") for their group sessions.

◎   *Structure tasks so that group members are dependent on one another for success.* We should structure cooperative learning activities in such a way that each student's success depends on the help and participation of other group members; furthermore, each student must believe it is to

FIGURE 13.6 To be effective, cooperative groups should work toward common goals. Here eighth-grade history teacher Mark Nichols identifies several things that students need to accomplish as they prepare their group presentations about colonial America.

<u>Colonial Economies</u>

Textbook Chapters:
   Planting Colonies—Chapter 4

      -Spain Builds a Large Empire (Mr. Nichols)
      -French and Dutch Colonies (Group 1)
      -English Settlers in Virginia (Group 2)
      -The Pilgrims at Plymouth (Group 3)

   English Colonies Take Root—Chapter 5

      -New England Colonies (Group 4)
      -Middle Colonies (Group 5)
      -Southern Colonies (Group 6)
      -Governing the Colonies (Group 7)

Group Responsibilities:

   Groups will be established with 3-4 students.

   Each group will be responsible for reading and thoroughly understanding their assigned sub-chapter.

   Each group will prepare an outline of the chapter which will be typed in final draft format. Copies will be made for each student in class.

   Each group will create an artistic example of their material and a board game to be played at the end of the presentations.

   The day before your group presentation you are to instruct the class to read your sub-chapter and prepare a homework assignment for the class.

   A presentation of the material will be made to the class, which will include going over the homework assignment, the outline, and explanation of your creative display of the sub-chapter information. Class members are required to question the presenting group on their material.

   An open note test will be given at the end of this unit in order to ensure understanding of the material.

his or her advantage that other group members do well (M. Deutsch, 1993; Karau & Williams, 1995; Lou et al., 1996). Tasks that involve creative problem solving and have more than one right answer are especially likely to encourage students to work cooperatively with one another (Blumenfeld et al., 1996). In some situations each student might have a unique and essential function within the group, perhaps serving as group leader, critic, bookkeeper, summarizer, and so on (A. L. Brown & Palincsar, 1989; D. W. Johnson & Johnson, 1991). In other situations the **jigsaw technique** is useful: New information is divided equally among all group members, and each student must teach his or her portion to the others (E. Aronson & Patnoe, 1997). Still another approach is to assign projects that require such a wide range of talents and skills that every group member is likely to have something truly unique and useful to contribute to the group's overall success (E. G. Cohen, 1994; Schofield, 1995).

When students are novices at cooperative learning, it is often helpful to give them a set of steps (a "script" to follow) that guides their interaction (Gillies, 2003; A. M. O'Donnell, 1999; N. M. Webb & Palincsar, 1996). In one approach, known as **scripted cooperation**, students work together in pairs to read and study expository text. One member of the pair might act as "recaller," summarizing the contents of a textbook passage. The other student acts as "listener," correcting any errors and recalling additional important information. For the next passage, the two students switch roles. Such an approach can help students improve such learning strategies as elaboration, summarizing, and comprehension monitoring (Dansereau, 1988; A. M. O'Donnell, 1999).

◎   *Serve more as a resource and monitor than as a "director."* During any cooperative learning activity, we should continually monitor each group to be sure that interactions are productive and

■ **jigsaw technique** Instructional technique in which materials are divided among members of a cooperative group, with different students being responsible for learning different material and teaching it to other group members.

■ **scripted cooperation** Technique in which cooperative groups follow a set of steps or "script" that guides members' verbal interactions.

socially appropriate (D. W. Johnson & Johnson, 1991; Meloth & Deering, 1999). For instance, we might consider issues such as these:

- Are students working toward a common goal?
- Are they all actively participating?
- Are they listening to one another's perspectives?
- Are they asking one another questions when they don't understand?
- Are they criticizing ideas rather than people?

We might also offer assistance in situations where group members are unable to provide information or insights that are critical for accomplishing the group's goal. Too much intervention can be counterproductive, however: Students tend to talk less with one another when their teacher joins the group (E. G. Cohen, 1994).

◎ *Make students individually accountable for their achievement, but also reinforce them for group success.* Students are more likely to learn assigned classroom subject matter during cooperative learning activities when they know they will have to demonstrate individual mastery or accomplishment of the group's goal—for example, answering questions in class, taking a quiz, or making a unique and easily identifiable contribution to an overall group product. Such an approach minimizes the likelihood that some students will do most or all of the work while others get a "free ride" (Finn, Pannozzo, & Achilles, 2003; Karau & Williams, 1995; N. M. Webb & Palincsar, 1996).

■ Observe the combination of individual accountability and group rewards in the "Cooperative Learning" clip on Video CD 2.

In addition to holding students accountable for their own learning and achievement, we might also reinforce group members for the success of the group as a whole—a group contingency in action (Lou et al., 1996; Slavin, 1990; Stipek, 1996). Such group rewards often promote higher achievement overall, perhaps because students have a vested interest in helping one another learn and so make a concerted effort to help fellow group members understand the subject matter (R. J. Stevens & Slavin, 1995). One commonly used approach is to give students a quiz over material they have studied in their cooperative groups and then award bonus points when all group members perform at or above a certain level. You can find an example of this strategy in the "Cooperative Learning" clip on Video CD 2.

It is important to note, however, that not all researchers have found group rewards to be beneficial. In particular, students may sometimes learn better when they focus on using effective learning strategies than when they focus on obtaining a group reward (Meloth & Deering, 1992, 1994). As we've discovered in our earlier discussions of behaviorism and self-determination (Chapters 9 and 12), the effects of extrinsic reinforcers can be a mixed bag.

◎ *At the end of an activity, have the groups evaluate their effectiveness.* Once cooperative groups have accomplished their goals, we should have them look analytically and critically (perhaps with our assistance) at the ways in which they have functioned effectively and the ways in which they need to improve (E. G. Cohen, 1994; M. Deutsch, 1993; D. W. Johnson & Johnson, 1991). We might ask them to consider some of the same issues we kept in mind as we monitored the activity—for instance, whether everyone participated equally, whether group members asked one another questions when they didn't understand, and whether everyone criticized ideas rather than people.

In Figure 13.7, 12-year-old Amaryth reflects on her group's effectiveness in a collaborative task. Notice her concerns: "not really focused," "not really listening, "yelling a lot." As you can see, members of her group still have much to learn about how to work well together.

The Into the Classroom feature "Enhancing the Effectiveness of Cooperative Learning" reviews and illustrates many of the strategies we've just discussed. One of the reasons that cooperative learning is so often effective is that students tutor one another in the subject matter they are studying. In the next section we look at peer tutoring more closely.

Peer Tutoring

As teachers, we can't always devote as much time as we'd like to one-on-one instruction. **Peer tutoring**, in which students who have mastered a topic help those who have not, can provide an effective alternative for teaching fundamental knowledge and skills (A. L. Brown & Palincsar, 1987; Durkin, 1995; Greenwood, Carta, & Hall, 1988; Pigott et al., 1986). For example, we might have students within a single class tutor one another. Alternatively, we might have older students teaching younger ones; for instance, fourth or fifth graders might tutor students in

■ **peer tutoring** Approach to instruction in which students who have mastered a topic teach those who have not.

kindergarten or first grade (A. L. Brown & Campione, 1994; Inglis & Biemiller, 1997; Kermani & Moallem, 1997).

Like mastery learning, direct instruction, and computer-based instruction, peer tutoring sessions give students many opportunities to make the active responses that, from a behaviorist perspective, are so essential to learning. From a cognitive framework, tutoring encourages students to organize and elaborate on what they have already learned in order to make the material clear to someone else. And cross-age tutoring is consistent with Vygotsky's belief that older and more competent individuals are invaluable in promoting the cognitive development of younger children.

In some cases peer tutoring leads to greater academic gains than either mastery learning or more traditional whole-class instruction (D. Fuchs, Fuchs, Mathes, & Simmons, 1997; Greenwood et al., 1988). One possible reason for its effectiveness is that it provides a context in which struggling students may be more comfortable asking questions when they don't understand something. In one study (Graesser & Person, 1994), students asked 240 times as many questions during peer tutoring as they did during whole-class instruction!

Peer tutoring typically benefits tutors as well as those being tutored (D. Fuchs et al., 1997; Inglis & Biemiller, 1997; Semb et al., 1993; N. M. Webb & Palincsar, 1996). When students study material with the expectation that they will be teaching it to someone else, they are more intrinsically motivated to learn it, find it more interesting, process it in a more meaningful way, and remember it longer (Benware & Deci, 1984; Semb et al., 1993). Furthermore, in the process of

FIGURE 13.7 In an entry in her class journal, 12-year-old Amaryth reflects on the effectiveness of a cooperative group (she misspells *group* as "gobe").

INTO THE CLASSROOM

Enhancing the Effectiveness of Cooperative Learning

Form groups of students who are likely to work together productively.

An elementary school teacher divides her class into cooperative groups of four or five students each. He makes sure that each group includes boys and girls, students of various ethnic backgrounds, and students who will be able to contribute different skills to the task at hand.

Provide clear goals toward which groups should work.

In a unit on Shakespeare, an English teacher asks cooperative groups to identify attitudes toward Jewish people expressed in *The Merchant of Venice*, as reflected in the actions and statements of Shylock and other characters.

Give each group member a different role or task within the group.

A biology teacher asks cooperative groups to prepare for an upcoming class debate on the pros and cons of mosquito control in the community. She gives each student a unique function. One student acts as *reader* of information about the issue, another acts as *recorder* of group members' arguments, a third acts as *checker* to determine whether all group members agree with each argument, and so on.

Monitor group interactions.

A social studies teacher asks cooperative groups to identify an effective way of helping the homeless find suitable housing. When he hears one student disparaging another because of a difference of opinion, he reminds the group that students should criticize ideas rather than people.

Provide critical information and insights when (but only when) a group is unlikely or unable to provide such information and insights for itself.

The same social studies teacher tells a group, "The solution you have developed assumes that most taxpayers would be willing to pay much higher taxes than they do now. Is that realistic?"

Make students individually accountable for their achievement.

A mathematics teacher has incorporated cooperative learning into a unit on calculating the area of squares, rectangles, and triangles. Later, she gives all students a quiz to assess their individual mastery of the subject.

Reinforce group success.

The same math teacher awards bonus points to students whose entire group performs at or above a certain test score.

Ask students to evaluate their effectiveness in working as a group.

After cooperative groups have completed their assigned tasks, a teacher asks the groups to answer questions such as these: "Did all group members actively participate?" "Did they ask questions when they didn't understand one another?" "Did they criticize ideas rather than people?"

When one student tutors another, the tutor often learns as much from the experience as the student being tutored.

directing and guiding other students' learning and problem solving, tutors may, in a Vygotskian fashion, internalize these processes and so become better able to direct and guide their *own* learning and problem solving; in other words, peer tutoring can foster greater self-regulation (Biemiller et al., 1998).

Peer tutoring has nonacademic benefits as well. Cooperation and other social skills improve, behavior problems diminish, and friendships form among students of different ethnic groups and between students with and without disabilities (DuPaul, Ervin, et al., 1998; Greenwood et al., 1988).

Like other interactive approaches to instruction, peer tutoring is most effective when teachers follow certain guidelines in its use. Here are several suggestions for using peer tutoring effectively:

◎ *Make sure tutors have mastered the material they are teaching and use sound instructional techniques.* Good tutors have a meaningful understanding of the subject matter they are teaching and provide explanations that focus on such understanding; poor tutors are more likely to describe procedures without explaining why the procedures are useful (L. S. Fuchs et al., 1996). Good tutors also use teaching strategies that are likely to promote learning: They ask questions, give hints, scaffold responses when necessary, provide feedback, and so on (Lepper, Aspinwall, Mumme, & Chabay, 1990).

Students don't always have the knowledge and skills that will enable them to become effective tutors, especially at the elementary school level (Greenwood et al., 1988; Kermani & Moallem, 1997; D. Wood, Wood, Ainsworth, & O'Malley, 1995). It is essential, then, that tutoring sessions be limited to subject matter that the tutors know well. Training in effective tutoring skills is also helpful; for example, we might show tutors how to establish a good relationship with the students they are tutoring, how to break a task into simple steps, how and when to give feedback, and so on (Fueyo & Bushell, 1998; Inglis & Biemiller, 1997; Kermani & Moallem, 1997).

◎ *Provide a structure for students' interactions.* Providing a structure for tutoring sessions can often help students tutor their classmates more effectively (Fantuzzo, King, & Heller, 1992; L. S. Fuchs et al., 1996; Mathes, Torgesen, & Allor, 2001). As an example, in one study (D. Fuchs et al., 1997), 20 second- through sixth-grade classes participated in a project called Peer-Assisted Learning Strategies (PALS), designed to foster more effective reading comprehension skills. In each class, students were ranked by reading ability, and the ranked list was divided in two. The first-ranked student in the top half of the list was paired with the first-ranked student in the bottom half of the list, the second student in the top half was paired with the second student in the bottom half, and so on down the line; through this procedure, students who were paired together had moderate but not extreme differences in their reading levels. Each pair read text at the level of the weaker reader and engaged in the following activities:

- *Partner reading with retell.* The stronger reader read aloud for five minutes, then the weaker reader read the same passage of text. Reading something that had previously been read presumably enabled the weaker reader to read the material easily. After the double reading, the weaker reader described the material just read.
- *Paragraph summary.* The students both read a passage one paragraph at a time. Then, with help from the stronger reader, the weaker reader tried to identify the subject and main idea of the paragraph.
- *Prediction relay.* Both students read a page of text, and then, with help from the stronger reader, the weaker reader would summarize the text and also make a prediction about what the next page would say. The students would read the following page, then the weaker reader would confirm or disconfirm the prediction, summarize the new page, make a new prediction, and so on.

Such a procedure enabled students in the PALS program to make significantly more progress in reading than students who had traditional reading instruction, even though the amount of class time devoted to reading was similar for both groups. The researchers speculated that the PALS students performed better because they had more frequent opportunities to make verbal responses to what they were reading, received more frequent feedback about their performance and, in general, were more frequently encouraged to use effective reading strategies.

At the secondary school levels, we can incorporate a tutoring component into paired study sessions by teaching students the kinds of questions to ask one another as they jointly study science, social studies, and other academic disciplines. In one approach (A. King, 1997, 1999), students are given "starters" to help them formulate questions that encourage meaningful learning, elaboration, critical thinking, self-reflection, and other effective strategies. Here are some examples:

- Describe . . . in your own words.
- What is the difference between . . . and . . . ?
- What do you think would happen to . . . if . . . happened?
- How did you figure that out? (A. King, 1997, pp. 229–231)

When we give students guidance in formulating good questions, highly effective tutoring sessions can result. Following is an example in which two seventh graders are following a prescribed questioning procedure as they study biology:

Jon:	How does the muscular system work, Kyle?
Kyle:	Well . . . it retracts and contracts when you move.
Jon:	Can you tell me more?
Kyle:	Um . . . well . . .
Jon:	Um, why are muscles important, Kyle?
Kyle:	They are important because if we didn't have them we couldn't move around.
Jon:	But . . . how do muscles work? Explain it more.
Kyle:	Um, muscles have tendons. Some muscles are called skeletal muscles. They are in the muscles that—like—in your arms—that have tendons that hold your muscles to your bones—to make them move and go back and forth. So you can walk and stuff.
Jon:	Good. All right! How are the skeletal muscles and the cardiac muscles the same?
Kyle:	Uhh—the cardiac and the smooth muscles?
Jon:	The cardiac and the skeletal.
Kyle:	Well, they're both a muscle. And they're both pretty strong. And they hold things. I don't really think they have much in common.
Jon:	Okay. Why don't you think they have much in common?
Kyle:	Because the smooth muscle is—I mean the skeletal muscle is voluntary and the cardiac muscle is involuntary. Okay, I'll ask now. What do you think would happen if we didn't have smooth muscles?
Jon:	We would have to be chewing harder. And so it would take a long time to digest food. We would have to think about digesting because the smooth muscles—like the intestines and stomach—are *in*voluntary.
Kyle:	Have you really thought about it?
Jon:	Yeah.
Kyle:	Yeah, well—um—but, do you think it would *hurt* you if you didn't have smooth muscles?
Jon:	Well, yeah—because you wouldn't have muscles to push the food along—in the stomach and intestines—you'd get plugged up! Maybe you'd hafta drink liquid—just liquid stuff. Yuk. (A. King, Staffieri, & Adelgais, 1998, p. 141)

Notice how Jon and Kyle ask questions that encourage the other to go beyond the material he has specifically learned (e.g., "How are the skeletal muscles and the cardiac muscles the same?" "Do you think it would hurt you if you didn't have smooth muscles?"). Also, the boys ask each other questions that encourage them to think about their thinking and thereby may promote metacognition (e.g., "Why don't you think they have much in common?" "Have you really thought about it?"). Through such structured interactions, even students at the same grade and ability levels can provide valuable scaffolding for one another's learning efforts (A. King, 1998).

◎ *Be careful that your use of higher-achieving students to tutor lower-achieving students is not excessive or exploitative.* As we have seen, tutors often gain just as much from tutoring sessions as the students they are tutoring. Nevertheless, we must not assume that high-achieving students will always learn from a tutoring session; we should regularly monitor the effects of a peer tutoring program to make sure that all students are reaping its benefits.

◎ *Use peer tutoring to help students with special educational needs.* Peer tutoring has been used effectively to help students with learning disabilities, physical disabilities, and other special educational needs (Cushing & Kennedy, 1997; DuPaul, Ervin, et al., 1998; D. Fuchs et al., 1997). In one study (Cushing & Kennedy, 1997), low-achieving students were assigned as tutors for

■ Have you ever tutored a student who had a disability? If so, what benefits did *you* gain from the experience?

classmates who had moderate or severe intellectual or physical disabilities. The student tutors clearly benefited from their tutoring assignments: They became more attentive in class, completed classroom tasks more frequently, and participated in class more regularly. I suspect that the opportunity to tutor classmates less capable than themselves may have enhanced their own self-efficacy for learning classroom subject matter, which in turn encouraged them to engage in the kinds of behaviors that would ensure academic success.

◎   *Make sure that all students have experience tutoring their classmates.* Ideally, we should make sure that *all* of our students have an opportunity to tutor others at one time or another (Greenwood, 1991). This is often easier said than done, as a few students may show consistently lower achievement than most of their peers. One potentially effective strategy in such situations is to teach those students specific tasks or procedures that they can share with their higher-achieving, but in this case uninformed, classmates (E. G. Cohen, Lockheed, & Lohman, 1976; N. M. Webb & Palincsar, 1996).

In fact, how we can best accommodate student diversity must be a top consideration no matter which instructional strategy we use. We turn now to a more focused discussion of individual and group differences and their potential implications for various instructional strategies.

TAKING STUDENT DIVERSITY INTO ACCOUNT

The instructional strategies we choose will to some degree depend on students' ages and developmental levels. Strategies that involve teaching well-defined topics requiring a great deal of active student responding and strategies that provide frequent feedback (e.g., mastery learning, direct instruction, computer-based instruction) will often be more appropriate for younger students than for older ones (Rosenshine & Stevens, 1986). Lectures (which are often somewhat abstract) and homework assignments tend to be more effective with older students (Ausubel et al., 1978; H. Cooper & Valentine, 2001).

The knowledge and skills that students bring to a topic should also be a consideration (Gustafsson & Undheim, 1996; Rosenshine & Stevens, 1986). Structured, teacher-directed approaches are probably most appropriate when students know little or nothing about the subject matter. But when students have mastered basic knowledge and skills, and particularly when they are self-regulating learners, they should begin directing some of their own learning, perhaps in group discussions, authentic activities, or use of hypermedia and the Internet.

In general, however, *all* students should have experience with a wide variety of instructional methods. For instance, although some students may need to spend considerable time on basic skills, too much time in structured, teacher-directed activities may minimize opportunities to choose what and how to study and learn and, as a result, may prevent students from developing a sense of self-determination (Battistich et al., 1995). In addition, authentic activities, though often unstructured and complex, give students of all levels a greater appreciation for the relevance and meaningfulness of classroom subject matter than may be possible with more traditional classroom tasks.

Some instructional strategies adapt themselves readily to a wide variety of student abilities and needs. For example, mastery learning provides a means through which students can learn at their own pace. Computer-based instructional programs often tailor instruction to students' prior knowledge and skills. Homework assignments can be easily individualized for the amount and kinds of practice that different students need.

Considering Group Differences

Students' ethnic and cultural backgrounds may sometimes guide our choice of instructional strategies. Recent immigrants from some Asian countries may be more accustomed to teacher-directed instruction than to learner-directed classroom activities (Igoa, 1995). Yet students from cultures that place a high premium on interpersonal cooperation (e.g., as is true in many Hispanic and Native American communities) are apt to achieve at higher levels in classrooms with many interactive and collaborative activities (García, 1994, 1995; McAlpine & Taylor, 1993; N. M. Webb & Palincsar, 1996). In situations where students have limited English skills, technology can often come to our assistance, perhaps in the form of English-language tutorials, computer programs that "read" electronic "books" to a student, and word processing programs with spell checkers and grammar checkers (P. F. Merrill et al., 1996).

Collaborative and cooperative approaches to instruction may also be helpful for our female students. Small-group discussions and activities encourage girls to participate more actively than they typically do during whole-class instruction (Théberge, 1994). We should note, however, that boys sometimes take control during small-group activities. If we regularly see such male dominance, we may occasionally want to form all-female groups; by doing so, we are likely to increase girls' participation in group activities and to encourage them to take leadership roles (Fennema, 1987; MacLean et al., 1995).

Our choice of instructional strategies may be especially critical when we work in schools in low-income, inner-city neighborhoods. Students in such schools often have more than their share of drill-and-practice work in basic skills—work that is hardly conducive to fostering excitement about academic subject matter (Duke, 2000; R. Ferguson, 1998; Portes, 1996). Mastering basic knowledge and skills is essential, to be sure, but we can often incorporate them into engaging lessons that ask students to apply what they're learning to personal interests and real-world contexts (Lee-Pearce et al., 1998; M. McDevitt & Chaffee, 1998). For example, in a curriculum called "Kids Voting USA," students in kindergarten through grade 12 have age-appropriate lessons about voting, political parties, and political issues, and they relate what they learn to local election campaigns (M. McDevitt & Chaffee, 1998). Depending on the grade level, they might conduct their own mock elections, analyze candidates' attacks of opponents, or give speeches about particular propositions on the ballot. Students who participate in the program are more likely to attend regularly to media reports about an election, initiate discussions about the election with friends and family members, and be knowledgeable about candidates and election results. In fact, their knowledge and excitement about politics is contagious, because even their *parents* begin to pay more attention to the news, talk more frequently about politics, and gain greater knowledge about candidates and political issues.

Interactive strategies are especially valuable when our instructional goals include promoting social development as well as academic achievement. Peer tutoring encourages friendly relationships across ethnic and racial lines (Greenwood et al., 1988). Cooperative learning groups, especially when students work on tasks involving a number of different skills and abilities, can foster an appreciation for the various strengths that students with diverse backgrounds are likely to contribute (E. G. Cohen, 1994; E. G. Cohen & Lotan, 1995). And virtually any collaborative approach to instruction—cooperative learning, reciprocal teaching, peer tutoring—may help students begin to recognize that despite the obvious diversity among them, they are ultimately more similar to one another than they are different (Schofield, 1995).

Accommodating Students with Special Needs

We may sometimes want to tailor our instructional goals to students' specific cognitive abilities or disabilities; for example, we may need to modify our expectations in some academic areas for students with learning disabilities, and we may find it beneficial to set more challenging goals for students who are gifted. In addition, different instructional strategies may be more or less useful for students with special educational needs. For instance, strictly expository instruction (e.g., a lecture) may provide a quick and efficient means of presenting new ideas to students who think abstractly and process information quickly yet be incomprehensible and overwhelming to students with low cognitive ability. Similarly, discovery learning is often effective in enhancing the academic achievement of students with high ability; however, it may actually be detrimental to the achievement of lower-ability students who have not yet mastered basic concepts and skills (Corno & Snow, 1986). And mastery learning and direct instruction have been shown to be effective with students who have learning difficulties, including many students with special educational needs, yet they may prevent rapid learners from progressing at a rate commensurate with their abilities (Arlin, 1984; Leinhardt & Pallay, 1982; Rosenshine & Stevens, 1986).

We will often need to adapt instructional strategies to the unique strengths and weaknesses of particular students with special needs. For example, when students have difficulty with certain aspects of information processing (e.g., when they have certain learning disabilities), it may be especially important to provide a variety of supports (advance organizers, visual aids, study guides, etc.) during expository instruction (Mercer, 1997). When students have social or behavioral problems, we may need to provide close supervision and frequent encouragement and feedback during independent in-class assignments. Table 13.4 provides a "memory refresher" for some of the characteristics of students with special needs that we've considered in previous chapters; it also presents some instructional strategies we can use to accommodate these characteristics.

TABLE 13.4   S T U D E N T S   I N   I N C L U S I V E   S E T T I N G S

Identifying Instructional Goals and Strategies Especially Suitable for Students with Special Educational Needs

CATEGORY	CHARACTERISTICS YOU MIGHT OBSERVE	SUGGESTED CLASSROOM STRATEGIES
Students with specific cognitive or academic difficulties	• Uneven patterns of achievement • Difficulty with complex cognitive tasks in some content domains • Difficulty processing or remembering information presented in particular modalities • Poor listening skills, reading skills, or both • Greater-than-average difficulty in completing homework	• Establish challenging yet realistic goals; tailor goals to individual students' strengths and weaknesses. • Use an information processing analysis to identify the specific cognitive skills involved in a complex task; consider teaching each skill separately. • Use mastery learning, direct instruction, computer-based instruction, cooperative learning, and peer tutoring to help students master basic knowledge and skills. • During expository instruction, provide information through multiple modalities (e.g., with videotapes, audiotapes, graphic materials), and provide advance organizers and study guides. • Have students use computer tools (e.g., grammar and spell checkers) to compensate for areas of weakness. • Assign homework that provides additional practice in basic skills; individualize assignments for students' unique abilities and needs; provide extra scaffolding (e.g., solicit parents' help, explicitly teach effective study habits). • Use reciprocal teaching to promote listening and reading comprehension.
Students with social or behavioral problems	• Frequent off-task behavior • Inability to work independently for extended periods • Poor social skills	• Provide small-group direct instruction and peer tutoring as ways of providing one-on-one attention. • Keep unsupervised seatwork assignments to a minimum. • Use cooperative learning to foster social skills and friendships. • Give explicit guidelines about how to behave during interactive learning sessions. (As appropriate, also use strategies listed for students with specific cognitive or academic difficulties.)
Students with general delays in cognitive and social functioning	• Difficulty with complex tasks • Difficulty thinking abstractly • Need for a great deal of repetition and practice of basic information and skills • Difficulty transferring information and skills to new situations	• Identify realistic goals in both the academic and social arenas. • Use task analysis to break complex behaviors into simpler responses that students can more easily learn. • Present information as concretely as possible (e.g., by engaging students in hands-on experiences). • Use direct instruction, computer-assisted instruction, and in-class activities to provide extended practice in basic skills. • Embed basic skills within authentic tasks to promote transfer to the outside world. • Use peer tutoring as a means of promoting friendships with nondisabled classmates; identify skills that students have mastered and can teach to their classmates or to younger students.
Students with physical or sensory challenges	• Average intelligence in most instances • Tendency to tire easily (for some) • Limited motor skills (for some) • Difficulty with speech (for some)	• Aim for instructional goals similar to those for nondisabled students unless there is a compelling reason to do otherwise. • Allow frequent breaks from strenuous or intensive activities. • Use computer-based instruction (with any needed mechanical adaptations) to allow students to progress through material at their own pace and make active responses during instruction. • When students have difficulty speaking, provide another means of enabling them to participate actively in class discussions and cooperative learning groups (perhaps through technology).
Students with advanced cognitive development	• Greater frequency of responses at higher levels of Bloom's taxonomy (e.g., analysis, evaluation) • Rapid learning • Greater ability to think abstractly; appearance of abstract thinking at a younger age • Greater conceptual understanding of classroom material • Ability to learn independently	• Identify goals and standards that challenge students and encourage them to develop to their full potential. • Provide opportunities to pursue topics in greater depth (e.g., through assigned readings, computer-based instruction, or homogeneous cooperative groups). • Teach strategies that enable students to learn on their own (e.g., library skills, scientific methods, use of hypermedia and the Internet). • Ask predominantly higher-level questions. • Introduce students to safe Internet outlets where they can communicate with others who have similar interests and abilities. • Use advanced students as peer tutors only if both tutors and learners will benefit.

Sources: T. Bryan, Burstein, & Bryan, 2001; Carnine, 1989; DuNann & Weber, 1976; DuPaul, Barkley, & Connor, 1998; Fiedler et al., 1993; Greenwood et al., 1988; Heward, 2003; C. C. Kulik et al., 1990; Mercer, 1997; P. F. Merrill et al., 1996; Morgan & Jenson, 1988; Piirto, 1999; A. Robinson, 1991; Ruef et al., 1998; Schiffman, Tobin, & Buchanan, 1984; Spicker, 1992; R. J. Stevens & Slavin, 1995; Tarver, 1992; R. Turnbull et al., 2004; J. W. Wood & Rosbe, 1985.

THE BIG PICTURE

Historically, many theorists and practitioners have looked for—and in some cases decided that they've found—the single "best" way to teach children and adolescents. The result has been a series of movements in which educators advocate a particular instructional approach and then, a few years later, advocate a very different approach (K. R. Harris & Alexander, 1998; Sfard, 1998). I've often wondered why the field of education is characterized by such "pendulum swings," and I've developed several hypotheses. Perhaps some people are looking for a teaching *algorithm*—a specific procedure they can follow to guarantee high achievement. Perhaps they confuse theory with fact, thinking that the latest theoretical fad must inevitably be the "correct" explanation of how children learn or develop, and so conclude that the teaching implications they derive from the theory must also be correct. Or maybe they just have an overly simplistic view of what the goals of our educational system should be.

When we consider which instructional strategies to use in our classrooms, we must remember that *there is no single best approach to classroom instruction*. Each of the strategies we've examined has its merits, and each is useful in different situations and for different students. In general, our choice of an instructional strategy must depend on at least three things: the objective of the lesson, the nature of the subject matter, and the characteristics and abilities of students. Table 13.5 presents general conditions and specific examples in which each strategy might be most appropriate.

A successful classroom—one in which students are acquiring and using school subject matter in truly meaningful ways—is undoubtedly a classroom in which a variety of approaches to instruction can be found. As you gain experience as a classroom teacher, you will become increasingly adept at using many (perhaps all) of the strategies we've explored in this chapter. You will, I hope, experiment with different approaches to determine which ones work most effectively for your own instructional goals, academic discipline(s), and students. Furthermore, as noted in Chapter 1, you can continue to grow as a teacher if you keep yourself up to date both on the subject matter you are teaching and on theoretical and research perspectives on effective classroom instruction.

Yet knowing how to plan and implement instruction is not enough. Effective teachers also create a classroom environment conducive to student learning. Furthermore, they regularly monitor their students' progress toward achieving classroom goals and adapt instruction when warranted. We will consider the classroom environment and assessment strategies in the next three chapters.

CASE STUDY: *Uncooperative Students*

Ms. Mihara is beginning the unit "Customs in Other Lands" in her fourth-grade class. Having heard about the benefits of cooperative learning, she asks students to form groups of four that will work together throughout the unit. On Monday she assigns each group a particular country: Australia, Colombia, Ireland, Greece, Japan, or South Africa. She then instructs the groups, "Today we will go to the school library, where you can find information on the customs of your country and check out materials you think will be useful. Over the next two weeks, you will have time every day to work as a group. You should learn all you can about the customs of your country. A week from Friday, each group will give an oral report to the rest of the class."

During the next few class sessions, Ms. Mihara runs into many more problems than she anticipated. For example, when the students form their groups, she notices that high achievers have gotten together to form two groups and that many socially oriented, "popular" students have flocked to two others. The remaining two groups are comprised of whichever students are left over. Some groups get immediately to work on their task, others spend their group time sharing gossip and planning upcoming social events, and still others are neither academically nor socially productive.

As the unit progresses, Ms. Mihara hears more and more complaints from students about their task ("Janet and I are doing all the work; Karen and Mary Kay aren't helping at all," "Eugene thinks he can boss the rest of us around because we're studying Ireland and he's Irish, " "We're spending all this time but just can't seem to get anywhere!"). And the group reports at the end of the unit differ markedly in quality: Some are carefully planned and informative, whereas others are disorganized and lack substantive information.

(continued on page 480)

TABLE 13.5

COMPARE/CONTRAST

Choosing an Instructional Strategy

YOU MIGHT USE . . .	WHEN . . .	FOR EXAMPLE, YOU MIGHT . . .
Expository instruction (e.g., lectures, textbook readings)	• The *objective* is to acquire new information. • The *lesson* involves information best learned within a specific organizational structure. • *Students* are capable of abstract thought, have knowledge to which they can relate new material, and have adequate reading skills and learning strategies for assigned readings.	• Describe critical battles of World War I to advanced history students. • Demonstrate several defensive strategies to the varsity soccer team.
Mastery learning	• The *objective* is to learn knowledge or skills to mastery (perhaps to automaticity). • The *lesson* provides critical information or skills for later instructional units. • *Students* vary in the time they need to achieve mastery.	• Have each student in instrumental music practice the C major scale until he or she can do so perfectly. • Have students practice 100 single-digit addition facts until they can answer all the facts correctly within a five-minute period.
Direct instruction	• The *objective* is to learn a well-defined body of knowledge and skills. • The *lesson* provides critical information or skills for later instructional units. • *Students* need considerable guidance and practice in order to learn successfully.	• Explain how to add fractions with different denominators, and give students practice in adding such fractions both in class and through homework. • Demonstrate how to use a jigsaw, and watch carefully as students use the tool to cut irregularly shaped pieces of wood.
Computer-based instruction	• The *objective* is to acquire basic knowledge and skills. • The *lesson* involves information that students can learn from reading text or from watching and listening to multimedia presentations. • *Students* have some familiarity with computers and can work with only minimal guidance from their teacher.	• Use a typing-skills tutorial that helps students develop automaticity in keyboarding. • Assign a research project that requires the use of a computer-based, multimedia encyclopedia.
Online research	• The *objective* is to gain expertise in finding information available on the World Wide Web. • The *lesson* requires information not readily available in the classroom. • *Students* have some familiarity with Internet software (e.g., Web browsers) and search engines.	• Ask students to identify demographic differences among various regions of the United States using data from the U.S. Census Bureau. • Have students read about current events on Web sites of national news bureaus and newsmagazines.
Discovery learning	• The *objective* is to gain firsthand experience with a phenomenon. • The *lesson* involves information that can be correctly deduced from experimentation or other personal experience. • *Students* have enough knowledge to interpret findings correctly but may have trouble learning from strictly abstract material.	• Ask students to find out what happens when two primary colors of paint (red and yellow, red and blue, or yellow and blue) are mixed together. • Conduct an activity in which students discover firsthand how it feels to experience "taxation without representation."
In-class activities	• The *objective* is to gain practice in using new information or skills. • The *lesson* requires considerable teacher monitoring and scaffolding. • *Students* cannot yet work independently on the task.	• Have beginning tennis students practice their serves. • Have students work in pairs to draw portraits of classmates.
Computer simulations and applications	• The *objective* is to gain experience in a domain that can be explored more easily in a "virtual" world *or* to gain experience with computer tools. • The *lesson* involves any task for which simulation software is available *or* that lends itself to a computer application. • *Students* have some familiarity with computers and can work with only minimal teacher guidance.	• Have students explore human anatomy through a computer simulation that gives an inside "look" at various anatomical structures. • Have students write a résumé using a word processing program.

TABLE 13.5

COMPARE/CONTRAST

Continued

YOU MIGHT USE . . .	WHEN . . .	FOR EXAMPLE, YOU MIGHT . . .
Homework	• The *objective* is to learn new yet simple material, obtain additional practice with familiar information and procedures, or relate classroom subject matter to the outside world. • The *lesson* is one that students can complete with little if any help from others. • *Students* exhibit enough self-regulation to complete the task independently.	• Have students read the next chapter in their health book and answer several questions about its content. • In a unit on migration, have students find out what state, province, or country their parents and grandparents were born in.
Authentic activities	• The *objective* is to apply class material to real-world situations. • The *lesson* involves synthesizing and applying a variety of knowledge and skills. • *Students* have mastered the knowledge and skills necessary to perform the task.	• Have students grow sunflowers using varying amounts of water, plant food, and sunlight. • Have students construct maps of their local community, using appropriate symbols to convey direction, scale, and natural and manmade features.
Teacher questions	• The *objective* is to understand and elaborate on a topic in greater depth. • The *lesson* involves complex material, such that frequent monitoring of students' learning is essential, mental elaboration of ideas is beneficial, or both. • *Students* are not likely to elaborate spontaneously or to monitor their own comprehension effectively.	• Ask questions that promote recall and review of the previous day's lesson. • Ask students for examples of how nonrenewable resources are recycled in their own community.
Class discussion	• The *objective* is to achieve greater conceptual understanding, acquire a multisided perspective of a topic, or both. • The *lesson* involves complex and possibly controversial issues. • *Students* have sufficient knowledge about the topic to offer informed ideas and opinions.	• Ask students to discuss the ethical implications of the United States' decision to drop an atomic bomb on Hiroshima. • Ask groups of four or five students to prepare arguments for an upcoming debate on the pros and cons of increasing the minimum wage.
Reciprocal teaching	• The *objective* is to develop reading comprehension and learning strategies. • The *lesson* requires students to cognitively process material in relatively complex ways. • *Students* have poor reading comprehension and learning strategies.	• Model four types of questions—summarizing, questioning, clarifying, and predicting—as students read aloud a passage from a textbook. • Ask students to take turns being "teacher" and ask similar questions of their classmates.
Technology-based discussion	• The *objective* is to construct new knowledge as a group and to evaluate and refine emerging understandings. • The *lesson* involves a topic that is sufficiently multifaceted that all students have something to contribute. • *Students* have adequate reading comprehension skills to learn independently or in small groups, as well as adequate computer literacy to exchange information electronically.	• In a community where students have easy access to computers and the Internet, set up an electronic bulletin board that allows students to share their questions and ideas about homework assignments. • On the classroom computer's desktop, create several "folders" in which students can save essays for one another to read and critique.
Cooperative learning	• The *objective* is to develop the ability to work cooperatively with others on academic tasks. • The *lesson* involves tasks that are too large or difficult for a single student to accomplish independently. • *Students'* cultural backgrounds emphasize cooperation rather than competition.	• Have groups of two or three students work together on mathematical "brain teasers." • Have students in a Spanish class work in small groups to write and videotape a soap opera spoken entirely in Spanish.
Peer tutoring	• The *objective* is to learn basic knowledge or skills. • The *lesson* contains material that can effectively be taught by students. • *Students* vary in their mastery of the material, yet even the most advanced can gain increased understanding by teaching it to someone else.	• Have students work in pairs to practice conjugating irregular French verbs. • Have some students help others work through simple mathematical word problems.

"So much for this cooperative learning stuff," Ms. Mihara mumbles to herself. "If I want students to learn something, I'll just have to teach it to them myself."

Why have Ms. Mihara's cooperative learning groups not been as productive as she had hoped? Considering the strategies for promoting cooperative learning that we examined in this chapter, what did Ms. Mihara do wrong?

How might you orchestrate the cooperative learning unit differently than Ms. Mihara?

Once you have answered these questions, compare your responses with those presented in Appendix B.

KEY CONCEPTS

teacher-directed instruction (p. 435)
learner-directed instruction (p. 435)
instructional goal (p. 436)
instructional objective (p. 436)
standards (p. 436)
Bloom's taxonomy (p. 439)
task analysis (p. 441)
expository instruction (p. 443)
advance organizer (p. 444)

mastery learning (p. 446)
direct instruction (p. 447)
computer-based instruction (CBI) (p. 449)
hypertext (p. 449)
hypermedia (p. 449)
distance learning (p. 450)
discovery learning (p. 451)
authentic activity (p. 456)

lower-level question (p. 458)
higher-level question (p. 458)
reciprocal teaching (p. 463)
cooperative learning (p. 466)
base group (p. 466)
jigsaw technique (p. 469)
scripted cooperation (p. 469)
peer tutoring (p. 470)

PRAXIS Turn to Appendix C, "Matching Book and Ancillary Content to the Praxis Principles of Learning and Teaching Tests," to discover sections of this chapter that may be especially applicable to the Praxis tests.

Companion Website

Now go to our Companion Website at **www.prehall. com/ormrod** to assess your understanding of chapter content with "Multiple-Choice Questions," apply comprehension in "Essay Questions," broaden your knowledge of educational psychology with related "Web Links," gain greater insight about classroom learning in "Learning in the Content Areas," and analyze and assess classroom work in the "Student Artifact Library."

*T*hink back to your elementary and secondary school years. In which teachers' classrooms were you most likely to work hard and stay on task? In which teachers' classrooms were you most likely to misbehave? What strategies did your best teachers use to help you be productive?

Effective teachers not only choose instructional strategies that promote effective learning and cognitive processing, but they also create an environment that keeps students productively engaged in classroom activities. In this chapter we will consider how we can create a classroom environment conducive to students' learning and achievement. As we do so, we will address questions such as these:

- What kinds of teacher-student relationships are most likely to enhance students' learning, development, and emotional well-being?
- How can we best keep students on task and minimize disruptive behavior?
- How should we deal with misbehaviors?
- What strategies have been shown to be effective in addressing aggression and violence at school?
- How can we work effectively with students' parents?

CASE STUDY: *A Contagious Situation*

Ms. Cornell received her teaching certificate in May; soon after, she accepted a position as a fifth-grade teacher at Twin Pines Elementary School. She spent the summer planning her classroom curriculum: She identified her instructional goals for the year and developed numerous activities to help students achieve those goals. She now feels well prepared for her first year in the classroom.

After the long, hot summer, most of Ms. Cornell's students seem happy to be back at school. On the first day of school, Ms. Cornell jumps headlong into the curriculum she has planned. But three problems quickly present themselves—problems in the form of Eli, Jake, and Vanessa.

These three students seem determined to disrupt the class at every possible opportunity. They move about the room without permission, making a point of annoying others as they walk to the pencil sharpener or wastebasket. They talk out of turn, sometimes being rude and disrespectful to their teacher and classmates and at other times belittling the activities Ms. Cornell has so carefully planned. They rarely complete in-class assignments, preferring instead to engage in horseplay or practical jokes. They seem especially prone to misbehavior during downtimes in the daily schedule—for example, at the beginning and end of the school day, before and after recess and lunch, and on occasions when Ms. Cornell is preoccupied with other students.

Ms. Cornell continues to follow her daily lesson plans, ignoring her problem students and hoping they will begin to shape up. Yet with the three of them egging one another on, the disruptive behavior continues. Furthermore, it begins to spread to other students. By the middle of October, Ms. Cornell's classroom is a three-ring circus, and instructional objectives are rarely accomplished. The few students who still seem intent on learning something are having a difficult time doing so.

- In what ways has Ms. Cornell planned for her classroom in advance? In what ways has she *not* planned?

- Why are Eli, Jake, and Vanessa so disruptive right from the start? Can you think of possible reasons related to how Ms. Cornell has begun the school year? Can you think of possible reasons related to our discussion of motivation in Chapters 11 and 12? Can you think of possible reasons related to the activities Ms. Cornell has planned?

- Why does the misbehavior of the three problem students continue? Why does it spread to other students in the classroom? Why is it particularly common during downtimes in the school day? Can you answer these questions using learning principles presented in earlier chapters?

CREATING AN ENVIRONMENT CONDUCIVE TO LEARNING

As a first-year teacher, Ms. Cornell is well prepared in some respects but not at all prepared in others. She has carefully identified her instructional goals and planned relevant lessons. But she has neglected to think about how she might keep students on task or how she might adjust her lessons based on how students are progressing. And she has not considered how she might nip behavior problems in the bud, before they begin to interfere with students' learning. In the absence of such planning, no curriculum—not even one grounded firmly in contemporary theories of learning and development—can be very effective.

Students learn more in some classroom environments than in others. Consider these four classes as examples:

- Mr. Aragon's class is calm and orderly. The students are working independently at their seats, and all of them appear to be concentrating on their assigned tasks. Occasionally students approach Mr. Aragon to seek clarification of an assignment or to get feedback about a task they've completed, and he confers quietly with them.
- Mr. Boitano's class is chaotic and noisy. A few students are doing their schoolwork, but most are engaged in very nonacademic activities. One girl is painting her nails behind a large dictionary propped up on her desk, a boy nearby is picking wads of gum off the underside of his desk, several students are exchanging the latest school gossip, and a group of boys is reenacting the Battle of Waterloo with rubber bands and paper clips.
- Mr. Cavalini's class is as noisy as Mr. Boitano's. But rather than exchanging gossip or waging war, students are debating (often loudly and passionately) about the pros and cons of nuclear energy. After twenty minutes of heated discussion, Mr. Cavalini stops them, lists their various arguments on the board, and then explains in simple philosophical terms why there is no easy or "correct" resolution of the issue.
- Mr. Durocher believes that students learn most effectively when rules for their behavior are clearly spelled out. So he has rules for almost every conceivable occasion—fifty-three rules in all. Following is a small sample:
  > Be in your seat before the bell rings.
  > Use a ballpoint pen with blue or black ink for all assignments.
  > Use white lined paper with straight edges; do not use paper with loose-leaf holes or spiral notebook "fringe."
  > Raise your hand if you wish to speak, and then speak only when called upon.
  > Do not ask questions unrelated to the topic being studied.
  > Never leave your seat without permission.

  Mr. Durocher punishes each infraction severely enough that students follow the rules to the letter. So his students are a quiet and obedient (if somewhat anxious) bunch, but they never seem to learn as much as Mr. Durocher knows they are capable of learning.

Two of these classrooms are quiet and orderly; the other two are active and noisy. Yet as you can see, the activity and noise levels are not good indicators of how much students are learning. Students are learning both in Mr. Aragon's quiet class and in Mr. Cavalini's rambunctious one. At the same time, neither the students in Mr. Boitano's loud, chaotic battlefield nor those in Mr. Durocher's peaceful military dictatorship seem to be learning much at all.

Effective **classroom management**—creating and maintaining a classroom environment conducive to learning and achievement—has little to do with noise or activity level. A well-managed classroom is one in which students are consistently engaged in productive learning activities and in which students' behaviors rarely interfere with the achievement of instructional goals (W. Doyle, 1990; Emmer & Evertson, 1981).

Creating and maintaining an environment in which students are continually engaged in productive activities can be a challenging task indeed. After all, we must tend to the unique needs of many different students, we must sometimes coordinate several activities at the same time, and we must often make quick decisions about how to respond to unanticipated events (W. Doyle, 1986a). Furthermore, we must vary our classroom management techniques considerably depending on the particular instructional strategies (e.g., expository, hands-on, or interactive) we are using (Emmer & Stough, 2001). So it is not surprising that many beginning teachers mention classroom management as their number one concern (Jones, 1996; Veenman, 1984).

■ Is it possible to *over*manage a classroom? If so, what might be the negative ramifications of doing so?

■ **classroom management** Establishment and maintenance of a classroom environment conducive to learning and achievement.

To create and maintain a productive learning environment, effective teachers typically

- Physically arrange the classroom in a way that minimizes distractions and facilitates teacher-student interaction
- Create a climate in which students feel they belong and are intrinsically motivated to learn
- Set reasonable limits for behavior
- Plan activities that encourage on-task behavior
- Continually monitor what students are doing
- Modify instructional strategies when necessary

In the pages that follow, we will identify specific ways to implement each of these strategies. We will then consider how individual and developmental differences enter into the picture.

A well-managed classroom is one in which students are consistently engaged in learning. It is not necessarily one in which everyone is quiet.

Arranging the Classroom

Good management begins well before the first day of class. As we arrange classroom furniture, decide where to put instructional materials and equipment, and think about where each student might sit, we should consider the effects that various arrangements are likely to have on students' behavior. Ultimately, we want a situation in which we can

- Minimize distractions
- Interact easily with every student
- Survey the entire class at any given time

Minimizing Distractions   Stuart is more apt to poke a classmate with his pencil if he has to brush past the classmate to get to the pencil sharpener. Marlene is more likely to fiddle with instructional materials at inappropriate times if they are within easy reach of her desk. David is more likely to gossip with a friend if the friend is sitting right beside him. As teachers, we should arrange our classrooms in ways that minimize the probability that such off-task behaviors will occur (Emmer, Evertson, Clements, & Worsham, 1994; Sabers, Cushing, & Berliner, 1991). For example, we can establish traffic patterns that allow students to move around the classroom without disturbing one another, keep intriguing materials out of sight and reach until they need to be used, and situate overly chatty friends on opposite sides of the room.

Facilitating Teacher-Student Interaction   Ideally, we should arrange desks, tables, and chairs so that we can easily interact and converse with students (G. A. Davis & Thomas, 1989). Students seated near us are more likely to pay attention, interact with us, and become actively involved in classroom activities; hence, we may want to place chronically misbehaving or uninvolved students close at hand (W. Doyle, 1986a; Woolfolk & Brooks, 1985).

Surveying the Entire Class   As we proceed through various lessons and activities—even when working with a single individual or small group—we should ideally be able to see *all* students (Emmer et al., 1994). By occasionally surveying the classroom for possible signs of confusion, frustration, or boredom, we can more easily detect minor student difficulties and misbehaviors before they develop into serious problems.

Creating an Effective Classroom Climate

Think back on your many years as a student. Can you recall a class in which you were afraid of being ridiculed if you asked a "stupid" question? Can you recall one in which you and your classmates spent more time goofing off than getting your work done because no one seemed to take the class seriously? Can you recall one in which you never knew what to expect because your instructor was continually changing expectations and giving last-minute assignments without warning?

In addition to the classroom's physical environment, we must also consider the psychological environment, or **classroom climate**, we create. Ideally, we want a classroom in which students feel safe and secure, make their own learning a high priority, and are willing to take the risks and make the mistakes so critical for long-term academic success (e.g., Brand, Felner,

■ **classroom climate** Overall psychological atmosphere of the classroom.

■ Observe the supportive classroom climates in the "Author's Chair" and "Scarlet Letter" clips on Video CD 2.

Shim, Seitsinger, & Duman, 2003). The "Author's Chair" and "Scarlet Letter" clips on Video CD 2 present two examples of supportive classroom climates (one each at the elementary and secondary levels) that facilitate learning and encourage risk taking.

In the following sections, we'll look at several general strategies for creating and maintaining a classroom climate conducive to learning:

- Forming and maintaining a productive relationship with every student
- Establishing a businesslike yet nonthreatening atmosphere
- Communicating appropriate messages about school subject matter
- Giving students some control over classroom activities
- Promoting a general sense of community and belongingness

Such strategies are especially important for students at risk for academic failure and dropping out of school (e.g., V. E. Lee & Burkam, 2003; Pianta, 1999; U.S. Dept. of Education, 1992).

Forming and Maintaining Productive Teacher-Student Relationships   As you should recall from Chapter 11, human beings seem to have a fundamental need to feel socially connected with others. In the classroom this *need for relatedness* may reveal itself in a variety of ways; for instance, students might eagerly seek our approval for something they've done well or, alternatively, misbehave to gain our attention (remember the case study of James at the beginning of Chapter 9). But in my own experiences as a teacher and school psychologist, I've never met a child or adolescent who, deep down, didn't want *positive, productive* relationships with school faculty.

To some extent, we can help students meet their need for relatedness by demonstrating, through the many little things we do, that we care about and respect them as people (Certo et al., 2002; Diamond, 1991; Spaulding, 1992). For example, we can give them a smile and warm greeting at the beginning of the day. We can compliment them when they get a new haircut, excel in an extracurricular activity, or receive recognition in the local newspaper. We can be good listeners when they come to school angry or upset. One high school student described caring teachers this way:

> They show it. You might see them in the hallway and they ask how you're doing, how was your last report card, is there anything you need. Or, maybe one day you're looking a little upset. They'll pull you to the side and ask you what's wrong, is there anything I can do. They just show a real concern for us students. (Certo et al., 2002, p. 15)

Such behaviors may be particularly beneficial for those students who have few caring relationships at home (Diamond, 1991).

Yet it's not enough simply to be "warm and fuzzy" in our interactions with students (L. H. Anderman, Patrick, Hruda, & Linnenbrink, 2002, p. 274; H. A. Davis, 2003). To show students we *truly* care about and respect them, we must also

- Be well prepared for class and in other ways demonstrate that we enjoy teaching and take our teaching responsibilities seriously
- Communicate high (yet realistic) expectations for student performance and provide the support students need to meet our expectations
- Include students in decision making and in evaluations of their work
- Acknowledge that students can occasionally have an "off" day and not hold it against them (Certo et al., 2002; H. A. Davis, 2003; H. A. Davis, Schutz, & Chambless, 2001)

Research consistently indicates that the quality of teacher-student relationships is one of the most important factors affecting students' motivation, emotional well-being, and achievement. More specifically, when students have positive, supportive relationships with teachers, they have higher self-efficacy and more intrinsic motivation to learn, engage in more self-regulated learning, are more likely to ask for help when they need it, are less apt to cheat on classroom assignments, and achieve at higher levels (Midgley, Middleton, Gheen, & Kumar, 2002; Murdock, Hale, Weber, Tucker, & Briggs, 1999; Pianta, 1999; Roeser, Eccles, & Sameroff, 2000; A. M. Ryan & Patrick, 2001).

Occasionally students will come to us with an apparent chip on the shoulder, distrusting us from day one because of previous hurtful relationships with parents or other adults (H. A. Davis, 2003; Pianta, 1999). At other times we may get relationships off to a bad start through our own actions—perhaps because we've incorrectly attributed low achievement to lack of effort rather than lack of skill or perhaps because we've accused a temperamentally high-energy child of being intentionally disobedient (Darch & Kame'enui, 2004; B. K. Keogh, 2003; Silverberg, 2003).

Regardless of how nonproductive relationships start, we must work hard to turn them into productive ones. The first step, of course, is to *identify* nonproductive relationships using such signs as these (Pianta, 1999):

- We have hostile feelings (e.g., dislike, anger) toward a student.
- We rarely interact with a student.
- Our messages to a student usually involve criticism or faultfinding.
- We have a sense of learned helplessness about our ability to work effectively with a student.

Once we have identified troublesome relationships, several strategies can help us repair them. One is to think actively—perhaps in a brainstorming session with one or more colleagues—about alternative hypotheses for why a student behaves as he or she does, being sure that our list of hypotheses offers potential solutions (Pianta, 1999; Silverberg, 2003). Another is to meet one-on-one with a student to talk openly about the problem and possible ways to fix it (we'll return to this point later in the chapter). Still another strategy, especially effective when working with young children, is simply to spend some time with a student in a noninstructional, noncontrolling, "fun" context that might allow more positive feelings to emerge (Pianta, 1999).

One strategy many teachers use to establish and maintain productive relationships with students is a two-way journal in which students regularly express their thoughts and feelings, ask questions, and ask for assistance. At least once a week—preferably more often—their teacher reads and responds to their entries. The following exercise provides an example.

Interpreting Student Artifacts and Behaviors

A Two-Way Journal

Midway through the school year, a first-grade teacher has her students begin *dialogue journals* that will allow them to communicate individually with her every day. Following are several entries in 6-year-old Matt's journal. Each entry is followed by a response (indented) from the teacher. As you read the journal, consider

- What we learn about Matt from his entries
- Whether Matt's writing skills are adequate to make the activity meaningful
- What purpose(s) this activity might serve

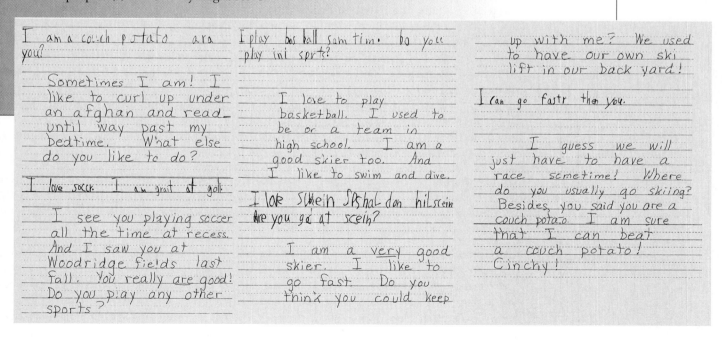

Despite his claim that he is a "couch potato," Matt clearly enjoys physical activity, including soccer, baseball, and skiing ("scein"). (This is the same Matt whose high school essay "Soccer, the Pride and Passion" appears in Figure 12.3.) We learn, too, that Matt feels comfortable enough with his teacher to tell her he is a better skier than she is ("I can go fastr then you"). Although Matt's writing skills are far from perfect—he leaves out some capital letters and periods and misspells many words (e.g., *especially downhill skiing* is "spshal don hilscein")—they are certainly adequate to communicate his thoughts.

The journal exchange serves both academic and social purposes: It allows the children to practice their reading and writing skills within an authentic task (actual communication with another person), and it provides a way for the teacher to express her unconditional regard and support for each student. Notice how the teacher does *not* correct Matt's misspellings. Her primary purposes are to encourage him to write and to open the lines of communication, and negative feedback about spelling might interfere with both of these goals. Instead, the teacher simply models correct spelling in her own entries.

■ How might the teacher adapt the journal assignment for students who cannot yet read and write?

Establishing a Businesslike, Nonthreatening Atmosphere   Although positive relationships with students are essential, we and our students must recognize that we are in school to get certain things accomplished. Accordingly, we should maintain a relatively businesslike atmosphere in the classroom most of the time (G. A. Davis & Thomas, 1989). This is not to say that classroom activities must be boring and tedious; on the contrary, they can often be exciting and engaging. But excitement and entertainment should not be thought of as goals in and of themselves. Rather, they are means to a more important goal: mastering academic subject matter.

Despite our emphasis on "business," the classroom atmosphere should never be uncomfortable or threatening. As noted in Chapter 11, students who are excessively anxious are unlikely to give us their best. How can we be businesslike without being threatening? Among other things, we can hold students accountable for achieving instructional objectives yet not place them under continual surveillance. We can point out their mistakes yet not make them feel like failures (C. R. Rogers, 1983). And we can admonish them for misbehavior yet not hold grudges against them from one day to the next (Spaulding, 1992).

Communicating Messages About School Subject Matter   In earlier chapters we've stressed the importance of making school subject matter relevant to students' lives. All too often, however, students view school activities and assignments more as things to "get done" than as things that will help them be successful over the long run (L. M. Anderson, Brubaker, Alleman-Brooks, & Duffy, 1985; Brophy & Alleman, 1991; Stodolsky et al., 1991).

As teachers, we give students messages about the value of school subject matter not only in what we say but also in what we do (W. Doyle, 1983). If we ask students to spend hours each day engaged in what seems like meaningless busy work, and if we assess learning primarily through tests that encourage rote memorization, we are indirectly telling students that classroom tasks are merely things that need to be "done." Furthermore, if we continually focus their attention on performance goals—what their test grades are, how their work compares to that of their classmates, and so on—we increase their anxiety about school subject matter and indirectly increase the frequency of disruptive behavior (Kumar et al., 2002; Marachi et al., 2001; A. M. Ryan & Patrick, 2001). If, instead, we continually demonstrate how classroom topics relate to the outside world, if we assess learning in ways that require meaningful learning and elaboration, and if we focus on how well each student is improving over time, we show students that the subject matter can potentially enhance the quality of their lives.

Giving Students a Sense of Control   To make sure students accomplish important instructional goals, we must control the direction of classroom events to some extent. Nevertheless, we can give students a sense that they, too, control some aspects of classroom life. For example, we can use strategies such as these (Spaulding, 1992):

- Give students advance notice of upcoming activities and assignments (enabling them to plan ahead).
- Create regular routines for accomplishing assignments (enabling students to complete the assignments successfully with only minimal guidance).
- Allow students to set some of their own deadlines for completing assignments (enabling them to establish a reasonable time frame for themselves).
- Provide occasional opportunities for students to make choices about how to complete assignments or spend class time (enabling them to set some of their own priorities).

■ In what sense do Eli, Jake, and Vanessa have control in Ms. Cornell's class? What might Ms. Cornell do to help them control their classroom lives in more productive ways?

By giving students opportunities to work independently and occasionally choose how best to learn and show mastery of classroom subject matter, we promote the sense of self-determination so important for intrinsic motivation (see Chapter 12). We also promote the self-regulated learning so essential for students' long-term academic success (see Chapter 10).

Promoting a Sense of Community and Belongingness   In the preceding chapter I described an activity in which cooperative groups in my daughter's high school Spanish class wrote and videotaped Spanish soap operas. Later the teacher awarded a variety of "Oscars" for these *teleno-velas*. She gave every student an Oscar for some aspect of his or her performance, but she also gave one group an Oscar for best telenovela. Occasionally, competition among *groups* of students can be productive *if* all groups have an equal chance of winning—for instance, if every group has diverse abilities and talents represented—and *if* the final outcome is determined more by student effort than by intelligence or other seemingly uncontrollable factors (Stipek, 1996).

In general, however, a competitive classroom environment is counterproductive when we consider principles of motivation presented in Chapter 12. For one thing, competitive situations focus students' attention on performance goals rather than mastery goals (Nicholls, 1984; Spaulding, 1992); hence, students are more likely to worry about how competent they appear to their teacher and classmates than about how well they understand classroom material. Second, competition creates a situation in which most students become losers rather than winners; their self-efficacy decreases as a result, and their intrinsic motivation to learn is undermined (Deci & Ryan, 1985, 1992). Finally, when students consistently see others performing more successfully than themselves, they are more likely to attribute their own failures to a lack of ability: They conclude that they simply don't have what it takes to succeed at classroom tasks (C. Ames, 1984).

Students achieve at higher levels in the classroom when they have a *sense of community*—that is, when they have shared goals and are respectful and supportive of one another's efforts.

Ideally, students will be more productive if they cooperate, rather than compete, with one another (C. Ames, 1984; Deci & Ryan, 1985). Not only can they support one another in their efforts to master classroom topics, but they can also nurture the peer relationships that, for many, are so important for social development and psychological well-being. Students have higher academic self-efficacy, are more motivated to learn and achieve, and are more consistently on task when they can collaborate with their classmates on assignments, believe that their peers accept and respect them, and have little fear that others will ridicule them if they make errors or ask for help (Osterman, 2000; A. M. Ryan & Patrick, 2001; A. M. Ryan et al., 2001).

In Chapter 7 we considered the concept of a *community of learners*, a classroom in which teacher and students consistently work together to help one another learn. Ultimately, we want to create a **sense of community** in the classroom—a sense that we and our students have shared goals, are mutually respectful and supportive of one another's efforts, and believe that everyone makes an important contribution to classroom learning (Hom & Battistich, 1995; D. Kim, Solomon, & Roberts, 1995; Lickona, 1991; Osterman, 2000). Creating a sense of community engenders feelings of **belongingness**: Students see themselves as important and valued members of the classroom (E. M. Anderman, 2002). In the following interview, a middle school student named Barnie describes how it feels *not* to belong at school:

Adult: Are there times when you feel you are really different from your classmates?
Barnie: Yeah, all the time. . . . Because they all answer the questions, when I raise my hand I always get it wrong. Last week I was in a group, a smart group and I am not that smart. And I mostly get all the wrong answers and they yell at me.
Adult: What do they say?
Barnie: "You're dumb! You're stupid!"
Adult: What do you tell them?
Barnie: That's the way I am.
Adult: Can you tell me about any other times when you felt different?
Barnie: When I am in the gym, I cannot run as fast as everybody and they all laugh at me. . . . It feels like I am the worst student ever. (dialogue from Kumar et al., 2002, p. 161)

Theorists have identified numerous strategies that can create a sense of classroom community and enhance students' feelings of belongingness:

- Make frequent use of interactive and collaborative teaching strategies (class discussions, cooperative learning activities, etc.).

■ **sense of community** Shared belief that teacher and students have common goals, are mutually respectful and supportive, and all make important contributions to classroom learning.

■ **belongingness** General sense that one is an important and valued member of the classroom.

- Solicit students' ideas and opinions, and incorporate them into classroom discussions and activities.
- Create mechanisms through which students can help make the classroom run smoothly and efficiently (e.g., assign various "helper" roles on a rotating basis).
- Emphasize such prosocial values as sharing and cooperation.
- Provide opportunities for students to help one another (e.g., by asking, "Who has a problem that someone else might be able to help you solve?").
- Institute a "no exclusion" policy in group activities (e.g., by insisting that any student who wants to be involved in a play activity *can* be involved).
- Encourage students to be on the lookout for classmates on the periphery of ongoing activities (perhaps students with disabilities) and to ask these children to join in.
- Work on social skills with those students whose interpersonal behaviors may alienate others.
- Provide public recognition of students' contributions to the overall success of the classroom.
- Convey the general message that *all* students deserve the respect of their classmates and are important members of the classroom community. (Emmer et al., 1994; D. Kim et al., 1995; Lickona, 1991; Osterman, 2000; A. M. Ryan & Patrick, 2001; Sapon-Shevin, Dobbelaere, Corrigan, Goodman, & Mastin, 1998; A. P. Turnbull et al., 2000)

When students share a sense of community, they are more likely to exhibit prosocial behavior, stay on task, express enthusiasm about classroom activities, and achieve at high levels. Furthermore, a sense of classroom community is associated with lower rates of emotional distress, disruptive classroom behavior, truancy, violence, drug use, and dropping out (D. C. Gottfredson, 2001; Hom & Battistich, 1995; D. Kim et al., 1995; Osterman, 2000; M. D. Resnick et al., 1997).

Setting Limits

In the opening case study, Ms. Cornell failed to provide guidelines for how students should behave—something she should have done in the first week. A class without guidelines for appropriate behavior is apt to be chaotic and unproductive. And students must learn that certain behaviors—especially those that cause injury, damage school property, or interfere with others' learning and performance—will simply not be tolerated. Setting reasonable limits on classroom behavior not only promotes a more productive learning environment but also contributes to students' socialization by encouraging them to develop behaviors essential for successful participation in the adult world.

■ Recall our discussion of *socialization* in Chapter 3.

Experienced educators have offered several suggestions for setting reasonable limits on students' classroom behavior. More specifically, they suggest that we

- Establish a few rules and procedures at the beginning of the year
- Present rules and procedures in an informational rather than controlling manner
- Periodically review the usefulness of existing rules and procedures
- Acknowledge students' feelings about classroom requirements
- Enforce rules consistently and equitably

As we consider these suggestions, we will also consider how we can preserve students' sense of control and self-determination.

Establishing Initial Rules and Procedures   The first few days and weeks of the school year are critical ones for establishing classroom procedures and setting expectations for student behavior. Effective classroom managers establish and communicate certain rules and procedures right from the start (Borko & Putnam, 1996; G. A. Davis & Thomas, 1989; W. Doyle, 1986a, 1990). They identify acceptable and unacceptable behaviors (e.g., see Figure 14.1). They develop consistent procedures and routines for such things as completing seatwork, asking for help, and turning in assignments. And they have procedures in place for nonroutine events such as school assemblies, field trips, and fire drills.

Ideally, students should understand that rules and procedures are not merely the result of our personal whims but are designed to help the classroom run smoothly and efficiently. One way of promoting such understanding is to include students in decision making about the rules and procedures by which the class will operate (G. A. Davis & Thomas, 1989; Fuller, 2001; Lickona, 1991). For example, we might solicit students' suggestions for making sure that unnecessary dis-

FIGURE 14.1 Beginning the school year with a few rules

Effective teachers typically begin the school year with a few rules that will help classroom activities run smoothly. Here are several examples of rules you might want to include in your list (based on Emmer et al., 1994):

Bring all needed materials to class. (Students should have books, homework assignments, permission slips, and any needed supplies for planned activities.)

Be in your seat and ready to work when the bell rings. (Students should be at their desks, have paper out and pencils sharpened, and be physically and mentally ready to work.)

Respect and be polite to all people. (Students should listen attentively when someone else is speaking, behave appropriately for a substitute teacher, and refrain from insults, fighting, and other disrespectful or hostile behavior.)

Respect other people's property. (Students should keep the classroom clean and neat, refrain from defacing school property, ask for permission to borrow another's possessions, and return those possessions in a timely fashion.)

Obey all school rules. (Students must obey the rules of the school building as well as the rules of the classroom.)

tractions are kept to a minimum and that everyone has a chance to speak during class discussions. By incorporating students' ideas and listening to their concerns about the limits we set, we help students understand the reasons for—and thereby help them adhere to—those limits (Emmer et al., 1994).

Once rules and procedures have been formulated, we should communicate them clearly and explicitly, describe the consequences of noncompliance, and enforce them consistently. Taking time to clarify and enforce rules and procedures seems to be especially important in the early elementary grades, when students may not be as familiar with "how things are done" at school (Evertson & Emmer, 1982; Gettinger, 1988).

Keep in mind that rules and procedures are easier to remember and therefore easier to follow if they are relatively simple and few in number (G. A. Davis & Thomas, 1989). Effective classroom managers tend to stress only the most important rules and procedures at the beginning of the school year; they introduce other rules and procedures later on as needed (W. Doyle, 1986a). Also keep in mind that although some order and predictability are essential for student productivity, *too much* order may make a classroom a rather boring, routine place—one without an element of fun and spontaneity. We don't necessarily need rules and procedures for everything!

■ Observe how one teacher communicates her rules in the "Classroom Rules" clip on Video CD 2.

The "Classroom Rules" clip on Video CD 2 shows how one second-grade teacher presents a short set of classroom rules in the first week of the school year. As you watch the clip, notice how the teacher solicits students' opinions about the rules and, in the process, gives them some sense of ownership regarding the rules.

Presenting Rules and Procedures as Information As we learned in Chapter 12, we are more likely to maintain students' sense of self-determination if we present rules and procedures as items of information instead of as forms of control. Figure 14.2 presents several examples of rules and procedures presented in an informational manner; each of these statements includes the reasons for imposing certain guidelines. The following scenario provides a simple illustration of how giving a reason can make all the difference in the world:

■ For additional benefits of providing reasons, see the discussion of *induction* in Chapter 3.

Gerard is a boy with a low tolerance for frustration. Whenever he asks Ms. Donnelly for assistance, he wants it *now*. If she is unable to help him immediately, he screams, "You're no good!" or "You don't care!" and shoves other students' desks as he walks angrily back to his seat.

At one point during the school year, the class has a unit on interpersonal skills. One lesson in the unit addresses *timing*—the most appropriate and effective time to ask for another person's assistance with a problem.

FIGURE 14.2 Presenting classroom rules and procedures as information

Students are more apt to be intrinsically motivated to follow classroom rules and procedures if we present them as items of information rather than as forms of control.

We might say this (information):	**... rather than this (control):**
"You'll get your independent assignments done more quickly if you get right to work."	"Please be quiet and do your own work."
"As we practice for our fire drill, it is important to line up quickly and be quiet so that we can hear the instructions we are given and will know what to do."	"When the fire alarm sounds, line up quickly and quietly, and then wait for further instructions."
"This assignment is designed to help you develop the writing skills you will need after you graduate. It is unfair to other authors to copy their work word for word, so we will practice putting ideas into our own words and giving credit to authors whose ideas we borrow. Passing off another's writing and ideas as your own can lead to suspension in college or a lawsuit in the business world."	"Cheating and plagiarism are not acceptable in this classroom."
"It's important that others can read your writing. If your words are illegible and your cross-outs are confusing, I may not be able to give you as high a grade as you deserve on an assignment."	"Use good penmanship on all assignments, and erase any errors carefully and completely. Points will be deducted for sloppy writing."

A week later, Gerard approaches Ms. Donnelly for help with a math problem. She is working with another student, but she turns briefly to Gerard and says, "Timing."

Ms. Donnelly waits expectantly for Gerard's usual screaming. Instead, he responds, "Hey, Ms. D., I get it! I can ask you at another time!" He returns to his seat with a smile on his face. (based on Sullivan-DeCarlo, DeFalco, & Roberts, 1998, p. 81)

Reviewing Existing Rules and Procedures   As the school year progresses, we may occasionally want to revise the rules and procedures we established earlier. For instance, we may find that rules about when students can and cannot move around the room are overly restrictive or that procedures for turning in homework don't adequately accommodate students who must sometimes leave class early for doctors' appointments, school athletic events, and the like.

Regularly scheduled class meetings provide one mechanism through which we and our students can periodically review classroom rules and procedures (D. E. Campbell, 1996; Glasser, 1969). Consider this scenario as an example:

> Every Friday at 2:00, Ms. Ayotte's students move their chairs into one large circle, and the weekly class meeting begins. First on the agenda is a review of the past week's successes, including both academic achievements and socially productive events. Next, the group identifies problems that have emerged during the week and brainstorms possible ways to avert such problems in the future. Finally, the students consider whether existing classroom rules and procedures are serving their purpose. They may decide to modify existing rules and procedures or may establish new ones.
>
> During the first few class meetings, Ms. Ayotte leads the group discussions. But once students have gotten the hang of things, she begins to relinquish control of the meetings to one or another of her students on a rotating basis.

By providing frequent opportunities for students to review classroom policies, we find another way of giving them a sense of ownership about such policies. Furthermore, perhaps because of the authoritative atmosphere and the conversations about moral dilemmas that student decision making may entail, more advanced moral reasoning may result (Power et al., 1989; Power & Power, 1992; also see the discussion of moral development in Chapter 3).

■ Do you see parallels between *authoritative parenting* (Chapter 3) and the guidelines for setting limits described in this chapter?

Acknowledging Students' Feelings   There will undoubtedly be times when we must ask students to do something they would prefer not to do. Rather than pretend that such feelings don't exist, we are better advised to acknowledge them (Deci & Ryan, 1985). For example, we might tell students that we know how difficult it can be to sit quietly during an unexpectedly lengthy school assembly or to spend an entire evening on a particular homework assignment. At the same time, we can explain that the behaviors we request of them, though not always intrinsically enjoyable, do, in fact, contribute to their own long-term goals. By acknowledging students' feelings about tasks they would rather not do yet also pointing out the benefits of performing those tasks, we increase the likelihood that students will accept the limitations imposed on their behavior (Deci & Ryan, 1985).

Enforcing Rules Consistently and Equitably   In our earlier discussions of behaviorism, social cognitive theory, and motivation, we've seen the importance of consistency in how we respond to classroom behaviors; to refresh your memory, see the discussions of reinforcement and punishment in Chapter 9, the section "Nonoccurrence of Expected Consequences" in Chapter 10, and the discussion of attributions in Chapter 12. Our strategies for *preventing* behavior problems may differ from one student to the next (more about this point shortly), but as a general rule, the consequences of inappropriate behavior should be consistent for all students (W. Doyle, 1986a; Evertson & Emmer, 1982).

If you think back to your years in elementary and secondary school, you can probably recall at least one student who was "teacher's pet"—someone who was clearly a favorite and had special privileges. You might also recall a few students who were continually blamed for misdeeds, sometimes when they weren't the true culprits. As teachers, we will inevitably like some students more than others (e.g., we're apt to prefer high achievers), but we must keep our preferences to ourselves. Students can be quite resentful of teachers who grant special favors to, and perhaps overlook rule infractions of, a few "pet" students (Babad, 1995; Babad, Avni-Babad, & Rosenthal, 2003; J. Baker, 1999). And students who are unfairly accused or punished are, of course, even more resentful, as one high school student explains:

> Because like if you had a past record or whatever like in middle school if you got in trouble like at all, they would think that you're a slight trouble maker and if you got in trouble again, they would always . . . if you were anywhere that something bad happened or something against the rules or whatever, they pick you first because they think that you have a past. So they wouldn't like pick the kids that had never done anything. (Certo et al., 2002, p. 25)

Thus, consistency and equitable treatment for all students—or lack thereof—is apt to have a significant effect on teacher-student relationships and overall classroom climate (Babad et al., 2003; J. Baker, 1999; Certo et al., 2002).

Planning Activities That Keep Students on Task

As noted in Chapter 13, effective teachers plan their lessons ahead of time. Furthermore, they plan activities that not only facilitate students' learning and cognitive processing but also motivate students to *want* to learn. For instance, they think about how to make the subject matter interesting and relevant to things students find important (e.g., their values and goals). They also incorporate variety into lessons, perhaps by using colorful audiovisual aids, conducting novel activities (e.g., small-group discussions, class debates), or moving to a different location (e.g., the media center or school yard) (G. A. Davis & Thomas, 1989; Munn, Johnstone, & Chalmers, 1990).

As we plan upcoming classroom activities, then, we should simultaneously plan specific ways of keeping students on task. In addition to using the motivational strategies described in Chapters 11 and 12—especially those that promote *intrinsic motivation*—we should

- Be sure students will always be productively engaged
- Choose tasks at an appropriate academic level
- Provide a reasonable amount of structure for activities and assignments
- Make special plans for transition times in the school day

Keeping Students Productively Engaged

Experiencing FIRSTHAND · Take Five

For the next five minutes, you are going to be a student who has nothing to do. *Remain exactly where you are,* put your book aside, and *do nothing.* Time yourself so that you spend exactly five minutes on this "task." Let's see what happens.

· · · · · · ·

What kinds of responses did you make during your five-minute break? Did you fidget a bit, perhaps wiggling tired body parts, scratching newly detected itches, or picking at your nails? Did you "interact" in some way with something or someone else, perhaps tapping loudly on a table, turning on a radio, or talking to another person in the room? Did you get out of your seat altogether—something I specifically asked you *not* to do?

The exercise I just gave you was a somewhat artificial one, to be sure, and the things I am defining as "misbehaviors" in this instance (wiggling your toes, tapping the table, getting out of your seat, etc.) won't necessarily qualify as misbehaviors in the classroom. Yet the exercise has, I hope, shown you that it is very difficult to do *nothing at all* for any length of time. Like us, our students will be most apt to misbehave when they have a lot of free time on their hands.

Effective classroom managers make sure there is little "empty" time in which nothing is going on. As teachers, we can use numerous strategies to keep students productively engaged; as examples, we can

Students who are actively engaged in classroom activities rarely exhibit problem behaviors.

- Have something specific for students to do each day, even on the first day of class
- Have materials organized and equipment set up before class
- Have activities that ensure *all* students' involvement and participation
- Maintain a brisk pace throughout each lesson (but not so fast that students can't keep up)
- Ensure that students' comments are relevant and helpful but not excessively long-winded (perhaps by taking any chronic time-monopolizers aside for a private discussion about giving others a chance to speak)
- Spend only short periods of time assisting individual students during class unless other students are capable of working independently and productively in the meantime
- Have a system in place that ensures that students who finish an assigned task quickly have something else to do (perhaps writing in a class journal or reading a book)
(G. A. Davis & Thomas, 1989; W. Doyle, 1986a; Emmer et al., 1994; Evertson & Harris, 1992; Gettinger, 1988; Munn et al., 1990)

Choosing Tasks at an Appropriate Level   Students are more likely to get involved in their classwork, rather than in off-task behavior, when they have tasks and assignments appropriate for their ability levels (W. Doyle, 1986a; Mac Iver et al., 1995; J. W. Moore & Edwards, 2003). They are apt to misbehave when they are asked to do things that are probably too difficult for them—in other words, when they are incapable of completing assigned tasks successfully. Thus, classroom misbehaviors are more often observed in students who have a history of struggling in their coursework (W. Doyle, 1986a).

■ With this point in mind, how might Ms. Cornell (in the opening case study) have gotten the year off to a better start?

This is not to suggest that we should plan activities so easy that students are not challenged and learn nothing new in doing them. One workable strategy is to *begin* the school year with relatively easy tasks that students can readily complete. Such early tasks enable students to practice normal classroom routines and procedures; they also give students a sense that they can enjoy and be successful in classroom activities. Once a supportive classroom climate has been established and students are comfortable with classroom procedures, we can gradually introduce more difficult and challenging assignments (W. Doyle, 1990; Emmer et al., 1994; Evertson & Emmer, 1982). We might take a similar approach when introducing new instructional strategies; for instance, when we first ask students to engage in cooperative activities, we might have them work with relatively familiar content so that they can focus on mastering effective group interaction skills (asking for help, giving explanations, etc.) without being distracted by difficult subject matter (N. M. Webb & Farivar, 1999).

Providing Structure

Experiencing FIRSTHAND · Take Five More

Grab a blank sheet of paper and a pen or pencil, and complete these two tasks:

> *Task A:* Using short phrases, list six characteristics of an effective teacher.
> *Task B:* Describe *schooling*.

Don't continue reading until you've spent a total of at least *five minutes* on these tasks.

Once you have completed the two tasks, answer either "Task A" or "Task B" to each of the following questions:

1. For which task did you have a better understanding of what you were being asked to do?
2. During which task did your mind more frequently wander to irrelevant topics?
3. During which task did you engage in more off-task behaviors (e.g., looking around the room, doodling, getting out of your seat)?

· · · · · · ·

I am guessing that you found the first task relatively straightforward, whereas the second wasn't at all clear-cut. Did Task B's ambiguity lead to more irrelevant thoughts and off-task behaviors for you?

Off-task behavior in the classroom occurs more frequently when activities are so loosely structured that students don't have a clear sense of what they are supposed to do. Effective teachers tend to give assignments with some degree of structure. They also give clear directions about how to proceed with a task and a great deal of feedback about appropriate responses, especially during the first few weeks of class (W. Doyle, 1990; Evertson & Emmer, 1982; Munn et al., 1990; Weinert & Helmke, 1995).

Yet we need to strike a happy medium here. We don't want to structure classroom tasks to the point where students never make their own decisions about how to proceed or to the point where only lower-level thinking skills are required. Ultimately, we want students to develop and use higher-level processes—for example, to think analytically, critically, and creatively—and we must have classroom assignments and activities that promote such processes (W. Doyle, 1986a; Weinert & Helmke, 1995).

The concept of *scaffolding* (see Chapter 2) is helpful in this context: We can provide a great deal of structure for tasks early in the school year, gradually removing it as students become better able to structure tasks for themselves. For example, when introducing students to cooperative learning, we might structure initial group meetings by breaking down each group task into several subtasks, giving clear directions as to how each subtask should be carried out, and assigning every group member a particular role to serve in the group. As the school year progresses and students become more adept at learning cooperatively with their classmates, we gradually can become less directive about how group tasks are accomplished.

Planning for Transitions   In the opening case study, Eli, Jake, and Vanessa often misbehave at the beginning and end of the school day, as well as before and after recess and lunch. Transition times—as students end one activity and begin a second, or as they move from one classroom to another—are times when misbehaviors most frequently occur. Effective classroom managers take steps to ensure that transitions proceed quickly and without a loss of momentum (Arlin, 1979; W. Doyle, 1984; Emmer et al., 1994). For example, they establish procedures for moving from one activity to the next. They ensure that there is little slack time in which students have nothing to do. And especially at the secondary level, where students change classes every hour or so, effective classroom managers typically have a task for students to complete as soon as they enter the classroom.

■ Can you relate this strategy to *behavioral momentum* (Chapter 9)?

How might we plan for the various transitions that occur throughout the school day? Here are some examples:

- A physical education teacher has students begin each class session with five minutes of stretching exercises.

Effective teachers communicate *withitness*: They know what each student is doing at all times.

- An elementary school teacher has students follow the same procedure each day as lunchtime approaches. Students must (1) place completed assignments in a basket on the teacher's desk, (2) put away supplies they have been using, (3) get their lunches from the coatroom, and (4) line up quietly by the door.
- A middle school mathematics teacher has students copy the new homework assignment as soon as they come to class.
- A high school English composition teacher writes a topic or question (e.g., "My biggest pet peeve," "Whatever happened to hula hoops?") on the chalkboard at the beginning of each class period. Students know that when they come to class, they should immediately begin to write on the topic or question of the day.

All of these strategies, though very different in nature, share the common goal of keeping students focused on productive behaviors.

Monitoring What Students Are Doing

Effective teachers communicate something called **withitness**: They know (and their students *know* they know) what students are doing at all times in the classroom. They regularly scan the classroom and make frequent eye contact with individual students. They know what misbehaviors are occurring *when* those misbehaviors occur, and they know who the perpetrators are (G. A. Davis & Thomas, 1989; Hogan, Rabinowitz, & Craven, 2003; Kounin, 1970). Consider the following scenario as an example:

> An hour and a half of each morning in Mr. Rennaker's elementary school classroom is devoted to reading. Students know that, for part of this time, they will meet with Mr. Rennaker in their small reading groups. They spend the remainder of the time working on independent assignments tailored to their individual reading skills. As Mr. Rennaker works with each reading group in one corner of the classroom, he situates himself with his back to the wall so that he can simultaneously keep one eye on students working independently at their seats. He sends a quick and subtle signal—perhaps a stern expression, a finger to the lips, or a call of a student's name—to any student who begins to be disruptive.

When we demonstrate such withitness, especially at the beginning of the school year, students are more likely to stay on task and display appropriate classroom behavior (W. Doyle, 1986a; Woolfolk & Brooks, 1985). Not surprisingly, they are also more likely to achieve at high levels (W. Doyle, 1986a).

Modifying Instructional Strategies

As we have repeatedly seen, principles of effective classroom management go hand in hand with principles of learning and motivation. When students are learning and achieving successfully and when they clearly want to pursue the classroom's instructional goals, they are apt to be busily engaged in productive activities for most of the school day (W. Doyle, 1990). In contrast, when they have difficulty understanding classroom subject matter or when they have little interest in learning it, they are likely to exhibit the nonproductive or counterproductive classroom behaviors that result from frustration or boredom.

Research tells us that when students misbehave, beginning teachers often think about what the students are doing wrong. In contrast, experienced, "expert" teachers are more apt to think about what *they themselves* can do differently to keep students on task, and they modify their plans accordingly (Emmer & Stough, 2001; Sabers et al., 1991; H. L. Swanson, O'Connor, & Cooney, 1990). So when behavior problems crop up, we should start thinking as the experts do, by considering questions such as the following:

- How can I alter instructional strategies to capture students' interest and excitement?
- Are instructional materials so difficult that students are becoming frustrated? Or are they so easy that students are bored?

■ **withitness** Appearance that a teacher knows what all students are doing at all times.

CREATING A PRODUCTIVE CLASSROOM ENVIRONMENT

Creating Conditions in Which Students Can Effectively Learn

Physically arrange the classroom in a way that facilitates teacher-student interactions and keeps distracting influences to a minimum.

An elementary school teacher has arranged the twenty-eight student desks in his classroom into seven clusters of four desks each. The four-student clusters become base groups for many of the classroom's cooperative learning activities. The teacher occasionally asks students to move their chairs into a large circle for whole-class discussions.

Show students that you care about and respect them as human beings, and give them some say about what happens in the classroom.

A high school teacher realizes that she is continually admonishing one particular student for his off-task behavior. To establish a more positive relationship with the student, she makes a point to greet him warmly in the hallway before school every day. At the end of one day in which his behavior has been especially disruptive, she catches him briefly to express her concern, and the two agree to meet the following morning to discuss ways of helping him stay on task more regularly.

Set reasonable limits for student behavior.

After describing the objectives of an instrumental music class on the first day of school, a junior high school teacher tells students,

"There is one rule for this class to which I will hold firm. You must not engage in any behavior that will interfere with your own learning or with that of your classmates."

Plan classroom activities that encourage on-task behavior.

Before each class, a creative writing teacher writes the day's topic on the chalkboard. Her students know that when they arrive at class, they are to take out pencil and paper and begin an essay addressing that topic.

Show students you are continually aware of what they're doing.

While meeting with each reading group in one corner of the classroom, an elementary school teacher sits with his back to the wall so he can keep an eye on those students who are working together at the science table or independently at their desks.

Modify your plans for instruction when necessary.

A teacher discovers that students quickly complete the activity she thought would take them an entire class period. She wraps up the activity after fifteen minutes and then begins the lesson she had originally planned for the following day.

- What are students really concerned about? For example, are they more concerned about interacting with their classmates than in gaining new knowledge and skills?
- How can I address students' motives and goals (e.g., their desire to affiliate with peers) while simultaneously helping them achieve classroom objectives?

Answering such questions helps us focus our efforts on our ultimate goal: to help students *learn*.

Occasionally, current events on the international, national, or local scene (e.g., a terrorist attack, a presidential election, or a tragic car accident involving fellow students) may take priority. When students' minds are justifiably preoccupied with something other than the topic of instruction, they will have difficulty paying attention to that preplanned topic and are likely to learn little about it. In such extenuating circumstances, we may want to abandon our lesson plans altogether.

The Creating a Productive Classroom Environment feature "Creating Conditions in Which Students Can Effectively Learn" illustrates some of the strategies we've identified in the last few pages. We turn now to how individual and developmental differences come into play in classroom management.

■ From your own perspective, what are the key ingredients of a successfully managed classroom?

Taking Individual and Developmental Differences into Account

Earlier I mentioned the importance of consistency and equity in enforcing classroom rules. Yet as we consider how best to *prevent* off-task behavior, optimal strategies may differ considerably from one student to the next. For instance, during independent seatwork assignments, some students may work well even when classmates are seated close by, but others may be easily distracted unless they can work in a quiet spot, perhaps near a teacher's desk. During small-group work, some groups may function quite effectively on their own, whereas others may need considerable guidance and supervision.

One important source of individual differences affecting students' classroom behavior is *temperament*—the extent to which a student is energetic, adaptable, irritable, impulsive, and so on. In Chapter 5 we examined the nature of temperament and its implications for classroom management; to refresh your memory, you might want to revisit the section on temperament and the Creating a Productive Classroom Environment feature "Accommodating Students' Diverse

TABLE 14.1   D E V E L O P M E N T A L   T R E N D S

Effective Classroom Management at Different Grade Levels

GRADE LEVEL	AGE-TYPICAL CHARACTERISTICS	SUGGESTED STRATEGIES
K–2	• Lack of familiarity with unspoken rules about appropriate classroom behavior • Anxiety about being in school, especially in the first few weeks and especially for students without preschool experience • Short attention span and distractibility • Little self-regulation • Desire for teacher affection and approval • Considerable individual differences in social skills	• Invite students and their parents to visit the classroom before the school year begins. • Keep assignments relatively short and focused. • Create a "gathering" place (e.g., a carpet) where students can sit close at hand for whole-class discussions. • Create areas where students can work independently on tasks of their choosing (e.g., a "reading center" where students can listen to storybooks on tape). • Be explicit about acceptable classroom behavior; correct inappropriate behavior gently but consistently.
3–5	• Continuing desire for teacher approval, but with increasing concern about peer approval as well. • Greater attentiveness to teachers who are emotionally expressive (e.g., teachers who often smile and show obvious concern in times of distress) • Increasing self-regulation skills • Increasing ability to reflect on one's own and others' thoughts and motives (i.e., increasing social cognition) • Increasing disengagement from school if students have consistently encountered academic and social failures there	• Use two-way journals to communicate regularly with students about academic, social, and emotional issues. • In your words and actions, consistently show students that you are concerned about their academic progress and emotional well-being. • Provide increasing opportunities for independent work, but with enough structure to guide students' efforts. • In times of disagreement or conflict, ask students to reflect on one another's thoughts and feelings. • Make an extra effort to establish close, supportive relationships with students who seem to be "unmotivated" and socially disengaged.
6–8	• Considerable anxiety about the transition to middle school, including about the less close and less supportive relationships with teachers • Decrease in intrinsic motivation to learn academic subject matter • Increase in cheating behavior; cheating less common if students think teachers respect them and are committed to helping them learn • Heightened concern about ability to "fit in" and be accepted by peers • Increase in bullying behaviors	• Find occasions to see students outside of class (e.g., chaperone dances, attend sporting events). • Plan lessons that are engaging and relevant to students' lives and needs. • Provide sufficient academic support that students have no reason to cheat; nevertheless, be on the lookout for possible cheating (see Chapter 15). • Do not tolerate bullying; address its possible underlying causes (see "Aggression and Social Cognition" in Chapter 3). • Reach out to students who seem socially "unconnected" (e.g., invite them to join you for lunch in your classroom).
9–12	• Anxiety about the transition to high school, especially if seventh- and eighth-grade were part of elementary school (as in some small school districts) • Social and romantic relationships often a source of considerable distraction • Considerable self-regulation skills in some but not all students • High incidence of cheating, in part because peers think it's acceptable • Disdain for classmates who work too hard for teacher approval (i.e., "brownnosers") • Violence increasingly common, especially at schools in low-income neighborhoods	• Remember that even at the high school level, students achieve at higher levels when they have close, supportive relationships with teachers. • Regularly plan activities that involve social interaction; if possible, move desks and chairs to allow students to interact more easily. • Provide guidance and support for students who have few self-regulatory skills to keep them on task. • Describe what cheating is and why it's unacceptable (see Chapter 15). • Communicate approval privately rather than publicly. • Vigorously address violence (see the section "Addressing Aggression and Violence at School" in this chapter).

Sources: Some ideas based on Blugental, Lyon, Lin, McGrath, & Bimbela, 1999; Cizek, 2003; Fingerhut & Christoffel, 2002; Mehan, 1979; Murdock et al., 1999; Pellegrini, 2002; many others derived from discussions in earlier chapters.

Temperaments" (p. 150). To be truly effective classroom managers, we must realize that students' vastly different classroom behaviors may be due, in part, to biological predispositions not entirely within their control. Such a realization will influence our beliefs about why students are acting as they are—that is, it will influence our *attributions*—and these beliefs will, in turn, affect our willingness to adapt classroom strategies to foster productive classroom behavior (B. K. Keogh, 2003).

Developmental differences, too, will have something to say about our classroom management strategies. Many children in the early elementary grades haven't had enough experience with formal education to know all the unspoken "rules" that govern classroom interactions—for instance, that students should remain silent when a teacher or other adult is talking, that only the student who is called on should answer a question, and so on (Mehan, 1979). Children just beginning kindergarten or first grade may find their new school environment to be unsettling and anxiety arousing, as will many adolescents making the transition to middle school or high school (see Chapter 11). And, of course, children gain increasing social skills as they grow older, affecting their ability to interact effectively with their teacher and classmates (see Chapter 3). Table 14.1 presents these and other developmental differences, along with examples of how we might accommodate them in our classroom practices.

Despite our best efforts, however, students may sometimes behave in ways that significantly disrupt classroom activities and interfere with student learning. Effective teachers not only plan and structure a classroom that minimizes potential behavior problems but also deal with the misbehaviors that do occur (W. Doyle, 1990). What strategies are most effective in dealing with student misbehaviors? We turn to this question now.

Dealing with Misbehaviors

For purposes of our discussion, we will define a **misbehavior** as any action that can potentially disrupt classroom learning and planned classroom activities (W. Doyle, 1990). Some classroom misbehaviors are relatively minor ones that have little long-term impact on students' achievement. Such behaviors as talking out of turn, writing notes to classmates during a lecture, and submitting homework assignments after their due date—particularly if such behaviors occur infrequently—generally fall in this category. Other misbehaviors are far more serious, in that they definitely interfere with the learning and achievement of one or more students. For example, when students scream at their teachers, hit their classmates, or habitually refuse to participate in classroom activities, then classroom learning—certainly the learning of the "guilty party" and often the learning of other students as well—may be adversely affected. Furthermore, such behaviors may, in some cases, threaten the physical safety or psychological well-being of others in the classroom.

As teachers, we need to plan ahead about how to respond to the variety of misbehaviors we may see in the classroom. Although we must certainly be consistent in the consequences we impose for blatant rule infractions (again recall our earlier discussion of consistency and equity), different strategies for reducing disruptive behavior over the long run may be useful and appropriate under different circumstances. In the upcoming sections we'll examine six strategies that may be helpful at one time or another: ignoring a behavior, cueing a student, discussing a problem privately with a student, teaching self-regulation strategies, using behaviorist approaches, and conferring with parents.

Ignoring Behavior

Consider these situations:

- Dimitra rarely breaks classroom rules. But on one occasion, after you have just instructed students to work quietly and independently at their seats, you see her briefly whisper to the girl beside her. None of the other students seems to notice that Dimitra has disobeyed your instructions.
- Herb is careless in chemistry lab and accidentally knocks over a small container of liquid (a harmless one, fortunately). He quickly apologizes and cleans up the mess.

Will these behaviors interfere with Dimitra's or Herb's academic achievement? Are they "contagious" behaviors that will spread to other students, as the horseplay did in Ms. Cornell's class? The answer to both questions is "Probably not."

On some occasions our best course of action is *no* action, at least nothing of a disciplinary nature (G. A. Davis & Thomas, 1989; Silberman & Wheelan, 1980). Whenever we stop an instructional activity to deal with a misbehavior, even for a few seconds, we run the risk of disrupting the momentum of the activity and drawing students' attention to their misbehaving classmates (W. Doyle, 1986a). If we respond every time someone gets a little bit out of line, our own actions may be more distracting than the actions we are trying to curtail. Furthermore, by drawing class attention to a particular student's behavior, we may actually be reinforcing it rather than discouraging it.

■ **misbehavior** Action that has the potential to disrupt students' learning and planned classroom activities.

Dimitra's behavior—whispering briefly to a classmate during independent seatwork—is unlikely to spread to her classmates (they didn't see her do it) and is probably not an instance of cheating (it occurred before she began working on the assignment). Herb's behavior—knocking over a container of liquid in chemistry lab—has, in and of itself, resulted in an unpleasant consequence: He must clean up the mess. In both situations *ignoring* the misbehavior is probably the best thing to do. Following are some general circumstances in which ignoring misbehavior may be the wisest course of action:

- When the behavior is a rare occurrence and probably won't be repeated
- When the behavior is unlikely to spread to other students
- When unusual circumstances (e.g., the last day of school before a holiday, or an unsettling event in a student's personal life) elicit inappropriate behavior only temporarily
- When the behavior is typical for a particular age-group (e.g., when kindergartners become restless after sitting for an extended time, when sixth-grade boys and girls resist holding one another's hands during dance instruction)
- When the behavior's result (its natural consequence) is unpleasant enough to deter a student from repeating the behavior
- When the behavior is not seriously affecting classroom learning
  (G. A. Davis & Thomas, 1989; W. Doyle, 1986a; Dreikurs & Cassel, 1972; Munn et al., 1990; Silberman & Wheelan, 1980; Wynne, 1990)

Cueing a Student

Consider these misbehaviors:

- As you're explaining a difficult concept, Marjorie is busily writing. At first, you think she's taking notes, but then you see her pass the paper across the aisle to Kang. A few minutes later, you see Kang pass the same sheet back to Marjorie. It appears that the two students are writing personal notes to each other and possibly not hearing a word you're saying.
- You have separated your class into small groups for a cooperative learning exercise. One group seems more interested in discussing an upcoming school dance than in accomplishing assigned work. The group is not making the progress that other groups are making and probably won't complete the assignment if its members don't get down to business soon.

In some situations off-task behaviors, though not serious in nature, *do* interfere with classroom learning and so must be discouraged. Effective classroom managers handle such minor behavior problems as unobtrusively as possible: They don't stop the lesson, distract other students, or call unnecessary attention to the behavior they're trying to stop (W. Doyle, 1990; Emmer, 1987). In many cases they use **cueing**: They let the students know, through a signal of one kind or another, that they are aware of the misbehavior and would like it to stop.

In Chapter 9 we discussed a variety of possible cues—a flick of the overhead light switch, body language, verbal hints, and so on—that can get students back on task (see the sections "Effects of Antecedent Stimuli and Responses" and "Cueing Inappropriate Behaviors"). Ideally, we should focus students' attention on what *should* be done, rather than on what *isn't* being done (Emmer et al., 1994; Good & Brophy, 1994). Furthermore, although indirect requests are often effective for older students (e.g., "I see some art supplies that still need to be put away"), more explicit ones may be necessary for younger children (e.g., "Table 3 needs to clean up its art supplies before it can go to lunch") (see the section "Development of Listening Comprehension" in Chapter 2). In the "Reading Group" clip on Video CD 2, a second-grade teacher cues one student first indirectly, and then more directly, to get her to join her reading group: "I called the Tigers. Someone wasn't listening. Sema, the Tigers were called."

Discussing a Problem Privately with a Student

Consider these misbehaviors:

- Alonzo is almost always several minutes late to your third-period algebra class. When he finally arrives, he takes an additional two or three minutes pulling his textbook and other class materials out of his backpack. You have often reminded him about the importance of coming to class on time, yet the tardiness continues.

■ Can you relate *ignoring* to a specific concept in operant conditioning?

■ Why is ignoring *not* an effective strategy in Ms. Cornell's classroom?

■ Observe cueing in the "Reading Group" clip on Video CD 2.

■ **cueing**   Use of signals to indicate that a certain behavior is desired or that a certain behavior should stop.

- Trudy rarely completes classroom assignments; in fact, she often doesn't even *begin* them. On many occasions you have tried unsuccessfully to get her on task with explicit verbal cues (e.g., "Your book should be open to page 27," "Your cooperative group is brainstorming possible solutions to a difficult problem, and they could really use your ideas"). A few times, when you have looked Trudy in the eye and asked her point-blank to get to work, she has defiantly responded, "I'm not going to do it. You can't make me!"

Sometimes in-class signals are insufficient to change a student's misbehavior. In such situations, talking privately with the student is the next logical step. The discussion should be a *private* one for several reasons. First, as noted earlier, calling peers' attention to a problem behavior may actually reinforce the behavior rather than discourage it. Or, instead, the attention of classmates may cause a student to feel excessively embarrassed or humiliated—feelings that may make the student overanxious about being in the classroom in the future. Finally, when we spend too much class time dealing with a single misbehaving student, other students are apt to get off task as well (Scott & Bushell, 1974).

Conversations with individual students give us, as teachers, a chance to explain why certain behaviors are unacceptable and must stop. (As noted earlier, students are more apt to obey rules when they understand the reasons behind them.) Furthermore, teacher-student conversations give students a chance to explain why they behave as they do. To illustrate, when talking with Alonzo, we may discover that as a diabetic, he must check his blood sugar level between his second- and third-period classes. He can perform the procedure himself, but it takes a few minutes; besides, he would prefer to do it in the privacy of the nurse's office at the other end of the building. When speaking with Trudy about her refusal to do assigned work, she may express her frustration about not being able to read or understand the subject matter as well as her classmates do.

If cueing a misbehaving student is ineffective, a private conversation might be the best next step. From a motivational standpoint, how might private discussions with students be helpful?

Students' explanations can sometimes provide clues about how best to deal with their behavior over the long run. For example, given Alonzo's diabetes, we may not be able to change his ongoing tardiness to class; instead, we might reassign him to a seat by the door so he can join class unobtrusively when he arrives, and we might ask the student next to him to quietly fill him in on the lesson in progress. Trudy's frustrations with her schoolwork suggest that she needs additional scaffolding to help her succeed; they also hint at a possible undiagnosed learning disability that may warrant a referral to the school psychologist. In some cases our conversations with students may reveal maladaptive interpretations of social situations. For instance, a chronically aggressive student may express her belief that her classmates "are always trying to pick a fight" when we ourselves know that this perception is not accurate (recall our discussion of *hostile attributional bias* in Chapter 3). In such instances we might consult with the school counselor about how to help the student interpret social interactions more productively.

Yet students won't always provide explanations that lead to such logical solutions. For example, it may be that Alonzo is late to class simply because he wants to spend a few extra minutes hanging out with friends in the hall. Or perhaps Trudy tells you she doesn't want to do her assignments because she's "sick and tired" of other people telling her what to do all the time. In such circumstances it is essential that we not get in a power struggle—a situation where one person "wins" by dominating over the other in some way (Diamond, 1991; Emmer et al., 1994). Several strategies can minimize the likelihood of a power struggle:

- Listen empathetically to what the student has to say, being openly accepting of the student's feelings and opinions (e.g., "I get the impression that you don't enjoy classroom activities very much; I'd really like to hear what your concerns are").
- Summarize what you think the student has told you, and seek clarification if necessary (e.g., "It sounds as if you'd rather not let your friends know how much trouble you're having with your schoolwork. Is that the problem, or is it something else?").
- Describe the effects of the problem behavior, including your own reactions to it (e.g., "When you come to class late every day, I worry that you are getting further and further behind, and sometimes I even feel a little hurt that you don't seem to value your time in my classroom").
- Give the student a choice of some sort (e.g., "Would you rather try to work quietly at your group's table, or would it be easier if you sat somewhere by yourself to complete your work?"). (derived from suggestions by Emmer et al., 1994)

Ultimately, we must communicate our interest in the student's long-term school achievement, our concern that the misbehavior is interfering with that achievement, and our commitment to working cooperatively with the student to alleviate the problem.

Teaching Self-Regulation Strategies

Sometimes, in addition to exploring reasons for a student's misbehavior and its unacceptability in the classroom, we may also want to develop a long-term plan for changing the student's behavior. Consider the following situations as examples:

- Brian doesn't seem to be making much progress in his academic work; for instance, his performance on assignments and tests is usually rather low. As Brian's teacher, you know he's capable of better work, because he occasionally turns in an assignment or test paper of exceptionally high quality. The root of Brian's problem seems to be that he is off task most of the time. When he should be paying attention to a lesson or doing an assignment, he is instead sketching pictures of sports cars and airplanes, fiddling with whatever objects he has found on the floor, or daydreaming. Brian would really like to improve his academic performance but doesn't seem to know how to do it.
- Georgia frequently speaks out without permission. She blurts out answers to your questions, preventing anyone else from answering them first. She rudely interrupts other students' comments with her own point of view. And she initiates conversations with classmates at the most inopportune times. You have talked with Georgia several times; she readily acknowledges the problem and vows to restrain herself. After each discussion with you, her behavior improves for a short time, but within a few days her mouth is off and running once again.

Brian's off-task behavior interferes with his own academic achievement, and Georgia's excessive chattiness interferes with the learning of her classmates. Cueing and private discussions haven't led to any improvement. But both Brian and Georgia have something going for them: They *want* to change their behavior. When students genuinely want to improve their own behavior, why not teach them ways to bring about desired changes *themselves*?

In Chapter 10 we examined a variety of strategies for promoting self-regulated behavior, learning, and problem solving, and several of them might be useful with Brian and Georgia. *Self-monitoring* is especially useful when students need a reality check about the severity of the problem. Brian may think he's on task far more often than he really is; thus, we might give him a timer set to beep every five minutes and ask him to write down whether he has been on task each time he hears a beep. Georgia may not realize how frequently she prevents her classmates from speaking; thus, we might ask her to make a check mark on a tally sheet every time she talks without permission. In fact, both Brian's and Georgia's behavior problems have been successfully addressed through self-monitoring alone (Broden, Hall, & Mitts, 1971; K. R. Harris, 1986; Mace et al., 1989; Mace & Kratochwill, 1988).

If, by itself, self-monitoring doesn't do the trick, we might give Georgia *self-instructions* that she can use whenever she wants to contribute to a classroom discussion:

1. *Button* my lips (by holding them tightly together).
2. *Raise* my hand.
3. *Wait* until I'm called on.

And we can use *self-imposed contingencies* to give both students a motivational boost. For example, we might ask Brian to give himself a point for each five-minute period he's been on task, and we might instruct Georgia to give herself a point for every fifteen-minute period in which she's spoken only when called on. By accumulating a certain number of points, the students could earn the right to engage in a favorite activity.

Self-regulatory strategies have several advantages. They help us avoid power struggles with students about who's "in charge." They increase students' sense of self-determination and so also increase their intrinsic motivation to learn and achieve in the classroom. Furthermore, self-regulation techniques benefit students over the long run, promoting productive behaviors that are apt to continue long after students have moved on from a particular classroom or school. And of course, when we teach students to monitor and modify their own behavior, rather than to depend on us to do it for them, we become free to do other things—for example, to *teach*!

At this point, let's look at how teachers at one school try to encourage good behavior through self-regulation.

<table>
<tr><td colspan="4" style="text-align:right">**Analyzing Teacher Strategies**</td></tr>
</table>

What Did I Do?
Teachers at an elementary school use the form to the right to encourage productive behaviors and minimize unproductive ones. As you examine the form, think about

- Its potential strength(s)
- Its potential drawback(s)

Scoring: 2 = great effort 1 = OK effort 0 = effort needs improvement	9:00–10:30	11:00–12:30	1:30–3:00
Did I listen when the teacher or adult was speaking?			
Did I try my hardest and have a positive attitude?			
Did I stay in my seat during listening and work time?			
Total			

In theory, at least, the form should encourage students to self-monitor a variety of on-task behaviors. However, it has several drawbacks that will limit its effectiveness. First, trying "my hardest" and having "a positive attitude" are virtually impossible to evaluate objectively. Even *listening* (in the first question) may be difficult to judge accurately: Young children in particular are apt to think of listening as sitting quietly and not interrupting, rather than as actually paying attention to and understanding what is being said (see Chapter 2). A second drawback is the time interval involved: Ninety minutes is so long that students may have trouble recalling how they've behaved for the entire time. A third weakness is that the form attempts to be a one-size-fits-all rating sheet, when such is probably not possible. If we want students to monitor their own behavior, we should tailor the forms they use to the particular responses of concern for each student (e.g., see Figure 10.6 in Chapter 10).

Using Behaviorist Approaches

Occasionally students may be either unwilling or unable to change their own behavior. Consider these situations:

- Tucker is out of his chair so often that, at times, you have to wonder whether he knows where his chair *is*. He finds many reasons to roam about the room—he "has to" sharpen a pencil, "has to" get his homework out of his backpack, "has to" get a drink of water, and so on. Naturally, Tucker gets very little work done, and his classmates are continually distracted by his perpetual motion.
- Janet's verbal abusiveness is getting out of hand. She regularly insults her classmates by using sexually explicit language, and she frequently likens you to a female dog or a certain body part. You have tried praising her on occasions when she's pleasant to others, and she seems to appreciate your doing so, yet her abusive remarks continue unabated.

Imagine that both Tucker and Janet are in your class. You've already spoken with each of them about their inappropriate behavior, yet you've seen no improvement. You've suggested methods of self-regulation, but the two students don't seem interested in changing for the better. So what do you do now?

When a misbehavior is clearly interfering with one or more students' learning and achievement and when such other strategies as cueing and self-regulating techniques don't seem to have an effect, then a more intensive intervention is in order. The behaviorist approaches described in Chapter 9 are often quite useful in such circumstances. Behaviorist approaches can be especially effective when combined with other interventions—for instance, fostering perspective-taking ability and other aspects of social cognition, teaching effective social skills, and providing self-regulatory strategies (e.g., D. C. Gottfredson, 2001; T. R. Robinson, Smith, Miller, & Brownell, 1999). Combining behaviorist principles with other, more "cognitive" techniques is sometimes called *cognitive behavioral therapy*.

How might we use behaviorist techniques to improve Tucker's classroom behavior? One approach would be to identify one or more effective reinforcers (given Tucker's constant fidgeting,

Sometimes misbehaviors help students satisfy certain needs or achieve certain goals. In such situations we may want to identify and encourage alternative behaviors that will enable students to accomplish the same ends.

■ What behaviorist techniques might Ms. Cornell use to help Eli, Jake, and Vanessa become more productive members of her classroom?

opportunities for physical activity might be reinforcing) and then gradually shape more sedentary behavior. Because some out-of-seat responses (e.g., getting a reference book from the bookshelf, delivering a completed assignment to the teacher's "In" basket) are quite appropriate, we might also give Tucker a reasonable allotment of out-of-seats he can use during the day. An alternative strategy might be to use functional analysis to determine the particular *purpose* that out-of-seat behavior serves for Tucker. Perhaps it allows him to avoid difficult tasks or to release the physical energy his body seems to overproduce. If we discover that Tucker acts out only when he expects challenging assignments (as was true for Samantha in Chapter 9), then we should provide the instruction and support he needs to accomplish those assignments successfully. If, instead, we find that Tucker's hyperactivity appears regularly regardless of the situation, we might instead suspect a physiological cause and so give him numerous opportunities to release pent-up energy during the school day.

A behaviorist approach may be helpful with Janet as well. In this case we might suspect that Janet has learned few if any social skills with which she can interact effectively with others; we might therefore need to begin by teaching her such skills through modeling, role playing, and so on (see "Fostering Social Skills" in Chapter 3). Once we know that Janet possesses effective interpersonal skills, we can begin to reinforce her for using those skills (perhaps with praise, as she has responded positively to such feedback in the past). Meanwhile, we should also punish (perhaps with a time-out) any relapses into old, abusive behavior patterns.

Conferring with Parents

Consider these problem behaviors:

- You assign short homework assignments almost every night; over the past three months, Carolyn has turned in only about a third of them. You're pretty sure she is capable of doing the work, and you know from previous teacher conferences that her parents give her the time and support she needs to get her assignments done. You've spoken with Carolyn about the situation on several occasions, but she shrugs you off as if she doesn't really care whether she does well in your class or not.
- Students have frequently found things missing from their tote trays or desks when Roger has been in the vicinity. A few students have told you they've seen Roger taking things that belong to others. Many of the missing objects have later turned up in Roger's possession. When you confront him about your suspicion that he's been stealing from classmates, he adamantly denies it. He says he has no idea how Cami's gloves or Marvin's baseball trading cards ended up in his desk.

As we deal with classroom misbehaviors, we may sometimes need to involve students' parents, especially when the misbehaviors show a pattern over time and have serious implications for students' long-term academic or social success. In some instances a simple telephone call may be sufficient (Emmer et al., 1994); for example, Carolyn's parents may be unaware that she hasn't been doing her homework (she's been telling them she doesn't have any) and may be able to take the steps necessary to ensure it gets done. In other cases a school conference may be more productive; for example, you may want to discuss Roger's stealing habits with both Roger and his parent(s) together—something you can do more effectively when you all sit face-to-face in the same room. A little later in the chapter, we'll identify strategies for discussing problem behavior with students' parents.

Table 14.2 summarizes the six general strategies just described. Some of them are especially useful in addressing aggression and violence, as we shall see now.

ADDRESSING AGGRESSION AND VIOLENCE AT SCHOOL

Aggression among children and adolescents occurs more frequently at school, especially in areas where adult supervision is minimal (e.g., hallways, restrooms, parking lots), than at any other location (Astor, Meyer, & Behre, 1999; Casella, 2001b; Finkelhor & Ormrod, 2000). The relative prevalence of aggression at school is almost certainly due to two factors. First, young people

TABLE 14.2

Strategies for Dealing with Student Misbehavior

STRATEGY	SITUATIONS IN WHICH IT'S APPROPRIATE	POSSIBLE EXAMPLES
Ignoring the behavior	• The misbehavior is unlikely to be repeated. • The misbehavior is unlikely to spread to other students. • Unusual circumstances elicit the misbehavior temporarily. • The misbehavior does not seriously interfere with learning.	• One student surreptitiously passes a note to another student just before the end of class. • A student accidentally drops her books, startling other students and temporarily distracting them from their work. • An entire class is hyperactive on the last afternoon before spring break.
Cueing the student	• The misbehavior is a minor infraction yet interferes with students' learning. • The behavior is likely to change with a subtle reminder.	• A student forgets to close his notebook at the beginning of a test. • A cooperative learning group is talking unnecessarily loudly. • Several students are exchanging jokes during an independent seatwork assignment.
Discussing the problem privately with the student	• Cueing has been ineffective in changing the behavior. • The reasons for the misbehavior, if made clear, might suggest possible strategies for reducing it.	• A student is frequently late to class. • A student refuses to do certain kinds of assignments. • A student shows a sudden drop in motivation for no apparent reason.
Promoting self-regulation	• The student has a strong desire to improve his or her behavior.	• A student doesn't realize how frequently she interrupts her classmates. • A student seeks help in learning to control his anger. • A student wants to develop more regular study habits.
Using behaviorist techniques	• The misbehavior has continued over a period of time and significantly interferes with student learning. • The student seems unwilling or unable to use self-regulation techniques.	• A student has unusual difficulty sitting still for reasonable periods of time. • A student's obscene remarks continue even though her teacher has spoken with her about the behavior on several occasions. • A member of the football team displays unsportsmanlike conduct that is potentially dangerous to other players.
Conferring with parents	• The source of the problem may lie outside school walls. • Parents are likely to work collaboratively with school personnel to bring about a behavior change.	• A student does well in class but rarely turns in required homework assignments. • A student is caught stealing, vandalizing school property, or engaging in other unethical or illegal behavior. • A student falls asleep in class almost every day.

spend a great deal of time at school—more so than in any other place except for home. Second, the sheer number of students attending even the smallest of schools makes some interpersonal conflict almost inevitable.

In recent years, news media have focused considerable attention on violent school crime, especially on school shootings, leading many to believe that violence in our schools is on the rise. In reality, violent crime involving serious injury or death is relatively rare on school grounds and, in the United States at least, has *declined* over the past ten years (DeVoe et al., 2003). In fact, if we consider more violent forms of aggression (those that cause serious injury or death), then school is probably the safest place that young people can be (Burstyn & Stevens, 2001; DeVoe et al., 2003; Garbarino, Bradshaw, & Vorrasi, 2002). Most aggression at school involves psychological harm, minor physical injury, or destruction of property; for instance, it might involve sexual or racial harassment, bullying, or vandalization of student lockers (G. Bender, 2001; Casella, 2001b; Pellegrini, 2002).

The roots of school aggression and violence are many and diverse. As we discovered in Chapter 3, a variety of cognitive factors (lack of perspective taking, misinterpretation of social cues, poor social problem-solving skills, etc.) predispose some students to aggressive behavior. Furthermore, perhaps because of the home or neighborhood environment in which they live, some students believe that aggression is an appropriate and effective way of resolving conflicts. Developmental factors come into play as well; for instance, many young children and a few adolescents have poor impulse control, and in early adolescence the unsettling transition to middle school may lead some students to bully weaker age-mates as a way of regaining social status with peers (Bronson, 2000; Espelage et al., 2003; Pellegrini, 2002). The school culture is also involved; for instance, at some high schools it is acceptable practice to threaten or fight with a peer who tries to steal one's boyfriend or girlfriend (K. M. Williams, 2001a, 2001b). Finally, aggression is a common reaction to frustration, and some students are repeatedly frustrated in their efforts to be academically and socially successful at school (G. Bender, 2001; Casella, 2001b; Miles, Stipek, & Strobel, 2003).

Regardless of the roots of the behavior, we must obviously not tolerate *any* form of aggression or violence on school grounds. Students can learn and achieve at optimal levels only if they know they are both physically and psychologically safe at school. Furthermore, if they *don't* feel safe, they're more likely to drop out before high school graduation (Rumberger, 1995). To be truly effective in combating aggression and violence, we must attack it on three levels (Dwyer & Osher, 2000). First, we must create an overall, schoolwide environment that makes aggression and violence unlikely. Second, we must intervene early and provide extra support for children who are at risk for academic failure or behavior problems. And third, we must provide intensive interventions for a few students who show clear signs of being in trouble. Figure 14.3 graphically depicts these three levels. Let's look at each one more closely.[1]

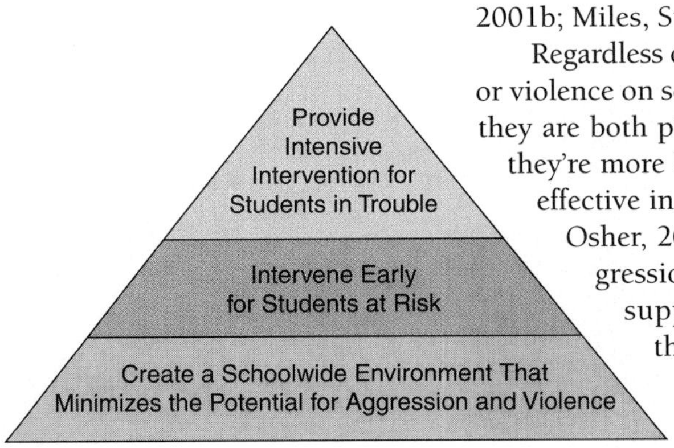

FIGURE 14.3 A three-level approach to preventing aggression and violence in schools

Based on a figure in *Safeguarding Our Children: An Action Guide* (p. 3), by K. Dwyer and D. Osher, 2000, Washington, DC: U.S. Departments of Education and Justice, American Institutes for Research.

Creating a Nonviolent School Environment

One-shot "anti-violence" campaigns have little lasting effect on school aggression and violence (Burstyn & Stevens, 2001). Instead, creating a peaceful, nonviolent school environment must be a long-term effort that includes the following:

- Schoolwide commitment to supporting *all* students' academic and social success
- A challenging and engaging curriculum
- Caring, trusting faculty-student relationships
- Genuine and equal respect—among students as well as faculty—for students of diverse backgrounds, races, and ethnicities
- Schoolwide policies and practices that promote appropriate behavior (e.g., clear guidelines for behavior, consistently applied consequences for infractions, instruction in effective social interaction and problem-solving skills)
- Student participation in school decision making
- Mechanisms through which students can communicate their concerns openly and without fear of reprisal
- Emphasis on prosocial behaviors (e.g., sharing, helping, cooperation)
- Close working relationships with community agencies and families
- Open discussion of safety issues
  (Burstyn & Stevens, 2001; Dwyer & Osher, 2000; Dwyer, Osher, & Warger, 1998; Learning First Alliance, 2001; Meehan, Hughes, & Cavell, 2003; Pellegrini, 2002)

With the exception of the last two items on the list, these strategies should look familiar, as they've surfaced frequently throughout the book, either in this chapter or in our earlier discussions of cognitive and social development (Chapters 2 and 3), group differences (Chapter 4), behaviorism (Chapter 9), social cognitive theory (Chapter 10), and motivation (Chapters 11 and 12). We'll take up the second-to-last strategy—working closely with community agencies and family—a bit later in this chapter.

The final strategy on the list—an open discussion of safety issues—encompasses a variety of more specific strategies. For example, we should explain what bullying is (i.e., that it involves harassing and intimidating peers who cannot easily defend themselves) and why it is unaccept-

---

[1] For a more in-depth discussion of the three levels, I urge you to read *Safeguarding Our Children: An Action Guide* by K. Dwyer and D. Osher (2000). You can download a copy from a variety of Internet Web sites, such as www.ed.gov/admins/lead/safety/actguide/index.html or www.air.org.cecp/guide/actionguide.htm.

able. We can solicit students' input on potentially unsafe areas (perhaps an infrequently used restroom or back stairwell) that require more faculty supervision. And our willingness to listen to students' complaints about troublesome classmates can give us important clues about which children and adolescents are most in need of our assistance and intervention.

Intervening Early for Students at Risk

In our earlier discussion of students at risk in Chapter 4, we focused largely on students at risk for *academic* failure. Yet students can be at risk for *social* failure as well. For instance, they may have few if any friends, be overtly bullied or rejected by many of their peers, or in other ways find themselves excluded from the social "life" of the school (e.g., G. Bender, 2001).

Perhaps 10 to 15 percent of our students will need some sort of intervention to help them interact effectively with peers, establish good working relationships with teachers, and become bona fide members of the school community (Dwyer & Osher, 2000). Such intervention cannot be a one-size-fits-all approach but must instead be tailored to students' particular strengths and needs. For some students it might take the form of social skills training. In other cases it might mean getting students actively involved in school clubs or extracurricular activities. In still others, it may require well-planned, systematic efforts to encourage and reinforce productive behaviors, perhaps through functional analysis and positive behavioral support (see Chapter 9). But regardless of their nature, interventions are more effective when they occur *early* in the game—before students go too far down the path of antisocial behavior—and when they are developed by a multidisciplinary team of teachers and other professionals who bring various areas of expertise to the planning table (Dryfoos, 1997; Dwyer & Osher, 2000).

Providing Intensive Intervention for Students in Trouble

For a variety of reasons, minor interventions will not always be sufficient when students are predisposed to be aggressive and violent. For instance, some students have serious mental illnesses that interfere with their ability to think rationally, cope appropriately with everyday frustrations, and control impulses (e.g., see the case study of Kirk in the section "Emotional and Behavioral Disorders" in Chapter 5). Typically, schools must work closely and collaboratively with other community groups—perhaps mental health clinics, police and probation officers, and social services—to help students at high risk for aggression and violence (Dwyer & Osher, 2000; Greenberg et al., 2003).

As teachers, our frequent interactions with students put us in an ideal position to identify those who may need intensive intervention to get them back on track for academic and social success. Especially as we get some teaching experience under our belts, we will begin to get a good sense of what characteristics are and are not normal for a particular age-group. We should also be on the lookout for the early warning signs of violence presented in Figure 14.4.

Although we must be ever vigilant about indicators that a student may be planning to cause harm to others, it is essential that we keep several points in mind. First, as I mentioned earlier, extreme violence is *very rare* in schools; unreasonable paranoia about potential school violence will prevent us from working effectively with students. Second, the great majority of students who exhibit one or a few of the warning signs on the list will *not* become violent. And most importantly, we must *never* use the warning signs as a reason to unfairly accuse, isolate, or punish a student (Dwyer et al., 1998). These signs provide a means of getting students help if they need it, not of excluding them from the education that all children and adolescents deserve.

TAKING STUDENT DIVERSITY INTO ACCOUNT

As we plan for a productive classroom environment, we must always take the diverse characteristics and needs of our students into account. For example, we should make an extra effort to establish a supportive classroom climate when working with students from ethnic minority groups or with students from lower-income neighborhoods. We must also be aware that some cultural and ethnic groups may have views about "appropriate" and "inappropriate" behaviors that are different from our own. Finally, we may often have to make special accommodations for students with special educational needs. Let's look briefly at each of these issues.

FIGURE 14.4 Early warning signs of violent behavior

Experts have identified numerous warning signs that a student may possibly be contemplating violent actions against others (Dwyer et al., 1998; O'Toole, 2000). Any one of them alone is unlikely to signal a violent attack, but several of them *in combination* should lead us to consult with school administrators and specially trained professionals about the student(s) of concern.

Social withdrawal. Over time, a student interacts less and less frequently with teachers and all or most peers.

Excessive feelings of isolation, rejection, or persecution. A student may directly or indirectly express the belief that he or she is friendless, disliked, or unfairly "picked on."

Rapid decline in academic performance. A student shows a dramatic change in academic performance and seems unconcerned about doing well; cognitive and physical factors (e.g., learning disabilities, ineffective study skills, brain injury) have been ruled out as the cause of the decline.

Poor coping skills. A student has little ability to deal effectively with frustration, takes the smallest affront personally, and has trouble "bouncing back" after minor disappointments.

Lack of anger control. A student frequently responds with uncontrolled anger to even the slightest injustice and may misdirect anger at innocent bystanders.

Sense of superiority, self-centeredness, and lack of empathy. A student depicts himself or herself as "smarter" or in some other way better than peers, is preoccupied with his or her own needs, and has little regard for the needs of others.

Lengthy grudges. A student is unforgiving of others' transgressions, even after considerable time has elapsed.

Violent themes in drawings and written work. Violence predominates in a student's artwork, stories, and journal entries, and perhaps certain individuals (e.g., a parent or particular classmate) are regularly targeted in these fantasies. (Keep in mind that *occasional* violence in writing and art is not unusual, especially for boys.)

Intolerance of individual and group differences. A student shows intense disdain and prejudice toward people of a certain race, ethnicity, gender, sexual orientation, religion, or disability.

History of violence, aggression, and other discipline problems. A student has a long record of seriously inappropriate behavior extending over several years.

Association with violent peers. A student associates regularly with a gang or other antisocial peer group.

Inappropriate role models. A student may speak with admiration about Hitler, Satan, or some other malevolent figure.

Excessive alcohol or drug use. A student who abuses alcohol or drugs may have reduced self-control; in some cases substance abuse signals significant mental illness.

Inappropriate access to firearms. A student has easy access to guns and ammunition and may regularly practice using them.

Threats of violence. A student has openly expressed an intent to harm someone else. *This warning sign alone requires immediate action.*

Creating a Supportive Climate

Earlier in the chapter we noted the value of creating a warm, supportive classroom atmosphere. Such an atmosphere may be especially important for students from ethnic minority groups (García, 1995; Ladson-Billings, 1994a; Meehan et al., 2003). For example, African American students in one eighth-grade social studies class were asked why they liked their teacher so much. Their responses were quite revealing:

> "She lets us express our opinions!"
> "She looks us in the eye when she talks to us!"
> "She smiles at us!"
> "She speaks to us when she sees us in the hall or in the cafeteria!" (Ladson-Billings, 1994a, p. 68)

Simple gestures such as these go a long way toward establishing the kinds of teacher-student relationships that lead to a productive learning environment. It's essential, too, that we create a sense of community in the classroom—a sense that we and our students share common goals and are mutually supportive of everyone's reaching those goals. This sense of community is consistent with the cooperative spirit evident in many Hispanic, Native American, and African American groups (Cazden, 1988; Ladson-Billings, 1994a).

When working with students from lower-socioeconomic backgrounds, we should also take special pains to create a classroom that feels affectionate, safe, and orderly (Becker & Luthar, 2002; Levine & Lezotte, 1995; Roderick & Camburn, 1999). Some students from lower-income neighborhoods are exposed to crime and violence almost daily; their outside world may be one in which they can rarely control the course of events. A classroom that is caring, dependable, and predictable can enhance their self-worth and elicit a sense of self-determination that they may not experience in any other environment. Hence, it can be a place to which they look forward to coming each day.

A warm, supportive classroom climate may be especially important for students from diverse ethnic backgrounds.

Defining and Responding to Misbehaviors

As we determine which behaviors are truly unacceptable in our classrooms, we must remember that some behaviors that our own culture deems inappropriate may be quite appropriate in another culture. In the following exercise, we look at some examples.

Experiencing FIRSTHAND · Identifying Misbehaviors

Read each of the scenarios at the bottom of this exercise and consider

- Whether you would classify it as a misbehavior
- What group(s) might find the behavior appropriate (draw on the discussion of group differences in Chapter 4)
- How you might deal with the behavior

1. A student is frequently late for school, sometimes arriving more than an hour after the school bell has rung.
2. Two students are sharing answers as they take a quiz.
3. Several students are exchanging insults that become increasingly more derogatory.

· · · · · · ·

Tardiness (example 1) interferes with learning, in that the student loses valuable instructional time. A student who is chronically tardy may live in a community that doesn't observe strict schedules and timelines, a pattern common in some Hispanic and Native American communities. Furthermore, arrival time may not be entirely within the student's control; for instance, perhaps the student has household responsibilities or transportation issues that make punctuality difficult. A private conversation with the student, perhaps followed up by a conference with family members, would be the most effective way to determine the root of the problem and identify potential solutions.

Sharing answers during a quiz (example 2) is a misbehavior *if* students have been specifically instructed to do their own work: Because a quiz helps a teacher determine what students have and have not learned, inaccurate quiz scores affect the teacher's instructional planning and so indirectly affect future learning. (Cheating also lowers the validity of the quiz scores; we'll discuss this concept in Chapter 15.) Although the behavior represents cheating to many people, it may reflect the cooperative spirit and emphasis on group achievement evident in the cultures of many Native American and Mexican American students. *If* we have previously explained what we mean by "cheating" in a way that students understand and *if* we have clearly described the situations in which collaboration is and is not appropriate—in other words, if the students know full well that their behavior violates classroom policy and interferes with their learning—then an adverse consequence is in order. But if we have *not* laid such groundwork, we must take the incident as a lesson about what we must do to prevent such behavior from occurring again.

Trading insults (example 3) might be psychologically harmful for the students involved and adversely affect the overall classroom climate, or it might simply be an instance of "playing the dozens," a playful verbal interaction common in some African American communities. How we handle the situation depends on the spirit in which the students seem to view the exchange. Their body language—whether they are smiling or scowling, whether they seem relaxed or tense—will tell us a great deal. If the insults truly signal escalating hostilities, then immediate intervention (separating the students, imposing an appropriate consequence, and perhaps following up with a private conference or peer mediation) is in order. If, instead, the insults reflect creative verbal play, we may simply need to establish reasonable boundaries (e.g., "indoor" voices should be used, racial or ethnic slurs are unacceptable).

■ You can find an example of playing the dozens in the section "Navigating Different Cultures at Home and at School" in Chapter 4.

Accommodating Students with Special Needs

As we create a classroom environment that promotes student learning, we must take into account any special educational needs that students may have. In general, an orderly classroom—one in which procedures for performing certain tasks are specified, expectations for student behavior are clear, and misbehaviors are treated consistently—makes it easier for students with special needs to adapt comfortably to a general education setting (Pfiffner & Barkley, 1998; M. C. Reynolds & Birch, 1988; Scruggs & Mastropieri, 1994).

When students have a history of behavior problems (e.g., as those with emotional and behavioral disorders often do), we may need to provide a great deal of guidance and support to help them develop productive classroom behavior. Furthermore, many students with special needs may need explicit feedback about their classroom performance. When praising desirable behavior, rather than saying "well done" or "nice work," we should describe exactly what responses we are praising. For example, we might say, "You did a good job following my instructions on your math assignment today," or "Thank you for remembering to sign yourself out when you went down the hall to use the drinking fountain." Similarly, when students display inappropriate behavior, we should tell them exactly what they've done wrong. For example, when speaking with a student with chronic behavior problems, we might say, "You borrowed Austin's book without asking him first. You know that taking other students' possessions without their permission is against the class rules we all agreed on at the beginning of the year." Additional suggestions for accommodating students with special needs are presented in Table 14.3.

Earlier in the chapter I mentioned that consistency and equitable treatment for all students is critical for establishing effective teacher-student relationships and a positive classroom climate. How do we reconcile this point with the need to accommodate individual differences, especially the often challenging behaviors of students with emotional and behavioral disorders? The key lies in knowing *when* and *how* to accommodate students' unique needs. To behave appropriately, students with special needs sometimes need more guidance and support than their nondisabled classmates. But unless there are extenuating circumstances, they must incur the same consequences as everyone else when their behaviors are out of line.

COORDINATING EFFORTS WITH OTHERS

As we work to promote students' learning and development, we will be far more effective if we coordinate our efforts with the other people in students' lives. In particular, we must work cooperatively with other teachers, with the community at large and, most importantly, with parents.

Working with Other Teachers

Although teachers spend much of the school day working in individual classrooms, they are far more effective when they

- Communicate and collaborate regularly with other classroom teachers and with specialists (e.g., librarians, counselors)
- Have common goals regarding what students should learn and achieve
- Work together to identify obstacles to students' learning and to develop strategies for overcoming those obstacles
- Are committed, as a group, to promoting equality and multicultural sensitivity throughout the school community
  (Battistich, Solomon, Watson, & Schaps, 1997; D. C. Gottfredson, 2001; J. A. Langer, 2000; Levine & Lezotte, 1995)

Ideally, we should not only create a sense of community within our individual classrooms but also create an overall **sense of school community** (Battistich, et al., 1995; Battistich et al., 1997). Students should get the same message from every member of the faculty—that we are working together to help them become informed, successful, and productive citizens and that they can and should *help one another* as well. Alicia, a tenth grader, reveals a sense of school community when she describes her high school:

> This school is something else! The teachers, they're friendlier, they're easier to work with. If you need help, they'll bend over backwards to help you, if it's after school, before school, anything— they'll do it. I know just about every teacher here. . . .

■ **sense of school community** Shared belief that all faculty and students within a school are working together to help everyone learn and succeed.

Maintaining a Productive Classroom Environment for Students with Special Educational Needs

CATEGORY	CHARACTERISTICS YOU MIGHT OBSERVE	SUGGESTED CLASSROOM STRATEGIES
Students with specific cognitive or academic difficulties	• Difficulty staying on task • Misbehaviors such as hyperactivity, impulsiveness, disruptiveness, inattentiveness (in some students) • Poor time management skills, a disorganized approach to accomplishing tasks, or both (in some students)	• Closely monitor students during independent assignments. • Make sure students understand their assignments; if appropriate, give them extra time to complete the assignments. • Make expectations for behavior clear, and enforce classroom rules consistently. • Cue students regarding appropriate behavior. • Reinforce (e.g., praise) desired behaviors immediately. • For hyperactive students, plan short activities that help them settle down after periods of physical activity (e.g., after recess, lunch, or physical education). • For impulsive students teach self-instructions (see Chapter 10). • Teach strategies for organizing time and work (e.g., tape a schedule of daily activities to students' desks, provide folders students can use to carry assignments between school and home).
Students with social or behavioral problems	• Frequent overt misbehaviors, such as acting out, aggression, noncompliance, destructiveness, or stealing (in some students) • Difficulty inhibiting impulses • Misbehaviors triggered by changes in the environment or daily routine or by sensory overstimulation (for students with autism) • Difficulty interacting effectively with classmates • Difficulty staying on task • Tendency to engage in power struggles with teachers (for some students)	• Specify in precise terms what behaviors are acceptable and unacceptable in the classroom; establish and enforce rules for behavior. • Maintain a predictable schedule; warn students ahead of time about changes in the routine. • Use self-regulation techniques and behaviorist approaches to promote productive classroom behaviors. • Teach social skills (see Chapter 3). • Closely monitor students during independent assignments. • Give students a sense of self-determination about some aspects of classroom life; minimize use of coercive techniques. • Make an extra effort to show students that you care about them as human beings.
Students with general delays in cognitive and social functioning	• Occasionally disruptive classroom behavior • Dependence on others for guidance about how to behave • More appropriate classroom behavior when expectations are clear	• Establish clear, concrete rules for classroom behavior. • Cue students regarding appropriate behavior; keep directions simple. • Use self-regulation techniques and behaviorist approaches to promote desired behaviors. • Give explicit feedback about what students are and are not doing appropriately.
Students with physical or sensory challenges	• Social isolation from classmates (for some students) • Difficulty accomplishing tasks as quickly as other students • Difficulty interpreting spoken messages (if students have hearing loss)	• Establish a strong sense of community within the classroom. • When appropriate, give extra time to complete assignments. • Keep unnecessary classroom noise to a minimum if one or more students have hearing loss.
Students with advanced cognitive development	• Off-task behavior in some students, often due to boredom during easy assignments and activities	• Assign tasks appropriate to students' cognitive abilities.

Sources: Achenbach & Edelbrock, 1981; Barkley, 1998; Beirne-Smith et al., 2002; Buchoff, 1990; B. Clark, 1997; Dempster & Corkill, 1999; Diamond, 1991; Friedel, 1993; Granger, Whalen, Henker, & Cantwell, 1996; Heward, 2003; Koegel et al., 1996; Landau & McAninch, 1993; Mercer, 1997; Morgan & Jenson, 1988; Ogden & Germinario, 1988; Patton et al., 1996; Pellegrini & Horvat, 1995; Piirto, 1999; M. C. Reynolds & Birch, 1988; R. Turnbull et al., 2004; Winner, 1997.

If I were not in this school right now, I would be in a group home. This is the only reason that I'm trying to work things out with my mom, cause I got so much going on here. . . .

They don't teach the way other high schools do. I can ask a question ten, eleven, twelve times, and they will still be there without getting hostile. They're not like, "Why haven't you gotten this through your head by now?" They'll go, "Why don't we try it a different way?" (From *Kids and School Reform,* pp. 10–11, by P. A. Wasley, R. L. Hample, & R. W. Clark, 1997, San Francisco: Jossey-Bass. Copyright 1997 by Jossey-Bass. This material is used by permisson of John Wiley & Sons, Inc.)

When teachers and students share an overall sense of school community, students have more positive attitudes toward school, are more motivated to achieve at high levels, exhibit more prosocial behavior, and are more likely to interact with peers from diverse backgrounds. Furthermore, teachers have higher expectations for students' achievement and a greater sense of self-efficacy about their teaching effectiveness (Battistich et al., 1995, 1997; J. A. Langer, 2000). In fact, when teachers work together, they may have higher *collective self-efficacy*—a belief that, working as a group, they can definitely have an impact on students' learning and achievement—and this collective self-confidence is indeed related to students' performance (Bandura, 2000; Goddard et al., 2000). Such a "team spirit" has an additional advantage for beginning teachers: It provides the support structure (scaffolding) they may need, especially when working with students who are at risk for school failure. New teachers report greater confidence in their ability to help their students learn and achieve when they collaborate regularly with their colleagues (Chester & Beaudin, 1996).

Working with the Community at Large

Students almost always have regular contact with other institutions besides school—possibly with youth groups, community organizations, social services, churches, hospitals, mental health clinics, or local judicial systems. And some of them are probably growing up in cultural environments unfamiliar to many teachers.

As teachers, we will be most effective if we understand the environments within which our students live and if we think of ourselves as part of a larger team that promotes their long-term development. For example, we must educate ourselves about students' cultural backgrounds, perhaps by taking coursework or getting involved in local community events after school hours (Hadaway, Florez, Larke, & Wiseman, 1993; Ladson-Billings, 1994a). We must also keep in contact with other people and institutions that play major roles in students' lives, coordinating our efforts whenever possible (J. L. Epstein, 1996). As we noted earlier, such coordination is especially important for students who may be at risk for academic or social failure at school and, perhaps, also at risk for aggressive and violent behavior.

Working with Parents

Above all, we must work cooperatively with students' parents and other primary caregivers. We can best think of our relationship with these individuals as a *partnership* in which we collaborate to promote students' long-term development and learning (Hidalgo et al., 1995). Such a relationship may be especially important when working with students from diverse cultural backgrounds (Hidalgo et al., 1995; Salend & Taylor, 1993). And it is *essential* when working effectively with students who have special educational needs (see Chapter 5).

Not all students come from traditional two-parent families, such as this one drawn by 5-year-old Haley (her teacher has labeled each person). Many children have single parents, grandparents, aunts and uncles, foster parents, or other individuals as their primary caregivers.

It is important to recognize that families come in a variety of forms and that students' primary caregivers are not always their parents. For example, in some ethnic minority communities, grandmothers take primary responsibility for raising children (Stack & Burton, 1993; M. Wilson, 1989). For simplicity, I will use the term *parents* in upcoming discussions, but I am in fact referring to all primary caregivers.

Communicating with Parents   At the very minimum, we must stay in regular contact with parents about the progress their children are making. We must inform them of their children's accomplishments and alert them about behaviors that are consistently interfering with learning and achievement. Regular communication also provides a means through which parents can give *us* information. Such information might suggest ideas about how we can best assist or motivate their children; at the least, it will help us understand why students sometimes behave as they do. Finally, we can coordinate our classroom strategies with those that parents use at home; our efforts to help students succeed will almost certainly yield greater returns if expectations for academic performance and social behavior are similar both in and out of school. Following are several ways in which we can communicate regularly with parents.

Parent-teacher conferences. In most school districts, formal parent-teacher conferences are scheduled one or more times a year. In the following exercise, we see some of the information that can emerge from such a conference.

Interpreting Student Artifacts and Behaviors

Goals Conference
In October of Todd's third-grade year, his mother, teacher, and student teacher met to discuss Todd's progress. The three adults brainstormed both the strengths and challenges for Todd. As you look at the teacher's notes from the conference, consider

- Possible ways in which instruction might build on Todd's strengths
- Possible strategies for addressing Todd's challenges

<u>Strengths</u>
Sports "dimension" - really enjoys them.
Curious - asks questions. Likes to see how things work - takes things apart.
Sensitive to his own feelings
Accepts the consequences.
Figures out the best result for himself.
Math -
"Fun" to write. New interest.
Reading - became comfortable with reading to himself last year (2nd)
Independent work -

<u>Challenges</u>
Embarassed by sensitivity
Will seek negative rewards.
Language - articulation.
Social communication.
When he doesn't feel good about himself he may put others down.
Cooperative group work - doesn't wait or help
Worries about image - insecure?

Some of the teacher's notes are vague or ambiguous, and her term "negative rewards" is an apparent oxymoron to someone who hasn't observed Todd's behavior in class. Nevertheless, we can see patterns in the group's observations. Todd has a number of strengths on which his teachers can build. He is strong in math and has recently discovered that it is fun to write. His teachers and mother might encourage more reading by providing fiction and nonfiction related to sports, and they might engage his interest in science by providing hands-on experiences with mechanical objects he can manipulate and take apart. Todd appears to have developed some self-regulatory behaviors (he does well at independent work), and he accepts the consequences when he behaves inappropriately. Todd's primary areas of challenge are in classroom behavior and interpersonal relationships: He sometimes acts out to gain teacher attention (this is the intended meaning of "negative rewards"), seems easily embarrassed, occasionally belittles others, and doesn't work well in cooperative groups. Todd could use guidance on how to get attention more productively, and he would probably benefit from explicit training in social skills (e.g., through role-playing activities).

Oftentimes we may want to include students in conferences—essentially making them parent-teacher-student conferences—and in some instances we might even ask students to *lead* them (Popham, 1995; Stiggins, 2001). By holding student-led conferences, we increase the likelihood that parents will come to the conferences, we encourage students to reflect on their own academic progress, and we give them practice in communication and leadership skills.

FIGURE 14.5 Conducting effective parent-teacher conferences

Suggestions for any conference:

- Schedule each conference at a time that accommodates parents' work schedules and other obligations.
- Prepare for the conference ahead of time; for example, organize your notes, review information you have about the student, plan an agenda for your meeting, and have examples of the student's work at hand.
- Create a warm, nonjudgmental atmosphere. For example, express your appreciation that the parents have come, actively encourage them to express their thoughts and perspectives, and give them enough time to do so. Remember that your objective is to work cooperatively and constructively together to create the best educational program possible for the student.
- Express your thoughts clearly, concisely, and honestly.
- Avoid educational jargon with which parents may be unfamiliar; describe the student's performance in ways a noneducator can understand.

- End the conference on a positive note—for instance, with a review of a student's many strengths and the progress he or she has made.
- After the conference, follow through with anything you have said you will do.

Additional suggestions for a student-led conference:

- Meet with the student ahead of time to agree on appropriate work samples to share.
- Model and role-play effective conferences in class, and give students time to practice with their classmates.
- Schedule a backup "audience" (e.g., one of the student's former teachers, a trusted friend) who can sit in if the parents don't show up.
- Offer additional time in which you can meet without the student present if the parents so desire.
- Talk with the student afterward about what went well and about how, together, you might improve the next conference.

Sources: R. L. Linn & Miller, 2005; Polloway & Patton, 1993; Salend & Taylor, 1993; Stiggins, 2001.

Furthermore, teachers, students, and parents alike are apt to leave such meetings with a shared understanding of the progress that has been made and the steps to be taken next. Several suggestions for conducting effective conferences are presented in Figure 14.5.

When a student's parents speak a language other than English, we will of course, want to include in the conversation someone who can converse fluently with the parents in their native tongue (and ideally, someone whom the parents trust). In cultures in which extended families play a key role in children's lives, we may want to include other family members (perhaps grandparents, aunts, or uncles) as well.

Written communication. Written communication can take a variety of forms. It can be a regularly scheduled, teacher-constructed checklist or grade sheet that documents a student's academic progress. It can be a quick, informal note acknowledging a significant accomplishment. Or it can be a general newsletter describing noteworthy classroom activities. All of these have something in common: They let parents know what is happening at school while also conveying our intention to stay in touch on an ongoing basis.

A letter from second-grade teacher Ann Reilly, shown in Figure 14.6, provides an illustration. Ms. Reilly sends a letter home to parents every Friday. This one was written on September 14, 2001, just three days after the terrorist attacks on the World Trade Center and Pentagon and during a week when her students were taking a districtwide standardized test. With the letter, Ms. Reilly communicates a great deal of information: what topics the class is studying, how parents will get results of the standardized testing, and why the class is not talking much about the terrorist attacks. She communicates attitudes as well; for instance, she is eager to keep the lines of communication with parents open, is approachable (she signs the letter "Ann"), and cares about how well her students are doing (e.g., "I don't like telling them that they are on their own" during the classroom assessments). She also suggests several simple ways in which parents might contribute to the class: volunteering to help with spelling assessment, donating tissues or baby wipes, and providing instructions for making baby wipes. Because she teaches in a school district where most parents have Internet access either at home or at work, she gives parents her e-mail address. Suggesting the use of e-mail would, of course, be inappropriate in communities where many families cannot afford computers or where parents have limited knowledge of English.

Telephone conversations. Telephone calls are useful when issues require immediate attention. We might call a parent to express concern when a student's behavior deteriorates unexpectedly

FIGURE 14.6 Example of a parent letter

9/14/01

Dear Parents,

I have been lucky so far and have not had to go back for jury duty. I have two more weeks to go [in terms of possibly being summoned for duty] and hope I will continue to be in the classroom.

We have been trying to keep the routine pretty regular, despite one or two testing sessions per day. The children have been pretty focused, although it is difficult when they are unfamiliar with the format and look to us for help. I don't like telling them that they are on their own! We are done, thank goodness. I believe you will receive results in the mail.

Homework and spelling will resume next week. I could also use my regular volunteers to help get through the spelling assessments. The times you have been coming are still fine. Call or e-mail me if you need the available times for helping.

We finished our unit on germs and sanitation, although we did not get into any discussions about Anthrax. It seems that you are keeping the children protected at home from details of the scary news, as we are at school. We kept our discussions to common illnesses that they are aware of and how they can avoid them with proper sanitation.

A few classrooms are doing activities to raise money for many of the children involved in the tragedy. Sarah [the teacher intern] and I decided not to work with our children on a fundraiser because we don't want to get into anxiety-producing discussions. It is hard to help young children understand that they are safe where they are and that it is unlikely that they will be involved in such things.

Next week, we will be starting a Nutrition Unit and beginning to read some Halloween stories. We will continue working to become automatic with math facts, along with our regular routine of phonics lessons, DOL [daily oral language], reading, writing, spelling, etc.

We are running out of Kleenex and could use some donations. We would also like some boxes of baby wipes to use in cleaning hands and desks when there is not time for the entire class to wash. Someone mentioned to me that there is a homemade recipe for baby wipes out there somewhere. Is there a parent who knows and would be willing to share?

Have a great weekend.

Ann

and without apparent provocation. But we might also call to express excitement about an important step forward. Parents, too, should feel free to call us. Keep in mind that many parents are at work during the school day; hence, it is often helpful to accept and encourage calls at home during the early evening hours.

Parent discussion groups. In some instances we may want to assemble a group of parents to discuss issues of mutual interest or concern. For example, we might use such a group as a sounding board when we can pick and choose among topics to include in the classroom curriculum, or perhaps when we are thinking about assigning controversial yet potentially valuable works of literature (e.g., Rudman, 1993). Alternatively, we might want to use a discussion group as a mechanism through which we can all share ideas about how best to promote students' academic, personal, and social development (e.g., J. L. Epstein, 1996). Some teachers have successfully used parent "coffee nights" during which they explain a new instructional strategy or "author teas" during which students read the poetry or short stories they have written (e.g., Fosnot, 1996).

None of the communication strategies just described will, in and of itself, guarantee a successful working relationship with parents. Parent-teacher conferences and parent discussion groups typically occur infrequently. Written communication is ineffective with parents who have limited literacy skills. And, of course, not everyone has a telephone. Ideally, we want not only to communicate with parents but to get them actively involved in school activities as well.

Getting Parents Involved in School Activities   Effective teachers get parents and other important family members (e.g., grandparents, older siblings) actively involved in school life and in children's learning (G. A. Davis & Thomas, 1989; J. L. Epstein, 1996; Levine & Lezotte, 1995). Students whose parents are involved in school activities have better attendance records, higher achievement, and more positive attitudes toward school. Although the reasons for the relationship are not entirely clear, it appears to be partly due to the fact that by becoming actively involved in school activities, parents have a better idea about how to help their children with academic skills at home (J. L. Epstein, 1996; N. E. Hill & Craft, 2003; Mattingly, Prislin, McKenzie, Rodrigues, & Kayzar, 2002).

Most parents become involved in school activities only when they have a specific invitation to do so and when they know that school personnel genuinely *want* them to be involved (A. A. Carr, 1997; Hoover-Dempsey & Sandler, 1997). For example, we might invite parents to an open house or choir performance in the evening, or we might request their help with a fund-raiser on a Saturday afternoon. We might seek volunteers to help with field trips, special projects, or individual tutoring during the school day. And we should certainly use parents and other community members as resources to give us a multicultural perspective of the community in which we work (McCarty & Watahomigie, 1998; Minami & Ovando, 1995; H. L. Smith, 1998).

Yet some parents, especially those from some minority groups, may not take our invitations seriously. Consider one African American parent's explanation of why she rarely attends school events:

> If we are talking about slavery times . . . the slaves were all around, plantation owner came to the plantation [and said] "Oh, we're having a party over next door, come on over!" He would say, "Come on over," there was an invitation without any qualification as to who was to come. The African Americans, the slaves would not come because they knew the invitation was not for them. . . . They were not expected to participate. (A. A. Carr, 1997, p. 2)

In such cases a personal invitation can often make a difference, as this parent's statement demonstrates:

> The thing of it is, had someone not walked up to me and asked me specifically, I would not hold out my hand and say, "I'll do it." . . . "You get parents here all the time, black parents that are willing, but maybe a little on the shy side and wouldn't say I really want to serve on this subject. You may send me the form, I may never fill the form out. Or I'll think about it and not send it back. But you know if that principal, that teacher, my son's math teacher called and asked if I would . . . (A. A. Carr, 1997, p. 2)

Encouraging "Reluctant" Parents   Despite our best efforts, a few parents will remain uninvolved in their children's education; for example, some parents may rarely if ever attend scheduled parent-teacher conferences. Before we jump too quickly to the conclusion that these parents are also *uninterested* in their children's education, we must recognize several possible reasons why parents might be reluctant to make contact with us. Some may have an exhausting work schedule or lack adequate child care. Others may have difficulty communicating in English or finding their way through the school system to the people they most need to talk with (H.-Z. Ho, Hinckley, Fox, Brown, & Dixon, 2001; Salend & Taylor, 1993). Still others may believe that it's inappropriate to bother teachers with questions about their children's progress or to offer information and suggestions (Hidalgo et al., 1995; Olneck, 1995; Pérez, 1998). And a few may simply have had bad experiences with school when they themselves were children (Salend & Taylor, 1993).

Experienced educators have offered numerous suggestions for getting reluctant parents more involved in their children's schooling:

- Make an extra effort to establish parents' trust and confidence—for instance, by demonstrating that we value their input and would never make them appear foolish.
- Encourage parents to be assertive when they have questions or concerns.
- Invite other important family members (e.g., grandparents, aunts, uncles) to participate in school activities, especially if a student's cultural background is one that places high value on the extended family.
- Give parents suggestions about learning activities they can easily do with their children at home.
- Find out what parents do exceptionally well (e.g., carpentry, cooking), and ask them to share their talents with the students.
- Provide opportunities for parents to volunteer for jobs that don't require them to leave home (e.g., to be someone students can call when unsure of homework assignments).
- Identify specific individuals (e.g., bilingual parents) who can translate for those who speak little or no English.
- Conduct parent-teacher conferences or parent discussions at times and locations more convenient for families; make use of home visits *if* such visits are welcomed.

- Offer resources for parents at the school building (e.g., contacts with social and health services; classes in English, literacy, home repairs, arts and crafts). (J. L. Epstein, 1996; Finders & Lewis, 1994; Hidalgo et al., 1995; H.-Z. Ho et al., 2001; Howe, 1994; G. R. López, 2001; Salend & Taylor, 1993; Sanders, 1996)

Another potentially effective strategy is to reinforce *parents* as well as students when the students do well at school. One administrator at a school with a large population of immigrant students put it this way:

> One of the things we do . . . is that we identify those students that had perfect attendance, those students that passed all areas of the [statewide achievement tests] and were successful. We don't honor the student, we honor the parents. We give parents a certificate. Because, we tell them, "through your efforts, and through your hard work, your child was able to accomplish this." (G. R. López, 2001, p. 273)

Discussing Problem Behaviors with Parents   As noted earlier, we may sometimes need to speak with parents about a chronic behavior problem at school. Put yourself in a parent's shoes in the following exercise.

Experiencing FIRSTHAND ·Putting Yourself in a Parent's Shoes

Imagine you're the parent of a seventh grader named Tommy. As you and your son are eating dinner one evening, the telephone rings. You get up to answer the phone.

You:	Hello?
Ms. J.:	Hi. This is Ms. Johnson, Tommy's teacher. May I talk with you for a few minutes?
You:	Of course. What can I do for you?
Ms. J.:	Well, I'm afraid I've been having some trouble with your son, and I thought you ought to know about it.
You:	Really? What seems to be the problem?
Ms. J.:	For one thing, Tommy hardly ever gets to class on time. When he does arrive, he spends most of his time talking and laughing with his friends, rather than paying attention to what I'm saying. It seems as if I have to speak to him three or four times every day about his behavior.
You:	How long has all this been going on?
Ms. J.:	For several weeks now. And the problem is getting worse rather than better. I'd really appreciate it if you'd talk with Tommy about the situation.
You:	Well, thank you for letting me know about this, Ms. Johnson.
Ms. J.:	You're most welcome. Good night.
You:	Good night, Ms. Johnson.

Take a few minutes to jot down some of the things that, as a parent, you might be thinking after this telephone conversation.

· · · · · · ·

You may have had a variety of reactions to your conversation with Ms. Johnson. Here are some of the possibilities:

- Why isn't Tommy taking his schoolwork more seriously?
- Isn't Tommy doing anything *right*?
- Has Ms. Johnson tried anything else besides reprimanding Tommy for his behavior? Or is she laying all of this on *my* shoulders?
- Tommy's a good kid; I should know, because I raised him. For some reason, Ms. Johnson doesn't like him, and so she'll find fault with *anything* he does.

Notice how Ms. Johnson focused strictly on the "negatives" of Tommy's classroom performance. As a result, you (as Tommy's parent) may possibly have felt anger at your son or guilt about your ineffective parenting skills. Alternatively, you may have maintained your confidence in your son's scholastic abilities and in your own ability to parent; if so, you may have begun to wonder about Ms. Johnson's ability to teach and motivate seventh graders.

We will be more effective when working with parents if we set a positive, upbeat tone in any communication. For one thing, we will always want to couch negative aspects of a student's classroom performance within the context of the many things the student does *well*. (For example, rather than starting out by complaining about Tommy's behavior, Ms. Johnson might have begun by saying that Tommy is a bright and capable young man with many friends and a good sense of humor.) And we must be clear about our commitment to working *together* with parents to help a student succeed in the classroom.

Ideally, discussions about problem behaviors are initiated within the context of a relationship that is characterized by mutual trust and respect and a shared concern for students' learning and well-being. Sadly, too many teachers reach out to parents only to talk about students' weaknesses—never their strengths—as the following interview with Jamal illustrates:

■ How might a chronically abusive parent react to the conversation with Ms. Johnson?

Adult:	Has your grandpa [Jamal's primary caregiver] come to school?
Jamal:	Yup, when the teachers call him.
Adult:	What did they call him for?
Jamal:	The only time they call him is when I am being bad, the teacher will call him, he will come up here and have a meeting with the teacher.
Adult:	If you are being good do the teachers call?
Jamal:	No. (dialogue from Kumar et al., 2002, p. 164)

Following are some additional suggestions for enhancing your chances for a successful outcome when you must speak with a parent about a problem behavior:

- *Don't place blame; instead, acknowledge that raising children is rarely easy.* Parents are more apt to respond constructively to your concerns if you don't blame them for their child's misbehavior.
- *Express your desire for whatever support they can give you.* Parents are more likely to be cooperative if you present the problem as one that can be effectively addressed if everyone works together to understand and solve it.
- *Ask for information and be a good listener.* If you show that you truly want to hear their perspective, parents are more likely to share their ideas regarding possible causes of the problem and possible ways of addressing it.
- *Agree on a strategy.* You are more likely to bring about an improvement in behavior if both you and a student's parents have similar expectations for behavior and similar consequences when those expectations are not met. Some parents, if making decisions on their own, may administer excessive or ineffective forms of punishment; agreement during your discussion as to what consequences are appropriate may avert such a situation. (derived from suggestions by Emmer et al., 1994)

Considering Group Differences When Working with Parents   As we work with students' parents, we must be aware that people from different cultural and ethnic groups sometimes have radically different ideas about what behaviors are problematic and how children should be disciplined. As an example, let's return to the opening case study in Chapter 4. Jack, a Native American seventh grader, had been absent from school for an entire week. Not only were his parents seemingly unconcerned, but they didn't even go looking for him until they needed him at home to help with the family farm. Their attitudes and actions make sense only when we understand that they knew their son was probably safe with neighbors and believed that, as a young adolescent, Jack was essentially an adult and responsible for his own decisions. In contrast, many parents from Asian cultures believe that Western schools are too lavish with their praise and too *lenient* in their efforts to correct misbehavior (Dien, 1998; Hidalgo et al., 1995; Tudge et al., 1999). In some cultures (including some Native American and Asian groups), ostracism is common practice: If a child's misbehaviors are seen as bringing shame on the family or community, the child is ignored for an extended period of time (Pang, 1995; Salend & Taylor, 1993).

Ultimately, we must recognize that the vast majority of parents want what's best for their children and recognize the value of a good education (Gallimore & Goldenberg, 2001; Hidalgo et al., 1995; Okagaki, 2001). It's essential, then, that we not leave them out of the loop when we're concerned how their children are performing in school. As we talk with them, we must listen to their attitudes and opinions with an open mind and try to find common ground on which to develop strategies for helping their children thrive in the classroom (Good & Nichols, 2001; Salend & Taylor, 1993).

Working Effectively with Parents

 Confer with parents if a collaborative effort might bring about a behavior change.

At a parent-teacher conference, a high school math teacher expresses his concern that a student is not turning in her homework assignments. Her parents are surprised to hear this, saying that "Carolyn usually tells us that she doesn't *have* any homework." Together they work out a strategy for communicating about what assignments have been given and when they are due.

 Use a variety of formats to communicate with parents.

A middle school language arts teacher works with her students to produce a monthly newsletter for parents. Two versions of the newsletter are created, one in English and one in Spanish.

Encourage parents and other family members to get involved in school activities.

Several elementary school classes decide to coordinate their efforts to help flood victims in a nearby town. They ask parents to contribute old clothing and household items and, if possible, to assist with collecting, organizing, or distributing the items.

 Tell parents about children's many strengths, even when communicating information about their shortcomings.

A teacher talks on the phone with the father of one of her students. She describes several areas in which the student has made considerable progress and then asks for advice about strategies for helping him stay on task and be more careful in his work.

 Acknowledge the strengths of families' varying backgrounds.

When planning a lesson on the history of farming in Colorado, a middle school social studies teacher asks a student's mother if she would be willing to talk about her own childhood experiences as a member of an immigrant family that harvested crops every summer.

 Be sensitive to parents' concerns about the limits of their influence.

A high school teacher talks with worried parents of a 16-year-old girl who has begun smoking cigarettes and is possibly experimenting with illegal drugs. Thinking about the girl's keen interest in photography, the teacher seeks an opening in an after-school photography club, with hopes that the companionship of more academically oriented peers might get her back on the right track. The teacher also consults with the school counselor about services at school and in the community that may be appropriate and beneficial.

THE BIG PICTURE

When it comes to classroom management, an ounce of prevention is worth a pound of cure. We will be far more effective classroom managers if we are proactive in our thinking—that is, if we consider in advance how we can best keep students on task throughout the school day. In this chapter we've identified a variety of strategies for keeping students focused on accomplishing instructional goals: arranging the classroom to facilitate interaction, creating a climate in which students feel safe and respected, setting reasonable limits for behavior, planning activities that keep students productively engaged with classroom subject matter, continually monitoring students' activities, and being somewhat flexible in our instructional strategies.

Yet despite our best efforts, students will sometimes exhibit behaviors that interfere with either their own or their classmates' learning. Regardless of the roots of these misbehaviors—whether they result from students' temperaments, family circumstances, peer influences, prior schooling, cognitive or emotional disabilities, or recent events in the classroom—we can nevertheless do many things to bring about positive changes in students' conduct. In other words, we *can make a difference* in students' behavioral development as well as in their cognitive and social development. Different approaches will be effective with different students, of course; some will respond favorably to subtle cues or brief conversations, whereas others may need planned, long-term interventions. All students ultimately want to succeed at school, and virtually all of them respond favorably to teachers who clearly care for and respect them and have their best interests at heart.

As teachers, we will be most effective in helping children and adolescents if we realize we are just one part (albeit a very important part) of a team of faculty, parents, and other community members who are helping children and adolescents acquire behaviors that will serve them well in the adult world. It is especially important that we keep in regular contact with students' parents, sharing information in both directions about the progress students are making and coordinating efforts at school with those on the home front.

CASE STUDY: *Old Friends*

Mr. Schulak has wanted to be a teacher for as long as he can remember. In his many volunteer activities over the years—coaching a girls' basketball team, assisting in a Boy Scout troop, teaching Sunday school—he has discovered how much he enjoys working with children. Children obviously enjoy working with him as well: Many occasionally call or stop by his home to shoot baskets, talk over old times, or just say hello. Some of them even call him by his first name.

Now that he has completed his college degree and obtained his teaching certificate, Mr. Schulak is a first-year teacher at his hometown's junior high school. He is delighted to find that he already knows many of his students—he has coached them, taught them, or gone to school with their older brothers and sisters—and so he spends the first few days of class renewing his friendships with them. But by the end of the week, he realizes that he and his students have accomplished little of an academic nature.

The following Monday, Mr. Schulak vows to get down to business. He begins each of his six class sessions by describing his instructional goals for the weeks to come; he then begins the first lesson. He is surprised to discover that many of his students—students with whom he has such a good rapport—are resistant to settling down and getting to work. They want to move from one seat to another, talk with their friends, toss wadded-up paper "baseballs" across the room and, in fact, do anything *except* the academic tasks that Mr. Schulak has in mind. In his second week as a new teacher, Mr. Schulak has already lost control of his classroom.

* Why is Mr. Schulak having so much difficulty bringing his classroom to order? What critical things has Mr. Schulak not done in his first week of teaching?

* Given that Mr. Schulak has gotten the school year off on the wrong foot, what might he do now to remedy the situation?

Once you have answered these questions, compare your responses with those presented in Appendix B.

KEY CONCEPTS

classroom management (p. 484)
classroom climate (p.485)
sense of community (p. 489)

belongingness (p. 489)
withitness (p. 496)
misbehavior (p. 499)

cueing (p. 500)
sense of school community (p. 510)

PRAXIS Turn to Appendix C, "Matching Book and Ancillary Content to the Praxis Principles of Learning and Teaching Tests," to discover sections of this chapter that may be especially applicable to the Praxis tests.

Companion Website

Now go to our Companion Website at **www. prenhall. com/ormrod** to assess your understanding of chapter content with "Multiple-Choice Questions," apply comprehension in "Essay Questions," broaden your knowledge of educational psychology with related "Web Links," gain greater insight about classroom learning in "Learning in the Content Areas," and analyze and assess classroom work in the "Student Artifact Library."

Chapter 15

Classroom Assessment Strategies

In your many years as a student, in what various ways have teachers assessed your achievement? In general, has your performance on classroom assessments accurately reflected what you've learned in class? Can you recall a situation in which a test or other classroom assessment seemed to have little or no relationship to important instructional goals?

As teachers, we will often need to assess students' learning and achievement so that we can make informed decisions. When we begin a new topic, we will want to identify existing knowledge and skills so we can gear instruction to an appropriate level. We will also want to monitor students' progress as we go along so that we can address trouble spots. And ultimately, we must determine what each student has accomplished during the school year. According to one estimate, we may spend one-third of our time, possibly even more, in assessment-related activities (Stiggins & Conklin, 1992).

It is essential that we use assessment techniques that accurately tell us what students know and can do; it is equally essential that such techniques promote students' learning and achievement over the long run. In this chapter we will examine basic concepts and principles of assessment and identify a variety of potentially effective assessment strategies. As we do so, we will address questions such as these:

- What do we mean by *assessment*, and what different forms might it take?
- For what reasons might we need to assess students' achievement and abilities? In what ways do classroom assessments actually *affect* students' achievement and abilities?
- What qualities do good assessment instruments and procedures have in common?
- In what situations is informal assessment most appropriate and useful?
- What steps should we take as we plan and design a test, assignment, or other formal assessment of achievement?
- Under what circumstances are paper-pencil measures useful? When are performance tasks preferable? How can we design good paper-pencil and performance measures?
- How and why might we get students actively involved in assessing their own learning?
- What issues must we consider as we assess students with diverse backgrounds and needs?

In Chapter 16 we will look at ways to summarize students' overall achievement.

CASE STUDY: *The Math Test*

Ms. Ford is teaching mathematics to a class of middle school students with low mathematical ability. She has just returned a set of test papers she has scored. The following class discussion ensues:

Ms. Ford:	When I corrected these papers, I was really, really shocked at some of the scores. And I think you will be too. I thought there were some that were so-so, and there were some that were devastating, in my opinion.
Student:	[Noise increasing.] Can we take them over?
Ms. Ford:	I am going to give them back to you. This is what I would like you to do: Every single math problem that you got wrong, for homework tonight and tomorrow, it is your responsibility to correct these problems and turn them in. In fact, I will say this, I want this sheet back to me by Wednesday at least. All our math problems that we got wrong I want returned to me with the correct answer.
Student:	Did anybody get 100?
Ms. Ford:	No.
Student:	Nobody got 100? [Groans]
Ms. Ford:	OK, boys and girls, shhh. I would say, on this test in particular, boys and girls, if you received a grade below 75 you definitely have to work on it. I do expect this quiz to be returned with Mom or Dad's signature on it. I want Mom and Dad to be aware of how we're doing.
Student:	No!
Student:	Do we have to show our parents? Is it a requirement to pass the class?
Ms. Ford:	If you do not return it with a signature, I will call home. (dialogue from J. C. Turner, Meyer, et al., 1998, pp. 740–741)

What information have the test results actually given Ms. Ford? What inferences does Ms. Ford make based on this information?

 What effects might this class discussion have on students' future motivation in class?

ASSESSMENTS AS TOOLS

The one thing Ms. Ford knows for sure is that her students have performed poorly on their recent math test. From this fact she assumes that they have not mastered the knowledge and skills the test was designed to assess. Ms. Ford appears to be angry rather than sympathetic about the test results; if we consider our discussion of teacher attributions in Chapter 12, we might reasonably conclude that she attributes the poor performance to a lack of effort or some other factor that students can control.

If Ms. Ford motivates her students to work harder on their math at all, she is certainly not promoting *intrinsic* motivation to master it. By focusing on students' test scores, she is fostering performance goals rather than mastery goals. Furthermore, notice how controlling, even threatening, some of her statements are: "it is your responsibility to correct these problems and turn them in. . . . All our math problems that we got wrong I want returned to me with the correct answer. . . . If you do not return it with a signature, I will call home." Such comments will almost certainly undermine students' sense of self-determination, and they are hardly going to endear students to the subject of mathematics. How Ms. Ford attempts to communicate students' test performance to their parents is yet another issue; we'll return to this point in Chapter 16.

Our assessment practices influence many other aspects of classroom functioning (recall Figure 13.1). They affect our future planning and instruction (e.g., what we teach and how we teach it), the classroom climate (e.g., whether it feels threatening or psychologically "safe"), and students' motivation and affect (e.g., whether students develop mastery or performance goals, whether they feel confident or anxious). Only when we consider the very integral role that assessment plays in the classroom can we truly harness its benefits to help our students achieve important instructional goals.

Paper-pencil tests, such as the one that Ms. Ford has given, provide one means through which we can assess student achievement. Yet not all classroom assessment involves paper and pencil. The statements students make in class, the ways they respond to questions, the questions *they* ask—all of these tell us something about what they have learned. Nonverbal behaviors give us information as well: We can observe how well students use a pair of scissors, how carefully they set up laboratory equipment, or how they perform on physical fitness tasks. Some forms of assessment take only a few seconds, whereas others may take several hours or even several days. Some are planned and developed in advance; others occur spontaneously during the course of a lesson or classroom activity.

What exactly do we mean by *assessment*? The following definition sums up its major features:

> **Assessment** is a process of observing a sample of a student's behavior and drawing inferences about the student's knowledge and abilities.

Several parts of the definition are important to note. First, we are looking at students' *behavior*. As behaviorists have pointed out, it's impossible to look inside students' heads and see what knowledge lurks there; we can see only how students actually respond in the classroom. Second, we typically use just a *sample* of classroom behavior; we certainly cannot observe and keep track of every single thing that every single student does during the school day. Finally, we must draw *inferences* from the specific behaviors we do observe to make judgments about students' overall classroom achievement—a tricky business at best. As we proceed through this chapter and the next, we will discover how to select behaviors that can give us a reasonably accurate estimate of what students know and can do.

Notice that our definition of assessment doesn't include anything about decision making. Assessment instruments do not, in and of themselves, dictate the decisions that should be made. Instead, *people*—teachers, administrators, government officials, parents, and sometimes even students themselves—interpret assessment results and make judgments based on them. When

Some tests involve paper and pencil, but others do not. In this industrial arts class, the students have designed and constructed rockets, and their teacher assesses how well each rocket performs.

■ Can you think of classroom tests you've taken that were probably *not* good samples of what they were supposed to measure?

■ **assessment** Process of observing a *sample* of a *student's* behavior and drawing inferences about the *student's* knowledge and abilities.

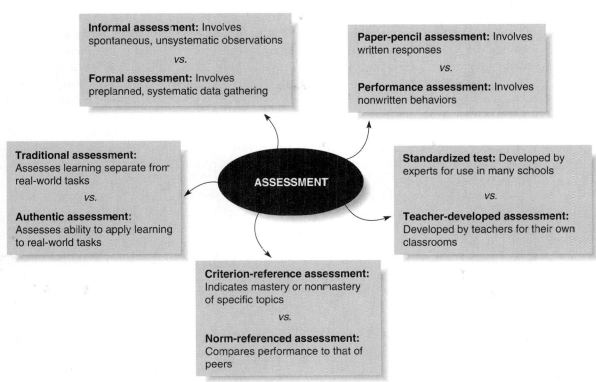

FIGURE 15.1   The various forms that educational assessment can take

people use classroom assessments for the wrong purpose, or when they interpret assessment results as those results were never meant to be interpreted, then it is the people, rather than the assessment instruments, who are to blame.

Assessments are *tools* that can help us make informed decisions about how best to help our students learn and achieve. The usefulness of these tools depends on how well matched they are to the circumstances in which we are using them. In the upcoming pages we will explore the many forms that assessment might take and the situations in which each might be helpful.

THE VARIOUS FORMS OF EDUCATIONAL ASSESSMENT

Figure 15.1 summarizes several distinctions that educators often make regarding educational assessment instruments. Let's look more closely at each one.

Informal versus formal assessment. Spontaneous, day-to-day observations of how students perform in class constitute **informal assessment**. When we conduct an informal assessment, we don't always have a specific agenda in mind, and we are likely to learn different things about different students. For instance, we may discover that Tony has a misconception about gravity when he asks, "How come people in Australia don't fall into space?" We may wonder if Jaffa needs an appointment with the eye doctor when we see her continually squinting at the chalkboard. And we may conclude that Marty has a high need for approval when he is constantly seeking our attention and praise.

In contrast, **formal assessment** is typically planned in advance and used for a specific purpose—perhaps to determine what students have learned from a geography unit, whether they can solve word problems requiring addition and subtraction, or how their strength and agility compare with those of students nationwide. It is "formal" in the sense that a particular time is set aside for it, students can prepare for it ahead of time, and it is intended to yield information about particular instructional objectives or content area standards.

Paper-pencil versus performance assessment. As teachers, we may sometimes choose **paper-pencil assessment**, in which we present questions to answer, topics to address, or problems to solve, and our students must write their responses on paper. Yet we may also find it helpful to use **performance assessment**, in which students demonstrate (*perform*) their abilities—for example, by giving an oral presentation, using a computer spreadsheet, jumping hurdles, or identifying acids and bases in a chemistry lab.

■ **informal assessment** Assessment that results from teachers' spontaneous, day-to-day observations of how students behave and perform in class.

■ **formal assessment** Preplanned, systematic attempt to ascertain what students have learned.

■ **paper-pencil assessment** Assessment in which students provide written responses to written items.

■ **performance assessment** Assessment in which students demonstrate their knowledge and skills in a nonwritten fashion.

Traditional versus authentic assessment. Historically, educational assessment instruments have focused on measuring basic knowledge and skills in relative isolation from tasks typically found in the outside world. Spelling quizzes, mathematics word problems, and physical fitness tests are examples of such **traditional assessment**. Yet ultimately students must be able to apply their knowledge and skills to complex tasks outside the classroom. The notion of **authentic assessment**—measuring the actual knowledge and skills we want students to demonstrate in an "authentic," real-life context—is gaining increasing popularity among educators (Darling-Hammond, 1991; Lester, Lambdin, & Preston, 1997; Paris & Paris, 2001; Valencia, Hiebert, & Afflerbach, 1994). Keep in mind that the distinction I've just made represents a *continuum* rather than an either-or situation: Assessment tasks can resemble real-world situations to varying degrees.

In some situations authentic assessment involves paper and pencil. For example, we might ask students to write a letter to a friend or develop a school newspaper. But in many cases it is based on nonwritten performance and closely integrated with instruction. For example, we might assess students' ability to present a persuasive argument, bake a cake, converse in a foreign language, design and build a bookshelf, or successfully maneuver a car into a parallel parking space. As teachers, we must consider what our students should be able to do when they join the adult world, and our assessment practices must, to some extent, reflect those real-life tasks.[1]

Standardized tests versus teacher-developed assessments. Sometimes classroom assessments involve tests developed by test construction experts and published for use in many different schools and classrooms. Such instruments, commonly called **standardized tests**, can be quite helpful in measuring general scholastic achievement and abilities. Thus school administrators often use them to track students' general progress in various content domains, and school psychologists, counselors, and other specialists use them to identify students with special educational needs. Unfortunately, however, standardized tests typically assess such broad abilities that they yield little information about what students specifically have and have not learned. When we want to assess students' learning and achievement related to specific instructional objectives—for example, whether students have mastered long division or whether they can apply what they've just learned in a social studies lesson—we will usually want to construct our own **teacher-developed assessment instruments**.

We will consider numerous strategies for constructing teacher-developed assessments later in this chapter. We will look more closely at the nature of standardized tests in Chapter 16.

Criterion-referenced versus norm-referenced assessments. Some assessment instruments are designed to tell us what students have and have not accomplished relative to predetermined standards or criteria; these are **criterion-referenced assessments**. Other assessment instruments indicate how well each student's performance compares with the performance of peers, perhaps that of classmates or that of age-mates across the nation. Rather than tell us specifically what a student has or has not learned, such **norm-referenced assessments** tell us how well a student stacks up against others at the same age or grade level.

Strictly speaking, any assessment has the potential to tell us *both* what students have learned and how they compare with peers. In reality, however, experienced educators tend to construct the two types of assessments somewhat differently. Ideally, questions and tasks on a criterion-referenced assessment are closely tied to the particular knowledge and skills that we hope students have acquired. If all students have mastered the subject matter to the same degree, it is entirely possible that they would all get the same score. If we want to know how students *differ* from one another—and we'll soon identify some circumstances in which we would want to do that—we must have an instrument that will yield considerable variability in scores. In such an instrument, we are apt to have questions and tasks that vary widely in difficulty level, including some that only a few students can respond to correctly.

---

[1] Educators are not in complete agreement in their use of the terms *performance assessment* and *authentic assessment*, and many treat them more or less as synonyms. I find it useful to consider separately whether an assessment involves *performance* (rather than paper and pencil) and whether it involves a complex, real-world (*authentic*) task. In the discussion here, then, I do *not* use the two terms interchangeably.

■ **traditional assessment** Assessment that focuses on measuring basic knowledge and skills in relative isolation from tasks more typical of the outside world.

■ **authentic assessment** Assessment of students' knowledge and skills in a "real-life" context.

■ **standardized test** Test constructed by experts and published for use in many different schools and classrooms.

■ **teacher-developed assessment instrument** Assessment tool developed by an individual teacher for use in his or her own classroom.

■ **criterion-referenced assessment** Assessment instrument designed to determine what students know and can do relative to predetermined standards or criteria.

■ **norm-referenced assessment** Assessment instrument that indicates how students perform relative to a peer group.

USING ASSESSMENT FOR DIFFERENT PURPOSES

On some occasions we will engage in **formative evaluation**: We will assess what students know and can do *before or during instruction*. Ongoing formative evaluation can help us determine how well students understand the topic at hand, what misconceptions they have, whether they need further practice on a particular skill, and so on. We can then develop or revise our lesson plans accordingly.

At other times we will engage in **summative evaluation**: We will conduct an assessment *after instruction* to make final decisions about what students have achieved. Summative evaluations are used to determine whether students have mastered the content of a lesson or unit, what final grades to assign, which students are eligible for more advanced classes, and the like.

With these two basic kinds of evaluation in mind, let's consider how teachers and other school personnel might use educational assessments for one or more of the following purposes: (a) promoting learning, (b) guiding instructional decision making, (c) diagnosing learning and performance problems, (d) promoting self-regulation, and (e) determining what students have learned.

Promoting Learning

When we use formative evaluation to develop or modify our lesson plans, we are obviously using assessment to facilitate students' learning. Yet summative evaluation can influence learning as well. More specifically, summative assessments can motivate students to study and learn, provide an opportunity to review previously learned material, influence how students cognitively process information, offer new ways to use and apply classroom subject matter, and provide feedback to help students enhance their knowledge and skills. Let's look more closely at each of these effects.

Assessments as motivators. On average, students study class material more and learn it better when they are told they will be tested on it or in some other way held accountable for it, rather than when they are simply told to learn it (Blumenfeld, Hamilton, Bossert, Wessels, & Meece, 1983; N. Frederiksen, 1984b; Halpin & Halpin, 1982). Yet *how* students are assessed is as important as *whether* they're assessed. Assessments are especially effective as motivators when they are criterion-referenced, are closely aligned with instructional goals and objectives, and challenge students to do their best (Maehr & Anderman, 1993; Mac Iver et al., 1995; Natriello & Dornbusch, 1984). Students' self-efficacy and attributions affect their perceptions of the "challenge," of course: Students must believe that success on an assigned task is possible if they exert reasonable effort and use appropriate strategies.

Although regular classroom assessments can be highly motivating, we must remember that, in and of themselves, they are *extrinsic* motivators. Thus, they may direct students' attention to performance goals and undermine any intrinsic motivation to learn (Grolnick & Ryan, 1987; Paris & Turner, 1994). They are especially likely to have this adverse effect when students perceive them as being primarily an evaluation of their performance rather than as a mechanism for helping them learn (Spaulding, 1992).

Assessments as mechanisms for review. As we discovered in Chapter 6, long-term memory is not necessarily "forever": for a variety of reasons, human beings tend to forget things as time goes on. Students have a better chance of remembering classroom subject matter over the long run when they review it at a later time. Studying for formal assessments provides one way of reviewing material related to important instructional goals (Dempster, 1991; Kiewra, 1989).

Assessments as influences on cognitive processing. Students will draw inferences about our instructional goals from the ways we assess their learning, and different assessment tasks may lead them to study and learn quite differently (J. R. Frederiksen & Collins, 1989; N. Frederiksen, 1984b; Lundeberg & Fox, 1991; L. A. Shepard, 2000). For instance, students will typically spend more time studying the things they think will be on a test than the things they think the test won't cover. Their expectations about the kinds of tasks they will need to perform and the questions they will need to answer also will influence whether they memorize isolated facts, on the one hand, or learn a meaningful, integrated body of information, on the other. Unfortunately, many students believe (incorrectly) that trying to learn information meaningfully—that is, trying to understand and make sense of what they study—interferes with their ability to do well on classroom tests that emphasize knowledge of isolated facts (Crooks, 1988).

What I already know about the Moon:

Solar ~~lunar~~ eclipse: Sun, Earth and ~~moon~~
are all in a line.
It is big.
Gravitational pull effects tides.
It has craters, people have seen on it.
It looks like a face.
It can be blue and yellow.

Assessments are sometimes conducted before a lesson to determine a starting point for instruction. Here 8-year-old Richard reveals his current knowledge and beliefs about the moon.

■ Do *you* study more when you know you will be tested on the subject matter?

■ **formative evaluation** Evaluation conducted before or during instruction to facilitate instructional planning and enhance students' learning.

■ **summative evaluation** Evaluation conducted after instruction to assess students' final achievement.

■ You can refresh your memory about epistemological beliefs by rereading the section "Factors Affecting Strategy Use" in Chapter 8.

How we assess students' learning is also likely to affect their views about the nature of various academic disciplines—that is, their *epistemological beliefs*. For example, if we give quizzes that assess knowledge of specific facts, students are apt to conclude that a discipline is just that: a collection of undisputed facts. If we instead ask students to take a position on a controversial issue and justify their position with evidence and logic, we give them a very different message: The discipline involves an integrated set of understandings that must be supported with reasoning and are subject to change over time.

Assessments as learning experiences. You can probably recall classroom assessments that actually taught you something. Perhaps an essay question asked you to compare two things you hadn't compared before and so helped you discover similarities you hadn't noticed earlier. Or perhaps a test problem asked you to apply a scientific principle to a situation you hadn't realized was related to that principle. Such assessment tasks not only measured what you learned, they also *helped* you learn.

In general, the very process of completing an assessment on class material helps students learn the material better, particularly if the assessment tasks ask students to elaborate on it in some way (Fall, Webb, & Chudowsky, 2000; Foos & Fisher, 1988; N. Frederiksen, 1984b). But two qualifications are important to note here. First, an assessment helps students learn only the material it specifically addresses (N. Frederiksen, 1984b). Second, when we present *incorrect* information on an assessment (as we often do in true-false and multiple-choice questions), students may eventually remember that misinformation as being true rather than false (A. S. Brown, Schilling, & Hockensmith, 1999; Voss, 1974).

What and how students study is influenced by how they expect their learning to be assessed.

Assessments as feedback. Regular classroom assessments can give students valuable feedback about which things they have and have not mastered. But simply knowing one's final assessment score (e.g., knowing the percentage of items answered correctly) is not terribly helpful. To facilitate students' learning—and ultimately to enhance their self-efficacy for mastering the subject matter—assessment results must include concrete information about where students have succeeded and where they've had difficulty (Baron, 1987; Krampen, 1987; Pintrich & Schunk, 2002).

The Into the Classroom feature "Using Assessment to Promote Students' Learning and Achievement" presents several examples of how we might use classroom assessments to foster effective cognitive processes and enhance student learning.

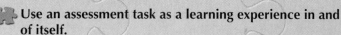

INTO THE CLASSROOM

Using Assessment to Promote Students' Learning and Achievement

 Give a formal or informal pretest to determine where to begin instruction.

When beginning a new unit on cultural geography, a teacher gives a pretest designed to identify misconceptions that students may have about various cultural groups—misconceptions he can then address during instruction.

 Choose or develop an assessment instrument that reflects the actual knowledge and skills you want students to achieve.

When planning how to assess his students' achievement, a teacher initially decides to use questions from the set of test items (test bank) that accompanies his textbook. When he looks more closely at the test bank, however, he discovers that the items measure only knowledge of isolated facts. Instead, he develops several authentic assessment tasks that better reflect his primary instructional goal: Students should be able to apply what they've learned to real-world problems.

Construct assessment instruments that reflect how you want students to process information when they study.

A teacher tells her students, "As you study for next week's vocabulary test, remember that the test questions will ask you to

put definitions in your own words and give your own examples to show what each word means."

 Use an assessment task as a learning experience in and of itself.

A high school science teacher has students collect samples of the local drinking water and test them for bacterial content. She is assessing her students' ability to use procedures she has taught them, but she also hopes they will learn something about their community's natural resources.

Use an assessment to give students specific feedback about what they have and have not mastered.

As he grades students' persuasive essays, a teacher writes numerous notes in the margins of the papers to indicate places where students have analyzed a situation correctly or incorrectly, identified a relevant or irrelevant example, proposed an appropriate or inappropriate solution, and so on.

Provide criteria that students can use to evaluate their *own* performance.

The teacher of a "foods and nutrition" class gives her students a checklist of qualities to look for in the pies they have baked.

Guiding Instructional Decision Making

As noted earlier, we may sometimes want to assess students' knowledge and understanding *before* we teach a topic; for instance. a quick pretest can help us determine a suitable point at which to begin instruction. We will also want to monitor students' learning throughout a lesson or unit (through either formal assessments or more informal means) to get ongoing information about the appropriateness of our instructional goals and the effectiveness of our instructional strategies. For example, if we find that almost all students are completing assignments quickly and easily, we might set our goals a bit higher. If we discover that many students are struggling with material we have presented in class lectures, we might consider trying a different instructional approach—perhaps a more concrete, hands-on one.

■ Is the emphasis on formative evaluation or summative evaluation here?

FORMATIVE

Diagnosing Learning and Performance Problems

Why is Louis having trouble learning to read? Why is Gretel misbehaving in class? Why does Martin seem excessively anxious during exams? We ask such questions when we suspect that certain students might learn differently from their classmates and may possibly require special educational services. Many standardized tests have been designed specifically to identify the special academic, social, and emotional needs that some students have. Most of these tests require explicit training in their use and so are often administered and interpreted by specialists (school psychologists, counselors, speech and language pathologists, etc.). As a general rule, they tend to be norm-referenced rather than criterion-referenced so as to identify students who are outside the "average" range for their age-group with respect to certain characteristics or abilities.

Yet teacher-developed assessment instruments can provide considerable diagnostic information as well, especially when they suggest where students are going wrong and why. In other words, they can, and ideally they *should*, give us information we can use to help students improve (Baek, 1994; Baxter, Elder, & Glaser, 1996; Covington, 1992). Furthermore, when we pass such diagnostic information on to students, it can promote greater self-regulation—our next topic of discussion.

Promoting Self-Regulation

In our discussion of self-regulation in Chapter 10. we noted the importance of *self-monitoring* (students must be aware of how well they are doing as they study and learn) and *self-evaluation* (students must be able to assess their final performance accurately). An important function of our classroom assessment practices should be to help students engage in such self-regulating processes (Covington, 1992; Paris & Ayres, 1994; Vye et al., 1998). We will look at strategies for promoting self-regulation in the section "Including Students in the Assessment Process" later in the chapter.

Determining What Students Have Learned

We will almost certainly use one or more formal assessments to determine whether students have achieved instructional objectives or met certain content area standards. Such information will be essential if we are using a mastery-learning approach to instruction; it will also be important as we assign final grades. School counselors and administrators, too, may use assessment results for making placement decisions, such as deciding which students are most likely to do well in advanced classes, which might need additional coursework in basic skills, and so on.

In some cases, assessments of students' achievement are used to make major decisions about students, teachers, and schools. For instance, some school districts use one or more assessments to determine which students graduate, which teachers get raises, and which schools get extra funds and other resources. As you might guess, such *high-stakes* assessments are a source of considerable controversy, and so we will look at them more closely in Chapter 16.

Let's now apply what we have learned to a critique of an actual classroom assessment instrument.

Analyzing Teacher Strategies

A. Write whether each of the rocks shown at the front of the room is a sedimentary, igneous, or metamorphic rock.

1. _____
2. _____
3. _____

B. The following are various stages of the rock cycle. Number them from 1 to 9 to indicate the order in which they occur.

____ Heat and pressure
____ Crystallization and cooling
____ Igneous rock forms
____ Magma
____ Weathering and erosion into sediments
____ Melting
____ Sedimentary rock forms
____ Pressure and cementing
____ Metamorphic rock forms

C. Write the letter for the correct definition of each rock group.

1. ____ Igneous
2. ____ Sedimentary
3. ____ Metamorphic

a. Formed when particles of eroded rock are deposited together and become cemented.
b. Produced by extreme pressures or high temperatures below the earth's surface.
c. Formed by the cooling of molten rock material from within the earth.

D. Fill in the blanks in each sentence.

1. The process of breaking down rock by the action of water, ice, plants, animals, and chemical changes is called _____ .
2. All rocks are made of _____ .
3. The hardness of rocks can be determined by a _____ .
4. Continued weathering of rock will eventually produce _____ .
5. Every rock has a _____ .

[The test continues with several additional fill-in-the-blank and short-answer items.]

Geology Test

A sixth-grade science teacher gives a test on a unit on rocks. As you examine the test, think about

- What purpose the teacher had in mind for the test
- What effects the test is apt to have on students' future learning efforts
- What the answer to the last question might be

The teacher used the test for summative evaluation: to assess students' final knowledge and understanding of basic principles of rock formation before moving to a different topic. Part A (identifying rocks shown at the front of the room) may be assessing either basic knowledge or transfer, depending on whether the students have seen those particular rocks before. The rest of the test clearly focuses on memorized facts—stages of the rock cycle, definitions of terms, and so on—and is likely to encourage students to engage in rote learning as they study for future tests. For instance, consider the last item, "Every rock has a _____." Students can answer this item correctly *only* if they have learned the material verbatim: The missing word here is "story."

Especially when we use classroom assessments to make final decisions about individual students—decisions related to class grades, graduation, and so on—we must be sure our assessments accurately reflect what students have achieved. How do we know when our assessment instruments and procedures are giving us accurate information? We'll answer this question as we consider four characteristics of good assessment.

IMPORTANT QUALITIES OF GOOD ASSESSMENT

As a student, have you ever been assessed in a way you thought was unfair? If so, *why* was it unfair? For example:

1. Did the teacher evaluate students' responses inconsistently?
2. Were some students assessed under more favorable conditions than others?
3. Was the assessment a poor measure of what you had learned?
4. Was the assessment so time-consuming that, after a while, you no longer cared how well you performed?

In light of your experiences, what characteristics do *you* think are essential for a good classroom assessment instrument?

The four numbered questions just posed reflect, respectively, four "RSVP" characteristics of good classroom assessment: *reliability, standardization, validity,* and *practicality.* These characteristics are summarized in Table 15.1.

■ A quick review: What do we call a memory aid such as *RSVP?* (You can find the answer in Chapter 6.)

TABLE 15.1

The RSVP Characteristics of Good Assessment

CHARACTERISTIC	DEFINITION	RELEVANT QUESTIONS TO CONSIDER
Reliability	The extent to which the assessment instrument yields consistent results for each student	• How much are students' scores affected by temporary conditions unrelated to the characteristic being measured (*test-retest reliability*)? • Do different people score students' performance similarly (*scorer reliability*, also known as *interrater reliability*)? • Do different parts of a single assessment instrument lead to similar conclusions about a student's achievement (*internal consistency reliability*)?
Standardization	The extent to which assessment procedures are similar for all students	• Are all students assessed on identical or similar content? • Do all students have the same types of tasks to perform? • Are instructions the same for everyone? • Do all students have similar time constraints? • Is everyone's performance evaluated using the same criteria?
Validity	The extent to which an assessment instrument measures what it is intended to measure	• Does the assessment tap into a representative sample of the content domain being assessed (*content validity*)? • Do students' scores predict their later success in a domain (*predictive validity*)? • Does the instrument measure a particular psychological or educational characteristic (*construct validity*)?
Practicality	The extent to which an assessment is easy and inexpensive to use	• How much class time does the assessment take? • How quickly and easily can students' responses be scored? • Is special training required to administer or score the assessment? • Does the assessment require specialized materials that must be purchased?

Reliability

Experiencing FIRSTHAND ·Fowl Play

Consider the following sequence of events:

- *Monday.* After a unit on the bone structures of both birds and dinosaurs, Ms. Fowler asks her students to write an essay explaining why many scientists believe that birds are descended from dinosaurs. After school, she tosses the pile of essays on the back seat of her cluttered '57 Chevy.
- *Tuesday.* Ms. Fowler looks high and low for the essays both at home and in her classroom, but she can't find them anywhere.
- *Wednesday.* Because Ms. Fowler wants to use the essay to determine what her students have learned, she asks the class to write the same essay a second time.
- *Thursday.* Ms. Fowler discovers Monday's essays on the back seat of her Chevy.
- *Friday.* Ms. Fowler grades both sets of essays. She is surprised to find little consistency between them: Students who wrote the best essays on Monday did not necessarily do well on Wednesday, and some of Monday's poorest performers did quite well on Wednesday.

Which results should Ms. Fowler use, Monday's or Wednesday's?

· · · · · · ·

The **reliability** of an assessment technique is the extent to which it yields consistent information about the knowledge, skills, or characteristics we are trying to measure. When we assess students' learning and achievement, we must be confident that our conclusions will be essentially the same regardless of whether we give the assessment Monday or Wednesday, whether the weather is sunny or rainy, and whether we evaluate students' responses while in a good mood or a foul frame of mind. Ms. Fowler's assessment technique has poor reliability: The results are completely different from one day to another. So which day's results should she use? I've asked you a trick question—we have no way of knowing which set is more appropriate to use.

■ **reliability** Extent to which an assessment instrument yields consistent information about the knowledge, skills, or characteristics being assessed.

Informal observations of student performance can give us valuable information about how students are progressing. But ultimately we should draw firm conclusions about students' achievement only when we know that our assessment methods are *reliable*—for instance, when they yield consistent results about individual students time after time.

The same assessment instrument will rarely give us *exactly* the same results for the same student on two different occasions, even if the knowledge or ability we're assessing (e.g., the extent to which a student knows basic addition facts, can execute a swan dive, or can compare the bone structures of birds and dinosaurs) remains the same. Many temporary conditions unrelated to what we are trying to measure—distractions in the classroom, variability in instructions and time limits, inconsistencies in rating students' responses, and so on—are apt to affect students' performance and almost inevitably lead to some fluctuation in assessment results.

What temporary conditions might have differentially affected students' performance on Ms. Fowler's essay on Monday and Wednesday? Following are a few possibilities:

- *Day-to-day changes in students*—for example, changes in health, motivation, mood, and energy level

    The 24-hour Netherlands Flu was making the rounds in Ms. Fowler's classroom.

- *Variations in the physical environment*—for example, variations in room temperature, noise level, and outside distractions

    On Monday, students who sat by the window in Ms. Fowler's classroom enjoyed peace and quiet; on Wednesday, those who sat by the window worked while noisy construction machinery tore up the pavement outside.

- *Variation in administration of the assessment*—for example, variations in instructions, timing, and the teacher's responses to students' questions

    On Monday, a few students had to write the essay after school because of play rehearsal during class time; Ms. Fowler explained the task more clearly than she had during class and gave students as much time as they needed to finish. On Wednesday, a different group of students had to write the essay after school because of a band concert during class time; Ms. Fowler explained the task very hurriedly and collected the essays before students had finished.

- *Characteristics of the assessment instrument*—for example, the length, clarity, and difficulty of tasks (longer tasks tend to be more reliable, because small errors have less of an impact on overall results; ambiguous and very difficult tasks increase students' tendency to guess randomly)

    The essay topic, "Explain why many scientists believe that birds are descended from dinosaurs," was a vague one that students interpreted differently from one day to the next.

- *Subjectivity in scoring*—for example, judgments made when the teacher must determine the "rightness" or "wrongness" of responses and when responses are scored on the basis of vague, imprecise criteria

    Ms. Fowler graded both sets of essays while she watched "Chainsaw Murders at Central High" on television Friday night; she gave higher scores during kissing scenes, lower scores during stalking scenes.

Whenever we draw conclusions about students' learning and achievement, we must be confident that the information on which we've based our conclusions is not overly distorted by temporary factors irrelevant to what we are trying to assess. How do we determine the reliability of an assessment instrument? We begin by getting two scores on the same instrument for the same group of students. We can derive these two scores in different ways, and each approach gives us a somewhat different angle on the instrument's reliability. If we assess students using the same instrument on two different occasions (as Ms. Fowler did), we get information about *test-retest reliability*, the extent to which the instrument yields similar information over a short time interval. If we ask two or more people to judge students' performance (to grade the same set of essay papers, rate the same performance of gymnastic skills, etc.), we get information about *scorer reliability*, the extent to which different experts agree in their judgments. If we compute two or more subscores for different items on the same instrument and look at how similar those subscores are, we get information about *internal consistency reliability*, the extent to which different parts of the instrument are all measuring the same characteristic.

Once we have two sets of scores for a group of students, we can determine how similar they are by computing a statistic known as a *correlation coefficient* (described in Appendix A); in this case it is more frequently called a **reliability coefficient**. The coefficient will typically range from 0 to +1.[2] A number close to +1 indicates high reliability: The two sets of test scores are very similar. Although a perfect reliability coefficient of 1.00 is rare, many published achievement and intelligence tests have reliabilities of .90 or above, reflecting a high degree of consistency in the scores they yield. As reliability coefficients decrease, they indicate more error in the assessment results—error due to temporary, and in most cases irrelevant, factors. Publishers of regional and national achievement and ability tests typically calculate and report reliability coefficients for the various scores and subscores that the tests yield.

Estimating Error in Assessment Results   A reliability coefficient tells us, in general, the degree to which temporary errors contribute to fluctuations in students' assessment results. But how much error is apt to be present in a *single* score? In other words, how close is a particular student's score to what it really should be? The **standard error of measurement (SEM)** allows us to estimate how close or far off the score might be. (The standard error of measurement is calculated from the reliability coefficient; see Anastasi & Urbina [1997] or R. M. Thorndike [1997] for details.)

Let's look at a concrete example. Imagine that Susan takes an academic achievement test known as the Basic Skills Test; we'll call it the BST. Imagine, too, that given how well Susan can read, she *should* get a score of 40 on the BST's Reading subtest. Susan's ideal score of 40 is her **true score**: This is what she would theoretically get if we could measure her reading achievement with *complete accuracy*. But Susan misinterprets a few test items, answering them incorrectly when in fact she knows the correct answers, so she actually gets a score of only 37. We cannot see inside Susan's head, so we have no way of determining what her true score is; we know only that she's gotten a 37 on the test. To estimate the amount of error in her score, we consult the BST test manual to find the standard error of measurement for the Reading subtest: 5 points. We can then guess that Susan's true score probably lies somewhere within a range that is one SEM to either side of her test score: 37±5, or 32–42.

Because almost any assessment score includes a certain amount of error, assessment results are sometimes reported not as a specific score, but as a range, or **confidence interval**, extending one SEM to either side of the actual test score.[3] Figure 15.2 shows how we might report Susan's scores on the Reading and other subtests of the BST. Notice that the confidence intervals for the different subtests are different lengths, because each subtest has a different standard error of measurement.

Enhancing the Reliability of Classroom Assessments   As classroom teachers, we will probably not have the time (and some teachers may not have the expertise) to mathematically determine

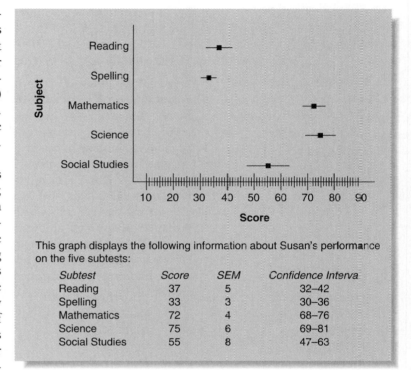

This graph displays the following information about Susan's performance on the five subtests:

Subtest	Score	SEM	Confidence Interval
Reading	37	5	32–42
Spelling	33	3	30–36
Mathematics	72	4	68–76
Science	75	6	69–81
Social Studies	55	8	47–63

FIGURE 15.2   A graphic representation of Susan's scores on the Basic Skills Test (BST)

■ **reliability coefficient** Numerical index of reliability; ranges from 0 to 1, with higher numbers indicating higher reliability.

■ **standard error of measurement (SEM)** Statistic estimating the amount of error in a test score or other assessment result.

■ **true score** Hypothetical score a student would obtain if an assessment measured a characteristic with complete accuracy.

■ **confidence interval** Range around an assessment score that reflects the probable amount of error in the score.

---

[2] Theoretically, reliability coefficients can range from +1 to −1. A negative coefficient would be obtained only when an inverse relationship between the two sets of scores exists—that is, when students who get the highest scores one time get the lowest scores the other time, and vice versa. Such an outcome is highly unlikely.

[3] When we use a single standard error of measurement (SEM) to determine the confidence interval, there is a 68 percent chance that the student's true score lies within that interval. If we instead use two SEMs to determine the interval (for Susan's reading score, identifying an interval of 27 to 47), we can be 95 percent confident that the true score lies within it. If you have some knowledge of descriptive statistics, it may help you to know that the SEM is the standard deviation for the hypothetical distribution of all possible scores that a student with a particular true score might get.

the reliability of every classroom assessment instrument we use. Even so, we must take precautions to maximize the extent to which any single instrument gives us reliable results. For instance, we should

- Include several tasks in each instrument, and look for consistency in students' performance from one task to another
- Define each task clearly enough that students know exactly what they are being asked to do
- Identify specific, concrete criteria with which to evaluate students' performance
- Try not to let expectations for students' performance influence judgments
- Avoid assessing students' learning when they are obviously ill, tired, or out of sorts
- Administer the assessment in similar ways and under similar conditions for all students

My last recommendation suggests that our assessment procedures be *standardized*—a characteristic we turn to now.

Standardization

A second important characteristic of good assessment is **standardization**: The assessment involves similar content and format and is administered and scored in the same way for everyone. In most situations students should all be given the same instructions, perform identical or similar tasks, have the same time limits, and work under the same constraints. Furthermore, students' responses should be scored as consistently as possible; for example, unless there are extenuating circumstances, we shouldn't use tougher standards for one student than for another.

As noted earlier, many tests constructed and published by testing experts are called *standardized* tests; this label indicates that such tests have explicit procedures for administration and scoring that are consistently applied wherever the tests are used. Yet standardization is important in our own classroom assessments as well: It reduces the error in our assessment results, especially error due to variation in test administration or subjectivity in scoring. The more an assessment is standardized for all students, then, the higher its reliability. Equity is an additional consideration: Under most circumstances, it is only fair to ask all students to be evaluated under similar conditions. We find an obvious exception to this guideline in the assessment of students with special educational needs. We'll consider appropriate accommodations for such students near the end of the chapter.

Validity

Experiencing FIRSTHAND · FTOI

A few minutes ago, you read about *reliability*. Let's see whether you can apply (transfer) your understanding of that concept to this situation:

> I have developed a new test called the FTOI: the Fathead Test of Intelligence. It consists of only a tape measure and a table of norms describing how others have performed on the test. Administration of the FTOI is quick and easy: You measure a student's head circumference just above the eyebrows (firmly but not too tightly) and compare your measure against the table of norms. Large heads (comparatively speaking) receive high IQ scores. Smaller heads receive low scores.

Does the FTOI have high reliability? Answer the question before you read further.

· · · · · · ·

No matter how often you measure a person's head circumference, you are going to get a similar score: Fatheads will continue to be fatheads, and pinheads will always be pinheads. So the answer to my question is yes: The FTOI has high reliability because it yields consistent results. If you answered no, you were probably thinking that the FTOI isn't a very good measure of intelligence—but that's a problem with the instrument's *validity*, not with its reliability.

The **validity** of an assessment instrument is the extent to which it measures what it is intended to measure. Does the FTOI measure intelligence? Are scores on a standardized, multiple-choice achievement test a good indication of how much students have learned during the school year? Does students' performance at a school concert reflect what they have achieved in their instrumental music class? When our assessments don't do these things well—when they are poor measures of students' knowledge and abilities—then we have a validity problem.

■ **standardization** Extent to which assessment instruments and procedures involve similar content and format and are administered and scored similarly for everyone.

■ **validity** Extent to which an assessment instrument actually measures what it is intended to measure.

As noted earlier, numerous irrelevant factors are likely to influence how well students perform in assessment situations. Some of these—students' health, classroom distractions, errors in scoring, and so on—are temporary conditions that lead to fluctuation in assessment results and thereby lower reliability. But other irrelevant factors—perhaps reading ability, self-efficacy, or trait anxiety—are more stable, and so their effects on assessment results will be relatively constant. For example, if Joe has poor reading skills, he may get consistently low scores on paper-pencil, multiple-choice achievement tests regardless of how much he has actually achieved in science, math, or social studies. If Jane suffers debilitating anxiety whenever she performs in front of an audience, her performance at a public concert may not be a good reflection of how well she can play the cello. When our assessment results continue to be affected by the same irrelevant variables, then we must question the validity of our instruments.

Psychologists distinguish among different kinds of validity, each of which is important in different situations. Three kinds of particular interest to educators and other practitioners are content validity, predictive validity, and construct validity.

Content validity. As classroom teachers, we will usually be most concerned with **content validity**, the extent to which the tasks we ask students to perform are a representative sample of the knowledge and skills we are trying to assess. In an assessment instrument with high content validity, test items and performance tasks reflect all parts of the content domain in appropriate proportions and require the particular behaviors and skills identified in instructional objectives or content area standards. As an illustration, Table 15.2 revisits the California state standards for reading comprehension presented in Chapter 13. The table's right-hand column offers examples of assessment strategies that might address those standards.

High content validity is *essential* whenever we are using an assessment instrument for summative evaluation purposes—that is, to determine what students have learned during their time in our classrooms. We maximize content validity when the tasks we ask students to perform are as similar as possible to the things we ultimately want them to be able to do—in other words, when they reflect our instructional objectives. In some situations, such as when the desired outcome is simple recall of facts, we might ask students to respond to multiple-choice or short-answer questions on a paper-pencil test. In other situations—for instance, when our goal is for students to critique a literary work or to explain everyday phenomena by using principles of physics—essay questions that require students to follow a logical line of reasoning are appropriate. *If* we can truly assess knowledge of a domain by having students respond in writing, then a paper-pencil assessment is a good choice.

Yet many skills—cooking a hard-boiled egg, executing a front dismount from the parallel bars, identifying specific microorganisms through a microscope—are difficult (perhaps impossible) to assess with paper and pencil. In such situations only performance assessment can give us reasonable content validity. Performance assessment can also be especially useful when we are concerned about students' ability to apply classroom subject matter to real-world situations. In the end, we may find that we can best assess students' achievement with a combination of paper-pencil and performance tasks (Messick, 1994; Stiggins, 2001; D. B. Swanson, Norman, & Linn, 1995).

Most classroom assessment activities, even paper-pencil ones, can give us only a small sample of what students know and can do. How can we make sure that our sample is truly *representative* of the content domain we are assessing? The most widely recommended strategy is to construct a blueprint that identifies the specific things we want to measure and the proportion of the instrument that should address each one. This blueprint frequently takes the form of a **table of specification**: a two-way grid that indicates both the topics to be covered and the behaviors associated with them (i.e., the things that students should be able to *do* with each topic). In each cell of the grid, we indicate the relative importance of each topic-behavior combination, perhaps as a particular number or percentage of tasks or test items to be included in the overall assessment. Figure 15.3 shows two examples, one for a paper-pencil test on addition and a second for a combined paper-pencil and performance assessment on simple machines. Once we have created a table of specifications, we can develop paper-pencil items or performance tasks that reflect both the topics and the behaviors we want to assess and have some confidence that our assessment instrument has content validity for the domain it is intended to represent.

Content validity is important not only for teacher-developed assessments but also for any published achievement tests we use in our schools. Because these tests have already been

■ **content validity** Extent to which an assessment includes a representative sample of tasks within the domain being assessed.

■ **table of specifications** Two-way grid indicating the topics to be covered in an assessment and the things students should be able to do with those topics.

TABLE 15.2

Matching Assessment Tasks to the California State Standards for Reading Comprehension at Different Grade Levels

GRADE LEVEL	EXAMPLES OF GRADE-SPECIFIC STANDARDS	EXAMPLES OF ASSESSMENT TASKS THAT ADDRESS ONE OR MORE STANDARDS
Grade 1	• Respond to who, what, when, where, and how questions. • Use context to resolve ambiguities about word and sentence meanings. • Relate prior knowledge to textual information. • Retell the central ideas of simple expository or narrative passages.	• Ask specific questions about a story's characters, setting, and plot. • Ask students to draw inferences about characters' thoughts and feelings based on their own experiences in similar situations. • Have students describe what they've just learned from a book about animal camouflage. • Have students act out a story they've recently read.
Grade 4	• Use appropriate strategies when reading for different purposes (e.g., full comprehension, location of information, personal enjoyment). • Make and confirm predictions about text by using prior knowledge and ideas presented in the text itself, including illustrations, titles, topic sentences, important words, and foreshadowing clues. • Evaluate new information and hypotheses by testing them against known information and ideas. • Distinguish between cause and effect and between fact and opinion in expository text.	• Ask students to use a book's index to quickly locate information about a particular topic. • Ask students to use the headings and subheadings in their science textbook to identify specific questions that each section will probably answer. • Modify a text passage so that it includes several inconsistent statements; ask students to find the inconsistencies. • Present a paragraph from an age-appropriate persuasive essay, and ask students to underline facts with a red pencil and opinions with a green pencil.
Grade 7	• Understand and analyze the differences in structure and purpose between various categories of informational materials (e.g., textbooks, newspapers, instructional materials, signs). • Identify and trace the development of an author's argument, point of view, or perspective in text. • Understand and explain the use of a simple mechanical device by following technical directions. • Assess the adequacy, accuracy, and appropriateness of the author's evidence to support claims and assertions, noting instances of bias and stereotyping.	• Have students identify similarities and differences between two descriptions of the same historical event: (a) a newspaper article written during or immediately after the event and (b) a description of the event in a history textbook. • Present an opinion piece from *Reader's Digest*, and have students identify the author's main point and supporting arguments. • Ask students to use written directions to construct a functioning electromagnet. • Give students an advertisement for a self-improvement product (e.g., a diet pill or exercise equipment); ask them to evaluate any evidence of the product's effectiveness presented in the ad.
Grades 11–12	• Analyze the way in which clarity of meaning is affected by the patterns of organization, hierarchical structures, repetition of the main ideas, syntax, and word choice in the text. • Verify and clarify facts presented in other types of expository texts by using a variety of consumer, workplace, and public documents. • Analyze an author's implicit and explicit philosophical assumptions and beliefs about a subject. • Critique the power, validity, and truthfulness of arguments set forth in public documents; their appeal to both friendly and hostile audiences; and the extent to which the arguments anticipate and address reader concerns and counterclaims (e.g., appeal to reason, to authority, to pathos and emotion).	• Ask students to find examples of a particular theme (e.g., ethnic stereotyping) or literary technique (e.g., foreshadowing) in the dialogue of a Shakespearean play. • Search the Internet for a personal Web site that presents information about a topic of general interest (e.g., air pollution or use of vitamin supplements); ask students to search the library for sources that either verify or discredit the author's claims. • Present a history book's description of the Battle of the Alamo and ask students to identify the author's assumptions and biases in writing it. • Give students an editorial from the local newspaper and ask them to describe (a) what kinds of people are apt to agree with the piece and (b) what kinds of people are apt to disagree with it, and for what reasons.

Note: Standards (middle column) are from a Web site maintained by California State University Northridge: *California Academic Content Standards Site: English and Language Arts* (n.d.). Retrieved August 18, 2004, from http://www.csun.edu/~hcbio027/k12standards/standards/lang-arts.pdf

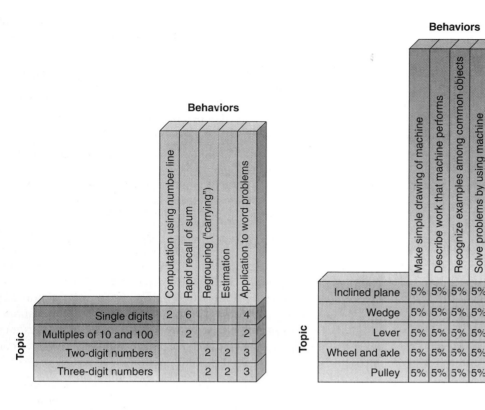

FIGURE 15.3   Two examples of a table of specifications. *Left:* This table provides specifications for a thirty-item paper-pencil test on addition. It assigns different weights (different numbers of items) to different topic-behavior combinations, with some combinations not being measured at all. *Right:* This table provides specifications for a combination paper-pencil and performance assessment on simple machines. It assigns equal importance (the same percentage of points) to each topic-behavior combination.

constructed, we can follow the steps for ensuring content validity in reverse order. By looking at the items on the test, we can identify the topics covered and the behaviors (e.g., recalling information, applying procedures, solving problems) required. Once again we can construct a table of specifications, indicating the number of test items that fall in each cell. (Sometimes such a table appears in the test manual or can be obtained from the test publisher.) We can then decide whether the table of specifications matches our curriculum closely enough that the test has content validity for our particular situation—that is, whether the test represents what we actually do in our classrooms.

Predictive validity. Shantel is thinking about a career in mathematics. But even though she is doing well in her eighth-grade math class, she worries that she will eventually have trouble with advanced courses in trigonometry and calculus. To get an idea of her chances for future math success, Shantel takes the Mathematics Aptitude Test (we'll call it the MAT) that her school counselor makes available to her. She does quite well on the MAT, renewing her confidence that she will succeed in a mathematics career. But does the MAT actually measure a student's potential for future success in math? This is a question of **predictive validity**, the extent to which an assessment instrument predicts future performance in some arena.

Publishers of norm-referenced ability tests often determine the accuracy with which test scores predict later success in certain domains. To do so, they first give a test to a group of people; a few months or years later, they measure the same group's success or competence in the behavior being predicted (the criterion behavior). They then calculate the correlation coefficient between the test scores and the criterion behavior. As is true for a reliability coefficient, this **validity coefficient** is typically a number between 0 and +1, with higher numbers indicating greater predictive validity. Tests with relatively high predictive validity for a particular behavior (validity coefficients in the .60s or .70s are usually considered high) predict that behavior fairly well. Those with lower predictive validity (e.g., coefficients in the .30s or .40s) are less accurate and will lead to more errors in our predictions.

Keep in mind that a test has no *single* predictive validity. Its validity in a given situation depends on the specific behavior being predicted, the age-group being tested (tests often have greater predictive validity for older students than for younger ones), and the amount of time between the test and the predicted performance.

Construct validity. In psychology, a *construct* is an hypothesized internal trait that cannot be directly observed but must instead be inferred from the consistencies we see in people's behavior.

■ Why are tests used to make predictions usually norm-referenced rather than criterion-referenced?

■ **predictive validity** Extent to which the results of an assessment predict future performance.

■ **validity coefficient** Numerical index of predictive validity; ranges from 0 to 1, with higher numbers indicating more accurate predictions.

This teacher may be making inferences about her student's motivation to master basic writing skills. When we want to draw conclusions about underlying traits such as motivation, we must consider the *construct validity* of our assessment methods.

Motivation, *self-esteem*, *intelligence*, and *visual-spatial ability* are all constructs; we can't actually *see* any of these things but must instead draw conclusions about them from what students do and don't do. For example, we might use our observations of students' on-task and off-task behavior in class to make inferences about their motivation to learn academic subject matter. Similarly, we might use tasks that ask them to reason abstractly to make inferences about their intelligence.

By **construct validity**, then, we mean the extent to which an assessment instrument actually measures a general, abstract characteristic. Construct validity is of most concern when we are trying to draw general conclusions about students' traits and abilities so that we can better adapt instructional methods and materials to meet their individual needs.

How do we determine whether a test or other assessment instrument measures something we cannot see? Assessment experts have developed a variety of strategies for doing so. For instance, they might determine how well assessment results correlate with other measures of the same trait (e.g., do scores on one intelligence test correlate with scores on other IQ tests?). They might find out whether older students perform better than younger students on instruments measuring traits that presumably increase with age (e.g., do 12-year-olds correctly answer more items on an intelligence test than 6-year-olds?). They might compare the performance of two groups who are known to be different with respect to the trait in question (e.g., do nondisabled 12-year-olds perform better on an intelligence test than 12-year-olds with mental retardation?). When data from a variety of sources are consistent with what we would expect if the instrument were a measure of the characteristic in question, we conclude that it probably does have construct validity.

One principle that applies to all three forms of validity is this: *An assessment tool may be more valid for some purposes than for others.* A mathematics achievement test may be a valid measure of how well students can add and subtract but a terrible measure of how well they can use addition and subtraction in real-life situations. A paper-pencil test on the rules of tennis may accurately assess students' knowledge of how many games are in a set, what *deuce* means, and so on, but it probably won't tell us much about how well students can actually play the game.

We should note, too, that *reliability is a necessary condition for validity*: Assessments can yield valid results only when they also yield consistent results—results that are only minimally affected by variations in administration, subjectivity in scoring, and so on. Reliability does not guarantee validity, however, as the FTOI exercise you did earlier illustrates.

Practicality

The last of the four RSVP characteristics is **practicality**, the extent to which assessment instruments and procedures are relatively easy to use.[4] Practicality includes concerns such as these:

- How much time will it take to develop the instrument?
- Can the assessment be administered to many students at once?
- Are expensive materials involved?
- How much time will the assessment take away from instructional activities?
- How quickly and easily can students' performance be evaluated?

There is often a trade-off between practicality and such other characteristics as validity and reliability. For example, a true-false test on tennis will be easier to construct and administer, but a performance assessment in which students actually demonstrate their tennis skills—even though it takes more time and energy—is undoubtedly a more valid measure of how well students have mastered the game.

Of our four RSVP characteristics, validity is the most important: We *must* have an assessment technique that measures what we want it to measure. Reliability ensures the dependability of our assessment results (in doing so, it indirectly affects their validity), and standardization can enhance the reliability of those results. Practicality should be a consideration only when validity, reliability, and standardization are not seriously jeopardized.

Now that we've examined desirable characteristics of any classroom assessment, we're in a good position to explore both informal and formal classroom assessment strategies. As we go

■ **construct validity** Extent to which an assessment accurately measures an unobservable educational or psychological characteristic.

■ **practicality** Extent to which an assessment instrument or procedure is inexpensive and easy to use and takes only a small amount of time to administer and score.

---

[4] Many psychologists use the term *usability*, but I think *practicality* better communicates the idea here.

along, we'll consider the goals and standards for which various strategies might be most appropriate and the RSVP characteristics of each one.

INFORMAL ASSESSMENT

From our daily observations of students' verbal and nonverbal behaviors, we can often draw conclusions about what students have and have not learned and make reasonable decisions about how future instruction should proceed. Such informal assessment takes many forms, including the following:

Assessment of verbal behaviors:
- Asking questions
- Listening to whole-class and small-group discussions
- Having students write daily or weekly entries in personal journals
- Holding brief conferences with individual students

Assessment of nonverbal behaviors:
- Observing how well students perform physical skills
- Looking at the relative frequency of on-task and off-task behaviors
- Identifying the activities in which students engage voluntarily
- Watching the "body language" that may reflect students' feelings about classroom tasks

The Into the Classroom feature "Asking Questions to Assess Learning and Achievement Informally" offers several suggestions for using in-class questions to assess students' knowledge and beliefs. When using such strategies, we should remember that students from some cultural backgrounds may find it disconcerting that we are asking questions for which we already know the answers (see Chapter 4).

Informal assessment has several advantages (Airasian, 1994; Stiggins, 2001). First and foremost, it gives us continuing feedback about the effectiveness of the day's instructional tasks and activities. Second, it is easily adjusted at a moment's notice; for example, when students express misconceptions about a particular topic, we can ask follow-up questions that probe their beliefs and reasoning processes. Third, it provides information that may either support or call into question the data we obtain from more formal assessments such as paper-pencil tests. Finally, informal procedures provide clues about social, emotional, and motivational factors affecting students' classroom performance and may often be the only practical means through which we can assess such goals as "shows courtesy" or "enjoys reading." In the portfolio excerpt shown in Figure 15.4, a kindergarten teacher describes 6-year-old Meghan's progress in work habits and social skills—areas that the teacher can probably assess only through informal observation.

■ Without looking back at Table 15.1, test yourself by describing the four characteristics of good assessment.

INTO THE CLASSROOM

Asking Questions to Assess Learning and Achievement Informally

Direct questions to the entire class, not just to a few who seem eager to respond.

The girls in a high school science class rarely volunteer when their teacher asks questions. Although the teacher often calls on students who raise their hands, he occasionally calls on those who do not, and he makes sure that he calls on *every* student at least once a week.

Have students "vote" when a question has only a few possible answers.

When beginning a lesson on dividing one fraction by another, a middle school math teacher writes this problem on the chalkboard:

$$\frac{3}{4} \div \frac{1}{2} = ?$$

She asks, "Before we talk about how we solve this problem, how many of you think the answer will be less than 1? How many think it will be greater than 1? How many think it will be *exactly* 1?" She tallies the number of hands that go up after each question and then says, "Hmmm, most of you think the answer will be less than 1. Let's look at how we solve a problem like this. Then each of you will know whether you were right or wrong."

Ask follow-up questions to probe students' reasoning.

In a geography lesson on Canada, a fourth-grade teacher points out the St. Lawrence River on a map. "Which way does the water flow, toward the ocean or away from it?" One student shouts out, "Away from it." "Why do you think so?" the teacher asks. The student's explanation reveals a common misconception: that rivers can flow only from north to south, never vice versa.

Group Participation and Work Habits

☺ **Demonstrates attentiveness as a listener through body language or facial expressions-** Meghan is still developing this skill. Sometimes it is difficult for her to listen when she is sitting near her friends.

☺ **Follows directions.**

☺ **Enters ongoing discussion on the subject.** -Sometimes needs to be encouraged to share her ideas.

☺ **Makes relevant contributions to ongoing activities.**

☺ **Completes assigned activities.** -Meghan is very responsible about her assignments.

☺ **Shows courtesy in conversations and discussions by waiting for turn to speak.**

Meghan enjoys lunch with her friends.

FIGURE 15.4 A kindergarten teacher's assessment of 6-year-old Meghan's work habits and social skills

■ **halo effect** Phenomenon in which people are more likely to perceive positive behaviors in someone they like or admire.

RSVP Characteristics of Informal Assessment

When we get information about students' characteristics and achievements through informal means, we must be aware of the strengths and limitations of this approach with respect to reliability, standardization, validity, and practicality.

Reliability   Most informal assessments are quite short; for example, we may notice that Naomi is off task during an activity, listen to Manuel's answer to a question, or have a brief conversation with Jacquie after school. But such snippets of students' behavior can be unreliable indicators of their overall accomplishments and dispositions. Perhaps we happen to look at Naomi during the *only* time she is off task. Perhaps we ask Manuel one of the few questions to which he *doesn't* know the answer. Perhaps we misinterpret what Jacquie is trying to say during a conversation with her. When we use informal assessment to draw conclusions about what students know and can do, we should base our conclusions on many observations over a long period (Airasian, 1994).

Furthermore, we should keep in mind a principle from cognitive psychology: Long-term memory is not a totally accurate or dependable record of previous experience (see Chapter 6). We will remember some student behaviors but not recall others. If we depend heavily on in-class observations of students, we should keep ongoing, written records of what we see and hear (R. L. Linn & Miller, 2005; Stiggins, 2001).

Standardization   Our informal assessments will rarely, if ever, be standardized; for example, we will ask different questions of different students, and we will probably observe each student's behavior in different contexts. Hence such assessments will definitely *not* give us the same information for each student. In most cases, then, we cannot make legitimate comparisons among students merely on the basis of a few casual observations.

Validity   Even if we see consistency in students' behavior over time, we will not always get accurate data about what they have learned (Airasian, 1994; Stiggins, 2001). For instance, Tom may intentionally answer questions incorrectly so that he doesn't look "smart" in front of his friends. Margot may be reluctant to say anything because of a chronic stuttering problem. In general, when we use in-class questions to assess students' learning, we must be aware that some students (especially females and students from certain ethnic minority groups) will be less eager to respond than others (B. Kerr, 1991; Sadker & Sadker, 1994; Villegas, 1991).

Principles from our discussion of knowledge construction (Chapter 7) are also relevant to the validity of informal assessment: We impose meanings on the things we see and hear, and those meanings are influenced by the things we already know or believe to be true. Our own biases and expectations will affect our interpretations of students' behaviors, inevitably affecting the accuracy of our conclusions (Farwell & Weiner, 1996; Ritts et al., 1992; Stiggins, 2001). We may expect academic or social competence from a student we like or admire and so are likely to perceive that student's actions in a positive light—a phenomenon known as the **halo effect**. In much the same way, we might expect inappropriate behavior from a student with a history of misbehavior, and our observations may be biased accordingly (we could call this the "horns effect").

As we discovered in Chapter 12, teachers' expectations for students are sometimes influenced by students' ethnicity, gender, and socioeconomic status, and such expectations may unfairly bias teachers' judgments of student performance. An experiment by Darley and Gross (1983) provides an example. Undergraduate students were told that they were participating in a study on teacher evaluation methods and were asked to view a videotape of a fourth grader named Hannah. Two versions of the videotape gave differing impressions about Hannah's socioeconomic status: Her clothing, the kind of playground on which she played, and information about her parents' occupations indirectly conveyed to some students that she was from a high socioeconomic background and to others that she was from a low socioeconomic background. All students watched Hannah taking an oral achievement test (one on which she performed at grade level) and were asked to rate Hannah on several characteristics. Students who had been led to believe that Hannah came

Interesting

from wealthy surroundings rated her ability well above grade level, whereas students believing that she came from a poor family evaluated her as being below grade level. The two groups of students also rated Hannah's work habits, motivation, social skills, and general maturity differently.

Practicality   The greatest strength of informal assessment is its practicality. It involves little if any of our time either beforehand or after the fact (except when we keep written records of our observations). Furthermore, it is flexible: We can adapt our assessment procedures on the spur of the moment, altering them as events in the classroom change.

Despite the practicality of informal assessment, we have noted serious problems regarding its reliability, standardization, and validity. Hence we should treat any conclusions we draw only as *hypotheses* that we must either confirm or disconfirm through other means. In the end, we must rely more heavily on formal assessment techniques to determine whether our students have achieved our instructional objectives and met content area standards.

PAPER-PENCIL ASSESSMENT

When we need to conduct a formal assessment, paper-pencil assessment is typically easier and faster—and so has greater practicality—than performance assessment. Unfortunately, however, many teacher-developed paper-pencil tests focus primarily on lower-level skills, perhaps because such tests are the easiest to write (J. R. Frederiksen & Collins, 1989; Nickerson, 1989; Poole, 1994; Silver & Kenney, 1995).

Questions that require brief responses, such as short-answer, matching, true-false, and multiple-choice, are often suitable for assessing students' knowledge of single, isolated facts. Paper-pencil tasks that require extended responses—essays, for instance—lend themselves more easily to assessing such higher-level skills as problem solving, critical thinking, and synthesis of ideas (J. R. Frederiksen & Collins, 1989; Popham, 1995; Stiggins, 2001). Yet item type alone does not tell us whether we are assessing lower-level or higher-level skills. Although many classroom teachers use multiple-choice items primarily to assess knowledge of basic facts, we can also construct multiple-choice items that assess higher-level skills, as the following example illustrates:

> An inventor has just designed a new device for cutting paper. Without knowing anything else about his invention, we can predict that it is probably which type of machine?
> a. A lever
> b. A movable pulley
> c. An inclined plane
> d. A wedge
>
> (The correct answer is *d*.)

With a little ingenuity, we can even develop relatively "authentic" paper-pencil tasks that assess students' ability to apply classroom subject matter to real-world tasks (Gronlund, 1993; D. B. Swanson et al., 1995). Here is an example:

> You are to play the role of an advisor to President Nixon after his election to office in 1968. As his advisor, you are to make a recommendation about the United States' involvement in Vietnam.
>
> Your paper is to be organized around three main parts: An introduction that shows an understanding of the Vietnam War up to this point by explaining who is involved in the war and what their objectives are; also in the Introduction, you are to state a recommendation in one or two sentences to make the advice clear.
>
> The body of the paper should be written to convince the President to follow your advice by discussing: (a) the pros of the advice, including statistics, dates, examples, and general information . . . ; (b) the cons of the advice, letting the President know that the advisor is aware of how others might disagree. Anticipate one or two recommendations that others might give, and explain why they are not the best advice.
>
> The conclusion makes a final appeal for the recommendation and sells the President on the advice. (Newmann, 1997, p. 368)

An additional consideration is whether recognition or recall tasks better match our instructional objectives. **Recognition tasks** ask students to identify correct answers within the context of incorrect statements or irrelevant information; examples include multiple-choice, true-false, and matching questions. **Recall tasks** require students to generate the correct answers

■ **recognition task** Memory task in which one must identify correct information among irrelevant information or incorrect statements.

■ **recall task** Memory task in which one must retrieve information in its entirety from long-term memory.

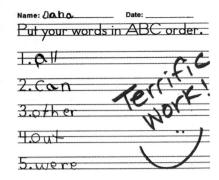

Even in the early grades, we can often use paper-pencil tasks to assess students' ability to apply what they've learned. Here 6-year-old Dana shows that she can put several new spelling words in alphabetical order.

themselves; examples include short-answer questions, essays, and word problems. As noted in Chapter 6, recognition tasks are typically easier than recall tasks because they provide more retrieval cues to aid recall of relevant information from long-term memory.

Recognition and recall tasks each have advantages and disadvantages. Students can often answer many recognition questions in a short time; hence, such questions allow us to sample a wide range of knowledge and skills. In addition, we can score students' responses quickly and consistently, thus addressing our needs for practicality and reliability. However, recognition tasks tend to overestimate achievement: Students can sometimes guess correctly when they don't know the material very well. Furthermore, as noted earlier, students who see incorrect statements in true-false and multiple-choice items may recall them later as being actual facts.

When we want to assess students' ability to remember knowledge and skills without the benefit of having the correct answer in front of them, then recall tasks obviously have greater validity. Furthermore, recall tasks are better suited to assessing students' ability to organize information, follow a line of reasoning, design an experiment, or justify their position on a controversial topic. Yet because students may require considerable time to respond to each item, we will be able to ask fewer items in a single assessment session (affecting reliability) and tap a more limited sample of the content domain (affecting content validity). In addition, we will typically take longer to score such items (a practicality issue) and make more errors in scoring them (an additional reliability issue).

We must weigh such advantages and disadvantages when deciding whether to use recognition items, recall items, or a combination of the two. We must also keep in mind that in some content domains—for example, when assessing writing skills—recognition tasks may simply not yield the same kind of information that recall tasks do (Traub, 1993).

Constructing the Assessment Instrument

Writing good paper-pencil assessment items, especially those that assess higher-level thinking skills, takes considerable time and practice. In the following pages, we will look at several formats:

Recognition Tasks	**Recall Tasks**
• Alternative-response items	• Short-answer items
• Matching items	• Completion items
• Multiple-choice items	• Problems
	• Interpretive exercises
	• Essays

■ Students tend to study more for essay tests than for multiple-choice tests (D'Ydewalle, Swerts, & De Corte, 1983; G. Warren, 1979). Why might this be so?

We will then identify several general guidelines for constructing a paper-pencil assessment instrument.

Alternative-Response Items   An *alternative-response item* is one for which there are only two or three possible answers, perhaps *true* versus *false*, or *fact* versus *opinion*. Such items are typically used to assess knowledge of discrete facts, although they can also be used for assessing such higher-level skills as discriminating between facts and opinions or identifying cause-effect relationships (R. L. Linn & Miller, 2005). The following items illustrate the use of an alternative-response format for assessing students' ability to identify cause and effect in science:

In each of the following statements, both parts of the statement are true. You are to decide whether the second part explains why the first part is true. If it does, circle Yes. If it does not, circle No.

Yes   (No)   1. Leaves are essential *because* they shade the tree trunk.
Yes   (No)   2. Whales are mammals *because* they are large.
(Yes)   No   3. Some plants do not need sunlight *because* they get their food from other plants.
(R. L. Linn & Miller, 2005, p. 174)

If the subject matter lends itself easily to assessment in an either-or fashion, alternative-response items allow us to ask a large number of questions in a short time and so can enhance our ability to sample the domain in question. Yet many subject areas cannot be assessed with this format, and students can get about half of the items correct simply by guessing. Furthermore, writing *good* alternative-response items is more difficult than you might think; following are a few guidelines:

◎   *Rephrase ideas presented in class or the textbook.* When students know that assessment items will be taken word for word from class material, they may try to learn the material verbatim. When they instead know that we will check for understanding by using different words and phrases to express the same idea, they will be more apt to engage in meaningful learning.

◎   *Make statements that clearly reflect one alternative or the other* (e.g., *statements that are clearly true or false*). A knowledgeable student should be able to respond to each item with certainty. When items are "sort of" true or "possibly" false, or they contain words with imprecise meanings (e.g., *sometimes, often*), then even the best students must resort to guessing what we had in mind when we wrote the items. Such guessing leads to a higher error factor in students' overall performance and so leads to lower test reliability.

◎   *Avoid excessive use of negatives, especially for false statements.* Consider these true-false items:

The south poles of two magnets don't repel each other.

In the history of human civilization, the beginning of animal domestication was unrelated to human settlement patterns.

Were these questions difficult to answer? Did the negatives (the *don't* in the first item and the *un-* in the second one) confuse you? Negative words and prefixes in true-false items (e.g., *no, not, never, un-, mis-*) often lead to confusion, especially when the statements themselves are false. By the way, both of the items just presented are false.

Matching Items   A matching item presents two columns of words, phrases, or data; students must match each item in the first column with an appropriate item in the second. Matching items lend themselves most readily to ideas that can be easily paired—words and their meanings, countries and their capitals, parts of the body and their functions, and so on. When our instructional goals truly involve such factual knowledge, matching items provide an efficient way of assessing it. Following are two guidelines to keep in mind when constructing these items:

◎   *Keep the items in each column homogeneous.* Consider this matching task from a world history test:

Match each item on the right with its description on the left:

a. German battleship that sank numerous British ships   1. George Patton
b. Year in which the Japanese attacked Pearl Harbor   2. The *Graf Spee*
c. Country invaded by Germany in 1939   3. Poland
d. General who led American troops into Italy   4. 1941

Even if you know nothing about World War II, you should be able to match the items easily. The first item in the right-hand column is a person, and there is only one description of a person on the left. Similarly, there is only one country, one year, and one "name of something" (in italics), so the correct responses are easy to deduce. Instead, the items in each column should be members of the same category (perhaps dates, generals, capital cities, or word definitions), so as to give students few clues about how to respond.

◎   *Have more items in one column than in the other.* Consider this matching item about the human digestive system:

Match each function with the component of the digestive system where it occurs. Items on the right can be used only once.

1. Production of enzyme secreted to the mouth   a. Pancreas
2. Mixing of food with digestive enzymes   b. Liver
3. Production of bile   c. Stomach
4. Production of insulin   d. Salivary glands

Even if you don't know much about human digestion, you can probably identify some of the correct answers here. If you can figure out three of the four items correctly, you know the last one by a simple process of elimination. But consider an alternative version of the same question:

Match each function with the component of the digestive system where it occurs. Items on the right can be used more than once.

1. Production of enzyme secreted to the mouth
2. Mixing of food with digestive enzymes
3. Production of bile
4. Production of insulin
5. Storage place for food

a. Colon
b. Gall bladder
c. Stomach
d. Salivary glands
e. Liver
f. Large intestine
g. Pancreas

Here the process of elimination doesn't work. "Stomach" is the correct choice for both 2 and 5, and three terms on the right aren't correct responses at all.

Multiple-Choice Items   A multiple-choice item consists of a question or incomplete statement (the *stem*) followed by a series of alternatives. In most cases only one alternative correctly answers the question or completes the statement; the other (incorrect) alternatives are *distractors*.

Of the various recognition items we might use, most assessment experts recommend multiple-choice items for two reasons. First, the number of items that students get correct simply by guessing is relatively low, especially in comparison with true-false and other alternative-response items (e.g., when multiple-choice items have four possible answers, students can get only about 25% of them correct through guessing alone). Second, of all the recognition item types, the multiple-choice format lends itself most readily to measuring higher-level thinking skills. These items cannot assess *everything*, of course; for instance, they can't assess students' ability to organize and express ideas coherently, nor can they assess what students would actually do in a real-life situation.

If a multiple-choice format is appropriate for the knowledge or skills you wish to assess, following are several guidelines to keep in mind:

◎ *Present distractors that are clearly wrong to students who know the material but plausible to students who haven't mastered it.* Distractors should not be obviously incorrect. Instead, they should reflect common errors and misunderstandings, as the following item illustrates:

John takes an achievement test and gets a percentile rank of 65. This score means that John has:

a. Mastered course objectives
b. Failed to master course objectives
c. Performed better than the average student
d. Answered 65 percent of the questions correctly

The correct answer is *c*: John's score indicates that he has performed better than the average student—in fact, better than 65 percent of students who've taken the test (we'll discuss percentile ranks in Chapter 16). Buried in the three distractors are two misconceptions that many students have: A percentile rank reflects the number of items correctly answered (distractor *d*), and norm-referenced test scores can give us information about mastery and nonmastery (distractors *a* and *b*).

◎ *Avoid putting negatives in both the stem and the alternatives.* Having negatives such as *not* and *don't* in two places at once amounts to a double negative that students have trouble understanding. Consider the following question, modeled after one actually found in the publisher's suggested test items, or **test bank**, for an educational psychology textbook:

Which one of the following is *not* a characteristic of most gifted children (in comparison with their classmates)?

a. They are not as old.
b. They are physically uncoordinated.
c. They do not feel uncomfortable in social situations.
d. They do not perform poorly on standardized achievement tests.

Confused? It's difficult to sort through all the *nots* and *uns* in order to determine which statement is true and which three are false. The answer in this case is *b*: Contrary to a popular stereotype, students who are gifted are just as coordinated as their nongifted peers.

◎ *Use "all of the above" or "none of the above" seldom if at all.* Listing three correct answers and then adding "all of the above" as the fourth choice is certainly an easy way to write a multiple-choice question. Yet my own experiences as a test-taker have taught me that "all of the above" is

Developing paper-pencil items that reflect important instructional goals often takes considerable thought and creativity.

■ **test bank** Collection of test items for a particular content domain; often provided by textbook publishers.

the correct choice more often than not, and many of my students tell me that they have learned likewise. Furthermore, when we tell students to choose the "best" or "most accurate" answer and then give them "all of the above" or "none of the above" as an alternative, they may understandably become confused about how they should respond.

◎ *Avoid giving logical clues about the correct answer.* To get a sense of how a student might use simple logic to answer multiple-choice questions, try the following exercise.

Experiencing FIRSTHAND · Califractions

Imagine you are enrolled in a course called Califractions. Early in the semester, your instructor gives you a surprise quiz before you've had a chance to do the assigned readings. Nevertheless you must take the quiz. Following are the first three quiz items; choose the single best answer for each one.

1. Because they are furstier than other califractions, califors are most often used to:
   a. Reassignment of matherugs
   b. Disbobble a fwing
   c. Mangelation
   d. In the burfews

2. Calendation is a process of:
   a. Combining two califors
   b. Adding two califors together
   c. Joining two califors
   d. Taking two califors apart

3. The furstiest califraction is the:
   a. Califor
   b. Calderost
   c. Calinga
   d. Calidater

· · · · · · ·

You may have found that you were able to answer the questions even though you knew nothing whatsoever about califractions. Because the first item says "califors are most often used to . . . ," the answer must begin with a verb. Alternatives *a* and *c* apparently begin with nouns ("reassign*ment*" and "mangela*tion*"), and *d* begins with a preposition ("in"), so *b* is the only possible correct answer. Item 2 presents three alternatives (*a*, *b*, and *c*) that all say the same thing, so because there can be only one right answer, the correct choice must be *d*. And the answer to item 3 (the "furstiest califraction") must be *a* (a califor) because item 1 has already stated that califors are furstier than other califractions.

Following are several ways to avoid giving logical clues about the correct alternative:

- Make all alternatives grammatically consistent with the stem, so that each one, when combined with the stem, forms a complete sentence.
- Make all alternatives different in meaning (don't present two or more alternatives that say essentially the same thing).
- Don't present information in one item that gives away the answer to another.
- Make all alternatives equally long and precise. (Novice test writers tend to make the correct alternative longer and more specific than the distractors.)

Short-Answer and Completion Items A short-answer item poses a question to be answered with a single word or number, a phrase, or a couple of sentences. A completion item presents a sentence with a blank for students to fill in. Both formats require recall (rather than recognition) of information, but they lend themselves most readily to measuring lower-level skills, and scoring students' responses becomes more subjective, thereby decreasing reliability. Following are two guidelines to keep in mind when writing short-answer and completion items:

◎ *Indicate the type of response required.* Consider this item from a middle school science test:

Explain why it is colder in winter than in summer.

A student could conceivably write several paragraphs on this topic. Fortunately, the teacher who wrote the item gave students some guidance about how to respond to it and the other short-answer items on her test:

Provide a short answer (1–2 sentences) for each of the following questions. You must use complete and clearly stated sentences. Please use part of the question to introduce your response.

◎ *For completion items, include only one or two blanks per item.* Too many blanks make an item difficult, and sometimes impossible, to interpret. To see what I mean, try filling in the blanks in this statement concerning material presented earlier in the chapter:

> Constructing an assessment instrument with high _____ can be accomplished by developing a _____ that describes both the _____ and the _____.

Are you having trouble filling in the blanks? If so, I'm not surprised. There are so many blanks that it's hard to know what information is being called for. (The answers I had in mind are "content validity," "table of specifications," "topic to be covered," and "student behaviors related to each topic," or words to that effect.)

Problems and Interpretive Exercises In a *problem*, students must manipulate or synthesize data and develop a solution to a new problem situation. We most often see this item type as word problems in mathematics, but we can use it in other subject areas as well; following is an example for science:

> You have a four-liter container of hot water (60°C) and a one-liter container of cold water (10°C). If you mix the water in the two containers together, what temperature will the water be?

In an *interpretive exercise*, students are given new material (e.g., a table, graphs, map, or paragraph of text) and asked to analyze and draw conclusions from it (R. L. Linn & Miller, 2005)[5].Figure 15.5 presents one example; Figure 8.7 in Chapter 8 provides another.

Problems and interpretive exercises are especially suitable for assessing students' ability to transfer what they've learned to new situations; such items may also involve such higher-level skills as analysis, synthesis, and critical thinking. They can be time-consuming to develop, but the time is well spent if we gain greater validity in assessing important instructional goals. The following two guidelines apply to both problems and interpretive exercises:

◎ *Use new examples and situations.* When you present problems or interpretive material that students have already encountered, students may respond correctly simply because they've memorized the answers. We can truly assess transfer only when we ask students to apply what they've learned to a novel context.

◎ *Include irrelevant information.* What is the area of this parallelogram?

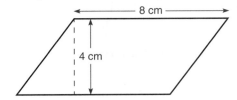

Even if you have completely forgotten how to compute the area of a parallelogram, you might be able to solve the problem correctly simply because you are given only two pieces of information. Calculating area typically involves multiplication, and you have only two numbers to multiply, so *voila!* you get the correct answer of 32 square centimeters. But now imagine that you instead see this figure:

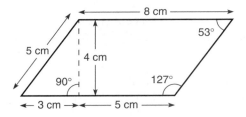

---

[5] R. L. Linn and Miller (2005) suggest using true-false or multiple-choice questions in interpretive exercises, making them recognition rather than recall tasks. In fact, the questions we ask in both problems and interpretive exercises could be *either* recognition or recall in format.

If you couldn't remember how to calculate the area of a parallelogram, you might be led astray by some of the information the figure provides.

Our purpose in adding extraneous information isn't necessarily to make a problem or exercise more difficult; rather, it is to make an assessment activity as similar as possible to real-life situations. The outside world typically presents a great deal of information that has little or nothing to do with the task at hand, and students must ultimately be able to determine what is relevant.

Essay Tasks An essay task requires a student to write a lengthy verbal response—at least a paragraph and perhaps as much as several pages. Essays are especially useful when we want students to show their writing ability or to demonstrate higher-level thinking skills (e.g., to analyze a piece of literature or compare and contrast two points of view) in a written format. Essay items have two serious limitations, however. First, students can respond to only a small number of questions in a single assessment, thereby limiting sampling of the content domain (and hence limiting content validity). Second, scoring is time-consuming and subjective (so somewhat unreliable), especially when the questions require lengthy, relatively unstructured responses. The guidelines that follow are designed to maximize the information we can get from students' essays while simultaneously ensuring reasonable validity and reliability:

◎ *Ask for several essays requiring short responses rather than one essay requiring a lengthy response.* The more items an assessment instrument includes, the more widely it can sample from the content domain it is meant to represent and the more reliable it is likely to be. In most situations an assessment consisting of only one or two essay questions cannot cover the breadth of knowledge and skills that we expect students to have acquired, and errors in our scoring can seriously impact overall test scores. Unless we are confident that one or two essay questions *do* provide a representative sample of the domain being assessed and, furthermore, that each question yields responses that can be scored consistently, we probably want to use one of two alternatives: (a) having several shorter essay questions or (b) combining one or two lengthy essays with other item types that can be answered quickly and easily.

◎ *Give students a structure for responding.* You may remember essay tests you've taken that provided little information or structure about how to respond; for example, perhaps you had to respond to an item such as this one:

List the causes of the American Civil War.

You may recall other tests that gave you clear guidance about the nature of the responses required, such as this item does:

Identify three policies or events between 1850 and 1860 that contributed to the outbreak of the American Civil War. For each of the three things you identify, explain in three to five sentences how it increased tension between the North and the South.

When we ask a totally unstructured question, students' responses may go in so many different directions that we will have difficulty scoring them consistently and reliably. Especially in situations where a great deal of material is potentially relevant, we should give students some

FIGURE 15.5 Example of an interpretive exercise

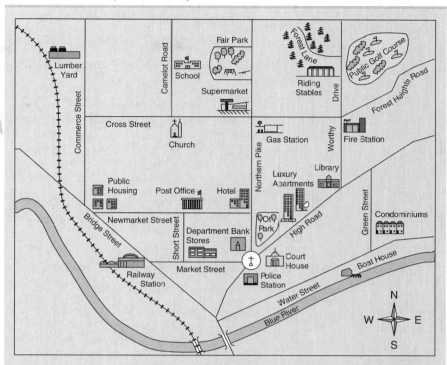

Here is a map of a small city named Riverdale. Apply principles of geography to answer the following questions. In each case, explain your reasoning.

1. Where in the city would you be most likely to find a steel mill?
2. Where would you be most likely to find upper-income, single-family homes?
3. Which area of the city appears to be undergoing urban renewal?
4. Where in the city would you expect traffic to be heaviest?

Answer key: (1) between the river and the railroad tracks, where both water and transportation are easily accessible; (2) near the riding stables and golf course, as horseback riding and golf are popular but expensive forms of recreation; (3) the southeastern part of the city, as evidenced by the luxury apartments and condominiums; (4) in the south central area, which appears to be the central business district.

Note: Map adapted from "Reconceptualizing Map Learning" by J. E. Ormrod, R. K. Ormrod, E. D. Wagner, and R. C. McCallin, 1988, *American Journal of Psychology, 101,* p. 428. Adapted with permission of the University of Illinois Press.

guidance about the length and completeness of the desired response and about the things they should specifically address. My second essay question concerning the Civil War illustrates how we might guide students toward responding in particular ways without giving the answer away.

◎   *Ask questions that can clearly be scored as correct or incorrect.* Consider this essay question:

How can the dilemma of the world's diminishing rain forests best be solved?

The question asks for students' opinions, which will be difficult to score as right or wrong. We do not necessarily have to limit our essay questions to those with only one correct answer, however. Consider this revision of the "rain forest" question:

Develop and explain a possible solution to the problem of the world's diminishing rain forests. Show how your solution addresses at least two of the economic, social, or political factors contributing to rain forest devastation.

Students' responses can be judged on how well their proposed solutions address factors that contribute to deforestation—factors that were presumably discussed in class or presented in the textbook.

General Guidelines for Constructing Paper-Pencil Assessments

Experiencing FIRSTHAND · Assessing Assessment

Your educational psychology instructor gives you a test that includes these questions:

1. List four qualities of a good classroom assessment instrument.
2. Summarize the purposes of classroom assessment.

Take a few minutes to think about how you might answer each question. Jot down your thoughts about what you would include in your responses.

· · · · · · ·

Was your answer to question 1 as simple as "reliability, standardization, validity, and practicality"? Did you think you would need to explain each of the RSVP characteristics? Did you identify legitimate qualities of "goodness" other than the four RSVP characteristics? And what about question 2? What purposes did you focus on, and how long do you think your actual summary might be? Words such as *list*, *qualities*, and *summarize* are difficult to interpret and can even be misleading.

Regardless of the kinds of items we use, we should follow several guidelines as we construct and administer a paper-pencil assessment instrument:

◎   *Define tasks clearly and unambiguously.* Contrary to what some teachers believe, little is to be gained from assigning ambiguous tasks to assess students' learning and achievement (Sax, 1989). Whether or not students know how to respond to assessment tasks, they should at least understand what we are asking them to do.

◎   *Decide whether students should have access to reference materials.* In some cases we may want students to have only one resource—their own long-term memory—as they carry out an assessment activity. But in others, it may be appropriate to let them use reference materials (perhaps a dictionary, an atlas, or a magazine article) as they work. An assessment task in which reference materials are allowed is especially appropriate when our objective is for students to locate, use, or analyze information rather than memorize it.

◎ *Specify scoring criteria in advance.* We will typically want to identify correct responses at the same time that we develop our assessment items. In situations where there will be more than one correct answer (as may be true for an essay), we should identify the components of a good response. In many situations we will want to share our scoring criteria with students; doing so gives them guidance about how they can best prepare and maximize their performance. Furthermore, we should develop policies to guide our scoring when students give partially correct answers, respond correctly but include additional *incorrect* information, or write responses with numerous grammatical and spelling errors.

◎   *Place easier and shorter items at the beginning of the instrument; place more challenging ones near the end.* Some students approach tests very strategically, answering quick and easy

Having students use reference materials during a formal assessment is quite appropriate when instructional goals focus on the ability to find and apply, rather than recall, information.

items first regardless of the order in which the items are sequenced. But other students answer items in the order they appear, sometimes spending so much time on one item (perhaps a lengthy essay) that they leave little time to tackle other, shorter ones. By beginning an assessment with short, relatively easy items, we put students at ease (thereby keeping test anxiety at a facilitative level) and ensure that they show us some of what they know before they get bogged down in an especially challenging task. Other things being equal, students perform better on paper-pencil assessments when items are arranged in order from easy to difficult (Gronlund, 1993; Sax & Cromack, 1966).

◎ *Set parameters for students' responses.* Students cannot always read our minds about how we expect them to respond to items on a paper-pencil assessment. So in addition to constructing the items themselves, we should develop directions that specify the following:

- *Time limits*—for example, how long students should spend on each item and whether they have a limited time to complete the overall assessment
- *Nature of desired responses*—for example, whether they should choose a single best answer on each multiple-choice question or instead mark all correct alternatives
- *Method of recording responses*—for example, whether students should indicate their answers on the instrument itself or on a separate answer sheet
- *Acceptability of guessing*—for example, whether students should guess if they're not sure or, instead, will be penalized for wrong answers

■ Subtracting points for wrong answers is controversial; see the supplementary reading "Correcting for Guessing in Paper-Pencil Assessments" in the *Study Guide and Reader.*

Administering the Assessment

Our concern about maximizing the validity of a paper-pencil assessment instrument should not end once we've created the instrument. We must also consider validity as we administer the instrument and score students' responses. For instance, we are more likely to get valid indicators of what students know and can do if their anxiety remains at a facilitative level (more on this point later in the chapter). Following are three additional strategies that should increase the validity of our results as we administer an assessment:

◎ *Provide a quiet and comfortable environment.* Students are more likely to perform at their best when they complete an assessment in a comfortable environment with acceptable room temperature, adequate lighting, reasonable workspace, and minimal distractions. This comfort factor may be especially important for students who are easily distracted, unaccustomed to formal assessments, or unmotivated to exert much effort; for example, it may be especially important for students at risk (Popham, 1990).

◎ *Encourage students to ask questions when tasks are not clear.* As noted earlier, students need to know what we are asking them to do. Yet despite our best intentions, we may present a task or question that is unclear, ambiguous, or even misleading. (Even with thirty years' experience developing assignments and exams, I still have students occasionally interpreting them in ways I didn't anticipate.) To increase the likelihood that students will respond in the ways we had in mind, we should encourage them to ask for clarification whenever they are uncertain about a task. Such encouragement is especially important for students from ethnic minority groups, many of whom may be reluctant to ask questions during a formal assessment situation (L. R. Cheng, 1987).

◎ *Take steps to discourage cheating.* The prevalence of cheating increases as students get older, and by high school, the great majority of students are apt to cheat at one time or another (Cizek, 2003). In fact, in the high school grades, many students think that occasional cheating is "no big deal" and report that some of their teachers seem unconcerned about it when it occurs (Cizek, 2003). In fact, cheating *is* a big deal, and its occurrence should concern us quite a bit. Not only does cheating render assessment results invalid, but it also can be habit-forming when students discover that it enables them to get good grades with minimal effort (Cizek, 2003).

Students cheat for a variety of reasons. For instance, they may be more interested in doing well on an assessment than in actually learning the subject matter; that is, performance goals predominate over mastery goals. Students may believe that teachers' or parents' expectations for their performance are so high as to be unattainable and that success is out of their control unless they *do* cheat. They may perceive certain assessments (tests especially) to be poorly constructed, arbitrarily graded, or in some other way a poor reflection of what they have learned. Furthermore, peer group norms may tell them that cheating is quite acceptable (E. M. Anderman et al., 1998; Cizek, 2003; E. D. Evans & Craig, 1990; Urdan et al., 2002).

The best approach is prevention—making sure students don't cheat in the first place. For instance, we can take the following precautions:

In the weeks or days before the assessment:
- Focus students' attention on mastery rather than performance goals
- Make success without cheating a realistic possibility
- Construct assessment instruments with obvious validity for important instructional goals
- Explain exactly what cheating is and why it is unacceptable
- Explain what the consequence for cheating will be

During the assessment:
- Use two or more assessment instruments that are equivalent in form and content but have different answers
- Have teacher-chosen assigned seats during any assessments that require individual (rather than group) work
- Seat students as far away from one another as possible

If, despite reasonable precautions, cheating does occur, we must administer the consequence we have previously described. This consequence should be severe enough to discourage a student from cheating again, yet not so severe that the student's motivation and chances for academic success are affected over the long run; for instance, what I have typically done is to require a student to redo the task, perhaps for less credit than he or she would have earned otherwise. Our final grades should ultimately reflect what a student has and has not learned, however. For this reason, one expert (Stiggins, 2001) recommends that the consequence for cheating *not* be a low (or failing) grade for an entire course in which a student has, in other graded assignments, demonstrated mastery of the subject matter.

■ Do you agree with Stiggins? Why or why not?

Scoring Students' Responses

Interpreting Student Artifacts and Behaviors

The Magic Baseball Bat
Imagine you are a fourth-grade teacher. You have asked your class to write short stories. Following is 9-year-old Seth's story. As you read it, consider

- What letter grade (A, B, C, D, or F) you might give it
- What criteria you would use to make your decision

The Magic Baseball Bat
One April 3 I sined up for baseball. A week later we started baseball. On the first pratice we lernd how to hit the ball. When I was up I hit a homer and I havent even hit a ball in my life. I was suprised that I hit it. All the other pratices until the game I hit the ball. When we had the first game I used anther bat and struk out so I dicitid to use that one bat. At the next game I use that one bat and hit a homer it was ausum. The kid after me used the bat and he hit a homer to then are wholl team used the the bat. Other teams wanted to trade bat but we didnt want to. Are team was the best, top, higesd. I couldnt believe it and no nonk had playd befor. One of the team we played cheatid. They put a magi in the ball and bat. But we fond out because when one of their players was up the bat broke. At the end of the seaon we were the top team. It trnd out are bat was magic. After the last game we had a treat at Burgr King it was fun and cool. Next seaon the wholl team is going to sine up and I hope were togeth er agin. Tonight are team is going to have a party at are coaches house it will be fun. Tomara my fanly and I are going to play baseball for fun

THE
H N
END

How did you grade the story about the magic baseball bat? What criteria did you use when you made your decision? How important was the student's development of plot? the student's creativity? the grammar, spelling, and punctuation? Different teachers might weigh each of these criteria differently, and their grades for the same story would differ as a result. In fact, in another month, you might grade the story differently than you did today.

The more variable and complex students' responses on a paper-pencil assessment instrument are, the greater difficulty we will have scoring those responses objectively and reliably, and the more our expectations for students' performance may bias our judgments. As an example, imagine that we have one student, Mary, who consistently performs well in her classwork, and another, Susan, who more typically turns in sloppy, incomplete assignments. Let's say that both girls turn in an essay of marginal quality. We are likely to *over*rate Mary's performance and *under*rate Susan's—an example of the *halo effect* mentioned earlier.

Several strategies can help us score students' responses in an objective, reliable, and standardized manner:

◎ *Specify scoring criteria in concrete terms*. Whenever an assessment task involves subjective evaluation of a complex performance—for instance, when it involves scoring lengthy essay responses—we should list the components that a correct response must include or the characteristics we will consider as we judge it. Such a list is sometimes known as a **rubric**. Figure 15.6 shows a rubric that one fourth-grade teacher uses for judging students' performance on mathematics word problems; notice how she provides spaces for both herself and the student to evaluate the performance (more about students' self-assessments later).

◎ *Unless specifically assessing writing skills, score grammar and spelling separately from the content of students' responses to the extent possible*. This recommendation is especially important when assessing students with limited English proficiency (Hamp-Lyons, 1992; Scarcella, 1990).

◎ *Skim a sample of students' responses ahead of time, looking for unanticipated responses and revising the criteria if necessary*. If we need to change our scoring criteria for unexpected reasons, we are more likely to score student responses consistently, fairly, and reliably if we change those criteria *before* we begin scoring rather than midway through a stack of papers.

◎ *Score item by item rather than paper by paper*. When students' responses involve some subjectivity in scoring, we can score them more reliably when we score them item by item—for example, scoring all students' responses to the first question, then all their responses to the second question, and so on.

◎ *Try not to let prior expectations for students' performance influence judgments of their actual performance*. Strategies such as shuffling papers after grading one question and using small self-stick notes to cover up students' names can help us keep our expectations from inappropriately influencing our judgments.

◎ *Accompany any overall scores with detailed feedback*. As we score students' responses, we should remember that our assessments should promote students' future learning as well as determine current achievement levels. Accordingly, we should give students detailed comments about their responses that tell them what they did well, where their weaknesses lie, and how they can improve (Bangert-Drowns et al., 1991; Deci & Ryan, 1985; Krampen, 1987).

◎ *Keep students' scores confidential*. Under *no* circumstances should we make students' individual assessment scores public—for instance, by announcing them in class or posting them beside students' names on the bulletin board. In Chapter 16 we'll consider reasons why confidentiality of assessment results—not only for paper-pencil classroom assessments but also for performance assessments, class grades, and standardized tests—is so important.

FIGURE 15.6 Example of a rubric for evaluating performance on mathematics word problems

Elements	Possible Points	Points Earned	
		Self	Teacher
1. You highlighted the question(s) to solve.	2	___	___
2. You picked an appropriate strategy.	2	___	___
3. Work is neat and organized.	2	___	___
4. Calculations are accurate.	2	___	___
5. Question(s) answered.	2	___	___
6. You have explained in words how you solved the problem.	5	___	___
Total	___	___	___

■ **rubric** List of components that a student's performance on an assessment task should ideally include.

RSVP Characteristics of Paper-Pencil Assessment

How do paper-pencil assessments measure up in terms of the four RSVP characteristics? Let's consider each characteristic in turn.

Reliability   When we have tasks and questions with definite right and wrong answers—that is, when we have objectively scorable responses—we can evaluate students' responses with a high degree of consistency and reliability. When we must make subjective judgments about the relative rightness or wrongness of students' responses, reliability will inevitably go down.

Standardization   As a general rule, paper-pencil instruments are easily standardized. We can present similar tasks and instructions to all students, provide similar time limits and environmental conditions, and score everyone's responses in more or less the same way. Nevertheless, we probably don't want to go overboard in this respect. For example, we might sometimes allow students to choose a writing topic, perhaps as a way of increasing their sense of self-determination (see Chapter 12). We may also need to tailor assessment tasks to the particular abilities and disabilities of our students with special needs.

Validity   When we ask questions that require only short, simple responses (e.g., true-false, multiple-choice, and matching questions), we can sample students' knowledge about many topics within a relatively short period of time. In this sense, then, such questions can give us greater content validity. Yet in some situations such items may not accurately reflect our instructional objectives. To assess our students' ability to apply what they've learned to new situations, or to find out how well students can solve problems (especially the ill-defined ones so common in the adult world), we may need to be satisfied with a few tasks requiring lengthy responses.

Practicality   Paper-pencil assessment is typically more practical than performance assessment; for instance, we will usually require no "equipment" other than paper and writing implements, and we can easily assess the knowledge and skills of all students at the same time. Some paper-pencil assessments have the additional advantage of being relatively quick and easy to score.

Because paper-pencil assessment is so practical, it should generally be our method of choice *if* it can also yield a valid measure of what students know and can do. But in situations where paper-pencil tasks are clearly not a good reflection of what students have learned, we may need to sacrifice such practicality to gain the greater validity that a performance assessment provides. Before we turn to that topic, however, let's apply what we've learned to a science test.

Analyzing Teacher Strategies

Life Functions

Following is a three-part test given in a high school biology class. As you look at the test, consider the extent to which it has the four RSVP characteristics.

Test on Life Functions

1. Column A lists terms. Column B lists definitions. Print the letter from column B that <u>best matches</u> each term in column A.

    ____ Enzymes   a. Passage of simple substances into the internal parts of plants and animals

    ____ Locomotion   b. Matter that was never alive

    ____ Self-repair   c. Changing digested food into new living material

    .   .

    .   .

[20 terms and 20 definitions are listed]

2. A paramecium is a single-celled organism. Name three more single-celled organisms.

    _____ _____ _____

3. List any five life functions and describe how the paramecium performs each one.

The biology test is certainly practical: It can be easily administered and scored. It should also be easy to administer in a consistent, standardized fashion for everyone. Items 1 and 2 can be scored consistently and reliably, in that answers are definitely right or wrong. Item 3 can probably be scored reliably as well: A paramecium is a simple enough organism that descriptions of basic life functions (how it reproduces, how it moves, how it excretes waste products, etc.) are fairly straightforward. The big problem with this test is its validity: Items 1 and 2 require nothing more than rote memorization. Whether item 3 assesses rote learning or more effective learning processes (e.g., meaningful learning, elaboration) depends on whether the class has specifically studied how a paramecium exhibits various life functions. We can reasonably assume that the instructional goals of a high school science class would *not* be limited to lower-level skills, yet the test focuses almost exclusively on them.

PERFORMANCE ASSESSMENT

A wide variety of performance tasks can be used to assess students' mastery of classroom subject matter. Here are just a few of the many possibilities:

- Playing a musical instrument
- Conversing in a foreign language
- Identifying an unknown chemical substance
- Engaging in a debate about social issues
- Fixing a malfunctioning machine
- Role-playing a job interview
- Performing a workplace routine
- Creating a computer simulation of a real-world task
  (Gronlund, 1993; C. Hill & Larsen, 1992; D. B. Swanson et al., 1995)

■ Are most performance tasks *recognition* or *recall* tasks?

Performance assessment lends itself especially well to the assessment of complex achievements, such as those that involve coordinating a number of skills simultaneously. It may also be quite helpful in assessing such higher-level cognitive skills as problem solving, creativity, and critical thinking. Furthermore, performance tasks are often more meaningful, thought-provoking, and authentic, and so often more motivating, than paper-pencil tasks (Khattri & Sweet, 1996; Paris & Paris, 2001; D. P. Resnick & Resnick, 1996). The following problem, which has been used to assess fourth graders' math and literacy skills, is an example of an assessment task that students find highly motivating:

> In a letter from the principal, it is announced that the fourth-grade classroom will be getting a 30-gallon aquarium. The students in that classroom have the responsibility of buying fish for the tank. The class will receive $25 to spend on fish and a *Choosing Fish for Your Aquarium* brochure. The brochure provides the necessary information about the size of each type of fish, how much each costs, and the special needs of each fish. The students are instructed to choose as many different kinds of fish as possible and then to write a letter explaining which fish were chosen. In the letter, the students must indicate how many of each kind of fish were selected and the reasons why they were chosen, demonstrate that the fish will not be overcrowded in the aquarium, and provide that the purchases maintain the limited budget of $25. (D. P. Resnick & Resnick, 1996, pp. 30–31)

Of course, we can also assess complex skills in ways that don't entail the expense and long-term commitment that maintaining a classroom aquarium would. In the upcoming pages we will examine various kinds of performance tasks we might use to assess students' learning and achievement. We will then identify strategies for developing, administering, and scoring performance assessments and consider how well these assessments reflect the RSVP characteristics.

Choosing Appropriate Performance Tasks

As we select tasks for a performance assessment, we must have a clear purpose in mind: We must identify the specific conclusions we wish to draw from students' performance. We must also consider whether a particular task will enable us to make reasonable generalizations about what our students know and can do in the content domain in question (Popham, 1995; Wiggins, 1992). Let's look at four distinctions that can help us zero in on the tasks most appropriate for our purposes: products versus processes, individual versus group performance, restricted versus extended performance, and static versus dynamic assessment.

Products versus processes. In performance assessment we can focus on products, processes, or both (E. H. Hiebert, Valencia, & Afflerbach, 1994; Messick, 1994; Paris & Paris, 2001). In some situations we can look at tangible *products* that students have created—perhaps a pen-and-ink drawing, scientific invention, or poster display. In situations with no tangible product, we must instead look at the specific *processes and behaviors* that students exhibit—perhaps giving an oral presentation, demonstrating a forward roll, or playing an instrumental solo.

Some skills, such as the ability to converse with others in a foreign language, can be assessed only with performance tasks.

When we look at processes rather than products, we may in some instances be interested in examining students' *thinking processes*. For instance, if we want to determine whether students have developed some of the concrete operational or formal operational abilities that Piaget described (conservation, multiple classification, separation and control of variables, etc.), we might present tasks similar to those Piaget used and ask students to explain their reasoning (De Corte et al., 1996). And we can often learn a great deal about how students conceptualize and reason about scientific phenomena when we ask them to manipulate physical objects (e.g., chemicals in a chemistry lab, electrical circuit boards in a physics class), make predictions about what will happen under varying circumstances, and then explain their results (Magnusson, Boyle, & Templin, 1994; Quellmalz & Hoskyn, 1997).

Individual versus group performance. Many performance tasks require *individual* students to complete them with little or no assistance from others. Other tasks are sufficiently complex that they are best accomplished by a *group* of students. For instance, we might assess high school students' mastery of a unit on urban geography using a field-based cooperative group project such as this one:

> First, select one of the neighborhoods marked on the city map. Second, identify its current features by doing an inventory of its buildings, businesses, housing, and public facilities. Also, identify current transportation patterns and traffic flow. From the information made available, identify any special problems this neighborhood has, such as dilapidated housing, traffic congestion, or a high crime rate. Third, as a group, consider various plans for changing and improving your neighborhood. (Newmann, 1997, p. 369)

Such a task requires students to collect data systematically, use the data to draw conclusions and make predictions and, more generally, think as an urban planner would think (Newmann, 1997).

One challenge in using group tasks for assessment purposes is determining how to evaluate each student's contribution. Often teachers consider individual students' behaviors and achievements (what and how much a student contributes to the group effort, how much the student has learned by the end of the project, etc.) in addition to, or perhaps instead of, the entire group's accomplishments (Lester et al., 1997; Stiggins, 2001).

Restricted versus extended performance. Some performance tasks are quite short; that is, they involve *restricted performance*. For instance, in a beginning instrumental music class, we might ask each student to play the C major scale to make sure that everyone has mastered the scale on his or her respective instrument. In a chemistry class we might ask students to demonstrate mastery of basic safety procedures before beginning their lab experiments.

We assess *extended performance* when we want to determine what students are capable of doing over several days or weeks (Alleman & Brophy, 1997; De Corte et al., 1996; Lester et al., 1997). Extended performance tasks might provide opportunities for students to collect data, engage in collaborative problem solving, and edit and revise their work. Many extended performance tasks embody authentic assessment: They closely resemble the situations and problems that students may eventually encounter in the outside world. Because extended performance tasks take a great deal of time, we should use them only for assessing achievement related to our most important and central instructional goals.

Static versus dynamic assessment. Most assessments, whether paper-pencil or performance tasks, focus on identifying students' existing abilities and achievements. When used in isolation from other assessments, they do not specifically address how students learn and change over time; thus, you might think of them as *static* indicators. Static assessment is consistent with Vygotsky's concept of a child's *actual developmental level*, reflecting the tasks that the child can easily do on his or her own (see Chapter 2).

In recent years some theorists have suggested an approach that instead focuses on assessing students' ability to learn in new situations, perhaps with the assistance of a teacher or other more competent individual (Feuerstein, Feuerstein, & Gross, 1997; L. A. Shepard, 2000; H. L. Swanson & Lussier, 2001). Such an approach, sometimes called **dynamic assessment**, reflects Vygotsky's *zone of proximal development* and can give us an idea of what our students are likely to be

■ **dynamic assessment** Systematic examination of how a student's knowledge or reasoning may change as a result of learning or performing a specific task.

able to accomplish with appropriate structure and guidance. Hence it is most appropriate for formative (rather than summative) evaluation.

Currently we have little hard data about the validity and reliability of dynamic assessment techniques (H. L. Swanson & Lussier, 2001; Tzuriel, 2000). However, this approach can be quite helpful in assessing students' cognitive processes and deficiencies, as well as in gathering information about students' dispositions and motivation (Feuerstein et al., 1997; Hamers & Ruijssenaars, 1997; Tzuriel, 2000). Furthermore, it often yields more optimistic evaluations of students' cognitive abilities than traditional assessment tasks do and may be particularly useful in assessing the abilities of students from diverse cultural backgrounds and those from lower-income families (Feuerstein, 1979; Tzuriel, 2000).

Planning and Administering the Assessment

Several of the guidelines presented in the section on paper-pencil assessment are equally relevant for performance assessment; in particular, we should

- Define tasks clearly and unambiguously
- Specify scoring criteria in advance (more about this point shortly)
- Standardize administration procedures as much as possible
- Encourage students to ask questions when tasks are not clear

Three additional guidelines pertain specifically to conducting performance assessments:

◎ *Consider incorporating the assessment into normal instructional activities.* Some theorists and practitioners recommend that we incorporate performance assessments into everyday instructional activities (Baxter et al., 1996; Boschee & Baron, 1993; Kennedy, 1992; Stiggins, 2001). We make more efficient use of our limited time with students if we can combine instruction and assessment into one activity. In addition, we may reduce the "evaluative" climate in our classroom; as you may recall from Chapter 12, external evaluation lowers students' sense of self-determination and can discourage risk taking. In the following exercise, we see a simple example of what an "incorporated" assessment might look like.

Interpreting Student Artifacts and Behaviors

Birthday Graph

In a unit on graphs early in the school year, first-grade teacher Susan O'Byrne distributes a table that lists the twelve months. She asks her students to circulate around the room, gathering everyone else's signature in a box beside his or her birthday month; in this way, students will have a graph showing how many class members were born in each month of the year. To the right is one student's completed graph. As you look at the graph, consider

- Which students understand the nature of the task and which do not
- What common sources of difficulty seem to be

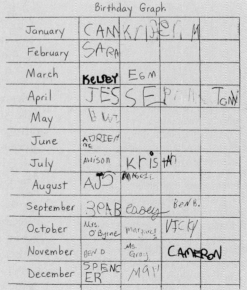

Many of the students seem to have the hang of the idea; for instance, Cam, Sara, Kelsey, Adrienne, and Spencer all write their names inside a single box in the table. However, a few students (Kristen, Jesse, Kristah, and Cameron) use *two* cells to write their names, perhaps because (a) they haven't mastered the idea that one person equals one box in the table, or (b) they can't write small enough to fit their name inside a box and don't know how to solve this problem. (Notice that Adrienne and Spencer *do* address the "fit" issue by writing their names in two lines within a box.) Meg (one of the March children) has a different problem: writing the letters of her name in the traditional left-to-right manner.

When we incorporate performance assessments into instructional activities, we must keep in mind that we will not be able to completely standardize conditions for all students, and we will not necessarily see students' best work. Furthermore, although it is quite appropriate to give students assistance or feedback during instruction, it may often be *in*appropriate to do

In some situations we can incorporate assessment into everyday instructional activities.

so during a summative evaluation of what they have achieved (L. M. Carey, 1994). In some situations, then, we may want to conduct an assessment separately from instructional activities, announce it in advance, and give students some guidance as to how they can maximize their performance (Stiggins, 2001).

◎   *Provide an appropriate amount of structure.* Especially during a summative evaluation, we will probably want to structure performance tasks to some degree. For example, we can provide detailed directions about what we want students to accomplish, what materials and equipment they can use, and how we will evaluate their performance (Gronlund, 1993; E. H. Hiebert, Valencia, & Afflerbach, 1994; Stiggins, 2001). Such structure helps to standardize the assessment and so enables us to evaluate students' performance more reliably. Yet too much structure will reduce the authenticity of a task if performance conditions become less like those in the outside world. Thus we must consider both reliability and validity as we determine the appropriate amount of structure to impose in any performance assessment.

◎   *Plan classroom management strategies for the assessment activity.* As we conduct a performance assessment, we should put into practice two important principles of classroom management presented in Chapter 14: Effective teachers are continually aware of what their students are doing (the notion of *withitness*), and they make sure that all students are busy and engaged. When we can assess only a few students (or perhaps only one) at a time, we must make sure other students are actively involved in a learning activity (L. M. Carey, 1994). For example, in an English class, when one student is giving an oral presentation, we might have the other students jot down notes about the topic being presented, including facts they find interesting, ideas they disagree with, and questions they wonder about. In a unit on soccer, when a few students are demonstrating their ability to dribble and pass the ball as they run down the field, we might have other students work in pairs to practice their footwork.

Scoring Students' Responses

Occasionally responses to performance assessment tasks are objectively scorable; for example, we can easily count the errors on a typing test or time students' performance in a 100-meter dash. But more often than not, we will find ourselves making somewhat subjective decisions when we assess performance. There are no clear-cut right or wrong responses when students give oral reports, create clay sculptures, or engage in heated debates on controversial issues. If we aren't careful, our judgments may be unduly influenced by our expectations for each student (L. M. Carey, 1994; Stiggins, 2001).

Especially for summative evaluations, we should carefully consider the criteria to use as we judge students' responses and develop a rubric that identifies these criteria. A rubric can guide us during the evaluation process, and later on, it can serve as a written record of what we have observed. The following strategies can help us design and use scoring rubrics effectively when we conduct performance assessments:

◎   *Consider using checklists, rating scales, or both in your rubric.* Some tasks lend themselves well to **checklists**, with which we evaluate student performance by indicating whether specific behaviors or qualities are present or absent. Other tasks are more appropriately evaluated with **rating scales**, with which we evaluate student performance by rating aspects of the performance on one or more continua (see Figure 15.7). Both approaches enhance the reliability of scoring and have instructional benefits as well: They identify specific areas of difficulty and so give students feedback about how performance can be improved.

◎   *Decide whether analytic or holistic scoring better serves your purpose(s) in conducting the assessment.* When we need detailed information about students' performance, we may want to use **analytic scoring**, in which we evaluate various aspects of the performance separately, perhaps with a checklist or several rating scales. In contrast, when we need to summarize students' performance in a single score, we should probably use **holistic scoring**, in which we consider all relevant criteria when making a single judgment; for instance, we might have a single 1-to-5 rating scale that describes typical overall performance at various points along the scale. Analytic scoring tends to be more useful in conducting formative evaluations and promoting students' learning, whereas holistic scoring is often used in summative evaluation.

■ **checklist** Assessment tool with which a teacher evaluates student performance by indicating whether specific behaviors or qualities are present or absent.

■ **rating scale** Assessment tool with which a teacher evaluates student performance by rating aspects of the performance on one or more continua.

■ **analytic scoring** Scoring a student's performance on an assessment by evaluating various aspects of it separately.

■ **holistic scoring** Summarizing a student's performance on an assessment with a single score.

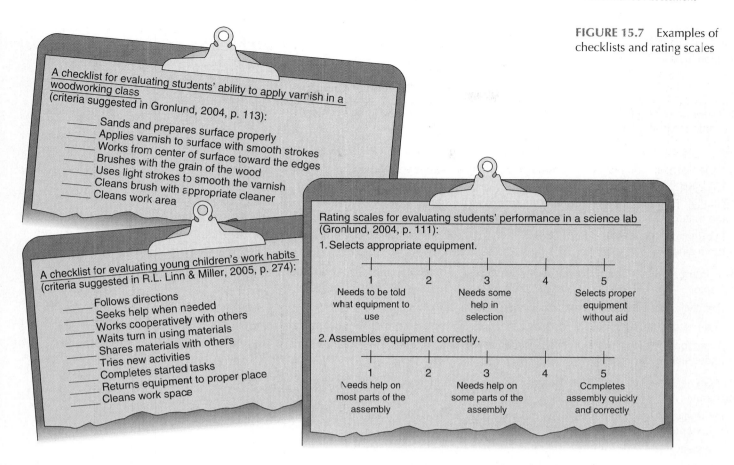

FIGURE 15.7   Examples of checklists and rating scales

◎   *Limit the criteria to the most important aspects of the desired response.* Our criteria should focus on aspects of the performance that are critical for a "good" response and most relevant to our instructional objectives (Stiggins, 2001; Wiggins, 1992). They should also be relatively few in number (perhaps five or six at the most) so that we can keep track of them as we observe each student's performance (Airasian, 1994; Gronlund, 1993; Popham, 1995).

■ Use the concept of *working memory* (Chapter 6) to explain the value of having only a few criteria.

◎   *Describe the criteria as explicitly and concretely as possible.* Criteria such as "excellent" and "needs improvement" don't tell us very much, nor do they offer much feedback for students. We can score students' performance more objectively and reliably, and provide more constructive feedback, when our criteria focus on specific, observable qualities of students' products or behaviors (R. L. Linn & Miller, 2005; Stiggins, 2001; Wiggins, 1992). For example, Chapter 13 describes a cooperative group activity that an eighth-grade history teacher uses in a unit on colonial America (see Figure 13.6). Figure 15.8 presents the rubric that the same teacher uses to evaluate students' performance in various aspects of this activity.

◎   *Make note of any other significant aspects of a student's performance that the rubric doesn't address.* Rubrics are rarely perfect. Whenever we break down students' performance on a complex task into discrete behaviors, we can lose valuable information in the process (Delandshere & Petrosky, 1998). When we use rubrics to assist us in scoring performance, then, we may occasionally want to jot down other noteworthy characteristics of students' performance. This aspect of our scoring process will be neither standardized nor reliable, of course, but it can sometimes be useful in identifying students' unique strengths and needs and can therefore assist us in future instructional planning.

RSVP Characteristics of Performance Assessment

Compared with traditional paper-pencil assessment, performance assessment techniques are relative newcomers on the educational scene; hence psychologists and educators are only beginning to address concerns related to reliability, standardization, validity, and practicality. Let's look at the data that researchers report, as well as at strategies for enhancing each of the four RSVP characteristics.

FIGURE 15.8   Eighth-grade history teacher Mark Nichols uses this rubric to evaluate students' performance in cooperative group projects about colonial America. The projects themselves are described in Figure 13.6 in Chapter 13.

Colonial Economies Rubric

The following rubric will help the student to understand the expectations for each component of the group project. The number value represents the level of mastery. Higher numbers reflect greater mastery.

Outline: The outline is organized and concise while summarizing important information.

Organization: The outline is formatted according to the style discussed in class and aligned with the book.	5	4	3	2	1
Clarity: The text of the outline is organized in a manner which helps students to fully understand the material.	5	4	3	2	1
Information: The outline information is to the point and does not exceed 1 sheet of paper (both sides).	5	4	3	2	1

Artistic Interpretation: The creative project displays some of the important information within the subchapter.

Creativity: The product reflects prior thought, effort, and artistry.	5	4	3	2	1
Interpretation: The product properly represents the material within the subchapter.	5	4	3	2	1
Attraction: The final product reflects organization and engages the audience through color, size, and a high level of quality.	5	4	3	2	1

Board Game: The board game is designed to entertain and teach 3–4 students at one time for approximately 10 minutes about the information in the subchapter.

Information: The game provides a means to test the players' knowledge about the assigned subchapter.	5	4	3	2	1
Creativity: The game reflects prior thought, artistry, and imagination.	5	4	3	2	1
Application: The game effectively helps students to apply their knowledge of the subchapter through the rules and organization of play.	5	4	3	2	1

Homework: The homework is assigned to the class the day prior to the presentation. Students are instructed to read the text and complete an assignment.

Organization: The assignment holds each student in class responsible for understanding key information.	5	4	3	2	1
Originality: The assignment shows imagination and effort along with innovative ways to help students learn.	5	4	3	2	1
Information: The homework assignment is clearly stated and focuses on important information which will help students to understand the material.	5	4	3	2	1

Presentations:

Preparedness: The group members are each prepared for the presentation with thorough knowledge of the material. They show preparedness through a sense of confidence in their presentation.	5	4	3	2	1
Clarity: The information presented is well organized and clearly stated. Members of the group make eye contact with the class and engage each student with understanding of the material.	5	4	3	2	1
Organization: The members of the group successfully organize the presentation so that there is an order and a pace which will enable students to gain a clear understanding of the material.	5	4	3	2	1

Reliability   Researchers have reported varying degrees of reliability in performance assessments; assessment results are often inconsistent over time, and different teachers may rate the same performance differently (S. Burger & Burger, 1994; R. L. Linn, 1994; Shavelson, Baxter, & Pine, 1992; D. B. Swanson et al., 1995). There are probably several reasons for the low reliability of many performance assessments (L. M. Carey, 1994; Wiley & Haertel, 1996). First, students don't always behave consistently; even in a task as simple as shooting a basketball, a student is likely to make a basket on some occasions but not others. Second, we sometimes need to evaluate various aspects of complex behaviors rather quickly; things may happen so fast that we miss important parts of a student's performance. If we have no tangible product, we cannot reevaluate the performance. Finally, one form of reliability, *internal consistency* (see Table 15.1), is simply inappropriate for complex, multifaceted behaviors.

Given these limitations, a single performance assessment may very well *not* be a reliable indicator of what students have achieved. Accordingly, we should ask students to demonstrate behaviors related to important instructional goals on more than one occasion (Airasian, 1994; L. M. Carey, 1994). And whenever possible, we should have more than one rater evaluate each student's performance (Stiggins, 2001; R. M. Thorndike, 1997).

Standardization   Some performance assessments are easily standardized, but others are not. If we want to assess typing ability, we can easily make the instructions, time limits, and material the same for everyone. In contrast, if we want to assess artistic creativity, we may want to give students free rein regarding the materials they use and the particular products they create. In such nonstandardized situations, it is especially important to use multiple assessments and look for consistency in students' performance across several occasions.

Validity   As previously noted, performance assessment tasks may sometimes provide more valid indicators of what students have accomplished relative to instructional goals. Researchers are finding, however, that students' responses to a *single* performance assessment task are frequently *not* a good indication of their overall achievement (Koretz, Stecher, Klein, & McCaffrey, 1994; R. L. Linn, 1994; Shavelson et al., 1992; D. B. Swanson et al., 1995). Content validity is at stake here: If we have time for students to perform only one or two complex tasks, we may not get a representative sample of what they have learned and can do. In addition, any biases that affect our judgments (e.g., beliefs we have about particular students' abilities) can distort our evaluations of students' performance (Airasian, 1994; L. M. Carey, 1994).

As a general rule, then, we will typically want to administer several *different* performance assessments, or perhaps administer the same task under different conditions, to ensure that our conclusions are reasonably valid (R. L. Linn, 1994; Messick, 1994; Stiggins, 2001). For efficiency, we may want to incorporate some of these assessment activities into everyday instructional activities (Shavelson & Baxter, 1992).

Practicality   Unfortunately, performance assessments are often less practical than more traditional paper-pencil assessments (L. M. Carey, 1994; Hambleton, 1996; Popham, 1995). Administering an assessment can be quite time-consuming, especially when we observe students one at a time or when they perform relatively complex (perhaps authentic) tasks. In addition, we may need considerable equipment to conduct the assessment, perhaps enough that every student has his or her own set. Furthermore, performance assessments used in large-scale, high-stakes testing are much more expensive than traditional paper-pencil tests (Hardy, 1996). Clearly, then, we must carefully consider whether the benefits of a performance assessment outweigh its impracticality (Messick, 1994; Tzuriel, 2000; Worthen & Leopold, 1992).

As we have just seen, performance assessments can be unreliable and impractical, and they may tap an insufficient sample of what students have learned. Yet in many situations they may more closely resemble the long-term goals we have for students, and in this sense they may be more valid indicators of students' achievement. As educators gain experience in the use of performance assessment in the years to come, increasingly valid, reliable, and practical measures of student performance will undoubtedly emerge. In the meantime, the most reliable, valid, and practical assessment strategy overall may be to use *both* paper-pencil and performance assessments when drawing conclusions about students' achievement (Gronlund, 1993; R. L. Linn, 1994).

At this point, you should be in a fairly good position to distinguish useful and dependable assessments from less valid and reliable ones. In the following exercise, you can apply what you have learned to an actual assessment instrument.

Interpreting Student Artifacts and Behaviors

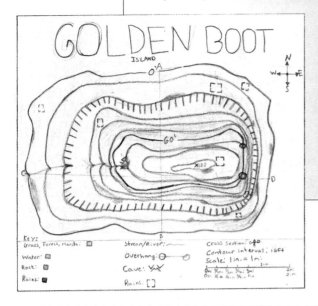

Golden Boot Island

A seventh-grade social studies class is learning techniques and conventions for depicting elevation and topography. Below is a take-home assignment for the unit.

Twelve-year-old Francisco's responses to the assignment (an aerial view of "Golden Boot Island" and two side views of the same island) appear to the left. As you look at the artifacts:

- Evaluate the assessment task in terms of its RSVP characteristics
- Identify strengths and weaknesses in Francisco's responses

Island Map Assignment

1. Using a contour interval of 15 feet and a scale of one inch to one mile, construct a contour map of an island that
   a. Is 6 miles from east to west and 4 miles from north to south
   b. Has a maximum elevation of 124 feet, but rises to at least 105 feet
   c. Is steepest on the east side
   d. Has a stream running into the ocean on the west shore, with its source at an elevation of 90 feet
2. Draw two profile maps of your island, one showing the island from west to east and the other showing it from north to south.

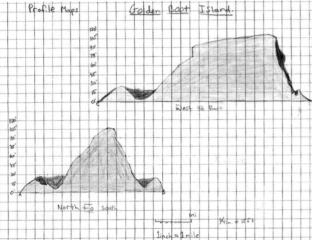

Students' maps must conform to certain measurements, and the teacher can probably ascertain whether they do with some objectivity and reliability. Predetermined scoring criteria can nevertheless enhance scorer reliability, given the variation and creativity the task allows. The task is standardized in some but not all respects: Students all have the same assignment and directions but are completing it at home, where some of them have greater access to resources (including helpful family members) than others. Content validity is probably a strong point: Although we don't know the teacher's instructional objectives, we can reasonably assume that they include not only knowledge of mapping techniques but also the ability to apply those techniques to realistic situations. The task is certainly practical, in that it involves minimal materials, very little in-class time (the task is completed at home), and probably would not take very much time to score.

Can you recall enough about mapping procedures to evaluate Francisco's island? He has been meticulous in his drawings, and he makes good use of a key to show various features (vegetation, rocks, ruins, etc.). He goes beyond the minimal specifications for the task (e.g., the island has a moat-shaped body of water). The island is indeed 6 miles from west to east and 4 miles from north to south, and it is steepest on the east side. The three views of the island are inconsistent in total elevation, depicting the summit as being 122, 105, or about 110 feet high. Nor is Francisco consistent in his use of contour lines (the concentric "circles" in the aerial view): Those marking lower elevations show 10-foot increments, but those above 60 feet appear to show 20-foot increments. It's not clear at what elevation the stream begins, but the source appears to be below the 90-foot level the assignment specifies. In general, it appears that Francisco has a good overall grasp of mapping techniques but may need some fine-tuning with respect to scale, elevation, and contour lines.

Table 15.3 presents a summary of our RSVP analyses of informal assessment, formal paper-pencil assessment, and formal performance assessment. We now turn our attention to strategies for including students in the assessment process.

TABLE 15.3

Evaluating the RSVP Characteristics of Different Kinds of Assessment

KIND OF ASSESSMENT	RELIABILITY	STANDARDIZATION	VALIDITY	PRACTICALITY
Informal assessment	A single, brief assessment is not a reliable indicator of achievement. We must look for consistency in a student's performance across time and in different contexts.	Informal observations are rarely, if ever, standardized. Thus, we should not compare one student to another on the basis of informal assessment alone.	Students' "public" behavior in the classroom is not always a valid indicator of their achievement (e.g., some may try to hide high achievement from peers).	Informal assessment is definitely practical: It is flexible and can occur spontaneously during instruction.
Formal paper-pencil assessment	Objectively scorable items are highly reliable. We can enhance the reliability of subjectively scorable items by specifying scoring criteria in concrete terms.	In most instances paper-pencil instruments are easily standardized for all students. Giving students choices (e.g., about topics to write about or questions to answer) may increase motivation, but it reduces standardization.	Using numerous questions that require short, simple responses can make an assessment a more representative sample of the content domain. But tasks requiring lengthier responses may sometimes more closely match objectives.	Paper-pencil assessment is usually practical: All students can be assessed at once, and no special materials are required.
Formal performance assessment	It is often difficult to score performance assessment tasks reliably. We can enhance reliability by specifying scoring criteria in concrete terms.	Some performance assessment tasks are easily standardized, whereas others are not.	Performance tasks may sometimes be more consistent with instructional objectives than paper-pencil tasks. A single performance task may not provide a representative sample of the content domain; several tasks may be necessary to ensure content validity.	Performance assessment is typically less practical than other approaches: It may involve special materials, and it can take a fair amount of class time, especially if students must be assessed one at a time.

INCLUDING STUDENTS IN THE ASSESSMENT PROCESS

Earlier in the chapter we noted that classroom assessments are extrinsic motivators: They provide an externally imposed reason for learning school subject matter and achieving instructional goals. Ideally, however, we want students to be *intrinsically* motivated to learn and achieve in the classroom, and they are more likely to be so if they have some sense of self-determination about classroom activities (see Chapter 12). Furthermore, if students are to become successful self-regulating learners, they must acquire skills in self-monitoring and self-evaluation (see Chapter 10). For such reasons, students should be regular and active participants in the assessment of their learning and performance. As teachers, we should think of assessment as something we do *with* students rather than *to* them.

Students become increasingly skillful in self-assessment as they grow older (van Kraayenoord & Paris, 1997), but even students in the elementary grades have some ability to evaluate their own performance if they have the tools and guidance to do so (e.g., see Figure 15.9 and the "Portfolio" clip on Video CD 1). Following are several strategies for including students in the assessment process and helping them develop important self-monitoring and self-evaluation skills:

■ Observe a second grader assess her progress in writing in the "Portfolio" clip on Video CD 1.

- Make evaluation criteria explicit and easily observable (e.g., the criteria in Figure 15.8 are given to students at the beginning of their "Colonial Economies" activity).
- Provide examples of "good" and "poor" products, and ask students to compare them on the basis of several criteria.
- Solicit students' ideas about evaluation criteria and rubric design.
- Have students compare self-ratings with teacher ratings (e.g., note the "Self" and "Teacher" columns in the word problem rubric in Figure 15.6).
- Have students keep ongoing records of their performance and chart their progress over time.
- Have students reflect on their work in daily or weekly journal entries, where they can keep track of knowledge and skills they have and have not mastered, as well as learning strategies that have and have not been effective.

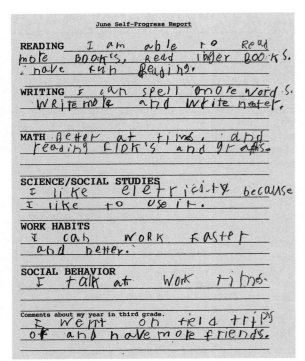

June Self-Progress Report

READING   I am able to Read more BOOK's, Read longer BOOKs. i have fun Reading.

WRITING   I can spell more words. WRite more and WRite neater.

MATH   Better at times, and reading LiBK's and graphs.

SCIENCE/SOCIAL STUDIES   I like eletricity because I like to use it.

WORK HABITS   I can work FASTer and better.

SOCIAL BEHAVIOR   I talk at work time.

Comments about my year in third grade.   I went on field trips of and have more friends.

FIGURE 15.9 At the end of his third-grade year, 9-year-old Philip reviewed his work over the course of the year and identified his strengths and weaknesses.

- Ask students to write practice questions similar to those they expect to see on upcoming quizzes and tests.
- Ask students to lead parent conferences (see Chapter 14, especially Figure 14.5). (A. L. Brown & Campione, 1996; R. L. Linn & Miller, 2005; Paris & Ayres, 1994; L. A. Shepard, 2000; Stiggins, 2001; Valencia et al., 1994)

An additional strategy is having students compile portfolios of their work; we will look at portfolios more closely in Chapter 16.

ENCOURAGING RISK TAKING

Not only should students be actively involved in assessing their own learning and performance, but they should also feel comfortable enough about the assessment process that they feel free to take risks and make mistakes. Only under these circumstances will students tackle the challenging tasks that can maximize their learning and cognitive development (Clifford, 1990). We encourage risk taking—and lower anxiety levels as well—when our assessment strategies give students some leeway to be wrong without penalty (Clifford, 1990). And certainly no single assessment should ever be "sudden death" for those who earn low scores.

Over the years, educators have developed a variety of strategies for encouraging risk taking and ensuring a reasonable comfort level about classroom assessments. Three important ones are frequent assessments, allowing retakes, and providing opportunities to correct errors.

Frequent assessments. Frequent assessment of students' learning and achievement is important for several reasons. First, it provides ongoing information to both students and ourselves about the progress that students are making and about areas of weakness that need attention. Second, students are less likely to experience debilitating anxiety when they have a number of assessments that each contribute only a small amount to their final grades (e.g., Sax, 1989). Third, frequent assessment motivates students, especially those with lower ability, to study regularly (Sax, 1989). Fourth, with the pressure off to perform well on every single test and assignment, students are less likely to cheat to obtain good grades (E. D. Evans & Craig, 1990). The bottom line is that students who are assessed frequently learn and achieve at higher levels than students who are assessed infrequently (Crooks, 1988; Gaynor & Millham, 1976; Glover, 1989).

Retakes. As noted in the discussion of mastery learning in Chapter 13, some students will invariably need more time to master a topic than others and may therefore need to be assessed on the same material more than once. In addition, students are less likely to have debilitating test anxiety when they know they will have a second try at an assessment task if they need one. Yet allowing retakes has disadvantages as well. When students know they can eventually retake an assessment if they get a low score the first time, they may prepare less well than they would otherwise. Furthermore, students who are allowed to retake the *same* instrument may study the specific things that it covers without studying equally important but nonassessed material (remember, most assessment tasks can be only small samples of the domain being assessed).

If we truly want students to master course material but also to take risks in their learning and classroom performance, then we may want to make retakes a regular practice. To encourage students to take the first assessment seriously and to discourage them from focusing only on the content of that assessment as they study for the retake, we can construct two assessment instruments for the same content domain, using one as the initial assessment and the other for retakes. If this strategy will be too time-consuming to be practical, we can allow students to redo the same assessment a second time but then average the two scores earned.

Opportunities to correct errors. Particularly when an assessment includes most or all of the content domain in question, students may learn as much—possibly even more—by correcting the errors they've made on an assessment task. One high school mathematics teacher, Dan Wagner, uses what he calls a *mastery reform* as a way of allowing students to make mistakes and then learn from them. When it is clear from classroom assessments that students haven't demonstrated mastery of a mathematical procedure, Dan has them complete an assignment that includes the following:

1. *Identification of the error.* Students describe in a short paragraph exactly what it is that they do not yet know how to do.
2. *Statement of the process.* Students explain the steps involved in the procedure they are trying to master; in doing so, they must demonstrate their understanding by using words rather than mathematical symbols.
3. *Practice.* Students show their mastery of the procedure with three new problems similar to the problem(s) they previously solved incorrectly.
4. *Statement of mastery.* Students state in a sentence or two that they have now mastered the procedure.

By completing the four prescribed steps, students can replace a grade on a previous assessment with the higher one they earn by attaining mastery. Such assignments can have long-term benefits as well: Dan tells me that many of his students eventually incorporate the four steps into their regular, more internalized learning strategies.

Throughout much of our discussion so far, we have considered what we can learn about our students when we give an assessment. Yet we should also learn something about our assessment practices, as we shall see now.

To encourage risk taking and reduce anxiety about classroom assessments, assess frequently and provide opportunities for students to correct errors. Here a teacher uses a student's errors on a paper-pencil assessment to guide her future studying efforts.

EVALUATING AN ASSESSMENT TOOL THROUGH ITEM ANALYSIS

In the process of scoring students' performance on an assessment instrument, we may discover that some items or tasks simply don't provide the information we had hoped they would. For instance, it may become obvious that one item is not measuring the knowledge or skill we had in mind (a validity problem) and that another is hard to score consistently (a reliability problem that indirectly affects validity as well). We can't always predict ahead of time which items and tasks are going to be good ones and which are not. For this reason, assessment experts frequently recommend an **item analysis** after an assessment has been administered and scored. Such an analysis typically involves an examination of both the difficulty level and discriminative power of each item on the assessment instrument.

Item difficulty. We can determine the difficulty of each item simply by finding out how many students responded to it correctly. The **item difficulty (p)** of an item is the proportion of students responding correctly relative to the total number of students who took the assessment:

$$p = \frac{\text{Number of students getting the item correct}}{\text{Number of students taking the assessment}}$$

This formula yields a number between 0.0 and 1.0. A high p value indicates that the item was a relatively easy one for students; for example, a p of .85 means that 85 percent of the students answered it correctly. A low p value indicates that the item was difficult; for example, a p of .10 means that only 10 percent gave a correct response.

On norm-referenced assessments, p values tell us which items have a difficulty level that is best for comparing the performance of individual students. In this situation, ideal p values are somewhere between .30 and .70, indicating that the items are difficult enough that some, but not all, students get them wrong. In contrast, when almost all students answer an item in the same way—either correctly (a very high p) or incorrectly (a very low p)—we get little if any information about how the students differ from one another.

In contrast, on criterion-referenced assessments, there is no "best" item difficulty value. In this case p values help us determine how effectively we are accomplishing our instructional objectives. If most students have responded to an item correctly, and if we can rule out other factors (e.g., guessing or implausible distractors) that may have contributed to the high success rate, we can conclude that students have mastered the knowledge or skill the item represents. A low p value tells us either that students haven't learned what we are assessing or that the item doesn't accurately reflect what students *did* learn.

Item discrimination. Imagine that you have just given your class a thirty-item multiple-choice test and are scoring students' test papers. You notice that the best students, although they have done well on most of the test, answered question 12 incorrectly. You also notice that several students who got very low test scores got question 12 *correct*. This doesn't make sense: You would expect the students who do well on any one item to be the same ones who perform well on the

■ **item analysis** Post-hoc analysis of patterns in students' responses to various items on an assessment instrument.

■ **item difficulty (p)** Proportion of students getting a particular assessment item correct.

test overall. When the "wrong" students are getting an item correct—when the item "discriminates" among informed and uninformed students inaccurately—we have a problem with **item discrimination (D)**.

Item discrimination (D) is determined using the approach I have just described. More specifically, we identify two groups of students, those who have gotten the highest overall scores and those who have gotten the lowest scores, putting about 20 to 30 percent of the total number of students in each group. We then compare the proportions of students in the two groups getting each item correct, like this:

$$D = \frac{\text{Number of high-scoring}}{\text{Total number of high-scoring students}} - \frac{\text{Number of low-scoring}}{\text{Total number of low-scoring students}}$$

The D formula yields a number ranging from −1.0 to +1.0. Positive D values tell us that a greater proportion of high-scoring students have done well on an item than low-scoring students; in other words, the item discriminates between knowledgeable and unknowledgeable students, which is exactly the situation we want. In contrast, negative D values reflect a situation like that of question 12 on the multiple-choice test described earlier: Low-scoring students are answering the item correctly, but high-scoring students are not. A negative D is often a sign that something is wrong with the item; perhaps it misleads knowledgeable students to choose what was intended to be an incorrect response, or perhaps we have marked an incorrect answer on the answer key.

But let's return to an assumption we made earlier: Students who do well on any single item should be the same ones who perform well overall. Here we are talking about *internal consistency reliability*, the extent to which different parts of an assessment instrument are all measuring more or less the same thing. When the items or tasks on an assessment instrument are all designed to measure very *different* things (as is often true for performance assessment), then D values are less helpful in evaluating an item's effectiveness.

Many teachers save their good assessment items in an item file for use on future occasions. For example, they might paste each item on an index card, with scoring criteria and item analysis data listed on the reverse side, or they might save the items in a specially marked folder on their computer. As they continue to add items to their files over the years, they eventually have a large enough collection that they don't have to use any one item very often.

TAKING STUDENT DIVERSITY INTO ACCOUNT IN CLASSROOM ASSESSMENTS

As we have seen, standardization of assessment instruments and procedures is important for fairness, reliability, and (indirectly) validity in our assessment results. Yet standardization has a downside: It limits our ability to accommodate students' diverse backgrounds and needs, capitalize on their individual strengths, and help them compensate for areas of weakness.

Standardization in classroom assessment practices is essential if, for some reason, we need to compare a student's performance to the performance of others. In many other situations—for example, when we are trying to ascertain appropriate starting points for instruction or specific weaknesses that each student needs to address—standardization is less critical. In some instances, in fact, we may find that the best way of assessing one student's learning is a relatively *in*effective way of assessing another's.

In the upcoming sections we'll look at two areas of individual difference—test anxiety and testwiseness—and a variety of group differences that can affect students' performance on classroom assessments. We'll then consider how we can accommodate the diverse characteristics and abilities of students with special educational needs.

Test Anxiety

How anxious do you get when you know you will be taking a test in class? Do you worry the night before, wondering if you've read all the assigned readings? Do you become nervous while the test is being handed out, fretting that maybe you don't know everything as well as you should? Do you have a lot of trouble remembering things you knew perfectly well when you

■ **item discrimination (D)** Relative proportion of high-scoring and low-scoring students getting a particular assessment item correct.

TABLE 15.4

Keeping Students' Anxiety at a Facilitative Level during Classroom Assessments

WHAT TO DO	WHAT *NOT* TO DO
Point out the value of the assessment as a feedback mechanism to improve learning.	Stress the fact that students' competence is being evaluated.
Administer a practice assessment or pretest that gives students an idea of what the final assessment instrument will be like.	Keep the nature of the assessment a secret until the day it is administered.
Encourage students to do their best.	Remind students that failing will have dire consequences.
Provide or allow the use of memory aids (e.g., a list of formulas or a single note card containing key facts) when instructional goals do not require students to commit information to memory.	Insist that students commit even trivial facts to memory.
Eliminate time limits unless speed is an important part of the skill being measured.	Give more questions or tasks than students can possibly respond to in the time allotted.
Continually survey the room and be available to answer students' questions.	Hover over students, watching them closely as they respond.
Use unannounced ("pop") quizzes only for formative evaluation (e.g., to determine an appropriate starting point for instruction).	Give occasional pop quizzes to motivate students to study regularly and to punish those who do not.
Use the results of several assessments to make decisions (e.g., to assign grades).	Evaluate students on the basis of a single assessment.

Sources: Brophy, 1986; Cizek, 2003; Gaudry & Bradshaw, 1971; K. T. Hill, 1984; K. T. Hill & Wigfield, 1984; Popham, 1990; Sax, 1989; Sieber, Kameya, & Paulson, 1970.

studied them? Do you get in such a panic that you can barely read the test questions at all? If your answer to any of these questions is yes, then you, like most students, experience **test anxiety**.

Students are typically not anxious about learning new knowledge and skills. But as we discovered in Chapter 11, many of them *are* anxious at the thought that they will be evaluated and judged and perhaps found to be "stupid" or in some other way inadequate. A little bit of test anxiety can be a good thing: Students are more likely to prepare for an assessment and to respond to questions and tasks carefully if they are concerned about how well they are going to perform (Shipman & Shipman, 1985). But their performance is apt to be impaired when they are *very* test anxious, particularly when assigned tasks require them to use what they have learned in a flexible and creative manner (Hagtvet & Johnsen, 1992; Kirkland, 1971). In cases of extreme test anxiety, students may have difficulty retrieving things from long-term memory and may not even be able to understand what we are asking them to do.

We will see debilitating test anxiety more frequently in older students, students from some minority groups, and students from lower socioeconomic backgrounds (K. T. Hill, 1984; Kirkland, 1971; Pang, 1995; B. N. Phillips et al., 1980). Often students with the highest test anxiety are those who have performed poorly in school in the past (Kirkland, 1971; Tryon, 1980). An important strategy for helping students overcome excessive test anxiety, then, is to help them master course material in the first place (Covington, 1992; Naveh-Benjamin, 1991; Tryon, 1980).

We don't necessarily want to eliminate test anxiety altogether; we just want to keep it at a facilitative level. Fortunately, we have considerable control over how we administer our own classroom assessment instruments. For example, we can eliminate time limits when we aren't trying to measure how *quickly* students can do something (K. T. Hill & Wigfield, 1984). We can let students use notes or other resources when there is no inherent value in committing certain information (e.g., formulas, trivial facts) to memory (Brophy, 1986; Stipek, 1993). We can describe assessments more as opportunities to increase knowledge and improve skills than as occasions for evaluation (Spaulding, 1992). And by making statements such as "We're here to learn, and you can't do that without making mistakes" (Brophy, 2004, p. 274), we can help students keep a healthy perspective on their imperfections. Table 15.4 distinguishes between classroom assessment practices that are likely to lead to facilitating anxiety and those that may elicit debilitating anxiety.

■ **test anxiety** Excessive anxiety about a particular test or about assessment in general.

Testwiseness

If you did well on the "califractions" quiz I gave you earlier in the chapter, then you have some degree of **testwiseness**: You use test-taking strategies that enhance your test performance. Testwiseness includes strategies such as these:

- *Using time efficiently*—for example, allocating enough time for each task and saving difficult items for last
- *Avoiding sloppy errors*—for example, checking answers a second time and erasing any stray pencil marks on a computer-scored answer sheet
- *Deductive reasoning*—for example, eliminating two alternatives that say the same thing and using information from one question to answer another
- *Guessing*—for example, eliminating obviously wrong alternatives and then guessing one of the others, and guessing randomly if time runs out and there is no penalty for guessing (Millman, Bishop, & Ebel, 1965; Petersen, Sudweeks, & Baird, 1990)

Because you have come as far as you have in our educational system, you probably have considerable testwiseness, in part because you've had a great deal of experience taking a wide variety of tests and other assessments. But we must remember that many students—especially younger ones and those whose prior schooling has been in a different culture—may have had little experience with assessment formats such as true-false and multiple-choice questions. In some instances we may be able to make our classroom assessment tasks similar to those with which students have had previous experience. When this is not possible or appropriate, we should give students ample practice with the format of any test items or performance tasks we use (Popham, 1990).

Accommodating Group Differences

Let's remind ourselves of a few sources of diversity identified in Chapter 4 (remember that these are *average* differences):

- Boys tend to talk more in class than girls.
- Girls tend to work harder on classroom assignments than boys.
- Some students who have been raised in other cultures have only a limited command of English.
- Mainstream Western culture values individual achievement, but students from some cultural backgrounds are more accustomed to working as a group than to working alone.
- Many students raised in mainstream Western culture are quite accustomed to showing others what they know and can do, but students from some cultural backgrounds are accustomed to practicing skills in private until they have achieved mastery.
- Students from very poor families may lack adequate nutrition and health care to perform at their best in the classroom.
- Students at risk for academic failure may find little relevance in academic subject matter for their own lives.

Furthermore, as noted in Chapter 7, students from different backgrounds invariably have different knowledge bases that they use to make sense of new situations and events. All these factors will, of course, affect students' ability to learn and achieve in the classroom. But they may also affect how students perform on our informal and formal assessments *independently* of their learning and achievement. This is just one of the many reasons why we should consider multiple measures—as well as several different kinds of measures—whenever we are using our classroom assessment results to assign grades and make other important decisions. We should also scrutinize our assessment tasks to be sure that they don't unfairly put some students at a disadvantage because of diversity in their life experiences; such inequity reflects *cultural bias*, a concept we'll look at more closely in Chapter 16. Ultimately, our assessment practices must be fair and equitable for students of all backgrounds and groups.

Accommodating Students with Special Needs

In Chapter 5 we discovered that, in the United States, the Individuals with Disabilities Education Act (IDEA) mandates that schools make appropriate accommodations for students with physical, mental, social, or emotional disabilities. This mandate applies not only to our instructional

■ **testwiseness** Test-taking know-how that enhances test performance.

practices but to our assessment practices as well. We may sometimes have to disregard our concern about standardization so that we can gain more *valid* assessments of what students with special needs know and can do.

The specific modifications to assessment instruments and procedures must, of course, be tailored to students' particular disabilities. For example, we may need to read paper-pencil test questions to students with limited reading skills (e.g., to some students with learning disabilities). We may need to break a lengthy assessment task into several shorter tasks for students with a limited attention span (e.g., for some students with ADHD or emotional and behavioral disorders). And we may have to construct individualized assessment instruments when instructional goals differ for some of our students (e.g., as may often be the case for students with mental retardation). Additional accommodations for students with special needs are presented in Table 15.5.

TABLE 15.5   STUDENTS IN INCLUSIVE SETTINGS

Using Classroom Assessments with Students Who Have Special Educational Needs

CATEGORY	CHARACTERISTICS YOU MIGHT OBSERVE	SUGGESTED CLASSROOM STRATEGIES
Students with specific cognitive or academic difficulties	• Poor listening, reading, and/or writing skills • Inconsistent performance due to off-task behaviors (for some students with learning disabilities or ADHD) • Difficulty processing specific kinds of information • Higher than average test anxiety	• Make paper-pencil instruments easy to respond to; for instance, type (rather than hand-write) tests, space items far apart, and have students respond directly on their test papers rather than on separate answer sheets. • Minimize reliance on reading and writing skills if appropriate. • Let students take tests in a quiet place (e.g., the school's resource room). • Give explicit directions. • Be sure students are motivated to do their best but are not overly anxious. • Provide extra time to complete assessments. • Score responses separately for content and quality of writing. • Look at students' errors for clues about processing difficulties. • Use informal assessments to either confirm or disconfirm results of formal assessments.
Students with social or behavioral problems	• Inconsistent performance on classroom assessments due to off-task behaviors or lack of motivation (for some students)	• Make modifications in assessment procedures as necessary (see strategies presented above for students with specific cognitive or academic difficulties). • Use informal assessments to either confirm or disconfirm results of formal classroom assessments.
Students with general delays in cognitive and social functioning	• Slow learning and cognitive processing • Limited if any reading skills • Poor listening skills	• Be explicit about what you are asking students to do. • Make sure any reading materials are appropriate for students' reading level. • Use performance assessments that require little reading or writing. • Allow sufficient time for students to complete assigned tasks.
Students with physical or sensory challenges	• Mobility problems (for some students with physical challenges) • Tendency to tire easily (for some students with physical challenges) • Less developed language abilities (for some students with hearing loss)	• Use written rather than oral assessments (for students with hearing loss). • Minimize reliance on visual materials (for students with visual impairments). • Use appropriate technology to facilitate students' performance. • Provide extra time to complete assessments. • Limit assessments to short time periods, and give frequent breaks. • Use simple language if students have language difficulties.
Students with advanced cognitive development	• Greater ability to perform exceptionally complex tasks • Unusual, sometimes creative, responses to classroom assessment instruments • Tendency in some students to hide giftedness to avoid possible ridicule by peers	• Use performance assessments to assess complex activities. • Establish scoring criteria that allow unusual and creative responses. • Provide opportunities for students to demonstrate their achievements privately. • Keep assessment results confidential.

Sources: Barkley, 1998; Beirne-Smith et al. 2002; D. Y. Ford & Harris, 1992; Mercer, 1997; D. P. Morgan & Jenson, 1988; Piirto, 1999; R. Turnbull et al., 2004.

THE BIG PICTURE

We must give considerable thought to how we can best determine what students are learning and devote considerable time and effort to designing assessment instruments. Let's review the ways in which our assessment practices are likely to affect students' learning and motivation. We will then identify several general strategies that can guide our classroom assessment practices.

LEARNING, MOTIVATION, AND ASSESSMENT

Our assessments will indirectly affect students' learning and achievement through their influences on planning, instruction, and the classroom environment. But they will also have several more direct effects on learning and motivation:

- They will communicate messages about how students should study and what things are most important to learn.
- They will convey impressions about the nature of an academic discipline (e. g., whether it is a collection of discrete facts or an integrated body of knowledge).
- They will provide opportunities for students to review, practice, and apply what they've learned.
- They will give feedback that can foster improvement.
- If students play an active role in the assessment process, assessments can enhance self-regulation skills.
- They may foster a focus on either performance goals (if any single assessment has major consequences) or mastery goals (if assessments are treated as mechanisms for helping students learn and if students have input into the assessment criteria).
- They may encourage students either to strive for increasingly complex knowledge and skills (if they are challenging yet take students' existing abilities into account) or to lose interest in classroom subject matter (if they are too easy or exceptionally difficult).
- They can either enhance or diminish self-efficacy for academic subject matter, depending not only on whether students perform well or poorly on them but also on whether they provide concrete feedback that helps students improve.

As we develop our classroom assessment instruments, then, we should continually ask ourselves questions such as these:

- Do our assessment tasks reflect knowledge and skills essential for students' long-term academic and personal success?
- Are our scoring criteria stringent enough to ensure that important instructional goals are achieved yet not so stringent that success is impossible?
- Do our assessment practices allow students to take risks and make mistakes as they study and learn?
- Are we involving students in assessing their own performance often enough that they are acquiring the skills they will ultimately need to be self-regulating learners?

GENERAL GUIDELINES FOR CLASSROOM ASSESSMENT

Following are several general suggestions that should apply to any assessment:

◎ *Match assessment instruments and practices to important instructional goals and objectives.* Classroom assessments are worthless if they don't tell us what we really need to know. In fact, they're counterproductive if they encourage students to adopt ineffective learning strategies (e.g., memorization of isolated facts) rather than strategies and processes that are likely to serve them well over the long run.

◎ *Consider the RSVP characteristics of every assessment.* Informal assessment, paper-pencil assessment, and performance assessment have different strengths and weaknesses. Informal assessments are practical, in that they take little time and effort, but they are rarely standardized and may not be reliable or valid reflections of more general characteristics and achievements. Paper-pencil assessment instruments with recognition items (e.g., multiple-choice) are easily standardized and can be both reliable and practical; when writing such items, however, many teachers focus primarily on knowledge of basic facts, limiting validity for assessing higher-level processes. More open-ended types of paper-pencil tasks lend themselves more readily to measuring higher-level skills (especially when they involve extended responses), but often at the expense of reliability and practicality. Performance assessments are typically less reliable and practical than paper-pencil assessments, yet they may be the only valid means of measuring some types of knowledge and skills. Clearly, then, we will have difficulty maximizing all four RSVP characteristics at once. Our ultimate concern must be *content validity*: Assessment tasks should provide a representative sample of what students have accomplished relative to our instructional objectives.

◎ *Specify scoring criteria as explicitly as possible.* When scoring criteria are explicit, we can evaluate students' responses more reliably and can more easily determine whether students are achieving instructional objectives. Meanwhile, students have clear targets to shoot for as they study and practice.

◎ *Look at students' errors for clues about where their difficulties lie.* Knowing where students are having difficulty is often more useful than knowing what they do well, provided that we use their errors as a guide for helping them improve.

◎ *Evaluate assessment instruments after the fact.* Even after considerable experience we may occasionally write items that students misinterpret (as reflected in low p or D values in an item analysis) and identify scoring criteria that don't adequately capture the knowledge and skills we want to assess. Ultimately we must learn from our mistakes and be careful not to make the same ones in future assessments.

Learning how to develop good classroom assessments may be one of your most challenging tasks as a teacher, and you, too, will make mistakes as you go along. The ending case study indicates just how much one teacher still has to learn.

CASE STUDY: *Pick and Choose*

Knowing that frequent review of class material leads to higher achievement and that a paper-pencil test is one way of providing such review, Mr. Bloskas tells his middle school science students that they will have a quiz every Friday. As a first-year teacher, he has had little experience developing test questions, so he decides to use the questions in the test bank that accompanies the class textbook. The night before the first quiz, Mr. Bloskas types thirty multiple-choice and true-false items from the test bank, making sure they cover the specific topics that he has covered in class.

His students complain that the questions are "picky." As he looks carefully at his quiz, he realizes that the students are right: The quiz measures nothing more than memorization of trivial details. So when he prepares the second quiz, Mr. Bloskas casts the test bank aside and writes two essay questions asking students to apply scientific principles they have studied to real-life situations. He's proud of his efforts: His quiz clearly assesses higher-level thinking skills.

The following Friday, his students complain even more loudly about the second quiz than they had about the first ("This is too hard!" "We never studied this stuff!" "I liked the first quiz better!"). As Mr. Bloskas scores the essays, he is appalled to discover how poorly his students have performed. "Back to the test bank," he tells himself.

- What mistakes does Mr. Bloskas make in developing the first quiz? What mistakes does he make in developing the second quiz? Are the quizzes likely to have content validity? Why or why not?

- Why do the students react as negatively as they do to the second quiz?

Once you have answered these questions, compare your responses with those presented in Appendix B.

KEY CONCEPTS

assessment (p. 524)
informal assessment (p. 525)
formal assessment (p. 525)
paper-pencil assessment (p. 525)
performance assessment (p. 525)
traditional assessment (p. 526)
authentic assessment (p. 526)
standardized test (p. 526)
teacher-developed assessment instrument (p. 526)
criterion-referenced assessment (p. 526)
norm-referenced assessment (p. 526)
formative evaluation (p. 527)
summative evaluation (p. 527)

reliability (p. 531)
reliability coefficient (p. 533)
standard error of measurement (SEM) (p. 533)
true score (p. 533)
confidence interval (p. 533)
standardization (p. 534)
validity (p. 534)
content validity (p. 535)
table of specifications (p. 535)
predictive validity (p. 537)
validity coefficient (p. 537)
construct validity (p. 538)
practicality (p. 538)
halo effect (p. 540)

recognition task (p. 541)
recall task (p. 541)
test bank (p. 544)
rubric (p. 551)
dynamic assessment (p. 554)
checklist (p. 556)
rating scale (p. 556)
analytic scoring (p. 556)
holistic scoring (p. 556)
item analysis (p. 563)
item difficulty (p) (p. 563)
item discrimination (D) (p. 564)
test anxiety (p. 565)
testwiseness (p. 566)

PRAXIS Turn to Appendix C, "Matching Book and Ancillary Content to the Praxis Principles of Learning and Teaching Tests," to discover sections of this chapter that may be especially applicable to the Praxis tests.

Now go to our Companion Website at **www.prenhall.com/ormrod** to assess your understanding of chapter content with "Multiple-Choice Questions," apply comprehension in "Essay Questions," broaden your knowledge of educational psychology with related "Web Links," gain greater insight about classroom learning in "Learning in the Content Areas," and analyze and assess classroom work in the "Student Artifact Library."

Chapter 16
Summarizing Student Achievement

Think about the final course grades you've gotten over the years. What do they say about what you've achieved in your classes? What do they *not* say about your achievement? Do you think your high school and college grade point averages are good indications of how much you've learned so far? Why or why not?

As teachers, we lose a great deal of information whenever we summarize students' learning as a single course grade, and we lose even more when we combine each student's course grades into a single grade point average (Delandshere & Petrosky, 1998). But for purposes of educational decision making—determining which students move forward to the next grade level, which ones earn their high school diplomas, which ones go on to highly selective universities, and so on—we must summarize students' accomplishments in some way. It would be highly impractical to list everything that each student knows and can do, because we would spend all our time keeping records rather than helping students learn.

In this chapter we'll explore several ways of summarizing achievement. We'll begin by looking at how we might combine the information obtained from a single assessment into an overall test score. We'll then look at three widely used ways of summarizing students' achievement over a lengthy period: course grades, portfolios, and standardized test scores. Finally, we'll identify the circumstances under which we can communicate students' assessment results to others. As we address these topics, we'll answer the following questions:

- In what various ways might we represent students' performance on an assessment as a single score?
- What advice do experts offer about how best to compute final class grades?
- What forms might portfolios take, and what purposes might they serve?
- What kinds of tests are available from test publishers, and what information can they give us?
- What are the ramifications of using standardized tests to hold students and teachers accountable for classroom learning?
- How can we accommodate group differences and special educational needs when we administer standardized tests?
- Who should know the results of students' performance on tests and other assessments, and how can we best communicate those results?

CASE STUDY: *B in History*

Twelve-year-old Ellie is the top student in Ms. Davidson's sixth-grade class at West Elementary School. She is very bright, highly motivated, and quite conscientious about completing her in-class work and homework assignments. It's not surprising, then, that Ellie has consistently earned straight As on report cards in previous years.

At the end of the school day one Friday in mid-November, Ms. Davidson tells her class, "As you all know, our first-quarter grading period ended last week. Today I have your report cards to take home to your parents. I'm especially proud of one student who always puts forth her best effort, and her grades are almost perfect." She smiles at Ellie with obvious affection and hands her a report card. "Here you are. Just one B, Ellie, in history. I'm sure you'll be able to bring it up to an A next quarter."

Despite the praise, Ellie seems devastated. She is blindsided by the B in history; she has had no idea it was coming. She successfully fights back the tears but looks down at her desk while Ms. Davidson distributes the other report cards. When the final school bell rings, she quickly gathers her coat and books and heads out the door, foregoing the usual after-school good-byes to her friends.

- Why might Ellie be so upset? Can you think of at least two possible explanations?
- Was it appropriate for Ms. Davidson to announce Ellie's grades to the class? Why or why not?

REVISITING SELF-REGULATION AND THE RSVP CHARACTERISTICS

Although Ellie knows she's made occasional errors on history quizzes and assignments, she's apparently been unaware of how those errors might add up to a B rather than an A. And with her past straight-A record, she's set an extremely high standard for herself. Only perfection is good enough—an unrealistic standard that characterizes perhaps 25 percent of high-achieving sixth graders (Parker, 1997). In addition, Ms. Davidson has announced Ellie's imperfection to the entire class. As a young adolescent, Ellie is not sure which is worse: that her peers know she's gotten the highest grades in the class or that they know she's *not* perfect in history. As we'll discover near the end of the chapter, announcing a student's grades violates the student's right to confidentiality.

Did you wonder if Ellie's parents might impose harsh consequences for the B? Although some overly perfectionist parents certainly would, in fact Ellie's parents are perfectly comfortable with their daughter's getting an occasional B. (They are far more concerned about Ellie's younger brother, a second grader who is still struggling with reading and probably has an undiagnosed learning disability.) Ellie's high standards for achievement are entirely self-imposed, perhaps in part because she's been able to meet them in past years when the subject matter has been less challenging. Although setting high goals is certainly commendable, students' goals must also be attainable. Perfection rarely *is* attainable, and it precludes the errors that are an inevitable part of mastering challenging tasks.

However we summarize students' achievement, our summaries should never come as a surprise. Throughout the school year students should have a good idea of how they are progressing and how their achievement is likely to be reflected in test scores and overall class grades. As we have seen in earlier chapters, it is essential that we include students in the assessment process; in doing so, we teach them how to monitor and evaluate their own performance and so help them acquire important self-regulation skills.

In choosing a way to summarize achievement, it is equally important that we consider the four RSVP characteristics. In particular, an overall indicator of achievement should be *reliable*, reflecting a consistent pattern of achievement rather than a rare, chance occurrence. It should be *standardized*: Except for extenuating circumstances (e.g., for certain students who have been identified as having special needs), the same criteria should apply to everyone. It should be *valid*; that is, it should accurately reflect what students have learned and achieved. And finally, it must be *practical* in terms of the time and effort it requires.

Our first order of business in this chapter is to consider how we might summarize students' performance on a single assessment instrument. After that, we'll consider ways to summarize students' achievement on a broader scale.

SUMMARIZING THE RESULTS OF A SINGLE ASSESSMENT

One way to summarize the results of a single assessment instrument is to condense them into a brief verbal description of what things a student has done well and what things the student needs to work on. Such a description can capture the multidimensional nature of a student's performance and provide the feedback students ultimately need to gain greater mastery of a content domain. If done regularly, however, writing summaries of every student's performance on every classroom assessment would be extremely time-consuming (a practicality issue). More often, teachers use numbers or letter grades to summarize how students have performed on individual classroom assessments. To simplify our discussion, we'll focus on numbers, which we'll call *scores*. But we should keep in mind that teachers frequently use scores to assign letter grades, and they sometimes translate letter grades into numbers they can later use to compute final class grades.

Scores on individual assessments, whether teacher-developed instruments or standardized tests, typically take one of three forms described in Table 16.1: raw scores, criterion-referenced scores, and norm-referenced scores.

Raw Scores

Sometimes a score is simply the number or percentage of items to which a student has responded correctly. At other times it is the sum of the points a student has earned for various items (2 points for one item, 5 for another, etc.). A score based solely on the number or point value of correct responses is a **raw score**.

■ **raw score** Score based solely on the number or point value of correctly answered items.

TABLE 16.1

Summarizing the Results of an Assessment with a Single Score

TYPE OF SCORE	HOW SCORE IS DETERMINED	USES	POTENTIAL DRAWBACKS
Raw score	By counting the number (or calculating a percentage) of correct responses or points earned	Often used in teacher-developed assessment instruments	Scores may be difficult to interpret without knowledge of how performance relates either to a specific criterion or to a norm group.
Criterion-referenced score	By comparing performance to one or more criteria or standards for success	Useful when determining whether specific instructional objectives or standards have been achieved	Concrete criteria for assessing mastery of complex skills are sometimes difficult to identify.
Age or grade equivalent (norm-referenced)	By equating a student's performance to the average performance of students at a particular age or grade level	Useful when explaining norm-referenced test performance to people unfamiliar with standard scores	Scores are frequently misinterpreted, especially by parents; may be inappropriately used as a standard that all students must meet; are often inapplicable when achievement at the secondary level or higher is being assessed.
Percentile rank (norm-referenced)	By determining the percentage of students at the same age or grade level who obtained lower scores	Useful when explaining norm-referenced test performance to people unfamiliar with standard scores	Scores overestimate differences near the mean and underestimate differences at the extremes.
Standard score (norm-referenced)	By determining how far the performance is from the mean (for the age or grade level) with respect to standard deviation units	Useful when describing a student's standing within the norm group	Scores are not easily understood by people who don't have some basic knowledge of statistics.

Raw scores are easy to calculate, and they appear to be easy to understand. But in fact, we sometimes have trouble knowing what raw scores really mean. Is 75 percent a good score or a bad one? Without knowing what kinds of tasks an assessment instrument includes or how other students have performed on the same assessment, we have no way to determine how good or bad a score of 75 percent really is. For this reason, raw scores are not always as useful as criterion-referenced or norm-referenced scores.

Criterion-Referenced Scores

As you might guess, criterion-referenced scores and norm-referenced scores are used, respectively, with criterion-referenced and norm-referenced assessment instruments. More specifically, a **criterion-referenced score** tells us what students have achieved in relation to specific instructional objectives or standards. Many criterion-referenced scores are "either-or" scores: They indicate that a student has passed or failed a unit, mastered or not mastered a skill, or met or not met an objective. Others indicate various levels of competence or achievement. For example, a criterion-referenced score on a fifth-grade test of written composition might reflect four levels of writing ability, three of which reflect mastery of essential writing skills, as follows:

In Progress: Is an underdeveloped and/or unfocused message.

Essential: Is a series of related ideas. The pattern of organization and the descriptive or supporting details are adequate and appropriate.

Proficient: Meets Essential Level criteria and contains a logical progression of ideas. The pattern of organization and the transition of ideas flow. Word choice enhances the writing.

Advanced: Meets Proficient Level criteria and contains examples of one or more of the following: insight, creativity, fluency, critical thinking, or style. (adapted from "District 6 Writing Assessment, Narrative and Persuasive Modes, Scoring Criteria, Intermediate Level" [Working Copy] by School District 6 [Greeley/Evans, CO], 1993; adapted by permission)

If a particular assessment instrument is designed to assess only one instructional objective or standard, then it may yield a single score. If it is designed to assess several areas of achievement

■ **criterion-referenced score** Score that specifically indicates what a student knows or can do.

Springside Parks and Recreation Department Beginner Swimmer Class

Students must demonstrate proficiency in each of the following:

☐ Jump into chest-deep water
☐ Hold breath under water for 8 seconds
☐ Float in prone position for 10 seconds
☐ Glide in prone position with flutter kick
☐ Float on back for 10 seconds
☐ Glide on back with flutter kick
☐ Demonstrate crawl stroke and rhythmic breathing while standing in chest-deep water
☐ Show knowledge of basic water safety rules

FIGURE 16.1 In this swimming class, students' performance is reported in a criterion-referenced fashion.

FIGURE 16.2 Hypothetical norm-group data for the Reading Achievement Test (RAT)

Norms for Grade Levels		Norms for Age Levels	
Grade	Average Raw Score	Age	Average Raw Score
5	19	10	18
6	25	11	24
7	30	12	28
8	34	13	33
9	39	14	37
10	43	15	41
11	46	16	44
12	50	17	48

■ **norm-referenced score** Score that indicates how a student's performance on an assessment compares with the average performance of peers.

■ **norms** Data regarding the typical performance of various groups of students on a standardized test or other norm-referenced assessment.

■ **grade-equivalent score** Score indicating the grade level of students to whom a student's performance is most similar.

■ **age-equivalent score** Score indicating the age level of students to whom a student's performance is most similar.

■ **percentile rank (percentile)** Score indicating the percentage of peers in the norm group getting a raw score less than or equal to a particular student's raw score.

simultaneously, a student's performance may be reported as a list of the various skills mastered and not mastered. As an example, a student's performance in a swimming class is often reported in a criterion-referenced fashion (see Figure 16.1).

We will often want to use a criterion-referenced approach to summarize what students have learned, especially when assessing basic skills that are essential prerequisites for later learning. Only through criterion-referenced assessment can we determine what specific objectives students have attained, what particular skills they have mastered, and where their individual weaknesses lie.

Norm-Referenced Scores

A **norm-referenced score** is derived by comparing a student's performance on an assessment with the performance of others, perhaps that of classmates or that of age-mates or grade-mates in a nationwide *norm group*. The set of scores obtained from the comparison group comprises the **norms** for the assessment. A norm-referenced score tells us little about what a student specifically knows and can do; instead, it tells us whether a student's performance is typical or unusual for the age or grade level.

We may occasionally find it appropriate to use norm-referenced scores for the assessment instruments we develop for our own classrooms (more about this point shortly). Furthermore, most scores on published standardized tests are norm-referenced scores. In some cases the scores are derived by comparing a student's performance with the performance of students at a variety of grade or age levels; such comparisons give us grade or age equivalents. In other cases the scores are based on comparisons only with students of the *same* age or grade; these comparisons give us either percentile scores or standard scores.

Grade-Equivalent and Age-Equivalent Scores Imagine that Shawn takes a standardized test, the Reading Achievement Test (RAT). He gets 46 of the 60 test items correct; thus 46 is his raw score. We turn to the norms reported in the test manual and find the average raw scores for students at different grade and age levels, shown in Figure 16.2. Shawn's raw score of 46 is the same as the average score of eleventh graders in the norm group, so he has a **grade-equivalent score** of 11. His score is halfway between the average score of 16-year-old and 17-year-old students, so he has an **age-equivalent score** of about 16½. Shawn is 13 years old and in eighth grade, so he has obviously done well on the RAT.

More generally, grade- and age-equivalent scores are determined by matching a student's raw score to a particular grade or age level in the norm group. A student who performs as well as the average second grader on a reading test will get a grade-equivalent score of 2, regardless of what grade level the student is actually in. A student who gets the same raw score as the average 10-year-old on a physical fitness test will get an age-equivalent score of 10, regardless of whether that student is 5, 10, or 15 years old.

Grade- and age-equivalent scores are frequently used because they seem so simple and straightforward. But they have a serious drawback: They give us no idea of the typical *range* of performance for students at a particular grade or age level. For example, a raw score of 34 on the RAT gives us a grade-equivalent score of 8, but obviously not all eighth graders will get raw scores of exactly 34. It is possible, and in fact quite likely, that many "normal" eighth graders will get raw scores several points above or below 34, thus getting a grade-equivalent score of 9 or 7 (perhaps even 10 or higher, or 6 or lower). Yet grade-equivalent scores are often used inappropriately as a standard for performance: Parents, school personnel, government officials, and the public at large may believe that *all* students should perform at grade level on an achievement test. Given the normal variability within most classrooms, this goal is probably impossible to meet.

Percentile Ranks A different approach is to compare students only with others at the same age or grade level. One way of making such a peer-based comparison is using a **percentile rank**: the percentage of people getting a raw score less than or equal to the student's raw score. (Such a score is sometimes known simply as a *percentile*.) To illustrate, let's once again consider Shawn's performance on the RAT. Because Shawn is in eighth grade, we would turn to the eighth-grade norms in the RAT test manual. Perhaps we discover that a raw score of 46 is at the 98th percentile for eighth graders. This means that Shawn has done as well as or better than 98 percent of eighth graders in the norm group. Similarly, a student getting a percentile rank of 25 has performed better than 25 percent of the norm group, and a student getting a score at the 60th percentile has done better than 60 percent. It is important to note that percentile ranks refer to a percentage of *people*, not to the percentage of correct items—a common misconception among teacher education students (Lennon et al., 1990).

Because percentile ranks are relatively simple to understand, they are used frequently in reporting test results. But they have a major weakness: They distort actual differences among students. As an illustration, consider the percentile ranks of these four boys on the RAT:

Student	Percentile Rank
Ernest	45
Frank	55
Giorgio	89
Wayne	99

In *actual achievement* (as measured by the RAT), Ernest and Frank are probably very similar to one another even though their percentile ranks are 10 points apart. Yet a 10-point difference at the upper end of the scale probably reflects a substantial difference in achievement: Giorgio's percentile rank of 89 tells us that he knows quite a bit, but Wayne's percentile rank of 99 tells us that he knows an exceptional amount. In general, percentiles tend to *over*estimate differences in the middle range of the characteristic being measured: Scores a few points apart reflect similar achievement or ability. Meanwhile, they *under*estimate differences at the lower and upper extremes: Scores only a few points apart often reflect significant differences in achievement or ability. We avoid this problem when we use standard scores.

Standard Scores   The school nurse measures the heights of all 25 students in Ms. Oppenheimer's third-grade class. The students' heights are presented on the left side of Figure 16.3. The nurse then makes a graph of the children's heights, as you can see on the right side of Figure 16.3. Notice that the graph is high in the middle and low on both ends. This shape tells us that most of Ms. Oppenheimer's students are more or less average in height, with only a handful of very short students (e.g., Pat, Amy, and Wil) and just a few very tall ones (e.g., Hal, Roy, and Jan).

Many psychologists believe that educational and psychological characteristics (including academic achievement and abilities) typically follow the same pattern we see for height: Most people are close to average, with fewer and fewer people as we move farther from this average. This theoretical pattern of educational and psychological characteristics, known as the **normal distribution** (or **normal curve**), is shown to the right. **Standard scores** are test scores that reflect this normal distribution: Many students get scores in the middle range, and only a few get very high or very low scores.

Before we examine standard scores in more detail, we need to understand two numbers used to derive these scores—the mean and standard deviation. The **mean (M)** is the average of a set of scores: We add all the scores together and divide by the total number of scores (or people). For example, if we add the heights of all 25 students in Ms. Oppenheimer's class and then divide by 25, we get a mean height of 50 inches (see the calculation at the bottom of Figure 16.3).

The **standard deviation (SD)** indicates the *variability* of a set of scores. A small number tells us that, generally speaking, the scores are close together, and a large number tells us that they are

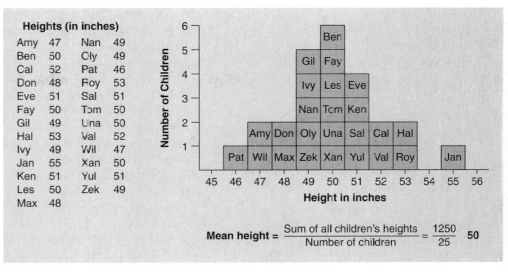

Heights (in inches)			
Amy	47	Nan	49
Ben	50	Cly	49
Cal	52	Pat	46
Don	48	Roy	53
Eve	51	Sal	51
Fay	50	Tom	50
Gil	49	Una	50
Hal	53	Val	52
Ivy	49	Wil	47
Jan	55	Xan	50
Ken	51	Yul	51
Les	50	Zek	49
Max	48		

$$\text{Mean height} = \frac{\text{Sum of all children's heights}}{\text{Number of children}} = \frac{1250}{25} = 50$$

FIGURE 16.3   Heights of children in Ms. Oppenheimer's third-grade class

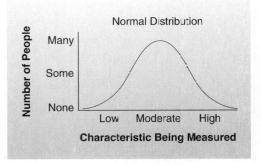

- **normal distribution (normal curve)** Theoretical pattern of educational and psychological characteristics in which most individuals lie in the middle range and only a few lie at either extreme.

- **standard score** Score that indicates how far a student's performance is from the mean with respect to standard deviation units.

- **mean (M)** Mathematical average of a set of scores.

- **standard deviation (SD)** Statistic indicating the variability of a set of scores.

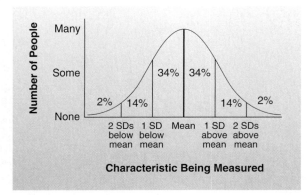

FIGURE 16.4 Normal distribution divided by the mean and standard deviation

spread far apart. For example, third graders tend to be more similar in height than eighth graders (some eighth graders are less than five feet tall, whereas others may be almost six feet tall). The standard deviation for the heights of third graders is therefore smaller than the standard deviation for the heights of eighth graders. The procedure for computing a standard deviation is more complex than that for computing a mean. If you are curious, you can find the details in the supplementary reading "Calculating Standard Deviations" in the *Study Guide and Reader* that accompanies this book.

The mean and standard deviation can be used to divide the normal distribution into several parts, as shown in Figure 16.4. The vertical line at the middle of the curve shows the mean; for a normal distribution, it is at the midpoint and highest point of the curve. The thinner lines to either side reflect the standard deviation: We count out a standard deviation's worth higher and lower than the mean and mark those spots with two lines, and then count another standard deviation to either side and draw two more lines. When we divide the normal distribution in this way, the percentages of students getting scores in each part are always the same. Approximately two-thirds (68%) get scores within one standard deviation of the mean (34% in each direction). As we go farther away from the mean, we find fewer and fewer students, with 28 percent lying between one and two standard deviations away (14% on each side) and only 4 percent being more than two standard deviations away (2% at each end).

Now that we better understand the normal distribution and two statistics that describe it, let's return to standard scores. A standard score reflects a student's position in the normal distribution: It tells us how far the student's performance is from the mean with respect to standard deviation units. Unfortunately, not all standard scores use the same scale: Different scores have different means and standard deviations. Four commonly used standard scores, depicted graphically in Figure 16.5, are the following:

- **IQ scores.** IQ scores are frequently used to report students' performance on intelligence tests. They have a *mean of 100* and, for most tests, a *standard deviation of 15*. (If you look back at Figure 5.1 in Chapter 5, you'll see that I've broken that curve up by thirds of a standard deviation unit. The lines for 85 and 115 reflect one standard deviation from the mean; those for 70 and 130 reflect two SDs from the mean.)

- **ETS scores.** ETS scores are used on tests published by the Educational Testing Service, such as the Scholastic Assessment Test (SAT) and the Graduate Record Examination (GRE). They have a *mean of 500* and a *standard deviation of 100*; however, no scores fall below 200 or above 800.

■ **IQ score** Standard score with a mean of 100 and a standard deviation of 15.

■ **ETS score** Standard score with a mean of 500 and a standard deviation of 100.

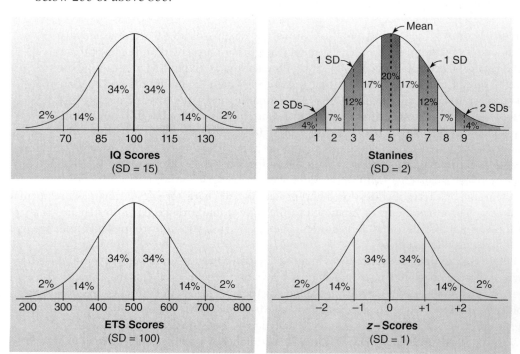

FIGURE 16.5 Distributions of four types of standard scores

- **Stanines.** Stanines (short for *standard nines*) are often used to report standardized achievement test results. They have a *mean of 5* and a *standard deviation of 2*. Because they are always reported as whole numbers, each score reflects a *range* of test performance (reflected by the shaded and nonshaded portions of the upper right-hand curve in Figure 16.5).
- **z-scores.** Standard scores known as z-scores are often used by statisticians. They have a *mean of 0* and a *standard deviation of 1*.

Using Criterion-Referenced Versus Norm-Referenced Scores in the Classroom

For teacher-developed assessments, norm-referenced scores may occasionally be appropriate. Such comparative scores may be necessary when designating "first chair" in an instrumental music class or choosing the best entries for a regional science fair. We may also need to resort to a norm-referenced approach when assessing complex skills that are difficult to describe as "mastered." Some complex tasks—for example, writing poetry, demonstrating advanced athletic skills, or critically analyzing works of literature—can sometimes be evaluated more easily by comparing students with one another than by specifying an absolute level of accomplishment. When we assign norm-referenced scores on teacher-developed assessment instruments, the norm group is likely to be all the students in a class: We give high scores to students who exhibit the best performance and low scores to students who, comparatively speaking, perform poorly. To use common lingo, we are "grading on the curve."

Most experts urge us to use criterion-referenced scores more frequently than norm-referenced scores when evaluating students' work. Why are criterion-referenced scores usually a better choice?

We should probably *not* use norm-referenced scores on a regular basis, however. For one thing, they create a competitive situation: Students do well only if their performance surpasses that of their classmates. As we discovered in Chapters 10 and 12, competitive situations create many more losers than winners and so are likely to undermine students' self-efficacy and intrinsic motivation to learn classroom material. Norm-referenced scores also focus students' attention primarily on performance goals—and may possibly encourage them to cheat on assessment tasks—rather than on mastery goals (E. M. Anderman et al., 1998; Mac Iver et al., 1995). Furthermore, they are inconsistent with the *sense of community* discussed in Chapter 14.

In most instances criterion-referenced scores communicate what teachers and students alike most need to know: whether instructional objectives and content area standards have been achieved. In doing so, they focus attention on mastery goals and, by showing improvement over time, should enhance students' self-efficacy for learning academic subject matter.

■ Some educators believe that classroom assessment scores should *always* be criterion-referenced. What do you think?

Eventually, of course, we must boil down classroom assessment results and other information we've gathered into more general indicators of what students have learned and achieved. Two widely used approaches are *final class grades* and *portfolios*.

DETERMINING FINAL CLASS GRADES

Over the years, teachers' grading practices have been a source of considerable controversy. Fueling the fire are several problems inherent in traditional grading procedures. First, because individual assessment instruments have less than perfect validity and reliability, grades based on these measures may also be somewhat inaccurate. Second, different teachers use different criteria to assign grades; for instance, some are more lenient than others, and some stress rote memorization whereas others stress higher-level skills. Third, in heterogeneous classes (e.g., those that include students from diverse backgrounds and students with special educational needs), different students may be working to accomplish different instructional goals. Fourth, typical grading practices promote performance goals rather than mastery goals and may encourage students to go for the "easy A" rather than take risks (Stipek, 1993; S. Thomas & Oldfather, 1997). Finally, students under pressure to achieve high grades may resort to undesirable behaviors (e.g., cheating, plagiarism) to attain those grades (Cizek, 2003).

Despite such problems, final grades continue to be the most common method of summarizing students' classroom achievement, in large part because school districts need an economical way of keeping track of students' overall performance to assist in decision making and communication with parents and colleges (e.g., Cizek, 2003). As teachers, we can take several steps to ensure that the grades we assign are as accurate a reflection of what each student has accomplished as we can possibly make them:

◎ *Take the job of grading seriously.* Consider these scenarios:

- A high school mathematics teacher who uses a formula to determine final grades makes numerous errors in his calculations. As a result, some students get lower grades than they've earned.

■ **stanine** Standard score with a mean of 5 and a standard deviation of 2.

■ **z-score** Standard score with a mean of 0 and a standard deviation of 1.

- A middle school Spanish teacher asks her teenage son to calculate her students' final grades. Some of the columns in her grade book are for scores students have earned when they've taken a test a second time to improve their record; students who did well on exams the first time have blanks in these columns. Not understanding the teacher's system, her son treats all blank spaces as a "zero." The highest achievers—those students who have many blank spots in the teacher's grade book—are quite surprised to discover that they've earned a D or F for the semester.

■ What are students likely to conclude about these two teachers?

A mathematics teacher who makes mathematical errors? A Spanish teacher who relies on a teenager to determine final grades? Preposterous? No, both scenarios are true stories. Here we have teachers who assign grades that are totally meaningless. Students' final class grades are often the *only* data that appear in their school records. We must take the time and make the effort to ensure that those grades are accurate.

Many computer software packages are now available to assist with record keeping and grading. In addition to helping us keep track of a sizable body of assessment information, such software makes it easier to share our records with students regularly (e.g., see Figure 16.6). We cannot use grading software mindlessly, however. For example, if we make errors when entering information or don't take into account the idiosyncrasies of our record-keeping system, we might as well have the Spanish teacher's son calculate our grades for us!

◎ *Base grades on achievement.* Tempting as it might be to reward well-behaved, cooperative students with good grades and punish chronic misbehavers with Ds or Fs, we must remember that grades should reflect how much students have *learned.* Awarding good grades simply for good behavior may mislead students and their parents to believe that students are making better progress than they actually are (Brookhart, 2004). Awarding low grades as punishment for disruptive behavior leads students to conclude—perhaps with good reason—that their teacher's grading system is arbitrary and meaningless (Cizek, 2003).

◎ *Base grades on hard data.* Subjective teacher judgments typically correlate with actual student achievement, but they are imperfect assessments at best, and some teachers are better judges than others (Gaines & Davis, 1990; Hoge & Coladarci, 1989). Furthermore, although teachers can generally judge the achievement of high-ability students with some accuracy, they are less accurate when they subjectively assess the achievement of low-ability students (Hoge & Coladarci, 1989). Teachers are especially likely to underestimate the achievement of students from minority groups and those from low socioeconomic backgrounds (Gaines & Davis, 1990). For these reasons and for the sake of our students (who learn more and achieve at higher levels when we tell them what we expect in concrete terms), we should base grades on objective and observable information derived from formal assessment instruments, *not* from our subjective impressions of how well students have done in our classes.

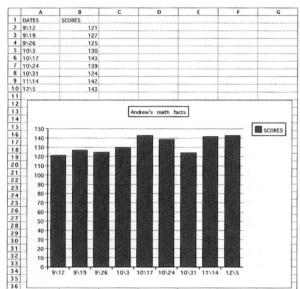

FIGURE 16.6 Computer software can often help us keep track of students' performance on classroom assessments. Here we see 10-year-old Andrew's performance on regular quizzes of math facts. Each quiz is worth 150 points.

◎ *Be selective about the assessments used to determine grades.* Using multiple assessments to determine final grades can help us compensate for the imperfect reliability and validity of any single assessment instrument. At the same time, we probably don't want to consider everything students do. As noted in the preceding chapter, we must create an atmosphere in which students feel free to take risks and make mistakes. Thus we may not want to include students' early efforts at new tasks, which are likely to involve some trial and error on their part (Brookhart, 2004; Canady & Hotchkiss, 1989). And many assessments may be more appropriately used for formative evaluation purposes—to help students learn—than for summative evaluation (Frisbie & Waltman, 1992).

◎ *Identify a reasonable grading system and stick to it.* Consider this situation:

Ms. Giroux tells her middle school students that class grades will be based solely on quiz and test scores throughout the semester. After a couple of months, she realizes that most students are struggling with her exams and will probably get Ds or Fs as a result. So near the end of the semester, she asks students to turn in all their homework assignments; completed assignments will contribute 20 percent to students' final grades. Believing that she is being quite generous, she is surprised when her students protest loudly and angrily. Many of them, thinking that there was no reason to keep their completed homework assignments, have already discarded their previous work.

If most students are getting Ds and Fs, something is definitely wrong. Perhaps Ms. Giroux didn't take students' prior knowledge into account when she chose a starting point for instruction. Perhaps she's moving too quickly through the curriculum and so students never achieve mastery of a topic. Perhaps her instructional methods aren't as effective as other approaches might be. Perhaps her quizzes and tests are extremely difficult and reflect unrealistic expectations about what her students can do.

As teachers, we can't always anticipate how best to teach a new topic or how well students will perform on our classroom assessment instruments. Nevertheless, if we want to give students a sense that they have some control over their grades (recall the discussion of attribution theory in Chapter 12), we must tell them early in the semester or school year what our grading criteria will be. In addition, by giving them concrete information about how we will be assigning grades, we avoid unpleasant surprises when students actually receive their grades (recall Ellie's sense of devastation in the opening case study). If we find that our criteria are overly stringent, we may need to "lighten up" in some way, perhaps by adjusting cutoffs or allowing retakes of critical assessments. But we must never change our criteria midstream in a way that unfairly penalizes some students or imposes additional, unanticipated requirements.

◎ *Accompany grades with qualitative information.* Whether they take the form of letter grades or specific numbers, final grades are at best only general indicators of the "quantity" of what students have learned. It is often helpful to accompany them with additional, more qualitative information—for instance, information about students' particular academic strengths, work habits, attitudes, social skills, unique contributions to the classroom community, and so on. Examples of what one second-grade teacher wrote to her students are shown in Figure 16.7. Students and parents alike often find such qualitative feedback just as informative as—sometimes even more informative than—final class grades. It should be fairly explicit, however; comments such as "a pleasure to have in class" communicate little (Brookhart, 2004, p. 183).

■ For ideas on possible grading systems you might use, see the supplementary reading "Combining Assessment Results to Determine Final Grades" in the *Study Guide and Reader.*

FIGURE 16.7   Examples of the qualitative feedback one second-grade teacher gave her students at the end of the school year

- To Amanda: You are a good friend to everyone in the class. You look out for people's feelings and work hard to make others feel good.

- To Andrea: You have a beautiful singing voice and are a very animated performer. You show self-confidence in all that you do.

- To Angus: You are always willing to lend a hand to teachers and peers alike. You have practical advice and reasonable solutions to many questions and situations that arise.

- To Charlotte: You are a very thoughtful worker. You always give 100% on everything you do. Your positive attitude and great work ethic are a wonderful addition to the class.

- To Colin: I love your sense of humor. You make me laugh with your great riddles and jokes. The humor in your stories is very creative and keeps your audience wanting to know more about the story.

Considering Improvement, Effort, and Extra Credit

Our discussion so far has been based on the assumption that class grades should reflect students' achievement of instructional goals. Yet some educators suggest that students be graded on the basis of how much they improve, how hard they try, or how much extra work they do (e.g., Kane, 1983). Let's consider the implications of incorporating each of these factors into final class grades.

Grading improvement. Assessment experts have made two good arguments against basing final grades solely on students' improvement over the course of a semester or school year. First, some students come to the first day of class already possessing some of the knowledge and skills in the year's curriculum, and so there is little room for improvement. Second, when we use improvement as a criterion, students trying to "beat the system" may quickly learn that they can achieve high grades simply by performing as poorly as possible at the beginning of the year (Airasian, 1994; Sax, 1989).

Yet as we discovered in our discussions of self-efficacy and intrinsic motivation in Chapters 10 and 12, motivation theorists stress the importance of focusing students' attention on their own improvement, rather than on how their performance compares with that of peers. So how do we balance what assessment experts recommend, on the one hand, with what motivation theorists recommend, on the other? One reasonable approach is to assign greater weight to assessments conducted at the end of the semester or school year, after *all* students have had a reasonable opportunity to achieve instructional goals (Lester et al., 1997). Two other strategies are ones mentioned in the preceding chapter: administering retakes (perhaps using items or tasks different from those presented the first time) and giving students a chance to correct their errors and, in

■ Observe a strategy for rewarding improvement in the "Cooperative Learning" clip on Video CD 2.

the process, demonstrate their mastery of the subject matter. Another approach—one used for determining team points and group rewards in cooperative learning activities but not necessarily in determining final class grades—is shown in the "Cooperative Learning" clip on Video CD 2.

Grading effort. Most assessment experts recommend that we *not* base final grades on the amount of effort that students appear to exert in the classroom. For one thing, students who begin the year already performing at a high level are penalized because they may not have to work as hard as their less knowledgeable classmates. Furthermore, "effort" is something that we can evaluate only subjectively and imprecisely at best (Brookhart, 2004; R. L. Linn & Miller, 2005; Stiggins, 2001).

An alternative approach is to have students work for individualized instructional goals appropriate for their existing knowledge and skills (Brookhart, 2004; Mac Iver, Stipek, & Daniels, 1991). By basing students' grades on individually tailored goals, we challenge them all to stretch their abilities. Such an individualized approach is quite workable if, when we report students' final grades, we also report the instructional goals on which the grades are based. In fact, it is widely used for students with special educational needs, whose goals are often described in their individualized education programs (IEPs; see Chapter 5, especially Figure 5.3).

Obviously, we enhance students' motivation when we acknowledge their effort, and so we may often want to communicate our informal assessment of it to students and their parents (Brookhart, 2004; Pintrich & Schunk, 2002). Some school systems have multidimensional grading systems that allow teachers to assign separate grades to the various aspects of students' classroom performance. Such mechanisms as letters to parents, parent-teacher conferences, and letters of recommendation provide an additional means by which we can describe the multifaceted nature of students' classroom performance.

Giving extra credit. To my knowledge, researchers have not yet investigated the effect of extra-credit assignments on students' long-term academic success, but my own experience leads me to argue against using extra-credit work to bolster students' grades. Over the years, I have occasionally had students appear at my office door, asking, sometimes begging, for an opportunity to improve their grades by completing extra-credit projects. Usually these students are failing one of my courses and are desperately trying to save their grade point average at the last minute. My response is invariably no, and for a very good reason: My course grades are based on the extent to which students achieve instructional goals for the course, as determined by their performance on tests and assignments that are the same or equivalent (therefore standardized and fair) for all students. Extra-credit projects assigned to only one or two students (typically those achieving at low levels) are insufficient to demonstrate mastery of the subject matter, and they are not standardized for the entire class.

■ Would a student who does little work all semester but pulls off a passing grade by doing an extra-credit project "learn a lesson" and develop more regular study habits? Why or why not?

We can certainly consider some extra-credit work as we assign grades, provided that the work relates to classroom objectives and all students are given the same opportunity to complete it. But incorporating extra credit into final evaluations is not the most appropriate way to help a failing student—one who has not met course goals—achieve a passing grade.

Choosing Criterion-Referenced or Norm-Referenced Grades

Many experts recommend that, as a general rule, final grades should reflect mastery of classroom subject matter and instructional goals; in other words, our grades should be criterion-referenced (e.g., Stiggins, 2001; Terwilliger, 1989). Criterion-referenced grades are especially appropriate during the elementary years: Much of the elementary curriculum consists of basic skills that are either mastered or not mastered, and there is little need to use grades as a basis for comparing students to one another.

The issue becomes more complicated at the secondary level: Students' grades are sometimes used to choose college applicants, award scholarships, and so on. My personal recommendation is that high school grades be criterion-referenced to the extent that such is possible. The most critical decisions for which grades are used—decisions about promotion and graduation—should be based on students' mastery or nonmastery of the school curriculum, not on their standing relative to others. Furthermore, different classes of students often differ in ability level; if grading were strictly norm-referenced, then a student's performance in one class (e.g., honors math) might be graded as C, whereas the same performance in another class (e.g., general math) might warrant an A. (Under such circumstances a student striving for a high grade point average would be a fool to enroll in the honors section.) Finally, only a very few students (the highest achievers) find a norm-referenced grading system motivating; most students quickly resign themselves to achieving at an average level at best (Wlodkowski, 1978; also see Chapter 12).

When setting up a criterion-referenced grading system, we must determine as concretely as possible what we want each grade to communicate about students' achievement. For example, if assigning traditional letter grades, we might use criteria such as the following:

Grade	Criteria
A	The student has a firm command of both basic and advanced knowledge and skills in the content domain. He or she is well prepared for future learning tasks.
B	The student has mastered all basic knowledge and skills; mastery at a more advanced level is evident in some, but not all, areas. In most respects, he or she is ready for future learning tasks.
C	The student has mastered basic knowledge and skills but has difficulty with more advanced aspects of the subject matter. He or she lacks a few of the prerequisites critical for future learning tasks.
D	The student has mastered some but not all of the basics in the content domain. He or she lacks many prerequisites for future learning tasks.
F	The student shows little if any mastery of instructional objectives and cannot demonstrate the most elementary knowledge and skills. He or she lacks most of the prerequisites essential for success in future learning tasks. (based on criteria described by Frisbie & Waltman, 1992)

Only when students' final grades reflect criteria such as these can they legitimately be used for instructional decision making.

Including Students in the Grading Process

Let's return to the opening case study, in which Ellie is completely blindsided by her B in history. Obviously, Ellie has been aware of her scores on history assignments and quizzes, but she has apparently *not* been aware of how those scores would be combined into an overall grade. Although her teacher has presumably been tracking her progress over time, she herself has not.

In previous chapters we have repeatedly seen the benefits of self-assessment for self-regulation and motivation. But how much involvement should students have in determining final grades? Before we address this question, let's look at one student's self-assessment.

Interpreting Student Artifacts and Behaviors

Self-Assessment

Students in a high school literature class write papers relating a poem of their choice to their own lives. After they've completed their papers, their teacher asks them to write two paragraphs in which they (a) assess their poetry analyses and (b) indicate and justify the grade they think they've earned for the nine-week term. In the artifact shown here, 15-year-old Lexee evaluates her written analysis of Jane Kenyon's poem "Killing the Plants" and then explains why she believes she's earned an A for the term. (The artifact also includes a few teacher comments.) As you read Lexee's self-assessment:

- Identify the criteria she's using to evaluate her paper
- Identify the criteria she's using to self-assign a grade

① Assessment:
I would not give this paper/poem a high, but I wouldn't give it an average either. If I had to choose between the two I would probably go for the higher grade, just because I like that grade. I think that the easiest part of writing this paper was when I related the poem to my life. Pretty much everything else was hard for me. [a little vague too] I don't know why, but it was very hard for me. It could've been because I had too big tests today (3/31) too. I just hope that it's ok! [wonderful!] [True!]

② I think that I deserve an A+ for this term. I tried my best, just some of the grammar things were hard for me so I got a few lower grades. oops! I'll list the other two reasons.
— I got everything in on time.
— I tried to participate as much as possible in class.

— Sorry about the paragraph and the few typos that I made. [we need to capitalize]

In evaluating her paper, Lexee knows that her skill in relating a poem to her own life must be an important criterion. Unfortunately, this is the *only* criterion she applies, and she acknowledges that other (unspecified) skills are "very hard for me." In giving herself an undefined "high" grade for the paper, she considers two other issues that are not, in and of themselves, indicators of quality of a paper: she would like a higher grade, and she had tests in two other courses on the same day that the paper was due. In the second paragraph, in which she gives herself an overall class grade, Lexee focuses on effort, punctuality, and amount

Meghan makes arrangements of six in math.

Meghan displays her collection of 100.

FIGURE 16.8 In a kindergarten portfolio, Meghan and her teacher included these two digital photographs to illustrate Meghan's developing math skills.

■ Observe Keenan assess her writing progress in the "Portfolio" clip on Video CD 1.

■ **portfolio** Collection of a student's work compiled systematically over a lengthy time period.

of class participation. Such things are important, to be sure, but they do not necessarily reflect mastery of the subject matter.

Not only do sixth graders (like Ellie) have trouble tracking their progress and evaluating their achievement, but so, too, do many high school students (like Lexee). Almost without exception, *we* must be the ones to determine students' final grades. At the same time, such grades should not, in students' minds, come out of the blue. Students must know, in advance and in concrete terms, our criteria for assigning grades, and we must frequently update them about their progress toward earning the grades they want (e.g., as is done in the computer printout in Figure 16.6). Under such conditions students *can* have a say in the grades they earn—in particular, by working hard to master classroom subject matter.

Even when we use explicit grading criteria, however, single letter grades communicate very little about what students specifically have learned and can do. An alternative gaining increasing popularity is the use of *portfolios* to capture the multifaceted nature of students' accomplishments. As you will see, portfolios also allow considerably more student input than is possible with letter grades.

USING PORTFOLIOS

A **portfolio** is a collection of a student's work compiled systematically over a lengthy period. It need not be limited to paper-pencil products that students have developed; it might also include photographs, audiotapes, videotapes, or objects that a student has created. Some portfolios are "developmental" in nature: Various products are included to show how a student has improved over a period of time. Others may include only the student's best work as a reflection of his or her final achievement (Spandel, 1997; Winograd & Jones, 1992). Figure 16.8 shows a page from a developmental portfolio, which 5-year-old Meghan and her kindergarten teacher created to show Meghan's progress in basic skills. (Another excerpt from Meghan's portfolio appears in Figure 15.4 in Chapter 15).

Portfolios have several advantages (C. Hill & Larsen, 1992; Paris & Paris, 2001; Paulson, Paulson, & Meyer, 1991; Popham, 1995; Spandel, 1997). First, they capture the complex nature of students' achievement, often over a prolonged period, in ways that single letter grades can't possibly do. Second, they provide a mechanism through which we can easily intertwine assessment with instruction: Students typically include products that we may have assigned primarily for instructional purposes. Third, the process of constructing a portfolio encourages students to reflect on and evaluate their accomplishments (e.g., the "Portfolio" clip on Video CD 1 shows 8-year-old Keenan reviewing her writing progress over the past year). And fourth, portfolios sometimes influence the very nature of the instruction that takes place; because the focus is on complex skills, teachers are more likely to *teach* those skills (Koretz et al., 1994).

RSVP characteristics are often a source of concern for portfolios, however, particularly if they are used to evaluate, rather than simply communicate, students' learning and achievement. When portfolios must be scored in some way, such scoring is often unreliable: There may be little agreement among teachers about how any particular portfolio should be rated (Koretz et al., 1994; Popham, 1995). In addition, we have an obvious standardization problem: Because each portfolio will include a unique set of products, we will be evaluating each student on the basis of different information. Validity may or may not be a problem: A portfolio must include enough work samples to adequately represent what students have accomplished relative to instructional goals (Arter & Spandel, 1992; Koretz et al., 1994). Last but not least, we must realize that portfolios, if used properly, are apt to take a great deal of our time, both during class and after hours (Airasian, 1994; Koretz et al., 1994; Popham, 1995); in this sense at least, they are less practical than other methods of summarizing achievement. All this is not to say that we should shy away from using portfolios. But we should make sure the potential benefits outweigh the disadvantages when we ask students to compile them, and we must use them cautiously when they serve as summative evaluations of what students have accomplished.

Advocates of portfolios have offered several suggestions for using portfolios effectively:

◎ *Consider the specific purpose for which a portfolio will be used.* Different kinds of portfolios are useful for different purposes. Developmental portfolios, which include products from the entire school year or perhaps from an even longer period, are most useful when we want to see whether students are making reasonable progress toward long-term instructional goals. Such portfolios are also invaluable for showing students *themselves* how much they've improved. In contrast, "best work" portfolios are more useful for summarizing students' final achievement, perhaps as a way of communicating students' accomplishments to parents, students' future teachers, or college admissions officers (Spandel, 1997).

◎   *Involve students in the selection of a portfolio's contents.* In most cases students should decide for themselves which products to include in their portfolios (Paulson et al., 1991; Popham, 1995; Spandel, 1997). Such practice gives students a sense of "ownership" of their portfolios and can enhance their sense of self-determination and intrinsic motivation to learn. We can help students make appropriate choices by scheduling periodic one-on-one conferences in which we jointly discuss the products that best reflect their achievements (Popham, 1995). We might also show them examples of portfolios created by other students; however, we should do so only if those students and their parents have given permission or if a portfolio's creator can truly remain confidential (Paulson et al., 1991; Stiggins, 2001).

◎   *Identify the criteria by which products should be selected and evaluated.* Students are more likely to make wise selections when they have guidelines for making their choices and (if applicable) when they know the criteria by which their portfolio will eventually be evaluated (Popham, 1995; Spandel, 1997; Stiggins, 2001). (If we are using portfolios for final evaluations, we will also want to develop a rubric for scoring it.) In some instances we may want to include students themselves in the process of identifying the criteria to be used (Popham, 1995). Such a strategy further enhances their sense of self-determination; it can also enhance their ability to self-evaluate in future projects and assignments.

◎   *Ask students to reflect on the products they include.* In addtion to examples of students' work, many portfolios include documentation that describes each product and the reason it was included. For example, in Figure 16.9, 14-year-old Kurt describes and evaluates the writing samples he has included in a portfolio for his eighth-grade language arts class (note that his portfolio includes two or more drafts of each piece of writing). Such documentation encourages students to reflect on and judge their own work in ways that teachers typically do (Airasian, 1994; Arter & Spandel, 1992; Popham, 1995). Thus it is likely to promote the self-monitoring and self-evaluation skills so essential for self-regulated learning.

Students have more ownership of a portfolio when they have played a role in selecting its contents.

FIGURE 16.9   In this self-reflection 14-year-old Kurt explains why he has chosen certain pieces to include in his eighth-grade language arts portfolio.

SELF-EVALUATION

The three pieces of writing in my portfolio that best represent who I am are: 1) "Author Ben Hoff," which is a story in the language of Ben Hoff; 2) "Quotes from The Tao of Pooh"; and 3) "Discrimination."

What "Author Ben Hoff" shows about me as a learner or a writer is that I am able to analyze and absorb the types and styles of an author and then transfer what I learn onto paper in a good final understandable piece of writing. This piece has good description, a good plot line, gets the point across, has a basic setting, and is understandable. I did not change too much of this piece from one draft to the next except punctuation, grammar and spelling. I did, however, add a quote from The Tao of Pooh.

"Quotes from The Tao of Pooh" shows that I am able to pull out good and significant quotes from a book, understand them, and put them into my own words. Then I can make them understandable to other people. This piece gets the point across well and is easy to understand. I really only corrected spelling and punctuation from one draft to the next.

"Discrimination" shows me that I am learning more about discrimination and how it might feel (even though I have never experienced really bad discrimination). I found I can get my ideas across through realistic writing. This piece has good description and was well written for the assignment. Besides correcting some punctuation and spelling, I changed some wording to make the story a little more clear.

For all three pieces, the mechanics of my writing tend to be fairly poor on my first draft, but that is because I am writing as thoughts come into my mind rather than focusing on details of grammar. Then my final drafts get better as I get comments and can turn my attention to details of writing.

The four most important things that I'm able to do as a writer are to: 1) get thoughts pulled into a story; 2) have that story understandable and the reader get something from it; 3) have the reader remember it was a good piece of writing; and 4) like the piece myself.

Summarizing Students' Classroom Achievement

 Assign criterion-referenced grades unless there is a compelling reason to do otherwise.

A teacher assigns criterion-referenced grades for Algebra I, knowing that those grades will be used by school counselors to determine an appropriate math class for each student next year.

 Base final grades on objective and observable data.

Carolyn always sits passively at the back of the classroom and never contributes to class discussions. Her teacher is surprised when she earns high scores on his first two classroom tests. He eventually realizes that, despite her lack of class participation, Carolyn is definitely achieving his instructional objectives and so grades her accordingly.

 Evaluate actual achievement separately from such other factors as effort, improvement, and extra-credit projects.

At a parent-teacher-student conference, a teacher describes Stan's performance this way: "Stan has gotten all Bs and Cs this term—grades that indicate adequate but not exceptional achievement. I have noticed a great deal of inconsistency in his classroom performance. When he puts forth the effort, he learns class material quite well; otherwise, he does poorly. Stan, can you help us understand why you don't always seem to be on top of your game?

Perhaps if we put our heads together, we can identify some strategies for helping you earn a few As next time."

 Use as many sources of data as is reasonably possible to determine grades.

When determining semester grades, a high school teacher considers her students' performance on five paper-pencil tests, three formal performance assessments, a research paper, and numerous smaller assignments.

 Don't count everything.

A teacher frequently assigns homework as a way of encouraging students to practice new skills. He gives students feedback on their work but does not consider these assignments when determining course grades.

 Use portfolios to summarize students' accomplishment of complex, multifaceted tasks.

A teacher has students develop portfolios of their fiction and nonfiction writing. These portfolios, which document students' mastery of some writing skills and their progress on others, are shared with parents at the end of the school year.

The Into the Classroom feature "Summarizing Students' Classroom Achievement" illustrates some of the strategies we've identified for describing and communicating what students have learned in a particular classroom. We now look at a very different approach—standardized testing—that assesses students' achievement and abilities more generally.

STANDARDIZED TESTS

Standardized tests are *standardized* in several ways: All students are given the same instructions and time limits, respond to the same (or very similar) questions or tasks, and have their responses evaluated in accordance with the same criteria. Standardized tests come with test manuals that describe the instructions to give students, the time limits to impose, and explicit scoring criteria to use. If the tests are norm-referenced (and most standardized tests are), their manuals provide norms for various age or grade levels. Often the manuals also provide information about test reliability for various populations and age-groups, as well as information from which we can draw inferences about test validity for our own purpose and situation.

In the upcoming sections we'll look at the general nature of standardized achievement and ability tests and at recent technological innovations in standardized testing. We'll then consider guidelines for choosing and using standardized tests and interpreting their results.

Types of Standardized Tests

A wide variety of standardized tests is currently available on the market.[1] Four kinds that school districts use frequently are tests of achievement, scholastic aptitude and intelligence, specific aptitude, and school readiness. Table 16.2 summarizes the general nature of each category.

Achievement Tests   Standardized achievement tests are designed to assess how much students have learned from the things they have specifically been taught. Test items are, at least in theory, written to reflect the curriculum common to most schools; for example, a history test will focus

---

[1] You can find descriptions of several widely used standardized tests at http://www.ctb.com (for CTB and McGraw-Hill), http://www.riverpub.com (for Riverside Publishing), and http://www.harcourt.com (for Harcourt Assessment and Psychological Corporation).

TABLE 16.2

Comparing Various Kinds of Standardized Tests

KIND OF TEST	PURPOSE	RELIABILITY AND VALIDITY	SPECIAL CONSIDERATIONS
Achievement tests	To assess how much students have learned from what they have specifically been taught	• *Reliability* coefficients are often .90 or higher; they are typically higher for secondary students than for elementary students. Coefficients may be somewhat lower for subtest scores. • *Content validity* must be determined for each situation.	• These tests are usually more appropriate for measuring broad areas of achievement than specific knowledge or skills.
Scholastic aptitude and intelligence tests	To assess students' general capability to learn; to predict their general academic success over the short run	• *Reliability* coefficients are often .90 or higher; they are typically higher for secondary students than for elementary students. • *Predictive validity* for academic success varies considerably, depending on the situation and population. Most validity coefficients are between .40 and .70.	• Test scores should not be construed as an indication of learning potential over the long run. • Individually administered tests (in which the tester works one-on-one with a particular student) are preferable when students' verbal skills are limited or when significant exceptionality is suspected.
Specific aptitude tests	To predict how well students are likely to perform in a specific content domain	• *Reliability* coefficients are often .90 or higher. • *Predictive validity* for academic success often falls below .50.	• Test scores should not be construed as an indication of learning potential over the long run.
School readiness tests	To determine whether students have the prerequisite cognitive skills to be successful in a typical kindergarten or first-grade curriculum	• *Reliability* coefficients tend to be lower than those for other standardized tests (e.g., in the .70s and .80s), in large part because of the young age-group with whom the tests are used. • *Predictive validity* varies considerably but is usually lower than .50; predictive validity for social and behavioral adjustment is especially low.	• Test scores should be used only in combination with other information about children. • Tests should be used primarily for instructional planning purposes, *not* for deciding whether students are ready to begin formal schooling.

on national or world history rather than the history of a particular state, province, or community. The overall test scores usually reflect achievement in a very broad sense: They tell us how much a student has learned about mathematics or language mechanics (relative to a norm group), but not necessarily whether the student knows how to multiply fractions or use commas appropriately.

Standardized achievement tests are useful in at least two ways (Ansley, 1997). First, they enable us to determine how well our own students' performance compares with that of students elsewhere; this information may indirectly tell us something about the effectiveness of our instructional programs. Second, they provide a means of tracking students' general progress over time and raising red flags about potential trouble spots. For example, if Lucas has been getting average test scores over the years, then suddenly performs well below average in eighth grade (even though the test and norm group are the same as in previous years), we have a signal that Lucas may possibly not be learning and performing at a level commensurate with his ability. At this point, we would want to ascertain whether the low performance was a fluke (perhaps due to illness on the test day or to some other temporary condition) or whether the relative decline in performance is due to other, longer-term factors that need our attention.

Content validity is our main concern when we assess achievement, and we need to determine each test's validity for our own situation. We can determine the content validity of a standardized achievement test by comparing a table of specifications (provided in the test manual or constructed ourselves) to our own curriculum. We should also scrutinize the actual test items to see whether they emphasize lower- or higher-level thinking skills; some commonly used achievement tests focus predominantly on lower-level skills (Alleman & Brophy, 1997; Marzano & Costa, 1988). A test has high content validity for our situation only if the topics and thinking skills emphasized in test items match the instructional goals or content area standards toward which we are aiming.

Scholastic Aptitude and Intelligence Tests   Achievement tests are designed to assess what students have specifically learned from the school curriculum. In contrast, **scholastic aptitude tests** are designed to assess a general *capacity* to learn. Traditionally, many of these tests have been called *intelligence tests* (recall our discussion of such tests in Chapter 5). However, some experts are beginning to shy away from the latter terminology because of the confusion about what "intelligence" is and the widespread misconception that IQ scores reflect inherited ability almost exclusively (R. L. Linn & Miller, 2005). Other commonly used terms are *general aptitude test*, *school ability test*, and *cognitive ability test*.

Regardless of what we call them, tests that fall in this category are used mainly for prediction—that is, to estimate how well students are likely to learn and perform in a future academic situation. One way to predict how well students will learn in the future is to assess what they have learned already, and in fact achievement tests can be quite useful as predictors of later academic performance (Jencks & Crouse, 1982; Sax, 1989; J. J. Stevens & Clauser, 1996). But rather than focus on what students have specifically been taught in school, scholastic aptitude tests typically assess how much students have learned and deduced from their general, everyday experiences. For example, many of these tests include vocabulary items designed to assess students' understanding of words they have presumably encountered over the years. They sometimes include analogies, intended to assess how well students can recognize similarities among well-known relationships. They may also ask students to analyze pictures or manipulate concrete objects. Most of them include measures of general knowledge as well as tasks requiring deductive reasoning and problem solving.

■ To get a sense of what items on scholastic aptitude tests might be like, revisit the "Mock Intelligence Test" exercise in Chapter 5 (p.141).

Specific Aptitude Tests   General scholastic aptitude tests are useful when we want to predict overall academic performance. But when we are interested in how well students are apt to perform in a particular area—perhaps in mathematics, art, music, or auto mechanics—then **specific aptitude tests** are more appropriate. Some aptitude tests are designed to predict future performance in just one content domain; others, called *multiple aptitude batteries*, yield subscores for a variety of domains simultaneously.

Aptitude tests are sometimes used by school personnel to select students for specific instructional programs—for example, to identify those students most likely to succeed in a particular course. They may also be used for counseling students about future educational plans and career choices. Aptitude tests are based on the notion that one's ability to learn in a specific area is fairly stable. In recent years, however, many educators have begun to argue that we should focus more on developing abilities in *all* students than on identifying the specific aptitudes that may be present in *some* students (Boykin, 1994; P. D. Nichols & Mittelholtz, 1997). Accordingly, specific aptitude tests now appear less frequently in wide-scale school testing programs than they once did.

Some standardized tests are administered one-on-one. Such tests enable the examiner to observe a student's attention span, motivation, and other factors that may affect academic performance. For this reason, individually administered tests are typically used when identifying special needs.

School Readiness Tests   Some standardized tests are designed to determine whether children have acquired cognitive skills—for instance, knowledge of colors, shapes, and letters—essential for success in kindergarten or first grade. Although widely used in school districts, these **school readiness tests** have come under fire in recent years, for several reasons. First, the scores they yield correlate only moderately at best with children's academic performance even a year or so later (La Paro & Pianta, 2000; C. E. Sanders, 1997; Stipek, 2002). Second, they typically assess only cognitive development, whereas social and emotional development should also be considerations in determining a child's readiness for formal education (Miller-Jones, 1989; Pellegrini, 1998). Finally, by age 5, most children are probably ready for *some* form of structured educational program (Stipek, 2002).

■ **scholastic aptitude test** Test designed to assess a general capacity to learn and used to predict future academic achievement.

■ **specific aptitude test** Test designed to predict future ability to succeed in a particular content domain.

■ **school readiness test** Test designed to assess cognitive skills important for success in a typical kindergarten or first-grade curriculum.

When used in combination with other information, school readiness tests can be quite helpful if we are looking for significant developmental delays that require immediate attention (Bracken & Walker, 1997; Lidz, 1991). They can also give us a rough idea of where to begin instruction with individual children. As a general rule, however, we should *not* use them to identify children who should postpone formal schooling. Rather than determining whether young children can adapt to a particular educational curriculum and environment, it is probably more beneficial to determine how we can adapt the school curriculum and environment to fit individual children's developmental progress and particular needs (Farran, 2001; Lidz, 1991; Stipek, 2002).

Technology and Assessment

The past few years have seen a rapid rise in the use of technology to administer and score standardized tests, and this trend will almost certainly continue. Computer technology and other technological advances provide several options that are either impractical or impossible with paper-pencil tests:

- They allow **adaptive testing**, which adjusts the difficulty level of items as students proceed through a test and can thereby zero in on students' specific strengths and weaknesses fairly quickly.
- They can include animations, simulations, videos, and audiotaped messages that greatly expand the kinds of knowledge and skills that can be assessed.
- They enable easy assessment of how students approach specific problems and how quickly they accomplish specific tasks.
- They allow the possibility of assessing students' abilities under varying levels of support (e.g., by providing one or more hints as needed to guide students' reasoning).
- They can provide on-the-spot, objective scoring and analyses of students' performance. (Anastasi & Urbina, 1997; R. L. Linn & Miller, 2005; Sattler, 2001)

Although computer-based assessment is still in its infancy, preliminary results indicate that it yields reliability and validity coefficients similar to those of traditional paper-pencil tests, often with less time and fewer items (Anastasi & Urbina, 1997). Its use should, of course, be limited to students who have adequate keyboarding skills and familiarity and comfort with computers.

Guidelines for Choosing and Using Standardized Tests

As teachers, we will sometimes have input into the selection of standardized tests for our districts, and we will often be involved in administering them. Following are some guidelines for choosing and using a standardized test appropriately:

◎ *Choose a test that has high validity for your particular purpose and high reliability for students similar to your own.* So far, we have talked about achievement, general scholastic aptitude, specific aptitude, and readiness tests as if they are all distinctly different entities, but in fact the differences among them are not always so clear-cut. To some extent, all of them assess what a student has already learned, and all of them can be used to predict future performance. Our best bet is to choose the test that has the best validity for our particular purpose, regardless of what the test might be called. Of course, we also want a test that has been shown to be highly reliable with a population similar to ours.

◎ *Make sure that the test's norm group is relevant to your own population.* Scrutinize the test manual's description of the norm group used for the test, with questions like this in mind:

- Is the norm group a representative sample of the population at large or in some other way appropriate for any comparisons you plan to make?
- Does it include students of the same age, educational level, and cultural background as your own students?
- Does it include students of both genders?
- Is it a large enough sample that the average scores reported are probably an accurate depiction of the population it represents?
- Have the normative data been collected recently enough that they reflect how students typically perform at the present time?

When we determine norm-referenced test scores by comparing students with an inappropriate norm group, those scores are meaningless. For example, I recall a situation in which teacher education students at a major state university were required to take basic skills tests in language and mathematics. The tests had been normed on a high school population, and so the university students' performance was compared to norms for high school seniors—a practice that made no sense whatsoever.

◎ *Take students' age and development into account.* As we discovered in Chapter 15, a variety of irrelevant factors—motivation, mood, energy level, and so on—affect students' performance on tests and other assessments. When factors such as these are relatively stable characteristics, they

■ **adaptive testing** Computer-based assessment in which students' performance on early items determines which items are presented subsequently.

affect the validity of an assessment instrument. When they are temporary and variable from day to day (perhaps even hour to hour), they affect an instrument's reliability and so indirectly affect its validity as well. Such sources of error in students' test scores and other assessment results are especially common in young children, who may have limited language skills, short attention spans, little motivation to do their best, and low tolerance for frustration (Bracken & Walker, 1997; Messick, 1983). Furthermore, young children's erratic behaviors may make it difficult to maintain standardized testing conditions (Wodtke, Harper, & Schommer, 1989).

FIGURE 16.10 Eight-year-old Connie describes how overwhelming test anxiety can be.

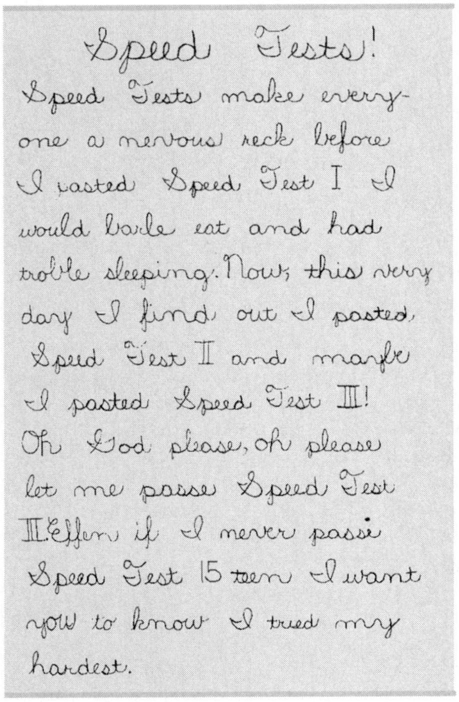

In adolescence, other variables can affect the validity of standardized test scores. Although students may get a bit nervous about tests in the elementary grades (e.g., see Figure 16.10), test anxiety increases in the middle school and high school grades, sometimes to the point of interfering with students' concentration during a test. Furthermore, especially in high school, some students become quite cynical about the validity and usefulness of standardized paper-pencil tests (Paris, Lawton, Turner, & Roth, 1991). When students see little point to taking a test, they may read test items superficially if at all, and a few may complete answer sheets simply by following a certain pattern (e.g., alternating between A and B) or making "pictures" as they fill in the bubbles (Paris et al., 1991). Table 16.3 describes these and other developmental differences affecting students' performance on standardized tests and offers suggestions for accommodating such differences.

◎ *Make sure students are adequately prepared to take the test.* In most instances we will want to prepare students ahead of time for any standardized test they will be taking. We can encourage them to get a full night's sleep and eat a good breakfast. We can explain the general nature of the test and the tasks it involves; for instance, we might mention that we don't expect students to know all the answers and point out that many students will not have enough time to answer every question (Popham, 1990). We can encourage students to do their best without describing the test as a life-or-death matter (Sax, 1989). And we can give them practice with the item types and format of a test—for example, by showing them how to answer multiple-choice questions and how to fill in computer-scored answer sheets (Kirkland, 1971; Sax, 1989).

To some degree, we can also help students prepare by teaching them useful test-taking strategies—temporarily skipping difficult items, double-checking to be sure they have marked their answers in the correct spots, and so on. We should keep in mind, however, that such testwiseness typically makes only a *small* difference in students' standardized test scores (Scruggs & Lifson, 1985). Furthermore, test-taking skills and student achievement are positively correlated: Students with many test-taking strategies tend to be higher achievers than students with few strategies. In other words, very few students get low test scores *only* because they are poor test takers (Scruggs & Lifson, 1985). In most cases we can better serve our students by teaching them the knowledge and skills that tests are designed to assess than spending an inordinate amount of time teaching them how to take tests (J. R. Frederiksen & Collins, 1989).

◎ *When administering the test, follow the directions closely and report any unusual circumstances.* Once the testing session begins, we should follow the test administration procedures to the letter, distributing test booklets as directed, asking students to complete any practice items provided, keeping time faithfully, and responding to questions in the prescribed manner. Remember, the test's norm group has taken the test under certain standardized conditions, and we must replicate those conditions as closely as possible. Occasionally, we will encounter events (a noisy construction project nearby, an unexpected power failure, etc.) that are beyond our control. When such events significantly alter the conditions under which our students are taking the test, they limit our ability to compare their performance with the norm group and so must be reported. We should also make note of any individual students who are behaving in ways unlikely to lead to maximum performance—students who appear exceptionally nervous, stare out the window for long periods, seem to be marking answers haphazardly, and so on (R. L. Linn, & Miller, 2005).

Interpreting Standardized Test Scores

As you've already learned, scores on most standardized tests are norm-referenced. Typically, the scores will be grade or age equivalents, percentile ranks, standard scores, or some combination of these. Yet we must be careful that we don't place too much stock in the specific scores that tests yield. Following are several guidelines to keep in mind when interpreting and using the scores:

TABLE 16.3   DEVELOPMENTAL TRENDS

Characteristics Affecting Standardized Test Performance at Different Grade Levels

GRADE LEVEL	AGE-TYPICAL CHARACTERISTICS	SUGGESTED STRATEGIES
K–2	• Short attention span; considerable individual differences in ability to stay focused on test items • Little intrinsic motivation to perform well on tests • Inconsistency in test performance from one occasion to another	• Do not use school readiness tests to determine which children are "ready" for elementary school; instead, plan early school experiences that can prepare students for future learning. • Leave assessment for diagnostic purposes (e.g., to identify students with special needs) in the hands of trained professionals who have experience in assessing young children. • Do not make long-term predictions about achievement based on standardized test scores.
3–5	• Unquestioning acceptance of standardized tests as valid measures of ability or achievement • Growing ability to stay focused on a paper-pencil assessment instrument • Growing facility with machine-scorable answer sheets • Considerable variability in testwiseness	• Stress the value of standardized tests for tracking students' progress and identifying areas in which students may need extra instruction and support. • Give students plenty of practice using machine-scorable answer sheets. • Explicitly teach basic test-taking strategies (e.g., skipping difficult test items and returning to them later if there is time).
6–8	• Increase in debilitating test anxiety (for some students) • Wide variability in test-taking strategies • Emerging skepticism about the value of standardized tests (for some students)	• Explain that standardized tests provide only a rough idea of what students know and can do; reassure students that test results will not be the only things affecting instructional decision making. • Encourage students to do their best on a test; assure them that test results will be used not to judge them but rather to help them learn more effectively. • Provide some practice in test-taking skills, but remember that students' performance depends more on their knowledge and abilities in content domains than on their general test-taking abilities.
9–12	• Increasing cynicism about the validity and usefulness of standardized tests (especially common in low-achieving students) • Decreasing motivation to perform well on standardized tests (e.g., students may mindlessly fill in answer sheet bubbles); may in some instances reflect self-handicapping as a way of justifying poor performance	• Acknowledge that standardized tests are not perfect, but explain that they *can* help teachers and administrators assess school effectiveness and plan future instruction. • Be alert for signs that a student may intentionally subvert an assessment or has already done so; speak privately with the student about his or her concerns and offer your support to enhance test performance.

Sources: Bracken & Walker, 1997; Dempster & Corkill, 1999; Lidz, 1991; Messick, 1983; Paris et al., 1991; Petersen et al., 1990 I. G. Sarason, 1980; Scruggs & Lifson, 1985; Stipek, 2002.

◎ *Have a clear and justifiable rationale for establishing cutoffs for "acceptable" performance.* If we want to use test results to make either-or decisions—for instance, whether a student should move to a more advanced math course, be exempt from a basic writing course, be awarded certification as a teacher, and so on—we must have a clear rationale for identifying the cutoff score. This process can be relatively easy for criterion-referenced scores, provided that they truly reflect mastery and nonmastery of the subject matter. It is far more difficult for norm-referenced scores: At what point does a student's performance become "acceptable"? At the 20th percentile? the 50th percentile? a stanine of 3? a stanine of 6? Without more information about what knowledge and skills such scores represent, there is no way of knowing.

◎ *Compare two standardized test scores only when those scores are derived from the same or equivalent norm group(s).* Because different standardized tests almost always have different norm groups, we cannot really compare students' performance on one test with their performance on another. For example, if Susan takes the Basic Skills Test (BST), we can compare her score on the BST Reading subtest with her score on the BST Mathematics subtest because both scores are from the same test and have been derived from the same norms. But we cannot compare Susan's BST scores with her scores on a *different* standardized achievement test, such as the Reading Achievement Test (RAT) that Shawn took, because the two sets of scores are likely to be based on entirely different norm groups.

When two or more scores are from the same test, we can use the confidence intervals for the scores to make meaningful comparisons. In the section on reliability in Chapter 15, Figure 15.2 depicts confidence intervals for Susan's scores on the BST; the intervals show how much error is apt to be in the scores as a result of imperfect test reliability. Test publishers often report confidence intervals for norm-referenced scores. Overlapping confidence intervals for any two subtests indicate that the student has performed equally well in the two areas. If the intervals show no overlap, we can reasonably conclude that the student has done better in one area than the other.

◎   *Never use a single test score to make important decisions.* As we have seen, no test, no matter how carefully constructed and widely used, has perfect reliability and validity. Every test is fallible, and students may do poorly on a test for a variety of reasons. Thus, we should never—and I do mean *never*—use a single assessment instrument or single test score to make important decisions about individual students. Nor should we use single test scores to make important decisions about large groups of students or about the teachers who teach them. We will look more closely at these issues in the following section on high-stakes testing and accountability. Before we do so, however, let's take a look at one student's standardized test results.

Interpreting Student Artifacts and Behaviors

A Computer Printout

Twelve-year-old Ingrid takes a standardized achievement test. At an after-school conference several weeks later, her teacher shares the results with Ingrid and her parents. As you look at the following computer printout, think about

- What the stanine and percentile scores tell us about Ingrid's achievement
- What the "national percentile bands" might refer to
- Which content areas are relative strengths and weaknesses for Ingrid
- Why the numbers in the bottom line (1, 5, 10, 20, etc.) are unevenly spaced

Quick reviews of the section on reliability in Chapter 15 and the section on percentile ranks earlier in this chapter can help you with some of the answers.

	STANINE	PERCENTILE	NATIONAL PERCENTILE BANDS
			WELL BELOW AVERAGE : BELOW AVERAGE : AVERAGE : ABOVE AVERAGE : WELL ABOVE AVERAGE :
			1 5 10 20 30 40 50 60 70 80 90 95 99
READING COMPREHENSION	8	92	XXXXXXXXXXXXX
SPELLING	4	39	XXXXXXXXXXXXX
MATH COMPUTATION	4	37	XXXXXXXXXX
MATH CONCEPTS	5	57	XXXXXXXXXXXXX
SCIENCE	8	90	XXXXXXXXXXXXXX
SOCIAL STUDIES	7	84	XXXXXXXX
			1 5 10 20 30 40 50 60 70 80 90 95 99

Ingrid's percentiles and stanines have been computed by comparing her raw scores with those of a national norm group. Ingrid appears to have achieved at average or below-average levels in spelling and math computation, at an average or above-average level in math concepts, and at well-above-average levels in reading comprehension, science, and social studies. The "national percentile bands" are confidence intervals that reflect the amount of error (due to imperfect reliability) that is apt to be in Ingrid's percentile scores. Ingrid's confidence intervals for spelling and math overlap, so even though she has gotten somewhat higher scores in math concepts than in spelling or math computation, the scores are not different *enough* to say that she is better at math concepts than in the other two areas. The confidence intervals for reading comprehension, science, and social studies overlap as well, so she performed similarly in these three areas. The confidence intervals for her three highest scores do *not* overlap with those for her lowest three scores. We can say, then, that Ingrid's relative strengths are in reading comprehension, science, and social studies; she has achieved at lower levels in spelling and math.

Why are the numbers for the percentile confidence intervals (the numbers on the bottom line) unevenly spaced? Remember, percentile ranks tend to overestimate differences near the mean and underestimate differences at the extremes. The uneven spacing is the test publisher's way of showing this fact: It squishes the middle percentile scores close together and spreads high and low percentile scores farther apart. In this way, it tries to give students and parents an idea about where students' test scores fall on a normal curve.

HIGH-STAKES TESTING AND ACCOUNTABILITY

Within the past two or three decades, many politicians, business leaders, and other public figures have lamented what appear to be low achievement levels among our students and have called for major overhauls of our educational system.[2] Many of these reform-minded individuals equate high achievement with high scores on standardized tests and, conversely, low achievement with low test scores. They have been putting considerable pressure on teachers and educational administrators to get the test scores up, and some threaten serious consequences (reduced funding, restrictions on salary, etc.) for those schools and school employees who do *not* get the scores up. Here we are talking about both **high-stakes testing**—making major decisions on the basis of single assessments—and **accountability**—a mandated obligation of teachers, administrators, and other school personnel to accept responsibility for students' performance on those assessments.

In the United States the No Child Left Behind Act of 2001[3] now mandates some form of accountability in all public elementary and secondary schools. It also mandates that all states establish

Challenging academic content standards in academic subjects that—
(I)   specify what children are expected to know and be able to do;
(II) contain coherent and rigorous content; and
(III) encourage the teaching of advanced skills (P.L. 107-110, Sec. 1111)

School districts must annually assess students in grades 3–8 to determine whether students are making "adequate yearly progress" in meeting state-determined standards. The nature of this "progress" is defined by the state (and so differs from state to state), but assessment results must clearly show that all students, including those from diverse racial and socioeconomic groups, are making such progress. (Students with significant cognitive disabilities may be given alternative assessments, but they must show improvement commensurate with their ability levels.) Schools that demonstrate progress receive rewards, such as teacher bonuses or increased budgets. Schools that do not are subject to sanctions and corrective actions (e.g., administrative restructuring), and students have the option of attending a better public school at the school district's expense.

Sometimes individual students, too, are held accountable for their performance on statewide or schoolwide assessments. Some school districts have used students' performance on tests or other assessments as a basis for promotion to the next grade level or for awarding high school diplomas (e.g., Boschee & Baron, 1993; Guskey, 1994).[4] Typically, school personnel begin by identifying certain content area standards (they sometimes use the word *competencies*) that students' final achievement should reflect. They then assess students' performance levels (sometimes known as *outcomes*) at the end of instruction, and only those students whose performance meets the predetermined standards and competencies move forward. In the United States, legislation in more than twenty states now requires that promotion or high school graduation be contingent on passing statewide or school district assessments (Jacob, 2003).

Such efforts to monitor schools' instructional effectiveness and students' academic progress are certainly well intentioned. Ideally, they can help schools determine whether instructional methods need revision and whether teachers need retooling, and they can help teachers identify students who are not acquiring the basic literacy and mathematics skills necessary for successful participation in the adult world. But the current emphasis on boosting students' test scores is

----

[2] In the United States a report entitled *A Nation at Risk*, published by the National Commission on Excellence in Education in 1983, has been especially influential.

[3] You can learn more about this legislation at the U.S. Department of Education's Website (http://www.ed.gov).

[4] Such approaches go by a variety of names; *outcomes-based education* and *minimum competency testing* are two common ones.

■ **high-stakes testing** Practice of using students' performance on a single assessment to make major decisions about students or school personnel.

■ **accountability** An obligation of teachers and other school personnel to accept responsibility for students' performance on high-stakes assessments; often mandated by policy makers calling for school reform.

fraught with difficulties, and solutions to these difficulties are only beginning to emerge. Let's consider both the problems and the potential solutions.

Problems with High-Stakes Testing

Experts have identified several problems with the heavy reliance on high-stakes tests to make decisions about students, teachers, and schools:

◎   *The tests don't always reflect important instructional goals.* Standardized achievement tests don't always have broad-based content validity for the contexts in which they're used. For one thing, they may reflect only a small portion of a school's curriculum and instructional goals (Stiggins, 2001). For instance, the emphasis in the No Child Left Behind Act and in some state-level and district-level assessments is primarily on achievement in literacy and mathematics, with little regard for achievement in science, social studies, and other disciplines (Jacob, 2003; Siskin, 2003a). Furthermore, the preponderance of multiple-choice and other objectively scorable items on many standardized tests limits the extent to which these tests assess higher-level thinking skills and performance on authentic, real-life tasks (Amrein & Berliner, 2002b; E. H. Hiebert & Raphael, 1996; L. A. Shepard, 2000).

◎   *Teachers spend a great deal of time teaching to the tests.* When teachers are being held accountable for their students' performance on a particular test, many of them understandably devote many class hours to the knowledge and skills that the test assesses, and students may focus their studying efforts accordingly (Jacob, 2003; R. L. Linn, 2000; L. B. Resnick & Resnick, 1992). The result is often that students perform at higher levels on a high-stakes test *without* improving their achievement and abilities more generally (Amrein & Berliner, 2002a, 2002b, 2002c; Jacob, 2003). If a test truly measures the things that are most important for students to learn—including such higher-level skills as transfer, problem solving, and critical thinking—then focusing on those things is quite appropriate. If the test primarily assesses rote knowledge and lower-level skills, however, then such emphasis may undermine the improvements we *really* want to see in students' achievement (Amrein & Berliner, 2002b; Kumar et al., 2002).

◎   *School personnel have disincentives to follow standardized testing procedures and to assess the progress of low achievers.* In a high-stakes situation, teachers and administrators sometimes conclude that *dishonesty* is the best policy. Imagine that as a teacher or school administrator, you want to maximize the average test scores of students in a particular class or at a particular grade level. What strategies might you use? Might you, say, give students more than the allotted time to finish the test? Might you provide hints about correct answers or possibly even *give* students correct answers? Might you find reasons to exempt certain students from taking the test—perhaps by finding a place for them in a special education program or retaining them at a grade level where they won't be assessed? Such practices *do* occur when teachers and administrators are under the gun to get their students' test scores up (Amrein & Berliner, 2002a; Jacob, 2003). As a result, average test scores can be misleading, and low-achieving students—those most in need of having their progress monitored—may be left out of the process altogether.

◎   *Different criteria lead to different conclusions about which students and schools are performing at high levels.* When we base school funding, salary increases, and other incentives on students' test performance, exactly what criterion do we use? A predetermined, absolute level of achievement? Improvement over time? Superior performance relative to other school districts? There is no easy answer to this question. Yet depending on which criterion we use, we will reach different conclusions as to which students and schools are and are not performing well (R. L. Linn, 2000). Compounding the problem is the fact that students in lower-income communities achieve (on average) at lower levels than those in higher-income communities even when both groups have excellent teachers and schools (R. L. Linn, 2000; McLoyd, 1998).

◎   *Too much emphasis is placed on punishing low-performing schools; not enough is placed on helping those schools improve.* Sadly, too many advocates of school reform think that a quick and easy "fix" to the low achievement levels of many students is simply to reward schools whose students do well and to punish schools whose students do not (L. A. Shepard, 2000). This strategy is unlikely to be effective, especially if some of the factors affecting students' academic performance (physical and mental health, family support, peer group norms, etc.) are beyond teachers' and administrators' control. In fact, at the present time there is no convincing evidence that holding school personnel accountable for students' performance on high-stakes assessments has a significant and positive influence on teachers' instructional strategies or on students' learning and achievement (Amrein & Berliner, 2002b; Firestone & Mayrowetz, 2000; R. L. Linn, 2000). Furthermore, the threat of harsh consequences for insufficient improvement in test scores can adversely affect teachers' morale and may lead some teachers (including some very good ones) to leave teaching altogether (Amrein & Berliner, 2002a; Chabrán, 2003; Kumar et al., 2002).

◎ *Students' motivation affects their performance on the tests, and consistently low test performance can affect their motivation.* For a variety of reasons—perhaps because they have low self-efficacy, attribute poor performance to factors beyond their control, or intentionally self-handicap so they can explain their poor performance—some students have little motivation to do well on high-stakes tests, and others become so anxious that they *can't* do as well as they should (Chabrán, 2003; Siskin, 2003b). Furthermore, when students get consistently low test scores, and especially when their scores pose obstacles to promotion and graduation, they may find little value in staying in school. In the majority of states that now require certain test scores for high school graduation, dropout rates have increased in recent years, especially for students from ethnic minority groups and students from low-income neighborhoods (Amrein & Berliner, 2002a, 2002b; Kumar et al., 2002).

Potential Solutions to the Problems

Public concern about students' achievement levels is not going away any time soon, nor should it. Many of our students *are* achieving at low levels, particularly those in low-income school districts, those with diverse cultural backgrounds, and those with special educational needs (see Chapters 4 and 5). So I offer several potential solutions—I say *potential* solutions because none of them is either easy or perfect—which, in combination, may alleviate the problems just identified:

◎ *We must identify and assess those things that are most important for students to know and do.* If we are going to base important decisions about students, teachers, and schools on assessment results, we must make sure that we are assessing aspects of achievement most critical for students' long-term success both in school and in the adult world.

◎ *We must educate the public about what standardized tests can and cannot do for us.* What I've seen and heard in the media leads me to think that many politicians and other policy makers overestimate how much standardized achievement tests can tell us: They assume that such instruments are highly accurate and comprehensive measures of students' overall academic achievement. True, these tests are usually developed by experts with considerable training in test construction, but no test is completely reliable, and its validity will vary considerably depending on the context in which it is being used. It behooves all of us—teachers, school administrators, parents, and so on—to learn for ourselves what the limitations of standardized tests are likely to be and to educate our fellow citizens accordingly.

◎ *We must look at alternatives to traditional objective tests.* Especially when a test is going to be administered to large numbers of students at a time, it is apt to be objective and machine-scorable in format, and multiple-choice items are often used. As we discovered in Chapter 15, well-constructed multiple-choice tests can certainly assess higher-level thinking skills. Nevertheless, paper-pencil tasks that ask students to choose from among four or five alternatives will inevitably limit how effectively we can assess important information and skills; for instance, they will tell us little about students' ability to write well (Traub, 1993). Thus some experts argue that we use authentic assessments either instead of or in addition to more traditional paper-pencil tests (e.g., L. B. Resnick & Resnick, 1992; L. A. Shepard, 2000). We should be aware, however, that those states and school districts that have begun to use authentic measures for large-scale assessments of students' achievement have encountered difficulties with reliability and validity, and so we must tread cautiously as we move in this direction (e.g., S. Burger & Burger, 1994; Khattri & Sweet, 1996; Koretz et al., 1994; R. L. Linn, 1994).

◎ *We must advocate for the use of multiple measures in any high-stakes decisions.* No matter what kind of assessment instruments we use, any one instrument is unlikely to give us a comprehensive picture of what students have learned and achieved. Even if an instrument could give us such a picture, perfect reliability is an elusive goal: Students' test results will inevitably be subject to temporary swings in motivation, attention, mood, health, and other factors. To base life-altering decisions about students on a single test score, then, is unconscionable.

TAKING STUDENT DIVERSITY INTO ACCOUNT

Whenever we administer high-stakes or other standardized tests of achievement and ability, we must remember that students often differ from one another in ways that affect their performance in assessment situations. If two students have *learned equally* yet *perform differently* on an assessment, then the information we obtain from the assessment has questionable validity. For example, in Chapter 11 we examined the phenomenon of *stereotype threat*, in which students from a stereotypically low-achieving group tend to perform more poorly on an assessment if they are aware of the stereotype. In Chapter 15 we found that test anxiety and testwiseness can also enter into the picture. Here we look at two additional factors—cultural bias and language differences—that can affect students' test scores. We will then consider how we might adapt standardized tests and classroom grading practices to accommodate students with special needs.

Cultural Bias

Experiencing FIRSTHAND · Predicting the Future

Imagine you are taking a test designed to predict your success in future situations. Following are the first three questions on the test:

1. When you enter a hogan, in which direction should you move around the fire?
2. Why is turquoise often attached to a baby's cradleboard?
3. If you need black wool for weaving a rug, how can you can obtain the blackest color? Choose one of the following:
   a. Dye the wool by using a mixture of sumac, ochre, and piñon gum.
   b. Dye the wool by using a mixture of indigo, lichen, and mesquite.
   c. Use the undyed wool of specially bred black sheep.

Try to answer these questions before you read further.

· · · · · · ·

Did you have trouble answering some or all of the questions? If so, your difficulty was probably due to the fact that the questions are written from the perspective of a particular culture—that of the Navajos. Unless you have had considerable exposure to Navajo culture, you would probably perform poorly on the test. By the way, the three answers are (1) clockwise, (2) to ward off evil, and (3) dye the wool by using a mixture of sumac, ochre, and piñon gum (Gilpin, 1968).

Is the test culturally biased? That depends. If the test is designed to assess your ability to succeed in a Navajo community, then the questions may be very appropriate. But if it's designed to assess your ability to accomplish instructional goals for which knowledge of Navajo culture is totally irrelevant, then such questions are culturally biased.

■ Notice that the term *cultural bias* includes biases related to gender and socioeconomic status as well as to culture and ethnicity.

An assessment instrument has **cultural bias** if any of its items either offend or unfairly penalize some students on the basis of their ethnicity, gender, or socioeconomic status (e.g., Popham, 1995). For example, imagine a test question that implies that boys are more competent than girls, and imagine another question that has a picture in which members of a particular ethnic group are engaging in criminal behavior. Such questions have cultural bias because some groups of students (girls in the first situation, and members of the depicted ethnic group in the second) may be offended by the questions and thus distracted from doing their best on the test. And consider these two assessment tasks:

Task 1: Would you rather swim in the ocean, a lake, or a swimming pool? Write a two-page essay defending your choice.

Task 2: Mary is making a patchwork quilt from 36 separate squares of fabric, as shown to the left. Each square of fabric has a perimeter of 20 inches. Mary sews the squares together, using a half-inch seam allowance. She then sews the assembled set of squares to a large piece of cotton that will serve as the flip side of the quilt, again using a half-inch seam allowance. How long is the perimeter of the finished quilt?

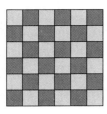

■ **cultural bias** Extent to which assessment tasks either offend or unfairly penalize some students because of their ethnicity, gender, or socioeconomic status.

Task 1 will obviously be difficult for students who haven't been swimming in all three environments and will be even more difficult for those who have never swum at all; students from low-income, inner-city families might easily fall into one of these two categories. Task 2 assumes a fair amount of knowledge about sewing (e.g., what a seam allowance is); this is knowledge that some students (especially girls) are more likely to have than others. Such tasks have cultural bias because some students will perform better than others because of differences in their background experiences, *not* because of differences in what they have learned in the classroom.

An assessment instrument isn't necessarily biased just because one group gets higher test scores than another group. It is biased only if the groups' scores are different when the characteristic we're trying to measure *isn't* different or if the instrument has higher predicitve validity for one group than for another. Yes, we may sometimes see group differences in students' performance on assessment instruments, but these differences often reflect inequities in students' previous experiences that will affect their future educational performance. For example, if high school girls earn lower scores on mathematics achievement tests than high school boys (on average), the difference may be partly due to the fact that the girls have had fewer "mathematical" toys and experiences than the boys (P. A. Campbell, 1986; Eccles & Jacobs, 1986; Kahle & Lakes, 1983). Similarly, if students from low-income families have had few opportunities to venture beyond their immediate neighborhoods (fewer museum trips, less travel, etc.), their more limited exposure to diverse environments is likely to impact both their test performance *and* their classroom achievement.

In fact, most companies that publish large-scale standardized tests now employ individuals who represent numerous minority groups, and they actively screen their test items for possible sources of bias (R. L. Linn & Miller 2005). Furthermore, most scholastic aptitude tests show similar predictive validity for various ethnic and cultural groups, provided that the members of those groups are native English speakers (R. T. Brown, Reynolds, & Whitaker, 1999; Sattler, 2001). Nevertheless, before using any standardized test, school personnel should scrutinize it carefully for any items that either gender or any cultural group may find offensive, as well as for items that might be more difficult for one group than another for reasons unrelated to the characteristic to be measured. And, of course, we should be continually on the lookout for any unintentional cultural bias in the assessment instruments that we ourselves construct.

Language Differences

In the preceding paragraph I said that most scholastic aptitude tests show similar predictive validity for various groups *provided that the members of those groups are native English speakers*. Without question, students' facility with the English language will affect their performance on English-based assessments of achievement and aptitude. Poor reading and writing skills are likely to interfere with success on paper-pencil tests; poor speaking skills may adversely influence students' ability to perform well on oral exams. If we are trying to assess students' achievement in areas unrelated to the language arts—perhaps achievement in mathematics, music, or physical education—then we may in some cases want to minimize our dependence on language to assess those areas.

In the United States the Individuals with Disabilities Education Act (IDEA) mandates that any tests and other assessments used to identify students with special needs be administered in the students' primary language (see the section "Public Law 94-142" in Chapter 5). Although this practice may be critical for an accurate appraisal of students' achievement and abilities, we will typically have little or no reliability and validity data for the tests in their translated forms, nor will we have appropriate norm groups to which we can compare our own students' performance (E. C. Lopez, 1997; Sattler, 2001). We must therefore be especially cautious in interpreting and using the results of standardized assessment instruments that have been translated for students with diverse language backgrounds.

Accommodating Students with Special Needs

We must keep students' unique needs and disabilities in mind whenever we summarize their overall classroom achievements. For instance, if the instructional goals for a student are different from those for the rest of the class, our grading criteria should be altered accordingly, perhaps to be in line with the student's IEP (Brookhart, 2004; Mastropieri & Scruggs, 2000; Venn, 2000). Yet letter grades alone communicate very little definitive information about what students have learned and achieved; if we change the criteria for a particular student, the grades communicate even *less* information. Portfolios (perhaps including teacher checklists, photographs, audiotapes, and videotapes, as well as students' written work) can be particularly helpful for conveying the progress and achievements of students with a variety of disabilities and special needs (Mastropieri & Scruggs, 2000; Venn, 2000).

■ Look again at the treehouse problem in Figure 8.4 in Chapter 8. Is this problem culturally biased? Why or why not?

■ Is this discussion of cultural bias consistent with your previous beliefs about the topic? If not, can you reconcile the inconsistencies?

We may also have to modify standardized testing procedures to accommodate students with special educational needs. IDEA mandates appropriate accommodations for students' disabilities. Such accommodations might involve one or more of the following:

- Modifying the presentation format of the assessment (e.g., using Braille or American Sign Language to present test items and other assessment tasks)
- Modifying the response format (e.g., dictating answers, using a word processor)
- Modifying the timing (e.g., giving extra time or frequent breaks)
- Modifying the assessment setting (e.g., having a student take a standardized paper-pencil test alone in a quiet room)
- Administering part but not all of an instrument
- Using instruments different from those given to nondisabled classmates, to be more compatible with students' ability levels and needs (American Educational Research Association, American Psychological Association, & National Council on Measurement in Education, 1999)

We can often use students' IEPs for guidance about appropriate accommodations for each student. Table 16.4 offers additional suggestions for using standardized tests with students who have special needs.

Whenever we modify educational assessment instruments for students with special needs, we must recognize that there is a trade-off between two of our RSVP characteristics. On the one hand, we are violating the idea that an assessment instrument should be standardized with respect to content, administration, and scoring criteria. On the other hand, if we fail to accommodate the disabilities that some students may have, we will inevitably get results that have little validity regarding the knowledge and skills that students have acquired. There is no magic formula for determining the right balance between standardization and validity for students with special needs; as teachers, we must use our best professional judgment (and perhaps seek the advice of specialists as well) in each situation.

We must keep in mind, too, that modifying assessment instruments or procedures for a standardized test may render the test's norms irrelevant, and hence any norm-referenced scores we derive may be uninterpretable. Standardized testing procedures and norm-referenced scores are sometimes appropriate for students with special needs when our purpose is to identify existing learning and performance difficulties. But when we are later concerned about how to modify instructional methods and materials to *address* those difficulties, criterion-referenced scores and a close inspection of students' responses to particular tasks and items may be more helpful.

CONFIDENTIALITY AND COMMUNICATION ABOUT ASSESSMENT RESULTS

How would you feel if your instructor

- Returned test papers in the order of students' test scores, so that those with highest scores were handed out first, and you received yours *last*?
- Told your other instructors how poorly you had done on the test, so that they could be on the lookout for other stupid things you might do?
- Looked through your school records and discovered that you scored 92 on an "IQ" test you took last year and furthermore that a personality test revealed some unusual sexual fantasies?

You would probably be outraged that your instructor would do any of these things. Likewise, recall the opening case study, in which Ellie is quite distressed when her teacher announces her grades to the entire class. Test results and class grades should be somewhat confidential. But exactly *how* confidential? When should people know the results of students' assessments, and who should know them?

In the United States we get legal guidance on these questions from the **Family Educational Rights and Privacy Act (FERPA)**, passed by the U.S. Congress in 1974. This legislation limits normal school testing practices primarily to the assessment of achievement and scholastic aptitude, two things that are clearly within the school's domain. Furthermore, it restricts knowledge of students' grades and test results to the few individuals who really need to know them: the students who earn them, their parents, and school personnel directly involved with students' education and well-being. School assessment results can be shared with other individuals (e.g., a

■ **Family Educational Rights and Privacy Act (FERPA)** U.S. legislation passed in 1974 that gives students and parents access to school records and limits others' access to those records.

TABLE 16.4   S T U D E N T S   I N   I N C L U S I V E   S E T T I N G S

Using Standardized Tests with Students Who Have Special Educational Needs

CATEGORY	CHARACTERISTICS YOU MIGHT OBSERVE	SUGGESTED CLASSROOM STRATEGIES
Students with specific cognitive or academic difficulties	• Poor listening, reading, and/or writing skills (for some students) • Tendency for test scores to underestimate overall achievement levels (if students have poor reading skills) • Inconsistent performance due to off-task behaviors (e.g., hyperactivity, inattentiveness), affecting reliability and validity of scores (for some students with learning disabilities or ADHD) • Higher-than-average test anxiety	• Modify test administration procedures to accommodate disabilities identified in students' IEPs (e.g., when administering a districtwide essay test, allow students with writing disabilities to use a word processor and spell checker). • Have students take tests in a room with minimal distractions. • Make sure students understand what they are being asked to do. • Be sure students are motivated to do their best but are not overly anxious. • Use classroom assessments (both formal and informal) to either confirm or disconfirm results of standardized test results. • Record and report all modifications made.
Students with social or behavioral problems	• Inconsistent performance due to off-task behaviors or lack of motivation, affecting reliability and validity of scores (for some students)	• Modify test administration procedures to accommodate disabilities identified in students' IEPs (e.g., when students are easily distracted, administer tests individually in a quiet room) • Use classroom assessments (both formal and informal) to either confirm or disconfirm results of standardized test results. • Record and report all modifications made.
Students with general delays in cognitive and social functioning	• Slow learning and cognitive processing • Limited if any reading skills • Poor listening skills	• Choose instruments appropriate for students' cognitive abilities and reading and writing skills. • Minimize use of instruments that are administered to an entire class at once; rely more on instruments that are administered to one student at a time. • Make sure students understand what they are being asked to do.
Students with physical or sensory challenges	• Mobility problems (for some students with physical challenges) • Tendency to tire easily (for some students with physical challenges) • Less developed language skills, affecting reading and writing ability (for some students with hearing loss)	• Obtain modified test materials for students with visual impairments (e.g., large-print or Braille test booklets). • Modify test administration procedures to accommodate students' unique needs (e.g., have a sign language interpreter give directions to students with hearing loss, have students with limited muscle control dictate their answers). • If reading and writing skills are impaired, read test items to students. • Break lengthy assessments into segments that can be administered on separate occasions. • Schedule tests at times when students feel rested and alert. • Record and report all modifications made. • Don't compare a student's performance to the norm group if significant modifications have been made.
Students with advanced cognitive development	• Greater interest and engagement in challenging tests • Tendency in some students to hide giftedness to avoid possible ridicule by peers (e.g., some minority students may want to avoid "acting White") • In some instances, ability levels beyond the scope of typical tests for the grade level	• Keep assessment results confidential. • When students consistently earn perfect or near-perfect scores (e.g., percentile ranks of 99), request individualized testing that can more accurately assess actual ability levels.

Sources. Barkley, 1998; Beirne-Smith et al., 2002; D. Y. Ford & Harris, 1992; A. W. Gottfried et al., 1994; Mastropieri & Scruggs, 2000; Mercer, 1997; M. S. Meyer, 2000; B. N. Phillips et al., 1980; Piirto, 1999; Pitoniak & Royer, 2001; R. Turnbull et al., 2004; Venn, 2000.

family doctor or a psychologist in private practice) *only* when parents or students (if at least 18 years old) give written permission.

This legislative mandate for confidentiality has several implications for school assessment practices. For example, we *cannot*

- Ask students to reveal their political affiliation, sexual behavior or attitudes, illegal or antisocial behavior, potentially embarrassing mental or psychological problems, or family income. (An exception: Questions about income are appropriate when used to determine eligibility for financial assistance.)

■ How often have your own teachers used practices prohibited by the Family Educational Rights and Privacy Act? How did such practices make you feel?

- Ask students to score one another's test papers.
- Post test scores in ways that allow students to learn one another's scores. For example, we cannot post scores according to birthdays, social security numbers, or code numbers that reflect the alphabetical order of students in the class.
- Distribute papers in any way that allows students to observe one another's scores. For example, we cannot let students search through a stack of scored papers to find their own.

Keeping students' test scores confidential makes educational as well as legal sense. Students getting low test scores may feel embarrassed or ashamed if classmates know their scores, and they may become more anxious about their future test performance than they would be otherwise. Students with high test scores may also suffer from having their scores made public: In many classrooms it isn't cool to be smart, and high achievers may perform at lower levels to avoid risking the rejection of peers. And, of course, publicizing students' assessment results focuses students' attention on performance goals—how they appear to others—rather than on mastering the subject matter.

An additional provision of FERPA is that parents and students (if at least 18 years old) have the right to review test scores and other school records. School personnel must present and interpret this information in a way that parents and students can understand. Let's look at some strategies for doing so.

Communicating Assessment Results to Students and Parents

Let's return to the opening case study in Chapter 15, in which Ms. Ford returns disappointing math papers to her students. Notice the approach she takes in communicating the test scores to the students' parents:

> *Ms. Ford:* OK, boys and girls, shhh. I would say, on this test in particular, boys and girls, if you received a grade below 75 you definitely have to work on it. I do expect this quiz to be returned with Mom or Dad's signature on it. I want Mom and Dad to be aware of how we're doing.
>
> *Student:* No!
>
> *Student:* Do we have to show our parents? Is it a requirement to pass the class?
>
> *Ms. Ford:* If you do not return it with a signature, I will call home. (dialogue from J. C. Turner, Meyer, et al., 1998, p. 741)

Ms. Ford obviously wants parents to know that their children are not doing well in her math class. However, there are three drawbacks to her approach. First, many students may find it easier to forge an adultlike signature than to deliver bad news to their parents. Second, parents who do see their children's test papers won't have much information to help them interpret the results (are the low scores due to low effort? to poor study strategies? to an undiagnosed learning disability? to insufficient instruction?). Finally, Ms. Ford focuses entirely on the problem—low achievement—without offering any suggestions for *solving* the problem.

Ultimately, we must think of ourselves as working in cooperation with students and parents for something that all of us want—students' academic success. Our primary goal in communicating assessment results is to share information that will help us achieve that end. As you have probably already discovered, the section "Working with Parents" in Chapter 14 includes several strategies for creating partnerships with parents to facilitate students' success at school.

When we need to report the results of standardized tests, we have a different challenge. How do we describe tests and test results to students and parents who, in all likelihood, have never read a chapter on assessment in an educational psychology textbook? Following are some general guidelines that experts offered many years ago yet still have relevance today (Durost, 1961; Ricks, 1959):

◎ *Make sure you understand the results yourself.* As teachers, we need to know something about a test's reliability and validity for the situation in which we have used it. We also need to know how the test scores have been derived. For example, we should know whether the scores are criterion-referenced or norm-referenced. If they're norm-referenced, we should also know something about the norm group that was used.

◎ *Remember that in many cases it is sufficient to describe the test and students' test performance in broad, general terms.* To illustrate, we might describe an achievement test as a general measure of how much a student has learned in mathematics compared to other students around the country, or we might describe a scholastic aptitude test as something that gives a rough idea about how well a student is likely to do in a particular instructional program. It's sometimes possible to describe a student's test performance without mentioning test scores at all. For example, we might say, "Your daughter scores like students who do well in college mathematics courses" or "Your son had more than average difficulty on the spelling portion of the achievement test; this is an area in which he may need extra help in the next few years." However, if parents want to know their child's specific test scores, in the United States the Family Educational Rights and Privacy Act requires that we reveal those scores and help parents understand what they mean.

◎ *When reporting specific test scores, use percentile ranks and stanines rather than grade equivalents or IQs.* Many parents mistakenly believe that a child's grade-equivalent score reflects the grade level that the child should actually be in, so they may argue for advanced placement of their high-achieving children or feel distressed that their low-achieving children are in over their heads. And many parents interpret IQ scores as reflecting a permanent, unchangeable ability rather than as just an estimate of a child's present cognitive functioning. By reporting test scores as percentile ranks or stanines instead, we are less likely to have parents jumping to such erroneous conclusions. Many parents are familiar with percentile ranks, and many others can easily grasp the notion of a percentile if it is explained to them. But because percentile ranks misrepresent actual differences between students (overestimating differences in the middle range and underestimating differences at the extremes), we may also want to provide stanine scores. Although most parents are unfamiliar with standard scores in general, we can often present stanines in a graphic and concrete fashion, such as I have done in Figure 16.11.

◎ *If you know the standard error of measurement, give parents the confidence interval for a test score.* By reporting confidence intervals along with specific test scores, you communicate an important point about the tests you give: Any test score has some error associated with it.

Whenever we assess students' achievement and abilities, we must remember that our primary purpose is to *help students learn and achieve more effectively* (Stiggins, 2001). When students perform well on our classroom assessments and standardized tests, we have cause for celebration, and we know that our instructional strategies are working as they should. But when students perform poorly, our primary concern, and that of students and parents as well, should be how to improve the situation.

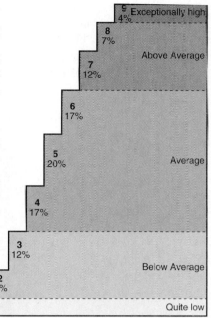

FIGURE 16.11 A graphic technique for explaining stanines to parents

Modeled after Durost, 1961.

THE BIG PICTURE

As we have seen, ongoing assessment of students' progress is—and *must* be—a critical part of our role as teachers. No matter whether we are using teacher-developed instruments or standardized tests to assess students' achievement and abilities, we must keep several general points in mind:

◎ *Classroom assessment practices have a significant influence on what and how students learn.* Regardless of our primary purpose in assessing students' learning and achievement, the nature of our assessment instruments—what topics they address, whether they focus on lower-level or higher-level skills, and so on—will communicate messages about what is most important for students to learn and about how students should study classroom subject matter. Assessing the knowledge and skills we truly want students to master is essential in any educational assessment, and particularly so for high-stakes assessments that may have a major impact on administrative decisions, educational policy, and students' lives.

◎ *Considerable information is lost when students' performance is summarized by a single grade or test score.* For practical and logistical reasons, we will often find it helpful to summarize students' performance with a number or letter grade. Yet by boiling down students' achievement into a single indicator, we lose valuable information about their specific strengths and weaknesses, in-

clinations and disinclinations, and so on. As we plan future lessons and determine how best to tailor instruction to meet students' unique needs, the nitty-gritty details of students' performance on assessment tasks—the specific things they do and do not know, the mistakes they make, the misconceptions they reveal—are apt to be more useful than overall test scores and class grades.

◎ *Most assessment instruments focus on cognitive factors affecting learning and achievement; they give short shrift to other factors that may be equally influential.* Most standardized tests and teacher-developed assessments are designed to assess students' competence in particular content domains. They may also require language skills (e.g., reading and writing ability), logical thinking skills, testwiseness, and other cognitive abilities. Occasionally, noncognitive factors (e.g., test anxiety) enter into the equation, but by and large, the assessment instruments we use will *not* reflect motivational and affective variables—goals, dispositions, interests, attitudes, and so on—that are important factors in students' learning and long-term success. No matter how valid and reliable our assessments may be, they are unlikely to give us a complete description of how well our students are doing and why.

◎ *Educational assessments are useful yet imperfect tools.* Teacher-developed assessments and standardized tests can tell us a great deal about what students know and can do and what students still need to learn and master. The usefulness of any assessment instrument depends on how well matched it is to the situation in which we want to use it and how reliable and valid it is for that situation. No assessment instrument ever has perfect reliability or va-

lidity, however, and so we must not take the results of any single assessment too seriously. As a general rule, we should think of any educational assessment instrument as a tool that, in combination with the other tools at our disposal, can help us improve classroom instruction and maximize students' learning and achievement.

CASE STUDY: *Can Johnny Read?*

Ms. Beaudry is serving on a committee to study reading curricula in her school district. As part of her work with the committee, she plans to administer a standardized reading achievement test to determine whether her sixth graders have mastered the reading skills she has been trying to teach them this year. She's been given the opportunity to select the test from three instruments approved for purchase in her district. She scrutinizes the test manuals carefully and eliminates one test when she sees that its test-retest reliability coefficient falls below .85. She analyzes the tables of specifications for the other two tests, comparing each one to her own sixth-grade curriculum. She eventually settles on the Colorado Reading Test (CRT) as being the most reliable and valid measure.

Ms. Beaudry gives the test to her class, following the prescribed administration procedures closely. Because the test consists entirely of multiple-choice items, she is able to score the results quickly and easily that night. She computes each student's raw score and then turns to the norms in the test manual to obtain stanine scores. Her students' stanines range from 3 to 8.

"Hmmm, what now?" she asks herself. "After all this, I still don't know if my students have learned what I've been trying to teach them."

■ Ms. Beaudry chooses the wrong test for her purpose. What specifically does she do wrong?

■ Is Ms. Beaudry's approach to determining test validity appropriate in this situation? Why or why not?

■ Ms. Beaudry eliminates one test on the basis of a reliability coefficient below .85. Is this a good decision? Why or why not?

Once you have answered these questions, compare your responses with those presented in Appendix B.

KEY CONCEPTS

raw score (p. 572)
criterion-referenced score (p. 573)
norm-referenced score (p. 574)
norms (p. 574)
grade-equivalent score (p. 574)
age-equivalent score (p. 574)
percentile rank (percentile) (p. 574)
normal distribution (normal curve) (p. 575)
standard score (p. 575)

mean (M) (p. 575)
standard deviation (SD) (p. 575)
IQ score (p. 576)
ETS score (p. 576)
stanine (p. 577)
z-score (p. 577)
portfolio (p. 582)
scholastic aptitude test (p. 586)

specific aptitude test (p. 586)
school readiness test (p. 586)
adaptive testing (p. 587)
high-stakes testing (p. 591)
accountability (p. 591)
cultural bias (p. 594)
Family Educational Rights and Privacy Act (FERPA) (p. 596)

PRAXIS Turn to Appendix C, "Matching Book and Ancillary Content to the Praxis Principles of Learning and Teaching Tests," to discover sections of this chapter that may be especially applicable to the Praxis tests.

Companion Website

Now go to our Companion Website at **www.prenhall. com/ormrod** to assess your understanding of chapter content with "Multiple-Choice Questions," apply comprehension in "Essay Questions," broaden your knowledge of educational psychology with related "Web Links," gain greater insight about classroom learning in "Learning in the Content Areas," and analyze and assess classroom work in the "Student Artifact Library."

Appendix A
Describing Associations
with Correlation Coefficients

- Do students with high self-esteem perform better in school than students with low self-esteem?
- Which students are more likely to answer questions correctly—those who answer questions quickly or those who are slow to respond?
- When students take two different intelligence tests at approximately the same time, how similar are their scores on the two tests likely to be?
- Are intellectually gifted students more emotionally well-adjusted than their classmates of average intelligence?

Each of these questions asks about an association between two variables—whether it be an association between self-esteem and school achievement, between speed and accuracy in answering questions, between two sets of intelligence test scores, or between giftedness and emotional adjustment. The nature of such associations is sometimes summarized by a statistic known as a **correlation coefficient**.

A correlation coefficient is a number between -1 and $+1$; most correlation coefficients are decimals (either positive or negative) somewhere between these two extremes. A correlation coefficient for two variables tells us about both the direction and strength of the association between those variables.

Direction. The direction of the association is indicated by the *sign* of the correlation coefficient—in other words, by whether the number is a positive or negative one. A positive number indicates a *positive correlation*: As one variable increases, the other variable also increases. For example, there is a positive correlation between self-esteem and school achievement: Students with higher self-esteem achieve at higher levels (e.g., H. W. Marsh, 1990a). In contrast, a negative number indicates a *negative correlation*: As one variable increases, the other variable decreases instead. For example, there is a negative correlation between speed and accuracy in answering questions: Students who take longer to answer questions tend to make fewer errors in answering them (e.g., Shipman & Shipman, 1985). Figure A.1 graphically depicts each of these relationships.

Strength. The strength of the association is indicated by the *size* of the correlation coefficient. A number close to either $+1$ or -1 (e.g., $+.89$ or $-.76$) indicates a *strong* correlation: The two variables are closely related, so knowing the level of one variable allows us to predict the level of the other variable with some accuracy. For example, we often find a strong relationship between two intelligence tests taken at the same time: Students tend to get similar scores on both tests, especially if both tests cover similar kinds of content (e.g., McGrew, Flanagan, Zeith, & Vanderwood, 1997). In contrast, a number close to 0 (e.g., $+.15$ or $-.22$) indicates a *weak* correlation: Knowing the level of one variable allows us to predict the level of the other variable, but we cannot predict with much accuracy. For example, there is a weak association between intellectual giftedness and emotional adjustment: In general, students with higher IQ scores show greater emotional maturity than students with lower scores (e.g., Janos & Robinson, 1985), but there are many students who are exceptions to this rule. Correlations in the middle range (e.g., those in the .40s and .50s—whether positive or negative) indicate a *moderate* correlation.

As teachers, we will often find correlation coefficients in research articles in our professional books and journals. For example, we might read that students' visual-spatial thinking ability is

■ **correlation coefficient** Statistic that indicates the strength and direction of an association between two variables.

FIGURE A.1   Positive and negative correlations

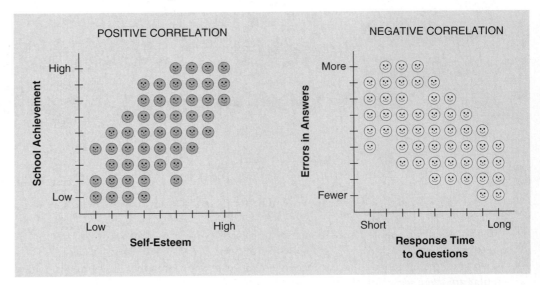

Each face in these two graphs represents one student in a group of fifty students. The location of the face tells the extent to which the student is high or low on the two characteristics indicated. There is a *positive correlation* between self-esteem and school achievement: Students with higher self-esteem tend to achieve at higher levels. There is a *negative correlation* between the length of time it takes for students to respond to questions and the number of errors in their answers: Students who take longer to answer questions tend to have fewer errors in their responses.

positively correlated with their success in a mathematics class or that there is a negative correlation between class size and students' achievement test scores. Whenever we see such evidence of correlation, we must remember one very important point: *Correlation does not necessarily indicate causation.* For example, we cannot say that visual-spatial thinking ability specifically *leads to* greater mathematical ability, nor can we say that class size specifically *interferes with* classroom achievement; both of these italicized phrases imply a causal relationship between one variable and another that does not necessarily exist. As Chapter 1 indicates, only carefully designed experimental studies enable us to draw conclusions about the extent to which one thing causes or influences another.

Many calculators are now programmed to compute correlation coefficients. Computing a correlation coefficient by hand is somewhat complicated but certainly not impossible. If you are curious, you can find the formula in most introductory statistics textbooks.

Appendix B
Analyses of the Ending Case Studies

CHAPTER 1: *MORE HARM THAN GOOD?* (P. 16)

Is the computer software somehow making mathematics more difficult for students? Or is there another possible explanation for students' lower scores?

We cannot say that the software is the cause of students' difficulty because we haven't eliminated other possible explanations for the differences between computer users and non-computer users. A number of factors probably influenced students' decisions to use or not use the computer lab—their involvement in other after-school activities, their access to transportation home in the late afternoon, and so on—and so the two groups of students are probably different in a variety of ways. One likely explanation for the computer users' lower scores is that students who used the software did so because they were having trouble understanding class material, whereas many nonusers were mastering the material on their own.

Which kind of study has Mr. Gualtieri conducted: descriptive, correlational, or experimental?

He has looked at the relationship between two things, computer use and class performance, as they occur naturally in the environment. Therefore, he has conducted a correlational study, which does not allow inferences about cause and effect.

Did Mr. Gualtieri make a good or a bad decision in advising his students to use the computer software? Is there any way to answer this question from the information he has obtained?

There is insufficient information to determine the effectiveness of the software on students' understanding of class material. To answer this question, Mr. Gualtieri would have to have insisted that some students use the software and that other students definitely not use it; the two groups would have to have been essentially the same in ability, motivation, and so on. By randomly assigning students to groups, he could assume that the two groups were similar (on average) to begin with; therefore, any achievement differences that emerged later would have been due to software use. Note, however, that conducting a study of this nature—one in which some students are denied access to potentially helpful software—would not be appropriate from a pedagogical or ethical standpoint. As a general rule, a teacher should provide as much instructional support as possible to *all* students.

CHAPTER 2: *IN THE EYE OF THE BEHOLDER* (P. 58)

What went wrong? Can you explain the students' inability to learn within the context of Piaget's theory of cognitive development? Can you explain it using some of Vygotsky's ideas? Can you explain it from an information processing perspective?

From Piaget's perspective, students may have assimilated the new information into their existing knowledge of how we see (i.e., we look *at* something) and so misinterpreted what Ms. Kontos actually said. From Vygotsky's perspective, the learning task may have been beyond students' zone of proximal development, or Ms. Kontos may have provided insufficient scaffolding to enable them to grasp the ideas she was presenting. From an information processing perspective, students may not have adequately processed what Ms. Kontos said; for instance, perhaps they weren't paying attention during the lesson, or perhaps they elaborated on the material inaccurately. Recall, too, that the students nodded when Ms. Kontos asked them if they understood her explanation; students of all ages often have difficulty assessing their own knowledge accurately (reflecting a weakness in metacognition).

In what ways might students' language capabilities have been insufficient to enable them to understand?
Ms. Kontos may have used vocabulary with which students were unfamiliar or complex sentence structures the students had difficulty interpreting.

What things might Ms. Kontos have done differently?
When Ms. Kontos asked her students, "Do you all understand how our eyes work?" the students nodded that they did. Although they may have *thought* they understood, many obviously did not. At a minimum, Ms. Kontos should have checked for comprehension by asking questions or presenting tasks that students could respond to correctly only if they had a true understanding of how light is involved in human sight.

CHAPTER 3: *THE SCARLET LETTER*   (P. 99)

What elements of a theory of mind and perspective taking are evident in the students' comments?
The students show an ability to make connections between people's behaviors, on the one hand, and their inner thoughts and feelings, on the other. Several of their comments reflect this ability:

- When Nicole observes Dimmesdale's tendency to act withdrawn, she speculates about his underlying motives: "He doesn't even want to be involved with the situation. He wants the other guy to question her, because he doesn't want to look her in the face and ask her to name *him*."
- Another student implies that the baby's focus on Dimmesdale reveals especially strong feelings for him.
- Mike interprets Dimmesdale's nervous behaviors (e.g., shaking) as revealing feelings of guilt. He also assumes that these feelings will be evident in Dimmesdale's facial expressions.
- Matt imagines that someone who feels as nervous and guilty as Dimmesdale does might be wiping his forehead.

Two students show a willingness to take Hester's perspective about the preacher:

- One student speculates about what Hester might have seen in Dimmesdale: "Maybe he's got a good personality."
- Another student speculates that Hester might have been drawn to his eyes.

What strategies does the teacher use to foster perspective taking, as well as social cognition more generally, as the students read the novel?
Ms. Southam does several things to help the students become more "people savvy":

- She presses them to look for behavioral clues that reveal Dimmesdale's guilt.
- She asks students to write about or draw characteristics "essential to understanding Dimmesdale's character."
- She suggests that Mike imagine himself directing a film about *The Scarlet Letter* and asks what characteristics the actor who plays Dimmesdale should have.
- She herself makes a connection between a behavior and an emotion: "[Dimmesdale is] holding his hand over his heart, as though he's somehow suffering some pain."
- She asks students to speculate about what Hester might have seen in Dimmesdale: "And if she was worth it, don't we also have to see him as somehow having been worthy of her risking *her* soul?"
- She speculates on how he affects the people in his congregation: "He apparently is, you know, a spellbinding preacher. He really can grab the crowd."

CHAPTER 4: *THE ACTIVE AND THE PASSIVE*   (P. 136)

What are some possible reasons why the girls and minority students are not participating in classroom activities?
Following are several possible reasons based on Chapter 4's discussion of ethnic and gender differences (you may have identified other reasons as well):

- Because some of the boys are responding to Ms. Stewart's questions almost immediately, there is little, if any, wait time that might allow the girls and minority students to speak up.

- Some of the minority students may find question-answer sessions inconsistent with their culture's preference for private conversations; others may find it odd that the teacher asks questions for which she already knows the answers.
- The teacher's question-answer sessions may create a competitive atmosphere in which some girls and students from minority cultures feel uncomfortable.
- The girls may be concerned that their public displays of science knowledge will be frowned on by their peers.
- When boys and girls work together on classroom tasks, it is typically the boys who take the more active role.
- By the secondary grade levels, girls are less confident about their ability to succeed in stereotypically male domains such as science and mathematics.

What strategies might Ms. Stewart use to increase their participation?
   Possible strategies to remedy the situation include these:

- Initially ignoring the hands that go up immediately and allowing sufficient time for other students to respond
- Incorporating cooperative learning activities into the weekly schedule
- Giving students opportunities to respond to questions in a more private manner (e.g., on paper)
- Forming all-male and all-female groups for laboratory activities
- Providing genuine success experiences that can help females and minorities gain self-confidence about their ability to succeed in science

CHAPTER 5: *QUIET AMY*   (P. 180)

Mr. Mahoney suspects that Amy may qualify for special educational services. If she does, in what category of special needs might she fall? Can you develop at least three different hypotheses as to where her difficulties may lie?
   Here are four possible hypotheses:

- A learning disability (see Figure 5.5 for specific possibilities)
- A communication disorder
- An emotional and behavioral disorder
- Hearing loss

We can probably rule out ADHD and mental retardation, because Amy can attend to arts and crafts projects for significant periods of time and performs at an appropriate age level on those projects. Before identifying Amy as belonging to *any* category of special needs, the interdisciplinary team should rule out the possibility that Amy's behaviors are simply the result of an environment that has encouraged and reinforced such behaviors.

Amy's evaluation will undoubtedly take several weeks to complete. In the meantime, what strategies might Mr. Mahoney try to improve Amy's classroom performance?
   Here are just a few possibilities (you might have identified others as well):

- Teach basic academic skills (e.g., letter recognition, basic number concepts) within the context of arts and crafts activities.
- Have Amy work one-on-one with an adult (e.g., a teacher aide or parent volunteer) on basic spoken language skills. Ideally, a specialist (e.g., speech pathologist) should be consulted for ideas about effective strategies.
- To promote interaction with classmates, design one or more activities in which students work in pairs; match Amy with a student who has strong social skills.

CHAPTER 6: *HOW TIME FLIES*   (P. 220)

Why might Ms. Llewellyn's students be having difficulty learning and remembering the things she is trying to teach them? Can you think of possible reasons related to the class curriculum? to Ms. Llewellyn's style of teaching? to Ms. Llewellyn's reading assignments?
   The *curriculum* includes too much material for a single school year. It necessitates such a fast pace and such superficial coverage that students probably don't have enough time

to learn the material meaningfully or elaborate on it effectively. The *teaching style* is almost exclusively lecture. Ms. Llewellyn presents so much information that students may have difficulty determining which things are important and which things are not. Furthermore, students may be experiencing information overload, to the point where they simply cannot store everything in working memory, let alone in long-term memory. And because Ms. Llewellyn seems to be doing most, if not all, of the talking, it is difficult to know how well students are paying attention. As for the *reading assignments*, the history textbook is probably suitable if it is truly written at the students' reading level. However, many high school students don't have the needed background knowledge, and possibly don't have the reading skills either, to gain much from reading articles in professional journals.

From the perspective of cognitive psychology, what would you do differently than Ms. Llewellyn?
    Here are some possible strategies:

- Plan more variety in teaching methods, including some that involve active student participation (discussions, debates, etc.). Also, incorporate many visual aids (maps, old newsreels, etc.) to complement verbal presentations.
- Make numerous connections between historical events and students' prior knowledge (e.g., relate emotions during the Civil War to emotions students might feel when embroiled in an argument with parents or peers about social or moral issues).
- Cut down the amount of information presented. If the district curriculum requires coverage of the entire time span Ms. Llewellyn is covering, then identify key events to focus on and downplay other, perhaps less important, aspects of history. Also, eliminate details that contribute little to students' overall understanding and so are needless sources of distraction.
- Eliminate the professional journals. Instead, assign readings that are likely to capture students' interest, such as newspaper clippings from various eras, excerpts from diaries (e.g., Anne Frank's *The Diary of a Young Girl*, *The Oregon Trail*), or novels set during particular time periods (e.g., *The Red Badge of Courage*, *From Here to Eternity*).

CHAPTER 7: *EARTH-SHAKING SUMMARIES*   (P. 251)

Why is Ms. Jewell not convinced that Frank and Mitchell have mastered the material? What critical aspects of the lesson did each boy omit in his response?
    Frank omits the idea that the earth's crust consists of separate pieces (plates). Both boys omit the idea that earthquakes result when two plates rub against each other as they move.

What pieces of information from the lesson did Adrienne, Toni, and Jonathan apparently use when answering Ms. Jewell's question? Can you explain their responses using the concept of knowledge construction?
    Adrienne apparently interprets *tectonics* as being related to technology (e.g., computers) and therefore infers that computers are involved in the scientific study of earthquakes. Toni interprets *plates* as eating utensils and deduces that such plates move during an earthquake. Jonathan hears the word *fault* and interprets it as a *person's* fault, deducing logically that earthquakes aren't caused by people's actions. All three of these ideas may be accurate, but none of them were presented in Ms. Jewell's lesson.

What instructional strategies might Ms. Jewell have used to help her students gain a better understanding of plate tectonics?
    There are numerous possible strategies that Ms. Jewell might use (see the section "Promoting Effective Knowledge Construction"). Following are two examples:

- She could have students experiment with a similar phenomenon on a small scale; perhaps she might give the students two sheets of cardboard with a small amount of sand or sugar placed on them and then have the students observe what happens when the edges of the two sheets are pressed against each other and shifted in opposite directions.
- She might ask her students to explain their interpretations of earthquakes to one another—a process through which they are likely to clarify their thinking and possibly find flaws in their own or their classmates' logic.

CHAPTER 8: *CHECKS AND BALANCES*   (P. 292)

How thoroughly have these students learned the material that Mr. Chen was trying to teach them? Why are they apparently unable to identify new examples of checks and balances?

Debra misunderstands "checks and balances." Mark has a vague idea about the system of checks and balances but can't describe it precisely or identify concrete examples. Neither Seth nor Karen has any notion of the material they have presumably studied. None of the four students, then, have really mastered the unit and so cannot effectively transfer what they've learned to a new situation (in this case, by generating a new example).

What evidence do you see that Mr. Chen's students have poor study skills? If you were teaching Mr. Chen's class, what might you do to help the students study and learn more effectively?

Two obvious pieces of evidence indicating that the students have poor study skills are Seth's omission of important information from his class notes and Karen's illusion of knowing the material. It appears that the students have a great deal to learn about note taking, meaningful learning, elaboration, and comprehension monitoring. This is hardly surprising: Many middle school students are quite naive about effective learning and study strategies. Mr. Chen can do many things to encourage and scaffold better strategies; the following are examples:

- Tell students which things are most important to learn and therefore to include in their notes.
- Provide an outline that helps students organize their notes.
- Give students questions to ask themselves as they read and study.
- Have students study the material in pairs or small groups, quizzing one another with lower-level and higher-level questions.

These and other strategies are presented in the sections "Effective Study Strategies" and "Factors Affecting Strategy Use" and in the right-hand column of Table 8.3. Additional strategies (e.g., teaching mnemonics) are presented in the discussion of long-term memory storage and retrieval in Chapter 6.

CHAPTER 9: *HOSTILE HELEN*   (P. 326)

In behaviorist terminology, what is Mr. Washington trying to do when he ignores Helen's inappropriate behavior? What are some possible reasons this approach isn't working?

Mr. Washington is trying to avoid reinforcing the behavior, hoping that *extinction* will occur. From an operant conditioning perspective, this approach may not be working for any one of several possible reasons:

- Perhaps other students (e.g., Helen's friends) are reinforcing the behavior.
- Perhaps Helen has been reinforced only intermittently for the behavior in the past; therefore, the behavior has become highly resistant to extinction.
- Perhaps Mr. Washington's attention has never been a reinforcer; instead, Helen simply has a very high baseline for such behavior.
- Perhaps Helen experiences some sort of intrinsic reinforcement for her behavior (e.g., physical aggression releases pent-up energy and so "feels good").

In behaviorist terminology, what is Mr. Washington trying to do when he praises Helen's appropriate behavior? What are some possible reasons this approach isn't working either?

Mr. Washington is trying to *reinforce an incompatible behavior.* Several factors may be interfering with the strategy's effectiveness:

- Perhaps Mr. Washington's praise is not a reinforcer for Helen.
- Perhaps Mr. Washington's praise would be effective if given in private, but it is not effective when given in front of Helen's peers.
- Perhaps Mr. Washington's praise is somewhat reinforcing, but the reinforcers Helen receives for behaving aggressively are more powerful.
- Reinforcement seldom occurs (Mr. Washington praises her only on "rare occasions").
- Reinforcement may be occurring inconsistently, because Mr. Washington can reinforce Helen only when he actually notices her behaving appropriately.
- Perhaps the praise is given in such a way that it undermines her sense of self-determination (see the discussion of limitations of behavioral approaches).

How might you use behaviorist learning principles to bring about a behavior change in Helen? Following are several suggestions:

- Specify the desired terminal behavior in precise, concrete terms.
- Identify a reinforcer that is clearly reinforcing for Helen (e.g., a favorite activity).
- Find a desired behavior that, although possibly not optimal, occurs frequently enough that you can reinforce it regularly.
- Use *shaping*, reinforcing small improvements over a period of time, rather than expecting overnight success.
- Monitor the effects of your reinforcer on Helen's behavior; choose a different one if you are seeing little or no change over a reasonable period of time.

CHAPTER 10: *TEACHER'S LAMENT*   (P. 363)

Why were students who had regularly been doing their homework so upset? Can you explain their reaction using social cognitive theory?

Mr. Adams is right that some students have home environments that are not terribly conducive to doing homework; for this and other reasons, homework should not be a major factor in assigning final grades (see Chapter 13). However, Mr. Adams has already told his students that homework will contribute 20 percent to final class grades. Students who have been doing their homework regularly are upset because the reinforcement they expected to receive for doing their homework did not occur.

From a social cognitive perspective, Mr. Adams inadvertently punished some students and reinforced others. Which students in the class were reinforced, and how? Which students were punished, and how?

Students who had not been doing their homework were reinforced: They did not receive the unpleasant consequences they had expected. Students who had been doing their homework were punished: They did not receive the reinforcement they had expected.

What might Mr. Adams do to encourage and help all students to complete homework assignments?

Research indicates that homework improves student achievement, at least at the middle school and secondary school grades (see Chapter 13), and so Mr. Adams should ideally find some way of enabling all his students to complete it. Following are several possible strategies (you might have thought of others as well):

- Middle school students often have few self-regulatory learning strategies, especially if they have few out-of-school role models with good study habits. Mr. Adams should probably teach and scaffold basic self-regulation behaviors, such as keeping track of homework assignments, developing a plan for accomplishing each assignment, and self-reinforcement for homework completion.
- If Mr. Adams' students live within walking distance of school, he might offer after-school homework sessions in his classroom.
- If some students live far enough away that they take the bus to and from school, he might confer with parents and guardians to see if, by working together on the problem, they can identify a quiet time and place for doing a small amount of homework every night.
- He and his fellow teachers could agree that some study hall periods would be specifically used for doing homework for certain classes.
- If Mr. Adams discovers too late that some students have not been doing their homework for reasons beyond their control, he should identify assignments that these students can reasonably complete to make up for the work that they have missed.

CHAPTER 11: *WHEN "PERFECT" ISN'T GOOD ENOUGH*   (P. 387)

Why might feedback such as "You sure are working hard" or "You can write beautifully in cursive" be more effective than feedback such as "Great" or "Perfect"? Use what you have learned about motivation to speculate.

The students in the experimental group appear to have more *intrinsic* motivation to write in cursive: They enjoy cursive writing more than those in the control group, and they use it more frequently in writing assignments. Feedback such as "You sure are working hard" and "You can write beautifully in cursive" probably enhances students' sense of competence and self-worth to a greater degree than "Great!" or "Perfect!," in that it specifically communicates the teacher's acknowledgment that the students themselves are responsible for their successes.

Making a connection between students' effort and abilities, on the one hand, and their success in cursive writing, on the other, is an example of an *attribution* (see Chapter 12).

Might the control group's feedback be more effective if Mrs. Gaskill used it for all, rather than just some, of her students? Explain your reasoning. (For help in answering this question, return to the section "Factors Influencing the Development of Self-Views" in Chapter 3.)

As noted in Chapter 3, how students evaluate their own performance depends partly on how it compares to that of their peers. In this situation, students in the control group are hearing some of their classmates get what appears to be more favorable feedback than they themselves are getting. If everyone were getting the same cryptic feedback they were, praise such as "Great!" and "Perfect!" would be interpreted quite positively.

CHAPTER 12: *WRITER'S BLOCK*   (P. 430)

How is Mr. Grunwald defining success in his English composition class? How are his students defining success? Are they focusing their attention on mastery goals or performance goals?

Mr. Grunwald is probably defining success as acquiring proficient writing skills—a mastery goal. His students are defining it as earning an A or B—a performance goal.

To what does Janis attribute her writing failure? What effect has her attribution had on her behavior?

She is attributing her failure to a general inability to write, which in her mind is an internal, stable, and uncontrollable characteristic. By believing that she has no control over her successes and failures in class, she is exhibiting learned helplessness. Learning to write is, in her view, a lost cause.

What strategies might Mr. Grunwald use to help his students become more intrinsically motivated to develop proficient writing skills?

Here are examples of strategies he might use:

- Downplay the importance of grades rather than threatening students with failing grades.
- Describe what he means by a "decent essay" in specific, concrete terms so that students have a clear goal toward which they can direct their efforts. For example, he might distribute copies of a scoring guide (rubric) he will use to evaluate students' papers. (See Chapter 15 for more about creating rubrics.)
- Give more specific feedback about what students are doing well and how they can improve.

Additional examples are presented in the Creating a Productive Classroom Environment feature "Promoting Intrinsic Motivation" on page 411.

CHAPTER 13: *UNCOOPERATIVE STUDENTS*   (P. 480)

Why have Ms. Mihara's cooperative learning groups not been as productive as she had hoped? Considering the strategies for promoting cooperative learning that we examined in this chapter, what did Ms. Mihara do wrong?

If we consider recommended procedures for conducting a cooperative learning activity, we can identify at least three things Ms. Mihara has done wrong:

- She let students form their own groups, so the groups were not necessarily ones that would be able to work effectively together.
- The objective of the activity was ambiguous. Students were told only to find information and give an oral report.
- She provided no structure to ensure that all students would participate actively in the activity.

How might you orchestrate the cooperative learning unit differently than Ms. Mihara?

You might

- Form the groups yourself, making sure that each one is heterogeneous in membership.
- Present a clear goal toward which each group should strive (e.g., to identify religious affiliations, national and religious holidays, typical diets, and so on).
- Create one or more unique roles for each group member (e.g., researcher, secretary, presenter, coordinator, and the like), so that each student's involvement is essential for overall group success.
- Assess what each student has learned (ensuring individual accountability).

CHAPTER 14: *OLD FRIENDS*   (P. 520)

Why is Mr. Schulak having so much difficulty bringing his classroom to order? What critical things has Mr. Schulak not done in his first week of teaching?

Mr. Schulak has not established a businesslike atmosphere; he has instead established one that seems to be all fun and games. Furthermore, he has not set any limits for behavior—something he should have done in the first week of class.

Given that Mr. Schulak has gotten the school year off on the wrong foot, what might he do now to remedy the situation?

He needs to emphasize that there are instructional goals his students must achieve this year and that it is time to get down to business. He might involve his classes in a discussion of some reasonable rules and procedures for accomplishing those goals; this strategy should be motivating for students in that it will enhance their sense of self-determination and give them ownership of the rules and procedures by which the class will operate. After his rocky start, Mr. Schulak should not expect overnight success; it may take a while for students to become focused on their schoolwork, and he will have to be consistent about enforcing the new rules and procedures.

CHAPTER 15: *PICK AND CHOOSE*   (P. 569)

What mistakes does Mr. Bloskas make in developing the first quiz? What mistakes does he make in developing the second quiz? Are the quizzes likely to have content validity? Why or why not?

In constructing the first quiz, Mr. Bloskas does not match his questions to his instructional goals, which presumably go beyond rote memorization of trivial details. He would be wise to construct a table of specifications first and then either find or construct quiz items that assess both the key ideas of the unit and the specific behaviors he wants students to demonstrate with regard to those ideas. In constructing the second quiz, Mr. Bloskas gives only two essay questions, which may not provide an adequate sample of the content domain. Both quizzes, then, may have questionable content validity—the first because it does not focus on desired behaviors, and the second because it is too restricted in the topics that it covers.

Why do the students react as negatively as they do to the second quiz?

Mr. Bloskas has neglected to consider the effects that classroom assessment practices have on students' future studying and learning. Expecting the second quiz to be similar to the first, his students probably studied for the quiz by memorizing trivial details rather than thinking about ways to apply what they had learned. Students should know what to expect on a classroom assessment instrument so that they can prepare accordingly. Any radical changes in the nature of assessment from one time to the next should be clearly described ahead of time; for example, a teacher might show students a few questions similar to those that will be on an upcoming quiz.

CHAPTER 16: *CAN JOHNNY READ?*   (P. 600)

Ms. Beaudry chooses the wrong test for her purpose. What specifically does she do wrong?

Ms. Beaudry apparently chooses a test that yields only stanines, norm-referenced scores that allow her to compare each student's performance to that of a national norm group of the same age or grade level. The test does not tell her specifically whether her students have acquired certain reading skills. To get such information, she should ideally use a test that yields criterion-referenced scores.

Is Ms. Beaudry's approach to determining test validity appropriate in this situation? Why or why not?

Yes, Ms. Beaudry's approach is appropriate. When measuring achievement in a particular content domain (such as reading), one should be most concerned with a test's *content* validity. The best way to determine content validity is to look at the match between the test and the curriculum, perhaps by using a table of specifications.

Ms. Beaudry eliminates one test on the basis of a reliability coefficient below .85. Is this a good decision? Why or why not?

Yes, it's a good decision. Many published achievement tests have reliability coefficients of .90 or above, so there is no reason to settle for anything less.

Appendix C
Matching Book and Ancillary Content to the Praxis® *Principles of Learning and Teaching Tests*

In the United States, state teacher licensing requirements in many states include passing Praxis® tests published by Educational Testing Service (ETS). Among the Praxis tests are four *Principles of Learning and Teaching* (PLT) tests, one each for teachers seeking licensure for early childhood and for grades K–6, 5–9, and 7–12. *Educational Psychology: Developing Learners* addresses most of the topics covered in the PLT tests. In the left column of Table C.1, I present the topics covered on the tests, as identified in the second edition of the *Study Guide for Principles of Learning and Teaching* (Educational Testing Service, 2003). In the middle column of the table, I indicate chapters and sections in *Educational Psychology: Developing Learners* that are relevant to these topics. In the right column, I suggest appropriate exercises and readings in the *Study Guide and Reader* that accompanies the textbook, as well as relevant videos on the two compact disks, *Video Examples to Accompany Educational Psychology: Developing Learners*, that are packaged with the book.

The Praxis Series: Professional Assessments for Beginning Teachers® (Praxis™)* tests involve reading and analyzing case studies. For this reason, the case studies presented in *Educational Psychology: Developing Learners* may be especially helpful as you prepare for these tests. The opening case in each chapter is addressed in several places throughout the chapter. The ending case poses questions that encourage you to apply chapter content; I urge you to develop your own answers to these questions before looking at how I answer them in Appendix B. You will find additional cases in the Interpreting Student Artifacts and Behaviors features in the textbook, on the *Video Examples* CDs, and in the Application Exercises in the *Study Guide and Reader*.

You may also want to obtain a copy of the study guide that ETS publishes to assist students as they prepare for the Praxis tests. This guide provides practice case studies and offers suggestions for analyzing them and responding to test questions. You can purchase a copy online at **http://www.ets.org/store**.html. Once there, select *Teaching and Learning* and, on the next screen, *Praxis Products*. On the following screen, scroll down until you find *Principles of Learning and Teaching Study Guide*.

TABLE C.1

Matching Book and Ancillary Content to the Praxis *Principles of Learning and Teaching* Tests

TOPICS IN THE PRAXIS PRINCIPLES OF LEARNING AND TEACHING TESTS	WHERE TOPICS APPEAR IN ORMROD'S *EDUCATIONAL PSYCHOLOGY* (5TH ED.)	WHERE TOPICS AND PRACTICE OPPORTUNITIES APPEAR IN STUDENT SUPPLEMENTS
I. Students as Learners		
A. Student Development and the Learning Process		
► Theoretical foundations about how learning occurs: how students construct knowledge, acquire skills, and develop habits of mind	**Chapters 6–10:** Entire chapters (pp. 182–363) **Chapter 2:** "An Information Processing View of Cognitive Development" (pp. 42–49)	**Study Guide and Reader:** Application Exercises 9–18 (pp. 95–100, 110–116, 129–132, 147–151, 163–168); Supplementary Reading 14, "Learning in the Content Areas" (pp. 343–406)
► Examples of important theorists: • Albert Bandura	**Chapter 10:** Entire chapter (pp. 328–363); especially see "Basic Assumptions of Social Cognitive Theory" (pp. 328–363)	**Study Guide and Reader:** Application Exercises 17, 18 (pp. 163–168)
• Jerome Bruner • John Dewey • Jean Piaget	**Chapter 2:** "Piaget's Theory of Cognitive Development" (pp. 24–34)	**Study Guide and Reader:** Application Exercises 3, 4 (pp. 33–38) **Video CD 2:** "Designing Experiments"
• Lev Vygotsky	**Chapter 2:** "Vygotsky's Theory of Cognitive Development" (pp. 33–42) **Chapter 10:** "Self-Instructions" (p. 349) **Chapter 13:** "Reciprocal Teaching" (pp. 462–464); "Peer Tutoring" (pp. 470–474)	**Study Guide and Reader:** Application Exercise 2 (pp. 31–32)
• Howard Gardner	**Chapter 5:** "Gardner's Theory of Multiple Intelligences"; Table 5.2 (pp. 144–145)	
• Abraham Maslow		**Study Guide and Reader:** Supplementary Reading 7, "Maslow's Hierarchy of Needs" (pp. 317–320)
• B. F. Skinner	**Chapter 9: "Case Study: The Attention Getter"** (p. 295); "Operant Conditioning" (pp. 301–310); "Shaping New Behaviors" (pp. 310–311); "Effects of Antecedent Stimuli and Responses" (pp. 311–314); "Using Intermittent Reinforcement" (pp. 320–321)	**Study Guide and Reader:** Application Exercises 15, 16 (pp. 147–151); Supplementary Reading 10, "A Shocking Lesson" (pp. 330–333)
► Important terms that relate to learning theory • Constructivism	**Chapter 2:** "Piaget's Basic Assumptions" (pp. 25–26); "Social Construction of Meaning" (pp. 37–39) **Chapter 3:** "General Themes in Personal, Social, and Moral Development" (pp. 98–99) **Chapter 6:** "Basic Assumptions of Cognitive Theory" (pp. 187–189); "Visual Imagery" (pp. 204–205); "Reconstruction Error" (p. 214) **Chapter 7: "Case Study: Pulling It All Together"** (pp. 223–224); "Constructive Processes in Learning and Memory" (pp. 224–226); "Knowledge Construction as a Social Process" (pp. 227–228); "When Knowledge Construction Goes Awry: Origins and Effects of Misconceptions" (pp. 235–238); "Considering Diversity in Constructive Processes" (pp. 250–251); **"Case Study: Earth-Shaking Summaries"** (pp. 251–252) **Chapter 13:** "Class Discussions" (pp. 460–462)	**Study Guide and Reader:** Application Exercises 11, 12 (pp. 110–116); Supplementary Reading 14, "Learning in the Content Areas" (pp. 343–406)
• Metacognition	**Chapter 2:** "Metacognition" (pp. 46–48) **Chapter 8: "Case Study: A Question of Speed"**; (p. 255); "Metacognition and Study Strategies" (pp. 257–269); **"Case Study: Checks and Balances"** (pp. 292–293) **Chapter 13:** "Reciprocal Teaching" (pp. 462–464); "Cooperative Learning" (pp. 465–470)	**Study Guide and Reader:** Application Exercise 13 (pp. 129–130); Supplementary Reading 14, "Learning in the Content Areas" (pp. 343–406) **Video CD 1:** "Memory and Metacognition"

TABLE C.1—continued

Matching Book and Ancillary Content to the Praxis *Principles of Learning and Teaching* Tests

TOPICS IN THE PRAXIS PRINCIPLES OF LEARNING AND TEACHING TESTS	WHERE TOPICS APPEAR IN ORMROD'S *EDUCATIONAL PSYCHOLOGY* (5TH ED.)	WHERE TOPICS AND PRACTICE OPPORTUNITIES APPEAR IN STUDENT SUPPLEMENTS
I. Students as Learners—continued		
A. Student Development and the Learning Process—continued		
• Readiness	**Chapter 2:** "Role of the Brain in Cognitive Development" (pp. 22–24); "Piaget's Basic Assumptions" (pp. 25–26) **Chapter 16:** "School Readiness Tests" (p. 586)	**Study Guide and Reader:** Application Exercise 32 (pp. 272–275)
• Schemata [schemas]	**Chapter 2:** "Piaget's Basic Assumptions" (pp. 25–26) **Chapter 7:** "Schemas and Scripts" (pp. 223–234)	**Study Guide and Reader:** Application Exercise 11 (pp. 110–112)
• Transfer	**Chapter 8:** "Transfer" (pp. 269–274)	**Study Guide and Reader:** Application Exercise 14 (pp. 131–132)
• Scaffolding	**Chapter 2:** "Current Perspectives on Vygotsky's Theory" (pp. 37–42) **Chapter 5:** "Mental Retardation" (pp. 169–170) **Chapter 8:** "Identifying Important Information" (pp. 259–260); "Retrieving Relevant Prior Knowledge" (p. 260); "Teaching Problem-Solving Strategies" (p. 278); "Accommodating Students with Special Needs" (pp. 290–291) **Chapter 13:** "Online Research" (pp. 450); Discovery Learning" (pp. 451–453); "Authentic Activities" (pp. 456–457); "Cooperative Learning" (pp. 465–470) **Chapter 14:** "Providing Structure" (p. 495)	**Study Guide and Reader:** Supplementary Reading 14, "Learning in the Content Areas" (pp. 343–406)
• Bloom's taxonomy	**Chapter 13:** "Identifying the Goals of Instruction" (pp. 436–440)	**Study Guide and Reader:** Supplementary Reading 8, "Using Taxonomies to Formulate Instructional Goals and Objectives" (pp. 321–325)
• Zone of proximal development	**Chapter 2:** "Vygotsky's Basic Assumptions" (pp. 34–37) **Chapter 5:** "Giftedness" (pp. 176–178) **Chapter 15:** "Static versus dynamic assessment" (pp. 554–555)	**Study Guide and Reader:** Application Exercise 2 (pp. 31–32)
• Intrinsic and extrinsic motivation	**Chapter 9:** "Reinforcement in the Classroom" (pp. 302–307); "Promoting Intrinsic Reinforcement" (p. 320); "Strengths and Potential Limitations of Behavioral Approaches" (pp. 324–326) **Chapter 10:** "How Self-Efficacy Affects Behavior and Cognition" (pp. 341–342) **Chapter 11: "Case Study: Quick Draw"** (p. 365); "Extrinsic Versus Intrinsic Motivation" (pp. 367–368) **Chapter 12:** "Self-Perceptions and Intrinsic Motivation" (pp. 392–398); "Expectancies and Values" (pp. 398–400); "Interest" (pp. 400–403); "Goals" (pp. 403–410); "The Big Picture" (pp. 428–429) **Chapter 15:** "Assessments as Tools" (pp. 524–525)	**Study Guide and Reader:** Application Exercises 19–22 (pp. 178–181, 194–197) **Video CD 2:** "Motivation"
▶ Human development in the physical, social, emotional, moral, and cognitive domains	**Chapters 2–3:** Entire chapters (pp. 18–101) **Chapters 4–16:** "Developmental Trends" tables (pp. 120, 143, 206, 237, 258, 305, 348, 380, 416, 437, 498, 536, 589) **Chapter 4:** "Origins of Gender Differences" (pp. 121–124) **Chapter 5:** "Nature, Nurture, and Group Differences in Intelligence" (pp. 147–148) **Chapter 6:** "Developmental Trends in Storage Processes for Declarative Information" (pp. 205–206) **Chapter 10:** "Factors in the Development of Self-Efficacy" (pp. 342–344) **Chapter 12:** "Developmental Trends in Attributions" (pp. 415–417); "Factors Influencing the Development of Attributions" (pp. 417–418) **Chapter 14:** "Taking Individual and Developmental Differences into Account" (pp. 497–499) **Chapter 16:** "Guidelines for Choosing and Using Standardized Tests" (pp. 587–588)	**Study Guide and Reader:** Application Exercises 2–6 (pp. 31–38, 50–53); Supplementary Reading 2, "Physical Development Across Childhood and Adolescence" (pp. 295–304); Supplementary Reading 4, "Parenting Styles and Children's Behavior" (pp. 309–312; Supplementary Reading 14, "Learning in the Content Areas" (especially see **"Case Study: The Birth of a Nation"** and "Developmental Changes" sections, pp. 344–345, 352–353, 364–365, 377–378, 368–369, 396) **Video CD 1:** "Cognitive Development"; "Memory and Metacognition"; "Friendships"; "Emotions"; "Motivation"; "Moral Reasoning"

continued

TABLE C.1—continued

Matching Book and Ancillary Content to the Praxis *Principles of Learning and Teaching* Tests

TOPICS IN THE PRAXIS PRINCIPLES OF LEARNING AND TEACHING TESTS	WHERE TOPICS APPEAR IN ORMROD'S *EDUCATIONAL PSYCHOLOGY* (5TH ED.)	WHERE TOPICS AND PRACTICE OPPORTUNITIES APPEAR IN STUDENT SUPPLEMENTS
I. Students as Learners—continued		
A. Student Development and the Learning Process—continued		
• The theoretical contributions of important theorists such as Erik Erikson, Lawrence Kohlberg, Carol Gilligan, Jean Piaget, Abraham Maslow, Albert Bandura, and Lev Vygotsky	**Chapter 2:** "Piaget's Theory of Cognitive Development" (pp. 24–34); "Vygotsky's Theory of Cognitive Development" (pp. 33–42); "An Information Processing View of Cognitive Development" (pp. 42–49); "Theoretical Perspectives on Language Development" (pp. 49–55) **Chapter 3:** "Erikson's Eight Stages of Psychosocial Development" (Figure 3.2; p. 69); "Development of Moral Reasoning: Kohlberg's Theory" (pp. 89–91); "Possible Gender Differences in Moral Reasoning: Gilligan's Theory" (pp. 91–92) **Chapter 10:** Entire chapter (pp. 328–363)	**Study Guide and Reader:** Application Exercises 2–6 (pp. 31–38, 50–55), 17–20 (pp. 163–168, 178–181); Supplementary Reading 3, "Ecological Systems Perspectives of Child Development" (pp. 305–308); Supplementary Reading 7, "Maslow's Hierarchy of Needs" (pp. 317–320)
• The major progressions in each developmental domain and the ranges of individual variation within each domain	**Chapters 2–16:** "Developmental Trends" tables (pp. 51, 72, 78, 87, 120, 143, 206, 237, 258, 305, 348, 380, 416, 437, 498, 536, 589) **Chapter 2:** "Piaget's Stages of Cognitive Development" (pp. 26–31); "Current Perspectives on Piaget's Theory" (pp. 31–33); "An Information Processing View of Cognitive Development" (pp. 42–49); "Trends in Language Development" (pp. 50–53) **Chapter 3:** "Developmental Changes in Sense of Self" (pp. 68–72); "Peer Relationships" (pp. 73–77); "Perspective Taking" (pp. 77–81); "Developmental Trends in Morality and Prosocial Behavior" (pp. 87–89); "Development of Moral Reasoning: Kohlberg's Theory" (pp. 89–91)	**Study Guide and Reader:** Application Exercises 3, 5 (pp. 33–36, 50–53); Supplementary Reading 2, "Physical Development Across Childhood and Adolescence" (pp. 295–304) **Video CD 1:** "Cognitive Development"; "Memory and Metacognition"; "Friendships"; "Emotions"; "Motivation"; "Moral Reasoning" **Video CD 2:** "Designing Experiments"
• The impact of students' physical, social, emotional, moral, and cognitive development on their learning and how to address these factors when making instructional decisions	**Chapter 2:** "Piaget's Stages of Cognitive Development" (pp. 26–31); "Current Perspectives on Piaget's Theory" (pp. 31–33); "An Information Processing View of Cognitive Development" (pp. 42–49); "Trends in Language Development" (pp. 50–53) **Chapter 3:** "Development of a Sense of Self" (pp. 65–72); "Social Development" (pp. 72–86); "Moral and Prosocial Development" (pp. 86–95); **"Case Study: *The Scarlet Letter*"** (pp. 99–100) **Chapter 5:** "Temperament" (pp. 149–151); "Emotional and Behavioral Disorders" (pp. 163–166); "Mental Retardation" (pp. 169–170)	**Study Guide and Reader:** Application Exercises 4, 6, 20 (pp. 37–38, 54–55, 180–181); Supplementary Reading 14, "Learning in the Content Areas" (pp. 343–406) **Video CD 1:** "Memory and Metacognition"; "Motivation"; "Moral Reasoning"
• How development in one domain, such as physical, may affect performance in another domain, such as social	**Chapter 2:** "Role of the Brain in Cognitive Development" (pp. 22–24) **Chapter 3:** "Developmental Changes in Sense of Self" (pp. 68–72); "Perspective Taking" (pp. 77–81); "Development of Moral Reasoning: Kohlberg's Theory" (pp. 89–91) **Chapter 4:** "Characteristics of Students at Risk" (p. 130) **Chapter 5:** "Temperament" (pp. 149–151) **Chapter 6:** "Learning and the Brain" (pp. 186–187)	**Study Guide and Reader:** Supplementary Reading 2, "Physical Development Across Childhood and Adolescence" (pp. 295–304) **Video CD 1:** "Emotions"; "Motivation" **Video CD 2:** "Scarlet Letter"
B. Students as Diverse Learners		
▶ Differences in the ways students learn and perform	**Chapters 2–16:** "Diversity" sections (pp. 55–56, 95–98, 133–135, 178–179, 217–219, 250–251, 290–291, 323–325, 359–361, 383–386, 424–428, 474–477, 507–511, 564–567, 594–597) **Chapter 2:** "Learning a Second Language" (pp. 53–55) **Chapter 3:** "Effects of Parenting" (p. 62); "Effects of Culture" (pp. 62–63) **Chapters 4–5:** Entire chapters (pp. 102–181)	**Study Guide and Reader:** Application Exercise 7 (pp. 64–67); Supplementary Reading 14, "Learning in the Content Areas" (pp. 343–406) **Video CD 1:** "Memory and Metacognition"
• Learning styles	**Chapter 2:** "Learning Strategies" (pp. 44–45) **Chapter 6:** "Accommodating Diversity in Cognitive Processes" (pp. 217–219)	

TABLE C.1—continued

Matching Book and Ancillary Content to the Praxis *Principles of Learning and Teaching* Tests

TOPICS IN THE PRAXIS PRINCIPLES OF LEARNING AND TEACHING TESTS	WHERE TOPICS APPEAR IN ORMROD'S *EDUCATIONAL PSYCHOLOGY* (5TH ED.)	WHERE TOPICS AND PRACTICE OPPORTUNITIES APPEAR IN STUDENT SUPPLEMENTS
I. Students as Learners—continued		
B. Students as Diverse Learners—continued		
• Multiple intelligences	**Chapter 5:** "Gardner's Theory of Multiple Intelligences" (pp. 144–145)	
• Performance modes – Concrete operational thinkers – Visual and aural learners	**Chapter 1:** "An Example: Research on Visual-Spatial Thinking" (pp. 8–9) **Chapter 2:** "Concrete Operations Stage" (pp. 28–29); Table 2.1 (p. 28); Table 2.2 (p. 29) **Chapter 5:** "Learning Disabilities" (pp. 155–159) **Chapter 6:** "The Various Forms of Knowledge" (pp. 196–197); "Visual Imagery" (pp. 204–205)	**Video CD 2:** "Designing Experiments"
• Gender differences	**Chapter 3:** "Possible Gender Differences in Moral Reasoning: Gilligan's Theory" (pp. 91–92); "Gender Differences" (p. 96) **Chapter 4:** "Gender Differences" (pp. 116–124); **"Case Study: The Active and the Passive"** (p. 136) **Chapter 5:** "Temperament" (pp. 149–151) **Chapter 10:** "Characteristics of Effective Models" (pp. 337–338) **Chapter 11:** "Gender Differences" (p. 385) **Chapter 12:** "Gender Differences" (p. 425) **Chapter 13:** "Considering Group Differences" (pp. 474–475) **Chapter 16:** "Cultural Bias" (pp. 594–595)	**Study Guide and Reader:** Application Exercise 7 (pp. 64–67) **Video CD 1:** "Emotions: Late Adolescence"; "Friendships"
• Cultural expectations and styles	**Chapter 1:** **"Case Study: Hidden Treasure"** (pp. 3–4) **Chapter 2:** "Vygotsky's Basic Assumptions" (pp. 34–37); "Considering Diversity in Cognitive and Linguistic Development" (pp. 55–56) **Chapter 3:** "Effects of Culture" (pp. 62–63); "Group Membership and Achievements" (pp. 67–68); "Ethnic Differences" (pp. 95–96) **Chapter 4:** **"Case Study: Why Jack Wasn't in School"** (pp. 103–104); "Cultural and Ethnic Differences" (pp. 105–116); **"Case Study: The Active and the Passive"** (p. 136) **Chapter 11:** "Cultural and Ethnic Differences" (pp. 384–385) **Chapter 12:** "Ethnic Differences" (pp. 424–425) **Chapter 13:** "Considering Group Differences" (pp. 474–475) **Chapter 14:** "Defining and Responding to Misbehaviors" (p. 509) **Chapter 16:** "Cultural Bias" (pp. 594–595)	**Study Guide and Reader:** Application Exercise 7 (pp. 64–67)
▶ Areas of exceptionality in students' learning	**Chapter 5:** Entire chapter (pp. 138–180); especially see **"Case Study: Tim"** (pp. 139–140) and **"Case Study: Quiet Amy"** (pp. 180–181) **Chapters 1–16:** "Students in Inclusive Settings" tables (pp. 12, 56, 97–98, 134, 156, 218, 250, 290, 325, 361, 386, 427, 476–477, 511, 567, 597) **Chapters 2–3, 6–16:** "Accommodating Students with Special Needs" sections (pp. 55–56, 97–98, 218–219, 250–251, 290–291, 324–325, 360–361, 385–386, 427–428, 475–477, 510–511, 566–567, 595–597)	**Study Guide and Reader:** Application Exercise 8 (pp. 80–82)
• Visual and perceptual difficulties	**Chapter 5:** Figure 5.5 (p. 157)	
• Special physical or sensory challenges	**Chapter 5:** "Students with Physical and Sensory Challenges" (pp. 170–175)	**Video CD 2:** "Bilingual Classroom"
• Learning disabilities	**Chapter 5:** "Learning Disabilities" (pp. 155–159) **Chapter 10:** "Factors in the Development of Self-Efficacy" (pp. 342–344)	**Study Guide and Reader:** Supplementary Reading 14, "Learning in the Content Areas" (pp. 343–406)

continued

TABLE C.1—continued

Matching Book and Ancillary Content to the Praxis *Principles of Learning and Teaching* Tests

TOPICS IN THE PRAXIS PRINCIPLES OF LEARNING AND TEACHING TESTS	WHERE TOPICS APPEAR IN ORMROD'S *EDUCATIONAL PSYCHOLOGY* (5TH ED.)	WHERE TOPICS AND PRACTICE OPPORTUNITIES APPEAR IN STUDENT SUPPLEMENTS
I. Students as Learners—continued		
B. Students as Diverse Learners—continued		
• Attention Deficit Disorder (ADD); Attention Deficit-Hyperactivity Disorder (ADHD)	**Chapter 5: "Case Study: Tim"** (pp. 139–140); "Attention-Deficit Hyperactivity Disorder (ADHD)" (pp. 159–161)	**Study Guide and Reader:** Supplementary Reading 14, "Learning in the Content Areas" (pp. 343–406)
• Functional mental retardation	**Chapter 5:** "Mental Retardation" (pp. 169–170)	**Study Guide and Reader:** Supplementary Reading 5, "Adaptive Behaviors and Mental Retardation" (p. 313)
• Behavioral disorders	**Chapter 5:** "Emotional and Behavioral Disorders" (pp. 163–166)	
• Developmental delays	**Chapter 5:** "Students with General Delays in Cognitive and Social Functioning" (pp. 168–170)	
▶ Legislation and institutional responsibilities relating to exceptional students		
• Americans with Disabilities Act (ADA)		
• Individuals with Disabilities Education Act (IDEA)	**Chapter 5:** "Public Law 94-142: The Individuals with Disabilities Education Act (IDEA)" (pp. 151–153)	
• Inclusion, mainstreaming, and "Least Restrictive Environment"	**Chapters 1–16:** "Students in Inclusive Settings" tables (pp. 12, 56, 97–98 134, 156, 218, 250, 290, 325, 361, 386, 427, 476–477, 511, 567, 597) **Chapter 5:** "Educating Students with Special Needs in General Education Classrooms" (pp. 151–154)	
• IEP (Individual Education Plan), including what, by law, must be included in each IEP	**Chapter 5:** "Individualized education program (IEP)" (p. 152) **Chapter 16:** "Grading effort" (p.580); "Accommodating Students with Special Needs" (pp. 595–597)	
• Section 504 of the Rehabilitation Act		
• Due process	**Chapter 5:** "Due process" (pp. 152–153)	
• Family involvement	**Chapter 5:** "Fair and nondiscriminatory evaluation" (p. 151); "Due process" (pp. 152–153) **Chapter 14:** "Working with Parents" (pp. 512–519)	
▶ Approaches for accommodating various learning styles, intelligences, or exceptionalities, including:	**Chapters 2–16:** "Students in Inclusive Settings" tables (pp. 56, 97–98, 134, 156, 218, 250, 290, 325, 361, 386, 427, 476–477, 511, 567, 597) **Chapter 5:** Entire chapter (pp. 138–181) **Chapter 6:** "Accommodating Diversity in Cognitive Processes" (pp. 217–219)	
• Differentiated instruction	**Chapters 2–16:** "Diversity" sections (pp. 55–56, 95–98, 133–135, 178–179, 217–219, 250–251, 290–291, 324–325, 359–361, 383–386, 424–428, 474–477, 507–511, 564–567, 594–597); "Students in Inclusive Settings" tables (pp. 56, 97–98, 134, 156, 218, 250, 290, 325, 361, 386, 427, 476–477, 511, 567, 597)	**Video CD 1:** "Portfolio"
• Alternative assessments	**Chapter 5:** "Considering Diversity When Identifying and Addressing Special Needs" (pp. 178–179) **Chapter 15:** "Informal Assessment" (pp. 539–541); "Performance Assessment" (pp. 553–559) **Chapter 16:** "Using Portfolios" (pp. 582–584)	
• Testing modifications	**Chapter 15:** Table 15.5 (p. 567) **Chapter 16:** "Accommodating Students with Special Needs" (pp. 595–597)	

Matching Book and Ancillary Content to the Praxis *Principles of Learning and Teaching* Tests

TABLE C.1—continued

Matching Book and Ancillary Content to the Praxis *Principles of Learning and Teaching* Tests

TOPICS IN THE PRAXIS PRINCIPLES OF LEARNING AND TEACHING TESTS	WHERE TOPICS APPEAR IN ORMROD'S *EDUCATIONAL PSYCHOLOGY* (5TH ED.)	WHERE TOPICS AND PRACTICE OPPORTUNITIES APPEAR IN STUDENT SUPPLEMENTS
I. Students as Learners—continued		
B. Students as Diverse Learners—continued		
▶ The process of second language acquisition and strategies to support the learning of students for whom English is not a first language	**Chapter 2:** "Learning a Second Language" (pp. 53–55) **Chapter 16:** "Language Differences" (p. 595)	**Video CD 2:** "Bilingual Classroom"
▶ How students' learning is influenced by individual experiences, talents, and prior learning, as well as language, culture, family, and community values, including:	**Chapter 1: "Case Study: Hidden Treasure"** (pp. 3–4) **Chapter 3: "Case Study: The Bad Apple"** (p. 61) **Chapter 4: "Case Study: Why Jack Wasn't in School"** (pp. 103–104) **Chapter 5:** "Considering Diversity When Identifying and Addressing Special Needs" (pp. 178–179) **Chapter 6: "Case Study: Darren's Day at School"** (pp. 183–184); "Prior Knowledge and Working Memory in Long-Term Memory Storage" (pp. 207–208) **Chapter 7:** "Construction in Storage" (pp. 224–226); "When Knowledge Construction Goes Awry" (pp. 235–238)	**Study Guide and Reader:** Supplementary Reading 3, "Ecological Systems Perspectives of Child Development" (pp. 305–308); Supplementary Reading 4, "Parenting Styles and Children's Behavior" (pp. 309–312)
• Multicultural backgrounds	**Chapter 2:** "Vygotsky's Theory of Cognitive Development" (pp. 33–42) **Chapter 3:** "Effects of Culture" (pp. 62–63); "Promoting Social Interaction Among Diverse Groups" (pp. 85–86) **Chapter 4: "Case Study: Why Jack Wasn't in School"** (pp. 103–104); "Cultural and Ethnic Differences" (pp. 105–116) **Chapter 6:** "Accomodating Diversity in Cognitive Processes" (pp. 217–219) **Chapter 7:** "Considering Diversity in Constructive Processes" (pp. 250–251) **Chapter 15:** "Testwiseness" (p. 566) **Chapter 16:** "Cultural Bias" (pp. 594–595)	**Study Guide and Reader:** Application Exercise 7 (pp. 64–67)
• Age-appropriate knowledge and behavior	**Chapter 2: "Case Study: Economic Activities"** (pp. 19–20); "Piaget's Stages of Cognitive Development" (pp. 26–31); "An Information Processing View of Cognitive Development" (pp. 42–49); "Trends in Language Development" (pp. 50–53)	**Video CD 2:** "Charles's Law"; "Civil War"; "Properties of Air"; "Reading Group"; "Scarlet Letter"
• The student culture at school	**Chapter 3:** "Peer Relationships" (pp. 73–77); "Promoting Social Interaction Among Diverse Groups" (pp. 85–86) **Chapter 4:** "Navigating Different Cultures at Home and at School" (pp. 105–107)	**Video CD 1:** "Friendships"; "Emotions"
• Family backgrounds	**Chapter 3:** "Effects of Parenting" (p. 62) **Chapter 4:** "Socioeconomic Differences" (pp. 124–129)	**Study Guide and Reader:** Supplementary Reading 4, "Parenting Styles and Children's Behavior" (pp. 309–312)
• Linguistic patterns and differences	**Chapter 2:** "Linguistic Development" (pp. 49–55) **Chapter 5:** "Speech and Communication Disorders" (pp. 161–162) **Chapter 16:** "Language Differences" (p. 595)	**Study Guide and Reader:** Application Exercise 7 (pp. 64–67)
• Cognitive patterns and differences	**Chapter 6:** "Accommodating Diversity in Cognitive Processes" (pp. 217–219) **Chapter 7:** "Considering Diversity in Constructive Processes" (pp. 250–251)	
• Social and emotional issues	**Chapter 3:** "Social Cognition" (pp. 77–83); "Determinants of Moral and Prosocial Behavior" (pp. 92–93) **Chapter 5:** "Temperament" (pp. 149–151); "Emotional and Behavioral Disorders" (pp. 163–166) **Chapter 11:** "Affect and Its Effects" (pp. 374–383) **Chapter 15:** "Test Anxiety" (pp. 564–565)	**Study Guide and Reader:** Application Exercise 19 (pp. 178–179) **Video CD 1:** "Friendships"; "Emotions"

continued

TABLE C.1—continued

Matching Book and Ancillary Content to the Praxis *Principles of Learning and Teaching* Tests

TOPICS IN THE PRAXIS PRINCIPLES OF LEARNING AND TEACHING TESTS	WHERE TOPICS APPEAR IN ORMROD'S *EDUCATIONAL PSYCHOLOGY* (5TH ED.)	WHERE TOPICS AND PRACTICE OPPORTUNITIES APPEAR IN STUDENT SUPPLEMENTS
I. Students as Learners—continued		
C. Student Motivation and the Learning Environment		
▶ Theoretical foundations about human motivation and behavior	**Chapters 11, 12:** Entire chapters (pp. 364–430)	**Study Guide and Reader:** Application Exercises 19–24 (pp. 178–181, 194–201)
• Abraham Maslow		**Study Guide and Reader:** Supplementary Reading 7, "Maslow's Hierarchy of Needs" (pp. 317–320)
• Albert Bandura	**Chapter 10:** Entire chapter (pp. 328–363)	**Study Guide and Reader:** Application Exercises 17–18, 22 (pp. 163–168, 196–197)
• B. F. Skinner	**Chapter 9:** "Operant Conditioning" (pp. 301–310); "Shaping New Behaviors" (pp. 310–311)	**Study Guide and Reader:** Application Exercises 15, 16 (pp. 147–151); Supplementary Reading 10, "A Shocking Lesson" (pp. 330–333)
▶ Important terms that relate to motivation and behavior		
• Hierarchy of needs		**Study Guide and Reader:** Supplementary Reading 7, "Maslow's Hierarchy of Needs" (pp. 317–320)
• Correlational and causal relationships	**Chapter 12: "Case Study: Passing Algebra"** (pp. 391–392); "Attributions: Perceived Causes of Success and Failure" (pp. 412–419)	**Study Guide and Reader:** Application Exercise 23 (pp. 198–199)
• Intrinsic motivation	**Chapter 9:** "Positive Reinforcement" (pp. 304–305); "Promoting Intrinsic Reinforcement" (p. 320); "Strengths and Potential Limitations of Behavioral Approaches" (pp. 324–326) **Chapter 10:** "How Self-Efficacy Affects Behavior and Cognition" (pp. 341–342) **Chapter 11: "Case Study: Quick Draw"** (p. 365); "Extrinsic Versus Intrinsic Motivation" (pp. 367–368) **Chapter 12:** "Self-Perceptions and Intrinsic Motivation" (pp. 392–398); "Expectancies and Values" (pp. 398–400); "Interest" (pp. 400–403); "Achievement Goals" (pp. 404–407); "Dispositions" (pp. 410–412); "The Big Picture" (pp. 428–429)	**Study Guide and Reader:** Application Exercises 19–22 (pp. 178–181, 194–197) **Video CD 1:** "Motivation" **Video CD 2:** "Properties of Air"
• Extrinsic motivation	**Chapter 9:** "Operant Conditioning" (pp. 301–310) **Chapter 11:** "Extrinsic Versus Intrinsic Motivation" (pp. 367–368) **Chapter 12:** "Achievement Goals" (pp. 404–407) **Chapter 15:** "Assessments as motivators" (p. 527)	**Study Guide and Reader:** Application Exercises 16, 19–22 (pp. 147–151, 178–181, 194–197)
• Learned helplessness	**Chapter 12:** "Mastery Orientation Versus Learned Helplessness" (pp. 418–419); **"Case Study: Writer's Block"** (p. 430)	
• Self-efficacy	**Chapter 3:** "Development of a Sense of Self" (pp. 65–72) **Chapter 10: "Case Study: Parlez-Vous Français?"** (p. 329); "Self-Efficacy" (pp. 340–346); "Teacher Self-Efficacy" (p. 346); "Using Diverse Models to Promote Success and Self-Efficacy" (p. 359) **Chapter 12:** "Self-Efficacy" (pp. 393–394)	**Study Guide and Reader:** Application Exercises 17, 18, 22 (pp. 163–168, 196–197) **Video CD 1:** "Portfolio"
• Operant conditioning	**Chapter 9:** "Operant Conditioning" (pp. 301–310); "Shaping New Behaviors" (pp. 310–311)	**Study Guide and Reader:** Application Exercises 15, 16 (pp. 147–151)
• Reinforcement	**Chapter 9: "Case Study: The Attention Getter"** (p. 295); "Reinforcement in the Classroom" (pp. 302–307); "Using Reinforcement Effectively" (pp. 307–310); "Reinforcing Incompatible Behaviors" (p. 315) **Chapter 10: "Case Study: Teacher's Lament"** (p. 363); "Vicarious Experiences" (pp. 332); "Nonoccurrence of Expected Consequences" (pp. 333–334) **Chapter 14:** "Using Behaviorist Approaches" (pp. 503–504)	**Study Guide and Reader:** Application Exercises 15, 16 (pp. 147–151) **Video CD 2:** "Cooperative Learning"; "Reading Group"

TABLE C.1—continued

Matching Book and Ancillary Content to the Praxis *Principles of Learning and Teaching* Tests

TOPICS IN THE PRAXIS PRINCIPLES OF LEARNING AND TEACHING TESTS	WHERE TOPICS APPEAR IN ORMROD'S *EDUCATIONAL PSYCHOLOGY* (5TH ED.)	WHERE TOPICS AND PRACTICE OPPORTUNITIES APPEAR IN STUDENT SUPPLEMENTS
I. Students as Learners—continued		
C. Student Motivation and the Learning Environment—continued		
• Positive reinforcement	**Chapter 9:** "Positive reinforcement" (pp. 304–305)	**Study Guide and Reader:** Application Exercises 15, 16 (pp. 147–151)
• Negative reinforcement	**Chapter 9:** "Negative reinforcement" (pp. 305–306)	**Study Guide and Reader:** Application Exercise 15 (pp. 147–148)
• Shaping successive approximations	**Chapter 9:** "Shaping New Behaviors" (pp. 310–311)	**Study Guide and Reader:** Supplementary Reading 10, "A Shocking Lesson" (pp. 330–333)
• Prevention	**Chapter 9:** "Functional Analysis and Positive Behavioral Support" (pp. 322–323) **Chapter 14:** "Creating an Environment Conducive to Learning" (pp. 484–499); "Creating a Nonviolent School Environment" (pp. 506–507); Figure 14.4 (p. 508)	**Study Guide and Reader:** Application Exercises 27, 28 (pp. 230–236)
• Extinction	**Chapter 9:** "Reducing and Eliminating Undesirable Behaviors" (pp. 314–319); **"Case Study: Hostile Helen"** (pp. 326–327) **Chapter 14:** "Ignoring Behavior" (pp. 499–500)	**Study Guide and Reader:** Application Exercise 15 (pp. 147–148)
• Punishment	**Chapter 9:** "Punishment" (pp. 315–319) **Chapter 10: "Case Study: Teacher's Lament"** (p. 363); "Vicarious Experiences" (p. 332); "Nonoccurrence of Expected Consequences" (pp. 333–334)	**Study Guide and Reader:** Application Exercise 28 (pp. 233–236)
• Continuous reinforcement	**Chapter 9:** "Using Reinforcement Effectively" (pp. 307–310)	**Study Guide and Reader:** Application Exercise 16 (pp. 149–151)
• Intermittent reinforcement	**Chapter 9:** "Using Intermittent Reinforcement" (pp. 320–321)	**Study Guide and Reader:** Application Exercise 16 (pp. 149–151)
▶ How knowledge of human motivation and behavior should influence strategies for organizing and supporting individual and group work in the classroom	**Chapters 11–12:** Entire chapters (pp. 364–430)	**Study Guide and Reader:** Application Exercises 16, 20, 22, 24 (pp. 149–151, 180–181, 196–197, 200–201) **Video CD 2:** "Author's Chair"; "Cooperative Learning"
▶ Factors and situations that are likely to promote or diminish students' motivation to learn; how to help students to become self-motivated	**Chapter 10:** "Self-Regulation" (pp. 346–356); "Promoting Self-Regulation in Students at Risk" (p. 360) **Chapters 11–12:** Entire chapters (pp. 364–430) **Chapter 14:** "Teaching Self-Regulation Strategies" (pp. 502–503)	**Study Guide and Reader:** Application Exercises 18–24 (pp. 166–168, 178–181, 194–201) **Video CD 1:** "Motivation"
▶ Principles of effective classroom management and strategies to promote positive relationships, cooperation, and purposeful learning	**Chapters 3–5, 9–12, 14:** "Creating a Productive Classroom Environment" features (pp. 83, 132, 150, 168, 313, 320, 334, 375, 411, 497) **Chapter 3:** "Fostering Social Skills" (pp. 83–84); "Promoting Social Interaction Among Diverse Groups" (pp. 85–86); "Promoting Moral and Prosocial Behavior in the Classroom" (pp. 93–95)	**Study Guide and Reader:** Application Exercise 27 (pp. 230–232) **Video CD 2:** "Author's Chair"; "Cooperative Learning"; "Group Work"
• Establishing daily procedures and routines	**Chapter 14:** Entire chapter (p. 482–520) **Chapter 14:** "Giving Students a Sense of Control" (p. 488); **"Case Study: Old Friends"** (p. 520)	
• Establishing classroom rules	**Chapter 10:** "Expectations" (pp. 331–332); "Nonoccurrence of Expected Consequences" (pp. 333–334) **Chapter 14:** "Setting Limits" (pp. 490–493)	**Video CD 2:** "Classroom Rules"
• Using natural and logical consequences	**Chapter 9:** "Logical consequences" (p. 317)	
• Providing positive guidance	**Chapter 3:** "Fostering Social Skills" (pp. 83–84) **Chapter 9:** "Shaping New Behaviors" (pp. 310–311); "Reducing and Eliminating Undesirable Behaviors" (pp. 314–319); "Addressing Especially Difficult Classroom Behaviors" (pp. 321–323)	**Video CD 2:** "Author's Chair"; "Reading Group" **Video CD 2:** "Author's Chair"; "Reading Group"

continued

TABLE C.1—continued

Matching Book and Ancillary Content to the Praxis *Principles of Learning and Teaching* Tests

TOPICS IN THE PRAXIS PRINCIPLES OF LEARNING AND TEACHING TESTS	WHERE TOPICS APPEAR IN ORMROD'S *EDUCATIONAL PSYCHOLOGY* (5TH ED.)	WHERE TOPICS AND PRACTICE OPPORTUNITIES APPEAR IN STUDENT SUPPLEMENTS
I. Students as Learners—continued		
C. Student Motivation and the Learning Environment—continued		
• Modeling conflict resolution, problem solving, and anger management	**Chapter 10:** "Self-Regulated Problem Solving" (pp. 355–356) **Chapter 14:** "Addressing Aggression and Violence at School" (pp. 504–507)	
• Giving timely feedback	**Chapter 9:** "Positive Versus Negative Reinforcement" (pp. 303–307); "Cueing Inappropriate Behaviors" (pp. 314–315) **Chapter 11: "Case Study: When 'Perfect' Isn't Good Enough"** (pp. 387–388) **Chapter 14:** "Cueing a Student" (p. 500); "Discussing a Problem Privately with a Student" (pp. 500–502) **Chapter 15:** "Scoring Students' Responses" (two sections, on pp. 550–551 and 556–557)	
• Maintaining accurate records	**Chapter 15:** "Informal Assessment" (pp. 539–541) **Chapter 16:** "Determining Final Class Grades" (pp. 577–582)	
• Communicating with parents and caregivers	**Chapter 14:** "Conferring with Parents" (p. 504); "Working with Parents" (pp. 512–519) **Chapter 16:** "Communicating Assessment Results to Students and Parents" (pp. 598–599)	
• Using objective behavior descriptions	**Chapter 5:** "General Recommendations for Students with Social or Behavioral Problems" (pp. 167–168) **Chapter 9:** "Using Reinforcement Effectively" (pp. 307–310); "Addressing Especially Difficult Classroom Behaviors" (pp. 321–323) **Chapter 14:** "Using Behaviorist Approaches" (pp. 503–504); "Accommodating Students with Special Needs" (pp. 510–511)	
• Responding to student misbehavior	**Chapter 9:** "Addressing Especially Difficult Classroom Behaviors" (pp. 321–323) **Chapter 14:** "Dealing with Misbehaviors" (pp. 499–504); "Addressing Aggression and Violence at School" (pp. 504–507); "Defining and Responding to Misbehaviors" (p. 509)	**Study Guide and Reader:** Application Exercise 28 (pp. 233–236) **Video CD 2:** "Reading Group"
• Arranging of classroom space	**Chapter 14:** "Arranging the Classroom" (p. 485)	
• Pacing and structuring the lesson	**Chapter 5:** "Mental Retardation" (pp. 169–170) **Chapter 6: "Case Study: How Time Flies"** (p. 220) **Chapter 13:** "Conducting a Task Analysis" (pp. 440–442); Table 13.3 (p. 444) **Chapter 14:** "Planning Activities That Keep Students on Task" (pp. 493–496)	
II. Instruction and Assessment		
A. Instructional Strategies		
▶ The major cognitive processes associated with student learning, including:	**Chapters 6–8:** Entire chapters (pp. 182–293) **Chapter 13: "Case Study: Oregon Trail"** (pp. 433–434)	**Study Guide and Reader:** Application Exercises 9–14 (pp. 95–100, 110–16, 129–132); Supplementary Reading 14, "Learning in the Content Areas" (pp. 343–406)
• Critical thinking	**Chapter 8:** "Critical Thinking" (pp. 287–289)	
• Creative thinking	**Chapter 8:** "Creativity" (pp. 284–287)	
• Higher-order thinking	**Chapter 8:** Entire chapter (pp. 254–293) **Chapter 12:** "Dispositions" (pp. 410–412) **Chapter 13:** "Formulating Useful Goals and Objectives" (pp. 438–440)	**Video CD 1:** "Memory and Metacognition" **Video CD 2:** "Civil War"; "Group Work"; "Scarlet Letter"

TABLE C.1—continued

Matching Book and Ancillary Content to the Praxis *Principles of Learning and Teaching* Tests

TOPICS IN THE PRAXIS PRINCIPLES OF LEARNING AND TEACHING TESTS	WHERE TOPICS APPEAR IN ORMROD'S *EDUCATIONAL PSYCHOLOGY* (5TH ED.)	WHERE TOPICS AND PRACTICE OPPORTUNITIES APPEAR IN STUDENT SUPPLEMENTS
II. Instruction and Assessment—continued		
A. Instructional Strategies—continued		
• Inductive and deductive thinking	**Chapter 2:** "Piaget's Stages of Cognitive Development" (pp. 26–31) **Chapter 8:** "Critical Thinking" (pp. 287–289)	**Study Guide and Reader:** Supplementary Reading 14, "Learning in the Content Areas" (pp. 343–406) **Video CD 1:** "Cognitive Development"
• Problem-structuring and problem-solving	**Chapter 8:** "Problem Solving" (pp. 274–284)	**Study Guide and Reader:** Application Exercise 14 (pp. 131–132); Supplementary Reading 14, "Learning in the Content Areas" (pp. 343–406) **Video CD 2:** "Charles's Law"
• Invention	**Chapter 8:** "Creativity" (pp. 284–287)	
• Memorization and recall	**Chapter 6:** Entire chapter (pp. 182–221)	**Study Guide and Reader:** Application Exercise 9–12 (pp. 95–100, 110–116) **Video CD 1:** "Memory and Metacognition"
• Social reasoning	**Chapter 3:** "Social Cognition" (pp. 77–83); "Developmental Trends in Morality and Prosocial Behavior" (pp. 87–89); "Development of Moral Reasoning" (pp. 89–91); "Possible Gender Differences in Moral Reasoning" (pp. 91–92); **"Case Study: *The Scarlet Letter*"** (pp. 99–100)	**Video CD 1:** "Friendships"; "Emotions" **Video CD 2:** "Civil War"; "Scarlet Letter"
• Representation of ideas	**Chapter 6:** "The Nature of Long-Term Memory" (p. 195); "Long-Term Memory Storage" (pp. 196–210) **Chapter 7:** "Organizing Knowledge" (pp. 228–235)	**Video CD 2:** "Group Work"; "Scarlet Letter"
▶ Major categories of instructional strategies, including:	**Chapter 13:** Entire chapter (pp. 432–481)	**Study Guide and Reader:** Application Exercise 26 (pp. 215–219)
• Cooperative learning	**Chapter 7:** "Benefits of Joint Meaning-Making with Peers" (pp. 227–228) **Chapter 13:** "Cooperative Learning" (pp. 465–470); **Case Study: Uncooperative Students** (p. 480)	**Video CD 2:** "Cooperative Learning"; "Group Work"
• Direct instruction	**Chapter 13:** "Direct Instruction" (pp. 447–448)	**Video CD 2:** "Charles's Law"; "Reading Group"
• Discovery learning	**Chapter 13:** "Discovery Learning" (pp. 451–453)	**Video CD 2:** "Charles's Law"; "Designing Experiments"; "Properties of Air"
• Whole-group discussion	**Chapter 7:** "Benefits of Joint Meaning-Making with Peers" (pp. 227–228); "Promoting Dialogue" (pp. 241–242) **Chapter 13:** "Class Discussions" (pp. 460–462)	**Study Guide and Reader:** Supplementary Reading 14, "Learning in the Content Areas" (pp. 343–406) **Video CD 2:** "Author's Chair"; "Properties of Air"; "Scarlet Letter"
• Independent study	**Chapter 5:** "Giftedness" (pp. 176–178) **Chapter 13:** "Computer-Based Instruction" (pp. 449–450); "Online Research" (p. 450); "Homework" (pp. 455–456)	**Study Guide and Reader:** Supplementary Reading 6, "Promoting Information Literacy Skills" (pp. 314–316); Supplementary Reading 10, "A Shocking Lesson" (pp. 330–333)
• Interdisciplinary instruction	**Chapter 6:** "Making Multiple Connections with Existing Knowledge" (p. 211) **Chapter 8:** "Factors Affecting Transfer" (pp. 271–273)	
• Concept mapping	**Chapter 8:** "Organizing Information" (pp. 261–263) **Chapter 13:** Table 13.3 (p. 444)	
• Inquiry method	**Chapter 7:** "Providing Opportunities for Experimentation" (pp. 238–239)	**Study Guide and Reader:** Supplementary Reading 14, "Learning in the Content Areas" (pp. 343–406)
• Questioning	**Chapter 4:** "Questions" (p. 109) **Chapter 8:** "The Nature of Higher-Level Thinking" (pp. 256–257); "Fostering Creativity" (pp. 285–287) **Chapter 13:** "Teacher Questions" (pp. 458–460)	**Video CD 2:** All videos

continued

TABLE C.1—continued

Matching Book and Ancillary Content to the Praxis *Principles of Learning and Teaching* Tests

TOPICS IN THE PRAXIS PRINCIPLES OF LEARNING AND TEACHING TESTS	WHERE TOPICS APPEAR IN ORMROD'S *EDUCATIONAL PSYCHOLOGY* (5TH ED.)	WHERE TOPICS AND PRACTICE OPPORTUNITIES APPEAR IN STUDENT SUPPLEMENTS
II. Instruction and Assessment—continued		
A. Instructional Strategies—continued		
• Play	**Chapter 2:** "Vygotsky's Basic Assumptions" (pp. 33–42)	
• Learning centers		
• Small group work	**Chapter 13:** "Cooperative Learning" (pp. 465–470); "Peer Tutoring" (pp. 470–474)	**Video CD 2:** "Cooperative Learning"; "Designing Experiments"; "Group Work"
• Revisiting	**Chapter 6:** "Using Knowledge Frequently" (p. 212)	
• Reflection	**Chapter 10:** "Self-Evaluation" (pp. 350–351) **Chapter 15:** "Including Students in the Assessment Process" (pp. 561–562)	**Video CD 1:** "Portfolio"
• Project approach	**Chapter 7:** "Using Authentic Activities" (pp. 242–243) **Chapter 13:** "Authentic Activities" (pp. 456–457)	
▶ Principles, techniques, and methods associated with various instructional strategies, including:	**Chapter 13:** Entire chapter (pp. 432–481)	**Study Guide and Reader:** Application Exercises 10, 26 (pp. 97–100, 215–219)
• Direct instruction	**Chapter 13:** "Direct Instruction" (pp. 447–448)	
– Madeline Hunter's "Effective Teaching Model"		
– David Ausubel's "Advance Organizers"	**Chapter 13:** Table 13.3 (p. 444)	**Study Guide and Reader:** Application Exercise 26 (pp. 215–219) **Video CD 2:** "Civil War"
– Mastery learning	**Chapter 13:** "Mastery Learning" (pp. 446–447)	
– Demonstrations	**Chapter 10:** "Helping Students Learn from Models" (pp. 338–340); "Successes and Failures of Others" (p. 343)	**Study Guide and Reader:** Application Exercises 17, 18 (pp. 163–168) **Video CD 2:** "Charles's Law"; "Properties of Air"
– Mnemonics	**Chapter 5:** "Learning Disabilities" (pp. 155–159) **Chapter 6:** "Using Mnemonics in the Absence of Relevant Prior Knowledge" (pp. 208–210)	**Video CD 1:** "Memory and Metacognition: Middle Childhood"; "Memory and Metacognition: Late Adolescence" **Video CD 2:** "Group Work"
– Note-taking	**Chapter 8:** "Taking Notes" (pp. 260–261)	**Study Guide and Reader:** Application Exercise 13 (pp. 129–130)
– Outlining	**Chapter 8:** "Organizing Information" (pp. 261–263)	
– Use of visual aids	**Chapter 5:** "Visual Impairments" (pp. 171–172) **Chapter 6:** "Visual Imagery" (pp. 204–205) **Chapter 13:** Table 13.3 (p. 444)	**Study Guide and Reader:** Application Exercise 10 (pp. 97–100) **Video CD 2:** "Civil War"
– Student-centered models	**Chapter 13:** "Overview of Instructional Strategies" (pp. 434–435)	**Study Guide and Reader:** Application Exercise 26 (pp. 215–219)
– Inquiry model	**Chapter 7:** "Providing Opportunities for Experimentation" (pp. 238–239)	
– Discovery learning	**Chapter 13:** "Discovery Learning" (pp. 451–453)	**Video CD 2:** "Designing Experiments"
– Cooperative learning (pair-share, jigsaw, STAD, teams, games, tournaments)	**Chapter 13:** "Cooperative Learning" (pp. 465–470)	**Video CD 2:** "Cooperative Learning"; "Group Work"
– Collaborative learning	**Chapter 13:** "Cooperative Learning" (pp. 465–470); "Peer Tutoring" (pp. 470–474)	

TABLE C.1—continued

Matching Book and Ancillary Content to the Praxis *Principles of Learning and Teaching* Tests

TOPICS IN THE PRAXIS PRINCIPLES OF LEARNING AND TEACHING TESTS	WHERE TOPICS APPEAR IN ORMROD'S *EDUCATIONAL PSYCHOLOGY* (5TH ED.)	WHERE TOPICS AND PRACTICE OPPORTUNITIES APPEAR IN STUDENT SUPPLEMENTS
II. Instruction and Assessment—continued		
A. Instructional Strategies—continued		
– Concept models (concept development, concept attainment, concept mapping)	**Chapter 7:** "Concepts" (pp. 228–232) **Chapter 8:** "Organizing Information" (pp. 261–263) **Chapter 13:** Table 13.3 (p. 444)	**Study Guide and Reader:** Application Exercises 11, 12 (pp. 110–116)
– Discussion models	**Chapter 7:** "Creating a Community of Learners" (pp. 243–245) **Chapter 13:** "Class Discussions" (pp. 460–462); "Technology-Based Discussions" (p. 465)	**Video CD 2:** "Scarlet Letter"
– Laboratories		**Study Guide and Reader:** Supplementary Reading 14, "Learning in the Content Areas" (see "Case Study: All Charged Up," pp. 405–406)
– Project-based learning	**Chapter 7:** "Using Authentic Activities" (pp. 242–243) **Chapter 13:** "Authentic Activities" (pp. 456–457)	**Video CD 2:** "Designing Experiments"
– Simulations	**Chapter 13:** "Computer Simulations and Applications" (p. 454)	**Study Guide and Reader:** Application Exercise 26 (pp. 215–219)
▶ Methods for enhancing student learning through the use of a variety of resources and materials		
• Computers, Internet resources, Web pages, e-mail	**Chapter 5:** "General Recommendations for Students with Physical and Sensory Challenges" (pp. 174–175) **Chapter 7:** "Creating a Community of Learners" (pp. 243–245) **Chapter 8:** "Using Computer Technology to Promote Problem Solving" (pp. 283–284) **Chapter 13:** "Computer-Based Instruction" (pp. 449–450); "Online Research" (p. 450); "Computer Simulations and Applications" (p. 454); "Technology-Based Discussions" (p. 465)	**Study Guide and Reader:** Application Exercise 26 (pp. 215–219); Supplementary Reading 10, "A Shocking Lesson" (pp. 330–333)
• Audio-visual technologies such as videotapes and compact discs	**Chapter 8:** "Using Computer Technology to Promote Problem Solving" (pp. 283–284) **Chapter 10:** "Using Diverse Models to Promote Success and Self-Efficacy" (p. 359)	
• Local experts	**Chapter 5:** "Giftedness" (pp. 176–178)	
• Primary documents and artifacts		**Study Guide and Reader:** Supplementary Reading 14, "Learning in the Content Areas" (pp. 343–406)
• Field trips	**Chapter 5:** "Students with Physical and Sensory Challenges" (pp. 170–175)	**Study Guide and Reader:** Chapter 13 (see "Answers to Selected Margin Notes," pp. 211–212)
• Libraries		**Study Guide and Reader:** Supplementary Reading 6, "Promoting Information Literacy Skills" (pp. 314–316)
• Service learning	**Chapter 3:** "Promoting Moral Development in the Classroom" (pp. 93–95)	
B. Planning Instruction		
▶ Techniques for planning instruction to meet curriculum goals, including the incorporation of learning theory, subject matter, curriculum development, and student development	**Chapter 13:** "Planning for Instruction" (pp. 435–443) **Chapter 14:** "**Case Study: A Contagious Situation**" (p. 483)	

continued

TABLE C.1—continued

Matching Book and Ancillary Content to the Praxis *Principles of Learning and Teaching* Tests

TOPICS IN THE PRAXIS PRINCIPLES OF LEARNING AND TEACHING TESTS	WHERE TOPICS APPEAR IN ORMROD'S *EDUCATIONAL PSYCHOLOGY* (5TH ED.)	WHERE TOPICS AND PRACTICE OPPORTUNITIES APPEAR IN STUDENT SUPPLEMENTS
II. Instruction and Assessment—continued		
B. Planning Instruction—continued		
• National and state learning standards	**Chapter 13:** "Aligning Instructional Goals with State and National Standards" (pp. 436–438) **Chapter 15:** Table 15.2 (p. 536)	
• State and local curriculum frameworks	**Chapter 13:** Table 13.1 (p. 437) **Chapter 15:** Table 15.2 (p. 536) **Chapter 16:** "Criterion-Referenced Scores" (pp. 573–574)	
• State and local curriculum guides		
• Scope and sequence in specific disciplines	**Chapter 13:** "Formulating Useful Goals" (pp. 438–440); "Conducting a Task Analysis" (pp. 440–442)	**Study Guide and Reader:** Supplementary Reading 8, "Using Taxonomies to Formulate Instructional Goals and Objectives" (pp. 321–325)
• Units and lessons—rationale for selecting content topics	**Chapter 13:** "Developing a Lesson Plan" (pp. 442–443)	**Study Guide and Reader:** Supplementary Reading 9, "Example of a Lesson Plan" (pp. 326–329)
• Behavioral objectives: affective, cognitive, psychomotor	**Chapter 13:** "Formulating Useful Goals" (pp. 438–440); "Conducting a Task Analysis" (pp. 440–442)	**Study Guide and Reader:** Supplementary Reading 8, "Using Taxonomies to Formulate Instructional Goals and Objectives" (pp. 321–325)
• Learner objectives and outcomes	**Chapter 12:** "Achievement Goals" (pp. 404–407) **Chapter 13:** "Identifying the Goals of Instruction" (pp. 436–440) **Chapter 15:** "Content Validity" (pp. 535–537)	**Study Guide and Reader:** Application Exercise 25 (pp. 213–214)
• Emergent curriculum		
• Anti-bias curriculum	**Chapter 4:** "Creating a More Multicultural Classroom Environment" (pp. 113–116)	
• Themes/projects	**Chapter 7:** "Emphasizing Conceptual Understanding" (pp. 239–241)	
• Curriculum webbing		
▶ Techniques for creating effective bridges between curriculum goals and students' experiences	**Chapter 13:** "Planning for Instruction" (pp. 435–443)	
• Modeling	**Chapter 10:** "Modeling" (pp. 334–340); "Using Diverse Models to Promote Success and Self-Efficacy" (p. 359)	**Study Guide and Reader:** Application Exercises 17, 18 (pp. 163–168)
• Guided practice	**Chapter 2:** "Scaffolding" (pp. 39–41); "Guided Participation" (p. 41); "Apprenticeships" (pp. 41–42)	**Video CD 2:** "Group Work"
• Independent practice, including homework	**Chapter 10:** "Self-Regulated Learning" (pp. 352–355) **Chapter 13:** "Homework" (pp. 455–456)	**Study Guide and Reader:** Application Exercise 26 (pp. 215–219)
• Transitions	**Chapter 14:** "Planning for Transitions" (pp. 495–496)	
• Activating students' prior knowledge	**Chapter 6:** "Moving Information to Long-Term Memory: Connecting New Information with Prior Knowledge" (pp. 194–195); "Prior Knowledge and Working Memory in Long-Term Memory Storage" (pp. 207–208) **Chapter 8:** "Retrieving Relevant Prior Knowledge" (p. 260) **Chapter 13:** Table 13.3 (p. 444)	**Study Guide and Reader:** Application Exercise 10 (pp. 97–100) **Video CD 2:** "Charles's Law"; "Civil War"; "Properties of Air"
• Anticipating preconceptions	**Chapter 2: "Case Study: In the Eye of the Beholder"** (p. 58) **Chapter 7:** "When Knowledge Construction Goes Awry" (pp. 235–238); "Promoting Conceptual Change" (pp. 247–249)	**Study Guide and Reader:** Application Exercise 12 (pp. 113–116) **Video CD 2:** "Properties of Air"

TABLE C.1—continued

Matching Book and Ancillary Content to the Praxis *Principles of Learning and Teaching* Tests

TOPICS IN THE PRAXIS PRINCIPLES OF LEARNING AND TEACHING TESTS	WHERE TOPICS APPEAR IN ORMROD'S *EDUCATIONAL PSYCHOLOGY* (5TH ED.)	WHERE TOPICS AND PRACTICE OPPORTUNITIES APPEAR IN STUDENT SUPPLEMENTS
II. Instruction and Assessment—continued		
B. Planning Instruction—continued		
• Encouraging exploration and problem-solving	**Chapter 2:** "Piaget's Basic Assumptions" (pp. 25–26) **Chapter 7:** "Providing Opportunities for Experimentation" (pp. 238–239) **Chapter 8:** "Problem Solving" (pp. 274–284) **Chapter 10:** "Self-Regulated Problem Solving" (pp. 355–356) **Chapter 13:** "Discovery Learning" (pp. 451–453)	**Study Guide and Reader:** Application Exercise 8 (pp. 80–82)
• Building new skills on those previously acquired	**Chapter 4:** "Building on Students' Strengths" (p. 129) **Chapter 6:** "How Procedural Knowledge Is Learned" (pp. 206–207) **Chapter 9:** "Shaping New Behaviors" (pp. 310–311) **Chapter 13:** "Mastery Learning" (pp. 446–447)	
• Predicting		**Study Guide and Reader:** Supplementary Reading 14, "Learning in the Content Areas" (pp. 343–406) **Video CD 2:** "Properties of Air"
C. Assessment Strategies		
▶ Measurement theory and assessment-related issues	**Chapters 1–16:** "Interpreting Student Artifacts and Behaviors" exercises **Chapters 15–16:** Entire chapters (pp. 522–600)	**Study Guide and Reader:** Application Exercises 29–32 (pp. 250–257, 270–275)
• Types of assessments	**Chapter 15:** "The Various Forms of Educational Assessment" (pp. 525–526)	
– Standardized tests, norm-referenced or criterion-referenced	**Chapter 15:** "The Various Forms of Educational Assessment" (pp. 525–526) **Chapter 16:** "Standardized Tests" (pp. 584–591); "High-Stakes Testing and Accountability" (pp. 591–593)	**Study Guide and Reader:** Application Exercise 32 (pp. 272–275)
– Achievement tests	**Chapter 16:** "Achievement Tests" (pp. 584–585); **"Case Study: Can Johnny Read?"** (p. 600)	
– Aptitude tests	**Chapter 16:** "Scholastic Aptitude and Intelligence Tests" (p. 586); "Specific Aptitude Tests" (p. 586)	
– Structured observations	**Chapter 15:** "Planning and Administering the [Performance] Assessment" (pp. 555–556)	
– Anecdotal notes	**Chapter 15:** "Informal Assessment" (pp. 539–541)	
– Assessments of prior knowledge	**Chapter 15:** "Guiding Instructional Decision Making" (p. 529)	
– Student responses during a lesson	**Chapter 15:** "Informal Assessment" (pp. 539–541)	
– Portfolios	**Chapter 16:** "Using Portfolios" (pp. 582–584)	**Study Guide and Reader:** Application Exercise 32 (pp. 272–275) **Video CD 1:** "Portfolio"
– Essays written to prompts	**Chapter 15:** "Essay Tasks" (pp. 547–548)	**Study Guide and Reader:** Application Exercise 30 (pp. 252–257)
– Journals	**Chapter 14:** "Forming and Maintaining Productive Teacher-Student Relationships" (pp. 486–488) **Chapter 15:** "Including Students in the Assessment Process" (pp. 561–562)	
– Self-evaluations	**Chapter 10:** "Self-Evaluation" (pp. 350–351) **Chapter 15:** "Including Students in the Assessment Process" (pp. 561–562) **Chapter 16:** "Including Students in the Grading Process" (pp. 581–582); "Using Portfolios" (pp. 582–584)	**Video CD 1:** "Portfolio"

continued

TABLE C.1—continued

Matching Book and Ancillary Content to the Praxis *Principles of Learning and Teaching* Tests

TOPICS IN THE PRAXIS PRINCIPLES OF LEARNING AND TEACHING TESTS	WHERE TOPICS APPEAR IN ORMROD'S *EDUCATIONAL PSYCHOLOGY* (5TH ED.)	WHERE TOPICS AND PRACTICE OPPORTUNITIES APPEAR IN STUDENT SUPPLEMENTS
II. Instruction and Assessment—continued		
C. Assessment Strategies—continued		
– Performance assessments	**Chapter 15:** "Performance Assessment" (pp. 553–559)	**Study Guide and Reader:** Application Exercise 30 (pp. 252–257)
• Characteristics of assessments	**Chapter 15: "Case Study: Pick and Choose"** (p. 569) **Chapter 16: "Case Study: Can Johnny Read?"** (p. 600)	
– Validity	**Chapter 15:** "Validity" (pp. 534–538); "RSVP Characteristics of Informal Assessment" (pp. 540–541); "RSVP Characteristics of Paper-Pencil Assessment" (pp. 552–553); "RSVP Characteristics of Performance Assessment" (pp. 557–559) **Chapter 16:** "Using Portfolios" (pp. 582–584)	**Study Guide and Reader:** Application Exercises 29, 30 (pp. 250–257)
– Reliability	**Chapter 15:** "Reliability" (pp. 531–534); "RSVP Characteristics of Informal Assessment" (pp. 540–541); "RSVP Characteristics of Paper-Pencil Assessment" (pp. 552–553); "RSVP Characteristics of Performance Assessment" (pp. 557–559) **Chapter 16:** "Using Portfolios" (pp. 582–584)	**Study Guide and Reader:** Application Exercise 29 (pp. 250–251)
– Norm-referenced	**Chapter 15:** "Criterion-referenced versus norm-referenced assessments" (p. 526) **Chapter 16:** "Norm-Referenced Scores" (pp. 574–577); "Using Criterion-Referenced Versus Norm-Referenced Scores in the Classroom" (p. 577); "Choosing Criterion-Referenced or Norm-Referenced Grades" (pp. 580–581)	
– Criterion-referenced	**Chapter 15:** "Criterion-referenced versus norm-referenced assessments" (p. 526) **Chapter 16:** "Criterion-Referenced Scores" (pp. 573–574); "Using Criterion-Referenced Versus Norm-Referenced Scores in the Classroom" (p. 577); "Choosing Criterion-Referenced or Norm-Referenced Grades" (pp. 580–581)	**Study Guide and Reader:** Application Exercise 32 (pp. 272–275)
– Mean, median, mode	**Chapter 16:** "Standard Scores" (pp. 575–577)	
– Sampling strategy	**Chapter 15:** "Content validity" (pp. 535–537)	**Study Guide and Reader:** Application Exercise 30 (pp. 252–257)
• Scoring assessments	**Chapter 15:** "Reliability" (pp. 531–534); "Scoring Students' Responses" (two sections, pp. 550–551 and 556–557)	**Study Guide and Reader:** Application Exercise 30 (pp. 252–257)
– Analytical scoring	**Chapter 15:** "Performance Assessment," especially the section "Scoring Students' Responses" (pp. 556–557)	
– Holistic scoring	**Chapter 15:** "Performance Assessment," especially the section "Scoring Students' Responses" (pp. 556–557)	
– Rubrics	**Chapter 15:** "Paper-Pencil Assessment," especially the section "Scoring Students' Responses" (pp. 550–551); Figure 15.6 (p. 551); Figure 15.7 (p. 557); Figure 15.8 (p. 558)	**Study Guide and Reader:** Application Exercise 30 (pp. 252–257)

– Reporting assessments results
  Percentile rank
  Stanines
  Mastery levels
  Raw score
  Scaled score
  Grade equivalent score
  Standard deviation
  Standard error of measurement
	Chapter 15: "Estimating Error in Assessment Results" (p. 533) **Chapter 16: "Case Study: B in History"** (p. 571); "Summarizing the Results of a Single Assessment" (pp. 572–577); "Confidentiality and Communication About Assessment Results" (pp. 596–599)	**Study Guide and Reader:** Application Exercise 31, 32 (pp. 270–275); Supplementary Reading 11, "Correcting for Guessing in Paper-Pencil Assessments" (pp. 334–335); Supplementary Reading 12, "Calculating Standard Deviations" (pp. 336–340)

TABLE C.1—continued

Matching Book and Ancillary Content to the Praxis *Principles of Learning and Teaching* Tests

TOPICS IN THE PRAXIS PRINCIPLES OF LEARNING AND TEACHING TESTS	WHERE TOPICS APPEAR IN ORMROD'S *EDUCATIONAL PSYCHOLOGY* (5TH ED.)	WHERE TOPICS AND PRACTICE OPPORTUNITIES APPEAR IN STUDENT SUPPLEMENTS
II. Instruction and Assessment—continued		
C. Assessment Strategies—continued		
• Uses of assessments	**Chapters 1–16:** Interpreting Student Artifacts and Behaviors exercises **Chapter 15:** "Using Assessment for Different Purposes" (pp. 527–530)	
– Formative evaluation	**Chapter 15:** "Using Assessment for Different Purposes," especially the introductory paragraphs (p. 527) and the sections "Promoting Learning" (pp. 527–528) and "Guiding Instructional Decision Making" (p. 529)	
– Summative evaluation	**Chapter 15:** "Determining What Students Have Learned" (p. 529)	**Study Guide and Reader:** Application Exercises 30, 32 (pp. 252–257, 272–275); Supplementary Reading 13, "Combining Assessment Results to Determine Final Grades" (pp. 341–342)
– Diagnostic evaluation	**Chapter 15:** "Diagnosing Learning and Performance Problems" (p. 529)	
• Understanding measurement theory and assessment-related issues	**Chapter 15:** "Important Qualities of Good Assessment" (pp. 530–539); "Evaluating an Assessment Tool Through Item Analysis (pp. 563–564); "Test Anxiety" (pp. 564–565); "Testwiseness" (p. 566) **Chapter 16:** "Considering Improvement, Effort, and Extra Credit" (pp. 579–580); "High-Stakes Testing and Accountability" (pp. 591–593); "Cultural Bias" (pp. 594–595)	**Study Guide and Reader:** Application Exercises 30, 32 (pp. 252–257, 272–275)
• Interpreting and communicating results of assessments	**Chapter 16:** "Confidentiality and Communication About Assessment Results" (pp. 596–599)	**Study Guide and Reader:** Application Exercise 32 (pp. 272–275)
III. Communication Techniques		
▶ Basic, effective verbal and nonverbal communication techniques	**Chapter 4:** "Supporting Students at Risk" (pp. 131–133) **Chapter 5:** "Classifying Students with Special Needs" (pp. 154–155) **Chapter 11: "Case Study: When 'Perfect' Isn't Good Enough"** (pp. 387–388) **Chapter 12:** "Self-Determination" (pp. 394–398); "Forming Productive Expectations and Attributions for Student Performance" (pp. 421–424) **Chapter 14:** "Creating an Effective Classroom Climate" (pp. 485–490); "Presenting Rules and Procedures as Information" (pp. 491–492); "Discussing a Problem Privately with a Student" (pp. 500–502); "Working with Parents" (pp. 512–519) **Chapter 15: "Case Study: The Math Test"** (pp. 523–524) **Chapter 16:** "Confidentiality and Communication About Assessment Results" (pp. 596–599)	**Video CD 2:** "Author's Chair"; "Bilingual Classroom"; "Group Work"; "Properties of Air"; "Scarlet Letter"
▶ The effect of cultural and gender differences on communications in the classroom	**Chapter 4:** "Examples of Cultural and Ethnic Diversity" (pp. 107–113)	
▶ Types of questions that can stimulate discussion in different ways for particular purposes	**Chapter 13:** "Teacher Questions" (pp. 458–460)	
• Probing for learner understanding	**Chapter 5:** "Hearing Loss" (pp. 172–174) **Chapter 6:** "Attention in the Classroom" (pp. 192–193) **Chapter 7:** "Promoting Conceptual Change" (pp. 247–249)	**Video CD 2:** "Charles's Law"

continued

TABLE C.1—continued

Matching Book and Ancillary Content to the Praxis *Principles of Learning and Teaching* Tests

TOPICS IN THE PRAXIS PRINCIPLES OF LEARNING AND TEACHING TESTS	WHERE TOPICS APPEAR IN ORMROD'S *EDUCATIONAL PSYCHOLOGY* (5TH ED.)	WHERE TOPICS AND PRACTICE OPPORTUNITIES APPEAR IN STUDENT SUPPLEMENTS
III. Communication Techniques—continued		
• Helping students articulate their ideas and thinking processes	**Chapter 6:** "Giving Students Time to Process: Effects of Increasing Wait Time" (pp. 216–217) **Chapter 7:** "Promoting Conceptual Change" (pp. 247–249)	**Video CD 2:** "Author's Chair"; "Scarlet Letter"
• Promoting risk-taking and problem-solving	**Chapter 8:** "Problem Solving" (pp. 274–284); "Creativity" (pp. 284–287)	**Video CD 2:** "Group Work"
• Facilitating factual recall	**Chapter 6:** "Factors Affecting Retrieval" (pp. 211–214); "Giving Students Time to Process: Effects of Increasing Wait Time" (pp. 216–217)	**Video CD 2:** "Charles's Law"
• Encouraging convergent and divergent thinking	**Chapter 6:** "Elaboration" (pp. 203–204) **Chapter 8:** "Creativity" (pp. 284–287)	**Video CD 2:** "Civil War"; "Group Work"; "Scarlet Letter"
• Stimulating curiosity	**Chapter 12:** "Situational Versus Personal Interest" (pp. 401–402) **Chapter 13:** "Discovery Learning" (pp. 451–453)	**Video CD 2:** "Properties of Air"
• Helping students to question	**Chapter 8:** "Intentional Elaboration" (p. 263); "Monitoring Comprehension" (pp. 264–265); "Critical Thinking" (pp. 287–289)	**Video CD 2:** "Scarlet Letter"
• Promoting a caring community	**Chapter 7:** "Creating a Community of Learners" (pp. 243–245) **Chapter 11:** "Relatedness" (pp. 372–374) **Chapter 14:** "Creating an Effective Classroom Climate" (pp. 485–490)	**Video CD 2:** "Author's Chair" **Study Guide and Reader:** Application Exercise 1 (pp. 15–18)
IV. Profession and Community		
A. The Reflective Practitioner		
▶ Types of resources available for professional development and learning		
• Professional literature	**Chapter 1:** "Developing as a Teacher" (pp. 13–14) **Chapter 5:** "Classifying Students with Special Needs" (pp. 154–155)	
• Colleagues	**Chapter 14:** "Working with Other Teachers" (pp. 410–412)	
• Professional associations	**Chapter 5:** "Classifying Students with Special Needs" (pp. 154–155)	
• Professional development activities	**Chapter 1:** "Developing as a Teacher" (pp. 13–14)	
▶ Ability to read, understand, and apply articles and books about current research, views, ideas, and debates regarding best teaching practices	**Chapter 1:** "Using Research in Classroom Decision Making" (pp. 5–10); "Applying Psychological Theories in Classroom Decision Making" (p. 10); **"Case Study: More Harm Than Good?"** (pp. 16–17) **Chapter 6:** "Keeping an Open Mind About Theories of Learning" (p. 187)	
▶ Why personal reflection on teaching practices is critical, and approaches that can be used to reflect and evaluate	**Chapter 1: "Case Study: Hidden Treasure"** (pp. 3–4); "Developing as a Teacher" (pp. 13–14) **Chapter 4:** "Coming to Grips with Our Own Cultural Lenses" (p. 113) **Chapter 12:** "Teacher Expectations and Attributions" (pp. 419–424)	
• Code of ethics		
• Advocacy for learners	**Chapter 4:** "Supporting Students at Risk" (pp. 131–133)	

TABLE C.1—continued

Matching Book and Ancillary Content to the Praxis *Principles of Learning and Teaching* Tests

TOPICS IN THE PRAXIS PRINCIPLES OF LEARNING AND TEACHING TESTS	WHERE TOPICS APPEAR IN ORMROD'S *EDUCATIONAL PSYCHOLOGY* (5TH ED.)	WHERE TOPICS AND PRACTICE OPPORTUNITIES APPEAR IN STUDENT SUPPLEMENTS
IV. Profession and Community—continued		
B. The Larger Community		
► The role of the school as a resource to the larger community		
• Teacher as a resource	**Chapter 14:** "Working with Parents" (pp. 512–519)	
► Factors in the students' environment outside of school (family circumstances, community environments, health and economic conditions) that may influence students' life and learning	**Chapter 4: "Case Study: Why Jack Wasn't in School"** (pp. 103–104); "Navigating Different Cultures at Home and at School" (pp. 105–107); "Family Relationships and Expectations" (p. 111); "Socioeconomic Differences" (pp. 124–129); "Students at Risk" (pp. 129–133) **Chapter 5:** "Nature, Nurture and Group Differences in Intelligence" (pp. 147–148)	**Study Guide and Reader:** Application Exercise 7 (pp. 64–67); Supplementary Reading 3, "Ecological Systems Perspectives of Child Development" (pp. 305–308); Supplementary Reading 4, "Parenting Styles and Children's Behavior" (pp. 309–312)
► Basic strategies for developing and utilizing active partnerships among teachers, parents/guardians, and leaders in the community to support the educational process	**Chapter 5:** "Giftedness" (pp. 176–178); "The Big Picture" (pp. 179–180) **Chapter 14:** "Coordinating Efforts with Others" (pp. 510–519)	
• Shared ownership		
• Shared decision making	**Chapter 5:** "Public Law 94-142: The Individuals with Disabilities Education Act (IDEA)" (pp. 151–153)	
• Respectful/reciprocal communication	**Chapter 14:** "Communicating with Parents" (pp. 513–515)	
► Major laws related to students' rights and teacher responsibilities		
• Equal education	**Chapter 16:** "High-Stakes Testing and Accountability" (pp. 591–593)	
• Appropriate education for students with special needs	**Chapter 5:** "Public Law 94-142: The Individuals with Disabilities Education Act (IDEA)" (pp. 151–153) **Chapter 15:** "Accommodating Students with Special Needs" (pp. 566–567) **Chapter 16:** "Language Differences" (p. 595); "Accommodating Students with Special Needs" (pp. 595–597)	**Study Guide and Reader:** Application Exercise 32 (pp. 272–275)
• Confidentiality and privacy	**Chapter 16: "Case Study: B in History"** (p. 571); "Confidentiality and Communication About Assessment Results" (pp. 596–599)	**Study Guide and Reader:** Application Exercise 32 (pp. 272–275)
• Appropriate treatment of students		
• Reporting in situations related to possible child abuse	**Chapter 5:** "Emotional and Behavioral Disorders" (pp. 163–166)	**Study Guide and Reader:** Supplementary Reading 4, "Parenting Styles and Children's Behavior" (pp. 309–312)

Glossary

accommodation In Piaget's theory, dealing with a new event by either modifying an existing scheme or forming a new one.

accountability An obligation of teachers and other school personnel to accept responsibility for students' performance on high-stakes assessments; often mandated by policy makers calling for school reform.

achievement motivation The need for excellence for its own sake, without regard for external rewards that accomplishments might bring.

action research Research conducted by teachers and other school personnel to address issues and problems in their own schools or classrooms.

activation The degree to which something in memory is being actively attended to and mentally processed.

activity reinforcer An opportunity to engage in a favorite activity.

actual developmental level In Vygotsky's theory, the upper limit of tasks one can perform independently.

adaptive behavior Behavior related to daily living skills and appropriate conduct in social situations; a deficit in adaptive behavior is used as a criterion for identifying students with mental retardation.

adaptive testing Computer-based assessment in which students' performance on early items determines which items are presented subsequently; allows more rapid measurement of a characteristic or ability than is possible in traditional paper-pencil testing.

advance organizer An introduction to a lesson that provides an overall organizational scheme for the lesson.

affect The feelings, emotions, and moods that an individual brings to bear on a task.

African American English A dialect of some African American communities that includes some pronunciations, grammatical constructions, and idioms different from those of Standard English.

age-equivalent score A score that indicates the age level of students to whom a student's performance is most similar.

aggressive behavior An action intentionally taken to hurt another either physically or psychologically.

algorithm A prescribed sequence of steps that guarantees a correct problem solution.

analytic scoring Scoring a student's performance on an assessment by evaluating various aspects of the performance separately.

antecedent response A response that increases the likelihood that a certain other response will follow.

antecedent stimulus A stimulus that increases the likelihood that a particular response will follow.

anxiety A feeling of uneasiness and apprehension concerning a situation with an uncertain outcome.

applied behavior analysis (ABA) The systematic application of behaviorist principles in educational and therapeutic settings; sometimes known as *behavior modification*.

apprenticeship A situation in which a learner works intensively with an expert to learn how to accomplish complex tasks in a particular domain.

assessment The process of observing a sample of a student's behavior and drawing inferences about the student's knowledge and abilities.

assimilation In Piaget's theory, dealing with a new event in a way that is consistent with an existing scheme.

attachment A strong, affectionate bond formed between a child and another individual (e.g., a parent); usually formed early in the child's life.

attention The focusing of mental processes on particular stimuli.

attention-deficit hyperactivity disorder (ADHD) A category of special needs marked either by inattention or by both hyperactivity and impulsive behavior (or by all three of these); such characteristics probably have a biological origin.

attribution A personally constructed causal explanation for one's own or another's success or failure.

authentic activity A classroom activity similar to one that students are apt to encounter in the outside world.

authentic assessment Assessment of students' knowledge and skills in an authentic, "real-life" context; in many cases, an integral part of instruction rather than a separate activity.

authoritative parenting A parenting style characterized by emotional warmth, high expectations and standards for behavior, consistent enforcement of rules, explanations of the reasons behind these rules, and inclusion of children in decision making.

autism A category of special needs characterized by impaired social interaction and communication, repetitive behaviors, restricted interests, and a strong need for a predictable environment; underlying the condition may be either an undersensitivity or an oversensitivity to sensory stimulation.

automaticity The ability to respond quickly and efficiently while mentally processing or physically performing a task.

backup reinforcer A reinforcer that a student can "purchase" with one or more tokens earned in a token economy.

base group A cooperative learning group in which students work together for an entire semester or school year to provide mutual support for one another's learning.

baseline The frequency of a response before operant conditioning begins.

behavioral momentum An increased tendency for a learner to make a particular response immediately after making similar responses.

behaviorism A theoretical perspective in which learning and behavior are described and explained in terms of stimulus-response relationships. Adherents to this perspective are called **behaviorists**.

behavior modification See *applied behavior analysis*.

belongingness A general sense that one is an important and valued member of the classroom.

bilingual education An approach to second-language instruction in which students are instructed in academic subject areas in their native language while simultaneously being taught to speak and write in the second language. The amount of instruction delivered in the native language decreases as students become more proficient in the second language.

Bloom's taxonomy A taxonomy of six cognitive processes, varying in complexity, that lessons might be designed to foster.

challenge A situation in which a learner believes that success is possible with sufficient effort.

checklist An assessment tool with which a teacher evaluates student performance by indicating whether specific behaviors or qualities are present or absent.

classical conditioning A form of learning in which a new, involuntary response is acquired as a result of two stimuli being presented at the same time.

classroom climate The overall psychological atmosphere of the classroom.

classroom management The establishment and maintenance of a classroom environment conducive to learning and achievement.

clique A moderately stable friendship group of perhaps three to ten members.

cognitive apprenticeship A mentorship in which a teacher and a student work together to accomplish a challenging task or solve a difficult problem; in the process, the teacher provides guidance about how to think about the task or problem.

cognitive dissonance A feeling of mental discomfort caused by new information that conflicts with current knowledge or beliefs.

cognitive modeling Demonstrating how to think about as well as how to do a task.

cognitive processes The ways in which one thinks about (processes) information.

cognitive psychology A theoretical perspective that focuses on the mental processes underlying learning and behavior. Adherents to this perspective are sometimes called **cognitivists.**

cognitive tool A concept, symbol, strategy, or other culture-based mechanism that helps people think and act more effectively.

collective self-efficacy People's beliefs about their ability to be successful when they work together on a task.

community of learners A class in which teacher(s) and students actively and collaboratively work to help one another learn.

comprehension monitoring The process of checking oneself to be sure one understands information being read or heard.

computer-based instruction (CBI) Instruction provided via computer technology.

concept A mental grouping of objects or events that have something in common.

concept map A diagram of concepts and their interrelationships.

conceptual change Revision of one's understanding of a topic in response to new information.

conceptual understanding Knowledge acquired in an integrated and meaningful fashion.

concrete operations stage Piaget's third stage of cognitive development, in which adult-like logic appears but is limited to concrete reality.

concrete reinforcer A reinforcer that can be touched.

conditioned response (CR) A response that, through classical conditioning, begins to be elicited by a particular (conditioned) stimulus.

conditioned stimulus (CS) A stimulus that, through classical conditioning, begins to elicit a particular response.

conditioning Another word for learning; commonly used by behaviorists.

confidence interval A range around an assessment score that reflects the amount of error likely to be affecting the score's accuracy.

confirmation bias The tendency to seek information that confirms rather than discredits current beliefs.

conservation The realization that if nothing is added or taken away, amount (e.g., number, mass) stays the same regardless of any alterations in shape or arrangement.

construction A mental process in which a learner takes many separate pieces of information and uses them to build an overall understanding or interpretation.

constructivism A theoretical perspective that proposes that learners construct (rather than absorb) a body of knowledge from their experiences—knowledge that may or may not be an accurate representation of external reality. Adherents to this perspective are called **constructivists.**

construct validity The extent to which an assessment accurately measures an unobservable educational or psychological characteristic.

content validity The extent to which an assessment includes a representative sample of tasks within the content domain being assessed.

contiguity The occurrence of two or more events at the same time. **Contiguous** is the adjective used to refer to events having contiguity.

contingency A situation in which one event happens only after another event has already occurred. One event is **contingent** on another's prior occurrence.

contingency contract A formal agreement between a teacher and a student that identifies behaviors the student will exhibit and the reinforcers that will follow those behaviors.

continuous reinforcement Reinforcement of a response every time it occurs.

control group A group of people in a research study who are given either no treatment or a presumably ineffective (placebo) treatment. The subsequent performance of this group is compared to the performance of one or more treatment groups.

conventional morality Acceptance of society's conventions regarding right and wrong; behaving to please others or to live up to society's expectations for appropriate behavior.

conventional transgression An action that violates a culture's general expectations regarding socially appropriate behavior.

convergent thinking The process of pulling several pieces of information together to draw a conclusion or solve a problem.

cooperative learning An approach to instruction in which students work with a small group of peers to achieve a common goal and help one another learn.

core goal A long-term goal that drives much of what a person does.

co-regulated learning A process through which an adult and child share responsibility for directing various aspects of the child's learning.

correlation The extent to which two variables are associated, such that when one variable increases, the other either increases or decreases somewhat predictably.

correlational feature A characteristic present in many positive instances of a concept but not essential for concept membership.

correlational study A research study that explores possible relationships among variables. Such a study enables researchers to predict one variable on the basis of their knowledge of another but not to draw a conclusion about a cause-effect relationship.

correlation coefficient Statistic that indicates the strength and direction of an association between two variables.

cortex The upper part of the brain; site of conscious and higher-level thinking processes.

creativity New and original behavior that yields an appropriate and productive result.

criterion-referenced assessment An assessment instrument designed to determine what students know and can do relative to predetermined standards or criteria.

criterion-referenced score A score that specifically indicates what a student knows or can do.

critical thinking The process of evaluating the accuracy and worth of information and lines of reasoning.

crowd A large, loose-knit social group that shares common interests and attitudes.

cueing The use of signals to indicate that a certain behavior is desired or that a certain behavior should stop.

cultural bias The extent to which assessment tasks either offend or unfairly penalize some students because of their ethnicity, gender, or socioeconomic status.

cultural mismatch A situation in which a child's home culture and the school culture hold conflicting expectations for the child's behavior.

culture The behaviors and belief systems of a long-standing social group.

culture shock A sense of confusion when a student encounters a culture with behavioral expectations very different from those previously learned.

debilitating anxiety Anxiety of sufficient intensity that it interferes with performance.

decay A hypothesized weakening over time of information stored in long-term memory, especially if the information is used infrequently or not at all.

declarative knowledge Knowledge related to "what is"—that is, to the nature of how things are, were, or will be (as opposed to *procedural knowledge*, which relates to how to do something).

deductive reasoning Drawing a logical inference about something that must be true, given other information that has already been presented as true.

defining feature In concept learning, a characteristic that must be present in all positive instances of a concept.

delay of gratification The ability to forego small, immediate reinforcers in order to obtain larger ones later on.

descriptive study A research study that enables researchers to draw conclusions about the current state of affairs but not about correlational or cause-effect relationships.

developmental milestone The appearance of a new, developmentally more advanced behavior.

dialect A form of English or other language characteristic of a particular region or ethnic group.

direct instruction An approach to instruction that uses a variety of techniques (e.g., explanations, questions, guided and independent practice) to promote learning of basic skills.

discovery learning An approach to instruction in which students develop an understanding of a topic through firsthand interaction with the environment.

discrimination A phenomenon in operant conditioning in which a student learns that a response is reinforced in the presence of one stimulus but not in the presence of another, similar stimulus.

disequilibrium In Piaget's theory, an inability to explain new events by using existing schemes.

disposition A general inclination to approach and think about a task in a particular way.

distance learning Technology-based instruction in which students are at a location physically separate from their instructor.

distributed cognition A process whereby learners think about an issue or problem together, sharing ideas and working collaboratively to draw conclusions or develop solutions.

distributed intelligence The idea that people are more likely to act "intelligently" when they have physical, symbolic, and/or social support systems to assist them.

distributive justice Beliefs about what constitutes people's fair share of a commodity.

divergent thinking The process of proceeding in a variety of directions from a single idea.

drive A motivational state in which something necessary for optimal functioning (food, water, etc.) is missing.

dynamic assessment A systematic examination of how a student's knowledge or reasoning may change as a result of learning or performing a specific task.

educational psychology A discipline encompassing psychological principles and theories related to learning, child and adolescent development, motivation, individual and group differences, and psychological assessment, especially as these topics relate to classroom practice.

egocentric speech Act of speaking without taking the perspective and knowledge of the listener into account.

elaboration A cognitive process in which learners expand on new information based on what they already know.

emotional and behavioral disorders A category of special needs characterized by emotional states and behaviors that are present over a substantial period of time and significantly disrupt students' academic learning and performance.

empathy The experience of sharing the same feelings as someone in unfortunate circumstances.

encoding Changing the format of new information as it is being stored in memory.

entity view of intelligence The belief that intelligence is a "thing" that is relatively permanent and unchangeable.

epistemological beliefs Beliefs about the nature of knowledge and knowledge acquisition.

equilibration In Piaget's theory, the movement from equilibrium to disequilibrium and back to equilibrium, a process that promotes development of more complex thought and understandings.

equilibrium In Piaget's theory, a state of being able to explain new events by using existing schemes.

equity (in instruction) Instruction without favoritism or bias toward particular individuals or groups of students.

ethnic group A group of people who have common historical roots, values, beliefs, and behaviors and who share a sense of interdependence. The group's roots either precede the creation of or are external to the country in which the group resides.

ethnic identity Awareness of one's membership in a particular ethnic or cultural group and willingness to adopt certain behaviors characteristic of the group.

ETS score A standard score with a mean of 500 and a standard deviation of 100.

exemplar A specific example that is an important part of a learner's general knowledge and understanding of a concept. Several exemplars taken together give the learner a sense of the variability that exists within any category of objects or events.

expectancy In motivation theory, the belief that as a result of both personal ability and external circumstances, one will be successful in accomplishing a task or achieving a goal.

experimental study (experiment) A research study that involves the manipulation of one variable to determine its possible effect on another variable. It enables researchers to draw conclusions about cause-effect relationships.

expository instruction An approach to instruction in which information is presented in more or less the same form in which students are expected to learn it.

externalizing behavior A symptom of an emotional or behavioral disorder that has direct or indirect effects on other people (e.g., aggression, disobedience, stealing).

extinction The gradual disappearance of an acquired response. In classical conditioning, results from repeated presentation of a conditioned stimulus in the absence of the unconditioned stimulus; in operant conditioning, results from repeated lack of reinforcement for the response.

extrinsic motivation Motivation promoted by factors external to the individual and unrelated to the task being performed.

extrinsic reinforcer A reinforcer that comes from the outside environment, rather than from within the individual.

facilitating anxiety Anxiety that enhances performance. Relatively low levels of anxiety are usually facilitating.

failure to store Failure to mentally process information in ways that promote its storage in long-term memory.

Family Educational Rights and Privacy Act (FERPA) U.S. legislation passed in 1974 mandating that teachers and other school personnel (a) restrict access to students' test results and school records only to students, their parents, and school employees directly involved in the students' education; (b) upon request, make test scores and other information in students' records available for inspection by students and parents; and (c) help students and parents appropriately interpret this information.

flow An intense form of intrinsic motivation, involving complete absorption in and concentration on a challenging activity.

formal assessment A preplanned, systematic attempt to ascertain what students have learned.

formal discipline A view of transfer suggesting that the study of rigorous subjects enhances one's ability to learn other, unrelated things.

formal operational egocentrism The inability of individuals in Piaget's formal operations stage to separate their own abstract logic from the perspectives of others and from practical considerations.

formal operations stage Piaget's fourth and final stage of cognitive development, in which logical reasoning processes are applied to abstract ideas as well as to concrete objects.

formative evaluation An evaluation conducted before or during instruction to facilitate instructional planning and enhance students' learning.

functional analysis The examination of a student's inappropriate behavior, as well as its antecedents and consequences, to determine the function(s) that the behavior might serve for the student.

g A theoretical *general factor* in intelligence that influences one's ability to learn in a wide variety of contexts and content domains.

gang A cohesive social group characterized by initiation rites, distinctive colors and symbols, territorial orientation, and feuds with rival groups.

gender schema A self-constructed, organized body of beliefs about the traits and behaviors of males or females.

generalization A phenomenon in which a person learns a response to a particular stimulus and then makes the same response to similar stimuli. In classical conditioning, involves making a conditioned response to stimuli similar to a conditioned stimulus; in operant conditioning, involves making a voluntary response to stimuli similar to a stimulus antecedent to a response-reinforcement contingency.

general transfer An instance of transfer in which the original learning task and the transfer task are different in content.

giftedness A category of special needs characterized by unusually high ability in one or more areas, to the point where students require special educational services to help them meet their full potential.

grade-equivalent score A score that indicates the grade level of students to whom a student's performance is most similar.

group contingency A situation in which everyone in a group must make a particular response before reinforcement occurs.

group differences Consistently observed differences (on average) among diverse groups of students (e.g., students of different genders or ethnic backgrounds).

guided participation A child's performance, with guidance and support, of an activity in the adult world.

guilt A feeling of discomfort when one knows one has caused someone else pain or distress.

halo effect A phenomenon in which people are more likely to perceive positive behaviors in someone they like or admire.

hearing loss A category of special needs characterized by malfunction of the ears or associated nerves that interferes with the perception of sounds within the frequency range of normal human speech.

heuristic A general strategy that facilitates problem solving but does not always yield a problem solution.

higher-level question A question that requires students to do something new with information they have learned—for example, to apply, analyze, synthesize, or evaluate it.

higher-level thinking Thinking that involves going well beyond information specifically learned (e.g., analyzing, applying, or evaluating it).

high-stakes testing Practice of using students' performance on a single assessment instrument to make major decisions about students or school personnel.

holistic scoring Summarizing a student's performance on an assessment with a single score.

hostile attributional bias A tendency to interpret others' behaviors (especially ambiguous ones) as reflecting hostile or aggressive intentions.

hot cognition Learning or cognitive processing that is emotionally charged.

hypermedia A collection of multimedia, computer-based instructional material (e.g., text, pictures, sound, animations) that students can examine in a sequence of their own choosing.

hypertext A collection of computer-based reading material that allows students to proceed from one topic to another, related one in a self-chosen sequence.

identity A self-constructed definition of who a person thinks he or she is and what things are important in life.

ill-defined problem A problem in which the desired goal is unclear, information needed to solve the problem is missing, and/or several possible solutions to the problem exist.

illusion of knowing Thinking that one knows something that one actually does *not* know.

imaginary audience The belief that one is the center of attention in any social situation.

immersion An approach to second-language instruction in which students hear and speak that language almost exclusively in the classroom.

inability to retrieve Failure to locate information that currently exists in long-term memory.

incentive A hoped-for, but not guaranteed, consequence of behavior.

inclusion The practice of educating all students, including those with severe and multiple disabilities, in neighborhood schools and general education classrooms.

incompatible behaviors Two or more behaviors that cannot be performed simultaneously.

incremental view of intelligence The belief that intelligence can and does improve with effort and practice.

individual constructivism A theoretical perspective that focuses on how people, as individuals, construct meaning from the events around them.

individual differences Variability in abilities and characteristics (intelligence, personality, etc.) among students at a particular age.

individualized education program (IEP) A written description of an appropriate instructional program for a student with special needs. In the United States an IEP is mandated by the Individuals with Disabilities Education Act (IDEA) for all students with disabilities.

Individuals with Disabilities Education Act (IDEA) U.S. legislation granting educational rights to people with cognitive, emotional, or physical disabilities from birth until age 21; it guarantees a free and appropriate education, fair and nondiscriminatory evaluation, education in the least restrictive environment, an individualized education program, and due process.

induction Explanation why a certain behavior is unacceptable, often with a focus on the pain or distress that someone has caused another.

informal assessment Assessment that results from teachers' spontaneous, day-to-day observations of how students behave and perform in class.

information processing theory A theoretical perspective that focuses on the specific ways in which learners mentally think about (process) new information and events.

inner speech Process of "talking" to oneself mentally rather than aloud.

in-school suspension A form of punishment in which a student is placed in a quiet, boring room within the school building. It often lasts one or more school days and involves close adult supervision.

instructional goal A desired long-term outcome of instruction.

instructional objective A desired outcome of a lesson or unit.

intelligence The ability to modify and adjust one's behaviors in order to accomplish new tasks successfully. It involves many different mental processes and may vary in nature depending on one's culture.

intelligence test A general measure of current cognitive functioning, used primarily to predict academic achievement over the short run.

interest A feeling that a topic is intriguing or enticing.

interference A phenomenon whereby something stored in long-term memory inhibits one's ability to remember something else correctly.

intermittent reinforcement Reinforcement of a response only occasionally, with some occurrences of the response going unreinforced.

internalization In Vygotsky's theory, the process through which social activities evolve into mental activities.

internalized motivation The adoption of others' priorities and values as one's own.

internalizing behavior Symptom of an emotional or behavioral disorder that primarily affects the student with the disorder, with little or no effect on others (e.g., anxiety, depression).

intrinsic motivation The internal desire to perform a particular task.

intrinsic reinforcer A reinforcer provided by oneself or inherent in the task being performed.

IQ score A score on an intelligence test, determined by comparing one's performance on the test with the performance of others in the same age-group. For most tests, it is a standard score with a mean of 100 and a standard deviation of 15.

IRE cycle An adult-child interaction marked by adult *i*nitiation (e.g., a question), child *r*esponse, and adult *e*valuation.

item analysis Post-hoc analysis of patterns in students' responses to various items on an assessment instrument.

item difficulty (p) The proportion of students getting a particular assessment item correct. A high p value indicates an easy item; a low p value indicates a difficult item.

item discrimination (D) The relative proportion of high-scoring and low-scoring students getting a particular assessment item correct. A positive D indicates that an item appears to discriminate between knowledgeable and unknowledgeable students; a negative D indicates that the item may be providing misinformation about what students know and can do.

jigsaw technique An instructional technique in which instructional materials are divided among members of a cooperative learning group, with individual students being responsible for learning different material and then teaching it to other group members.

keyword method A mnemonic technique in which an association is made between two ideas by forming a visual image of one or more concrete objects (*keywords*) that either sound similar to, or symbolically represent, those ideas.

knowledge base One's knowledge about specific topics and the world in general.

learned helplessness A general belief that one is incapable of accomplishing tasks and has little or no control of the environment.

learned industriousness The recognition that one can succeed at some tasks only with effort, persistence, and well-chosen strategies.

learner-directed instruction An approach to instruction in which students have considerable say in the issues they address and how to address them.

learning A relatively permanent change, due to experience, either in behavior or in mental representations or associations.

learning disabilities A category of special needs characterized by deficiencies in one or more specific cognitive processes rather than in overall cognitive functioning.

learning strategy One or more cognitive processes used intentionally for a particular learning task.

least restrictive environment The most typical and standard educational environment that can reasonably meet the needs of a student with a disability.

level of potential development In Vygotsky's theory, the upper limit of tasks one can perform with the assistance of a more competent individual.

limited English proficiency (LEP) A limited ability to understand and communicate in oral or written English, usually because English is not one's native language.

live model An individual whose behavior is observed "in the flesh."

logical consequence A consequence that follows naturally or logically from a student's misbehavior; in other words, a punishment that fits the crime.

long-term memory The component of memory that holds knowledge and skills for a relatively long period of time.

lower-level question A question that requires students to express what they have learned in essentially the same way they learned it—for example, by reciting a textbook's definition of a concept or describing an application their teacher presented in class.

maintenance rehearsal See *rehearsal*.

mastery goal A desire to acquire additional knowledge or master new skills.

mastery learning An approach to instruction in which students learn one topic thoroughly before moving to a subsequent one.

mastery orientation A general belief that one is capable of accomplishing challenging tasks.

maturation The unfolding of genetically controlled changes as a child develops.

mean (M) The mathematical average of a set of scores. It is calculated by adding all the scores and then dividing by the total number of people who have obtained those scores.

meaningful learning A cognitive process in which learners relate new information to things they already know.

meaningful learning set An attitude that one can make sense of the information one is studying.

mediated learning experience An interaction in which an adult helps a child make sense of a phenomenon or event.

memory A learner's ability to save something (mentally) that he or she has previously learned, *or* the mental "location" where such information is saved.

mental retardation A category of special needs characterized by significantly below-average general intelligence and deficits in adaptive behavior.

mental set An inclination to encode a problem in a way that excludes potential problem solutions.

metacognition One's knowledge and beliefs about one's own cognitive processes and one's resulting attempts to regulate those cognitive processes to maximize learning and memory.

metalinguistic awareness The extent to which one is able to think about the nature of language.

misbehavior An action that has the potential to disrupt students' learning and planned classroom activities.

misconception A belief inconsistent with commonly accepted scientific explanations.

mnemonic A memory aid or trick designed to help students learn and remember a specific piece of information.

model A person who demonstrates a behavior for someone else.

modeling Demonstrating a behavior for another, *or* observing and imitating another's behavior.

moral dilemma A situation in which there is no clear-cut answer regarding the morally correct action.

morality One's general standards about right and wrong.

moral transgression An action that causes harm or infringes on the needs and rights of others.

motivation A state that energizes, directs, and sustains behavior.

multicultural education Instruction that integrates perspectives and experiences of numerous cultural groups throughout the curriculum.

myelination Growth of a fatty sheath (myelin) around neurons, enabling faster transmission of messages.

naive theory An early (and possibly inaccurate) theory developed by a child who has limited knowledge about the phenomenon involved.

need for affiliation The tendency to seek out friendly relationships with others.

need for approval A desire to gain acceptance and positive judgments from others.

need for relatedness A basic need to feel socially connected to others and to secure others' love and respect.

negative instance A nonexample of a concept.

negative reinforcement A consequence that brings about the increase of a behavior through the removal (rather than the presentation) of a stimulus.

negative transfer A phenomenon in which something learned at one time interferes with learning or performance at a later time.

neglected students Students whom peers rarely select as people they would either really like or really *not* like to do something with; students about whom most peers have no strong feelings, either positive or negative.

neuron A cell in the brain or another part of the nervous system that transmits information to other cells.

neurotransmitter A chemical substance through which one neuron sends a message to another.

neutral stimulus A stimulus that does not elicit any particular response.

normal distribution (normal curve) A theoretical pattern of educational and psychological characteristics in which most individuals lie somewhere in the middle range and only a few lie at either extreme.

norm-referenced assessment An assessment instrument that indicates how students perform relative to a peer group.

norm-referenced score A score that indicates how a student's performance on an assessment compares with the average performance of peers (i.e., with the performance of a norm group).

norms Data regarding the typical performance of various groups of students on a standardized test or other norm-referenced assessment.

observational learning effect A phenomenon in which an observer acquires a new behavior after watching someone else demonstrate it.

operant conditioning A form of learning in which a response increases in frequency as a result of its being followed by reinforcement.

organization A cognitive process in which learners find connections (e.g., by forming categories, identifying hierarchies, determining cause-effect relationships) among the various pieces of information they need to learn.

overgeneralization An overly broad meaning for a word that includes some situations where the word is not appropriate; an overly broad view of what objects or events a concept includes.

paper-pencil assessment An assessment in which students provide written responses to written items.

pedagogical content knowledge Knowledge about effective methods of teaching a specific content area.

peer mediation An approach to conflict resolution in which a student (mediator) asks peers in conflict to express their differing viewpoints and then work together to identify an appropriate compromise.

peer pressure A phenomenon whereby agemates strongly encourage some behaviors and discourage others.

peer tutoring An approach to instruction in which students who have mastered a topic teach those who have not.

people-first language Language in which a student's disability is identified *after* the student is named (e.g., "student with a learning disability" rather than "learning disabled student").

percentile rank (percentile) A score that indicates the percentage of people in the norm group getting a raw score less than or equal to a particular student's raw score.

performance-approach goal A desire to look good and receive favorable judgments from others.

performance assessment Assessment in which students demonstrate their knowledge and skills in a nonwritten fashion.

performance-avoidance goal A desire not to look bad or receive unfavorable judgments from others.

performance goal A desire to demonstrate high ability and make a good impression.

personal fable The belief that one is completely unlike anyone else and so cannot be understood by others.

personal interest A long-term, relatively stable interest in a particular topic or activity.

personal space A personally or culturally preferred distance between two people during social interaction.

perspective taking The ability to look at a situation from someone's else viewpoint.

physical aggression An action that can potentially cause bodily injury.

physical and health impairments A category of special needs characterized by general physical or medical conditions (usually long-term) that interfere with students' school performance to such an extent that special instruction, curricular materials, equipment, or facilities are needed.

popular students Students whom many peers like and perceive to be kind and trustworthy.

portfolio A collection of a student's work compiled systematically over a lengthy period of time.

positive behavioral support A variation of traditional applied behavior analysis that includes identifying the purposes that undesirable behaviors serve for a student and providing a more appropriate way for the student to accomplish those purposes.

positive feedback A message that an answer is correct or a task has been well done.

positive instance A specific example of a concept.

positive reinforcement A consequence that brings about the increase of a behavior through the presentation (rather than removal) of a stimulus.

positive transfer A phenomenon in which something learned at one time facilitates learning or performance at a later time.

postconventional morality Behaving in accordance with self-developed, abstract principles regarding right and wrong.

practicality The extent to which an assessment instrument or procedure is inexpensive and easy to use and takes only a small amount of time to administer and score.

pragmatics Knowledge about culture-specific social conventions guiding verbal interactions.

preconventional morality A lack of internalized standards about right and wrong; making decisions based solely on what is best for oneself, without regard for others' needs and feelings.

predictive validity The extent to which the results of an assessment predict future performance.

Premack principle A phenomenon in which students do less-preferred activities in order to engage in more-preferred activities.

preoperational egocentrism In Piaget's theory, the inability of children in the preoperational stage to view situations from another person's perspective.

preoperational stage Piaget's second stage of cognitive development, in which children can think about objects beyond their immediate view but do not yet reason in logical, adultlike ways.

presentation punishment A form of punishment involving the presentation of a new stimulus, presumably one a learner finds unpleasant.

primary reinforcer A consequence that satisfies a biologically built-in need.

prior knowledge activation Process of reminding students of things they have already learned relative to a new topic.

private speech See *self-talk*.

proactive aggression Deliberate aggression against another as a means of obtaining a desired goal.

procedural knowledge Knowledge concerning how to do something (as opposed to *declarative knowledge*, which relates to how things are).

process goal A desire to perfect the form or procedure that a skill involves.

product goal A desire to attain a certain, concrete standard of excellence.

prosocial behavior Behavior directed toward promoting the well-being of another.

prototype A mental representation of a "typical" positive instance of a concept.

proximal goal A concrete goal that one can accomplish within a short time period; may be a stepping stone toward a longer-range goal.

psychological punishment A consequence that seriously threatens a student's self-esteem.

punishment A consequence (stimulus) that decreases the frequency of the response it follows.

rating scale An assessment tool with which a teacher evaluates student performance by rating aspects of the performance on one or more continua.

raw score A score based solely on the number or point value of correctly answered items.

reactive aggression An aggressive response to frustration or provocation.

recall task A memory task in which one must retrieve information in its entirety from long-term memory.

reciprocal causation The interdependence of environment, behavior, and personal variables as these three factors influence learning and development.

reciprocal teaching An approach to teaching reading and listening comprehension in which students take turns asking teacherlike questions of their classmates.

recognition task A memory task in which one must identify correct information among irrelevant information or incorrect statements.

reconstruction error Construction of a logical but incorrect "memory" by using information retrieved from long-term memory plus one's general knowledge and beliefs about the world.

reflective teaching Regular, ongoing examination and critique of one's assumptions and instructional strategies, and revision of them as necessary to enhance students' learning and development.

rehearsal A cognitive process in which information is repeated over and over as a possible way of learning and remembering it. When it is used to keep information "fresh" in working memory, it is called **maintenance rehearsal**.

reinforcement The act of following a particular response with a reinforcer and thereby increasing the frequency of that response.

reinforcer A consequence (stimulus) of a response that leads to increased frequency of that response.

rejected students Students whom many peers identify as being undesirable social partners.

relational aggression An act of aggression that can adversely affect interpersonal relationships.

reliability The extent to which an assessment instrument yields consistent information about the knowledge, skills, or characteristics being assessed.

reliability coefficient A numerical index of an assessment tool's reliability; ranges from 0 to 1, with higher numbers indicating higher reliability.

removal punishment A form of punishment involving removal of an existing stimulus, presumably one a learner views as desirable and doesn't want to lose.

resilient self-efficacy The belief that one can perform a task successfully even after experiencing setbacks; includes the belief that effort and perseverance are essential for success.

resilient students Students who succeed in school and in life despite exceptional hardships at home.

response (R) A specific behavior that an individual exhibits.

response cost The loss either of a previously earned reinforcer or of an opportunity to obtain reinforcement.

response disinhibition effect A phenomenon in which an observer displays a previously forbidden or punished behavior more frequently after seeing someone else do it without adverse consequences.

response facilitation effect A phenomenon in which an observer displays a previously learned behavior more frequently after seeing someone else being reinforced for it.

response inhibition effect A phenomenon in which an observer displays a previously learned behavior less frequently after seeing someone else being punished for it.

retrieval The process of "finding" information previously stored in memory.

retrieval cue A hint about where to "look" for a piece of information in long-term memory.

rote learning Learning information in a relatively uninterpreted form, without making sense of it or attaching much meaning to it.

rubric A list of components that a student's performance on an assessment task should ideally include.

scaffolding A support mechanism, provided by a more competent individual, that helps a learner successfully perform a task within his or her zone of proximal development.

schema In contemporary cognitive psychology, an organized body of knowledge about a specific topic.

scheme In Piaget's theory, an organized group of similar actions or thoughts.

scholastic aptitude test A test designed to assess one's general capacity to learn; typically used to predict students' success in future learning situations.

school readiness test A test designed to assess cognitive skills important for success in a typical kindergarten or first-grade curriculum.

script A schema that involves a predictable sequence of events related to a common activity.

scripted cooperation In cooperative learning, a technique in which cooperative groups follow a set of steps or "script" that guides members' verbal interactions.

secondary reinforcer A consequence that becomes reinforcing over time through its association with another reinforcer.

self-concept See *sense of self*.

self-determination A sense that one has some choice and control regarding the future course of one's life.

self-efficacy The belief that one is capable of executing certain behaviors or reaching certain goals.

self-esteem See *sense of self*.

self-evaluation Judgment of one's own performance or behavior.

self-explanation A process of occasionally stopping to verbalize to oneself (and hence to better understand) material being read or studied.

self-fulfilling prophecy A situation in which one's expectations for an outcome either directly or indirectly lead to the expected result.

self-handicapping Undermining one's own success, often as a way of protecting one's sense of self-worth when being asked to perform difficult tasks.

self-imposed contingency Self-reinforcement or self-punishment that follows a behavior.

self-instructions Instructions that one gives oneself (aloud or mentally) while performing a complex behavior.

self-monitoring The process of observing and recording one's own behavior.

self-questioning The process of asking oneself questions as a way of checking one's understanding of a topic.

self-regulated behavior Self-chosen behavior that leads to the fulfillment of personally chosen standards and goals.

self-regulated learning The regulation of one's own cognitive processes in order to learn successfully; includes such things as goal setting, planning, attention control, self-motivation, flexible use of learning strategies, self-monitoring, asking for help when needed, and self-evaluation.

self-regulated problem solving The employment of self-directing strategies to address one's own problems.

self-regulation The process of setting standards and goals for oneself and engaging in behaviors and cognitive processes that lead to meeting the standards and accomplishing the goals.

self-socialization The tendency to integrate personal observations and others' input into self-constructed standards for behavior and to choose actions accordingly.

self-talk Process of talking to oneself as a way of guiding oneself through a task; also known as *private speech*.

self-worth Beliefs about one's own general ability to deal effectively with the environment.

semantics The meanings of words and word combinations.

sense of community In the classroom, a widely shared belief that teacher and students have common goals, are mutually respectful and supportive, and all make important contributions to classroom learning.

sense of school community A widely shared belief that all faculty and students within a school are working together to help everyone learn and succeed.

sense of self Perceptions, beliefs, judgments, and feelings about oneself (includes *self-concept* and *self-esteem*).

sensitive period An age range during which a certain aspect of a child's development is especially susceptible to environmental conditions.

sensorimotor stage Piaget's first stage of cognitive development, in which schemes are based on behaviors and perceptions.

sensory register A component of memory that holds incoming information in an unanalyzed form for a very brief period of time (perhaps a second or less).

setting event In behaviorism, a complex environmental condition in which a particular behavior is most likely to occur.

severe and multiple disabilities A category of special needs in which students have two or more disabilities, the combination of which requires significant adaptations and highly specialized services in students' educational programs.

shame A feeling of embarrassment or humiliation after failing to meet standards for moral behavior that adults have set.

shaping A process of reinforcing successively closer and closer approximations to a desired terminal behavior.

short-term memory See *working memory*.

situated cognition Knowledge and thinking skills that are acquired and used primarily within certain contexts, with limited if any transfer to other contexts.

situated motivation A phenomenon in which aspects of the immediate environment enhance motivation to learn particular things or behave in particular ways.

situational interest Interest evoked temporarily by something in the environment.

social cognition The process of thinking about how other people are likely to think, act, and react.

social cognitive theory A theoretical perspective in which learning by observing others is the focus of study.

social constructivism A theoretical perspective that focuses on people's collective efforts to impose meaning on the world.

social information processing Mental processes involved in understanding and responding to social events.

socialization The process of molding a child's behavior to be appropriate for his or her cultural group.

social reinforcer A gesture or sign that one person gives another, often to communicate positive regard.

sociocultural perspective A theoretical perspective that emphasizes the importance of society and culture for promoting cognitive development.

socioeconomic status (SES) One's general social and economic standing in society, encompassing such variables as family income, occupation, and level of education.

specific aptitude test A test designed to predict students' future ability to learn in a particular content domain.

specific transfer An instance of transfer in which the original learning task and the transfer task overlap in content.

speech and communication disorders A category of special needs characterized by impairments in spoken language or language comprehension that significantly interfere with students' classroom performance.

stage theory A theory that depicts development as a series of relatively discrete periods (*stages*), with relatively slow growth within each stage and more rapid growth during the transition from one stage to another.

standard deviation (SD) A statistic that reflects how close together or far apart a set of scores are and thereby indicates the variability of the scores.

Standard English The form of English generally considered acceptable at school, as reflected in textbooks and grammar instruction.

standard error of measurement (SEM) A statistic estimating the amount of error likely to be present in a particular test score or other assessment result.

standardization The extent to which assessment instruments and procedures involve similar content and format and are administered and scored in the same way for everyone.

standardized test A test developed by test construction experts and published for use in many different schools and classrooms.

standards General statements regarding the knowledge and skills that students should gain and the characteristics that their accomplishments should reflect.

standard score A score that indicates how far a student's performance is from the mean with respect to standard deviation units.

stanine A standard score with a mean of 5 and a standard deviation of 2; it is always reported as a whole number.

state anxiety A temporary feeling of anxiety elicited by a threatening situation.

stereotype A rigid, simplistic, and erroneous caricature of a particular group of people.

stereotype threat Awareness of a negative stereotype about one's own group and accompanying uneasiness that low performance will confirm the stereotype; leads (often unintentionally) to a reduction in performance.

stimulus (S) (pl. stimuli) A specific object or event that influences an individual's learning or behavior.

storage The process of "putting" new information into memory.

students at risk Students who have a high probability of failing to acquire the minimal academic skills necessary for success in the adult world.

students with special needs Students who are different enough from their peers that they require specially adapted instructional materials and practices.

subculture A group that resists the ways of the dominant culture and adopts its own norms for behavior.

summative evaluation An evaluation conducted after instruction is completed to assess students' final achievement.

superimposed meaningful structure A familiar shape, word, sentence, poem, or story imposed on information in order to facilitate recall; used as a *mnemonic*.

symbolic model A real or fictional character portrayed in the media (television, books, etc.) that influences an observer's behavior.

symbolic thought The ability to represent and think about external objects and events in one's mind.

sympathy A feeling of sorrow or concern for another person's problems or distress.

synapse A junction between two neurons that allows transmission of messages from one to the other.

synaptic pruning A universal process in brain development in which many previously formed synapses wither away.

synaptogenesis A universal process in early brain development in which many new synapses spontaneously appear.

syntax The set of rules that one uses (often unconsciously) to put words together into sentences.

table of specifications A two-way grid that indicates both the topics to be covered in an assessment and the things that students should be able to do with those topics.

task analysis A process of identifying the specific knowledge, behaviors, or cognitive processes necessary to master a particular subject area or skill.

teacher-developed assessment instrument An assessment tool developed by an individual teacher for use in his or her own classroom.

teacher-directed instruction An approach to instruction in which the teacher is largely in control of the course of the lesson.

temperament A genetic predisposition to respond in particular ways to one's physical and social environments.

terminal behavior The form and frequency of a desired response that a teacher or other practitioner hopes to foster through operant conditioning.

test anxiety Excessive anxiety about a particular test or about assessment in general.

test bank A collection of test items for a particular content domain; often provided by publishers of classroom textbooks.

testwiseness Test-taking know-how that enhances test performance.

theory An integrated set of concepts and principles developed to explain a particular phenomenon.

theory of mind Understanding of one's own and other people's mental and psychological states (thoughts, feelings, etc.).

threat A situation in which a learner believes there is little or no chance of success.

time on task The amount of time that students are actively engaged in a learning activity.

time-out A form of punishment in which a student is placed in a dull, boring situation with no opportunity to obtain reinforcement or interact with others.

token economy A technique in which desired behaviors are reinforced by tokens that learners can use to "purchase" a variety of other reinforcers.

traditional assessment Assessment that focuses on measuring basic knowledge and skills in relative isolation from tasks more typical of the outside world.

trait anxiety A pattern of responding with anxiety even in nonthreatening situations.

trait theory (of motivation) A theoretical perspective portraying motivation as involving enduring personality characteristics that learners have to a greater or lesser degree.

transfer A phenomenon in which something a student has learned at one time affects how the student learns or performs in a later situation.

treatment group A group of people in a research study who are given a particular experimental treatment (e.g., a particular method of instruction).

true score The hypothetical score a student would obtain if an assessment instrument could measure a characteristic with complete accuracy.

unconditioned response (UCR) A response that, without prior learning, is elicited by a particular (unconditioned) stimulus.

unconditioned stimulus (UCS) A stimulus that, without prior learning, elicits a particular response.

undergeneralization An overly restricted meaning for a word that excludes some situations to which the word does, in fact, apply; an overly narrow view of what objects or events a concept includes.

universals (in development) Similar patterns in how children change and progress over time regardless of the specific environment in which they are raised.

validity The extent to which an assessment instrument actually measures what it is intended to measure.

validity coefficient A numerical index of an assessment tool's predictive validity; ranges from 0 to 1, with higher numbers indicating more accurate predictions.

value The belief that an activity has direct or indirect benefits.

verbal mediator A word or phrase that forms a logical connection or "bridge" between two pieces of information; used as a *mnemonic*.

verbal reprimand A scolding for inappropriate behavior.

vicarious punishment A phenomenon in which a response decreases in frequency when another (observed) person is punished for that response.

vicarious reinforcement A phenomenon in which a response increases in frequency when another (observed) person is reinforced for that response.

visual imagery The process of forming mental pictures of objects or ideas.

visual impairment Malfunction of the eyes or optic nerves that prevents normal vision even with corrective lenses.

visual-spatial thinking The ability to imagine and mentally manipulate two- and three-dimensional figures.

wait time The length of time a teacher pauses, either after asking a question or hearing a student's comment, before saying something.

well-defined problem A problem in which the goal is clearly stated, all information needed to solve the problem is present, and only one correct answer exists.

withitness The appearance that a teacher knows what all students are doing at all times.

work-avoidance goal A desire either to avoid classroom tasks or to complete them with only minimal effort.

working memory A component of memory that holds and actively thinks about and processes a limited amount of information; also known as *short-term memory*.

zone of proximal development (ZPD) In Vygotsky's theory, the range of tasks between one's actual developmental level and one's level of potential development—that is, the range of tasks that one cannot yet perform independently but can perform with the help and guidance of others.

z-score A standard score with a mean of 0 and a standard deviation of 1.

References

Abdul-Jabbar, K., & Knobles, P. (1983). *Giant steps: The autobiography of Kareem Abdul-Jabbar.* New York: Bantam Books.

Abery, B., & Zajac, R. (1996). Self-determination as a goal of early childhood and elementary education. In D. J. Sands & M. L. Wehmeyer (Eds.), *Self-determination across the life span: Independence and choice for people with disabilities.* Baltimore: Brookes.

Abi-Nader, J. (1993). Meeting the needs of multicultural classrooms: Family values and the motivation of minority students. In M. J. O'Hair & S. J. Odell (Eds.), *Diversity and teaching: Teacher education yearbook I.* Fort Worth, TX: Harcourt Brace Jovanovich.

Ablard, K. E., & Lipschultz, R. E. (1998). Self-regulated learning in high-achieving students: Relations to advanced reasoning, achievement goals, and gender. *Journal of Educational Psychology, 90,* 94–101.

Achenbach, T. M. (1974). *Developmental psychopathology.* New York: Ronald Press.

Achenbach, T. M., & Edelbrock, C. S. (1981). Behavioral problems and competencies reported by parents of normal and disturbed children aged four through sixteen. *Monographs of the Society for Research in Child Development, 46*(1, Serial No. 138).

Adalbjarnardottir, S., & Selman, R. L. (1997). "I feel I have received a new vision": An analysis of teachers' professional development as they work with students on interpersonal issues. *Teaching and Teacher Education, 13,* 409–428.

Adams, P. A., & Adams, J. K. (1960). Confidence in the recognition and reproduction of words difficult to spell. *American Journal of Psychology, 73,* 544–552.

Adelman, H. S. (1996). Appreciating the classification dilemma. In W. Stainback & S. Stainback (Eds.), *Controversial issues confronting special education: Diverse perspectives.* Boston: Allyn & Bacon.

Airasian, P. W. (1994). *Classroom assessment* (2nd ed.). New York: McGraw-Hill.

Alapack, R. (1991). The adolescent first kiss. *Humanistic Psychologist, 19,* 48–67.

Alberto, P. A., & Troutman, A. C. (2003). *Applied behavior analysis for teachers* (6th ed.). Upper Saddle River, NJ: Merrill/Prentice Hall.

Alderman, M. K. (1990). Motivation for at-risk students. *Educational Leadership, 48*(1), 27–30.

Alexander, K. L., Entwisle, D. R., & Dauber, S. L. (1995). *On the success of failure.* New York: Cambridge University Press.

Alexander, K. L., Entwisle, D. R., & Thompson, M. (1987). School performance, status relations, and the structure of sentiment: Bringing the teacher back in. *American Sociological Review, 52,* 665–682.

Alexander, P. A. (1997). Mapping the multidimensional nature of domain learning: The interplay of cognitive, motivational, and strategic forces. In P. R. Pintrich & M. L. Maehr (Eds.), *Advances in motivation and achievement* (Vol. 10). Greenwich, CT: JAI Press.

Alexander, P. A., Graham, S., & Harris, K. R. (1998). A perspective on strategy research: Progress and prospects. *Educational Psychology Review, 10,* 129–154.

Alexander, P. A., & Jetton, T. L. (1996). The role of importance and interest in the processing of text. *Educational Psychology Review, 8,* 89–121.

Alexander, P. A., & Judy, J. E. (1988). The interaction of domain-specific and strategic knowledge in academic performance. *Review of Educational Research, 58,* 375–404.

Alexander, P. A., Kulikowich, J. M., & Schulze, S. K. (1994). How subject-matter knowledge affects recall and interest. *American Educational Research Journal, 31,* 313–337.

Alfassi, M. (1998). Reading for meaning: The efficacy of reciprocal teaching in fostering reading comprehension in high school students in remedial reading classes. *American Educational Research Journal, 35,* 309–332.

Algozzine, B., Browder, D., Karvonen, M., Test, D. W., & Wood, W. M. (2001). Effects of interventions to promote self-determination for individuals with disabilities. *Review of Educational Research, 71,* 219–277.

Alleman, J., & Brophy, J. (1992). Analysis of the activities in a social studies curriculum. In J. Brophy (Ed.), *Advances in research on teaching: Vol. 3. Planning and managing learning tasks and activities.* Greenwich, CT: JAI Press.

Alleman, J., & Brophy, J. (1997). Elementary social studies: Instruments, activities, and standards. In G. D. Phye (Ed.), *Handbook of classroom assessment: Learning, achievement, and adjustment.* San Diego, CA: Academic Press.

Alleman, J., & Brophy, J. (1998, April). *Strategic learning opportunities during out-of-school hours.* Paper presented at the annual meeting of the American Educational Research Association, San Diego, CA.

Allen, J. P., McElhaney, K. B., Land, D. J., Kuperminc, G. P., Moore, C. W., O'Beirne-Kelly, H., & Kilmer, S. L. (2003). A secure base in adolescence: Markers of attachment security in the mother-adolescent relationship. *Child Development, 74,* 292–307.

Allen, K. D. (1998). The use of an enhanced simplified habit-reversal procedure to reduce disruptive outbursts during athletic performance. *Journal of Applied Behavior Analysis, 31,* 489–492.

Alley, G., & Deshler, D. (1979). *Teaching the learning disabled adolescent: Strategies and methods.* Denver, CO: Love.

Allington, R. L., & Weber, R. (1993). Questioning questions in teaching and learning from texts. In B. K. Britton, A. Woodward, & M. Binkley (Eds.), *Learning from textbooks: Theory and practice.* Mahwah, NJ: Erlbaum.

Altermatt, E. R., Jovanovic, J., & Perry, M. (1998). Bias or responsivity? Sex and achievement-level effects on teachers' classroom questioning practices. *Journal of Educational Psychology, 90,* 516–527.

Altmann, E. M. & Gray, W. D. (2002). Forgetting to remember: The functional relationship of decay and interference. *Psychological Science, 13,* 27–33.

Amabile, T. M., & Hennessey, B. A. (1992). The motivation for creativity in children. In A. K. Boggiano & T. S. Pittman (Eds.), *Achievement and motivation: A social-developmental perspective.* Cambridge, England: Cambridge University Press.

Ambrose, D., Allen, J., & Huntley, S. B. (1994). Mentorship of the highly creative. *Roeper Review, 17,* 131–133.

American Educational Research Association, American Psychological Association, & National Council on Measurement in Education. (1999). *Standards for Educational and Psychological Testing* (2nd ed.). Washington, DC: American Educational Research Association.

American Psychiatric Association. (1994). *Diagnostic and statistical manual of mental disorders* (4th ed.). Washington, DC: Author.

Ames, C. (1984). Competitive, cooperative, and individualistic goal structures: A cognitive-motivational analysis. In R. Ames & C. Ames (Eds.), *Research on motivation in education: Vol. 1. Student motivation.* San Diego, CA: Academic Press.

Ames, C. (1992). Classrooms: Goals, structures, and student motivation. *Journal of Educational Psychology, 84,* 261–271.

Ames, C., & Archer, J. (1988). Achievement goals in the classroom: Students' learning strategies and motivation processes. *Journal of Educational Psychology, 80,* 260–267.

Ames, R. (1983). Help-seeking and achievement orientation: Perspectives from attribution theory. In A. Nadler, J. Fisher, & B. DePaulo (Eds.), *New directions in helping* (Vol. 2). New York: Academic Press.

Amrein, A. L., & Berliner, D. C. (2002a, December). *An analysis of some unintended and negative consequences of high- stakes testing* (Report EPSL-0211-125-EPRU). Tempe: Educational Policy Study Laboratory, Arizona State University. Retrieved April 28, 2003, from http://www.asu.edu/educ/epsl/EPRU/epru_2002_Research_Writing.htm

Amrein, A. L., & Berliner, D. C. (2002b, March 28). High-stakes testing, uncertainty, and student learning. *Education Policy Analysis Archives, 10*(18). Retrieved April 9, 2002, from http://epaa.asu.edu/epaa/v10n18/.

Amrein, A. L., & Berliner, D. C. (2002c). The impact of high-stakes tests on student academic performance: An analysis of NAEP results in states with high-stakes tests and ACT, SAT, and AP test results in states with high school graduation exams. Retrieved April 28, 2003, from Arizona State University, Education Policy Studies Laboratory Web site: http://www.asu.edu/educ/epsl/EPRU/epru_2002_Research_Writing.htm.

Anand, P., & Ross, S. (1987). A computer-based strategy for personalizing verbal problems in teaching mathematics. *Educational Communication and Technology Journal, 35,* 151–162.

Anastasi, A., & Urbina, S. (1997). *Psychological testing.* Upper Saddle River, NJ: Prentice Hall.

Anderman, E. M. (2002). School effects on psychological outcomes during adolescence. *Journal of Educational Psychology, 94,* 795–809.

Anderman, E. M. Griesinger, T., & Westerfield, G. (1998). Motivation and cheating during early adolescence. *Journal of Educational Psychology, 90,* 84–93.

Anderman, E. M. & Maehr, M. L. (1994). Motivation and schooling in the middle grades. *Review of Educational Research, 64,* 287–309.

Anderman, L. H., & Anderman, E. M. (1999). Social predictors of changes in students' achievement goal orientation. *Contemporary Educational Psychology, 25,* 21–37.

Anderman, L. H., Patrick, H., Hruda, L. Z., & Linnenbrink, E. A. (2002). Observing classroom goal structures to clarify and expand goal theory. In C. Midgley (Ed.), *Goals, goal structures, and patterns of adaptive learning* (pp 243–278). Mahwah, NJ: Erlbaum.

Anderson, C. A., Berkowitz, L., Donnerstein, E., Huesmann, L. R., Johnson, J. D., Linz, D., Malamuth, N. M., & Wartella, E. (2003). The influence of media violence on youth. *Psychological Science in the Public Interest, 4,* 81–110.

Anderson, J. R. (1983). *The architecture of cognition.* Cambridge, MA: Harvard University Press.

Anderson, J. R. (1987). Skill acquisition: Compilation of weak-method problem solutions. *Psychological Review, 94,* 192–210.

Anderson, J. R. (1990). *Cognitive psychology and its implications* (3rd ed.). New York: Freeman.

Anderson, J. R. (1995). *Learning and memory: An integrated approach.* New York: Wiley.

Anderson, J. R., Greeno, J. G., Reder, L. M., & Simon, H. A. (2000). Perspectives on learning, thinking, and activity. *Educational Researcher, 29*(4), 11–13.

Anderson, J. R., Reder, L. M., & Simon, H. A. (1996). Situated learning and education. *Educational Researcher, 25*(4), 5–11.

Anderson, L. H. (1999). *Speak.* New York: Puffin Books.

Anderson, L. M. (1993). Auxiliary materials that accompany textbooks: Can they promote "higher-order" learning? In B. K. Britton, A. Woodward, & M. Binkley (Eds.), *Learning from textbooks: Theory and practice.* Mahwah, NJ: Erlbaum.

Anderson, L. M., Brubaker, N. L., Alleman-Brooks, J., & Duffy, G. (1985). A qualitative study of seatwork in first-grade classrooms. *Elementary School Journal, 86,* 123–140.

Anderson, L. W., Krathwohl, D. R., Airasian, P. W., Cruikshank, K. A., Mayer, R. E., Pintrich, P. R., Raths, J., & Wittrock, M. C. (Eds.). (2001). *A taxonomy for learning, teaching, and assessing: A revision of Bloom's taxonomy of educational objectives.* New York: Longman.

Anderson, L. W., & Pellicer, L. O. (1998). Toward an understanding of unusually successful programs for economically disadvantaged students. *Journal of Education for Students Placed at Risk, 3,* 237–263.

Anderson, R. C., Nguyen-Jahiel, K., McNurlen, B., Archodidou, A., Kim, S. Y., Reznitskaya, A., Tillmanns, M., & Gilbert, L. (2001). The snowball phenomenon: Spread of ways of talking and ways of thinking across groups of children. *Cognition and Instruction, 19,* 1–46.

Anderson, R. C., Reynolds, R. E., Schallert, D. L., & Goetz, E. T. (1977). Frameworks for comprehending discourse. *American Educational Research Journal, 14,* 367–381.

Anderson, V., & Hidi, S. (1988/1989). Teaching students to summarize. *Educational Leadership, 46*(4), 26–28.

Andre, T. (1986). Problem solving and education. In G. D. Phye & T. Andre (Eds.), *Cognitive classroom learning: Understanding, thinking, and problem solving.* San Diego, CA: Academic Press.

Andre, T., & Windschitl, M. (2003). Interest, epistemological belief, and intentional conceptual change. In G. M. Sinatra & P. R. Pintrich (Eds.), *Intentional conceptual change* (pp. 173–197). Mahwah, NJ: Erlbaum.

Anglin, J. M. (1977). *Word, object, and conceptual development.* New York: Norton.

Ansley, T. (1997). The role of standardized achievement tests in grades K–12. In G. D. Phye (Ed.), *Handbook of classroom assessment: Learning, achievement, and adjustment.* San Diego, CA: Academic Press.

Anzai, Y. (1991). Learning and use of representations for physics expertise. In K. A. Ericsson & J. Smith (Eds.), *Toward a general theory of expertise: Prospects and limits.* Cambridge, England: Cambridge University Press.

Archer, S. L. (1982). The lower age boundaries of identity development. *Child Development, 53,* 1551–1556.

Ardoin, S. P., Martens, B. K., & Wolfe, L. A. (1999). Using high-probability instructional sequences with fading to increase student compliance during transitions. *Journal of Applied Behavior Analysis, 32,* 339–351.

Arenz, B. W., & Lee, M. J. (1990, April). *Gender differences in the attitude, interest and participation of secondary students in computer use.* Paper presented at the annual meeting of the American Educational Research Association, Boston.

Arlin, M. (1979). Teacher transitions can disrupt time flow in classrooms. *American Educational Research Journal, 16,* 42–56.

Arlin, M. (1984). Time, equality, and mastery learning. *Review of Educational Research, 54,* 65–86.

Armstrong, T. (1994). *Multiple intelligences in the classroom.* Alexandria, VA: Association for Supervision and Curriculum Development.

Arnett, J. (1995). The young and the reckless: Adolescent reckless behavior. *Current Directions in Psychological Science, 4,* 67–71.

Arnett, J. J. (1999). Adolescent storm and stress, reconsidered. *American Psychologist, 54,* 317–326.

Arnold, M. L. (2000). Stage, sequence, and sequels: Changing conceptions of morality, post-Kohlberg. *Educational Psychology Review, 12,* 365–383.

Aronson, E., & Patnoe, S. (1997). *The jigsaw classroom: Building cooperation in the classroom* (2nd ed.). New York: Longman.

Aronson, J., Lustina, M. J., Good, C., Keough, K., Steele, C. M., & Brown, J. (1999). When white men can't do math: Necessary and sufficient factors in stereotype threat. *Journal of Experimental Social Psychology, 35,* 29–46.

Arter, J. A., & Spandel, V. (1992). Using portfolios of student work in instruction and assessment. *Educational Measurement: Issues and Practice, 11*(1), 36–44.

Ashcraft, M. H. (2002). Math anxiety: Personal, educational, and cognitive consequences. *Current Directions in Psychological Science, 11,* 181–184.

Asher, S. R., & Parker, J. G. (1989). Significance of peer relationship problems in childhood. In B. H. Schneider, G. Attili, J. Nadel, & R. P. Weissberg (Eds.), *Social competence in developmental perspective.* Dordrecht, Netherlands: Kluwer.

Asher, S. R., & Renshaw, P. D. (1981). Children without friends: Social knowledge and social skill training. In S. R. Asher & J. M. Gottman (Eds.), *The development of children's friendships.* New York: Cambridge University Press.

Ashton, P. (1985). Motivation and the teacher's sense of efficacy. In C. Ames & R. Ames (Eds.), *Research on motivation in education: Vol. 2. The classroom milieu.* San Diego, CA: Academic Press.

Assor, A., & Connell, J. P. (1992). The validity of students' self-reports as measures of performance affecting self-appraisals. In D. H. Schunk & J. L. Meece (Eds.), *Student perceptions in the classroom.* Mahwah, NJ: Erlbaum.

Astington, J. W., & Pelletier, J. (1996). The language of mind: Its role in teaching and learning. In D. R. Olson & N. Torrance (Eds.), *The handbook of education and human development: New models of learning, teaching, and schooling.* Cambridge, MA: Blackwell.

Astor, R. A. (1994). Children's moral reasoning about family and peer violence: The role of provocation and retribution. *Child Development, 65,* 1054–1067.

Astor, R. A., Meyer, H. A., & Behre, W. J. (1999). Unowned places and times: Maps and interviews about violence in high schools. *American Educational Research Journal, 36,* 3–42.

Atkinson, J. W., & Feather, N. T. (Eds.). (1966). *A theory of achievement motivation.* New York: Wiley.

Atkinson, R. C., & Shiffrin, R. M. (1968). Human memory: A proposed system and its control processes. In K. W. Spence & J. T. Spence (Eds.), *The psychology of learning and motivation: Advances in research and theory* (Vol. 2). San Diego, CA: Academic Press.

Atkinson, R. K., Derry, S. J., Renkl, A., & Wortham, D. (2000). Learning from examples: Instructional principles from the worked examples research. *Review of Educational Research, 70,* 181–214.

Atkinson, R. K., Levin, J. R., Kiewra, K. A., Meyers, T., Kim, S., Atkinson, L. A., Renandya, W. A., & Hwang, Y. (1999). Matrix and mnemonic text-processing adjuncts: Comparing and combining their components. *Journal of Educational Psychology, 91,* 342–357.

Attie, I., Brooks-Gunn, J., & Petersen, A. (1990). A developmental perspective on eating disorders and eating problems. In M. Lewis & S. M. Miller (Eds.), *Handbook of developmental psychopathology* (pp. 409–420). New York: Plenum Press.

Au, K. H. (1980). Participation structures in a reading lesson with Hawaiian children: Analysis of a culturally appropriate instructional event. *Anthropology and Education Quarterly, 11,* 91–115.

Au, T. K., Knightly, L. M., Jun, S., & Oh, J. S. (2002). Overhearing a language during childhood. *Psychological Science, 13,* 238–243.

Aulls, M. W. (1998). Contributions of classroom discourse to what content students learn during curriculum enactment. *Journal of Educational Psychology, 90,* 56–69.

Ausubel, D. P., Novak, J. D., & Hanesian, H. (1978). *Educational psychology: A cognitive view* (2nd ed.). New York: Holt, Rinehart & Winston.

Babad, E. (1993). Teachers' differential behavior. *Educational Psychology Review, 5,* 347–376.

Babad, E. (1995). The "teacher's pet phenomenon," students' perceptions of teachers' differential behavior, and students' morale. *Journal of Educational Psychology, 87,* 361–374.

Babad, E., Avni-Babad, D., & Rosenthal, R. (2003). Teachers' brief nonverbal behaviors in defined instructional situations can predict students' evaluations. *Journal of Educational Psychology, 95,* 553–562.

Bachevalier, J., Malkova, L., & Beauregard, M. (1996). Multiple memory systems: A neuropsychological and developmental perspective. In G. R. Lyon & N. A. Krasnegor (Eds.), *Attention, memory, and executive function* (pp. 185–198). Baltimore: Brookes.

Baddeley, A. (1999). *Essentials of human memory.* Philadelphia: Psychology Press.

Baddeley, A. D. (2001). Is working memory still working? *American Psychologist, 56,* 851–864.

Baek, S. (1994). Implications of cognitive psychology for educational testing. *Educational Psychology Review, 6,* 373–389.

Bahrick, H. P., Bahrick, L. E., Bahrick, A. S., & Bahrick, P. E. (1993). Maintenance of foreign language vocabulary and the spacing effect. *Psychological Science, 4,* 316–321.

Baillargeon, R. (2004). Infants' physical worlds. *Current Directions in Psychological Science, 13,* 89–94.

Baker, J. (1999). Teacher-student interaction in urban at-risk classrooms: Differential behavior, relationship quality, and student satisfaction with school. *The Elementary School Journal, 100,* 57–70.

Baker, L. (1989). Metacognition, comprehension monitoring, and the adult reader. *Educational Psychology Review, 1,* 3–38.

Baker, L., & Brown, A. L. (1984). Metacognitive skills of reading. In D. Pearson (Ed.), *Handbook of reading research.* White Plains, NY: Longman.

Balla, D. A., & Zigler, E. (1979). Personality development in retarded persons. In N. R. Ellis (Ed.), *Handbook of mental deficiency: Psychological theory and research* (2nd ed.). Mahwah, NJ: Erlbaum.

Ballenger, C. (1992). Because you like us: The language of control. *Harvard Educational Review, 62,* 199–208.

Bandura, A. (1965). Influence of models' reinforcement contingencies on the acquisition of imitative responses. *Journal of Personality and Social Psychology, 1,* 589–595.

Bandura, A. (1977). *Social learning theory.* Upper Saddle River, NJ: Prentice Hall.

Bandura, A. (1982). Self-efficacy mechanism in human agency. *American Psychologist, 37,* 122–147.

Bandura, A. (1986). *Social foundations of thought and action: A social cognitive theory.* Upper Saddle River, NJ: Prentice Hall.

Bandura, A. (1989). Human agency in social cognitive theory. *American Psychologist, 44,* 1175–1184.

Bandura, A. (1997). *Self-efficacy: The exercise of control.* New York: Freeman.

Bandura, A. (2000). Exercise of human agency through collective efficacy. *Current Directions in Psychological Science, 9,* 75–78.

Bandura, A., Barbaranelli, C., Caprara, G. V., & Pastorelli, C. (2001). Self-efficacy beliefs as shapers of children's aspirations and career trajectories. *Child Development, 72,* 187–206.

Bandura, A., Ross, D., & Ross, S. A. (1963). Imitation of film-mediated aggressive models. *Journal of Abnormal and Social Psychology, 66,* 3–11.

Bandura, A., & Schunk, D. H. (1981). Cultivating competence, self-efficacy, and intrinsic interest through proximal self-motivation. *Journal of Personality and Social Psychology, 41,* 586–598.

Bangert-Drowns, R. L., Kulik, C. C., Kulik, J. A., & Morgan, M. (1991). The instructional effect of feedback in test-like events. *Review of Educational Research, 61,* 213–238.

Banks, J. A. (1991). Multicultural literacy and curriculum reform. *Educational Horizons, 69*(3), 135–140.

Banks, J. A. (1994). *An introduction to multicultural education.* Needham Heights, MA: Allyn & Bacon.

Banks, J. A. (1995). Multicultural education: Historical development, dimensions, and practice. In J. A. Banks & C. A. M. Banks (Eds.), *Handbook of research on multicultural education.* New York: Macmillan.

Banks, J. A., & Banks, C. A. M. (Eds.). (1995). *Handbook of research on multicultural education.* New York: Macmillan.

Barab, S. A., & Landa, A. (1997). Designing effective interdisciplinary anchors. *Educational Leadership, 54*(6), 52–55.

Barab, S. A., & Plucker, J. A. (2002). Smart people or smart contexts? Cognition, ability, and talent development in an age of situated approaches to knowing and learning. *Educational Psychologist, 37,* 165–182.

Barbetta, P. M. (1990). GOALS: A group-oriented adapted levels system for children with behavior disorders. *Academic Therapy, 25,* 645–656.

Barbetta, P. M., Heward, W. L., Bradley, D. M., & Miller, A. D. (1994). Effects of immediate and delayed error correction on the acquisition and maintenance of sight words by students with developmental disabilities. *Journal of Applied Behavior Analysis, 27,* 177–178.

Barga, N. K. (1996). Students with learning disabilities in education: Managing a disability. *Journal of Learning Disabilities, 29,* 413–421.

Barkley, R. A. (1996). Linkages between attention and executive functions. In G. R. Lyon & N. A. Krasnegor (Eds.), *Attention, memory, and executive function.* Baltimore: Brookes.

Barkley, R. A. (1998). *Attention-deficit hyperactivity disorder: A handbook for diagnosis and treatment* (2nd ed.). New York: Guilford Press.

Barnes, D. (1976). *From communication to curriculum.* London: Penguin.

Barnett, J. E. (2001, April). *Study strategies and preparing for exams: A survey of middle and high school students.* Paper presented at the annual meeting of the American Educational Research Association, Seattle, WA.

Barnett, J. E., Di Vesta, F. J., & Rogozinski, J. T. (1981). What is learned in note taking? *Journal of Educational Psychology, 73,* 181–192.

Baron, J. B. (1987). Evaluating thinking skills in the classroom. In J. B. Baron & R. J. Sternberg (Eds.), *Teaching thinking skills: Theory and practice.* New York: Freeman.

Baron-Cohen, S., Tager-Flusberg, H., & Cohen, D. J. (1993). *Understanding other minds: Perspectives from autism.* Oxford, England: Oxford University Press.

Barrish, H. H., Saunders, M., & Wolf, M. M. (1969). Good behavior game: Effects of individual contingencies for group consequences on disruptive behavior in a classroom. *Journal of Applied Behavior Analysis, 2,* 119–124.

Barron, B. (2000). Problem solving in video-based microworlds: Collaborative and individual outcomes of high-achieving sixth-grade students. *Journal of Educational Psychology, 92,* 391–398.

Bartlett, F. C. (1932). *Remembering: A study in experimental and social psychology.* Cambridge, England: Cambridge University Press.

Basinger, K. S., Gibbs, J. C., & Fuller, D. (1995). Context and the measurement of moral judgment. *International Journal of Behavioral Development, 18,* 537–556.

Bassett, D. S., Jackson, L., Ferrell, K. A., Luckner, J., Hagerty, P. J., Bunsen, T. D., & MacIsaac, D. (1996). Multiple perspectives on inclusive education: Reflections of a university faculty. *Teacher Education and Special Education, 19,* 355–386.

Basso, K. (1972). To give up on words: Silence in western Apache culture. In P. Giglioli (Ed.), *Language and social context.* New York: Penguin Books.

Bassok, M. (1990). Transfer of domain-specific problem-solving procedures. *Journal of Experimental Psychology: Learning, Memory, and Cognition, 16,* 522–533.

Bassok, M. (1997). Two types of reliance on correlations between content and structure in reasoning about word problems. In L. D. English (Ed.), *Mathematical reasoning: Analogies, metaphors, and images* (pp. 221–246). Mahwah, NJ: Erlbaum.

Bates, E., & MacWhinney, B. (1987). Competition, variation, and language learning. In B. MacWhinney (Ed.), *Mechanisms of language acquisition.* Mahwah, NJ: Erlbaum.

Batshaw, M. L., & Shapiro, B. K. (1997). Mental retardation. In M. L. Batshaw (Ed.), *Children with disabilities* (4th ed.). Baltimore: Brookes.

Batson, C. D. (1991). *The altruism question: Toward a social-psychological answer.* Hillsdale, NJ: Erlbaum.

Batson, C. D., & Thompson, E. R. (2001). Why don't moral people act morally? Motivational considerations. *Current Directions in Psychological Science, 10,* 54–57.

Battin-Pearson, S., Newcomb, M. D., Abbott, R. D., Hill, K. G., Catalano, R. F., & Hawkins, J. D. (2000). Predictors of early high school dropout: A test of five theories. *Journal of Educational Psychology, 92,* 568–582.

Battistich, V., Solomon, D., Kim, D., Watson, M., & Schaps, E. (1995). Schools as communities, poverty levels of student populations, and students' attitudes, motives, and performance: A multilevel analysis. *American Educational Research Journal, 32,* 627–658.

Battistich, V., Solomon, D., Watson, M., & Schaps, E. (1997). Caring school communities. *Educational Psychologist, 32,* 137–151.

Baumeister, A. A. (1989). Mental retardation. In C. G. Lask & M. Hersen (Eds.), *Handbook of child psychiatric diagnosis.* New York: Wiley.

Baumeister, R. F., Campbell, J. D., Krueger, J. I., & Vohs, K. D. (2003). Does high self-esteem cause better performance, interpersonal success, happiness, or healthier lifestyles? *Psychological Science in the Public Interest, 4*(1), 1–44.

Baumeister, R. F., Smart, L., & Boden, J. M. (1996). Relation of threatened egotism to violence and aggression: The dark side of high self-esteem. *Psychological Review, 103,* 5–33.

Baumrind, D. (1971). Current patterns of parental authority. *Developmental Psychology Monograph, 4*(1, Pt. 2).

Baumrind, D. (1989). Rearing competent children. In W. Damon (Ed.), *Child development today and tomorrow.* San Francisco: Jossey-Bass.

Baxter, G. P., Elder, A. D., & Glaser, R. (1996). Knowledge-based cognition and performance assessment in the science classroom. *Educational Psychologist, 31,* 133–140.

Bay-Hinitz, A. K., Peterson, R. F., & Quilitch, H. R. (1994). Cooperative games: A way to modify aggressive and cooperative behaviors in young children. *Journal of Applied Behavior Analysis, 27,* 435–446.

Bebko, J. M., Burke, L., Craven, J., & Sarlo, N. (1992). The importance of motor activity in sensorimotor development: A perspective from children with physical handicaps. *Human Development, 35*(4), 226–240.

Beck, I. L., & McKeown, M. G. (1994). Outcomes of history instruction: Paste-up accounts. In M. Carretero & J. F. Voss (Eds.), *Cognitive and instructional processes in history and the social sciences* (pp. 237–256). Mahwah, NJ: Erlbaum.

Becker, B. E., & Luthar, S. S. (2002). Social-emotional factors affecting achievement outcomes among disadvantaged students: Closing the achievement gap. *Educational Psychologist, 37,* 197–214.

Bédard, J., & Chi, M. T. H. (1992). Expertise. *Current Directions in Psychological Science, 1,* 135–139.

Begg, I., Anas, A., & Farinacci, S. (1992). Dissociation of processes in belief: Source recollection, statement familiarity, and the illusion of truth. *Journal of Experimental Psychology: General, 121,* 446–458.

Behr, M., & Harel, G. (1988, April). Cognitive conflict in procedure applications. In D. Tirosh (Chair), *The role of inconsistent ideas in learning mathematics.* Symposium conducted at the annual meeting of the American Educational Research Association, New Orleans, LA.

Behrmann, M. (2000). The mind's eye mapped onto the brain's matter. *Current Directions in Psychological Science, 9,* 50–54.

Beirne-Smith, M., Ittenbach, R. F., & Patton, J. R. (2002). *Mental retardation* (6th ed.). Upper Saddle River, NJ: Merrill/Prentice Hall.

Belfiore, P. J., & Hornyak, R. S. (1998). Operant theory and application to self-monitoring in adolescents. In D. H. Schunk and B. J. Zimmerman (Eds.), *Self-regulated learning: From teaching to self-reflective practice.* New York: Guilford Press.

Belfiore, P. J., Lee, D. L., Vargas, A. U., & Skinner, C. H. (1997). Effects of high-preference single-digit mathematics problem completion on multiple-digit mathematics problem performance. *Journal of Applied Behavior Analysis, 30,* 327–330.

Bell, L. A. (1989). Something's wrong here and it's not me: Challenging the dilemmas that block girls' success. *Journal for the Education of the Gifted, 12,* 118–130.

Bell, P., & Linn, M. C. (2002). Beliefs about science: How does science instruction contribute? In B. K. Hofer & P. R. Pintrich (Eds.), *Personal epistemology: The psychology of beliefs about knowledge and knowing* (pp. 321–346). Mahwah, NJ: Erlbaum.

Bellezza, F. S. (1986). Mental cues and verbal reports in learning. In G. H. Bower (Ed.), *The psychology of learning and motivation: Advances in research and theory* (Vol. 20). San Diego, CA: Academic Press.

Bem, S. L. (1981). Gender schema theory: A cognitive account of sex typing. *Psychological Review, 88,* 354–364.

Bem, S. L. (1983). Gender schema theory and its implications for child development: Raising gender-aschematic children in a gender-schematic society. *Signs: Journal of Women in Culture and Society, 8,* 598–616.

Bem, S. L. (1984). Androgyny and gender schema theory: A conceptual and empirical integration. In R. A. Dienstbier & T. B. Sonderegger (Eds.). *Nebraska Symposium on Motivation* (Vol. 34). Lincoln: University of Nebraska Press.

Bender, G. (2001). Resisting dominance? The study of a marginalized masculinity and its construction within high school walls. In J. N. Burstyn, G. Bender, R. Casella, H. W. Gordon, D. P. Guerra, K. V. Luschen, R. Stevens, & K. M. Williams, *Preventing violence in schools: A challenge to American democracy* (pp. 61–77). Mahwah, NJ: Erlbaum.

Bender, T. A. (1997). Assessment of subjective well-being during childhood and adolescence. In G. D. Phye (Ed.), *Handbook of classroom assessment: Learning, achievement, and adjustment.* San Diego, CA: Academic Press.

Benenson, J. F., & Christakos, A. (2003) The greater fragility of females' versus males' closest same-sex friendships. *Child Development, 74,* 1123–1129.

Benenson, J. F., Maiese, R., Dolenszky, E., Dolensky, N., Sinclair, N., & Simpson, A. (2002). Group size regulates self-assertive versus self-deprecating responses to interpersonal competition. *Child Development, 73,* 1818–1829.

Bennett, G. K., Seashore, H. G., & Wesman, A. G. (1982). *Differential Aptitude Tests.* San Antonio, TX: Psychological Corporation.

Bennett, R. E., Gottesman, R. L., Rock, D. A., & Cerullo, F. (1993). Influence of behavior perceptions and gender on teachers' judgments of students' academic skill. *Journal of Educational Psychology, 85,* 347–356.

Benware, C., & Deci, E. L. (1984). Quality of learning with an active versus passive motivational set. *American Educational Research Journal, 21,* 755–765.

Bereiter, C. (1995). A dispositional view of transfer. In A. McKeough, J. Lupart, & A. Marini (Eds.), *Teaching for transfer: Fostering generalization in learning.* Mahwah, NJ: Erlbaum.

Bereiter, C., & Scardamalia, M. (1987). *The psychology of written composition.* Mahwah, NJ: Erlbaum.

Berk, L. E. (1994). Why children talk to themselves. *Scientific American, 271,* 78–83.

Berk, L. E. (2003). *Child development* (6th ed.). Boston: Allyn & Bacon.

Berk, L. E., & Potts, M. K. (1991). Development and functional significance of private speech among attention-deficit hyperactivity disorder and normal boys. *Journal of Abnormal Child Psychology, 19,* 357–377.

Berkowitz, M. W., Guerra, N., & Nucci, L. (1991). Sociomoral development and drug and alcohol abuse. In W. M. Kurtines & J. L. Gewirtz (Eds.), *Moral behavior and development: Vol. 3. Application.* Mahwah, NJ: Erlbaum.

Berliner, D. C. (1988, February). *The development of expertise in pedagogy.* Paper presented at the American Association of Colleges for Teacher Education, New Orleans, LA.

Berliner, D. C. (1997, March). Discussant's comments. In H. Borko (Chair), *Educational psychology and teacher education: Perennial issues.* Symposium conducted at the annual meeting of the American Educational Research Association, Chicago.

Berlyne, D. E. (1960). *Conflict, arousal, and curiosity.* New York: McGraw-Hill.

Berndt, T. J. (1992). Friendship and friends' influence in adolescence. *Current Directions in Psychological Science, 1*, 156–159.

Berndt, T. J. (2002). Friendship quality and social development. *Current Directions in Psychological Science, 11*, 7–10.

Berndt, T. J., Hawkins, J. A., & Jiao, Z. (1999). Influences of friends and friendships on adjustment to junior high school. *Merrill Palmer Quarterly, 45*, 13–41.

Berndt, T. J., & Keefe, K. (1996). Friends' influence on school adjustment: A motivational analysis. In J. Juvonen & K. R. Wentzel (Eds.), *Social motivation: Understanding children's school adjustment* (pp. 248–278). Cambridge, England: Cambridge University Press.

Berndt, T. J., Laychak, A. E., & Park, K. (1990). Friends' influence on adolescents' academic achievement motivation: An experimental study. *Journal of Educational Psychology, 82*, 664–670.

Berzonsky, M. D. (1988). Self-theorists, identity status, and social cognition. In D. K. Lapsley & F. C. Power (Eds.), *Self, ego, and identity: Integrative approaches* (pp. 243–261). New York: Springer-Verlag.

Beyer, B. K. (1985). Critical thinking: What is it? *Social Education, 49*, 270–276.

Bialystok, E. (1994a). Representation and ways of knowing: Three issues in second language acquisition. In N. C. Ellis (Ed.), *Implicit and explicit learning of languages.* London: Academic Press.

Bialystok, E. (1994b). Towards an explanation of second language acquisition. In G. Brown, K. Malmkjær, A. Pollitt, & J. Williams (Eds.), *Language and understanding.* Oxford, England: Oxford University Press.

Bialystok, E. (2001). *Bilingualism in development: Language, literacy, and cognition.* Cambridge, England: Cambridge University Press.

Bidell, T. R., & Fischer, K. W. (1997). Between nature and nurture: The role of human agency in the epigenesis of intelligence. In R. J. Sternberg & E. L. Grigorenko (Eds.), *Intelligence, heredity, and environment* (pp. 193–242). Cambridge, England: Cambridge University Press.

Biemiller, A., Shany, M., Inglis, A., & Meichenbaum, D. (1998). Factors influencing children's acquisition and demonstration of self-regulation on academic tasks. In D. H. Schunk & B. J. Zimmerman (Eds.), *Self-regulated learning: From teaching to self-reflective practice* (pp. 203–224). New York: Guilford Press.

Bierman, K. L., Miller, C. L., & Stabb, S. D. (1987). Improving the social behavior and peer acceptance of rejected boys: Effect of social skill training with instructions and prohibitions. *Journal of Consulting and Clinical Psychology, 55*, 194–200.

Bigler, R. S., Brown, C. S., & Markell, M. (2001). When groups are not created equal: Effects of group status on the formation of intergroup attitudes in children. *Child Development, 72*, 1151–1162.

Binder, L. M., Dixon, M. R., & Ghezzi, P. M. (2000). A procedure to teach self-control to children with attention deficit hyperactivity disorder. *Journal of Applied Behavior Analysis, 33*, 233–237.

Binns, K., Steinberg, A., Amorosi, S., & Cuevas, A. M. (1997). *The Metropolitan Life survey of the American teacher 1997: Examining gender issues in public schools.* New York: Louis Harris and Associates.

Bivens, J. A., & Berk, L. E. (1990). A longitudinal study of the development of elementary school children's private speech. *Merrill-Palmer Quarterly, 36*, 443–463.

Bjorklund, D. F. (1987). How age changes in knowledge base contribute to the development of children's memory: An interpretive review. *Developmental Review, 7*, 93–130.

Bjorklund, D. F., & Coyle, T. R. (1995). Utilization deficiencies in the development of memory strategies. In F. E. Weinert & W. Schneider (Eds.), *Research on memory development: State of the art and future directions.* Mahwah, NJ: Erlbaum.

Bjorklund, D. F., & Green, B. L. (1992). The adaptive nature of cognitive immaturity. *American Psychologist, 47*, 46–54.

Bjorklund, D. F., & Jacobs, J. W. (1985). Associative and categorical processes in children's memory: The role of automaticity in the development of organization in free recall. *Journal of Experimental Child Psychology, 39*, 599–617.

Bjorklund, D. F., Muir-Broaddus, J. E., & Schneider, W. (1990). The role of knowledge in the development of strategies. In D. F. Bjorklund (Ed.), *Children's strategies: Contemporary views of cognitive development.* Mahwah, NJ: Erlbaum.

Bjorklund, D. F., Schneider, W., Cassel, W. S., & Ashley, E. (1994). Training and extension of a memory strategy: Evidence for utilization deficiencies in high- and low-IQ children. *Child Development, 65*, 951–965.

Blair, C. (2002). School readiness: Integrating cognition and emotion in a neurobiological conceptualization of children's functioning at school entry. *American Psychologist, 57*, 111–127.

Blake, S. B., & Clark, R. E. (1990, April). *The effects of metacognitive selection on far transfer in analogical problem-solving tasks.* Paper presented at the annual meeting of the American Educational Research Association, Boston.

Blanchard, F. A., Lilly, T., & Vaughn, L. A. (1991). Reducing the expression of racial prejudice. *Psychological Science, 2*, 101–105.

Blasi, A. (1980). Bridging moral cognition and moral action: A critical review of the literature. *Psychological Bulletin, 88*, 593–637.

Blasi, A. (1995). Moral understanding and the moral personality: The process of moral integration. In W. M. Kurtines & J. L. Gewirtz (Eds.), *Moral development: An introduction.* Boston: Allyn & Bacon.

Block, J. H. (1980). Promoting excellence through mastery learning. *Theory into Practice, 19*, 66–74.

Block, J. H. (1983). Differential premises arising from differential socialization of the sexes: Some conjectures. *Child Development, 54*, 1335–1354.

Block, J. H., & Burns, R. B. (1976). Mastery learning. In L. Shulman (Ed.), *Review of research in education* (Vol. 4). Itasca, IL: Peacock.

Blok, H., Oostdam, R., Otter, M. E., & Overmaat, M. (2002). Computer-assisted instruction in support of beginning reading instruction: A review. *Review of Educational Research, 72*, 101–103.

Bloom, B. S. (1981). *All our children learning.* New York: McGraw-Hill.

Bloom, B. S., Englehart, M. D., Furst, E. J., Hill, W. H., & Krathwohl, D. R. (1956). *Taxonomy of educational objectives. The classification of educational goals: Handbook I. Cognitive domain.* New York: David McKay.

Bloom, L., & Tinker, E. (2001). The intentionality model and language acquisition. *Monographs of the Society for Research in Child Development, 66*(4, Serial No. 267).

Blugental, D. B., Lyon, J. E., Lin, E. K., McGrath, E. P., & Bimbela, A. (1999). Children "tune out" to the ambiguous communication style of powerless adults. *Child Development, 70*, 214–230.

Blumenfeld, P. C. (1992). The task and the teacher: Enhancing student thoughtfulness in science. In J. Brophy (Ed.), *Advances in research on teaching: Vol. 3. Planning and managing learning tasks and activities.* Greenwich, CT: JAI Press.

Blumenfeld, P., Hamilton, V. L., Bossert, S., Wessels, K., & Meece, C. (1983). Teacher talk and student thought: Socialization into the student role. In J. Levine & U. Wang (Eds.), *Teacher and student perceptions: Implications for learning.* Mahwah, NJ: Erlbaum.

Blumenfeld, P. C., Marx, R. W., Soloway, E., & Krajcik, J. (1996). Learning with peers: From small group cooperation to collaborative communities. *Educational Researcher, 25*(8), 37–40.

Boggiano, A. K., & Pittman, T. S. (Eds.). (1992). *Achievement and motivation: A social-developmental perspective.* Cambridge, England: Cambridge University Press.

Boldizar, J. P., Perry, D. G., & Perry, L. C. (1989). Outcome values and aggression. *Child Development, 60*, 571–579.

Bolger, K. E., & Patterson, C. J. (2001). Developmental pathways from child maltreatment to peer rejection. *Child Development, 72*, 549–568.

Bolles, R. C. (1975). *Theory of motivation* (2nd ed.). New York: Harper & Row.

Bong, M. (2001). Between- and within-domain relations of academic motivation among middle and high school students: Self-efficacy, task-value, and achievement goals. *Journal of Educational Psychology, 93*, 23–34.

Bong, M., & Skaalvik, E. M. (2003). Academic self-concept and self-efficacy: How different are they really? *Educational Psychology Review, 15*, 1–40.

Boom, J., Brugman, D., & van der Heijden, P. G. M. (2001). Hierarchical structure of moral stages assessed by a sorting task. *Child Development, 72*, 535–548.

Borko, H., & Putnam, R. T. (1996). Learning to teach. In D. C. Berliner & R. C. Calfee (Eds.), *Handbook of educational psychology.* New York: Macmillan.

Borkowski, J. G., & Burke, J. E. (1996). Theories, models, and measurements of executive functioning. In G. R. Lyon & N. A. Krasnegor (Eds.), *Attention, memory, and executive function* (pp. 235–261). Baltimore: Brookes.

Borkowski, J. G., Carr, M., Rellinger, E., & Pressley, M. (1990). Self-regulated cognition: Interdependence of metacognition, attributions, and self-esteem. In B. F. Jones & L. Idol (Eds.), *Dimensions of thinking and cognitive instruction.* Mahwah, NJ: Erlbaum.

Born, D. G., & Davis, M. L. (1974). Amount and distribution of study in a personalized instruction course and in a lecture course. *Journal of Applied Behavior Analysis, 7*, 365–375.

Bornholt, L. J., Goodnow, J. J., & Cooney, G. H. (1994). Influences of gender stereotypes on adolescents' perceptions of their own achievement. *American Educational Research Journal, 31*, 675–692.

Bortfeld, H., & Whitehurst, G. J. (2001). Sensitive periods in first language acquisition. In D. B. Bailey, Jr., J. T. Bruer, F. J. Symons, & J. W. Lichtman (Eds.), *Critical thinking about critical periods* (pp. 173–192). Baltimore: Brookes.

Bosacki, S. L. (2000). Theory of mind and self-concept in preadolescents: Links with gender and language. *Journal of Educational Psychology, 92*, 709–717.

Boschee, F., & Baron, M. A. (1993). *Outcome-based education: Developing programs through strategic planning.* Lancaster, PA: Technomic.

Bouchard, T. J., Jr. (1997). IQ similarity in twins reared apart: Findings and responses to critics. In R. J. Sternberg & E. L. Grigorenko (Eds.), *Intelligence, heredity, and environment* (pp. 126–160). Cambridge, England: Cambridge University Press.

Bourne, L. E., Jr., Dominowski, R. L., Loftus, E. F., & Healy, A. F. (1986). *Cognitive processes* (2nd ed.). Englewood Cliffs, NJ: Prentice Hall.

Bousfield, W. A. (1953). The occurrence of clustering in the recall of randomly arranged associates. *Journal of General Psychology, 49*, 229–240.

Boutte, G. S., & McCormick, C. B. (1992). Authentic multicultural activities: Avoiding pseudomulticulturalism. *Childhood Education, 68*, 140–144.

Bower, G. H. (1994). Some relations between emotions and memory. In P. Ekman & R. J. Davidson (Eds.), *The nature of emotion: Fundamental questions.* New York: Oxford University Press.

Bower, G. H., Black, J. B., & Turner, T. J. (1979). Scripts in memory for text. *Cognitive Psychology, 11*, 177–220.

Bower, G. H., & Clark, M. C. (1969). Narrative stories as mediators for serial learning. *Psychonomic Science, 14*, 181–182.

Bower, G. H., Clark, M. C., Lesgold, A. M., & Winzenz, D. (1969). Hierarchical retrieval schemes in recall of categorized word lists. *Journal of Verbal Learning and Verbal Behavior, 8*, 323–343.

Bower, G. H., & Forgas, J. P. (2001). Mood and social memory. In J. P. Forgas (Ed.), *Handbook of affect and social cognition* (pp. 95–120). Mahwah, NJ: Erlbaum.

Bower, G. H., Karlin, M. B., & Dueck, A. (1975). Comprehension and memory for pictures. *Memory and Cognition, 3*, 216–220.

Bowey, J. (1986). Syntactic awareness and verbal performance from preschool to fifth grade. *Journal of Psycholinguistic Research, 15*, 285–308.

Bowman, L. G., Piazza, C. C., Fisher, W. W., Hagopian, L. P., & Kogan, J. S. (1997). Assessment of preference for varied versus constant reinforcers. *Journal of Applied Behavior Analysis, 30,* 451–458.

Boyatzis, R. E. (1973). Affiliation motivation. In D. C. McClelland & R. S. Steele (Eds.), *Human motivation: A book of readings.* Morristown, NJ: General Learning Press.

Boykin, A. W. (1994). Harvesting talent and culture: African-American children and educational reform. In R. J. Rossi (Ed.), *Schools and students at risk: Context and framework for positive change.* New York: Teachers College Press.

Braaksma, M. A. H., Rijlaarsdam, G., & van den Bergh, H. (2002). Observational learning and the effects of model-observer similarity. *Journal of Educational Psychology, 94,* 405–415.

Bracken, B. A., McCallum, R. S., & Shaughnessy, M. F. (1999). An interview with Bruce A. Bracken and R. Steve McCallum, authors of the Universal Nonverbal Intelligence Test (UNIT). *North American Journal of Psychology, 1,* 277–288.

Bracken, B. A., & Walker, K. C. (1997). The utility of intelligence tests for preschool children. In D. P. Flanagan, J. L. Genshaft, & P. L. Harrison (Eds.), *Contemporary intellectual assessment: Theories, tests, and issues* (pp. 484–502). New York: Guilford Press.

Braden, J. P. (1992). Intellectual assessment of deaf and hard-of-hearing people: A quantitative and qualitative research synthesis. *School Psychology Review, 21,* 82–94.

Bradley, L., & Bryant, P. E. (1991). Phonological skills before and after learning to read. In S. A. Brady & D. P. Shankweiler (Eds.), *Phonological processes in literacy.* Mahwah, NJ: Erlbaum.

Bradley, R. H., & Caldwell, B. M. (1984). The relation of infants' home environments to achievement test performance in first grade: A follow-up study. *Child Development, 55,* 803–809.

Brainerd, C. J. (2003). Jean Piaget, learning research, and American education. In B. J. Zimmerman & D. H. Schunk (Eds.), *Educational psychology: A century of contributions* (pp. 251–287). Mahwah, NJ: Erlbaum.

Brainerd, C. J., Reyna, V. F., Howe, M. L., & Kingma, J. (1990). The development of forgetting and reminiscence. *Monographs of the Society for Research in Child Development, 55*(3–4, Serial No. 222).

Branch, C. (1999). Race and human development. In R. H. Sheets & E. R. Hollins (Eds.), *Racial and ethnic identity in school practices: Aspects of human development* (pp. 7–28). Mahwah, NJ: Erlbaum.

Brand, S., Felner, R., Shim, M., Seitsinger, A., & Duman, T. (2003). Middle school improvement and reform: Development and validation of a school-level assessment of climate, cultural pluralism, and school safety. *Journal of Educational Psychology, 95,* 570–588.

Bransford, J. D., & Franks, J. J. (1971). The abstraction of linguistic ideas. *Cognitive Psychology, 2,* 331–350.

Bransford, J. D., Franks, J. J., Vye, N. J., & Sherwood, R. D. (1989). New approaches to instruction: Because wisdom can't be told. In S. Vosniadou & A. Ortony (Eds.), *Similarity and analogical reasoning.* Cambridge, England: Cambridge University Press.

Bransford, J. D., & Johnson, M. K. (1972). Contextual prerequisites for understanding: Some investigations of comprehension and recall. *Journal of Verbal Learning and Verbal Behavior, 11,* 717–726.

Brantlinger, E. (1997). Using ideology: Cases of nonrecognition of the politics of research and practice in special education. *Review of Educational Research, 67,* 425–459.

Braukmann, C. J., Kirigin, K. A., & Wolf, M. M. (1981). Behavioral treatment of juvenile delinquency. In S. W. Bijou & R. Ruiz (Eds.), *Behavior modification: Contributions to education.* Mahwah, NJ: Erlbaum.

Braun, L. J. (1998). *The cat who saw stars.* New York: G. P. Putnam's Sons.

Brenner, M. E., Mayer, R. E., Moseley, B., Brar, T., Durán, R., Reed, B. S., & Webb, D. (1997). Learning by understanding: The role of multiple representations in learning algebra. *American Educational Research Journal, 34,* 663–689.

Bressler, S. L. (2002). Understanding cognition through large-scale cortical networks. *Current Directions in Psychological Science, 11,* 58–61.

Brigham, F. J., & Scruggs, T. E. (1995). Elaborative maps for enhanced learning of historical information: Uniting spatial, verbal, and imaginal information. *Journal of Special Education, 28,* 440.

Britton, B. K., Stimson, M., Stennett, B., & Gülgöz, S. (1998). Learning from instructional text: Test of an individual differences model. *Journal of Educational Psychology, 90,* 476–491.

Broden, M., Hall, R. V., & Mitts, B. (1971). The effect of self-recording on the classroom behavior of two eighth-grade students. *Journal of Applied Behavior Analysis, 4,* 191–199.

Brody, G. H., & Shaffer, D. R. (1982). Contributions of parents and peers to children's moral socialization. *Developmental Review, 2,* 31–75.

Brody, N. (1992). *Intelligence* (2nd ed.). San Diego, CA: Academic Press.

Brody, N. (1997). Intelligence, schooling, and society. *American Psychologist, 52,* 1046–1050.

Bronson, M. B. (2000). *Self-regulation in early childhood: Nature and nurture.* New York: Guilford Press.

Brooke, R. R., & Ruthren, A. J. (1984). The effects of contingency contracting on student performance in a PSI class. *Teaching of Psychology, 11,* 87–89.

Brookhart, S. M. (2004). *Grading.* Upper Saddle River, NJ: Merrill/Prentice Hall.

Brooks, L. W., & Dansereau, D. F. (1987). Transfer of information: An instructional perspective. In S. M. Cormier & J. D. Hagman (Eds.), *Transfer of learning: Contemporary research and applications.* San Diego, CA: Academic Press.

Brooks-Gunn, J. (2003). Do you believe in magic?: What we can expect from early childhood intervention programs. *Social Policy Report of the Society for Research in Child Development, 17*(1), 3–14.

Brooks-Gunn, J., Klebanov, P. K., & Duncan, G. J. (1996). Ethnic differences in children's intelligence test scores: Role of economic deprivation, home environment, and maternal characteristics. *Child Development, 67,* 396–408.

Brooks-Gunn, J., & Paikoff, R. L. (1993). "Sex is a gamble, kissing is a game": Adolescent sexuality and health promotion. In S. G. Millstein, A. C. Petersen, & E. O. Nightingale (Eds.), *Promoting the health of adolescents: New directions for the twenty-first century* (pp. 180–208). New York: Oxford University Press.

Brophy, J. E. (1986). *On motivating students* (Occasional Paper No. 101). East Lansing: Michigan State University, Institute for Research on Teaching.

Brophy, J. E. (1987). Synthesis of research on strategies for motivating students to learn. *Educational Leadership, 45*(2), 40–48.

Brophy, J. E. (1988). Research linking teacher behavior to student achievement: Potential implications for instruction of Chapter 1 students. *Educational Psychologist, 23,* 235–286.

Brophy, J. E. (Ed.). (1991). *Advances in research on teaching: Vol. 2. Teachers' knowledge of subject matter as it relates to their teaching practice.* Greenwich, CT: JAI Press.

Brophy, J. E. (1992a). Conclusions: Comments on an emerging field. In J. Brophy (Ed.), *Advances in research on teaching: Vol. 3. Planning and managing learning tasks and activities.* Greenwich, CT: JAI Press.

Brophy, J. E. (1992b). Probing the subtleties of subject-matter teaching. *Educational Leadership, 49*(7), 4–8.

Brophy, J. E. (2004). *Motivating students to learn* (2nd ed.). Mahwah, NJ: Erlbaum.

Brophy, J. E., & Alleman, J. (1991). Activities as instructional tools: A framework for analysis and evaluation. *Educational Researcher, 20*(4), 9–23.

Brophy, J. E., & Alleman, J. (1992). Planning and managing learning activities: Basic principles. In J. Brophy (Ed.), *Advances in research on teaching: Vol. 3. Planning and managing learning tasks and activities.* Greenwich, CT: JAI Press.

Brophy, J. E., & Alleman, J. (1996). *Powerful social studies for elementary students.* Fort Worth, TX: Harcourt, Brace.

Brophy, J. E., & Good, T. L. (1986). Teacher effects. In M. C. Wittrock (Ed.), *Handbook of research on teaching* (3rd ed.). New York: Macmillan.

Brophy, J. E., & VanSledright, B. (1997). *Teaching and learning history in elementary schools.* New York: Teachers College Press.

Brown, A. L., & Campione, J. C. (1994). Guided discovery in a community of learners. In K. McGilly (Ed.), *Classroom lessons: Integrating cognitive theory and classroom practice.* Cambridge, MA: MIT Press.

Brown, A. L., & Campione, J. C. (1996). Psychological theory and the design of innovative learning environments: On procedures, principles, and systems. In L. Schauble & R. Glaser (Eds.), *Innovations in learning: New environments for education.* Mahwah, NJ: Erlbaum.

Brown, A. L., Campione, J., & Day, J. (1981). Learning to learn: On training students to learn from texts. *Educational Researcher, 10*(2), 14–21.

Brown, A. L., & Palincsar, A. S. (1987). Reciprocal teaching of comprehension strategies: A natural history of one program for enhancing learning. In J. Borkowski & J. D. Day (Eds.), *Cognition in special education: Comparative approaches to retardation, learning disabilities, and giftedness.* Norwood, NJ: Ablex.

Brown, A. L., & Palincsar, A. S. (1989). Guided, cooperative learning and individual knowledge acquisition. In L. B. Resnick (Ed.), *Knowing, learning, and instruction: Essays in honor of Robert Glaser.* Mahwah, NJ: Erlbaum.

Brown, A. L., & Reeve, R. A. (1987). Bandwidths of competence: The role of supportive contexts in learning and development. In L. S. Liben (Ed.), *Development and learning: Conflict or congruence?* Mahwah, NJ: Erlbaum.

Brown, A. L., Smiley, S. S., Day, J. D., Townsend, M. A. R., & Lawton, S. C. (1977). Intrusion of a thematic idea in children's comprehension and retention of stories. *Child Development, 48,* 1454–1466.

Brown, A. S., Schilling, H. E. H., & Hockensmith, M. L. (1999). The negative suggestion effect: Pondering incorrect alternatives may be hazardous to your knowledge. *Journal of Educational Psychology, 91,* 756–764.

Brown, B. B. (1990). Peer groups. In S. Feldman & G. Elliott (Eds.), *At the threshold: The developing adolescent* (pp. 171–196). Cambridge, MA: Harvard University Press.

Brown, B. B. (1993). School culture, social politics, and the academic motivation of U.S. students. In T. M. Tomlinson (Ed.), *Motivating students to learn: Overcoming barriers to high achievement.* Berkeley, CA: McCutchan.

Brown, B. B. (1999). "You're going out with *who*?" Peer group influences on adolescent romantic relationships. In W. Furman, B. B. Brown, & C. Feiring (Eds.), *The development of romantic relationships in adolescence* (pp. 291–329). Cambridge, England: Cambridge University Press.

Brown, B. B., Eicher, S. A., & Petrie, S. (1986). The importance of peer group ("crowd") affiliation in adolescence. *Journal of Adolescence, 9,* 73–96.

Brown, B. B., Feiring, C., & Furman, W. (1999). Missing the love boat: Why researchers have shied away from adolescent romance. In W. Furman, B. B. Brown, & C. Feiring (Eds.), *The development of romantic relationships in adolescence* (pp. 1–16). Cambridge, England: Cambridge University Press.

Brown, J. S., Collins, A., & Duguid, P. (1989). Situated cognition and the culture of learning. *Educational Researcher, 18*(1), 32–42.

Brown, L. M., Tappan, M. B., & Gilligan, C. (1995). Listening to different voices. In W. M. Kurtines & J. L. Gewirtz (Eds.), *Moral development: An introduction.* Boston: Allyn & Bacon.

Brown, R., & McNeill, D. (1966). The "tip of the tongue" phenomenon. *Journal of Verbal Learning and Verbal Behavior, 5,* 325–337.

Brown, R. D., & Bjorklund, D. F. (1998). The biologizing of cognition, development, and education: Approach with cautious enthusiasm. *Educational Psychology Review, 10,* 355–373.

Brown, R. T. (1989). Creativity: What are we to measure? In J. A. Glover, R. R. Ronning, & C. R. Reynolds (Eds.), *Handbook of creativity*. New York: Plenum Press.

Brown, R. T., Reynolds, C. R., & Whitaker, J. S. (1999). Bias in mental testing since *Bias in Mental Testing*. *School Psychology Quarterly, 14,* 208–238.

Brown, W. H., Fox, J. J., & Brady, M. P. (1987). Effects of spatial density on 3- and 4-year-old children's socially directed behavior during freeplay: An investigation of a setting factor. *Education and Treatment of Children, 10,* 247–258.

Brownell, M. T., Mellard, D. F., & Deshler, D. D. (1993). Differences in the learning and transfer performance between students with learning disabilities and other low-achieving students on problem-solving tasks. *Learning Disabilities Quarterly, 16,* 138–156.

Brown-Mizuno, C. (1990). Success strategies for learners who are learning disabled as well as gifted. *Teaching Exceptional Children, 23*(1), 10–12.

Bruer, J. T. (1999). *The myth of the first three years: A new understanding of early brain development and life-long learning.* New York: Free Press.

Bruer, J. T., & Greenough, W. T. (2001). The subtle science of how experience affects the brain. In D. B. Bailey, Jr., J. T. Bruer, F. J. Symons, & J. W. Lichtman (Eds.), *Critical thinking about critical periods* (pp. 209–232). Baltimore: Brookes.

Bruner, J. S. (1961). The act of discovery. *Harvard Educational Review, 31,* 21–32.

Bruner, J. S. (1966). *Toward a theory of instruction.* Cambridge, MA: Harvard University Press.

Bruner, J. S., Goodnow, J., & Austin, G. (1956). *A study of thinking.* New York: Wiley.

Bruning, R. H., Schraw, G. J., & Ronning, R. R. (1995). *Cognitive psychology and instruction* (2nd ed.). Upper Saddle River, NJ: Merrill/Prentice Hall.

Bryan, J. H. (1975). Children's cooperation and helping behaviors. In E. M. Hetherington (Ed.), *Review of child development research* (Vol. 5). Chicago: University of Chicago Press.

Bryan, T. (1991). Social problems and learning disabilities. In B. Y. L. Wong (Ed.), *Learning about learning disabilities.* San Diego, CA: Academic Press.

Bryan, T., Burstein, K., & Bryan, J. (2001). Students with learning disabilities: Homework problems and promising practices. *Educational Psychologist, 36,* 167–180.

Buchoff, T. (1990). Attention deficit disorder: Help for the classroom teacher. *Childhood Education, 67,* 86–90.

Budwig, N. (1995). *A developmental-functionalist approach to child language.* Mahwah, NJ: Erlbaum.

Buehl, M. M., & Alexander, P. A. (2001). Beliefs about academic knowledge. *Educational Psychology Review, 13,* 385–418.

Bugelski, B. R., & Alampay, D. A. (1961). The role of frequency in developing perceptual sets. *Canadian Journal of Psychology, 15,* 205–211.

Buhrmester, D. (1992). The developmental courses of sibling and peer relationships. In F. Boer and J. Dunn (Eds.), *Children's sibling relationships: Developmental and clinical issues.* Mahwah, NJ: Erlbaum.

Bulgren, J. A., Deshler, D. D., Schumaker, J. B., & Lenz, B. K. (2000). The use and effectiveness of analogical instruction in diverse secondary content classrooms. *Journal of Educational Psychology, 92,* 426–441.

Bulgren, J. A., Schumaker, J. B., & Deshler, D. D. (1994). The effects of a recall enhancement routine on the test performance of secondary students with and without learning disabilities. *Learning Disabilities Research and Practice, 9,* 2–11.

Burger, H. G. (1973). Cultural pluralism and the schools. In C. S. Brembeck & W. H. Hill (Eds.), *Cultural challenges to education: The influence of cultural factors in school learning.* Lexington, MA: Heath.

Burger, S., & Burger, D. (1994). Determining the validity of performance-based assessment. *Educational Measurement: Issues and Practice, 13*(1), 9–15.

Burhans, K. K., & Dweck, C. S. (1995). Helplessness in early childhood: The role of contingent worth. *Child Development, 66,* 1719–1738.

Burstyn, J. N., & Stevens, R. (2001). Involving the whole school in violence prevention. In J. N. Burstyn, G. Bender, R. Casella, H. W. Gordon, D. P. Guerra, K. V. Luschen, R. Stevens, & K. M. Williams, *Preventing violence in schools: A challenge to American democracy* (pp. 139–158). Mahwah, NJ: Erlbaum.

Bushman, B. J., & Anderson, C. A. (2001). Media violence and the American public: Scientific facts versus media misinformation. *American Psychologist, 56,* 477–489.

Bussey, K., & Bandura, A. (1992). Self-regulatory mechanisms governing gender development. *Child Development, 63,* 1236–1250.

Butler, D. L., & Winne, P. H. (1995). Feedback and self-regulated learning: A theoretical synthesis. *Review of Educational Research, 65,* 245–281.

Butler, R. (1989). Mastery versus ability appraisal: A developmental study of children's observations of peers' work. *Child Development, 60,* 1350–1361.

Butler, R. (1990). The effects of mastery and competitive conditions on self-assessment at different ages. *Child Development, 61,* 201–210.

Butler, R. (1994). Teacher communication and student interpretations: Effects of teacher responses to failing students on attributional inferences in two age groups. *British Journal of Educational Psychology, 64,* 277–294.

Butler, R. (1998a). Age trends in the use of social and temporal comparison for self-evaluation: Examination of a novel developmental hypothesis. *Child Development, 69,* 1054–1073.

Butler, R. (1998b). Determinants of help seeking: Relations between perceived reasons for classroom help-avoidance and help-seeking behaviors in an experimental context. *Journal of Educational Psychology, 90,* 630–644.

Butterfield, E. C., & Ferretti, R. P. (1987). Toward a t heoretical integration of cognitive hypotheses about intellectual differences among children. In J. G. Borkowski & J. D. Day (Eds.), *Cognition in special children: Approaches to retardation, learning disabilities, and giftedness.* Norwood, NJ: Ablex.

Byrne, B. M. (2002). Validating the measurement and structure of self-concept: Snapshots of past, present, and future research. *American Psychologist, 57,* 897–909.

Byrnes, J. P. (1988). Formal operations: A systematic reformulation. *Developmental Review, 8,* 66–87.

Byrnes, J. P. (2001). *Minds, brains, and learning: Understanding the psychological and educational relevance of neuroscientific research.* New York: Guilford Press.

Byrnes, J. P. (2003). Factors predictive of mathematics achievement in White, Black, and Hispanic 12th graders. *Journal of Educational Psychology, 95,* 316–326.

Byrnes, J. P., & Fox, N. A. (1998). The educational relevance of research in cognitive neuroscience. *Educational Psychology Review, 10,* 297–342.

Cacioppo, J. T., Petty, R. E., Feinstein, J. A., & Jarvis, W. B. G. (1996). Dispositional differences in cognitive motivation: The life and times of individuals varying in need for cognition. *Psychological Bulletin, 119,* 197–253.

Cairns, H. S.(1996). *The acquisition of language* (2nd ed.). Austin, TX: Pro-Ed.

Calderhead, J. (1996). Teachers: Beliefs and knowledge. In D. C. Berliner & R. C. Calfee (Eds.), *Handbook of educational psychology.* New York: Macmillan.

Caldwell, C. H., Zimmerman, M. A., Bernat, D. H., Sellers, R. M., & Notaro, P. C. (2002). Racial identity, maternal support, and psychological distress among African American adolescents. *Child Development, 73,* 1322–1336.

Calfee, R. (1981). Cognitive psychology and educational practice. In D. C. Berliner (Ed.), *Review of research in education* (Vol. 9). Washington, DC: American Educational Research Association.

Calfee, R., Dunlap, K., & Wat, A. (1994). Authentic discussion of texts in middle grade schooling: An analytic-narrative approach. *Journal of Reading, 37,* 546–556.

Callanan, M. A., & Oakes, L. M. (1992). Preschoolers' questions and parents' explanations: Causal thinking in everyday activity. *Cognitive Development, 7,* 213–233.

Cameron, J. (2001). Negative effects of reward on intrinsic motivation—a limited phenomenon: Comment on Deci, Koestner, and Ryan (2001). *Review of Educational Research, 71,* 29–42.

Cameron, J., & Pierce, W. D. (1994). Reinforcement, reward, and intrinsic motivation: A meta-analysis. *Review of Educational Research, 64,* 363–423.

Campbell, A. (1984). *The girls in the gang: A report from New York City.* New York: Blackwell.

Campbell, D. E. (1996). *Choosing democracy: A practical guide to multicultural education.* Upper Saddle River, NJ: Merrill/Prentice Hall.

Campbell, F. A., & Ramey, C. T. (1994). Effects of early intervention on intellectual and academic achievement: A follow-up study of children from low-income families. *Child Development, 65,* 684–698.

Campbell, F. A., & Ramey, C. T. (1995). Cognitive and school outcomes for high-risk African-American students at middle adolescence: Positive effects of early intervention. *American Educational Research Journal, 32,* 742–772.

Campbell, L., Campbell, B., & Dickinson, D. (1998). *Teaching and learning through multiple intelligences* (2nd ed.). Boston: Allyn & Bacon.

Campbell, P. A. (1986). What's a nice girl like you doing in a math class? *Phi Delta Kappan, 67,* 516–520.

Campione, J. C., Brown, A. L., & Bryant, N. R. (1985). Individual differences in learning and memory. In R. J. Sternberg (Ed.), *Human abilities: An information-processing approach.* New York: Freeman.

Campione, J. C., Shapiro, A. M., & Brown, A. L. (1995). Forms of transfer in a community of learners: Flexible learning and understanding. In A. McKeough, J. Lupart, & A. Marini (Eds.), *Teaching for transfer: Fostering generalization in learning.* Mahwah, NJ: Erlbaum.

Canady, R. L., & Hotchkiss, P. R. (1989). It's a good score! Just a bad grade. *Phi Delta Kappan, 71,* 68–71.

Candler-Lotven, A., Tallent-Runnels, M. K., Olivárez, A., & Hildreth, B. (1994, April). *A comparison of learning and study strategies of gifted, average-ability, and learning-disabled ninth-grade students.* Paper presented at the annual meeting of the American Educational Research Association, New Orleans, LA.

Caprara, G. V., Barbaranelli, C., Pastorelli, C., Bandura, A., & Zimbardo, P. G. (2000). Prosocial foundations of children's academic achievement. *Psychological Science, 11,* 302–306.

Capron, C., & Duyme, M. (1989). Assessment of effects of socio-economic status on IQ in a full cross-fostering study. *Nature, 340,* 552–554.

Carey, L. M. (1994). *Measuring and evaluating school learning* (2nd ed.). Needham Heights, MA: Allyn & Bacon.

Carey, S. (1978). The child as word learner. In M. Halle, J. Bresnan, & G. A. Miller (Eds.), *Linguistic theory and psychological reality.* Cambridge, MA: MIT Press.

Carey, S. (1985). *Conceptual change in childhood.* Cambridge, MA: MIT Press.

Carey, S. (1986). Cognitive science and science education. *American Psychologist, 41,* 1123–1130.

Carlson, B. E. (1984). The father's contribution to child care: Effects on children's perceptions of parental roles. *American Journal of Orthopsychiatry, 54,* 123–136.

Carlson, R., Chandler, P., & Sweller, J. (2003). Learning and understanding science instructional material. *Journal of Educational Psychology, 95,* 629–640.

Carlson, S. M., & Moses, L. J. (2001). Individual differences in inhibitory control and children's theory of mind. *Child Development, 72,* 1032–1053.

Carmichael, C. A., & Hayes, B. K. (2001). Prior knowledge and exemplar encoding in children's concept acquisition. *Child Development, 72,* 1071–1090.

Carney, R. N., & Levin, J. R. (2002). Pictorial illustrations *still* improve students' learning from text. *Educational Psychology Review, 14,* 5–26.

Carnine, D. (1989). Teaching complex content to learning disabled students: The role of technology. *Exceptional Children, 55*, 524–533.

Carnoy, M., Elmore, R., & Siskin, L. S. (Eds.). (2003). *The new accountability: High schools and high-stakes testing.* New York: RoutledgeFalmer.

Carpenter, P. A., & Just, M. A. (1986). Cognitive processes in reading. In J. Orasanu (Ed.), *Reading comprehension: From research to practice.* Mahwah, NJ: Erlbaum.

Carpenter, T. P., & Moser, J. M. (1984). The acquisition of addition and subtraction concepts in grades one through three. *Journal for Research in Mathematics Education, 15*, 179–202.

Carr, A. A. (1997, March). *The participation "race": Kentucky's site based decision teams.* Paper presented at the annual meeting of the American Educational Research Association, Chicago.

Carr, E. G., Levin, L., McConnachie, G., Carlson, J. I., Kemp, D. C., & Smith, C. E. (1994). *Communication-based intervention for problem behavior: A user's guide for producing positive change.* Baltimore: Brookes.

Carr, M., & Biddlecomb, B. (1998). Metacognition in mathematics from a constructivist perspective. In D. J. Hacker, J. Dunlosky, & A. C. Graesser (Eds.), *Metacognition in educational theory and practice* (pp. 69–91). Mahwah, NJ: Erlbaum.

Carr, M., & Borkowski, J. G. (1989). Attributional training and the generalization of reading strategies with underachieving children. *Learning and Individual Differences, 1*, 327–341.

Carr, M., Kurtz, B. E., Schneider, W., Turner, L. A., & Borkowski, J. G. (1989). Strategy acquisition and transfer among American and German children: Environmental influences on metacognitive development. *Developmental Psychology, 25*, 765–771.

Carraher, T. N., Carraher, D. W., & Schliemann, A. D. (1985). Mathematics in the streets and in the schools. *British Journal of Developmental Psychology, 3*, 21–29.

Carrasco, R. L. (1981). Expanded awareness of student performance: A case study in applied ethnographic monitoring in a bilingual classroom. In H. T. Trueba, G. P. Guthrie, & K. H. Au (Eds.), *Culture and the bilingual classroom: Studies in classroom ethnography.* Rowley, MA: Newbury House.

Carter, K. R. (1991). Evaluation of gifted programs. In N. Buchanan & J. Feldhusen (Eds.), *Conducting research and evaluation in gifted education: A handbook of methods and applications.* New York: Teachers College Press.

Carter, K. R., & Ormrod, J. E. (1982). Acquisition of formal operations by intellectually gifted children. *Gifted Child Quarterly, 26*, 110–115.

Cartledge, G., & Milburn, J. F. (1995). *Teaching social skills to children and youth: Innovative approaches* (3rd ed.). Needham Heights, MA: Allyn & Bacon.

Carver, C. S., & Scheier, M. F. (1990). Origins and functions of positive and negative affect: A control-process view. *Psychological Review, 97*, 19–35.

Casanova, U. (1987). Ethnic and cultural differences. In V. Richardson-Koehler (Ed.), *Educator's handbook: A research perspective.* White Plains, NY: Longman.

Case, R., & Okamoto, Y., in collaboration with Griffin, S., McKeough, A., Bleiker, C., Henderson, B., & Stephenson, K. M. (1996). The role of central conceptual structures in the development of children's thought. *Monographs of the Society for Research in Child Development, 61*(1, Serial No. 246).

Caseau, D., Luckasson, R., & Kroth, R. L. (1994). Special education services for girls with serious emotional disturbance: A case of gender bias? *Behavioral Disorders, 20*, 51–60.

Casella, R. (2001a). The cultural foundations of peer mediation: Beyond a behaviorist model of urban school conflict. In J. N. Burstyn, G. Bender, R. Casella, H. W. Gordon, D. P. Guerra, K. V. Luschen, R. Stevens, & K. M. Williams, *Preventing violence in schools: A challenge to American democracy* (pp. 159–179). Mahwah, NJ: Erlbaum.

Casella, R. (2001b). What is violent about "school violence"? The nature of violence in a city high school.

In J. N. Burstyn, G. Bender, R. Casella, H. W. Gordon, D. P. Guerra, K. V. Luschen, R. Stevens, & K. M. Williams, *Preventing violence in schools: A challenge to American democracy* (pp. 15–46). Mahwah, NJ: Erlbaum.

Casey, B. J. (2001). Disruption of inhibitory control in developmental disorders: A mechanistic model of implicated frontostriatal circuitry. In J. L. McClelland & R. S. Siegler (Eds.), *Mechanisms of cognitive development: Behavioral and neural perspectives* (pp. 327–349). Mahwah, NJ: Erlbaum.

Casey, W. M., & Burton, R. V. (1982). Training children to be consistently honest through verbal self-instructions. *Child Development, 53*, 911–919.

Caspi, A., & Silva, P. A. (1995). Temperamental qualities at age three predict personality traits in young adulthood: Longitudinal evidence from a birth cohort. *Child Development, 66*, 486–498.

Caspi, A., Taylor, A., Moffitt, T. E., & Plomin, R. (2000). Neighborhood deprivation affects children's mental health: Environmental risks identified in a genetic design. *Psychological Science, 11*, 338–342.

Cassady, J. C. (2002, April). *The impact of test anxiety on expository text passage comprehension and recall.* Paper presented at the annual meeting of the American Educational Research Association, New Orleans.

Casserly, P. L. (1980). Factors affecting female participation in Advanced Placement programs in mathematics, chemistry, and physics. In L. H. Fox, L. Brody, & D. Tobin (Eds.), *Women and the mathematical mystique.* Baltimore: Johns Hopkins University Press.

Cassidy, J., Ziv, Y., Mehta, T. G., & Feeney, B. C. (2003). Feedback seeking in children and adolescents: Associations with self-perceptions, attachment representations, and depression. *Child Development, 74*, 612–628.

Cauce, A. M., Mason, C., Gonzales, N., Hiraga, Y., & Liu, G. (1994). Social support during adolescence: Methodological and theoretical considerations. In F. Nestemann & K. Hurrelmann (Eds.), *Social networks and social support in childhood and adolescence.* Berlin, Germany: Aldine de Gruyter.

Cazden, C. B. (1976). Play with language and metalinguistic awareness: One dimension of language experience. In J. Bruner, A. Jolly, & K. Sylva (Eds.), *Play: Its role in development and evolution.* New York: Basic Books.

Cazden, C. B. (1988). *Classroom discourse: The language of teaching and learning.* Portsmouth, NJ: Heinemann.

Ceci, S. J. (2003). Cast in six ponds and you'll reel in something: Looking back on 25 years of research. *American Psychologist, 58*, 855–864.

Center for the Future of Children. (1997). Executive summary: Children and poverty, *The Future of Children, 7*(2), 1–7.

Certo, J., Cauley, K. M., & Chafin, C. (2002, April). *Students' perspectives on their high school experience.* Paper presented at the annual meeting of the American Educational Research Association, New Orleans, LA.

Chabrán, M. (2003). Listening to talk from and about students on accountability. In M. Carnoy, R. Elmore, & L. S. Siskin (Eds.), *The new accountability: High schools and high-stakes testing* (pp. 129–145). New York: RoutledgeFalmer.

Chafel, J. A. (1997). Schooling, the hidden curriculum, and children's conceptions of poverty. *Social Policy Report of the Society for Research in Child Development, 11*(1), 1–18.

Chalfant, J. C. (1989). Learning disabilities: Policy issues and promising approaches. *American Psychologist, 44*, 392–398.

Chall, J. S. (1996). *Stages of reading development* (2nd ed.). Fort Worth, TX: Harcourt Brace.

Chalmers, D. J. (1996). *The conscious mind: In search of a fundamental theory.* New York: Oxford University Press.

Chalmers, J., & Townsend, M. (1990). The effects of training in social perspective taking on socially maladjusted girls. *Child Development, 61*, 178–190.

Chambliss, M. J. (1994). Why do readers fail to change their beliefs after reading persuasive text? In

R. Garner & P. A. Alexander (Eds.), *Beliefs about text and instruction with text.* Mahwah, NJ: Erlbaum.

Chambliss, M. J., Calfee, R. C., & Wong, I. (1990, April). *Structure and content in science textbooks: Where is the design?* Paper presented at the annual meeting of the American Educational Research Association, Boston.

Champagne, A. B., Klopfer, L. E., & Gunstone, R. F. (1982). Cognitive research and the design of science instruction. *Educational Psychologist, 17*, 31–53.

Chandler, M. (1987). The Othello effect: Essay on the emergence and eclipse of skeptical doubt. *Human Development, 30*, 137–159.

Chandler, M., & Boyes, M. (1982). Social-cognitive development. In B. Wolman (Ed.), *Handbook of developmental psychology.* Upper Saddle River, NJ: Prentice Hall.

Chandler, M. J., Hallett, D., & Sokol, B. W. (2002). Competing claims about competing knowledge claims. In B. K. Hofer & P. R. Pintrich (Eds.), *Personal epistemology: The psychology of beliefs about knowledge and knowing* (pp. 145–168). Mahwah, NJ: Erlbaum.

Chang, L. (2003) Variable effects of children's aggression, social withdrawal, and prosocial leadership as functions of teacher beliefs and behaviors. *Child Development, 74*, 535–548.

Chao, R. K. (1994). Beyond parental control and authoritarian parenting style: Understanding Chinese parenting through the cultural notion of training. *Child Development, 65*, 1111–1119.

Chapman, J. W. (1988). Learning disabled children's self-concepts. *Review of Educational Research, 58*, 347–371.

Chapman, J. W., Tunmer, W. E., & Prochnow, J. E. (2000). Early reading-related skills and performance, reading self-concept, and the development of academic self-concept: A longitudinal study. *Journal of Educational Psychology, 92*, 703–708.

Chavous, T. M., Bernat, D. H., Schmeelk-Cone, K., Caldwell, C. H., Kohn-Wood, L., & Zimmerman, M. A. (2003). Racial identity and academic attainment among African American adolescents. *Child Development, 74*, 1076–1090.

Chen, X., Rubin, K. H., & Sun, Y. (1992). Social reputation and peer relationships in Chinese and Canadian children: A cross-cultural study. *Child Development, 63*, 1336–1343.

Chen, Z. (1999). Schema induction in children's analogical problem solving. *Journal of Educational Psychology, 91*, 703–715.

Cheng, L. R. (1987). *Assessing Asian language performance.* Rockville, MD: Aspen.

Cheng, P. W. (1985). Restructuring versus automaticity: Alternative accounts of skill acquisition. *Psychological Review, 92*, 414–423.

Cherry, E. C. (1953). Some experiments on the recognition of speech, with one and with two ears. *Journal of the Acoustical Society of America, 25*, 975–979.

Chester, M. D., & Beaudin, B. Q. (1996). Efficacy beliefs of newly hired teachers in urban schools. *American Educational Research Journal, 33*, 233–257.

Cheyne, J. A., & Walters, R. H. (1970). Punishment and prohibition: Some origins of self-control. In T. M. Newcomb (Ed.), *New directions in psychology.* New York: Holt, Rinehart & Winston.

Chi, M. T. H. (1978). Knowledge structures and memory development. In R. S. Siegler (Ed.), *Children's thinking: What develops?* Mahwah, NJ: Erlbaum.

Chi, M. T. H., Feltovich, P., & Glaser, R. (1981). Categorization and representation of physics problems by experts and novices. *Cognitive Science, 5*, 121–152.

Chinn, C. A., & Brewer, W. F. (1993). The role of anomalous data in knowledge acquisition: A theoretical framework and implications for science instruction. *Review of Educational Research, 63*, 1–49.

Chinn, C. A., & Malhotra, B. A. (2002). Children's responses to anomalous scientific data: How is conceptual change impeded? *Journal of Educational Psychology, 94*, 327–343.

Chisholm, J. S. (1996). Learning "respect for everything": Navajo images of development. In C. P.

Hwant, M. E. Lamb, & I. E. Sigel (Eds.), *Images of childhood* (pp. 167–183). Mahwah, NJ: Erlbaum.

Chomsky, N. (1965). *Aspects of the theory of syntax.* Cambridge, MA: MIT Press.

Chomsky, N. (1972). *Language and mind* (enlarged ed.). San Diego, CA: Harcourt Brace Jovanovich.

Christenson, S. L., & Thurlow, M. L. (2004). School dropouts: Prevention, considerations, interventions, and challenges. *Current Directions in Psychological Science, 13,* 36–39.

Christie, J. F., & Johnsen, E. P. (1983). The role of play in social-intellectual development. *Review of Educational Research, 53,* 93–115.

Christmann, E., Badgett, J., & Lucking, R. (1997). Microcomputer-based computer- assisted instruction within differing subject areas: A statistical deduction. *Journal of Educational Computing Research, 16,* 281–296.

Church, M. A., Elliot, A. J., & Gable, S. L. (2001). Perceptions of classroom environment, achievement goals, and achievement outcomes. *Journal of Educational Psychology, 93,* 43–54.

Cizek, G. J. (2003). *Detecting and preventing classroom cheating: Promoting integrity in assessment.* Thousand Oaks, CA: Corwin.

Clark, A.-M., Anderson, R. C., Kuo, L., Kim, I., Archodidou, A., & Nguyen-Jahiel, K. (2003). Collaborative reasoning: Expanding ways for children to talk and think in school. *Educational Psychology Review, 15,* 181–198.

Clark, B. (1997). *Growing up gifted* (5th ed.). Upper Saddle River, NJ: Merrill/ Prentice Hall.

Clark, C. C. (1992). Deviant adolescent subcultures: Assessment strategies and clinical interventions. *Adolescence, 27*(106), 283–293.

Clark, C. M., & Peterson, P. L. (1986). Teachers' thought processes. In M. C. Wittrock (Ed.), *Handbook on research on teaching* (3rd ed.). New York: Macmillan.

Clark, E. V. (1971). On the acquisition of the meaning of "before" and "after." *Journal of Verbal Learning and Verbal Behavior, 10,* 266–275.

Clark, J. M., & Paivio, A. (1991). Dual coding theory and education. *Educational Psychology Review, 3,* 149–210.

Clark, R. E. (1983). Reconsidering research on learning from media. *Review of Educational Research, 53,* 445–459.

Clark, R. M. (1983). *Family life and school achievement: Why poor black children succeed or fail.* Chicago: University of Chicago Press.

Clarke, S., Dunlap, G., Foster-Johnson, L., Childs, K. E., Wilson, D., White, R., & Vera, A. (1995). Improving the conduct of students with behavioral disorders by incorporating student interests into curricular areas. *Behavioral Disorders, 20,* 221–237.

Clarke-Stewart, K. A. (1988). Parents' effects on children's development: A decade of progress? *Journal of Applied Developmental Psychology, 9,* 41–84.

Claude, D., & Firestone, P. (1995). The development of ADHD boys: A 12–year follow-up. *Canadian Journal of Behavioural Science, 27,* 226–249.

Clawson, D. L., & Fisher, J. S. (1998). *World regional geography: A development approach* (6th ed.). Upper Saddle River, NJ: Prentice Hall.

Clifford, M. M. (1990). Students need challenge, not easy success. *Educational Leadership, 48*(1), 22–26.

Cobb, P., Wood, T., Yackel, E., Nicholls, J., Wheatley, G., Trigatti, B., & Perlwitz, M. (1991). Assessment of a problem centered second-grade mathematics project. *Journal for Research in Mathematics Education, 22,* 3–29.

Cobb, P., & Yackel, E. (1996). Constructivist, emergent, and sociocultural perspectives in the context of developmental research. *Educational Psychologist, 31,* 175–190.

Cochran, K. F., & Jones, L. L. (1998). The subject matter knowledge of preservice science teachers. In B. J. Fraser & K. G. Tobin (Eds.), *International handbook of science education* (Pt. II). Dordrecht, Netherlands: Kluwer.

Cochran-Smith, M., & Lytle, S. (1993). *Inside out: Teacher research and knowledge.* New York: Teachers College Press.

Coe, J., Salamon, L., & Molnar, J. (1991). *Homeless children and youth.* New Brunswick, NJ: Transaction.

Cognition and Technology Group at Vanderbilt. (1990). Anchored instruction and its relationship to situated cognition. *Educational Researcher, 19*(6), 2–10.

Cognition and Technology Group at Vanderbilt. (1993). Anchored instruction and situated cognition revisited. *Educational Technology, 33*(3), 52–70.

Cognition and Technology Group at Vanderbilt. (1996). Looking at technology in context: A framework for understanding technology and education research. In D. C. Berliner & R. C. Calfee (Eds.), *Handbook of educational psychology* (pp. 807–840). New York: Macmillan.

Cognition and Technology Group at Vanderbilt. (1997). *The Jasper project: Lessons in curriculum, instruction, assessment, and professional development.* Mahwah, NJ: Erlbaum.

Cohen, E. G. (1994). Restructuring the classroom: Conditions for productive small groups. *Review of Educational Research, 64,* 1–35.

Cohen, E. G., Lockheed, M. E., & Lohman, M. R. (1976). The center for interracial cooperation: A field experiment. *Sociology of Education, 59,* 47–58.

Cohen, E. G., & Lotan, R. A. (1995). Producing equal-status interaction in the heterogeneous classroom. *American Educational Research Journal, 32,* 99–120.

Cohen, R. L. (1989). Memory for action events: The power of enactment. *Educational Psychology Review, 1,* 57–80.

Coie, J. D., & Cillessen, A. H. N. (1993). Peer rejection: Origins and effects on children's development. *Current Directions in Psychological Science, 2,* 89–92.

Coie, J. D., & Dodge, K. A. (1998). Aggression and antisocial behavior. In W. Damon (Series Ed.) & N. Eisenberg (Vol. Ed.), *Handbook of child psychology: Vol. 3. Social, emotional, and personality development* (5th ed., pp. 779–862). New York: Wiley.

Colby, A., & Kohlberg, L. (1984). Invariant sequence and internal consistency in moral judgment stages. In W. M. Kurtines & J. L. Gewirtz (Eds.), *Morality, moral behavior, and moral development.* New York: Wiley.

Colby, A., Kohlberg, L., Gibbs, J., & Lieberman, M. (1983). A longitudinal study of moral judgment. *Monographs of the Society for Research in Child Development, 48*(1–2, Serial No. 200).

Cole, D. A., Martin, J. M., Peeke, L. A., Seroczynski, A. D., & Fier, J. (1999). Children's over- and underestimation of academic competence: A longitudinal study of gender differences, depression, and anxiety. *Child Develop- ment, 70,* 459–473.

Cole, D. A., Maxwell, S. E., Martin, J. M., Peeke, L. G., Seroczynski, A. D., Tram, J. M., Hoffman, K. B., Ruiz, M. D., Jacquez, F., & Maschman, T. (2001). The development of multiple domains of child and adolescent self-concept: A cohort sequential longitudinal design. *Child Development, 72,* 1723–1746.

Cole, N. S. (1990). Conceptions of educational achievement. *Educational Researcher, 19*(3), 2–7.

Cole, P. M., Bruschi, C. J., & Tamang, B. L. (2002). Cultural differences in children's emotional reactions to difficult situations. *Child Development, 73,* 983–996.

Collie, R., & Hayne, H. (1999). Deferred imitation by 6- and 9-month-old infants: More evidence for declarative memory. *Developmental Psychobiology, 35,* 83–90.

Collier, V. P. (1992). The Canadian bilingual immersion debate: A synthesis of research findings. *Studies in Second Language Acquisition, 14,* 87–97.

Collins, A., Brown, J. S., & Newman, S. E. (1989). Cognitive apprenticeship: Teaching the crafts of reading, writing, and mathematics. In L. B. Resnick (Ed.), *Knowing, learning, and instruction: Essays in honor of Robert Glaser.* Mahwah, NJ: Erlbaum.

Collins, W. A., Maccoby, E. E., Steinberg, L., Hetherington, E. M., & Bornstein, M. H. (2000). Contemporary research on parenting: The case for nature and nurture. *American Psychologist, 55,* 218–232.

Combs, A. W., Richards, A. C., & Richards, F. (1976). *Perceptual psychology: A humanistic approach to the study of persons.* New York: Harper & Row.

Condon, J. C., & Yousef, F. S. (1975). *An introduction to intercultural communication.* Indianapolis, IN: Bobbs-Merrill.

Cone, T. E., Wilson, L. R., Bradley, C. M., & Reese, J. H. (1985). Characteristics of LD students in Iowa: An empirical investigation. *Learning Disability Quarterly, 8,* 211–220.

Conlon, C. J. (1992). New threats to development: Alcohol, cocaine, and AIDS. In M. L. Batshaw & Y. M. Perret (Eds.), *Children with disabilities: A medical primer* (3rd ed.). Baltimore: Brookes.

Connell, J. P., & Wellborn, J. G. (1991). Competence, autonomy, and relatedness: A motivational analysis of self-system processes. In M. R. Gunnar & L. A. Sroufe (Eds.), *Self processes and development: The Minnesota Symposia on Child Psychology* (Vol. 23). Mahwah, NJ: Erlbaum.

Connolly, F. W., & Eisenberg, T. E. (1990). The feedback classroom: Teaching's silent friend. *T.H.E. Journal, 17*(5), 75–77.

Connolly, J., & Goldberg, A. (1999). Romantic relationships in adolescence: The role of friends and peers in their emergence and development. In W. Furman, B. B. Brown, & C. Feiring (Eds.), *The development of romantic relationships in adolescence* (pp. 266–290). Cambridge, England: Cambridge University Press.

Conte, R. (1991). Attention disorders. In B. Y. L. W.ong (Ed.), *Learning about learning disabilities.* San Diego, CA: Academic Press.

Cook, B., & Semmel, M. (1999). Peer acceptance of included students with disabilities as a function of severity of disability and classroom composition. *Journal of Special Education, 33,* 50–62.

Cook, T. D., Herman, M. R., Phillips, M., & Settersten, R. A., Jr. (2002). Some ways in which neighborhoods, nuclear families, friendship groups, and schools jointly affect changes in early adolescent development. *Child Development, 73,* 1283–1309.

Cooney, C. (1997). *Wanted.* New York: Scholastic.

Cooney, J. B. (1991). Reflections on the origin of mathematical intuition and some implications for instruction. *Learning and Individual Differences, 3,* 83–107.

Cooper, C. R., Jackson, J. F., Azmitia, M., Lopez, E., & Dunbar, N. (1995). Bridging students' multiple worlds: African American and Latino youth in academic outreach programs. In R. F. Macias & R. G. Garcia-Ramos (Eds.), *Changing schools for changing students: An anthology of research on language minorities* (pp. 211–234). Santa Barbara: University of California Linguistic Minority Research Institute.

Cooper, H. (1989). Synthesis of research on homework. *Educational Leadership, 47*(3), 85–91.

Cooper, H., Lindsay, J. J., Nye, B., & Greathouse, S. (1998). Relationships among attitudes about homework, amount of homework assigned and completed, and student achievement. *Journal of Educational Psychology, 90,* 70–83.

Cooper, H., & Valentine, J. C. (2001). Using research to answer practical questions about homework. *Educational Psychologist, 36,* 143–153.

Cooper, H. M., & Good, T. (1983). *Pygmalion grows up: Studies in the expectation communication process.* White Plains, NY: Longman.

Corkill, A. J. (1992). Advance organizers: Facilitators of recall. *Educational Psychology Review, 4,* 33–67.

Cormier, S. M. (1987). The structural processes underlying transfer of training. In S. M. Cormier & J. D. Hagman (Eds.), *Transfer of learning: Contemporary research and applications.* San Diego, CA: Academic Press.

Cornell, D. G., Pelton, G. M., Bassin, L. E., Landrum, M., Ramsay, S. G., Cooley, M. R., Lynch, K. A., & Hamrick, E. (1990). Self-concept and peer status among gifted program youth. *Journal of Educational Psychology, 82,* 456–463.

Corno, L. (1993). The best-laid plans: Modern conceptions of volition and educational research. *Educational Researcher, 22*(2), 14–22.

Corno, L. (1996). Homework is a complicated thing. *Educational Researcher, 25*(8), 27–30.

Corno, L., Cronbach, L. J., Kupermintz, H., Lohman, D. F., Mandinach, E. B., Porteu, A. W., & Talbert, J. E. (2002). *Remaking the concept of aptitude: Extending the legacy of Richard E. Snow.* Mahwah, NJ: Erlbaum.

Corno, L., & Rohrkemper, M. M. (1985). The intrinsic motivation to learn in classrooms. In C. Ames & R. Ames (Eds.), *Research on motivation in education: Vol. 2. The classroom milieu.* San Diego, CA: Academic Press.

Corno, L., & Snow, R. E. (1986). Adapting teaching to individual differences among learners. In M. C. Wittrock (Ed.), *Handbook of research on teaching* (3rd ed.). New York: Macmillan.

Cosden, M., Morrison, G., Albanese, A. L., & Macias, S. (2001). When homework is not home work: After-school programs for homework assistance. *Educational Psychologist, 36,* 211–221.

Cothern, N. B., Konopak, B. C., & Willis, E. L. (1990). Using readers' imagery of literary characters to study text meaning construction. *Reading Research and Instruction, 30,* 15–29.

Council for Exceptional Children. (1995). *Toward a common agenda: Linking gifted education and school reform.* Reston, VA: Author.

Courchesne, E., Townsend, J., Akshoomoff, N. A., Saitoh, O., Yeung-Courchesne, R., Lincoln, A. J., James, H. E., Haas, R. H., Schreibman, L., & Lau, L. (1994). Impairment of shifting attention in autistic and cerebellar patients. *Behavioral Neuroscience, 108,* 848–865.

Covington, M. V. (1987). Achievement motivation, self-attributions, and the exceptional learner. In J. D. Day & J. G. Borkowski (Eds.), *Intelligence and exceptionality.* Norwood, NJ: Ablex.

Covington, M. V. (1992). *Making the grade: A self-worth perspective on motivation and school reform.* Cambridge, England: Cambridge University Press.

Covington, M. (2000). Intrinsic versus extrinsic motivation in schools: A reconciliation. *Current Directions in Psychological Science, 9,* 22–25.

Covington, M. V., & Beery, R. M. (1976). *Self-worth and school learning.* New York: Holt, Rinehart & Winston.

Covington, M. V., & Müeller, K. J. (2001). Intrinsic versus extrinsic motivation: An approach/avoidance reformulation. *Educational Psychology Review, 13,* 157–176.

Covington, M. V., & Omelich, C. L. (1991). Need achievement revisited: Verification of Atkinson's original 2 x 2 model. In C. D. Spielberger, I. G. Sarason, Z. Kulcsar, & G. L. Van Heck (Eds.), *Stress and emotion* (Vol. 14). New York: Hemisphere.

Cowan, N. (1995). *Attention and memory: An integrated framework.* New York: Oxford University Press.

Cox, B. D. (1997). The rediscovery of the active learner in adaptive contexts: A developmental-historical analysis of transfer of training. *Educational Psychologist, 32,* 41–55.

Craft, M. (1984). Education for diversity. In M. Craft (Ed.), *Educational and cultural pluralism.* London: Falmer Press.

Craft, M. A., Alberg, S. R., & Heward, W. L. (1998). Teaching elementary students with developmental disabilities to recruit teacher attention in a general education classroom: Effects on teacher praise and academic productivity. *Journal of Applied Behavior Analysis, 31,* 399–415.

Crago, M. B. (1988). *Cultural context in the communicative interaction of young Inuit children.* Unpublished doctoral dissertation, McGill University.

Crago, M. B., Annahatak, B., & Ningiuruvik, L. (1993). Changing patterns of language socialization in Inuit homes. *Anthropology and Education Quarterly, 24,* 205–223.

Craik, F. I. M., & Watkins, M. J. (1973). The role of rehearsal in short-term memory. *Journal of Verbal Learning and Verbal Behavior, 12,* 598–607.

Crain, S. (1993). Language acquisition in the absence of experience. In P. Bloom (Ed.), *Language acquisition: Core readings.* Cambridge, MA: MIT Press.

Creasey, G. L., Jarvis, P. A., & Berk, L. E. (1998). Play and social competence. In O. N. Saracho & B. Spodek (Eds.). *Multiple perspectives on play in early childhood education.* Albany: State University of New York Press.

Crick, N. R., & Dodge, K. A. (1994). A review and reformulation of social information-processing mechanisms in children's social adjustment. *Psychological Bulletin, 115,* 74–101.

Crick, N. R., & Dodge, K. A. (1996). Social information-processing mechanisms in reactive and proactive aggression. *Child Development, 67,* 993–1002.

Crick, N. R., Grotpeter, J. K., & Bigbee, M. A. (2002). Relationally and physically aggressive children's intent attributions and feelings of distress for relational and instrumental peer provocation. *Child Development, 73,* 1134–1142.

Crockett, L., Losoff, M., & Peterson, A. C. (1984). Perceptions of the peer group and friendship in early adolescence. *Journal of Early Adolescence, 4,* 155–181.

Cromer, R. F. (1993). Language growth with experience without feedback. In P. Bloom (Ed.), *Language acquisition: Core readings.* Cambridge, MA: MIT Press.

Crone, D. A., & Horner, R. H. (2003). *Building positive behavior support systems in schools: Functional behavioral assessment.* New York: Guilford Press.

Crook, C. (1995). On resourcing a concern for collaboration within peer interactions. *Cognition and Instruction, 13,* 541–547.

Crooks, T. J. (1988). The impact of classroom evaluation practices on students. *Review of Educational Research, 58,* 438–481.

Cross, D. R., & Paris, S. G. (1988). Developmental and instructional analyses of children's metacognitive and reading comprehension. *Journal of Educational Psychology, 80,* 131–142.

Cross, W. E., Jr., Strauss, L., & Fhagen-Smith, P. (1999). African American identity development across the life span: Educational implications. In R. H. Sheets & E. R. Hollins (Eds.), *Racial and ethnic identity in school practices: Aspects of human development* (pp. 29–47). Mahwah, NJ: Erlbaum.

Crowder, R. (1993). Short-term memory: Where do we stand? *Memory and Cognition, 21,* 142–145.

Crowley, K., & Siegler, R. S. (1999). Explanation and generalization in young children's strategy learning. *Child Development, 70,* 304–316.

Crowne, D. P., & Marlowe, D. (1964). *The approval motive: Studies in evaluative dependence.* New York: Wiley.

Csikszentmihalyi, M. (1990). *Flow: The psychology of optimal experience.* New York: HarperPerennial.

Csikszentmihalyi, M. (1996). *Creativity: Flow and the psychology of discovery and invention.* New York: HarperCollins.

Csikszentmihalyi, M., & Nakamura, J. (1989). The dynamics of intrinsic motivation: A study of adolescents. In C. Ames & R. Ames (Eds.), *Research on motivation in education: Vol. 3. Goals and cognitions.* San Diego, CA: Academic Press.

Cunningham, C. E., & Cunningham, L. J. (1998). Student-mediated conflict resolution programs. In R. A. Barkley, *Attention-deficit hyperactivity disorder: A handbook for diagnosis and treatment* (2nd ed., pp. 491–509). New York: Guilford Press.

Cunningham, T. H., & Graham, C. R. (2000). Increasing native English vocabulary recognition through Spanish immersion: Cognate transfer from foreign to first language. *Journal of Educational Psychology, 92,* 37–49.

Curtis, K. A., & Graham, S. (1991, April). *Altering beliefs about the importance of strategy: An attributional intervention.* Paper presented at the annual meeting of the American Educational Research Association, Chicago.

Cushing, L. S., & Kennedy, C. H. (1997). Academic effects of providing peer support in general education classrooms on students without disabilities. *Journal of Applied Behavior Analysis, 30,* 139–151.

d'Ailly, H. (2003). Children's autonomy and perceived control in learning: A model of motivation and achievement in Taiwan. *Journal of Educational Psychology, 95,* 84–96.

Daley, T. C., Whaley, S. E., Sigman, M. D., Espinosa, M. P., & Neumann, C. (2003). IQ on the rise: The Flynn effect in rural Kenyan children. *Psychological Science, 14,* 215–219.

Dalrymple, N. J. (1995). Environmental supports to develop flexibility and independence. In K. A. Quill (Ed.), *Teaching children with autism: Strategies to enhance communication and socialization.* New York: Delmar.

Damasio, A. R. (1994). *Descartes' error: Emotion, reason, and the human brain.* New York: Avon Books.

D'Amato, R. C., Chitooran, M. M., & Whitten, J. D. (1992). Neuropsychological consequences of malnutrition. In D. I. Templer, L. C. Hartlage, & W. G. Cannon (Eds.), *Preventable brain damage: Brain vulnerability and brain health.* New York: Springer.

Damon, W. (1977). *The social world of the child.* San Francisco: Jossey-Bass.

Damon, W. (1980). Patterns of change in children's social reasoning: A two-year longitudinal study. *Child Development, 51,* 1010–1017.

Damon, W. (1988). *The moral child: Nurturing children's natural moral growth.* New York: Free Press.

Damon, W. (1991). Putting substance into self-esteem: A focus on academic and moral values. *Educational Horizons, 70(1),* 12–18.

Damon, W., & Hart, D. (1988). *Self-understanding from childhood and adolescence.* New York: Cambridge University Press.

Danner, F. W., & Day, M. C. (1977). Eliciting formal operations. *Child Development, 48,* 1600–1606.

Danner, F. W., & Lonky, E. (1981). A cognitive-developmental approach to the effects of rewards on intrinsic motivation. *Child Development, 52,* 1043–1052.

Dansereau, D. F. (1988). Cooperative learning strategies. In C. E. Weinstein, E. T. Goetz, & P. A. Alexander (Eds.), *Learning and study strategies: Issues in assessment, instruction, and evaluation.* San Diego, CA: Academic Press.

Dansereau, D. F. (1995). Derived structural schemas and the transfer of knowledge. In A. McKeough, J. Lupart, & A. Marini (Eds.), *Teaching for transfer: Fostering generalization in learning.* Mahwah, NJ: Erlbaum.

Darch, C. B., & Kame'enui, E. J. (2004). *Instructional classroom management: A proactive approach to behavior management* (2nd ed.). Upper Saddle River, NJ: Merrill/Prentice Hall.

Darley, J. M., & Gross, P. H. (1983). A hypothesis-confirming bias in labeling effects. *Journal of Personality and Social Psychology, 44,* 20–33.

Darling-Hammond, L. (1991). The implications of testing policy for quality and equality. *Phi Delta Kappan, 73,* 220–225.

Darling-Hammond, L. (1995). Inequality and access to knowledge. In J. A. Banks & C. A. M. Banks (Eds.), *Handbook of research on multicultural education.* New York: Macmillan.

Das, J. P., Naglieri, J. A., & Kirby, J. R. (1994). *Assessment of cognitive processes.* Needham Heights, MA: Allyn & Bacon.

Davenport, E. C., Jr., Davison, M. L., Kuang, H., Ding, S., Kim, S., & Kwak, N. (1998). High school mathematics course-taking by gender and ethnicity. *American Educational Research Journal, 35,* 497–514.

Davidson, F. H. (1976). Ability to respect persons compared to ethnic prejudice in childhood. *Journal of Personality and Social Psychology, 34,* 1256–1267.

Davidson, F. H., & Davidson, M. M. (1994). *Changing childhood prejudice: The caring work of the schools.* Westport, CT: Bergin & Garvey.

Davidson, J. E., & Sternberg, R. J. (1998). Smart problem solving: How metacognition helps. In D. J. Hacker, J. Dunlosky, & A. C. Graesser (Eds.), *Metacognition in educational theory and practice* (pp. 47–68). Mahwah, NJ: Erlbaum.

Davis, G. A., & Rimm, S. B. (1998). *Education of the gifted and talented* (4th ed.). Boston: Allyn & Bacon.

Davis, G. A., & Thomas, M. A. (1989). *Effective schools and effective teachers.* Needham Heights, MA: Allyn & Bacon.

Davis, H. A. (2003). Conceptualizing the role and influence of student-teacher relationships on children's social and cognitive development. *Educational Psychologist, 38,* 207–234.

Davis, H. A., Schutz, P. A., & Chambless, C. B. (2001, April). *Uncovering the impact of social relationships in the classroom: Viewing relationships with teachers from different lenses.* Paper presented at the annual meeting of the American Educational Research Association, Seattle, WA.

Davis, L. E., Ajzen, I., Saunders, J., & Williams, T. (2002). The decision of African American students to complete high school: An application of the theory of planned behavior. *Journal of Educational Psychology, 94,* 810–819.

Davis-Kean, P. E., & Sandler, H. M. (2001). A meta-analysis of measures of self-esteem for young children: A framework for future measures. *Child Development, 72,* 887–906.

Deaux, K. (1984). From individual differences to social categories: Analysis of a decade's research on gender. *American Psychologist, 39,* 105–116.

DeCasper, A. J., & Spence, M. J. (1986). Prenatal maternal speech influences newborns' perception of speech sounds. *Infant Behavior and Development, 9,* 133–150.

deCharms, R. (1972). Personal causation training in the schools. *Journal of Applied Social Psychology, 2,* 95–113.

Deci, E. L. (1992). The relation of interest to the motivation of behavior: A self-determination theory perspective. In K. A. Renninger, S. Hidi, & A. Krapp (Eds.), *The role of interest in learning and development.* Mahwah, NJ: Erlbaum.

Deci, E. L. (1998). The relation of interest to motivation and human needs: The self-determination theory viewpoint. In L. Hoffman, A. Krapp, K. Renninger, & J. Baumert (Eds.), *Interest and learning: Proceedings of the Seeon Conference on Interest and Gender* (pp. 146–163). Keil, Germany: IPN.

Deci, E. L., Koestner, R., & Ryan, R. M. (1999). A meta-analytic review of experiments examining the effects of extrinsic rewards on intrinsic motivation. *Psychological Bulletin, 125,* 627–688.

Deci, E. L., Koestner, R., & Ryan, R. M. (2001). Extrinsic rewards and intrinsic motivation in education: Reconsidered once again. *Review of Educational Research. 71,* 1–27.

Deci, E. L., & Ryan, R. M. (1985). *Intrinsic motivation and self-determination in human behavior.* New York: Plenum Press.

Deci, E. L., & Ryan, R. M. (1992). The initiation and regulation of intrinsically motivated learning and achievement. In A. K. Boggiano & T. S. Pittman (Eds.), *Achievement and motivation: A social-developmental perspective.* Cambridge, England: Cambridge University Press.

Deci, E. L., & Ryan, R. M. (1995). Human autonomy: The basis for true self-esteem. In M. H. Kernis (Ed.), *Efficacy, agency, and self-esteem.* New York: Plenum Press.

De Corte, E. (2003). Transfer as the productive use of acquired knowledge, skills, and motivations. *Current Directions in Psychological Science, 12,* 142–146.

De Corte, E., Greer, B., & Verschaffel, L. (1996). Mathematics teaching and learning. In D. C. Berliner & R. C. Calfee (Eds.), *Handbook of educational psychology.* New York: Macmillan.

Dee-Lucas, D., & Larkin, J. H. (1991). Equations in scientific proofs: Effects on comprehension. *American Educational Research Journal, 28,* 661–682.

DeGrandpre, R. J. (2000). A science of meaning: Can behaviorism bring meaning to psychological science? *American Psychologist, 55,* 721–739.

de Jong, T., & van Joolingen, W. R. (1998). Scientific discovery learning with computer simulations of conceptual domains. *Review of Educational Research, 68,* 179–201.

DeLain, M. T., Pearson, P. D., & Anderson, R. C. (1985). Reading comprehension and creativity in black language use: You stand to gain by playing the sounding game! *American Educational Research Journal, 22,* 155–173.

Delandshere, G., & Petrosky, A. R. (1998). Assessment of complex performances: Limitations of key measurement assumptions. *Educational Researcher, 27*(2), 14–24.

deLeeuw, N., & Chi, M. T. H. (2003). Self-explanation: Enriching a situation model or repairing a domain model? In G. M. Sinatra & P. R. Pintrich (Eds.), *Intentional conceptual change* (pp. 55–78). Mahwah, NJ: Erlbaum.

Delgado-Gaitan, C. (1994). Socializing young children in Mexican-American families: An intergenerational perspective. In P. M. Greenfield & R. R. Cocking (Eds.), *Cross-cultural roots of minority child development.* Mahwah, NJ: Erlbaum.

De Lisi, R., & Golbeck, S. L. (1999). Implications of Piagetian theory for peer learning. In A. M. O'Donnell & A. King (Eds.), *Cognitive perspectives on peer learning* (pp. 3–37). Mahwah, NJ: Erlbaum.

DeLisle, J. R. (1984). *Gifted children speak out.* New York: Walker.

DeLoache, J. S., & Todd, C. M. (1988). Young children's use of spatial categorization as a mnemonic strategy. *Journal of Experimental Child Psychology, 46,* 1–20.

Delval, J. (1994). Stages in the child's construction of social knowledge. In M. Carretero & J. F. Voss (Eds.), *Cognitive and instructional processes in history and the social sciences* (pp. 77–102). Mahwah, NJ: Erlbaum.

DeMarie-Dreblow, D., & Miller, P. H. (1988). The development of children's strategies for selective attention: Evidence for a transitional period. *Child Development, 59,* 1504–1513.

Demetriou, A., Christou, C., Spanoudis, G., & Platsidou, M. (2002). The development of mental processing: Efficiency, working memory, and thinking. *Monographs of the Society for Research in Child Development, 67*(1, Serial No. 268).

Dempster, F. N. (1985). Proactive interference in sentence recall: Topic-similarity effects and individual differences. *Memory and Cognition, 13,* 81–89.

Dempster, F. N. (1991). Synthesis of research on reviews and tests. *Educational Leadership, 48*(7), 71–76.

Dempster, F. N. (1992). The rise and fall of the inhibitory mechanism: Toward a unified theory of cognitive development and aging. *Developmental Review, 12,* 45–75.

Dempster, F. N., & Corkill, A. J. (1999). Interference and inhibition in cognition and behavior: Unifying themes for educational psychology. *Educational Psychology Review, 11,* 1–88.

Denkla, M. B. (1986). New diagnostic criteria for autism and related behavioral disorders: Guidelines for research protocols. *Journal of the American Academy of Child Psychiatry, 25,* 221–224.

Dennis, T. A., Cole, P. M., Zahn-Waxler, C., & Mizuta, I. (2002). Self in context: Autonomy and relatedness in Japanese and U.S. mother-preschooler dyads. *Child Development, 73,* 1803–1817.

DeRidder, L. M. (1993). Teenage pregnancy: Etiology and educational interventions. *Educational Psychology Review, 5,* 87–107.

Derry, S. J. (1996). Cognitive schema theory in the constructivist debate. *Educational Psychologist, 31,* 163–174.

Derry, S. J., Levin, J. R., Osana, H. P., & Jones, M. S. (1998). Developing middle school students' statistical reasoning abilities through simulation gaming. In S. P. Lajoie (Ed.), *Reflections on statistics: Learning, teaching, and assessment in grades K–12* (pp. 175–195). Mahwah, NJ: Erlbaum.

Desberg, P., & Taylor, J. H. (1986). *Essentials of task analysis.* Lanham, MD: University Press of America.

Deshler, D. D., & Schumaker, J. B. (1988). An instructional model for teaching students how to learn. In J. L. Graden, J. E. Zins, & M. J. Curtis (Eds.), *Alternative educational delivery systems: Enhancing instructional options for all students.* Washington, DC: National Association of School Psychologists.

Deutsch, F. M., Ruble, N., Fleming, A., & Brooks-Gunn, J. (1988). Information-seeking and maternal self-definition during the transition to motherhood. *Journal of Personality and Social Psychology, 55,* 420–431.

Deutsch, M. (1993). Educating for a peaceful world. *American Psychologist, 48,* 510–517.

DeVault, G., Krug, C., & Fake, S. (1996, September). Why does Samantha act that way: Positive behavioral support leads to successful inclusion. *Exceptional Parent,* 43–47.

Devine, P. G. (1995). Prejudice and out-group perception. In A. Tesser (Ed.), *Advanced social psychology.* New York: McGraw-Hill.

DeVoe, J. F., Peter, K., Kaufman, P., Ruddy, S. A., Miller, A. K., Planty, M., Snyder, T. D., & Rand, M. R. (2003). *Indicators of school crime and safety: 2003* (NCES 2004–004/NCJ 201257). Washington, DC: U.S. Departments of Education and Justice. Retrieved February 27, 2004, from http://nces.ed.gov/

DeVries, R. (1997). Piaget's social theory. *Educational Researcher, 26*(2), 4–17.

DeVries, R., & Zan, B. (1996). A constructivist perspective on the role of the sociomoral atmosphere in promoting children's development. In C. T. Fosnot (Ed.), *Constructivism: Theory, perspectives, and practice.* New York: Teachers College Press.

Dewhurst, S. A., & Conway, M. A. (1994). Pictures, images, and recollective experience. *Journal of Experimental Psychology: Learning, Memory, and Cognition, 20,* 1088–1098.

Deyhle, D., & LeCompte, M. (1999). Cultural differences in child development: Navajo adolescents in middle schools. In R. H. Sheets & E. R. Hollins (Eds.), *Racial and ethnic identity in school practices: Aspects of human development* (pp. 123–139). Mahwah, NJ: Erlbaum.

Deyhle, D., & Margonis, F. (1995). Navajo mothers and daughters: Schools, jobs, and the family. *Anthropology and Education Quarterly, 26,* 135–167.

Diamond, S. C. (1991). What to do when you can't do anything: Working with disturbed adolescents. *Clearing House, 64,* 232–234.

Diaz, R. M. (1983). Thought and two languages: The impact of bilingualism on cognitive development. In E. W. Gordon (Ed.), *Review of research in education* (Vol. 10). Washington, DC: American Educational Research Association.

Diaz, R. M., & Berk, L. E. (1995) A Vygotskian critique of self-instructional training. *Development and Psychopathology, 7,* 369–392.

Diaz, R. M., & Klinger, C. (1991). Toward an explanatory model of the interaction between bilingualism and cognitive development. In E. Bialystok (Ed.), *Language processing in bilingual children.* Cambridge, England: Cambridge University Press.

Dien, T. (1998). Language and literacy in Vietnamese American communities. In B. Pérez (Ed.), *Sociocultural contexts of language and literacy.* Mahwah, NJ: Erlbaum.

Dillon, A., & Gabbard, R. (1998). Hypermedia as an educational technology: A review of the quantitative research literature on learner comprehension, control, and style. *Review of Educational Research, 68,* 322–349.

Dirks, J. (1982). The effect of a commercial game on children's Block Design scores on the WISC–R test. *Intelligence, 6,* 109–123.

diSessa, A. A. (1996). What do "just plain folk" know about physics? In D. R. Olson & N. Torrance (Eds.), *The handbook of education and human development: New models of learning, teaching, and schooling.* Cambridge, MA: Blackwell.

Dishion, T. J., McCord, J., & Poulin, F. (1999). When interventions harm: Peer groups and problem behavior. *American Psychologist, 54,* 755–764.

Di Vesta, F. J., & Gray, S. G. (1972). Listening and note-taking. *Journal of Educational Psychology, 63,* 8–14.

Di Vesta, F. J., & Peverly, S. T. (1984). The effects of encoding variability, processing activity and rule example sequences on the transfer of conceptual rules. *Journal of Educational Psychology, 76,* 108–119.

Di Vesta, F. J., & Smith, D. A. (1979). The pausing principle: Increasing the efficiency of memory for ongoing events. *Contemporary Educational Psychology, 4,* 288–296.

Dodge, K. A. (1986). A social information processing model of social competence in children. In M. Perlmutter (Ed.), *Minnesota Symposia on Child Psychology: Vol. 18. Cognitive perspectives in children's social and behavioral development.* Mahwah, NJ: Erlbaum.

Dodge, K. A., Asher, S. R., & Parkhurst, J. T. (1989). Social life as a goal-coordination task. In C. Ames & R. Ames (Eds.), *Research on motivation in education: Vol. 3. Goals and cognitions.* San Diego: Academic Press.

Dodge, K. A., Lansford, J. E., Burks, V. S., Bates, J. E., Pettit, G. S., Fontaine, R., & Price, J. M. (2003). Peer rejection and social information-processing factors in the development of aggressive behavior problems in children. *Child Development, 74,* 374–393.

Dodge, K. A., Lochman, J. E., Harnish, J. D., Bates, J. E., & Pettit, G. S. (1997). Reactive and proactive aggression in school children and psychiatrically impaired chronically assaultive youth. *Journal of Abnormal Psychology, 106,* 37–51.

Doescher, S. M., & Sugawara, A. I. (1989). Encouraging prosocial behavior in young children. *Childhood Education, 65,* 213–216.

Dole, J. A., Duffy, G. G., Roehler, L. R., & Pearson, P. D. (1991). Moving from the old to the new: Research on reading comprehension instruction. *Review of Educational Research, 61,* 239–264.

Dominowski, R. L. (1998). Verbalization and problem solving. In D. J. Hacker, J. Dunlosky, & A. C. Graesser (Eds.), *Metacognition in educational theory and practice* (pp. 25–45). Mahwah, NJ: Erlbaum.

Donaldson, M. (1978). *Children's minds.* New York: Norton.

Donaldson, S. K., & Westerman, M. A. (1986). Development of children's understanding of ambivalence and causal theories of emotion. *Developmental Psychology, 22,* 655–662.

Donnelly, C. M., & McDaniel, M. A. (1993). Use of analogy in learning scientific concepts. *Journal of Experimental Psychology: Learning, Memory, and Cognition, 19,* 975–987.

Dorris, M. (1989). *The broken cord.* New York: Harper & Row.

Dovidio, J. F., & Gaertner, S. L. (1999). Reducing prejudice: Combating intergroup biases. *Current Directions in Psychological Science, 8,* 101–105.

Dovidio, J. F., Kawakami, K., & Gaertner, S. L. (2000). Reducing contemporary prejudice: Combating explicit and implicit bias at the individual and intergroup level. In S. Oskamp (Ed.), *Reducing prejudice and discrimination* (pp. 137–163). Mahwah, NJ: Erlbaum.

Dowson, M., & McInerney, D. M. (2001). Psychological parameters of students' social and work avoidance goals: A qualitative investigation. *Journal of Educational Psychology, 93,* 35–42.

Doyle, A. (1982). Friends, acquaintances, and strangers: The influence of familiarity and ethnolinguistic backgrounds on social interaction. In K. Rubin & H. Ross (Eds.), *Peer relationships and social skills in childhood.* New York: Springer-Verlag.

Doyle, W. (1983). Academic work. *Review of Educational Research, 53,* 159–199.

Doyle, W. (1984). How order is achieved in classrooms: An interim report. *Journal of Curriculum Studies, 16,* 259–277.

Doyle, W. (1986a). Classroom organization and management. In M. C. Wittrock (Ed.), *Handbook of research on teaching* (3rd ed.). New York: Macmillan.

Doyle, W. (1986b). Content representation in teachers' definitions of academic work. *Journal of Curriculum Studies, 18,* 365–379.

Doyle, W. (1990). Classroom management techniques. In O. C. Moles (Ed.), *Student discipline strategies: Research and practice.* Albany: State University of New York Press.

Dreikurs, R. (1998). *Maintaining sanity in the classroom: Classroom management techniques* (2nd ed.). Bristol, PA: Hemisphere.

Dreikurs, R., & Cassel, P. (1972). *Discipline without tears* (2nd ed.). New York: Dutton.

Drevno, G. E., Kimball, J. W., Possi, M. K., Heward, W. L., Gardner, R., III, & Barbetta, P. M. (1994). Effects of active student responding during error correction on the acquisition, maintenance, and generalization of science vocabulary by elementary students: A systematic replication. *Journal of Applied Behavior Analysis, 27,* 179–180.

Driver, B. L. (1996). Where do we go from here? Sustaining and maintaining co-teaching relationships. *Learning Disabilities Forum, 21*(2), 29–32.

Driver, R. (1995). Constructivist approaches to science teaching. In L. P. Steffe & J. Gale (Eds.), *Constructivism in education.* Mahwah, NJ: Erlbaum.

Driver, R., Asoko, H., Leach, J., Mortimer, E., & Scott, P. (1994). Constructing scientific knowledge in the classroom. *Educational Researcher, 23*(7), 5–12.

Dryfoos, J. G. (1997). The prevalence of problem behaviors: Implications for programs. In R. P. Weissberg, T. P. Gullotta, R. L. Hampton, B. A. Ryan, & G. R. Adams (Eds.), *Enhancing children's wellness* (Vol. 8, pp. 17–46). Thousand Oaks, CA: Sage.

DuBois, D. L., Burk-Braxton, C., Swenson, L. P., Tevendale, H. D., & Hardesty, J. L. (2002). Race and gender influences on adjustment in early adolescence: Investigation of an integrative model. *Child Development, 73,* 1573–1592.

DuBois, N. F., Kiewra, K. A., & Fraley, J. (1988, April). *Differential effects of a learning strategy course.* Paper presented at the annual meeting of the American Educational Research Association, New Orleans, LA.

Duchardt, B. A., Deshler, D. D., & Schumaker, J. B. (1995). A strategy intervention for enabling students with learning disabilities to identify and change their ineffective beliefs. *Learning Disability Quarterly, 18,* 186–201.

Duit, R. (1991). Students' conceptual frameworks: Consequences for learning science. In S. M. Glynn, R. H. Yeany, & B. K. Britton (Eds.), *The psychology of learning science.* Mahwah, NJ: Erlbaum.

Duke, N. K. (2000). For the rich it's richer: Print experiences and environments offered to children in very low- and very high-socioeconomic status first-grade classrooms. *American Educational Research Journal, 37,* 441–478.

DuNann, D. G., & Weber, S. J. (1976). Short- and long-term effects of contingency managed instruction on low, medium, and high GPA students. *Journal of Applied Behavior Analysis, 9,* 375–376.

Duncker, K. (1945). On problem solving. *Psychological Monographs, 58* (Whole No. 270).

Dunlap, G., dePerczel, M., Clarke, S., Wilson, D., Wright, S., White, R., & Gomez, A. (1994). Choice making to promote adaptive behavior for students with emotional and behavioral challenges. *Journal of Applied Behavior Analysis, 27,* 505–518.

DuPaul, G. J., Barkley, R. A., & Connor, D. F. (1998). Stimulants. In R. A. Barkley, *Attention-deficit hyperactivity disorder: A handbook for diagnosis and treatment* (2nd ed., pp. 510–551). New York: Guilford Press.

DuPaul, G. J., & Eckert, T. L. (1994). The effects of social skills curricula: Now you see them, now you don't. *School Psychology Quarterly, 9,* 113–132.

DuPaul, G. J., Ervin, R. A., Hook, C. L., & McGoey, K. E. (1998). Peer tutoring for children with attention deficit hyperactivity disorder: Effects on classroom behavior and academic perfor- mance. *Journal of Applied Behavior Analysis, 31,* 579–592.

Duran, B. J., & Weffer, R. E. (1992). Immigrants' aspirations, high school process, and academic outcomes. *American Educational Research Journal, 29,* 163–181.

Durkin, K. (1995). *Developmental social psychology: From infancy to old age.* Cambridge, MA: Blackwell.

Durost, W. N. (1961). How to tell parents about standardized test results. *Test Service Notebook* (No. 26). New York: Harcourt, Brace, & World.

Dweck, C. S. (1975). The role of expectations and attributions in the alleviation of learned helplessness. *Journal of Personality and Social Psychology, 31,* 674–685.

Dweck, C. S. (1978). Achievement. In M. E. Lamb (Ed.), *Social and personality development.* New York: Holt, Rinehart & Winston.

Dweck, C. S. (1986). Motivational processes affecting learning. *American Psychologist, 41,* 1040–1048.

Dweck, C. S. (2000). *Self-theories: Their role in motivation, personality, and development.* Philadelphia: Psychology Press.

Dweck, C. S., & Elliott, E. S. (1983). Achievement motivation. In E. M. Hetherington (Ed.), *Handbook of child psychology: Vol. 4. Socialization, personality, and social development* (4th ed., pp. 643–691). New York: Wiley.

Dweck, C. S., Goetz, T. E., & Strauss, N. L. (1980). Sex differences in learned helplessness: IV. An experimental and naturalistic study of failure generalization and its mediators. *Journal of Personality and Social Psychology, 38,* 441–452.

Dweck, C. S., & Leggett, E. L. (1988). A social-cognitive approach to motivation and personality. *Psychological Review, 95,* 256–273.

Dwyer, K., & Osher, D. (2000). *Safeguarding our children: An action guide.* Washington, DC: U.S. Departments of Education and Justice, American Institutes for Research. Retrieved February 26, 2004, from http://www. ed.gov/pubs/edpubs.html.

Dwyer, K., Osher, D., & Warger, C. (1998). *Early warning, timely response: A guide to safe schools.* Washington, DC: U.S. Department of Education. Retrieved February 26, 2004, from http://www.ed.gov/offices/OSERS/OSEP/earlywrn.htm.

D'Ydewalle, G., Swerts, A., & De Corte, E. (1983). Study time and test performance as a function of test expectations. *Contemporary Educational Psychology, 8*(1), 55–67.

Dyer, H. S. (1967). The discovery and development of educational goals. *Proceedings of the 1966 Invitational Conference on Testing Problems.* Princeton, NJ: Educational Testing Service.

Eacott, M. J. (1999). Memory for the events of early childhood. *Current Directions in Psychological Science, 8,* 46–49.

Eaton, J. F., Anderson, C. W., & Smith, E. L. (1984). Students' misconceptions interfere with science learning: Case studies of fifth-grade students. *Elementary School Journal, 84,* 365–379.

Eaton, W. O., & Enns, L. R. (1986). Sex differences in human motor activity level. *Psychological Bulletin, 100,* 19–28.

Eccles, J. S. (1989). Bringing young women to math and science. In M. Crawford & M. Gentry (Eds.), *Gender and thought: Psychological perspectives.* New York: Springer-Verlag.

Eccles, J. S., & Jacobs, J. E. (1986). Social forces shape math attitudes and performance. *Signs: Journal of Women in Culture and Society, 11,* 367–380.

Eccles, J. S., Jacobs, J., Harold, R., Yoon, K. S., Arbreton, A., & Freedman-Doan, C. (1993). Parents and gender-related socialization during the middle childhood and adolescent years. In S. Oskamp & M. Costanzo (Eds.), *Gender issues in contemporary society.* Newbury Park, CA: Sage.

Eccles, J. S., Jacobs, J., Harold-Goldsmith, R., Jayaratne, T., & Yee, D. (1989, April). *The relations between parents' category-based and target-based beliefs: Gender roles and biological influences.* Paper presented at the Society for Research in Child Development, Kansas City, MO.

Eccles, J. S., & Midgley, C. (1989). Stage-environment fit: Developmentally appropriate classrooms for young adolescents. In C. Ames & R. Ames (Eds.), *Research on motivation in education: Vol. 3. Goals and cognition.* San Diego, CA: Academic Press.

Eccles, J. S., & Wigfield, A. (1985). Teacher expectations and student motivation. In J. B. Dusek (Ed.), *Teacher expectancies.* Mahwah, NJ: Erlbaum.

Eccles, J. S., Wigfield, A., & Flanagan, C., Miller, C., Reuman, D., & Yee, D. (1989). Self-concepts, domain values, and self-esteem: Relations and changes at early adolescence. *Journal of Personality, 57,* 283–310.

Eccles, J. S., Wigfield, A., & Schiefele, U. (1998). Motivation to succeed. In W. Damon (Series Ed.) & N. Eisenberg (Vol. Ed.), *Handbook of child psychology: Vol. 3. Social, emotional, and personality development* (5th ed., pp. 1017–1095). New York: Wiley.

Eccles (Parsons), J. S. (1983). Expectancies, values, and academic behaviors. In J. T. Spence (Ed.), *Achievement and achievement motivation.* San Francisco: Freeman.

Eccles (Parsons), J. S. (1984). Sex differences in mathematics participation. In M. Steinkamp & M. Maehr (Eds.), *Women in science.* Greenwich, CT: JAI Press.

Echols, L. D., West, R. F., Stanovich, K. E., & Kehr, K. S. (1996). Using children's literacy activities to predict growth in verbal cognitive skills: A longitudinal investigation. *Journal of Educational Psychology, 88,* 296–304.

Eckert, P. (1989). *Jocks and burnouts: Social categories and identity in the high school.* New York: Teachers College Press.

Eden, G. F., Stein, J. F., & Wood, F. B. (1995). Verbal and visual problems in reading disability. *Journal of Learning Disabilities, 28,* 272–290.

Edens, K. M., & Potter, E. F. (2001). Promoting conceptual understanding through pictorial representation. *Studies in Art Education, 42,* 214–233.

Educational Testing Service (2003). *Study Guide for Principles of Learning and Teaching* (2nd ed.). Princeton, NJ: Author.

Eeds, M., & Wells, D. (1989). Grand conversations: An explanation of meaning construction in literature study groups. *Research in the Teaching of English, 23,* 4–29.

Eilam, B. (2001). Primary strategies for promoting homework performance. *American Educational Research Journal, 38,* 691–725.

Eisenberg, N. (1982). The development of reasoning regarding prosocial behavior. In N. Eisenberg (Ed.), *The development of prosocial behavior.* San Diego, CA: Academic Press.

Eisenberg, N. (1987). The relation of altruism and other moral behaviors to moral cognition: Methodological and conceptual issues. In N. Eisenberg (Ed.), *Contemporary topics in developmental psychology* (pp. 165–189). New York: Wiley.

Eisenberg, N. (1995). Prosocial development: A multifaceted model. In W. M. Kurtines & J. L. Gewirtz (Eds.), *Moral development: An introduction.* Boston: Allyn & Bacon.

Eisenberg, N., Carlo, G., Murphy, B., & Van Court, N. (1995). Prosocial development in late adolescence: A longitudinal study. *Child Development, 66,* 1179–1197.

Eisenberg, N., & Fabes, R. A. (1991). Prosocial behavior: A multimethod developmental perspective. In M. S. Clark (Ed.), *Review of personality and social psychology* (Vol. 2, pp. 34–61). Newbury Park, CA: Sage.

Eisenberg, N., & Fabes, R. A. (1998). Prosocial development. In W. Damon (Series Ed.) & N. Eisenberg (Vol. Ed.), *Handbook of child psychology: Vol. 3. Social, emotional, and personality development* (5th ed., pp. 701–778). New York: Wiley.

Eisenberg, N., Lennon, R., & Pasternack, J. F. (1986). Altruistic values and moral judgment. In N. Eisenberg (Ed.), *Altruistic emotion, cognition, and behavior.* Mahwah, NJ: Erlbaum.

Eisenberg, N., Martin, C. L., & Fabes, R. A. (1996). Gender development and gender effects. In D. C. Berliner & R. C. Calfee (Eds.), *Handbook of educational psychology.* New York: Macmillan.

Eisenberg, N., Pidada, S., & Liew, J. (2001). The relations of regulation and negative emotionality to Indonesian children's social functioning. *Child Development, 72,* 1747–1763.

Eisenberg, N., Zhou, Q., & Koller, S. (2001). Brazilian adolescents' prosocial moral judgment and behavior: Relations to sympathy, perspective taking, gender-role orientation, and demographic characteristics. *Child Development, 72,* 518–534.

Eisenberger, R. (1992). Learned industriousness. *Psychological Review, 99,* 248–267.

Elder, A. D. (2002). Characterizing fifth grade students' epistemological beliefs in science. In B. K. Hofer & P. R. Pintrich (Eds.), *Personal epistemology: The psychology of beliefs about knowledge and knowing* (pp. 347–363). Mahwah, NJ: Erlbaum.

Elia, J. P. (1994). Homophobia in the high school: A problem in need of a resolution. *Journal of Homosexuality, 77*(1), 177–185.

Elkind, D. (1981). *Children and adolescents: Interpretive essays on Jean Piaget* (3rd ed.). New York: Oxford University Press.

Ellenwood, S., & Ryan, K. (1991). Literature and morality: An experimental curriculum. In W. M. Kurtines & J. L. Gewirtz (Eds.), *Moral behavior and development: Vol. 3. Application.* Mahwah, NJ: Erlbaum.

Elliot, A. J., & McGregor, H. A. (2000, April). Approach and avoidance goals and autonomous-controlled regulation: Empirical and conceptual relations. In A. Assor (Chair), *Self-determination theory and achievement goal theory: Convergences, divergences, and educational implications.* Symposium conducted at the annual meeting of the American Educational Research Association, New Orleans, LA.

Elliot, A. J., & Thrash, T. M. (2001). Achievement goals and the hierarchical model of achievement motivation. *Educational Psychology Review, 13,* 139–156.

Elliott, D. J. (1995). *Music matters: A new philosophy of music education.* New York: Oxford University Press.

Elliott, S. N., & Busse, R. T. (1991). Social skills assessment and intervention with children and adolescents. *School Psychology International, 12,* 63–83.

Ellis, E. S., & Friend, P. (1991). Adolescents with learning disabilities. In B. Y. L. Wong (Ed.), *Learning about learning disabilities.* San Diego, CA: Academic Press.

Ellis, H. C., & Hunt, R. R. (1983). *Fundamentals of human memory and cognition* (3rd ed.). Dubuque, IA: Wm. C. Brown.

Ellis, N. C. (Ed.). (1994). *Implicit and explicit learning of languages.* London: Academic Press.

Ellis, N. R. (Ed.). (1979). *Handbook of mental deficiency: Psychological theory and research.* Mahwah, NJ: Erlbaum.

Elrich, M. (1994). The stereotype within. *Educational Leadership, 51*(8), 12–15.

Emmer, E. T. (1987). Classroom management and discipline. In V. Richardson-Koehler (Ed.), *Educators' handbook: A research perspective.* White Plains, NY: Longman.

Emmer, E. T. (1994, April). *Teacher emotions and classroom management.* Paper presented at the annual meeting of the American Educational Research Association, New Orleans, LA.

Emmer, E. T., & Evertson, C. M. (1981). Synthesis of research on classroom management. *Educational Leadership, 38*(4), 342–347.

Emmer, E. T., Evertson, C. M., Clements, B. S., & Worsham, M. E. (1994). *Classroom management for secondary teachers* (3rd ed.). Needham Heights, MA: Allyn & Bacon.

Emmer, E. T., & Stough, L. M. (2001). Classroom management: A critical part of educational psychology, with implications for teacher education. *Educational Psychologist, 36,* 103–112.

Engle, R. W. (2002). Working memory capacity as executive attention. *Current Directions in Psychological Science, 11,* 19–23.

Englemann, S., & Carnine, D. (1982). *Theory of instruction: Principles and applications.* New York: Irvington.

Entwisle, N. J., & Ramsden, P. (1983). *Understanding student learning.* London: Croom Helm.

Epstein, J. L. (1983). Longitudinal effects of family-school-person interactions on student outcomes. *Research in Sociology of Education and Socialization, 4,* 101–127.

Epstein, J. L. (1986). Friendship selection: Developmental and environmental influences. In E. Mueller & C. Cooper (Eds.), *Process and outcome in peer relationships* (pp. 129–160). New York: Academic Press.

Epstein, J. L. (1989). Family structures and student motivation. In R. E. Ames & C. Ames (Eds.), *Research on motivation in education: Vol. 3. Goals and cognitions* (pp. 259–295). New York: Academic Press.

Epstein, J. L. (1996). Perspectives and previews on research and policy for school, family, and community partnerships. In A. Booth & J. F. Dunn (Eds.), *Family-school links: How do they affect educational outcomes?* Mahwah, NJ: Erlbaum.

Epstein, J. L., & Van Voorhis, F. L. (2001). More than minutes: Teachers' roles in designing homework. *Educational Psychologist, 36,* 181–193.

Epstein, J. S. (1998). Introduction: Generation X, youth culture, and identity. In J. S. Epstein (Ed.), *Youth culture: Identity in a postmodern world.* Malden, MA: Blackwell.

Epstein, T. (2000). Adolescents' perspectives on racial diversity in U.S. history: Case studies from an urban classroom. *American Educational Research Journal, 37,* 185–214.

Erdelyi, M. H. (1985). *Psychoanalysis: Freud's cognitive psychology.* New York: Freeman.

Erdley, C. A., & Asher, S. R. (1996). Children's social goals and self-efficacy perceptions as influences on their responses to ambiguous provocation. *Child Development, 67,* 1329–1344.

Erdley, C. A., Qualey, L. L., & Pietrucha, C. A. (1996, April). *Boys' and girls' attributions of intent and legitimacy of aggression beliefs as predictors of their social behavior.* Paper presented at the annual meeting of the American Educational Research Association, New York.

Ericsson, K. A., & Chalmers, N. (1994). Expert performance: Its structure and acquisition. *American Psychologist, 49,* 725–747.

Eriks-Brophy, A., & Crago, M. B. (1994). Transforming classroom discourse: An Inuit example. *Language and Education, 8*(3), 105–122.

Erikson, E. H. (1963). *Childhood and society* (2nd ed.). New York: Norton.

Erikson, E. H. (1972). Eight ages of man. In C. S. Lavatelli & F. Stendler (Eds.), *Readings in child behavior and child development.* San Diego, CA: Harcourt Brace Jovanovich.

Eron, L. D. (1980). Prescription for reduction of aggression. *American Psychologist, 35,* 244–252.

Erwin, P. (1993). *Friendship and peer relations in children.* Chichester, England: Wiley.

Eslinger, P. J. (1996). Conceptualizing, describing, and measuring components of executive function: A summary. In G. R. Lyon & N. A. Krasnegor (Eds.), *Attention, memory, and executive function* (pp. 367–395). Baltimore: Brookes.

Espelage, D. L., Holt, M. K., & Henkel, R. R. (2003). Examination of peer-group contextual effects on aggression during early adolescence. *Child Development, 74,* 205–220.

Esquivel, G. B. (1995). Teacher behaviors that foster creativity. *Educational Psychology Review, 7,* 185–202.

Evans, E. D., & Craig, D. (1990). Teacher and student perceptions of academic cheating in middle and senior high schools. *Journal of Educational Research, 84*(1), 44–52.

Evans, G. W., & English, K. (2002). The environment of poverty: Multiple stressor exposure, psychophysiological stress, and socioemotional adjustment. *Child Development, 73,* 1238–1248.

Evertson, C. M., & Emmer, E. T. (1982). Effective management at the beginning of the year in junior high classes. *Journal of Educational Psychology, 74,* 485–498.

Evertson, C. M., & Harris, A. H. (1992). What we know about managing classrooms. *Educational Leadership, 49*(7), 74–78.

Eysenck, M. W. (1992). *Anxiety: The cognitive perspective.* Hove, England: Erlbaum.

Eysenck, M. W., & Keane, M. T. (1990). *Cognitive psychology: A student's handbook.* Hove, England: Erlbaum.

Fabes, R. A., Martin, C. L., & Hanish, L. D. (2003). Young children's play qualities in same-, other-, and mixed-sex peer groups. *Child Development, 74,* 921–932.

Fabos, B., & Young, M. D. (1999). Telecommunication in the classroom: Rhetoric versus reality. *Review of Educational Research, 69,* 217–259.

Fagot, B. I. (1985). Beyond the reinforcement principle: Another step toward understanding sex role development. *Developmental Psychology, 21,* 1097–1104.

Fagot, B. I., Hagan, R., Leinbach, M. D., & Kronsberg, S. (1985). Differential reactions to assertive and communicative acts of toddler boys and girls. *Child Development, 56,* 1499–1505.

Fairchild, H. H., & Edwards-Evans, S. (1990). African American dialects and schooling: A review. In A. M. Padilla, H. H. Fairchild, & C. M. Valadez (Eds.), *Bilingual education: Issues and strategies.* Newbury Park, CA: Sage.

Fall, R., Webb, N. M., & Chudowsky, N. (2000). Group discussion and large-scale language arts assessment:

Effects on students' comprehension. *American Educational Research Journal, 37*, 911–941.

Fantuzzo, J. W., King, J., & Heller, L. R. (1992). Effects of reciprocal peer tutoring on mathematics and school adjustment: A component analysis. *Journal of Educational Psychology, 84*, 331–339.

Farber, B., Mindel, C. H., & Lazerwitz, B. (1988). The Jewish American family. In C. H. Mindel, R. W. Habenstein, & R. Wright (Eds.), *Ethnic families in America: Patterns and variations.* New York: Elsevier.

Farmer, T. W., Leung, M.-C., Pearl, R., Rodkin, P. C., Cadwallader, T. W., & Van Acker, R. (2002). Deviant or diverse peer groups? The peer affiliations of aggressive elementary students. *Journal of Educational Psychology, 94*, 611–620.

Farran, D. C. (2001). Critical periods and early intervention. In D. B. Bailey, Jr., J. T. Bruer, F. J. Symons, & J. W. Lichtman (Eds.), *Critical thinking about critical periods* (pp. 233–266). Baltimore: Brookes.

Farrell, E. (1990). *Hanging in and dropping out: Voices of at-risk high school students.* New York: Teachers College Press.

Farver, J. A. M., & Branstetter, W. H. (1994). Preschoolers' prosocial responses to their peers' distress. *Developmental Psychology, 30*, 334–341.

Farwell, L., & Weiner, B. (1996). Self-perception of fairness in individual and group contexts. *Personality and Social Psychology Bulletin, 22*, 867–881.

Feather, N. T. (1982). *Expectations and actions: Expectancy-value models in psychology.* Mahwah, NJ: Erlbaum.

Feingold, A. (1992). Sex differences in variability in intellectual abilities: A new look at an old controversy. *Review of Educational Research, 62*, 61–84.

Feld, S., Ruhland, D., & Gold, M. (1979). Developmental changes in achievement motivation. *Merrill-Palmer Quarterly, 25*, 43–60.

Feldhusen, J. F. (1989). Synthesis of research on gifted youth. *Educational Leadership, 26*(1), 6–11.

Feldhusen, J. F., & Treffinger, D. J. (1980). *Creative thinking and problem solving in gifted education.* Dubuque, IA: Kendall/Hunt.

Feldhusen, J. F., Treffinger, D. J., & Bahlke, S. J. (1970). Developing creative thinking: The Purdue Creativity Program. *Journal of Creative Behavior, 4*, 85–90.

Feldhusen, J. F., Van Winkle, L., & Ehle, D. A. (1996) Is it acceleration or simply appropriate instruction for precocious youth? *Teaching Exceptional Children, 28*(3), 48–51.

Feltz, D. L., Chase, M. A., Moritz, S. E. & Sullivan, P. J. (1999). A conceptual model of coaching efficacy: Preliminary investigation and instrument development. *Journal of Educational Psychology, 91*, 765–776.

Fennema, E. (1987). Sex-related differences in education: Myths, realities, and interventions. In V. Richardson-Koehler (Ed.), *Educators' handbook: A research perspective.* White Plains, NY: Longman.

Ferguson, E. L., & Hegarty, M. (1995). Learning with real machines or diagrams: Application of knowledge to real-world problems. *Cognition and Instruction, 13*, 129–160.

Ferguson, R. (1998). Can schools narrow the Black-White test score gap? In C. Jencks & M. Phillips (Eds.), *The Black-White test score gap* (pp. 318–374). Washington, DC: Brookings Institute.

Ferrari, M., & Elik, N. (2003). Influences on intentional conceptual change. In G. M. Sinatra & P. R. Pintrich (Eds.), *Intentional conceptual change* (pp. 21–54). Mahwah, NJ: Erlbaum.

Fessler, M. A., Rosenberg, M. S., & Rosenberg, L. A. (1991). Concomitant learning disabilities and learning problems among students with behavioral/emotional disorders. *Behavioral Disorders, 16*, 97–106.

Feuerstein, R. (1979). *The dynamic assessment of retarded performers: The Learning Potential Assessment Device, theory, instruments, and techniques.* Baltimore: University Park Press.

Feuerstein, R. (1990). The theory of structural cognitive modifiability. In B. Z. Presseisen (Ed.), *Learning and thinking styles: Classroom interaction.* Washington, DC: National Education Association.

Feuerstein, R., Feuerstein, R., & Gross, S. (1997). The Learning Potential Assessment Device. In D. P. Flanagan, J. L. Genshaft, & P. L. Harrison (Eds.), *Contemporary intellectual assessment: Theories, tests, and issues* (pp. 297–313). New York: Guilford Press.

Feuerstein, R., Klein, P. R., & Tannenbaum, A. (Eds.). (1991). *Mediated learning experience: Theoretical, psychosocial, and learning implications.* London: Freund.

Fey, M. E., Catts, H., & Larrivee, L. (1995). Preparing preschoolers for the academic and social challenges of school. In M. E. Fey, J. Windsor, & S. F. Warren (Eds.), *Language intervention: Preschool through elementary years.* Baltimore: Brookes.

Fiedler, E. D., Lange, R. E., & Winebrenner, S. (1993). In search of reality: Unraveling the myths about tracking, ability grouping and the gifted. *Roeper Review, 16*(1), 4–7.

Field, D. (1987). A review of preschool conservation training: An analysis of analyses. *Developmental Review, 7*, 210–251.

Field, T. F., Woodson, R., Greenberg, R., & Cohen, D. (1982). Discrimination and imitation of facial expressions by neonates. *Science, 218*, 179–181.

Finders, M., & Lewis, C. (1994). Why some parents don't come to school. *Educational Leadership, 51*(8), 50–54.

Fingerhut, L. A., & Christoffel, K. K. (2002). Firearm-related death and injury among children and adolescents. *The Future of Children, 12*(2), 25–37.

Finke, R. A., & Bettle, J. (1996). *Chaotic cognition: Principles and applications.* Mahwah, NJ: Erlbaum.

Finkelhor, D., & Ormrod, R. (2000, December). *Juvenile victims of property crimes.* Washington, DC: U.S. Department of Justice, Office of Justice Programs, Office of Juvenile Justice and Delinquency Prevention.

Finn, J. D. (1989). Withdrawing from school. *Review of Educational Research, 59*, 117–142.

Finn, J. D. (1991). How to make the dropout problem go away. *Educational Researcher, 20*(1), 28–30.

Finn, J. D., Pannozzo, G. M., & Achilles, C. M. (2003). The "why's" of class size: Student behavior in small classes. *Review of Educational Research, 73*, 321–368.

Firestone, W. A., & Mayrowetz, D. (2000). Rethinking "high stakes": Lessons from the United States and England and Wales. *Teachers College Record, 102*, 724–749.

Fischer, K. W., & Bidell, T. (1991). Constraining nativist inferences about cognitive capacities. In S. Carey & R. Gelman (Eds.), *The epigenesis of mind: Essays on biology and cognition.* Mahwah, NJ: Erlbaum.

Fischer, K. W., & Rose, S. P. (1996). Dynamic growth cycles of brain and cognitive development. In R. Thatcher, G. R. Lyon, J. Rumsey, & N. Krasnegor (Eds.), *Developmental neuroimaging: Mapping the development of brain and behavior.* New York: Academic Press.

Fisher, W. W., & Mazur, J. E. (1997). Basic and applied research on choice responding. *Journal of Applied Behavior Analysis, 30*, 387–410.

Fivush, R., Haden, C., & Adam, S. (1995). Structure and coherence of preschoolers' personal narratives over time: Implications for childhood amnesia. *Journal of Experimental Child Psychology, 60*, 32–56.

Flanagan, C. A., & Faison, N. (2001). Youth civic development: Implications of research for social policy and programs. *Social Policy Report of the Society for Research in Child Development, 15*(1), 1–14.

Flanagan, C. A., & Tucker, C. J. (1999). Adolescents' explanations for political issues: Concordance with their views of self and society. *Developmental Psychology, 35*, 1198–1209.

Flavell, J. H. (1994). Cognitive development: Past, present, and future. In R. D. Parke, P. A. Ornstein, J. J. Rieser, & C. Zahn-Waxler (Eds.), *A century of developmental psychology.* Washington, DC: American Psychological Association.

Flavell, J. H. (1996). Piaget's legacy. *Psychological Science, 7*, 200–203.

Flavell, J. H. (2000). Development of children's knowledge about the mental world. *International Journal of Behavioral Development, 24*(1), 15–23.

Flavell, J. H., Friedrichs, A. G., & Hoyt, J. D. (1970). Developmental changes in memorization processes. *Cognitive Psychology, 1*, 324–340.

Flavell, J. H., Green, F. L., & Flavell, E. R. (1995). Young children's knowledge about thinking. *Monographs of the Society for Research in Child Development, 60*(1, Serial No. 243).

Flavell, J. H., & Miller, P. H. (1998). Social cognition. In W. Damon (Series Ed.), D. Kuhn, & R. S. Siegler (Vol. Eds.), *Handbook of child psychology: Vol. 2. Cognition, perception, and language* (5th ed.). New York: Wiley.

Flavell, J. H., Miller, P. H., & Miller, S. A. (1993). *Cognitive development* (3rd ed.). Upper Saddle River, NJ: Prentice Hall.

Fletcher, K. L., & Bray, N. W. (1995). External and verbal strategies in children with and without mild mental retardation. *American Journal on Mental Retardation, 99*, 363–375.

Flood, W. A., Wilder, D. A., Flood, A. L., & Masuda, A. (2002). Peer-mediated reinforcement plus prompting as treatment for off-task behavior in children with attention deficit hyperactivity disorder. *Journal of Applied Behavior Analysis, 35*, 199–204.

Flynn, J. R. (1987). Massive IQ gains in 14 nations: What IQ tests really measure. *Psychological Bulletin, 101*, 171–191.

Flynn, J. R. (2003). Movies about intelligence: The limitations of g. *Current Directions in Psychological Science, 12*, 95–99.

Foos, P. W., & Fisher, R. P. (1988). Using tests as learning opportunities. *Journal of Educational Psychology, 80*, 179–183.

Ford, D. Y. (1996). *Reversing underachievement among gifted black students.* New York: Teachers College Press.

Ford, D. Y., & Harris, J. J. (1992). The American achievement ideology and achievement differentials among preadolescent gifted and nongifted African American males and females. *The Journal of Negro Education, 61*(1), 45–64.

Ford, M. E. (1992). *Motivating humans: Goals, emotions, and personal agency beliefs.* Newbury Park, CA: Sage.

Ford, M. E. (1996). Motivational opportunities and obstacles associated with social responsibility and caring behavior in school contexts. In J. Juvonen & K. R. Wentzel (Eds.), *Social motivation: Understanding children's school adjustment* (pp. 126–153). Cambridge, England: Cambridge University Press.

Ford, M. E., & Nichols, C. W. (1991). Using goal assessments to identify motivational patterns and facilitate behavioral regulation and achievement. In M. Maehr & P. R. Pintrich (Eds.), *Advances in motivation and achievement: Vol. 7. Goals and self-regulatory processes.* Greenwich, CT: JAI Press.

Fordham, S., & Ogbu, J. U. (1986). Black students' school success: Coping with "the burden of 'acting white.'" *The Urban Review, 18*, 176–206.

Forgas, J. P. (2000). The role of affect in social cognition. In J. Forgas (Ed.), *Feeling and thinking: The role of affect in social cognition* (pp. 1–28). New York: Cambridge University Press.

Forsyth, J. P., & Eifert, G. H. (1998). Phobic anxiety and panic: An integrative behavioral account of their origin and treatment. In J. J. Plaud & G. H. Eifert (Eds.), *From behavior theory to behavior therapy* (pp. 38–67). Needham Heights, MA: Allyn & Bacon.

Fosnot, C. T. (1996). Constructivism: A psychological theory of learning. In C. T. Fosnot (Ed.), *Constructivism: Theory, perspectives, and practice.* New York: Teachers College Press.

Foster-Johnson, L., Ferro, J., & Dunlap, G. (1994). Preferred curriculum activities and reduced problem behaviors in students with intellectual disabilities. *Journal of Applied Behavior Analysis, 27*, 493–504.

Fowler, S. A., & Baer, D. M. (1981). "Do I have to be good all day?" The timing of delayed reinforcement as a factor in generalization. *Journal of Applied Behavior Analysis, 14*, 13–24.

Fox, N. A., Henderson, H. A., Rubin, K. H., Calkins, S. D., & Schmidt, L. A. (2001). Continuity and discontinuity of behavioral inhibition and exuberance:

Psychophysical and behavioral influences across the first four years of life. *Child Development, 72,* 1–21.

Fox, P. W., & LeCount, J. (1991, April). *When more is less: Faculty misestimation of student learning.* Paper presented at the annual meeting of the American Educational Research Association, Chicago.

Frankenberger, K. D. (2000). Adolescent egocentrism: A comparison among adolescents and adults. *Journal of Adolescence, 23,* 343–354.

Frasier, M. M. (1989). Identification of gifted black students: Developing new perspectives. In C. J. Maker & S. W. Schiever (Eds.), *Critical issues in gifted education: Vol. 2. Defensible programs for cultural and ethnic minorities.* Austin, TX: Pro-Ed.

Frederiksen, J. R., & Collins, A. (1989). A systems approach to educational testing. *Educational Researcher, 18*(9), 27–32.

Frederiksen, N. (1984a). Implications of cognitive theory for instruction in problem-solving. *Review of Educational Research, 54,* 363–407.

Frederiksen, N. (1984b). The real test bias: Influences of testing on teaching and learning. *American Psychologist, 39,* 193–202.

Freedman, B. A. (2003, April). *Boys and literacy: Why boys? Which boys? Why now?* Paper presented at the annual meeting of the American Educational Research Association, Chicago.

Freedman, S. G. (1990). *Small victories: The real world of a teacher, her students, and their high school.* New York: Harper & Row.

Freeland, J. T., & Noell, G. H. (1999). Maintaining accurate math responses in elementary school students: The effects of delayed intermittent reinforcement and programming common stimuli. *Journal of Applied Behavior Analysis, 32,* 211–215.

Freeman, K. E., Gutman, L. M., & Midgley, C. (2002). Can achievement goal theory enhance our understanding of the motivation and performance of African American young adolescents? In C. Midgley (Ed.), *Goals, goal structures, and patterns of adaptive learning* (pp. 175–204). Mahwah, NJ: Erlbaum.

French, D. C., Jansen, E. A., & Pidada, S. (2002). United States and Indonesian children's and adolescents' reports of relational aggression by disliked peers. *Child Development, 73,* 1143–1150.

French, E. G. (1956). Motivation as a variable in work partner selection. *Journal of Abnormal and Social Psychology, 53,* 96–99.

Freund, L. (1990). Maternal regulation of children's problem solving behavior and its impact on children's performance. *Child Development, 61,* 113–126.

Friedel, M. (1993). *Characteristics of gifted/creative children.* Warwick, RI: National Foundation for Gifted and Creative Children.

Friedman, L. (1995). The space factor in mathematics: Gender differences. *Review of Educational Research, 65,* 22–50.

Friedrich, L. K., & Stein, A. H. (1973). Aggressive and pro-social television programs and the natural behavior of preschool children. *Society for Research in Child Development Monographs, 38* (Whole No. 151).

Frisbie, D. A., & Waltman, K. K. (1992). Developing a personal grading plan. *Educational Measurement: Issues and Practice, 11*(3), 35–42. Reprinted in K. M. Cauley, F. Linder, & J. H. McMillan (Eds.), (1994), *Educational psychology 94/95.* Guilford, CT: Dushkin.

Frost, J. L., Shin, D., & Jacobs, P. J. (1998). Physical environments and children's play. In O. N. Saracho & B. Spodek (Eds.), *Multiple perspectives on play in early childhood education.* Albany: State University of New York Press.

Frydenberg, E., & Lewis, R. (2000). Teaching coping to adolescents: When and to whom? *American Educational Research Journal, 37,* 727–745.

Fuchs, D., Fuchs, L. S., Mathes, P. G., & Simmons, D. C. (1997). Peer-assisted learning strategies: Making classrooms more responsive to diversity. *American Educational Research Journal, 34,* 174–206.

Fuchs, L. S., Fuchs, D., Hamlett, C. L., & Karns, K. (1998). High-achieving students' interactions and performance on complex mathematical tasks as a function of homogeneous and heterogeneous pairings. *American Educational Research Journal, 35,* 227–267.

Fuchs, L. S., Fuchs, D., Karns, K., Hamlett, C. L., Dutka, S., & Katzaroff, M. (1996). The relation between student ability and the quality and effectiveness of explanations. *American Educational Research Journal, 33,* 631–664.

Fuchs, L. S., Fuchs, D., Karns, K., Hamlett, C. L., Katzaroff, M., & Dutka, S. (1997). Effects of task-focused goals on low-achieving students with and without learning disabilities. *American Educational Research Journal, 34,* 513–543.

Fuchs, L. S., Fuchs, D., Prentice, K., Burch, M., Hamlett, C. L., Owen, R., Hosp, M., & Jancek, D. (2003). Explicitly teaching for transfer: Effects on third-grade students' mathematical problem solving. *Journal of Educational Psychology, 95,* 295–305.

Fueyo, V., & Bushell, D., Jr. (1998). Using number line procedures and peer tutoring to improve the mathematics computation of low-performing first graders. *Journal of Applied Behavior Analysis, 31,* 417–430.

Fujimura, N. (2001). Facilitating children's proportional reasoning: A model of reasoning processes and effects of intervention on strategy change. *Journal of Educational Psychology, 93,* 589–603.

Fuligni, A. J. (1998). The adjustment of children from immigrant families. *Current Directions in Psychological Science, 7,* 99–103.

Fuller, M. L. (2001). Multicultural concerns and classroom management. In C. A. Grant & M. L. Gomez, *Campus and classroom: Making schooling multicultural* (2nd ed., pp. 109–134). Upper Saddle River, NJ: Merrill/Prentice Hall.

Funder, D. C. (1991). Global traits: A neo-Allportian approach to personality. *Psychological Science, 2,* 31–39.

Furman, W., Brown, B. B., & Feiring, C. (Eds.). (1999). *The development of romantic relationships in adolescence..* Cambridge, England: Cambridge University Press.

Furman, W., & Buhrmester, D. (1992). Age and sex differences in perceptions of networks and personal relationships. *Child Development, 63,* 103–115.

Furman, W., & Simon, V. A. (1999). Cognitive representations of adolescent romantic relationships. In W. Furman, B. B. Brown, & C. Feiring (Eds.), *The development of romantic relationships in adolescence* (pp. 75–98). Cambridge, England: Cambridge University Press.

Furnham, A., & Mak, T. (1999). Sex-role stereotyping in television commercials: A review and comparison of fourteen studies done on five continents over 25 years. *Sex Roles, 41,* 413–437.

Furrer, C., & Skinner, E. (2003). Sense of relatedness as a factor in children's academic engagement and performance. *Journal of Educational Psychology, 95,* 148–162.

Gabriele, A. J., & Boody, R. M. (2001, April). *The influence of achievement goals on the constructive activity of low achievers during collaborative problem solving.* Paper presented at the annual meeting of the American Educational Research Association, Seattle, WA.

Gabriele, A. J., & Montecinos, C. (2001). Collaborating with a skilled peer: The influence of achievement goals and perceptions of partner's competence on the participation and learning of low-achieving students. *Journal of Experimental Education, 69,* 152–178.

Gage, N. L. (1991). The obviousness of social and educational research results. *Educational Researcher, 20*(1), 10–16.

Gagné, E. D. (1985). *The cognitive psychology of school learning.* Boston: Little, Brown.

Gagné, R. M. (1985). *The conditions of learning and theory of instruction* (4th ed.). New York: Holt, Rinehart & Winston.

Gagné, R. M., Briggs, L. J., & Wager, W. W. (1992). *Principles of instructional design* (4th ed.). Fort Worth, TX: Harcourt Brace Jovanovich.

Gaines, M. L., & Davis, M. (1990, April). *Accuracy of teacher prediction of elementary student achievement.* Paper presented at the annual meeting of the American Educational Research Association, Boston.

Galambos, N. L., Barker, E. T., & Almeida, D. M. (2003). Parents *do* matter: Trajectories of change in externalizing and internalizing problems in early adolescence. *Child Development, 74,* 578–594.

Gallagher, J. J. (1991). Personal patterns of underachievement. *Journal for the Education of the Gifted, 14,* 221–233.

Gallimore, R., & Goldenberg, C. (2001). Analyzing cultural models and settings to connect minority achievement and school improvement research. *Educational Psychologist, 36,* 45–56.

Gallimore, R., & Tharp, R. (1990). Teaching mind in society: Teaching, schooling, and literate discourse. In L. C. Moll (Ed.), *Vygotsky and education: Instructional implications and applications of sociohistorical psychology.* Cambridge, England: Cambridge University Press.

Gallini, J. (2000, April). *An investigation of self-regulation developments in early adolescence: A comparison between non- at-risk and at-risk students.* Paper presented at the annual meeting of the American Educational Research Association, New Orleans, LA.

Garbarino, J., Bradshaw, C. P., & Vorrasi, J. A. (2002). Mitigating the effects of gun violence on children and youth. *The Future of Children, 12*(2), 73–85.

García, E. E. (1992). "Hispanic" children: Theoretical, empirical, and related policy issues. *Educational Psychology Review, 4,* 69–93.

García, E. E. (1994). *Understanding and meeting the challenge of student cultural diversity.* Boston: Houghton Mifflin.

García, E. E. (1995). Educating Mexican American students: Past treatment and recent developments in theory, research, policy, and practice. In J. A. Banks & C. A. M. Banks (Eds.), *Handbook of research on multicultural education.* New York: Macmillan.

Gardner, H. (1983). *Frames of mind: The theory of multiple intelligences.* New York: Basic Books.

Gardner, H. (1995). Reflections on multiple intelligences: Myths and messages. *Phi Delta Kappan, 77,* 200–209.

Gardner, H. (1998, April). *Where to draw the line: The perils of new paradigms.* Paper presented at the annual meeting of the American Educational Research Association, San Diego, CA.

Gardner, H. (1999). *Intelligence reframed: Multiple intelligences for the 21st century.* New York: Basic Books.

Gardner, H. (2000). *The disciplined mind: Beyond facts and standardized tests, the K–12 education that every child deserves.* New York: Penguin Books.

Gardner, H., & Hatch, T. (1990). Multiple intelligences go to school: Educational implications of the theory of multiple intelligences. *Educational Researcher, 18*(8), 4–10.

Gardner, H., Torff, B., & Hatch, T. (1996). The age of innocence reconsidered: Preserving the best of the progressive traditions in psychology and education. In D. R. Olson & N. Torrance (Eds.), *The handbook of education and human development: New models of learning, teaching, and schooling.* Cambridge, MA: Blackwell.

Garhart, C., & Hannafin, M. J. (1986). The accuracy of cognitive monitoring during computer-based instruction. *Journal of Computer-Based Instruction, 13,* 88–93.

Garibaldi, A. M. (1992). Educating and motivating African American males to succeed. *The Journal of Negro Education, 61*(1), 4–11.

Garibaldi, A. M. (1993). Creating prescriptions for success in urban schools: Turning the corner on pathological explanations for academic failure. In T. M. Tomlinson (Ed.), *Motivating students to learn: Overcoming barriers to high achievement.* Berkeley, CA: McCutchan.

Garner, R. (1998). Epilogue: Choosing to learn or not-learn in school. *Educational Psychology Review, 10,* 227–237.

Garner, R., Alexander, P. A., Gillingham, M. G., Kulikowich, J. M., & Brown, R. (1991). Interest and learning from text. *American Educational Research Journal, 28,* 643–659.

Garner, R., Brown, R., Sanders, S., & Menke, D. J. (1992). "Seductive details" and learning from text. In

K. A. Renninger, S. Hidi, & A. Krapp (Eds.), *The role of interest in learning and development*. Mahwah, NJ: Erlbaum.

Garnier, H. E., Stein, J. A., & Jacobs, J. K. (1997). The process of dropping out of high school: A 19-year perspective. *American Educational Research Journal, 34*, 395–419.

Garrison, L. (1989). Programming for the gifted American Indian student. In C. J. Maker & S. W. Schiever (Eds.), *Critical issues in gifted education: Vol. 2. Defensible programs for cultural and ethnic minorities*. Austin, TX: Pro-Ed.

Gaskill, P. J. (2001, April). *Differential effects of reinforcement feedback and attributional feedback on second-graders' self-efficacy*. Paper presented at the annual meeting of the American Educational Research Association, Seattle, WA.

Gathercole, S. E., & Hitch, G. J. (1993). Developmental changes in short-term memory: A revised working memory perspective. In A. F. Collins, S. E. Gathercole, M. A. Conway, & P. E. Morris (Eds.), *Theories of memory*. Hove, England: Erlbaum.

Gaudry, E., & Bradshaw, G. D. (1971). The differential effect of anxiety on performance in progressive and terminal school examinations. In E. Gaudry & C. D. Spielberger (Eds.), *Anxiety and educational achievement*. Sydney, Australia: Wiley.

Gauntt, H. L. (1991, April). *The roles of prior knowledge of text structure and prior knowledge of content in the comprehension and recall of expository text*. Paper presented at the annual meeting of the American Educational Research Association, Chicago.

Gauvain, M. (1999). Everyday opportunities for the development of planning skills: Sociocultural and family influences. In A. Göncü (Ed.) *Children's engagement in the world: Sociocultural perspectives* (pp. 173–201). Cambridge, England: Cambridge University Press.

Gauvain, M. (2001). *The social context of cognitive development*. New York: Guilford Press.

Gavin, L. A., & Fuhrman, W. (1989). Age differences in adolescents' perceptions of their peer groups. *Developmental Psychology, 25*, 827–834.

Gay, J., & Cole, M. (1967). *The new mathematics and an old culture*. New York: Holt, Rinehart & Winston.

Gayford, C. (1992). Patterns of group behavior in open-ended problem solving in science classes of 15-year-old students in England. *International Journal of Science Education, 14*, 41–49.

Gaynor, J., & Millham, J. (1976). Student performance and evaluation under variant teaching and testing methods in a large college course. *Journal of Educational Psychology, 68*, 312–317.

Gazelle, H., & Ladd, G. W. (2003). Anxious solitude and peer exclusion: A diathesis-stress model of internalizing trajectories in childhood. *Child Development, 74*, 257–278.

Gearheart, B. R., Weishahn, M. W., & Gearheart, C. J. (1992). *The exceptional child in the regular classroom* (5th ed.). Upper Saddle River, NJ: Merrill/Prentice Hall.

Geary, D. C. (1998). What is the function of mind and brain? *Educational Psychology Review, 10*, 377–387.

Gelman, R., & Baillargeon, R. (1983). A review of some Piagetian concepts. In J. H. Flavell & E. M. Markman (Eds.), *Handbook of child psychology: Vol. 3. Cognitive development*. New York: Wiley.

Genova, W. J., & Walberg, H. J. (1984). Enhancing integration in urban high schools. In D. E. Bartz & M. L. Maehr (Eds.), *Advances in motivation and achievement: Vol 1. The effects of school desegregation on motivation and achievement*. Greenwich, CT: JAI Press.

Gentry, M., Gable, R. K., & Rizza, M. G. (2002). Students' perceptions of classroom activities: Are there grade-level and gender differences? *Journal of Educational Psychology, 94*, 539–544.

Gerst, M. S. (1971). Symbolic coding processes in observational learning. *Journal of Personality and Social Psychology, 19*, 7–17.

Gettinger, M. (1988). Methods of proactive classroom management. *School Psychology Review, 17*, 227–242.

Giaconia, R. M. (1988). Teacher questioning and wait-time (Doctoral dissertation, Stanford University, 1988). *Dissertation Abstracts International, 49*, 462A.

Giaconia, R. M., & Hedges, L. V. (1982). Identifying features of effective open education. *Review of Educational Research. 52*, 579–602.

Giangreco, M. F. (1997). Responses to Nietupski et al. *Journal of Special Education, 31*, 56–57.

Gibbs, J. C. (1995). The cognitive developmental perspective. In W. M. Kurtines & J. L. Gewirtz (Eds.), *Moral development: An introduction*. Boston: Allyn & Bacon.

Gick, M. L., & Holyoak, K. J. (1987). The cognitive basis of knowledge transfer. In S. M. Cormier & J. D. Hagman (Eds.), *Transfer of learning: Contemporary research and applications*. San Diego, CA: Academic Press.

Gillberg, I. C., & Coleman, M. (1996). Autism and medical disorders: A review of the literature. *Developmental Medicine and Child Neurology, 38*, 191–202.

Gillies, R. M. (2003). The behaviors, interactions, and perceptions of junior high school students during small-group learning. *Journal of Educational Psychology, 95*, 137–147.

Gillies, R. M., & Ashman, A. D. (1998). Behavior and interactions of children in cooperative groups in lower and middle elementary grades. *Journal of Educational Psychology, 90*, 746–757.

Gilligan, C. F. (1982). *In a different voice*. Cambridge, MA: Harvard University Press.

Gilligan, C. F. (1985, March). Keynote address. Conference on Women and Moral Theory, Stony Brook, NY.

Gilligan, C. F. (1987). Moral orientation and moral development. In E. F. Kittay & D. T. Meyers (Eds.), *Women and moral theory*. Totowa, NJ: Rowman & Littlefield.

Gilligan, C., & Attanucci, J. (1988). Two moral orientations: Gender differences and similarities. *Merrill-Palmer Quarterly, 34*, 223–237.

Gilliland, H. (1988). Discovering and emphasizing the positive aspects of the culture. In H. Gilliland & J. Reyhner (Eds.), *Teaching the Native American*. Dubuque, IA: Kendall/Hunt.

Gilpin, L. (1968). *The enduring Navaho*. Austin: University of Texas Press.

Ginsberg, D., Gottman, J. M., & Parker, J. G. (1986). The importance of friendship. In J. M. Gottman & J. G. Parker (Eds.), *Conversations of friends: Speculations on affective development* (pp. 3–48). Cambridge, England: Cambridge University Press.

Girotto, V., & Light, P. (1993). The pragmatic bases of children's reasoning. In P. Light & G. Butterworth (Eds.), *Context and cognition: Ways of learning and knowing*. Mahwah, NJ: Erlbaum.

Glanzer, M., & Nolan, S. D. (1986). Memory mechanisms in text comprehension. In G. H. Bower (Ed.), *The psychology of learning and motivation: Advances in research and theory* (Vol. 20). San Diego, CA: Academic Press.

Glaser, D. (2000). Child abuse and neglect and the brain: A review. *Journal of Child Psychology and Psychiatry and Allied Disciplines, 41*, 97–116.

Glass, A. L., & Holyoak, K. J. (1975). Alternative conceptions of semantic memory. *Cognition, 3*, 313–339.

Glass, A. L., Holyoak, K. J., & Santa, J. L. (1979). *Cognition*. Reading, MA: Addison-Wesley.

Glasser, W. (1969). *Schools without failure*. New York: Harper & Row.

Glover, J. A. (1989). The "testing" phenomenon: Not gone but nearly forgotten. *Journal of Educational Psychology, 81*, 392–399.

Glover, J. A., Ronning, R. R., & Reynolds, C. R. (Eds.). (1989). *Handbook of creativity*. New York: Plenum Press.

Glucksberg, S., & Krauss, R. M. (1967). What do people say after they have learned to talk? Studies of the development of referential communication. *Merrill-Palmer Quarterly, 13*, 309–316.

Glynn, S. M., Yeany, R. H., & Britton, B. K. (1991). A constructive view of learning science. In S. M. Glynn, R. H. Yeany, & B. K. Britton (Eds.), *The psychology of learning science*. Mahwah, NJ: Erlbaum.

Gnepp, J. (1989). Children's use of personal information to understand other people's feelings. In C. Saarni & P. L. Harris (Eds.), *Children's understanding of emotion*. Cambridge, England: Cambridge University Press.

Goddard, R. D. (2001). Collective efficacy: A neglected construct in the study of schools and student achievement. *Journal of Educational Psychology, 93*, 467–476.

Goddard, R. D., Hoy, W. K., & Woolfolk Hoy, A. (2000). Collective teacher efficacy: Its meaning, measure, and impact on student achievement. *American Educational Research Journal, 37*, 479–507.

Goldenberg, C. (1992). The limits of expectations: A case for case knowledge about teacher expectancy effects. *American Educational Research Journal, 29*, 517–544.

Goldenberg, C. (2001). Making schools work for low-income families in the 21st century. In S. B. Neuman & D. K. Dickinson (Eds.), *Handbook of early literacy research* (pp. 211–231). New York: Guilford Press.

Goldenberg, C., Gallimore, R., Reese, L., & Garnier, H. (2001). Cause or effect? A longitudinal study of immigrant Latino parents' aspirations and expectations, and their children's school performance. *American Educational Research Journal, 38*, 547–582.

Goldstein, N. E., Arnold, D. H., Rosenberg, J. L., Stowe, R. M., & Ortiz, C. (2001). Contagion of aggression in day care classrooms as a function of peer and teacher responses. *Journal of Educational Psychology, 93*, 708–719.

Gollnick, D. M., & Chinn, P. C. (2002). *Multicultural education in a pluralistic society* (6th ed.). Upper Saddle River, NJ: Merrill/Prentice Hall.

Good, T. L., & Brophy, J. E. (1994). *Looking in classrooms* (6th ed.). New York: HarperCollins.

Good, T. L., McCaslin, M. M., & Reys, B. J. (1992). Investigating work groups to promote problem solving in mathematics. In J. Brophy (Ed.), *Advances in research on teaching: Vol. 3. Planning and managing learning tasks and activities*. Greenwich, CT: JAI Press.

Good, T. L., & Nichols, S. L. (2001). Expectancy effects in the classroom: A special focus on improving the reading performance of minority students in first-grade classrooms. *Educational Psychologist, 36*, 113–126.

Goodenow, C. (1993). Classroom belonging among early adolescent students: Relationships to motivation and achievement. *Journal of Early Adolescence, 13*, 21–43.

Goodman, C. S., & Tessier-Lavigne, M. (1997). Molecular mechanisms of axon guidance and target recognition. In W. M. Cowan, T. M. Jessell, & S. L. Zipursky (Eds.), *Molecular and cellular approaches to neural development* (pp. 108–137). New York: Oxford University Press.

Goodnow, J. J. (1992). *Parental belief systems: The psychological consequences for children*. Mahwah, NJ: Erlbaum.

Gootman, M. E. (1998). Effective in-house suspension. *Educational Leadership, 56*(1), 39–41.

Gopnik, A., & Meltzoff, A. N. (1997). *Words, thoughts and theories*. Cambridge, MA: MIT Press.

Gopnik, M. (Ed.). (1997). *The inheritance and innateness of grammars*. New York: Oxford University Press.

Gottfredson, D. C. (2001). *Schools and delinquency*. Cambridge, England: Cambridge University Press.

Gottfredson, D. C., Fink, C. M., & Graham, N. (1994). Grade retention and problem behavior. *American Educational Research Journal, 31*, 761–784.

Gottfredson, G. D., & Gottfredson, D. C. (1985). *Victimization in schools*. New York: Plenum Press.

Gottfredson, L. S. (1981). Circumscription and compromise: A developmental theory of occupational aspirations. *Journal of Counseling Psychology Monograph, 28*, 545–579.

Gottfried, A. E. (1990). Academic intrinsic motivation in young elementary school children. *Journal of Educational Psychology, 82*, 525–538.

Gottfried, A. E., Fleming, J. S., & Gottfried, A. W. (1994). Role of parental motivational practices in children's academic intrinsic motivation and achievement. *Journal of Educational Psychology, 86*, 104–113.

Gottfried, A. E., Fleming, J. S., & Gottfried, A. W. (2001). Continuity of academic intrinsic motivation from childhood through late adolescence: A longitudinal study. *Journal of Educational Psychology, 93,* 3–13.

Gottfried, A. W., Gottfried, A. E., Bathurst, K., & Guerin, D. W. (1994). *Gifted IQ: Early developmental aspects.* New York: Plenum Press.

Gottlieb, G. (2000). Environmental and behavioral influences on gene activity. *Current Directions in Psychological Science, 9,* 93–97.

Gottman, J. M. (1986). The world of coordinated play: Same- and cross-sex friendship in young children. In J. M. Gottman & J. G. Parker (Eds.), *Conversations of friends: Speculations on affective development* (pp. 139–191). Cambridge, England: Cambridge University Press.

Gottman, J. M., & Mettetal, G. (1986). Speculations about social and affective development: Friendship and acquaintanceship through adolescence. In J. M. Gottman & J. G. Parker (Eds.), *Conversations of friends: Speculations on affective development* (pp. 192–237). Cambridge, England: Cambridge University Press.

Gould, E., Beylin, A., Tanapat, P., Reeves, A., & Shors, T. J. (1999). Learning enhances adult neurogenesis in the hippocampal formation. *Nature Neuroscience, 2,* 260–265.

Grabe, M. (1986). Attentional processes in education. In G. D. Phye & T. Andre (Eds.), *Cognitive classroom learning: Understanding, thinking, and problem solving.* San Diego, CA: Academic Press.

Graesser, A., & Person, N. K. (1994). Question asking during tutoring. *American Educational Research Journal, 31,* 104–137.

Graham, S. (1989). Motivation in Afro-Americans. In G. L. Berry & J. K. Asamen (Eds.), *Black students: Psychosocial issues and academic achievement.* Newbury Park, CA: Sage.

Graham, S. (1990). Communicating low ability in the classroom: Bad things good teachers sometimes do. In S. Graham & V. S. Folkes (Eds.), *Attribution theory: Applications to achievement, mental health, and interpersonal conflict.* Mahwah, NJ: Erlbaum.

Graham, S. (1991). A review of attribution theory in achievement contexts. *Educational Psychology Review, 3,* 5–39.

Graham, S. (1994). Motivation in African Americans. *Review of Educational Research, 64,* 55–117.

Graham, S. (1997). Using attribution theory to understand social and academic motivation in African American youth. *Educational Psychologist, 32,* 21–34.

Graham, S., & Golen, S. (1991). Motivational influences on cognition: Task involvement, ego involvement, and depth of information processing. *Journal of Educational Psychology, 83,* 187–194.

Graham, S., & Harris, K. R. (1996). Addressing problems in attention, memory, and executive functioning. In G. R. Lyon & N. A. Krasnegor (Eds.), *Attention, memory, and executive function* (pp. 349–365). Baltimore: Brookes.

Graham, S., Harris, K. R., & Fink, B. (2000). Is handwriting causally related to learning to write? Treatment of handwriting problems in beginning writers. *Journal of Educational Psychology, 92,* 620–633.

Graham, S., & Hudley, C. (1994). Attributions of aggressive and nonaggressive African-American male early adolescents: A study of construct accessibility. *Developmental Psychology, 30,* 365–373.

Graham, S., & Weiner, B. (1996). Theories and principles of motivation. In D. C. Berliner & R. C. Calfee (Eds.), *Handbook of educational psychology.* New York: Macmillan.

Grandin, T. (1995). *Thinking in pictures and other reports of my life with autism.* New York: Random House.

Granger, D. A., Whalen, C. K., Henker, B., & Cantwell, C. (1996). ADHD boys' behavior during structured classroom social activities: Effects of social demands, teacher proximity, and methylphenidate. *Journal of Attention Disorders, 1*(1), 16–30.

Grant, C. A., & Gomez, M. L. (2001). *Campus and classroom: Making schooling multicultural* (2nd ed.). Upper Saddle River, NJ: Merrill/Prentice Hall.

Gray, C., & Garaud, J. D. (1993). Social stories: Improving responses of students with autism with accurate social information. *Focus on Autistic Behavior, 8,* 1–10.

Gray, W. D., & Orasanu, J. M. (1987). Transfer of cognitive skills. In S. M. Cormier & J. D. Hagman (Eds.), *Transfer of learning: Contemporary research and applications.* San Diego, CA: Academic Press.

Green, L., Fry, A. F., & Myerson, J. (1994). Discounting of delayed rewards: A life-span comparison. *Psychological Science, 5,* 33–36.

Greenberg, M. T., Weissberg, R. P., O'Brien, M. U., Zins, J. E., Fredericks, L., Resnik, H., & Elias, M. J. (2003). Enhancing school-based prevention and youth development through coordinated social, emotional, and academic learning. *American Psychologist, 58,* 466–474.

Greene, B. A. (1994, April). *Instruction to enhance comprehension of unfamiliar text: Should it focus on domain-specific or strategy knowledge?* Paper presented at the annual meeting of the American Educational Research Association, New Orleans, LA.

Greenfield, P. M. (1994). Independence and interdependence as developmental scripts: Implications for theory, research, and practice. In P. M. Greenfield & R. R. Cocking (Eds.), *Cross-cultural roots of minority child development.* Mahwah, NJ: Erlbaum.

Greeno, J. G. (1997). On claims that answer the wrong questions. *Educational Researcher, 26*(1), 5–17.

Greenough, W. T., Black, J. E., & Wallace, C. S. (1987). Experience and brain development. *Child Development, 58,* 539–559.

Greenspan, S., & Granfield, J. M. (1992). Reconsidering the construct of mental retardation: Implications of a model of social competence. *American Journal of Mental Retardation, 96,* 442–453.

Greenwood, C. R. (1991). Classwide peer tutoring: Longitudinal effects on the reading, language, and mathematics achievement of at-risk students. *Journal of Reading, Writing, and Learning Disabilities International, 7*(2), 105–123.

Greenwood, C. R., Carta, J. J., & Hall, R. V. (1988). The use of peer tutoring strategies in classroom management and educational instruction. *School Psychology Review, 17,* 258–275.

Gregg, M., & Leinhardt, G. (1994, April). *Constructing geography.* Paper presented at the annual meeting of the American Educational Research Association, New Orleans, LA.

Gresham, F. M., & MacMillan, D. L. (1997). Social competence and affective characteristics of students with mild disabilities. *Review of Educational Research, 67,* 377–415.

Griffin, M. M., & Griffin, B. W. (1994, April). *Some can get there from here: Situated learning, cognitive style, and map skills.* Paper presented at the annual meeting of the American Educational Research Association, New Orleans, LA.

Griffin, S. A., Case, R., & Capodilupo, A. (1995). Teaching for understanding: The importance of the central conceptual structures in the elementary mathematics curriculum. In A. McKeough, J. Lupart, & A. Marini (Eds.), *Teaching for transfer: Fostering generalization in learning.* Mahwah, NJ: Erlbaum.

Grinberg, D., & McLean-Heywood, D. (1999). *Perceptions of behavioural competence in depressed and non-depressed children with behavioural difficulties.* Paper presented at the annual meeting of the American Educational Research Association, Montreal, Canada.

Grissmer, D. W., Williamson, S., Kirby, S. N., & Berends, M. (1998). Exploring the rapid rise in Black achievement scores in the United States (1970–1990). In U. Neisser (Ed.), *The rising curve: Long-term gains in IQ and related measures* (pp. 251–285). Washington, DC: American Psychological Association.

Griswold, K. S., & Pessar, L. F. (2000). Management of bipolar disorder. *American Family Physician, 62,* 1343–1356.

Grodzinsky, G. M., & Diamond, R. (1992). Frontal lobe functioning in boys with attention-deficit hyperactivity disorder. *Developmental Neuropsychology, 8,* 427–445.

Grolnick, W. S., & Ryan, R. M. (1987). Autonomy in children's learning: An experimental and individual difference investigation. *Journal of Personality and Social Psychology, 52,* 890–898.

Gronlund, N. E. (1993). *How to make achievement tests and assessments* (5th ed.). Needham Heights, MA: Allyn & Bacon.

Gronlund, N. E. (2000). *How to write and use instructional objectives* (6th ed.). Upper Saddle River, NJ: Merrill/Prentice Hall.

Gronlund, N. E. (2004). *Writing instructional objectives for teaching and assessment* (7th ed.). Upper Saddle River, NJ: Merrill/Prentice Hall.

Grossman, H. L. (1994). *Classroom behavior management in a diverse society.* Mountain View, CA: Mayfield.

Grusec, J. E., & Redler, E. (1980). Attribution, reinforcement, and altruism. *Developmental Psychology, 16,* 525–534.

Guay, F., Boivin, M., & Hodges, E. V. E. (1999). Social comparison processes and academic achievement: The dependence of the development of self-evaluations on friends' performance. *Journal of Educational Psychology, 91,* 564–568.

Guay, F., Marsh, H. W. & Boivin, M. (2003). Academic self-concept and academic achievement: Developmental perspectives on their causal ordering. *Journal of Educational Psychology, 95,* 124–136.

Guerra, N. G., Huesmann, L. R., & Spindler, A. (2003). Community violence exposure, social cognition, and aggression among urban elementary school children. *Child Development, 74,* 1561–1576.

Guerra, N. G., & Slaby, R. G. (1990). Cognitive mediators of aggression in adolescent offenders: 2. Intervention. *Developmental Psychology, 26,* 269–277.

Guess, D., Roberts, S., Siegel-Causey, E., & Rues, J. (1995). Replication and extended analysis of behavior state, environmental events, and related variables among individuals with profound disabilities. *American Journal on Mental Retardation, 100,* 36–51.

Guinee, K. (2003, April). *Comparison of second-graders' narrative stories written using paper-and-pencil and a multimedia computer-based writing tool.* Paper presented at the annual meeting of the American Educational Research Association, Chicago.

Gulley, V., Northup, J., Hupp, S., Spera, S., LeVelle, J., & Ridgway, A. (2003). Sequential evaluation of behavioral treatments and methylphenidate dosage for children with attention deficit hyperactivity disorder. *Journal of Applied Behavior Analysis, 36,* 375–378.

Gunstone, R. F. (1994). The importance of specific science content in the enhancement of metacognition. In P. J. Fensham, R. F. Gunstone, & R. T. White (Eds.), *The content of science: A constructivist approach to its teaching and learning.* London: Falmer Press.

Guskey, T. R. (1985). *Implementing mastery learning.* Belmont, CA: Wadsworth.

Guskey, T. R. (1994, April). *Outcome-based education and mastery learning: Clarifying the differences.* Paper presented at the annual meeting of the American Educational Research Association, New Orleans, LA.

Guskey, T. R., & Sparks, D. (2002, April). *Linking professional development to improvements in student learning.* Paper presented at the annual meeting of the American Educational Research Association, New Orleans, LA.

Gustafsson, J., & Undheim, J. O. (1996). Individual differences in cognitive functions. In D. C. Berliner & R. C. Calfee (Eds.), *Handbook of educational psychology.* New York: Macmillan.

Guthrie, P. (2001). "Catching sense" and the meaning of belonging on a South Carolina Sea island. In S. S. Walker (Ed.), *African roots/American cultures: Africa in the creation of the Americas* (pp. 275–283). Lanham, MD: Rowman & Littlefield.

Gutiérrez, K. D., & Rogoff, B. (2003). Cultural ways of learning: Individual traits or repertoires of practice. *Educational Researcher, 32*(5), 19–25.

Guzzetti, B. J., Snyder, T. E., Glass, G. V., & Gamas, W. S. (1993). Promoting conceptual change in science: A comparative meta-analysis of instructional interventions from reading education and science education. *Reading Research Quarterly, 28,* 117–159.

Hacker, D. J. (1998a). Definitions and empirical foundations. In D. J. Hacker, J. Dunlosky, & A. C. Graesser (Eds.), *Metacognition in educational theory and practice* (pp. 1–23). Mahwah, NJ: Erlbaum.

Hacker, D. J. (1998b). Self-regulated comprehension during normal reading. In D. J. Hacker, J. Dunlosky, & A. C. Graesser (Eds.), *Metacognition in educational theory and practice* (pp. 165–191). Mahwah, NJ: Erlbaum.

Hacker, D. J., Bol, L., Horgan, D. D., & Rakow, E. A. (2000). Test prediction and performance in a classroom context. *Journal of Educational Psychology, 92*, 160–170.

Hacker, D. J., & Tenent, A. (2002). Implementing reciprocal teaching in the classroom: Overcoming obstacles and making modifications. *Journal of Educational Psychology, 94*, 699–718.

Hadaway, N. L., Florez, V., Larke, P. J., & Wiseman, D. (1993). Teaching in the midst of diversity: How do we prepare? In M. J. O'Hair & S. J. Odell (Eds.), *Diversity and teaching: Teacher education yearbook I*. Fort Worth, TX: Harcourt Brace Jovanovich.

Haenan, J. (1996). Piotr Gal'perin's criticism and extension of Lev Vygotsky's work. *Journal of Russian and East European Psychology, 34*(2), 54–60.

Hagen, J. W., & Stanovich, K. G. (1977). Memory: Strategies of acquisition. In R. V. Kail, Jr., & J. W. Hagen (Eds.), *Perspectives on the development of memory and cognition*. Mahwah, NJ: Erlbaum.

Hagger, M. S., Chatzisarantis, N. L. D., Culverhouse, T., & Biddle, S. J. H. (2003). The processes by which perceived autonomy support in physical education promotes leisure-time physical activity intentions and behavior: A trans-contextual model. *Journal of Educational Psychology, 95*, 784–795.

Hagtvet, K. A., & Johnsen, T. B. (Eds.). (1992). *Advances in test anxiety research* (Vol. 7). Amsterdam: Swets & Zeitlinger.

Hahn, H. (1989). The politics of special education. In D. K. Lipsky & A. Gartner (Eds.), *Beyond separate education: Quality education for all*. Baltimore: Brookes.

Haier, R. J. (2001). PET studies of learning and individual differences. In J. L. McClelland & R. S. Siegler (Eds.), *Mechanisms of cognitive development: Behavioral and neural perspectives* (pp. 123–145). Mahwah, NJ: Erlbaum.

Hakuta, K. (2001). A critical period for second language acquisition? In D. B. Bailey, Jr., J. T. Bruer, F. J. Symons, & J. W. Lichtman (Eds.), *Critical thinking about critical periods* (pp. 193–205). Baltimore: Brookes.

Hakuta, K., Bialystok, E., & Wiley, E. (2003). Critical evidence: A test of the critical-period hypothesis for second-language acquisition. *Psychological Science, 14*, 31–38.

Hale, G. A. (1983). Students' predictions of prose forgetting and the effects of study strategies. *Journal of Educational Psychology, 75*, 708–715.

Hale-Benson, J. E. (1986). *Black children: Their roots, culture, and learning styles*. Baltimore: Johns Hopkins University Press.

Halford, G. S. (1989). Cognitive processing capacity and learning ability: An integration of two areas. *Learning and Individual Differences, 1*, 125–153.

Hall, R. H., & O'Donnell, A. (1994, April). *Alternative materials for learning: Cognitive and affective outcomes of learning from knowledge maps*. Paper presented at the annual meeting of the American Educational Research Association, New Orleans, LA.

Hallenbeck, M. J. (1996). The cognitive strategy in writing: Welcome relief for adolescents with learning disabilities. *Learning Disabilities Research and Practice, 11*, 107–119.

Haller, E. P., Child, D. A., & Walberg, H. J. (1988). Can comprehension be taught? A quantitative synthesis of "metacognitive" studies. *Educational Researcher, 17*(9), 5–8.

Hallinan, M. T., & Teixeira, R. A. (1987). Opportunities and constraints: Black-white differences in the formation of interracial friendships. *Child Development, 58*, 1358–1371.

Hallowell, E. (1996). *When you worry about the child you love*. New York: Simon and Schuster.

Halpern, D. F. (1992). *Sex differences in cognitive abilities* (2nd ed.). Mahwah, NJ: Erlbaum.

Halpern, D. F. (1997a). *Critical thinking across the curriculum: A brief edition of thought and knowledge*. Mahwah, NJ: Erlbaum.

Halpern, D. F. (1997b). Sex differences in intelligence: Implications for education. *American Psychologist, 52*, 1091–1102.

Halpern, D. F. (1998). Teaching critical thinking for transfer across domains. *American Psychologist, 53*, 449–455.

Halpern, D. F., & LaMay, M. L. (2000). The smarter sex: A critical review of sex differences in intelligence. *Educational Psychology Review, 12*, 229–246.

Halpin, G., & Halpin, G. (1982). Experimental investigations of the effects of study and testing on student learning, retention, and ratings of instruction. *Journal of Educational Psychology, 74*, 32–38.

Halvorsen, A. T., & Sailor, W. (1990). Integration of students with severe and profound disabilities: A review of research. In R. Gaylord-Ross (Ed.), *Issues and research in special education* (Vol. 1, pp. 110–172). New York: Teachers College Press.

Hambleton, R. K. (1996). Advances in assessment models, methods, and practices. In D. C. Berliner & R. C. Calfee (Eds.), *Handbook of educational psychology*. New York: Macmillan.

Hamers, J. H. M., & Ruijssenaars, A. J. J. M. (1997). Assessing classroom learning potential. In G. D. Phye (Ed.), *Handbook of academic learning: Construction of knowledge*. San Diego, CA: Academic Press.

Hamman, D., Berthelot, J., Saia, J., & Crowley, E. (2000). Teachers' coaching of learning and its relation to students' strategic learning. *Journal of Educational Psychology, 92*, 342–348.

Hamman, D., Shell, D. F., Droesch, D., Husman, J., Handwerk, M., Park, Y., & Oppenheim, N. (1995, April). *Middle school readers' on-line cognitive processes: Influence of subject-matter knowledge and interest during reading*. Paper presented at the annual meeting of the American Educational Research Association, San Francisco.

Hammer, D. (1997). Discovery learning and discovery teaching. *Cognition and Instruction, 15*, 485–529.

Hamp-Lyons, L. (1992). Holistic writing assessment for L.E.P. students. In *Focus on evaluation and measurement* (Vol. 2). Washington, DC: U.S. Department of Education.

Hampton, J. A. (1981). An investigation of the nature of abstract concepts. *Memory and Cognition, 9*, 149–156.

Hanich, L. B., Jordan, N. C., Kaplan, D., & Dick, J. (2001). Performance across different areas of mathematical cognition in children with learning difficulties. *Journal of Educational Psychology, 93*, 615–626.

Hansen, J., & Pearson, P. D. (1983). An instructional study: Improving the inferential comprehension of good and poor fourth-grade readers. *Journal of Educational Psychology, 75*, 821–829.

Hardre, P. L., & Reeve, J. (2003). A motivational model of rural students' intentions to persist in, versus drop out of, high school. *Journal of Educational Psychology, 95*, 347–356.

Hardy, M. S. (2002). Behavior-oriented approaches to reducing youth gun violence. *The Future of Children, 12*(2), 101–117.

Hardy, R. (1996). Performance assessment: Examining the costs. In M. B. Kane & R. Mitchell (Eds.), *Implementing performance assessment: Promises, problems, and challenges* (pp. 107–117). Mahwah, NJ: Erlbaum.

Hareli, S., & Weiner, B. (2002). Social emotions and personality inferences: A scaffold for a new direction in the study of achievement motivation. *Educational Psychologist, 37*, 183–193.

Harlow, H. F., & Zimmerman, R. R. (1959). Affectional responses in the infant monkey. *Science, 130*, 421–432.

Harmon-Jones, E. (2001). The role of affect in cognitive-dissonance processes. In J. P. Forgas (Ed.), *Handbook of affect and social cognition* (pp. 237–255). Mahwah, NJ: Erlbaum.

Harnishfeger, K. K. (1995). The development of cognitive inhibition: Theories, definitions, and research evidence. In F. N. Dempster & C. J. Brainerd (Eds.), *Interference and inhibition in cognition*. San Diego, CA: Academic Press.

Harp, S. F., & Mayer, R. E. (1998). How seductive details do their damage: A theory of cognitive interest in science learning. *Journal of Educational Psychology, 90*, 414–434.

Harris, A. C. (1986). *Child development*. St. Paul, MN: West.

Harris, C. R. (1991). Identifying and serving the gifted new immigrant. *Teaching Exceptional Children, 23*(4), 26–30.

Harris, J. R. (1995). Where is the child's environment? A group socialization theory of development. *Psychological Review, 102*, 458–489.

Harris, J. R. (1998). *The nurture assumption: Why children turn out the way they do*. New York: Free Press.

Harris, K. R. (1982). Cognitive-behavior modification: Application with exceptional students. *Focus on Exceptional Children, 15*, 1–16.

Harris, K. R. (1986). Self-monitoring of attentional behavior versus self-monitoring of productivity: Effects of on-task behavior and academic response rate among learning disabled children. *Journal of Applied Behavior Analysis, 19*, 417–423.

Harris, K. R., & Alexander, P. A. (1998). Integrated, constructivist education: Challenge and reality. *Educational Psychology Review, 10*, 115–127.

Harris, M. (1992). *Language experience and early language development: From input to uptake*. Hove, England: Erlbaum.

Harris, M. B. (1997). Preface: Images of the invisible minority. In M. B. Harris (Ed.), *School experiences of gay and lesbian youth: The invisible minority* (pp. xiv–xxii). Binghamton, NY: Harrington Park Press.

Harris, M. J., & Rosenthal, R. (1985). Mediation of interpersonal expectancy effects: 31 meta-analyses. *Psychological Bulletin, 97*, 363–386.

Harris, R. J. (1977). Comprehension of pragmatic implications in advertising. *Journal of Applied Psychology, 62*, 603–608.

Hart, C. H., Ladd, G. W., & Burleson, B. (1990). Children's expectations of the outcomes of social strategies: Relations with sociometric status and maternal disciplinary styles. *Child Development, 61*, 127–137.

Hart, D. (1988). The adolescent self-concept in social context. In D. K. Lapsley & F. C. Power (Eds.), *Self, ego, and identity: Integrative approaches* (pp. 71–90). New York: Springer-Verlag.

Hart, D., Atkins, R., & Fegley, S. (2003). Personality and development in childhood: A person-centered approach. *Monographs of the Society for Research in Child Development, 68*(1, Serial No. 272).

Hart, D., & Fegley, S. (1995). Prosocial behavior and caring in adolescence: Relations to self-understanding and social judgment. *Child Development, 66*. 1346–1359.

Hart, E. L., Lahey, B. B., Loeber, R., Applegate, B., & Frick, P. J. (1995). Developmental changes in attention-deficit hyperactivity disorder in boys: A four-year longitudinal study. *Journal of Abnormal Child Psychology, 23*, 729–750.

Hart, E. R., & Speece, D. L. (1998). Reciprocal teaching goes to college: Effects for postsecondary students at risk for academic failure. *Journal of Educational Psychology, 90*, 670–681.

Harter, S. (1975). Mastery motivation and the need for approval in older children and their relationship to social desirability response tendencies. *Developmental Psychology, 11*, 186–196.

Harter, S. (1978). Pleasure derived from challenge and the effects of receiving grades on children's difficulty level choices. *Child Development, 49*, 788–799.

Harter, S. (1983). Children's understanding of multiple emotions: A cognitive-developmental approach. In W. F. Overton (Ed.), *The relationship between social and cognitive development*. Mahwah, NJ: Erlbaum.

Harter, S. (1988). The construction and conservation of the self: James and Cooley revisited. In D. K. Lapsley & F. C. Power (Eds.), *Self, ego, and identity: Integrative approaches* (pp. 43–69). New York: Springer-Verlag.

Harter, S. (1990). Causes, correlates, and the functional role of global self-worth: A life-span perspective. In

R. J. Sternberg & J. Kolligian, Jr. (Eds.), *Competence considered.* New Haven, CT: Yale University Press.

Harter, S. (1992). The relationship between perceived competence, affect, and motivational orientation within the classroom: Processes and patterns of change. In A. K. Boggiano & T. S. Pittman (Eds.), *Achievement and motivation: A social-developmental perspective.* Cambridge, England: Cambridge University Press.

Harter, S. (1996). Teacher and classmate influences on scholastic motivation, self-esteem, and level of voice in adolescents. In J. Juvonen & K. Wentzel (Eds.), *Social motivation: Understanding children's school adjustment.* New York: Cambridge University Press.

Harter, S. (1999). *The construction of the self: A developmental perspective.* New York: Guilford Press.

Harter, S., & Jackson, B. J. (1992). Trait vs. nontrait conceptualizations of intrinsic/ extrinsic motivational orientation. *Motivation and Emotion, 16,* 209–230.

Harter, S., & Whitesell, N. R. (1989). Developmental changes in children's understanding of single, multiple, and blended emotion concepts. In C. Saarni & P. Harris (Eds.), *Children's understanding of emotion* (pp. 81–116). Cambridge, England: Cambridge University Press.

Harter, S., Whitesell, N. R., & Junkin, L. J. (1998). Similarities and differences in domain-specific and global self-evaluations of learning-disabled, behaviorally disordered, and normally achieving adolescents. *American Educational Research Journal, 35,* 653–680.

Harter, S., Whitesell, N. R., & Kowalski, P. (1992). Individual differences in the effects of educational transitions on young adolescents' perceptions of competence and motivational orientation. *American Educational Research Journal, 29,* 777–807.

Hartley, J., & Trueman, M. (1982). The effects of summaries on the recall of information from prose: Five experimental studies. *Human Learning, 1,* 63–82.

Hartley, K., & Bendixen, L. D. (2001). Educational research in the Internet age: Examining the role of individual characteristics. *Educational Researcher, 30*(9), 22–26.

Hartup, W. W. (1983). Peer relations. In E. M. Hetherington (Ed.), *Handbook of child psychology: Vol. 4. Socialization, personality, and social development* (4th ed., pp. 103–196). New York: Wiley.

Hartup, W. W. (1989). Social relationships and their developmental significance. *American Psychologist, 44,* 120–126.

Hartup, W. W. (1992). Friendships and their developmental significance. In H. McGurk (Ed.), *Contemporary issues in childhood social development.* London: Routledge.

Harwood, R. L., Miller, J. G., & Irizarry, N. L. (1995). *Culture and attachment: Perceptions of the child in context.* New York: Guilford Press.

Haseman, A. L. (1999, April). *Cross talk: How students' epistemological beliefs impact the learning process in a constructivist course.* Paper presented at the annual meeting of the American Educational Research Association, Montreal, Canada.

Hatano, G., & Inagaki, K. (1991). Sharing cognition through collective comprehension activity. In L. B. Resnick, J. M. Levine, & S. D. Teasley (Eds.), *Perspectives on socially shared cognition.* Washington, DC: American Psychological Association.

Hatano, G., & Inagaki, K. (1993). Desituating cognition through the construction of conceptual knowledge. In P. Light & G. Butterworth (Eds.), *Context and cognition: Ways of learning and knowing.* Mahwah, NJ: Erlbaum.

Hatano, G., & Inagaki, K. (1996). Cognitive and cultural factors in the acquisition of intuitive biology. In D. R. Olson & N. Torrance (Eds.), *The handbook of education and human development: New models of learning, teaching, and schooling.* Cambridge, MA: Blackwell.

Hatano, G., & Inagaki, K. (2003). When is conceptual change intended? A cognitive-sociocultural view. In G. M. Sinatra & P. R. Pintrich (Eds.), *Intentional conceptual change* (pp. 407–427). Mahwah, NJ: Erlbaum.

Hathaway, W., Dooling-Litfin, J. K., & Edwards, G. (1998). Integrating the results of an evaluation: Eight clinical cases. In R. A. Barkley, *Attention-deficit hyperactivity disorder: A handbook for diagnosis and treatment* (pp. 312–344). New York: Guilford Press.

Hattie, J., Biggs, J., & Purdie, N. (1996). Effects of learning skills interventions on student learning: A meta-analysis. *Review of Educational Research, 66,* 99–136.

Hauser-Cram, P., Sirin, S. R., & Stipek, D. (2003). When teachers' and parents' values differ: Teachers' ratings of academic competence in children from low-income families. *Journal of Educational Psychology, 95,* 813–820.

Hawkins, F. P. L. (1997). *Journey with children: The autobiography of a teacher.* Niwot: University Press of Colorado.

Haxby, J. V., Gobbini, M. I., Furey, M. L., Ishai, A., Schouten, J. L., & Pietrini, P. (2001). Distributed and overlapping representations of faces and objects in ventral temporal cortex. *Science, 293,* 2425–2430.

Hay, I., Ashman, A. F., van Kraayenoord, C. E., & Stewart, A. L. (1999). Identification of self-verification in the formation of children's academic self-concept. *Journal of Educational Psychology, 91,* 225–229.

Hayes, S. C., Rosenfarb, I., Wulfert, E., Munt, E. D., Korn, Z., & Zettle, R. D. (1985). Self-reinforcement effects: An artifact of social standard setting? *Journal of Applied Behavior Analysis, 18,* 201–214.

Hayes-Roth, B., & Thorndyke, P. W. (1979). Integration of knowledge from text. *Journal of Verbal Learning and Verbal Behavior, 18,* 91–108.

Hayslip, B., Jr. (1994). Stability of intelligence. In R. J. Sternberg (Ed.), *Encyclopedia of human intelligence* (Vol. 2). New York: Macmillan.

Hearold, S. (1986). A synthesis of 1,043 effects of television on social behavior. In G. Comstock (Ed.), *Public communication and behavior* (Vol. 1). New York: Academic Press.

Heath, S. B. (1980). Questioning at home and at school: A comparative study. In G. Spindler (Ed.), *The ethnography of schooling: Educational anthropology in action.* New York: Holt, Rinehart & Winston.

Heath, S. B. (1989). Oral and literate traditions among black Americans living in poverty. *American Psychologist, 44,* 367–373.

Heck, A., Collins, J., & Peterson, L. (2001). Decreasing children's risk taking on the playground. *Journal of Applied Behavior Analysis, 34,* 349–352.

Hedges, L. V., & Nowell, A. (1995). Sex differences in mental test scores, variability, and numbers of high-scoring individuals. *Science, 269,* 41–45.

Hegarty, M., & Kozhevnikov, M. (1999). Types of visual-spatial representations and mathematical problem solving. *Journal of Educational Psychology, 91,* 684–689.

Hegland, S., & Andre, T. (1992). Helping learners construct knowledge. *Educational Psychology Review, 4,* 223–240.

Heindel, P., & Kose, G. (1990). The effects of motoric action and organization on children's memory. *Journal of Experimental Child Psychology, 50,* 416–428.

Heller, J. I., & Hungate, H. N. (1985). Implications for mathematics instruction of research on scientific problem solving. In E. A. Silver (Ed.), *Teaching and learning mathematical problem solving: Multiple research perspectives.* Mahwah, NJ: Erlbaum.

Helton, G. B., & Oakland, T. D. (1977). Teachers' attitudinal responses to differing characteristics of elementary school students. *Journal of Educational Psychology, 69,* 261–266.

Helwig, C. C. (1995). Adolescents' and young adults' conceptions of civil liberties: Freedom of speech and religion. *Child Development, 66,* 152–166.

Helwig, C. C., & Jasiobedzka, U. (2001). The relation between law and morality: Children's reasoning about socially beneficial and unjust laws. *Child Development, 72,* 1382–1393.

Helwig, C. C., Zelazo, P. D., & Wilson, M. (2001). Children's judgments of psychological harm in normal and noncanonical situations. *Child Development, 72,* 66–81.

Hembree, R. (1988). Correlates, causes, effects, and treatment of test anxiety. *Review of Educational Research, 58,* 47–77.

Hennessey, B. A. (1995). Social, environmental, and developmental issues and creativity. *Educational Psychology Review, 7,* 163–183.

Hennessey, B. A., & Amabile, T. M. (1987). *Creativity and learning.* Washington, DC: National Education Association.

Hennessey, M. G. (2003). Metacognitive aspects of students' reflective discourse: Implications for intentional conceptual change teaching and learning. In G. M. Sinatra & P. R. Pintrich (Eds.), *Intentional conceptual change* (pp. 103–132). Mahwah, NJ: Erlbaum.

Herbert, J., Stipek, D., & Miles, S. (2003, April). *Gender differences in perceptions of ability in elementary school students: The role of parents, teachers and achievement.* Paper presented at the annual meeting of the American Educational Research Association, Chicago.

Hernandez, D. J. (1997). Child development and the social demography of childhood. *Child Development, 68,* 149–169.

Herrenkohl, L. R., & Guerra, M. R. (1998). Participant structures, scientific discourse, and student engagement in fourth grade. *Cognition and Instruction, 16,* 431–473.

Herrnstein, R. J., & Murray, C. (1994). *The bell curve: Intelligence and class structure in American life.* New York: Free Press.

Hertel, P. T. (1994). Depression and memory: Are impairments remediable through attentional control? *Current Directions in Psychological Science, 3,* 190–193.

Hess, G. A., Jr., Lyons, A., & Corsino, L. (1990, April). *Against the odds: The early identification of dropouts.* Paper presented at the annual meeting of the American Educational Research Association, Boston.

Hess, R. D., Chih-Mei, C., & McDevitt, T. M. (1987). Cultural variations in family beliefs about children's performance in mathematics: Comparisons among People's Republic of China, Chinese-American, and Caucasian-American families. *Journal of Educational Psychology, 79,* 179–188.

Hess, R. D., & Holloway, S. D. (1984). Family and school as educational institutions. In R. D. Parke, R. N. Emde, H. P. McAdoo, & G. P. Sackett (Eds.), *Review of child development research* (Vol. 7). Chicago: University of Chicago Press.

Hess, R. D., & McDevitt, T. M. (1989). Family. In E. Barnouw (Ed.), *International encyclopedia of communications.* New York: Oxford University Press.

Hettinger, H. R., & Knapp, N. F. (2001). Potential, performance, and paradox: A case study of J.P., a verbally gifted, struggling reader. *Journal for the Education of the Gifted, 24,* 248–289.

Heuer, F., & Reisberg, D. (1992). Emotion, arousal, and memory for detail. In S. Christianson (Ed.), *Handbook of emotion and memory.* Hillsdale, NJ: Erlbaum.

Heward, W. L. (2003). *Exceptional children: An introduction to special education* (7th ed.). Upper Saddle River, NJ: Merrill/Prentice Hall.

Hewitt, J., Brett, C., Scardamalia, M., Frecker, K., & Webb, J. (1995, April). *Schools for thought: Transforming classrooms into learning communities.* Paper presented at the annual meeting of the American Educational Research Association, San Francisco.

Hewitt, J., & Scardamalia, M. (1996, April). *Design principles for the support of distributed processes.* Paper presented at the annual meeting of the American Educational Research Association, New York.

Hewitt, J., & Scardamalia, M. (1998). Design principles for distributed knowledge building processes. *Educational Psychology Review, 10,* 75–96.

Heymann, S. J., & Earle, A. (2000). Low-income parents: How do working conditions affect their opportunity to help school-age children at risk? *American Educational Research Journal, 37,* 833–848.

Hickey, D. T. (1997). Motivation and contemporary socio-constructivist instructional perspectives. *Educational Psychologist, 32,* 175–193.

Hickey, D. T., Moore, A. L., & Pellegrino, J. W. (2001). The motivational and academic consequences of elementary mathematics environments: Do constructivist innovations and reforms make a difference? *American Educational Research Journal, 38,* 611–652.

Hicks, L. (1997). Academic motivation and peer relationships—how do they mix in an adolescent world? *Middle School Journal, 28,* 18–22.

Hidalgo, N. M., Siu, S., Bright, J. A., Swap, S. M., & Epstein, J. L. (1995). Research on families, schools, and communities: A multicultural perspective. In J. A. Banks & C. A. M. Banks (Eds.), *Handbook of research on multicultural education.* New York: Macmillan.

Hidi, S. (1990). Interest and its contribution as a mental resource for learning. *Review of Educational Research, 60,* 549–571.

Hidi, S., & Anderson, V. (1986). Producing written summaries: Task demands, cognitive operations, and implications for instruction. *Review of Educational Research, 86,* 473–493.

Hidi, S., & Anderson, V. (1992). Situational interest and its impact on reading and expository writing. In K. A. Renninger, S. Hidi, & A. Krapp (Eds.), *The role of interest in learning and development.* Mahwah, NJ: Erlbaum.

Hidi, S., & Harackiewicz, J. M. (2000). Motivating the academically unmotivated: A critical issue for the 21st century. *Review of Educational Research, 70,* 151–179.

Hidi, S., & McLaren, J. (1990). The effect of topic and theme interestingness on the production of school expositions. In H. Mandl, E. De Corte, N. Bennett, & H. F. Friedrich (Eds.), *Learning and instruction in an international context.* Oxford, England: Pergamon Press.

Hidi, S., Weiss, J., Berndorff, D., & Nolan, J. (1998). The role of gender, instruction, and a cooperative learning technique in science education across formal and informal settings. In L. Hoffman, A. Krapp, K. Renninger, & J. Baumert (Eds.), *Interest and learning: Proceedings of the Seeon Conference on Interest and Gender* (pp. 215–227). Kiel, Germany: IPN.

Hiebert, E. H., & Fisher, C. W. (1992). The tasks of school literacy: Trends and issues. In J. Brophy (Ed.), *Advances in research on teaching: Vol. 3. Planning and managing learning tasks and activities.* Greenwich, CT: JAI Press.

Hiebert, E. H., & Raphael, T. E. (1996). Psychological perspectives on literacy and extensions to educational practice. In D. C. Berliner & R. C. Calfee (Eds.), *Handbook of educational psychology.* New York: Macmillan.

Hiebert, E. H., Valencia, S. W., & Afflerbach, P. P. (1994). Definitions and perspectives. In S. W. Valencia, E. H. Hiebert, & P. P. Afflerbach (Eds.), *Authentic reading assessment: Practices and possibilities.* Newark, DE: International Reading Association.

Hiebert, J., Carpenter, T. P., Fennema, E., Fuson, K. C., Wearne, D., Murray, H., Olivier, A., & Human, P. (1997). *Making sense: Teaching and learning mathematics with understanding.* Portsmouth, NH: Heinemann.

Hiebert, J., & Lefevre, P. (1986). Conceptual and procedural knowledge in mathematics: An introductory analysis. In J. Hiebert (Ed.), *Conceptual and procedural knowledge: The case of mathematics.* Mahwah, NJ: Erlbaum.

Hiebert, J., & Wearne, D. (1996). Instruction, understanding, and skill in multidigit addition and subtraction. *Cognition and Instruction, 14,* 251–283.

Higgins, A. (1995). Educating for justice and community: Lawrence Kohlberg's vision of moral education. In W. M. Kurtines & J. L. Gewirtz (Eds.), *Moral development: An introduction.* Boston: Allyn & Bacon.

Higgins, A. T., & Turnure, J. E. (1984). Distractibility and concentration of attention in children's development. *Child Development, 55,* 1799–1810.

Hill, C. (1994). Testing and assessment: An applied linguistic perspective. *Educational Assessment, 2*(3), 179–212.

Hill, C., & Larsen, E. (1992). *Testing and assessment in secondary education: A critical review of emerging practices.* Berkeley: University of California, National Center for Research in Vocational Education.

Hill, K. T. (1984). Debilitating motivation and testing: A major educational problem, possible solutions, and

policy applications. In R. Ames & C. Ames (Eds.), *Research on motivation in education: Vol. 1. Student motivation.* San Diego, CA: Academic Press.

Hill, K. T., & Sarason, S. B. (1966). The relation of test anxiety and defensiveness to test and school performance over the elementary school years: A further longitudinal study. *Monographs for the Society of Research in Child Development, 31*(2, Serial No. 104).

Hill, K. T., & Wigfield, A. (1984). Test anxiety: A major educational problem and what can be done about it. *Elementary School Journal, 85,* 105–126.

Hill, N. E., Bush, K. R., & Roosa, M. W. (2003). Parenting and family socialization strategies and children's mental health: Low-income Mexican-American and Euro-American mothers and children. *Child Development, 74,* 189–204.

Hill, N. E., & Craft, S. A. (2003). Parent-school involvement and school performance: Mediated pathways among socioeconomically comparable African American and Euro-American families. *Journal of Educational Psychology, 95,* 74–83.

Hine, P., & Fraser, B. J. (2002, April). *Combining qualitative and quantitative methods in a study of Australian students' transition from elementary to high school.* Paper presented at the annual meeting of the American Educational Research Association, New Orleans, LA.

Hines, M., Golombok, S., Rust, J., Johnston, K. J., Golding, J., & the Avon Longitudinal Study of Parents and Children Study Team. (2002). Testosterone during pregnancy and gender role behavior of preschool children: A longitudinal, population study. *Child Development, 73,* 1678–1687.

Hinkley, J. W., McInerney, D. M., & Marsh, H. W. (2001, April). *The multi-faceted structure of school achievement motivation: A case for social goals.* Paper presented at the annual meeting of the American Educational Research Association, Seattle, WA.

Hirsch, E. D., Jr. (1996). *The schools we need and why we don't have them.* New York: Doubleday.

Hirschfeld, L. A. & Gelman, S. A. (Eds.). (1994). *Mapping the mind: Domain specificity in cognition and culture.* Cambridge, England: Cambridge University Press.

Ho, D. Y. F. (1986). Chinese pattern of socialization: A critical review. In M. H. Bond (Ed.), *The psychology of Chinese people.* Oxford, England: Oxford University Press.

Ho, D. Y. F. (1994). Cognitive socialization in Confucian heritage cultures. In P. M. Greenfield & R. R. Cocking (Eds.), *Cross-cultural roots of minority child development.* Mahwah, NJ: Erlbaum.

Ho, H.-Z., Hinckley, H. S., Fox, K. R., Brown, J. H., & Dixon, C. N. (2001, April). *Family literacy: Promoting parent support strategies for student success.* Paper presented at the annual meeting of the American Educational Research Association, Seattle, WA.

Hobbs, N. (1980). An ecologically oriented service-based system for the classification of handicapped children. In E. Salzinger, J. Antrobus, & J. Glick (Eds.), *The ecosystem of the "sick" child.* New York: Academic Press.

Hocevar, D., & Bachelor, P. (1989). A taxonomy and critique of measurements used in the study of creativity. In J. A. Glover, R. R. Ronning, & C. R. Reynolds (Eds.), *Handbook of creativity.* New York: Plenum Press.

Hodges, E., Malone, J., & Perry, D. (1997). Individual risk and social risk as interacting determinants of victimization in the peer group. *Developmental Psychology, 32,* 1033–1039.

Hofer, B. K. (2001). Personal epistemology research: Implications for learning and teaching. *Educational Psychology Review, 13,* 353–383.

Hofer, B. K., & Pintrich, P. R. (1997). The development of epistemological theories: Beliefs about knowledge and knowing and their relation to learning. *Review of Educational Research, 67,* 88–140.

Hofferth, S. L. (1990). Trends in adolescent sexual activity, contraception, and pregnancy in the United States. In J. Bancroft & J. M. Reinisch (Eds.), *Adolescence and puberty* (pp. 217–233). New York: Oxford University Press.

Hoff-Ginsberg, E. (1997). *Language development.* Pacific Grove, CA: Brooks/Cole.

Hoffman, M. L. (1970). Moral development. In P. H. Mussen (Ed.). *Carmichael's manual of child psychology* (Vol. 2). New York: Wiley.

Hoffman, M. L. (1975). Altruistic behavior and the parent-child relationship. *Journal of Personality and Social Psychology, 31,* 937–943.

Hoffman, M. L. (1984). Interaction of affect and cognition in empathy. In C. E. Izard, J. Kagan, & R. B. Zajonc (Eds.), *Emotions, cognition, and behavior.* Cambridge, England: Cambridge University Press.

Hoffman, M. L. (1991). Empathy, social cognition, and moral action. In W. M. Kurtines & J. L. Gewirtz (Eds.), *Moral behavior and development: Vol. 1. Theory* (pp. 275–301). Mahwah, NJ: Erlbaum.

Hogan, D. M., & Tudge, J. R. H. (1999). Implications of Vygotsky's theory for peer learning. In A. M. O'Donnell & A. King (Eds.), *Cognitive perspectives on peer learning* (pp. 39–65). Mahwah, NJ: Erlbaum.

Hogan, K., Nastasi, B. K., & Pressley, M. (2000). Discourse patterns and collaborative scientific reasoning in peer and teacher-guided discussions. *Cognition and Instruction, 17,* 379–432.

Hogan, T., Rabinowitz, M., & Craven, J. A., III. (2003). Representation in teaching: Inferences from research of expert and novice teachers. *Educational Psychologist, 38,* 235–247.

Hogdon, L. A. (1995). *Visual strategies for improving communication. Vol. 1: Practical supports for school and home.* Troy, MI: Quirk Roberts.

Hoge, R. D., & Coladarci, T. (1989). Teacher-based judgments of academic achievement: A review of literature. *Review of Educational Research, 59,* 297–313.

Hoge, R. D., & Renzulli, J. S. (1993). Exploring the link between giftedness and self-concept. *Review of Educational Research, 63,* 449–465.

Holley, C. D., & Dansereau, D. F. (1984). *Spatial learning strategies: Techniques, applications, and related issues.* San Diego, CA: Academic Press.

Holliday, B. G. (1985). Towards a model of teacher-child transactional processes affecting black children's academic achievement. In M. B. Spencer, G. K. Brookins, & W. R. Allen (Eds.), *Beginnings: The social and affective development of black children.* Mahwah, NJ: Erlbaum.

Hollins, E. R. (1996). *Culture in school learning: Revealing the deep meaning.* Mahwah, NJ: Erlbaum.

Hollon, R. E., Roth, K. J., & Anderson, C. W. (1991). Science teachers' conceptions of teaching and learning. In J. Brophy (Ed.), *Advances in research on teaching: Vol. 2. Teachers' knowledge of subject matter as it relates to their teaching practice.* Greenwich, CT: JAI Press.

Holt-Reynolds, D. (1992). Personal history-based beliefs as relevant prior knowledge in course work. *American Educational Research Journal, 29,* 325–349.

Hom, A., & Battistich, V. (1995, April). *Students' sense of school community as a factor in reducing drug use and delinquency.* Paper presented at the annual meeting of the American Educational Research Association, San Francisco.

Homme, L. E., deBaca, P. C., Devine, J. V., Steinhorst, R., & Rickert, E. J. (1963). Use of the Premack principle in controlling the behavior of nursery school children. *Journal of the Experimental Analysis of Behavior, 6,* 544.

Hong, Y., Chiu, C., & Dweck, C. S. (1995). Implicit theories of intelligence: Reconsidering the role of confidence in achievement motivation. In M. H. Kernis (Ed.), *Efficacy, agency, and self-esteem.* New York: Plenum Press.

Hong, Y., Morris, M. W., Chiu, C., & Benet-Martínez, V. (2000). Multicultural minds: A dynamic constructivist approach to culture and cognition. *American Psychologist, 55,* 709–720.

Hoover-Dempsey, K. V., Battiato, A. C., Walker, J. M. T., Reed, R. P., DeJong, J. M., & Jones, K. P. (2001). Parental involvement in homework. *Educational Psychologist, 36,* 195–209.

Hoover-Dempsey, K. V., & Sandler, H. M. (1997). Why do parents become involved in their children's education? *Review of Educational Research, 57,* 3–42.

Horgan, D. (1990, April). *Students' predictions of test grades: Calibration and metacognition.* Paper presented at the annual meeting of the American Educational Research Association, Boston.

Horgan, D. D. (1995). *Achieving gender equity: Strategies for the classroom.* Needham Heights, MA: Allyn & Bacon.

Horgan, D. D., Hacker, D., & Huffman, S. (1997, May). *How students predict their exam performance.* Paper presented at the annual meeting of the Southern Society for Philosophy and Psychology, Atlanta, GA.

Hosmer, E. (1987, June). Paradise lost: The ravaged rainforest. *Multinational Monitor, 8*(6), 6–8.

Hossler, D., & Stage, F. K. (1992). Family and high school experience influences on the postsecondary educational plans of ninth-grade students. *American Educational Research Journal, 29,* 425–451.

Houtz, J. C. (1990). Environments that support creative thinking. In C. Hedley, J. Houtz, & A. Baratta (Eds.), *Cognition, curriculum, and literacy.* Norwood, NJ: Ablex.

Howe, C. K. (1994). Improving the achievement of Hispanic students. *Educational Leadership, 51*(8), 42–44.

Howe, C., Tolmie, A., Greer, K., & Mackenzie, M. (1995). Peer collaboration and conceptual growth in physics: Task influences on children's understanding of heating and cooling. *Cognition and Instruction, 13,* 483–503.

Howie, J. D. (2002, April). *Effects of audience, gender, and achievement level on adolescent students' communicated attributions and affect in response to academic success and failure.* Paper presented at the annual meeting of the American Educational Research Association, New Orleans, LA.

Hudley, C., & Graham, S. (1993). An attributional intervention to reduce peer-directed aggression among African American boys. *Child Development, 64,* 124–138.

Huff, J. A. (1988). Personalized behavior modification: An in-school suspension program that teaches students how to change. *School Counselor, 35,* 210–214.

Hughes, F. P. (1998). Play in special populations. In O. N. Saracho & B. Spodek (Eds.), *Multiple perspectives on play in early childhood education* (pp. 171–193). Albany: State University of New York Press.

Hughes, J. N. (1988). *Cognitive behavior therapy with children in schools.* New York: Pergamon Press.

Hulme, C., & Joshi, R. M. (Eds.). (1998). *Reading and spelling: Development and disorders.* Mahwah, NJ: Erlbaum.

Humphreys, L. G. (1992). What both critics and users of ability tests need to know. *Psychological Science, 3,* 271–274.

Hunt, P., & Goetz, L. (1997). Research on inclusive educational programs, practices, and outcomes for students with severe disabilities. *Journal of Special Education, 31,* 3–29.

Hunter, M. (1982). *Mastery teaching.* El Segundo, CA: TIP.

Husman, J., & Freeman, B. (1999, April). *The effect of perceptions of instrumentality on intrinsic motivation.* Paper presented at the annual meeting of the American Educational Research Association, Montreal, Canada.

Huston, A. C. (1983). Sex-typing. In E. M. Hetherington (Ed.), *Handbook of child psychology: Vol. 4. Socialization, personality, and social development* (4th ed.). New York: Wiley.

Huston, A. C., Donnerstein, E., Fairchild, H., Feshbach, N. D., Katz, P. A., Murray, J. P., Rubenstein, E. A., Wilcox, B. L., & Zuckerman, D. (1992). *Big world, small screen: The role of television in American society.* Lincoln: University of Nebraska Press.

Huston, A. C., Watkins, B. A., & Kunkel, D. (1989). Public policy and children's television. *American Psychologist, 44,* 424–433.

Hutt, S. J., Tyler, S., Hutt, C., & Christopherson, H. (1989). *Play, exploration, and learning: A natural history of the pre-school.* London: Routledge.

Huttenlocher, P. R., & Dabholkar, A. S. (1997). Regional differences in synaptogenesis in human cerebral cortex. *Journal of Comparative Neurology, 387,* 167–178.

Hymel, S. (1986). Interpretations of peer behavior: Affective bias in childhood and adolescence. *Child Development, 57,* 431–445.

Hymel, S., Comfort, C., Schonert-Reichl, K., & McDougall, P. (1996). Academic failure and school dropout: The influence of peers. In J. Juvonen & K. R. Wentzel (Eds.), *Social motivation: Understanding children's school adjustment* (pp. 313–345). Cambridge, England: Cambridge University Press.

Hynd, C. (1998a). Conceptual change in a high school physics class. In B. Guzzetti & C. Hynd (Eds.), *Perspectives on conceptual change: Multiple ways to understand knowing and learning in a complex world* (pp. 27–36). Mahwah, NJ: Erlbaum.

Hynd, C. (1998b). Observing learning from different perspectives: What does it mean for Barry and his understanding of gravity? In B. Guzzetti & C. Hynd (Eds.), *Perspectives on conceptual change: Multiple ways to understand knowing and learning in a complex world* (pp. 235–244). Mahwah, NJ: Erlbaum.

Hynd, C. (2003). Conceptual change in response to persuasive messages. In G. M. Sinatra & P. R. Pintrich (Eds.), *Intentional conceptual change* (pp. 291–315). Mahwah, NJ: Erlbaum.

Igoa, C. (1995). *The inner world of the immigrant child.* Mahwah, NJ: Erlbaum.

Igoe, A. R., & Sullivan, H. (1991, April). *Gender and grade-level differences in student attributes related to school learning and motivation.* Paper presented at the annual meeting of the American Educational Research Association, Chicago.

Inglehart, M., Brown, D. R., & Vida, M. (1994). Competition, achievement, and gender: A stress theoretical analysis. In P. R. Pintrich, D. R. Brown, & C. E. Weinstein (Eds.), *Student motivation, cognition, and learning: Essays in honor of Wilbert J. McKeachie.* Mahwah, NJ: Erlbaum.

Inglis, A., & Biemiller, A. (1997, March). *Fostering self-direction in mathematics: A cross-age tutoring program that enhances math problem solving.* Paper presented at the annual meeting of the American Educational Research Association, Chicago.

Inhelder, B., & Piaget, J. (1958). *The growth of logical thinking from childhood to adolescence* (A. Parsons & S. Milgram, Trans.). New York: Basic Books.

Irujo, S. (1988). An introduction to intercultural differences and similarities in nonverbal communication. In J. S. Wurzel (Ed.), *Toward multiculturalism: A reader in multicultural education.* Yarmouth, ME: Intercultural Press.

Iwata, B. A., & Bailey, J. S. (1974). Reward versus cost token systems: An analysis of the effects on students and teacher. *Journal of Applied Behavior Analysis, 7,* 567–576.

Izard, C., Fine, S., Schultz, D., Mostow, A., Ackerman, B., & Youngstrom, E. (2001). Emotion knowledge as a predictor of social behavior and academic competence in children at risk. *Psychological Science, 12,* 18–23.

Jackson, D. L., & Ormrod, J. E. (1998). *Case studies: Applying educational psychology.* Upper Saddle River, NJ: Merrill/Prentice Hall.

Jacob, B. A. (2003). Accountability, incentives, and behavior: The impact of high- stakes testing in the Chicago Public Schools. *Education Next, 3*(1). Retrieved March 10, 2004, from http:// www.education-next.org/unabridged/20031/jacob.pdf.

Jacobs, J. E., & Klaczynski, P. A. (2002). The development of judgment and decision making during childhood and adolescence. *Current Directions in Psychological Science, 11,* 145–149.

Jacobs, J. E., Lanza, S., Osgood, D. W., Eccles, J. S., & Wigfield, A. (2002). Changes in children's self-competence and values: Gender and domain differences across grades one through twelve. *Child Development, 73,* 509–527.

Jacobsen, B., Lowery, B., & DuCette, J. (1986). Attributions of learning disabled children. *Journal of Educational Psychology, 78,* 59–64.

Jacoby, R., & Glauberman, N. (Eds.). (1995). *The bell curve debate: History, documents, opinions.* New York: Random House.

Jagacinski, C. M., & Nicholls, J. G. (1984). Conceptions of ability and related affects in task involvement and ego involvement. *Journal of Educational Psychology, 76,* 909–919.

Jagacinski, C. M., & Nicholls, J. G. (1987). Competence and affect in task involvement and ego involvement: The impact of social comparison information. *Journal of Educational Psychology, 79,* 107–114.

James, W. (1890). *Principles of psychology.* New York: Holt.

Janos, P. M., & Robinson, N. M. (1985). Psychosocial development in intellectually gifted children. In F. D. Horowitz & M. O'Brien (Eds.), *The gifted and talented: Developmental perspectives.* Washington, DC: American Psychological Association.

Janosz, M., Le Blanc, M., Boulerice, B., & Tremblay, R. E. (2000). Predicting different types of school dropouts: A typological approach with two longitudinal samples. *Journal of Educational Psychology, 92,* 171–190.

Jencks, C., & Crouse, J. (1982). Should we relabel the SAT . . . or replace it? In W. Shrader (Ed.), *New directions for testing and measurement: Measurement, guidance, and program improvement* (No. 13). San Francisco: Jossey-Bass.

Jenlink, C. L. (1994, April). *Music: A lifeline for the self-esteem of at-risk students.* Paper presented at the annual meeting of the American Educational Research Association, New Orleans, LA.

Jimerson, S., Egeland, B., & Teo, A. (1999). A longitudinal study of achievement trajectories: Factors associated with change. *Journal of Educational Psychology, 91,* 116–126.

Johanning, D. I., D'Agostino, J. V., Steele, D. F., & Shumow, L. (1999, April). *Student writing, post-writing group collaboration, and learning in pre-algebra.* Paper presented at the annual meeting of the American Educational Research Association, Montreal, Canada.

Johnson, D. W., & Johnson, R. T. (1985). Classroom conflict: Controversy versus debate in learning groups. *American Educational Research Journal, 22,* 237–256.

Johnson, D. W., & Johnson, R. T. (1988). Critical thinking through structured controversy. *Educational Leadership, 45*(8), 58–64.

Johnson, D. W., & Johnson, R. T. (1991). *Learning together and alone: Cooperative, competitive, and individualistic learning* (3rd ed.). Upper Saddle River, NJ: Prentice Hall.

Johnson, D. W., & Johnson, R. T. (1996). Conflict resolution and peer mediation programs in elementary and secondary schools: A review of the research. *Review of Educational Research, 66,* 459–506.

Johnson, D. W., & Johnson, R. T. (2001, April). *Teaching students to be peacemakers: A meta-analysis.* Paper presented at the annual meeting of the American Educational Research Association, Seattle, WA.

Johnson, D. W., Johnson, R., Dudley, B., Ward, M., & Magnuson, D. (1995). The impact of peer mediation training on the management of school and home conflicts. *American Educational Research Journal, 32,* 829–844.

Johnson, H. C., & Friesen, B. (1993). Etiologies of mental and emotional disorders in children. In H. Johnson (Ed.), *Child mental health in the 1990s: Curricula for graduate and undergraduate.* Washington, DC: U.S. Department of Health and Human Services.

Johnson, M. H., & de Haan, M. (2001). Developing cortical specialization for visual-cognitive function: The case of face recognition. In J. L. McClelland & R. S. Siegler (Eds.), *Mechanisms of cognitive development: Behavioral and neural perspectives* (pp. 253–270). Mahwah, NJ: Erlbaum.

Johnson-Glenberg, M. C. (2000). Training reading comprehension in adequate decodes/poor comprehenders: Verbal versus visual strategies. *Journal of Educational Psychology, 92,* 772–782.

John-Steiner, V. (1997). *Notebooks of the mind: Explorations of thinking* (Rev. ed.). New York: Oxford University Press.

John-Steiner, V., & Mahn, H. (1996). Sociocultural approaches to learning and development: A Vygotskian framework. *Educational Psychologist, 31,* 191–206.

Johnstone, A. H., & El-Banna, H. (1986). Capacities, demands and processes—a predictive model for science education. *Education in Chemistry, 23*, 80–84.

Jonassen, D. H. (1996). *Computers in the classroom: Mindtools for critical thinking.* Upper Saddle River, NJ: Merrill/Prentice Hall.

Jonassen, D. H., Hannum, W. H., & Tessmer, M. (1989). *Handbook of task analysis procedures.* New York: Praeger.

Jones, D., & Christensen, C. A. (1999). Relationship between automaticity in handwriting and students' ability to generate written text. *Journal of Educational Psychology, 91*, 44–49.

Jones, E. E., & Berglas, S. (1978). Control of attributions about the self through self-handicapping strategies: The appeal of alcohol and the role of underachievement. *Personality and Social Psychology Bulletin, 4*, 200–206.

Jones, K. M., Drew, H. A., & Weber, N. L. (2000). Noncontingent peer attention as treatment for disruptive classroom behavior. *Journal of Applied Behavior Analysis, 33*, 343–346.

Jones, M. C. (1924). The elimination of children's fears. *Journal of Experimental Psychology, 7*, 382–390.

Jones, M. S., Levin, M. E., Levin, J. R., & Beitzel, B. D. (2000). Can vocabulary-learning strategies and pair-learning formats be profitably combined? *Journal of Educational Psychology, 92*, 256–262.

Jones, V. (1996). Classroom management. In J. Sikula, T. J. Buttery, & E. Guyton (Eds.), *Handbook of research on teacher education* (2nd ed., pp. 503–521). New York: Macmillan.

Joshi, M. S., & MacLean, M. (1994). Indian and English children's understanding of the distinction between real and apparent emotion. *Child Development, 65*, 1372–1384.

Josselson, R. (1988). The embedded self: I and Thou revisited. In D. K. Lapsley & F. C. Power (Eds.), *Self, ego, and identity: Integrative approaches* (pp. 91–106). New York: Springer-Verlag.

Jovanovic, J., & King, S. S. (1998). Boys and girls in the performance-based science classroom: Who's doing the performing? *American Educational Research Journal, 35*, 477–496.

Jozefowicz, D. M., Arbreton, A. J., Eccles, J. S., Barber, B. L., & Colarossi, L. (1994, April). *Seventh grade student, parent, and teacher factors associated with later school dropout or movement into alternative educational settings.* Paper presented at the annual meeting of the American Educational Research Association, New Orleans, LA.

Judd, C. H. (1932). Autobiography. In C. Murchison (Ed.), *History of psychology in autobiography* (Vol. 2). Worcester, MA: Clark University Press.

Jussim, L., Eccles, J., & Madon, S. (1996). Social perception, social stereotypes, and teacher expectations: Accuracy and the quest for the powerful self-fulfilling prophecy. In L. Berkowitz (Ed.), *Advances in experimental social psychology.* New York: Academic Press.

Just, M. A., Carpenter, P. A., Keller, T. A., Emery, L., Zajac, H., & Thulborn, K. R. (2001). Interdependence of nonoverlapping cortical systems in dual cognitive tasks. *NeuroImage, 14*, 417–426.

Juvonen, J. (1991). Deviance, perceived responsibility, and negative peer reactions. *Developmental Psychology, 27*, 672–681.

Juvonen, J. (1996). Self-presentation tactics promoting teacher and peer approval: The function of excuses and other clever explanations. In J. Juvonen & K. R. Wentzel (Eds.), *Social motivation: Understanding children's school adjustment* (pp. 43–65). Cambridge, England: Cambridge University Press.

Juvonen, J. (2000). The social functions of attributional face-saving tactics among early adolescents. *Educational Psychology Review, 12*, 15–32.

Juvonen, J., & Hiner, M. (1991, April). *Perceived responsibility and annoyance as mediators of negative peer reactions.* Paper presented at the annual meeting of the American Educational Research Association, Chicago.

Juvonen, J., Nishina, A., & Graham, S. (2000). Peer harassment, psychological adjustment, and school functioning in early adolescence. *Journal of Educational Psychology, 92*, 349–359.

Juvonen, J., & Weiner, B. (1993). An attributional analysis of students' interactions: The social consequences of perceived responsibility. *Educational Psychology Review, 5*, 325–345.

Kagan, J. (1998). Biology and the child. In W. Damon (Series Ed.) & N. Eisenberg (Vol. Ed.), *Handbook of child psychology: Vol. 3. Social, emotional, and personality development* (5th ed., pp. 177–235). New York: Wiley.

Kahl, B., & Woloshyn, V. E. (1994). Using elaborative interrogation to facilitate acquisition of factual information in cooperative learning settings: One good strategy deserves another. *Applied Cognitive Psychology, 8*, 465–478.

Kahle, J. B. (1983). *The disadvantaged majority: Science education for women.* Burlington, NC: Carolina Biological Supply Co.

Kahle, J. B., & Lakes, M. K. (1983). The myth of equality in science classrooms. *Journal of Research in Science Teaching, 20*, 131–140.

Kail, R. (1990). *The development of memory in children* (3rd ed.). New York: Freeman.

Kail, R. V. (1998). *Children and their development.* Upper Saddle River, NJ: Prentice Hall.

Kail, R. (2000). Speed of information processing: Developmental change and links to intelligence. *Journal of School Psychology, 38*, 51–61.

Kane, R. J. (1983). In defense of grade inflation. *Today's Education, 67*(4), 41.

Kaplan, A. (1998, April). *Task goal orientation and adaptive social interaction among students of diverse cultural backgrounds.* Paper presented at the annual meeting of the American Educational Research Association, San Diego, CA.

Kaplan, A., & Midgley, C. (1999). The relationship between perceptions of the classroom goal structure and early adolescents' affect in school: The mediating role of coping strategies. *Learning and Individual Differences, 11*, 187–212.

Karau, S. J., & Williams, K. D. (1995). Social loafing: Research findings, implications, and future directions. *Current Directions in Psychological Science, 4*, 134–140.

Kardash, C. A. M., & Amlund, J. T. (1991). Self-reported learning strategies and learning from expository text. *Contemporary Educational Psychology, 16*, 117–138.

Kardash, C. A. M., & Scholes, R. J. (1996). Effects of preexisting beliefs, epistemological beliefs, and need for cognition on interpretation of controversial issues. *Journal of Educational Psychology, 88*, 260–271.

Karmiloff-Smith, A. (1979). Language development after five. In P. Fletcher & M. Garman (Eds.), *Language acquisition: Studies in first language development.* Cambridge, England: Cambridge University Press.

Karmiloff-Smith, A. (1993). Innate constraints and developmental change. In P. Bloom (Ed.), *Language acquisition: Core readings.* Cambridge, MA: MIT Press.

Karplus, R., Pulos, S., & Stage, E. K. (1983). Proportional reasoning of early adolescents. In R. Lesh & M. Landau (Eds.), *Acquisition of mathematics concepts and processes.* San Diego, CA: Academic Press.

Karpov, Y. V., & Haywood, H. C. (1998). Two ways to elaborate Vygotsky's concept of mediation: Implications for instruction. *American Psychologist, 53*, 27–36.

Katayama, A. D., & Robinson, D. H. (2000). Getting students "partially" involved in note-taking using graphic organizers. *Journal of Experimental Education, 68*, 119–133.

Katchadourian, H. (1990). Sexuality. In S. S. Feldman & G. R. Elliott (Eds.), *At the threshold: The developing adolescent* (pp. 330–351). Cambridge, MA: Harvard University Press.

Katkovsky, W., Crandall, V. C., & Good, S. (1967). Parental antecedents of children's beliefs in internal-external control of reinforcements in intellectual achievement situations. *Child Development, 38*, 765–776.

Katz, L. (1993). All about me: Are we developing our children's self-esteem or their narcissism? *American Educator, 17*(2), 18–23.

Kearins, J. M. (1981). Visual spatial memory in Australian aboriginal children of desert regions. *Cognitive Psychology, 13*, 434–460.

Kehle, T. J., Clark, E., & Jenson, W. R. (1996). Interventions for students with traumatic brain injury: Managing behavioral disturbances. *Journal of Learning Disabilities, 29*, 633–642.

Kehle, T. J., Clark, E., Jenson, W. R., & Wampold, B. (1986). Effectiveness of the self-modeling procedure with behaviorally disturbed elementary age children. *School Psychology Review, 15*, 289–295.

Keil, F. C. (1986). The acquisition of natural kind and artifact terms. In W. Demopolous & A. Marras (Eds.), *Language learning and concept acquisition.* Norwood, NJ: Ablex.

Keil, F. C. (1987). Conceptual development and category structure. In U. Neisser (Ed.), *Concepts and conceptual development: Ecological and intellectual factors in categorization.* Cambridge, England: Cambridge University Press.

Keil, F. C. (1989). *Concepts, kinds, and cognitive development.* Cambridge, MA: MIT Press.

Keil, F. C. (1991). Theories, concepts, and the acquisition of word meaning. In S. A. Gelman & J. P. Byrnes (Eds.), *Perspectives on language and thought: Interrelations in development.* Cambridge, England: Cambridge University Press.

Keil, F. C. (1994). The birth and nurturance of concepts by domains: The origins of concepts of living things. In L. A. Hirschfeld & S. A. Gelman (Eds.), *Mapping the mind: Domain specificity in cognition and culture.* New York: Cambridge University Press.

Keil, F. C., & Silberstein, C. S. (1996). Schooling and the acquisition of theoretical knowledge. In D. R. Olson & N. Torrance (Eds.), *The handbook of education and human development: New models of learning, teaching, and schooling.* Cambridge, MA: Blackwell.

Kelemen, D. (1999). Why are rocks pointy? Children's preference for teleological explanations of the natural world. *Developmental Psychology, 35*, 1440–1452.

Keller, J. M. (1987). Development and use of the ARCS model of instructional design. *Journal of Instructional Development, 10*(3), 2–10.

Kelley, M. L., & Carper, L. B. (1988). Home-based reinforcement procedures. In J. C. Witt, S. N. Elliott, & F. M. Gresham (Eds.), *Handbook of behavior therapy in education.* New York: Plenum Press.

Kelly, A., & Smail, B. (1986). Sex stereotypes and attitudes to science among eleven-year-old children. *British Journal of Educational Psychology, 56*, 158–168.

Kelly, G. J., & Chen, C. (1998, April). *The sound of music: Experiment, discourse, and writing of science as sociocultural practices.* Paper presented at the annual meeting of the American Educational Research Association, San Diego, CA.

Kennedy, R. (1992). What is performance assessment? *New Directions for Education Reform, 1*(2), 21–27.

Keogh, B. A., & Becker, L. D. (1973). Early detection of learning problems: Questions, cautions, and guidelines. *Exceptional Children, 39*, 5–11.

Keogh, B. K. (2003). *Temperament in the classroom.* Baltimore: Brookes.

Keogh, B. K., & MacMillan, D. L. (1996). Exceptionality. In D. C. Berliner & R. C. Calfee (Eds.), *Handbook of educational psychology.* New York: Macmillan.

Kermani, H., & Moallem, M. (1997, March). *Cross-age tutoring: Exploring features and processes of peer-mediated learning.* Paper presented at the annual meeting of the American Educational Research Association, Chicago.

Kern, L., Dunlap, G., Childs, K. E., & Clark, S. (1994). Use of a classwide self-management program to improve the behavior of students with emotional and behavioral disorders. *Education and Treatment of Children, 17*, 445–458.

Kerns, L. L., & Lieberman, A. B. (1993). *Helping your depressed child.* Rocklin, CA: Prima.

Kerr, B. (1991). Educating gifted girls. In N. Coangelo & G. A. Davis (Eds.), *Handbook of gifted education.* Needham Heights, MA: Allyn & Bacon.

Kerr, M. M., & Nelson, C. M. (1989). *Strategies for managing behavior problems in the classroom* (2nd ed.). Upper Saddle River, NJ: Merrill/Prentice Hall.

Khattri, N., & Sweet, D. (1996). Assessment reform: Promises and challenges. In M. B. Kane & R. Mitchell

(Eds.), *Implementing performance assessment: Promises, problems, and challenges* (pp. 1–21). Mahwah, NJ: Erlbaum.

Kiewra, K. A. (1985). Investigating notetaking and review: A depth of processing alternative. *Educational Psychologist, 20,* 23–32.

Kiewra, K. A. (1989). A review of note-taking: The encoding-storage paradigm and beyond. *Educational Psychology Review, 1,* 147–172.

Kim, D., Solomon, D., & Roberts, W. (1995, April). *Classroom practices that enhance students' sense of community.* Paper presented at the annual meeting of the American Educational Research Association, San Francisco.

Kim, J. M., & Turiel, E. (1996). Korean and American children's concepts of adult and peer authority. *Social Development, 5,* 310–329.

Kimberg, D. Y., D'Esposito, M., & Farah, M. J. (1997). Cognitive functions in the prefrontal cortex—working memory and executive control. *Current Directions in Psychological Science, 6,* 185–192.

Kimble, G. A. (2000). Behaviorism and unity in psychology. *Current Directions in Psychological Science, 9,* 208–212.

Kindermann, T. A., McCollam, T., & Gibson, E. (1996). Peer networks and students' classroom engagement during childhood and adolescence. In J. Juvonen & K. Wentzel (Eds.), *Social motivation: Understanding children's school adjustment.* Cambridge, England: Cambridge University Press.

King, A. (1992). Comparison of self-questioning, summarizing, and notetaking-review as strategies for learning from lectures. *American Educational Research Journal, 29,* 303–323.

King, A. (1994). Guiding knowledge construction in the classroom: Effects of teaching children how to question and how to explain. *American Educational Research Journal, 31,* 338–368.

King, A. (1997). ASK to THINK—TEL WHY®©: A model of transactive peer tutoring for scaffolding higher level complex learning. *Educational Psychologist, 32,* 221–235.

King, A. (1998). Transactive peer tutoring: Distributing cognition and metacognition. *Educational Psychology Review, 10,* 57–74.

King, A. (1999). Discourse patterns for mediating peer learning. In A. M. O'Donnell & A. King (Eds.), *Cognitive perspectives on peer learning* (pp. 87–115). Mahwah, NJ: Erlbaum.

King, A., Staffieri, A., & Adelgais, A. (1998). Mutual peer tutoring: Effects of structuring tutorial interaction to scaffold peer learning. *Journal of Educational Psychology, 90,* 134–152.

King, N. J., & Ollendick, T. H. (1989). Children's anxiety and phobic disorders in school settings: Classification, assessment, and intervention issues. *Review of Educational Research, 59,* 431–470.

King, P. M., & Kitchener, K. S. (2002). The reflective judgment model: Twenty years of research on epistemic cognition. In B. K. Hofer & P. R. Pintrich (Eds.), *Personal epistemology: The psychology of beliefs about knowledge and knowing* (pp. 37–61). Mahwah, NJ: Erlbaum.

Kintsch, W. (1998). *Comprehension: A paradigm for cognition.* Cambridge, England: Cambridge University Press.

Kirk, S. A. (1972). Ethnic differences in psycholinguistic abilities. *Exceptional Children, 39,* 112–118.

Kirkland, M. C. (1971). The effect of tests on students and schools. *Review of Educational Research, 41,* 303–350.

Kirschenbaum, R. J. (1989). Identification of the gifted and talented American Indian student. In C. J. Maker & S. W. Schiever (Eds.), *Critical issues in gifted education: Vol. 2. Defensible programs for cultural and ethnic minorities.* Austin, TX: Pro-Ed.

Kitsantas, A., Zimmerman, B. J., & Cleary, T. (2000). The role of observation and emulation in the development of athletic self-regulation. *Journal of Educational Psychology, 92,* 811–817.

Klaczynski, P. A. (2001). Analytic and heuristic processing influences on adolescent reasoning and decision-making. *Child Development, 72,* 844–861.

Kladopoulos, C. N., & McComas, J. J. (2001). The effects of form training on foul-shooting performance in members of a women's college basketball team. *Journal of Applied Behavior Analysis, 34,* 329–332.

Klassen, R. (2002). Writing in early adolescence: A review of the role of self-efficacy beliefs. *Educational Psychology Review, 14,* 173–203.

Klein, J. D. (1990, April). *The effect of interest, task performance, and reward contingencies on self-efficacy.* Paper presented at the annual meeting of the American Educational Research Association, Boston.

Kletzien, S. B. (1988, April). *Achieving and non-achieving high school readers' use of comprehension strategies for reading expository text.* Paper presented at the annual meeting of the American Educational Research Association, New Orleans, LA.

Klin, A., Volkmar, F. R., & Sparrow, S. S. (Eds.). (2000). *Asperger syndrome.* New York: Guilford Press.

Klinger, E. (1996). Emotional influences on cognitive processing, with implications for theories of both. In P. M. Gollwitzer & J. A. Bargh (Eds.), *The psychology of action: Linking cognition and motivation to behavior* (pp. 168–189). New York: Guilford Press.

Kluger, A. N., & DeNisi, A. (1998). Feedback interventions: Toward the understanding of a double-edged sword. *Current Directions in Psychological Science, 7,* 67–72.

Knapp, M. S., Turnbull, B. J., & Shields, P. M. (1990). New directions for educating the children of poverty. *Educational Leadership, 48*(1), 4–9.

Knapp, M. S., & Woolverton, S. (1995). Social class and schooling. In J. A. Banks & C. A. M. Banks (Eds.), *Handbook of research on multicultural education.* New York: Macmillan.

Knowlton, D. (1995). Managing children with oppositional behavior. *Beyond Behavior, 6*(3), 5–10.

Knutson, D. J., & Mantzicopoulos, P. Y. (1999, April). *Contextual factors of geographic mobility and their relation to the achievement and adjustment of children.* Paper presented at the annual meeting of the American Educational Research Association, Montreal, Canada.

Kochanska, G., Gross, J. N., Lin, M.-H., & Nichols, K. E. (2002). Guilt in young children: Development, determinants, and relations with a broader system of standards. *Child Development, 73,* 461–482.

Koegel, L. K. (1995). Communication and language intervention. In R. L. Koegel & L. K. Koegel (Eds.), *Strategies for initiating positive interactions and improving learning opportunities.* Baltimore: Brookes.

Koegel, L. K., Koegel, R. L., & Dunlap, G. (Eds.). (1996). *Positive behavioral support: Including people with difficult behavior in the community.* Baltimore: Brookes.

Koeppel, J., & Mulrooney, M. (1992). The Sister Schools Program: A way for children to learn about cultural diversity—when there isn't any in their school. *Young Children, 48*(1), 44–47.

Koestner, R., Ryan, R. M., Bernieri, F., & Holt, K. (1984). Setting limits in children's behavior: The differential effects of controlling versus informational styles on intrinsic motivation and creativity. *Journal of Personality, 52,* 233–248.

Kogan, N. (1983). Stylistic variation in childhood and adolescence: Creativity, metaphor, and cognitive style. In J. H. Flavell & E. M. Markman (Eds.), *Handbook of child psychology: Vol. 3. Cognitive development.* New York: Wiley.

Kohlberg, L. (1963). Moral development and identification. In H. W. Stevenson (Ed.), *Child psychology: 62nd yearbook of the National Society for the Study of Education* (pp. 277–332). Chicago: University of Chicago Press.

Kohlberg, L. (1975). The cognitive-developmental approach to moral education. *Phi Delta Kappan, 57,* 670–677.

Kohlberg, L. (1976). Moral stages and moralization: The cognitive-developmental approach. In T. Lickona (Ed.), *Moral development and behavior: Theory, research, and social issues.* New York: Holt, Rinehart & Winston.

Kohlberg, L. (1981). *The philosophy of moral development: Moral stages and the idea of justice.* San Francisco: Harper & Row.

Kohlberg, L. (1984). *The psychology of moral development: The nature and validity of moral stages.* San Francisco: Harper & Row.

Kohlberg, L. (1986). A current statement on some theoretical issues. In S. Modgil & C. Modgil (Eds.), *Lawrence Kohlberg: Consensus and controversy.* Philadelphia: Falmer Press.

Kohlberg, L., & Candee, D. (1984). The relationship of moral judgment to moral action. In W. M. Kurtines & J. L. Gewirtz (Eds.), *Morality, moral behavior, and moral development.* New York: Wiley.

Kohn, A. (1993). Choices for children: Why and how to let students decide. *Phi Delta Kappan, 75*(1), 8–20.

Kohut, S., Jr. (1988). *The middle school: A bridge between elementary and high schools* (2nd ed.). Washington, DC: National Education Association.

Kolb, B., Gibb, R., & Robinson, T. E. (2003). Brain plasticity and behavior. *Current Directions in Psychological Science, 12,* 1–5.

Kolb, B., & Whishaw, I. Q. (1990). *Fundamentals of human neurophychology* (3rd ed.). New York: Freeman.

Kolodner, J. (1985). Memory for experience. In G. H. Bower (Ed.), *The psychology of learning and motivation: Advances in research and theory* (Vol. 19). San Diego, CA: Academic Press.

Koretz, D., Stecher, B., Klein, S., & McCaffrey, D. (1994). The Vermont portfolio assessment program: Findings and implications. *Educational Measurement: Issues and Practice, 13*(3), 5–16.

Kosslyn, S. M. (1985). Mental imagery ability. In R. J. Sternberg (Ed.), *Human abilities: An information-processing approach.* New York: Freeman.

Kounin, J. S. (1970). *Discipline and group management in classrooms.* New York: Holt, Rinehart & Winston.

Kovacs, D. M., Parker, J. G., & Hoffman, L. W. (1996). Behavioral, affective, and social correlates of involvement in cross-sex friendship in elementary school. *Child Development, 67,* 2269–2286.

Koyanagi, C., & Gaines, S. (1993). *All systems failure: An examination of the results of neglecting the needs of children with serious emotional disturbance.* Alexandria, VA: National Mental Health Association.

Krajcik, J. S. (1991). Developing students' understanding of chemical concepts. In S. M. Glynn, R. H. Yeany, & B. K. Britton (Eds.), *The psychology of learning science.* Mahwah, NJ: Erlbaum.

Kramarski, B., & Mevarech, Z. R. (2003). Enhancing mathematical reasoning in the classroom: The effects of cooperative learning and metacognitive training. *American Educational Research Journal, 40,* 281–310.

Krampen, G. (1987). Differential effects of teacher comments. *Journal of Educational Psychology, 79,* 137–146.

Krashen, S. D. (1996). *Under attack: The case against bilingual education.* Culver City, CA: Language Education Associates.

Krebs, D. L., & Van Hesteren, F. (1994). The development of altruism: Toward an integrative model. *Developmental Review, 14,* 103–158.

Krumboltz, J. D., & Krumboltz, H. B. (1972). *Changing children's behavior.* Upper Saddle River, NJ: Prentice Hall.

Kucan, L., & Beck, I. L. (1997). Thinking aloud and reading comprehension research: Inquiry, instruction, and social interaction. *Review of Educational Research, 67,* 271–299.

Kuhl, J. (1985). Volitional mediators of cognition-behavior consistency: Self-regulatory processes and actions versus state orientation. In J. Kuhl & J. Beckmann (Eds.), *Action control: From cognition to behavior.* Berlin, Germany: Springer-Verlag.

Kuhl, J., & Kraska, K. (1989). Self-regulation and meta-motivation: Computational mechanisms, development, and assessment. In R. Kanfer, P. L. Ackerman, & R. Cudeck (Eds.), *Abilities, motivation, and methodology: The Minnesota Symposium on Learning and Individual Differences* (pp. 343–374). Mahwah, NJ: Erlbaum.

Kuhn, D. (2001a). How do people know? *Psychological Science, 12,* 1–8.

Kuhn, D. (2001b). Why development does (and does not) occur: Evidence from the domain of inductive reasoning. In J. L. McClelland & R. S. Siegler (Eds.), *Mechanisms of cognitive development: Behavioral and neural perspectives* (pp. 221–249). Mahwah, NJ: Erlbaum.

Kuhn, D., Amsel, E., & O'Loughlin, M. (1988). *The development of scientific thinking skills.* San Diego, CA: Academic Press.

Kuhn, D., Daniels, S., & Krishnan, A. (2003, April). *Epistemology and intellectual values as core metacognitive constructs.* Paper presented at the annual meeting of the American Educational Research Association, Chicago.

Kuhn, D., Garcia-Mila, M., Zohar, A., & Andersen, C. (1995). Strategies of knowledge acquisition. *Monographs of the Society for Research in Child Development, 60* (Whole No. 245).

Kuhn, D., Shaw, V., & Felton, M. (1997). Effects of dyadic interaction on argumentative reasoning. *Cognition and Instruction, 15,* 287–315.

Kuhn, D., & Weinstock, M. (2002). What is epistemological thinking and why does it matter? In B. K. Hofer & P. R. Pintrich (Eds.), *Personal epistemology: The psychology of beliefs about knowledge and knowing* (pp. 121–144). Mahwah, NJ: Erlbaum.

Kuklinski, M. R., & Weinstein, R. S. (2001). Classroom and developmental differences in a path model of teacher expectancy effects. *Child Development, 72,* 1554–1578.

Kulhavy, R. W., Lee, J. B., & Caterino, L. C. (1985). Conjoint retention of maps and related discourse. *Contemporary Educational Psychology 10,* 28–37.

Kulik, C. C., Kulik, J. A., & Bangert-Drowns, R. L. (1990). Effectiveness of mastery learning programs: A meta-analysis. *Review of Educational Research, 60,* 265–299.

Kulik, J. A., & Kulik, C. C. (1988). Timing of feedback and verbal learning. *Review of Educational Research, 58,* 79–97.

Kulik, J. A., & Kulik, C. C. (1997). Ability grouping. In N. Colangelo & G. Davis (Eds.), *Handbook of gifted education* (2nd ed., pp. 230–242). Boston: Allyn & Bacon.

Kulik, J. A., Kulik, C. C., & Cohen, P. A. (1979). A meta-analysis of outcome studies of Keller's Personalized System of Instruction. *American Psychologist, 34,* 307–318.

Kulik, J. A., Kulik, C. C., & Cohen, P. A. (1980). Effectiveness of computer-based college teaching: A meta-analysis of findings. *Review of Educational Research, 50,* 525–544.

Kumar, R., Gheen, M. H., & Kaplan, A. (2002). Goal structures in the learning environment and students' disaffection from learning and schooling. In C. Midgley (Ed.), *Goals, goal structures, and patterns of adaptive learning* (pp. 143–173). Mahwah, NJ: Erlbaum.

Kunc, N. (1984). Integration: Being realistic isn't realistic. *Canadian Journal for Exceptional Children, 1*(1), 4–8.

Kunzinger, E. L., III. (1985). A short-term longitudinal study of memorial development during early grade school. *Developmental Psychology, 21,* 642–646.

Kupersmidt, J. B., Buchele, K. S., Voegler, M. E., & Sedikides, C. (1996). Social self-discrepancy: A theory relating peer relations problems and school maladjustment. In J. Juvonen & K. R. Wentzel (Eds.), *Social motivation: Understanding children's school adjustment* (pp. 66–97). Cambridge, England: Cambridge University Press.

Kupersmidt, J. B., & Coie, J. D. (1990). Preadolescent peer status, aggression, and school adjustment as predictors of externalizing problems in adolescence. *Child Development, 61,* 1350–1362.

Kurtines, W. M., Berman, S. L., Ittel, A., & Williamson, S. (1995). Moral development: A co-constructivist perspective. In W. M. Kurtines & J. L. Gewirtz (Eds.), *Moral development: An introduction.* Boston: Allyn & Bacon.

Kyle, W. C., & Shymansky, J. A. (1989, April). Enhancing learning through conceptual change teaching. *NARST News, 31,* 7–8.

LaBar, K. S., & Phelps, E. A. (1998). Arousal-mediated memory consolidation: Role of the medial temporal lobe in humans. *Psychological Science, 9,* 490–493.

LaBlance, G. R., Steckol, K. F., & Smith, V. L. (1994). Stuttering: The role of the classroom teacher. *Teaching Exceptional Children, 26*(2), 10–12.

Laboratory of Human Cognition. (1982). Culture and intelligence. In R. J. Sternberg (Ed.), *Handbook of human intelligence.* Cambridge, England: Cambridge University Press.

Labov, W. (1973). The boundaries of words and their meanings. In C.-J. N. Bailey & R. W. Shuy (Eds.), *New ways of analyzing variations in English.* Washington, DC: Georgetown University Press.

Ladson-Billings, G. (1994a). *The dreamkeepers: Successful teachers of African American children.* San Francisco: Jossey-Bass.

Ladson-Billings, G. (1994b). What we can learn from multicultural education research. *Educational Leadership, 51*(8), 22–26.

Ladson-Billings, G. (1995). Toward a theory of culturally relevant pedagogy. *American Educational Research Journal, 32,* 465–491.

LaFromboise, T., Coleman, H. L. K., & Gerton, J. (1993). Psychological impact of biculturalism: Evidence and theory. *Psychological Bulletin, 114,* 395–412.

Lahey, B. B., & Carlson, C. L. (1991). Validity of the diagnostic category of attention deficit disorder without hyperactivity: A review of the literature. *Journal of Learning Disabilities, 24,* 110–120.

Lajoie, S. P., & Derry, S. J. (Eds.). (1993). *Computers as cognitive tools.* Mahwah, NJ: Erlbaum.

Lamborn, S. D., Mounts, N. S., Steinberg, L., & Dornbusch, S. M. (1991). Patterns of competence and adjustment among adolescents from authoritative, authoritarian, indulgent, and neglectful families. *Child Development, 62,* 1049–1065.

Lamon, M., Chan, C., Scardamalia, M., Burtis, P. J., & Brett, C. (1993, April). *Beliefs about learning and constructive processes in reading: Effects of a computer supported intentional learning environment (CSILE).* Paper presented at the annual meeting of the American Educational Research Association, Atlanta, GA.

Lampert, M. (1990). When the problem is not the question and the solution is not the answer: Mathematical knowing and teaching. *American Educational Research Journal, 27,* 29–63.

Lampert, M., Rittenhouse, P., & Crumbaugh, C. (1996). Agreeing to disagree: Developing sociable mathematical discourse. In D. R. Olson & N. Torrance (Eds.), *The handbook of education and human development: New models of learning, teaching, and schooling.* Cambridge, MA: Blackwell.

Lan, W. Y., Repman, J., Bradley, L., & Weller, H. (1994, April). *Immediate and lasting effects of criterion and payoff on academic risk taking.* Paper presented at the annual meeting of the American Educational Research Association, New Orleans, LA.

Landau, S., & McAninch, C. (1993). Young children with attention deficits. *Young Children, 48*(4), 49–58.

Landesman, S., & Ramey, C. (1989). Developmental psychology and mental retardation: Integrating scientific principles with treatment practices. *American Psychologist, 44,* 409–415.

Lane, D. M., & Pearson, D. A. (1982). The development of selective attention. *Merrill-Palmer Quarterly, 28,* 317–337.

Langer, E. J. (1997). *The power of mindful learning.* Reading, MA: Addison-Wesley.

Langer, E. J. (2000). Mindful learning. *Current Directions in Psychological Science, 9,* 220–223.

Langer, J. A. (2000). Excellence in English in middle and high school: How teachers' professional lives support student achievement. *American Educational Research Journal 37,* 397–439.

Lanza, A., & Roselli, T. (1991). Effect of the hypertextual approach versus the structured approach on students' achievement. *Journal of Computer-Based Instruction, 18*(2), 48–50.

Lapan, R. T., Tucker, B., Kim, S.-K., & Kosciulek, J. F. (2003). Preparing rural adolescents for post-high

school transitions. *Journal of Counseling and Development, 81,* 329–342.

La Paro, K. M., & Pianta, R. C. (2000). Predicting children's competence in the early school years: A meta-analytic review. *Review of Educational Research, 70,* 443–484.

Lapsley, D. K. (1993). Toward an integrated theory of adolescent ego development: The "new look" at adolescent egocentrism. *American Journal of Orthopsychiatry, 63,* 562–571.

Larkin, R. W. (1979). *Suburban youth in cultural crisis.* New York: Oxford University Press.

Larson, R. W. (2000). Toward a psychology of positive youth development. *American Psychologist, 55,* 170–183.

Larson, R. W., Clore, G. L., & Wood, G. A. (1999). The emotions of romantic relationships: Do they wreak havoc on adolescents? In W. Furman, B. B. Brown, & C. Feiring (Eds.), *The development of romantic relationships in adolescence* (pp. 19–49). Cambridge, England: Cambridge University Press.

Larson, R. W., Moneta, G., Richards, M. H., & Wilson, S. (2002). Continuity, stability, and change in daily emotional experience across adolescence. *Child Development, 73,* 1151–1165.

Laupa, M., & Turiel, E. (1995). Social domain theory. In W. M. Kurtines & J. L. Gewirtz (Eds.), *Moral development: An introduction.* Boston: Allyn & Bacon.

Lave, J. (1993). Word problems: A microcosm of theories of learning. In P. Light & G. Butterworth (Eds.), *Context and cognition: Ways of learning and knowing.* Mahwah, NJ: Erlbaum.

Lave, J., & Wenger, E. (1991). *Situated learning: Legitimate peripheral participation.* Cambridge, England: Cambridge University Press.

Lazarus, R. S. (1991). *Emotion and adaptation.* New York: Oxford University Press.

Learning First Alliance. (2001). *Every child learning: Safe and supportive schools.* Washington, DC: Association for Supervision and Curriculum Development.

Learning Technology Center, Vanderbilt University. (1996). *Jasper in the Classroom* (videodisc). Mahwah, NH: Erlbaum.

Leary, M. R. (1999). Making sense of self-esteem. *Current Directions in Psychological Science, 8,* 32–35.

Leary, M. R., & Hill, D. A. (1996). Moving on: Autism and movement disturbance. *Mental Retardation, 34,* 39–53.

LeBlanc, L. A., Coates, A. M., Daneshvar, S., Charlop-Christy, M. H., Morris, C., & Lancaster, B. M. (2003). Using video modeling and reinforcement to teach perspective-taking skills to children with autism. *Journal of Applied Behavior Analysis, 36,* 253–257.

Lee, C. D., & Slaughter-Defoe, D. T. (1995). Historical and sociocultural influences on African and American education. In J. A. Banks & C. A. M. Banks (Eds.), *Handbook of research on multicultural education.* New York: Macmillan.

Lee, J. F., Jr., & Pruitt, K. W. (1984). *Providing for individual differences in student learning: A mastery learning approach.* Springfield, IL: Charles C Thomas.

Lee, O. (1999). Science knowledge, world views, and information sources in social and cultural contexts: Making sense after a natural disaster. *American Educational Research Journal, 36,* 187–219.

Lee, S. (1985). Children's acquisition of conditional logic structure: Teachable? *Contemporary Educational Psychology, 10,* 14–27.

Lee, V. E., & Burkam, D. T. (2003). Dropping out of high school: The role of school organization and structure. *American Educational Research Journal, 40,* 353–393.

Lee-Pearce, M. L., Plowman, T. S., & Touchstone, D. (1998). Starbase-Atlantis, a school without walls: A comparative study of an innovative science program for at-risk urban elementary students. *Journal of Education for Students Placed at Risk, 3,* 223–235.

Leffert, J. S., Siperstein, G. N., & Millikan, E. (1999). *Social perception and strategy generation: Two key social cognitive processes in children with mental retardation.* Paper presented at the biennial meeting of the

Society for Research in Child Development, Albuquerque, NM.

Lehrer, R. (1993). Authors of knowledge: Patterns of hypermedia design. In S. P. Lajoie & S. J. Derry (Eds.), *Computers as cognitive tools* (pp. 197–227). Mahwah, NJ: Erlbaum.

Leichtman, M. D., & Ceci, S. J. (1995). The effects of stereotypes and suggestions on preschoolers' reports. *Developmental Psychology, 31,* 568–578.

Lein, L. (1975). Black American immigrant children: Their speech at home and school. *Council on Anthropology and Education Quarterly, 6,* 1–11.

Leinhardt, G. (1994). History: A time to be mindful. In G. Leinhardt, I. L. Beck, & C. Stainton (Eds.), *Teaching and learning in history.* Mahwah, NJ: Erlbaum.

Leinhardt, G., & Pallay, A. (1982). Restrictive educational settings: Exile or haven? *Review of Educational Research, 52,* 557–578.

Leiter, J., & Johnsen, M. C. (1997). Child maltreatment and school performance declines: An event-history analysis. *American Educational Research Journal, 34,* 563–589.

Lejuez, C. W., Schaal, D. W., & O'Donnell, J. (1998). Behavioral pharmacology and the treatment of substance abuse. In J. J. Plaud & G. H. Eifert (Eds.), *From behavior theory to behavior therapy* (pp. 116–135). Needham Heights, MA: Allyn & Bacon.

Lenneberg, E. H. (1967). *Biological foundations of language.* New York: Wiley.

Lennon, R., Eisenberg, N., & Carroll, J. L. (1983). The assessment of empathy in early childhood. *Journal of Applied Developmental Psychology, 4,* 295–302.

Lennon, R., Ormrod, J. E., Burger, S. F., & Warren, E. (1990, October). *Belief systems of teacher education majors and their possible influences on future classroom performance.* Paper presented at the Northern Rocky Mountain Educational Research Association, Greeley, CO.

Lentz, F. E. (1988). Reductive procedures. In J. C. Witt, S. N. Elliott, & F. M. Gresham (Eds.), *Handbook of behavior therapy in education.* New York: Plenum Press.

Lepper, M. R. (1981). Intrinsic and extrinsic motivation in children: Detrimental effects of superfluous social controls. In W. A. Collins (Ed.), *Minnesota Symposia on Child Psychology* (Vol. 14). Mahwah, NJ: Erlbaum.

Lepper, M. R., Aspinwall, L. G., Mumme, D. L., & Chabay, R. W. (1990). Self-perception and social perception processes in tutoring: Subtle social control strategies of expert tutors. In J. M. Olson & M. P. Zanna (Eds.), *Self-inference processes: The Ontario Symposium.* Mahwah, NJ: Erlbaum.

Lepper, M. R., & Gurtner, J. (1989). Children and computers: Approaching the twenty-first century. *American Psychologist, 44,* 170–178.

Lepper, M. R., & Hodell, M. (1989). Intrinsic motivation in the classroom. In C. Ames & R. Ames (Eds.), *Research on motivation in education: Vol. 3. Goals and cognitions.* San Diego, CA: Academic Press.

Lerman, D. C., & Iwata, B. A. (1995). Prevalence of the extinction burst and its attenuation during treatment. *Journal of Applied Behavior Analysis, 28,* 93–94.

Lerman, D. C., Kelley, M. E., Vorndran, C. M., Kuhn, S. A. C., & LaRue, R. H., Jr. (2002). Reinforcement magnitude and responding during threatment with differential reinforcement. *Journal of Applied Behavior Analysis, 35,* 29–48.

Lerman, D. C., & Vorndran, C. M. (2002). On the status of knowledge for using punishment: Implications for treating behavior disorders. *Journal of Applied Behavior Analysis, 35,* 431–464.

Lerner, J. W. (1985). *Learning disabilities: Theories, diagnosis, and teaching strategies* (4th ed.). Boston: Houghton Mifflin.

Lesgold, A. M. (2001). The nature and methods of learning by doing. *American Psychologist, 56,* 965–973.

Lester, F. K., Jr., Lambdin, D. V., & Preston, R. V. (1997). A new vision of the nature and purposes of assessment in the mathematics classroom. In G. D. Phye (Ed.), *Handbook of classroom assessment: Learning, achievement, and adjustment.* San Diego, CA: Academic Press.

Levay, S., Wiesel, T. N., & Hubel, D. H. (1980). The development of ocular dominance columns in normal and visually deprived monkeys, *Journal of Comparative Neurology, 19,* 11–51.

Leventhal, T., & Brooks-Gunn, J. (2000). The neighborhoods they live in: The effects of neighborhood residence upon child and adolescent outcomes. *Psychological Bulletin, 126,* 309–337.

Levin, H. M. (1998). Educational performance standards and the economy. *Educational Researcher, 27*(4), 4–10.

Levin, J. R., & Mayer, R. E. (1993). Understanding illustrations in text. In B. K. Britton, A. Woodward, & M. Binkley (Eds.), *Learning from textbooks: Theory and practice.* Mahwah, NJ: Erlbaum.

Levine, D. U., & Lezotte, L. W. (1995). Effective schools research. In J. A. Banks & C. A. M. Banks (Eds.), *Handbook of research on multicultural education.* New York: Macmillan.

Levitt, M. J., Guacci-Franco, N., & Levitt, J. L. (1993). Convoys of social support in childhood and early adolescence: Structure and function. *Developmental Psychology, 29,* 811–818.

Levitt, M. J., Levitt, J. L., Bustos, G. L., Crooks, N. A., Santos, J. D., Telan, P., & Silver, M. E. (1999, April). *The social ecology of achievement in pre-adolescents: Social support and school attitudes.* Paper presented at the annual meeting of the American Educational Research Association, Montreal, Canada.

Levstik, L. S. (1994). Building a sense of history in a first-grade classroom. In J. Brophy (Ed.), *Advances in research on teaching: Vol. 4. Case studies of teaching and learning in social studies.* Greenwich, CT: JAI Press.

Levy, I., Kaplan, A., & Patrick, H. (2000, April). *Early adolescents' achievement goals, intergroup processes, and attitudes towards collaboration.* Paper presented at the annual meeting of the American Educational Research Association, New Orleans, LA.

Lewis, M. (1991). Self-knowledge and social influence. In M. Lewis & S. Feinman (Eds.), *Social influences and socialization in infancy: Vol. 6. Genesis of behavior* (pp. 111–134). New York: Plenum Press.

Lewis, R. B., & Doorlag, D. H. (1991). *Teaching special students in the mainstream* (3rd ed.). Upper Saddle River, NJ: Merrill/Prentice Hall.

Lewit, E. M. Terman, D. L., & Behrman, R. E. (1997). Children and poverty: Analysis and recommendations. *The Future of Children: Children and Poverty, 7,* 4–24.

Liben, L. S., & Bigler, R. S. (2002). The developmental course of gender differentiation: Conceptualizing, measuring, and evaluating constructs and pathways. *Monographs of the Society for Research in Child Development, 67*(2, Serial No. 269).

Liben, L. S., Bigler, R. S., & Krogh, H. R. (2002). Language at work: Children's gendered interpretations of occupational titles. *Child Development, 73,* 810–828.

Liben, L. S., & Downs, R. M. (1989). Understanding maps as symbols: The development of map concepts in children. In H. W. Reese (Ed.), *Advances in child development and behavior* (Vol. 22). San Diego, CA: Harcourt Brace Jovanovich.

Lichtman, J. W. (2001). Developmental neurobiology overview: Synapses, circuits, and plasticity. In D. B. Bailey, Jr., J. T. Bruer, F. J. Symons, & J. W. Lichtman (Eds.), *Critical thinking about critical periods* (pp. 27–42). Baltimore: Brookes.

Lickona, T. (1991). Moral development in the elementary school classroom. In W. M. Kurtines & J. L. Gewirtz (Eds.), *Moral behavior and development: Vol. 3. Application.* Mahwah, NJ: Erlbaum.

Lidz, C. S. (1991). Issues in the assessment of preschool children. In B. A. Bracken (Ed.), *The psychoeducational assessment of preschool children* (2nd ed., pp. 18–31). Boston: Allyn & Bacon.

Light, J. G., & Defries, J. C. (1995). Comorbidity of reading and mathematics disabilities: Genetic and environmental etiologies. *Journal of Learning Disabilities, 28,* 96–106.

Light, P., & Butterworth, G. (Eds.). (1993). *Context and cognition: Ways of learning and knowing.* Mahwah, NJ: Erlbaum.

Lillard, A. S. (1997). Other folks' theories of mind and behavior. *Psychological Science, 8,* 268–274.

Lind, G. (1994, April). *Why do juvenile delinquents gain little from moral discussion programs?* Paper presented at the annual meeting of the American Educational Research Association, New Orleans, LA.

Lindberg, M. (1991). A taxonomy of suggestibility and eyewitness memory: Age, memory process, and focus of analysis. In J. L. Doris (Ed.), *The suggestibility of children's recollections.* Washington, DC: American Psychological Association.

Linderholm, T., Gustafson, M., van den Broek, P., & Lorch, R. F., Jr. (1997, March). *Effects of reading goals on inference generation.* Paper presented at the annual meeting of the American Educational Research Association, Chicago.

Linn, M. C., Clement, C., Pulos, S., & Sullivan, P. (1989). Scientific reasoning during adolescence: The influence of instruction in science knowledge and reasoning strategies. *Journal of Research in Science Teaching, 26,* 171–187.

Linn, M. C., & Hyde, J. S. (1989). Gender, mathematics, and science. *Educational Researcher, 18*(8), 17–19, 22–27.

Linn, M. C., Songer, N. B., & Eylon, B. (1996). Shifts and convergences in science learning and instruction. In D. C. Berliner & R. C. Calfee (Eds.), *Handbook of educational psychology.* New York: Macmillan.

Linn, R. L. (1994). Performance assessment: Policy promises and technical measurement standards. *Educational Researcher, 23*(9), 4–14.

Linn, R. L. (2000). Assessments and accountability. *Educational Researcher, 29*(2), 4–16.

Linn, R. L., & Miller, M. D. (2005). *Measurement and assessment in teaching* (9th ed.). Upper Saddle River, NJ: Merrill/Prentice Hall.

Linnenbrink, E. A., & Pintrich, P. R. (2002). Achievement goal theory and affect: An asymmetrical bidirectional model. *Educational Psychologist, 37,* 69–78.

Linnenbrink, E. A., & Pintrich, P. R. (2003). Achievement goals and intentional conceptual change. In G. M. Sinatra & P. R. Pintrich (Eds.), *Intentional conceptual change* (pp. 347–374). Mahwah, NJ: Erlbaum.

Lipka, J., with Mohatt, G. V., & the Ciulistet Group. (1998). *Transforming the culture of schools: Yup'ik Eskimo examples.* Mahwah, NJ: Erlbaum.

Lippa, R. A. (2002). *Gender, nature, and nurture.* Mahwah, NJ: Erlbaum.

Lipson, M. Y. (1983). The influence of religious affiliation on children's memory for text information. *Reading Research Quarterly, 18,* 448–457.

Liss, M. B. (1983). Learning gender-related skills through play. In M. B. Liss (Ed.), *Social and cognitive skills: Sex roles and children's play.* San Diego, CA: Academic Press.

Little, L. (2002). Middle class mothers' perceptions of peer and sibling victimization among children with Asperger's syndrome and nonverbal learning disorders. *Comprehensive Pediatric Nursing, 25,* 43–57.

Littlewood, W. T. (1984). *Foreign and second language learning: Language-acquisition research and its implications for the classroom.* Cambridge, England: Cambridge University Press.

Liu, J., Golinkoff, R. M., & Sak, K. (2001). One cow does not an animal make: Young children can extend novel words at the superordinate level. *Child Development, 72,* 1674–1694.

Liu, L. G. (1990, April). *The use of causal questioning to promote narrative comprehension and memory.* Paper presented at the annual meeting of the American Educational Research Association, Boston.

Lochman, J. E., & Dodge, K. A. (1994). Social-cognitive processes of severely violent, moderately aggressive, and nonaggressive boys. *Journal of Consulting and Clinical Psychology, 62,* 366–374.

Locke, E. A., & Latham, G. P. (1990). *A theory of goal setting and task performance.* Upper Saddle River, NJ: Prentice Hall.

Locke, E. A., & Latham, G. P. (2002). Building a practically useful theory of goal setting and task motivation: A 35-year odyssey. *American Psychologist, 57,* 705–717.

Lockhart, K. L., Chang, B., & Story, T. (2002). Young children's beliefs about the stability of traits: Protective optimism? *Child Development, 73*, 1408–1430.

Lodico, M. G., Ghatala, E. S., Levin, J. R., Pressley, M., & Bell, J. A. (1983). The effects of strategy monitoring training on children's selection of effective memory strategies. *Journal of Experimental Child Psychology, 35*, 273–277.

Loeber, R., & Stouthamer-Loeber, M. (1998). Development of juvenile aggression and violence. *American Psychologist, 53*, 242–259.

Loftus, E. F. (1991). Made in memory: Distortions in recollection after misleading information. In G. H. Bower (Ed.), *The psychology of learning and motivation: Advances in research and theory* (Vol. 27). San Diego, CA: Academic Press.

Loftus, E. F., & Loftus, G. R. (1980). On the permanence of stored information in the human brain. *American Psychologist, 35*, 409–420.

Logan, K. R., Alberto, P. A., Kana, T. G., & Waylor-Bowen, T. (1994). Curriculum development and instructional design for students with profound disabilities. In L. Sternberg (Ed.), *Individuals with profound disabilities: Instructional and assistive strategies* (3rd ed.). Austin, TX: Pro-Ed.

Lomawaima, K. T. (1995). Educating Native Americans. In J. A. Banks & C. A. M. Banks (Eds.), *Handbook of research on multicultural education*. New York: Macmillan.

Lopez, A. M. (2003). Mixed-race school-age children: A summary of census 2000 data. *Educational Researcher, 32*(6), 25–37.

Lopez, E. C. (1997). The cognitive assessment of limited English proficient and bilingual children. In D. P. Flanagan, J. L. Genshaft, & P. L. Harrison (Eds.), *Contemporary intellectual assessment: Theories, tests, and issues* (pp. 503–516). New York: Guilford Press.

López, G. R. (2001). Redefining parental involvement: Lessons from high-performing migrant-impacted schools. *American Educational Research Journal, 38*, 253–288.

Loranger, A. L. (1994). The study strategies of successful and unsuccessful high school students. *Journal of Reading Behavior, 26*, 347–360.

Lorch, E. P., Diener, M. B., Sanchez, R. P., Milich, R., Welsh, R., & van den Broek, P. (1999). The effects of story structure on the recall of stories in children with attention deficit hyperactivity disorder. *Journal of Educational Psychology, 91*, 273–283.

Lorch, R. F., Jr., Lorch, E. P., & Inman, W. E. (1993). Effects of signaling topic structure on text recall. *Journal of Educational Psychology, 85*, 281–290.

Losey, K. M. (1995). Mexican American students and classroom interaction: An overview and critique. *Review of Educational Research, 65*, 283–318.

Lou, Y., Abrami, P. C., & d'Apollonia, S. (2001). Small group and individual learning with technology: A meta-analysis. *Review of of Educational Research, 71*, 449–521.

Lou, Y., Abrami, P. C., Spence, J. C., Poulsen, C., Chambers, B., & d'Apollonia, S. (1996). Within-class grouping: A meta-analysis. *Review of Educational Research, 66*, 423–458.

Lounsbury, J. H. (Ed.). (1984). *Perspectives: Middle school education 1964–1984*. Columbus, OH: National Middle School Association.

Lovell, K. (1979). Intellectual growth and the school curriculum. In F. B. Murray (Ed.), *The impact of Piagetian theory: On education, philosophy, psychiatry, and psychology*. Baltimore: University Park Press.

Lovett, S. B., & Flavell, J. H. (1990). Understanding and remembering: Children's knowledge about the differential effects of strategy and task variables on comprehension and memorization. *Child Development, 61*, 1842–1858.

Lovitt, T. C., Guppy, T. E., & Blattner, J. E. (1969). The use of free-time contingency with fourth graders to increase spelling accuracy. *Behaviour Research and Therapy, 7*, 151–156.

Lowry, R., Sleet, D., Duncan, C., Powell, K., & Kolbe, L. (1995). Adolescents at risk for violence. *Educational Psychology Review, 7*, 7–39.

Lubart, T. I. (1994). Creativity. In R. J. Sternberg (Ed.), *Thinking and problem solving*. San Diego, CA: Academic Press.

Lucariello, J., Kyratzis, A., & Nelson, K. (1992). Taxonomic knowledge: What kind and when? *Child Development, 63*, 978–998.

Luchins, A. S. (1942). Mechanization in problem solving: The effect of Einstellung. *Psychological Monographs, 54* (Whole No. 248).

Luchins, A. S., & Luchins, E. H. (1950). New experimental attempts at preventing mechanization in problem solving. *Journal of General Psychology, 42*, 279–297.

Luck, S. J., & Vogel, E. K. (1997). The capacity of visual working memory for features and conjunctions. *Nature, 390*, 279–281.

Luckasson, R., Borthwick-Duffy, S., Buntinx, W. H. E., Coulter, D. L., Craig, E. M., Reeve, A., Schalock, R. L., Snell, M. E., Spitalnik, D. M., Spreat, S., & Tassé, M. J. (Eds.). (2002). *Mental retardation: Definition, classification, and systems of supports* (10th ed.). Washington, DC: American Association on Mental Retardation.

Lueptow, L. B. (1984). *Adolescent sex roles and social change*. New York: Columbia University Press.

Lundeberg, M. A., & Fox, P. W. (1991). Do laboratory findings on test expectancy generalize to classroom outcomes? *Review of Educational Research, 61*, 94–106.

Lupart, J. L. (1995). Exceptional learners and teaching for transfer. In A. McKeough, J. Lupart, & A. Marini (Eds.), *Teaching for transfer: Fostering generalization in learning*. Mahwah, NJ: Erlbaum.

Luque, M. L. (2003). The role of domain-specific knowledge in intentional conceptual change. In G. M. Sinatra & P. R. Pintrich (Eds.), *Intentional conceptual change* (pp. 133–170). Mahwah, NJ: Erlbaum.

Lustig, C., & Hasher, L. (2001). Implicit memory is vulnerable to proactive interference. *Psychological Science, 12*, 408–412.

Luthar, S. S., & Becker, B. E. (2002). Privileged but pressured? A study of affluent youth. *Child Development, 73*, 1593–1610.

Lyon, G. R., & Krasnegor, N. A. (Eds.). (1996). *Attention, memory, and executive function*. Baltimore: Brookes.

Lyon, M. A. (1984). Positive reinforcement and logical consequences in the treatment of classroom encopresis. *School Psychology Review, 13*, 238–243.

Lytton, H., & Romney, D. M. (1991). Parents' differential socialization of boys and girls: A meta-analysis. *Psychological Bulletin, 109*, 267–296.

Ma, X., & Kishor, N. (1997). Attitude toward self, social factors, and achievement in mathematics: A meta-analytic review. *Educational Psychology Review, 9*, 89–120.

Maccoby, E. E. (2002). Gender and group process: A developmental perspective. *Current Directions in Psychological Science, 11*, 54–58.

Maccoby, E. E., & Hagen, J. W. (1965). Effects of distraction upon central versus incidental recall: Developmental trends. *Journal of Experimental Child Psychology, 2*, 280–289.

Maccoby, E. E., & Martin, J. A. (1983). Socialization in the context of the family: Parent-child interaction. In E. M. Hetherington (Ed.), *Handbook of child psychology: Vol. 4. Socialization, personality, and social development* (4th ed.). New York: Wiley.

Mace, F. C., Belfiore, P. J., & Shea, M. C. (1989). Operant theory and research on self-regulation. In B. J. Zimmerman & D. H. Schunk (Eds.), *Self-regulated learning and academic achievement: Theory, research, and practice*. New York: Springer-Verlag.

Mace, F. C., Hock, M. L., Lalli, J. S., West, B. J., Belfiore, P., Pinter, E., & Brown, D. K. (1988). Behavioral momentum in the treatment of noncompliance. *Journal of Applied Behavior Analysis, 21*, 123–141.

Mace, F. C., & Kratochwill, T. R. (1988). Self-monitoring. In J. C. Witt, S. N. Elliott, & F. M. Gresham (Eds.), *Handbook of behavior therapy in education*. New York: Plenum Press.

Machiels-Bongaerts, M., Schmidt, H. G., & Boshuizen, H. P. A. (1991, April). *The effects of prior knowledge*

activation on free recall and study time allocation. Paper presented at the annual meeting of the American Educational Research Association, Chicago.

Mac Iver, D. J., Reuman, D. A., & Main, S. R. (1995). Social structuring of the school: Studying what is, illuminating what could be. In J. T. Spence, J. M. Darley, & D. J. Foss (Eds.), *Annual review of psychology* (Vol. 46, pp. 375–400). Palo Alto, CA: Annual Review, Inc.

Mac Iver, D. J., Stipek, D. J., & Daniels, D. H. (1991). Explaining within-semester changes in student effort in junior high school and senior high school courses. *Journal of Educational Psychology, 83*, 201–211.

MacLean, D. J., Sasse, D. K., Keating, D. P., Stewart, B. E., & Miller, F. K. (1995, April). *All-girls' mathematics and science instruction in early adolescence: Longitudinal effects*. Paper presented at the annual meeting of the American Educational Research Association, San Francisco.

MacMillan, D. L., & Meyers, C. E. (1979). Educational labeling of handicapped learners. In D. C. Berliner (Ed.), *Review of research in education* (No. 7). Washington, DC: American Educational Research Association.

Madden, N. A., & Slavin, R. E. (1983). Mainstreaming students with mild handicaps: Academic and social outcomes. *Review of Educational Research, 53*, 519–569.

Maehr, M. L. (1984). Meaning and motivation: Toward a theory of personal investment. In R. Ames & C. Ames (Eds.), *Research on motivation in education: Vol. 1. Student motivation*. San Diego, CA: Academic Press.

Maehr, M. L., & Anderman, E. M. (1993). Reinventing schools for early adolescents: Emphasizing task goals. *Elementary School Journal, 93*, 593–610.

Maehr, M. L., & Meyer, H. A. (1997). Understanding motivation and schooling: Where we've been, where we are, and where we need to go. *Educational Psychology Review, 9*, 371–409.

Magnusson, S. J., Boyle, R. A., & Templin, M. (1994, April). *Conceptual development: Re-examining knowledge construction in science*. Paper presented at the annual meeting of the American Educational Research Association, New Orleans, LA.

Mahoney, J. L., Cairns, B. D., & Farmer, T. W. (2003). Promoting interpersonal competence and educational success through extracurricular activity participation. *Journal of Educational Psychology, 95*, 409–418.

Maker, C. J. (1993). Creativity, intelligence, and problem solving: A definition and design for cross-cultural research and measurement related to giftedness. *Gifted Education International, 9*(2), 68–77.

Maker, C. J., & Schiever, S. W. (Eds.). (1989). *Critical issues in gifted education: Vol. 2. Defensible programs for cultural and ethnic minorities*. Austin, TX: Pro-Ed.

Mandler, G., & Pearlstone, Z. (1966). Free and constrained concept learning and subsequent recall. *Journal of Verbal Learning and Verbal Behavior, 5*, 126–131.

Manis, F. R. (1996). Current trends in dyslexia research. In B. J. Cratty & R. L. Goldman (Eds.), *Learning disabilities: Contemporary viewpoints*. Amsterdam: Harwood Academic.

Manset, G., & Semmel, M. I. (1997). Are inclusive programs for students with mild disabilities effective? A comparative review of model programs. *Journal of Special Education, 31*, 155–180.

Marachi, R., Friedel, J., & Midgley, C. (2001, April). *"I sometimes annoy my teacher during math": Relations between student perceptions of the teacher and disruptive behavior in the classroom*. Paper presented at the annual meeting of the American Educational Research Association, Seattle, WA.

Maratsos, M. (1998). Some problems in grammatical acquisition. In W. Damon (Series Ed.), D. Kuhn, & R. S. Siegler (Vol. Eds.), *Handbook of child psychology: Vol. 2. Cognition, perception, and language* (5th ed.). New York: Wiley.

Marcia, J. E. (1980). Identity in adolescence. In J. Adelson (Ed.), *Handbook of adolescent psychology*. New York: Wiley.

Marcia, J. E. (1988). Common processes underlying ego identity, cognitive/moral development, and individuation. In D. K. Lapsley & F. C. Power (Eds.), *Self, ego, and identity: Integrative approaches* (pp. 211–225). New York: Springer-Verlag.

Marcus, R. F. (1980). Empathy and popularity of preschool children. *Child Study Journal, 10,* 133–145.

Maria, K. (1998). Self-confidence and the process of conceptual change. In B. Guzzetti & C. Hynd (Eds.), *Perspectives on conceptual change: Multiple ways to understand knowing and learning in a complex world* (pp. 7–16). Mahwah, NJ: Erlbaum.

Markman, E. M. (1977). Realizing that you don't understand: A preliminary investigation. *Child Development, 48,* 986–992.

Markman, E. M. (1979). Realizing that you don't understand: Elementary school children's awareness of inconsistencies. *Child Development, 50,* 643–655.

Marks, H. M. (2000). Student engagement in instructional activity: Patterns in the elementary, middle, and high school years. *American Educational Research Journal, 37,* 153–184.

Marks, J. (1995). *Human biodiversity: Genes, race, and history.* New York: Aldine de Gruyter.

Markus, H. R., & Kitayama, S. (1991). Culture and the self: Implications for cognition, emotion, and motivation. *Psychological Review, 98,* 224–253.

Marsh, H. W. (1989). Age and sex effect in multiple dimensions of self-concept: Preadolescence to early-adulthood. *Journal of Educational Psychology, 81,* 417–430.

Marsh, H. W. (1990a). Causal ordering of academic self-concept and academic achievement: A multiwave, longitudinal panel analysis. *Journal of Educational Psychology, 82,* 646–656.

Marsh, H. W. (1990b). A multidimensional, hierarchical model of self-concept: Theoretical and empirical justification. *Educational Psychology Review, 2,* 77–172.

Marsh, H. W., & Craven, R. (1997). Academic self-concept: Beyond the dustbowl. In G. D. Phye (Ed.), *Handbook of classroom assessment: Learning, achievement, and adjustment.* San Diego, CA: Academic Press.

Marsh, H. W., & Hau, K. T. (2003). Big-fish–little-pond effect on academic self-concept: A cross-cultural (26-country) test of the negative effects of academically selective schools. *American Psychologist, 58,* 364–376.

Marsh, H. W., Hau, K.-T., & Kong, C. K. (2002). Multilevel causal ordering of academic self-concept and achievement: Influence of language of instruction (English compared with Chinese) for Hong Kong students. *American Educational Research Journal, 39,* 727–763.

Marsh, H. W., Parada, R. H., Yeung, A. S., & Healey, J. (2001). Aggressive school troublemakers and victims: A longitudinal model examining the pivotal role of self-concept. *Journal of Educational Psychology, 93,* 411–419.

Marshall, H. H. (1981). Open classrooms: Has the term outlived its usefulness? *Review of Educational Research, 51,* 181–192.

Marshall, H. H. (1992). *Redefining student learning: Roots of educational change.* Norwood, NJ: Ablex.

Martin, A. J., Marsh, H. W., & Debus, R. L. (2001). A quadripolar need achievement representation of self-handicapping and defensive pessimism. *American Educational Research Journal, 38,* 583–610.

Martin, A. J., Marsh, H. W., Williamson, A., & Debus, R. L. (2003). Self-handicapping, defensive pessimism, and goal orientation: A qualitative study of university students. *Journal of Educational Psychology, 95,* 617–628.

Martin, C. L. (2000). Cognitive theories of gender development. In T. Eckes & H. Trautner (Eds.), *The developmental social psychology of gender* (pp. 91–121). Mahwah, NJ: Erlbaum.

Martin, C. L., & Halverson, C. F. (1987). The roles of cognition in sex role acquisition. In D. B. Carter (Ed.), *Current conceptions of sex roles and sex typing: Theory and research.* New York: Praeger.

Martin, S. S., Brady, M. P., & Williams, R. E. (1991). Effects of toys on the social behavior of preschool children in integrated and nonintegrated groups: Investigation of a setting event. *Journal of Early Intervention, 15,* 153–161.

Marzano, R. J., & Costa, A. L. (1988). Question: Do standardized tests measure general cognitive skills? Answer: No. *Educational Leadership, 45*(8), 66–71.

Maslow, A. H. (1973). Theory of human motivation. In R. J. Lowry (Ed.), *Dominance, self-esteem, self-actualization: Germinal papers of A. H. Maslow.* Monterey, CA: Brooks/Cole.

Maslow, A. H. (1987). *Motivation and personality* (3rd ed.). New York: Harper & Row.

Mason, L. (2003). Personal epistemologies and intentional conceptual change. In G. M. Sinatra & P. R. Pintrich (Eds.), *Intentional conceptual change* (pp. 199–236). Mahwah, NJ: Erlbaum.

Massialas, B. G., & Zevin, J. (1983). *Teaching creatively: Learning through discovery.* Malabar, FL: Krieger.

Masten, A. S. (2001). Ordinary magic: Resilience processes in development. *American Psychologist, 56,* 227–238.

Masten, A. S., & Coatsworth, J. D. (1998). The development of competence in favorable and unfavorable environments. *American Psychologist, 53,* 205–220.

Mastropieri, M. A., & Scruggs, T. E. (1992). Science for students with disabilities. *Review of Educational Research, 62,* 377–411.

Mastropieri, M. A., & Scruggs, T. E. (2000). *The inclusive classroom: Strategies for effective instruction.* Upper Saddle River, NJ: Merrill/Prentice Hall.

Mastropieri, M. A., Scruggs, T. E., & Butcher, K. (1997). How effective is inquiry learning for students with mild disabilities? *Journal of Special Education, 31,* 199–211.

Masur, E. F., McIntyre, C. W., & Flavell, J. H. (1973). Developmental changes in apportionment of study time among items in a multitrial free recall task. *Journal of Experimental Child Psychology, 15,* 237–246.

Mathes, P. G., Torgesen, J. K., & Allor, J. H. (2001). The effects of peer-assisted literacy strategies for first-grade readers with and without additional computer-assisted instruction. *American Educational Research Journal, 38,* 371–410.

Mattingly, D. J., Prislin, R., McKenzie, T. L., Rodrigues, J. L., & Kayzar, B. (2002). Evaluating evaluations: The case of parent involvement programs. *Review of Educational Research, 72,* 549–576.

Maughan, A., & Cicchetti, D. (2002). Impact of child maltreatment and interadult violence on children's emotion regulation abilities and socioemotional adjustment. *Child Development, 73,* 1525–1542.

Maxmell, D., Jarrett, O. S., & Dickerson, C. (1998, April). *Are we forgetting the children's needs? Recess through the children's eyes.* Paper presented at the annual meeting of the American Educational Research Association, San Diego, CA.

Mayer, R. E. (1974). Acquisition processes and resilience under varying testing conditions for structurally different problem-solving procedures. *Journal of Educational Psychology, 66,* 644–656.

Mayer, R. E. (1984). Aids to text comprehension. *Educational Psychologist, 19,* 30–42.

Mayer, R. E. (1985). Implications of cognitive psychology for instruction in mathematical problem solving. In E. A. Silver (Ed.), *Teaching and learning mathematical problem solving: Multiple research perspectives.* Mahwah, NJ: Erlbaum.

Mayer, R. E. (1986). Mathematics. In R. F. Dillon & R. J. Sternberg (Eds.), *Cognition and instruction.* San Diego, CA: Academic Press.

Mayer, R. E. (1987). *Educational psychology: A cognitive approach.* Boston: Little, Brown.

Mayer, R. E. (1989). Models for understanding. *Review of Educational Research, 59,* 43–64.

Mayer, R. E. (1992). *Thinking, problem solving, cognition* (2nd ed.). New York: Freeman.

Mayer, R. E. (1996). Learning strategies for making sense out of expository text: The SOI model for guiding three cognitive processes in knowledge construction. *Educational Psychology Review, 8,* 357–371.

Mayer, R. E. (1998). Does the brain have a place in educational psychology? *Educational Psychology Review, 10,* 389–396.

Mayer, R. E. (2004). Should there be a three-strikes rule against pure discovery learning? *American Psychologist, 59,* 14–19.

Mayer, R. E., & Gallini, J. (1990). When is an illustration worth ten thousand words? *Journal of Educational Psychology, 82,* 715–726.

Mayer, R. E., & Wittrock, M. C. (1996). Problem-solving transfer. In D. C. Berliner & R. C. Calfee (Eds.), *Handbook of educational psychology.* New York: Macmillan.

Mayfield, K. H., & Chase, P. N. (2002). The effects of cumulative practice on mathematics problem solving. *Journal of Applied Behavior Analysis, 35,* 105–123.

McAlpine, L. (1992). Language, literacy and education: Case studies of Cree, Inuit and Mohawk communities. *Canadian Children, 17*(1), 17–30.

McAlpine, L., & Taylor, D. M. (1993). Instructional preferences of Cree, Inuit, and Mohawk teachers. *Journal of American Indian Education, 33*(1), 1–20.

McAshan, H. H. (1979). *Competency-based education and behavioral objectives.* Englewood Cliffs, NJ: Educational Technology.

McCall, R. B. (1994). Academic underachievers. *Current Directions in Psychological Science, 3,* 15–19.

McCall, R. B., & Plemons, B. W. (2001). The concept of critical periods and their implications for early childhood services. In D. B. Bailey, Jr., J. T. Bruer, F. J. Symons, & J. W. Lichtman (Eds.), *Critical thinking about critical periods* (pp. 267–287). Baltimore: Brookes.

McCallum, R. S., & Bracken, B. A. (1993). Interpersonal relations between school children and their peers, parents, and teachers. *Educational Psychology Review, 5,* 155–176.

McCarty, T. L., & Watahomigie, L. J. (1998). Language and literacy in American Indian and Alaska Native communities. In B. Pérez (Ed.), *Sociocultural contexts of language and literacy.* Mahwah, NJ: Erlbaum.

McCaslin, M., & Good, T. L. (1996). The informal curriculum. In D. C. Berliner & R. C. Calfee (Eds.), *Handbook of educational psychology.* New York: Macmillan.

McClelland, D. C., Atkinson, J. W., Clark, R. A., & Lowell, E. L. (1953). *The achievement motive.* New York: Appleton-Century-Crofts.

McCloskey, M. E., & Glucksberg, S. (1978). Natural categories: Well-defined or fuzzy sets? *Memory and Cognition, 6,* 462–472.

McClowry, S. G. (1998). The science and art of using temperament as the basis for intervention. *School Psychology Review, 27,* 551–563.

McComas, J. J., Thompson, A., & Johnson, L. (2003). The effects of presession attention on problem behavior maintained by different reinforcers. *Journal of Applied Behavior Analysis, 36,* 297–307.

McCombs, B. L. (1988). Motivational skills training: Combining metacognitive, cognitive, and affective learning strategies. In C. E. Weinstein, E. T. Goetz, & P. A. Alexander (Eds.), *Learning and study strategies: Issues in assessment, instruction, and evaluation.* San Diego: Harcourt Brace Jovanovich.

McCombs, B. L. (1996). Alternative perspectives for motivation. In L. Baker, P. Afflerbach, & D. Reinking (Eds.), *Developing engaged readers in school and home communities.* Hillsdale, NJ: Erlbaum.

McCoy, K. (1994). *Understanding your teenager's depression.* New York: Perigee.

McCoy, L. P. (1990, April). *Correlates of mathematics anxiety.* Paper presented at the annual meeting of the American Educational Research Association, Boston.

McCutchen, D. (1996). A capacity theory of writing: Working memory in composition. *Educational Psychology Review, 8,* 299–325.

McDaniel, L. (1997). *For better, for worse, forever.* New York: Bantam.

McDaniel, M. A., & Einstein, G. O. (1989). Material-appropriate processing: A contextualist approach to reading and studying strategies. *Educational Psychology Review, 1,* 113–145.

McDaniel, M. A., & Masson, M. E. J. (1985). Altering memory representations through retrieval. *Journal of Experimental Psychology: Learning, Memory, and Cognition, 11,* 371–385.

McDaniel, M. A., & Schlager, M. S. (1990). Discovery learning and transfer of problem-solving skills. *Cognition and Instruction, 7,* 129–159.

McDaniel, M. A., Waddill, P. J., & Einstein, G. O. (1988). A contextual account of the generation effect: A three-factor theory. *Journal of Memory and Language, 27,* 521–536.

McDaniel, M. A., Waddill, P. J., Finstad, K., & Bourg, T. (2000). The effects of text-based interest on attention and recall. *Journal of Educational Psychology, 92,* 492–502.

McDevitt, M., & Chaffee, S. H. (1998). Second chance political socialization: "Trickle-up" effects of children on parents. In T. J. Johnson, C. E. Hays, & S. P. Hays (Eds.), *Engaging the public: How government and the media can reinvigorate American democracy* (pp. 57–66).

McDevitt, T. M. (1990). Encouraging young children's listening skills. *Academic Therapy, 25,* 569–577.

McDevitt, T. M., & Ford, M. E. (1987). Processes in young children's communicative functioning and development. In M. E. Ford & D. H. Ford (Eds.), *Humans as self-constructing living systems: Putting the framework to work.* Mahwah, NJ: Erlbaum.

McDevitt, T. M., & Ormrod, J. E. (2004). *Child development: Educating and working with children and adolescents* (2nd ed.). Upper Saddle River, NJ: Merrill/Prentice Hall.

McDevitt, T. M., Spivey, N., Sheehan, E. P., Lennon, R., & Story, R. (1990). Children's beliefs about listening: Is it enough to be still and quiet? *Child Development, 61,* 713–721.

McGee, K. D., Knight, S. L., & Boudah, D. J. (2001, April). *Using reciprocal teaching in secondary inclusive English classroom instruction.* Paper presented at the annual meeting of the American Educational Research Association, Seattle, WA.

McGee, L. M. (1992). An exploration of meaning construction in first graders' grand conversations. In C. K. Kinzer & D. J. Leu (Eds.), *Literacy research, theory, and practice: Views from many perspectives.* Chicago: National Reading Conference.

McGill, P. (1999). Establishing operations: Implications for the assessment, treatment, and prevention of problem behavior. *Journal of Applied Behavior Analysis, 32,* 393–418.

McGinn, P. V., Viernstein, M. C., & Hogan, R. (1980). Fostering the intellectual development of verbally gifted adolescents. *Journal of Educational Psychology, 72,* 494–498.

McGlynn, S. M. (1998). Impaired awareness of deficits in a psychiatric context: Implications for rehabilitation. In D. J. Hacker, J. Dunlosky, & A. C. Graesser (Eds.), *Metacognition in educational theory and practice* (pp. 221–248). Mahwah, NJ: Erlbaum.

McGowan, R. J., & Johnson, D. L. (1984). The mother-child relationship and other antecedents of childhood intelligence: A causal analysis. *Child Development, 55,* 810–820.

McGregor, H. A., & Elliot, A. J. (2002). Achievement goals as predictors of achievement-relevant processes prior to task engagement. *Journal of Educational Psychology, 94,* 381–395.

McGrew, K. S., Flanagan, D. P., Zeith, T. Z., & Vanderwood, M. (1997). Beyond g: The impact of Gf–Gc specific cognitive abilities research on the future use and interpretation of intelligence tests in the schools. *School Psychology Review, 26,* 189–210.

McGue, M., Bouchard, T. J., Jr., Iacono. W. G., & Lykken, D. T. (1993). Behavioral genetics of cognitive ability: A life-span perspective. In R. Plomin & G. E. McClearn (Eds.), *Nature, nurture, and psychology.* Washington, DC: American Psychological Association.

McKeon, D. (1994). When meeting "common" standards is uncommonly difficult. *Educational Leadership, 51*(8), 45–49.

McKeown, M. G., & Beck, I. L. (1990). The assessment and characterization of young learners' knowledge of a topic in history. *American Educational Research Journal, 27,* 688–726.

McKown, C., & Weinstein, R. S. (2003). The development and consequences of stereotype consciousness in middle childhood. *Child Development, 74,* 498–515.

McLeod, D. B., & Adams, V. M. (Eds.). (1989). *Affect and mathematical problem solving: A new perspective.* New York: Springer-Verlag.

McLoyd. V. C. (1998). Socioeconomic disadvantage and child development. *American Psychologist, 53,* 185–204.

McMillan, J. H., & Reed, D. F. (1994). At-risk students and resiliency: Factors contributing to academic success. *Clearing House, 67*(3), 137–140.

McMillan, J. H., Singh, J., & Simonetta, L. G. (1994). The tyranny of self-oriented self-esteem. *Educational Horizons, 72*(3), 141–145.

McNamara, D. S. & Healy, A. F. (1995). A generation advantage for multiplication skill training and nonword vocabulary acquisition. In A. F. Healy & L. E. Bourne, Jr. (Eds.), *Learning and memory of knowledge and skills: Durability and specificity.* Thousand Oaks, CA: Sage

McNamara, E. (1987). Behavioural approaches in the secondary school. In K. Wheldall (Ed.), *The behaviourist in the classroom.* London: Allen & Unwin.

McNeil, N. M., & Alibali, M. W. (2000). Learning mathematics from procedural instruction: Externally imposed goals influence what is learned. *Journal of Educational Psychology, 92,* 734–744.

McRobbie, C., & Tobin, K. (1995). Restraints to reform: The congruence of teacher and student actions in a chemistry classroom. *Journal of Research in Science Teaching. 32,* 373–385.

McWhiter, C. C. & Bloom, L. A. (1994). The effects of a student-operated business curriculum on the on-task behavior of students with behavioral disorders. *Behavioral Disorders, 19,* 136–141.

Meece, J. L. (1994). The role of motivation in self-regulated learning. In D. H. Schunk & B. J. Zimmerman (Eds.), *Self-regulation of learning and performance: Issues and educational applications.* Mahwah, NJ: Erlbaum.

Meece, J. L., & Holt, K. (1993). A pattern analysis of students' achievement goals. *Journal of Educational Psychology, 85,* 582–590.

Meehan, B. T., Hughes, J. N., & Cavell, T. A. (2003). Teacher-student relationships as compensatory resources for aggressive children. *Child Development, 74,* 1145–1157.

Mehan. H. (1979). *Social organization in the classroom.* Cambridge, MA: Harvard University Press.

Meichenbaum, D. (1977). *Cognitive-behavior modification: An integrative approach.* New York: Plenum Press.

Meichenbaum, D. (1985). Teaching thinking: A cognitive-behavioral perspective. In S. F. Chipman, J. W. Segal, & R. Glaser (Eds.), *Thinking and learning skills: Vol. 2. Research and open questions.* Mahwah, NJ: Erlbaum.

Meichenbaum, D., & Goodman, J. (1971). Training impulsive children to talk to themselves: A means of developing self-control. *Journal of Abnormal Psychology, 77,* 115–126.

Mellers, B. A., & McGraw, A. P. (2001). Anticipated emotions as guides to choice. *Current Directions in Psychological Science, 10,* 210–214.

Meloth, M. S., & Deering, P. D. (1992). Effects of two cooperative conditions on peer-group discussions, reading comprehension, and metacognition. *Contemporary Educational Psychology, 17,* 175–193.

Meloth, M. S., & Deering, P. D. (1994). Task talk and task awareness under different cooperative learning conditions. *American Educational Research Journal, 31,* 138–165.

Meloth, M. S., & Deering, P. D. (1999). The role of the teacher in promoting cognitive processing during collaborative learning. In A. M. O'Donnell & A. King (Eds.), *Cognitive perspectives on peer learning* (pp. 235–255). Mahwah, NJ: Erlbaum.

Menéndez. R. (Director). (1988). *Stand and deliver* [Motion picture]. United States: Warner Studios.

Menyuk, P., & Menyuk, D. (1988). Communicative competence: A historical and cultural perspective. In J. S. Wurzel (Ed.), *Toward multiculturalism: A reader in multicultural education.* Yarmouth, ME: Intercultural Press.

Mercer, C. D. (1997). *Students with learning disabilities* (5th ed.). Upper Saddle River, NJ: Merrill/Prentice Hall.

Mercer, C. D., Jordan, L., Allsopp, D. H., & Mercer, A. R. (1996). Learning disabilities definitions and criteria used by state education departments. *Learning Disabilities Quarterly, 19,* 217–231.

Merrill, M. D., & Tennyson, R. D. (1977). *Concept teaching: An instructional design guide.* Englewood Cliffs, NJ: Educational Technology.

Merrill, M. D., & Tennyson, R. D. (1978). Concept classification and classification errors as a function of relationships between examples and non-examples. *Improving Human Performance, 7.* 351–364.

Merrill, P. F., Hammons, K., Vincent, B. R., Reynolds, P. L., Christensen, L., & Tolman, M. N. (1996). *Computers in education* (3rd ed.). Needham Heights, MA: Allyn & Bacon.

Mervis, C. B. (1987). Child-basic object categories and early lexical development. In U. Neisser (Ed.), *Concepts and conceptual development: Ecological and intellectual factors in categorization.* Cambridge, England: Cambridge University Press.

Merzenich, M. M. (2001). Cortical plasticity contributing to child development. In J. L. McClelland & R. S. Siegler (Eds.), *Mechanisms of cognitive development: Behavioral and neural perspectives* (pp. 67–95). Mahwah, NJ: Erlbaum.

Messick, S. (1983). Assessment of children. In W. Kessen (Ed.), *Handbook of child psychology* (Vol. 1). New York: Wiley.

Messick, S. (1994). The interplay of evidence and consequences in the validation of performance assessments. *Educational Researcher, 23*(2), 13–23.

Metz, K. E. (1995). Reassessment of developmental constraints on children's science instruction. *Review of Educational Research, 65,* 93–127.

Meyer, B. J. F., Brandt, D. H., & Bluth, G. J. (1980). Use of top-level structure in text: Key for reading comprehension of ninth-grade students. *Reading Research Quarterly, 16,* 72–103.

Meyer, D. K., & Turner, J. C. (2002). Discovering emotion in classroom motivation research. *Educational Psychologist, 37,* 107–114.

Meyer, K. A. (1999). Functional analysis and treatment of problem behavior exhibited by elementary school children. *Journal of Applied Behavior Analysis, 32,* 229–232.

Meyer, M. S. (2000). The ability-achievement discrepancy: Does it contribute to an understanding of learning disabilities? *Educational Psychology Review, 12,* 315–337.

Meyers, D. T. (1987). The socialized individual and individual autonomy: An intersection between philosophy and psychology. In E. F. Kittay and D. T. Meyers (Eds.). *Women and moral theory.* Totowa, NJ: Rowman & Littlefield.

Michael, J. (2000). Implications and refinements of the establishing operation concept. *Journal of Applied Behavior Analysis, 33,* 401–410.

Middleton, M. J. (1999, April). *Classroom effects on the gender gap in middle school students' math self-efficacy.* Paper presented at the annual meeting of the American Educational Research Association. Montreal, Canada.

Middleton, M. J., & Midgley, C. (1997). Avoiding the demonstration of lack of ability: An under-explored aspect of goal theory. *Journal of Educational Psychology, 89,* 710–718.

Middleton, M. J., & Midgley, C. (2002). Beyond motivation: Middle school students' perceptions of press for understanding in math. *Contemporary Educational Psychology. 27,* 373–391.

Midgley, C. (1993). Motivation and middle level schools. In M. Maehr & P. R. Pintrich (Eds.), *Advances in motivation and achievement* (Vol. 8, pp. 217–274). Greenwich, CT: JAI Press.

Midgley, C. (Ed.). (2002). *Goals, goal structures, and patterns of adaptive learning.* Mahwah, NJ: Erlbaum.

Midgley, C., Kaplan, A., & Middleton, M. (2001). Performance-approach goals: Good for what, for whom, under what circumstances, and at what cost? *Journal of Educational Psychology, 93,* 77–86.

Midgley, C., Kaplan, A., Middleton, M., Maehr, M., Urdan, T., Anderman, L., Anderman, E., & Roeser, R. (1998). The development and validation of scales assessing students' achievement goal orientations. *Contemporary Educational Psychology, 23,* 113–131.

Midgley, C., Middleton, M. J., Gheen, M. H., & Kumar, R. (2002). Stage-environment fit revisited: A goal theory approach to examining school transitions. In C. Midgley (Ed.), *Goals, goal structures, and patterns of adaptive learning* (pp. 109–142). Mahwah, NJ: Erlbaum.

Mikaelsen, B. (1996). *Countdown.* New York: Hyperion Books for Children.

Milch-Reich, S., Campbell, S. B., Pelham, W. E., Jr., Connelly, L. M., & Geva, D. (1999). Developmental and individual differences in children's on-line representations of dynamic social events. *Child Development, 70,* 413–431.

Miles, S. B., Stipek, D. J., & Strobel, K. R. (2003, April). *Fighting in school: Exploring relations between aggression, prosocial behavior, and reading achievement during elementary school.* Paper presented at the annual meeting of the American Educational Research Association, Chicago.

Miller, B. C., & Benson, B. (1999). Romantic and sexual relationship development during adolescence. In W. Furman, B. B. Brown, & C. Feiring (Eds.), *The development of romantic relationships in adolescence* (pp. 99–121). Cambridge, England: Cambridge University Press.

Miller, D. L., & Kelley, M. L. (1994). The use of goal setting and contingency contracting for improving children's homework performance. *Journal of Applied Behavior Analysis, 27,* 73–84.

Miller, G. A. (1956). The magical number seven, plus or minus two: Some limits on our capacity for processing information. *Psychological Review, 63,* 81–97.

Miller, J. G., & Bersoff, D. M. (1992). Culture and moral judgment: How are conflicts between justice and interpersonal responsibilities resolved? *Journal of Personality and Social Psychology, 62,* 541–554.

Miller, L. S. (1995). *An American imperative: Accelerating minority educational advancement.* New Haven, CT: Yale University Press.

Miller, N. E., & Dollard, J. C. (1941). *Social learning and imitation.* New Haven, CT: Yale University Press.

Miller, P., & Seier, W. (1994). Strategy utilization deficiencies in children: when, where, and why. In H. Reese (Ed.), *Advances in child development and behavior* (Vol. 25). New York: Academic Press.

Miller, P. A., Eisenberg, N., Fabes, R. A., & Shell, R. (1996). Relations of moral reasoning and vicarious emotion to young children's prosocial behavior toward peers and adults. *Developmental Psychology, 32,* 210–219.

Miller, P. H. (1993). Focus on the interface of cognition, social-emotional behavior and motivation. In P. H. Miller (Ed.), *Theories of developmental psychology* (3rd ed.). New York: Freeman.

Miller, R. R., & Barnet, R. C. (1993). The role of time in elementary associations. *Current Directions in Psychological Science, 2,* 106–111.

Miller, S. D., Heafner, T., Massey, D., & Strahan, D. B. (2003, April). *Students' reactions to teachers' attempts to create the necessary conditions to promote the acquisition of self-regulation skills.* Paper presented at the annual meeting of the American Educational Research Association, Chicago.

Miller-Jones, D. (1989). Culture and testing. *American Psychologist, 44,* 360–366.

Millman, J., Bishop, C. H., & Ebel, R. (1965). An analysis of test-wiseness. *Educational and Psychological Measurement, 25,* 707–726.

Mills, G. E. (2003). *Action research: A guide for the teacher researcher* (2nd ed.). Upper Saddle River, NJ: Merrill/Prentice Hall.

Milroy, L. (1994). Sociolinguistics and second language learning: Understanding speakers from different speech communities. In G. Brown, K. Malmkjær, A. Pollitt, & J. Williams (Eds.), *Language and understanding.* Oxford, England: Oxford University Press.

Minami, M., & McCabe, A. (1996). Compressed collections of experiences: Some Asian American traditions. In A. McCabe (Ed.), *Chameleon readers: Some problems cultural differences in narrative structure pose for multicultural literacy programs* (pp. 72–97). New York: McGraw-Hill.

Minami, M., & Ovando, C. J. (1995). Language issues in multicultural contexts. In J. A. Banks & C. A. M. Banks (Eds.), *Handbook of research on multicultural education.* New York: Macmillan.

Minstrell, J., & Stimpson, V. (1996). A classroom environment for learning: Guiding students' reconstruction of under- standing and reasoning. In L. Schauble & R. Glaser (Eds.), *Innovations in learning: New environments for education.* Mahwah, NJ: Erlbaum.

Mintzes, J. J., Trowbridge, J. E., Arnaudin, M. W., & Wandersee, J. H. (1991). Children's biology: Studies on conceptual development in the life sciences. In S. M. Glynn, R. H. Yeany, & B. K. Britton (Eds.), *The psychology of learning science.* Mahwah, NJ: Erlbaum.

Mintzes, J. J., Wandersee, J. H., & Novak, J. D. (1997). Meaningful learning in science: The human constructivist perspective. In G. D. Phye (Ed.), *Handbook of academic learning: Construction of knowledge.* San Diego, CA: Academic Press.

Mischel, W., & Grusec, J. E. (1966). Determinants of the rehearsal and transmission of neutral and aversive behaviors. *Journal of Personality and Social Psychology, 3,* 197–205.

Mischel, W., & Shoda, Y. (1995). A cognitive- affective system theory of personality: Reconceptualizing situations, dispositions, dynamics, and invariance in personality structure. *Psychological Review, 102,* 246–268.

Mistry, R. S., Vandewater, E. A., Huston, A. C., & McLoyd, V. C. (2002). Economic well-being and children's social adjustment: The role of family process in an ethnically diverse low-income sample. *Child Development, 73,* 935–951.

Mitchell, M. (1993). Situational interest: Its multifaceted structure in the secondary school mathematics classroom. *Journal of Educational Psychology, 85,* 424–436.

Mithaug, D. K., & Mithaug, D. E. (2003). Effects of teacher-directed versus student-directed instruction on self-management of young children with disabilities. *Journal of Applied Behavior Analysis, 36,* 133–136.

Mohatt, G., & Erickson, F. (1981). Cultural differences in teaching styles in an Odawa school: A sociolinguistic approach. In H. T. Trueba, G. P. Guthrie, & K. H. Au (Eds.), *Culture and the bilingual classroom: Studies in classroom ethnography.* Rowley, MA: Newbury House.

Moje, E. B., & Shepardson, D. P. (1998). Social interactions and children's changing understanding of electric circuits: Exploring unequal power relations in "peer"-learning groups. In B. Guzzetti & C. Hynd (Eds.), *Perspectives on conceptual change: Multiple ways to understand knowing and learning in a complex world* (pp. 225–234). Mahwah, NJ: Erlbaum.

Moles, O. C. (Ed.). (1990). *Student discipline strategies: Research and practice.* Albany: State University of New York Press.

Montagu, A. (Ed.). (1999). *Race and IQ* (expanded ed.). New York: Oxford University Press.

Montgomery, D. (1989). Identification of giftedness among American Indian people. In C. J. Maker & S. W. Schiever (Eds.), *Critical issues in gifted education: Vol. 2. Defensible programs for cultural and ethnic minorities.* Austin, TX: Pro-Ed.

Moon, S. M., Feldhusen, J. F., & Dillon, D. R. (1994). Long-term effects of an enrichment program based on the Purdue Three-Stage Model. *Gifted Child Quarterly, 38,* 38–48.

Mooney, C. M. (1957). Age in the development of closure ability in children. *Canadian Journal of Psychology, 11,* 219–226.

Moore, D. S., & Erickson, P. I. (1985). Age, gender, and ethnic differences in sexual and contraceptive knowledge, attitudes, and behavior. *Family and Community Health, 8,* 38–51.

Moore, J. W., & Edwards, R. P. (2003). An analysis of aversive stimuli in classroom demand contexts. *Journal of Applied Behavior Analysis, 36,* 339–348.

Moran, C. E., & Hakuta, K. (1995). Bilingual education: Broadening research perspectives. In J. A. Banks & C. A. M. Banks (Eds.), *Handbook of research on multicultural education.* New York: Macmillan.

Moran, S. (1991). Creative reading: Young adults and paperback books. *Horn Book Magazine, 67,* 437–441.

Moreno, R., Mayer, R. E., Spires, H. A., & Lester, J. C. (2001). The case for social agency in computer-based teaching: Do students learn more deeply when they interact with animated pedagogical agents? *Cognition and Instruction, 19,* 177–213.

Morgan, D. P., & Jenson, W. R. (1988). *Teaching behaviorally disordered students: Preferred practices.* Upper Saddle River, NJ: Merrill/Prentice Hall.

Morris, C. D., Bransford, J. D., & Franks, J. J. (1977). Levels of processing versus transfer appropriate processing. *Journal of Verbal Learning and Verbal Behavior, 16,* 519–533.

Morrison, G., Furlong, M., & Smith, G. (1994). Factors associated with the experience of school violence among general education, leadership class, opportunity class, and special day class pupils. *Education and Treatment of Children, 17,* 356–369.

Morrow, S. L. (1997). Career development of lesbian and gay youth: Effects of sexual orientation, coming out, and homophobia. In M. B. Harris (Ed.), *School experiences of gay and lesbian youth: The invisible minority* (pp. 1–15). Binghamton, NY: Harrington Park Press.

Mostow, A. J., Izard, C. E., Fine, S., & Trantacosta, C. J. (2002). Modeling emotional, cognitive, and behavioral predictors. *Child Development, 73,* 1775–1787.

Mueller, J. H. (1980). Test anxiety and the encoding and retrieval of information. In I. G. Sarason (Ed.), *Test anxiety: Theory, research, and applications.* Mahwah, NJ: Erlbaum.

Munn, P., Johnstone, M., & Chalmers, V. (1990, April). *How do teachers talk about maintaining effective discipline in their classrooms?* Paper presented at the annual meeting of the American Educational Research Association, Boston.

Murdock, T. B. (1999). The social context of risk: Status and motivational predictors of alienation in middle school. *Journal of Educational Psychology, 91,* 62–75.

Murdock, T. B. (2000). Incorporating economic context into educational psychology: Methodological and conceptual challenges. *Educational Psychologist, 35,* 113–124.

Murdock, T. B., Hale, N., Weber, M. J., Tucker, V., & Briggs, W. (1999, April). *Relations of cheating to social and academic motivation among middle school students.* Paper presented at the annual meeting of the American Educational Research Association, Montreal, Canada.

Murphy, D. M. (1996). Implications of inclusion for general and special education. *Elementary School Journal, 96,* 469–492.

Murphy, P. K., & Alexander, P. A. (2000). A motivated exploration of motivation terminology. *Contemporary Educational Psychology, 25,* 3–53.

Murray, C. B., & Jackson, J. S. (1982/1983). The conditioned failure model of black educational underachievement. *Humboldt Journal of Social Relations, 10,* 276–300.

Murray, F. B. (1978). Teaching strategies and conservation training. In A. M. Lesgold, J. W. Pellegrino, S. D. Fokkema, & R. Glaser (Eds.), *Cognitive psychology and instruction.* New York: Plenum Press.

Nadel, L., & Jacobs, W. J. (1998). Traumatic memory is special. *Current Directions in Psychological Science, 7,* 154–157.

Narvaez, D. (1998). The influence of moral schemas on the reconstruction of moral narratives in eighth graders and college students. *Journal of Educational Psychology, 90,* 13–24.

Narvaez, D. (2002). Does reading moral stories build character? *Educational Psychology Review, 14,* 155–171.

Narváez, D., & Rest, J. (1995). The four components of acting morally. In W. M. Kurtines & J. L. Gewirtz (Eds.), *Moral development: An introduction.* Boston: Allyn & Bacon.

National Association of Bilingual Education. (1993). Census reports sharp increase in number of non-English-speaking Americans. *NABE News, 16*(6), 1, 25.

National Commission on Excellence in Education. (1983). *A nation at risk: The imperative for educational reform.* Washington, DC: U.S. Government Printing Office.

National Joint Committee on Learning Disabilities. (1994). Learning disabilities: Issues on definition, a position paper of the National Joint Committee on Learning Disabilities. In *Collective perspectives on issues affecting learning disabilities: Position papers and statements.* Austin, TX: Pro-Ed.

Natriello, G., & Dornbusch, S. M. (1984). *Teacher evaluative standards and student effort.* White Plains, NY: Longman.

Naveh-Benjamin, M. (1991). A comparison of training programs intended for different types of text-anxious students: Further support for an information-processing model. *Journal of Educational Psychology, 83,* 134–139.

NCSS Task Force on Ethnic Studies Curriculum Guidelines. (1992). Curriculum guidelines for multicultural education. *Social Education, 56,* 274–294.

Neel, R. S., Jenkins, Z. N., & Meadows, N. (1990). Social problem-solving behaviors and aggression in young children: A descriptive observational study. *Behavioral Disorders, 16,* 39–51.

Neisser, U. (1967). *Cognitive psychology.* New York: Appleton-Century-Crofts.

Neisser, U. (1998a). Introduction: Rising test scores and what they mean. In U. Neisser (Ed.), *The rising curve: Long-term gains in IQ and related measures* (pp. 3–22). Washington, DC: American Psychological Association.

Neisser, U. (Ed.). (1998b). *The rising curve: Long-term gains in IQ and related measures).* Washington, DC: American Psychological Association.

Neisser, U., Boodoo, G., Bouchard, T. J., Boykin, A. W., Brody, N., Ceci, S. J., Halpern, D. F., Loehlen, J. C., Perloff, R., Sternberg, R. J., & Urbina, S. (1996). Intelligence: Knowns and unknowns. *American Psychologist, 51,* 77–101.

Nell, V. (2002). Why young men drive dangerously: Implications for injury prevention. *Current Directions in Psychological Science, 11,* 75–79.

Nelson, J. R., Smith, D. J., Young, R. K., & Dodd, J. M. (1991). A review of self-management outcome research conducted with students who exhibit behavioral disorders. *Behavioral Disorders, 16,* 169–179.

Nelson, T. O., & Dunlosky, J. (1991). When people's judgments of learning (JOLs) are extremely accurate at predicting subsequent recall: The "delayed-JOL effect." *Psychological Science, 2,* 267–270.

Nelson-Barber, S., & Estrin, E. (1995). Bringing Native American perspectives to mathematics and science teaching. *Theory into Practice, 34,* 174–185.

Nesdale, D., & Flesser, D. (2001). Social identity and the development of children's group attitudes. *Child Development, 72,* 506–517.

Neubauer, G., Mansel, J., Avrahami, A., & Nathan, M. (1994). Family and peer support of Israeli and German adolescents. In F. Nestemann & K. Hurrelmann (Eds.), *Social networks and social support in childhood and adolescence.* Berlin, Germany: Aldine de Gruyter.

Neville, H. J., & Bavelier, D. (2001). Variability of developmental plasticity. In J. L. McClelland & R. S. Siegler (Eds.), *Mechanisms of cognitive development: Behavioral and neural perspectives* (pp. 271–287). Mahwah, NJ: Erlbaum.

Nevin, J. A., Mandell, C., & Atak, J. R. (1983). The analysis of behavioral momentum. *Journal of the Experimental Analysis of Behavior, 39,* 49–59.

Newby, T. J., Ertmer, P. A., & Stepich, D. A. (1994, April). *Instructional analogies and the learning of concepts.* Paper presented at the annual meeting of the American Educational Research Association, New Orleans, LA.

Newcomb, A. F., & Bagwell, C. L. (1995). Children's friendship relations: A meta-analysis review. *Psychological Bulletin, 117,* 306–347.

Newcombe, N., & Huttenlocher, J. (1992). Children's early ability to solve perspective-taking problems. *Developmental Psychology, 28,* 635–643.

Newman, L. S. (1990). Intentional and unintentional memory in young children: Remembering vs. playing. *Journal of Experimental Child Psychology, 50,* 243–258.

Newman, R. S. (1998). Students' help seeking during problem solving: Influences of personal and contextual achievement goals. *Journal of Educational Psychology, 90,* 644–658.

Newman, R. S., & Schwager, M. T. (1995). Students' help seeking during problem solving: Effects of grade, goal, and prior achievement. *American Educational Research Journal, 32,* 352–376.

Newmann, F. M. (1981). Reducing student alienation in high schools: Implications of theory. *Harvard Educational Review, 51,* 546–564.

Newmann, F. M. (1997). Authentic assessment in social studies: Standards and examples. In G. D. Phye (Ed.), *Handbook of classroom assessment: Learning, achievement, and adjustment.* San Diego, CA: Academic Press.

Newmann, F. M., & Wehlage, G. G. (1993). Five standards of authentic instruction. *Educational Leadership, 50*(7), 8–12.

Newport, E. L. (1993). Maturational constraints on language learning. In P. Bloom (Ed.), *Language acquisition: Core readings.* Cambridge, MA: MIT Press.

Nicholls, J. G. (1979). Development of perception of own attainment and causal attributions for success and failure in reading. *Journal of Educational Psychology, 71,* 94–99.

Nicholls, J. G. (1984). Conceptions of ability and achievement motivation. In R. Ames & C. Ames (Eds.), *Research on motivation in education: Vol 1. Student motivation.* San Diego, CA: Academic Press.

Nicholls, J. G. (1990). What is ability and why are we mindful of it? A developmental perspective. In R. J. Sternberg & J. Kolligian (Eds.), *Competence considered.* New Haven, CT: Yale University Press.

Nicholls, J. G., Cobb, P., Yackel, E., Wood, T., & Wheatley, G. (1990). Students' theories of mathematics and their mathematical knowledge: Multiple dimensions of assessment. In G. Kulm (Ed.), *Assessing higher order thinking in mathematics.* Washington, DC: American Association for the Advancement of Science.

Nichols, J. D. (1996). The effects of cooperative learning on student achievement and motivation in a high school geometry class. *Contemporary Educational Psychology, 21,* 467–476.

Nichols, J. D., Ludwin, W. G., & Iadicola, P. (1999). A darker shade of gray: A year-end analysis of discipline and suspension data. *Equity and Excellence in Education, 32*(1), 43–55.

Nichols, M. L., & Ganschow, L. (1992). Has there been a paradigm shift in gifted education? In N. Coangelo, S. G. Assouline, & D. L. Ambroson (Eds.), *Talent development: Proceedings from the 1991 Henry B. and Jocelyn Wallace National Research Symposium on Talent Development.* New York: Trillium.

Nichols, P. D., & Mittelholtz, D. J. (1997). Constructing the concept of aptitude: Implications for the assessment of analogical reasoning. In G. D. Phye (Ed.), *Handbook of academic learning: Construction of knowledge.* San Diego, CA: Academic Press.

Nickerson, R. S. (1989). New directions in educational assessment. *Educational Researcher, 18*(9), 3–7.

Nickerson, R. S., & Adams, M. J. (1979). Long-term memory for a common object. *Cognitive Psychology, 1,* 287–307.

Nieto, S. (1995). A history of the education of Puerto Rican students in U.S. mainland schools: "Losers," "outsiders," or "leaders"? In J. A. Banks & C. A. M. Banks (Eds.), *Handbook of research on multicultural education.* New York: Macmillan.

Nippold, M. A. (1988). The literate lexicon. In M. A. Nippold (Ed.), *Later language development: Ages nine through nineteen.* Boston: Little, Brown.

Nist, S. L., Simpson, M. L., Olejnik, S., & Mealey, D. L. (1991). The relation between self-selected study processes and test performance. *American Educational Research Journal, 28,* 849–874.

Nix, R. L., Pinderhughes, E. E., Dodge, K. A., Bates, J. E., Pettit, G. S., & McFadyen-Ketchum, S. A. (1999). The relation between mothers' hostile attribution tendencies and children's externalizing behavior problems: The mediating role of mothers' harsh discipline practices. *Child Development, 70,* 896–909.

Noddings, N. (1985). Small groups as a setting for research on mathematical problem solving. In E. A. Silver (Ed.), *Teaching and learning mathematical problem solving: Multiple research perspectives.* Mahwah, NJ: Erlbaum.

Nolen, S. B. (1996). Why study? How reasons for learning influence strategy selection. *Educational Psychology Review, 8,* 335–355.

Nolen-Hoeksema, S. (2001). Gender differences in depression. *Current Directions in Psychological Science, 10,* 173–176.

Norman, D. A. (1969). *Memory and attention: An introduction to human information processing.* New York: Wiley.

Northup, J. (2000). Further evaluation of the accuracy of reinforcer surveys: A systematic replication. *Journal of Applied Behavior Analysis, 33,* 335–338.

Northup, J., Broussard, C., Jones, K., George, T., Vollmer, T. R., & Herring, M. (1995). The differential effects of teachers and peer attention on the disruptive classroom behavior of three children with a diagnosis of attention deficit hyperactivity disorder. *Journal of Applied Behavior Analysis, 28,* 227–228.

Novak, J. D. (1998). *Learning, creating, and using knowledge: Concept maps as facilitative tools in schools and corporations.* Mahwah, NJ: Erlbaum.

Novak, J. D., & Gowin, D. B. (1984). *Learning how to learn.* Cambridge, England: Cambridge University Press.

Novak, J. D., & Musonda, D. (1991). A twelve-year longitudinal study of science concept learning. *American Educational Research Journal, 28.* 117–153.

Nucci, L. P., & Nucci, M. S. (1982). Children's social interactions in the context of moral and conventional transgressions. *Child Development, 53,* 403–412.

Nucci, L. P., & Weber, E. K. (1995). Social interactions in the home and the development of young children's conceptions of the personal. *Child Development, 66,* 1438–1452.

Nunner-Winkler, G. (1984). Two moralities? A critical discussion of an ethic of care and responsibility versus an ethic of rights and justice. In W. M. Kurtines & J. L. Gewirtz (Eds.), *Morality, moral behavior, and moral development.* New York: Wiley.

Nussbaum, N., & Bigler, E. (1990). *Identification and treatment of attention deficit disorder.* Austin, TX: Pro-Ed.

Nuthall, G. (1996). Commentary: Of learning and language and understanding the complexity of the classroom. *Educational Psychologist, 31,* 207–214.

Oakes, J., & Guiton, G. (1995). Matchmaking: The dynamics of high school tracking decisions. *American Educational Research Journal, 32,* 3–33.

O'Boyle, M. W., & Gill, H. S.(1998). On the relevance of research findings in cognitive neuroscience to educational practice. *Educational Psychology Review, 10,* 397–409.

Ochs, E. (1982). Talking to children in western Samoa. *Language and Society, 11,* 77–104.

Ochsner, K. N., & Lieberman, M. D. (2001). The emergence of social cognitive neuroscience. *American Psychologist, 56,* 717–734.

O'Donnell, A. M. (1999). Structuring dyadic interaction through scripted cooperation. In A. M. O'Donnell & A. King (Eds.), *Cognitive perspectives on peer learning* (pp. 179–196). Mahwah, NJ: Erlbaum.

O'Donnell, A. M., & O'Kelly, J. (1994). Learning from peers: Beyond the rhetoric of positive results. *Educational Psychology Review, 6,* 321–349.

O'Donnell, D. A., Schwab-Stone, M. E., & Muyeed, A. Z. (2002). Multidimensional resilience in urban children exposed to community violence. *Child Development, 73*, 1265–1282.

Ogbu, J. U. (1992). Understanding cultural diversity and learning. *Educational Researcher, 21*(8), 5–14, 24.

Ogbu, J. U. (1994). From cultural differences to differences in cultural frame of reference. In P. M. Greenfield & R. R. Cocking (Eds.), *Cross-cultural roots of minority child development*. Mahwah, NJ: Erlbaum.

Ogbu, J. U. (1999). Beyond language: Ebonics, proper English, and identity in a Black-American speech community. *American Educational Research Journal, 36*, 147–184.

Ogden, E. H., & Germinario, V. (1988). *The at-risk student: Answers for educators*. Lancaster, PA: Technomic.

O'Grady, W. (1997). *Syntactic development*. Chicago: University of Chicago.

Okagaki, L. (2001). Triarchic model of minority children's school achievement. *Educational Psychologist, 36*, 9–20.

O'Leary, K. D., Kaufman, K. F., Kass, R. E., & Drabman, R. S. (1970). The effects of loud and soft reprimands on the behavior of disruptive students. *Exceptional Children, 37*, 145–155.

O'Leary, K. D., & O'Leary, S. G. (Eds.). (1972). *Classroom management: The successful use of behavior modification*. New York: Pergamon Press.

Olneck, M. R. (1995). Immigrants and education. In J. A. Banks & C. A. M. Banks (Eds.), *Handbook of research on multicultural education*. New York: Macmillan.

Onosko, J. J. (1989). Comparing teachers' thinking about promoting students' thinking. *Theory and Research in Social Education, 17*, 174–195.

Onosko, J. J. (1996). Exploring issues with students despite the barriers. *Social Education, 60*(1), 22–27.

Onosko, J. J., & Newmann, F. M. (1994). Creating more thoughtful learning environments. In J. N. Mangieri & C. C. Block (Eds.), *Advanced educational psychology: Enhancing mindfulness*. Fort Worth, TX: Harcourt Brace Jovanovich.

Oppenheimer, L. (1986). Development of recursive thinking: Procedural variations. *International Journal of Behavioral Development, 9*, 401–411.

Ormrod, J. E. (2004). *Human learning* (4th ed.). Upper Saddle River, NJ: Merrill/ Prentice Hall.

Ormrod, J. E., & Jenkins, L. (1989). Study strategies in spelling: Correlations with achievement and developmental changes. *Perceptual and Motor Skills, 68*, 643–650.

Ormrod, J. E., Ormrod, R. K., Wagner, E. D., & McCallin, R. C. (1988). Reconceptualizing map learning. *American Journal of Psychology, 101*, 425–433.

Ormrod, J. E., & Wagner, E. D. (1987, October). *Spelling conscience in undergraduate students: Ratings of spelling accuracy and dictionary use*. Paper presented at the annual meeting of the Northern Rocky Mountain Educational Research Association, Park City, UT.

Ornstein, R. (1997). *The right mind: Making sense of the hemispheres*. San Diego, CA: Harcourt Brace.

Orobio de Castro, B., Veerman, J. W., Koops, W., Bosch, J. D., & Monshouwer, H. J. (2002). Hostile attribution of intent and aggressive behavior: A meta-analysis. *Child Development, 73*, 916–934.

Osborne, J. W., & Simmons, C. M. (2002, April). *Girls, math, stereotype threat, and anxiety: Physiological evidence*. Paper presented at the annual meeting of the American Educational Research Association, New Orleans, LA.

Oskamp, S. (Ed.). (2000). *Reducing prejudice and discrimination*. Mahwah, NJ: Erlbaum.

Osterman, K. F. (2000). Students' need for belonging in the school community. *Review of Educational Research, 70*, 323–367.

O'Sullivan, J. T., & Joy, R. M. (1990, April). *Children's theories about reading difficulty: A developmental study*. Paper presented at the annual meeting of the American Educational Research Association, Boston.

Otero, J., & Kintsch, W. (1992). Failures to detect contradictions in a text: What readers believe versus what they read. *Psychological Science, 3*, 229–235.

O'Toole, M. E. (2000). *The school shooter: A threat assessment perspective*. Quantico, VA: Federal Bureau of Investigation. Retrieved February 26, 2004, from http://www.fbi.gov/publications/school/ school2.pdf.

Owens, R. E., Jr. (1995). *Language disorders: A functional approach to assessment and intervention* (2nd ed.). Boston: Allyn & Bacon.

Owens, R. E., Jr. (1996). *Language development* (4th ed.). Boston: Allyn & Bacon.

Padilla, A. M. (1994). Bicultural development: A theoretical and empirical examination. In R. G. Malgady & O. Rodriguez (Eds.), *Theoretical and conceptual issues in Hispanic mental health* (pp. 20–51). Malabar, FL: Krieger.

Paget, K. F., Kritt, D., & Bergemann, L. (1984). Understanding strategic interactions in television commercials: A developmental study. *Journal of Applied Developmental Psychology, 5*, 145–161.

Page-Voth, V., & Graham, S. (1999). Effects of goal setting and strategy use on the writing performance and self-efficacy of students with writing and learning problems. *Journal of Educational Psychology, 91*, 230–240.

Pajares, F., & Schunk, D. H. (2002). Self and self-belief in psychology and education: A historical perspective. In J. Aronson & D. Cordova (Eds.), *Improving academic achievement: Impact of psychological factors on education* (pp. 3–21). New York: Academic Press.

Pajares, F., & Valiante, G. (1999). *Writing self-efficacy of middle school students: Relation to motivation constructs, achievement, gender, and gender orientation*. Paper presented at the annual meeting of the American Educational Research Association, Montreal, Canada.

Paley, V. G. (1984). *Boys and girls: Superheroes in the doll corner*. Chicago: University of Chicago Press.

Palincsar, A. S., & Brown, A. L. (1984). Reciprocal teaching of comprehension-fostering and comprehension-monitoring activities. *Cognition and Instruction, 1*, 117–175.

Palincsar, A. S., & Brown, A. L. (1989). Classroom dialogues to promote self-regulated comprehension. In J. Brophy (Ed.), *Advances in research on teaching* (Vol. 1). Greenwich, CT: JAI Press.

Palincsar, A. S., & Herrenkohl, L. R. (1999). Designing collaborative contexts: Lessons from three research programs. In A. M. O'Donnell & A. King (Eds.), *Cognitive perspectives on peer learning* (pp. 151–177). Mahwah, NJ: Erlbaum.

Palmer, D. J., & Goetz, E. T. (1988). Selection and use of study strategies: The role of the studier's beliefs about self and strategies. In C. E. Weinstein, E. T. Goetz, & P. A. Alexander (Eds.), *Learning and study strategies: Issues in assessment, instruction, and evaluation*. San Diego: Academic Press.

Palmer, E. L. (1965). Accelerating the child's cognitive attainments through the inducement of cognitive conflict: An interpretation of the Piagetian position. *Journal of Research in Science Teaching, 3*, 324.

Pang, V. O. (1995). Asian Pacific American students: A diverse and complex population. In J. A. Banks & C. A. M. Banks (Eds.), *Handbook of research on multicultural education*. New York: Macmillan.

Paris, S. G. (1988). Models and metaphors of learning strategies. In C. E. Weinstein, E. T. Goetz, & P. A. Alexander (Eds.), *Learning and study strategies: Issues in assessment, instruction, and evaluation*. San Diego, CA: Academic Press.

Paris, S. G., & Ayres, L. R. (1994). *Becoming reflective students and teachers with portfolios and authentic assessment*. Washington, DC: American Psychological Association.

Paris, S. G., & Byrnes, J. P. (1989). The constructivist approach to self-regulation and learning in the classroom. In B. J. Zimmerman & D. H. Schunk (Eds.), *Self-regulated learning and academic achievement: Theory, research, and practice*. New York: Springer-Verlag.

Paris, S. G., & Cunningham, A. E. (1996). Children becoming students. In D. C. Berliner & R. C. Calfee (Eds.), *Handbook of educational psychology*. New York: Macmillan.

Paris, S. G., Lawton, T. A., Turner, J. C., & Roth, J. L. (1991). A developmental perspective on standardized achievement testing. *Educational Researcher, 20*(5), 12–20, 40.

Paris, S. G., & Paris, A. H. (2001). Classroom applications of research on self-regulated learning. *Educational Psychologist, 36*, 89–101.

Paris, S. G., & Turner, J. C. (1994). Situated motivation. In P. R. Pintrich, D. R. Brown, & C. E. Weinstein (Eds.), *Student motivation, cognition, and learning: Essays in honor of Wilbert J. McKeachie*. Mahwah, NJ: Erlbaum.

Paris, S. G., & Winograd, P. (1990). How metacognition can promote academic learning and instruction. In B. F. Jones & L. Idol (Eds.), *Dimensions of thinking and cognitive instruction*. Mahwah, NJ: Erlbaum.

Parke, R. D. (1974). Rules, roles, and resistance to deviation: Explorations in punishment, discipline, and self-control. In A. Pick (Ed.), *Minnesota Symposia on Child Psychology* (Vol. 8). Minneapolis: University of Minnesota Press.

Parker, W. D. (1997). An empirical typology of perfectionism in academically talented children. *American Educational Research Journal, 34*, 545–562.

Parkhurst, J. T., & Hopmeyer, A. (1998). Sociometric popularity and peer-perceived popularity: Two distinct dimensions of peer status. *Journal of Early Adolescence, 18*, 125–144.

Parks, C. P. (1995). Gang behavior in the schools: Reality or myth? *Educational Psychology Review, 7*, 41–68.

Parnes, S. J. (1967). *Creative behavior guidebook*. New York: Scribner's.

Parsons, J. E., Kaczala, C. M., & Meece, J. L. (1982). Socialization of achievement attitudes and beliefs: Classroom influences. *Child Development, 53*, 322–339.

Pascarella, E. T., & Terenzini, P. T. (1991). *How college affects students: Findings and insights from twenty years of research*. San Francisco: Jossey-Bass.

Patrick, H. (1997). Social self-regulation: Exploring the relations between children's social relationships, academic self-regulation, and school performance. *Educational Psychologist, 32*, 209–220.

Patrick, H., Anderman, L. H., & Ryan, A. M. (2002). Social motivation and the classroom social environment. In C. Midgley (Ed.), *Goals, goal structures, and patterns of adaptive learning* (pp. 85–108). Mahwah, NJ: Erlbaum.

Patterson, C. J. (1995). Sexual orientation and human development: An overview. *Developmental Psychology, 31*, 3–11.

Patterson, G. R., DeBaryshe, B. D., & Ramsey, E. (1989). A developmental perspective on antisocial behavior. *American Psychologist, 44*, 329–335.

Patterson, G. R., Littman, R., & Bricker, W. (1967). Assertive behavior in children: A step toward a theory of aggression. *Monographs of the Society for Research in Child Development, 32* (Serial No. 113).

Patton, J. R., Blackbourn, J. M., & Fad, K. S. (1996). *Exceptional individuals in focus* (6th ed.). Upper Saddle River, NJ: Merrill/Prentice Hall.

Paulson, F. L., Paulson, P. R., & Meyer, C. A. (1991). What makes a portfolio a portfolio? *Educational Leadership, 49*(5), 60–63.

Paus, T., Zijdenbos, A., Worsley, K., Collins, D. L., Blumenthal, J., Giedd, J. N., Rapoport, J. L., & Evans, A. C. (1999). Structural maturation of neural pathways in children and adolescents: In vivo study. *Science, 283*, 1908–1911.

Pavlov, I. P. (1927). *Conditioned reflexes* (G. V. Anrep, Trans.). London: Oxford University Press.

Pawlas, G. E. (1994). Homeless students at the school door. *Educational Leadership, 51*(8), 79–82.

Paxton, R. J. (1999). A deafening silence: History textbooks and the students who read them. *Review of Educational Research, 69*, 315–339.

Pea, R. D. (1993). Practices of distributed intelligence and designs for education. In G. Salomon (Ed.), *Distributed cognitions: Psychological and educational considerations*. Cambridge, England: Cambridge University Press.

Pellegrini, A. D. (1998). Play and the assessment of young children. In O. N. Saracho & B. Spodek (Eds.), *Multiple perspectives on play in early childhood education*. Albany: State University of New York Press.

Pellegrini, A. D. (2002). Bullying, victimization, and sexual harassment during the transition to middle school. *Educational Psychologist, 37*, 151–163.

Pellegrini, A. D., & Bartini, M. (2000). A longitudinal study of bullying, victimization, and peer affiliation during the transition from primary school to middle school. *American Educational Research Journal, 37*, 699–725.

Pellegrini, A. D., Bartini, M., & Brooks, F. (1999). School bullies, victims, and aggressive victims: Factors relating to group affiliation and victimization in early adolescence. *Journal of Educational Psychology, 91*, 216–224.

Pellegrini, A. D., & Bjorklund, D. F. (1997). The role of recess in children's cognitive performance. *Educational Psychologist, 32*, 35–40.

Pellegrini, A. D., & Horvat, M. (1995). A developmental contextualist critique of attention deficit hyperactivity disorder. *Educational Researcher, 24*(1), 13–19.

Pellegrini, A. D., Huberty, P. D., & Jones, I. (1995). The effects of recess timing on children's playground and classroom behaviors. *American Educational Research Journal, 32*, 845–864.

Pellegrini, A. D., Kato, K., Blatchford, P., & Baines, E. (2002). A short-term longitudinal study of children's playground games across the first year of school: Implications for social competence and adjustment to school. *American Educational Research Journal, 39*, 991–1015.

Penner, A. M. (2003). International gender X item difficulty interactions in mathematics and science achievement tests. *Journal of Educational Psychology, 95*, 650–655.

Pérez, B. (1998). *Sociocultural contexts of language and literacy.* Mahwah, NJ: Erlbaum.

Perkins, D. N. (1990). The nature and nurture of creativity. In B. F. Jones & L. Idol (Eds.), *Dimensions of thinking and cognitive instruction.* Mahwah, NJ: Erlbaum.

Perkins, D. N. (1992). *Smart schools: From training memories to educating minds.* New York: Free Press/Macmillan.

Perkins, D. N. (1995). *Outsmarting IQ: The emerging science of learnable intelligence.* New York: Free Press.

Perkins, D. N., & Salomon, G. (1987). Transfer and teaching thinking. In D. N. Perkins, J. Lochhead, & J. Bishop (Eds.), *Thinking: The second international conference.* Mahwah, NJ: Erlbaum.

Perkins, D. N., & Salomon, G. (1989). Are cognitive skills context-bound? *Educational Researcher, 18*(1), 16–25.

Perkins, D. N., & Simmons, R. (1988). Patterns of misunderstanding: An integrative model for science, math, and programming. *Review of Educational Research, 58*, 303–326.

Perner, J., & Wimmer, H. (1985). "John *thinks* that Mary *thinks* that . . ." Attribution of second-order beliefs by 5- to 10-year-old children. *Journal of Experimental Child Psychology, 39*. 437–471.

Perry, D. G., & Perry, L. C. (1983). Social learning, causal attribution, and moral internalization. In J. Bisanz, G. L. Bisanz, & R. Kail (Eds.), *Learning in children: Progress in cognitive development research.* New York: Springer-Verlag.

Perry, N. E. (1998). Young children's self-regulated learning and contexts that support it. *Journal of Educational Psychology, 90*, 715–729.

Perry, N. E., VandeKamp, K. O., Mercer, L. K., & Nordby, C. J. (2002). Investigating teacher-student interactions that foster self-regulated learning. *Educational Psychologist, 37*, 5–15.

Perry, R. P. (1985). Instructor expressiveness: Implications for improving teaching. In J. G. Donald & A. M. Sullivan (Eds.), *Using research to improve teaching* (pp. 35–49). San Francisco: Jossey-Bass.

Petersen, G. A., Sudweeks, R. R., & Baird, J. H. (1990, April). *Test-wise responses of third-, fifth-, and sixth-grade students to clued and unclued multiple-choice science items.* Paper presented at the annual meeting of the American Educational Research Association, Boston.

Peterson, C. (1990). Explanatory style in the classroom and on the playing field. In S. Graham & V. S. Folkes (Eds.), *Attribution theory: Applications to achievement, mental health, and interpersonal conflict.* Mahwah, NJ: Erlbaum.

Peterson, C. C. (2002). Drawing insight from pictures: The development of concepts of false drawing and false belief in children with deafness, normal hearing, and autism. *Child Development, 73*, 1442–1459.

Peterson, C., Maier, S., & Seligman, M. (1993). *Learned helplessness: A theory for the age of personal control.* New York: Oxford University Press.

Peterson, L. R., & Peterson, M. J. (1959). Short-term retention of individual items. *Journal of Experimental Psychology, 58*, 193–198.

Peterson, P. L. (1979). Direct instruction reconsidered. In P. L. Peterson & H. L. Walberg (Eds.), *Research on teaching: Concepts, findings and implications.* Berkeley, CA: McCutchan.

Peterson, P. L. (1988). Teachers' and students' cognitional knowledge for classroom teaching and learning. *Educational Researcher, 17*(5), 5–14.

Peterson, P. L. (1992). Revising their thinking: Keisha Coleman and her third-grade mathematics class. In H. H. Marshall (Ed.), *Redefining student learning: Roots of educational change.* Norwood, NJ: Ablex.

Peterson, S. E. (1993). The effects of prior achievement and group outcome on attributions and affect in cooperative tasks. *Contemporary Educational Psychology, 18*, 479–485.

Petrill, S. A., & Wilkerson, B. (2000). Intelligence and achievement: A behavioral genetic perspective. *Educational Psychology Review, 12*, 185–199.

Petterson, S. M., & Albers, A. B. (2001). Effects of poverty and maternal depression on early child development. *Child Development, 72*, 1794–1813.

Pettigrew, T. F., & Pajonas, P. J. (1973). The social psychology of heterogeneous schools. In C. S. Brembeck & W. H. Hill, *Cultural challenges to education: The influence of cultural factors in school learning.* Lexington, MA: Heath.

Pettito, A. L. (1985). Division of labor: Procedural learning in teacher-led small groups. *Cognition and Instruction, 2*, 233–270.

Peverly, S. T., Broost, K. E., Graham, M., & Shaw, R. (2003). College adults are not good at self-regulation: A study on the relationship of self-regulation, note taking, and test taking. *Journal of Educational Psychology, 95*, 335–346.

Pezdek, K., & Banks, W. P. (Eds.). (1996). *The recovered memory/false memory debate.* San Diego: Academic Press.

Pfeifer, M., Goldsmith, H. H., Davidson, R. J., & Rickman, M. (2002). Continuity and change in inhibited and uninhibited children. *Child Development, 73*, 1474–1485.

Pfiffner, L. J., & Barkley, R. A. (1998). Treatment of ADHD in school settings. In R. A. Barkley, *Attention-deficit hyperactivity disorder: A handbook for diagnosis and treatment* (2nd ed., pp. 458–490). New York: Guilford Press.

Pfiffner, L. J., & O'Leary, S. G. (1993). School-based psychological treatments. In J. L. Matson (Ed.), *Handbook of hyperactivity in children* (pp. 234–255). Boston: Allyn & Bacon.

Pfiffner, L. J., Rosen, L. A., & O'Leary, S. G. (1985). The efficacy of an all-positive approach to classroom management. *Journal of Applied Behavior Analysis, 18*, 257–261.

Phelan, P., Davidson, A. L., & Cao, H. T. (1991). Students' multiple worlds: Negotiating the boundaries of family, peer, and school cultures. *Anthropology and Education Quarterly, 22*, 224–250.

Phelan, P., Yu, H. C., & Davidson, A. L. (1994). Navigating the psychosocial pressures of adolescence: The voices and experiences of high school youth. *American Educational Research Journal, 31*, 415–447.

Phillip, R. A., Flores, A., Sowder, J. T., & Schappelle, B. P. (1994). Conceptions and practices of extraordinary mathematics teachers. *Journal of Mathematical Behavior, 13*, 155–180.

Phillips, B. N., Pitcher, G. D., Worsham, M. E., & Miller, S. C. (1980). Test anxiety and the school environ-ment. In I. G. Sarason (Ed.), *Test anxiety: Theory, research, and applications.* Mahwah, NJ: Erlbaum.

Phillips, D., & Zimmerman, M. (1990). The developmental course of perceived competence and incompetence among competent children. In R. Sternberg & J. Kolligian (Eds.), *Competence considered* (pp. 41–66). New Haven, CT: Yale University Press.

Phillips, G., McNaughton, S., & McDonald, S. (2004). Managing the mismatch: Enhancing early literacy progress for children with diverse language and cultural identities in mainstream urban schools in New Zealand. *Journal of Educational Psychology, 96*, 309–323.

Phinney, J. (1989). Stages of ethnic identity development in minority group adolescents. *Journal of Early Adolescence, 9*, 34–39.

Phinney, J. S. (1990). Ethnic identity in adolescents and adults: Review of research. *Psychological Bulletin, 108*, 499–514.

Phye, G. D. (1997). Classroom assessment: A multidimensional perspective. In G. D. Phye (Ed.), *Handbook of classroom assessment: Learning, achievement, and adjustment.* San Diego, CA: Academic Press.

Piaget, J. (1928). *Judgment and reasoning in the child* (M. Warden, Trans.). New York: Harcourt, Brace.

Piaget, J. (1929). *The child's conception of the world.* New York: Harcourt, Brace.

Piaget, J. (1960). *The moral judgment of the child* (M. Gabain, Trans.). Glencoe, IL: Free Press. (First published in 1932)

Piaget, J. (1952). *The origins of intelligence in children* (M. Cook, Trans.). New York: Norton.

Piaget, J. (1959). *The language and thought of the child* (3rd ed.; M. Gabain, Trans.). London: Routledge & Kegan Paul.

Piaget, J. (1970). Piaget's theory. In P. H. Mussen (Ed.), *Carmichael's manual of psychology.* New York: Wiley.

Piaget, J. (1980). *Adaptation and intelligence: Organic selection and phenocopy* (S. Eames, Trans.). Chicago: University of Chicago Press.

Pianta, R. C. (1999). *Enhancing relationships between children and teachers.* Washington, DC: American Psychological Association.

Piersel, W. C. (1987). Basic skills education. In C. A. Maher & S. G. Forman (Eds.), *A behavioral approach to education of children and youth.* Mahwah, NJ: Erlbaum.

Pietsch, J., Walker, R., & Chapman, E. (2003). The relationship among self-concept, self-efficacy, and performance in mathematics during secondary school. *Journal of Educational Psychology, 95*, 589–603.

Pigott, H. E., Fantuzzo, J. W., & Clement, P. W. (1986). The effects of reciprocal peer tutoring and group contingencies on the academic performance of elementary school children. *Journal of Applied Behavior Analysis, 19*, 93–98.

Piirto, J. (1999). *Talented children and adults: Their development and education* (2nd ed.). Upper Saddle River, NJ: Merrill/Prentice Hall.

Pillow, B. H. (2002). Children's and adults' evaluation of the certainty of deductive inferences, inductive inferences, and guesses. *Child Development, 73*, 779–792.

Pine, K. J., & Messer, D. J. (2000). The effect of explaining another's actions on children's implicit theories of balance. *Cognition and Instruction, 18*, 35–51.

Pinker, S. (1987). The bootstrapping problem in language acquisition. In B. MacWhinney (Ed.), *Mechanisms of language acquisition.* Mahwah, NJ: Erlbaum.

Pintrich, P. R. (2000). Multiple goals, multiple pathways: The role of goal orientation in learning and achievement. *Journal of Educational Psychology, 92*, 544–555.

Pintrich, P. R. (2003). Motivation and classroom learning. In W. M. Reynolds, G. E. Miller (Vol. Eds.) & I B. Weiner (Editor-in-Chief), *Handbook of psychology: Vol. 7. Educational psychology* (pp. 103–122). New York: Wiley.

Pintrich, P. R., & De Groot, E. V. (1990). Motivational and self-regulated learning components of classroom academic performance. *Journal of Educational Psychology, 82*, 33–40.

Pintrich, P. R., & Garcia, T. (1994). Regulating motivation and cognition in the classroom: The role of self-schemas and self-regulatory strategies. In D. Schunk & B. Zimmerman (Eds.), *Self-regulation of learning and performance: Issues and educational applications*. Mahwah, NJ: Erlbaum.

Pintrich, P. R., Garcia, T., & De Groot, E. (1994, April). *Positive and negative self-schemas and self-regulated learning*. Paper presented at the annual meeting of the American Educational Research Association, New Orleans, LA.

Pintrich, P. R., Marx, R. W., & Boyle, R. A. (1993). Beyond cold conceptual change: The role of motivational beliefs and classroom contextual factors in the process of conceptual change. *Review of Educational Research, 63*, 167–199.

Pintrich, P. R., & Schrauben, B. (1992). Students' motivational beliefs and their cognitive engagement in academic tasks. In D. Schunk & J. Meece (Eds.), *Students' perceptions in the classroom: Causes and consequences*. Mahwah, NJ: Erlbaum.

Pintrich, P. R., & Schunk, D. H. (2002). *Motivation in education: Theory, research, and applications* (2nd ed.). Upper Saddle River, NJ: Merrill/Prentice Hall.

Piontkowski, D., & Calfee, R. (1979). Attention in the classroom. In G. A. Hale & M. Lewis (Eds.), *Attention and cognitive development*. New York: Plenum Press.

Pipher, M. (1994). *Reviving Ophelia: Saving the selves of adolescent girls*. New York: Putnam.

Pitner, R. O., Astor, R. A., Benbenishty, R., Haj-Yahia, M. M., & Zeira, A. (2003). The effects of group stereotypes on adolescents' reasoning about peer retribution. *Child Development, 74*, 413–425.

Pitoniak, M. J., & Royer, J. M. (2001). Testing accommodations for examinees with disabilities: A review of psychometric, legal, and social policy issues. *Review of Educational Research, 71*, 53–104.

Pittman, K., & Beth-Halachmy, S. (1997, March). *The role of prior knowledge in analogy use*. Paper presented at the annual meeting of the American Educational Research Association, Chicago.

Plomin, R. (1989). Environment and genes: Determinants of behavior. *American Psychologist, 44*, 105–111.

Plomin, R. (1994). *Genetics and experience: The interplay between nature and nurture*. Thousand Oaks, CA: Sage.

Plomin, R., Fulker, D. W., Corley, R., & DeFries, J. C. (1997). Nature, nurture, and cognitive development from 1 to 16 years: A parent-offspring adoption study. *Psychological Science, 8*, 442–447.

Plumert, J. M. (1994). Flexibility in children's use of spatial and categorical organizational strategies in recall. *Developmental Psychology, 30*, 738–747.

Poche, C., Yoder, P., & Miltenberger, R. (1988). Teaching self-protection to children using television techniques. *Journal of Applied Behavior Analysis, 21*, 253–261.

Pogrow, S., & Londer, G. (1994). The effects of an intensive general thinking program on the motivation and cognitive development of at-risk students: Findings from the HOTS program. In H. F. O'Neil, Jr., & M. Drillings (Eds.), *Motivation: Theory and research*. Mahwah, NJ: Erlbaum.

Polloway, E. A., & Patton, J. R. (1993). *Strategies for teaching learners with special needs* (5th ed.). Upper Saddle River, NJ: Merrill/Prentice Hall.

Pomerantz, E. M. Altermatt, E. R., & Saxon, J. L. (2002). Making the grade but feeling distressed: Gender differences in academic performance and internal distress. *Journal of Educational Psychology, 94*, 396–404.

Pomerantz, E. M. & Saxon, J. L. (2001). Conceptions of ability as stable and self-evaluative processes: A longitudinal examination. *Child Development, 72*, 152–173.

Poole, D. (1994). Routine testing practices and the linguistic construction of knowledge. *Cognition and Instruction, 12*, 125–150.

Popham, W. J. (1990). *Modern educational measurement: A practitioner's perspective* (2nd ed.). Upper Saddle River, NJ: Prentice Hall.

Popham, W. J. (1995). *Classroom assessment: What teachers need to know*. Needham Heights, MA: Allyn & Bacon.

Porath, M. (1988, April). *Cognitive development of gifted children: A neo-Piagetian perspective*. Paper presented at the annual meeting of the American Educational Research Association, New Orleans, LA.

Porter, A. C. (1989). A curriculum out of balance: The case of elementary school mathematics. *Educational Researcher, 18*(5), 9–15.

Portes, P. R. (1996). Ethnicity and culture in educational psychology. In D. C. Berliner & R. C. Calfee (Eds.), *Handbook of educational psychology*. New York: Macmillan.

Posner, G. J., Strike, K. A., Hewson, P. W., & Gertzog, W. A. (1982). Accommodation of a scientific conception: Toward a theory of conceptual change. *Science Education, 66*, 211–227.

Postman, L., & Underwood, B. J. (1973). Critical issues in interference theory. *Memory and Cognition, 1*, 19–40.

Poulin, F., & Boivin, M. (1999). Proactive and reactive aggression and boys' friendship quality in mainstream classrooms. *Journal of Emotional and Behavioral Disorders, 7*, 168–177.

Powell, B. M. (1990, April). *Children's perceptions of classroom goal orientation: Relationship to learning strategies and intrinsic motivation*. Paper presented at the annual meeting of the American Educational Research Association, Boston.

Powell, G. J. (1983). *The psychosocial development of minority children*. New York: Brunner/Mazel.

Powell, S., & Nelson, B. (1997). Effects of choosing academic assignments on a student with attention deficit hyperactivity disorder. *Journal of Applied Behavior Analysis, 30*, 181–183.

Power, F. C., Higgins, A., & Kohlberg, L. (1989). *Lawrence Kohlberg's approach to moral education*. New York: Columbia University Press.

Power, F. C., & Power, M. R. (1992). A raft of hope: Democratic education and the challenge of pluralism. *Journal of Moral Education, 21*, 193–205.

Powers, L. E., Sowers, J. A., & Stevens, T. (1995). An exploratory, randomized study of the impact of mentoring on the self-efficacy and community-based knowledge of adolescents with severe physical challenges. *Journal of Rehabilitation, 61*(1), 33–41.

Powers, L. E., Wilson, R., Matuszewski, J., Phillips, A., Rein, C., Schumacher, D., & Gensert, J. (1996). Facilitating adolescent self-determination. In D. J. Sands & M. L. Wehmeyer (Eds.), *Self-determination across the life span: Independence and choice for people with disabilities*. Baltimore: Brookes.

Powers, S. I., Hauser, S. T., & Kilner, L. A. (1989). Adolescent mental health. *American Psychologist, 44*, 200–208.

Prawat, R. S. (1989). Promoting access to knowledge, strategy, and disposition in students: A research synthesis. *Review of Educational Research, 59*, 1–41.

Prawat, R. S. (1992). From individual differences to learning communities: Our changing focus. *Educational Leadership, 49*(7), 9–13.

Prawat, R. S. (1993). The value of ideas: Problems versus possibilities in learning. *Educational Researcher, 22*(6), 5–16.

Premack, D. (1959). Toward empirical behavior laws: I. Positive reinforcement. *Psychological Review, 66*, 219–233.

Premack, D. (1963). Rate differential reinforcement in monkey manipulation. *Journal of Experimental Analysis of Behavior, 6*, 81–89.

Prentice, N. M. (1972). The influence of live and symbolic modeling on prompting moral judgments of adolescent delinquents. *Journal of Abnormal Psychology, 80*, 157–161.

Presseisen, B. Z., & Beyer, F. S. (1994, April). *Facing history and ourselves: An instructional tool for constructivist theory*. Paper presented at the annual meeting of the American Educational Research Association, New Orleans, LA.

Pressley, M. (1982). Elaboration and memory development. *Child Development, 53*, 296–309.

Pressley, M., with McCormick, C. B. (1995). *Advanced educational psychology for educators, researchers, and policymakers*. New York: HarperCollins.

Pressley, M., Borkowski, J. G., & Schneider, W. (1987). Cognitive strategies: Good strategy users coordinate metacognition and knowledge. In R. Vasta (Ed.), *Annals of child development* (Vol. 4). Greenwich, CT: JAI Press.

Pressley, M., El-Dinary, P. B., Marks, M. B., Brown, R., & Stein, S. (1992). Good strategy instruction is motivating and interesting. In K. A. Renninger, S. Hidi, & A. Krapp (Eds.), *The role of interest in learning and development*. Mahwah, NJ: Erlbaum.

Pressley, M., Harris, K. R., & Marks, M. B. (1992). But good strategy instructors are constructivists! *Educational Psychology Review, 4*, 3–31.

Pressley, M., Levin, J. R., & Delaney, H. D. (1982). The mnemonic keyword method. *Review of Educational Research, 52*, 61–91.

Pressley, M., Snyder, B. L., & Cariglia-Bull, T. (1987). How can good strategy use be taught to children? Evaluation of six alternative approaches. In S. M. Cormier & J. D. Hagman (Eds.), *Transfer of learning: Contemporary research and applications*. San Diego, CA: Academic Press.

Pressley, M., Woloshyn, V., Lysynchuk, L. M., Martin, V., Wood, E., & Willoughby, T. (1990). A primer of research on cognitive strategy instruction: The important issues and how to address them. *Educational Psychology Review, 2*, 1–58.

Pressley, M., Yokoi, L., van Meter, P., Van Etten, S., & Freebern, G. (1997). Some of the reasons why preparing for exams is so hard: What can be done to make it easier? *Educational Psychology Review, 9*, 1–38.

Price-Williams, D. R., Gordon, W., & Ramirez, M. (1969). Skill and conservation. *Developmental Psychology, 1*, 769.

Pritchard, R. (1990). The effects of cultural schemata on reading processing strategies. *Reading Research Quarterly, 25*, 273–295.

Proctor, R. W., & Dutta, A. (1995). *Skill acquisition and human performance*. Thousand Oaks, CA: Sage.

Pruitt, R. P. (1989). Fostering creativity: The innovative classroom environment. *Educational Horizons, 68*(1), 51–54.

Pugh, K. J., Bergin, D. A., & Rocks, J. (2003, April). *Motivation and transfer: A critical review*. Paper presented at the annual meeting of the American Educational Research Association, Chicago.

Pulos, S., & Linn, M. C. (1981). Generality of the controlling variables scheme in early adolescence. *Journal of Early Adolescence, 1*, 26–37.

Purcell-Gates, V. (1995). *Other people's words: The cycle of low literacy*. Cambridge, MA: Harvard University Press.

Purdie, N., & Hattie, J. (1996). Cultural differences in the use of strategies for self-regulated learning. *American Educational Research Journal, 33*, 845–871.

Purdie, N., Hattie, J., & Carroll, A. (2002). A review of the research on interventions for attention deficit hyperactivity disorder: What works best? *Review of Educational Research, 72*, 61–99.

Purdie, N., Hattie, J., & Douglas, G. (1996). Student conceptions of learning and their use of self-regulated learning strategies: A cross-cultural comparison. *Journal of Educational Psychology, 88*, 87–100.

Putnam, R. T. (1992). Thinking and authority in elementary-school mathematics tasks. In J. Brophy (Ed.), *Advances in research on teaching: Vol. 3. Planning and managing learning tasks and activities*. Greenwich, CT: JAI Press.

Qian, G., & Pan, J. (2002). A comparison of epistemological beliefs and learning from science text between American and Chinese high school students. In B. K. Hofer & P. R. Pintrich (Eds.), *Personal epistemology: The psychology of beliefs about knowledge and knowing* (pp. 365–385). Mahwah, NJ: Erlbaum.

Qin, Z., Johnson, D. W., & Johnson, R. T. (1995). Cooperative versus competitive efforts and problem solving. *Review of Educational Research, 65*, 129–143.

Quellmalz, E., & Hoskyn, J. (1997). Classroom assessment of reading strategies. In G. D. Phye (Ed.), *Handbook of classroom assessment: Learning, achievement, and adjustment*. San Diego, CA: Academic Press.

Quill, K. A. (1995). Visually cued instruction for children with autism and pervasive developmental disorders. *Focus on Autistic Behavior, 10*(3), 10–20.

Quinn, P. C. (2002). Category representation in young infants. *Current Directions in Psychological Science, 11,* 66–70.

Raber, S. M. (1990, April). *A school system's look at its dropouts: Why they left school and what has happened to them.* Paper presented at the annual meeting of the American Educational Research Association, Boston.

Rabinowitz, M., & Glaser, R. (1985). Cognitive structure and process in highly competent performance. In F. D. Horowitz & M. O'Brien (Eds.), *The gifted and the talented: Developmental perspectives.* Washington, DC: American Psychological Association.

Rachlin, H. (1991). *Introduction to modern behaviorism* (3rd ed.). New York: Freeman.

Radke-Yarrow, M., Zahn-Waxler, C., & Chapman, M. (1983). Children's prosocial dispositions and behavior. In E. M. Hetherington (Ed.), *Handbook of child psychology: Vol. 4. Socialization, personality, and social development* (4th ed.). New York: Wiley.

Radziszewska, B., & Rogoff, B. (1991). Children's guided participation in planning imaginary errands with skilled adult or peer partners. *Developmental Psychology, 27,* 381–389.

Raine, A., Reynolds, C., & Venables, P. H. (2002). Stimulation seeking and intelligence: A prospective longitudinal study. *Journal of Personality and Social Psychology, 82,* 663–674.

Raine, A., & Scerbo, A. (1991). Biological theories of violence. In J. S. Milner (Ed.), *Neuropsychology of aggression* (pp. 1–25). Boston: Kluwer.

Rakow, S. J. (1984). What's happening in elementary science: A national assessment. *Science and Children, 21*(4), 39–40.

Ramey, C. T. (1992). High-risk children and IQ: Altering intergenerational patterns. *Intelligence, 16,* 239–256.

Ramey, C. T., & Ramey, S. L. (1998). Early intervention and early experience. *American Psychologist, 53,* 109–120.

Ramsey, P. G. (1987). *Teaching and learning in a diverse world: Multicultural education for young children.* New York: Teachers College Press.

Ramsey, P. G. (1995). Growing up with the contradictions of race and class. *Young Children, 50,* 18–22.

Rapport, M. D., Murphy, H. A., & Bailey, J. S. (1982). Ritalin vs. response cost in the control of hyperactive children: A within-subject comparison. *Journal of Applied Behavior Analysis, 15,* 205–216.

Raudenbush, S. W. (1984). Magnitude of teacher expectancy effects on pupil IQ as a function of credibility induction: A synthesis of findings from 18 experiments. *Journal of Educational Psychology, 76,* 85–97.

Rawsthorne, L. J., & Elliot, A. J. (1999). Achievement goals and intrinsic motivation: A meta-analytic review. *Personality and Social Psychology Review, 3,* 326–344.

Rayner, K., Foorman, B. R., Perfetti, C. A., Pesetsky, D., & Seidenberg, M. S. (2001). How psychological science informs the teaching of reading. *Psychological Science in the Public Interest, 2,* 31–74.

Raynor, J. O. (1981). Future orientation and achievement motivation: Toward a theory of personality functioning and change. In G. Ydewalle & W. Lens (Eds.), *Cognition in human motivation and learning* (pp. 199–231). Hillsdale, NJ: Erlbaum.

Redfield, D. L., & Rousseau, E. W. (1981). A meta-analysis of experimental research on teacher questioning behavior. *Review of Educational Research, 51,* 237–245.

Reeve, J., Bolt, E., & Cai, Y. (1999). Autonomy-supportive teachers: How they teach and motivate students. *Journal of Educational Psychology, 91,* 537–548.

Reeve, R. E. (1990). ADHD: Facts and fallacies. *Intervention in School and Clinic, 26*(2), 70–78.

Reich, P. A. (1986). *Language development.* Upper Saddle River, NJ: Prentice Hall.

Reid, N. (1989). Contemporary Polynesian conceptions of giftedness. *Gifted Education International, 6*(1), 30–38.

Reimann, P., & Schult, T. J. (1996). Turning examples into cases: Acquiring knowledge structures for analogical problem solving. *Educational Psychologist, 31,* 123–132.

Reimer, J., Paolitto, D. P., & Hersh, R. H. (1983). *Promoting moral growth: From Piaget to Kohlberg* (2nd ed.). White Plains, NY: Longman.

Reiner, M., Slotta, J. D., Chi, M. T. H., & Resnick, L. B. (2000). Naive physics reasoning: A commitment to substance-based conceptions. *Cognition and Instruction, 18,* 1–34.

Reis, S. M. (1989). Reflections on policy affecting the education of gifted and talented students: Past and future perspectives. *American Psychologist, 44,* 399–408.

Reisberg, D. (1997). *Cognition: Exploring the science of the mind.* New York: Norton.

Reisberg, D., & Heuer, F. (1992). Remembering the details of emotional events. In E. Winograd & U. Neisser (Eds.), *Affect and accuracy in recall: Studies of "flashbulb" memories.* Cambridge, England: Cambridge University Press.

Reiter, S. N. (1994). Teaching dialogically: Its relationship to critical thinking in college students. In P. R. Pintrich, D. R. Brown, & C. E. Weinstein (Eds.), *Student motivation, cognition, and learning: Essays in honor of Wilbert J. McKeachie.* Mahwah, NJ: Erlbaum.

Renkl, A., & Atkinson, R. K. (2003). Structuring the transition from example study to problem solving in cognitive skill acquisition: A cognitive load perspective. *Educational Psychologist, 38,* 15–22.

Renkl, A., Mandl, H., & Gruber, H. (1996). Inert knowledge: Analyses and remedies. *Educational Psychologist, 31,* 115–121.

Renninger, K. A., Hidi, S., & Krapp, A. (Eds.). (1992). *The role of interest in learning and development.* Mahwah, NJ: Erlbaum.

Renzulli, J. S. (1978). What makes giftedness? Reexamining a definition. *Phi Delta Kappan, 60,* 180–184.

Renzulli, J. S. (2002). Emerging conceptions of giftedness: Building a bridge to the new century. *Exceptionality, 10*(2), 67–75.

Rescorla, R. A. (1967). Pavlovian conditioning and its proper control procedures. *Psychological Review, 74,* 71–80.

Rescorla, R. A. (1988). Pavlovian conditioning: It's not what you think it is. *American Psychologist, 43,* 151–160.

Resnick, D. P., & Resnick, L. B. (1996). Performance assessment and the multiple functions of educational measurement. In M. B. Kane & R. Mitchell (Eds.), *Implementing performance assessment: Promises, problems, and challenges* (pp. 23–38). Mahwah, NJ: Erlbaum.

Resnick, L. B. (1983). Mathematics and science learning: A new conception. *Science, 220,* 477–478.

Resnick, L. B. (1988). Treating mathematics as an ill-structured discipline. In R. I. Charles & E. A. Silver (Eds.), *The teaching and assessing of mathematical problem solving* (pp. 32–60). Mahwah, NJ: Erlbaum.

Resnick, L. B. (1989). Developing mathematical knowledge. *American Psychologist, 44,* 162–169.

Resnick, L. B., & Resnick, D. P. (1992). Assessing the thinking curriculum: New tools for educational reform. In B. G. Gifford & M. C. O'Connor (Eds.), *Changing assessments: Alternative views of aptitude, achievement and instruction* (pp. 37–75). Boston: Kluwer Academic.

Resnick, M. D., Bearman, P. S., Blum, R. W., Bauman, K. E., Harris, K. M., Jones, J., Tabor, J., Beuhring, T., Sieving, R. E., Shew, M., Ireland, M., Bearinger, L. H., & Udry, J. R. (1997). Protecting adolescents from harm: Findings from the National Longitudinal Study on Adolescent Health. *Journal of the American Medical Association, 278,* 823–832.

Rest, J., Narvaez, D., Bebeau, M., & Thoma, S. (1999). A neo-Kohlbergian approach: The DIT and schema theory. *Educational Psychology Review, 11,* 291–324.

Reusser, K. (1990, April). *Understanding word arithmetic problems: Linguistic and situational factors.* Paper presented at the annual meeting of the American Educational Research Association, Boston.

Reyna, C. (2000). Lazy, dumb, or industrious: When stereotypes convey attribution information in the classroom. *Educational Psychology Review, 12,* 85–110.

Reyna, C., & Weiner, B. (2001). Justice and utility in the classroom: An attributional analysis of the goals of teachers' punishment and intervention strategies. *Journal of Educational Psychology, 93,* 309–319.

Reynolds, M. C. (1984). Classification of students with handicaps. In E. W. Gordon (Ed.), *Review of research in education* (No. 11). Washington, DC: American Educational Research Association.

Reynolds, M. C., & Birch, J. W. (1988). *Adaptive mainstreaming: A primer for teachers and principals* (3rd ed.). White Plains, NY: Longman.

Reynolds, R. E., & Shirey, L. L. (1988). The role of attention in studying and learning. In C. E. Weinstein, E. T. Goetz, & P. A. Alexander (Eds.), *Learning and study strategies: Issues in assessment, instruction, and evaluation.* San Diego, CA: Academic Press.

Reynolds, R. E., Taylor, M. A., Steffensen, M. S., Shirey, L. L., & Anderson, R. C. (1982). Cultural schemata and reading comprehension. *Reading Research Quarterly, 17,* 353–366.

Ricciuti, H. N. (1993). Nutrition and mental development. *Current Directions in Psychological Science, 2,* 43–46.

Rice, M., Hadley, P. A., & Alexander, A. L. (1993). Social biases toward children with speech and language impairments: A correlative causal model of language limitations. *Applied Psycholinguistics, 14,* 445–471.

Richards, C. M., Symons, D. K., Greene, C. A., & Szuszkiewicz, T. A. (1995). The bidirectional relationship between achievement and externalizing behavior disorders. *Journal of Learning Disabilities, 28,* 8–17.

Ricks, J. H. (1959). On telling parents about test results. *Test Service Bulletin* (No. 59). New York: Psychological Corporation.

Riggs, J. M. (1992). Self-handicapping and achievement. In A. K. Boggiano & T. S. Pittman (Eds.), *Achievement and motivation: A social-developmental perspective.* Cambridge, England: Cambridge University Press.

Rimm, D. C., & Masters, J. C. (1974). *Behavior therapy: Techniques and empirical findings.* San Diego, CA: Academic Press.

Ripple, R. E. (1989). Ordinary creativity. *Contemporary Educational Psychology, 14,* 189–202.

Ritts, V., Patterson, M. L., & Tubbs, M. E. (1992). Expectations, impressions, and judgments of physically attractive students: A review. *Review of Educational Research, 62,* 413–426.

Ritvo, E. R., & Freeman, B. J. (1978). National Society for Autistic Children definition of the syndrome of autism. *Journal of Autism and Childhood Schizophrenia, 8,* 162–167.

Roberts, G. C., Treasure, D. C., & Kavussanu, M. (1997). Motivation in physical activity contexts: An achievement goal perspective. *Advances in Motivation and Achievement, 10,* 413–447.

Roberts, T., & Kraft, R. (1987). Reading comprehension performance and laterality: Evidence for concurrent validity of dichotic, haptic, and EEG laterality measures. *Neuropsychologia, 25,* 817–828.

Robertson, J. S. (2000). Is attribution training a worthwhile classroom intervention for K–12 students with learning difficulties? *Educational Psychology Review, 12,* 111–134.

Robins, R. W., Gosling, S. D., & Craik, K. H. (1999). An empirical analysis of trends in psychology. *American Psychologist, 54,* 117–128.

Robinson, A. (1991). Cooperation or exploitation? The argument against cooperative learning for talented students. *Journal for the Education of the Gifted, 14,* 9–27.

Robinson, T. R., Smith, S. W., Miller, M. D., & Brownell, M. T. (1999). Cognitive behavior modification of hyperactivity-impulsivity and aggression: A meta-analysis of school-based studies. *Journal of Educational Psychology, 91,* 195–203.

Roblyer, M. D. (2003). *Integrating educational technology into teaching* (3rd ed.). Upper Saddle River, NJ: Merrill/Prentice Hall.

Roderick, M. (1994). Grade retention and school dropout: Investigating the association. *American Educational Research Journal, 31*, 729–759.

Roderick, M., & Camburn, E. (1999). Risk and recovery from course failure in the early years of high school. *American Educational Research Journal, 36*, 303–343.

Roediger, H. L., III, & McDermott, K. B. (2000). Tricks of memory. *Current Directions in Psychological Science, 9*, 123–127.

Roeser, R. W., Eccles, J. S., & Sameroff, A. J. (2000). School as a context of early adolescents' academic social-emotional development: A summary of research findings. *The Elementary School Journal, 100*, 443–471.

Roeser, R. W., Marachi, R., & Gehlbach, H. (2002). A goal theory perspective on teachers' professional identities and the contexts of teaching. In C. Midgley (Ed.), *Goals, goal structures, and patterns of adaptive learning* (pp. 205–241). Mahwah, NJ: Erlbaum.

Rogers, C. R. (1983). *Freedom to learn for the 80's.* Upper Saddle River, NJ: Merrill/ Prentice Hall.

Rogers, T. B., Kuiper, N. A., & Kirker, W. S. (1977). Self-reference and the encoding of personal information. *Journal of Personality and Social Psychology, 35*, 677–688.

Rogoff, B. (1990). *Apprenticeship in thinking: Cognitive development in social context.* New York: Oxford University Press.

Rogoff, B. (1991). Social interaction as apprenticeship in thinking: Guidance and participation in spatial planning. In L. B. Resnick, J. M. Levine, & S. D. Teasley (Eds.), *Perspectives on socially shared cognition.* Washington, DC: American Psychological Association.

Rogoff, B. (1994, April). *Developing understanding of the idea of communities of learners.* Paper presented at the annual meeting of the American Educational Research Association, New Orleans, LA.

Rogoff, B. (2001). *Everyday cognition: Its development in social context.* New York: Replica Books.

Rogoff, B. (2003). *The cultural nature of human development.* Oxford, England: Oxford University Press.

Rogoff, B., Matusov, E., & White, C. (1996). Models of teaching and learning: Participation in a community of learners. In D. R. Olson & N. Torrance (Eds.), *The handbook of education and human development: New models of learning, teaching, and schooling.* Cambridge, MA: Blackwell.

Rogoff, B., & Waddell, K. J. (1982). Memory for information organized in a scene by children from two cultures. *Child Development, 53*, 1224–1228.

Rohner, R. P. (1998). Father love and child development: History and current evidence. *Current Directions in Psychological Science, 7*, 157–161.

Rohrbeck, C. A., Ginsburg-Block, M. D., Fantuzzo, J. W., & Miller, T. R. (2003). Peer-assisted learning interventions with elementary school students: A meta-analytic review. *Journal of Educational Psychology, 95*, 240–257.

Roid, G. (2003). *Stanford-Binet Intelligence Scales* (5th ed.). Itasca, IL: Riverside.

Roopnarine, J. L., Lasker, J., Sacks, M., & Stores, M. (1998). The cultural contexts of children's play. In O. N. Saracho & B. Spodek (Eds.), *Multiple perspectives on play in early childhood education.* Albany: State University of New York Press.

Root, M. P. P. (1999). The biracial baby boom: Understanding ecological constructions of racial identity in the 21st century. In R. H. Sheets & E. R. Hollins (Eds.), *Racial and ethnic identity in school practices: Aspects of human development* (pp. 67–89). Mahwah, NJ: Erlbaum.

Rortvedt, A. K., & Miltenberger, R. G. (1994). Analysis of a high-probability instructional sequence and time-out in the treatment of child noncompliance. *Journal of Applied Behavior Analysis, 27*, 327–330.

Rosch, E. H. (1973a). Natural categories. *Cognitive Psychology, 4*, 328–350.

Rosch, E. H. (1973b). On the internal structure of perceptual and semantic categories. In T. E. Moore (Ed.), *Cognitive development and the acquisition of language.* San Diego, CA: Academic Press.

Rosch, E. H. (1977). Human categorization. In N. Warren (Ed.), *Advances in cross-cultural psychology* (Vol. 1). San Diego, CA: Academic Press.

Rosch, E. H., Mervis, C. B., Gray, W. D., Johnson, D. M., & Boyes-Braem, P. (1976). Basic objects in natural categories. *Cognitive Psychology, 8*, 382–439.

Rose, A. J. (2002). Co-rumination in the friendship of girls and boys. *Child Development, 73*, 1830–1843.

Rose, R. J., Viken, R. J., Dick, D. M., Bates, J. E., Pulkkinen, L., & Kaprio, J. (2003). It *does* take a village: Nonfamiliar environments and children's behavior. *Psychological Science, 14*, 273–277.

Rose, S. C., & Thornburg, K. R. (1984). Mastery motivation and need for approval in young children: Effects of age, sex, and reinforcement condition. *Educational Research Quarterly, 9*(1), 34–42.

Rosenberg, E. L. (1998). Levels of analysis and the organization of affect. *Review of General Psychology, 2*, 247–270.

Rosenshine, B., & Meister, C. (1992). The use of scaffolds for teaching higher-level cognitive strategies. *Educational Leadership, 49*(7), 26–33.

Rosenshine, B., & Meister, C. (1994). Reciprocal teaching: A review of the research. *Review of Educational Research, 64*, 479–530.

Rosenshine, B., Meister, C., & Chapman, S. (1996). Teaching students to generate questions: A review of the intervention studies. *Review of Educational Research, 66*, 181–221.

Rosenshine, B. V., & Stevens, R. (1986). Teaching functions. In M. C. Wittrock (Ed.), *Handbook of research on teaching* (3rd ed.). New York: Macmillan.

Rosenthal, R. (1994). Interpersonal expectancy effects: A 30-year perspective. *Current Directions in Psychological Science, 3*, 176–179.

Rosenthal, R. (2002). Covert communication in classrooms, clinics, courtrooms, and cubicles. *American Psychologist, 57*, 839–849.

Rosenthal, R., & Jacobson, L. (1968). *Pygmalion in the classroom: Teacher expectation and pupils' intellectual development.* New York: Holt, Rinehart & Winston.

Rosenthal, T. L., Alford, G. S., & Rasp, L. M. (1972). Concept attainment, generalization, and retention through observation and verbal coding. *Journal of Experimental Child Psychology, 13*, 183–194.

Rosenthal, T. L., & Bandura, A. (1978). Psychological modeling: Theory and practice. In S. L. Garfield & A. E. Begia (Eds.), *Handbook of psychotherapy and behavior change: An empirical analysis* (2nd ed.). New York: Wiley.

Rosenthal, T. L., & Zimmerman, B. J. (1978). *Social learning and cognition.* San Diego, CA: Academic Press.

Rosenzweig, M. R. (1986). Multiple models of memory. In S. L. Friedman, K. A. Klivington, & R. W. Peterson (Eds.), *The brain, cognition, and education.* Orlando, FL: Academic Press.

Ross, B. H., & Spalding, T. L. (1994). Concepts and categories. In R. J. Sternberg (Ed.), *Handbook of perception and cognition* (Vol. 12). New York: Academic Press.

Ross, J. A. (1988). Controlling variables: A meta-analysis of training studies. *Review of Educational Research, 58*, 405–437.

Rosser, R. (1994). *Cognitive development: Psychological and biological perspectives.* Needham Heights, MA: Allyn & Bacon.

Rotenberg, K. J., & Mayer, E. V. (1990). Delay of gratification in Native and White children: A cross-cultural comparison. *International Journal of Behavioral Development, 13*, 23–30.

Roth, K. J. (1990). Developing meaningful conceptual understanding in science. In B. F. Jones & L. Idol (Eds.), *Dimensions of thinking and cognitive instruction.* Mahwah, NJ: Erlbaum.

Roth, K. J., & Anderson, C. (1988). Promoting conceptual change learning from science textbooks. In P. Ramsden (Ed.), *Improving learning: New perspectives.* London: Kogan Page.

Roth, W., & Bowen, G. M. (1995). Knowing and interacting: A study of culture, practices, and resources in a grade 8 open-inquiry science classroom guided by a cognitive apprenticeship metaphor. *Cognition and Instruction, 13*, 73–128.

Rothbaum, F., Weisz, J., Pott, M., Miyake, K., & Morelli, G. (2000). Attachment and culture: Security in the United States and Japan. *American Psychologist, 55*, 1093–1104.

Roughead, W. G., & Scandura, J. M. (1968). What is learned in mathematical discovery. *Journal of Educational Psychology, 59*, 283–289.

Rowe, D. C., Almeida, D. M., & Jacobson, K. C. (1999). School context and genetic influences on aggression in adolescence. *Psychological Science, 10*, 277–280.

Rowe, E. (1999, April). *Gender differences in math self-concept development: The role of classroom interaction.* Paper presented at the annual meeting of the American Educational Research Association, Montreal, Canada.

Rowe, M. B. (1974). Wait-time and rewards as instructional variables, their influence on language, logic, and fate control: Part one—wait time. *Journal of Research in Science Teaching, 11*, 81–94.

Rowe, M. B. (1978). *Teaching science as continuous inquiry.* New York: McGraw-Hill.

Rowe, M. B. (1987). Wait-time: Slowing down may be a way of speeding up. *American Educator, 11*, 38–43, 47.

Rubin, K. H. (1982). Nonsocial play in preschoolers: Necessarily evil? *Child Development, 53*, 651–657.

Rubin, K. H., Bukowski, W., & Parker, J. G. (1998). Peer interactions, relationships, and groups. In W. Damon (Series Ed.) & N. Eisenberg (Vol. Ed.), *Handbook of child psychology: Vol. 3. Social, emotional, and personality development* (5th ed.). New York: Wiley.

Rubin, K. H., & Krasnor, L. R. (1986). Social-cognitive and social behavioral perspectives on problem solving. In M. Perlmutter (Ed.), *Minnesota Symposia on Child Psychology: Vol. 18. Cognitive perspectives on children's social and behavioral development.* Mahwah, NJ: Erlbaum.

Ruble, D. N. (1988). Sex-role development. In M. H. Bornstein & M. E. Lamb (Eds.), *Developmental psychology: An advanced textbook* (2nd ed.). Mahwah, NJ: Erlbaum.

Ruble, D. N., & Ruble, T. L. (1982). Sex stereotypes. In A. G. Miller (Ed.), *In the eye of the beholder.* New York: Praeger.

Rudman, M. K. (1993). Multicultural children's literature: The search for universals. In M. K. Rudman (Ed.), *Children's literature: Resource for the classroom* (2nd ed.). Norwood, MA: Christopher-Gordon.

Rudolph, K. D., Lambert, S. F., Clark, A. G., & Kurlakowsky, K. D. (2001). Negotiating the transition to middle school: The role of self-regulatory processes. *Child Development, 72*, 929–946.

Rueda, R., & Moll, L. C. (1994). A sociocultural perspective on motivation. In H. F. O'Neil, Jr., & M. Drillings (Eds.), *Motivation: Theory and research.* Mahwah, NJ: Erlbaum.

Ruef, M. B., Higgins, C., Glaeser, B., & Patnode, M. (1998). Positive behavioral support: Strategies for teachers. *Intervention in School and Clinic, 34*(1), 21–32.

Rueger, D. B., & Liberman, R. P. (1984). Behavioral family therapy for delinquent substance-abusing adolescents. *Journal of Drug Abuse, 14*, 403–418.

Ruffman, T., Slade, L., & Crowe, E. (2002). The relation between children's and mothers' mental state language and theory-of-mind understanding. *Child Development, 73*, 734–751.

Rumberger, R. W. (1995). Dropping out of middle school: A multilevel analysis of students and schools. *American Educational Research Journal, 32*, 583–625.

Rumelhart, D. E., & Ortony, A. (1977). The representation of knowledge in memory. In R. C. Anderson, R. J. Spiro, & W. E. Montague (Eds.), *Schooling and the acquisition of knowledge.* Mahwah, NJ: Erlbaum.

Rummel, N., Levin, J. R., & Woodward, M. M. (2003). Do pictorial mnemonic text-learning aids give students something worth writing about? *Journal of Educational Psychology, 95*, 327–334.

Runco, M. A., & Chand, I. (1995). Cognition and creativity. *Educational Psychology Review, 7*, 243–267.

Rushton, J. P. (1980). *Altruism, socialization, and society.* Upper Saddle River, NJ: Prentice Hall.

Rushton, J. P. (1982). Social learning theory and the development of prosocial behavior. In N. Eisenberg (Ed.), *The development of prosocial behavior.* New York: Academic Press.

Russ, S. W. (1993). *Affect and creativity: The role of affect and play in the creative process.* Mahwah, NJ: Erlbaum.

Ryan, A. M. (2000). Peer groups as a context for the socialization of adolescents' motivation, engagement, and achievement in school. *Educational Psychologist, 35*, 101–111.

Ryan, A. M. (2001). The peer group as a context for the development of young adolescent motivation and achievement. *Child Development, 72*, 1135–1150.

Ryan, A. M., Hicks, L., & Midgley, C. (1997). Social goals, academic goals, and avoiding help seeking in the classroom. *Journal of Early Adolescence, 17*, 152–171.

Ryan, A. M., & Patrick, H. (2001). The classroom social environment and changes in adolescents' motivation and engagement during middle school. *American Educational Research Journal, 38*, 437–460.

Ryan, A. M., Pintrich, P. R., & Midgley, C. (2001). Avoiding seeking help in the classroom: Who and why? *Educational Psychology Review, 13*, 93–114.

Ryan, R. M., Connell, J. P., & Grolnick, W. S. (1992). When achievement is *not* intrinsically motivated: A theory of internalization and self-regulation in school. In A. K. Boggiano & T. S. Pittman (Eds.), *Achievement and motivation: A social-developmental perspective.* Cambridge, England: Cambridge University Press.

Ryan, R. M., & Deci, E. L. (2000). Self-determination theory and the facilitation of intrinsic motivation, social development, and well-being. *American Psychologist, 55*, 68–78.

Ryan, R. M., & Kuczkowski, R. (1994). The imaginary audience, self-consciousness, and public individuation in adolescence. *Journal of Personality, 62*, 219–237.

Ryan, R. M., & Lynch, J. H. (1989). Emotional autonomy versus detachment: Revisiting the vicissitudes of adolescence and young adulthood. *Child Development, 60*, 340–356.

Ryan, R. M., Mims, V., & Koestner, R. (1983). Relation of reward contingency and interpersonal context to intrinsic motivation: A review and test using cognitive evaluation theory. *Journal of Personality and Social Psychology, 45*, 736–750.

Ryan, R. M., Stiller, J. D., & Lynch, J. H. (1994). Representations of relationships to teachers, parents, and friends as predictors of academic motivation and self-esteem. *Journal of Early Adolescence, 14*, 226–249.

Ryan, S., Ormond, T., Imwold, C. & Rotunda, R. J. (2002). The effects of a public address system on the off-task behavior of elementary physical education students. *Journal of Applied Behavior Analysis, 35*, 305–308.

Sabers, D. S., Cushing, K. S., & Berliner, D. C. (1991). Differences among teachers in a task characterized by simultaneity, multidimensionality, and immediacy. *American Educational Research Journal, 28*, 63–88.

Sadker, M. P., & Miller, D. (1982). *Sex equity handbook for schools.* White Plains, NY: Longman.

Sadker, M. P., & Sadker, D. (1994). *Failing at fairness: How our schools cheat girls.* New York: Touchstone.

Sadker, M. P., Sadker, D., & Klein, S. (1991). The issue of gender in elementary and secondary education. In G. Grant (Ed.), *Review of research in education.* Washington, DC: American Educational Research Association.

Sadoski, M., Goetz, E. T., & Fritz, J. B. (1993). Impact of concreteness on comprehensibility, interest, and memory for text: Implications for dual coding theory and text design. *Journal of Educational Psychology, 85*, 291–304.

Sadoski, M., & Paivio, A. (2001). *Imagery and text: A dual coding theory of reading and writing.* Mahwah, NJ: Erlbaum.

Salend, S. J., & Taylor, L. (1993). Working with families: A cross-cultural perspective. *Remedial and Special Education, 14*(5), 25–32, 39.

Salisbury, C. L., Evans, I. M., & Palombaro, M. M. (1997). Collaborative problem solving to promote the inclusion of young children with significant disabilities in primary grades. *Exceptional Children, 63*, 195–210.

Saljo, R., & Wyndhamn, J. (1992). Solving everyday problems in the formal setting: An empirical study of the school as context for thought. In S. Chaiklin & J. Lave (Eds.), *Understanding practice.* New York: Cambridge University Press.

Salomon, G. (1993). No distribution without individuals' cognition: A dynamic interactional view. In G. Salomon (Ed.), *Distributed cognitions: Psychological and educational considerations* (pp. 111–138). Cambridge, England: Cambridge University Press.

Saltz, E. (1971). *The cognitive bases of human learning.* Homewood, IL: Dorsey.

Sameroff, A. J., Seifer, R., Baldwin, A., & Baldwin, C. (1993). Stability of intelligence from preschool to adolescence: The influence of social and family risk factors. *Child Development, 64*, 80–97.

Sanborn, M. P. (1979). Counseling and guidance needs of the gifted and talented. In A. H. Passow (Ed.), *The gifted and the talented: Their education and development. The seventy-eighth yearbook of the National Society for the Study of Education.* Chicago: University of Chicago Press.

Sanchez, F., & Anderson, M. L. (1990). Gang mediation: A process that works. *Principal, 69*(4), 54–56.

Sanders, C. E. (1997). Assessment during the preschool years. In G. D. Phye (Ed.), *Handbook of classroom assessment: Learning, achievement, and adjustment.* San Diego, CA: Academic Press.

Sanders, M. G. (1996). Action teams in action: Interviews and observations in three schools in the Baltimore School–Family–Community Partnership Program. *Journal of Education for Students Placed at Risk, 1*, 249–262.

Sanders, S. (1987). Cultural conflicts: An important factor in academic failures of American Indian students. *Journal of Multicultural Counseling and Development, 15*(2), 81–90.

Sands, D. J., & Wehmeyer, M. L. (Eds.). (1996). *Self-determination across the life span: Independence and choice for people with disabilities.* Baltimore: Brookes.

Sapolsky, R. M. (1999). Glucocorticoids, stress, and their adverse neurological effects: Relevance to aging. *Experimental Gerontology, 34*, 721–732.

Sapon-Shevin, M., Dobbelaere, A., Corrigan, C., Goodman, K., & Mastin, M. (1998). Everyone here can play. *Educational Leadership, 56*(1), 42–45.

Sarason, I. G. (Ed.). (1980). *Test anxiety: Theory, research, and applications.* Mahwah, NJ: Erlbaum.

Sarason, S. B. (1972). What research says about test anxiety in elementary school children. In A. R. Binter & S. H. Frey (Eds.), *The psychology of the elementary school child.* Chicago: Rand McNally.

Sasso, G. M., & Rude, H. A. (1987). Unprogrammed effects of training high-status peers to interact with severely handicapped children. *Journal of Applied Behavior Analysis, 20*, 35–44.

Sattler, J. M. (2001). *Assessment of children: Cognitive applications* (4th ed.). San Diego, CA: Author.

Sawyer, R. J., Graham, S., & Harris, K. R. (1992). Direct teaching, strategy instruction, and strategy instruction with explicit self-regulation: Effects on the composition skills and self-efficacy of students with learning disabilities. *Journal of Educational Psychology, 84*, 340–352.

Sax, G. (1989). *Principles of educational and psychological measurement and evaluation* (3rd ed.). Belmont, CA: Wadsworth.

Sax, G., & Cromack, T. R. (1966). The effects of various forms of item arrangements on test performance. *Journal of Educational Measurement, 3*, 309–311.

Scarcella, R. (1990). *Teaching language-minority students in the multicultural classroom.* Upper Saddle River, NJ: Prentice Hall.

Scardamalia, M., & Bereiter, C. (1985). Fostering the development of self-regulation in children's knowledge processing. In S. F. Chipman, J. W. Segal, & R. Glaser (Eds.), *Thinking and learning skills: Vol. 2. Research and open questions.* Mahwah, NJ: Erlbaum.

Scarr, S., & Weinberg, R. A. (1976). IQ test performance of black children adopted by white families. *American Psychologist, 31*, 726–739.

Scevak, J. J., Moore, P. J., & Kirby, J. R. (1993). Training students to use maps to increase text recall. *Contemporary Educational Psychology, 18*, 401–413.

Schacter, D. L. (1999). The seven sins of memory: Insights from psychology and neuroscience. *American Psychologist, 54*, 182–203.

Schacter, J. (2000). Does individual tutoring produce optimal learning? *American Educational Research Journal, 37*, 801–829.

Schank, R. C. (1979). Interestingness: Controlling inferences. *Artificial Intelligence, 12*, 273–297.

Schank, R. C., & Abelson, R. P. (1995). Knowledge and memory: The real story. In R. S. Wyer, Jr. (Ed.), *Advances in social cognition: Vol. 8 Knowledge and memory: The real story.* Mahwah, NJ: Erlbaum.

Schauble, L. (1990). Belief revision in children: The role of prior knowledge and strategies for generating evidence. *Journal of Experimental Child Psychology, 49*, 31–57.

Schiefele, U. (1991). Interest, learning, and motivation. *Educational Psychologist, 26*, 299–323.

Schiefele, U. (1992). Topic interest and levels of text comprehension. In K. A. Renninger, S. Hidi, & A. Krapp (Eds.), *The role of interest in learning and development.* Mahwah, NJ: Erlbaum.

Schiefele, U. (1998). Individual interest and learning: What we know and what we don't know. In L. Hoffman, A. Krapp, K. Renninger, & J. Baumert (Eds.), *Interest and learning: Proceedings of the Seeon Conference on Interest and Gender* (pp. 91–104). Kiel, Germany: IPN.

Schiefele, U., Krapp, A., & Winteler, A. (1992). Interest as a predictor of academic achievement: A meta-analysis of research. In K. A. Renninger, S. Hidi, & A. Krapp (Eds.), *The role of interest in learning and development.* Mahwah, NJ: Erlbaum.

Schiefele, U., & Wild, K. (1994, April). *Motivational predictors of strategy use and course grades.* Paper presented at the annual meeting of the American Educational Research Association, New Orleans, LA.

Schiffman, G., Tobin, D., & Buchanan, B. (1984). Microcomputer instruction for the learning disabled. *Annual Review of Learning Disabilities, 2*, 134–136.

Schimmoeller, M. A. (1998, April). *Influence of private speech on the writing behaviors of young children: Four case studies.* Paper presented at the annual meeting of the American Educational Research Association, San Diego, CA.

Schirmer, B. R. (1994). *Language and literacy development in children who are deaf.* Needham Heights, MA: Allyn & Bacon.

Schlaefli, A., Rest, J. R., & Thoma, S. J. (1985). Does moral education improve moral judgment? A meta-analysis of intervention studies using the defining issues test. *Review of Educational Research, 55*, 319–352.

Schliemann, A. D., & Carraher, D. W. (1993). Proportional reasoning in and out of school. In P. Light & G. Butterworth (Eds.), *Context and cognition: Ways of learning and knowing.* Mahwah, NJ: Erlbaum.

Schloss, P. J., & Smith, M. A. (1994). *Applied behavior analysis in the classroom.* Needham Heights, MA: Allyn & Bacon.

Schmidt, R. A., & Bjork, R. A. (1992). New conceptualizations of practice: Common principles in three paradigms suggest new concepts for training. *Psychological Science, 3*, 207–217.

Schneider, W. (1993). Domain-specific knowledge and memory performance in children. *Educational Psychology Review, 5*, 257–273.

Schneider, W., & Pressley, M. (1989). *Memory development between 2 and 20.* New York: Springer-Verlag.

Schoenfeld, A. H. (1985). Metacognitive and epistemological issues in mathematical understanding. In E. A.

Silver (Ed.), *Teaching and learning mathematical problem solving: Multiple research perspectives.* Mahwah, NJ: Erlbaum.

Schoenfeld, A. H., & Hermann, D. J. (1982). Problem perception and knowledge structure in expert and novice mathematical problem solvers. *Journal of Experimental Psychology: Learning, Memory, and Cognition, 8,* 484–494.

Schofield, J. W. (1995). Improving intergroup relations among students. In J. A. Banks & C. A. M. Banks (Eds.), *Handbook of research on multicultural education.* New York: Macmillan.

Schommer, M. (1994a). An emerging conceptualization of epistemological beliefs and their role in learning. In R. Garner & P. A. Alexander (Eds.), *Beliefs about text and instruction with text.* Mahwah, NJ: Erlbaum.

Schommer, M. (1994b). Synthesizing epistemological belief research: Tentative understandings and provocative confusions. *Educational Psychology Review, 6,* 293–319.

Schommer, M. (1997). The development of epistemological beliefs among secondary students: A longitudinal study. *Journal of Educational Psychology, 89,* 37–40.

Schommer-Aikins, M. (2001). An evolving theoretical framework for an epistemological belief system. In B. K. Hofer & P. R. Pintrich (Eds.), *Personal epistemology: The psychology of beliefs about knowledge and knowing.* Mahwah, NJ: Erlbaum.

Schonert-Reichl, K. A. (1993). Empathy and social relationships in adolescents with behavioral disorders. *Behavioral Disorders, 18,* 189–204.

Schraw, G., & Lehman, S. (2001). Situational interest: A review of the literature and directions for future research. *Educational Psychology Review, 13,* 23–52.

Schraw, G., & Moshman, D. (1995). Metacognitive theories. *Educational Psychology Review, 7,* 351–371.

Schraw, G., & Wade, S. (1991, April). *Selective learning strategies for relevant and important text information.* Paper presented at the annual meeting of the American Educational Research Association, Chicago.

Schreibman, L. (1988). *Autism.* Newbury Park, CA: Sage.

Schubert, J. G. (1986). Gender equity in computer learning. *Theory into Practice, 25,* 267–275.

Schult, C. A. (2002). Children's understanding of the distinction between intentions and desires. *Child Development, 73,* 1727–1747.

Schultz, G. F., & Switzky, H. N. (1990). The development of intrinsic motivation in students with learning problems: Suggestions for more effective instructional practice. *Preventing School Failure, 34*(2), 14–20.

Schultz, K., Buck, P., & Niesz, T. (2000). Democratizing conversations: Racialized talk in a post-desegregated middle school. *American Educational Research Journal, 37,* 33–65.

Schultz, K., & Lochhead, J. (1991). A view from physics. In M. U. Smith (Ed.), *Toward a unified theory of problem solving: Views from the content domains.* Mahwah, NJ: Erlbaum.

Schumaker, J. B., & Hazel, J. S. (1984). Social skill assessment and training for the learning disabled: Who's on first and what's on second? (Pt. 1). *Journal of Learning Disabilities, 17,* 422–431.

Schunk, D. H. (1981). Modeling and attributional effects on children's achievement: A self-efficacy analysis. *Journal of Educational Psychology, 73,* 93–105.

Schunk, D. H. (1983a). Ability versus effort attributional feedback: Differential effects on self-efficacy and achievement. *Journal of Educational Psychology, 75,* 848–856.

Schunk, D. H. (1983b). Developing children's self-efficacy and skills: The roles of social comparative information and goal setting. *Contemporary Educational Psychology, 8,* 76–86.

Schunk, D. H. (1987). Peer models and children's behavioral change. *Review of Educational Research, 57,* 149–174.

Schunk, D. H. (1989a). Self-efficacy and achievement behaviors. *Educational Psychology Review, 1,* 173–208.

Schunk, D. H. (1989b). Self-efficacy and cognitive skill learning. In C. Ames & R. Ames (Eds.), *Research on motivation in education: Vol. 3. Goals and cognitions.* San Diego, CA: Academic Press.

Schunk, D. H. (1989c). Social cognitive theory and self-regulated learning. In B. J. Zimmerman & D. H. Schunk (Eds.), *Self-regulated learning and academic achievement: Theory, research, and practice.* New York: Springer-Verlag.

Schunk, D. H. (1990, April). *Socialization and the development of self-regulated learning: The role of attributions.* Paper presented at the annual meeting of the American Educational Research Association, Boston.

Schunk, D. H. (1991). *Learning theories: An educational perspective.* Upper Saddle River, NJ: Merrill/Prentice Hall.

Schunk, D. H. (1996). Goal and self-evaluative influences during children's cognitive skill learning. *American Educational Research Journal, 33,* 359–382.

Schunk, D. H. (1998). Teaching elementary students to self-regulate practice of mathematical skills with modeling. In D. H. Schunk & B. J. Zimmerman (Eds.), *Self-regulated learning: From teaching to self-reflective practice* (pp. 137–159). New York: Guilford Press.

Schunk, D. H., & Hanson, A. R. (1985). Peer models: Influence on children's self-efficacy and achievement. *Journal of Educational Psychology, 77,* 313–322.

Schunk, D. H., Hanson, A. R., & Cox, P. D. (1987). Peer-model attributes and children's achievement behaviors. *Journal of Educational Psychology, 79,* 54–61.

Schunk, D. H., & Swartz, C. W. (1993). Goals and progress feedback: Effects on self-efficacy and writing achievement. *Contemporary Educational Psychology, 18,* 337–354.

Schunk, D. H., & Zimmerman, B. J. (1997). Social origins of self-regulatory competence. *Educational Psychologist, 32,* 195–208.

Schutz, P. A. (1994). Goals as the transactive point between motivation and cognition. In P. R. Pintrich, D. R. Brown, & C. E. Weinstein (Eds.), *Student motivation, cognition, and learning: Essays in honor of Wilbert J. McKeachie.* Mahwah, NJ: Erlbaum.

Schwartz, B., & Reisberg, D. (1991). *Learning and memory.* New York: Norton.

Schwartz, D., Dodge, K. A., Coie, J. D., Hubbard, J. A., Cillesen, A. H., Lemerise, E. A., & Bateman, H. (1998). Social-cognitive and behavioral correlates of aggression and victimization in boys' play groups. *Journal of Abnormal Child Psychology, 26,* 431–440.

Schwartz, D., Dodge, K. A., Pettit, G. S., & Bates, J. E. (1997). The early socialization of aggressive victims of bullying. *Child Development, 68,* 665–675.

Schwartz, D., McFadyen-Ketchum, S., Dodge, K. A., Pettit, G. S., & Bates, J. E. (1999). Early behavior problems as a predictor of later peer victimization: Moderators and mediators in the pathways of social risk. *Journal of Abnormal Child Psychology, 27,* 191–201.

Schwarz, B. B., Neuman, Y., & Biezuner, S. (2000). Two wrongs may make a right . . . if they argue together! *Cognition and Instruction, 18,* 461–494.

Schwebel, A. I., & Cherlin, D. L. (1972). Physical and social distancing in teacher-pupil relationships. *Journal of Educational Psychology, 63,* 543–550.

Scott, J., & Bushell, D. (1974). The length of teacher contacts and students' off-task behavior. *Journal of Applied Behavior Analysis, 7,* 39–44.

Scott-Jones, D. (1984). Family influences on cognitive development and school achievement. In E. W. Gordon (Ed.), *Review of research in education* (Vol. 11). Washington, DC: American Educational Research Association.

Scruggs, T. E., & Lifson, S. A. (1985). Current conceptions of test-wiseness: Myths and realities. *School Psychology Review, 14,* 339–350.

Scruggs, T. E., & Mastropieri, M. A. (1989). Mnemonic instruction of learning disabled students: A field-based evaluation. *Learning Disabilities Quarterly, 12,* 119–125.

Scruggs, T. E., & Mastropieri, M. A. (1992). Classroom applications of mnemonic instruction: Acquisition, maintenance, and generalization. *Exceptional Children, 58,* 219–229.

Scruggs, T. E., & Mastropieri, M. A. (1994). Successful mainstreaming in elementary science classes: A qualitative study of three reputational cases. *American Educational Research Journal, 31,* 785–811.

Seaton, E., Rodriguez, A., Jacobson, L., Taylor, R., Cantic, R., & Dale, P. (1999, April). *Influence of economic resources on family organization and achievement in economically disadvantaged African-American families.* Paper presented at the annual meeting of the American Educational Research Association, Montreal, Canada.

Seeley, K. (1989). Facilitators for the gifted. In J. Feldhusen, J. VanTassel-Baska, & K. Seeley, *Excellence in educating the gifted.* Denver, CO: Love.

Seligman, M. E. P. (1975). *Helplessness: On depression, development, and death.* San Francisco: Freeman.

Seligman, M. E. P. (1991). *Learned optimism.* New York: Knopf.

Selkow, P. (1984). Effects of maternal employment on kindergarten and first-grade children's vocational aspirations. *Sex Roles, 11,* 677–690.

Selman, R. L. (1980). *The growth of interpersonal understanding.* San Diego, CA: Academic Press.

Semb, G. B., & Ellis, J. A. (1994). Knowledge taught in school: What is remembered? *Review of Educational Research, 64,* 253–286.

Semb, G. B., Ellis, J. A., & Araujo, J. (1993). Long-term memory for knowledge learned in school. *Journal of Educational Psychology, 85,* 305–316.

Serbin, L., & Karp, J. (2003). Intergenerational studies of parenting and the transfer of risk from parent to child. *Current Directions in Psychological Science, 12,* 138–142.

Sergeant, J. (1996). A theory of attention: An information processing perspective. In G. R. Lyon & N. A. Krasnegor (Eds.), *Attention, memory, and executive function* (pp. 57–69). Baltimore: Brookes.

Sfard, A. (1998). On two metaphors for learning and the dangers of choosing just one. *Educational Researcher, 27*(2), 4–13.

Shabani, D. B., Katz, R. C., Wilder, D. A., Beauchamp, K., Taylor, C. R., & Fischer, K. J. (2002). Increasing social initiations in children with autism: Effects of a tactile prompt. *Journal of Applied Behavior Analysis, 35,* 79–83.

Shachar, H., & Sharan, S. (1994). Talking, relating, and achieving: Effects of cooperative learning and whole-class instruction. *Cognition and Instruction, 12,* 313–353.

Shavelson, R. J., & Baxter, G. P. (1992). What we've learned about assessing hands-on science. *Educational Leadership, 49*(8), 20–25.

Shavelson, R. J., Baxter, G. P., & Pine, J. (1992). Performance assessments: Political rhetoric and measurement reality. *Educational Researcher, 21*(4), 22–27.

Sheets, R. H. (1999). Human development and ethnic identity. In R. H. Sheets & E. R. Hollins (Eds.), *Racial and ethnic identity in school practices: Aspects of human development* (pp. 91–101). Mahwah, NJ: Erlbaum.

Sheets, R. H., & Hollins, E. R. (Eds.). (1999). *Racial and ethnic identity in school practices: Aspects of human development.* Mahwah, NJ: Erlbaum.

Sheffield, F. D., Wulff, J. J., & Backer, R. (1951). Reward value of copulation without sex drive reduction. *Journal of Comparative and Physiological Psychology, 44,* 3–8.

Sheldon, A. (1974). The role of parallel function in the acquisition of relative clauses in English. *Journal of Verbal Learning and Verbal Behavior, 13,* 272–281.

Shepard, L. A. (2000). The role of assessment in a learning culture. *Educational Researcher, 29*(7), 4–14.

Shepard, R. N., & Metzler, J. (1971). Mental rotation of three-dimensional objects. *Science, 171,* 701–703.

Shepperd, J. A., & McNulty, J. K. (2002). The affective consequences of expected and unexpected outcomes. *Psychological Science, 13,* 85–88.

Sherif, M., Harvey, O. J., White, B. J., Hood, W. R., & Sherif, C. (1961). *Inter-group conflict and cooperation: The Robbers Cave experiment.* Norman: University of Oklahoma Press.

Sherman, D. K., & Cohen, G. L. (2002). Accepting threatening information: Self-affirmation and the reduction of defensive biases. *Current Directions in Psychological Science, 11,* 119–123.

Shernoff, D. J., & Hoogstra, L. A. (2001, April). *Exploring continuing interest: How engagement in high school classes relates to subsequent commitment.* Paper presented at the annual meeting of the American Educational Research Association, Seattle, WA.

Shernoff, D. J., Knauth, S., & Makris, E. (2000). The quality of classroom experiences. In M. Csikszentmihalyi & B. Schneider, *Becoming adult: How teenagers prepare for the world of work.* New York: Basic Books.

Shernoff, D. J., Schneider, B., & Csikszentmihalyi, M. (2001, April). *An assessment of multiple influences on student engagement in high school classrooms.* Paper presented at the annual meeting of the American Educational Research Association, Seattle, WA.

Sheveland, D. E. (1994, April). *Motivational factors in the development of independent readers.* Paper presented at the annual meeting of the American Educational Research Association, New Orleans, LA.

Shih, S.-S., & Alexander, J. M. (2000). Interacting effects of goal setting and self- or other-referenced feedback on children's development of self-efficacy and cognitive skill within the Taiwanese classroom. *Journal of Educational Psychology, 92,* 536–543.

Shipman, S., & Shipman, V. C. (1985). Cognitive styles: Some conceptual, methodological, and applied issues. In E. W. Gordon (Ed.), *Review of research in education* (Vol. 12). Washington, DC: American Educational Research Association.

Shoda, Y., Mischel, W., & Peake, P. K. (1990). Predicting adolescent cognitive and self-regulatory competencies from preschool delay of gratification: Identifying diagnostic conditions. *Developmental Psychology, 26,* 978–986.

Short, E. J., Schatschneider, C. W., & Friebert, S. E. (1993). Relationship between memory and metamemory performance: A comparison of specific and general strategy knowledge. *Journal of Educational Psychology, 85,* 412–423.

Shrager, L., & Mayer, R. E. (1989). Note-taking fosters generative learning strategies in novices. *Journal of Educational Psychology, 81,* 263–264

Shrigley, R. L. (1979). Strategies in classroom management. *NASSP Bulletin, 63*(428), 1–9.

Shrum, W., & Cheek, N. H. (1987). Social structure during the school years: Onset of the degrouping process. *American Sociological Review, 52,* 218–223.

Shuell, T. J. (1996). Teaching and learning in a classroom context. In D. C. Berliner & R. C. Calfee (Eds.), *Handbook of educational psychology.* New York: Macmillan.

Shulman, L. S. (1986). Those who understand: Knowledge growth in teaching. *Educational Researcher, 15*(2), 4–14.

Shulman, L. S., & Quinlan, K. M. (1996). The comparative psychology of school subjects. In D. C. Berliner & R. C. Calfee (Eds.), *Handbook of educational psychology.* New York: Macmillan.

Shulman, S., Elicker, J., & Sroufe, L. A. (1994). Stages of friendship growth in preadolescence as related to attachment history. *Journal of Social and Personal Relationships, 11,* 341–361.

Shure, M. B., & Spivack, G. (1980). Interpersonal problem-solving as a mediator of behavioral adjustment in preschool and kindergarten children. *Journal of Applied Developmental Psychology, 1,* 29–44.

Shweder, R. A., Goodnow, J., Hatano, G., Levine, R. A., Marcus, H., & Miller, P. (1998). The cultural psychology of development: One mind, many mentalities. In W. Damon (Editor-in-Chief) & R. M. Lerner (Vol. Ed.), *Handbook of child psychology: Vol. 1. Theoretical models of human development* (5th ed., pp. 865–937). New York: Wiley.

Shweder, R. A., Mahapatra, M., & Miller, J. G. (1987). Culture and moral development. In J. Kagan & S. Lamb (Eds.), *The emergence of morality in young children* (pp. 1–83). Chicago: University of Chicago Press.

Shymansky, J. A., Hedges, L. V., & Woodworth, G. (1990). A reassessment of the effects of inquiry-based science curricula of the 60s on student performance. *Journal of Research in Science Teaching, 27,* 127–144.

Sidel, R. (1996). *Keeping women and children last: America's war on the poor.* New York: Penguin Books.

Sieber, J. E., Kameya, L. I., & Paulson, F. L. (1970). Effect of memory support on the problem-solving ability of test-anxious children. *Journal of Educational Psychology, 61,* 159–168.

Siegler, R. S. (1996). *Emerging minds: The process of change in children's thinking.* New York: Oxford University Press.

Siegler, R. S. (1998). *Children's thinking* (3rd ed.). Upper Saddle River, NJ: Prentice Hall.

Siegler, R. S., & Richards, D. D. (1982). The development of intelligence. In R. J. Sternberg (Ed.), *Handbook of human intelligence.* Cambridge, England: Cambridge University Press.

Sigman, M., & Whaley, S. E. (1998). The role of nutrition in the development of intelligence. In U. Neisser (Ed.), *The rising curve: Long-term gains in IQ and related measures* (pp. 155–182). Washington, DC: American Psychological Association.

Silberman, M. L., & Wheelan, S. A. (1980). *How to discipline without feeling guilty: Assertive relationships with children.* Champaign, IL: Research Press.

Silver, E. A., & Kenney, P. A. (1995). Sources of assessment information for instructional guidance in mathematics. In T. Romberg (Ed.), *Reform in school mathematics and authentic assessment.* Albany, NY: State University of New York Press.

Silverberg, R. P. (2003, April). *Developing relational space. Teachers who came to understand themselves and their students as learners.* Paper presented at the annual meeting of the American Educational Research Association, Chicago.

Simon, H. A. (1974). How big is a chunk? *Science, 183,* 482–488.

Simons, R. L., Whitbeck, L. B., Conger, R. D., & Conger, K. J. (1991). Parenting factors, social skills, and value commitments as precursors to school failure, involvement with deviant peers, and delinquent behavior. *Journal of Youth and Adolescence, 20,* 645–664.

Simonton, D. K. (2000). Creativity: Cognitive, personal, developmental, and social aspects. *American Psychologist, 55,* 151–158.

Simonton, D. K. (2001). Talent development as a multidimensional, multiplicative, and dynamic process. *Current Directions in Psychological Science, 10,* 39–42.

Sinatra, G. M., & Pintrich, P. R. (Eds.). (2003a). *Intentional conceptual change.* Mahwah, NJ: Erlbaum.

Sinatra, G. M., & Pintrich, P. R. (2003b). The role of intentions in conceptual change learning. In G. M. Sinatra & P. R. Pintrich (Eds.), *Intentional conceptual change* (pp. 1–18). Mahwah, NJ: Erlbaum.

Singer, D. G., & Singer, J. L. (1994). *Barney & Friends as education and entertainment: Phase 3. A national study: Can preschoolers learn through exposure to Barney & Friends?* New Haven, CT: Yale University Family Television Research and Consultation Center.

Singley, M. K., & Anderson, J. R. (1989). *The transfer of cognitive skill.* Cambridge, MA: Harvard University Press.

Sisk, D. A. (1989). Identifying and nurturing talent among American Indians. In C. J. Maker & S. W. Schiever (Eds.), *Critical issues in gifted education: Vol. 2. Defensible programs for cultural and ethnic minorities.* Austin, TX: Pro-Ed.

Siskin, L. S. (2003a). Outside the core: Accountability in tested and untested subjects. In M. Carnoy, R. Elmore, & L. S. Siskin (Eds.), *The new accountability: High schools and high-stakes testing* (pp. 87–98). New York: RoutledgeFalmer.

Siskin, L. S. (2003b). When an irresistible force meets an immovable object: Core lessons about high schools and accountability. In M. Carnoy, R. Elmore, & L. S. Siskin (Eds.), *The new accountability: High schools and high-stakes testing* (pp. 175–194). New York: RoutledgeFalmer.

Sitko, B. M. (1998). Knowing how to write: Metacognition and writing instruction. In D. J. Hacker, J. Dunlosky, & A. C. Graesser (Eds.), *Metacognition in educational theory and practice* (pp. 93–115). Mahwah, NJ: Erlbaum.

Sizer, T. R. (1992). *Horace's school: Redesigning the American high school.* Boston: Houghton Mifflin.

Skaalvik, E. (1997). Self-enhancing and self-defeating ego orientation: Relations with task avoidance orientation, achievement, self-perceptions, and anxiety. *Journal of Educational Psychology, 89,* 71–81.

Skiba, R., & Raison, J. (1990). Relationship between the use of time-out and academic achievement. *Exceptional Children, 57,* 36–46.

Skinner, B. F. (1953). *Science and human behavior.* New York: Macmillan.

Skinner, B. F. (1954). The science of learning and the art of teaching. *Harvard Educational Review, 24,* 86–97.

Skinner, B. F. (1968). *The technology of teaching.* New York: Appleton-Century-Crofts.

Slaughter-Defoe, D. T. (2001). A longitudinal case study of Head Start eligible children: Implications for urban education. *Educational Psychologist, 36,* 31–44.

Slavin, R. E. (1983). When does cooperative learning increase student achievement? *Psychological Bulletin, 94,* 429–445.

Slavin, R. E. (1987). Ability grouping and student achievement in elementary schools: A best-evidence synthesis. *Review of Educational Research, 57,* 293–336.

Slavin, R. E. (1989). Students at risk of school failure: The problem and its dimensions. In R. E. Slavin, N. L. Karweit, & N. A. Madden (Eds.), *Effective programs for students at risk.* Needham Heights, MA: Allyn & Bacon.

Slavin, R. E. (1990). *Cooperative learning: Theory, research, and practice.* Upper Saddle River, NJ: Prentice Hall.

Slavin, R. E., Karweit, N. L., & Madden, N. A. (Eds.). (1989). *Effective programs for students at risk.* Needham Heights, MA: Allyn & Bacon.

Sleeter, C. E., & Grant, C. A. (1999). *Making choices for multicultural education: Five approaches to race, class, and gender* (3rd ed.). Upper Saddle River, NJ: Merrill/Prentice Hall.

Slife, B. R., Weiss, J., & Bell, T. (1985). Separability of metacognition and cognition: Problem solving in learning disabled and regular students. *Journal of Educational Psychology, 77,* 437–445.

Slonim, M. B. (1991). *Children, culture, ethnicity: Evaluating and understanding the impact.* New York: Garland.

Slusher, M. P., & Anderson, C. A. (1996). Using causal persuasive arguments to change beliefs and teach new information: The mediating role of explanation availability and evaluation bias in the acceptance of knowledge. *Journal of Educational Psychology, 88,* 110–122.

Small, M. Y., Lovett, S. B., & Scher, M. S. (1993). Pictures facilitate children's recall of unillustrated expository prose. *Journal of Educational Psychology, 85,* 520–528.

Small, R. V., & Grabowski, B. L. (1992). An exploratory study of information-seeking behaviors and learning with hypermedia information systems. *Journal of Educational Multimedia and Hypermedia, 1,* 445–464.

Smetana, J. G. (1981). Preschool children's conceptions of moral and social rules. *Child Development, 52,* 1333–1336.

Smetana, J. G., & Braeges, J. L. (1990). The development of toddlers' moral and conventional judgments. *Merrill-Palmer Quarterly, 36,* 329–346

Smith, B. L., & MacGregor, J. T. (1992). What is collaborative learning? In A. Goodsell, M. Maher, & V. Tinto (Eds.), *Collaborative learning: A sourcebook for higher education.* University Park: National Center on

Postsecondary Teaching, Learning, and Assessment, The Pennsylvania State University.

Smith, C. L., Maclin, D., Grosslight, L., & Davis, H. (1997). Teaching for understanding: A study of students' preinstruction theories of matter and a comparison of the effectiveness of two approaches to teaching about matter and density. *Cognition and Instruction, 15*, 317–393.

Smith, D. C., & Neale, D. C. (1991). The construction of subject-matter knowledge in primary science teaching. In J. Brophy (Ed.), *Advances in research on teaching: Vol. 2. Teachers' knowledge of subject matter as it relates to their teaching practice.* Greenwich, CT: JAI Press.

Smith, D. J., Young, K. R., West, R. P., Morgan, R. P., & Rhode, G. (1988). Reducing the disruptive behavior of junior high school students: A classroom self-management procedure. *Behavioral Disorders, 13,* 231–239.

Smith, E. E. (2000). Neural bases of human working memory. *Current Directions in Psychological Science, 9,* 45–49.

Smith, H. L. (1998). Literacy and instruction in African American communities: Shall we overcome? In B. Pérez (Ed.), *Sociocultural contexts of language and literacy.* Mahwah, NJ: Erlbaum.

Smith, K., Johnson, D. W., & Johnson, R. T. (1981). Can conflict be constructive? Controversy versus concurrence seeking in learning groups. *Journal of Educational Psychology, 73,* 651–663.

Smith, P. B., & Bond, M. H. (1994). *Social psychology across cultures: Analysis and perspectives.* Needham Heights, MA: Allyn & Bacon.

Smith, R. E., & Smoll, F. L. (1997). Coaching the coaches: Youth sports as a scientific and applied behavioral setting. *Current Directions in Psychological Science, 6*(1), 16–21.

Smitherman, G. (1994). "The blacker the berry the sweeter the juice": African American student writers. In A. H. Dyson & C. Genishi (Eds.), *The need for story: Cultural diversity in classroom and community.* Urbana, IL: National Council of Teachers of English.

Snarey, J. (1995). In a communitarian voice: The sociological expansion of Kohlbergian theory, research, and practice. In W. M. Kurtines & J. L. Gewirtz (Eds.), *Moral development: An introduction.* Boston: Allyn & Bacon.

Sneider, C., & Pulos, S. (1983). Children's cosmographies: Understanding the earth's shape and gravity. *Science Education, 67,* 205–221.

Snow, C. E. (1990). Rationales for native language instruction: Evidence from research. In A. M. Padilla, H. H. Fairchild, & C. M. Valadez (Eds.), *Bilingual education: Issues and strategies.* Newbury Park, CA: Sage.

Snow, R. E., Corno, L., & Jackson, D., III (1996). Individual differences in affective and conative functions. In D. C. Berliner & R. C. Calfee (Eds.), *Handbook of educational psychology.* New York: Macmillan.

Sosniak, L. A., & Stodolsky, S. S. (1994). Making connections: Social studies education in an urban fourth-grade classroom. In J. Brophy (Ed.), *Advances in research on teaching: Vol. 4. Case studies of teaching and learning in social studies.* Greenwich, CT: JAI Press.

Southerland, S. A., & Sinatra, G. M. (2003). Learning about biological evolution: A special case of intentional conceptual change. In G. M. Sinatra & P. R. Pintrich (Eds.), *Intentional conceptual change* (pp. 317–345). Mahwah, NJ: Erlbaum.

Spandel, V. (1997). Reflections on portfolios. In G. D. Phye (Ed.), *Handbook of academic learning: Construction of knowledge.* San Diego, CA: Academic Press.

Spaulding, C. L. (1992). *Motivation in the classroom.* New York: McGraw-Hill.

Spear, L. P. (2000). Neurobehavioral changes in adolescence. *Current Directions in Psychological Science, 9,* 111–114.

Spearman, C. (1904). General intelligence, objectively determined and measured. *American Journal of Psychology, 15,* 201–293.

Spearman, C. (1927). *The abilities of man: Their nature and measurement.* New York: Macmillan.

Spencer, M. B., Noll, E., Stoltzfus, J., & Harpalani, V. (2001). Identity and school adjustment: Revisiting the "acting White" phenomenon. *Educational Psychologist, 36,* 21–30.

Spencer, S. J., Steele, C. M., & Quinn, D. M. (1999). Stereotype threat and women's math performance. *Journal of Experimental Social Psychology, 35,* 4–28.

Spicker, H. H. (1992). Identifying and enriching: Rural gifted children. *Educational Horizons, 70*(2), 60–65.

Spires, H. A., & Donley, J. (1998). Prior knowledge activation: Inducing engagement with informational texts. *Journal of Educational Psychology, 90,* 249–260.

Spires, H. A., Donley, J., & Penrose, A. M. (1990, April). *Prior knowledge activation: Inducing text engagement in reading to learn.* Paper presented at the annual meeting of the American Educational Research Association, Boston.

Spivey, N. N. (1997). *The constructivist metaphor: Reading, writing, and the making of meaning.* San Diego, CA: Academic Press.

Sprafkin, C., Serbin, L. A., Denier, C., & Connor, J. M. (1983). Sex-differentiated play: Cognitive consequences and early interventions. In M. B. Liss (Ed.), *Social and cognitive skills: Sex roles and children's play.* San Diego, CA: Academic Press.

Sroufe, L. A., Carlson, E., & Shulman, S. (1993). Individuals in relationships: Development from infancy through adolescence. In D. C. Funder, R. D. Parke, C. Tomlinson-Keasey, & K. Widaman (Eds.), *Studying lives through time: Personality and development* (pp. 315–342). Washington, DC: American Psychological Association.

Stacey, K. (1992). Mathematical problem solving in groups: Are two heads better than one? *Journal of Mathematical Behavior, 11,* 261–275.

Stack, C. B., & Burton, L. M. (1993). Kinscripts. *Journal of Comparative Family Studies, 24,* 157–170.

Stainback, S., & Stainback, W. (Eds.). (1985). *Integrating students with severe handicaps into regular schools.* Reston, VA: Council for Exceptional Children.

Stainback, S., & Stainback, W. (1990). Inclusive schooling. In W. Stainback & S. Stainback (Eds.), *Support networks for inclusive schooling: Interdependent integrated education.* Baltimore: Brookes.

Stainback, S., & Stainback, W. (1992). Schools as inclusive communities. In W. Stainback & S. Stainback (Eds.), *Controversial issues confronting special education: Divergent perspectives.* Boston: Allyn & Bacon.

Stainback, W., & Stainback, S. (1992). *Controversial issues confronting special education: Divergent perspectives.* Boston: Allyn & Bacon.

Standage, M., Duda, J. L., & Ntoumanis, N. (2003). A model of contextual motivation in physical education: Using constructs from self-determination and achievement goal theories to predict physical activity intentions. *Journal of Educational Psychology, 95,* 97–110.

Stanley, J. C. (1980). On educating the gifted. *Educational Researcher, 9*(3), 8–12.

Stanovich, K. E. (1999). *Who is rational? Studies of individual differences in reasoning.* Mahwah, NJ: Erlbaum.

Stanovich, K. E. (2000). *Progress in understanding reading: Scientific foundations and new frontiers.* New York: Guilford Press.

Stanovich, K. E., West, R. F., & Harrison, M. R. (1995). Knowledge growth and maintenance across the life span: The role of print exposure. *Developmental Psychology, 31,* 811–826.

Starr, E. J., & Lovett, S. B. (2000). The ability to distinguish between comprehension and memory: Failing to succeed. *Journal of Educational Psychology, 92,* 761–771.

Staub, D. (1998). *Delicate threads: Friendships between children with and without special needs in inclusive settings.* Bethesda, MD: Woodbine House.

Staub, E. (1995). The roots of prosocial and antisocial behavior in persons and groups: Environmental influence, personality, culture, and socialization. In W. M. Kurtines & J. L. Gewirtz (Eds.), *Moral development: An introduction.* Boston: Allyn & Bacon.

Steele, C. M. (1997). A threat in the air: How stereotypes shape intellectual identity and performance. *American Psychologist, 52,* 613–629.

Steffensen, M. S., Joag-Dev, C., & Anderson, R. C. (1979). A cross-cultural perspective on reading comprehension. *Reading Research Quarterly, 15,* 10–29.

Stein, D. M., & Reichert, P. (1990). Extreme dieting behaviors in early adolescence. *Journal of Early Adolescence, 10,* 108–121.

Steinberg, E. R. (1989). Cognition and learner control: A literature review, 1977–1988. *Journal of Computer-Based Instruction, 16*(4), 117–121.

Steinberg, L. (1996). *Beyond the classroom: Why school reform has failed and what parents need to do.* New York: Touchstone.

Steinberg, L., Blinde, P. L., & Chan, K. S. (1984). Dropping out among language minority youth. *Review of Educational Research, 54,* 113–132.

Steiner, H. H., & Carr, M. (2003). Cognitive development in gifted children: Toward a more precise understanding of emerging differences in intelligence. *Educational Psychology Review, 15,* 215–246.

Stepans, J. (1991). Developmental patterns in students' understanding of physics concepts. In S. M. Glynn, R. H. Yeany, & B. K. Britton (Eds.), *The psychology of learning science.* Mahwah, NJ: Erlbaum.

Stephens, T. M., Blackhurst, A. E., & Magliocca, L. A. (1988). *Teaching mainstreamed students* (2nd ed.). Oxford, England: Pergamon Press.

Sternberg, R. J. (1984). Toward a triarchic theory of human intelligence. *Behavioral and Brain Sciences, 7,* 269–287.

Sternberg, R. J. (1985). *Beyond IQ: A triarchic theory of human intelligence.* Cambridge, England: Cambridge University Press.

Sternberg, R. J. (1996a). Educational psychology has fallen, but it can get up. *Educational Psychology Review, 8,* 175–185.

Sternberg, R. J. (1996b). Myths, countermyths, and truths about intelligence. *Educational Researcher, 25*(2), 11–16.

Sternberg, R. J. (1997). The concept of intelligence and its role in lifelong learning and success. *American Psychologist, 52,* 1030–1037.

Sternberg, R. J. (1998). Teaching triarchically improves school achievement. *Journal of Educational Psychology, 90,* 374–384.

Sternberg, R. J. (2002). Raising the achievement of all students: Teaching for successful intelligence. *Educational Psychology Review, 14,* 383–393.

Sternberg, R. J., & Detterman, D. K. (Eds.). (1986). *What is intelligence? Contemporary views on its nature and definition.* Norwood, NJ: Ablex.

Sternberg, R. J., Forsythe, G. B., Hedlund, J., Horvath, J. A., Wagner, R. K., Williams, W. M., Snook, S. A., & Grigorenko, E. L. (2000). *Practical intelligence in everyday life.* Cambridge, England: Cambridge University Press.

Sternberg, R. J., & Frensch, P. A. (1993). Mechanisms of transfer. In D. K. Detterman & R. J. Sternberg (Eds.), *Transfer on trial: Intelligence, cognition, and instruction.* Norwood, NJ: Ablex.

Sternberg, R. J., & Horvath, J. A. (1995). A prototype view of expert teaching. *Educational Researcher, 24*(6), 9–17.

Sternberg, R. J., & Wagner, R. K. (Eds.). (1994). *Mind in context: Interactionist perspectives on human intelligence.* Cambridge, England: Cambridge University Press.

Sternberg, R. J., & Zhang, L. (1995). What do we mean by giftedness? A pentagonal implicit theory. *Gifted Child Quarterly, 39,* 88–94.

Stevahn, L., Oberle, K., Johnson, D. W., & Johnson, R. T. (2001, April). *Effects of role reversal training and use of integrative negotiation for classroom management on conflict resolution in kinder- garten.* Paper presented at the annual meeting of the American Educational Research Association, Seattle, WA.

Stevens, J. J., & Clauser, P. (1996, April). *Longitudinal examination of a writing portfolio and the ITBS.* Paper presented at the annual meeting of the American Educational Research Association, New York.

Stevens, R. J., & Slavin, R. E. (1995). The cooperative elementary school: Effects of students' achievement, attitudes, and social relations. *American Educational Research Journal, 32*, 321–351.

Stevenson, H. C., & Fantuzzo, J. W. (1986). The generality and social validity of a competency-based self-control training intervention for underachieving students. *Journal of Applied Behavior Analysis, 19*, 269–272.

Stevenson, H. W., Chen, C., & Uttal, D. H. (1990). Beliefs and achievement: A study of black, white, and Hispanic children. *Child Development, 61*, 508–523.

Stewart, L., & Pascual-Leone, J. (1992). Mental capacity constraints and the development of moral reasoning. *Journal of Experimental Child Psychology, 54*, 251–287.

Stice, E., & Barrera, M., Jr. (1995). A longitudinal examination of the reciprocal relations between perceived parenting and adolescents' substance use and externalizing behaviors. *Developmental Psychology, 31*, 322–334.

Stiggins, R. J. (2001). *Student-involved classroom assessment* (3rd ed.). Upper Saddle River, NJ: Merrill/Prentice Hall.

Stiggins, R. J., & Conklin, N. F. (1992). *In teachers' hands: Investigating the practices of classroom assessment.* Albany: State University of New York Press.

Stipek, D. J. (1984). Sex differences in children's attributions for success and failure on math and spelling tests. *Sex Roles, 11*, 969–981.

Stipek, D. J. (1993). *Motivation to learn: From theory to practice* (2nd ed.). Boston: Allyn & Bacon.

Stipek, D. J. (1996). Motivation and instruction. In D. C. Berliner & R. C. Calfee (Eds.), *Handbook of educational psychology.* New York: Macmillan.

Stipek, D. (2002). At what age should children enter kindergarten? A question for policy makers and parents. *Social Policy Report of the Society for Research in Child Development, 16*(2), 3–16.

Stipek, D. J., & Gralinski, H. (1990, April). *Gender differences in children's achievement-related beliefs and emotional responses to success and failure in math.* Paper presented at the annual meeting of the American Educational Research Association, Boston.

Stodolsky, S. S., Salk, S., & Glaessner, B. (1991). Student views about learning math and social studies. *American Educational Research Journal, 28*, 89–116.

Stone, N. J. (2000). Exploring the relationship between calibration and self-regulated learning. *Educational Psychology Review, 12*, 437–475.

Strayer, D. L., & Johnston, W. A. (2001). Driven to distraction: Dual-task studies of simulated driving and conversing on a cellular telephone. *Psychological Science, 12*, 462–466.

Stright, A. D., Neitzel, C., Sears, K. G., & Hoke-Sinex, L. (2001). Instruction begins in the home: Relations between parental instruction and children's self-regulation in the classroom. *Journal of Educational Psychology, 93*, 456–466.

Strike, K. A., & Posner, G. J. (1992). A revisionist theory of conceptual change. In R. A. Duschl & R. J. Hamilton (Eds.), *Philosophy of science, cognitive psychology, and educational theory and practice.* New York: State University of New York Press.

Stringer, E. (2004). *Action research in education.* Upper Saddle River, NJ: Prentice Hall.

Sue, D. W. (1990). Culture-specific strategies in counseling: A conceptual framework. *Professional Psychology: Research and Practice, 21*, 424–433.

Sue, S., & Chin, R. (1983). The mental health of Chinese-American children: Stressors and resources. In G. J. Powell (Ed.), *The psychosocial development of minority children.* New York: Brunner/Mazel.

Suina, J. H., & Smolkin, L. B. (1994). From natal culture to school culture to dominant society culture: Supporting transitions for Pueblo Indian students. In P. M. Greenfield & R. R. Cocking (Eds.), *Cross-cultural roots of minority child development.* Mahwah, NJ: Erlbaum.

Sullivan, J. S. (1989). Planning, implementing, and maintaining an effective in-school suspension program. *Clearing House, 62*, 409–410.

Sullivan, R. C. (1994). Autism: Definitions past and present. *Journal of Vocational Rehabilitation, 4*, 4–9.

Sullivan-DeCarlo, C., DeFalco, K., & Roberts, V. (1998). Helping students avoid risky behavior. *Educational Leadership, 56*(1), 80–82.

Sund, R. B. (1976). *Piaget for educators.* Upper Saddle River, NJ: Merrill/Prentice Hall.

Suskind, R. (1998). *A hope in the unseen: An American odyssey from the inner city to the Ivy League.* New York: Broadway Books.

Suttles, G. D. (1970). Friendship as a social institution. In G. J. McCall, M. McCall, N. K. Denzin, G. D. Suttles, & S. Kurth (Eds.), *Social relationships* (pp. 95–135). Chicago: Aldine de Gruyter.

Sutton-Smith, B. (Ed.). (1979). *Play and learning.* New York: Gardner Press.

Swan, K., Mitrani, M., Guerrero, F., Cheung, M., & Schoener, J. (1990, April). *Perceived locus of control and computer-based instruction.* Paper presented at the annual meeting of the American Educational Research Association, Boston.

Swanborn, M. S. L., & de Glopper, K. (1999). Incidental word learning while reading: A meta-analysis. *Review of Educational Research, 69*, 261–285.

Swanson, D. B., Norman, G. R., & Linn, R. L. (1995). Performance-based assessment: Lessons from the health professions. *Educational Researcher, 24*(5), 5–11, 35.

Swanson, H. L. (1993). An information processing analysis of learning disabled children's problem solving. *American Educational Research Journal, 30*, 861–893.

Swanson, H. L., Cooney, J. B., & O'Shaughnessy, T. E. (1998). Learning disabilities and memory. In B. Y. L. Wong (Ed.), *Learning about learning disabilities* (2nd ed.). San Diego, CA: Academic Press.

Swanson, H. L., & Lussier, C. M. (2001). A selective synthesis of the experimental literature on dynamic assessment. *Review of Educational Research, 71*, 321–363.

Swanson, H. L., Mink, J., & Bocian, K. M. (1999). Cognitive processing deficits in poor readers with symptoms of reading disabilities and ADHD: More alike than different? *Journal of Educational Psychology, 91*, 321–333.

Swanson, H. L., O'Connor, J. E., & Cooney, J. B. (1990). An information processing analysis of expert and novice teachers' problem solving. *American Educational Research Journal, 27*, 533–556.

Tamburrini, J. (1982). Some educational implications of Piaget's theory. In S. Modgil & C. Modgil (Eds.), *Jean Piaget: Consensus and controversy.* New York: Praeger.

Tarver, S. G. (1992). Direct Instruction. In W. Stainback & S. Stainback (Eds.), *Controversial issues confronting special education.* Boston: Allyn & Bacon.

Tate, W. F. (1995). Returning to the root: A culturally relevant approach to mathematics pedagogy. *Theory into Practice, 34*, 166–173.

Taylor, B. A., & Levin, L. (1998). Teaching a student with autism to make verbal initiations: Effects of a tactile prompt. *Journal of Applied Behavior Analysis, 31*, 651–654.

Taylor, I. A. (1976). A retrospective view of creativity investigation. In I. A. Taylor & J. W. Getzels (Eds.), *Perspectives in creativity.* Chicago: Aldine de Gruyter.

Taylor, J. C., & Romanczyk, R. G. (1994). Generating hypotheses about the function of student problem behavior by observing teacher behavior. *Journal of Applied Behavior Analysis, 27*, 251–265.

Taylor, S. M. (1994, April). *Staying in school against the odds: Voices of minority adolescent girls.* Paper presented at the annual meeting of the American Educational Research Association, New Orleans, LA.

Teasley, S. D., & Roschelle, J. (1993). Constructing a joint problem space: The computer as a tool for sharing information. In S. P. Lajoie & S. J. Derry (Eds.), *Computers as cognitive tools* (pp. 229–258). Hillsdale, NJ: Erlbaum.

Tennyson, R. D., & Cocchiarella, M. J (1986). An empirically based instructional design theory for teaching concepts. *Review of Educational Research, 56*, 40–71.

Terman, L. M., & Merrill, M. A. (1972). *Stanford-Binet Intelligence Scale* (3rd ed.). Boston: Houghton Mifflin

Terwilliger, J. S. (1989). Classroom standard setting and grading practices. *Educational Measurement: Issues and Practice, 8*(2), 15–19.

Tessler, M., & Nelson, K. (1994). Making memories: The influence of joint encoding on later recall by young children. *Consciousness and Cognition, 3*, 307–326.

Tharp, R. G. (1989). Psychocultural variables and constants: Effects on teaching and learning in schools. *American Psychologist, 44*, 349–359.

Tharp, R. G. (1994). Intergroup differences among Native Americans in socialization and child cognition: An ethnogenetic analysis. In P. M. Greenfield & R. R. Cocking (Eds.), *Cross-cultural roots of minority child development.* Mahwah, NJ: Erlbaum.

Théberge, C. L. (1994, April). *Small-group vs. whole-class discussion: Gaining the floor in science lessons.* Paper presented at the annual meeting of the American Educational Research Association, New Orleans, LA.

Thelen, E., & Smith, L. B. (1998). Dynamic systems theories. In W. Damon (Series Ed.) & R. M. Lerner (Vol. Ed.), *Handbook of child psychology: Vol. 1. Theoretical models of human development.* (5th ed.). New York: Wiley.

Themann, K. S., & Goldstein, H. (2001). Social stories, written text cues, and video feedback: Effects on social communication of children with autism. *Journal of Applied Behavior Analysis, 34*, 425–446.

Thomas, A., & Chess, S. (1977). *Temperament and development.* New York: Brunner/Mazel.

Thomas, H., & Kail, R. (1991). Sex differences in the speed of mental rotation and the X-linked genetic hypothesis. *Intelligence, 15*, 17–32.

Thomas, J. R., & French, K. E. (1985). Gender differences across age in motor performance: A meta-analysis. *Psychological Bulletin, 98*, 260–282.

Thomas, J. W. (1993a). Expectations and effort: Course demands, students' study practices, and academic achievement. In T. M. Tomlinson (Ed.), *Motivating students to learn: Overcoming barriers to high achievement.* Berkeley, CA: McCutchan.

Thomas, J. W. (1993b). Promoting independent learning in the middle grades: The role of instructional support practices. *Elementary School Journal, 93*, 575–591.

Thomas, S., & Oldfather, P. (1997). Intrinsic motivations, literacy, and assessment practices: "That's my grade. That's me." *Educational Psychologist, 32*, 107–123.

Thomas, S. P., Groër, M., & Droppleman, P. (1993). Physical health of today's school children. *Educational Psychology Review, 5*, 5–33.

Thomas, W. P., Collier, V. P., & Abbott, M. (1993). Academic achievement through Japanese, Spanish, or French: The first two years of partial immersion. *Modern Language Journal, 77*, 170–179.

Thompson, A. G., & Thompson, P. W. (1989). Affect and problem solving in an elementary school mathematics classroom. In D. B. McLeod & V. M. Adams (Eds.), *Affect and mathematical problem solving: A new perspective.* New York: Springer-Verlag.

Thompson, H., & Carr, M. (1995, April). *Brief metacognitive intervention and interest as predictors of memory for text.* Paper presented at the annual meeting of the American Educational Research Association, San Francisco.

Thompson, R. A. (1998). Early sociopersonality development. In W. Damon (Series Ed.) & N. Eisenberg (Vol. Ed.), *Handbook of child psychology: Vol. 3. Social, emotional, and personality development* (5th ed.). New York: Wiley.

Thompson, R. A., & Nelson, C. A. (2001). Developmental science and the media: Early brain development. *American Psychologist, 56*, 5–15.

Thompson, R. A., & Wyatt, J. M. (1999). Current research on child maltreatment: Implications for educators. *Educational Psychology Review, 11,* 173–201.

Thompson, R. F. (1985). *The brain: An introduction to neuroscience.* New York: Freeman.

Thompson, T. L., & Zerbinos, E. (1995). Gender roles in animated cartoons: Has the picture changed in 20 years? *Sex Roles, 32,* 651–673.

Thorkildsen, T. A. (1995). Conceptions of social justice. In W. M. Kurtines & J. L. Gewirtz (Eds.), *Moral development: An introduction.* Boston: Allyn & Bacon.

Thorndike, E. L. (1924). Mental discipline in high school studies. *Journal of Educational Psychology, 15,* 1–22, 83–98.

Thorndike, R. M. (1997). *Measurement and evaluation in psychology and education* (6th ed.). Upper Saddle River, NJ: Merrill/Prentice Hall.

Thorndike, R., Hagen, E., & Sattler, J. (1986). *Stanford-Binet Intelligence Scale* (4th ed.). Itasca, IL: Riverside.

Thousand, J. S., Villa, R. A., & Nevin, A. I. (1994). *Creativity and collaborative learning: A practical guide for empowering students and teachers.* Baltimore: Brookes.

Threadgill-Sowder, J. (1985). Individual differences and mathematical problem solving. In E. A. Silver (Ed.), *Teaching and learning mathematical problem solving: Multiple research perspectives.* Mahwah, NJ: Erlbaum.

Thurstone, L. L. (1938). *Primary mental abilities.* Chicago: University of Chicago Press.

Thurstone, L. L., & Jeffrey, T. E. (1956). *FLAGS: A test of space thinking.* Chicago: Industrial Relations Center.

Timm, P., & Borman, K. (1997). The soup pot don't stretch that far no more: Intergenerational patterns of school leaving in an urban Appalachian neighborhood. In M. Sellter & L. Weis (Eds.), *Beyond black and white: New faces and voices in U.S. schools.* Albany: State University of New York Press.

Tirosh, D., & Graeber, A. O. (1990). Evoking cognitive conflict to explore preservice teachers' thinking about division. *Journal for Research in Mathematics Education, 21,* 98–108.

Tisak, M. (1993). Preschool children's judgments of moral and personal events involving physical harm and property damage. *Merrill-Palmer Quarterly, 39,* 375–390.

Tobias, S. (1977). A model for research on the effect of anxiety on instruction. In J. E. Sieber, H. F. O'Neil, Jr., & S. Tobias (Eds.), *Anxiety, learning, and instruction.* Mahwah, NJ: Erlbaum.

Tobias, S. (1980). Anxiety and instruction. In I. G. Sarason (Ed.), *Test anxiety: Theory, research, and applications.* Mahwah, NJ: Erlbaum.

Tobias, S. (1985). Test anxiety: Interference, defective skills, and cognitive capacity. *Educational Psychologist, 20,* 135–142.

Tobias, S. (1994). Interest, prior knowledge, and learning. *Review of Educational Research, 64,* 37–54.

Tobin, K. (1987). The role of wait time in higher cognitive level learning. *Review of Educational Research, 57,* 69–95.

Tomasello, M. (2000). Culture and cognitive development. *Current Directions in Psychological Science, 9,* 37–40.

Tompkins, G. E., & McGee, L. M. (1986). Visually impaired and sighted children's emerging concepts about written language. In D. B. Yaden, Jr., & S. Templeton (Eds.), *Metalinguistic awareness and beginning literacy: Conceptualizing what it means to read and write.* Portsmouth, NH: Heinemann.

Torrance, E. P. (1970). *Encouraging creativity in the classroom.* Dubuque, IA: Wm. C. Brown.

Torrance, E. P. (1976). Creativity research in education: Still alive. In I. A. Taylor & J. W. Getzels (Eds.), *Perspectives in creativity.* Chicago: Aldine de Gruyter.

Torrance, E. P. (1989). A reaction to "Gifted black students: Curriculum and teaching strategies." In C. J. Maker & S. W. Schiever (Eds.), *Critical issues in gifted education: Vol. 2. Defensible programs for cultural and ethnic minorities.* Austin, TX: Pro-Ed.

Torrance, E. P. (1995). Insights about creativity: Questioned, rejected, ridiculed, ignored. *Educational Psychology Review, 7,* 313–322.

Torrance, E. P., & Myers, R. E. (1970). *Creative learning and teaching.* New York: Dodd, Mead.

Torres-Guzmán, M. E. (1998). Language, culture, and literacy in Puerto Rican communities. In B. Pérez (Ed.), *Sociocultural contexts of language and literacy.* Mahwah, NJ: Erlbaum.

Traub, R. E. (1993). On the equivalence of the traits assessed by multiple-choice and constructed-response tests. In R. E. Bennett & W. C. Ward (Eds.), *Construction versus choice in cognitive measurement: Issues in constructed response, performance testing, and portfolio assessment* (pp. 29–44). Mahwah, NJ: Erlbaum.

Trautner, H. M. (1992). The development of sex-typing in children: A longitudinal analysis. *German Journal of Psychology, 16,* 183–199.

Trautwein, U., & Köller, O. (2003). The relationship between homework and achievement—still much of a mystery. *Educational Psychology Review, 15,* 115–145.

Trawick-Smith, J. (2003). *Early childhood development: A multicultural perspective* (3rd ed.). Upper Saddle River, NJ: Merrill/Prentice Hall.

Treffert, D. A., & Wallace, G. L. (2002). Islands of genius. *Scientific American, 286*(6), 76–85.

Triandis, H. C. (1995). *Individualism and collectivism.* Boulder, CO: Westview Press.

Triona, L. M., & Klahr, D. (2003). Point and click or grab and heft: Comparing the influence of physical and virtual instructional materials on elementary school students' ability to design experiments. *Cognition and Instruction, 2,* 149–173.

Tryon, G. S. (1980). The measurement and treatment of anxiety. *Review of Educational Research, 50,* 343–372.

Tschannen-Moran, M., Woolfolk Hoy, A., & Hoy, W. K. (1998). Teacher efficacy: Its meaning and measure. *Review of Educational Research, 68,* 202–248.

Tucker, V. G., & Anderman, L. H. (1999, April). *Cycles of learning: Demonstrating the interplay between motivation, self-regulation, and cognition.* Paper presented at the annual meeting of the American Educational Research Association, Montreal, Canada.

Tudge, J., Hogan, D., Lee, S., Tammeveski, P., Meltsas, M., Kulakova, N., Snezhkova, I., & Putnam, S. (1999). Cultural heterogeneity: Parental values and beliefs and their preschoolers' activities in the United States, South Korea, Russia, and Estonia. In A. Göncü (Ed.), *Children's engagement in the world: Sociocultural perspectives* (pp. 62–96). Cambridge, England: Cambridge University Press.

Tulving, E. (1962). Subjective organization in free recall of "unrelated" words. *Psychological Review, 69,* 344–354.

Tulving, E. (1983). *Elements of episodic memory.* Oxford, England: Oxford University Press.

Tulving, E., & Thomson, D. M. (1973). Encoding specificity and retrieval processes in episodic memory. *Psychological Review, 80,* 352–373.

Tunstall, P., & Gipps, C. (1996). Teacher feedback to young children in formative assessment: A typology. *British Educational Research Journal, 22,* 389–404.

Turiel, E. (1983). *The development of social knowledge: Morality and convention.* Cambridge, England: Cambridge University Press.

Turiel, E. (1998). The development of morality. In W. Damon (Series Ed.) & N. Eisenberg (Vol. Ed.), *Handbook of child psychology: Vol. 3. Social, emotional, and personality development* (5th ed., pp. 863–932). New York: Wiley.

Turiel, E., Smetana, J. G., & Killen, M. (1991). Social contexts in social cognitive development. In W. M. Kurtines & J. L. Gewirtz (Eds.), *Moral behavior and development: Vol. 2. Research.* Mahwah, NJ: Erlbaum.

Turnbull, A. P. (1974). Teaching retarded persons to rehearse through cumulative overt labeling. *American Journal of Mental Deficiency, 79,* 331–337.

Turnbull, A. P., Pereira, L., & Blue-Banning, M. (2000). Teachers as friendship facilitators. *Teaching Exceptional Children, 32*(5), 66–70.

Turnbull, R., Turnbull, A., Shank, M., & Smith, S. J. (2004). *Exceptional lives: Special education in today's schools* (4th ed.). Upper Saddle River, NJ: Merrill/Prentice Hall.

Turner, J. C. (1995). The influence of classroom contexts on young children's motivation for literacy. *Reading Research Quarterly, 30,* 410–441.

Turner, J. C., Meyer, D. K., Cox, K. E., Logan, C., DiCintio, M., & Thomas, C. T. (1998). Creating contexts for involvement in mathematics. *Journal of Educational Psychology, 90,* 730–745.

Turner, J. C., Thorpe, P. K., & Meyer, D. K. (1998). Students' reports of motivation and negative affect: A theoretical and empirical analysis. *Journal of Educational Psychology, 90,* 758–771.

Turner, J. E., Husman, J., & Schallert, D. L. (2002). The importance of students' goals in their emotional experience of academic failure: Investigating the precursors and consequences of shame. *Educational Psychologist, 37,* 79–89.

Tuttle, D. W., & Tuttle, N. R. (1996). *Self-esteem and adjusting with blindness: The process of responding to life's demands* (2nd ed.). Springfield, IL: Charles C Thomas.

Tyler, B. (1958). Expectancy for eventual success as a factor in problem solving behavior. *Journal of Educational Psychology, 49,* 166–172.

Tzuriel, D. (2000). Dynamic assessment of young children: Educational and intervention perspectives. *Educational Psychology Review, 12,* 385–435.

Udall, A. J. (1989). Curriculum for gifted Hispanic students. In C. J. Maker & S. W. Schiever (Eds.), *Critical issues in gifted education: Vol. 2. Defensible programs for cultural and ethnic minorities.* Austin, TX: Pro-Ed.

Ulichny, P. (1994, April). *Cultures in conflict.* Paper presented at the annual meeting of the American Educational Research Association, New Orleans, LA.

Underwood, B. J. (1954). Studies of distributed practice: XII. Retention following varying degrees of original learning. *Journal of Experimental Psychology, 47,* 294–300.

Urdan, T. C. (1997). Achievement goal theory: Past results, future directions. In M. L. Maehr & P. R. Pintrich (Eds.), *Advances in motivation and achievement* (Vol. 10, pp. 99–141). Greenwich, CT: JAI Press.

Urdan, T. C., & Maehr, M. L. (1995). Beyond a two-goal theory of motivation and achievement: A case for social goals. *Review of Educational Research, 65,* 213–243.

Urdan, T., & Midgley, C. (2001). Academic self-handicapping: What we know, what more there is to learn. *Educational Psychology Review, 13,* 115–138.

Urdan, T. C., Midgley, C., & Anderman, E. M. (1998). The role of classroom goal structure in students' use of self-handicapping strategies. *American Educational Research Journal, 35,* 101–122.

Urdan, T., Ryan, A. M., Anderman, E. M. & Gheen, M. H. (2002). Goals, goal structures, and avoidance behaviors. In C. Midgley (Ed.), *Goals, goal structures, and patterns of adaptive learning* (pp. 55–83). Mahwah, NJ: Erlbaum.

U.S. Bureau of the Census. (1994). *Statistical abstract of the United States: 1994* (114th ed.). Washington, DC: Author.

U.S. Department of Education. (1992). *To assure the free appropriate public education of all children with disabilities: Fourteenth annual report to Congress on the implementation of the Individuals with Disabilities Education Act.* Washington, DC: Author.

U.S. Department of Education. (1993). *National excellence: A case for developing America's talent.* Washington, DC: Office of Educational Research and Improvement.

U.S. Department of Education. (1995). *To assure the free appropriate public education of all children with disabilities: Seventeenth annual report to Congress on the implementation of the Individuals with Disabilities Education Act.* Washington, DC: Author.

U.S. Department of Education. (1996). *To assure the free appropriate public education of all children with disabilities: Eighteenth annual report to Congress on the implementation of the Individuals with Disabilities Education Act.* Washington, DC: Author.

U.S. Department of Education. (1997). *To assure the free appropriate public education of all children with disabilities: Nineteenth annual report to Congress on the imple-*

mentation of the Individuals with Disabilities Education Act. Washington, DC: Author.

U.S. Department of Education, Office of Civil Rights. (1993). Annual report to Congress. Washington, DC: Author.

Valencia, S. W., Hiebert, E. H., & Afflerbach, P. P. (1994). Realizing the possibilities of authentic assessment: Current trends and future issues. In S. W. Valencia, E. H. Hiebert, & P. P. Afflerbach (Eds.), Authentic reading assessment: Practices and possibilities. Newark, DE: International Reading Association.

Valente, N. (2001). "Who cares about school?" A student responds to learning. Unpublished paper, University of New Hampshire, Durham.

Valentine, J. C., Cooper, H., Bettencourt, B. A., & DuBois, D. L. (2002). Out-of-school activities and academic achievement: The mediating role of self-beliefs. Educational Psychologist, 37, 245–256.

Vallerand, R. J., Fortier, M. S., & Guay, F. (1997). Self-determination and persistence in a real-life setting: Toward a motivational model of high school dropout. Journal of Personality and Social Psychology, 72, 1161–1176.

Van Camp, C. M., Lerman, D. C., Kelley, M. E., Roane, H. S., Contrucci, S. A., & Vorndran, C. M. (2000). Further analysis of idiosyncratic antecedent influences during the assessment and treatment of problem behavior. Journal of Applied Behavior Analysis, 33, 207–221.

Van Houten, R., Nau, P., MacKenzie-Keating, S., Sameoto, D., & Colavecchia, B. (1982). An analysis of some variables influencing the effectiveness of reprimands. Journal of Applied Behavior Analysis, 15, 65–83.

van Kraayenoord, C. E., & Paris, S. G. (1997). Australian students' self-appraisal of their work samples and academic progress. Elementary School Journal, 97, 523–537.

van Laar, C. (2000). The paradox of low academic achievement but high self-esteem in African American students: An attributional account. Educational Psychology Review, 12, 33–61.

van Merriënboer, J. J. G., Kirschner, P. A., & Kester, L. (2003). Taking the load off a learner's mind: Instructional design for complex learning. Educational Psychologist, 38, 5–13.

Van Meter, P. (2001). Drawing construction as a strategy for learning from text. Journal of Educational Psychology, 93, 129–140.

Van Meter, P., Yokoi, L., & Pressley, M. (1994). College students' theory of notetaking derived from their perceptions of notetaking. Journal of Educational Psychology, 86, 323–338.

Van Rossum, E. J., & Schenk, S. M. (1984). The relationship between learning conception, study strategy, and learning outcome. British Journal of Educational Psychology, 54, 73–83.

VanSledright, B., & Brophy, J. (1992). Storytelling, imagination, and fanciful elaboration in children's historical reconstructions. American Educational Research Journal, 29, 837–859.

Vasquez, J. A. (1988). Contexts of learning for minority students. Educational Forum, 6, 243–253.

Vaughn, B. J., & Horner, R. H. (1997). Identifying instructional tasks that occasion problem behaviors and assessing the effects of student versus teacher choice among these tasks. Journal of Applied Behavior Analysis, 30, 299–312.

Vaughn, S. (1991). Social skills enhancement in students with learning disabilities. In B. Y. L. Wong (Ed.), Learning about learning disabilities. San Diego, CA: Academic Press.

Veenman, S. (1984). Perceived problems of beginning teachers. Review of Educational Research, 54, 143–178.

Venn, J. J. (2000). Assessing students with special needs (2nd ed.). Upper Saddle River, NJ: Merrill/Prentice Hall.

Verdi, M. P., & Kulhavy, R. W. (2002). Learning with maps and texts: An overview. Educational Psychology Review, 14, 27–46.

Verdi, M. P., Kulhavy, R. W., Stock, W. A., Rittschof, K. A., & Johnson, J. T. (1996). Text learning using scien-

tific diagrams: Implications for classroom use. Contemporary Educational Psychology, 21, 487–499.

Vermeer, H. J., Boekaerts, M., & Seegers, G. (2000). Motivational and gender differences: Sixth-grade students' mathematical problem-solving behavior. Journal of Educational Psychology, 92, 308–315.

Vernon, P. A. (1993). Intelligence and neural efficiency. In D. K. Detterman (Ed.), Current topics in human intelligence (Vol. 3). Norwood, NJ: Ablex.

Veroff, J., McClelland, L., & Ruhland, D. (1975). Varieties of achievement motivation. In M. T. S. Mednick, S. S. Tangri, & L. W. Hoffman (Eds.), Women and achievement: Social and motivational analyses. New York: Halsted.

Villegas, A. (1991). Culturally responsive pedagogy for the 1990s and beyond. Princeton, NJ: Educational Testing Service.

Vitaro, F., Gendreau, P. L., Tremblay, R. E., & Oligny, P. (1998). Reactive and proactive aggression differentially predict later conduct problems. Journal of Child Psychology and Psychiatry and Allied Disciplines, 39, 377–385.

Volet, S. (1999). Learning across cultures: Appropriateness of knowledge transfer. International Journal of Educational Research, 31, 625–643.

Vollmer, T. R., & Hackenberg, T. D. (2001). Reinforcement contingencies and social reinforcement: Some reciprocal relations between basic and applied research. Journal of Applied Behavior Analysis, 34, 241–253.

Vorrath, H. (1985). Positive peer culture. New York: Aldine de Gruyter.

Vosniadou, S. (1994). Universal and culture-specific properties of children's mental models of the earth. In L. A. Hirschfeld & S. A. Gelman (Eds.), Mapping the mind: Domain specificity in cognition and culture. Cambridge, England: Cambridge University Press.

Vosniadou, S. (2003). Exploring the relationships between conceptual change and intentional learning. In G. M. Sinatra & P. R. Pintrich (Eds.), Intentional conceptual change (pp. 377–406). Mahwah, NJ: Erlbaum.

Vosniadou, S., & Brewer, W. F. (1987). Theories of knowledge restructuring in development. Review of Educational Research, 57, 51–67.

Voss, J. F. (1974). Acquisition and nonspecific transfer effects in prose learning as a function of question form. Journal of Educational Psychology, 66, 736–740.

Voss, J. F. (1987). Learning and transfer in subject-matter learning: A problem-solving model. International Journal of Educational Research, 11, 607–622.

Voss, J. F., Greene, T. R., Post, T. A., & Penner, B. D. (1983). Problem-solving skill in the social sciences. In G. H. Bower (Ed.), The psychology of learning and motivation (Vol. 17). San Diego, CA: Academic Press.

Voss, J. F., & Schauble, L. (1992). Is interest educationally interesting? An interest-related model of learning. In K. A. Renninger, S. Hidi, & A. Krapp (Eds.), The role of interest in learning and development. Mahwah, NJ: Erlbaum.

Vye, N. J., Schwartz, D. L., Bransford, J. D., Barron, B. J., Zech, L., & The Cognition and Technology Group at Vanderbilt. (1998). SMART environments that support monitoring, reflection, and revision. In D. J. Hacker, J. Dunlosky, & A. C. Graesser (Eds.), Metacognition in educational theory and practice (pp. 305–346). Mahwah, NJ: Erlbaum.

Vygotsky, L. S. (1962). Thought and language (E. Haufmann & G. Vakar, Eds. and Trans.). Cambridge, MA: MIT Press.

Vygotsky, L. S. (1978). Mind in society: The development of higher psychological pro- cesses. Cambridge, MA: Harvard University Press.

Vygotsky, L. S. (1987). The collected works of L. S. Vygotsky (Vol. 3; R. W. Rieber & A. S. Carton, Eds.). New York: Plenum Press.

Vygotsky, L. S. (1997). Educational psychology (R. Silverman, Trans.). Boca Raton, FL: St. Lucie Press.

Wade, S. E. (1992). How interest affects learning from text. In K. A. Renninger, S. Hidi, & A. Krapp (Eds.), The role of interest in learning and development. Mahwah, NJ: Erlbaum.

Wagner, R. K. (1996). From simple structure to complex function: Major trends in the development of theories, models, and measurements of memory. In G. R. Lyon & N. A. Krasnegor (Eds.), Attention, memory, and executive function (pp. 139–156). Baltimore: Brookes.

Wahlsten, D., & Gottlieb, G. (1997). The invalid separation of effects of nature and nurture: Lessons from animal experimentation. In R. J. Sternberg & E. L. Grigorenko (Eds.), Intelligence, heredity, and environment (pp. 163–192). Cambridge, England: Cambridge University Press.

Walberg, H. J., & Uguroglu, M. (1980). Motivation and educational productivity: Theories, results, and implications. In L. J. Fyans, Jr. (Ed.), Achievement motivation: Recent trends in theory and research. New York: Plenum Press.

Walker, E. F. (2002). Adolescent neurodevelopment and psychopathology. Current Directions in Psychological Science, 11, 24–28.

Walker, J. E., & Shea, T. M. (1995). Behavior management: A practical approach for educators (5th ed.). Upper Saddle River, NJ: Merrill/Prentice Hall.

Walker, J. M. T. (2001, April). A cross-sectional study of student motivation, strategy knowledge and strategy use during homework: Implications for research on self-regulated learning. Paper presented at the annual meeting of the American Educational Research Association, Seattle, WA.

Walker, L. J. (1991). Sex differences in moral reasoning. In W. M. Kurtines & J. L. Gewirtz (Eds.), Handbook of moral behavior and development: Vol. 2. Research (pp. 333–364). Mahwah, NJ: Erlbaum.

Walker, L. J. (1995). Sexism in Kohlberg's moral psychology? In W. M. Kurtines & J. L. Gewirtz (Eds.), Moral development: An introduction. Boston: Allyn & Bacon.

Wang, P. P., & Baron, M. A. (1997). Language and communication: Development and disorders. In M. L. Batshaw (Ed.), Children with disabilities (4th ed.). Baltimore: Brookes.

Want, S. C., & Harris, P. L. (2001). Learning from other people's mistakes: Causal understanding in learning to use a tool. Child Development, 72, 431–443.

Ward, T. B., Vela, E., & Haas, S. D. (1990). Children and adults learn family-resemblance categories analytically. Child Development, 61, 593–605.

Warren, A. R., & McCloskey, L. A. (1993). Pragmatics: Language in social contexts. In J. Berko Gleason (Ed.), The development of language (3rd ed.). New York: Macmillan.

Warren, G. (1979). Essay versus multiple-choice tests. Journal of Research in Science Teaching, 16, 563–567.

Warren, R. L. (1988). Cooperation and conflict between parents and teachers: A comparative study of three elementary schools. In H. T. Trueba & C. Delgado-Gaitan (Eds.), School and society: Learning content through culture. New York: Praeger.

Wasik, B. A., Karweit, N., Burns, L., & Brodsky, E. (1998, April). Once upon a time: The role of rereading and retelling in storybook reading. Paper presented at the annual meeting of the American Educational Research Association, San Diego, CA.

Wasley, P. A., Hampel, R. L., & Clark, R. W. (1997). Kids and school reform. San Francisco: Jossey-Bass.

Waters, H. S. (1982). Memory development in adolescence: Relationships between metamemory, strategy use, and performance. Journal of Experimental Child Psychology, 33, 183–195.

Way, N. (1998). Everyday courage: The lives and stories of urban teenagers. New York: New York University Press.

Weatherford, J. (1988). Indian givers: How the Indians of the Americas transformed the world. New York: Crown.

Weaver, C. A., III, & Kelemen, W. L. (1997). Judgments of learning at delays: Shifts in response patterns or increased metamemory accuracy? Psychological Science, 8, 318–321.

Webb, J. T., Meckstroth, E. A., & Tolan, S. S. (1982). Guiding the gifted child: A practical source for parents and teachers. Dayton, OH: Ohio Psychology Press.

Webb, N. M. (1989). Peer interaction and learning in small groups. *International Journal of Educational Research, 13*, 21–39.

Webb, N. M., & Farivar, S. (1994). Promoting helping behavior in cooperative small groups in middle school mathematics. *American Educational Research Journal, 31*, 369–395.

Webb, N. M., & Farivar, S. (1999). Developing productive group interaction in middle school mathematics. In A. M. O'Donnell & A. King (Eds.), *Cognitive perspectives on peer learning* (pp. 117–149). Mahwah, NJ: Erlbaum.

Webb, N. M., Nemer, K. M., Chizhik, A. W., & Sugrue, B. (1998). Equity issues in collaborative group assessment: Group composition and performance. *American Educational Research Journal, 35*, 607–651.

Webb, N. M., Nemer, K. M., & Zuniga, S. (2002). Short circuits or superconductors? Effects of group composition on high-achieving students' science assessment performance. *American Educational Research Journal, 39*, 943–989.

Webb, N. M., & Palincsar, A. S. (1996). Group processes in the classroom. In D. C. Berliner & R. C. Calfee (Eds.), *Handbook of educational psychology.* New York: Macmillan.

Webber, J., Scheuermann, B., McCall, C., & Coleman, M. (1993). Research on self-monitoring as a behavior management technique in special education classrooms: A descriptive review. *Remedial and Special Education, 14*(2), 38–56.

Wechsler, D. (2003). *Wechsler Intelligence Scale for Children* (4th ed.). San Antonio, TX: Psychological Corporation.

Wehmeyer, M. L. (1996). Self-determination as an educational outcome. In D. J. Sands & M. L. Wehmeyer (Eds.), *Self-determination across the life span: Independence and choice for people with disabilities.* Baltimore: Brookes.

Weiner, B. (1984). Principles for a theory of student motivation and their application within an attributional framework. In R. Ames & C. Ames (Eds.), *Research on motivation in education: Vol. 1. Student motivation.* San Diego, CA: Academic Press.

Weiner, B. (1986). *An attributional theory of motivation and emotion.* New York: Springer-Verlag.

Weiner, B. (1994). Ability versus effort revisited: The moral determinants of achievement evaluation and achievement as a moral system. *Educational Psychologist, 29*, 163–172.

Weiner, B. (1995). *Judgments of responsibility: Foundations for a theory of social conduct.* New York: Guilford Press.

Weiner, B. (2000). Intrapersonal and interpersonal theories of motivation from an attributional perspective. *Educational Psychology Review, 12*, 1–14.

Weiner, B., Russell, D., & Lerman, D. (1978). Affective consequences of causal ascriptions. In J. Harvey, W. Ickes, & R. Kidd (Eds.), *New directions in attribution research* (Vol. 2). Mahwah, NJ: Erlbaum.

Weinert, F. E., & Helmke, A. (1995). Learning from wise Mother Nature or Big Brother Instructor: The wrong choice as seen from an educational perspective. *Educational Psychologist, 30*, 135–142.

Weinstein, C. E., Goetz, E. T., & Alexander, P. A. (Eds.). (1988). *Learning and study strategies: Issues in assessment, instruction, and evaluation.* San Diego, CA: Academic Press.

Weinstein, C. E., Hagen, A. S., & Meyer, D. K. (1991, April). *Work smart . . . not hard: The effects of combining instruction in using strategies, goal using, and executive control on attributions and academic performance.* Paper presented at the annual meeting of the American Educational Research Association, Chicago.

Weinstein, R. S. (1993). Children's knowledge of differential treatment in school: Implications for motivation. In T. M. Tomlinson (Ed.), *Motivating students to learn: Overcoming barriers to high achievement.* Berkeley, CA: McCutchan.

Weinstein, R. S., Madison, S. M., & Kuklinski, M. R. (1995). Raising expectations in schooling: Obstacles

and opportunities for change. *American Educational Research Journal, 32*, 121–159.

Weisberg, R. W. (1993). *Creativity: Beyond the myth of genius.* New York: Freeman.

Weiss, M. R., & Klint, K. A. (1987). "Show and tell" in the gymnasium: An investigation of developmental differences in modeling and verbal rehearsal of motor skills. *Research Quarterly for Exercise and Sport, 58*, 234–241.

Weissberg, R. P. (1985). Designing effective social problem-solving programs for the classroom. In B. H. Schneider, K. H. Rubin, & J. E. Ledingham (Eds.), *Children's peer relations: Issues in assessment and intervention.* New York: Springer-Verlag.

Welch, G. J. (1985). Contingency contracting with a delinquent and his family. *Journal of Behavior Therapy and Experimental Psychiatry, 16*, 253–259.

Wellman, H. M. (1985). The child's theory of mind: The development of conceptions of cognition. In S. R. Yussen (Ed.), *The growth of reflection in children.* San Diego, CA: Academic Press.

Wellman, H. M. (1988). The early development of memory strategies. In F. Weinert & M. Perlmutter (Eds.), *Memory development: Universal changes and individual differences.* Mahwah, NJ: Erlbaum.

Wellman, H. M. (1990). *The child's theory of mind.* Cambridge, MA: MIT Press.

Wellman, H. M., Cross, D., & Watson, J. (2001). Meta-analysis of theory-of-mind development: The truth about false belief. *Child Development, 72*, 655–684.

Wellman, H. M., & Gelman, S. A. (1998). Acquisition of knowledge. In W. Damon (Series Ed.), D. Kuhn, & R. S. Siegler (Vol. Eds.), *Handbook of child psychology: Vol. 2. Cognition, perception, and language* (5th ed.). New York: Wiley.

Wellman, H. M., Phillips, A. T., & Rodriguez, T. (2000). Young children's understanding of perception, desire, and emotion. *Child Development, 71*, 895–912.

Wentzel, K. R. (1999). Social-motivational processes and interpersonal relationships: Implications for understanding motivation at school. *Journal of Educational Psychology, 91*, 76–97.

Wentzel, K. R., & Asher, S. R. (1995). The academic lives of neglected, rejected, popular, and controversial children. *Child Development, 66*, 754–763.

Wentzel, K. R., & Wigfield, A. (1998). Academic and social motivational influences on students' academic performance. *Educational Psychology Review, 10*, 155–175.

Werner, E. E. (1995). Resilience in development. *Current Directions in Psychological Science, 4*, 81–85.

Werner, E. E., & Smith, R. S. (1982). *Vulnerable but invincible: A longitudinal study of resilient children.* New York: McGraw-Hill. New York: Adams, Bannister, Cox.

Werner, E. E., & Smith, R. S. (2001). *Journeys from childhood to midlife: Risk, resilience, and recovery.* Ithaca, NY: Cornell University Press.

Wertsch, J. V. (1984). The zone of proximal development: Some conceptual issues. *Children's learning in the zone of proximal development: New directions for child development* (No. 23). San Francisco: Jossey-Bass.

West, C. K., Farmer, J. A., & Wolff, P. M. (1991). *Instructional design: Implications from cognitive science.* Upper Saddle River, NJ: Prentice Hall.

Whalen, C. K., Jamner, L. D., Henker, B., Delfino, R. J., & Lozano, J. M. (2002). The ADHD spectrum and everyday life: Experience sampling of adolescent moods, activities, smoking, and drinking. *Child Development, 73*, 209–227.

White, A. G., & Bailey, J. S. (1990). Reducing disruptive behaviors of elementary physical education students with sit and watch. *Journal of Applied Behavior Analysis, 23*, 353–359.

White, B. Y., & Frederiksen, J. R. (1998). Inquiry, modeling, and metacognition: Making science accessible to all students. *Cognition and Instruction, 16*, 3–118.

White, J. J., & Rumsey, S. (1994). Teaching for understanding in a third-grade geography lesson. In J. Brophy (Ed.), *Advances in research on teaching: Vol. 4.*

Case studies of teaching and learning in social studies. Greenwich, CT: JAI Press.

White, R. (1959). Motivation reconsidered: The concept of competence. *Psychological Review, 66*, 297–333.

White, R., & Cunningham, A. M. (1991). *Ryan White: My own story.* New York: Signet.

Whiting, B. B., & Edwards, C. P. (1988). *Children of different worlds.* Cambridge, MA: Harvard University Press.

Whitley, B. E., Jr., & Frieze, I. H. (1985). Children's causal attributions for success and failure in achievement settings: A meta-analysis. *Journal of Educational Psychology, 77*, 608–616.

Wideen, M., Mayer-Smith, J., & Moon, B. (1998). A critical analysis of the research on learning to teach: Making the case for an ecological perspective on inquiry. *Review of Educational Research, 68*, 130–178.

Wigfield, A. (1994). Expectancy-value theory of achievement motivation: A developmental perspective. *Educational Psychology Review, 6*, 49–78.

Wigfield, A. (1997). Reading motivation: A domain-specific approach to motivation. *Educational Psychologist, 32*, 59–68.

Wigfield, A., & Eccles, J. (1992). The development of achievement task values: A theoretical analysis. *Developmental Review, 12*, 265–310.

Wigfield, A., & Eccles, J. S. (1994). Children's competence beliefs, achievement values, and general self-esteem: Change across elementary and middle school. *Journal of Early Adolescence, 14*, 107–138.

Wigfield, A., & Eccles, J. (2000). Expectancy-value theory of achievement motivation. *Contemporary Educational Psychology, 25*, 68–81.

Wigfield, A., & Eccles, J. (2002). The development of competence beliefs, expectancies for success, and achievement values from childhood to adolescence. In A. Wigfield & J. Eccles (Eds.), *Development of achievement motivation* (pp. 91–120). San Diego, CA: Academic Press.

Wigfield, A., Eccles, J., Mac Iver, D., Reuman, D., & Midgley, C. (1991). Transitions at early adolescence: Changes in children's domain-specific self-perceptions and general self-esteem across the transition to junior high school. *Developmental Psychology, 27*, 552–565.

Wigfield, A., Eccles, J. S., & Pintrich, P. R. (1996). Development between the ages of 11 and 25. In D. C. Berliner & R. C. Calfee (Eds.), *Handbook of educational psychology.* New York: Macmillan.

Wigfield, A., & Meece, J. L. (1988). Math anxiety in elementary and secondary school students. *Journal of Educational Psychology, 80*, 210–216.

Wiggins, G. (1992). Creating tests worth taking. *Educational Leadership, 49*(8), 26–33.

Wilder, A. A., & Williams, J. P. (2001). Students with severe learning disabilities can learn higher order comprehension skills. *Journal of Educational Psychology, 93*, 268–278.

Wiles, J., & Bondi, J. (2001). *The new American middle school: Educating preadolescents in an era of change.* Upper Saddle River, NJ: Merrill/Prentice Hall.

Wiley, D. E., & Haertel, E. H. (1996). Extended assessment tasks: Purposes, definitions, scoring, and accuracy. In M. B. Kane & R. Mitchell (Eds.), *Implementing performance assessment: Promises, problems, and challenges* (pp. 61–89). Mahwah, NJ: Erlbaum.

Wilkinson, L. D., & Frazer, L. H. (1990, April). *Fine-tuning dropout prediction through discriminant analysis: The ethnic factor.* Paper presented at the annual meeting of the American Educational Research Association, Boston.

Will, M. C. (1986). Educating children with learning problems: A shared responsibility. *Exceptional Children, 52*, 411–415.

Williams, B., & Newcombe, E. (1994). Building on the strengths of urban learners. *Educational Leadership, 51*(8), 75–78.

Williams, D. (1996). *Autism: An inside-outside approach.* London: Jessica Kingsley.

Williams, J. P. (1991, November). *Comprehension of learning disabled and nondisabled students: Identification of narrative themes and idiosyncratic text representation.* Paper presented at the annual meeting of the National Reading Conference, Austin, TX.

Williams, K. M. (2001a). "Frontin' it": Schooling, violence, and relationships in the 'hood. In J. N. Burstyn, G. Bender, R. Casella, H. W. Gordon, D. P. Guerra, K. V. Luschen, R. Stevens, & K. M. Williams, *Preventing violence in schools: A challenge to American democracy* (pp. 95–108). Mahwah, NJ: Erlbaum.

Williams, K. M. (2001b). What derails peer mediation?. In J. N. Burstyn, G. Bender, R. Casella, H. W. Gordon, D. P. Guerra, K. V. Luschen, R. Stevens, & K. M. Williams, *Preventing violence in schools: A challenge to American democracy* (pp. 199–208). Mahwah, NJ: Erlbaum.

Willig, A. C. (1985). A meta-analysis of selected studies on the effectiveness of bilingual education. *Review of Educational Research, 55,* 269–317.

Willingham, D. B. (1998). A neuropsychological theory of motor skill learning. *Psychological Review, 105,* 558–584.

Willingham, D. T. (2004). *Cognition: The thinking animal* (2nd ed.). Upper Saddle River, NJ: Prentice Hall.

Wilson, B. L., & Corbett, H. D. (2001). *Listening to urban kids: School reform and the teachers they want.* Albany: State University of New York Press.

Wilson, C. C., Piazza, C. C., & Nagle, R. (1990). Investigation of the effect of consistent and inconsistent behavioral examples upon children's donation behaviors. *Journal of Genetic Psychology, 151,* 361–376.

Wilson, J. E. (1988). Implications of learning strategy research and training: What it has to say to the practitioner. In C. E. Weinstein, E. T. Goetz, & P. A. Alexander (Eds.), *Learning and study strategies: Issues in assessment, instruction, and evaluation.* San Diego, CA: Academic Press.

Wilson, M. (1989). Child development in the context of the black extended family. *American Psychologist, 44,* 380–383.

Wilson, P. S. (1988, April). The relationship of students' definitions and example choices in geometry. In D. Tirosh (Chair), *The role of inconsistent ideas in learning mathematics.* Symposium conducted at the annual meeting of the American Educational Research Association, New Orleans, LA.

Wilson, P. T., & Anderson, R. C. (1986). What they don't know will hurt them: The role of prior knowledge in comprehension. In J. Orasanu (Ed.), *Reading comprehension: From research to practice.* Mahwah, NJ: Erlbaum.

Wimmer, H., & Perner, J. (1983). Beliefs about beliefs: Representation and constraining function of wrong beliefs in young children's understanding of deception. *Cognition, 13,* 103–128.

Windschitl, M. (2002). Framing constructivism in practice as the negotiation of dilemmas: An analysis of the conceptual, pedagogical, cultural, and political challenges facing teachers. *Review of Educational Research, 72,* 131–175.

Wine, J. D. (1980). Cognitive-attentional theory of test anxiety. In I. G. Sarason (Ed.), *Test anxiety: Theory, research, and applications.* Mahwah, NJ: Erlbaum.

Wingfield, A., & Byrnes, D. L. (1981). *The psychology of human memory.* San Diego, CA: Academic Press.

Winn, W. (1991). Learning from maps and diagrams. *Educational Psychology Review, 3,* 211–247.

Winn, W. (2002). Current trends in educational technology research: The study of learning environments. *Educational Psychology Review, 14,* 331–351.

Winne, P. H. (1995). Inherent details in self-regulated learning. *Educational Psychologist, 30,* 173–187.

Winne, P. H., & Hadwin, A. F. (1998). Studying as self-regulated learning. In D. J. Hacker, J. Dunlosky, & A. C. Graesser (Eds.), *Metacognition in educational theory and practice* (pp. 277–304). Mahwah, NJ: Erlbaum.

Winne, P. H., & Marx, R. W. (1989). A cognitive-processing analysis of motivation with classroom tasks.

In C. Ames & R. Ames (Eds.), *Research on motivation in education* (Vol. 3). San Diego, CA: Academic Press.

Winner, E. (1988). *The point of words.* Cambridge, MA: Harvard University Press.

Winner, E. (1997). Exceptionally high intelligence and schooling. *American Psychologist, 52,* 1070–1081.

Winner, E. (2000a). Giftedness: Current theory and research. *Current Directions in Psychological Science, 9,* 153–156.

Winner, E. (2000b). The origins and ends of giftedness. *American Psychologist, 55,* 159–169.

Winograd, P., & Jones, D. L. (1992). The use of portfolios in performance assessment. *New Directions for Education Reform, 1*(2), 37–50.

Winsler, A., & Naglieri, J. (2003). Overt and covert verbal problem-solving strategies: Developmental trends in use, awareness, and relations with task performance in children aged 5 to 17. *Child Development, 74,* 659–678.

Wise, B. W., & Olson, R. K. (1998). Studies of computer-aided remediation for reading disabilities. In C. Hulme & R. M. Joshi (Eds.), *Reading and spelling: Development and disorders.* Mahwah, NJ: Erlbaum.

Witmer, S. (1996). Making peace, the Navajo way. *Tribal College Journal, 8,* 24–27.

Wittmer, D. S., & Honig, A. S. (1994). Encouraging positive social development in young children. *Young Children, 49*(5), 4–12.

Wittrock, M. C. (1994). Generative science teaching. In P. J. Fensham, R. F. Gunstone, & R. T. White (Eds.), *The content of science: A constructivist approach to its teaching and learning.* London: Falmer Press.

Wixson, K. K. (1984). Level of importance of postquestions and children's learning from text. *American Educational Research Journal, 21,* 419–433.

Wlodkowski, R. J. (1978). *Motivation and teaching. A practical guide.* Washington, DC: National Education Association.

Wlodkowski, R. J., & Ginsberg, M. B. (1995). *Diversity and motivation: Culturally responsive teaching.* San Francisco: Jossey-Bass.

Wodtke, K. H., Harper, F., & Schommer, M. (1989). How standardized is school testing? An exploratory observational study of standardized group testing in kindergarten. *Educational Evaluation and Policy Analysis, 11,* 223–235.

Wolf, R. M. (1998). National standards: Do we need them? *Educational Researcher, 27*(4), 22–24.

Wolpe, J. (1969). *The practice of behavior therapy.* Oxford, England: Pergamon Press.

Wolters, C. A. (1998). Self-regulated learning and college students' regulation of motivation. *Journal of Educational Psychology, 90,* 224–235.

Wolters, C. A. (2003). Regulation of motivation: Evaluating an underemphasized aspect of self-regulated learning. *Educational Psychologist, 38,* 189–205.

Wolters, C. A., & Rosenthal, H. (2000). The relation between students' motivational beliefs and their use of motivational regulation strategies. *International Journal of Educational Research, 33,* 801–820.

Woltz, D. J. (2003). Implicit cognitive processes as aptitudes for learning. *Educational Psychologist, 38,* 95–104.

Wong, B. Y. L. (1985). Self-questioning instructional research: A review. *Review of Educational Research, 55,* 227–268.

Wong, B. Y. L. (Ed.). (1991a). *Learning about learning disabilities.* San Diego, CA: Academic Press.

Wong, B. Y. L. (1991b). The relevance of metacognition to learning disabilities. In B. Y. L. Wong (Ed.), *Learning about learning disabilities.* San Diego, CA: Academic Press.

Wood, D., Bruner, J. S., & Ross, G. (1976). The role of tutoring in problem-solving. *Journal of Child Psychology and Psychiatry, 17,* 89–100.

Wood, D., Wood, H., Ainsworth, S., & O'Malley, C. (1995). On becoming a tutor: Toward an ontogenetic model. *Cognition and Instruction, 13,* 565–581.

Wood, E., Motz, M., & Willoughby, T. (1997, April). *Examining students' retrospective memories of strategy*

development. Paper presented at the annual meeting of the American Educational Research Association, Chicago.

Wood, E., Willoughby, T., McDermott, C., Motz, M., Kaspar, V., & Ducharme, M. J. (1999). Developmental differences in study behavior. *Journal of Educational Psychology, 91,* 527–536.

Wood, E., Willoughby, T., Reilley, S., Elliott, S., & DuCharme, M. (1994, April). *Evaluating students' acquisition of factual material when studying independently or with a partner.* Paper presented at the annual meeting of the American Educational Research Association, New Orleans, LA.

Wood, J. W. (1998). *Adapting instruction to accommodate students in inclusive settings* (3rd ed.). Upper Saddle River, NJ: Merrill/Prentice Hall.

Wood, J. W., & Rosbe, M. (1985). Adapting the classroom lecture for the mainstreamed student in the secondary schools. *Clearing House, 58,* 354–358.

Woolfe, T., Want, S. C., & Siegal, M. (2002). Signposts to development: Theory of mind in deaf children. *Child Development, 73,* 768–778.

Woolfolk, A. E., & Brooks, D. M. (1985). The influence of teachers' nonverbal behaviors on students' perceptions and performances. *Elementary School Journal, 85,* 513–528.

Woolley, J. D. (1995). The fictional mind: Young children's understanding of pretense, imagination, and dreams. *Developmental Review, 15,* 172–211.

Worthen, B. R., & Leopold, G. D. (1992). Impediments to implementing alternative assessment: Some emerging issues. *New Directions for Education Reform, 1*(2), 1–20.

Wright, L. S. (1982). The use of logical consequences in counseling children. *School Counselor, 30,* 37–49.

Wright, R. (1994). *The moral animal: The new science of evolutionary psychology.* New York: Pantheon Books.

Wright, S. C., & Taylor, D. M. (1995). Identity and the language of the classroom: Investigating the impact of heritage versus second-language instruction on personal and collective self-esteem. *Journal of Educational Psychology, 87,* 241–252.

Wright, S. C., Taylor, D. M., & Macarthur, J. (2000). Subtractive bilingualism and the survival of the Inuit language: Heritage- versus second-language education. *Journal of Educational Psychology, 92,* 63–84.

Wynne, E. A. (1990). Improving pupil discipline and character. In O. C. Moles (Ed.), *Student discipline strategies: Research and practice.* Albany: State University of New York Press.

Yarmey, A. D. (1973). I recognize your face but I can't remember your name: Further evidence on the tip-of-the-tongue phenomenon. *Memory and Cognition, 1,* 287–290.

Yates, M., & Youniss, J. (1996). A developmental perspective on community service in adolescence. *Social Development, 5,* 85–111.

Yau, J., & Smetana, J. G. (2003). Conceptions of moral, social-conventional, and personal events among Chinese preschoolers in Hong Kong. *Child Development, 74,* 647–658.

Yee, A. H. (1992). Asians as stereotypes and students: Misperceptions that persist. *Educational Psychology Review, 4,* 95–132.

Yee, D. K., & Eccles, J. S. (1988). Parent perceptions and attributions for children's math achievement. *Sex Roles, 19,* 317–333.

Yell, M. L., Robinson, T. R., & Drasgow, E. (2001). Cognitive behavior modification. In T. J. Zirpoli & K. J. Melloy, *Behavior management: Applications for teachers* (3rd ed., pp. 200–246). Upper Saddle River, NJ: Merrill/Prentice Hall.

Yerkes, R. M., & Dodson, J. D. (1908). The relation of strength of stimulus to rapidity of habit-formation. *Journal of Comparative Neurology of Psychology, 18,* 459–482.

Yip, T., & Fuligni, A. J. (2002). Daily variation in ethnic identity, ethnic behaviors, and psychological well-being among American adolescents of Chinese descent. *Child Development, 73,* 1557–1572.

Yokoi, L. (1997, March). *The developmental context of notetaking: A qualitative examination of notetaking at the secondary level.* Paper presented at the annual meeting of the American Educational Research Association, Chicago.

Youniss, J., & Volpe, J. (1978). A relational analysis of children's friendships. In W. Damon (Ed.), *New directions for child development: Vol. 1. Social cognition* (pp. 1–22). San Francisco: Jossey-Bass.

Youniss, J., & Yates, M. (1999). Youth service and moral-civic identity: A case for everyday morality. *Educational Psychology Review, 11,* 361–376.

Yu, S. L., Elder, A. D., & Urdan, T. C. (1995, April). *Motivation and cognitive strategies in students with a "good student" or "poor student" self-schema.* Paper presented at the annual meeting of the American Educational Research Association, San Francisco.

Yuker, H. E. (Ed.). (1988). *Attitudes toward persons with disabilities.* New York: Springer.

Zahn-Waxler, C., Radke-Yarrow, M., Wagner, E., & Chapman, M. (1992). Development of concern for others. *Developmental Psychology, 28,* 126–136.

Zahn-Waxler, C., & Robinson, J. (1995). Empathy and guilt: Early origins of feelings of responsibility. In J. P. Tangney & K. W. Fischer (Eds.), *Self-conscious emotions: The psychology of shame, guilt, embarrassment, and pride* (pp. 143–173). New York: Guilford Press.

Zahorik, J. A. (1994, April). *Making things interesting.* Paper presented at the annual meeting of the American Educational Research Association, New Orleans, LA.

Zajonc, R. B. (1980). Feeling and thinking: Preferences need no inferences. *American Psychologist, 35,* 151–175.

Zambo, D. (2003). *Uncovering the conceptual representations of students with learning disabilities.* Unpublished doctoral dissertation, Arizona State University, Tempe.

Zeaman, D., & House, B. J. (1979). A review of attention theory. In N. R. Ellis (Ed.), *Handbook of mental deficiency: Psychological theory and research* (2nd ed.). Mahwah, NJ: Erlbaum.

Zeidner, M. (1998). *Test anxiety: The state of the art.* New York: Plenum Press.

Zeldin, A. L., & Pajares, F. (2000). Against the odds: Self-efficacy beliefs of women in mathematical, scientific, and technological careers. *American Educational Research Journal, 37,* 215–246.

Zelli, A., Dodge, K. A., Lochman, J. E., & Laird, R. D. (1999). The distinction between beliefs legitimizing aggression and deviant processing of social cues: Testing measurement validity and the hypothesis that biassed processing mediates the effects of beliefs on aggression. *Journal of Personality and Social Psychology, 77,* 150–166.

Ziegert, D. I., Kistner, J. A., Castro, R., & Robertson, B. (2001). Longitudinal study of young children's responses to challenging achievement situations. *Child Development, 72,* 609–624.

Ziegler, S. G. (1987). Effects of stimulus cueing on the acquisition of groundstrokes by beginning tennis players. *Journal of Applied Behavior Analysis, 20,* 405–411.

Zigler, E. F., & Finn-Stevenson, M. (1992). Applied developmental psychology. In M. H. Bornstein & M. E. Lamb (Eds.), *Developmental psychology: An advanced textbook.* Mahwah, NJ: Erlbaum.

Zigler, E. F., & Seitz, V. (1982). Social policy and intelligence. In R. J. Sternberg (Ed.), *Handbook of human intelligence* (pp. 586–641). Cambridge, England: Cambridge University Press.

Zigmond, N., Jenkins, J., Fuchs, L. S., Deno, S., Fuchs, D., Baker, J. N., Jenkins, L., & Couthino, M. (1995, March). Special education in restructured schools: Findings from three multi-year studies. *Phi Delta Kappan,* 531–540.

Zimmerman, B. J. (1998). Developing self-fulfilling cycles of academic regulation: An analysis of exemplary instructional models. In D. H. Schunk & B. J. Zimmerman (Eds.), Self-regulated learning: From teaching to self-reflective practice (pp. 1–19). New York: Guilford Press.

Zimmerman, B. J., Bandura, A., & Martinez-Pons, M. (1992). Self-motivation for academic attainment: The role of self-efficacy beliefs and personal goal setting. *American Educational Research Journal, 29,* 663–676.

Zimmerman, B. J., & Kitsantas, A. (1997). Developmental phases in self-regulation: Shifting from process to outcome goals. *Journal of Educational Psychology, 89,* 29–36.

Zimmerman, B. J., & Risemberg, R. (1997). Self-regulatory dimensions of academic learning and motivation. In G. D. Phye (Ed.), *Handbook of academic learning: Construction of knowledge.* San Diego, CA: Academic Press.

Zirin, G. (1974). How to make a boring thing more boring. *Child Development, 45,* 232–236.

Zirpoli, T. J., & Melloy, K. J. (2001). *Behavior management: Applications for teachers.* Upper Saddle River, NJ: Merrill/Prentice Hall.

Zook, K. B. (1991). Effects of analogical processes on learning and misrepresentation. *Educational Psychology Review, 3,* 41–72.

Zook, K. B., & Di Vesta, F. J. (1991). Instructional analogies and conceptual misrepresentations. *Journal of Educational Psychology, 83,* 246–252.

Name Index

Subject Index